Douglas F. Robertson
University of Minnesota

Donald R. Robertson

Microcomputer Applications and Programming

A Complete Computer Course with DOS, WordPerfect 5.1, Lotus 1-2-3, dBASE IV, and BASIC

The Dryden Press
Harcourt Brace Jovanovich College Publishers
Fort Worth Philadelphia San Diego New York Orlando Austin San Antonio
Toronto Montreal London Sydney Tokyo

Acquisitions Editor: Richard Bonacci
Associate Editor: Ruth Rominger
Manuscript Editor: Joan Harlan
Production Editor: Michael Ferreira
Designer: Diana Jean Parks
Art Editor: Louise Sandy-Karkoutli
Production Manager: Diane Southworth

ISBN: 0-15-558372-7

Library of Congress Catalog Card Number: 91-75637

Printed in the United States of America

ILLUSTRATION CREDITS:

Cover Courtesy of International Business Machines Corporation.

Fig. 1 (top) Courtesy of International Business Machines Corporation; (bottom) Courtesy of Apple Computer, Inc. Photo by Will Mosgrove; (right) Courtesy of Zenith Data Systems.

Fig. 2, Fig. 3 Courtesy of International Business Machines Corporation.

Fig. 4 Photo by Paul Shambroom, Courtesy of Cray Research, Inc.

Fig. 5 © 1991 Larry Chapman. All Rights Reserved.

Fig. 6 HBJ Collection.

Fig. 7 © 1991 Larry Chapman. All Rights Reserved.

Fig. 8, Fig. 9, Fig. 18, Fig. 19 Courtesy of International Business Machines Corporation.

Fig. 20, Fig. 21 Courtesy of Intel Corporation.

Fig. 25 © 1991 Larry Chapman. All Rights Reserved.

Fig. 26 Photo courtesy of ITAC Systems.

Fig. 27 Summa Sketch II from Summagraphics Corporation.

Fig. 28, Fig. 29 Courtesy of International Business Machines Corporation.

Fig. 30 Reprinted with the permission of Merrill, an imprint of Macmillan Publishing Company, from *The Illustrated Computer Dictionary*, 3/e, by Donald A. Spencer. Copyright © 1986 by Merrill Publishing Company.

Fig. 35 Photo courtesy of Xerox Corporation.

Fig. 40 © 1986, 1988, 1991 by Harcourt Brace Jovanovich, Inc.; from *Living with Computers*, 3/e, by Patrick McKeown.

P. 157 Courtesy of Campbell Soup Company.

Preface

• Development and Audience •

This book is intended for students with little or no computer experience who would like to learn how to use the computer as a problem-solving tool. The main objective of the book is to provide students with hands-on experience in working with three widely used applications programs and to give them a brief introduction to programming using a high-level computer language. By the end of study, students will be able to use word-processing, spreadsheet, and database management software and to write elementary BASIC programs to help them solve problems in business and the social sciences. Such knowledge will serve as a genuine aid in their academic and later professional careers.

Many of the examples and homework exercises in this book are from the business sector but assume no prior business training and only an arithmetic background in mathematics. Because all of the homework exercises require computer output, students will have the opportunity to work directly on the computer as they progress through the course material.

This book was developed over the past six years to serve as the textbook for an introductory microcomputer applications and programming course sequence offered through the General College of the University of Minnesota. The mission of the General College is to develop, through teaching, research, and service, the potential for baccalaureate education in students who are serious about fulfilling their previously undeveloped or unrecognized academic promise. In essence, the General College provides entry to the University for students from a wide range of ethnic, social, academic, and economic backgrounds who would like to pursue a four-year degree, but who may not have yet developed strong academic skills. The approach used in this book should prove useful to instructors who, in a relatively short period of time (two quarters or semesters), must make students with a variety of educational backgrounds and problem-solving skills comfortable in the use of productivity software and elementary computer programming.

The material in this book has been tested with day school students, night school students, and students enrolled in correspondence study at the University of Minnesota. It has also been used with students at Anoka-Ramsey Community College in Anoka, Minnesota and Liberty High School in Renton, Washington.

• Pedagogy •

The underlying pedagogy of this book is that students learn best when they are actively involved in the learning process so that they are *doing* as well as *reading about* computer operations. Throughout the book, it is assumed that students will work through the computer keystrokes as they are presented.

Many students find computing difficult and frustrating. Therefore, we have tried to reduce the potential for frustration by clearly marking keystrokes and including adjacent explanations and screen dumps so that students can see *why* a particular operation works as well as *how* it works.

• Software •

The software described in this book is DOS version 4.0, WordPerfect version 5.1, Lotus 1-2-3 Release 2.2, dBASE IV, and GW-BASIC version 3.0. The book assumes that the student will be using an IBM-compatible computer with the software installed on a hard drive, but notes are also provided on how to do the work with a two-disk drive system. A minimum of 640K of RAM is needed to run the software.

Organization and Features

This book is divided into an introductory chapter, "Getting Started: Concepts," and four parts: WordPerfect and DOS, Lotus 1-2-3, dBASE IV, and BASIC. The material on DOS is split into two sections. The first section, in "Getting Started: Concepts," introduces students to the basics of DOS and guides them through the formatting of data disks, which will be used to store files created by the applications. The second section of DOS is presented in Part I, Chapter 4, right after the section on word processing. Instruction on DOS is divided in this way because students need only a brief introduction to DOS in order to get started in word processing. Then, after they have created a number of files, they are given more information on how to manage those files. Each part ends with an Appendix that summarizes selected features of the application.

Additional features of this book that make it different from other books include:

- Carefully laid out step-by-step instructions with detailed keystroke explanations for each example presented.
- A large number of screen dumps that show exactly how the screen should look as the student progresses through the examples.
- A reading level aimed at first-year college students.
- An active learning pedagogy employed throughout.
- Instruction that is tied to objectives stated at the beginning of each chapter.
- Definitions of important terms, which are presented at the beginning of each section to serve as advance organizers for student learning. These definitions and others are collected in an extensive Glossary.
- In later chapters, integrated information from WordPerfect, Lotus 1-2-3, and dBASE that will help students to see how these programs can be used as a complete office-management package rather than as three separate programs.
- An approach to BASIC programming that begins with simple concepts and evolves to a structured format for writing complex programs. This approach is developed in a natural way that convinces students that writing structured programs is an obvious and effective way to solve problems on the computer.
- Demonstrations of the relationship between applications packages and programming languages by having students work out some of the same exercises using Lotus 1-2-3 and BASIC and by using data from a dBASE database as input for a BASIC program.
- Detailed keyboard templates at the back of the book that can be cut out and placed directly on the keyboard for quick reference.
- A detailed index to help students locate items of interest quickly and easily.

Uses

A two-quarter (20-week) course sequence based on the material contained in this book has been taught at the University of Minnesota using a number of different formats.

- *Computers available for each student or small groups of students:* This is the way we are currently using the materials at the University of Minnesota. Students work through the material at their own pace in a computer lab setting with an instructor available to help students when they need it. If this method is used, it is important to pace the students so that they are able to finish the required work within the appropriate time frame. The *Instructor's Guide* includes the syllabus and other course materials that are used at the University of Minnesota.
- *Large lecture format with one computer and an overhead projection system such as* KODAK DataShow: This allows the instructor to go through the material in a demonstration mode so that students can be shown how to get around difficult parts of the course material. It

is not necessary to go through every keystroke with students but only the ones related to the important or difficult topics.

- *Large lecture format with no computer available in the classroom:* This requires the use of many overhead projection transparencies of the screen dumps so that the instructor may show students the highlights of the results of various operations. Students then must go to a computer lab to work out the homework assignments.
- *Self study:* In such a format, students work through the course material at home or in a computer lab on their own and communicate with the instructor only when problems arise and to turn in homework assignments. This type of instruction is found in many correspondence programs or where necessitated by lab space and student schedules.

• Acknowledgments •

Many people have helped in the preparation of this manuscript. We would like to express our appreciation to the following for their comments, suggestions, and support:

Molly Collins, Jay Heffernan, Dan Hollar, David Lin, Nader Mahmoodi, and Michael Schmitz for their thoughtful suggestions and tactful pointing out of errors in the manuscript. Bobby Moothedan for the meticulous care with which he checked the accuracy of the manuscript and constructed the homework keys. Andres Belalcazar, Eric Crane, Alex Gohar, Babak Hamidzaded, Jerry Horazdovsky, Suthep Madarasmi, and Andres Moreno for their suggestions and ideas and for testing the manuscript in their classes. Susan Gorman, Alice Ross, Sherri Tolk, and Mary Van Beusekom for their patience and help in numerous aspects of this writing project. Professor Carol Miller for her assistance in the WordPerfect sections of this book. Professor David Giese for his encouragement and support for this writing project and for his administrative accommodation in scheduling equipment, courses, students, and staff. Dr. Terry Lamb Robertson for the many hours she spent working through and editing the material. Dr. Maren Watson and Kathleen Wheeler for their helpful suggestions concerning the BASIC sections of this book. The reviewers who took the time to make careful and constructive criticisms of the manuscript: Mark Ciampa, Volunteer State Community College; Maurice L. Eggen, Trinity University; Robert S. Fritz, American River College; Barbara A. Gentry, Parkland College; Randy Goldberg, Marist College; Michael Goul, Arizona State University; Fran Goertzel Gustavson, Pace University; Donald C. Harris, Lincoln Land Community College; Colis Isaacs, Salem Community College; Catherine A. Kelly, Owens Technical College; Jeff Mock, Diablo Valley Community College; Jack Pesci, Owens Technical College; Leonard Presby, William Patterson State College of New Jersey; Judith A. Scheeren, Westmoreland County Community College; Robert S. Tannenbaum, University of Kentucky; David Van Over, University of Georgia; Karen L. Watterson, *Data Base Solutions;* H. Roland Weistroffer, Virginia Commonwealth University; Kathleen Wheeler, Pillsbury; John D. Witherspoon, Monroe Community College.

The excellent staff at Harcourt Brace Jovanovich who worked on this book: Richard Bonacci, Michael Ferreira, Joan Harlan, Diana Jean Parks, Ruth Rominger, Diane Southworth, Bill Teague, and Thomas Thompson.

The computer students of the General College, University of Minnesota; Anoka-Ramsey Community College, Anoka, Minnesota; and Liberty High School, Renton, Washington, for their suggestions and comments and willingness to use draft versions of this manuscript. Special thanks to Andrea Williams and Donald Plishke for their helpful suggestions on the chapters covering BASIC programming.

• User Comments •

If you find any errors in this book or if you have any comments or suggestions for change, please write to Professor Douglas Robertson, University of Minnesota, 128 Pleasant Street SE #340, Minneapolis, MN 55455. Thank you.

Douglas F. Robertson
Donald R. Robertson

Contents in Brief

Contents

Part II

Lotus 1-2-3 L1

To the memory of our grandfather

Professor C. H. Robertson

an extraordinary scholar, inventor, and humanitarian
who unselfishly taught thousands
of nontraditional students throughout Asia
the wonders of physics and mathematics.

Getting Started

Objectives *After you have completed this chapter, you should be able to*

- Define terms frequently encountered when talking about microcomputers.
- Describe the different types of computers and applications software.
- Describe the components of a microcomputer and the purpose of each.
- Describe the difference between RAM and ROM.
- Identify proper care for disks.
- Identify the functions of various keys on the computer keyboard.

CONCEPTS

- Define DOS and describe its purpose.
- Boot a microcomputer.
- Print what is displayed on the computer screen.
- Use `DIR` to list the directory of a disk.
- Use the `FORMAT` command to initialize a disk for use on an IBM or IBM-compatible computer.

Introduction

In this chapter we will discuss a brief history of the development and uses of computers, some of the concepts related to computers, and a general description of computer hardware (the physical components that make up the computer) and software (the sets of instructions provided by humans to guide the computer's operations).

Definitions

Before reading this chapter, you should familiarize yourself with some definitions of terms frequently encountered when talking about microcomputers:

Applications software . . . (C31) Programs (word processors, spreadsheets, database management programs, etc.) that enable the computer to analyze and manipulate data under the direction of the computer user.

Bit . . . (C13) A binary digit. The smallest unit that can be used to store data in the binary number system. A bit is either a 1 (meaning the electrical current is turned on) or a 0 (meaning the current is turned off).

Boot . . . (C32) The process of starting a computer by loading the system software into the main memory of the machine.

Byte . . . (C13) Typically, eight bits bundled together. A byte is a unit used to indicate the amount of data that can be stored on a disk or in the memory of a computer. A byte represents one character (letter, digit, punctuation mark, etc.).

Command . . . (C37) An instruction given to the computer (e.g., **DIR**).

Computer . . . (C6) An electronic device capable of receiving data, manipulating the data arithmetically and/or logically according to prescribed internally stored instructions, and then supplying the results of those manipulations (e.g., an IBM PS/2 or an Apple Macintosh).

Computer interface . . . (C18) The connection between the computer and some external device such as a printer.

Computer system . . . (C15) All the components needed to use a computer, including the user (human operator), hardware (physical components), software (programs), storage devices (disks), and data.

Cursor . . . (C33) A character (usually a blinking line) on the screen that indicates where characters will be displayed when typing begins.

Data . . . (C13) The raw unorganized facts that serve as the building blocks needed to construct meaningful information (the word data is actually a plural referring to more than one fact—the singular form of data is datum).

Database management program . . . (C12) A program that enables the user to enter, organize, modify, and retrieve large amounts of data (e.g., dBASE III PLUS).

Default . . . (C35) An assumption made by the computer system when the user has not indicated some specific choice. A default *drive* is the disk drive assumed by the computer system unless the user specifies another drive. A default *value* is a quantity that is assumed unless otherwise specified. For example, the default value for the size of paper used in a printer is $8\frac{1}{2}$ by 11 inches.

Directory . . . (C36) A listing of the names of files stored on a disk.

Disk drive . . . (C28) A mechanical device used to read data from disks and write data onto disks. Most disk drives have a small light on them that indicates when the drive is actively reading or writing information to the disk. Never try to remove a disk when the disk light is on because doing so might damage the drive mechanism.

Diskette . . . (C27) A flexible piece of plastic with a magnetic coating capable of storing data in a permanent fashion. Diskettes are also referred to as *disks*, *floppy diskettes*, and *floppies*. Diskettes can store from hundreds of thousands to millions of bytes of data. Older IBM computers (IBM PC, IBM XT) use $5\frac{1}{4}$-inch square diskettes, which can hold up to 1.2 million bytes of data. Newer models (IBM PS/2) use $3\frac{1}{2}$-inch square diskettes, which can hold up to 1.44 million bytes of data.

DOS (Disk Operating System) . . . (C31) A set of programs stored on a disk that act as the interface between the user and the computer hardware.

File . . . (C36) A collection of related information that is stored as a logical unit in the memory of the computer (e.g., a letter written in WordPerfect or a BASIC program).

Format . . . (C28) Preparing the magnetic material on a disk so that it matches the way in which data are stored by a given brand of computer. For example, a diskette formatted for use with an IBM PS/2 cannot be used in an Apple Macintosh without reformatting it for that machine.

Function keys . . . (C20) Keys labeled F1, F2, etc., that enable the user to perform specific tasks such as saving, printing, and formatting with a single keystroke.

Hard copy . . . (C26) A printed copy of information obtained from the computer.

Hard disk . . . (C30) A mechanical device that includes the magnetic disk and disk drive as a permanent fixture of the computer system. Hard disks can store millions to billions of bytes of data and the computer can access data much faster from a hard disk than from a floppy diskette.

Hardware . . . (C15) The physical components that make up a computer system (e.g., system unit, monitor, keyboard, disk drive, printer).

Input device . . . (C19) A device used to enter data into the computer (e.g., a keyboard).

Kilobyte . . . (C14) 1,024 bytes. A kilobyte is abbreviated with the letter K and is usually rounded off to the nearest thousand. Thus, 360K means 360,000 bytes.

Main memory . . . see RAM.

Microprocessor . . . (C16) An integrated circuit that contains the central processing unit (the "brain") of a computer. It determines the overall characteristics of the computer including performance and cost.

Operating system . . . (C31) Instructions (programs) that monitor and control the operations of the computer system. These programs tell the computer how to do specific tasks such as sending output to the monitor, receiving input from the keyboard, and driving the printer.

Output device . . . (C24) A device used to get information out of the computer (e.g., a monitor or printer).

Peripheral . . . (C18) An external device, such as a printer or a modem, that can be attached to the computer.

Programming language . . . (C13) Translators (e.g., BASIC) that provide the interface between human language (e.g., English) and the electronic language used by the computer.

RAM (random-access memory) . . . (C18) A part of the memory of the computer that temporarily holds instructions and data when the power to the computer is on. RAM is erased when the power is turned off. The contents of RAM can be changed by the computer user.

ROM (read-only memory) . . . (C18) A part of the memory of the computer that permanently holds instructions. ROM is not erased when the power to the computer is turned off. The contents of ROM cannot be changed by the user.

Root directory . . . (C36) The single main directory of a disk that is created when the disk is formatted.

Screen dump . . . (C35) A printed copy of the exact contents of the screen.

Software . . . (C31) The instructions that allow computers to carry out the wishes of the computer user (e.g., programs such as WordPerfect).

Spreadsheet program . . . (C12) A computer program set up to resemble an electronic ledger that allows users to enter text, numeric data, and formulas and then to manipulate them to construct summary information or make projections (e.g., Lotus 1-2-3).

Storage device . . . (C27) A device used to store data on a permanent basis (e.g., a hard disk or a floppy diskette).

Subdirectory . . . (C36) A listing of the files (i.e., a directory) that have been grouped together under a single heading (e.g., you might create one subdirectory to hold all WordPerfect files and another to hold all Lotus 1-2-3 files).

System unit . . . (C15) The main part of a microcomputer that contains the central processing unit, disk drives, power supply, and main memory.

Systems software . . . (C31) Sets of instructions that tell the computer's hardware how to work. Some of the instructions are continued in ROM (read-only memory) and some are contained in DOS (disk operating system).

Word-processing program . . . (C11) A computer program that enables a user to enter, manipulate, store, and print documents such as memos and reports (e.g., WordPerfect).

Types of Computers

A **computer** is an electronic device that is capable of receiving data, manipulating the data arithmetically and/or logically according to prescribed internally stored instructions, and then supplying the results of those manipulations. Computers are usually classified according to their size, speed, processing capabilities, and price.

- *Microcomputers* (also known as *micros*, *personal computers* or simply *PCs*) are small, low-priced machines (under $10,000) that are widely used in business and for personal computing. The IBM PS/2 and the Apple Macintosh (Fig. 1) are examples of well-known microcomputers. These computers come in different sizes including laptop computers (the size of a briefcase and weighing under eighteen pounds), portable computers (about the size of a suitcase and somewhat heavier than a laptop), desktop computers (the most common type of microcomputer), and floor models (large and powerful microcomputers designed to sit on the floor next to a desk).
- *Minicomputers* (Fig. 2) are larger and more expensive than micros (over $20,000) and can be used by more than one person at a time.

FIGURE 1

Three popular microcomputers: an IBM PS/2 Model 30 286 (*top*), a Zenith Data Systems Z-286 LP (*right*), and an Apple Macintosh IIfx (*bottom*).

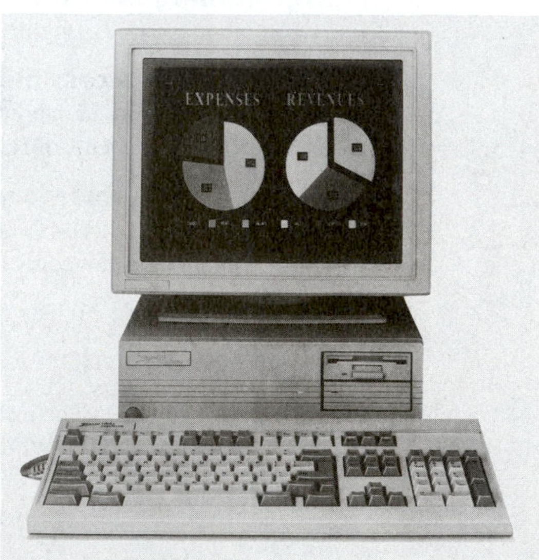

FIGURE 2

An IBM minicomputer.

- *Mainframe computers* (Fig. 3) are larger still and more expensive (hundreds of thousands to millions of dollars), can process large amounts of data at high speed, and can be used by more than one person at a time.

FIGURE 3

An IBM mainframe computer.

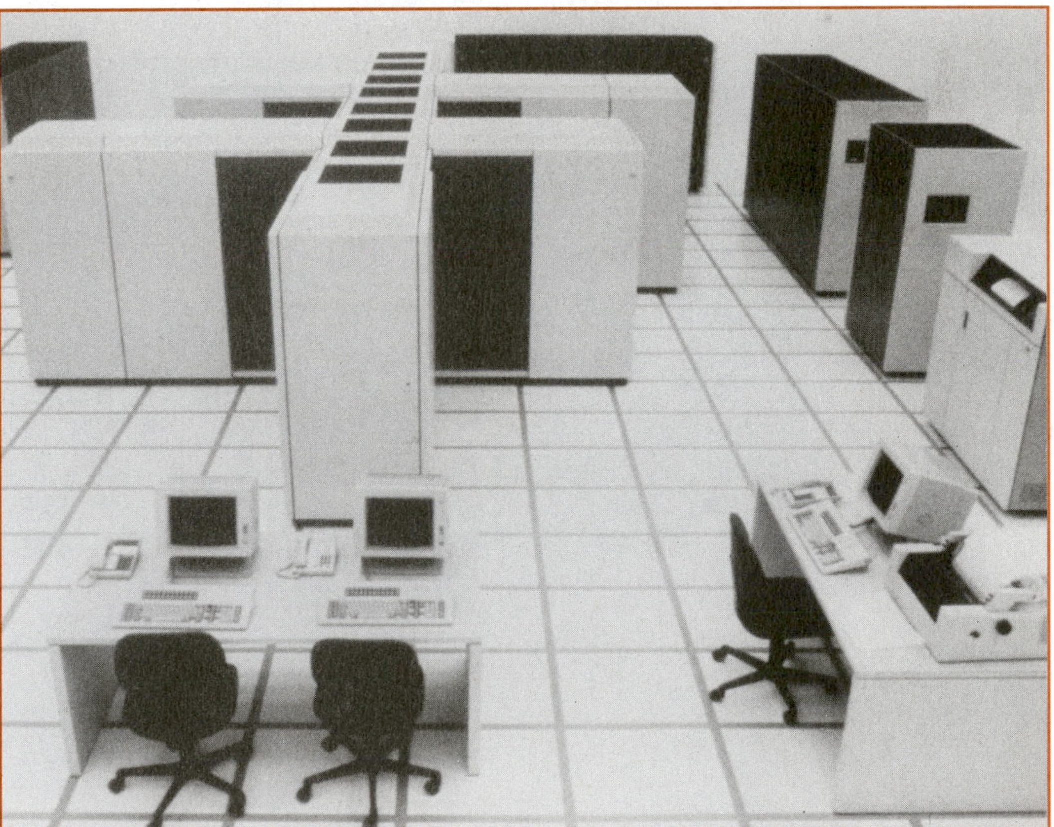

FIGURE 4

A Cray-2 System super computer.

- *Supercomputers* (Fig. 4) are the largest and most expensive systems (millions of dollars) and can process billions of instructions per second.

A Brief History of Computers

Counting devices have been used for thousands of years to help humans perform mathematical computations quickly and accurately. Prehistoric people used knots tied in rope to help them keep track of their animals and other possessions. Perhaps the earliest calculating machine was the Chinese abacus (Fig. 5)—a device that is still used today by many people.

FIGURE 5

The abacus, an ancient calculator, is still used today.

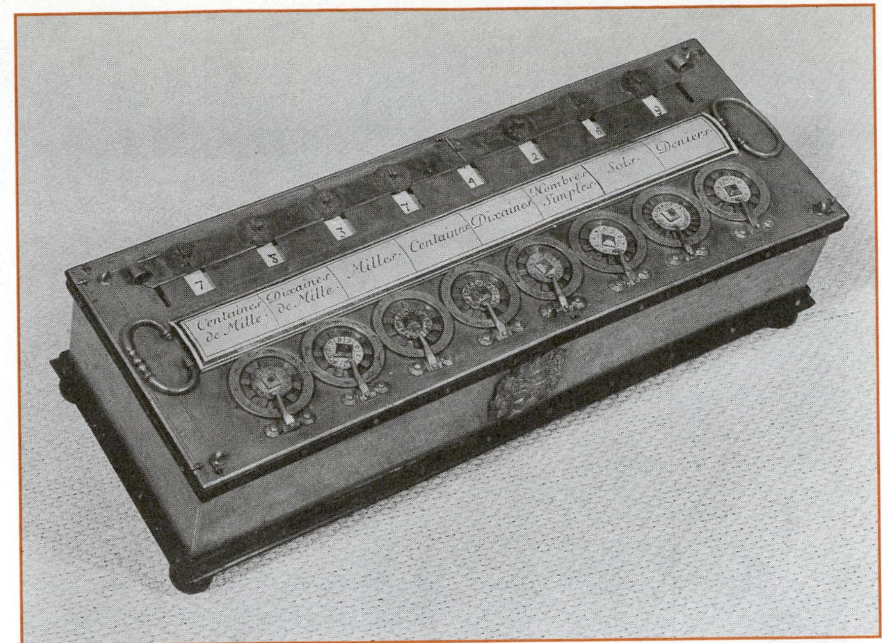

FIGURE 6

The Pascal calculator used mechanical gears to add and subtract numbers.

The first mechanical adding machine was developed in the 1640s by the French physicist and mathematician Blaise Pascal (after whom the computer language Pascal was named). His machine, called the *Pascal calculator* (Fig. 6), used mechanical gears to add and subtract numbers.

About 50 years later, a German mathematician, Gottfried Wilhelm von Leibnitz, improved on Pascal's ideas and developed a machine that could add, subtract, multiply, and divide numbers and find square roots.

In the early 1800s, Joseph Jacquard used cardboard cards with holes punched in them to control the action of weaving looms. Similar cards were used in the 1880s by Herman Hollerith to store census data. These *Hollerith cards* (Fig. 7) served as the basis for the punched cards used to store data and instructions for electronic computers from the 1950s through the 1970s. The cards are about the size of a dollar bill and contain 80 columns and 12 rows. Codes were developed to represent letters, numbers, and other characters so that holes punched into the cards could be interpreted by machines.

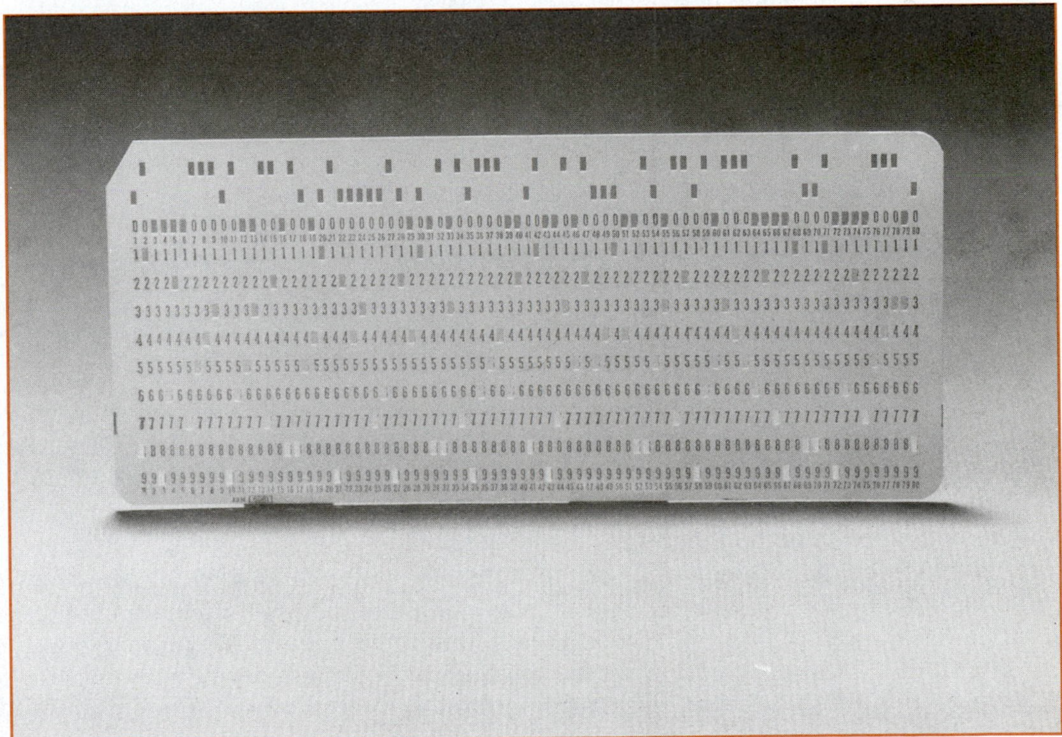

FIGURE 7

A Hollerith card was used to store data in a coded form.

FIGURE 8

The Babbage Difference Engine was an early form of a mechanical calculator.

Also in the early 1800s, while Jacquard was developing his card-controlled loom, Charles Babbage was developing a device called a *Difference Engine.* (Fig. 8).

The Difference Engine was designed to calculate and print mathematics tables. Unfortunately, the engine needed to rely on moving parts that had to be so precisely machined that the actual working engine could not be built at that time. However, Babbage's ideas and inventions contributed so much to the development of modern computers that he is known today as the "father of computers."

During the early 1900s many people worked on the development of calculating machines that could be used for business and scientific computations. The earliest machines used mechanical gears, but in the 1930s and 1940s electronic relays replaced many of the mechanical parts. In 1944, the ENIAC (Electronic Numerical Integrator and Calculator) was built with funding from the U.S. Army. This was the first electronic computer to be used for practical purposes and was considered an engineering marvel for its time. It contained 18,000 vacuum tubes, used 140,000 watts of power when operating, weighed 30 tons and was over 100 feet long and 10 feet high. It could multiply two ten-digit numbers in about three-thousandths of a second. For those days, this was blindingly fast but today a briefcase-sized 40 pound IBM PS/2 can do the same calculation much faster.

Over the years, as the need for quick and accurate calculation increased, the computer developed in step with advancing electronics technology. Computer scientists view the development of modern computers in four phases, called generations (Fig. 9):

- First generation (1951–1958) computers used vacuum tubes to process information, magnetic drums to store internal data and instructions, and punched (Hollerith) cards to store data externally. During this time period, IBM, which had been producing punch-card and other business equipment, began manufacturing computers.
- Second generation (1959–1964) computers used transistors in place of vacuum tubes and magnetic cores instead of magnetic drums. Because transistors are up to 200 times smaller than comparable vacuum tubes, the second generation computers were much smaller and used much less electricity than the first generation machines. These computers also used magnetic tapes and disks to store data externally.
- Third generation (1965–1970) computers used small (one-eighth inch square) integrated circuits in place of many transistors and other electronic components. Also during this period, minicomputers were introduced, which were smaller and less costly than their larger mainframe counterparts. In addition, remote typewriter-like terminals were developed, which allowed many users to interact with a single computer at one time.

FIGURE 9

As technology improved, vacuum tubes (*left*) were replaced by transistors (*right*) which were replaced by integrated circuits (*middle*) which were replaced by microprocessors (*front*).

- Fourth generation (1971–present) computers use LSI (large-scale integration) and VLSI (very large-scale integration) technology to place hundreds of thousands of electronic components on a single silicon chip. Also, the magnetic core memory system has been replaced by much more reliable and smaller silicon chip memory systems. This technology enabled the development of the microprocessor, the small silicon electronic chip that is the brain of today's microcomputers.

Uses of Computers

Computers are used most heavily in four areas: word processing, spreadsheet applications, database management, and programming using a high-level computer language such as BASIC, Pascal, and C.

Word-processing applications such as WordPerfect, WordStar, and Microsoft Word (Fig. 10) are programs that enable the user to enter text material in much the same way as has been done for years on mechanical or electric typewriters. Once information has been entered into the computer, the word-processing program allows the user to quickly and easily make additions, deletions, or modifications to the original text. The final text may then be printed on paper or other media or transmitted to other computers via telephone lines.

FIGURE 10

A word-processing (WordPerfect) document as displayed on the computer screen.

```
                         MEMORANDUM

DATE:      February 10, 1991

TO:        Bill Schwartz and Lisa Pearson

FROM:      Alec Benson

SUBJECT:   Preparation of Conference Room

                We need to prepare the conference room
           for a meeting of the BOARD OF DIRECTORS to be
           held from 9:00 am to 11:30 am on February 12,
           1991.

           Please call the people listed below to remind
           them of the meeting:

           Smith,    Jim,       555-2132
           Benson,   Geri,      553-3224
           Perez,    Juan,      545-8912
           Daniels,  Matt,      555-6672
           Wheeler,  Vanessa,   505-6540

A:\MRMPREP.V7                           Doc 1 Pg 1 Ln 4" Pos 2"
```

FIGURE 11

A spreadsheet (Lotus 1-2-3) worksheet as displayed on the computer screen.

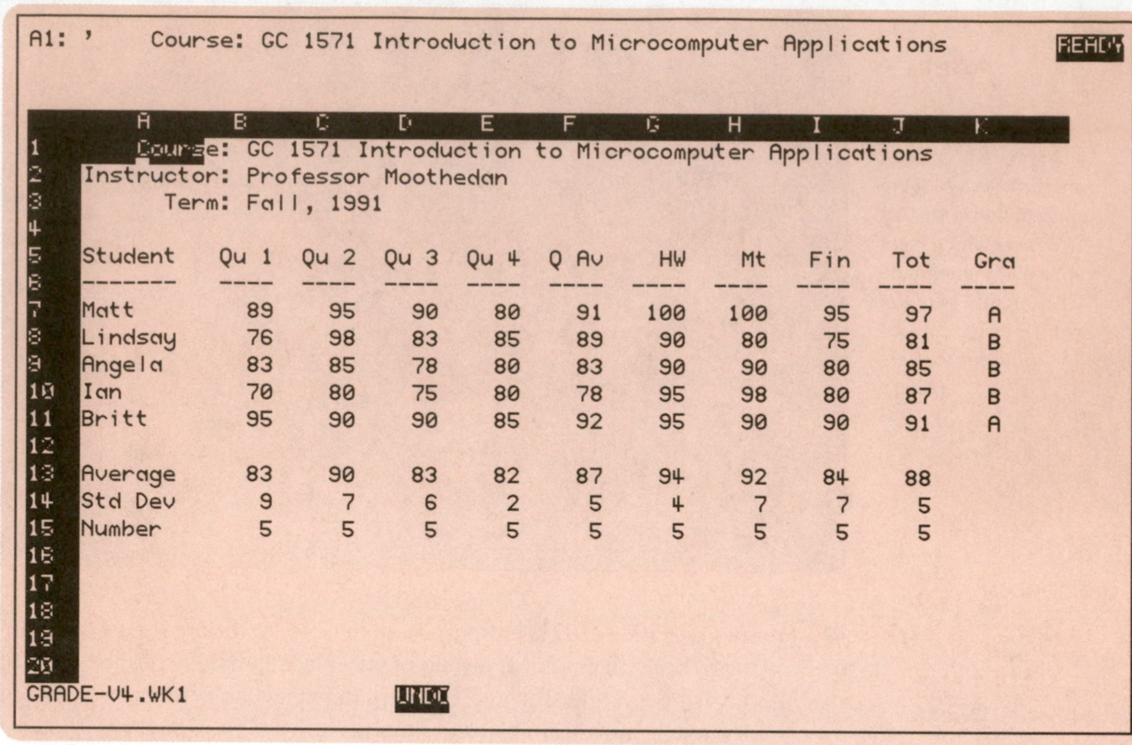

Spreadsheet programs such as Lotus 1-2-3, Excel, and Quattro (Fig. 11) are electronic ledgers that allow users to enter text and/or numeric data and formulas and then to manipulate them to construct summary information or make projections. The uses of spreadsheets in business might include forecasting the cost of introducing a new product, recording and tracking income and expenses for tax purposes, and gathering or manipulating data to make other business decisions that depend on finances.

Database management programs such as dBASE, R-Base, and Paradox (Fig. 12) allow users to maintain records of just about any type. Data are entered into the program and can then be reorganized in specific ways to generate reports covering a variety of topics. For example, a small business might keep its inventory of products on a database and use that data at the end of each month to produce reports detailing when the products were sold, what revenue they generated, and how many of each type are left in stock.

FIGURE 12

A database management program (dBASE III PLUS) as displayed on the computer screen.

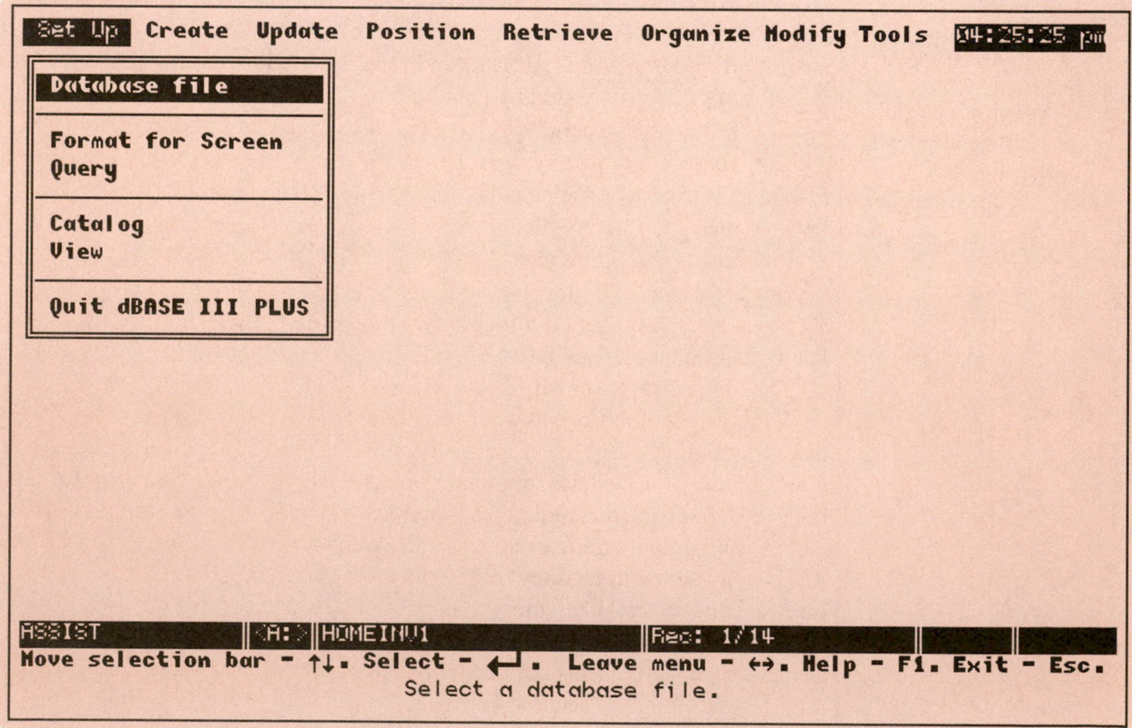

FIGURE 13

A BASIC program and resulting output as displayed on the computer screen.

```
LOAD"METRIC1
Ok
LIST
1100 A$ = "Inches  Centimeters  Meters"
1200 B$ = "  ##       ##.##      ##.##"
1300   PRINT A$
1400     FOR INCH = 0 TO 12 STEP 4
1500       PRINT USING B$;INCH,2.54*INCH,2.54*INCH/100
1600     NEXT INCH
Ok
RUN
Inches  Centimeters  Meters
   0        0.00       0.00
   4       10.16       0.10
   8       20.32       0.20
  12       30.48       0.30
Ok

_

1LIST  2RUN←  3LOAD"  4SAVE"  5CONT←  6,"LPT1  7TRON←  8TROFF←  9KEY  0SCREEN
```

Programming languages such as BASIC, Pascal, or C (Fig. 13) provide a way of instructing computers to do tasks that require the manipulation of numbers, text, and graphic material. Programming languages have the capability of accomplishing the same kinds of tasks as applications programs such as word processors, spreadsheets, and database management programs but they are much more flexible because they allow the user complete control over data entry, data processing, and data output. Of course, this increased flexibility means that the programming languages are a bit more difficult to work with than the applications programs.

How Computers View Data

Data can be thought of as the raw, unorganized facts that serve as the building blocks needed to construct meaningful information. For example, if we wanted to calculate the gas mileage of a particular make of automobile we would collect raw data such as the number of miles driven and the gallons of gas used to drive those miles. The data could then be processed into information (miles per gallon) by dividing the miles driven by the gallons of gas used. Computers are able to process data by using numerical representations for facts and instructions. These representations are then translated into electronic signals and processed by the computer's hardware.

While humans generally use a decimal (base 10) number system to do computations, computers use a binary (base 2) number system. The decimal number system is a logical choice for organisms (people) that have 10 fingers which can be used to help them count things. The binary system is a good choice for machines (computers) that have only two states (electric current is either on or off) to count things. There is also a third number system, called the hexadecimal (base 16) system, which computer scientists sometimes use. Figure 14 shows the relation between the binary, decimal, and hexadecimal representation of the numbers 0 through 20. For more information on number systems and how to convert from one to the other see Part IV, Chapter 2.

The binary digit (or **bit** for short) is the smallest unit that can be used to store data in the binary number system. A bit is either a 1 (meaning the electrical current is turned on) or a 0 (meaning the current is turned off). Bits are bundled together into larger units called **bytes** (typically, eight bits make a byte). In the United States, computer professionals have agreed upon a standard way in which bits are used to code characters and other functions typically done by computers. For most microcomputers, the code is called the American Standard Code for Information Interchange (or ASCII for short). Using ASCII (rhymes with passkey) eight bits are bundled together to code letters, digits, punctuation, and other special control characters. For example, the binary ASCII representation for the uppercase letter *A* is given as 01000001 (this corresponds to the decimal number 65) while the lowercase letter *a* is represented by 01100001 (this corresponds to the decimal number 97). The first digit on the left is usually used for checking the accuracy of the rest of the digits and the remaining seven digits can be used to

FIGURE 14

The correspondence between binary, decimal, and hexadecimal numbers.

Binary	Decimal	Hexadecimal
0	0	0
1	1	1
10	2	2
11	3	3
100	4	4
101	5	5
110	6	6
111	7	7
1000	8	8
1001	9	9
1010	10	A
1011	11	B
1100	12	C
1101	13	D
1110	14	E
1111	15	F
10000	16	10
10001	17	11
10010	18	12
10011	19	13
10100	20	14

represent 2^7 or 128 different characters. The example in Figure 15 shows the English, decimal ASCII, and binary ASCII representations of the word *Hello*.

FIGURE 15

The word *Hello* represented in English, ASCII decimal, and ASCII binary coding schemes. Mainframe computers often use a different scheme called EBCDIC (Extended Binary Coded Decimal Interchange Code) in place of ASCII.

English:

```
Hello
```

ASCII decimal (each group of three digits represents one letter):

```
072101108108111
```

ASCII binary (each group of eight digits represents one letter):

```
0100100001100101011011000110110001101111
```

To represent large numbers of bytes prefixes are used:

- 1 **kilobyte** (1K) means 2^{10} = 1,024 or about 1,000 bytes
- 1 **megabyte** (1Mb or 1 Meg) means 2^{20} = 1,048,576 or about 1 million bytes
- 1 **gigabyte** (1Gb or one Gig) means 2^{30} = 1,073,741,824 or about 1 billion bytes

Thus, a 720K floppy diskette can hold approximately 720,000 bytes of data while an 80Mb hard disk can hold approximately 80,000,000 bytes of data.

Components of a Microcomputer System

The physical devices that make up a computer system are referred to as the computer **hardware** (Fig. 16). Most computer systems contain four main parts: the *system unit*, which contains the *central processing unit* (*CPU*) or "brain" of the machine; the *input device*, which is used to enter data into the computer (e.g., a *keyboard*); the *output device*, which is used to get data out of the computer (e.g., a *monitor* or *printer*); and a *storage device*, which is used to store data on a permanent basis (e.g., a *hard disk* or a *floppy diskette*).

FIGURE 16

Components of a typical microcomputer.

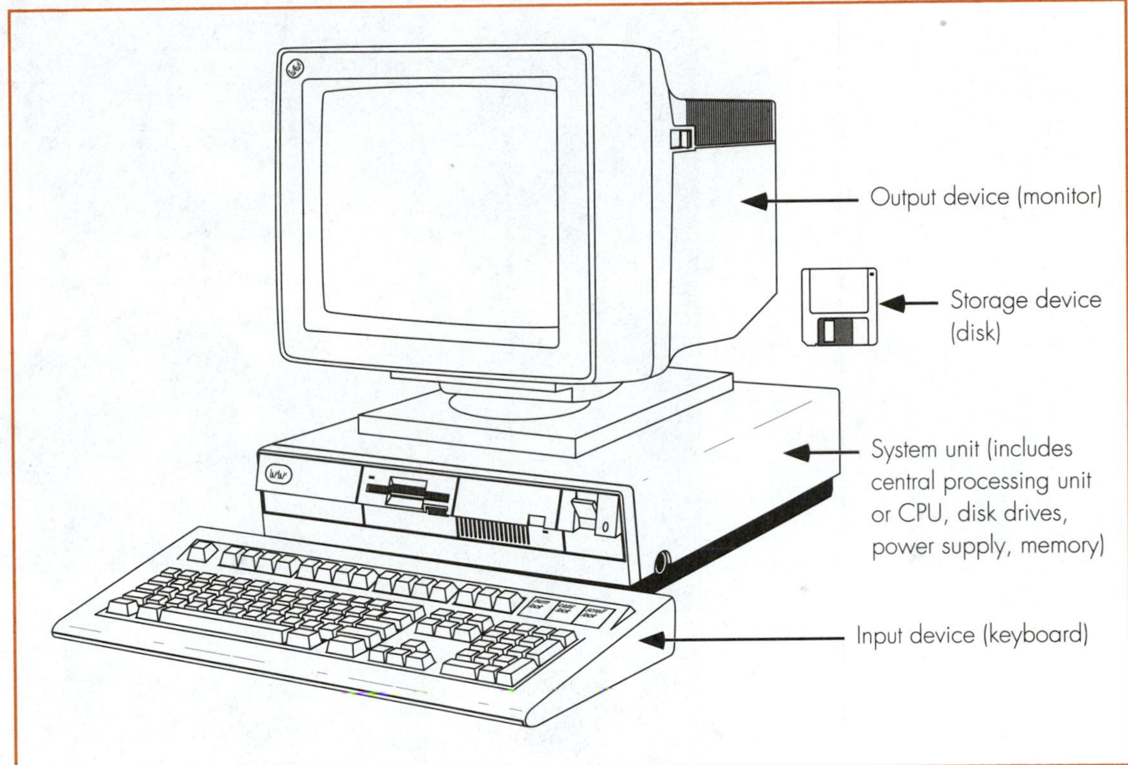

FIGURE 17

Outside view of a system unit.

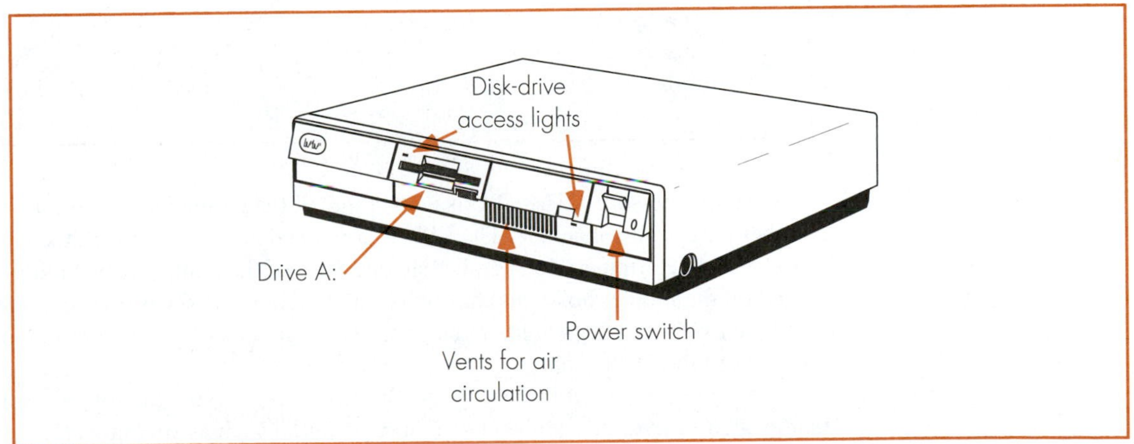

• System Unit •

The **system unit** (Figs. 17 and 18) is the large box that the monitor usually sits upon. It contains the central processing unit (CPU) on the main circuit board (also called the system or motherboard), the disk drives (usually one or two located side by side or stacked one on top of the other), memory, a power supply, and a fan to keep the electronic parts cool enough to work properly. The system unit also contains expansion slots that can be used to expand the capabilities of the computer by adding other electronic devices.

FIGURE 18

Inside view of a system unit.

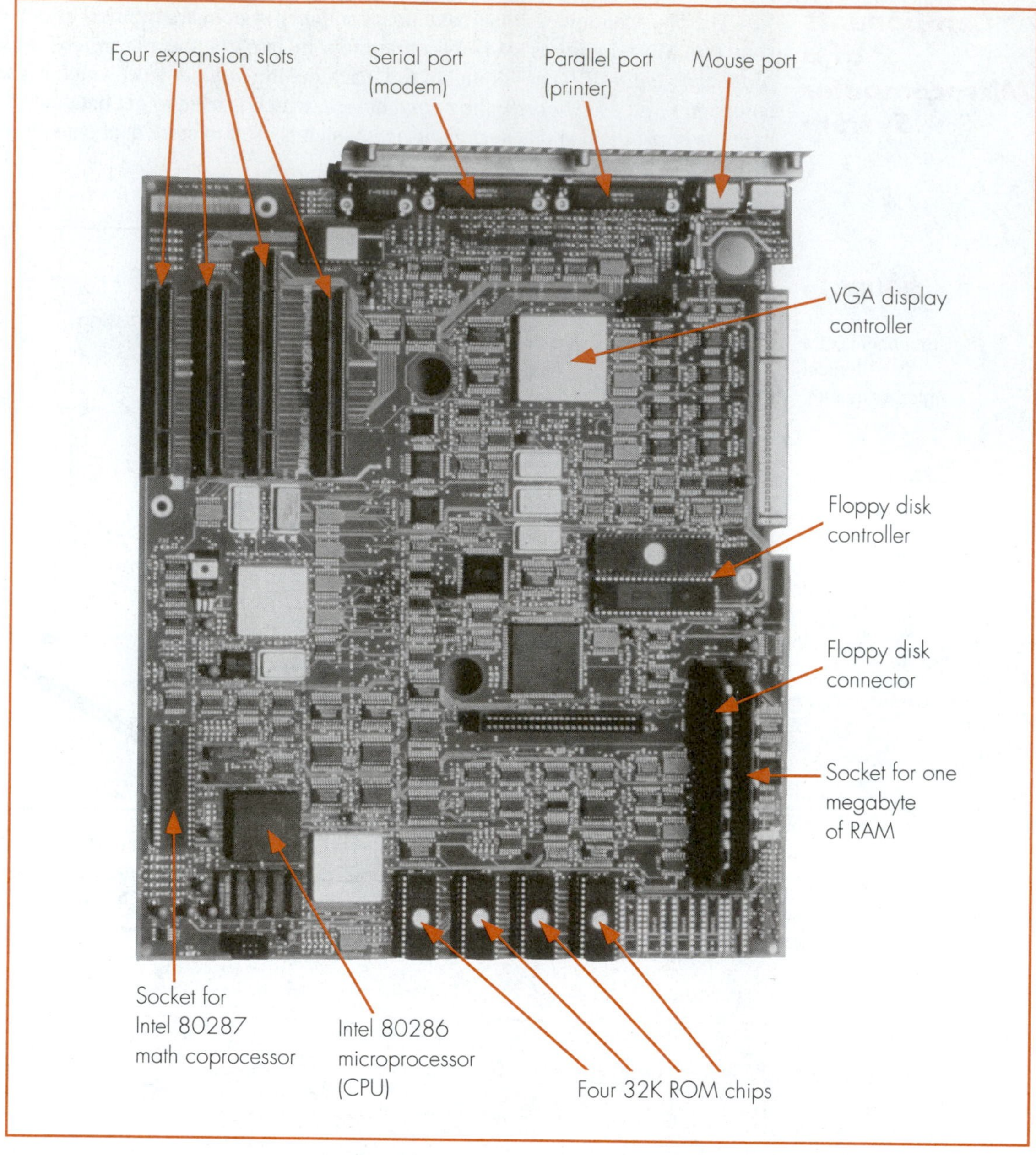

Microprocessors The CPU is the "brain" of the computer because it controls the functions of all the other parts of the machine. The CPU is contained in a single integrated circuit called a **microprocessor** and it determines the overall characteristics of the computer including performance and cost. It is located on the mother board and has two basic functions: it performs the arithmetic operations in a part called the *arithmetic logic unit*, and it controls the actions of the various components of the computer in a part called the *control unit*.

The *integrated circuit* (Figs. 19 and 20) that makes up the microprocessor is a small (about one-quarter inch square) piece of semiconductor material such as silicon that has been impregnated with thousands of electronic components such as transistors. The integrated circuit is placed in a hard plastic shell (Fig. 21) and connected to the outside world by a series of wires that extend from under the shell and plug into sockets in the motherboard.

Microprocessors generally use 8-bit, 16-bit, or 32-bit storage compartments (called registers) to do their internal processing. The larger the register the more data that can be processed at one time and hence the faster the machine. The speed at which the microprocessor runs also affects the overall processing speed of the computer. A system clock controls the timing of the computer operations and so the faster the clock speed the more operations that can be performed in a given time interval. Microcomputers typically use clock speeds that range from 4 MHz (million Hertz or cycles per second) to 50 MHz.

FIGURE 19

A magnified view of an integrated circuit.

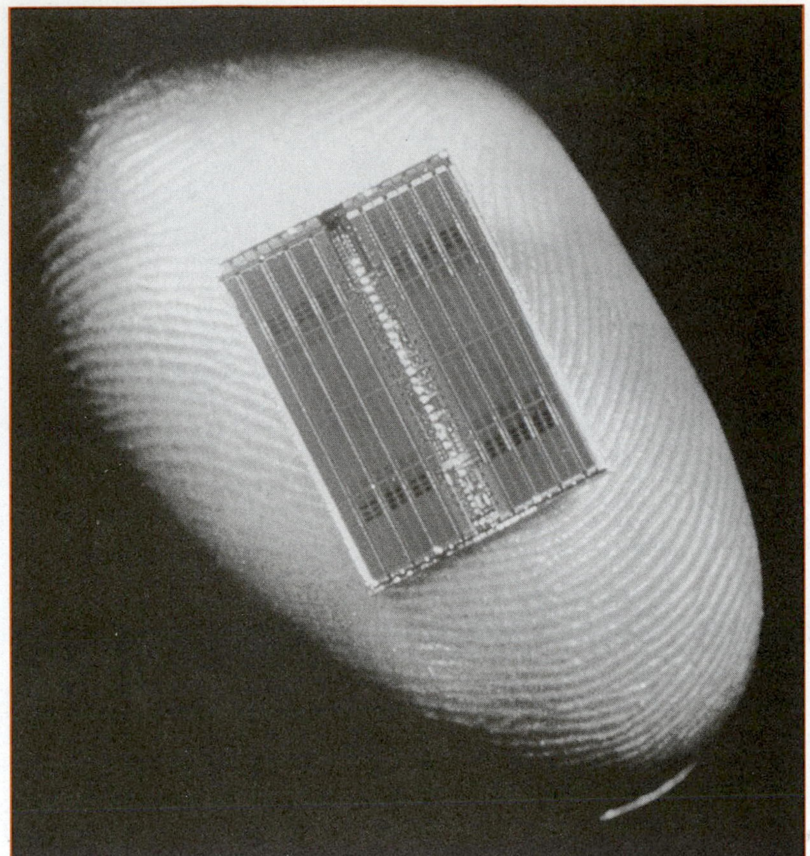

The Apple II microcomputer uses an 8-bit microprocessor running at 2 or 4 MHz, while the IBM PC uses a 16-bit microprocessor called the Intel 8088 running at 8 MHz. Newer machines, such as the the IBM PS/2 (model 80), use the Intel 80386, which is a 32-bit microprocessor that can run at speeds up to 25 MHz. This microprocessor enables users to run applications up to 20 times faster than is possible using the 8088 microprocessor. The fastest IBM microcomputers use the Intel 80486 microprocessor running at 50 MHz and can process millions of instructions per second.

FIGURE 20

The Intel 80386 integrated circuit.

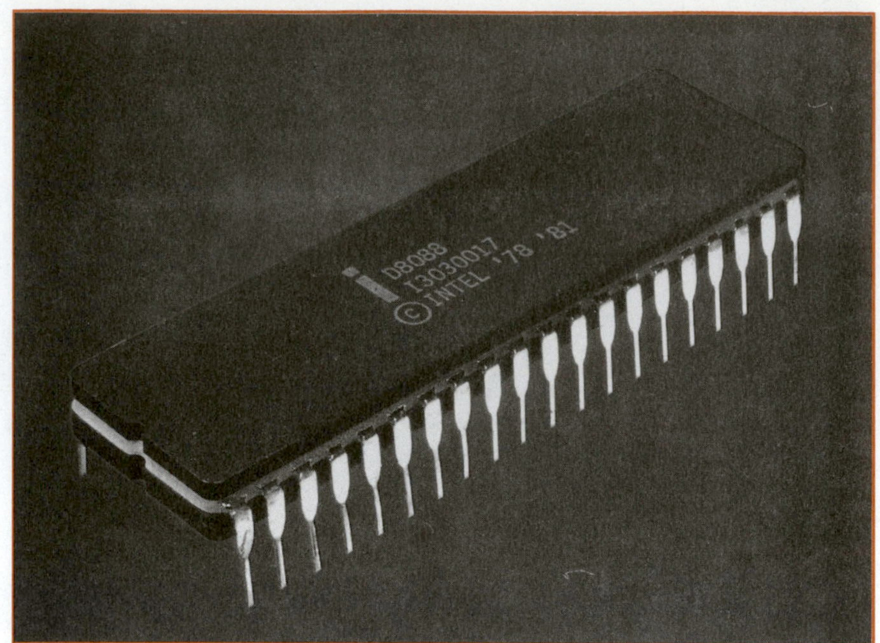

FIGURE 21

The Intel 8088 microprocessor inside its protective case.

Some microcomputers use a *coprocessor* in addition to the regular microprocessor. This is a specially designed microprocessor that can quickly perform specific tasks, such as mathematical operations, while the regular microprocessor attends to other tasks. Programs must be specifically designed to access a coprocessor; if they are not, the operations will be performed by the regular microprocessor and there will be no increase in speed. Lotus 1-2-3, for example, is designed to access a mathematics coprocessor, if one is available in the computer, to dramatically increase the speed of arithmetic calculations.

RAM and ROM Also located on the motherboard are microchips that contain two types of primary storage (memory): **random-access memory (RAM)** and **read-only memory (ROM)**. The RAM memory works only when the computer's power is on and is used to temporarily hold both data and program instructions. Information can be written to RAM or read from RAM. A typical IBM PC contains 640K of RAM. The K means 1,024, so 640K means that it can hold 640 × 1,024 or 655,360 bytes (pieces) of information—about 655,360 characters (letters, digits, punctuation marks). RAM is considered *volatile memory* because it is erased when the machine is turned off.

The amount of RAM that can be used by the computer depends, in part, on its microprocessor. Generally speaking, the more RAM a computer has the more powerful it is. However, RAM is expensive and may not be worth the extra cost because many programs and operating systems have a limit on the amount of RAM they can use. Buying a computer with 4 megabytes of RAM to run software that can only access 512 kilobytes is like buying a race car to drive on city streets—you are paying for a lot of power that you cannot use.

Read-only memory (ROM) is information that is permanently etched into the electronic parts of the computer and cannot be changed without physically removing hardware from the computer; information contained in ROM can only be read (hence the name read-only memory). The company which manufactured the computer put certain information into ROM that it felt would never have to be changed during the life of the computer. Unlike RAM, when the power is turned off, the information in ROM is not erased. Hence, ROM is referred to as *nonvolatile memory*.

Types of Interfaces An **interface** is the connection between the computer and some external device (called a **peripheral**) such as a printer or a modem (a device that can be used to transmit data from one computer to another). Three popular types of interfaces currently in use in microcomputers are the *serial interface*, the *parallel interface*, and the *small computer system interface*.

- *Serial interfaces* (or ports) transmit data in a stream one bit at a time. They are reliable and inexpensive but slow. You might think of a serial interface as a single door through which all the occupants of a building must pass to reach the outside. The RS-232 is a standard serial interface used by many microcomputers.

- *Parallel interfaces* (or ports) transmit data in parallel streams of bits (actually, 1 byte or 8 bits at a time). They are much faster than serial ports because they can transfer more data at one time. Parallel interfaces can be thought of as multiple doors through which the occupants of a building may pass simultaneously to reach the outside. The Centronics interface is a standard parallel interface used by many microcomputers.
- *Small Computer System Interface* (or *SCSI*, pronounced scuzzy) offers even faster transmission of data than does the parallel interface. This interface is often used to connect external hard disks to computers where data must be exchanged very rapidly.

• Input Devices •

An **input device** is a piece of equipment that can send information from the computer user to the central processing unit. Input devices include punch-card readers, magnetic tape readers, disk drives, and computer keyboards. You will use the keyboard as the primary input device.

Keyboard Standard keyboards (Fig. 22), usually found on older-model computers such as the IBM PC, have three main parts: a typewriter-like keypad, a set of special-purpose function keys, and a numeric keypad.

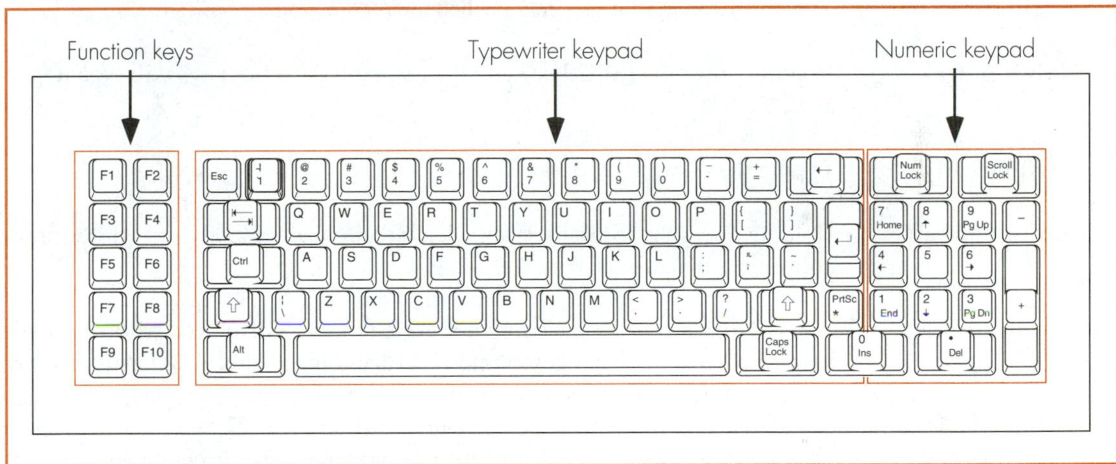

FIGURE 22

The standard keyboard.

The typewriter-like keypad contains the regular typing keys including letters, numerals, and such special characters as the comma, period, and semicolon. This part of the keyboard is used for entering text. The keys are usually arranged in a "QWERTY" configuration (Fig. 23). This arrangement gets its name from the letters of the keys in the upper left-hand side of the second row. This arrangement has

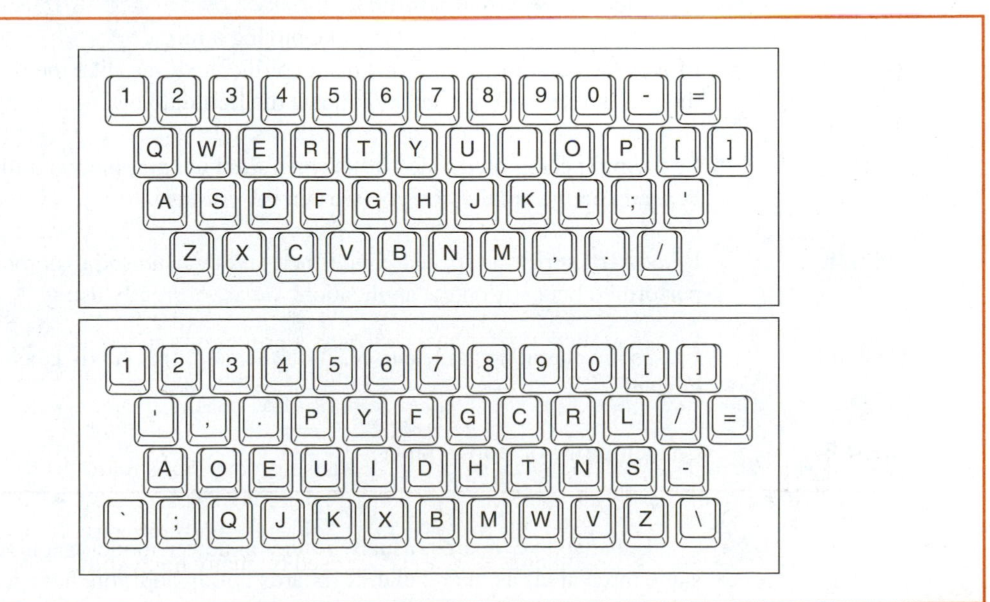

FIGURE 23

The standard QWERTY keyboard (*top*) and the more efficient Dvorak keyboard (*bottom*).

been in use since the first mechanical typewriters were developed over one hundred years ago. In fact, its awkward arrangement of keys was designed to slow down typists so that the old mechanical typewriters could keep up with the speed of the typists. Twenty words per minute was about the fastest that the old machines could handle. Other much more efficient keyboard arrangements, such as the Dvorak keyboard (Fig. 23), developed in 1936 by August Dvorak, have been designed. The Dvorak arrangement of keys reduces the distance fingers have to travel by a factor of about 16. Even though the new key arrangements are faster and less fatiguing they are not widely used because of the large number of people who already know the QWERTY keyboard arrangement.

The **function keypad** is used for entering special commands. These keys are labeled F1, F2, F3, F4, and so on. They have different effects depending on the program you are running. The **numeric keypad** looks like a calculator keypad. These keys are used for entering numeric data, inserting and deleting characters, and moving the cursor to different locations on the computer display.

Some of the keys and their functions are shown in the following table. (Note: In this book, specific keystrokes are set in boldface type and enclosed in brackets; for example, the "enter" key is represented as **[Enter]**.)

Keystroke	Purpose (action varies depending on program)
[Letter]	Typing lowercase (small) letters such as **a**, **b**, **c**, and so on.
[Shift-letter]	Holding down the **[Shift]** key and then tapping the letter keys will type uppercase (capital) letters such as **A**, **B**, **C**, **D**.
[Numeral]	Typing the digits **1**, **2**, **3**, **4**.
[Shift-numeral]	Holding down the **[Shift]** key and then tapping the numeral keys will display the special characters above the numerals such as **!**, **@**, **#**, **$**.
[Caps Lock]	Pressing this key once causes uppercase letters to be displayed without the use of the shift key. Pressing it again returns the letter keys to normal functioning. This is called a *toggle key* because it toggles (switches) between two states.
[Backspace]	Erases the character to the left of the cursor and moves the cursor one space to the left (back).
[Tab]	Acts like the tab on a typewriter. It moves the cursor to a preset location to the right of its current position.
[Shift-Tab]	Holding down the **[Shift]** key and then tapping the **[Tab]** key will move the cursor to a preset location to the left of its current position.
[Enter]	Moves the cursor to the left-hand side of the next line (like the return key of a typewriter). In this book, the symbol ↵ will be used to indicate the **[Enter]** key.
[Alt]	Performs special, predefined tasks when used in combination with other keys. The task performed depends on the application you are currently using.
[Ctrl]	Like **[Alt]**, performs special, predefined tasks when used in combination with other keys. The task performed depends on the application you are currently using.
[Delete]	Erases the character at the cursor. A duplicate of this key is labelled **[Del]** on the **[.]** key of the numeric keypad.
[Esc]	Cancels a line or stops a process.

Enhanced keyboards (usually found on newer-model machines such as the IBM PS/2) have the same three areas as the regular keyboards but, in addition, have a fourth set of keys called *special-*

FIGURE 24

An enhanced keyboard.

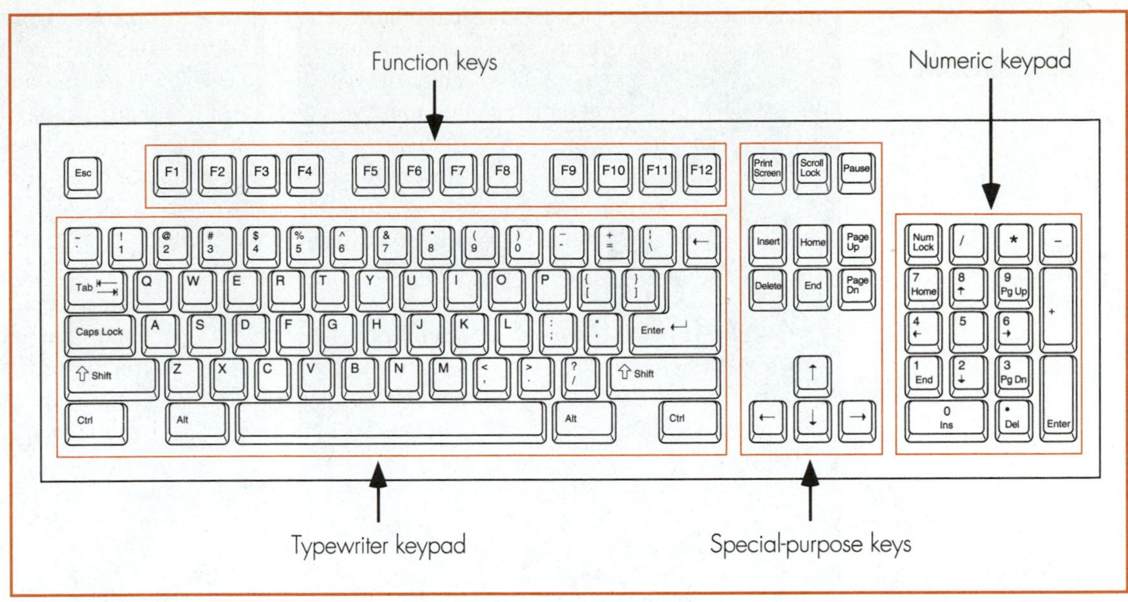

purpose keys (Fig. 24). These keys are located between the typewriter keypad and the numeric keypad. These keys are duplicates of some of the dual purpose keys on the numeric keypad.

In addition to the function keys, other special-purpose keys found on an enhanced keyboard include the following:

Keystroke	Action Resulting from Keystroke
[End]	Sends the cursor to the end of a line. A duplicate of this key is on the **[1]** key of the numeric keypad.
[Home]	Sends the cursor to the upper left-hand corner of the screen. A duplicate of this key is on the **[7]** key of the numeric keypad.
[Insert]	Toggles (turns on or off) insertion so that characters can be inserted at the cursor. A duplicate of this key is labelled **[Ins]** on the **[0]** key of the numeric keypad.
[PageUp]	Displays the previous screen. A duplicate of this key is labelled **[PgUp]** on the **[9]** key of the numeric keypad.
[PageDown]	Displays the next screen. A duplicate of this key is labelled **[PgDn]** on the **[3]** key of the numeric keypad.
[Pause]	Interrupts a process.
[Print Screen]	Sends the contents of the screen to the printer. On some keyboards, this key is labelled **[PrtSc]** and you may have to use it in conjunction with the **[Shift]** key.
←	Pressing once moves the cursor one character to the left. A duplicate of this key is on the **[4]** key of the numeric keypad.
→	Pressing once moves the cursor one character to the right. A duplicate of this key is on the **[6]** key of the numeric keypad.
↑	Pressing once moves the cursor one line up. A duplicate of this key is on the **[8]** key of the numeric keypad.
↓	Pressing once moves the cursor one line down. A duplicate of this key is on the **[2]** key of the numeric keypad.

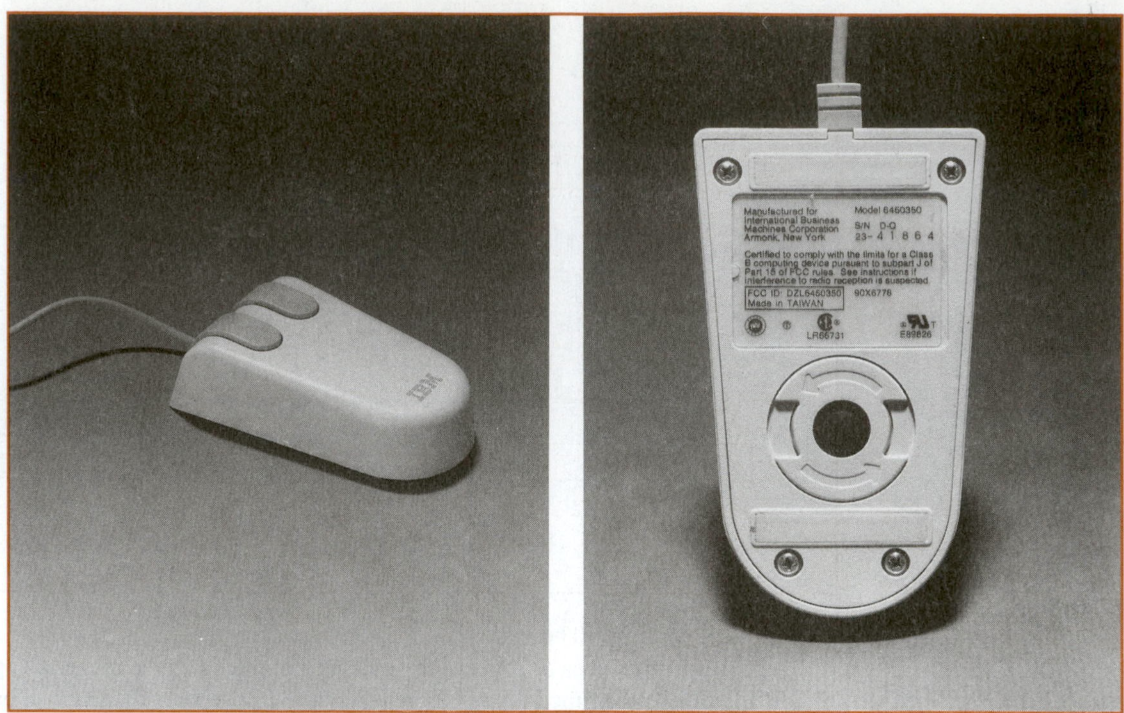

FIGURE 25

A mouse.

Although the keyboard is the most popular input device, it is not the only one. Any device that can enter data into the machine can be considered an input device.

Mouse A *mouse* (Fig. 25) is a device that is about the size and shape of a common field mouse (hence the name). It has a wire at one end, one, two, or three buttons on the top, and a ball sticking through a hole in the bottom. The mouse is grasped so that the index and middle fingers rest lightly on the buttons. Sliding the mouse along the desktop sends an electronic signal to the computer, which moves a pointer or cursor across the computer's display. The mouse is designed to supplement or even replace the **[arrow]** keys on the keyboard by providing an alternative way of locating the cursor on the screen.

Trackball A *trackball* (Fig. 26) is a device that looks like an upside-down mouse with an oversized ball. With this device, the ball is rotated by your fingers while the trackball case remains stationary. It has the same effect as that of a mouse.

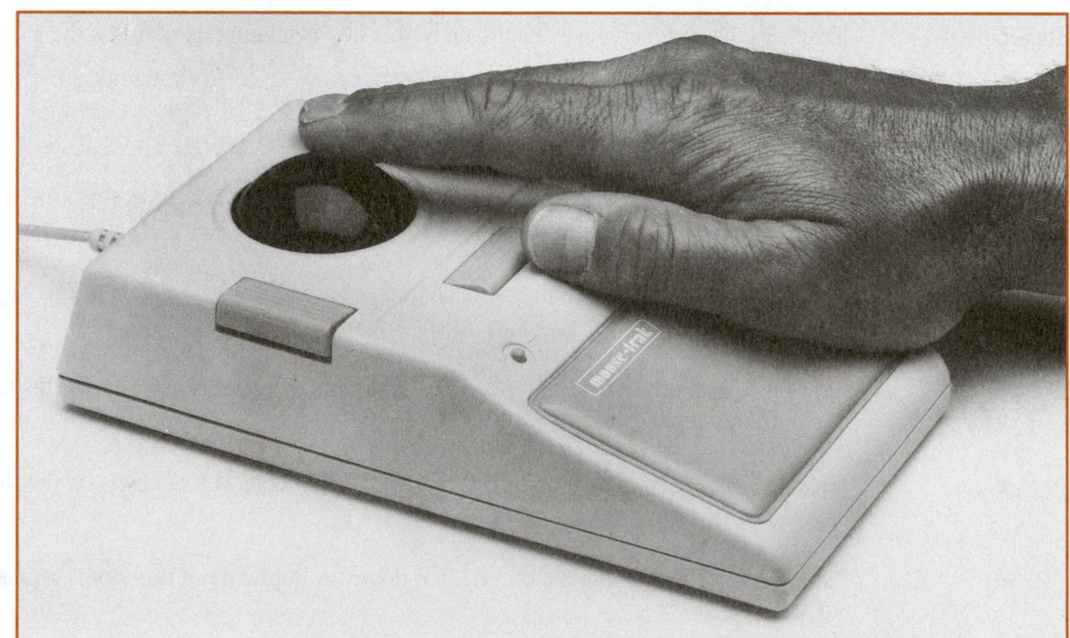

FIGURE 26

A trackball.

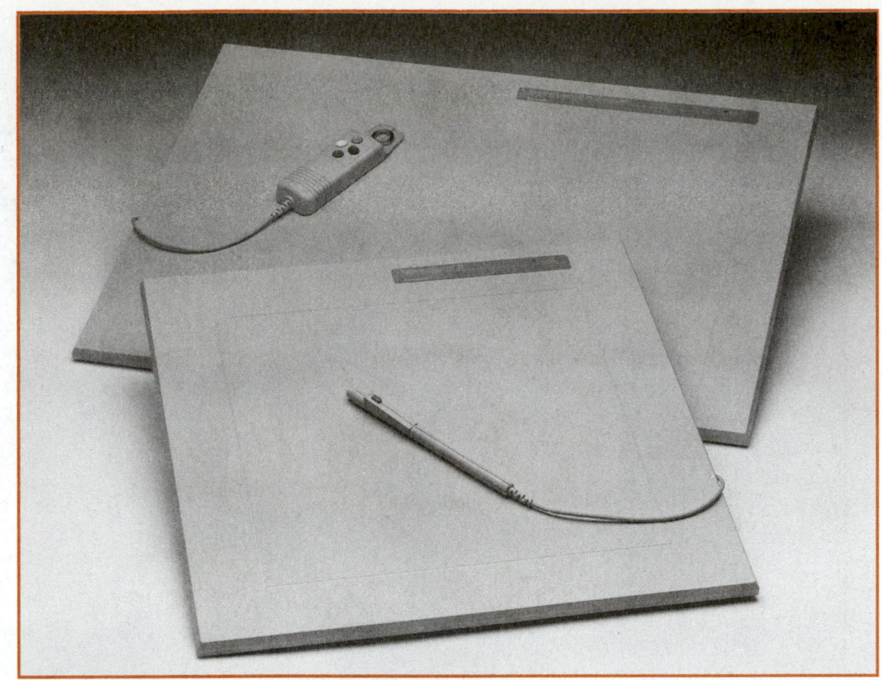

FIGURE 27

A graphics tablet.

Graphics Tablet A *graphics tablet* (Fig. 27) consists of a stylus much like a pencil and a flat surface that can record the location of the stylus in relation to a grid. The stylus may be used to draw graphic images, which are then encoded into binary data and sent to the computer to be stored as a graphic image.

Scanner A *scanner* (Fig. 28) is a device that can be used to convert graphics or text into a form that can be stored and/or interpreted by the computer. Scanners can be used to create computer graphics from photographs and drawings or they can be used to read and interpret typed or written textual material.

FIGURE 28

A scanner is used to convert graphics or text into a form that can be used or stored by the computer.

FIGURE 29

A touch screen allows the computer user to select objects or commands on the screen with the touch of a finger.

Touch Screen A *touchscreen* (Fig. 29) is a device that fits over the front of a computer's screen and allows the computer operator to select objects or commands on the screen by pointing with a finger. The location of the tip of the finger is recorded by measuring its horizontal and vertical coordinates, which then are interpreted by a microprocessor.

• *Output Devices* •

An **output device** takes data out of the computer and presents it to the user in some fashion. The monitor (sometimes called a *cathode ray tube* or *CRT*) and *printer* are examples of output devices.

Monitors Computer *monitors* work in much the same way as do television screens. An electron gun in the back of the monitor produces a beam of electrons which is directed toward the front of the screen by electromagnets (Fig. 30). When the electrons strike phosphor-coated dots on the inside of the screen, the dots glow for a short period of time. By using electromagnets to control the path of the electron beam, specific dots can be energized and appear on the front side of the screen to form characters or graphic images.

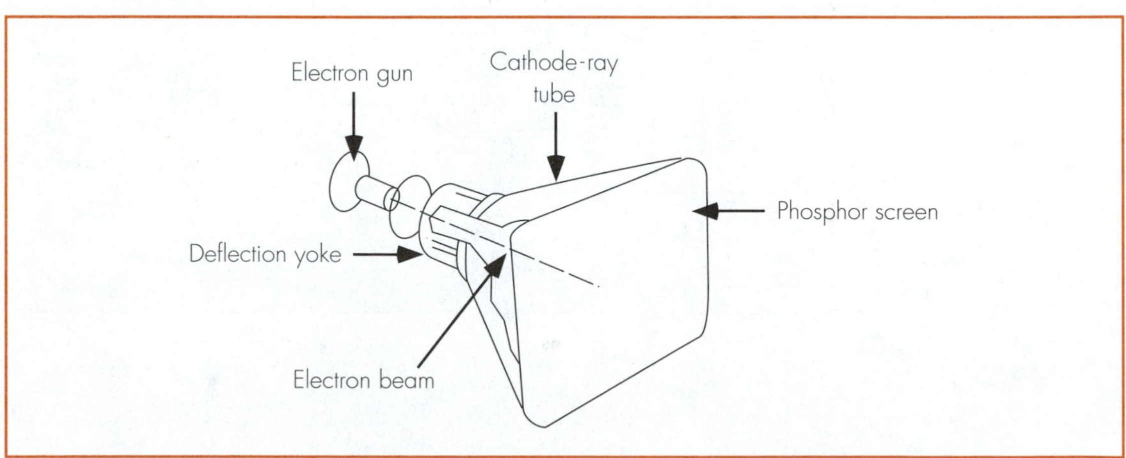

FIGURE 30

The inside of a cathode-ray tube.

FIGURE 31

Pixels energized to form the numeral 4.

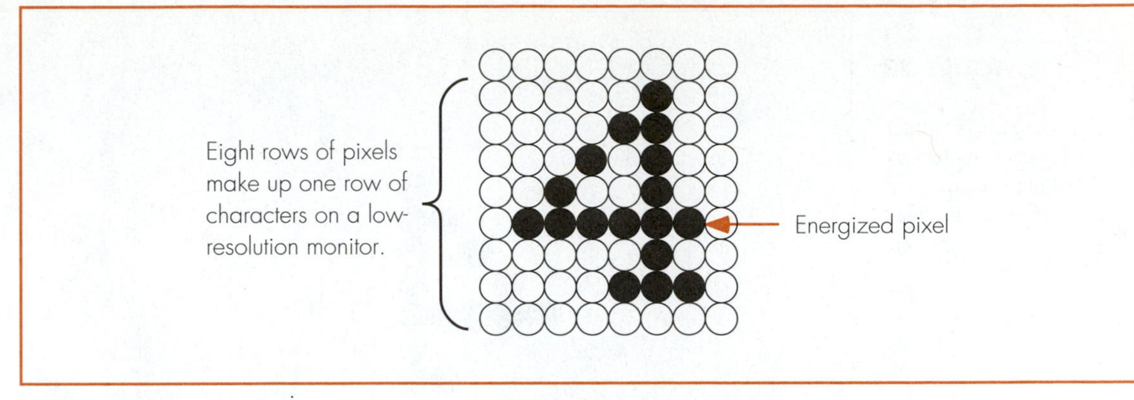

Each character displayed on the screen is made up of a number of dots called *pixels* (picture elements) (Fig. 31). Low-resolution monitors generally have pixels arranged in 160 columns by 200 rows, whereas medium-resolution monitors have a resolution of about 320 columns by 200 rows. High-resolution monitors may have as many as 640 columns by 480 rows and, therefore, have the sharpest images. Monitors generally display 25 rows and 80 columns of text for a total of 2000 characters on the screen at one time (Fig. 32).

The *refresh rate* of the monitor refers to the number of times per second that the beam of electrons sweeps across the screen to re-energize (refresh) the pixels. If the refresh rate is too low, the pixels will grow dim before they can be reenergized and the screen will appear to flicker. The higher the refresh rate the better and more stable the image. Refresh rates generally range from 15 to 30 times per second.

Monochrome monitors display only one color plus black (e.g., black and white, black and green, black and amber). *Text-only monochrome monitors* display crisp text but cannot display graphics without additional hardware. The original monitor for the IBM PC was a text-only monitor. *Composite monochrome monitors* can display both text and graphics. They tend to be inexpensive but the quality of the text is usually poor to fair.

Color monitors can display many different colors simultaneously. Some color monitors, called *RGB monitors*, have three electron guns, one each for red, green, and blue and three-color phosphors in the pixels. The three electron beams are aligned to strike the screen at the same location and by altering the intensity of the individual beams they may produce many different colors.

There are a number of different levels of resolution for color monitors. *CGA (Color Graphics Adapter) monitors* have the lowest resolution and can display only a limited number of colors at one time. *EGA (Enhanced Graphics Adapter) monitors* have a higher resolution and can display more colors. *VGA (Video Graphics Array) monitors* present the clearest images with the most colors.

FIGURE 32

Screen of a microcomputer's monitor.

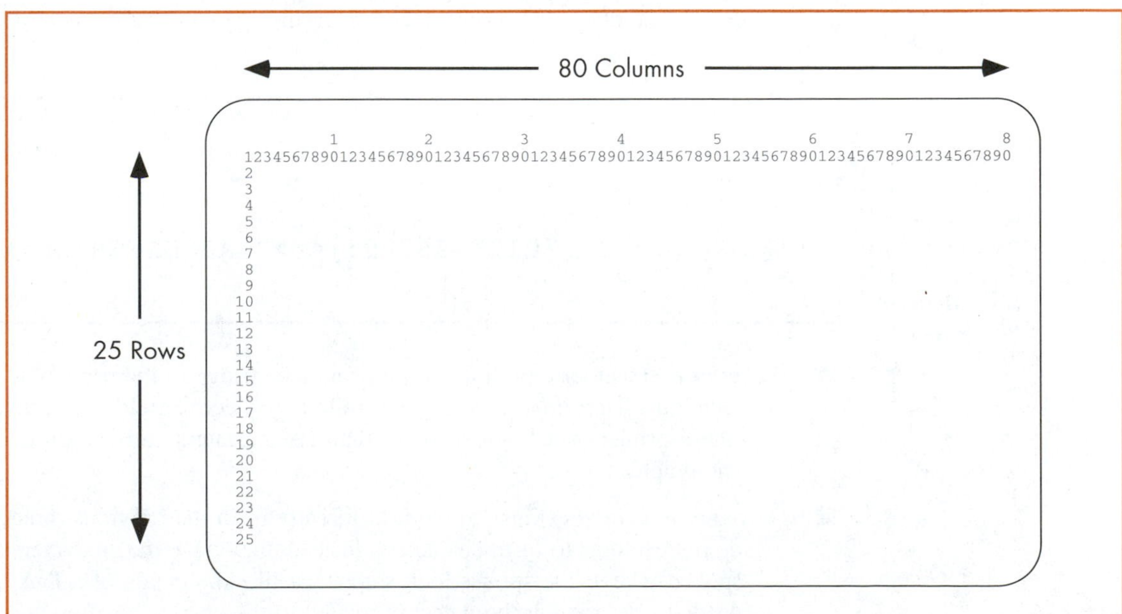

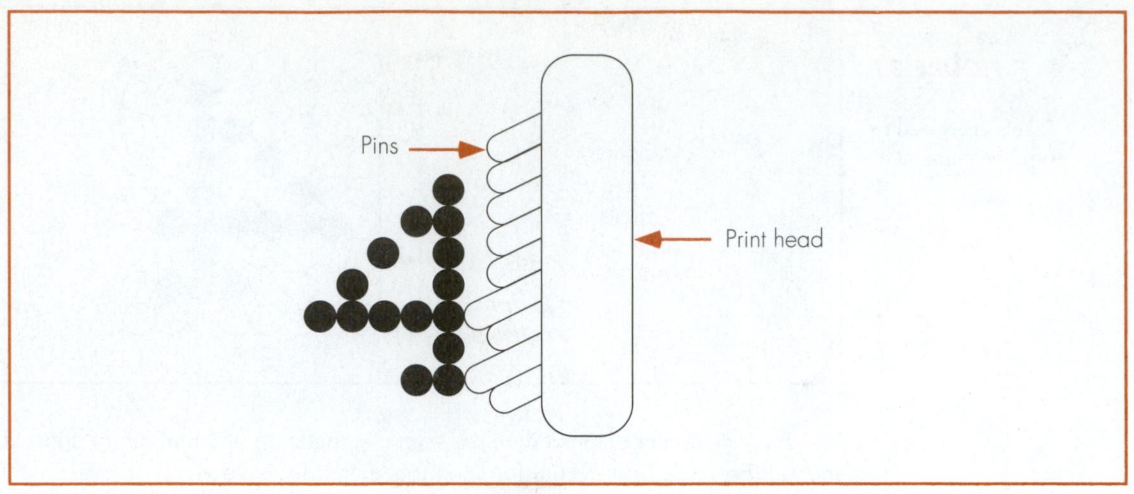

FIGURE 33

A dot matrix printer forms characters by striking selected pins through an inked ribbon.

Printers While monitors display images in a dynamic fashion, **hard copy** is obtained through the use of a printer. Like monitors, printers come in many types and resolutions.

- *Dot matrix printers* form images by printing small dots on the paper. The dots are formed by a vertical column of pins in a moving print head striking a piece of paper through an inked ribbon (Fig. 33). For each column of dots in the character, software and hardware instruct the printer head which pins to extend (to make a dot) and which to retract (to leave the dot uninked). Similar to the resolution of a monitor, the more pins used, the higher the quality of the printed output. Low-resolution dot matrix printers have 9 vertical pins while high-resolution printers have 24 vertical pins. The 24-pin models are called *near letter quality* because the dots are so small that the characters are almost indistinguishable from those produced by a typewriter. Dot matrix printers are the most common form of microcomputer printer used today. They typically print 50 to 250 dots per inch.
- *Laser printers* are similar to dot matrix printers in that they form images by printing dots (Fig. 34). However, instead of using mechanical pins and an inked ribbon, laser printers use a highly focused laser beam to electrostatically charge extremely small dots on a photosensitive drum. The drum then rotates across a reservoir containing tiny black dots called toner where only the charged parts of the drum pick up the toner. The drum rotates further across a piece of paper and deposits the toner, which is then bonded to the paper by heat. Standard laser printers have a resolution of 300 dots per inch and are quieter and faster than dot matrix printers. However, they generally are much more expensive.

FIGURE 34

```
!"#$%&'()*+,-./0123456789:;<=>?@ABCDEFGHIJKLMNOPQRSTUVWXYZ

!"#$%&'()*+,-./0123456789:;<=>?@ABCDEFGHIJKLMNOPQRSTUVWXYZ
```

Output from a dot matrix printer (*top*) and a laser printer (*bottom*).

- *Ink jet printers* shoot tiny drops of ink from a cartridge in the print head onto the paper. The location of the dots of ink is controlled by electric fields generated in the print head. These printers are less expensive than laser printers and can produce letter quality text and graphics.
- *Daisy wheel printers* (Fig. 35) work differently from the previous three printers in that they do not use dots to form characters. Instead, they have the characters already formed on a spoked wheel (the spokes look somewhat like the petals of a daisy). When a character needs to be printed, the wheel is rotated to the correct position and then a hammer hits the proper spoke which, in turn, strikes the page through an inked ribbon. Such printers,

FIGURE 35

A print wheel used on a daisy wheel printer.

like electric typewriters, are noisy and cannot print graphic images. The letters, however, are of very high quality.

• Storage Devices •

Storage devices are designed to hold data in some retrievable permanent or semipermanent form. Most microcomputers use magnetic disks in the form of floppy diskettes or hard disks. These magnetic disks are capable of permanently storing information by altering the magnetic field of a special coating on the surface of a plastic or metal-alloy disk-shaped platter.

Floppy **diskettes** (Fig. 36), also known as *flexible diskettes*, *floppies*, or simply *disks*, are small (usually $5\frac{1}{4}$ inches or $3\frac{1}{2}$ inches square), thin (.125 inch high), and flexible. Diskettes contain a very thin

FIGURE 36

Microcomputer $5\frac{1}{4}$-inch (*left*) and $3\frac{1}{2}$-inch (*right*) floppy diskettes.

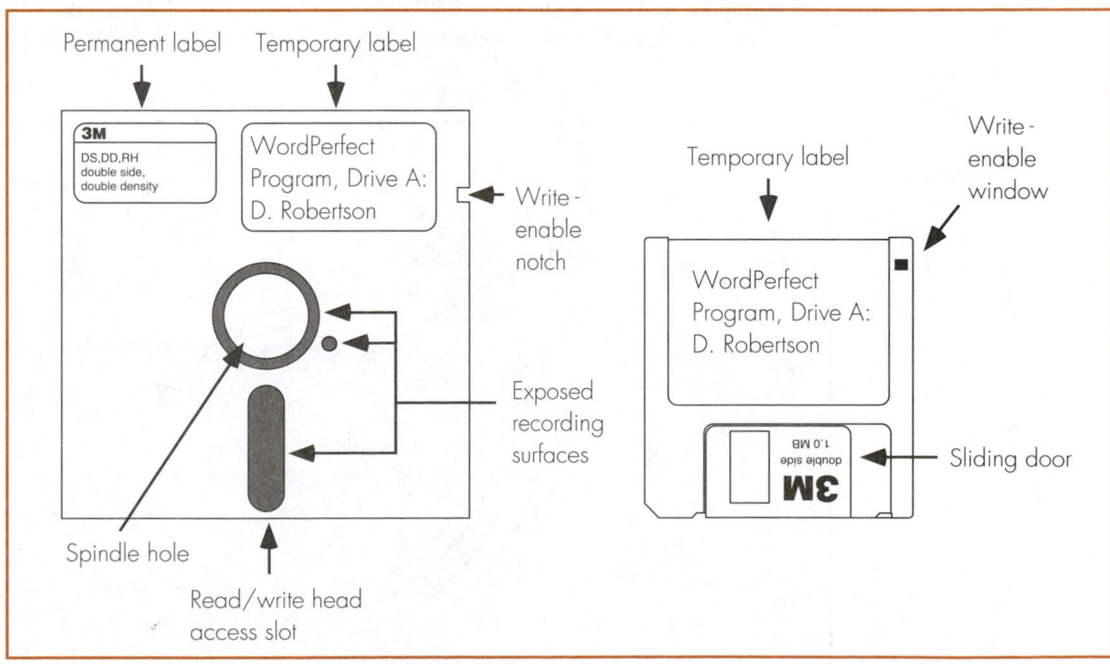

circular piece of plastic that is coated with an iron oxide capable of being magnetized. The $5\frac{1}{4}$-inch diskettes are encased in a flexible vinyl cover to protect them from dust and dirt while the $3\frac{1}{2}$-inch diskettes are enclosed in a stiff plastic case which affords even more protection and makes them less floppy (but more rugged).

The diskettes can be inserted into **disk drives**, which are mechanisms designed to read and write the magnetic codes in much the same way as a tape recorder reads and writes information on a recording tape. The IBM PC uses diskettes that are $5\frac{1}{4}$ inches on a side and can hold hundreds of thousands of characters of data. The IBM PS/2 microcomputers use diskettes that are $3\frac{1}{2}$ inches square and can store millions of characters of information. Table 1 lists the storage capacities of diskettes. Some microcomputers are capable of using both sizes of diskettes.

TABLE 1

Memory Capacities of $5\frac{1}{4}$-inch and $3\frac{1}{2}$-inch Floppy Diskettes

Physical Size	Specification	Approximate Capacity (in number of characters)
$5\frac{1}{4}$ inches	double sided double density	360K
$5\frac{1}{4}$ inches	high density	1,200K
$3\frac{1}{2}$ inches	double sided double density	720K
$3\frac{1}{2}$ inches	high density	1,440K

Before a diskette can be used to store information it must be electronically structured, or **formatted**, for use by a given brand and model of computer. The formatting process electronically partitions the diskette into invisible concentric circles called *tracks* and pie-shaped wedges called sectors. (Fig. 37) A $5\frac{1}{4}$-inch double-sided double-density diskette used by an IBM PC contains 40 tracks and 9 sectors on each side. Because each sector can hold 512,000 bytes of data the entire diskette can hold a total of 40 tracks x 9 sectors x 512 bytes per sector x 2 sides = 368,640 bytes of data. Such a diskette is referred to as a *360K diskette*.

When a diskette is inserted into a disk drive (Fig. 38) a part of the thin plastic inner disk is situated between the drive's *read/write heads* (two electromagnets attached to a moveable access arm). When information is to be written onto the diskette or read from it, the inner disk spins at high speed while the read/write head moves in and out in order to align itself with the proper location on the surface of the inner disk.

When information is to be read from the diskette, the electromagnets on the read/write head detect the magnetic field at various spots on the rotating inner disk. A magnetic field pointing in one direction on the inner disk will induce an electric current in a certain direction in the wires of the read/write head.

FIGURE 37

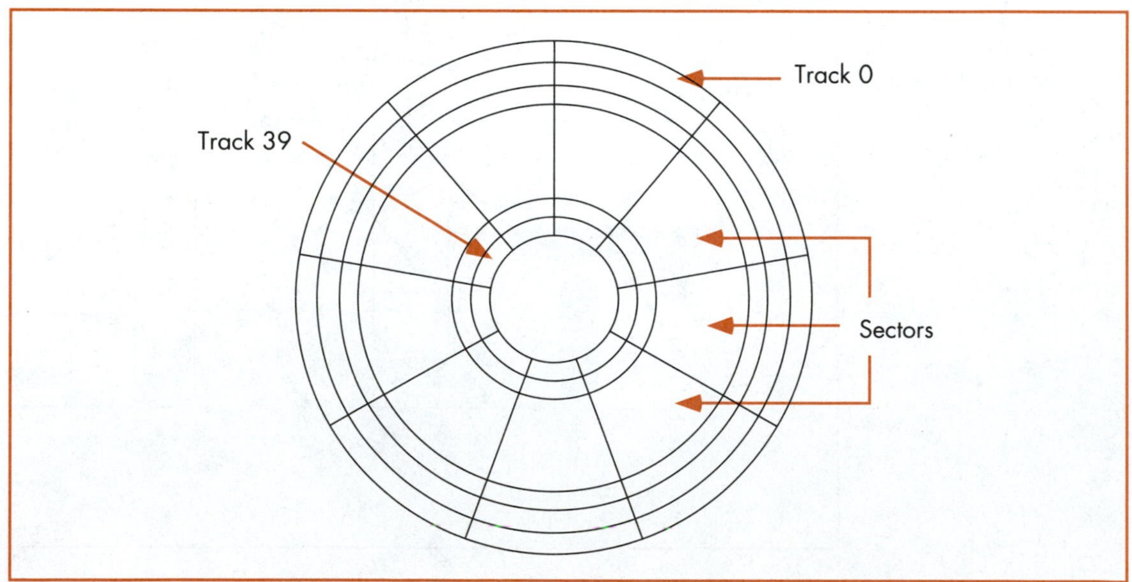

The electronic partitions of a $5\frac{1}{4}$-inch floppy diskette.

A magnetic field in the opposite direction on the inner disk will induce an electric current in the opposite direction in the read/write head. Current flowing in the two opposing directions corresponds to the 0s and 1s of a bit. This information is then interpreted by other hardware and software in the computer. When information is stored on the diskette during a write operation, the electromagnets in the read/write heads alter the directions of the magnetic fields on the inner disk at various spots and so store information at those locations.

Rules for Handling Floppy Diskettes Floppy diskettes are very fragile and must be given special care. If a diskette is "soiled" it is usually impossible to recover the information from it. If you spill a cup of coffee on a paper copy of a 50-page report you can still see the information, even though you may have to retype the report. If you spill coffee on a diskette that contains a 50-page report, the information is lost. Always keep the following rules in mind when handling floppy diskettes:

- If you are using a $5\frac{1}{4}$-inch diskette, be sure to hold it by the label end. If you touch any of the exposed recording surfaces the oils from your fingers may stick to the surface and make the information on that part of the inner disk unreadable. This is less of a problem with $3\frac{1}{2}$-inch diskettes because there are no exposed recording surfaces.
- Keep the diskette in its envelope or box when not in use. Laying the diskette on a desk top may allow dust to adhere to any exposed magnetic material and minute dust particles can cause errors when the diskette is read by the computer. Again, this is less of a problem with the $3\frac{1}{2}$-inch disks because of their protective cases. However, if the outside of your $3\frac{1}{2}$-inch diskette picks up dirt from a table top and then you insert the diskette into a disk drive, you may be transferring the dirt to the drive. This could damage the drive.
- If you are using a $5\frac{1}{4}$-inch diskette, only write on the diskette label using a felt tip pen. The force of writing with a ballpoint pen might go right through the vinyl cover and leave an impression on the magnetic material making that part of the inner disk unreadable by the computer.

FIGURE 38

Inside view of a $3\frac{1}{2}$-inch disk drive.

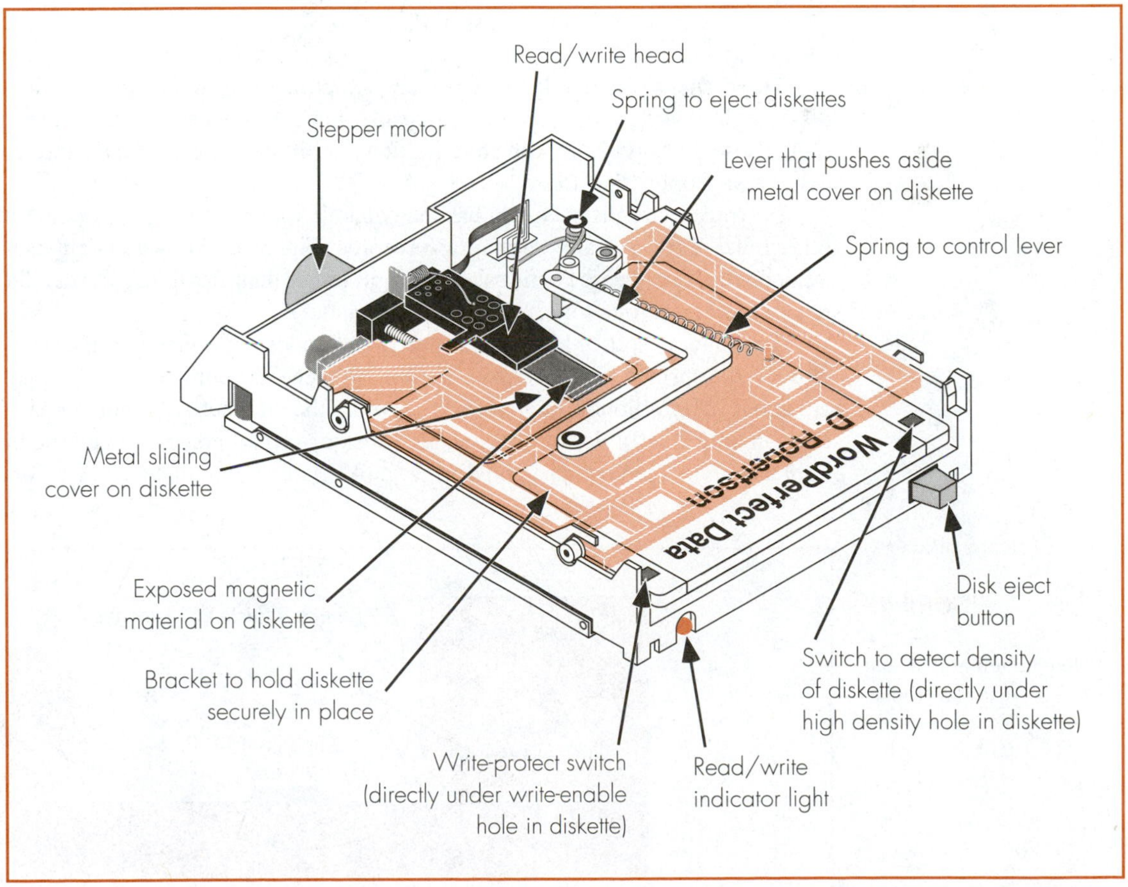

FIGURE 39

Inside view of a hard-disk drive.

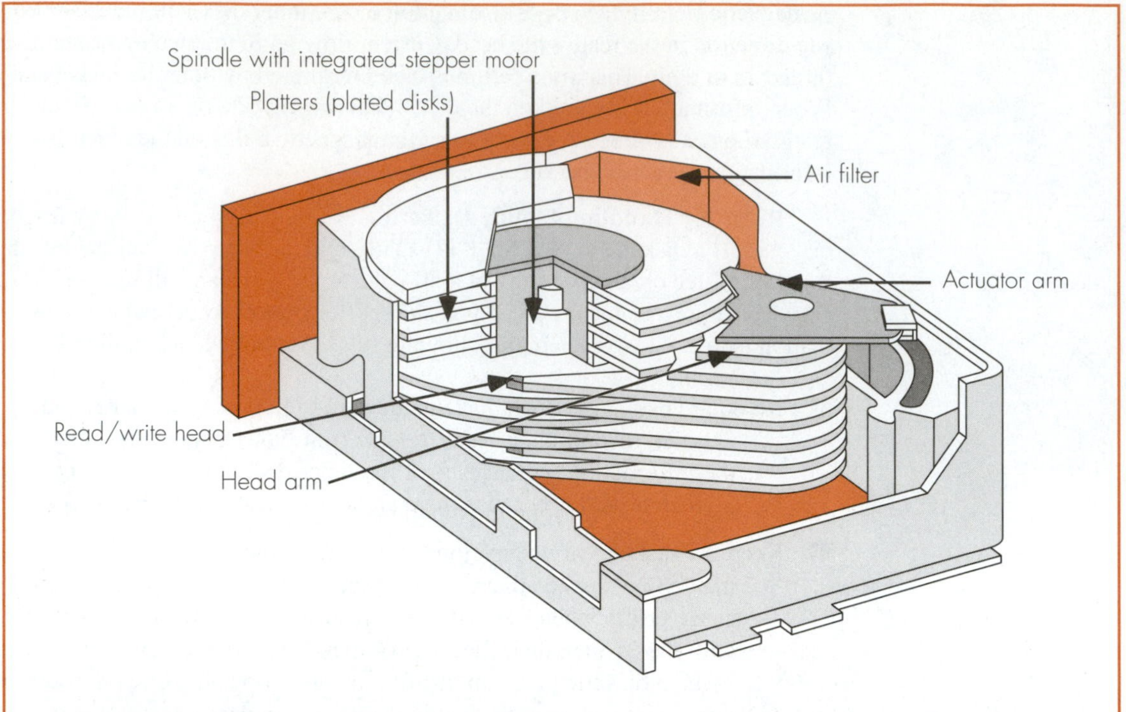

- Keep the diskette away from heat (e.g., radiators, the dashboard of your car), magnetic fields (magnets and motors), all liquids (coffee, water, cleaning liquids), and cigarette smoke (the smoke particles will coat the disk and the insides of the disk drive and could cause major problems).
- Do not bend the diskette. This can cause creases in the magnetic material on the inner disk and may result in the loss of data.

Hard Disks **Hard disks**, which are sometimes referred to as fixed disks, are similar to floppy diskettes in that they store data magnetically, but they are usually permanently encased in the system unit. These disks typically can store millions or billions of bits of data and read and write data much faster than floppy diskettes.

A typical hard disk actually has many parallel inner disks (called platters) stacked one on top of the other much like a stack of phonograph records (Fig. 39). The platters are usually made of aluminum treated with a magnetic coating and are rigid rather than flexible. Between the rows of platters are read/write heads (one for each side of each platter).

The platters spin at high speed (nearly 100 miles per hour) with the read/write heads floating very close to the surface (about 10 millionths of an inch). By comparison, a smoke particle and a fingerprint are about 250 millionths of an inch thick while the thickness of a human hair is about 4,000 millionths of an inch (Fig. 40). For this reason, hard-disk drive platters and read/write heads are enclosed in an air-tight casing to keep out dust and dirt. A smoke particle that makes its way onto a hard-disk platter could

FIGURE 40

Separation of disk and read/write head.

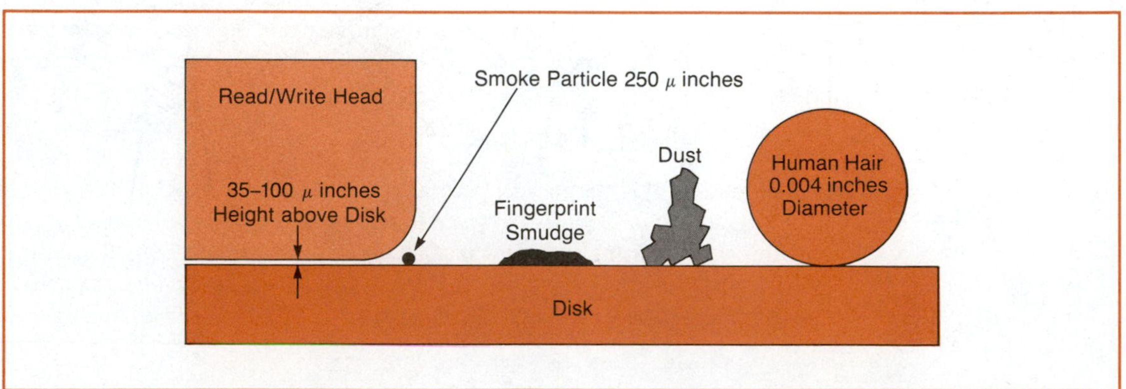

crash into the read/write head and cause it to destroy a part of the platter or the head itself (this is called a *head crash*). Also, care must be taken to ensure that the system unit containing the hard disk is not subjected to vibrations when the computer is operating. Vibration could also cause a head crash.

Computer Software

The set of instructions that direct the operation of the computer hardware are referred to as **software**. Software provides the interface between the hardware and the human operator. Examples of software include computer programs written in a high-level computer language such as BASIC or Pascal and applications programs including word processors such as WordPerfect, spreadsheets such as Lotus 1-2-3, and database management programs such as dBASE. There are two general types of computer programs: systems software and applications software.

• Systems Software •

Systems software are sets of instructions that tell the computer's hardware how to work. Some of the instructions are contained in the read only memory (ROM) of the computer and some are contained in the *disk operating system (DOS)* of the computer. They direct the actions of the printer, the CPU, the disk drives, the keyboard, and the monitor and help them run quickly and efficiently. They are usually written for a specific brand of machine and so cannot be transported to another brand. They are usually supplied by the manufacturer and are rarely modified by the computer user.

• Applications Software •

Applications software are sets of instructions that tell the computer how to solve specific types of problems. Word processing and spreadsheet programs are examples of applications software. They work in conjunction with the system software to enable the computer user to communicate with the hardware of the computer.

Operating System

The **operating system** is a special set of programs that monitors and controls the operations of the system. These programs tell the computer how to do specific tasks such as sending output to the monitor, receiving input from the keyboard, and driving the printer.

IBM microcomputers use operating system programs stored both in hardware and on disks. The programs in the hardware are in the ROM. These programs are available whenever the machine is switched on. The rest of the operating system programs are on disk. These are the so-called DOS programs. Such programs are needed to carry out complex operations. For more information on DOS, see pages C32–47.

Computers and Vending Machines

Before you begin to actually work on the computer, a word of advice is in order. Computers are electronic machines that cannot think for themselves—they can do only what you, the user, tell them to do. The clever men and women who designed, built, and programmed the computers that you will use did such a good job that the computer may sometimes seem to have a life of its own, with a mentality and an ability to reason. However, computers can only follow instructions.

It may help you to think of the computer as a vending machine. If you give it the correct instructions (push the right buttons), it will give you what you want. If you give it the wrong instructions, you will not get what you want and will probably become very frustrated. As with a vending machine, the only way you can damage the computer is to physically abuse it in some way. So, don't be afraid to experiment and try new things. Just think before you push the buttons.

As you work with the computer, keep this in mind. If you get confused or frustrated, you can always simply turn off the machine and start all over. Generally though, turning off the power is not a good idea; it is like stopping your car by running it into a tree. However, in an emergency (e.g., the brakes on your car have failed), you can do it. As long as the little red (or green) light on the disk drive is not on, you will not hurt the machine, although you may lose data and have to start over again.

Assumptions and Conventions Used in This Book

Because of their large size, programs such as WordPerfect, Lotus 1-2-3, and dBASE are designed to be operated on a hard-disk system. In this book, we will assume that you are working on such a system, that you are using version 4.0 of DOS (actually, any version 2.0 or higher will suffice), and that WordPerfect version 5.1 (version 5.0 can be used for most of the operations), Lotus 1-2-3 Release 2.2, and dBASE software have been installed on the hard disk. We will also assume that your computer has the following subdirectories (see p. C36 for more information on subdirectories) stored on it (your instructor may have set up the subdirectories differently for your school's computer lab):

DOS contains all DOS files.

WP51 contains all WordPerfect version 5.1 files.

123 contains all Lotus 1-2-3 files.

DB contains all dBASE files.

BA contains all BASIC files.

We will also provide pertinent information for those of you working on a two-drive system. In any case, your course instructor may give you different directions for accessing the programs or for saving data files for the particular system available to you in your school's computer lab.

We have included hundreds of sample screens (called **screen dumps**) that show you exactly how your computer's screen should look after completing various procedures. In those screen dumps we have used the following conventions in order to make things clearer:

- Text typed by the computer user (i.e., you) is underlined.
- The symbol ↵ means that the **[Enter]** key has been pressed.
- `Text that appears on the computer's screen is shown using this style of type.`
- **Our comments that appear in the screen dumps are in this style of type.**
- Sometimes, parts of the screen are enclosed in **dotted boxes** for illustration.

Introduction to DOS

For the rest of this chapter, and for all the chapters that follow, we will assume that you are sitting in front of a computer and that you will try the operations described. However, you will find it very helpful to quickly read through a few sections completely before actually attempting to do the keystrokes. This will give you an overview of the topic. It may seem like previewing the material will take longer that just sitting down and typing at the computer, but in the long run you will learn the material faster and with greater understanding and fewer mistakes.

• Booting the Computer •

To **boot** the computer means to start it by transferring instructions (usually part of the operating system) from a storage device (usually a floppy or hard disk) into the main memory of the machine. A *cold boot* occurs when the electrical power to the computer must be turned on in order to start the machine. If the power is already on, the startup process is called a *warm boot*.

To boot the computer do the following:

1. Begin with the power to the computer turned off.

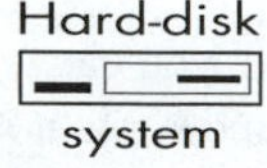

IF YOU ARE USING A HARD-DISK SYSTEM, be sure the floppy-diskette drive is empty before turning on the machine.

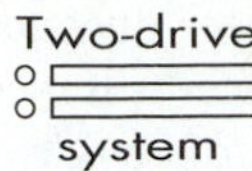

IF YOU ARE USING A TWO-DRIVE SYSTEM, you will have to insert the DOS diskette into the A: drive before turning on the machine. Depending on the particular computer you are using, the A: drive is the top drive or the left-hand drive.

- If you are using a $5\frac{1}{4}$-inch diskette you will have to open the door of the drive by gently flipping up a lever on the front of the drive (ask if you need help!). If you are using a $3\frac{1}{2}$-inch diskette, there is no lever on the disk drive.
- Grasp the DOS diskette by the label, with the label side up, and slowly insert the diskette all the way into the A: drive. Do not force the diskette—it should slide in fairly easily (ask if you need help!).
- If you are using a $5\frac{1}{4}$-inch diskette, close the disk-drive door by moving the lever again. There is no lever on $3\frac{1}{2}$-inch disk drives.

2. Turn on the system unit and the monitor. The power switch may be on the front, side, or back of the system unit; the monitor may have a separate power switch or it may get its electrical power directly from the system unit (ask if you need help!).
3. The computer will begin an internal check of its main memory. In a few seconds you will hear a beep, the light on the disk drive will go on, and you will hear the drive begin to spin. **Never remove or insert a diskette when the drive light is on or you may damage the disk drive.** The light means the computer is reading information from the disk or writing information to the disk.
4. What you see next will depend on the system you are using.

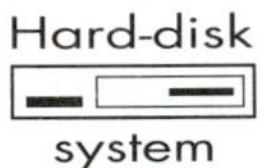

IF YOU ARE USING A HARD-DISK SYSTEM, your computer probably has a battery-operated clock that enables it to keep track of the date and time while the power is turned off. In that case, when the disk access light goes out some information will be displayed and then the system prompt **C:\>** will appear.

The blinking line to the right of the system prompt is called the **cursor**. It shows where text will appear on the screen when it is typed using the keyboard.

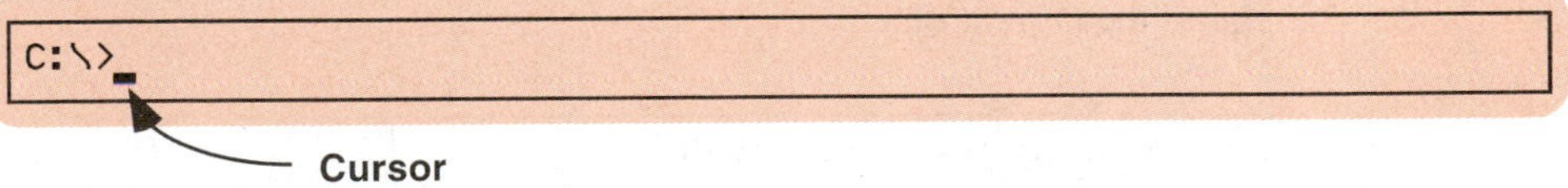

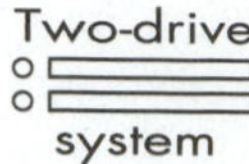

IF YOU ARE USING A TWO-DRIVE SYSTEM, your computer may not have a battery-operated clock that enables the computer to keep track of the date and time while the power is turned off. In that case, when the disk access light goes out the computer will ask you to provide the current date:

```
Current date is Tue 01-01-1980
Enter new date (mm-dd-yy): _   <-- Cursor
```

The blinking line is called the **cursor**. It shows where text will appear on the screen when it is typed using the keyboard. The computer is asking you to enter the current date in the form **mm-dd-yy** (i.e., two digits for the month, then a dash, then two digits for the day, then a dash, then two digits for the year). For example, if the current date is February 10, 1991, you would type **2-10-91**. After typing the date you must press the **[Enter]** key. This key is located on the right-hand side of the typewriter part of the keyboard and contains the symbol ↵. If you type a date that is not in the correct form of month-day-year (e.g., if you type **February 10, 1991**), the computer will respond with the following (the underlined parts were typed by the user and the rest was typed by the computer; the symbol ↵ means that you need to press **[Enter]**.):

```
Current date is Tue 01-01-1980
Enter new date (mm-dd-yy): February 10, 1991↵

Invalid date
Enter new date (mm-dd-yy): _
```

Date must be in the proper form or you will get an error message

If this happens, simply type the date again in the proper form (e.g., **2-10-91**).

If you notice that you have made a typing mistake before you press **[Enter]**, you can use the **[Backspace]** key (top row, right-hand side of the typewriter part of the keyboard) to back up and make changes.

5. After typing the date (if necessary) and pressing the **[Enter]** key, the computer may request the current time:

```
Current date is Tue 01-01-1980
Enter new date (mm-dd-yy): February 10, 1991↵

Invalid date
Enter new date (mm-dd-yy): 2-10-91↵
Current time is 12:00:44.48a
Enter new time: _
```

Computer may ask you to enter the current time of day

The time displayed (**12:00:44.48a**) is the time that has elapsed (44.48 seconds) since the computer was booted with the DOS disk (the computer assumes that it was booted at 12:00 midnight). The time is given in the form:

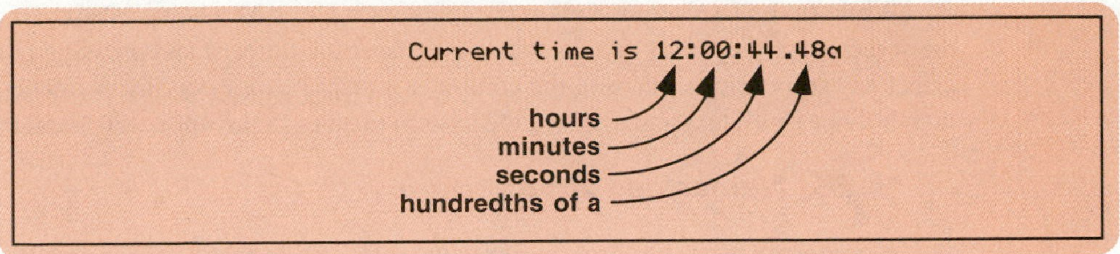

Type in the current time, using a 24-hour clock (e.g., **16:30** for 4:30 p.m.; it is not necessary to type the seconds). After you have pressed **[Enter]**, the following will be displayed:

```
Current date is Tue 01-01-1980
Enter new date (mm-dd-yy): February 10, 1991

Invalid date
Enter new date (mm-dd-yy): 2-10-91
Current time is 12:00:44.48a
Enter new time: 16:30


Microsoft(R) MS-DOS(R) Version 4.01
             (C)Copyright Microsoft Corp 1981-1988

A> <——————— System prompt is A> or A:\> for a two-drive system
```

The **C:\>** (or **A>**) at the bottom of the screen is called the *system prompt*. Its appearance means that you currently are in the *DOS environment* (see p. W4) and that the computer is ready to carry out the user's commands. It also indicates that if information is to be read from or written to a disk, that disk will be the one in the C: (or A:) drive. When the **C:\>** is displayed, we say that the C: drive is the *default* drive. You have now successfully booted the computer and are ready to use its power to help you solve problems.

For your information and reference, a summary of selected DOS commands appears on page W219 of the Appendix. Also, a keyboard template for DOS is located at the back of this book. If your keyboard has 12 function keys along the top, cut out the two halves of the template, tape the ends together, and place the template around the function keys. If your keyboard has 10 function keys along the left-hand side, you still may use the top half of the template, but the bottom half must be cut off.

• Printing the Contents of the Screen •

It is often useful to have a printed copy (called **hard copy**) of the computer display for future reference. In later chapters, we will discuss a number of different ways of getting hard copy. For now, the simplest way to print the contents of the displayed text is to use the **[Print Screen]** key. This key is located in different places depending on the keyboard you are using. On the standard keyboard, it is located on the lower right-hand side, between the letter keys and the numeric keypad, and is labeled **PrtSc**. On the enhanced keyboard, it is located on the right-hand side of the top row and is labeled **Print Screen**.

Before using the **[Print Screen]** key, you must be sure that a printer is attached to your computer, that the power to the printer is turned on, that the printer is properly loaded with paper, and that the "On Line" status light (if your printer has one) is on. The status light is used to indicate that the printer is able to receive instructions from the computer. If the light is off the printer will not be able to print. If your printer is shared with other computers you may have to select other switches before using it. See your instructor if you need help.

To actually print the contents of the display, press **[Print Screen]** (or **[PrtSc]**). (Note: On some keyboards and systems, you have to hold down **[Shift]** while you press **[Print Screen]**.) In a few seconds, the printer will produce a copy (screen dump) of the contents of the screen. Get a screen dump of the booting process now by turning on the power to the printer and then pressing **[Print Screen]**.

While in the DOS environment (i.e., while **C:\>** or **A>** is displayed) you can clear the contents of the screen by typing **CLS** (which stands for **CL**ear the **S**creen) and pressing **[Enter]**. **CLS** does not affect any information that is in the computer's main memory or any permanent information stored on disk but erases all text and displays the system prompt in the upper left-hand corner of the screen.

• File Names and Subdirectories •

A computer *file* is a collection of related information that is stored as a logical unit in the memory of the computer. Most users need to deal with only three types of files:

- System files, which contain instructions to enable the computer to carry out its normal operating procedures such as reading data from disks, displaying information on the screen, or sending information to the printer.
- Programs, which contain instructions for the computer to follow to accomplish specific tasks such as word processing or database management.
- Data files, which contain raw or processed data to be used by the programs. These might include memos you created using WordPerfect or worksheets you created using Lotus 1-2-3.

Hard disks can store thousands of files. In order to help organize the files so that they are readily accessible, the files on most hard disks are grouped into logical units called **subdirectories**. Think of a hard disk as a room that contains a number of filing cabinets, each of which contains a number of drawers, each of which contains many folders, which themselves contain many documents (Fig. 41). The **root (main) directory** can be thought of as the room itself while the file cabinets, drawers, and folders can be thought of as subdirectories.

In this book we will use files related to DOS, WordPerfect, Lotus 1-2-3, dBASE III PLUS, and BASIC. It would make sense to set up subdirectories for each of these so that if, for example, you want to find a WordPerfect memo, you (and the computer) do not have to search through all the file names on the hard disk; instead, you could simply go to the WordPerfect subdirectory and search for the memo there. This makes things much easier for both the user and the computer (it can operate faster with subdirectories). If you are using a two-drive system, you can think of each disk as a subdirectory (i.e., each

FIGURE 41

Subdirectories of the root (or main) directory help to keep files organized.

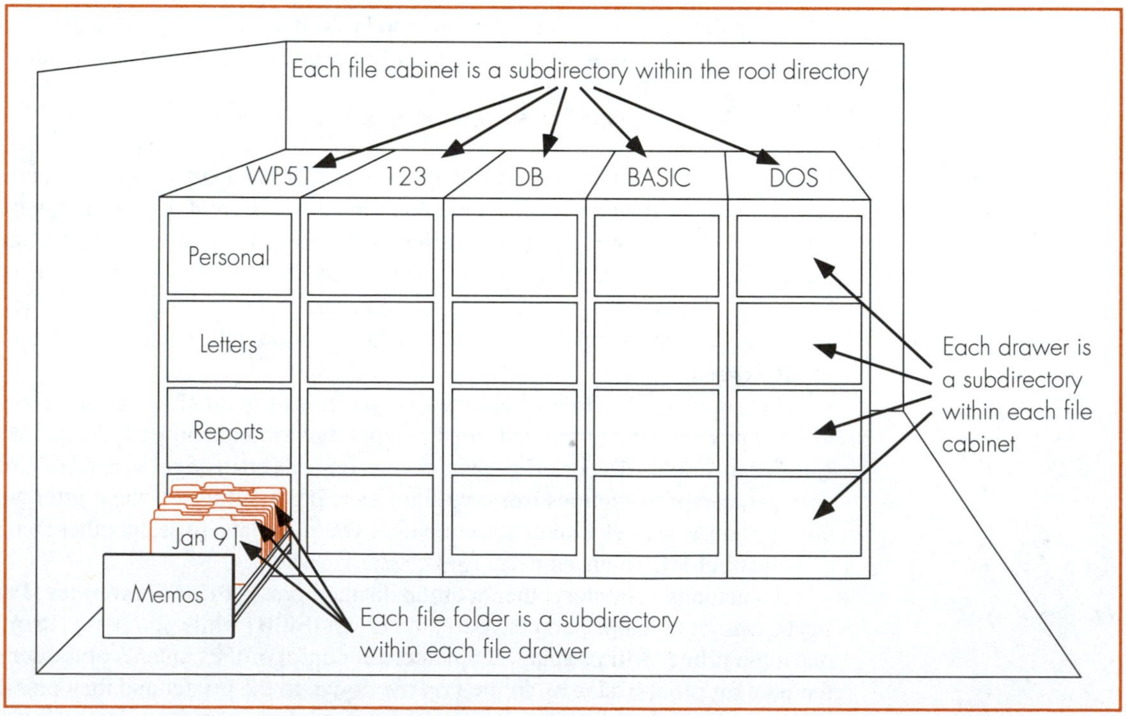

disk contains lots of related files). Subdirectories can be set up on floppy diskettes also. For more information on subdirectories (how to create, move between, and remove), see page W216 of the Appendix.

Aside from the obvious organizational advantage of subdirectories, they are necessary for storing large numbers of files on both floppy diskettes and hard drives. For example, the maximum number of files that can usually be stored in the root directory of a $5\frac{1}{4}$-inch double-sided double-density diskette is 112 (for a $3\frac{1}{2}$-inch high-density diskette the number is 224). This means that even if there is enough room on the diskette the operating system will not let you save more than 112 files (or 224 files for a high-density diskette). However, if you place some or all of the files in subdirectories you can exceed these numbers.

We have used the term *logical unit* when describing subdirectories. You should realize that grouping things into logical units may be quite different from grouping them into physical units. For example, the names listed in a telephone directory are grouped into a logical unit (alphabetical) even though the physical units (the people represented by the names) are not physically located next to each other. The organization of files and directories is analogous to this. The files in a single subdirectory may not be physically located next to each other on the disk (in fact, they probably are not). Likewise, the files themselves may be broken up into many physical units and stored in different parts of the disk (this is called *file fragmentation*). This physical arrangement is usually of no concern to the computer user. However, if a hard drive becomes highly fragmented (i.e., if many of the files are broken up into many separate physical units) it will take longer to access the files because the read/write head of the disk drive has to move to more locations to access the individual file pieces. When this happens, running a program called a disk optimizer, such as PC Tools Delux, will rearrange the files into a more efficient configuration.

• Listing Computer Files •

The directory (**DIR**) command can be used to get a listing of the names of files stored on the disk. For example, typing **DIR** ↵ will display something like the following (the exact contents of your display will be different):

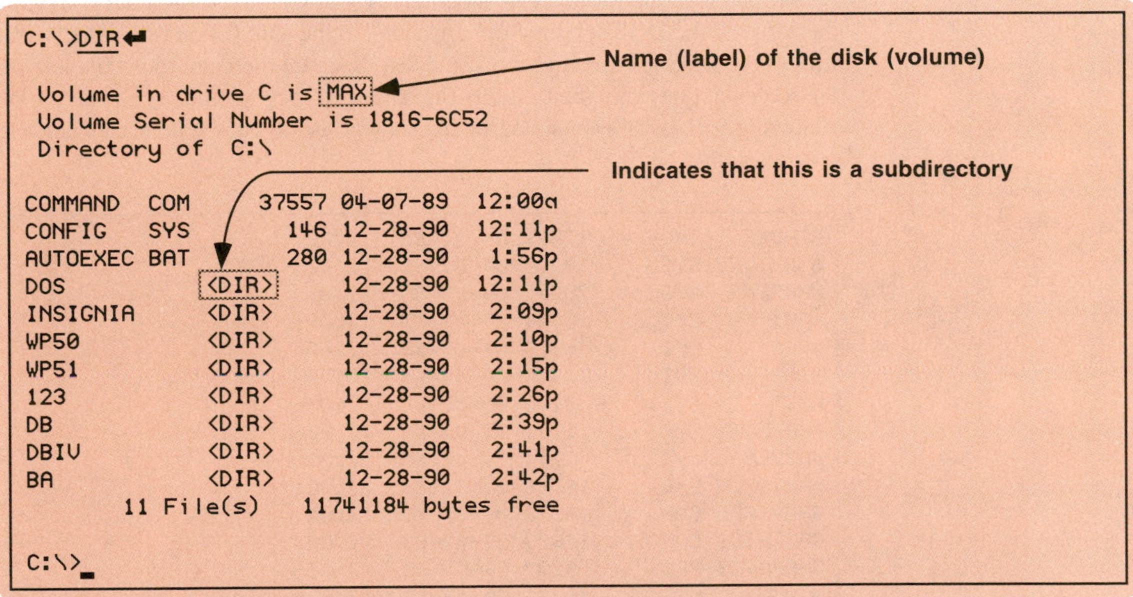

If you use **[Print Screen]**, you will get a screen dump (i.e., a hard copy) of the screen, which is required for Homework Exercise 1 (see p. C47).

The above screen displays the root or main directory of the hard drive C:. Notice that after the computer has listed the directory, the system prompt, **C:\>** (or **A>** or **A:\>**), is displayed and the computer is again ready to receive instructions.

The first line of the display, **Volume in drive C is MAX**, indicates that the **Volume** (DOS refers to a disk as a **Volume**) in the C: drive is called **MAX**. Giving each disk a name (which DOS refers to as a *label*) helps to distinguish one disk from another. The second line of the display, **Volume Serial Number is 1816-6C52** provides a unique reference number for the disk. The third line of the display **Directory of C:**, means that the computer is listing the contents of the root directory of the disk in the C: drive. The root directory is the single main directory of a disk (the other directories are referred to as subdirectories) and is indicated by the back slash, ****. The rest of the display contains information on the files and subdirectories stored on the disk. File names consist of one to eight characters, with an optional one-, two-, or three-character extension that is attached to the file name with a period. File names may contain the letters of the alphabet, the digits **0** through **9**, and some special characters including **#**, **$**, **&**, *****, **–**, **(**, and **)**. For example, **CONFIG.SYS**, **P#2**, **PAY(MAY).89**, and **IRS3** are allowable file names. The five columns in the list contain the following information:

Column	Example	Meaning
1	**COMMAND**	The name of the file is **COMMAND**.
2	**COM**	The extension is **COM**. The full name of the file is **COMMAND.COM** but the period between **COMMAND** and **COM** is not displayed in the directory listing.
3	**37577**	The size of this file is 37,577 bytes. Each byte represents one character (thus, file **COMMAND.COM** contains 37,577 characters).
4	**04-07-89**	The date the file was last modified. The date is given with the two digits on the left representing the month (**04** for April), the two middle digits representing the day (**07**), and two right-most digits representing the year (**89** for 1989).
5	**12:00a**	The time of day when the file was last modified.

The phrase, **11 File(s)   11741184 bytes free**, at the bottom of the screen indicates that 11 files and/or subdirectories are in this directory and that 11,741,184 bytes of space are available (**free**) on the disk. This means that you can store almost 12 million additional characters on the disk.

To get a listing of the DOS subdirectory you would use the **DIR** command again but this time with the name of the DOS subdirectory appended to the end. If you type **DIR \DOS ↵** the names of all the files in the DOS subdirectory will be listed. Because there are more file names than can be displayed on the screen at one time, the first few file names will *scroll* (move) off the top of the screen and only the following will remain (many of the names you see on your screen may be different from those illustrated here):

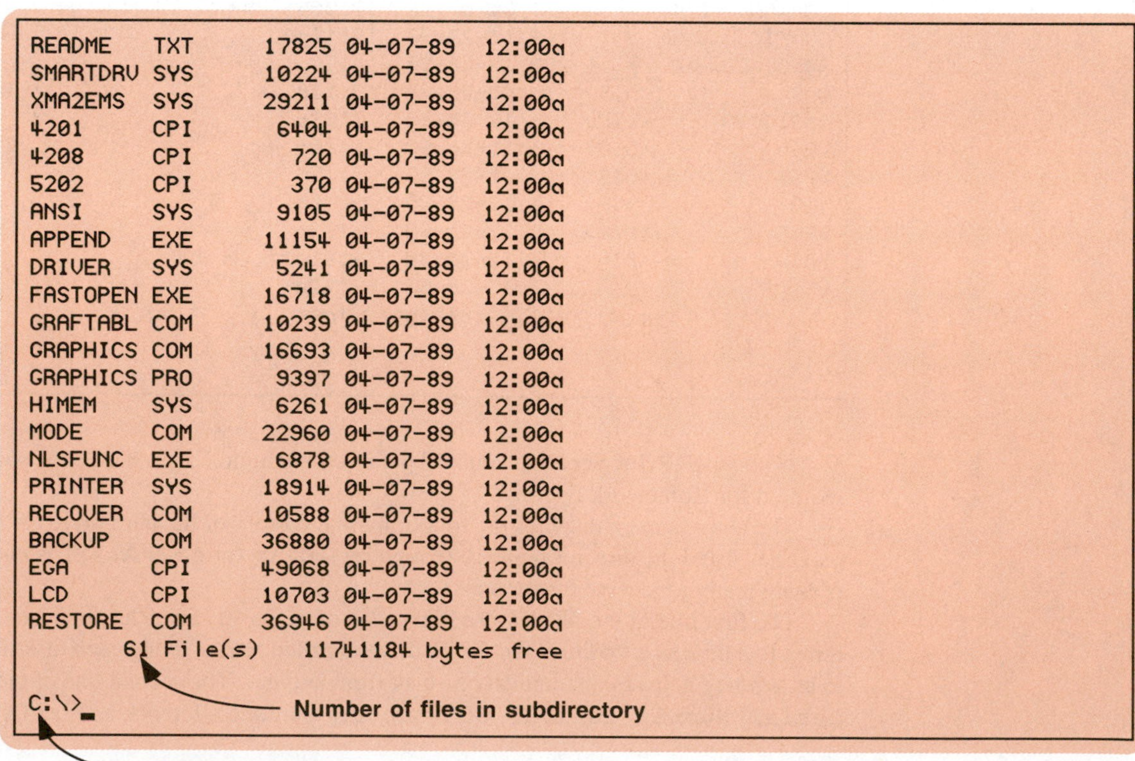
```
README   TXT     17825 04-07-89  12:00a
SMARTDRV SYS     10224 04-07-89  12:00a
XMA2EMS  SYS     29211 04-07-89  12:00a
4201     CPI      6404 04-07-89  12:00a
4208     CPI       720 04-07-89  12:00a
5202     CPI       370 04-07-89  12:00a
ANSI     SYS      9105 04-07-89  12:00a
APPEND   EXE     11154 04-07-89  12:00a
DRIVER   SYS      5241 04-07-89  12:00a
FASTOPEN EXE     16718 04-07-89  12:00a
GRAFTABL COM     10239 04-07-89  12:00a
GRAPHICS COM     16693 04-07-89  12:00a
GRAPHICS PRO      9397 04-07-89  12:00a
HIMEM    SYS      6261 04-07-89  12:00a
MODE     COM     22960 04-07-89  12:00a
NLSFUNC  EXE      6878 04-07-89  12:00a
PRINTER  SYS     18914 04-07-89  12:00a
RECOVER  COM     10588 04-07-89  12:00a
BACKUP   COM     36880 04-07-89  12:00a
EGA      CPI     49068 04-07-89  12:00a
LCD      CPI     10703 04-07-89  12:00a
RESTORE  COM     36946 04-07-89  12:00a
       61 File(s)   11741184 bytes free

C:\>_
```

If, for some reason you need to abort (stop) the **DIR** command (or most other commands) while it is executing, press **[Ctrl-C]** (i.e., hold down the **[Ctrl]** key and, while holding down the **[Ctrl]** key, tap the **[C]** key). This will display **^C** and then the system prompt **C:\>**.

To stop the first few file names from scrolling off the top of the screen, type **DIR \DOS/P ↵**. The **/P** stands for **P**aginate (to group the output into pages or screens of information). The following will be displayed:

```
.              <DIR>      04-05-90    8:37a
..             <DIR>      04-05-90    8:37a
DOSSHELL BAT          196 02-10-90    6:59p
COMMAND  COM        37557 04-07-89   12:00a
COUNTRY  SYS        12806 04-07-89   12:00a
DISKCOPY COM        10396 04-07-89   12:00a
DISPLAY  SYS        15692 04-07-89   12:00a
FDISK    EXE        60935 04-07-89   12:00a
FORMAT   COM        22875 04-07-89   12:00a
KEYB     COM        14727 04-07-89   12:00a
KEYBOARD SYS        23328 04-07-89   12:00a
REPLACE  EXE        19415 04-07-89   12:00a
SYS      COM        11456 04-07-89   12:00a
ASSIGN   COM         5753 04-07-89   12:00a
ATTRIB   EXE        18263 04-07-89   12:00a
CHKDSK   COM        17787 04-07-89   12:00a
COMP     COM         9459 04-07-89   12:00a
DEBUG    COM        21574 04-07-89   12:00a
DISKCOMP COM         9857 04-07-89   12:00a
EDLIN    COM        14069 04-07-89   12:00a
FC       EXE        15807 04-07-89   12:00a
FILESYS  EXE        11129 04-07-89   12:00a
FIND     EXE         5941 04-07-89   12:00a
Press any key to continue . . .
▬
```

Notice that only the first 23 names are listed and that the message **Press any key to continue** is displayed at the bottom of the screen. The computer will wait until a key (any key) is pressed before continuing to list the files. After **[Enter]** (or any other key) is pressed, the next 23 names will be displayed. Finally, when **[Enter]** (or any key) is pressed again, the end of the list will be displayed:

```
XMA2EMS  SYS        29211 04-07-89   12:00a
4201     CPI         6404 04-07-89   12:00a
4208     CPI          720 04-07-89   12:00a
5202     CPI          370 04-07-89   12:00a
ANSI     SYS         9105 04-07-89   12:00a
Press any key to continue . . .

APPEND   EXE        11154 04-07-89   12:00a
DRIVER   SYS         5241 04-07-89   12:00a
FASTOPEN EXE        16718 04-07-89   12:00a
GRAFTABL COM        10239 04-07-89   12:00a
GRAPHICS COM        16693 04-07-89   12:00a
GRAPHICS PRO         9397 04-07-89   12:00a
HIMEM    SYS         6261 04-07-89   12:00a
MODE     COM        22960 04-07-89   12:00a
NLSFUNC  EXE         6878 04-07-89   12:00a
PRINTER  SYS        18914 04-07-89   12:00a
RECOVER  COM        10588 04-07-89   12:00a
BACKUP   COM        36880 04-07-89   12:00a
EGA      CPI        49068 04-07-89   12:00a
LCD      CPI        10703 04-07-89   12:00a
RESTORE  COM        36946 04-07-89   12:00a
       61 File(s)   11741184 bytes free

C:\>_
```

The file names can be displayed horizontally by typing **DIR \DOS/W ↵**. **DIR** instructs the computer to list the directory, **\DOS** says to use the DOS subdirectory, and **/W** says to display the files in a wide format. When using this command, only the file names and extensions are displayed. After typing this command, the following will be displayed:

/W says to display the directory in wide format

```
C:\>DIR \DOS/W ↵

 Volume in drive C is MAX
 Volume Serial Number is 1816-6C52
 Directory of  C:\DOS

.                ..               DOSSHELL BAT     COMMAND  COM     COUNTRY  SYS
DISKCOPY COM     DISPLAY  SYS     FDISK    EXE     FORMAT   COM     KEYB     COM
KEYBOARD SYS     REPLACE  EXE     SYS      COM     ASSIGN   COM     ATTRIB   EXE
CHKDSK   COM     COMP     COM     DEBUG    COM     DISKCOMP COM     EDLIN    COM
FC       EXE     FILESYS  EXE     FIND     EXE     IFSFUNC  EXE     JOIN     EXE
LABEL    COM     MEM      EXE     MORE     COM     SHARE    EXE     SORT     EXE
SUBST    EXE     TREE     COM     XCOPY    EXE     EMM386   SYS     EXE2BIN  EXE
GWBASIC  EXE     LINK     EXE     PRINT    COM     RAMDRIVE SYS     README   TXT
SMARTDRV SYS     XMA2EMS  SYS     4201     CPI     4208     CPI     5202     CPI
ANSI     SYS     APPEND   EXE     DRIVER   SYS     FASTOPEN EXE     GRAFTABL COM
GRAPHICS COM     GRAPHICS PRO     HIMEM    SYS     MODE     COM     NLSFUNC  EXE
PRINTER  SYS     RECOVER  COM     BACKUP   COM     EGA      CPI     LCD      CPI
RESTORE  COM
       61 File(s)   11741184 bytes free

C:\>_
```

If you use **[Print Screen]**, you will get a screen dump (i.e., a hard copy) of the screen, which is required for Homework Exercise 2 (see p. C48).

If the directory contains a large number of files, the **/P** and **/W** listings may be combined by typing **DIR \DOS/W/P ↵**. This will produce a listing using the wide format but will pause each time the screen is filled.

• Printing More Than One Screen at a Time •

Recall that in order to print the contents of the screen the user must tap the **[Print Screen]** key. This works fine for output that can fit completely on the screen. However, the user may need to print something, such as the list of the file names in the DOS subdirectory, that is longer than the 25 lines the screen can display at one time. To do this, the user can either interrupt the output process (as with **DIR /P**) or use the *print screen toggle* function. The print screen toggle function is a way of telling the computer to turn on the printer (*toggle* it on) before typing a command that will produce more than 25 lines of output, so that all lines of output can be printed. This can be done by holding down the control, **[Ctrl]**, key while pressing **[Print Screen]**. The printer is then toggled on and everything displayed on the screen from then on will also be sent to the printer. To turn off this feature (i.e., to stop sending output to the printer) press **[Ctrl-PrintScreen]** again (i.e., hold down **[Ctrl]** and, while holding down **[Ctrl]**, tap the **[Print Screen]** key).

The print screen toggle can be used to produce a hard copy of the entire DOS subdirectory. Try this by doing the following (Homework Exercise 3 on p. C48 asks you to do just this):

1. Turn on the printer (use the on/off switch of the printer).
2. Toggle on the printer (press **[Ctrl-Print Screen]**).
3. Type **DIR \DOS** and press **[Enter]**.
4. When instructed to **Press any key to continue**, press the **[Enter]** key.
5. When the entire subdirectory has been printed, toggle off the printer (press **[Ctrl-Print Screen]** again).

• *Taking a Break* •

Throughout this book we will insert "TO TAKE A BREAK" notes like the following one to indicate where you might want to stop working on the computer and take a break (e.g., to go to your next class, to go to lunch, etc.). You may or may not want to turn off the power to the computer when you stop. As is the case with most electronic devices, it is better to leave the power on rather than switch it off and on repeatedly. Use this rule of thumb: If you or someone else will be using the computer in the next few hours, leave it on; otherwise, turn it off. If you are using someone else's computer, ask them whether you should turn off the power when you stop working.

TO TAKE A BREAK Hard drive: Turn off power, if appropriate. Two drive: Remove DOS diskette; turn off power, if appropriate. To resume . . . Hard drive: Turn on power, if necessary. Two drive: Insert DOS diskette; turn on power, if necessary.

• *Formatting a Data Diskette* •

Before a microcomputer can store information on a disk, the disk must be *formatted*. Recall from page C28 that formatting means preparing the magnetic material on the disk so that it matches the way in which data are stored by a given brand of computer. As an analogy, think of having to prepare a typesetting machine to print a book. If the book were written in English a certain set of printing characters would be used. However, if the book were written in Chinese, a completely different set of printing characters would be employed. The style of type used has to match the characteristics of the language in which the book was written. A typesetting machine set up to print a Chinese book would not be able to print one in English.

Brand-new disks (both floppy and hard) are completely blank and can be used by many different brands of microcomputers. However, once a disk has been formatted for use by one type of machine (e.g., an IBM or compatible) it cannot be used by a different type of machine (e.g., an Apple Macintosh) without reformatting. This is why a disk that contains the IBM version of WordPerfect will not work on a computer that is not IBM or IBM compatible. Even though a $3\frac{1}{2}$-inch diskette that contains the IBM version of WordPerfect will physically fit into the disk drive of an Apple Macintosh, the Macintosh will not be able to read the information on the diskette.

Finally, it should be noted that because the formatting process restructures the magnetic fields on the disk, it also erases all information on the disk. Thus, never format a disk that has important information on it.

For the purposes of this book, you will need to format some data diskettes that you can use to store your WordPerfect, Lotus 1-2-3, dBASE, and BASIC files. If you are using 360K diskettes it would be a good idea to store files from different applications on separate disks. If you are using 1440K diskettes, you probably will have enough room to store all your files on one diskette but you still may want to use more than one data diskette. We will assume that you will use a separate data diskette for each application.

To format a disk that will serve as your *WordPerfect Data* diskette, do the following:

1. Prepare a blank diskette for formatting by doing the following:

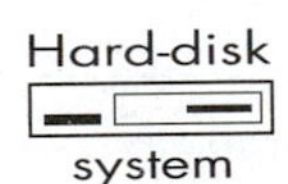

IF YOU ARE USING A HARD-DISK SYSTEM:

- Write *WordPerfect Data* and your name on a diskette label, attach the label to a new diskette, and insert the diskette into the A: drive.
- Type **CD\DOS** and press **[Enter]**. This will make the DOS subdirectory the default (the system prompt will appear as **C:\DOS>** to indicate this). If your computer does not have a subdirectory called **DOS** see your instructor for help.
- After you have formatted the diskette you may want to get back to the root (main) directory. To do this, type **CD** and press **[Enter]**. For more information on moving between subdirectories see page W217 of the Appendix.

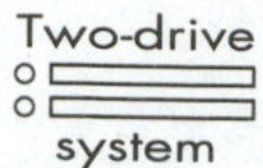
Two-drive
system

IF YOU ARE USING A TWO-DRIVE SYSTEM:

- If you are using a $5\frac{1}{4}$-inch DOS diskette, place a write-protect tab over the write-enable notch. If you are using a $3\frac{1}{2}$-inch DOS diskette, move the little button in the write-enable window so that the window is open. This will protect the DOS diskette from accidental erasure in the event that you make a mistake following the formatting directions.
- Place the DOS diskette in the B: drive. This is done so that the commands which follow will be the same as those for users with a hard-disk system.
- Type **B:** and press **[Enter]**. This will make the B: drive the default drive (the system prompt should be **B:\>** or **B>**).
- Write *WordPerfect Data/Boot* and your name on a diskette label, attach the label to a new diskette, and insert the diskette into the A: drive.

2. Insert the blank diskette into the A: drive. Check to see if the diskette in drive A: has any information on it by typing: **DIR A:** and pressing **[Enter]**. The **DIR** instructs the computer to list the names of the files on a disk and the **A:** instructs it to look at the diskette in the A: drive.

   Be sure to type the directory command correctly. For example, if the space between the **DIR** and the **A:** is left out, the following message would be displayed:

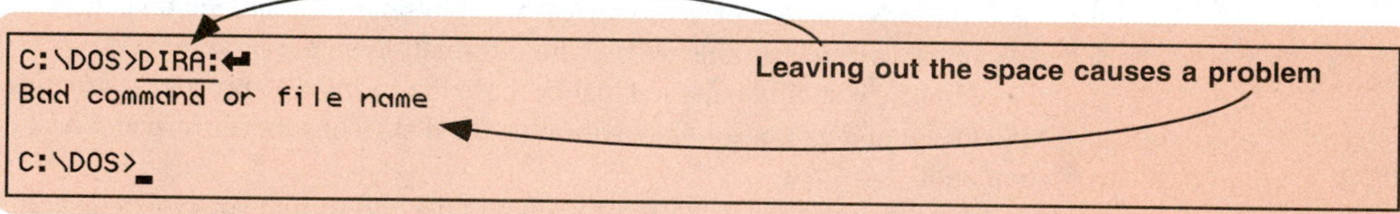
C:\DOS>DIRA:
Bad command or file name
C:\DOS>_
Leaving out the space causes a problem

   The message **Bad command or file name** means that the computer could not understand the instruction just typed and so has ignored it. Computers are designed to be very picky and, of course, cannot think. A human reading the command **DIRA:** would have been able to figure out what the user really wanted, but the computer could not. Making a mistake like this does not usually cause a problem. But because the computer ignored the command it must be typed again, in the correct form (**DIR A:**).

   If the colon at the end of the **A:** is left off, the computer will respond as follows:

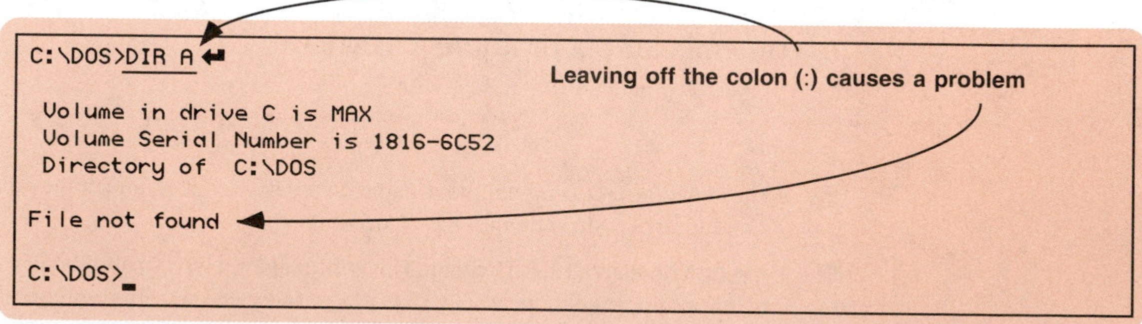
C:\DOS>DIR A
Leaving off the colon (:) causes a problem
Volume in drive C is MAX
Volume Serial Number is 1816-6C52
Directory of C:\DOS
File not found
C:\DOS>_

   Without the colon, the computer interpreted the command **DIR A** as if the user were looking for a file called A rather than for the directory listing of the disk in the A: drive.

If the disk has not been formatted for an IBM or compatible machine the computer will present the following message:

```
C:\DOS>DIR A: ↵

General failure reading drive A
Abort, Retry, Fail?_
```

The computer is stating that it could not read any information from the disk in drive A: (the disk is probably not formatted for use in an IBM computer). Three choices are given:

Type the letter **A** to **Abort** (stop) the command.

Type the letter **R** to have the computer **Retry** the command.

Type the letter **F** to select **Fail**.

Type the letter **A** to abort the command. The system prompt will be displayed again.

3. Use the **FORMAT** command to format the diskette in drive A:. Before doing this, you must determine the capacity of the diskette and the disk drive (360K, 720K, 1200K [1.2Mb] or 1440K [1.44Mb]; other combinations are possible). Do not attempt to format a high density (1200K or 1440K) diskette in a low density drive; see your instructor if you have questions. The exact form of the **FORMAT** command is different depending on the capacity of the diskette and the version of DOS you are using. If you are not sure which version of DOS you are using, type **VER** ↵.

```
C:\DOS>VER ↵

MS-DOS Version 4.01

C:\DOS>_
```

4. Now, format the diskette in drive A: by typing one of the following:

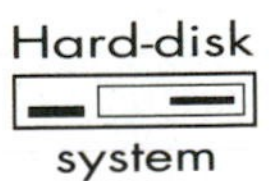

USING DOS VERSION 4

- $3\frac{1}{2}$-inch double-sided double-density (720K) diskette: **FORMAT A:/V/F:720** ↵

  or

- $3\frac{1}{2}$-inch high-density (1440K) diskette: **FORMAT A:/V/F:1440** ↵

  or

- $5\frac{1}{4}$-inch double-sided double-density (360K) diskette: **FORMAT A:/V/F:360** ↵

  or

- $5\frac{1}{4}$-inch high-density (1200K) diskette: **FORMAT A:/V/F:1200** ↵

Hard-disk system

USING DOS VERSION 3

- $3\frac{1}{2}$-inch double-sided double-density (720K) diskette: **FORMAT A:/V/T:80/N:9** ↵

  or
- $3\frac{1}{2}$-inch high-density (1440K) diskette: **FORMAT A:/V** ↵

  or
- $5\frac{1}{4}$-inch double-sided double-density (360K) diskette: **FORMAT A:/V/4** ↵

  or
- $5\frac{1}{4}$-inch high-density (1200K) diskette: **FORMAT A:/V** ↵

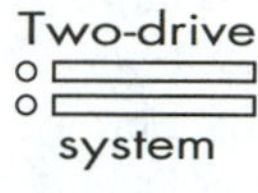

USING DOS VERSION 4

- $3\frac{1}{2}$-inch double-sided double-density (720K) diskette: **FORMAT A:/S/V/F:720** ↵

  or
- $3\frac{1}{2}$-inch high-density (1440K) diskette **FORMAT A:/S/V/F:1440** ↵

  or
- $5\frac{1}{4}$-inch double-sided double-density (360K) diskette: **FORMAT A:/S/V/F:360** ↵

  or
- $5\frac{1}{4}$-inch high-density (1200K) diskette: **FORMAT A:/S/V/F:1200** ↵

Two-drive system

USING DOS VERSION 3

- $3\frac{1}{2}$-inch double-sided double-density (720K) diskette: **FORMAT A:/S/V/T:80/N:9** ↵

  or
- $3\frac{1}{2}$-inch high-density (1440K) diskette: **FORMAT A:/S/V** ↵

  or
- $5\frac{1}{4}$-inch double-sided double-density (360K) diskette: **FORMAT A:/S/V/4** ↵

  or
- $5\frac{1}{4}$-inch high-density (1200K) diskette: **FORMAT A:/S/V** ↵

FORMAT instructs the computer to access the formatting program.

A: says to format the diskette in the A: drive.

/S says to transfer one of the System files (including a file called **COMMAND.COM**) to the new diskette (so that the computer can be booted using this diskette in the future). This is only needed for the two-drive systems.

/V says to ask the user for a Volume label for the diskette.

/F:*size* specifies the capacity (***size***) of the diskette to be formatted when using DOS version 4.

/T:80 specifies the number of tracks on the diskette when using DOS version 3.

/N:9 specifies the number of sectors per track on the diskette when using DOS version 3.

5. After typing the command and pressing **[Enter]**, the computer will ask you to insert a new diskette into the A: drive. Because there is a new diskette in drive A: already, simply press **[Enter]** and the formatting process will begin. After about a minute the computer will ask for a volume label (i.e., a name). The label can contain a maximum of 11 characters (letters, digits, and the dash). So that your disk can be distinguished from those of your fellow students, type your last name (e.g., **ROBERTSON**) and press **[Enter]**. Finally, the computer will ask whether another disk is to be formatted. Type **N** for **n**o and press **[Enter]**. The computer will display the system prompt.

If, for some reason you need to abort the **FORMAT** command (or most other commands) while it is executing, press **[Ctrl-C]** (i.e., hold down the **[Ctrl]** key and tap the **[C]** key). This will display **^C** and then the system prompt **C:\DOS>**.

The whole process, for formatting a high-density (1440K) diskette on a system with a hard disk would look like the following:

```
C:\DOS>FORMAT A:/V/F:1440↵
Insert new diskette for drive A:
and press ENTER when ready...

Format complete

Volume label (11 characters, ENTER for none)? ROBERTSON↵

   1457664 bytes total disk space
   1457664 bytes available on disk

       512 bytes in each allocation unit
      2847 allocation units available on disk

Volume Serial Number is 1D64-11E0

Format another (Y/N)?N↵
C:\DOS>_
```

Type your last name here

If you use **[Print Screen]** to get a screen dump, you will get a hard copy of the display, which is required for Homework Exercise 4 (see p. C48).

You may switch from one disk drive to another by simply typing the drive letter and then a colon. For example, to make drive A: the default drive, you would type **A:** and press **[Enter]**. It makes no difference whether you use uppercase letters (**A:**) or lowercase letters (**a:**). The computer will respond with **A:\>** to indicate that all information is now to be read or written to the diskette in the A: drive.

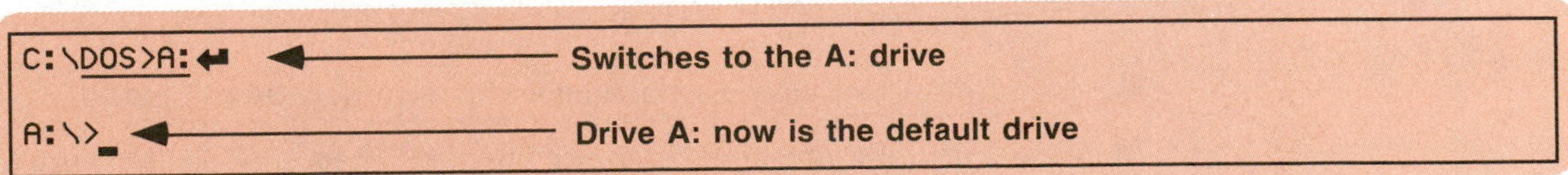
C:\DOS>A:↵
Switches to the A: drive
A:\>_
Drive A: now is the default drive

To get a listing of the directory of the diskette in drive A:, use the **DIR** command:

```
A:\>DIR

 Volume in drive A is ROBERTSON
 Volume Serial Number is 1D64-11E0
 Directory of  A:\

File not found

A:\>_
```

No files are currently stored on the disk in drive A:

To switch back to the C: (or B:) drive you would type **C:** (or **B:**) and press **[Enter]**.

```
A:\>C:

C:\DOS>_
```

• *Checking a Disk using* CHKDSK •

The **CHKDSK** command may be used to analyze the directories and files of a disk, fix some errors in the way data were written to the disk, and check the memory status of the computer. The report produced by **CHKDSK** will inform you if a portion of a disk is damaged in some way (this will result in the disk being able to store less data than you expect). Try using this command on the diskette in the A: drive by typing **CHKDSK A:/V ↵**.

CHKDSK says to call up the program called **CHKDSK** and to follow the instructions contained in that program.

A: says to check the disk in the A: drive.

/V says to display all the files on the disk and their paths.

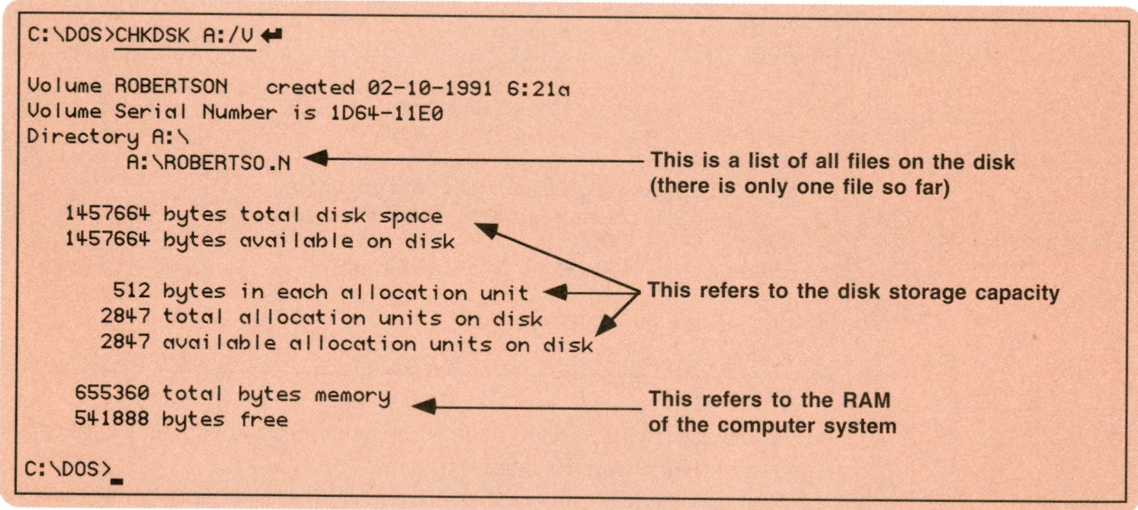

```
C:\DOS>CHKDSK A:/V

Volume ROBERTSON   created 02-10-1991 6:21a
Volume Serial Number is 1D64-11E0
Directory A:\
       A:\ROBERTSO.N

  1457664 bytes total disk space
  1457664 bytes available on disk

      512 bytes in each allocation unit
     2847 total allocation units on disk
     2847 available allocation units on disk

   655360 total bytes memory
   541888 bytes free

C:\DOS>_
```


In the above screen dump,

- Line 1 displays the volume label (**ROBERTSON**) and the date and time the disk was formatted.
- Line 2 displays a unique serial number for the disk (**1D64-11E0**).
- Line 3 identifies the directory being checked. The **A:** means the diskette in drive A: is being checked and the **** means the file name(s) listed on the next line(s) is in the root directory of the diskette.

- Line 4 displays the name of the file stored on the disk. Currently, there is only one file on this disk. The name of the file is **ROBERTSO** and the extension to the file name is **N**. This is a file that is used to store the name of the volume (**ROBERTSON**). It is called a *hidden* file because its name does not appear when the **DIR** command is given. If there had been more files (hidden or not) stored on the disk their names would have appeared also.
- Lines 5 through 9 show the total amount of memory available on the diskette (**1457664** bytes, which is correct for a 1.44 megabyte disk) and how the memory is allocated on the diskette.
- Lines 10 and 11 refer to the RAM of the computer. This machine has 640K of RAM (represented by the **655360**) and **541888** bytes are currently available for use by other programs. The difference between **655360** and **541888** is the RAM used by that part of DOS that is currently active.

If you use **[Print Screen]**, you will get a screen dump (i.e., a hard copy) of the screen, which is required for Homework Exercise 5 (see p. C48).

TO TAKE A BREAK Remove diskette(s) if necessary. To resume (hard disk): Insert *Word Perfect Data* diskette. To resume (two drive): Insert *WordPerfect Data/Boot* and DOS diskettes.

Homework Exercises

① Boot your computer and enter the correct time and date if requested to do so. Then, use the **DIR** command to display the root directory of the default disk drive. Use **[Print Screen]** to print out the contents of the computer screen (i.e., to get a screen dump). The output should look something like the following:

```
C:\>DIR↵

 Volume in drive C is MAX
 Volume Serial Number is 1816-6C52
 Directory of  C:\

COMMAND  COM     37557 04-07-89  12:00a
CONFIG   SYS       146 12-28-90  12:11p
AUTOEXEC BAT       280 12-28-90   1:56p
DOS          <DIR>     12-28-90  12:11p
INSIGNIA     <DIR>     12-28-90   2:09p
WP50         <DIR>     12-28-90   2:10p
WP51         <DIR>     12-28-90   2:15p
123          <DIR>     12-28-90   2:26p
DB           <DIR>     12-28-90   2:39p
DBIV         <DIR>     12-28-90   2:41p
BA           <DIR>     12-28-90   2:42p
       11 File(s)   11741184 bytes free

C:\>_
```

Your output will not look exactly like the above because not all computers and operating systems are set up in the same way. The important parts of the screen, however, should be present (the system prompt and the directory listing). It is the substance of the output that is important rather than the exact way it looks.

Continued . . .

② Use the **DIR /W** command to produce a listing of the DOS subdirectory (or diskette if you are using a two-drive system) in wide format. Do a screen dump of the directory listing.

---

③ Use the **DIR** command to produce a listing of the DOS subdirectory (or diskette if you are using a two-drive system) in regular format. To get a hard copy of the result, you must use the print screen toggle, **[Ctrl-Print Screen]**, because there will be more than 25 lines of output.

---

④ Following the directions given in this chapter, format a blank diskette for use as your *WordPerfect Data* disk. Do a screen dump to show the formatting process.

---

⑤ Use the **CHKDSK** command to produce a status report of the diskette you formatted in Exercise 4. Do a screen dump to show the **CHKDSK** status report.

PART

WordPerfect 5.1

Introduction to Word Processing

Objectives *After you have completed this chapter, you should be able to*

- Define commonly used terms associated with word processing and word-processing programs.
- Access the WordPerfect word-processing program.
- Identify the different parts of the WordPerfect screen.
- Access the WordPerfect on-line *Help* feature.
- Create a short document.
- Save a document to disk.
- Print a document.
- Use the WordPerfect *View* feature to display on the screen how a printed document will look.

CHAPTER 1

- Modify a document by:
  using typeover (overstrike),
  inserting text,
  reformatting paragraphs,
  deleting text,
  breaking up paragraphs,
  deleting entire lines of text,
  combining paragraphs.
- Switch between WordPerfect documents.
- Retrieve WordPerfect documents using the *List Files* feature.

Introduction

A word processor is a computer program that allows users to create, edit, and save written material easily and quickly. Most people are used to writing by hand or with a typewriter and may find using a word processor to be a bit awkward at first. However, after a little practice, most people prefer using a word processor for their writing tasks.

The word processor described in this book is called WordPerfect. It is powerful, easy to use, and is one of the most popular word-processing programs on the market today. Remember, however, that even though WordPerfect is an excellent program it can only follow the exact directions you give it. If the computer appears to make an error, check to see that you have given it the correct command (including spaces and punctuation).

Computer Environments

An environment is a surrounding. When we talk about our global environment we are talking about the land, air, and water of the planet. Within that global environment are many lesser environments such as oceans, mountains, plains, and woodlands. To survive in each of these, we must learn something about them and conduct our activities when in those environments according to what we have learned.

The computer can be thought of as possessing a number of different **environments** (or contexts) within which you work. In Getting Started, we discussed the DOS environment, which was indicated by the system prompt **`C:\>`** (or **`A>`** if you are working on a two-drive system). We can think of DOS as a global environment because it is always present. It serves as the intermediary between the hardware of the computer, the user, and application programs (like WordPerfect). When in the DOS environment, we can do certain things such as format disks (using the **`FORMAT`** command, see pp. C43–45) or display listings of directories (using the **`DIR`** command, see pp. C37–40).

In this chapter, we will focus attention on the WordPerfect environment, which exists within the larger DOS environment. We can do things while in the WordPerfect environment which, as we shall see, cannot be done while in the DOS environment, and vice versa. Even though we will be working in the WordPerfect environment and it will look like DOS has disappeared, DOS must always be present (in the form of the **`COMMAND.COM`** file), at least in the background, in order for the computer to operate.

Definitions

Before beginning a specific example, you should familiarize yourself with some definitions of terms frequently encountered when talking about word processing:

Access a program . . . (W6) To copy a program, such as WordPerfect, from a disk into the main memory of the computer so that the user can work with it.

Delete . . . (W30) To remove (erase) a character or group of characters.

Document . . . (W12) A file such as a memo, letter, or report created by WordPerfect. WordPerfect files are referred to as documents.

Edit . . . (W12) To modify (change, add to, or delete) a document or part of a document.

Environment . . . (W4) The context within which you are working. When in the DOS environment, the system prompt **`C:\>`** is displayed and you can execute DOS commands such as **`DIR`**. Likewise, when in the WordPerfect environment you may execute WordPerfect commands but not DOS commands.

File specification . . . (W14) The complete designation for a file including the disk drive where the file resides, the name of the file, and the file name extension (e.g., **`A:MRMPREP.V1`**).

Insert . . . (W28) To add a character or group of characters without replacing others. As the new characters are inserted, all characters to the right of the cursor are moved accordingly.

Justification . . . (W16) To line up text so that the edge of a paragraph appears even. With *left* justification, also called flush left or left align, only the left-hand margin is even; with *right* justification, also called flush right or right align, only the right-hand margin is even; with *full* justification, both left and right margins are even.

Load a document . . . (W26) To copy a document, such as a letter created by WordPerfect, from a disk into the main memory of the computer so that the user can work with it.

Menu . . . (W15) A list of commands or prompts presented on the screen. For example, in WordPerfect, users may select an operation such as print or save from a menu.

Retrieve a file . . . (W32) Read the contents of a file from a disk into the main memory of the computer. For example, when you retrieve a file from within WordPerfect, that file will appear on the screen so that you can work with it.

Save a file . . . (W13) Make a permanent copy of a file, usually on a disk. Later, saved files can be loaded into an application, modified, and saved again.

Status line . . . (W9) A line of text located at the bottom of the screen that provides information on the location of the cursor and the name of the document being edited.

Typeover . . . (W28) To replace one character with another.

Word wrap . . . (W12) To adjust automatically the number of words in a line, so that a word that would be displayed past the right margin of the line is placed at the left margin of the next line.

WordPerfect Versions 5.0 and 5.1

Like most other computer software, WordPerfect is continually evolving in response to consumer demand and advances in hardware technology. As the new versions are developed, WordPerfect Corporation attempts to keep the overall *feel* of the program the same while adding new features, enhancing others, and improving the user interface. This means that if you learn to use one version of the program it is usually not difficult to learn the next version when it becomes available. However, some of the keystrokes may change and some of the screens may be rearranged; when in doubt, consult the *WordPerfect Reference Manual.*

In this book, we will assume that you are running WordPerfect version 5.1 on a hard disk. However, pertinent information for two-drive systems is also given. We have included the notation USERS OF VERSION 5.0 in those relatively few places where version 5.1 differs from version 5.0. However, if the change is only cosmetic, we have not bothered to make note of it.

A major feature that was added when version 5.0 was upgraded to version 5.1 was support for pull-down menus (see p. W20) and a mouse (see p. W24). Other advanced features that were added include a mathematical equation editor, a link that allows you to import spreadsheet files directly, and a table generator.

System Requirements

The full WordPerfect package distributed by WordPerfect Corporation contains six 720K disks and a 1000-page reference book. In order to run WordPerfect as described in this book, your computer system must have two $3\frac{1}{2}$-inch floppy-diskette drives, or one floppy-diskette drive and a hard disk and a minimum of 512K of RAM (random-access memory).

For reference, a summary of selected WordPerfect features appears on page W226 of the Appendix. Also, keyboard templates for WordPerfect versions 5.0 and 5.1 are located at the back of this book. If your keyboard has 12 function keys along the top, cut out the two halves of the template, tape the ends together, and place the template around the function keys. If your keyboard has 10 function keys along the left-hand side, you still may use the top half of the template, but the bottom half must be cut off.

Because of their large size, programs such as WordPerfect, Lotus 1-2-3, and dBASE III PLUS are designed to be operated on a hard-disk system. We will assume that you are working on such a system and that the WordPerfect software has been installed on the hard disk in a subdirectory with path **C:\WP51** (or path **C:\WP50** if you are using version 5.0). However, we will also provide pertinent information for those of you working on a two-drive system. In either case, your course instructor may give you different directions for accessing the program and for saving data files for the particular computer system available to you in your school's computer lab.

Booting the Computer

Before turning on the computer, be sure you have the proper disks handy.

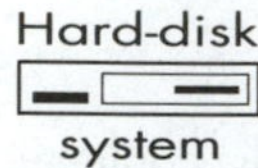

IF YOU ARE USING A HARD-DISK SYSTEM, you only need your formatted *WordPerfect Data* diskette. You will use this disk for storing WordPerfect documents. If you are using your own computer you do not need this disk (you will want to save files directly to the hard disk). Be sure the floppy-disk drive is empty before turning on the machine.

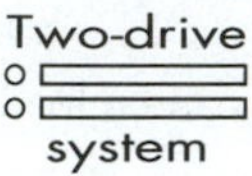

IF YOU ARE USING A TWO-DRIVE SYSTEM, you need the *WordPerfect Data/Boot* disk and the *WordPerfect Program* disk. Gently insert the *WordPerfect Data/Boot* diskette into the A: drive (the drive on the left or on top). Be sure to insert the diskette label-side up.

1. Turn on the system unit and the monitor.
2. The computer will take a few seconds to check its internal memory. When it has completed its check it will beep and begin to load the needed parts of the operating system from the disk.
3. If you are requested to do so, enter the date and then press **[Enter]**. If your system has a battery-operated clock you may not be asked for the date.
4. If you are requested to do so, enter the time and then press **[Enter]**. If your system has a battery-operated clock you may not be asked for the time.

At this point you should see the system prompt `C:\>` if you are using a hard-disk system or `A>` if you are using a two-drive system.

Accessing WordPerfect

The system prompt, `C:\>` (or `A>`), means that you are in the DOS environment and that the computer is ready to process your commands. To **access**, or load, the WordPerfect program into the main memory of the computer, do the following:

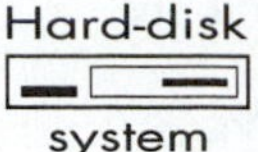

IF YOU ARE USING A HARD-DISK SYSTEM, insert the *WordPerfect Data* diskette into the A: drive and then type the following:

Keystroke	Action Resulting from Keystroke
A: ↵	Switches the default drive from C: to A:. This will ensure that the drive containing your *WordPerfect Data* diskette will be used as the default drive rather than the drive containing the WordPerfect program.
C:\WP51\WP ↵	Says to look in the subdirectory called **WP51** on the **C:** drive for a program called **WP**. Be careful when you enter the command to access WordPerfect. If you type **WORDPERFECT** or **WORDPERF** or **WPERF** or anything other than **WP** (or **wp**), the computer will respond with the phrase **Bad command or file name** and will wait for another command.

USERS OF VERSION 5.0 Your subdirectory name is probably **WP50** rather than **WP51**. If this is the case, type **C:\WP50\WP ↵** to access WordPerfect.

After typing the **WP** command, the following screen should be displayed. However, it may flash by so quickly that you do not see it.

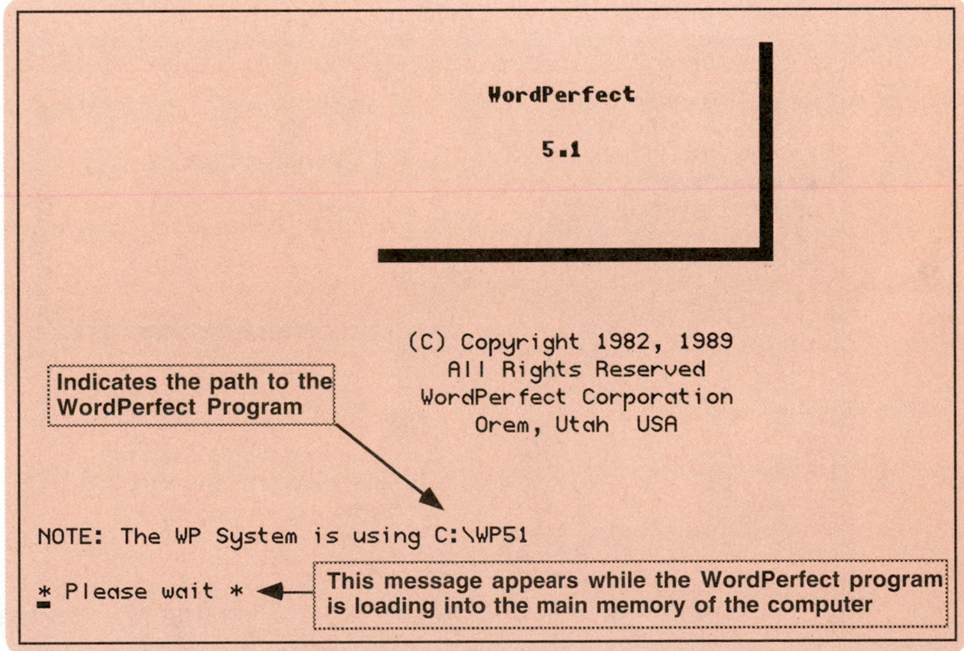

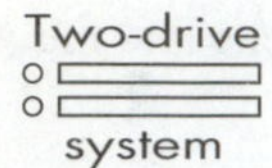

IF YOU ARE USING A TWO-DRIVE SYSTEM, place the *WordPerfect 1* diskette into the B: drive and type the following:

Keystroke	Action Resulting from Keystroke
A: ↵	Makes the **A:** drive the default drive. (If you just booted the computer from the diskette in the A: drive, this step is not needed because the A: drive will already be the default drive.) This will ensure that the drive containing your *WordPerfect Data* diskette will be used as the default drive rather than the drive containing the WordPerfect program.
B:WP ↵	Says to look on the B: drive for a program called **WP** and then to load that program into the main memory of the computer. Be careful when you enter the command to access WordPerfect. If you type **WORDPERFECT** or **WORDPERF** or **WPERF** or anything other than **WP** or **wp**, the computer will respond with the phrase **Bad command or file name** and will wait for another command.

After typing the **B:WP** command, the red light on the B: drive will light and you will hear the disk drive begin to spin. In a few seconds the following screen should be displayed. (You may see a message across the middle of the screen asking you to insert the *WordPerfect 2* diskette. In that case, replace the *WordPerfect 1* diskette with the *WordPerfect 2* diskette and press **[Enter]**.)

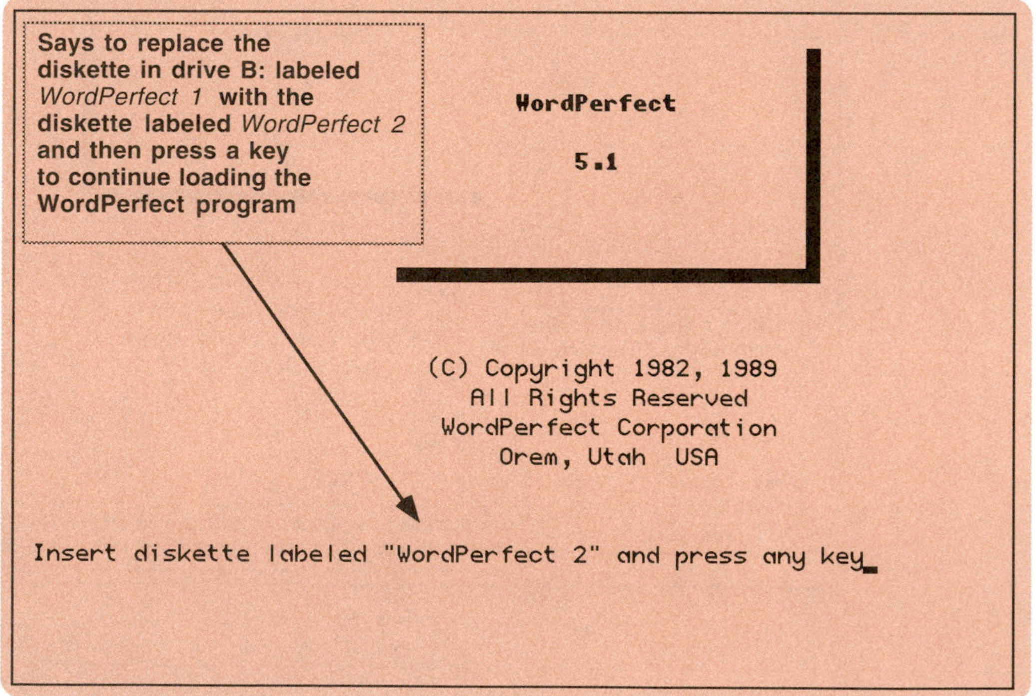

The above screen is called a *startup screen*. It shows the name of the program being used **(WordPerfect)** and the version number (**5.1**). If you or someone else had previously exited WordPerfect incorrectly (for example, if you had turned off the power to the computer before exiting WordPerfect) the following message would be displayed at the bottom of the screen:

```
Are other copies of WordPerfect currently running? (Y/N) _
```

If you see such a message, type **N** for **N**o and WordPerfect will continue to run.

At this point, the screen will be blank except for the blinking cursor in the upper left-hand corner (this indicates where the next character you type will be displayed) and the **status line**, which is the last line at the bottom of the screen. If you are using a color monitor, different parts of the screen may appear in different colors (e.g., the background may be blue with a dull white cursor and bright white letters on the status line, or you may see a black cursor on a white background with blue letters on the status line). If you are using a monochrome monitor, parts of the screen may be displayed white (or green or amber) on black while the rest may be black on white (this is called *reverse video*). The screen colors can be changed by using the *Setup* feature (see p. W222 of the Appendix). For now, it is probably a good idea to leave the settings alone, especially if you are not using your own computer. After you become familiar with WordPerfect you can try customizing it to suit your own needs and tastes.

In the display that follows, the numbers across the top and down the left-hand side of the editing screen are for reference only; they do not appear in the actual display.

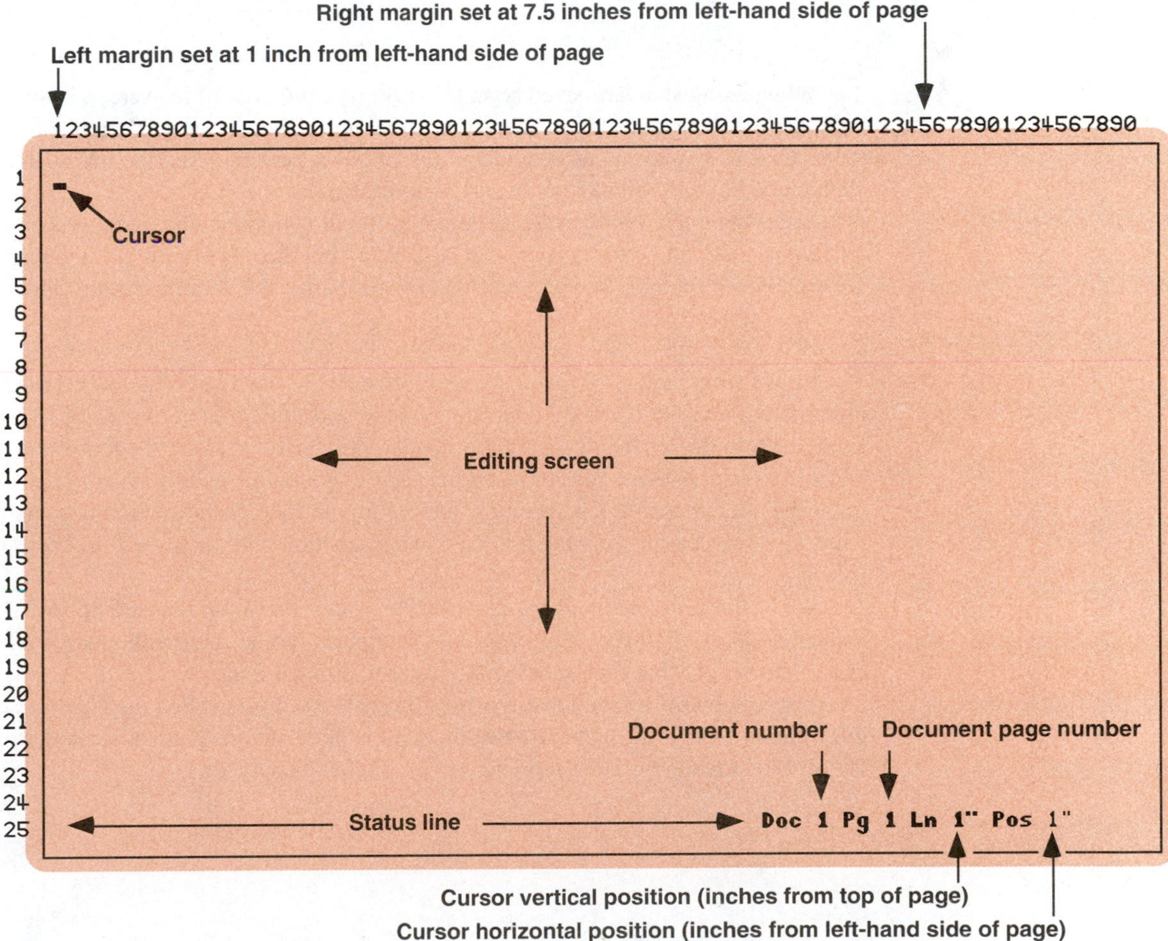

The status line provides information about the document you are working on:

Doc 1 means that the screen is displaying the contents of the first **Doc**ument. More than one document can be opened at one time.

Pg 1 means that the cursor is currently located in **Page 1** of the document.

Ln 1" means that the cursor is currently located at a **Lin**e that is **1** inch from the top of the page. For standard-sized type, 1 vertical inch represents six lines of text. For example, the following six characters would take up 1 inch of vertical space on the page:

```
1
2
3
4
5
6
```

Pos 1" says that the cursor is currently located at a **Pos**ition that is **1** inch from the left-hand edge of the paper. For standard-sized type, one horizontal inch represents ten characters. For example, the following ten characters would take up 1 inch of space horizontally on the page.

```
1234567890
```

When using standard-sized type, the main (typing) area of the screen is 80 positions (columns) wide and 24 lines (rows) high. This means that up to 24 lines of text can be displayed at one time and that each line displayed can be a maximum of 80 characters wide (the lines can be wider than 80 characters, but only 80 will be displayed at one time).

Unless you tell WordPerfect differently, it will automatically single space the document and set the left, right, top, and bottom margins to be 1 inch from the edge of the printed page. These initial settings are the default settings. We will discuss how to change the default settings later.

The Function Keys

Recall from page C20 that the keys labeled F1, F2, and so on are called function keys and are programmed to do specific tasks, depending on the application you are running. The function keys are located along the left-hand side of the standard keyboard or along the top of the extended keyboard. WordPerfect uses these keys to perform specific operations on documents such as checking spelling, moving text, enhancing text, printing, and saving. In fact, each function key can perform up to four different tasks depending on how it is used in conjunction with the modifying keys (**[Ctrl]**, **[Alt]**, and **[Shift]**).

We will discuss many of the function keys later. For now, you should find the keyboard template located at the back of this book, cut it out, and place it over the function keys. This template will serve as a reminder of what each function key is programmed to do.

Just to see how a function key works, press **[F3]** (this is called the *Help* key). This accesses information from a file called **WPHELP.FIL**, which contains a quick reminder of most of the WordPerfect features. The following screen will be displayed:

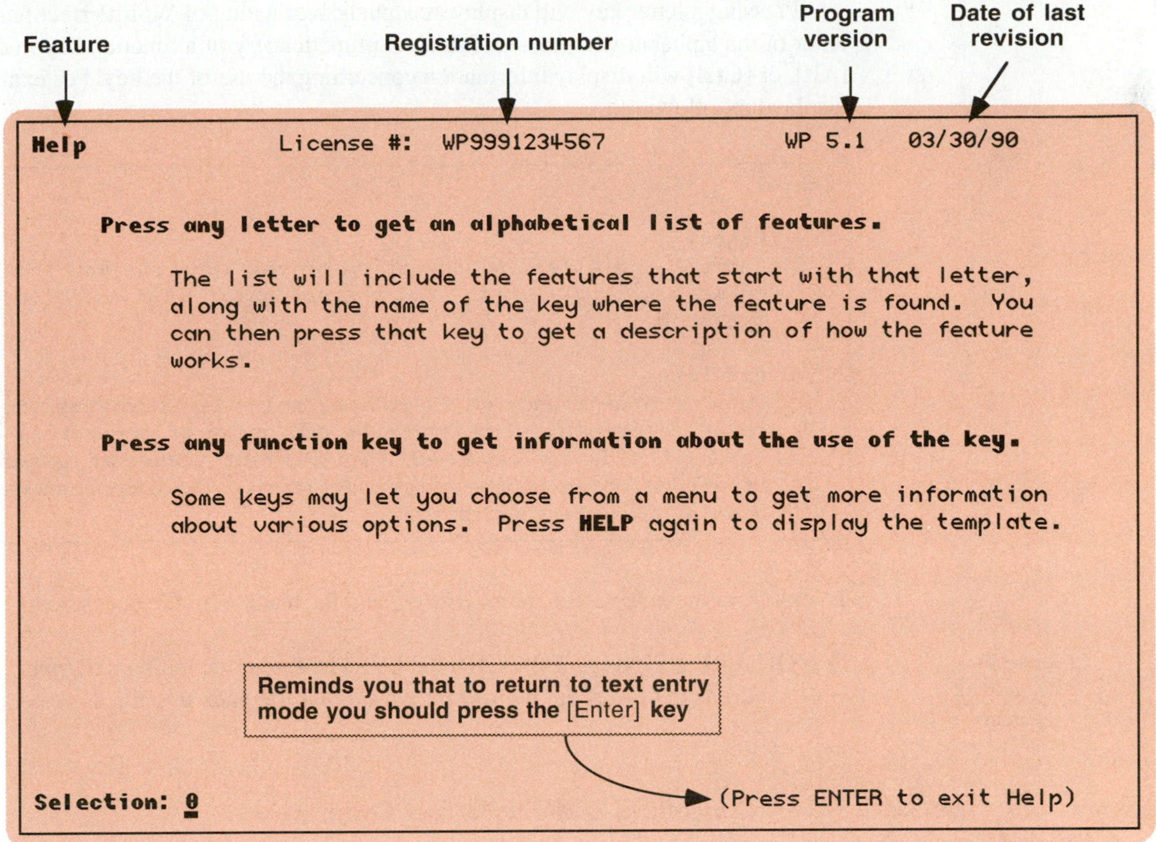

Feature
Registration number
Program version
Date of last revision
Help
License #: WP9991234567
WP 5.1
03/30/90
Press any letter to get an alphabetical list of features.
The list will include the features that start with that letter, along with the name of the key where the feature is found. You can then press that key to get a description of how the feature works.
Press any function key to get information about the use of the key.
Some keys may let you choose from a menu to get more information about various options. Press HELP again to display the template.
Reminds you that to return to text entry mode you should press the [Enter] key
Selection: 0
(Press ENTER to exit Help)

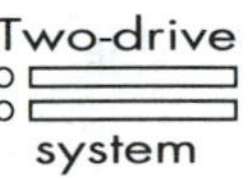

IF YOU ARE USING A TWO-DRIVE SYSTEM, the following message may appear at the bottom of the screen:

WPHELP.FIL not found. Insert the diskette and press drive letter: _

The file **WPHELP.FIL** is located on the WordPerfect 1 disk. Remove the *WordPerfect Data* diskette from the A: drive, insert the *WordPerfect 1* diskette and press the **[A]** key.

The top line of the screen contains the following information:

Help is the name of the feature you have accessed.

WP9991234567 is the registration number of the program (this identifies your copy).

WP 5.1 is the version of WordPerfect you are using.

03/30/90 is the revision number of version 5.1 of WordPerfect (version 5.1 has undergone a number of minor revisions since its introduction). In most instances, the revision number will be of no concern to us. However, if you are using a revision different from **03/30/90** (e.g., **11/06/89**) there may be minor differences in the appearance of some screens.

Pressing a letter key will display an alphabetical listing of WordPerfect features, beginning with the letter of the alphabet you pressed. Pressing a function key or a function key in combination with **[Shift]**, **[Alt]**, or **[Ctrl]** will display information concerning the use of the key. For example, press **[F1]** to display the following:

```
Cancel

    Cancel
    Cancels the effect or operation of any function key that displays a prompt
    or menu.  It will also stop the operation of a macro or merge before it is
    finished.

    Undelete
    When no other function is active, this key undeletes (restores) up to
    three deletions.  A deletion is any group of characters or codes erased
    before the cursor is moved.  WordPerfect temporarily inserts the most
    recent deletion at the cursor position.  You can then restore the text or
    display the previous deletion.
```

To exit from the help screen, press **[Enter]** and the blank WordPerfect screen will reappear.

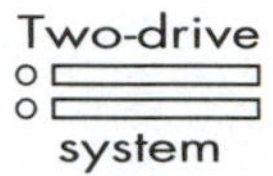

IF YOU ARE USING A TWO-DRIVE SYSTEM, remove the *WordPerfect 1* diskette from the A: drive and insert the *WordPerfect Data* diskette back into the drive.

Basic WordPerfect Operations

• Cancelling a WordPerfect Command •

The **[F1]** key is called the *cancel* key because it can be used to cancel many WordPerfect operations. This is particularly useful if you press a key by mistake and want to go back to where you were before you pressed the key. For example, suppose you wanted to bring up the help screen but you pressed **[F5]** instead of **[F3]**. In that case, the bottom of the screen would display the following message:

```
Dir A:\*.*                                      (Type = to change default Dir)
```

At this point, you do not understand what this message means. To undo the mistaken keystroke (i.e., to cancel its effect), simply press **[F1]**. The operation invoked by **[F5]** will be aborted and the screen will be returned to the way it was. (This usually works, but not always—ask if you need help.)

• Entering a WordPerfect Document •

Typing on a word processor is similar to typing on a typewriter, except that when the cursor gets to the right-hand side of the screen the user does not have to press **[Enter]**; the computer automatically goes to the next line as typing continues. This is called **word wrap** because the computer "wraps" the extra words around to the next line. The **[Enter]** key is used to insert blank lines.

As a first **document** (WordPerfect files are called documents), type the short memo displayed below. Don't worry about typographical errors or getting the wording exactly right because you can easily make changes to (**edit**) the document later. However, if you notice an error while typing, you can correct it using the **[Backspace]** key (located on the upper right-hand side of the typewriter part of the keyboard).

REMEMBER . . . If you make a few typing mistakes, don't worry. You will learn how to edit a document in the next section. If you really mess up your document and wish you could start over from scratch, you can do one of the following:

- Exit the current WordPerfect document but remain in the WordPerfect program by tapping the following three keys in succession:

  Tap **[F7]** (this is called the *Exit* key)
  Tap **[N]** for **N**o when you are asked **`Save document? Yes (No)`**
  Tap **[N]** for **N**o when you are asked **`Exit WP? No (Yes)`**

  This will discard your current document (i.e., all your typing in the document will be forgotten) and display a blank WordPerfect screen. Then, begin typing the memo again.

or (if you really panic)

- Hold down the **[Ctrl]** and **[Alt]** keys and tap the **[Del]** key. This will reboot the computer and allow you to begin again from the start.
- Follow the steps given on pages W7–8 for accessing WordPerfect and type the memo again.

After entering the memo, the editing screen should look like the following (the ↵ shows where the **[Enter]** key has been pressed). Again, don't worry if you have some mistakes—you can correct them later.

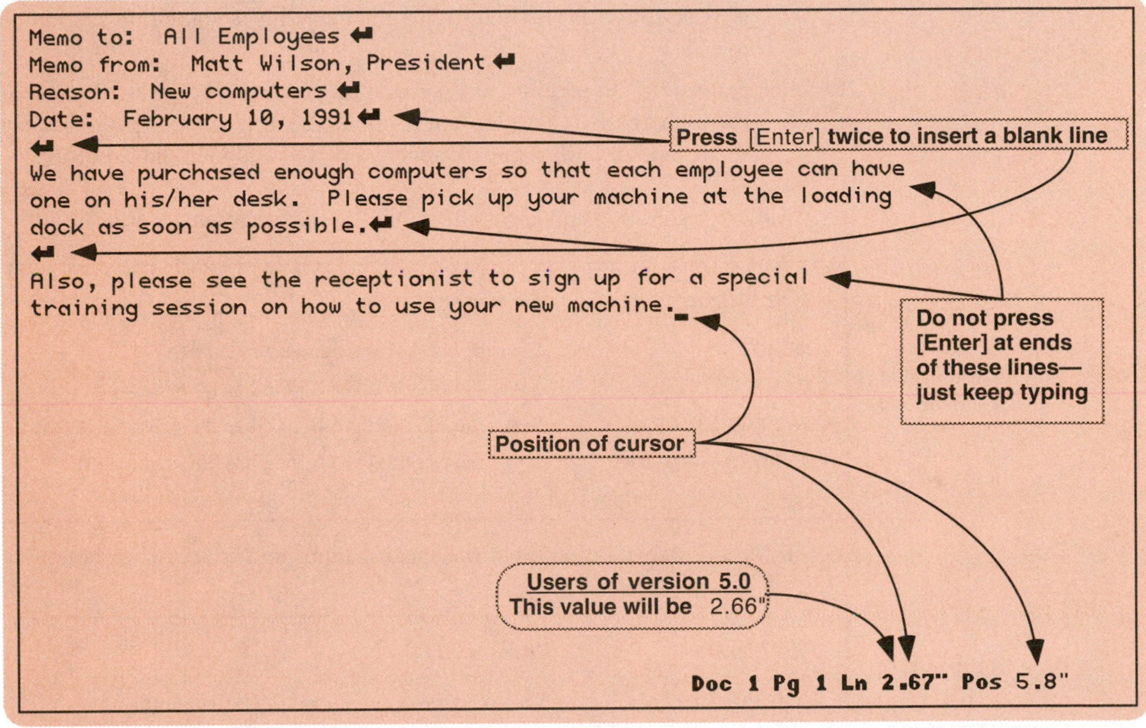

USERS OF VERSION 5.0 When showing the cursor location on the status line, version 5.0 truncates the values (e.g., **`2.66666"`** is displayed as **`2.66"`**) while version 5.1 rounds-off the values (e.g., **`2.66666"`** is displayed as **`2.67"`**). Therefore, throughout this book, the values displayed on the status line may differ from the values displayed on your screen by .01 inch.

• *Saving a Document* •

A copy of the memo you just entered is now in the main (RAM) memory of the computer. If something unexpected were to happen such as a power failure, a power surge from static electricity, a hardware malfunction, or a program error, you probably would lose all the work you have done on the document so far. It is therefore a good idea to save work about every ten minutes so that if something does go wrong, you will have lost only a small amount of work.

Let's make a permanent copy of the work completed so far by instructing WordPerfect to permanently **save** the document on your *WordPerfect Data* diskette. To do this, press **[F10]** (this key is located on the lower left-hand side of the standard keyboard or in the middle of the top row of the extended keyboard). WordPerfect will display the following at the bottom of the screen:

```
Document to be saved: _
```

The phrase **`Document to be saved:`** means that WordPerfect wants to know the file specification for the document. A **file specification** consists of three parts: a disk-drive designator, a file name, and an optional file name extension.

- Disk-drive designator A parameter, such as **A:,** that tells the computer on which disk to write the file. If a drive designator is not specified, the computer will use the default drive (i.e., the drive that was last indicated by the DOS system prompt, **`A>`** or **`C:\>`**, before the application was entered). When you entered WordPerfect the **`A>`** prompt was showing and, therefore, the current default drive is the A: drive.
- File name DOS allows you to give names to files so that they can be identified later. The names must be from one to eight characters in length and can contain letters **`A`** through **`Z`**, digits **`0`** through **`9`**, and some special characters including **`#`**, **`$`**, **`&`**, **`*`**, **`-`**, **`(`**, and **`)`**. Note that spaces are not allowed in file names. It is generally a good idea to make file names as descriptive as possible so that the name gives some information about the contents of the file.
- File extension In addition to a name, a file also may be given an *extension* of one-, two-, or three-character. The extension is optional, but if you choose to use one, it must be placed on the end of a file name by adding a period and then the extension.

Table 1-1 shows examples of allowable file specifications:

TABLE 1-1

Allowable File Specifications

File Name	*Comment*
`MEMO1`	Uses the default drive and no extension.
`C:P1`	Saves the file on drive C: and has no extension.
`B:PAGE12.CP1`	Saves the file on drive B: and has the extension **`CP1`**.
`A:WORD-PRG.BKU`	Saves the file on drive A: and has extension **`BKU`**.

Table 1-2 shows examples of file specifications that are *not* allowable:

TABLE 1-2

Non-allowable File Specifications

File Name	*Comment*
`A:MEMO 829.A`	A blank space is not allowed in a file name.
`B:P1+`	The character **+** is not allowed in a file name.
`PAGE12.CP12`	Extension too long—a maximum of three characters is allowed.
`WORD-PROG.BKU`	File name too long—a maximum of eight characters is allowed.

Save the document on the *WordPerfect Data* diskette using the name **`MEMO1`** by typing **`A:MEMO1`** and pressing **[Enter]**. The **`A:`** tells the computer to save the file on the diskette in drive A: (this is the data diskette), and the **`MEMO1`** specifies the name to use. For this example, the file name does not have an extension. The computer will save the document (the red light on the disk drive will glow and the message **`Saving A:\MEMO1`** will flash across the bottom of the screen—the **** means that the file is being saved on the root or main directory of the disk). After the document is saved, WordPerfect will display in the status line the name of the document as follows:

```
A:\MEMO1                                   Doc 1 Pg 1 Ln 2.67" Pos 5.8"
```

• *Printing a Document* •

WordPerfect allows you to print an entire document or only part of it. To illustrate this feature, let's print the document **MEMO1** by doing the following:

1. Be sure that a printer is connected to the computer, that it is properly loaded with paper, and that it is turned on.
2. Press **[Shift-F7]** (i.e., hold down **[Shift]** and tap **[F7]**). This will display a **menu** (a list of options or commands presented on the screen) related to printing:

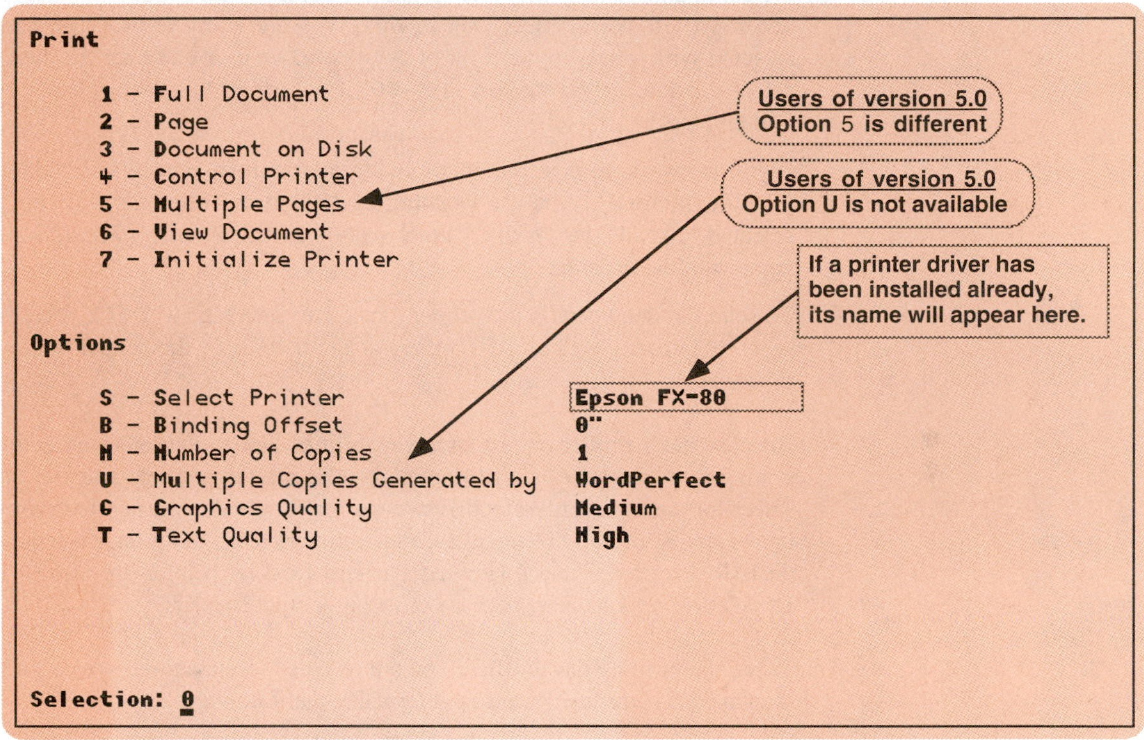

1 - Full Document prints the entire document.

2 - Page prints only the page that contains the cursor.

3 - Document on Disk allows you to print a document saved on disk (i.e., you can print one document while displaying and working on another document).

4 - Control Printer displays a screen that provides options to help you manage document printing (e.g., cancelling the printing of specific documents, rearranging the printing order of documents, displaying a list of documents waiting to be printed, and interrupting jobs currently being printed).

5 - Multiple Pages allows you to print selected pages of the document or a document summary (which can contain basic information such as the document's name, creation date, subject, author, and other comments).

6 - View Document allows you to see exactly how the output will appear on paper before you actually print it. In addition to the text which normally appears on the screen, headers, footers, footnotes, endnotes, page numbers, and graphics are displayed in their proper positions.

7 - Initialize Printer allows you to use different fonts (styles of type).

You may select an option from a menu in one of three ways:

- Type the number next to the option. For example, to select the option **1 - Full Document** you could tap the **[1]** key (use the number **[1]** key at the top of the keyboard rather than the number **[1]** key on the numeric keypad).

- Type the highlighted letter in the option. The letter **F** is highlighted in **1 - Full Document** so tapping the **[F]** key will select that option.
- Use your computer's mouse, if it has one, to position the mouse cursor on the option and then press the *left* mouse button. (For more information on using a mouse, see p. W24.)

WordPerfect can produce hard copy of documents by using many different printers (e.g., IBM Proprinter, IBM Graphics, Epson MX-80 Graphics, Hewlett Packard DeskJet). Each printer requires a driver (i.e., a program or list of instructions) to enable it to understand the commands sent to it by the computer. Before you can send a document to the printer, you must tell WordPerfect which printer you are going to use. The name of the printer selected will appear to the right of **S - Select Printer**. In the above screen, the selected printer is the **Epson FX-80**. If no printer has been selected, the printer name will be blank.

If you are working in a computer lab, a printer will have been selected already (if not, see your instructor). If you are working on your own computer or if no printer has been selected, consult the *Printer, Select* section of the *WordPerfect Reference Manual* that came with the program.

3. To send the document to the printer, press **1** to select **1 - Full Document**. The message ***Please Wait*** will appear at the bottom of the screen while the document is printed.

   Because each printer has its own capabilities and limitations, the actual appearance of your printed documents will depend on the printer you use and the printer driver you select for use by WordPerfect. However, for simple documents that contain only text, the hard copy is virtually identical for most printers (e.g., the printed version of **MEMO1** from an IBM Proprinter and a Hewlett Packard DeskJet printer are almost identical but the DeskJet copy looks nicer because of its higher quality print).

4. When the printing has finished, you are returned to the editing screen and the document is displayed. The printed output will look like the following:

```
Memo to:  All Employees
Memo from:  Matt Wilson, President
Reason:  New computers
Date:  February 10, 1991

We have purchased enough computers so that each employee can have
one on his/her desk.  Please pick up your machine  at the loading
dock as soon as possible.

Also,  please see  the  receptionist to  sign  up for  a  special
training session on how to use your new machine.
```

Notice that the printed output looks a bit different from the screen display. The screen display appears exactly as you typed it with an even left-hand margin but a ragged right-hand margin. However, the printed version has even margins on both the left-hand and right-hand sides. To line up text so that the edge or edges of a paragraph appear even is called **justification**. To *left* justify means only the left-hand margin is even; to *right* justify means only the right-hand margin is even. With *full* justification, both left- and right-hand margins are even. WordPerfect fully justifies printed output to give the document a more finished look. However, in order to line up both margins, WordPerfect must insert extra spaces into the document (e.g., in the second to last line, between the comma and **please**, between **see** and **the**, between **the** and **receptionist**, and so on). Some people find that this makes the document more difficult to read. Later, on page W78, we will discuss how to turn off the justification of printed documents.

```
Memo to:  All Employees
Memo from:  Matt Wilson, President
Reason:  New computers
Date:  February 10, 1991

We have purchased enough computers so that each employee can have
one on his/her desk.  Please pick up your machine at the loading
dock as soon as possible.

Also, please see the receptionist to sign up for a special
training session on how to use your new machine._
```

Displayed version — ragged right-hand margin

```
Memo to:  All Employees
Memo from:  Matt Wilson, President
Reason:  New computers
Date:  February 10, 1991

We have purchased enough computers so that each employee can have
one on his/her desk.  Please pick up your machine  at the loading
dock as soon as possible.

Also,  please see  the  receptionist to  sign  up for  a  special
training session on how to use your new machine.
```

Printed version — Even right-hand margin

• *Using View to Preview a Document* •

WordPerfect allows you to view the way a document will appear in final printed form without actually printing it. This is useful for setting **pagination** (adjusting text to fit on pages of fixed size) for longer documents and for documents that contain **headers** (text that appears at the top of every page), **footers** (text that appears at the bottom of every page), and **graphics** (nontext items such as pictures or graphs).

Use the *View* feature to display the document **`MEMO1`** by doing the following (begin this procedure from the normal editing screen):

Keystroke	*Action Resulting from Keystroke*
[Shift-F7]	Invokes the *Print* feature and displays its menu.
`V` (or **`6`**)	Selects **`6 - View Document`** from the menu and displays a picture of the page containing the cursor exactly as it would appear when printed. Depending on the quality of your monitor, you may have difficulty reading the text but you can see the overall attributes of the printed page.

The menu at the bottom of the screen allows you to view the document in one of four ways.

1 **`100%`** displays the document in its actual size as it would appear on the printed page. If you have a high resolution monitor you will be able to easily read the text. You may use the **[arrow keys]** to move up and down within the document.

2 **`200%`** displays the document at twice its normal size. This makes it easier to read on the screen but only shows a small portion of the page. You may use the following keystrokes to quickly move to different parts of the page:

Keystroke	**Movement**
[End]	Right side of page
[Home-Up Arrow]	Top of page
[Home-Down Arrow]	Bottom of page
[Home-Left Arrow]	Left side of page

Continued . . .

Keystroke	Action Resulting from Keystroke
	3 Full Page displays the document at a reduced size, one page at a time.

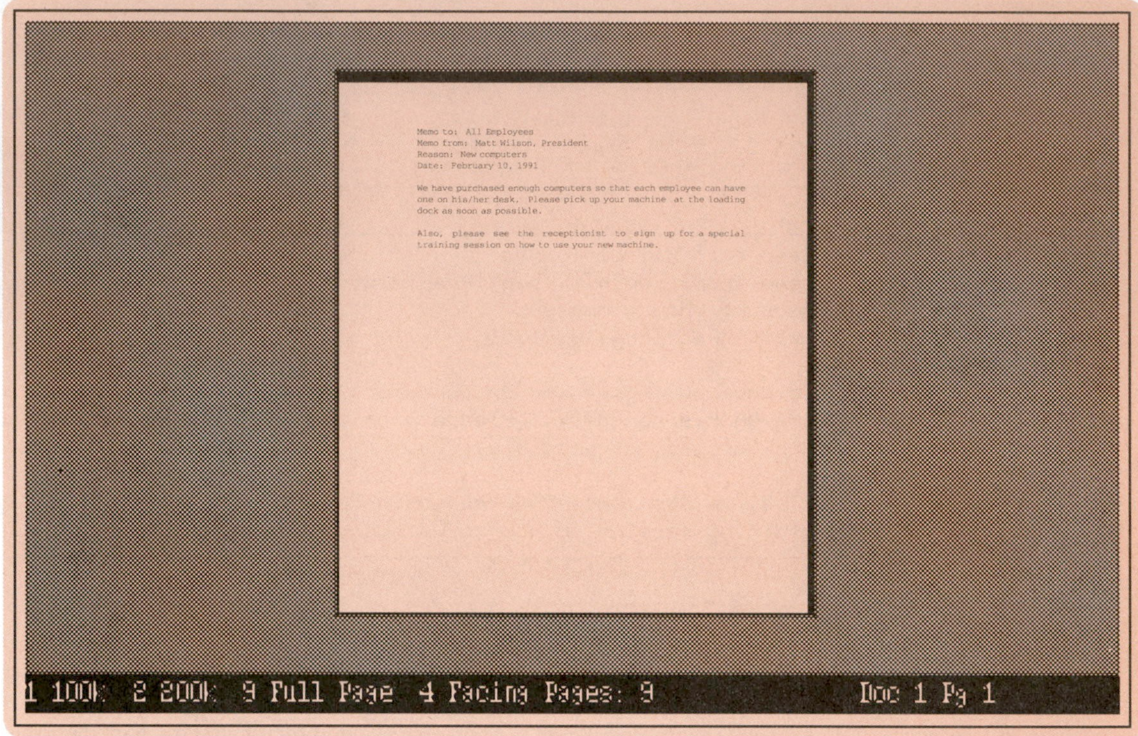

Keystroke	Action Resulting from Keystroke
	4 Facing Pages displays two pages at a time, in reduced size. Page 1 always begins as the right-hand page with a blank facing page. Because **MEMO1** is less than one page in length, only one page is displayed.
	You may not edit the document when in view mode but you can scroll through the document using the regular scrolling keys (**[arrow]**, **[Home]**, **[PageUp]**, **[PageDown]**).
	After viewing the page you may press **[F1]** (the cancel key) to return to the Print menu or **[F7]** (the exit key) to return to the editing screen.
[F7]	Exits the *View* feature and returns to the editing screen.

• *Exiting WordPerfect* •

To exit the WordPerfect environment and return to the DOS environment, do the following:

Keystroke	Action Resulting from Keystroke
[F7]	Specifies that you want to exit the word processor and return to DOS. WordPerfect responds with the following at the bottom of the screen:

```
Save document? Yes (No)                    (Text was not modified)
```

Continued . . .

If you have not made any changes to the document since it was last saved, you will see the message **(Text was not modified)** on the right-hand side of the status line. If you have made changes, this message will not appear.
You have three choices at this point:

- Typing **Y** specifies that **Y**es, you want to save the document. Notice that WordPerfect has underlined **Yes** for you. **Yes** is the default value (WordPerfect assumes that you want to save the document). Pressing **[Enter]** will have the same effect as typing **Y**.
- Typing **N** specifies that **N**o, you do not want to save the document.
- Pressing **[F1]** cancels the exit operation and returns you to the current document.

Y — Specifies that **Y**es, you want to save the document and displays the following message:

```
Document to be saved: A:\MEMO1
```

The file specification of the document is displayed as a reminder.

A: specifies the drive where the file is to be saved (this will be your *WordPerfect Data* diskette).

\ specifies that the file is in the root (main) directory of the disk. If you are interested or if you are storing your documents in a subdirectory, detailed information on subdirectories may be found in the Appendix on pages W216–19.

MEMO1 specifies the name of the file. Note that the file has no extension to the name (i.e., there is no **.xxx** in the file specification). If you want to save the document under a new name, you can type the new name. Otherwise, just press **[Enter]**. This will save the current document under the same name as before.

[Enter] — Specifies that the current document is to be saved using the same name as before and displays the following message:

```
Replace A:\MEMO1? No (Yes)
```

WordPerfect is asking if you want to replace the old version of the document with the new version.

You have three choices at this point:

- Typing **Y** specifies that **Y**es, you want to replace the old version of **MEMO1** with the current version. In this example, because there have been no modifications since the last save, these two versions are the same.
- Typing **N** specifies that **N**o, you do not want to replace the old version with the current version. In that case, you will be asked for a new name for the document. This is the default option (i.e., if you press **[Enter]** WordPerfect will assume you mean **No**).
- Pressing **[F1]** cancels the operation and then WordPerfect asks you for the name of the document to be saved. If you press **[F1]** again you will be returned to the current document.

Y — Specifies that **Y**es, the old version of the document is to be replaced by the new version and saves the document (the message **Saving A:\MEMO1** will flash across the screen while the file is being written to the disk). WordPerfect then displays the following message:

Continued . . .

Keystroke	Action Resulting from Keystroke

```
Exit WP? No (Yes)                    (Cancel to return to document)
```

You have three choices at this point:

- Typing **Y** exits WordPerfect and returns control to DOS.
- Typing **N** clears the screen and returns control to WordPerfect. In this case, you may begin to type a brand new document. This is the default option (i.e., if you press **[Enter]** WordPerfect will assume you mean **No**).
- Pressing **[F1]** cancels the exit operation and returns you to the current document.

Y — Specifies that **Y**es, you want to exit WordPerfect and returns control to DOS. The DOS system prompt, **A:\>**, now should be displayed on the screen.

TO TAKE A BREAK Remove diskette(s). To resume (hard disk): Insert *Data* diskette. To resume (two drive): Insert diskettes.

Pull-down Menus

Pull-down menus serve as an alternative to using the function keys to invoke WordPerfect features. A mouse (see p. W24), the **[arrow]** keys, or typing certain key letters can be used to "pull down" these menus from a menu bar at the top of the screen (the process is visually similar to pulling down a window shade, hence the name).

USERS OF VERSION 5.0 Version 5.0 does not have pull-down menus nor does it support a mouse.

WordPerfect can be set up to always display the pull-down menu bar at the top of the screen (see the *Setup* feature in the *WordPerfect Reference Manual*). This gives you one or two less lines of displayed text but keeps the menu visible for easy reference. As was the case with the screen colors, it is probably a good idea to leave the default settings alone, especially if you are not using your own computer.

If the menu bar is not visible at the top of the screen, you may display it by tapping **[Alt-=]** (i.e., hold down the **[Alt]** key and tap the **[=]** key). **[Alt-=]** is a toggle key. Pressing it switches (toggles) between the menu bar being displayed and not being displayed. If there is a mouse attached to your computer, the menu bar may be displayed by clicking the right button on the mouse.

You may use the **[arrow]** keys, letter keys, or a mouse to highlight and select options on the menu bar and the pull-down menus. You may use **[F1]**, **[Esc]**, or **[Spacebar]** to back out of a menu by one step.

Let's see how these menus work. If you are currently in DOS (i.e., if the system prompt **A:\>** or **C:\>** is currently displayed), load the WordPerfect program as before by doing the following:

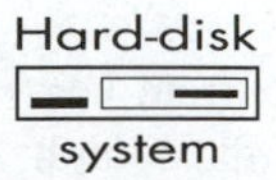

IF YOU ARE USING A HARD-DISK SYSTEM, be sure the *WordPerfect Data* diskette is in drive A: and then type the following:

Keystroke	Action Resulting from Keystroke
A: ↵	Ensures that the default drive will be A:.
C:\WP51\WP ↵	Loads the WordPerfect program.

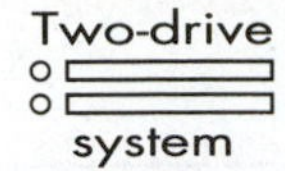

IF YOU ARE USING A TWO-DRIVE SYSTEM, be sure the *WordPerfect Data/Boot* diskette is in drive A:, place the *WordPerfect 1* diskette into drive B:, and then type the following:

Keystroke	Action Resulting from Keystroke
A: ↵	Ensures that the default drive will be A:.
B:WP ↵	Loads the WordPerfect program. If you are instructed to do so, insert the *WordPerfect 2* diskette into the B: drive and tap **[Enter]** to complete the loading process.

When the program has loaded, you will be presented with a blank WordPerfect screen. To display the menu bar, do the following:

Keystroke	Action Resulting from Keystroke
[Alt-=]	Displays the pull-down menu bar at the top of the screen.

```
File Edit Search Layout Mark Tools Font Graphics Help
```

Note that depending on how WordPerfect is set up on your computer, the menu bar may look slightly different (e.g., selections may be in different colors, the highlighting may be different, and the double horizontal line may be absent). The menu items, however, should be the same.

To highlight one of the nine menu items, you may use the **[left arrow]** and **[right arrow]** keys, a mouse, or simply tap the highlighted letter of the selection you want. For example, to pull down the **File** menu you would do the following:

Keystroke	Action Resulting from Keystroke
← or →	Use the **[left arrow]** or **[right arrow]** key, if necessary, to highlight the left-most option labeled **File**.
	To pull down the menu of the highlighted item, use the **[down arrow]** key.
↓	Pulls down the **File** menu and displays its options. Instead of using the **[arrow]** keys you could have simply tapped the letter **F** to select and pull down the **File** menu.

Continued . . .

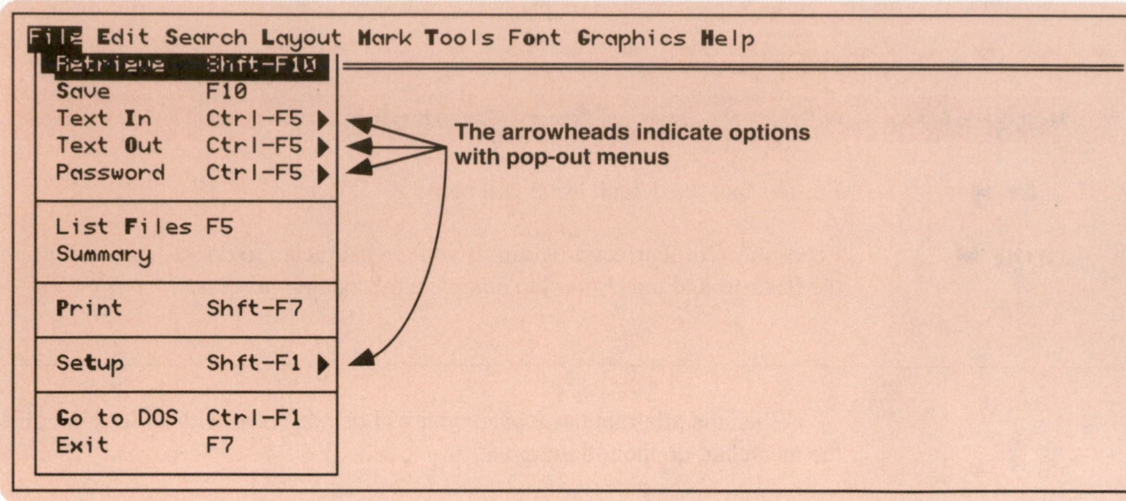

Some of the pull-down menu options have function keys displayed to their right (e.g., **`Retrieve Shft-F10`**). This reminds you which function keys you could press instead of using the menu (e.g., to retrieve a file you could select **`Retrieve`** from the menu or you could press the **[Shift-F10]** keys instead). Note that if you have an early revision of WordPerfect 5.1 the function key equivalents may not be displayed in the menu.

Some of the pull-down menu options also have a small arrowhead on the right-hand side to indicate that these options have submenus, called pop-out menus. To see one of the *pop-out* menus, do the following:

Keystroke	Action Resulting from Keystroke
↓	Use the **[down arrow]** key to highlight the third option (**`Text In`**). Instead of using the **[arrow]** key you could simply tap the letter **`I`** (the highlighted letter in **`Text In`**).
→	Use the **[right arrow]** key to highlight the first option of the **`Text In`** menu.

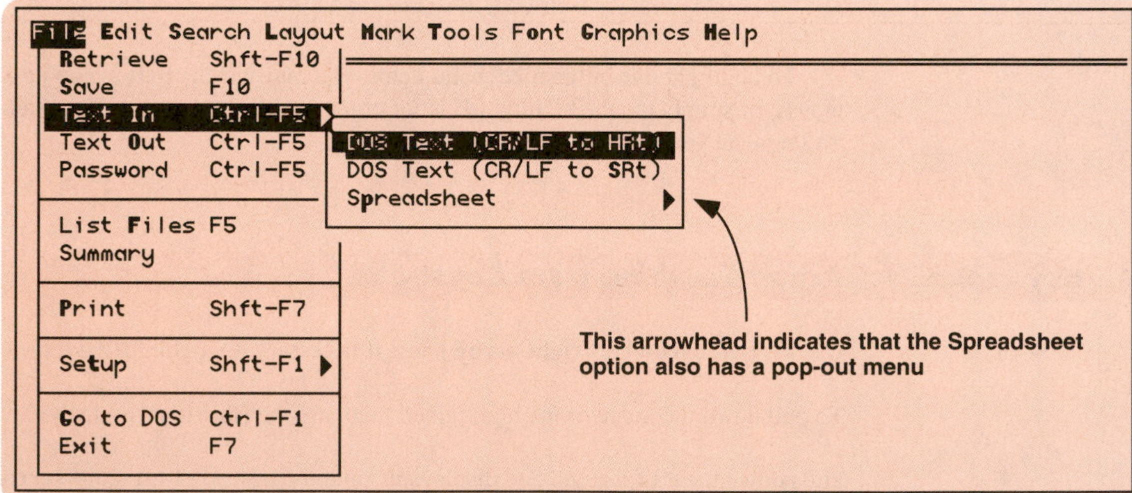

You may use **[F1]**, or **[Esc]** or **[Spacebar]** to back out of a menu one step at a time.

Keystroke	Action Resulting from Keystroke
[F1]	Removes the highlighting from the pop-out menu (i.e., it backs out of the **`Text In`** submenu).
[F1]	Backs out of the **`File`** menu and closes the menu. Only the menu bar at the top of the screen remains.

As a second example of pull-down menus, recall that on page W10 you used the **[F3]** key to invoke the *Help* feature. Let's carry out the same operation using the pull-down menus instead of the function keys.

Keystroke	Action Resulting from Keystroke
← or →	Use the **[left arrow]** or **[right arrow]** key to highlight the right-most option labeled **Help**.
	To pull down the menu of the highlighted item (**Help**), use the **[down arrow]** key.
↓	Pulls down the **Help** menu and displays its options. Instead of using the **[arrow]** keys you could have simply tapped the letter **H** to select and pull down the **Help** menu.

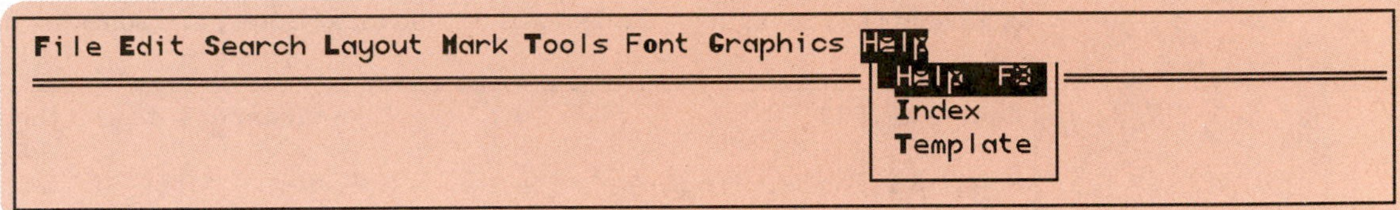

File Edit Search Layout Mark Tools Font Graphics Help
Help F3
Index
Template

The **Help** menu has three entries. The first is the help command that you used before when you pressed **[F3]**. (Note: If you are using an early revision of WordPerfect version 5.1 the **F3** reminder next to the word **Help** may be missing).

Keystroke	Action Resulting from Keystroke
↓ or ↑	If necessary, use the **[down arrow]** or **[up arrow]** key to highlight the top-most option labeled **Help**.
[Enter]	Displays the help screen. Note that instead of using the **[arrow]** keys to highlight **Help** and then pressing **[Enter]** to select it, you could have simply typed the letter **H**.

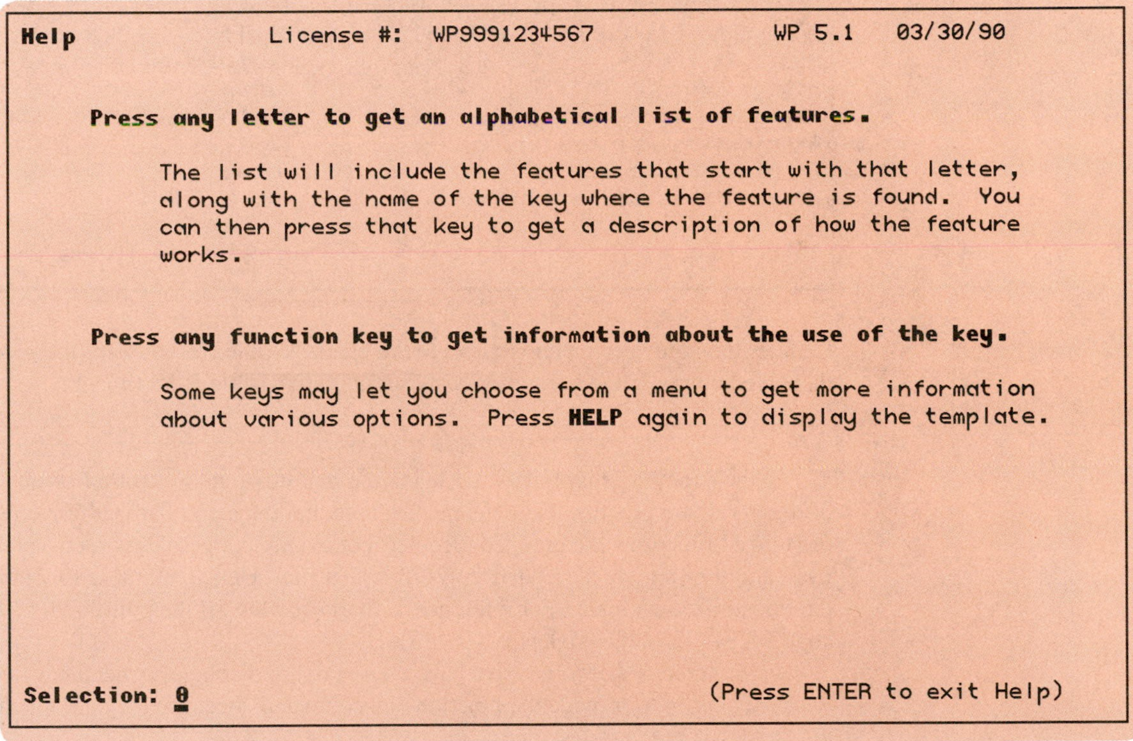

Help License #: WP9991234567 WP 5.1 03/30/90
Press any letter to get an alphabetical list of features.
The list will include the features that start with that letter, along with the name of the key where the feature is found. You can then press that key to get a description of how the feature works.
Press any function key to get information about the use of the key.
Some keys may let you choose from a menu to get more information about various options. Press HELP again to display the template.
Selection: 0
(Press ENTER to exit Help)

This is the same screen that you used **[F3]** to display on pages W10–11. In this case, it took a lot longer to use the pull-down menus than to press the single function key. However, if you could not remember which function key to press, using the pull-down menu would probably be faster than looking up the correct key in the index of this book. The choice is up to you.

Keystroke	Action Resulting from Keystroke
[Enter]	Cancels the help screen and returns to the blank WordPerfect screen (the menu bar will not be displayed unless it had been set up to be visible at all times).

Continued . . .

Keystroke	Action Resulting from Keystroke
[Alt-=]	Displays the pull-down menu bar again.
H	Selects the **Help** menu and displays its options. You could use the **[arrow]** keys or the mouse to accomplish the same thing.
I	Selects the middle option labeled **Index** and displays an alphabetical listing of all the WordPerfect features and the corresponding keystrokes. Note that instead of using the letter key you could have used the **[arrow]** key to highlight **Index** and then pressed **[Enter]** to display the list.

```
Features [A]                                WordPerfect Key   Keystrokes

Absolute Tab Settings                       Format            Shft-F8,1,8,t,1
Acceleration Factor (Mouse)                 Setup             Shft-F1,1,5
Add Password                                Text In/Out       Ctrl-F5,2
Additional Printers                         Print             Shft-F7,s,2
Advance (To Position, Line, etc.)           Format            Shft-F8,4,1
Advanced Macro Commands (Macro Editor)      Macro Commands    Ctrl-PgUp
Advanced Merge Codes                        Merge Codes       Shft-F9,6
Align/Decimal Character                     Format            Shft-F8,4,3
Align Text on Tabs                          Tab Align         Ctrl-F6
Alphabetize Text                            Merge/Sort        Ctrl-F9,2
Alt/Ctrl Key Mapping                        Setup             Shft-F1,5
Alt-=                                       Menu Bar          Alt-=
Appearance of Printed Text                  Font              Ctrl-F8
Append Text to a File (Block On)            Move              Ctrl-F4,1-3,4
Append to Clipboard (Block On)              Shell             Ctrl-F1,3
ASCII Text File                             Text In/Out       Ctrl-F5,1
Assign Keys                                 Setup             Shft-F1,5
Assign Variable                             Macro Commands    Ctrl-PgUp
Attributes, Printed                         Font              Ctrl-F8
Attributes, Screen                          Setup             Shft-F1,2,1
More... Press a to continue.

Selection: 0                                         (Press ENTER to exit Help)
```

Keystroke	Action Resulting from Keystroke
[Enter]	Cancels the index screen and returns to the blank WordPerfect screen (the menu bar will not be displayed unless it had been previously set up to be visible at all times).

In the examples that follow, try using the pull-down menus for a few operations just to get the feel of them. As you practice using the menus, note that the menu bar is arranged so that features that carry out related functions are grouped together. For example, operations such as retrieving, saving, listing files, and printing are all related to WordPerfect files. Hence, all these functions can be accessed from the File pull-down menu. For reference, a chart showing all the pull-down menu options is located on page W231–32 of the Appendix.

In the screens that follow, we have chosen not to display the menu bar in order to save space. Also, we have chosen to provide the function key commands because they are much faster to use than either the menu bar or the mouse.

The Mouse

A mouse is a piece of hardware that is about the size of a common field mouse (hence the name). It has a wire at one end (it looks like the mouse's tail), one, two, or three buttons on the top, and a ball sticking through a hole in the bottom. The mouse is grasped so that the index and middle fingers are resting lightly on the buttons. Sliding the mouse along a desk top moves a *mouse cursor* (this is different from the regular cursor) across the computer's display. The mouse is designed to supplement the **[arrow]** keys by giving you an alternative way of locating the cursor on the screen.

USERS OF VERSION 5.0 Version 5.0 does not support a mouse.

Before you can use a mouse, it must be installed both physically (i.e., plugged into the back of the computer) and electronically (i.e., a piece of software called a *mouse driver* must be run from within WordPerfect so that the program knows the type of mouse you are using).

If you are right handed it probably will be a little easier, at first, to operate the mouse with that hand. However, if you operate the mouse with your left hand you soon will gain skill with that hand leaving your right hand free to write or to use the **[PageUp]**, **[PageDown]**, **[Home]**, and **[End]** keys while keeping your left hand on the mouse. No matter which hand you use, operating the mouse will seem awkward at first, but you will get used to it.

The mouse has three main uses in WordPerfect 5.1:

- Feature and option selection Most of the features of version 5.1 may be invoked using the mouse in conjunction with pull-down menus.
- Cursor control You may position the cursor anywhere on the active area of the screen by moving the mouse cursor to the desired spot and then clicking the *left* mouse button.
- Blocking text You may block text (see p. W70) by positioning the mouse cursor at the beginning of the desired block, holding down the *left* mouse button, sliding the mouse until the mouse cursor is at the end of the desired block (this process is called a *drag*), and then letting up on the button. When you stop and let up the button, the block remains selected.

The Mouse and Pull-down Menus

Pull-down menus may be accessed using the mouse instead of the keys. For example, if you wanted to use the mouse to display a list of all the WordPerfect commands contained within the *Help* feature, you would do the following (begin from a blank WordPerfect screen):

1. Grasp the mouse so that your index and middle fingers are resting lightly on the buttons and slide it along your desk top. Notice how the mouse cursor (a black or orange rectangle) moves across the computer's display. To get a feel for the relation between the movement of the mouse and the movement of the mouse cursor, move the mouse so that the mouse cursor travels to the top of the screen; then move it to the bottom of the screen; then move it to the right-hand side of the screen; finally, move it to the left-hand side of the screen. Next, move the mouse in a circular motion and watch the resulting motion of the mouse cursor.

2. While holding the mouse perfectly still, click (quickly tap) the right mouse button. The menu bar should appear at the top of the screen. Clicking the right mouse button again removes the menu bar. Thus, the *right* mouse button is used to toggle the menu bar on and off.

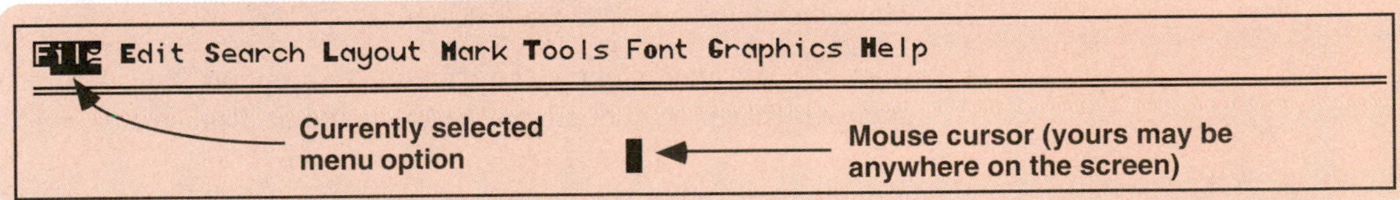

3. With the menu bar displayed, you may select one of its options by sliding the mouse along your desk top until the mouse cursor rests anywhere in the name of the option you want. The following display shows the mouse cursor on the letter **H** in the **Help** menu:

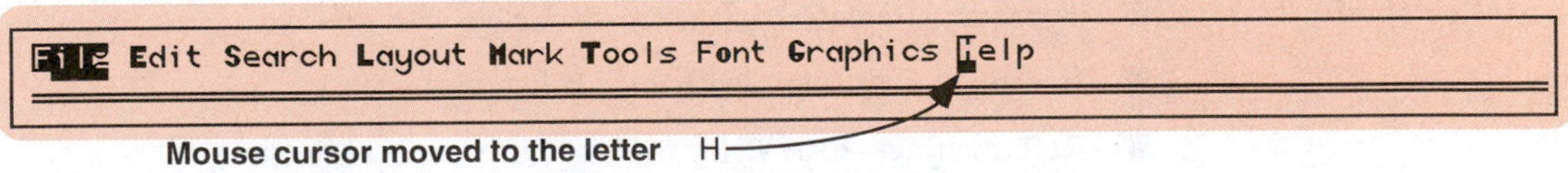

4. To pull down the **Help** menu, hold the mouse perfectly still and click the left mouse button. If you move the mouse while tapping the button the menu bar may disappear. In that case, simply begin at step 2 again. If you do it correctly, the pull-down menu for **Help** will be displayed.

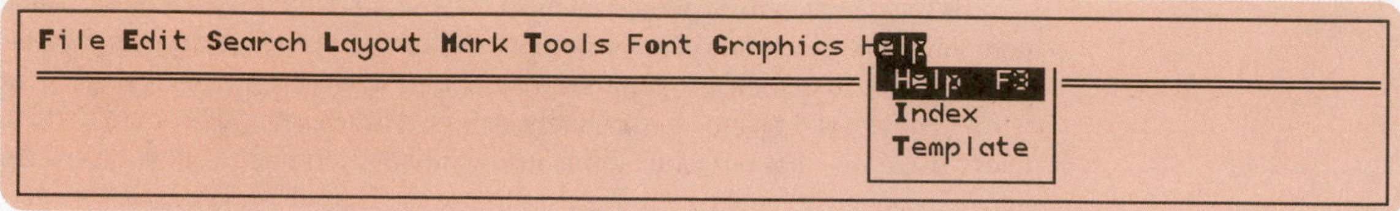

5. To select an option from a submenu, again slide the mouse until the mouse cursor is on the desired option name. For example, slide the mouse until the mouse cursor is located on the letter **I** in the word **Index** in the pull-down menu.

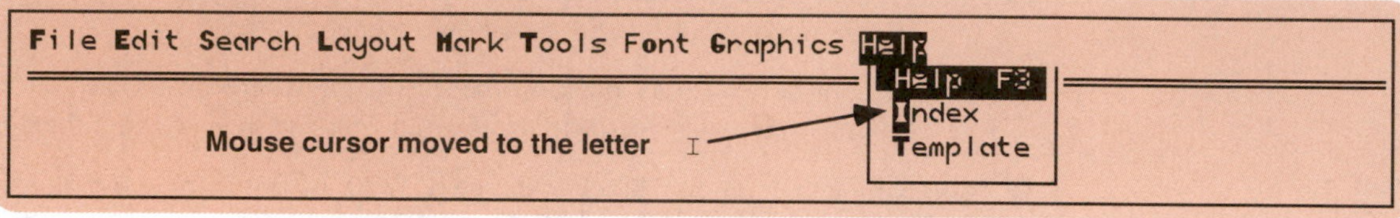

6. While holding the mouse perfectly still, click the left mouse button. The **Index** help screen will be displayed.
7. Press **[Enter]** to return to the blank WordPerfect screen (the menu bar will not be displayed).
8. To use the mouse and pull-down menus to return to the DOS environment do the following:
   a. Click the right mouse button to display the menu bar.
   b. Move the mouse cursor to the **File** option.
   c. Click the left mouse button to pull down the **File** menu.
   d. Move the mouse cursor to the **Exit** option.
   e. Click the left mouse button to select the **Exit** option. You will be asked if you want to save the document.
   f. Move the mouse cursor to the **No** option.
   g. Click the left mouse button to select the **No** option. You will be asked if you want to exit WordPerfect.
   h. Move the mouse cursor to the **Yes** option.
   i. Click the left mouse button to select the **Yes** option. You will be returned to the DOS environment (the system prompt **A:\>** should be displayed).

If you find it easier to use the **[arrow]** keys or the function keys to select some or all WordPerfect features, then by all means use them instead of the mouse; the choice is up to you. Just because your computer has a mouse do not feel that you have to use it for all operations.

Making Modifications

There are a number of ways to make modifications to a document, including:

- Typeover—replacing unwanted characters with new ones.
- Inserting—inserting new characters into the text.
- Reformatting—rearranging the way the paragraphs look.
- Deleting—removing unwanted characters.
- Breaking up paragraphs—separating single paragraphs into one or more paragraphs.
- Deleting whole lines of text.
- Combining paragraphs—making one paragraph out of two or more paragraphs.

Let's see how to make the changes described above to the document called **MEMO1**. Because you are beginning from the DOS environment, the computer first must read the WordPerfect program from the disk and place it into its main memory. Then, WordPerfect must read the document **MEMO1** from the *WordPerfect Data* diskette and load that document into memory.

To load WordPerfect and the document **MEMO1** at the same time, do the following:

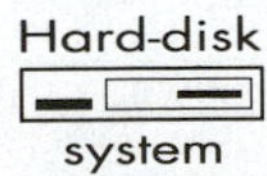

IF YOU ARE USING A HARD-DISK SYSTEM, be sure the *WordPerfect Data* diskette is in the A: drive and then type the following:

Keystroke	Action Resulting from Keystroke
A: ↵	Ensures that the default drive will be **A:**.
C:\WP51\WP A:MEMO1 ↵	Accesses the WordPerfect program from the **WP51** subdirectory on the **C:** drive and loads the document **MEMO1** from the diskette in drive **A:** into WordPerfect.

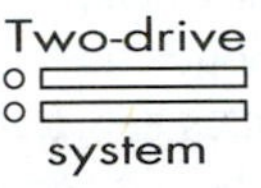

IF YOU ARE USING A TWO-DRIVE SYSTEM, be sure the *WordPerfect Data/Boot* diskette is in the A: drive, place the *WordPerfect 1* diskette in the B: drive, and type the following:

Keystroke	Action Resulting from Keystroke
A: ↵	Ensures that the default drive will be A:.
B:WP A:MEMO1 ↵	Accesses the WordPerfect program from the diskette in drive **B:** and loads the document **MEMO1** from the diskette in drive **A:** into WordPerfect.

In a few seconds the startup screen should appear. If you exited WordPerfect incorrectly when you last used it (e.g., if you turned off the power before exiting), you will see the message **Are other copies of WordPerfect currently running? (Y/N)**. If this happens, type **N** for **No**. Finally, the document **MEMO1** should appear on the screen.

REMEMBER . . . If you forget to type the drive specifications in the above commands, WordPerfect will look for the document **MEMO1** on the default drive. If it cannot find the document on that drive, WordPerfect will assume that you want to create a new document called **MEMO1** and so will present you with a blank screen. If this happens, press **[Shift-F10]** to load the file and then type the proper file specification (**A:MEMO1 ↵**).

To modify the document, you first must move the cursor to the appropriate location on the screen by using the **[arrow]** keys or the mouse. The **[arrow]** keys on the enhanced keyboard are located between the typewriter keyboard and the numeric keypad.

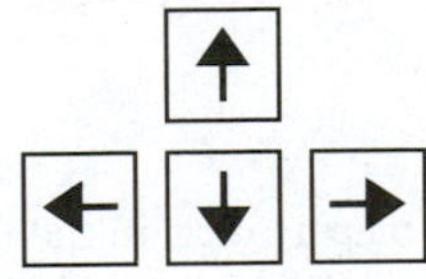

Pressing ↑ once moves the cursor one line up.

Pressing ↓ once moves the cursor one line down.

Pressing ← once moves the cursor one character to the left.

Pressing → once moves the cursor one character to the right.

If you have a standard keyboard, the cursor control keys are on the number keys of the numeric keypad.

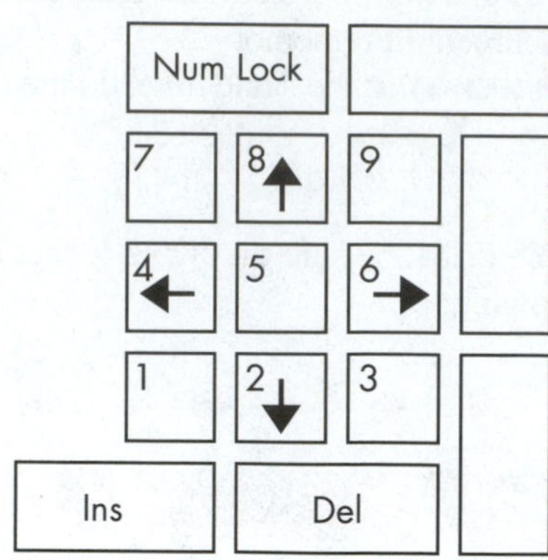

Pressing **[8]** (🡅) once moves the cursor one line up.

Pressing **[2]** (🡇) once moves the cursor one line down.

Pressing **[4]** (🡄) once moves the cursor one character to the left.

Pressing **[6]** (🡆) once moves the cursor one character to the right.

REMEMBER . . . If numbers are displayed rather than the cursor moving when these keys are pressed, the **[NumLock]** key on the numeric keypad must be pressed to change the keys from numeric entry mode to cursor control mode.

• *Typing Over* •

Use the **[arrow]** keys or the mouse to move the cursor to the first letter of the word **`President`** (the cursor location at the lower right-hand side of the screen should read **`Ln 1.17" Pos 3.5"`**). If you are using a mouse, simply move the mouse cursor to the desired location (the letter **`P`**) and click the left button. Then press the **[Insert]** key (or the **[Ins]** key on the numeric keypad) and notice how the word **`Typeover`** appears on the left-hand side of the status line. **Typeover** means that as new letters are entered, they are *typed over* existing letters. Now, type **`PRESIDENT`**. Notice that the old letters, **`President`**, are replaced by the new letters, **`PRESIDENT`**.

The screen will look like the following:

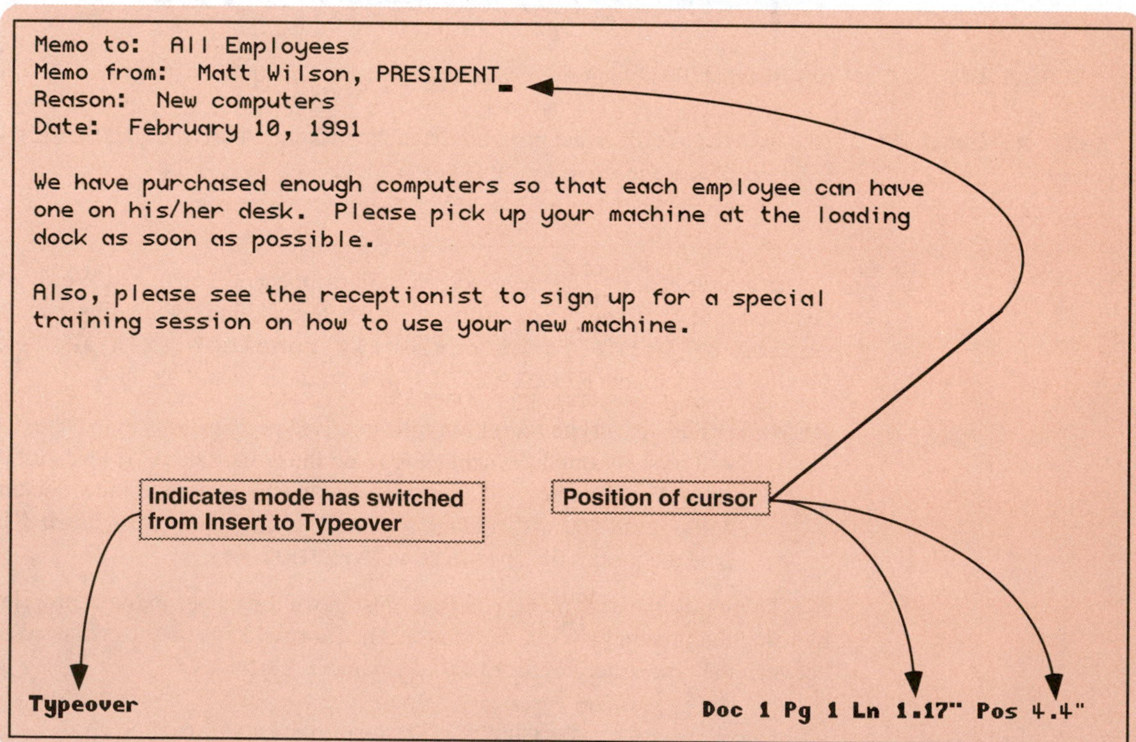

• *Inserting* •

Next, move the cursor to the first letter of the word **`computers`** in the first sentence (the cursor location is **`Ln 1.83" Pos 3.5"`**). Let's say that this needs to be changed to **`wonderful IBM`**

microcomputers. You cannot use typeover because you need to insert more letters, not just change those that are there. To insert letters, use the **[Insert]** key (or the **[Ins]** key on the numeric keypad) again. Press the **[Insert]** key and notice that the word **Typeover** disappears from the status line. The **[Insert]** key is referred to as a toggle key because it is used to switch (toggle) between two different states or modes of operation (typeover is either on or off). The **[NumLock]** key is another example of a toggle key because it is used to switch between entering numbers and cursor control on the numeric keypad. Now, type the words, **wonderful IBM micro**. Notice that as each letter is inserted, the words to the right of the cursor are moved farther to the right to make room for the extra letters. This makes some of the words move off the right-hand side of the screen, but that will be fixed in a minute. The screen will now look like the following:

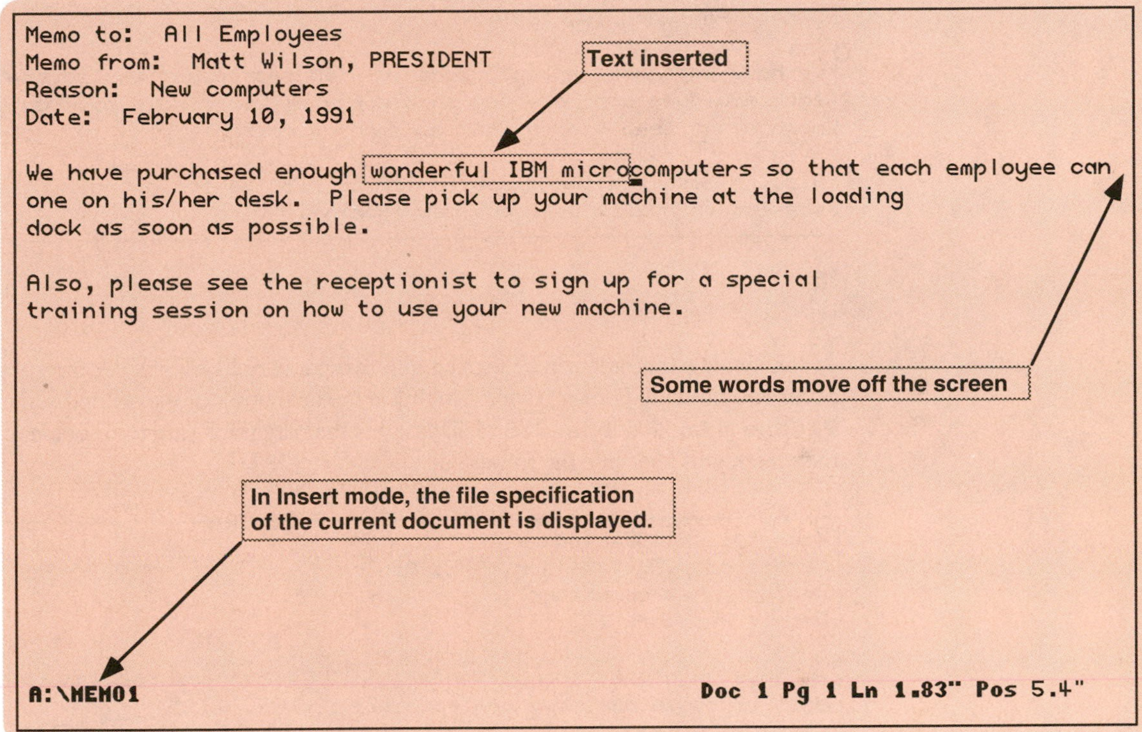

• *Reformatting* •

As soon as one of the **[arrow]** keys is pressed, WordPerfect will adjust the words in the paragraph so that they all fit between the right- and left-hand margins. This process is called *reformatting* the paragraph. Reformatting refers to changing the form of a paragraph so that all the characters fall between the right- and left-hand margins. As was mentioned earlier, WordPerfect automatically reformats (adjusts) paragraphs as needed whenever the cursor is moved to a new line of the text or whenever the **[Insert]** key is pressed (to toggle between insert and typeover mode). Press the **[down arrow]** key and the top of the screen will look like the following:

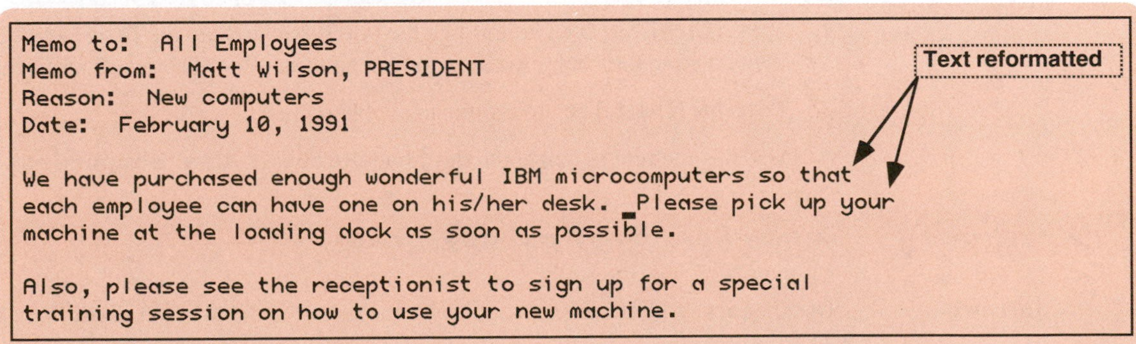

• Deleting •

Delete (erase) the word **`special`** in the middle of the second paragraph. To do this, move the cursor to the first letter in the word **`special`** (the cursor location is **`Ln 2.5" Pos 6.1"`**) and tap the **[Delete]** key (or **[Del]** key on the numeric keypad). One letter disappears each time the key is tapped and the rest of the text moves to the left to fill in the space made by the deleted letters. After deleting the word **`special`** and the blank space to its right, and then pressing the **[down arrow]** key, the top of the screen looks like the following:

```
Memo to:  All Employees
Memo from:  Matt Wilson, PRESIDENT
Reason:  New computers
Date:  February 10, 1991

We have purchased enough wonderful IBM microcomputers so that
each employee can have one on his/her desk.  Please pick up your
machine at the loading dock as soon as possible.

Also, please see the receptionist to sign up for a training
session on how to use your new machine._
```

The word `special` was deleted and the paragraph was reformatted

• Breaking up Paragraphs •

A single paragraph can be broken into two paragraphs by placing the cursor where the split is to occur and pressing **[Enter]** twice. Do this at the beginning of the second sentence (the letter **`P`** of **`Please`** at **`Ln 2" Pos 5.5"`**). This splits the paragraph into two separate paragraphs, and the top of the screen will look like the following:

```
Memo to:  All Employees
Memo from:  Matt Wilson, PRESIDENT
Reason:  New computers
Date:  February 10, 1991

We have purchased enough wonderful IBM microcomputers so that
each employee can have one on his/her desk.

Please pick up your machine at the loading dock as soon as
possible.

Also, please see the receptionist to sign up for a training
session on how to use your new machine.
```

Pressing [Enter] twice splits up paragraphs

• Deleting Entire Lines •

An entire line can be deleted by doing the following:

1. Locate the cursor on the left-hand side of the line to be deleted.
2. Press **[Ctrl-End]** (i.e., hold down the **[Ctrl]** key and tap the **[End]** key). This will erase all the text from the cursor location to the end of the line. The result will be a blank line.
3. Press the **[Delete]** key to eliminate the blank line.

Use this method to delete the third line (**`Reason: New computers`**) by doing the following:

Keystroke	Action Resulting from Keystroke
[arrow]	Use the **[arrow]** keys or mouse to move the cursor to the **`R`** in **`Reason`** (location **`Ln 1.33" Pos 1"`**).

Continued . . .

Keystroke	Action Resulting from Keystroke
[Ctrl-End]	Deletes all text from the cursor to the end of the line.
[Delete]	Deletes the resulting blank line.

The screen now should look like the following:

```
Memo to:  All Employees
Memo from:  Matt Wilson, PRESIDENT
Date:  February 10, 1991

We have purchased enough wonderful IBM microcomputers so that
each employee can have one on his/her desk.

Please pick up your machine at the loading dock as soon as
possible.

Also, please see the receptionist to sign up for a training
session on how to use your new machine.
```

Pressing [Ctrl-End] deletes all text from cursor to end of line

• Saving a Copy of the Modified Document •

Because a number of modifications have been made to the document, it would be a good idea at this time to save the modified copy. To save the document and continue to work with WordPerfect on the same document, do the following:

Keystroke	Action Resulting from Keystroke
[F10]	Specifies that you want to save the document and remain in WordPerfect. WordPerfect responds with the message **Document to be Saved: A:\MEMO1**. The name of the document is displayed as a reminder. If you want to save the document under a new name, you can type the new name. If you want to replace the old version of the document with the current (modified) version you would just press **[Enter]**. However, we want to save it using a new name, **MEMO2**.
[End]	Moves the cursor to the end of the line (just to the right of the **1** in **A:\MEMO1**).
[Backspace]	Deletes the **1**.
2	Replaces the **1** in **A:\MEMO1** with a **2**.
↵	The document now will be saved under the name **A:\MEMO2**. Saving the file under a new name means that two versions of the document will be on the disk: the original version under the name **MEMO1** and the modified version under the name **MEMO2**. If you mess up the editing of the current version or simply like the way the earlier version read, you will still have a copy of it. Eventually, as space on the disk becomes limited, you can erase all but one version (see p. W209). After pressing **[Enter]**, WordPerfect displays the document just as you left it, but the file specification **A:\MEMO2** now appears on the status line.

• Combining Paragraphs •

You can combine paragraphs using the **[Delete]** key. For example, to combine all three paragraphs into a single paragraph do the following:

Keystroke	Action Resulting from Keystroke
[arrow]	Use the [arrow] keys or mouse to move the cursor to the first letter in the second paragraph (the **P** in **Please pick up your machine...** at **Ln 2.17" Pos 1"**).
[Backspace] [Backspace]	Press the [Backspace] key twice (once to delete the blank line between the two paragraphs and again to move the word **Please** up into the first paragraph). You may also have to insert two blank spaces between the period and the word **Please**.
[arrow]	Use the [arrow] keys or mouse to move the cursor to the first letter in the last paragraph (the **A** in **Also, please see...** at **Ln 2.33" Pos 1"**).
[Backspace] [Backspace]	Press the [Backspace] key twice (once to delete the blank line between the two paragraphs and again to move the word **Also** up into the first paragraph). You may also have to insert two blank spaces between the period and the word **Also**.
↓	Reformats the new paragraph. Now, the screen should look as follows:

```
Memo to:  All Employees
Memo from:  Matt Wilson, PRESIDENT
Date:  February 10, 1991

We have purchased enough wonderful IBM microcomputers so that
each employee can have one on his/her desk.  Please pick up your
machine at the loading dock as soon as possible.  Also, please
see the receptionist to sign up for a training session on how to
use your new machine.
```

Switching Documents

Let's say that we are finished with this document and want to begin work on a brand new document. To do this, you first should exit the current document by using the **[F7]** key:

Keystroke	Action Resulting from Keystroke
[F7]	Specifies that you want to exit the document and displays the message **Save document? Yes (No)**.
N	Specifies that **N**o, the current document is not to be saved. If you had wanted to save the modified document you would type **Y** instead of **N** and then type a new file name.
	WordPerfect will now display the message **Exit WP? No (Yes)**.
N	Specifies that **N**o, you do not want to exit WordPerfect. At this point you will be presented with a blank WordPerfect screen. You now may begin typing and editing a new document.

Now suppose you want to edit the first document (or file; the words are interchangeable) you created, **MEMO1**. To do this, the contents of the file must be read into the computer's main memory. This is called **retrieving a file**. Retrieve the document from the *WordPerfect Data* diskette by doing the following:

Keystroke	Action Resulting from Keystroke
[F5]	Invokes the *List Files* feature and displays the following at the bottom of the screen:

```
Dir A:\*.*                                    (Type = to change default Dir)
```

`Dir A:\*.*` means that WordPerfect is about to display a **`Dir`**ectory listing of all of the files (`*.*`) on the diskette in drive **`A:`**. The asterisks (`*`) are called *global characters* (see pp. W199 and W206 for a discussion of asterisks in file names) and are used to represent all the names of all the files.

(**`Type = to change default Dir`**) means that if you want to change the default directory (i.e., the default disk drive and file names) to something else, tap **[=]** and then specify the new default directory.

↵ Requests the listing of the directory of the diskette in the A: drive and displays the following screen (the directory of your disk may be different from that shown below):

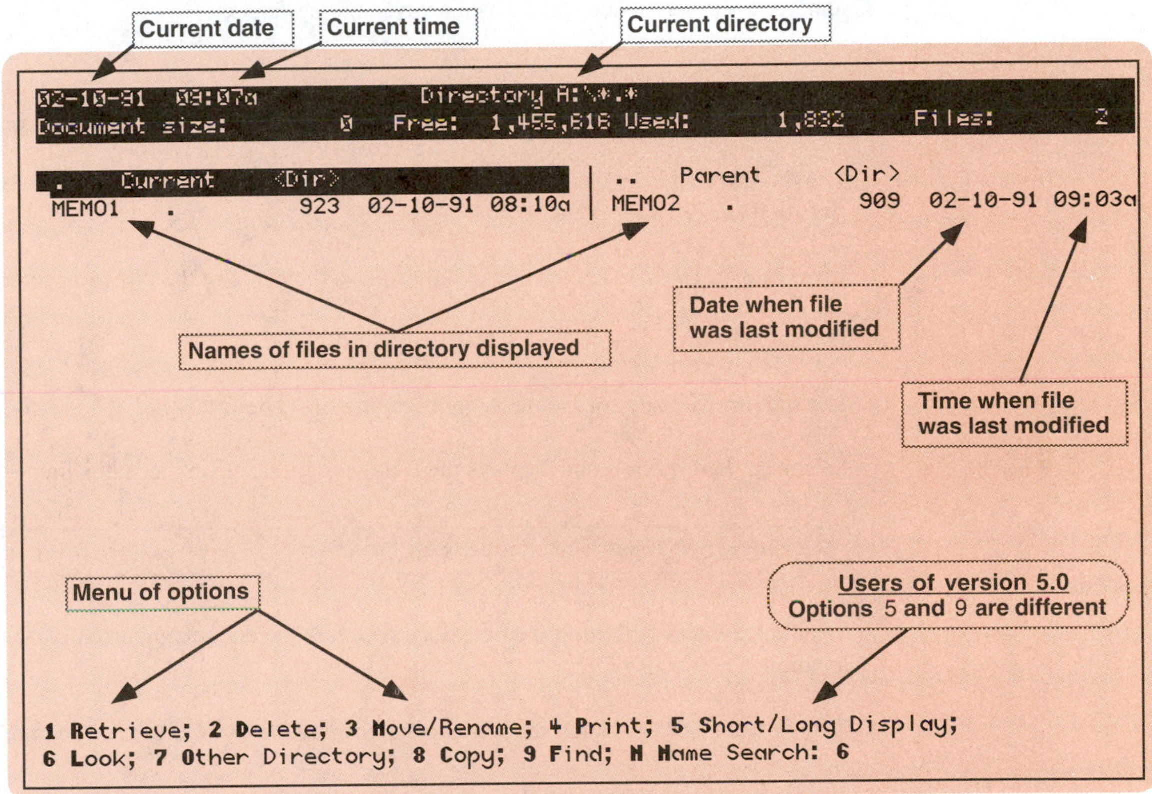

You may highlight any file in the display by using the **[arrow]** keys or mouse. The ten options at the bottom of the screen will be discussed later (see p. W108).

[arrow] Use the **[arrow]** keys or mouse to highlight the file called **`MEMO1`**.

R or **1** Selects **`1 Retrieve`**. The highlighted file (**`MEMO1`**) is retrieved and loaded into WordPerfect so that it can be edited. WordPerfect then returns to the editing screen and the file **`MEMO1`** is displayed.

Continued . . .

Keystroke	Action Resulting from Keystroke

```
Memo to:  All Employees
Memo from:  Matt Wilson, President
Reason:  New computers
Date:  February 10, 1991

We have purchased enough computers so that each employee can have
one on his/her desk.  Please pick up your machine at the loading
dock as soon as possible.

Also, please see the receptionist to sign up for a special
training session on how to use your new machine.
```

Be careful when you retrieve a document. WordPerfect will insert the contents of the retrieved document into the current document at the cursor location. Thus, if the screen is not blank, the new document will be inserted in the middle of the current document (i.e., the retrieved document does not replace the current one but is inserted into it). For example, observe what happens if you retrieve another document while **MEMO1** is displayed on the screen.

Keystroke	Action Resulting from Keystroke
[arrow]	Use the **[arrow]** keys or mouse to move the cursor to the blank line between the two paragraphs (location **Ln 2.33" Pos 1"**).
[F5]	Invokes the *List Files* feature again and displays the name of the directory to be listed.
↵	Displays the directory of the diskette in the A: drive.
[arrow]	Use the **[arrow]** keys or mouse to highlight the file called **MEMO2**.
R (or **1**)	Selects **1 Retrieve** and displays the following message on the status line:

```
Retrieve into current document? No (Yes)
```

Typing **Y** for **Y**es will insert the new document into the document currently on the screen at the cursor location.

Typing **N** for **N**o will cancel the retrieve and display the *List Files* screen again.

Just to see what happens, tap **Y**.

Y	Inserts the contents of the file **MEMO2** at the cursor location, and returns to the editing screen. The screen now looks like the following:

Continued . . .

Keystroke	Action Resulting from Keystroke

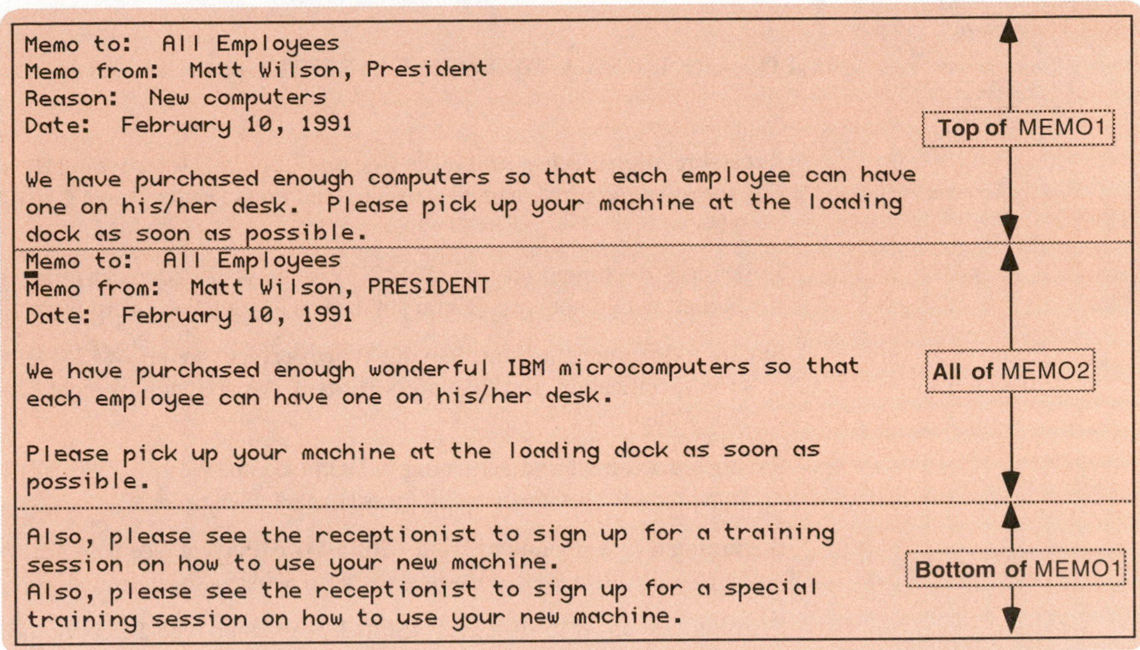

```
Memo to:  All Employees
Memo from:  Matt Wilson, President
Reason:  New computers
Date:  February 10, 1991

We have purchased enough computers so that each employee can have
one on his/her desk.  Please pick up your machine at the loading
dock as soon as possible.
Memo to:  All Employees
Memo from:  Matt Wilson, PRESIDENT
Date:  February 10, 1991

We have purchased enough wonderful IBM microcomputers so that
each employee can have one on his/her desk.

Please pick up your machine at the loading dock as soon as
possible.
Also, please see the receptionist to sign up for a training
session on how to use your new machine.
Also, please see the receptionist to sign up for a special
training session on how to use your new machine.
```


There are times when you might want to do this, but this is not one of them. To exit WordPerfect and return to DOS without saving the last change, do the following:

Keystroke	Action Resulting from Keystroke
[F7]	Specifies that you want to exit the document.
N	Specifies that **N**o, the current document is not to be saved.
Y	Specifies that **Y**es, you do want to exit WordPerfect. At this point you will be returned to the DOS environment and the system prompt **A:\>** will be displayed.

Summary of Operations and Commands

The following is a summary of the operations discussed in this chapter. WordPerfect has other features, but what we have just discussed is all that is needed to use the word processor for writing simple documents. As you practice with WordPerfect, you may want to keep your book open to this page. After you have practiced for a while, you will no longer need this reference sheet. Also, remember that many of the WordPerfect features are summarized in the Appendix (see pp. W226–32) and that there is a WordPerfect keyboard template at the end of this book.

Booting (see p. W6): This depends on your computer system:

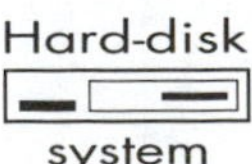

IF YOU ARE USING A HARD-DISK SYSTEM, be sure that the A: drive is empty before turning on the machine. When the DOS prompt appears, insert your *WordPerfect Data* diskette into the A: drive.

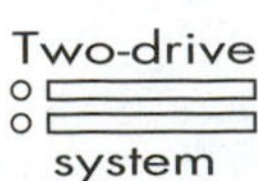

IF YOU ARE USING A TWO-DRIVE SYSTEM, insert your *WordPerfect Data/Boot* diskette into drive A: and then turn on the machine. Type the date and time if requested to do so. When the DOS prompt appears, insert the *WordPerfect 1* diskette into the B: drive.

Accessing WordPerfect (see pp. W6–7): This depends on your computer system:

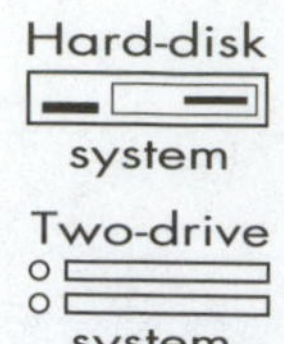

IF YOU ARE USING A HARD-DISK SYSTEM, type `A:` ↵ and then `C:\WP51\WP` ↵.

IF YOU ARE USING A TWO-DRIVE SYSTEM, type `A:` ↵ and then `B:WP` ↵.

Accessing WordPerfect and a file (see pp. W26–27): After typing `WP`, type a space, the file specification (drive:name.extension), and press **[Enter]** (e.g., `C:\WP51\WP A:MEMO1` ↵).

Entering a document (see pp. W12–13): Type your document in as you would on a typewriter, but do not press **[Enter]** at the end of each line (word wrap takes care of that).

Saving a document without leaving WordPerfect (see pp. W13–14): Press **[F10]**, type the file specification, and then press **[Enter]**. A maximum of eight characters may be used for a file name.

Saving a document and returning to DOS (see pp. W18–20): Press **[F7]**, then press `Y`, then type the file specification and press **[Enter]**, then press `Y`.

Beginning a new document from within WordPerfect (see p. W32): Press **[F7]**, then press `Y` (to save the current document) or `N` (to not save the current document), then press `N`.

Printing (see pp. W15–16): Press **[Shift-F7]** and then type `1` to print the entire document.

Typing over (see p. W28): Position the cursor at the proper location. If the word `Typeover` is not displayed in the status line, press **[Insert]**. Then, type the new information. To turn off typeover, press **[Insert]** again.

Inserting (see p. W28): Position the cursor at the proper location. If the word `Typeover` is displayed, press **[Insert]**. Then, type the information to be inserted. To turn off insertion, press **[Insert]** again.

Reformatting paragraphs (see p. W29): Paragraphs are automatically reformatted whenever the cursor is moved to a new line.

Deleting (see p. W30): To delete a character to the left of the cursor, position the cursor and press **[Backspace]**. To delete a character at the cursor, position the cursor and press **[Delete]**.

Breaking up paragraphs (see p. W30): Position the cursor where the break is to occur and press **[Enter]** twice.

Deleting entire lines (see p. W30): Position the cursor on the left-hand side of the line to be deleted and press **[Ctrl-End]**. If a blank line results, press **[Delete]** to remove it.

Exiting WordPerfect (see p. W18): Press **[F7]**.

Summary of Special Keys

The following list summarizes the functions of the special WordPerfect keys covered in this chapter. A more complete list appears in the Appendix on pages W226–32.

Key	Page	Explanation
↵ [Enter]	W12	Moves the cursor to the next line down and/or inserts a blank line.
↑ [up arrow]	W27	Moves the cursor up one line.
↓ [down arrow]	W27	Moves the cursor down one line.
← [left arrow]	W27	Moves the cursor one character to the left.
→ [right arrow]	W27	Moves the cursor one character to the right.
[Backspace]	W12	Deletes the character to the left of the cursor.
[Delete]	W30	Deletes the character at the cursor.
[Insert]	W28	Switches back and forth (toggles) between typeover mode and insert mode.
[End]	W31	Moves the cursor to the end of the line.
[Shift]	C20	Pressing this key in conjunction with a letter key will print the uppercase (capital) representation of the letter. Pressing this key in conjunction with a key that has two symbols will print the upper symbol on the key.
[F1]	W12	Cancels the current operation or restores text just deleted if no operation is active.
[F3]	W10	Displays a help screen.
[F5]	W33	Retrieves files saved on the disk.
[F7]	W18	Exits documents and WordPerfect.
[Shift-F7]	W15	Prints or views a document.
[F10]	W14	Saves a document.

TO TAKE A BREAK Remove diskette(s). To resume (hard disk): Insert Data diskette and type **A:** ↵ , then **C:\WP51\WP** ↵. To resume (two drive): Insert diskettes and Type **A:** ↵ , then **B:WP** ↵.

Homework Exercises

You are going to spend a significant amount of time working on the following homework exercises. Just to be on the safe side, while you are working on a homework exercise, it would be a good idea to save the document every so often using different file names. That way, if you make a major error, you will be able to call up a previous version of the document rather than having to retype the entire document. Also, if you discover an error later, you will be able to make minor corrections without having to redo the entire document. You should use file names that will enable you to tell which documents go with which homework problems. For example, save the first version of the document you create for Exercise 2 as **HWW1-02A** (**H**ome**W**ork for Chapter **1**, Exercise 0**2**, version **A**). Save the second version of the document as **HWW1-02B**, and so on. Save the final version (the one you will hand in for grading) as **HWW1-02**.

---

① Display the help screen for the **[F7]** function key and use the **[PrintScreen]** key to do a screen dump of the display.

---

② Write a personal letter to a friend describing a recent camping trip (or vacation, or business trip, etc.). The letter should include the date, a salutation (e.g., **Dear Fred**), at least two paragraphs describing the trip, and a closing (e.g., **Your friend, Beth**). Use **[F10]** to save the final version of the document under the name **HWW1-02FIN**. Use **[PrintScreen]** to get a hard copy of the document as it appears on the screen just after typing and saving. The screen dump should look something like the following:

```
February 10, 1991

Dear Fred:

Hi!  How are you?  I am having a wonderful time on my vacation.
We are staying at a ranch which is very near the mountains.
Every day we go riding and hiking.

Tomorrow we will go out on a five-day backpacking trip.  We hope
to hike to the base of Coco mountain and then try to climb to the
top (about 10,000 feet).  I'll send you pictures when I get back.

I have to go pack now.

Your friend,
Beth_

A:\HWW1-02FIN                                  Doc 1 Pg 1 Ln 3.5" POS 1.4"
```

CHAPTER ONE

③ Use the *View* feature (see p. W17) to display the printed version of the document you created in Exercise 2. Write a brief description of how the screen looks using the different view settings (**100%**, **200%**, **Full Page**, and **Facing Pages**).

---

④ Use **[Shift-F7]** to print the document you created in Exercise 2. The printed output should look something like the following:

```
February 10, 1991

Dear Fred:

Hi!  How are  you?  I am having a wonderful  time on my vacation.
We  are staying  at a  ranch which  is very  near the  mountains.
Every day we go riding and hiking.

Tomorrow we will go out on a five-day backpacking trip.   We hope
to hike to the base of Coco mountain and then try to climb to the
top (about 10,000 feet).  I'll send you pictures when I get back.

I have to go pack now.

Your friend,
Beth
```

Remember — Full justification is automatically turned on when document is printed.

Notice how the lines of text are fully justified in the printed version but are only left justified in the version on the screen.

---

⑤ Create a memo addressed to the director of parking services for your company noting that you have just been promoted and would like your parking space moved from the employee parking lot to the executive garage. Use **[F10]** to save the final version of the document under the name **HWW1-05FIN**. Use **[Shift-F7]** to print the final document. The printed output should look like the following:

```
  Memo to:  Director, Parking Services
Memo from:  Karen Brandt, International Sales Manager
   Reason:  Change in Parking Space
     Date:  February 10, 1991

I have recently been promoted  to International Sales Manager and
therefore am entitled to a parking space in the executive parking
garage.  Would you please attend to this matter immediately?  My
current parking spot is in lot C-27.

Thank  you  for attending  to  this  matter.   If you  have  any
questions, please call my office at 625-1902.
```

Continued . . .

CHAPTER ONE

⑥ Modify the memo you wrote in Exercise 5 so that it follows a more formal business letter format (i.e., include your return address, the address of the director, and a proper closing). The body of the letter should be the same as the body of the memo. Use **[F10]** to save the final version of the document under the name **HWW1-06FIN**. Use **[Shift-F7]** to print the final document. The printed output should look like the following:

```
                                        429 First Street SE
                                        Minneapolis, MN  55455
                                        February 10, 1991

Alex Gohar, Director
Parking Services
Ali Plumbing, Inc.
213 Apple Lane
Minneapolis, MN  55431

Dear Mr. Gohar:

I have recently been promoted to International Sales Manager  and
therefore am entitled to a parking space in the executive parking
garage.  Would you please attend to this matter immediately?  My
current parking spot is in lot C-27.

Thank  you  for  attending  to this  matter.   If  you  have any
questions, please call my office at 625-1902.

                                        Sincerely,

                                        Karen Brandt
                                        International Sales Manager
```

⑦ Use the *List Files* feature (see p. W33) to display the directory of all files on your *WordPerfect Data* diskette. Do a screen dump of the display.

CHAPTER ONE

⑧ Write a résumé that you could submit to a prospective employer. The résumé should include the following information:

Name

Address

Phone number

Employment objective Describe the type of job you are looking for in the short-term (the next few months) or the long-term (in a few years).

Education Describe your formal education including high school, college courses completed, grade point average, major, minor, and any honors received.

Work experience Describe your work history including summer, part-time, and full-time jobs. Briefly describe the work you did in each job

References Provide the names and addresses of two people who know you well enough to supply information about your abilities.

Use **[F10]** to save the final version of the document under the name `HWW1-08FIN`. Use **[Shift-F7]** to print the final document. The printed output should look something like the following:

```
Molly Collins
216 Pillsbury Drive SE
Minneapolis, MN  55455
612/373-2212

EMPLOYMENT OBJECTIVE
Long-term objective:  To become a nuclear physicist and work in a
large metropolitan hospital doing cancer research.

Short-term objective: To find summer employment in a physics lab.

EDUCATION
Graduated high school in  1988 with an  A average.  Completed  53
credits at the University of Minnesota, including calculus I, II,
and III, freshman English,  and 20 credits in liberal arts.  Math
and science GPA = 3.7/4.0, liberal arts GPA = 3.4/4.0.

WORK EXPERIENCE
1988-present:   Undergraduate  teaching assistant in  the General
College Computer Program.   Duties  include tutoring students  in
computer programming and grading papers.

REFERENCES
Dr. Geri Benson (current work supervisor)
117 Appleby Hall
Minneapolis, MN  55455
612/373-8832

Nader Mahmoodi
1 Penny Lane
Minneapolis, MN  55411
612/329-1023
```

More Word Processing

Objectives *After you have completed this chapter, you should be able to*

- Describe character enhancements as they relate to word processing.
- Describe page formatting options available when using a word processor.
- Use special keys to move around the WordPerfect screen.
- Explain what WordPerfect codes are and how they are used.
- Set tabs, margins, and indentations for WordPerfect documents.
- Execute DOS commands from within WordPerfect (drop to DOS).
- Double space documents.
- Perform operations such as moving, copying, and deleting blocks of text.
- Turn on and off WordPerfect document justification.

CHAPTER 2

- Number lines of text in WordPerfect printed output.
- Center lines of text.
- Convert the case of text to uppercase or lowercase.
- Highlight text with **boldface** or underline.
- Define page formats for entire documents.
- Create headers and footers for documents.
- Insert hard page breaks into WordPerfect documents.
- Use the WordPerfect *Spell* feature.
- Use the WordPerfect *Thesaurus* feature.

Introduction

By this time, you should have practiced with WordPerfect enough so that you can create simple documents with some degree of ease. In this chapter, we will discuss the process of working with a word processor (versus working with a typewriter) and how to make major revisions to your documents.

Definitions

Before beginning a specific example, you should familiarize yourself with some definitions of terms frequently encountered when talking about word processing.

Block . . . (W70) A specified section of text such as a word, group of words, sentence, or paragraph.

Block operation . . . (W70) An operation performed on a block of text, such as copying, deleting, or moving.

Boldface . . . (W45) Text that is darker than normal **(like this)**.

Character enhancements . . . (W45) Changes to characters that alter their appearance such as superscript (e.g., the 2 in x^2), boldface (e.g., **this phrase is in boldface**), italic (e.g., *this phrase is in italic*), subscript (e.g., the 2 in H_2O) and underline (e.g., <u>this phrase is underlined</u>).

Cutting text . . . (W72) Deleting a block of text from a document but saving the text temporarily in the main memory of the computer. Text which has been cut can be inserted (pasted) into a different location of the same document or a different document. This makes it easy to rearrange sentences or paragraphs of a document.

Codes . . . (W51) Markers that WordPerfect uses to keep track of and control how text will look on the screen and how it will be printed.

Footer . . . (W86) A portion of a document that automatically appears at the bottom (foot) of each page.

Format . . . (W45) To make a document look a certain way when completed, including spacing, pagination, character enhancements, margin settings, etc. Compare this with *format* when used in relation to initializing a disk (see p. W43).

Hanging paragraph . . . (W66) Positioning the first line of a paragraph at the left margin and indenting all subsequent lines.

Header . . . (W86) A portion of a document that automatically appears at the top (head) of each page.

Page break . . . (W91) A location in a document where WordPerfect tells the printer to continue printing on a new sheet of paper.

Paginate . . . (W86) To break up a document into pages of a specified size and to number the pages sequentially.

Pasting text . . . (W72) Inserting a block of text from a disk or the main memory of the computer.

Writing with a Word Processor

Once a writer has become familiar with the computer keyboard and the word-processing program, writing becomes less of a chore. The writer can concentrate on what he or she wants to say rather than having to pay attention to the exact form it will take or to spelling or punctuation.

For example, the authors used the following process for writing each chapter of this book. First, we thought about what it was we wanted to say (this is the difficult and time-consuming part). Next, we generated an outline of the content for the chapter. Then, a first draft of the text was typed on the word processor (the backspace key was used to correct any typographical errors detected while typing). The text was entered without much thought as to how the pages were to be formatted — the information just came out of our heads and went into the computer.

While typing the drafts, the text was saved to disk many times as we added more information. Repeated saving of a document as it evolves provides some insurance against accidental loss of data in the event of a power failure or the program or computer crashing unexpectedly. It is also a good idea to save copies of your drafts on different disks so that if one disk becomes damaged a backup copy is available. When the first draft of a chapter was completed, a copy was printed so that it could be read and edited. Many people prefer to edit the hard copy rather than the copy displayed on the screen because the editing can be done anywhere (you do not have to be sitting in front of the computer) and because you can see more of the text at one time than the 25 lines displayed on the computer monitor. Others find it more efficient to do the editing right on the computer screen.

During the editing process, passages were inserted, deleted, modified, and moved to different locations. The changes written on the hard copy were entered into the computer using the editing capabilities of the word processor and then the document was checked for spelling errors.

Once the final draft of the document has been entered into the computer, the appearance of the final printed version can be changed by adding character enhancements and page formatting.

The process just outlined is a good one to follow. However, document size and importance, time constraints, and your own personal preferences will determine which of the steps you want to follow.

Character Enhancements

Character enhancements are changes to the way in which the characters will appear when they are printed. Different word processors have varying capabilities; examples of some enhancements are as follows:

Enhancement	Example	Typical use
Underlining	Moby Dick	Underline titles of books.
Subscripts	H_2O	Mathematics and science.
Superscripts	X^2	Mathematical exponents, footnotes.
Boldface	**Profits Up**	Draws attention to words.
Italic	*Profits Up*	Draws attention to words.
Fonts	`Profits Up`	A font is a complete set of characters using a certain typeface. Some fonts make text easier to read while others make the text look "fancier." Some fonts are proportionally spaced (different characters take up different amounts of space; the letter *w*, for example, takes up more space than the letter *i*), while others are monospaced (each character takes up the same amount of space; for example, **`w`** and **`i`** are the same size). Two common fonts are displayed below (the Times font is proportionally spaced while the Courier font is monospaced). Both examples use the same size of type (12 point).

Font	Example
Times	The quick brown fox jumped over the lazy dog.
`Courier`	`The quick brown fox jumped over the lazy dog.`

Type Size	Example
Big profit	Draws attention to words. Type sizes are given in terms of points. A point is measured from the highest part of the tallest letter to the lowest descender (the part of a letter that falls below the line, such as the tail of the letter *g*).
9 point	The quick brown fox jumped over the lazy dog.
12 point	The quick brown fox jumped over the lazy dog.
24 point	The quick brown fox ...

Be careful when using character enhancements; it is easy to go overboard and put in so many different fonts and styles that the enhancements detract from the document. For example, a business letter that uses five different fonts, styles, and sizes would give the document too much of a "carnival" flavor. Which of the following two letters would you take more seriously?

Sample letter 1

843 22nd Avenue South
Minneapolis, MN 55455
10 February 1991

Computer Sales, Inc.
12 Benson Avenue
St. Paul, MN 55110

Dear Sir or Madam:

I would like to apply for the salesperson job which you listed in the *Computer Weekly* on 7 February. I am very interested in becoming more involved in retail sales of computers and I feel that my background matches the qualifications which you seek. My resume is attached.

Thank you for consideration of my application.

Sincerely,

Carol Bliss

Sample letter 2

843 22nd Avenue South
Minneapolis, MN 55455
10 February 1991

Computer Sales, Inc.
12 Benson Avenue
St. Paul, MN 55110

Dear Sir or Madam:

I would like to apply for the salesperson job which you listed in the Computer Weekly on 7 February. I am very interested in becoming more involved in retail sales of computers and I feel that my background matches the qualifications which you seek. My resume is attached.

Thank you for consideration of my application.

Sincerely,

Carol Bliss

Page Formatting

Page formatting refers to the way in which the printed pages will appear. This includes such things as setting the margins (wide, narrow, or anything in between), justifying the text (lining up margins on the left, right, or both sides), and printing headers and footers on each page. The following examples illustrate some of the ways in which pages can be formatted:

The justification can be set to *left justification* (*flush left*), as can be seen in this sentence where everything is lined up on the left-hand side of the page but the right-hand side has a ragged edge.

Or, the justification of the text can be set to *right justification* (*flush right*), as can be seen in this sentence where everything is lined up on the right-hand side of the page but the left-hand side has a ragged edge.

Or the text can be fully justified as in this paragraph. With *full justification*, the text is lined up on both the left-hand and right-hand sides. In order to do this, the computer has to insert extra spaces between the words. Some people find this makes reading the document more difficult and slower because the reader has to look at a lot of "extra" blank spaces. However, full justification gives the document a more finished or typeset look.

Lines can be centered, as in this sentence where everything is centered on the page between the left-hand and right-hand margins.

The between-line spacing can be adjusted, as in this sentence so that there is less space between lines of text.

The between-line spacing can be set to double space, as in this sentence where there is one blank line between lines of text. This makes the text appear less cramped and provides room for the reader to write comments about the text material right on the paper.

The spacing can be set to triple space, as in this sentence where there are two blank lines between lines of text. As with double spacing, this provides the reader with lots of room to write comments on the material. However, it may slow down reading because the text is so spread out.

Moving around the WordPerfect Screen

As documents become larger and as you do more editing, using the **[arrow]** keys or mouse to move around the document is sometimes time consuming. To increase your efficiency, WordPerfect employs special cursor-control key combinations that allow you to quickly move throughout a document or a screen.

To see how the cursor-control keys can save you time, you need a long document to work with. Create such a document by doing the following (this document will also be used in later sections):

1. Boot the computer and make A: the default drive by typing **A:** ↵. Access the WordPerfect program by typing **C:\WP51\WP** ↵ (for a hard-disk system) or **B:WP** ↵ (for a two-drive system).

2. After the blank WordPerfect screen appears, type the memo shown in Figure 2–1. To get you started, do the following:

FIGURE 2-1

```
MEMORANDUM

DATE:      February 10, 1991

TO:        Bill Schwartz and Lisa Pearson

FROM:      Alec Benson

SUBJECT:   Preparation of Conference Room

We need to prepare the conference room for a meeting of the Board
of Directors to be held from 9:00 am to 11:30 am on February 12,
1991.  The following have to be taken care of by that time:

1.  The room needs to be cleaned (call Quick Klean Company?).

2.  An overhead projector and a screen have to be rented (call
Readi Rents?) and set up at the front of the room.

3.  Name tags for the twenty participants need to be prepared.
See Jim Wilson for the list of names.

I would like us to meet tomorrow at 9:00 am in the conference
room to finalize the plans and make specific assignments.

This is a very important meeting for the future of our company so
I want everything to go smoothly.

If you have any questions before our meeting do not hesitate to
call me at 624-1128.

cc: Sara Nelson
Jill Smith
```

Use [Space bar] rather than [Tab] here

Only this much text can fit on the screen at one time

Keystroke	Action Resulting from Keystroke
MEMORANDUM ↵	Enters the first line of the document and moves the cursor to the second line.
↵	Enters a blank line and moves the cursor to the third line.
DATE:	Enters the first part of the third line.
[Spacebar]	Press the **[Spacebar]** five times to move the cursor to location **Ln 1.33" Pos 2"**. At this point you may type the date (e.g., **February 10, 1991**) or you may have WordPerfect enter it for you by using the Date feature. Let's do the latter.
[Shift-F5]	Selects the WordPerfect *Date* feature and displays the following menu at the bottom of the screen:

```
1 Date Text; 2 Date Code; 3 Date Format; 4 Outline; 5 Para Num; 6 Define: 0
```

This menu is more fully described on page W160. For now, you want to enter the date as text so press **T**.

T (or **1**)	Selects **Date Text** and inserts the date at the cursor. Note that the date inserted is that which is currently on the computer's clock. If it is incorrect you probably did not enter the proper date when you booted the computer. In that case, simply use the **[Backspace]** key to erase it and type in the correct date.

```
MEMORANDUM

DATE:      February 10, 1991_
```

Continue typing the rest of the memo. Note that the memo is more than 24 lines in length and therefore is too long to be entirely visible on the screen at one time. As you begin to type line 25, line 1 will scroll off the top of the screen (of course, it is still in the computer's main memory, but you cannot see it until you use the cursor-control keys to move up to that line).

When typing the memo, do not use the **[Tab]** key to adjust the spacing; use the **[Spacebar]** key. The **[Tab]** key inserts special codes into the document which would confuse things at this point. The **[Tab]** key and other codes will be discussed later.

3. Save the document under the name **MRMPREP.V1** by doing the following:

Keystroke	Action Resulting from Keystroke
[F10]	Specifies that you want to save the document. WordPerfect responds with the message **Document to be Saved:**.
A:MRMPREP.V1 ↵	Provides the file specification of the document to be saved and returns to the editing screen. The document is saved on the diskette in the **A:** drive under the name **MRMPREP** (for **M**emo on **R**oo**M** **PREP**aration) with the extension **V1** (for **V**ersion **1** of the memo). Note that WordPerfect displays the document just as you left it, but that now the file specification **A:\MRMPREP.V1** appears on the status line.

4. The WordPerfect cursor-control keys are summarized in the following table:

Key	Cursor Movement
←	Moves the cursor left one character.
→	Moves the cursor right one character.
↑	Moves the cursor up one line.
↓	Moves the cursor down one line.
↵	Moves the cursor down one line and to the left-hand margin (which adds one line).
[Ctrl ←]	Moves the cursor left one word on the same line.
[Ctrl →]	Moves the cursor right one word on the same line.
[Home] ←	Moves the cursor to the left end of the text on the same line.
[Home] →	Moves the cursor to the right end of the text on the same line.
[Home] ↑	Moves the cursor to the top line of the screen (this may not be the top of the document). The cursor does not move horizontally (i.e., its **Pos**ition remains the same).

Continued . . .

Key	Cursor Movement
[Home] ↓	Moves the cursor to the bottom line of the screen (this may not be the bottom of the document). The cursor does not move horizontally (i.e., its **Pos**ition remains the same).
[Home] [Home] ↑	Moves the cursor to the top of the document.
[Home] [Home] ↓	Moves the cursor to the bottom of the document.
[Ctrl-Home]	Moves the cursor to the top of the page specified by the user (this is called the *Go to* command).
[PageDown]	Moves the cursor to the first line of the next page.
[PageUp]	Moves the cursor to the first line of the previous page.
[+] (on numeric keypad)	Moves the cursor to the last line on the screen. If the cursor does not move but a plus sign is displayed, press the **[NumLock]** key.
[-] (on numeric keypad)	Moves the cursor to the first line on the screen. If the cursor does not move but a minus sign is displayed, press the **[NumLock]** key.
[Tab]	Moves the cursor right to the next tab stop.
[Shift-Tab]	Moves the cursor left to the previous tab stop.
[End]	Moves the cursor to the end of the current line.

5. To try out some of these key combinations, do the following:

Keystroke	Action Resulting from Keystroke
[Home] [Home] ↑	Moves the cursor to the top of the document. The status line should read **`Doc 1 Pg 1 Ln 1" Pos 1"`** and the cursor should be located under the first **`M`** in **`MEMORANDUM`**.
[End]	Moves the cursor to the end of the current line. The status line should read **`Doc 1 Pg 1 Ln 1" Pos 2"`** and the cursor should be located under the space just to the right of **`MEMORANDUM`**.
[Home] ↓	Moves the cursor to the bottom of the screen (this is not the bottom of the document). The status line should read **`Doc 1 Pg 1 Ln 4.83" Pos 2"`** and the cursor should be located under the **`n`** in **`finalize`**.
[Ctrl →]	Moves the cursor to the next word on the same line. The status line should read **`Doc 1 Pg 1 Ln 4.83" Pos 2.7"`** and the cursor should be located under the **`t`** in **`the plans and...`**
[PageDown]	Moves the cursor to the first line of the next page. However, because the current document does not have a page two, the cursor is sent to the bottom of the document rather than to the top of page two. The status line should read **`Doc 1 Pg 1 Ln 6.5" Pos 1"`**. Remember—a page is 66 lines (11 inches) tall but a screen is only 24 lines (4 inches) tall.
[Home] [Home] ↑	Moves the cursor back to the top of the document.

WordPerfect Codes

The tabs, margins, indentations, and other characteristics of a document can be changed quickly and easily by using special WordPerfect codes. **Codes** are markers that WordPerfect uses to keep track of and control how text will look on the screen and how it will be printed. The codes, normally hidden from view, can be revealed when needed by pressing **[Alt-F3]**, the *Reveal Codes* feature.

Before using the *Reveal Codes* feature on **`MRMPREP.V1`**, be sure that the cursor is at the top of the document (press **[Home] [Home]** 🡅 if necessary). To show the codes which WordPerfect has inserted into the document, press **[Alt-F3]** (while holding down **[Alt]**, tap **[F3]**). This key combination is referred to as *Reveal Codes* because it will reveal the special formatting codes used by WordPerfect. The screen will appear as follows:

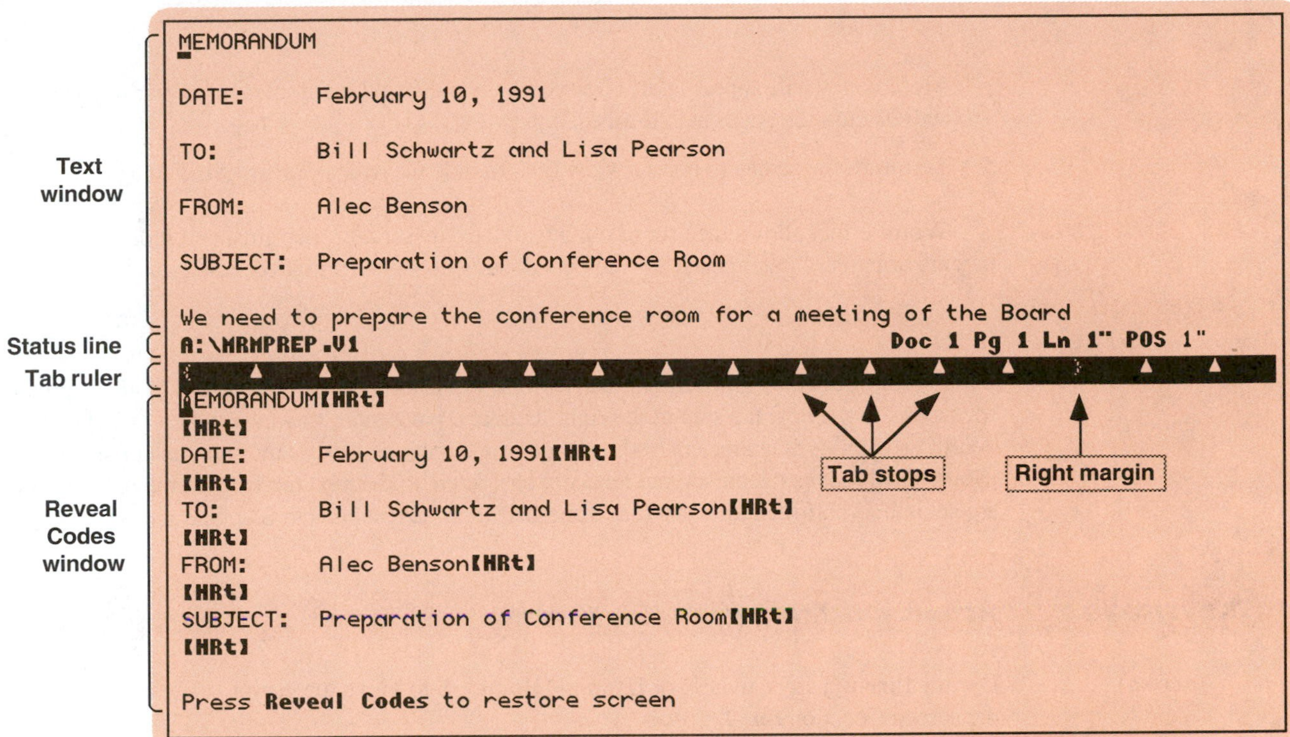

The screen is divided into four areas:

1. The top of the screen is called the *text window*. It shows up to five lines of text directly above and directly below the cursor. This window shows how the document normally appears on the screen.

2. The *status line* is displayed just below the text window. It shows the file specification, the document number, the page number, and the location of the cursor.

3. The *tab ruler* is just below the status line. It shows the locations of the left-hand margin, **{**, the tab stops, ▲ , and the right-hand margin, **}**. Braces, such as **{** or **}**, are used to indicate when a margin and a tab occur at the same position. Brackets, such as **[** or **]**, are used to indicate margins by themselves. Thus, in the ruler displayed above, the brace, **{**, at the left-hand margin indicates that there is a tab stop at that location also. The brace, **}**, at the right-hand margin indicates that this margin also coincides with a tab stop.

4. The bottom part of the screen is called the *Reveal Codes window*. Like the text window, this window shows the text; but in addition, it shows the normally hidden formatting codes. These codes are created in different ways, many of which will be discussed in detail later. They can be deleted in the same way as normal text (use **[Backspace]** and **[Delete]**). For this particular document, the following codes are shown:

Code	Description
M	The first letter of the word **MEMORANDUM** is displayed in reverse video. This indicates the location of the cursor in the same way as does the blinking line, ▬, in the text window.
[HRt]	This code stands for **H**ard **Ret**urn. It indicates where **[Enter]** has been pressed to move (return) the cursor to the left-hand margin. In contrast, a **S**oft **Ret**urn (shown as **[SRt]** when it appears in *Reveal Codes*) is where normal word wrap has been used to move (return) the cursor to the left-hand margin. Notice that two hard returns in a row show as a blank line in the document.

More codes will appear later, after you have enhanced the document in various ways. We will discuss the codes at that time.

5. To return the screen to normal view (i.e., to hide the codes), press **[Alt-F3]** again.

Tabs, Margins, and Indentations

WordPerfect allows the user to quickly and easily set tabs, margins, and indentations of entire documents or parts of documents. This allows documents to be formatted exactly as the user wishes.

• Tabs •

WordPerfect tabs function in a way similar to the tabs on a typewriter. If **[Tab]** is pressed, the cursor moves to the next tab stop to the right. Unlike a typewriter, however, when **[Tab]** is pressed, WordPerfect moves characters to the right of the cursor, as well as moving the cursor itself. Pressing **[Shift-Tab]** moves the cursor and adjacent characters to the next tab stop on the left. Initially, tab stops are set at one-half inch intervals (each one-half inch corresponds to five characters). For example:

Keystroke	Action Resulting from Keystroke
[arrow]	Use the **[arrow]** keys, mouse, or **[Home] [Home]** ↑ to move the cursor to the upper left-hand corner of the screen (location **Ln 1" Pos 1"**).
[Tab]	Press **[Tab]** and note how the cursor and the word **MEMORANDUM** both move five spaces to the right. This will happen each time **[Tab]** is pressed.
[Shift-Tab]	Moves the cursor and the word **MEMORANDUM** five spaces to the left.
	To actually see where the tab stops are, you may use the *Reveal Codes* feature (**[Alt-F3]**) as described in the previous section. For example:
[Alt-F3]	Reveals the codes and displays the following in the center of the screen just below the tab ruler:

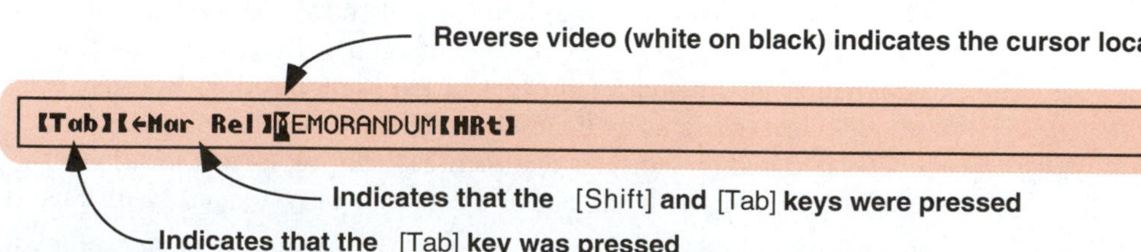
Reverse video (white on black) indicates the cursor location
[Tab][←Mar Rel]MEMORANDUM[HRt]
Indicates that the [Shift] and [Tab] keys were pressed
Indicates that the [Tab] key was pressed

Notice the two new codes just to the left of the word **MEMORANDUM**. These were inserted when you pressed **[Tab]** and **[Shift-Tab]**:

[TAB] indicates that the **[Tab]** key was pressed and instructs WordPerfect to move the text to the next tab stop on the right.

Continued . . .

Keystroke	Action Resulting from Keystroke
	`[<-Mar Rel]` indicates that **[Shift-Tab]** was pressed and shows that the **Mar**gin was **Rel**eased to the left (**<-**). The effect is to move one tab stop to the left.
[Alt-F3]	Hides the codes again.

To change the tab stops, you must use the *Format* feature. For example, change the tab stops on the last two lines of the document on page W48 so that there is a single tab setting 1.5 inches from the left-hand side of the page by doing the following:

Keystroke	Action Resulting from Keystroke
[Home] [Home] ↓	Moves the cursor to the bottom of the document.
[arrow]	Use the **[arrow]** keys or mouse to move the cursor to the first letter, **c**, in the second to last line (**cc: Sara Nelson**). This should be location **Ln 6.17" Pos 1"**.
[Shift-F8]	Selects the *Format* feature and displays the following screen:

```
Format

     1 - Line
              Hyphenation                     Line Spacing
              Justification                   Margins Left/Right
              Line Height                     Tab Set
              Line Numbering                  Widow/Orphan Protection

     2 - Page
              Center Page (top to bottom)     Page Numbering
              Force Odd/Even Page             Paper Size/Type
              Headers and Footers             Suppress
              Margins Top/Bottom

     3 - Document
              Display Pitch                   Redline Method
              Initial Codes/Font              Summary

     4 - Other
              Advance                         Overstrike
              Conditional End of Page         Printer Functions
              Decimal Characters              Underline Spaces/Tabs
              Language                        Border Options

Selection: 0
```

Users of version 5.0
One more option is given

Users of version 5.0
This option is missing

This menu is divided into four areas each of which has its own submenu. For those options under **1 - Line**, **2 - Page**, and **4 - Other**, any changes will affect text from the point of the cursor to the end of the document or the next format change. Changes listed under **3 - Document** will affect the entire document. Many of the options will be discussed in later sections of this book.

For now, we are interested in setting the tabs. This option is listed under **1 - Line**. Notice that the numeral **1** and the letter **L** are both highlighted. This means that you may tap either of these keys to select this option.

Continued . . .

Keystroke	Action Resulting from Keystroke
L (or **1**)	Selects **1 - Line** and displays the following screen:

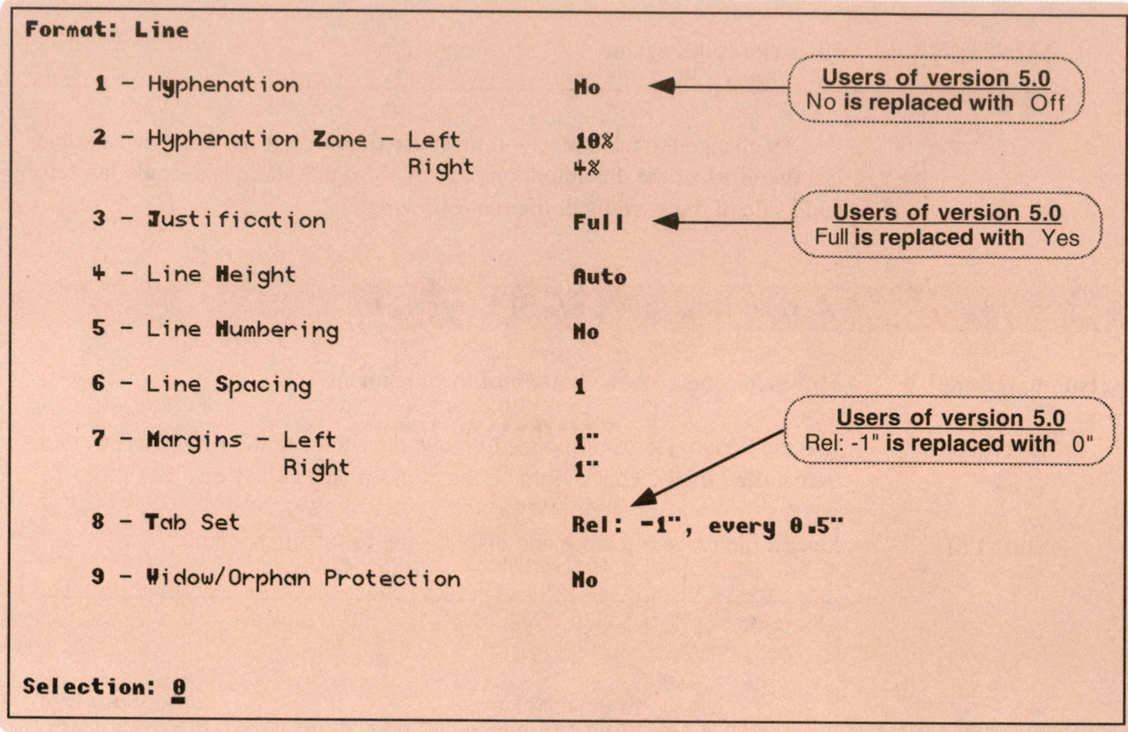

1 - Hyphenation allows you to hyphenate words.

2 - Hyphenation Zone, if hyphenation has been turned on, allows you to decide which words to hyphenate and which to wrap around to the next line.

3 - Justification allows you to turn right justification on or off.

4 - Line Height allows you to adjust the space assigned to (height of) each line of text.

5 - Line Numbering allows you to number lines of text.

6 - Line Spacing allows you to change the spacing of lines (i.e., single space, double space)

7 - Margins allows you to set the left-hand and right-hand margins.

8 - Tab Set allows you to set the tab stops.

9 - Widow/Orphan Protection allows you to determine whether or not you will allow single lines of a paragraph to appear at the top of a page (an orphan) or at the bottom of a page (a widow).

WordPerfect version 5.1 has two types of tabs: *absolute* and *relative*. Absolute tab stops are located in relation to the left edge of the paper (as they might be on a typewriter). If you change the margins of your document at some later time, the absolute tabs remain unchanged. For example, if you set an absolute tab stop at 1 inch and then later change the left margin to 2 inches, the tab stop will remain at 1 inch. Relative tabs, on the other hand, are always set relative to the current left margin rather than the left edge of the paper. This means that if you set the tabs and then later change the left margin setting, the tab stops will adjust automatically relative to the new margin. Thus, if you set a relative tab stop at 1 inch and then later move the left margin 2 inches to the right, the tab stop will be reset at 3 inches (the original 1 inch plus the 2 inches you moved the margin).

USERS OF VERSION 5.0 All tabs in version 5.0 are absolute tabs. Relative tabs are new to version 5.1.

The default setting for tabs is given as **`Rel: -1", every 0.5"`**. This means that the tabs are set relative to the left margin, beginning at –1" (i.e., 1 inch to the left of the left margin), and that a tab stop occurs every .5 inch.

To actually set the tabs, do the following:

Keystroke	*Action Resulting from Keystroke*
`T` (or **8**)	Selects **8 - `Tab Set`** and displays the following tabs ruler at the bottom of the screen:

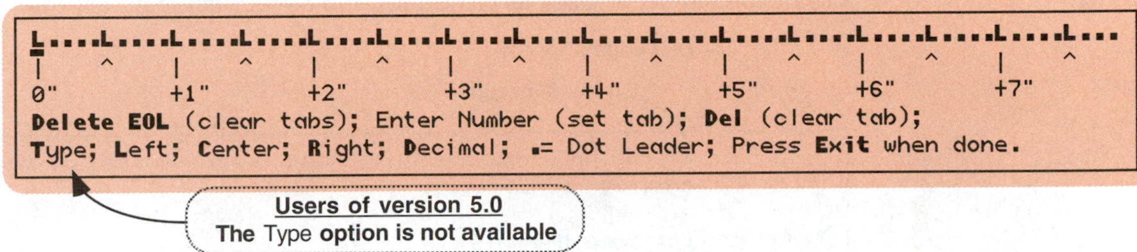

The current tab stops are indicated by the letter **`L`** to indicate **`L`**eft tabs. This means that words will be lined up on their left sides. By default the tabs are set every .5 inch (notice on the ruler that there is an L at 0", .5", 1", etc.)

The last two lines serve as a reminder of the different tab options:

`Delete EOL (clear tabs)` means that if you press **[Ctrl-End]** (this is the delete to the **`E`**nd **`O`**f the **`L`**ine key combination), all the tabs from the current cursor location to the end of the line will be deleted.

`Enter Number (set tab)` means that if you type a number (indicating the horizontal position where you want the tab) and then press **[Enter]**, a tab stop will be placed at that position. For example, typing **`2.6`** ↵ will place a tab 2.6 inches from the left margin (for relative tabs) or 2.6 inches from the left edge of the page (for absolute tabs).

`Del (clear tab)` means that you may clear an individual tab by using the **[arrow]** keys or mouse to move the cursor to the appropriate location and pressing **[Delete]**.

`Type` allows you to select either relative or absolute tabs.

`Left` means that the left sides of words line up on the tab stop.

`Center` means that the centers of words line up on the tab stop.

`Right` means that the right sides of words line up on the tab stop.

`Decimal` means that words are lined up by their alignment characters (the default alignment character is the decimal point). Using this type of tab allows you to set up columns of numbers with the decimal points (or any other specified character) lined up on the tab stop. WordPerfect allows you to change the alignment character to any character you wish.

Continued . . .

Keystroke	Action Resulting from Keystroke
	.= **Dot Leader** means that you may set up a dot leader for tabs. This fills the space preceding a tab with dots rather than blank spaces. To set up a dot leader, first set a tab and then type a period at the same location. The tab setting will appear in reverse video (so that it looks like this ▙) to indicate that it has been changed to a dot leader. Dot leaders are often used in the table of contents of books.
T (or **1**)	Selects **Type** and displays the following at the bottom of the screen:

```
Tab Type: 1 Absolute; 2 Relative to Margin: 0
```

Keystroke	Action Resulting from Keystroke
A (or **1**)	Selects **Absolute** and returns to the tabs ruler.
[Home] ←	Moves the cursor to the far left-hand side of the tabs ruler. Notice how the screen scrolls horizontally in order to display the **0"** marking on the ruler (this corresponds to the left edge of the paper).

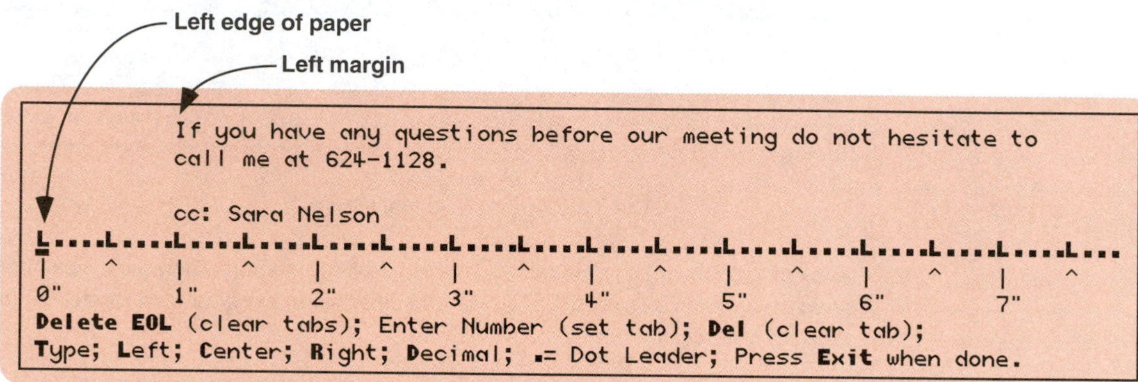

Keystroke	Action Resulting from Keystroke
[Ctrl-End]	Clears all the tab stops at and to the right of the cursor.
1.5 ↵	Inserts a left tab 1.5 inches from the left edge of the page. The tab now is set to this position for the rest of the document (actually, only one more line) or until a new ruler is encountered. The bottom few lines of the screen will look as follows:

```
        If you have any questions before our meeting do not hesitate to
        call me at 624-1128.

        cc: Sara Nelson
..............L...................................................
|    ^    |    ^    |    ^    |    ^    |    ^    |    ^    |    ^    |    ^
0"        1"        2"        3"        4"        5"        6"        7"
Delete EOL (clear tabs); Enter Number (set tab); Del (clear tab);
Type; Left; Center; Right; Decimal; .= Dot Leader; Press Exit when done.
```

Keystroke	Action Resulting from Keystroke
[F7]	Saves the changes to the ruler, exits *Tab Set*, and returns to the *Format* **Line** menu. If you had wanted to exit *Tab Set* and keep the ruler as it was, you would have pressed **[F1]**.
[F7]	Exits the *Format* **Line** menu and returns to the editing screen.
[arrow]	Use the **[arrow]** keys or mouse to move the cursor to the **S** in **Sara Nelson** (location **Ln 6.17" Pos 1.4"**).
[Tab]	Shifts **Sara Nelson** to the right until the next tab stop (at position **1.5"**).

Continued . . .

Keystroke	Action Resulting from Keystroke

[arrow] Use the **[arrow]** keys or mouse to move the cursor to the **J** in **Jill Smith** (location **Ln 6.33" Pos 1"**).

[Tab] Shifts **Jill Smith** to the right until the next tab stop (at position **1.5"**). The bottom of the screen should look as follows:

```
If you have any questions before our meeting do not hesitate to
call me at 624-1128.

cc:  Sara Nelson
     Jill Smith

A:\MRMPREP.V1                             Doc 1 Pg 1 Ln 6.33" Pos 1.5"
```

To show the new codes, use the *Reveal Codes* feature:

[Alt-F3] Reveals the codes and displays the following:

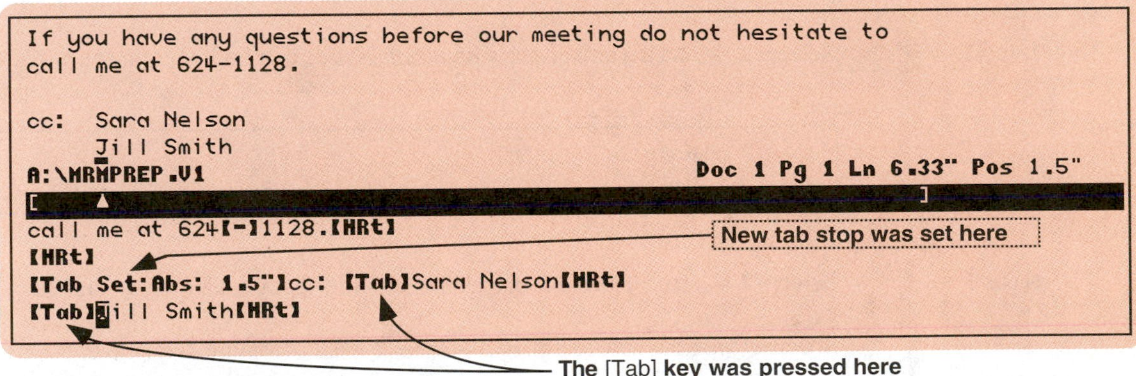
If you have any questions before our meeting do not hesitate to
call me at 624-1128.
cc: Sara Nelson
Jill Smith
A:\MRMPREP.V1
Doc 1 Pg 1 Ln 6.33" Pos 1.5"
call me at 624[-]1128.[HRt]
[HRt]
[Tab Set:Abs: 1.5"]cc: [Tab]Sara Nelson[HRt]
[Tab]Jill Smith[HRt]
New tab stop was set here
The [Tab] key was pressed here

Notice the second line from the bottom:

```
[Tab Set:Abs: 1.5"]cc: [Tab]Sara Nelson[HRt]
```

The **[Tab Set:Abs: 1.5"]** indicates that an absolute tab stop has been set at 1.5 inches for the rest of the document from this point on. This means that when **[Tab]** is pressed just before **Sara** and just before **Jill**, their names will be lined up 1.5 inches from the left edge of the page.

USERS OF VERSION 5.0 The tab code will not include the word **Abs:**. The code will read **[Tab Set: 1.5"]**.

[Alt-F3] Hides the codes again.

[F10] Saves the document. Use the name **MRMPREP.V1T**. It is a good idea to save your document often so that if your computer crashes you will not lose a lot of information and work.

• *Margins* •

The margins control where text will line up on the left- and right-hand sides of the page. The margins can be changed by inserting margin codes using the *Format* feature, **[Shift-F8]**. When you insert a margin code, all the margins in the document from that point on are changed until a new margin code is encountered or until the end of the document is reached. For example, if you change the margins of the first paragraph so that they are 2 inches from both the left- and right-hand sides of the page, then all paragraphs from that point on will have those margins (unless you change the margins back again later on).

To illustrate this, begin with the document **`MRMPREP.V1T`** and change the margins of the first paragraph **`(We need to prepare...)`** so that they are two inches from both sides of the page:

Keystroke	Action Resulting from Keystroke
[Home] [Home] ↑	Moves the cursor to the upper left-hand corner of the screen (location **`Ln 1" Pos 1"`**).
[arrow]	Use the **[arrow]** keys or mouse to move the cursor to the first letter of the first paragraph (location **`Ln 2.67" Pos 1"`**).
[Shift-F8]	Selects the *Format* feature and displays its menu.
`L` (or **1**)	Selects **`1 - Line`** and displays its menu. Notice that both margins have been preset to 1 inch.

```
     7 - Margins - Left              1"
                   Right             1"
```

Keystroke	Action Resulting from Keystroke
`M` (or **7**)	Selects **`7 - Margins`** and places the blinking cursor under the **`1"`** indicator for the left margin.
2	Specifies that the new left margin is to be **2** inches from the left side of the page.
↓	Moves the cursor down one line so that it is blinking under the right margin indicator.
2	Specifies that the new right margin is to be **2** inches from the right side of the page. For a standard-size 8.5-inch wide page, having both margins set at 2 inches leaves 4.5 inches for text.
[F7]	Exits the margin selection line.
[F7]	Exits the *Format* feature and returns to the editing screen. The screen may look a little strange at this point because WordPerfect has not yet reformatted the paragraph.
↓	Moves the cursor down one line and reformats the document. Notice that all text at and below the first paragraph now takes on the new margins:

Continued . . .

Keystroke **Action Resulting from Keystroke**

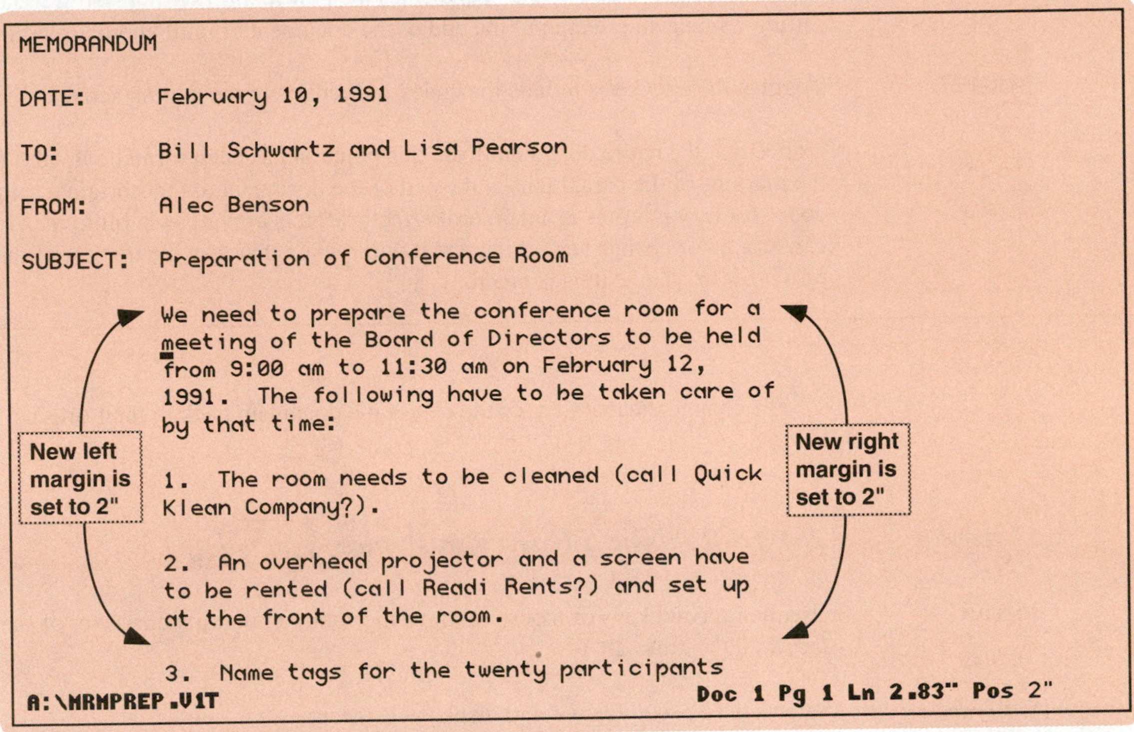

```
MEMORANDUM

DATE:      February 10, 1991

TO:        Bill Schwartz and Lisa Pearson

FROM:      Alec Benson

SUBJECT:   Preparation of Conference Room

           We need to prepare the conference room for a
           meeting of the Board of Directors to be held
           from 9:00 am to 11:30 am on February 12,
           1991.  The following have to be taken care of
           by that time:

           1.  The room needs to be cleaned (call Quick
           Klean Company?).

           2.  An overhead projector and a screen have
           to be rented (call Readi Rents?) and set up
           at the front of the room.

           3.  Name tags for the twenty participants
A:\MRMPREP.V1T                      Doc 1 Pg 1 Ln 2.83" Pos 2"
```


You can see how WordPerfect has coded the new margins by selecting *Reveal Codes* (**[Alt-F3]**).

[Alt-F3] Selects *Reveal Codes* and displays the following:

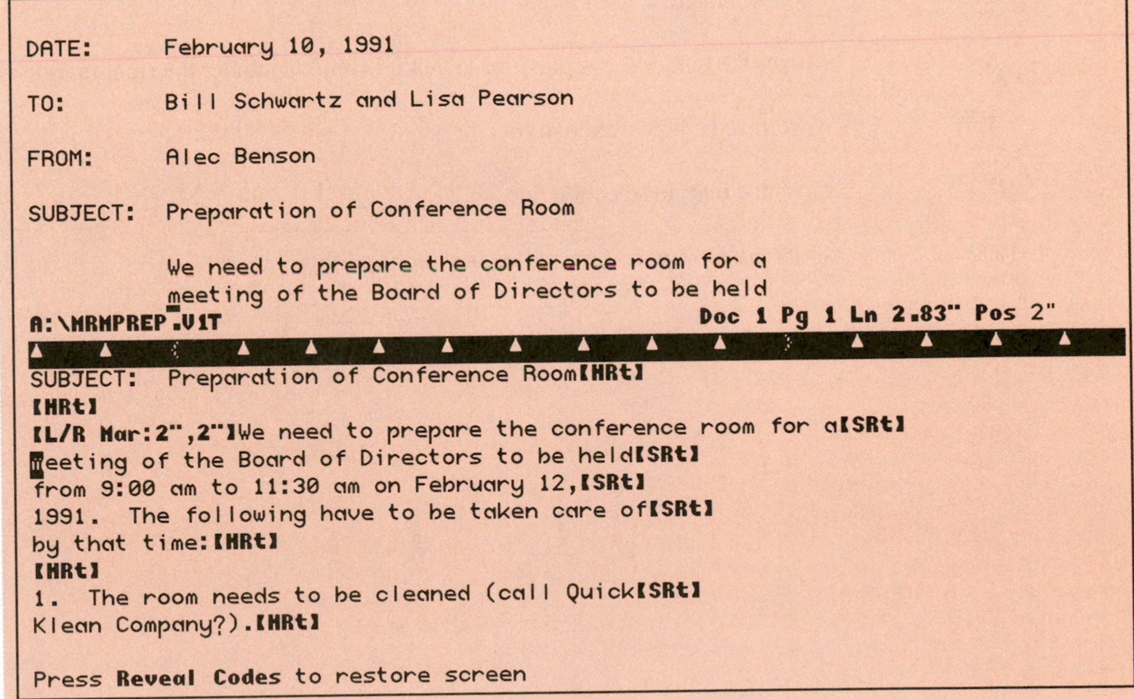

```
DATE:      February 10, 1991

TO:        Bill Schwartz and Lisa Pearson

FROM:      Alec Benson

SUBJECT:   Preparation of Conference Room

           We need to prepare the conference room for a
           meeting of the Board of Directors to be held
A:\MRMPREP.V1T                      Doc 1 Pg 1 Ln 2.83" Pos 2"
SUBJECT:   Preparation of Conference Room[HRt]
[HRt]
[L/R Mar:2",2"]We need to prepare the conference room for a[SRt]
meeting of the Board of Directors to be held[SRt]
from 9:00 am to 11:30 am on February 12,[SRt]
1991.  The following have to be taken care of[SRt]
by that time:[HRt]
[HRt]
1.  The room needs to be cleaned (call Quick[SRt]
Klean Company?).[HRt]

Press Reveal Codes to restore screen
```

Continued . . .

Keystroke	Action Resulting from Keystroke
	The code **`[L/R Mar:2",2"]`** indicates the new margin setting (left **`2"`** and right **`2"`**). This margin setting remains in effect until the end of the document or until another margin set is encountered.
[Alt-F3]	Toggles *Reveal Codes* to hide the codes and returns to the editing screen.
	Notice that the entire document from this point on has been formatted with the new margins. To restore the margins of the paragraphs at the end of the document to their original settings, you have to insert the codes for new margins again. WordPerfect uses this *toggle* (switching) idea in many of its features. You can turn on or change something and it will remain that way for the rest of the document or until you turn it off or change it back again.

To change the margins for the rest of the document back to their original 1-inch settings do the following:

Keystroke	Action Resulting from Keystroke
[arrow]	Use the **[arrow]** keys or mouse to move the cursor to the first character of the numbered items (location **`Ln 3.67" Pos 2"`**).
[Shift-F8]	Selects the *Format* feature and displays its menu.
`L` (or **`1`**)	Selects **`1 - Line`** and displays its menu.
`M` (or **`7`**)	Selects **`7 - Margins`** and places the blinking cursor under the **`2"`** indicator for the left margin.
`1`	Specifies the new left margin.
↓	Moves the cursor down one line so that it is blinking under the right margin indicator.
`1`	Specifies the new right margin.
[F7]	Exits the margin selection line.
[F7]	Exits the *Format* feature and returns to the editing screen.

Continued . . .

↓ Reformats the document. The entire memo now should look like the following (this is for reference only; the entire document will not fit on the screen at one time as shown here):

```
MEMORANDUM

DATE:     February 10, 1991

TO:       Bill Schwartz and Lisa Pearson

FROM:     Alec Benson

SUBJECT:  Preparation of Conference Room

          We need to prepare the conference room for a
          meeting of the Board of Directors to be held
          from 9:00 am to 11:30 am on February 12,
          1991.  The following have to be taken care of
          by that time:

1.  The room needs to be cleaned (call Quick Klean Company?).

2.  An overhead projector and a screen have to be rented (call
Readi Rents?) and set up at the front of the room.

3.  Name tags for the twenty participants need to be prepared.
See Jim Wilson for the list of names.

I would like us to meet tomorrow at 9:00 am in the conference
room to finalize the plans and make specific assignments.

This is a very important meeting for the future of our company so
I want everything to go smoothly.

If you have any questions before our meeting do not hesitate to
call me at 624-1128.

cc:  Sara Nelson
     Jill Smith
```

[F10] Saves the document. Use the name **`MRMPREP.V1M`**.

• *Indentations* •

The *Left-indent* feature allows you to indent a single paragraph from the left-hand side without changing the margins for other paragraphs. This is different from using the *Margin* feature because only one paragraph will be affected. When **[F4]** is pressed, the left-hand side of the paragraph moves right one tab stop (remember, the default setting for tab stops is every one-half inch).

For example, indent the fifth paragraph (**`I would like us...`**) one-half inch from its present margin by doing the following:

Keystroke	Action Resulting from Keystroke
[arrow]	Use the **[arrow]** keys or mouse to move the cursor to the first character of the paragraph (location `Ln 5" Pos 1"`). Be sure that the cursor is at the proper location before tapping **[F4]**. If the cursor is at some other location within the paragraph, the characters to the left of the cursor will remain where they are while the characters to the right of and below the cursor will be indented. (If that happens, move the cursor to the spot where it was when you pressed **[F4]** and press **[Backspace]**. This will remove the indent code from that location and restore the paragraph to its original margins.)
[F4]	Selects the indent option and shifts the text in the first line of the paragraph one-half inch to the right (actually, the text is shifted to the next tab stop, which is located at position `1.5"`). Be careful! Each time you press **[F4]** the paragraph is indented one more tab stop. Do not hold down the **[F4]** key or you will indent the paragraph more than once.

USERS OF VERSION 5.0 Press the **[down arrow]** key to reformat the paragraph.

The paragraph now should look as follows:

```
3.  Name tags for the twenty participants need to be prepared.
See Jim Wilson for the list of names.

     I would like us to meet tomorrow at 9:00 am in the
     conference room to finalize the plans and make specific
     assignments.

This is a very important meeting for the future of our company so
I want everything to go smoothly.

If you have any questions before our meeting do not hesitate to
call me at 624-1128.

cc:  Sara Nelson
     Jill Smith
```

You may use the *Double-indent* feature (the **[Shift-F4]** key) to indent both the left-hand and right-hand sides of a single paragraph. For example, in the sixth paragraph (**`This is a very important...`**), indent both sides of the paragraph by .5 inch by doing the following:

Keystroke	Action Resulting from Keystroke
[arrow]	Use the **[arrow]** keys or mouse to move the cursor to the letter **`T`** at the beginning of the paragraph (location `Ln 5.67" Pos 1"`).
[Shift-F4]	Selects the *Double-indent* feature and shifts the text in the first line of the paragraph one-half inch to the right.

USERS OF VERSION 5.0 Press the **[down arrow]** key to reformat the paragraph.

For this paragraph, the right-hand indentation may not be obvious because of the ragged edge. However, you can see the special indenting codes if you use the *Reveal Codes* feature.

Keystroke	Action Resulting from Keystroke
[arrow]	Use the **[arrow]** keys or mouse to move the cursor to the letter **`I`** at the beginning of the fifth paragraph (location `Ln 5." Pos 1.5"`).

Continued . . .

Keystroke	Action Resulting from Keystroke
[Alt-F3]	Selects *Reveal Codes* and displays the following:

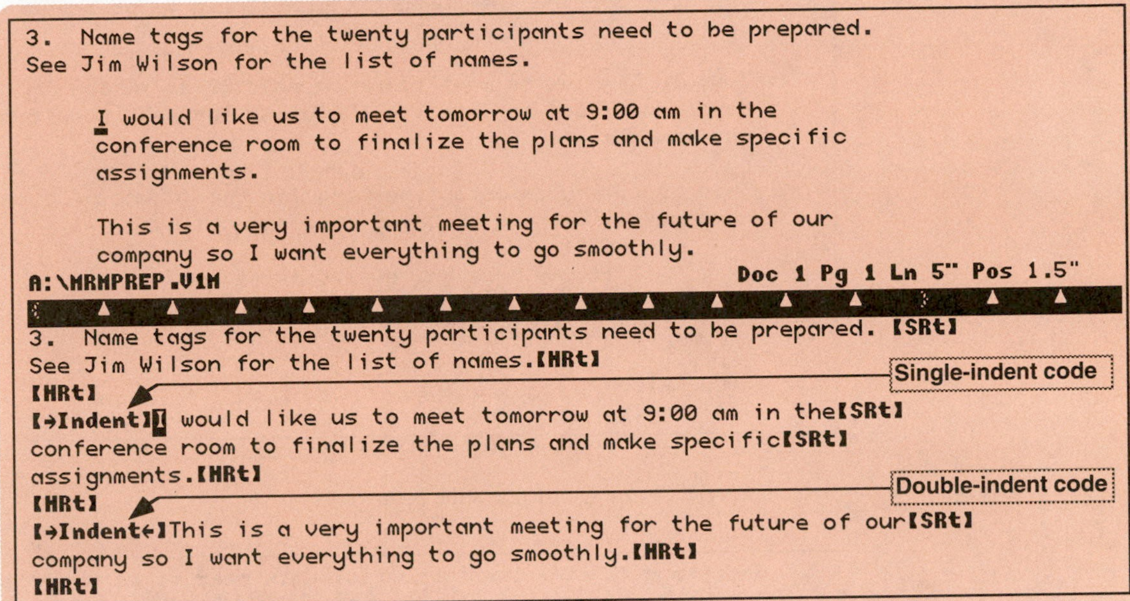

The **[->Indent<-]** at the beginning of the doubly indented paragraph in the *Reveal Codes* screen indicates that the paragraph has been indented in both directions (notice the **->** and the **<-**). The paragraph has been indented, but the margins have remained where they were (indicated by the **{** and the **}** in the tabs ruler).

[Alt-F3]	Toggles *Reveal Codes* to hide the codes again.

A paragraph may be indented more than once using **[F4]** or **[Shift-F4]**. For example, indent the last paragraph (**If you have any questions...**) so that all the text falls between positions **2.5"** and **6"** by doing the following:

Keystroke	Action Resulting from Keystroke
[arrow]	Use the **[arrow]** keys or mouse to move the cursor to the letter **I** at the beginning of the last paragraph (location **Ln 6.17" Pos 1"**).
[Shift-F4]	Selects the *Double-indent* feature and shifts the text in the first line of the paragraph one-half inch to the right. The first letter now should be at position **1.5"**.
[Shift-F4]	Selects the *Double-indent* feature and shifts the text in the first line of the paragraph another one-half inch to the right. The first letter now should be at position **2"**.
[Shift-F4]	Selects the *Double-indent* feature and shifts the text in the first line of the paragraph another .5 inch to the right. The first letter now should be at position **2.5"**.
	USERS OF VERSION 5.0 Press the **[down arrow]** key to reformat the paragraph.

Continued . . .

```
3.  Name tags for the twenty participants need to be prepared.
See Jim Wilson for the list of names.

     I would like us to meet tomorrow at 9:00 am in the
     conference room to finalize the plans and make specific
     assignments.

     This is a very important meeting for the future of our
     company so I want everything to go smoothly.

               If you have any questions before
               our meeting do not hesitate to call
               me at 624-1128.

cc:  Sara Nelson
     Jill Smith
```

[Alt-F3] Selects *Reveal Codes* and displays the following:

```
3.  Name tags for the twenty participants need to be prepared.
See Jim Wilson for the list of names.

     I would like us to meet tomorrow at 9:00 am in the
     conference room to finalize the plans and make specific
     assignments.

     This is a very important meeting for the future of our
     company so I want everything to go smoothly.

               If you have any questions before
A:\MRMPREP.V1M                              Doc 1 Pg 1 Ln 6.17" Pos 2.5"
[→Indent←]This is a very important meeting for the future of our[SRt]
company so I want everything to go smoothly.[HRt]
[HRt]                                         Three double-indent codes
[→Indent←][→Indent←][→Indent←]If you have any questions before[SRt]
our meeting do not hesitate to call[SRt]
me at 624[-]1128.[HRt]
[HRt]
[Tab Set:Abs: 1.5"]cc: [TAB]Sara Nelson[HRt]
[TAB]Jill Smith[HRt]

Press Reveal Codes to restore screen
```

There are three *Double-indent* codes at the beginning of the paragraph (one for each **[Shift-F4]** you pressed).

```
[→Indent←][→Indent←][→Indent←]If you have any questions before[SRt]
```

Remove two of the *Double-indent* codes by doing the following:

Keystroke	Action Resulting from Keystroke
[arrow]	Use the **[arrow]** keys or mouse, if necessary, to move the cursor in the *Reveal Codes* screen to the **I** in **If you have...** at **Ln 6.17" Pos 2.5"**).
[Backspace]	Deletes the indent code to the left.
[Backspace]	Deletes the next indent code to the left. Now only one indent code should be left on the line.

```
3.  Name tags for the twenty participants need to be prepared.
See Jim Wilson for the list of names.

     I would like us to meet tomorrow at 9:00 am in the
     conference room to finalize the plans and make specific
     assignments.

     This is a very important meeting for the future of our
     company so I want everything to go smoothly.

     If you have any questions before our meeting do not
A:\MRMPREP.V1H                              Doc 1 Pg 1 Ln 6.17" Pos 1.5"
[→Indent←]This is a very important meeting for the future of our[SRt]
company so I want everything to go smoothly.[HRt]
[HRt]
[→Indent←]If you have any questions before our meeting do not[SRt]
hesitate to call[SRt]
me at 624[-]1128.[HRt]
[HRt]
[Tab Set:Abs: 1.5"]cc: [TAB]Sara Nelson[HRt]
[TAB]Jill Smith[HRt]


Press Reveal Codes to restore screen
```

[Alt-F3]	Toggles *Reveal Codes* to hide the codes again. The bottom of the document should look like the following:

```
3.  Name tags for the twenty participants need to be prepared.
See Jim Wilson for the list of names.

     I would like us to meet tomorrow at 9:00 am in the
     conference room to finalize the plans and make specific
     assignments.

     This is a very important meeting for the future of our
     company so I want everything to go smoothly.

     If you have any questions before our meeting do not
     hesitate to call me at 624-1128.

cc:  Sara Nelson
     Jill Smith
```

[F10]	Saves the document. Use the name **MRMPREP.V1I**.

• Semiblock Form and Hanging Paragraphs •

To format paragraphs in a semiblock (first line indented) style, simply position the cursor and press **[Tab]**. For example, indent the first paragraph **(We need to prepare...)** by doing the following:

Keystroke	Action Resulting from Keystroke
[arrow]	Use the **[arrow]** keys or mouse to move the cursor to the first letter of the first paragraph (location **Ln 2.67" Pos 2"**).
[Tab]	Shifts the line to the next tab stop (one-half inch to the right).
↓	Reformats the paragraph.

The entire memo now looks likes the following:

```
MEMORANDUM

DATE:     February 10, 1991

TO:       Bill Schwartz and Lisa Pearson

FROM:     Alec Benson

SUBJECT:  Preparation of Conference Room

               We need to prepare the conference room
          for a meeting of the Board of Directors to be
          held from 9:00 am to 11:30 am on February 12,
          1991.  The following have to be taken care of
          by that time:

1.  The room needs to be cleaned (call Quick Klean Company?).

2.  An overhead projector and a screen have to be rented (call
Readi Rents?) and set up at the front of the room.

3.  Name tags for the twenty participants need to be prepared.
See Jim Wilson for the list of names.

     I would like us to meet tomorrow at 9:00 am in the
     conference room to finalize the plans and make specific
     assignments.

     This is a very important meeting for the future of our
     company so I want everything to go smoothly.

     If you have any questions before our meeting do not
     hesitate to call me at 624-1128.

cc:  Sara Nelson
     Jill Smith
```

The *Left-indent* feature allows you to create a *hanging paragraph* (also called a *hanging indentation* or an *outdent*) by positioning the first line of a paragraph at the left margin and indenting all subsequent lines. Create hanging paragraphs for the three numbered items in the middle of the memo by doing the following:

Keystroke	Action Resulting from Keystroke
[arrow]	Use the **[arrow]** keys or mouse to move the cursor to the **`T`** in **`The room needs...`** (location **`Ln 3.67" Pos 1.4"`**).
[F4]	Indents the paragraph to the next tab stop.
[arrow]	Use the **[arrow]** keys or mouse to move the cursor to the **`A`** in **`An overhead...`** (location **`Ln 4" Pos 1.4"`**). This also reformats the previous paragraph.
[F4]	Indents the paragraph to the next tab stop.
[arrow]	Use the **[arrow]** keys or mouse to move the cursor to the **`N`** in **`Name tags...`** (location **`Ln 4.5" Pos 1.4"`**).
[F4]	Indents the paragraph to the next tab stop.

USERS OF VERSION 5.0 Press the **[down arrow]** key to reformat the paragraph.

The document now should look as follows:

```
          MEMORANDUM

          DATE:       February 10, 1991

          TO:         Bill Schwartz and Lisa Pearson

          FROM:       Alec Benson

          SUBJECT:    Preparation of Conference Room

                           We need to prepare the conference room
                      for a meeting of the Board of Directors to be
                      held from 9:00 am to 11:30 am on February 12,
                      1991.  The following have to be taken care of
                      by that time:

          1.     The room needs to be cleaned (call Quick Klean Company?).

          2.     An overhead projector and a screen have to be rented (call
                 Readi Rents?) and set up at the front of the room.

          3.     Name tags for the twenty participants need to be prepared.
                 See Jim Wilson for the list of names.

                 I would like us to meet tomorrow at 9:00 am in the
                 conference room to finalize the plans and make specific
                 assignments.

                 This is a very important meeting for the future of our
                 company so I want everything to go smoothly.

                 If you have any questions before our meeting do not
                 hesitate to call me at 624-1128.

          cc:    Sara Nelson
                 Jill Smith
```

[F10]	Saves the document. Use the name **`MRMPREP.V2`**.

Dropping to DOS (Shell Feature)

The *Shell* feature **[Ctrl-F1]** allows DOS commands to be executed without exiting WordPerfect. This process is called *dropping to DOS* and is convenient if you are working on a document and need to return to DOS for just a moment (e.g., to format a disk).

NOTE . . . In order to do this section, the system file **COMMAND.COM** must be in the root directory of the drive you used to boot the computer. If it is not, the message **ERROR: Can't find COMMAND.COM** will be displayed when you try to drop to DOS. If this is the case, see your course instructor for help.

Let's see how this operation works by doing the following (the document **MRMPREP.V2** should be currently displayed on the screen):

Keystroke	Action Resulting from Keystroke
[Ctrl-F1]	Invokes the *Shell* feature and displays the following on the status line:

```
1 Go to DOS; 2 DOS Command: 0
```

1 **Go to DOS** suspends WordPerfect and transfers control to DOS. To return to WordPerfect you must type Exit and then press **[Enter]**.

2 **Dos Command** allows you to enter a single DOS command. The command is executed and then you are returned to WordPerfect after pressing any key.

Keystroke	Action Resulting from Keystroke
G (or **1**)	Suspends WordPerfect, enters the DOS environment, and displays the following screen (your screen may look somewhat different, depending on the version of DOS you are using):

```
Microsoft(R) MS-DOS(R) Version 4.01
             (C)Copyright Microsoft Corp 1981-1988

Enter 'EXIT' to return to WordPerfect
A:\>
```

If you get the message **ERROR: Can't find COMMAND.COM**, you will not be able to complete this section. In that case, control will automatically be returned to WordPerfect.

Notice that the reminder **Enter 'EXIT' to return to WordPerfect** is displayed along with the DOS system prompt, **A:\>**. From this point on, you can enter DOS commands. DOS commands will be explained in detail in Part I, Chapter 4. For now, use the **DIR** command to display the names of the files on the diskette in the A: drive.

Keystroke	Action Resulting from Keystroke
DIR A:/W↵	Lists the names of the files on the diskette in drive A: in wide format.

```
A:\>DIR A:/W↵

 Volume in drive A is ROBERTSON
 Directory of  A:\

MEMO1           MEMO2           HWW1-02         HWW1-05         HWW1-06
HWW1-08         MRMPREP  V1     MRMPREP  V1T    MRMPREP  V1M    MRMPREP  V1I
MRMPREP  V2
       11 File(s)    1440256 bytes free

Enter 'EXIT' to return to WordPerfect
A:\>_
```

Continued . . .

Keystroke	Action Resulting from Keystroke
EXIT ↵	Returns control to WordPerfect. The screen will appear exactly as you left it before pressing **[Ctrl-F1]**.
[F7]	Exits the current document, **MRMPREP.V2**. Because you have not modified the document since you last saved it, the message **(Text was not modified)** should appear on the status line. You need not save the document again.
N	Specifies that the current document is not to be saved again and asks if you want to exit WordPerfect.
Y	Specifies that **Y**es, you want to exit WordPerfect and returns control to DOS.

TO TAKE A BREAK Remove diskette(s). To resume (hard disk): Insert *Data diskette*, type **A: ↵**. To resume (two drive): Insert diskettes, type **A: ↵**.

Double Spacing Text

You can set the line spacing for text to double spacing by using the *Format* feature. If you are currently in DOS and you are using a hard-drive system, load WordPerfect and the document **MRMPREP.V2** by typing **C:\WP51\WP A:MRMPREP.V2 ↵**. If you are using a two-drive system, type **B:WP A:MRMPREP.V2 ↵**.

Keystroke	Action Resulting from Keystroke
[arrow]	Use the **[arrow]** keys or mouse to move the cursor to the first character in the third to last paragraph (the **I** in **I would like us to ...** at location **Ln 5" Pos 1.5"**).
[Shift-F8]	Selects the *Format* feature and displays its menu.
L (or **1**)	Selects **1 - Line** and displays its menu.
S (or **6**)	Selects **6 - Line Spacing** and locates the cursor under the line spacing value. The default setting is **1** (i.e., single spacing). To change this setting to double spacing, type **2**.
2 ↵	Sets the line spacing to **2**.
[F7]	Exits the **Line** menu and returns to the editing screen.

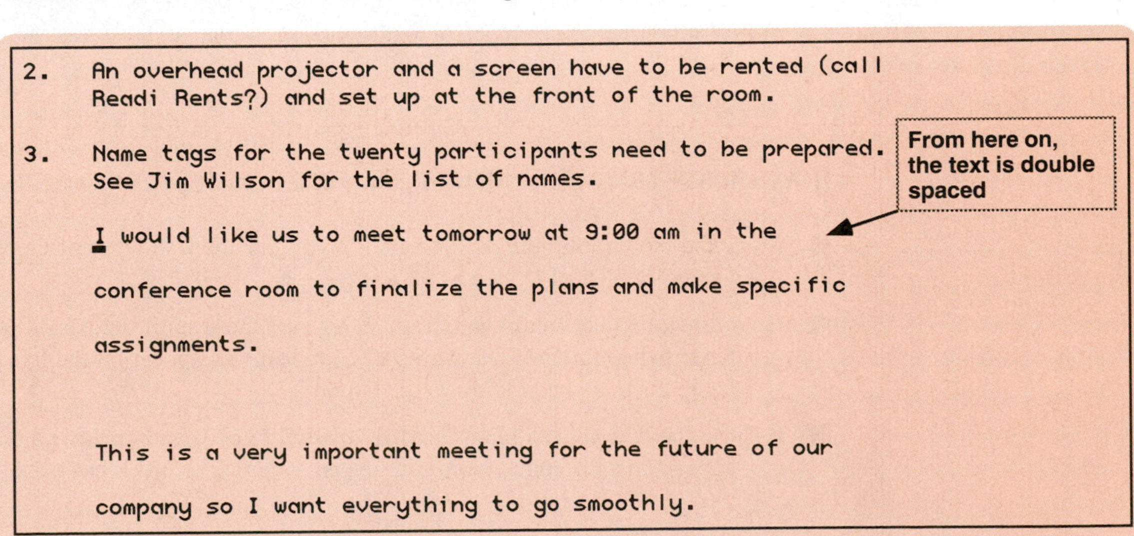

Continued . . .

Keystroke	Action Resulting from Keystroke
	WordPerfect has inserted a code at the cursor indicating that the document should be double spaced from that point on. Notice that above the cursor the document remains single spaced.
	To see the actual spacing code, use the *Reveal Codes* feature:
[Alt-F3]	Reveals the codes and displays the following screen:

```
2.    An overhead projector and a screen have to be rented (call
      Readi Rents?) and set up at the front of the room.

3.    Name tags for the twenty participants need to be prepared.
      See Jim Wilson for the list of names.

      I would like us to meet tomorrow at 9:00 am in the
A:\MRMPREP.V2                                    Doc 1 Pg 1 Ln 5" Pos 1.5"

3.  [→Indent]Name tags for the twenty participants need to be prepared. [SRt]
See Jim Wilson for the list of names.[HRt]
[HRt]
[→Indent][Ln Spacing:2]I would like us to meet tomorrow at 9:00 am in the[SRt]
conference room to finalize the plans and make specific[SRt]
assignments.[HRt]
[HRt]
```

Line spacing code has been set to 2 (i.e., double spacing)

	To remove the spacing code, use the **[Backspace]** key while still within *Reveal Codes*.
[Backspace]	Removes the spacing code. The text below the cursor changes back to single spacing.
[Alt-F3]	Returns to the editing screen.

Selecting and Moving Blocks of Text

A **block operation** is something done (an operation) to a selected portion of text (a block). For example, in the third paragraph from the bottom of the document, **`MRMPREP.V2`**, change the location of the phrase **`make specific assignments`** so that it appears before the words **`finalize the plans`** in the same paragraph. To do this, WordPerfect must be told three things: (1) what to move (select the block of text), (2) where to move it (move the cursor to the new location), (3) carry out the move.

1. Tell WordPerfect which block of text to move:

IF YOUR SYSTEM HAS A MOUSE, use it to select the block of text to be moved:

- Move the mouse until the mouse cursor highlights the first letter of the word **`make`** (the **`m`** at location **`Ln 5.17" Pos 5.7"`**).
- Hold down the left button and drag (slide) the mouse until the period at the end of the sentence is highlighted. The words **`Block on`** will appear on the left-hand side of the status line while you hold down the button.
- Release the button. The phrase **`make specific assignments`** is now highlighted (it appears in a different color or in reverse video). The block has been selected.

IF YOUR SYSTEM DOES NOT HAVE A MOUSE, do the following:

Keystroke	Action Resulting from Keystroke
[arrow]	Use the [arrow] keys to move the cursor to the first letter of the word **make** (the **m** at location **Ln 5.17" Pos 5.7"**).
[Alt-F4]	Specifies the beginning of the block. The words **Block on** will appear on the left-hand side of the status line.
[arrow]	Use the [arrow] keys to move the cursor to the period at the end of the sentence (location **Ln 5.33" Pos 2.6"**). The phrase **make specific assignments** is now highlighted (it appears in a different color or in reverse video). The block has been selected.

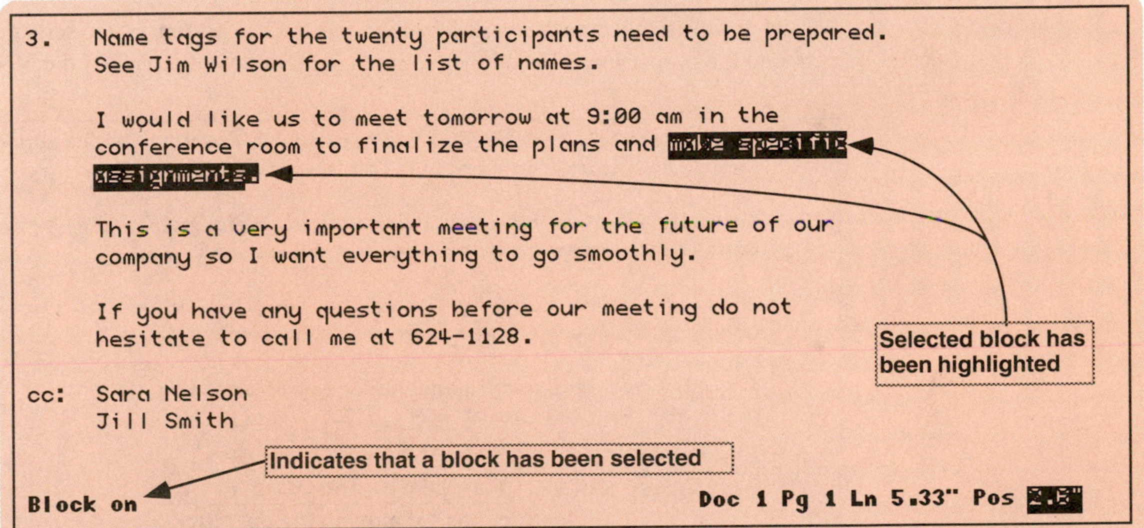

2. Tell WordPerfect what to do with the selected block of text:

Keystroke	Action Resulting from Keystroke
[Ctrl-F4]	Specifies that the selected block is to be operated on and displays a list of options in the status line:

```
Move: 1 Block; 2 Tabular Column; 3 Rectangle: 0
```

1 Block refers to a block of text such as the one you just defined.

2 Tabular Column refers to a column of text or numbers that has been defined by tabs, tab aligns, indents, or hard returns.

3 Rectangle refers to a rectangle of text that has been defined using its upper-left and lower-right corners.

Continued . . .

Keystroke	Action Resulting from Keystroke
	For this operation you want to move a block of text, so **1** is the proper choice.
B (or **1**)	Selects **1 Block** and displays the following menu:

```
1 Move; 2 Copy; 3 Delete; 4 Append: 0
```

1 Move will remove the text from its current location in the document but will keep a copy of it in the main memory of the computer until another move command is issued or until you exit WordPerfect. This is sometimes referred to as *cutting text* because the text is removed from (cut out of) the document.

2 Copy will not remove the text but will keep a copy of it in memory.

3 Delete will remove the text from the document but will retain a copy with up to two other blocks of deleted text. To restore deleted text, press **[F1]** and then choose **Restore**.

4 Append This option allows you to append the block to the end of another file that has been saved on a disk or to a new file.

Keystroke	Action Resulting from Keystroke
M (or **1**)	Selects **1 Move** and cuts the block from the screen. The bottom of the screen instructs you to move the cursor to the proper location and then to press the **[Enter]** key to insert the block:

```
3.   Name tags for the twenty participants need to be prepared.
     See Jim Wilson for the list of names.

     I would like us to meet tomorrow at 9:00 am in the
     conference room to finalize the plans and .

     This is a very important meeting for the future of our
     company so I want everything to go smoothly.

     If you have any questions before our meeting do not
     hesitate to call me at 624-1128.

cc:  Sara Nelson
     Jill Smith

Move cursor; press Enter to retrieve.          Doc 1 Pg 1 Ln 5.17" Pos 5.7"
```

Block has been cut from the screen.

Instructions for moving the cut block

3. Tell WordPerfect where to move the block of text.

Keystroke	Action Resulting from Keystroke
[arrow]	Use the **[arrow]** keys or mouse to move the cursor so that it is at the first letter of the word **finalize** (location **Ln 5.17" Pos 3.4"**).
[Enter]	Specifies that the block is to be moved and pastes it at the location of the cursor.
	The screen should now look as follows:

Continued . . .

Keystroke	Action Resulting from Keystroke

```
3.    Name tags for the twenty participants need to be prepared.
      See Jim Wilson for the list of names.

      I would like us to meet tomorrow at 9:00 am in the
      conference room to make specific assignmentsfinalize the
      plans and .

      This is a very important meeting for the future of our
      company so I want everything to go smoothly.

      If you have any questions before our meeting do not
      hesitate to call me at 624-1128.

cc:   Sara Nelson
      Jill Smith

A:\MRMPREP.V2                          Doc 1 Pg 1 Ln 5.17" Pos 3.4"
```

Block has been inserted at the cursor

The text needs to be cleaned up a bit. The word **and** and the blank space at the end of the sentence need to be deleted and inserted between **assignments** and **finalize**. Of course, you could do this with a block move, but because it is only one word it will be faster and easier to delete it and retype it in the proper location. After this is done, the bottom of the document looks like the following:

```
3.    Name tags for the twenty participants need to be prepared.
      See Jim Wilson for the list of names.

      I would like us to meet tomorrow at 9:00 am in the
      conference room to make specific assignments and finalize
      the plans._

      This is a very important meeting for the future of our
      company so I want everything to go smoothly.

      If you have any questions before our meeting do not
      hesitate to call me at 624-1128.

cc:   Sara Nelson
      Jill Smith

A:\MRMPREP.V2                          Doc 1 Pg 1 Ln 5.33" Pos 2.5"
```

Selecting and Moving Sentences and Paragraphs

If the block you want to move is a sentence, paragraph, or page, you may use special WordPerfect codes to select them quickly and easily. For example, move the third to last paragraph, **I would like us to...**, and make it the second to last paragraph by doing the following:

Keystroke	Action Resulting from Keystroke
[arrow]	If necessary, use the **[arrow]** keys or mouse to move the cursor to any location in the paragraph (e.g., location **`Ln 5.33" Pos 2.5"`**).
[Ctrl-F4]	Specifies that the block containing the cursor is to be operated on and displays the following menu in the status line:

```
Move: 1 Sentence; 2 Paragraph; 3 Page; 4 Retrieve: 0
```

You want to move the entire paragraph, so select **`2 Paragraph`**.

`P` (or **2**)	Selects **`2 Paragraph`**. The entire paragraph is highlighted and the following menu is displayed on the status line:

```
1 Move; 2 Copy; 3 Delete; 4 Append: 0
```

You want to move the paragraph from its present location to a new location, so select **`1 Move`**.

`M` (or **`1`**)	Selects **`1 Move`** and erases the paragraph from the screen but keeps a copy in memory.
[arrow]	Use the **[arrow]** keys or mouse to move the cursor so that it is to the left of the sentence **`If you have...`** (location **`Ln 5.5" Pos 1"`**). Be careful when you position the cursor! If you place the cursor at **`Ln 5.5" Pos 1.5"`** (i.e., at the **`I`** in **`If you have...`**), when you paste the paragraph it will be inserted to the right of the indentation code rather than to the left of the code. If that happens, you will end up with two indentation codes for the paragraph **`I would like...`** and none for the paragraph **`If you have....`** In that case, the bottom three paragraphs will look as follows (this is *not* what you want):

```
          This is a very important meeting for the future of our
          company so I want everything to go smoothly.

          _      I would like us to meet tomorrow at 9:00 am in the
                 conference room to make specific assignments and
                 finalize the plans.

     If you have any questions before our meeting do not hesitate to
     call me at 624-1128.

A:\MRMPREP.V2                               Doc 1 Pg 1 Ln 5.5" Pos 1.5"
```

Thus, be sure the cursor is at location **`Ln 5.5" Pos 1"`** before doing the next command.

[Enter]	Specifies that the paragraph is to be moved.
[F10]	Saves the document. Use the name **`MRMPREP.V3`**.

The entire document should look as follows:

```
MEMORANDUM

DATE:      February 10, 1991

TO:        Bill Schwartz and Lisa Pearson

FROM:      Alec Benson

SUBJECT:   Preparation of Conference Room

                We need to prepare the conference room
           for a meeting of the Board of Directors to be
           held from 9:00 am to 11:30 am on February 12,
           1991.  The following have to be taken care of
           by that time:

1.    The room needs to be cleaned (call Quick Klean Company?).

2.    An overhead projector and a screen have to be rented (call
      Readi Rents?) and set up at the front of the room.

3.    Name tags for the twenty participants need to be prepared.
      See Jim Wilson for the list of names.

      This is a very important meeting for the future of our
      company so I want everything to go smoothly.

      I would like us to meet tomorrow at 9:00 am in the
      conference room to make specific assignments and finalize
      the plans.

      If you have any questions before our meeting do not
      hesitate to call me at 624-1128.

cc:   Sara Nelson
      Jill Smith
```

Selecting and Copying Blocks of Text

Following a procedure similar to that outlined in the previous section, blocks, sentences, paragraphs, and pages of text can be copied from one part of a document (or even a different document) and then inserted at a new location. For example, in file **`MRMPREP.V3`**, copy the sentence **`This is a very important...`** from the third to the last paragraph (beginning at **`Ln 5" Pos 1.5"`**) so that it also appears as the second sentence of the first paragraph (beginning at **`Ln 3.17" Pos 2.7"`**).

Keystroke	Action Resulting from Keystroke
[arrow]	Use the **[arrow]** keys or mouse to move the cursor to any position in the sentence to be moved (e.g., the **`T`** at location **`Ln 5" Pos 1.5"`**).
[Ctrl-F4]	Specifies that the block containing the cursor is to be operated on and displays the following menu in the status line:

```
Move: 1 Sentence; 2 Paragraph; 3 Page; 4 Retrieve: 0
```

Continued . . .

Keystroke	Action Resulting from Keystroke
s (or **1**)	Selects **1 Sentence** and highlights the entire sentence. Because this sentence is also a complete paragraph, you may be tempted to select **2 Paragraph** at this point. However, selecting the paragraph will select the invisible indenting code as well as the text. This is not what you want (i.e., you do not want to copy the indenting code, only the text). The following menu is displayed on the status line:

```
1 Move; 2 Copy; 3 Delete; 4 Append: 0
```

You want to copy the sentence (as opposed to move or delete it) so select **2 Copy**.

c (or **2**) Selects **2 Copy** and displays the following message on the status line:

```
Move cursor; press Enter to retrieve.                  Doc 1 Pg 1 Ln 5.17" Pos 5.9"
```

The block of text (i.e., the sentence) remains on the screen but it is no longer highlighted. The text has been saved in the computer's main memory so that it can be pasted into the document in a new position. The block will remain in memory until it is replaced by another block or until WordPerfect is exited.

[arrow] Use the **[arrow]** keys or mouse to move the cursor so that it is at the first letter in the sentence **The following have to be...** (location **Ln 3.17" Pos 2.7"**) of the first paragraph.

[Enter] Specifies that the block is to be retrieved (inserted or pasted) at the cursor.

The only thing left to do is to insert two spaces after the period of the newly pasted sentence (location **Ln 3.5" Pos 4.5"**) and then to reformat the paragraph using an **[arrow]** key. After this is done, the screen appears as follows:

```
MEMORANDUM

DATE:      February 10, 1991

TO:        Bill Schwartz and Lisa Pearson

FROM:      Alec Benson

SUBJECT:   Preparation of Conference Room

                We need to prepare the conference room
           for a meeting of the Board of Directors to be
           held from 9:00 am to 11:30 am on February 12,
           1991.  This is a very important meeting for
           the future of our company so I want
           everything to go smoothly.  The following
           have to be taken care of by that time:

1.    The room needs to be cleaned (call Quick Klean Company?).

2.    An overhead projector and a screen have to be rented (call
      Readi Rents?) and set up at the front of the room.

3.    Name tags for the twenty participants need to be prepared.
A:\MRMPREP.V3                                  Doc 1 Pg 1 Ln 3.67" Pos 4.8"
```

Newly copied sentence

[F10] Saves the document. Use the name **MRMPREP.V4**.

Copying Rulers

Following a procedure similar to that used to copy text, rulers can be copied from one part of a document to another. For example, copy the ruler from the first paragraph in the memo **MRMPREP.V4** so that it affects the last two paragraphs by doing the following:

Keystroke	Action Resulting from Keystroke
[arrow]	Use the **[arrow]** keys or mouse to move the cursor to the left margin of the first paragraph (location **Ln 2.67" Pos 1"**).
[Alt-F3]	Reveals the hidden codes.
	REMEMBER . . . you can use your mouse to select the block and then skip the next two steps.
[Alt-F4]	Specifies the beginning of the block to be copied.
[right-arrow]	Press the **[right-arrow]** key once to highlight the margin code — the **[Tab]** code will be in reverse video when this is done and the margin code **[L/R Mar: 2", 2"]** is selected.
	`[Block][L/R Mar:2",2"][TAB]We need to prepare the conference room[SRt]`
[Ctrl-F4]	Specifies that the block (i.e., the margin code) is to be operated on and displays the following menu:
	`Move: 1 Block; 2 Tabular Column; 3 Rectangle: 0`
B (or **1**)	Selects **1 Block** and displays the following menu:
	`1 Move; 2 Copy; 3 Delete; 4 Append: 0`
	You want to copy the codes so select **2 Copy**.
C (or **2**)	Selects **2 Copy**.
[arrow]	Use the **[arrow]** keys or mouse to move the cursor so that it is at the left margin of the second to last paragraph, **I would like us to meet...** (location **Ln 5.83" Pos 1"**).
[Enter]	Specifies that the block is to be retrieved (inserted or pasted) at the cursor. Notice that the margin code **[L/R Mar:2",2"]** appears at the beginning of the paragraph and that the last two paragraphs are affected by this new margin.

Continued . . .

Keystroke	Action Resulting from Keystroke

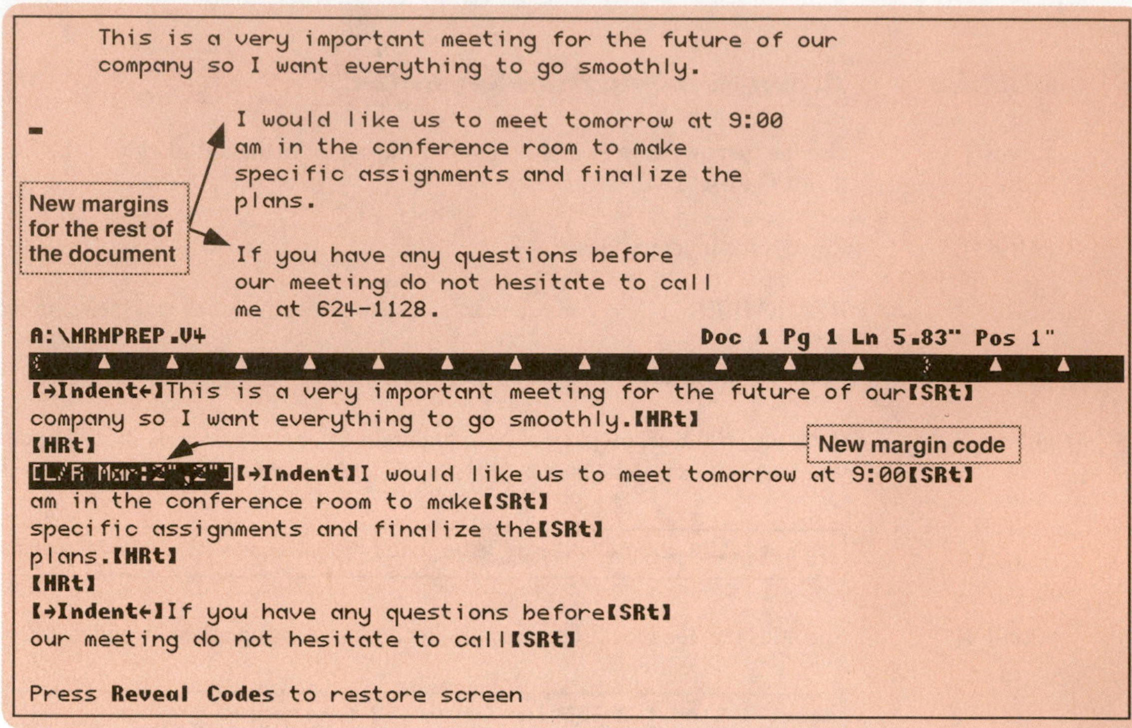

To erase the new ruler setting you simply delete the margin code **[L/R Mar:2",2"]**.

[arrow]	Use the **[arrow]** keys or mouse, if necessary, to move the cursor so that the margin code **[L/R Mar:2",2"]** is highlighted.
[Delete]	Deletes the code. The margins for the last part of the document return to their original positions.
[Alt-F3]	Hides the codes and returns the screen to normal view.

Document Justification and Line Numbering

Recall from page W47 that left justification (flush left) means that the text is lined up at the left-hand margin. Right justification (flush right) means that the text is lined up at the right-hand margin. Full justification (sometimes simply called justification) means that text at both the left-hand and right-hand margins is lined up. Full justification is accomplished by adding extra spaces between the words on each line. Some people find these extra spaces distracting because it slows down the reading process (the words are spread out so the reader's eyes have to cover more ground for a given amount of information). However, full justification gives the printed copy a more "finished" look.

In WordPerfect, documents appear left justified on the screen; but when they are printed, they are fully justified. You can change the document justification and other printer attributes (such as font, underlining, and line numbering) by using the same *Format* feature you used when you changed the margins and tabs. Note that when changes are made to the printer attributes, those changes affect text beginning at the cursor and continuing until the end of the document or until another printer control code of the same type is encountered.

To illustrate this, print the document **MRMPREP.V4** with the last ten lines left justified (i.e., turn off full justification) and the lines numbered.

Keystroke	Action Resulting from Keystroke
[arrow]	Use the **[arrow]** keys or mouse to move the cursor to the blank line just above the second to the last paragraph, **`I would like us to...`** (location **`Ln 5.67" Pos 1"`**).
[Shift-F8]	Displays the *Format* screen, which shows the default settings for **`Line`**, **`Page`**, **`Document`**, and **`Other`** categories. Remember, when you change a setting, a code is placed into the document at the current cursor location and that code will be in effect until the end of the document or until another code of the same type is encountered.
`L` (or **`1`**)	Selects **`1 - Line`** and displays its menu.
`J` (or **`3`**)	Selects **`3 - Justification`** and displays the following four choices for justification:

```
Justification: 1 Left; 2 Center; 3 Right; 4 Full: 0
```

USERS OF VERSION 5.0 Selecting **`3 - Justification`** places the cursor at the word **`Yes`**. Pressing **`Y`** (for **`Yes`**) turns on justification while pressing **`N`** (for **`No`**) turns off justification. Press **`N`** and skip the next step.

Keystroke	Action Resulting from Keystroke
`L` (or **`1`**)	Selects **`1 Left`** and turns on left justification.
`N` (or **`5`**)	Selects **`5 - Line Numbering`** and places the cursor under the word **`No`**. Pressing **`Y`** (for **`Yes`**) turns on line numbering while pressing **`N`** (for **`No`**) turns off line numbering.
`Y`	Turns on line numbering and displays the following menu:

```
Format: Line Numbering

     1 - Count Blank Lines                          Yes

     2 - Number Every n Lines, where n is           1

     3 - Position of Number from Left Edge          0.6"

     4 - Starting Number                            1

     5 - Restart Numbering on Each Page             Yes
```

The default settings will:

- include blank lines in the numbering process
- number every line
- display the line numbers .6 inches from the left edge of the page
- begin numbering the lines with 1
- restart the numbering at the beginning of each new page

To change a setting, simply type the highlighted letter or number of the corresponding item. For example, change the position of the number to .75 inch from the left edge of the page by doing the following:

Keystroke	Action Resulting from Keystroke
`P` (or **`3`**)	Selects **`3 - Position of Number from Left Edge`** and places the cursor under the 0 in 0.6".

Continued . . .

Keystroke	Action Resulting from Keystroke
`0.75` ↵	Changes the position to .75 inch.
[F7]	Accepts the rest of the default settings and returns to the editing screen.
[Shift-F7]	Displays the *Print* menu. If you have a printer available at this time, print the document. Otherwise, use the view option to look at a printed preview of the document.
`F` (or `1`)	Selects **`1 - Full Document`** and prints the document. If you prefer, press **`V`** (or **`6`**) to select **`6 - View Document`** (see pp. W17–18 for help with the view option).

The printed document will look as follows:

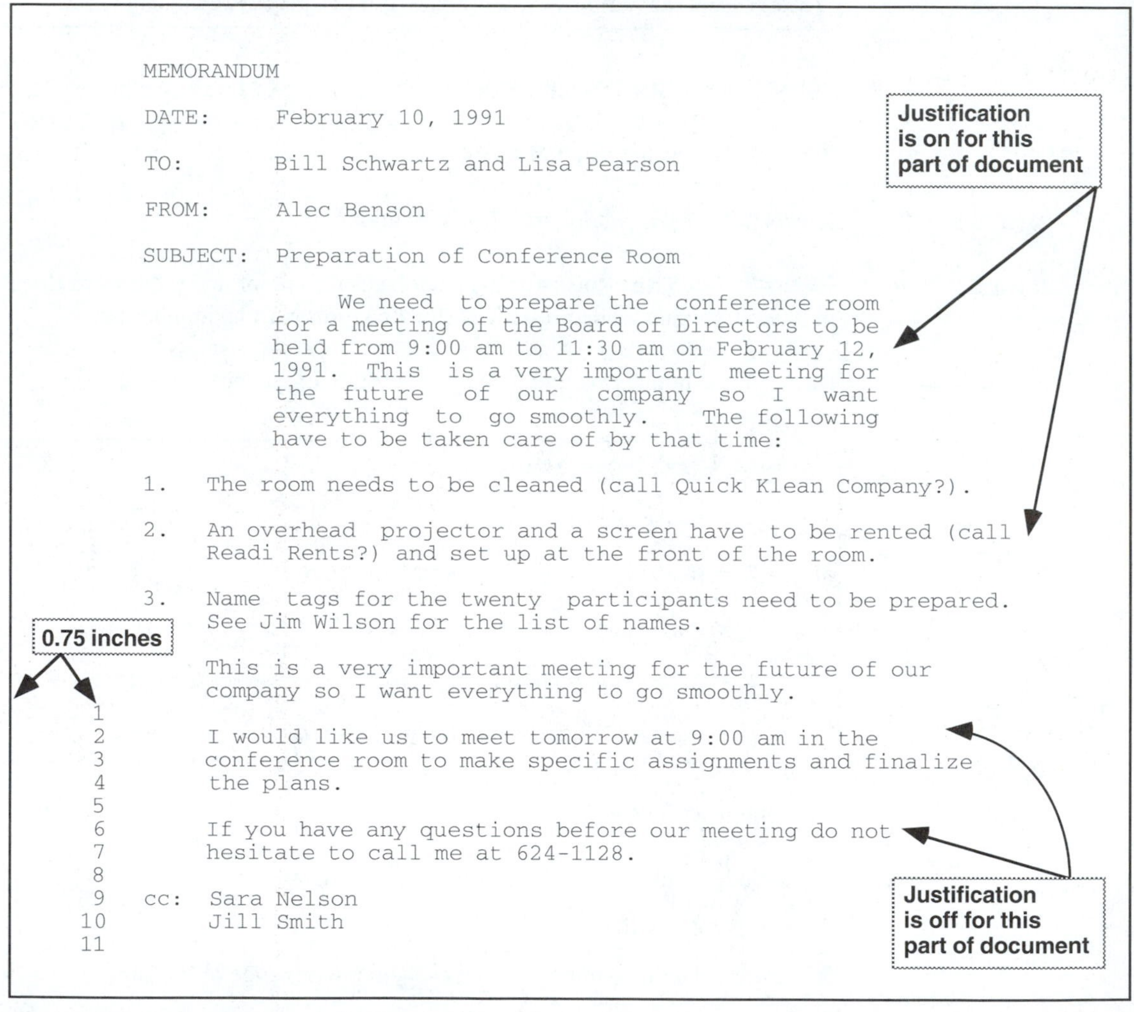

MEMORANDUM

DATE: February 10, 1991

TO: Bill Schwartz and Lisa Pearson

FROM: Alec Benson

SUBJECT: Preparation of Conference Room

We need to prepare the conference room for a meeting of the Board of Directors to be held from 9:00 am to 11:30 am on February 12, 1991. This is a very important meeting for the future of our company so I want everything to go smoothly. The following have to be taken care of by that time:

1. The room needs to be cleaned (call Quick Klean Company?).

2. An overhead projector and a screen have to be rented (call Readi Rents?) and set up at the front of the room.

3. Name tags for the twenty participants need to be prepared. See Jim Wilson for the list of names.

This is a very important meeting for the future of our company so I want everything to go smoothly.

I would like us to meet tomorrow at 9:00 am in the conference room to make specific assignments and finalize the plans.

If you have any questions before our meeting do not hesitate to call me at 624-1128.

cc: Sara Nelson
Jill Smith

If you used the **`View`** option, press **[F7]** to return to the editing screen.

To see the codes that WordPerfect has inserted into the document, use the *Reveal Codes* feature:

Keystroke	Action Resulting from Keystroke
[arrow]	Use the [arrow] keys or mouse to move the cursor, if it is not already there, to the blank line just above the second to the last paragraph, **I would like us to...** (location **Ln 5.67" Pos 1"**).
[Alt-F3]	Selects *Reveal Codes* and displays the following:

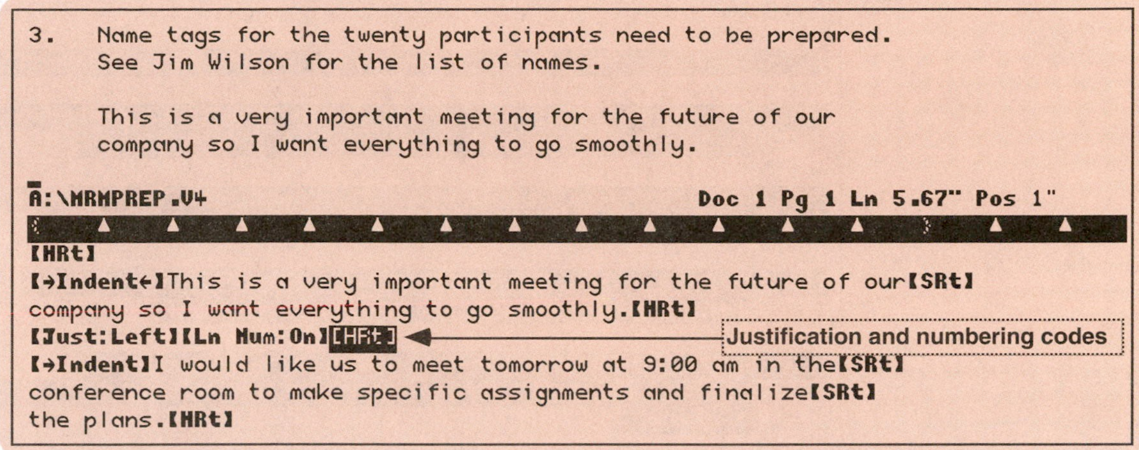

[Just:Left] means that left justification has been turned on. When printed, the text will appear with a ragged-right edge from this point on.

USERS OF VERSION 5.0 The first code will read **[Just Off]** indicating that full justification has been turned off (and, therefore, left justification has been turned on).

[Ln Num:On] means that line numbering has been turned on. When printed, line numbers will appear on the left-hand edge of the document from this point on.

Keystroke	Action Resulting from Keystroke
[Alt-F3]	Toggles *Reveal Codes* and returns to normal display.
[F10]	Saves the document. Use the name **MRMPREP.V5**.

TO TAKE A BREAK Press **[F7]**, type **N**, type **Y**, remove diskette(s). To resume (hard disk): Insert *Data* diskette, type **A: ↵**, type **C:\WP51\WP A:MRMPREP.V5 ↵**. To resume (two drive): Insert diskettes, type **A: ↵**, type **B:WP A:MRMPREP.V5 ↵**.

Selecting and Deleting Blocks of Text

Single characters of text may be deleted using **[Delete]** or **[Backspace]** and single lines may be deleted using **[Ctrl-End]** (see p. W30). However, it is faster to delete large areas of text using block operations. For example, in the file **MRMPREP.V5**, delete everything after the first sentence in the first paragraph (i.e., after the words **February 12, 1991**) by doing the following:

Keystroke	Action Resulting from Keystroke
[arrow]	Use the [arrow] keys or mouse to move the cursor to the first letter of the word **This** (the **T** at location **Ln 3.17" Pos 2.7**).

REMEMBER . . . you can use your mouse to select the block and then skip the next two steps. In this case, using the keyboard is probably easier.

Continued . . .

Keystroke	Action Resulting from Keystroke
[Alt-F4]	Specifies the beginning of the block. The words `Block on` will appear in the status line.
[Home] [Home] ↓	Moves the cursor to the last character in the file (you could use the **[arrow]** keys or mouse to do this, but **[Home] [Home] ↓** is faster). The block of text has been selected.

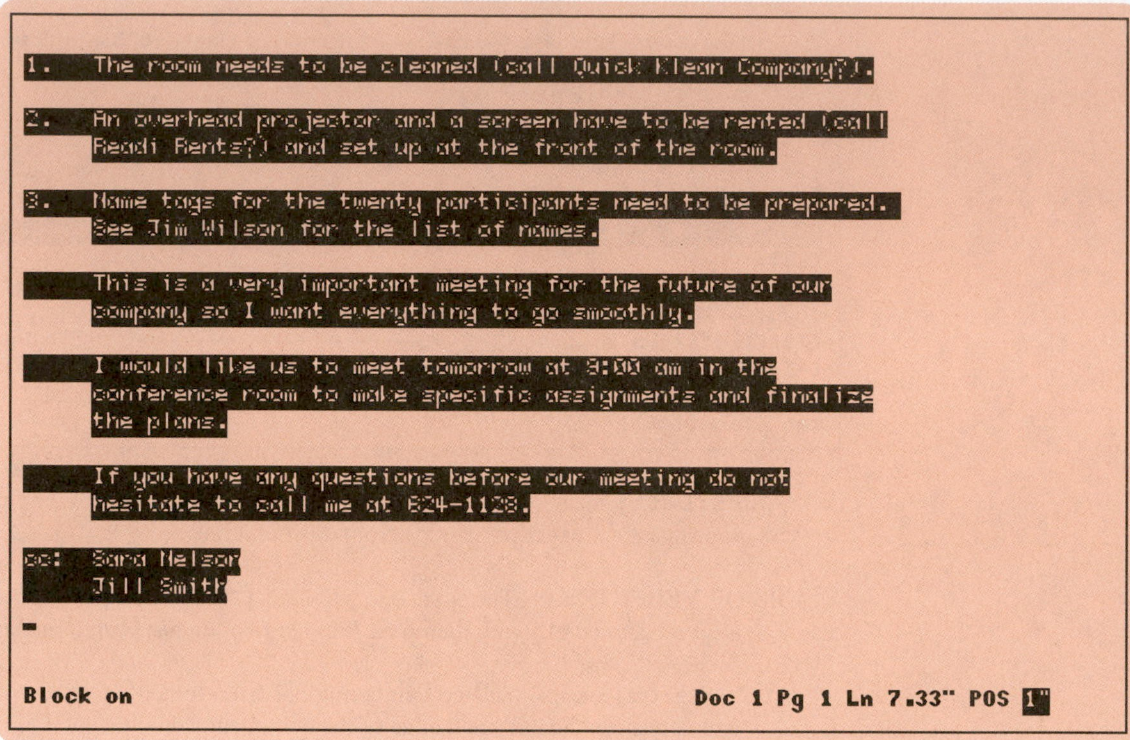

Keystroke	Action Resulting from Keystroke
[Delete]	Specifies that the block is to be deleted. As a precaution against the possibility of your deleting a large portion of text by mistake, WordPerfect displays the following message on the status line:

```
Delete Block? No (Yes)
```

Continued . . .

Keystroke	Action Resulting from Keystroke
Y	Specifies that **Y**es, you do want to delete the block. The block of text is deleted and the screen looks as follows:

```
MEMORANDUM

DATE:      February 10, 1991

TO:        Bill Schwartz and Lisa Pearson

FROM:      Alec Benson

SUBJECT:   Preparation of Conference Room

                We need to prepare the conference room
           for a meeting of the Board of Directors to be
           held from 9:00 am to 11:30 am on February 12,
           1991. _

A:\MRMPREP.V5                        Doc 1 Pg 1 Ln 3.17" Pos 2.7"
```

Centering

WordPerfect allows you to center a line of text between its left-hand and right-hand margins, center a heading over a column, or center each line individually in a block. Center the word **MEMORANDUM** in the first line of the document **MRMPREP.V5** by doing the following:

Keystroke	Action Resulting from Keystroke
[Home] [Home] ↑	Moves the cursor to the first character of the document (or use the **[arrow]** keys or mouse to move the cursor to location **Ln 1" Pos 1"**).
[Shift-F6]	Select the *Center* feature and insert the special center code **[Center]** at the cursor (this code can be seen only if you press **[Alt-F3]** to reveal the codes). The centering code affects only the line of text it is on. When the **[down arrow]** key is pressed, the word is exactly centered between the left and right margins. Note that the word may not be centered on the screen, but it will be centered on the printed version of the document.
↓	Reformats the line (the effect is that **MEMORANDUM** is centered).
[F10]	Saves the document. Use the name **MRMPREP.V6**.

To center a block of text rather than a single line, you would first select the block (by using **[Alt-F4]** or the mouse) and then press **[Shift-F6]**. If you do this, WordPerfect will display **`[Just:Center] ? No (Yes)`** on the status line. If you enter **`Y`** (for yes), WordPerfect will insert the special justification code **`[Just:Center]`** at the beginning of the block and **`[Just:Full]`** at the end to indicate where line centering is to begin and where it is to end.

Case Conversion

Sometimes you may want to emphasize a certain phrase or sentence by making all the letters uppercase (capitals). For example, in the file **`MRMPREP.V6`**, change all the letters in the phrase **`Board of Directors`** to uppercase **`(BOARD OF DIRECTORS)`** by doing the following:

Keystroke	Action Resulting from Keystroke
[arrow]	Use the **[arrow]** keys or mouse to move the cursor to the first letter of **`Board`** (location **`Ln 2.83" Pos 4.1"`**).
	REMEMBER . . . you can use your mouse to select the block and then skip the next two steps.
[Alt-F4]	Specifies the beginning of the block. The words **`Block on`** will appear on the status line.
[arrow]	Use the **[arrow]** keys to move the cursor to the space just to the right of the last letter of the word **`Directors`** (location **`Ln 2.83" Pos 5.9"`**).
[Shift-F3]	Selects the *Switch* feature and displays the following menu:

```
1 Uppercase; 2 Lowercase: 0
```

Keystroke	Action Resulting from Keystroke
`U` (or **`1`**)	Selects **`1 Uppercase`** from the menu and changes all the letters in the selected block to uppercase.

```
                         MEMORANDUM

DATE:     February 10, 1991

TO:       Bill Schwartz and Lisa Pearson

FROM:     Alec Benson

SUBJECT:  Preparation of Conference Room

               We need to prepare the conference room
          for a meeting of the BOARD OF DIRECTORS to be
          held from 9:00 am to 11:30 am on February 12,
          1991.
```

If you wanted to convert the letters to lowercase, you would follow the same procedure, except that you would select **`2 Lowercase`** from the *Switch* menu.

Highlighting (Boldface and Underline)

Blocks of text can be highlighted using **boldface** and underline. To illustrate this, underline the word **MEMORANDUM** and boldface the names of the persons to whom the memo is addressed by doing the following:

Keystroke	Action Resulting from Keystroke
[Home] [Home] ↑	Moves the cursor to the upper left-hand corner of the document (location **Ln 1" Pos 1"**).
	REMEMBER . . . you can use your mouse to select the block and then skip the next two steps.
[Alt-F4]	Specifies the beginning of the block. The words **Block on** will appear on the status line.
[End]	Moves the cursor to the end of the line (location **Ln 1" Pos 5"**). This selects the entire line that contains the word **MEMORANDUM**.
[F8]	Specifies that the highlighted text is to be underlined. Depending on your monitor, the word **MEMORANDUM** may appear in a new color or it may appear underlined.
[arrow]	Use the **[arrow]** keys or mouse to move the cursor to the first letter of the word **Bill** (the **B** at location **Ln 1.67" Pos 2"**).
	REMEMBER . . . you can use your mouse to select the block and then skip the next two steps.
[Alt-F4]	Specifies the beginning of the block.
[End]	Moves the cursor to the end of the line (location **Ln 1.67" Pos 5"**). This selects the entire line.
[F6]	Specifies that the highlighted text is to be printed in boldface. Depending on your monitor, the words **Bill Schwartz and Lisa Pearson** may appear in a new color or they may appear in boldface.
	When the document is printed, it will appear as follows:

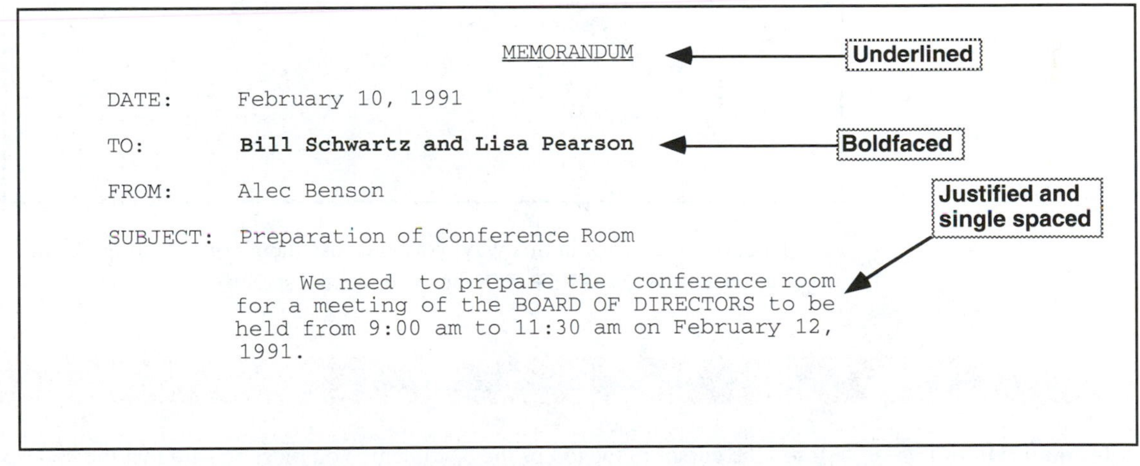

[F10]	Saves the document. Use the name **MRMPREP.V7**.

Defining Pages, Headers, and Footers

WordPerfect allows the user to define the structure of the pages of documents including centering text between the top and bottom of the page, numbering pages, using different paper sizes, including **headers** (text which appears at the top of each page), **footers** (text which appears at the bottom of each page), footnotes, and endnotes. The headers and footers can be printed on odd pages or even pages only, or different ones can be printed on odd and even pages.

For example, you might want to set up the pages for your documents so that they all will print on 8½ × 11-inch paper (this is equivalent to 66 lines of text per page when you use standard fonts), with 1-inch (six lines) margins at the top and bottom, a header that contains your name and your computer course number, and a footer that contains a page number. Such a document might look like the following:

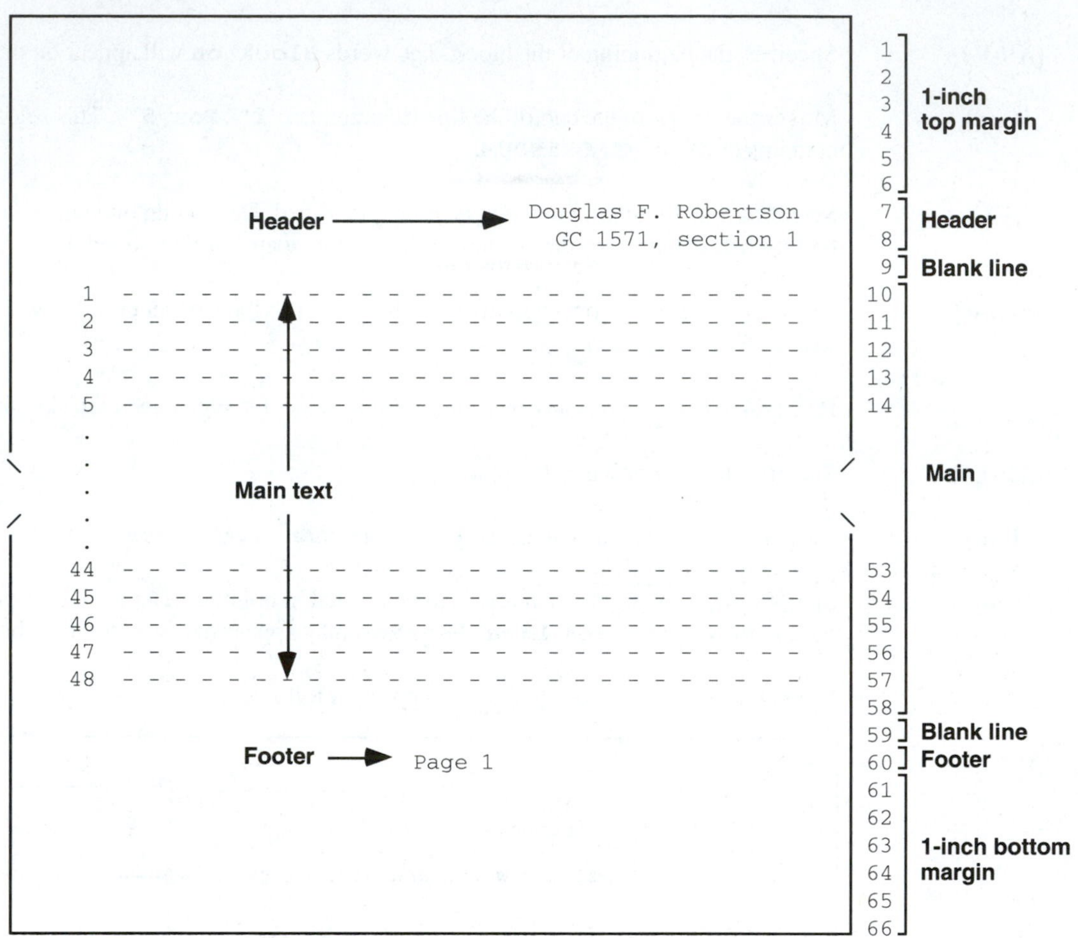

To define the pages in this way, you must use the *Format* feature. To illustrate this, do the following (the document **MRMPREP.V7** should be on the screen):

Keystroke	Action Resulting from Keystroke
[Home] [Home] ↑	Moves the cursor to the top of the document. You must be sure that the codes we are about to insert for the header and footer are not placed between the underline codes on the first line of the document. If they are, everything in the header and footer will be underlined! Use *Reveal Codes* to check this.

Continued . . .

Keystroke	Action Resulting from Keystroke

[Alt-F3] Reveals the codes.

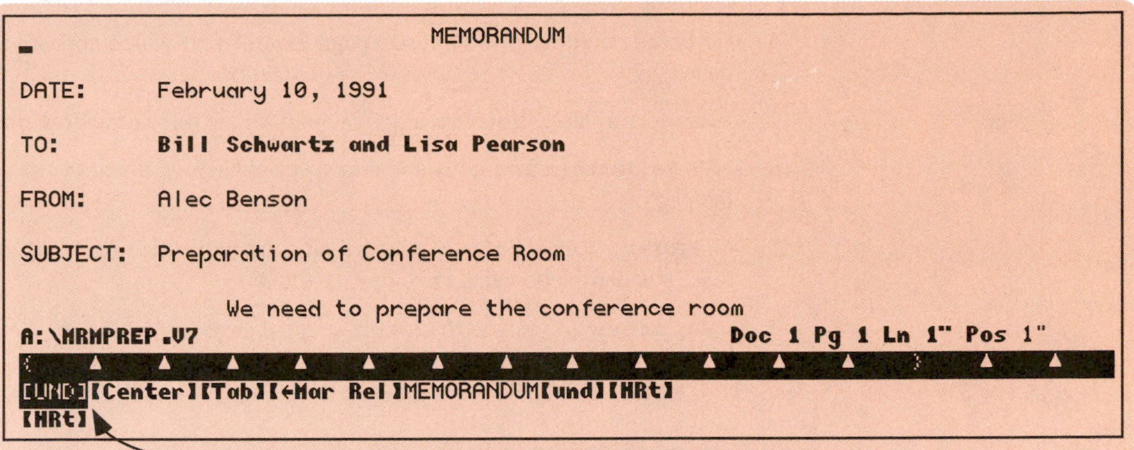

[arrow] Use the **[arrow]** keys or mouse, if necessary, to move the cursor so that the left-most code is highlighted. This will ensure that the header and footer codes will be read first by WordPerfect.

[Shift-F8] Displays the *Format* menu. This menu is broken down into four submenus. You have already used the **Line** submenu to set margins (pp. W58–61), tabs (pp. W52–57), text justification (pp. W78–79), line spacing (pp. W69–70) and line numbering (pp. W79–80). This time, you will use the **Page** submenu.

P (or **2**) Selects **2 - Page** and displays the following menu:

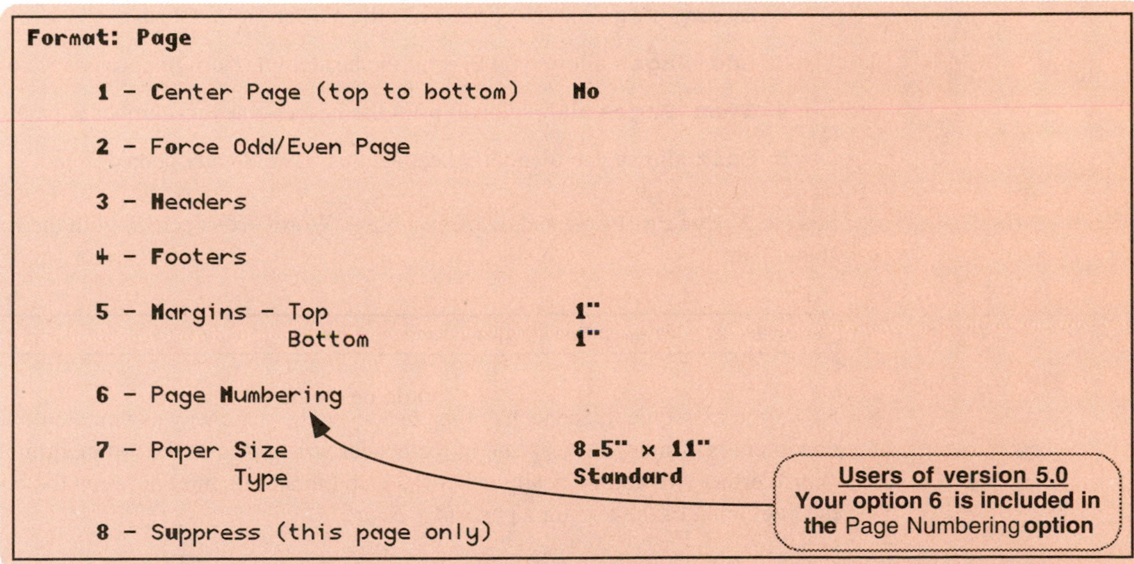

1 - Center Page allows you to center the text between the top and the bottom of the page.

2 - Force Odd/Even Page allows you to force the page number of the current page to be either odd or even.

Continued . . .

3 – **Headers** allows you to create page headers (text which appears at the top of each page).

4 – **Footers** allows you to create page footers (text which appears at the bottom of each page).

5 – **Margins Top/Bottom** allows you to set the top and bottom margins of the page.

6 – **Page Numbering** allows you to specify where you want page numbers to appear on the page.

7 – **Paper Size** allows you to specify the paper size (e.g., standard, legal) and type (e.g., standard, letterhead, envelope, labels).

8 – **Suppress** allows you to turn off selected page formatting for the current page.

H (or **3**) Selects **3 – Headers** and displays the following on the status line:

```
1 Header A; 2 Header B: 0
```

You may create up to two headers for a document.

A (or **1**) Selects **1 Header A** and displays the following on the status line.

```
1 Discontinue; 2 Every Page; 3 Odd Pages; 4 Even Pages; 5 Edit: 0
```

1 **Discontinue** allows you to discontinue a header within a document.

2 **Every Page** allows you to print the header on every page.

3 **Odd Pages** allows you to print the header on odd-numbered pages only.

4 **Even Pages** allows you to print the header on even-numbered pages only.

5 **Edit** allows you to modify headers that have already been defined.

P (or **2**) Selects **2 Every Page** and displays a blank WordPerfect screen with the following displayed on the status line:

```
Header A:  Press Exit when done                          Ln 1" Pos 1"
```

Now, you may type the contents of the header in the same way as you would any other text. When the document is printed, the first line of the header will appear at the top margin of the page. Also, WordPerfect will automatically insert .16 inch (about one line) between the bottom of the header and the beginning of the text for a particular page.

Type your name and computer course number on the right-hand side of the page. To align text to the right side of the page you could either insert blank spaces to the left of the text or use the *Flush Right* feature. We will do the latter:

Keystroke	Action Resulting from Keystroke
[Alt-F6]	Selects *Flush Right* and moves the cursor to the right-hand margin.
	Type the following text:

Douglas F. Robertson ↵

[Alt-F6]	Selects *Flush Right* again and moves the cursor to the right-hand margin.
	Type the following text:

GC 1571, section 1 ↵

	The header is now complete and so you can exit this screen.
[F7]	Exits the header definition. Notice that the phrase **HA Every page** now appears on the menu to the right of **3 - Headers**. This serves as a reminder that you have defined **Header A** and that it will be printed on every page of the document.
F (or **4**)	Selects **4 - Footers** and displays the following on the status line:

```
1 Footer A; 2 Footer B: 0
```

	You may create up to two footers for a document.
A (or **1**)	Selects **1 Footer A** and displays the following on the status line.

```
1 Discontinue; 2 Every Page; 3 Odd Pages; 4 Even Pages; 5 Edit: 0
```

P (or **2**)	Selects **2 Every Page** and displays a blank WordPerfect screen (with the words **Footer A:** on the status line). Now, you may type the contents of the footer. When the document is printed, the first line of the footer will appear at the bottom margin of the page. As was the case with the headers, WordPerfect will automatically insert .16 inch between the top of the footer and the last line of text for a particular page.
	To create the footer, type the word **Page** and then the WordPerfect page code in the center of the page by doing the following:
[Shift-F6]	Selects *Center* and moves the cursor to the center of the page.
	Type the following:
Page	Enters the word **Page** in the center of the page.
[Spacebar]	Inserts one blank space.
[Ctrl-B] ↵	This displays the special code (**^B**) used by WordPerfect to indicate that a page number is to be printed at this location. WordPerfect will number the pages automatically. The top of the screen should look like the following:

```
                    Page ^B
```

Continued . . .

Keystroke	Action Resulting from Keystroke
[F7]	Exits the footer definition. Notice that **FA Every page** now appears on the menu to the right of **4 - Footers**. This serves as a reminder that you have defined **Footer A** and that it will be printed on every page of the document.
[F7]	Exits the *Format* **Page** menu and returns to the editing screen.

```
                              MEMORANDUM
DATE:     February 10, 1991

TO:       Bill Schwartz and Lisa Pearson

FROM:     Alec Benson

SUBJECT:  Preparation of Conference Room

               We need to prepare the conference room
A:\MRMPREP.V7                                Doc 1 Pg 1 Ln 1.67" Pos 1"
[Header A:Every page;[Flsh Rgt]Douglas F. Robertson[HRt]
[Flsh Rgt]GC 1571, s ... ][Footer A:Every page;[Center]Page ^B][UND][Center][Tab
][←Mar Rel]MEMORANDUM[und][HRt]
```

Code for header

Code for footer

Keystroke	Action Resulting from Keystroke
[Alt-F3]	Hides the codes and returns to the normal editing screen.

To see the effect of the header and footer definitions, the document must be printed or use the view option.

Keystroke	Action Resulting from Keystroke
[F10]	Saves the document. Use the file specification **A:MRMPREP.VHF**.
[Shift-F7]	Selects the *Print* feature.
	If a printer is not available, use the view option (press **V** or **6** instead of **F** or **1** in the next step).
F (or **1**)	Selects **1 - Full Document** and sends the document to the printer.

Continued . . .

Keystroke	Action Resulting from Keystroke
	The printed document will look like the following:

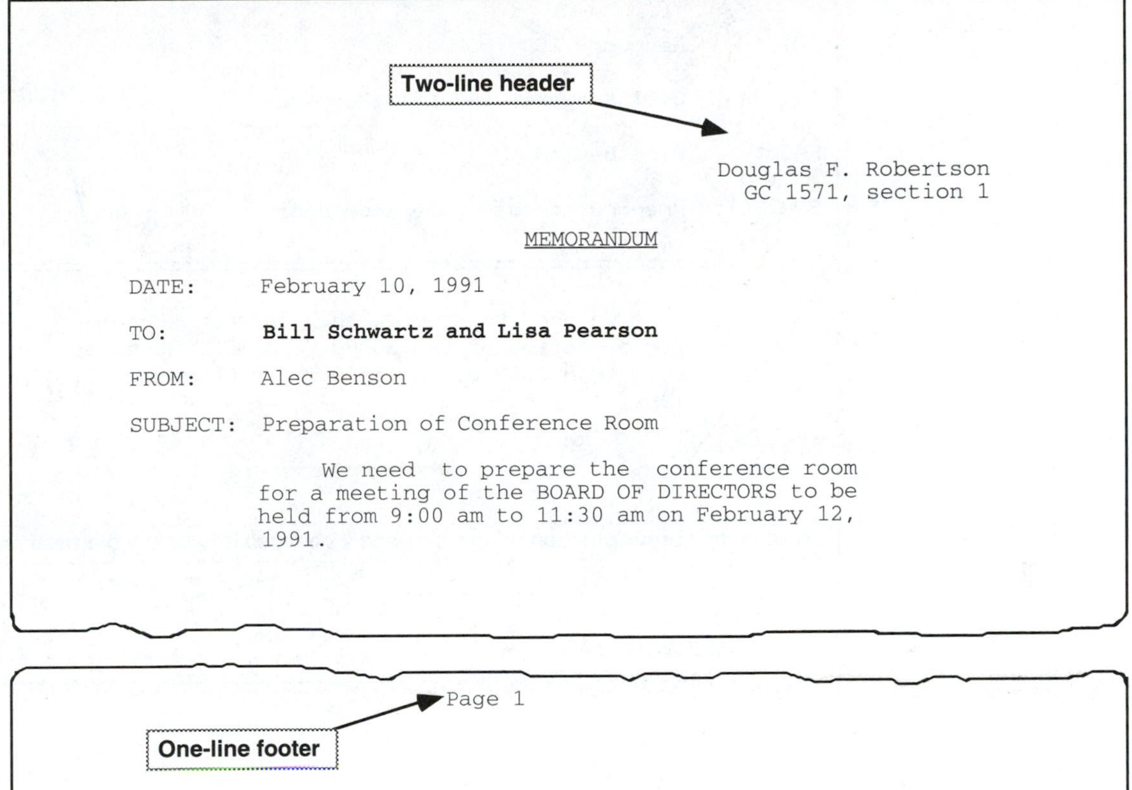

If you used the view option, press **[F7]** to exit to the editing screen.

Page Breaks

A page break is a location in a document where WordPerfect tells the printer to begin printing on a new sheet of paper. A *soft* page break is one that is automatically inserted by WordPerfect when the bottom margin of a page is reached. It appears as a line of dashes across the screen. A *hard* page break is one that you insert by pressing **[Ctrl-Enter]** wherever you wish. It appears as a line of equal signs across the screen.

To see how hard page breaks work, do the following (begin with the document **MRMPREP.VHF**):

Keystroke	Action Resulting from Keystroke
[arrow]	Use the **[arrow]** keys or mouse to move the cursor to the blank line just above the first paragraph (location **Ln 3.17" Pos 1"**).
[Ctrl-Enter]	Inserts a hard page break. A line of equal signs will appear across the screen.

Continued . . .

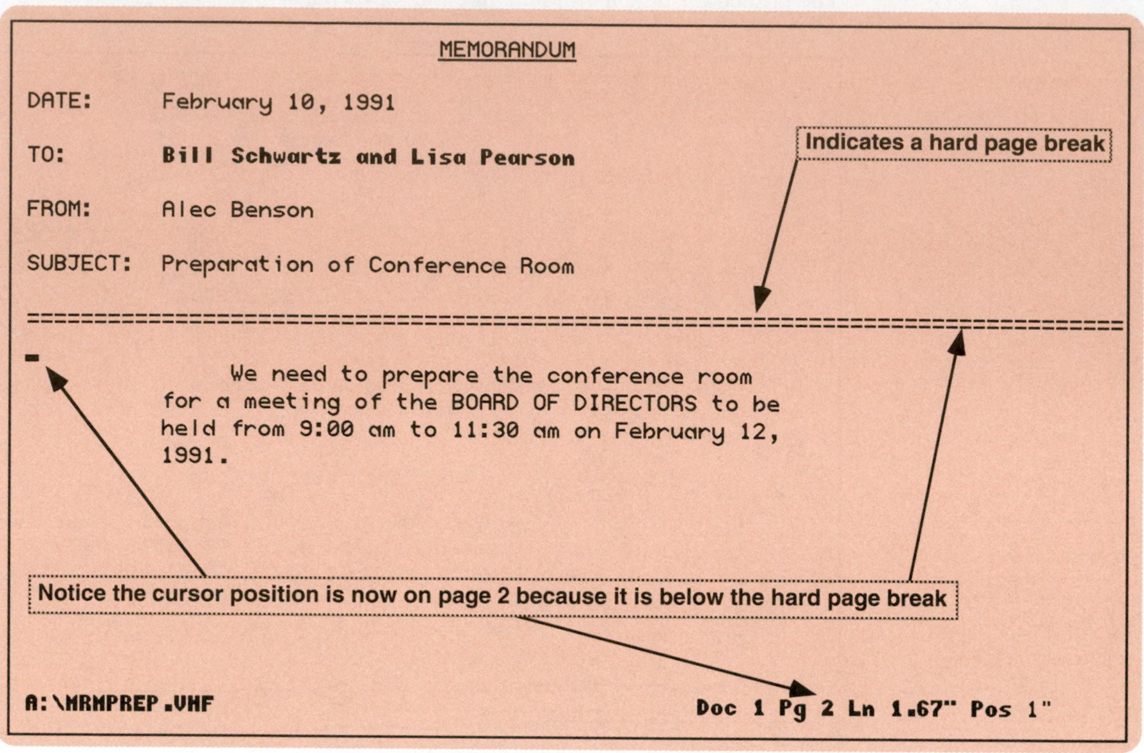

[Shift-F7]	Selects the *Print* feature.
	If a printer is not available, use the view option (press **6** (or **V**) instead of **1** (or **F**) in the next step).
F (or **1**)	Selects **1 - Full Document** and sends the document to the printer. Two pages will be printed. Each page will have a header and a footer.
	If you used the view option, press **[F7]** to exit to the editing screen.
[F7]	Exits this document.
N	Specifies that the file is not to be saved.
N	Specifies that **N**o, you do not want to exit WordPerfect.

TO TAKE A BREAK Press **[F7]**, type **N**, type **Y**, remove diskette(s). To resume (hard disk): Insert *Data* diskette, type **A: ↵**, type **C:\WP51\WP ↵**. To resume (two drive): Insert diskettes, type **A: ↵**, type **B:WP ↵**.

Using the Spell Feature

The WordPerfect *Spell* feature (sometimes called *spell checker* or *speller*) can be instructed to check the spelling of words by comparing each word in your document with the entries in a 115,000-word dictionary. If a match cannot be found, WordPerfect gives you a number of alternatives ranging from ignoring the word to selecting an alternative from a given list. The *Spell* feature also checks for some capitalization errors and double words such as *the the*.

We will use the document **MEMO2**, which you saved on page W31, to illustrate how the *Spell* feature works. Before checking the spelling in **MEMO2**, you first will have to retrieve it (begin from a blank WordPerfect screen).

Keystroke	Action Resulting from Keystroke
[Shift-F10]	Specifies that you want to retrieve (load) a WordPerfect file and displays the following on the status line:

```
Document to be retrieved: _
```

A:MEMO2 ↵	Provides the file specification for the document to be loaded.

To illustrate how the *Spell* feature works, you will need to modify **MEMO2** so that it includes a few errors. Use the regular editing techniques to modify the document so that it looks like the following:

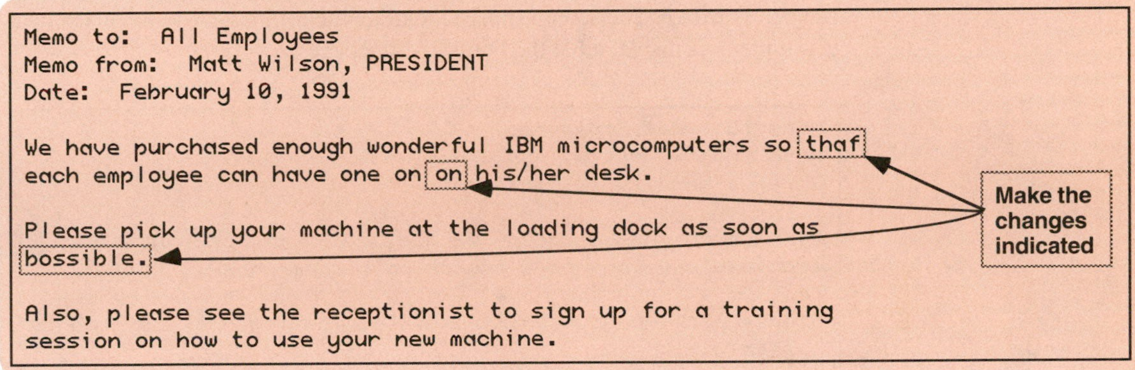

```
Memo to:  All Employees
Memo from:  Matt Wilson, PRESIDENT
Date:  February 10, 1991

We have purchased enough wonderful IBM microcomputers so thaf
each employee can have one on on his/her desk.

Please pick up your machine at the loading dock as soon as
bossible.

Also, please see the receptionist to sign up for a training
session on how to use your new machine.
```


After you have made the above modifications, save the document and begin the spell checking process by doing the following:

Keystroke	Action Resulting from Keystroke
[F10]	Saves the document.
A:SPELL1 ↵	Specifies the name of the document.
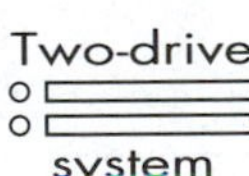 Two-drive system	**IF YOU ARE USING A TWO-DRIVE SYSTEM:** replace the *WordPerfect Data* diskette in drive A: with the diskette called *Speller*.
[Ctrl-F2]	Calls up the *Spell* feature and displays the following menu:

```
Check: 1 Word; 2 Page; 3 Document; 4 New Sup. Dictionary; 5 Look Up; 6 Count: 0
```

1 **Word** allows you to check the spelling of the word at the cursor only. If the word is in the dictionary, the cursor will move to the next word in the document. If the word is suspect, WordPerfect will alert you to that fact by displaying **Not Found** on the status line.

2 **Page** allows you to check the spelling of all the words on the page that contains the cursor (this is a printed page, not just what is displayed on a single screen).

3 **Document** allows you to check the spelling of the words in the entire document. This is the option you would normally pick.

Continued . . .

4 **New Sup. Dictionary** allows you to open and use alternative dictionaries. Sometimes, you may want to create dictionaries that have words which are used only in certain contexts (e.g., you are a dentist and want a special dictionary of dental terms, or you are a geophysicist and want a special dictionary of rock and mineral names). If you select this option, WordPerfect will ask you for the name of the file that contains the supplementary dictionary.

5 **Look Up** allows you to check the spelling of a word prior to entering it into the document. Just press **5**, type the word you want to check, and then press **[Enter]**.

6 **Count** allows you to count the number of words in the document.

D (or **3**) Selects **3 Document** and begins searching the document from the beginning. The first word that is flagged is **thaf**. The screen should look like the following (notice that **thaf** has been highlighted and that a menu is displayed at the bottom of the page):

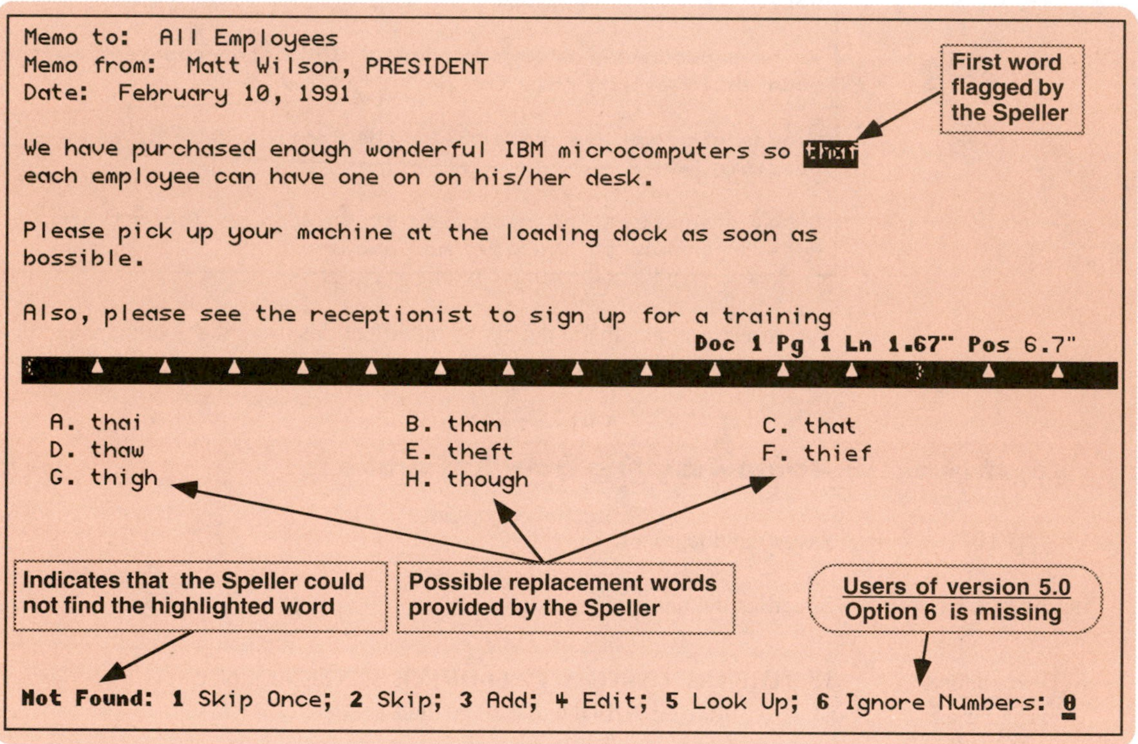

USERS OF VERSION 5.0 Your screen will look slightly different and option 6 is missing.

1 **Skip Once** allows you to skip over this word and continue with the process (i.e., you believe that the word is correctly spelled in this instance). If the word is encountered again, it will be flagged again.

2 **Skip** is similar to **Skip Once** except that the word will not be flagged again if it is encountered. The checking process continues.

Continued . . .

Keystroke	Action Resulting from Keystroke
	3 Add allows you to save the particular word in your own personal supplementary dictionary called **WP{WP}US.SUP**. This is useful if you have specialized words that you know are spelled correctly but those words are not in the regular WordPerfect dictionary. Later, those words can be added to the main dictionary if you so desire. **4 Edit** allows you to correct the spelling of the flagged word using the normal editing techniques. **5 Look Up** allows you to look up a word to see if it is in the main dictionary. **6 Ignore Numbers** instructs the speller to ignore words that contain numbers (e.g., if you select this option, then words such as **360K** will not be flagged). A list of possible replacement words is displayed in the lower half of the screen. These words are WordPerfect's guesses at what the flagged word should be. To replace the flagged word with one of the choices, type the appropriate letter (e.g., to replace **thaf** with **that**, press **C**).
c	Selects the word **that** to replace the flagged word and continues the checking process. WordPerfect then flags the double words **on on** and displays the following on the status line: `Double Word: 1 2 Skip; 3 Delete 2nd; 4 Edit; 5 Disable Double Word Checking_` **1 2 Skip** skips the double words and continues the checking process. **3 Delete 2nd** deletes the second word and continues the checking process. **4 Edit** allows you to change the highlighted text using the standard editing techniques. **5 Disable Double Word Checking** instructs WordPerfect to ignore double occurring words for the rest of the document.
3	Deletes the second word and continues the checking process. WordPerfect then flags the word **bossible** but this time does not display any suggested replacement words. Apparently the algorithm (procedure) used by WordPerfect to display alternatives was not good enough to make a good guess. Thus, the word must be manually edited.
4	Selects **4 Edit** and places the cursor at the first letter of the suspect word. The following reminder is displayed on the status line: `Spell Edit:  Press Exit when done                Doc 1 Pg 1 Ln 2.33" Pos 1"` This means that when you have finished editing the word you must press **[F7]** (this is the *Exit* key) to continue.
[Insert]	Toggles to typeover mode and displays **Typeover** on the status line as a reminder.
p	Replaces the letter **b** with the letter **p**.

Continued . . .

Keystroke	Action Resulting from Keystroke
[F7]	Exits *Spell* edit mode and continues checking the document. No more words are flagged and WordPerfect displays the number of words checked on the status line:

```
Word count: 61          Press any key to continue_
```

USERS OF VERSION 5.0 Because of a slight change in the way WordPerfect counts words, your word count will be 63 rather than 61.

Note that the number of words checked may be different from the number of words in the document. For example, you may have broken up one word into two or you may have checked only a part of the document rather than the entire document. In that case, the word count would be the number of words in the section checked rather than in the entire document. To get an accurate word count, select the count option from the first *Spell* menu (i.e., tap **[Ctrl-F2]** and then **6**).

Keystroke	Action Resulting from Keystroke
↵	Exits the *Spell* mode and returns to the editing screen.
Two-drive system	**IF YOU ARE USING A TWO-DRIVE SYSTEM:** replace the *Spell* diskette in drive A: with your *WordPerfect Data* diskette.
[F7]	Exits the current document.
N	Specifies that the document should not be saved. WordPerfect then asks if you want to exit the program.
N	Specifies that **N**o, you do not want to exit the program. WordPerfect will present you with an empty screen.

Using the Thesaurus Feature

In addition to a spelling checker, WordPerfect has a large thesaurus that can be used to help you find alternatives to individual words in your documents. Let's see how the *Thesaurus* feature can be used by doing the following:

Keystroke	Action Resulting from Keystroke
[Shift-F10]	Specifies that you want to retrieve (load) a WordPerfect file.
A:MEMO2 ↵	Indicates the file specification for the document to be loaded.
[arrow]	Use the **[arrow]** keys or mouse to move the cursor to the first letter of the word **wonderful** (location **Ln 1.67" Pos 3.5"**).
Two-drive system	**IF YOU ARE USING A TWO-DRIVE SYSTEM:** replace the *WordPerfect Data* diskette in drive A: with the diskette labeled *Thesaurus*.
[Alt-F1]	Calls up the *Thesaurus* screen:

Continued . . .

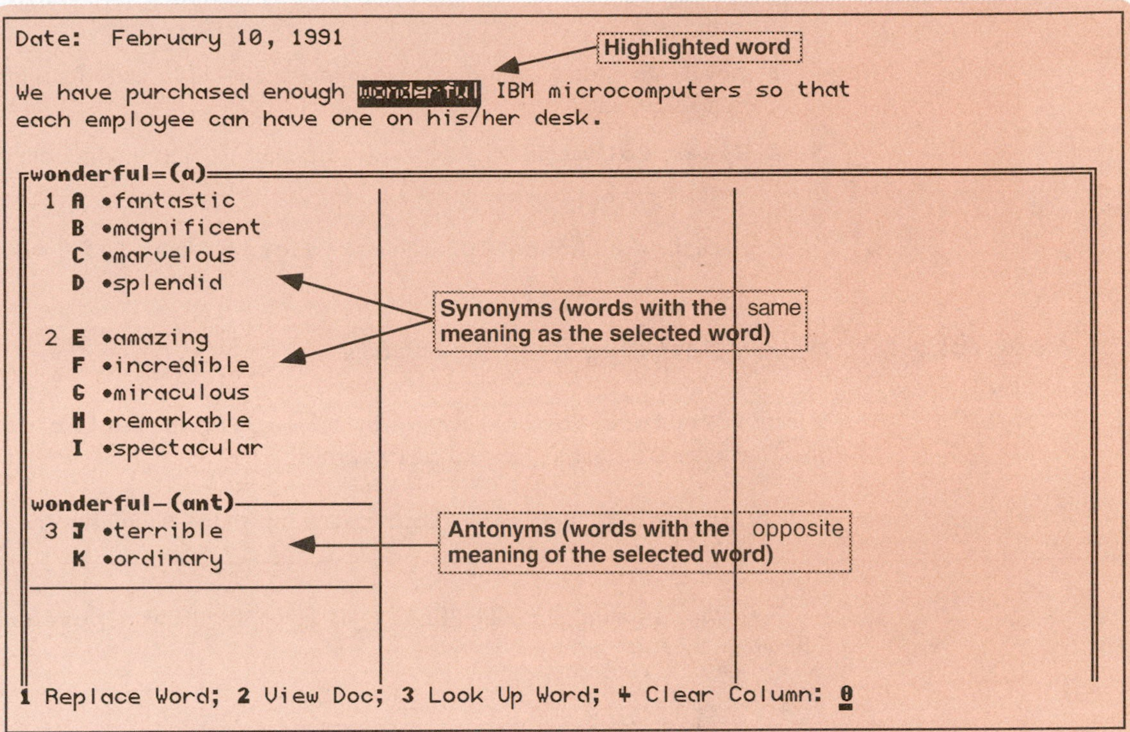

- The top of the screen shows a maximum of four lines of the document, including the word that has been selected.
- The middle of the screen shows a list of alternative choices found in the *Thesaurus*. Words that can be looked up in the *Thesaurus* (e.g., **wonderful**) are called *headwords*. Words listed under the headword (e.g., **fantastic**) are called *references* and are listed in groups as adjectives **(a)**, nouns **(n)**, verbs **(v)**, and antonyms **(ant)**. Each reference has a reference letter that can be used to select that word (e.g., the reference letter for **fantastic** is **A**). References marked with a bullet (e.g., **•fantastic**) are themselves headwords (i.e., they can be looked up in the *Thesaurus*).
- Because the word **wonderful** is an adjective, the alternative choices are listed under **wonderful (a)**.
- If the word could be used as a noun, the alternative choices would be listed under **wonderful (n)**. No such choices are listed.
- If the word could be used as a verb, the alternative choices would be listed under **wonderful (v)**. No such choices are listed.
- Antonyms (words having the opposite meaning) are listed under **wonderful (ant)**. These include **terrible** and **ordinary**.
- The bottom of the screen contains a menu listing possible actions you may take.

```
1 Replace Word; 2 View Doc; 3 Look Up Word; 4 Clear Column: 0
```

1 Replace Word allows you to replace the highlighted word **(wonderful)** with one of the choices listed. To do this, type the letter next to the word you want to select (e.g., to replace **wonderful** with **fantastic**, type **A**).

Continued . . .

Keystroke	Action Resulting from Keystroke
	2 View Doc allows you to use the **[arrow]** keys to scroll through the document to see other parts. **3 Look Up Word** allows you to display the *Thesaurus* entry for a different word than the one highlighted. **4 Clear Column** allows you to erase the contents of a column from the screen.

Replace the word **wonderful** with **marvelous** by doing the following:

Keystroke	Action Resulting from Keystroke
1	Selects **1 Replace Word** and displays the message **Press letter for word** on the status line. The letter **C** is next to the word **marvelous**.
C	Replaces **wonderful** with **marvelous** and returns to the editing screen.

Following a similar procedure, find a replacement for the word **purchased** by doing the following:

Keystroke	Action Resulting from Keystroke
[arrow]	Use the **[arrow]** keys or mouse to move the cursor to the first letter of the word **purchased** (location **Ln 1.67" Pos 1.8"**).
[Alt-F1]	Calls up the *Thesaurus* screen:

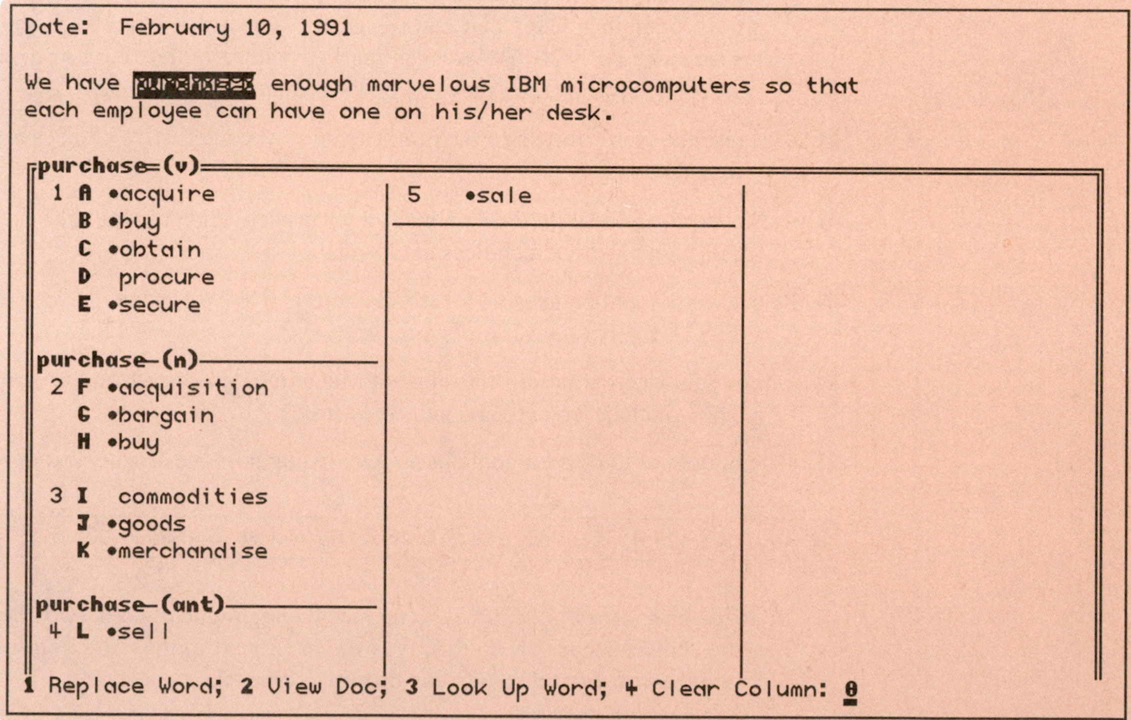

Recall that each word with a bullet is itself a headword and may be looked up in the *Thesaurus*. For example, display the entry for the word **acquire** by pressing **A**.

Keystroke	Action Resulting from Keystroke
A	Selects **acquire** and displays its alternatives in the second column.

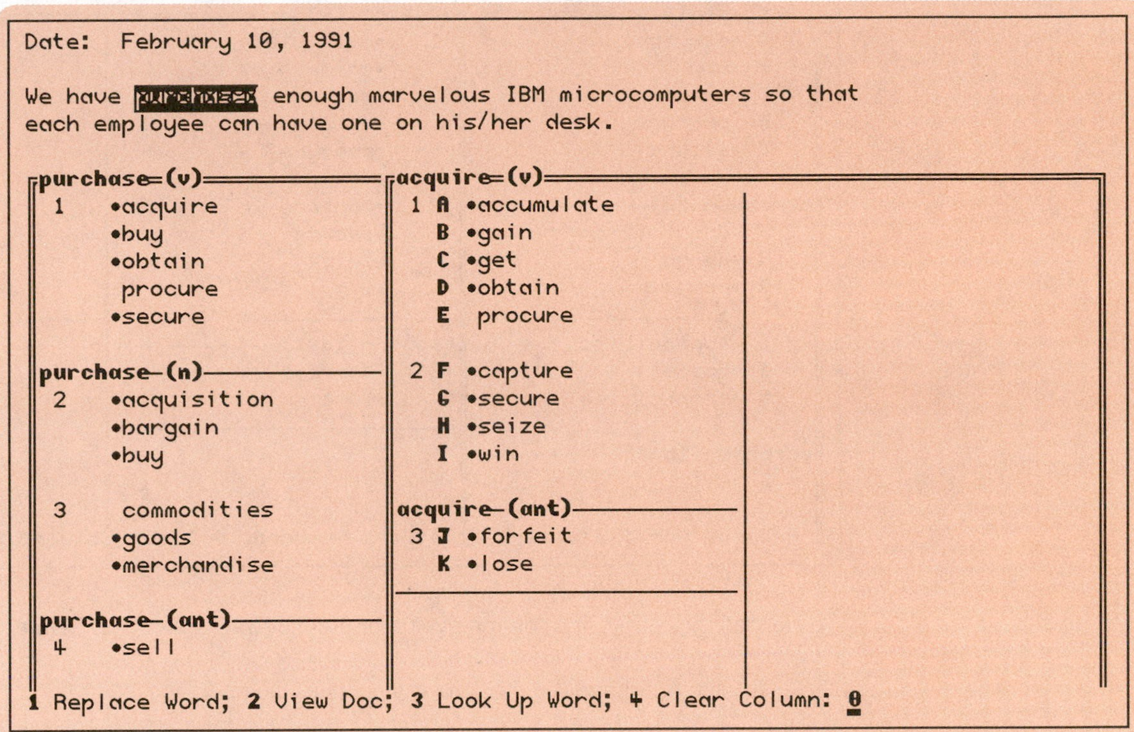

```
Date:  February 10, 1991

We have purchased enough marvelous IBM microcomputers so that
each employee can have one on his/her desk.

purchase=(v)=====================  acquire=(v)=================
 1    •acquire                      1 A •accumulate
      •buy                            B •gain
      •obtain                         C •get
       procure                        D •obtain
      •secure                         E  procure

purchase-(n)---------------------   2 F •capture
 2    •acquisition                    G •secure
      •bargain                        H •seize
      •buy                            I •win

 3     commodities                  acquire-(ant)---------------
      •goods                        3 J •forfeit
      •merchandise                    K •lose

purchase-(ant)-------------------
 4    •sell

1 Replace Word; 2 View Doc; 3 Look Up Word; 4 Clear Column: 0
```

Notice that the reference letters have moved to the second column so that you can select from the new list. To move the reference letters to a different column, use the **[left-arrow]** or **[right-arrow]** keys. For example, move the reference letters to the left-most column by pressing the **[left-arrow]**.

Keystroke	Action Resulting from Keystroke
←	Moves the reference letters left one column.

Continued . . .

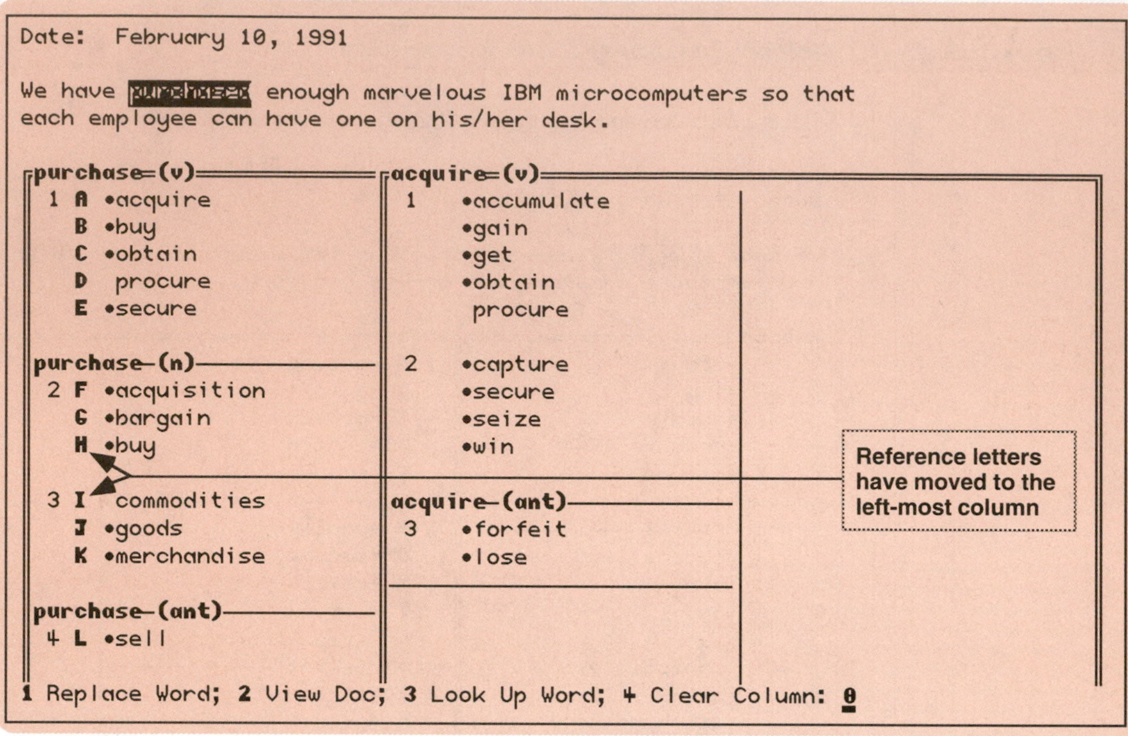

To clear all the entries in a column, type **4** or use the **[Backspace]** or **[Delete]** keys.

4 Clears the active column (i.e., the one that contains the reference letters).

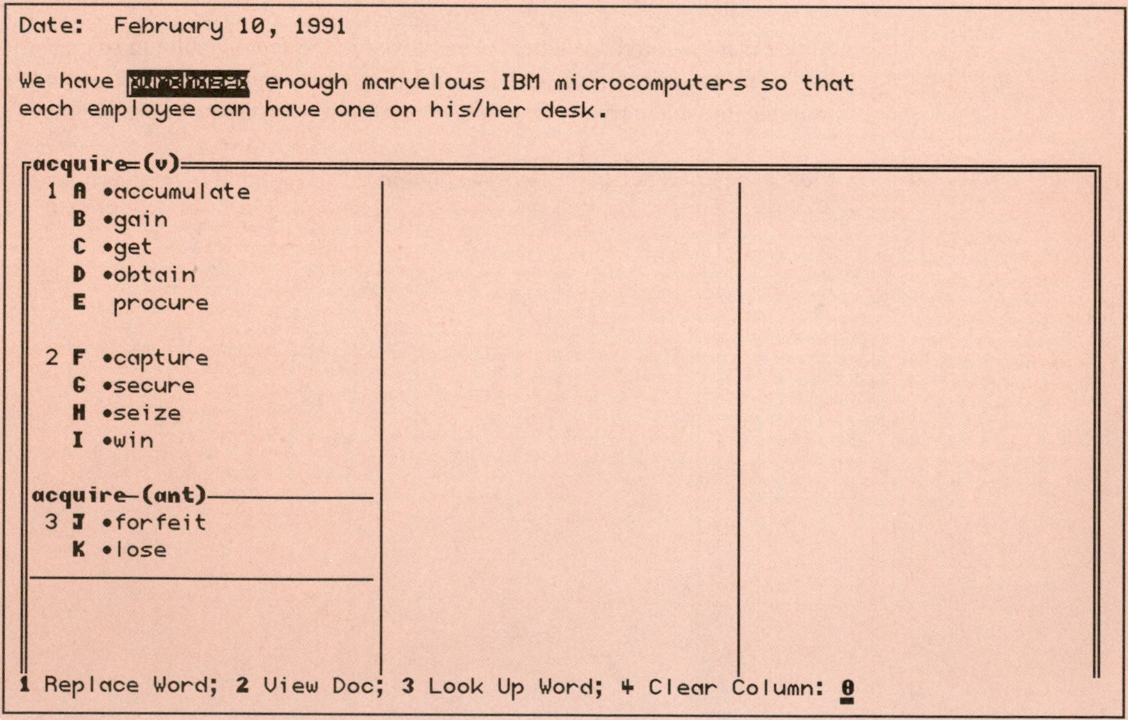

Continued . . .

Keystroke	Action Resulting from Keystroke
	Let's replace the word **purchase** with **procure**.
1	Selects **1 Replace Word** and asks for the reference letter of the replacement.
E	Replaces **purchased** with **procure** and returns to the editing screen. Notice that WordPerfect does not correctly change the tense of the verb (the correct replacement for **purchased** should be **procured**). You will have to fix that yourself. After making that change, the final document should look like the following:

```
Memo to:  All Employees
Memo from:  Matt Wilson, PRESIDENT
Date:  February 10, 1991

We have procured enough marvelous IBM microcomputers so that each
employee can have one on his/her desk.

Please pick up your machine at the loading dock as soon as
possible.

Also, please see the receptionist to sign up for a training
session on how to use your new machine.
```

Keystroke	Action Resulting from Keystroke
[F7]	Exits this document and asks if the document is to be saved.
Y	Specifies that the document is to be saved.
Two-drive system	**IF YOU ARE USING A TWO-DRIVE SYSTEM,** replace the *Thesaurus* diskette with your *WordPerfect Data* diskette.
A:THESAU1 ↵	Provides the file specification for the document.
Y	Specifies that you want to exit WordPerfect and return to DOS.

TO TAKE A BREAK Remove diskette(s). To resume (hard disk): Insert *Data* diskette, type **A: ↵**, type **C:\WP51\WP ↵**. To resume (two drive): Insert diskettes, type **A: ↵**, type **B:WP ↵**.

Homework Exercises

① Construct a letter to KeepGreen, Inc., the company that takes care of your lawn, stating that you no longer want to utilize their services. In a numbered list that employs hanging indentations, state at least three reasons why you are dissatisfied. In order to illustrate the hanging indentations, at least one of your reasons must be longer than one line. The letter should use a standard business style (your address, the date, a salutation, the text, and a closing), be at least two paragraphs in length, and include a listing of your concerns using numbered hanging indentations. Such a letter might look like the following:

```
123 Birch Lake Road
Blue Earth, MN  55012
11 February 1991

Customer Relations
KeepGreen, Inc.
88 Acorn Lane
White Pines, MN  55102

Dear Sir or Madam:

I would like to  cancel my lawn-care contract with  your company.
I am not satisfied with your service for the following reasons:

1.    You use a poor quality fertilizer.
2.    The service personnel who work on my lawn do not  show up on
      time and are quite rude.
3.    The price you charge is too high.

Please return my deposit as soon as possible.

Sincerely,

Tom Lamb
```

Save the final copy of the letter as **HWW2-01** and then print it.

② Show the indentation codes for the letter you created for Exercise 1 by moving the cursor to the first numbered reason and then using the *Reveal Codes* feature. Do a screen dump of the result.

③ Change the margins of the first paragraph in the letter you created in Exercise 1 so that both the left-hand and right-hand margins are set to 3 inches. Save the modified letter as **HWW2-03** and then print it.

④ While still in WordPerfect, drop to DOS and display a directory of the diskette in drive A:. Do a screen dump to show the process.

⑤ Print a double-spaced version of the document **HWW2-01** you created in Exercise 1. Save the double-spaced document as **HWW2-05**.

⑥ Use block movements to modify the letter **HWW2-01** from Exercise 1 so that the reasons listed are in reverse order (renumber them appropriately). Save the document as **HWW2-06** and then print it.

---

⑦ Print the letter **HWW2-01** from Exercise 1 with the text left justified (lined up on the left-hand side only) rather than fully justified (i.e., turn off full justification for the printed copy).

---

⑧ Use the line numbering option to number the last five lines of your document **HWW2-01** from Exercise 1. Save the document as **HWW2-08** and then print it.

---

⑨ Write an advertisement that could be posted on a bulletin board offering your services as a tutor for students who need help with word processing. The document should use the centering option to center your name, mailing address, and phone number at the top of the page. Below that, write the details on your experience, your price structure (how much do you charge? do you charge by the hour or by the size of the document? do you offer discounts to groups?), any other services you offer in connection with this (typing, checking spelling, saving, printing, pick up and delivery, etc.), and how to contact you. Save the document as **HWW2-09** and then print it.

---

⑩ Use the case conversion option to modify the advertisement from Exercise 9 so that your name and mailing address are all in uppercase letters. Save the document as **HWW2-10** and then print it.

---

⑪ Modify the advertisement from Exercise 10 so that your name is underlined and the price you charge is in boldface. Save the document as **HWW2-11** and then print it.

---

⑫ Retrieve the file **HWW2-01**, which you created in Exercise 1, and insert a hard page break in the middle of the document. Save the document as **HWW2-12** and then do a screen dump to show the location of the page break.

---

⑬ Create headers and footers for the document you created for Exercise 12. The header should include your name centered on the page and the footer should include the page number. Save the document as **HWW2-13** and then print it.

---

⑭ Check the spelling of the letter from Exercise 1 and do a screen dump when the first unknown word is flagged (this probably will be **KeepGreen**).

---

⑮ Use the *Thesaurus* feature to display alternatives for the word **Dear** from the document you created for Exercise 1. Do a screen dump when the alternatives are displayed.

Advanced Word Processing

Objectives *After you have completed this chapter, you should be able to*

- Use the *List Files* feature to view, search, copy, and retrieve files.
- Create text only (ASCII) files.
- Load text from one file into another.
- Open two WordPerfect documents at the same time.
- Cut (remove) blocks of text from one WordPerfect document and paste (add) them into another.
- Alphabetize a list of names from within WordPerfect.
- Search a document for specific strings and replace them with new ones.

CHAPTER 3

- Create personalized letters (*mail merge*) from a form letter and a list of names and addresses.
- Insert graphics into WordPerfect documents.
- Create mathematical and chemical equations for technical reports.
- Create and run simple programs, called macros, from within WordPerfect to do repetitive tasks such as changing rulers or entering text.
- Create and format a long document.
- Create a table of contents and index for a long document.

Introduction

In this chapter, we discuss advanced word-processing techniques that can be used to create complex documents and to improve efficiency when working with smaller documents. These techniques provide more control over the output produced by WordPerfect and allow the text from two or more documents to be combined into a single file.

Definitions

Before beginning a specific example, you should familiarize yourself with some definitions of terms frequently encountered when talking about word processing.

ASCII . . . (American Standard Code for Information Interchange) (W113) A standard coding scheme used by many computers. A file saved in ASCII by one application (e.g., Lotus 1-2-3) can be used by most other applications (e.g., WordPerfect), although some special codes (e.g., margins, character enhancements) will be lost. ASCII files are sometimes referred to as *text only* files because they have been stripped of all of their special codes.

Graphics . . . (W136) Non-text material such as pictures, tables, or charts.

Macro . . . (W148) A program (set of instructions) that tells an application to do a specified procedure. In their simplest form, WordPerfect macros are sets of keystrokes (including text and special WordPerfect keys) that the user has told WordPerfect to memorize. Those keystrokes can then be played back very quickly by pressing a single key.

Merge . . . (W128) To combine text or data from one document with that of another. Merge allows you to create a single *form* letter and then to make personalized copies for a large number of people by inserting their names and addresses into the form letter during the printing process.

Search . . . (W126) To scan a document for a specific set of characters (e.g., words or phrases).

Search and replace . . . (W126) To scan a document for a set of characters and replace the characters with another set.

Sort . . . (W120) Arrange (alphabetize) text according to a specified scheme.

Strings . . . (W124) Collections of characters (e.g., letters, digits, punctuation, blank spaces) that are treated as a group. For example, this sentence and paragraph can each be considered a string.

Listing Files

By this time, you have created a number of WordPerfect documents and saved them on your *WordPerfect Data* diskette. WordPerfect allows you to access those files quickly and easily using the *List Files* feature (see p. W33). This feature has many other options that can be used to perform operations such as deleting, moving, renaming, printing, copying, viewing, and combining documents. To more fully illustrate this feature, do the following (begin from DOS):

Keystroke	Action Resulting from Keystroke
A: ↵	Ensures that **A:** is the default drive.
C:\WP51\WP ↵	Accesses the WordPerfect program and presents a blank WordPerfect screen.
Two-drive system	**IF USING A TWO-DRIVE SYSTEM:** type **B:WP** ↵.
[F5]	Selects the *List Files* feature and displays the following in the status line:

```
Dir A:\*.*                                   (Type = to change default Dir)
```

Continued . . .

Keystroke	Action Resulting from Keystroke
	If you press **[Enter]**, the directory of the diskette in the A: drive will be displayed. If you press [=], WordPerfect will allow you to define a new disk drive as the default. Just to see how this works, press [=].
=	Specifies that that you want to switch the default drive and displays the following on the status line:

```
New directory = A:\
```

Keystroke	Action Resulting from Keystroke
C: ↵	Specifies that the root directory of **C:** is to be the new default drive.

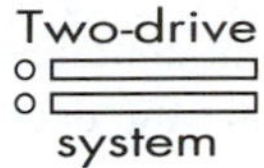

IF YOU ARE USING A TWO-DRIVE SYSTEM: Type **B:** ↵.

From now on, whenever you ask for a listing of the files, WordPerfect will assume you want to list the files in the root directory of the C: drive. The following is displayed on the status line:

```
Dir C:\*.*                                    (Type = to change default Dir)
```

Keystroke	Action Resulting from Keystroke
↵	Requests a listing of the root directory of the C: drive and displays the following screen (the directory of your disk will be different from that shown below):

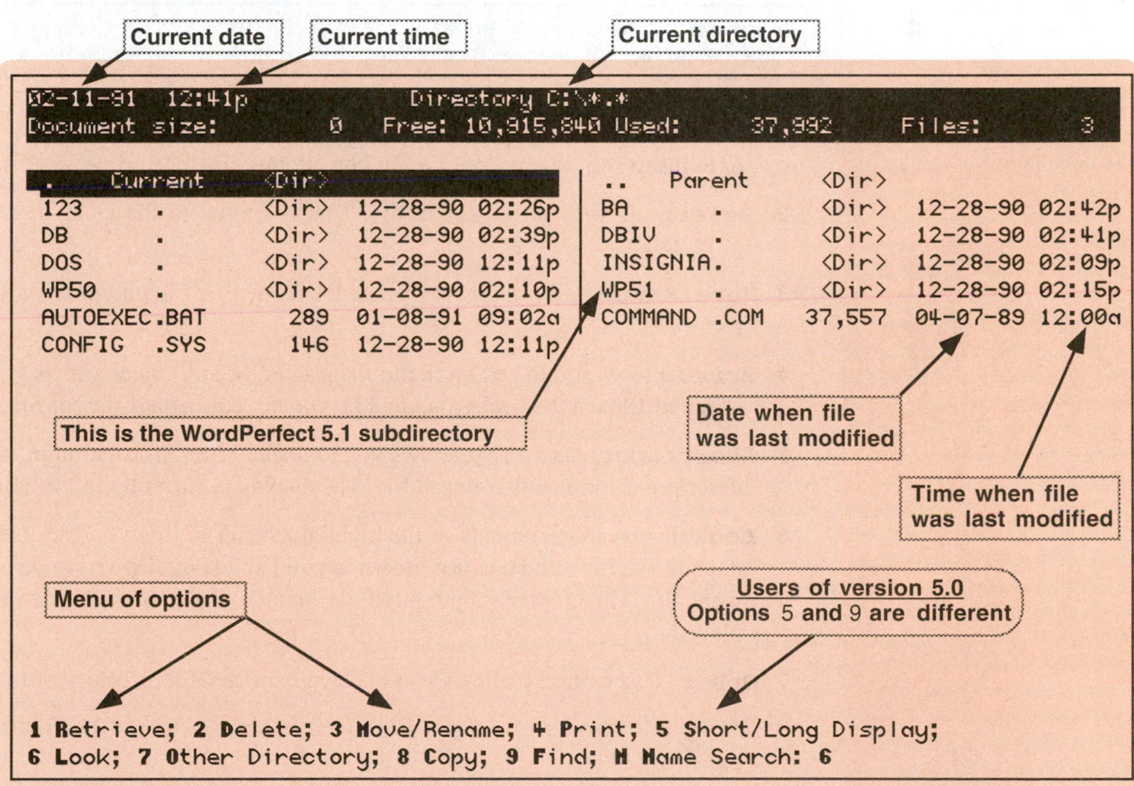

The screen consists of three parts:

1. A two-line header, which contains the following:
   - Date (**02-11-91**).
   - Time (**12:41p**).
   - Name of the directory displayed (**C:*.***) — this is the root directory of the **C:** drive.

- Size in bytes of the current document (this is **0** because the current document is blank).
- Number of bytes available for storage on the disk (**10,915,840**).
- Number of bytes used by the files in this directory (the total is **37992**), which is **289** (for the **AUTOEXEC.BAT** file) + **37557** (for the **COMMAND.COM** file) + **146** (for the **CONFIG.SYS** file).
- The number of file names displayed (there are three file names displayed — the rest of the names are for subdirectories, which are identified by **<DIR>**).

2. A list of subdirectories and files in the directory:

- The subdirectory names are listed first, in alphabetical order, and then the file names are listed alphabetically.
- For the subdirectories, the first column contains the name, the second column contains **<DIR>**, indicating that this is a subdirectory, and the last two columns contain the date and time of creation of the subdirectory.
- For the files, the first column contains the name, the second column contains the size in bytes, and the last two columns contain the date and time of the most recent modification to the file.

3. The following menu of options is displayed at the bottom of the screen:

```
1 Retrieve; 2 Delete; 3 Move/Rename; 4 Print; 5 Short/Long Display;
6 Look; 7 Other Directory; 8 Copy; 9 Find; N Name Search: 6
```

1 Retrieve allows you to load a WordPerfect document into a blank WordPerfect screen or to insert the contents of one file into another file (see pp. W33–35).

2 Delete allows you to erase a file. This is similar to the DOS **DELETE** command (see p. W209).

3 Move/Rename allows you to change the name of a file and/or to move it to a new subdirectory.

4 Print allows you to send a file to the printer. WordPerfect allows you to print a file or a group of files in the background while you are editing a different file.

5 Short/Long Display allows you to display file information in more detail including descriptive comments for each file. The display is currently in the **Short** form.

6 Look displays the contents of the highlighted file so that you can look at it, but you cannot edit the file. You can use **[down arrow]** and **[PageDown]** to scroll through the document. If a directory is highlighted, the names of the files in that directory will be displayed.

7 Other Directory allows you to change the default directory or to create a new one.

8 Copy allows you to copy a file. This is similar to the DOS **COPY** command (see pp. W205–207).

9 Find helps you to find a file that contains a specific word or phrase or that has a specific group of characters in its name. When you use this option, WordPerfect will display the names of files that meet the conditions you specify.

N Name Search allows you to select a file by typing its name rather than by using the **[arrow]** keys to select it. You need only type enough characters to uniquely define the name. As you type each character, WordPerfect highlights the first file name in the display that matches what you have typed so far.

Let's try a few of these features to see how they work. First, use the **Other Directory** option to display a listing of the directory of the *WordPerfect Data* diskette in drive A:.

Keystroke	Action Resulting from Keystroke
O (or **7**)	Selects **7 Other Directory** and displays the following at the bottom of the screen:

```
New directory = C:\
```

Keystroke	Action Resulting from Keystroke
A:\ ↵	Specifies that the directory is to be changed to the root directory of the diskette in drive A: and displays the following at the bottom of the screen:

```
Dir A:\*.*
```

Keystroke	Action Resulting from Keystroke
↵	Displays the root directory of the diskette in drive A: (the directory of your diskette may be different from that shown below):

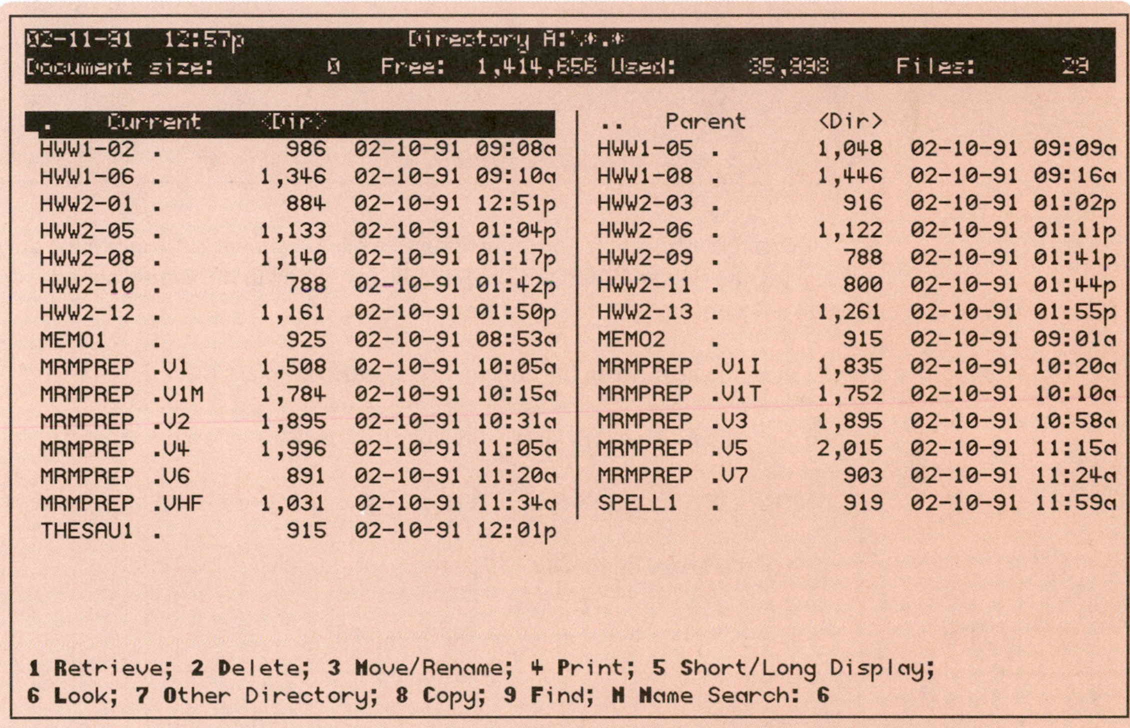

```
02-11-91  12:57p                  Directory A:\*.*
Document size:          0  Free:  1,414,656 Used:      35,888      Files:      29

 .    Current    <Dir>                   | ..    Parent     <Dir>
 HWW1-02  .        986  02-10-91 09:08a  | HWW1-05  .      1,048  02-10-91 09:09a
 HWW1-06  .      1,346  02-10-91 09:10a  | HWW1-08  .      1,446  02-10-91 09:16a
 HWW2-01  .        884  02-10-91 12:51p  | HWW2-03  .        916  02-10-91 01:02p
 HWW2-05  .      1,133  02-10-91 01:04p  | HWW2-06  .      1,122  02-10-91 01:11p
 HWW2-08  .      1,140  02-10-91 01:17p  | HWW2-09  .        788  02-10-91 01:41p
 HWW2-10  .        788  02-10-91 01:42p  | HWW2-11  .        800  02-10-91 01:44p
 HWW2-12  .      1,161  02-10-91 01:50p  | HWW2-13  .      1,261  02-10-91 01:55p
 MEMO1    .        925  02-10-91 08:53a  | MEMO2    .        915  02-10-91 09:01a
 MRMPREP  .V1    1,508  02-10-91 10:05a  | MRMPREP  .V1I   1,835  02-10-91 10:20a
 MRMPREP  .V1M   1,784  02-10-91 10:15a  | MRMPREP  .V1T   1,752  02-10-91 10:10a
 MRMPREP  .V2    1,895  02-10-91 10:31a  | MRMPREP  .V3    1,895  02-10-91 10:58a
 MRMPREP  .V4    1,996  02-10-91 11:05a  | MRMPREP  .V5    2,015  02-10-91 11:15a
 MRMPREP  .V6      891  02-10-91 11:20a  | MRMPREP  .V7      903  02-10-91 11:24a
 MRMPREP  .VHF   1,031  02-10-91 11:34a  | SPELL1   .        919  02-10-91 11:59a
 THESAU1  .        915  02-10-91 12:01p  |

1 Retrieve; 2 Delete; 3 Move/Rename; 4 Print; 5 Short/Long Display;
6 Look; 7 Other Directory; 8 Copy; 9 Find; N Name Search: 6
```

You may use the **[arrow keys]** or mouse to highlight the name of any file you wish to examine. For example, let's use the **Look** option to examine the contents of the file called **MEMO1**.

Keystroke	Action Resulting from Keystroke
[arrow]	Use the **[arrow]** keys or mouse to highlight the name **MEMO1**.
L (or **6**)	Selects **6 Look** and displays the following screen:

Continued . . .

Keystroke	Action Resulting from Keystroke

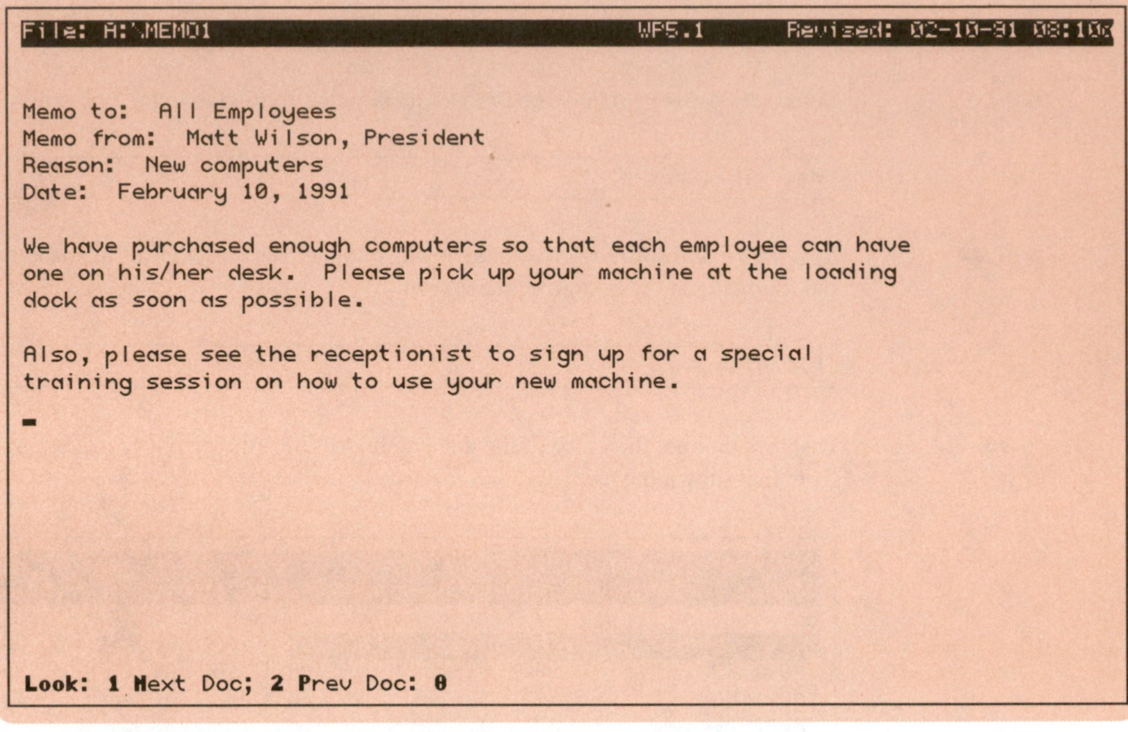
File: A:\MEMO1   WP5.1   Revised: 02-10-91 08:10

Memo to: All Employees
Memo from: Matt Wilson, President
Reason: New computers
Date: February 10, 1991

We have purchased enough computers so that each employee can have one on his/her desk. Please pick up your machine at the loading dock as soon as possible.

Also, please see the receptionist to sign up for a special training session on how to use your new machine.

Look: 1 Next Doc; 2 Prev Doc: 0

This feature is useful if you are working on one document but want to look at another one without leaving the first one. You may not edit the text while in this **Look** option (you may only view it). To edit a document, you must first **Retrieve** it.

To view the next file in the directory (i.e., **MEMO2**), press **N** (or **1**).

To view the previous file in the directory (i.e., **HWW2-13**), press **P** (or **2**).

USERS OF VERSION 5.0 The **Next Doc** and **Prev Doc** options are not available.

To exit the **Look** option, tap **[F7]**.

Keystroke	Action Resulting from Keystroke
[F7]	Exits **Look** and returns to the *List Files* screen.

The **Copy** option allows you to make copies of files without returning to DOS. For example, make a backup copy of the document **MEMO2** using the **Copy** option by doing the following:

Keystroke	Action Resulting from Keystroke
[arrow]	Use the **[arrow]** keys or mouse, if necessary, to highlight the name **MEMO2**.
C (or **8**)	Displays the following message at the bottom of the screen:

```
Copy this file to: _
```

Typing a file specification will make a backup copy of the highlighted file.

Continued . . .

Keystroke	Action Resulting from Keystroke
A:\MEMO2.BU ↵	Provides the file specification, makes a copy of the file under the new name, and returns to the *List Files* screen. The next time the *List Files* screen is updated, the name of the new file will appear in the list.
o (or **7**)	Selects **7 Other Directory** and displays **New directory = A:**.
↵	Accepts the name of the directory and displays **Dir A:*.***.
↵	Displays the directory specified. The file name **MEMO2.BU** now should appear in the list.

The **Find** option allows you to search the contents of every WordPerfect file listed in the directory for a specific word or phrase. Let's use the **Find** option to find the names of all WordPerfect documents on the diskette in drive A: that contain the name **Quick Klean**.

USERS OF VERSION 5.0 The **Find** option is named **Word Search**.

Keystroke	Action Resulting from Keystroke
F (or **9**)	Selects **9 Find** and displays the following at the bottom of the screen:

```
Find: 1 Name; 2 Doc Summary; 3 First Pg; 4 Entire Doc; 5 Conditions; 6 Undo: 0
```

USERS OF VERSION 5.0 Version 5.0 does not have the **Name** or **Undo** options.

1 **Name** allows you to search for a file by name or part of a name.

2 **Doc Summary** allows you to search the *document summary* of specific files for a particular phrase. This is very fast, but the document summaries for the files must first be created (we will not discuss this — see the *WordPerfect Reference Manual* for details).

3 **First Pg** allows you to search the first page of each document for a particular phrase (this saves time because the entire document is not searched).

4 **Entire Doc** allows you to search each document for a particular phrase (this can take quite some time if you have a lot of large documents on your disk).

5 **Conditions** allows you to enter specific conditions for the search process.

6 **Undo** allows you to return to the file list as it was before you began the search (i.e., it undoes the last **Find** command).

Keystroke	Action Resulting from Keystroke
E (or **4**)	Selects **4 Entire Doc** and requests the **Word pattern** to search for.
Quick Klean ↵	Specifies the phrase to be searched for and begins the search. WordPerfect then examines the contents of every file in the directory and displays the names of those files that contain the phrase **Quick Klean**. During the search, a message similar to the following will appear at the bottom of the screen:

```
Searching file  8_  of 26
```

Continued . . .

The search may take many minutes if you are using a hard disk that contains hundreds of files. When the search has been completed the screen should look like the following:

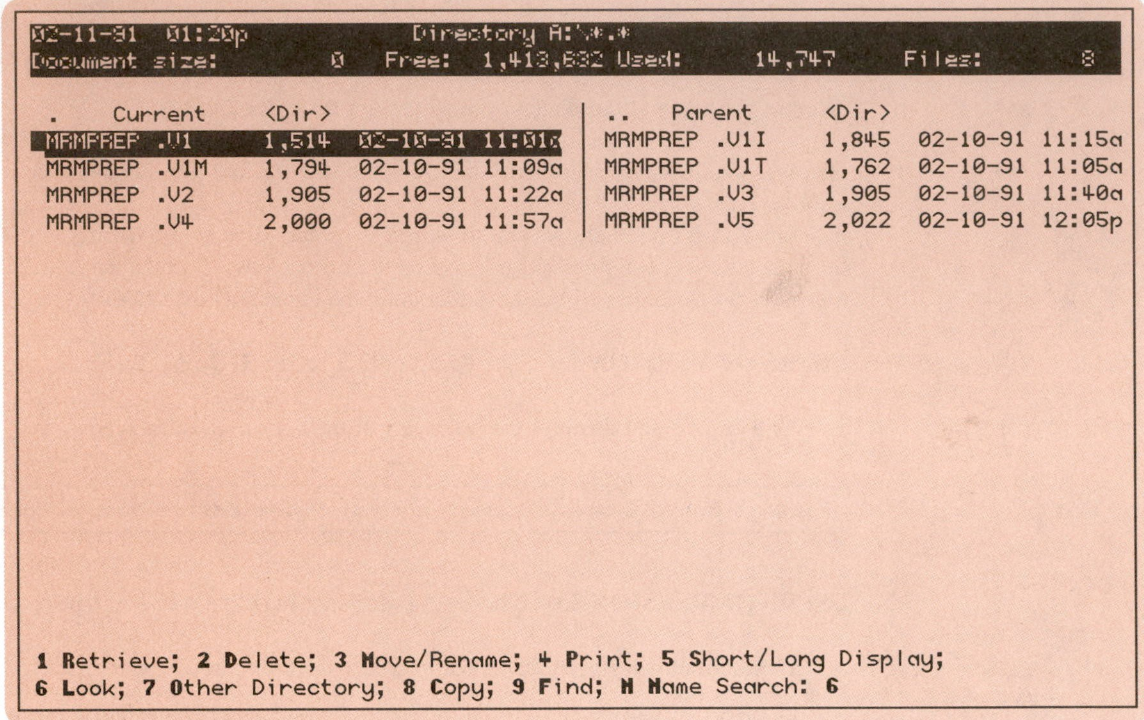

Only files **MRMPREP.V1** through **MRMPREP.V5** contain the specified words and thus they are the only ones that are listed.

USERS OF VERSION 5.0 Version 5.0 marks the file names in the *List Files* screen with an asterisk rather than listing the names of the selected files.

[F7] Exits the *List Files* screen and returns to a blank WordPerfect screen.

TO TAKE A BREAK Press **[F7]**, type **N**, type **Y**, remove diskette(s). To resume (hard disk): Insert *Data* diskette, type **A:** ↵, type **C:\WP51\WP** ↵. To resume (two drive): Insert diskettes, type **A:** ↵. Type **B:WP** ↵.

Creating a Text Only (ASCII) File

Like most other computer applications WordPerfect saves files in a *coded* format in order to increase speed of operation and to conserve space on the disk. Coding makes the information on a file more easily accessible by a specific program because it sets up the information in a way that is convenient for that program. This works well for WordPerfect documents if the only application that uses them is WordPerfect itself. However, there are many occasions where information created by one application needs to be used by others including other word processors (e.g., Microsoft Word), spreadsheets (e.g., Lotus 1-2-3), database management programs (e.g., dBASE), programming languages (e.g., BASIC) or even DOS.

When information needs to be shared by two different applications, you have three choices:

1. The information can be retyped into the new application. This could take a long time if there is a lot of information.

2. A translation program can be used to convert from one coding scheme into another. Such programs are available for most popular applications programs. For example, one of the authors of this book uses WordPerfect while the other author uses Microsoft Word. Using a translator, we can exchange files and edit each other's documents quite easily. Some programs even come with built-in translators. For example, WordPerfect comes with a program called **CONVERT** that can translate files created by WordStar and other applications into a form usable by WordPerfect.

3. Files can be written using a standard coding system that both applications understand. The system used by many applications is called **ASCII** (American Standard Code for Information Interchange). This coding scheme is convenient because most applications support (understand) it. However, special codes and characters sometimes become lost in the translation process (much like translating a phrase from English to German and then from German to Chinese—something usually gets lost in the translation).

In later chapters, we will discuss specific examples of translations between different applications. For now, let's see how to instruct WordPerfect to save a file using ASCII code instead of the usual WordPerfect code. For this example, begin from a blank WordPerfect screen and create the data file displayed below, which contains the names and phone numbers of five people. This file will be used later in this chapter and in chapters that follow. The last names should begin in column 1 (**Pos 1"**), the first names should begin in column 10 (**Pos 1.9"**), and the phone numbers should begin in column 20 (**Pos 2.9"**). Use the **[Spacebar]** rather than the **[Tab]** key to locate the names and numbers.

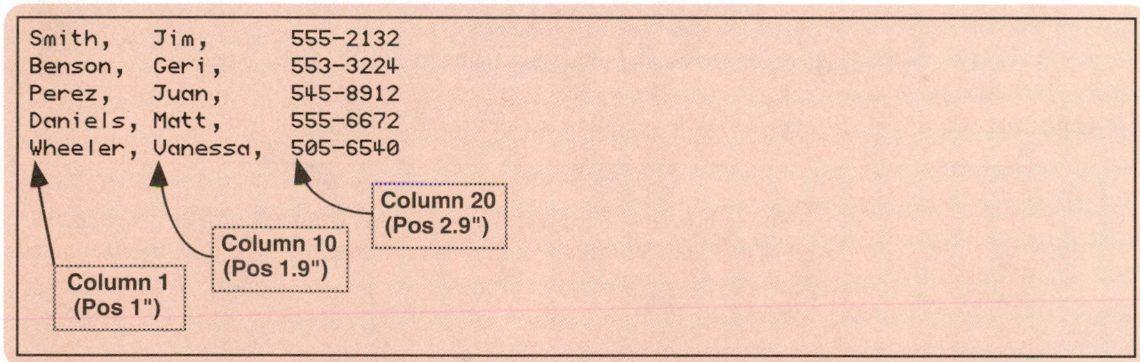
```
Smith,   Jim,      555-2132
Benson,  Geri,     553-3224
Perez,   Juan,     545-8912
Daniels, Matt,     555-6672
Wheeler, Vanessa,  505-6540
```


Now, use the *Text In/Out* feature to save the document as an ASCII text file. This process will retain all text, spaces, tabs, and carriage returns but will remove all formatting codes:

Keystroke	*Action Resulting from Keystroke*
[Ctrl-F5]	Invokes the *Text In/Out* feature and displays the following on the status line:

```
1 DOS Text; 2 Password; 3 Save As; 4 Comment; 5 Spreadsheet: 0
```

USERS OF VERSION 5.0 The **Save As** option is displayed as **Save Generic** and the **Spreadsheet** option is not available.

1 DOS Text allows you to save a file in ASCII text format.

2 Password allows you to assign a password to a document so that it may not be printed or retrieved without the password. This is useful for documents that contain confidential information.

Continued . . .

Keystroke	Action Resulting from Keystroke
	3 Save As allows you to save the document as a generic word-processing file, a WordPerfect version 4.2 file, or a WordPerfect version 5.0 file.
	4 Comment allows you to save a comment (an electronic note that will be displayed on the screen but will not be printed as part of the document).
	5 Spreadsheet allows you to directly import files created by Lotus 1-2-3, PlanPerfect, and Excel.
T (or **1**)	Selects **1 DOS Text** and displays the following on the status line:

```
1 Save; 2 Retrieve (CR/LF to [HRt]); 3 Retrieve (CR/LF to [SRt] in HZone): 0
```

Keystroke	Action Resulting from Keystroke
	1 Save saves the file as an ASCII text file.
	2 Retrieve (CR/LF to [HRt]) allows you to retrieve a file that was saved in ASCII mode. This option converts carriage returns into WordPerfect hard returns (the kind created when the **[Enter]** key is pressed).
	3 Retrieve (CR/LF to [SRt] in HZone) is similar to the previous retrieve except that carriage returns are converted into WordPerfect soft returns (the kind created when text wraps around to the next line as the cursor approaches the right margin).
S (or **1**)	Selects **1 Save** and requests a name for the file to be saved.
A:PHONETXT ↵	Provides the file specification and saves the file as an ASCII file.

To see how an ASCII text file is different from a WordPerfect coded file, let's also save the document as a regular WordPerfect file (call it **PHONEWP**) and then list the contents of the two files while in DOS.

Keystroke	Action Resulting from Keystroke
[F10]	Requests the name of the file to be saved.
A:PHONEWP ↵	Provides the file specification and saves the file using the normal WordPerfect coding.
[Ctrl-F1]	Suspends WordPerfect and enters the DOS environment.
G (or **1**)	Specifies that we want to drop to DOS.
TYPE A:PHONETXT ↵	Displays the contents of the file **PHONETXT**. (For more information on the **TYPE** command, see p. W203.)

Continued . . .

Keystroke	Action Resulting from Keystroke

```
Microsoft(R) MS-DOS(R) Version 4.01
              (C)Copyright Microsoft Corp 1981-1988

Enter 'EXIT' to return to WordPerfect
A:\>TYPE A:PHONETXT
Smith,   Jim,       555-2132
Benson,  Geri,      553-3224
Perez,   Juan,      545-8912
Daniels, Matt,      555-6672
Wheeler, Vanessa,   505-6540

Enter 'EXIT' to return to WordPerfect
A:\>_
```

This is how the file looks when saved as an ASCII text file

TYPE A:PHONEWP ↵ Displays the contents of the file **PHONEWP**.

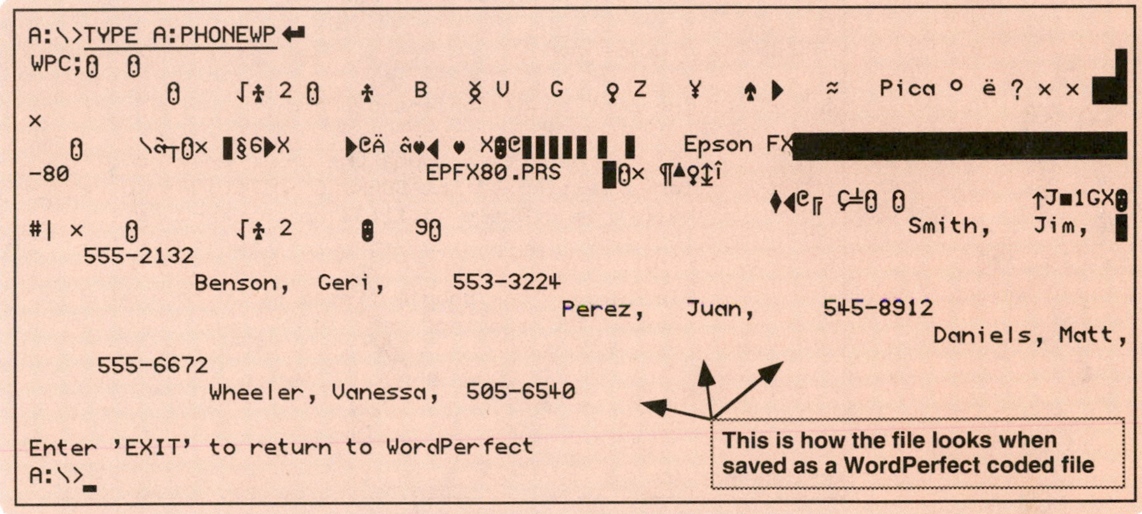

As you can see, the WordPerfect coded file includes many strange characters that WordPerfect uses to set margins, tabs, indentations, character enhancements, etc. These codes are generally unintelligible to other programs and to humans.

Exit ↵	Returns to WordPerfect.
[F7]	Exits the current document.
N	Specifies that **N**o, you do not want to save the document.
N	Specifies that **N**o, you do not want to exit WordPerfect and displays a blank WordPerfect screen.

Loading ASCII Text from Another File

As was discussed in the previous section, information stored on disk by one application may be used by other applications without the necessity of retyping it. For example, suppose you want to insert the names and phone numbers you saved in file **PHONETXT** into the memo **MRMPREP.V7**, which you created and modified on page W85. If **PHONETXT** were a WordPerfect coded file, you could use the *Retrieve* feature to make the modifications. However, because **PHONETXT** is an ASCII file it is better to use the *Text In/Out* feature.

Keystroke	Action Resulting from Keystroke
[Shift-F10]	Retrieves a file.
A:MRMPREP.V7 ↵	Indicates the file specification and loads the file into WordPerfect.
[Home] [Home] ↓	Moves the cursor to the bottom of the document.
↵ ↵	Moves the cursor down two lines. Type the following into the document:

Please call the people listed below to remind them of the meeting:

↵ ↵	Moves the cursor down two lines.

```
                         MEMORANDUM

DATE:     February 10, 1991

TO:       Bill Schwartz and Lisa Pearson

FROM:     Alec Benson

SUBJECT:  Preparation of Conference Room

               We need to prepare the conference room
          for a meeting of the BOARD OF DIRECTORS to be
          held from 9:00 am to 11:30 am on February 12,
          1991.

          Please call the people listed below to remind
          them of the meeting:

          _

A:\MRMPREP.V7                          Doc 1 Pg 1 Ln 4" Pos 2"
```

[Ctrl-F5]	Invokes the *Text In/Out* feature and displays the following on the status line:

```
1 DOS Text; 2 Password; 3 Save As; 4 Comment; 5 Spreadsheet: 0
```

T (or **1**)	Selects **1 DOS Text** and displays the following on the status line:

```
1 Save; 2 Retrieve (CR/LF to [HRt]); 3 Retrieve (CR/LF to [SRt] in HZone): 0
```

R (or **2**)	Selects **2 Retrieve** and asks for the name of the file to be retrieved.
A:PHONETXT ↵	Provides the file specification and inserts the file into the current document at the cursor.

Continued . . .

Keystroke	Action Resulting from Keystroke

```
                              MEMORANDUM

DATE:      February 10, 1991

TO:        Bill Schwartz and Lisa Pearson

FROM:      Alec Benson

SUBJECT:   Preparation of Conference Room

                We need to prepare the conference room
           for a meeting of the BOARD OF DIRECTORS to be
           held from 9:00 am to 11:30 am on February 12,
           1991.

           Please call the people listed below to remind
           them of the meeting:

           Smith,   Jim,       555-2132
           Benson,  Geri,      553-3224
           Perez,   Juan,      545-8912
           Daniels, Matt,      555-6672
           Wheeler, Vanessa,   505-6540

A:\MRMPREP.V7                          Doc 1 Pg 1 Ln 4" Pos 2"
```

[F7]	Exits the document and asks if it is to be saved.
Y	Specifies that **Y**es, the document is to be saved.
A:MRMPREP.V8 ↵	Specifies the name for the document.
N	Specifies that **N**o, you do not want to exit WordPerfect and displays a blank WordPerfect screen.

REMEMBER . . . to retrieve a file that was saved as a WordPerfect document (e.g., most of the documents you create using WordPerfect) use the *Retrieve* feature (press **[Shift-F10]** and then type the name of the file or press **[F5]** and then select the name from a list). To retrieve an ASCII text file (e.g., most of the data files you save using other programs for use with WordPerfect) use the *Text In/Out* feature (press **[Ctrl-F5]** and then select **DOS Text**).

Having Two Documents Open at the Same Time

WordPerfect allows you to open two documents at the same time. This is useful when you want to exchange information between files. For example, suppose you wanted to copy some information from **MRMPREP.V8** (the memo you just saved) and insert it into **MEMO2** (see p. W31). The easiest way to do that is to have both documents open at the same time. Begin the following from a blank WordPerfect screen:

Keystroke	Action Resulting from Keystroke
[Shift-F10]	Retrieves a file.
A:MRMPREP.V8 ↵	Indicates the file specification and loads the file into WordPerfect.

Continued . . .

Keystroke	Action Resulting from Keystroke
[Shift-F3]	Selects the *Switch* feature and creates (switches to) a new, blank WordPerfect document. Notice **Doc 2** now appears in the status line.
	To switch between two documents, use the switch key again:
[Shift-F3]	Switches from the blank document, which currently has no name, back to **MRMPREP.V8**. Notice **Doc 1** now appears in the status line. Each time **[Shift-F3]** is pressed, WordPerfect switches to the other document.
[Shift-F3]	Switches back to the other document (the blank screen) and displays **Doc 2** on the status line again.
[Shift-F10]	Retrieves a file.
A:MEMO2 ↵	Indicates the file specification and loads the file into WordPerfect.

Cutting and Pasting between Documents

Parts of one document can be copied or cut from that document and then pasted (inserted) into another document. This process is similar to the block operations discussed on pages W81–83 in Chapter 2. However, in this case, text is moved from one document to another document rather than moved within the same document.

To illustrate this, copy the list of names from the document **MRMPREP.V8** and insert it into the document **MEMO2** by doing the following (both documents should currently be opened with **MEMO2** displayed on the screen—see the previous section for details):

Keystroke	Action Resulting from Keystroke
[Home] [Home] ↓	Moves the cursor to the bottom of the document **MEMO2**.
↵ ↵	Pressing **[Enter]** twice inserts a blank line.
cc: ↵	**cc:** stands for **c**arbon **c**opy and is used to indicate that a copy of a memo is being sent to the persons listed next.
[Shift-F3]	Selects the *Switch* feature and displays the other document (i.e., **MRMPREP.V8**).
[arrow]	Use the **[arrow]** keys or mouse to move the cursor to the first letter in **Smith, Jim** (the right-hand side of the status line should display **Doc 1 Pg 1 Ln 4" Pos 2"**).
	REMEMBER . . . if your system has a mouse, you may use it to select the block of text to be copied:
	■ Be sure the mouse cursor is in the correct position (**Doc 1 Pg 1 Ln 4" Pos 2"**).
	■ Hold down the left button and drag (slide) the mouse until the end of the last line is highlighted (the status line should contain **Doc 1 Pg 1 Ln 4.67" Pos 4.7"**) . The words **Block on** will appear on the left-hand side of the status line while you hold down the button.
	■ Release the button. All the names and phone numbers should be highlighted.
	■ Skip the next two steps.
[Alt-F4]	Begins the definition of the block to be copied.

Continued . . .

Keystroke	Action Resulting from Keystroke
[arrow]	Use the **[arrow]** keys or mouse to move the cursor to the end of the last line (the status line should contain **`Doc 1 Pg 1 Ln 4.67" Pos 4.7"`**). All the names and phone numbers should be highlighted.
[Ctrl-F4]	Specifies that the selected block of text is to be operated on and displays a list of options on the status line:

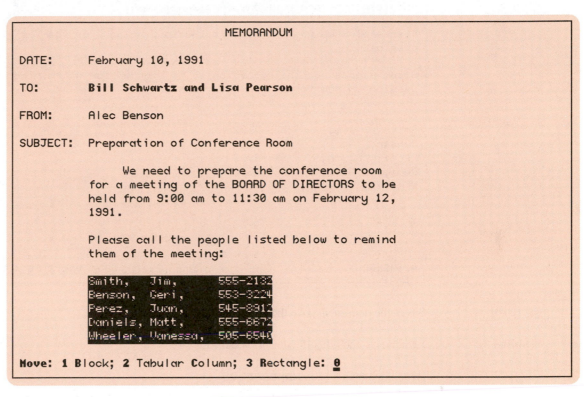

```
                              MEMORANDUM

DATE:      February 10, 1991

TO:        Bill Schwartz and Lisa Pearson

FROM:      Alec Benson

SUBJECT:   Preparation of Conference Room

                We need to prepare the conference room
           for a meeting of the BOARD OF DIRECTORS to be
           held from 9:00 am to 11:30 am on February 12,
           1991.

           Please call the people listed below to remind
           them of the meeting:

           Smith,    Jim,        555-2133
           Benson,   Geri,       553-3224
           Perez,    Juan,       545-8913
           Daniels, Matt,        555-8873
           Wheeler, Vanessa,     505-6540

Move: 1 Block; 2 Tabular Column; 3 Rectangle: 0
```

You want to move a **`Block`** so the correct option to select is **`1`**.

Keystroke	Action Resulting from Keystroke
`B` (or **`1`**)	Selects **`1 Block`** and displays the following on the status line:

```
1 Move; 2 Copy; 3 Delete; 4 Append: 0
```

Keystroke	Action Resulting from Keystroke
`C` (or **`2`**)	Selects **`2 Copy`**. The block of text is copied to the main memory of the computer (the block remains on the screen but it is no longer highlighted). The block will remain in memory until it is replaced by another block or until WordPerfect is exited. The status line should contain the following message:

```
Move cursor; press Enter to retrieve.              Doc 1 Pg 1 Ln 4.66" Pos 4.7"
```

This reminds you to move the cursor to the location where the text is to be inserted and then to press **[Enter]** to do the actual insertion.

Keystroke	Action Resulting from Keystroke
[Shift-F3]	Switches to the other document (**`MEMO2`**). The cursor should already be in the proper position (location **`Ln 3.33" Pos 1"`**).
[Enter]	Inserts the text at the cursor.

Continued . . .

Keystroke	Action Resulting from Keystroke

```
Memo to:  All Employees
Memo from:  Matt Wilson, PRESIDENT
Date:  February 10, 1991

We have purchased enough wonderful IBM microcomputers so that
each employee can have one on his/her desk.

Please pick up your machine at the loading dock as soon as
possible.

Also, please see the receptionist to sign up for a training
session on how to use your new machine.

cc:
Smith,   Jim,      555-2132
Benson,  Geri,     553-3224
Perez,   Juan,     545-8912
Daniels, Matt,     555-6672
Wheeler, Vanessa,  505-6540


A:\MEMO2                                Doc 2 Pg 1 Ln 3.33" Pos 1"
```

[F10]	Saves the document. Use the name **A:MEMO3**.
[Shift-F3]	Switches to the other document (**MRMPREP.V8**).
[F7]	Exits document 1 (i.e., **MRMPREP.V8**).
N	Specifies that you do not want to save the document. WordPerfect then will ask if you want to **Exit doc 1** (**MRMPREP.V8**).
Y	Specifies that you want to exit document 1 and displays document 2 again (**MEMO3**).

TO TAKE A BREAK Press **[F7]**, type **N**, type **Y**, remove diskette(s). To resume (hard disk): Insert *Data* diskette, type **A:** ↵, type **C:\WP51\WP A:MEMO3** ↵. To resume (two drive): Insert diskettes, type **A:** ↵, type **B:WP A:MEMO3** ↵.

Sorting Strings

WordPerfect may be used to **sort** (alphabetize) words, lines, or paragraphs, or to merge records (see pp. W128–36). For example, suppose you want to sort the lines that contain the names and phone numbers in the document **MEMO3** (i.e., you want to alphabetize the list by last name):

Keystroke	Action Resulting from Keystroke
[arrow]	If it is not already there, use the **[arrow]** keys or mouse to move the cursor to the first letter in **Smith** (location **Ln 3.33" Pos 1"**).
	REMEMBER . . . you can use your mouse to select the block and then skip the next two steps.

Continued . . .

Keystroke	Action Resulting from Keystroke
[Alt-F4]	Begins the definition of the block to be sorted.
[arrow]	Use the **[arrow]** keys or mouse to move the cursor to the end of the last line (location **Ln 4" Pos 3.7"**). All the names and phone numbers should be highlighted.
[Ctrl-F9]	Begins the sorting process and displays the sort menu in the lower half of the screen:

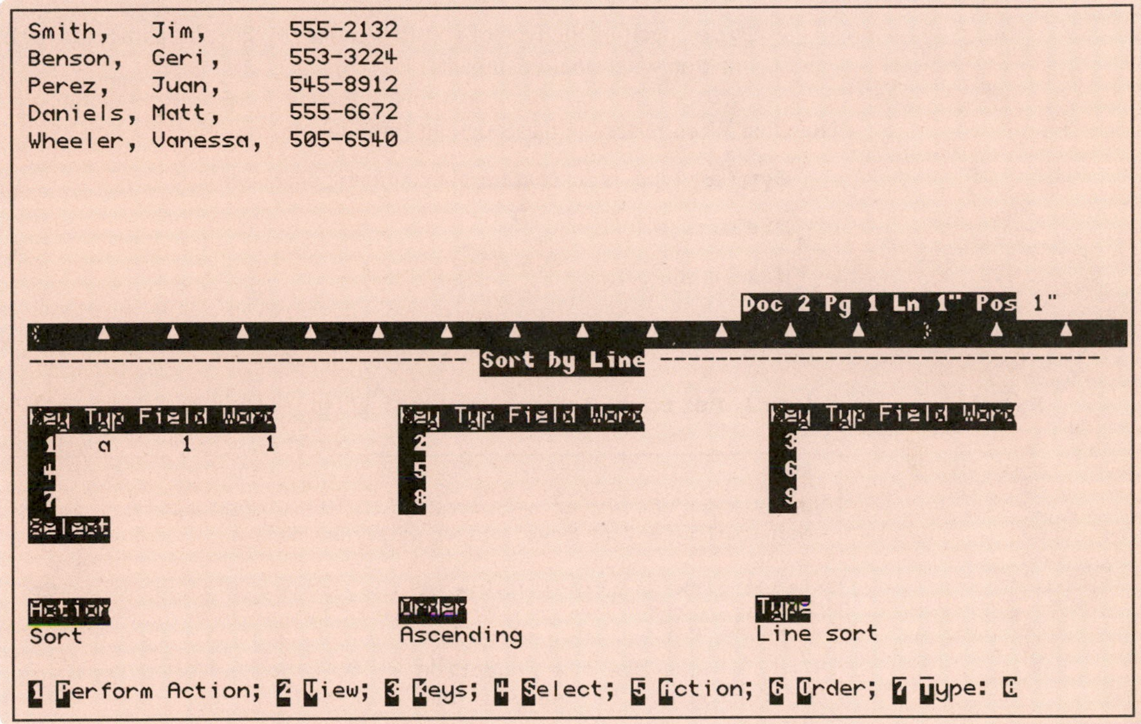

1 **Perform Action** begins the sorting process.

2 **View** allows you to scroll through the selected text using the **[arrow]** keys.

3 **Keys** The keys are the codes that WordPerfect will use to carry out the sort. Because there are nine keys available, you can sort using up to nine different levels. For example, you may want to sort by last name (this would be level one) and then, for people with the same last name, you may want to sort by first name (this would be level two); you could then sort by middle name (level three), etc. Each key has three parameters associated with it: **Typ**, **Field**, and **Word**.

Typ indicates the type of character to be sorted. Alphanumeric characters (use **a**) can be letters, numbers, or other characters. Numbers (use **n**) should include only digits but can include the dollar sign, commas, and decimal points. Letters in a numeric sort will be ignored.

Field is the location of the item you want to sort on. Fields are separated by tabs or indents. Because the block selected in **MEMO3** file has no tabs, there is only one field in this example.

Word is a group of characters separated from others by spaces. Each line of the selected block consists of three *words* (the first *word* is last name, the second *word* is first name, and the third *word* is phone number).

Continued . . .

Keystroke	Action Resulting from Keystroke

4 **Select** allows you to create logical statements to select data for inclusion based on specified criteria (e.g., you could select only those people who have a phone number that begins with 555).

5 **Action** is used in conjunction with **Select** and specifies whether to select and sort a block or only to select it.

6 **Order** specifies whether the sort will be ascending (**a** to **z**) or descending (**z** to **a**).

7 **Type** specifies the type of sort to be done (by line, by paragraph, or by merging the information with other documents).

Note that WordPerfect suggests default (initial) values for the first key:

Typ (key type) is set to **a** for alphanumeric characters.

Field is set to **1**.

Word is set to **1**.

For this example, the default values would sort the lines by last name in ascending order.

P (or **1**) Selects **1 Perform Action**, sorts the highlighted lines, and returns control to the editing screen.

```
We have purchased enough wonderful IBM microcomputers so that
each employee can have one on his/her desk.

Please pick up your machine at the loading dock as soon as
possible.

Also, please see the receptionist to sign up for a training
session on how to use your new machine.

cc:
Benson,  Geri,      553-3224
Daniels, Matt,      555-6672
Perez,   Juan,      545-8912
Smith,   Jim,       555-2132
Wheeler, Vanessa,   505-6540

A:\MEMO3                              Doc 2 Pg 1 Ln 3.33" Pos 1"
```

These lines were sorted by last name in ascending order

[F10] Saves the document. Use the name **A:MEMO4**.

Just for practice, sort the list of names by first name in descending order by doing the following:

Keystroke	Action Resulting from Keystroke
[arrow]	If it is not already there, use the [arrow] keys or mouse to move the cursor to the first letter in Benson (location `Ln 3.33" Pos 1"`).
	REMEMBER . . . you can use your mouse to select the block and then skip the next two steps.
[Alt-F4]	Begins the definition of the block to be sorted.
[arrow]	Use the [arrow] keys or mouse to move the cursor to the end of the last line (location `Ln 4" Pos 3.7"`). All the names and phone numbers should be highlighted.
[Ctrl-F9]	Begins the sorting process and displays the sort options.
K (or **3**)	Selects **3 Keys** from the menu and places the cursor at **Typ** (under the letter **a**).
a	Selects alphanumeric as the key type and moves the cursor to the **Field** key.
1 ↵	Selects the first field (actually, there is only one field because there are no tabs or indents in the lines to be sorted) and moves the cursor to the **Word** key.
2	Selects the second word in each line (i.e., the first name) as the key.
[F7]	Exits the **Key** menu.
O (or **6**)	Selects **6 Order** and asks if you want to sort in ascending or descending order.
D (or **2**)	Selects **2 Descending** order.
P (or **1**)	Selects **1 Perform Action**, sorts the highlighted lines, and returns to the editing screen. Note that the names now are listed by first name in descending order.

```
We have purchased enough wonderful IBM microcomputers so that
each employee can have one on his/her desk.

Please pick up your machine at the loading dock as soon as
possible.

Also, please see the receptionist to sign up for a training
session on how to use your new machine.

cc:
Wheeler, Vanessa,  505-6540
Daniels, Matt,     555-6672
Perez,   Juan,     545-8912
Smith,   Jim,      555-2132
Benson,  Geri,     553-3224
```

Names now are sorted by first name in descending order

Keystroke	Action Resulting from Keystroke
[F7]	Selects exit.
N	Specifies that the document is not to be saved.
N	Specifies that WordPerfect is not to be exited. This leaves you with a blank screen and **Doc 2** displayed on the status line.
[Shift-F3]	Switches to document 1 (also a blank document). This is not necessary but sometimes people think that if **Doc 2** is displayed on the status line, then there must be a **Doc 1** also currently active.

String Search

Strings are collections of characters (e.g., letters, digits, punctuation, blank spaces) that are treated as a group. In large documents, it is often desirable to be able to quickly and accurately locate particular strings so that they can be examined or modified. For example, let's say you have written a ten-page letter of recommendation for one of your employees, Barbara Wagner, and that throughout the letter you have referred to her as Barb. However, after you are finished, you decide that it would sound more professional to refer to her as Ms. Wagner. Using the **Search** feature, you can ask WordPerfect to locate all occurrences of **Barb** and, using the **Replace** feature, you can replace each **Barb** with **Ms. Wagner**.

When the *Search* feature is used, WordPerfect locates the specified string in a case-insensitive manner (i.e., it will treat **Yes**, **YES**, and **yes** as the same word). WordPerfect will also locate strings of characters that are a part of a word as well as strings of characters that are stand alone as words. For example, if you search for the word **for**, WordPerfect will locate **for**, **form**, **format,** etc. The *Search* feature also may be used to search for WordPerfect codes such as **[BOLD]** and **[UND]**.

To practice using the *Search* feature, locate all occurrences of the phrase **conference room** in the document **MRMPREP.V6** by doing the following:

Keystroke	Action Resulting from Keystroke
[Shift-F10]	Retrieves a document.
A:MRMPREP.V6 ↵	Indicates the file specification and loads the file into WordPerfect.
[F2]	Invokes the *Forward Search* feature and displays **-> Srch:** on the status line. WordPerfect is asking for the string of characters you want to locate.
conf	Specifies the string to be searched for. For this example, it makes no difference whether you use the entire string (**conference room**) or just a part of it (e.g., **conf**). This is because the computer does not speak English and so it can only search for the particular characters you specify by trying to match exactly what you have typed. Therefore, if the only occurrence of **conf** is in the string **conference room**, the computer will correctly locate the words. However, if there are words such as **confine**, **confound**, or **confuse**, they will also be found.
[F2]	Begins the forward search. WordPerfect will find the first occurrence of **conf** at **Conference** and place the cursor to the right of the string (i.e., at location **Ln 2.33" Pos 3.9"**). Pressing **[F2]** again will bring up the **-> Srch:** display again but, this time, it will already have the word **conf** entered. Each time **[F2]** is pressed twice, WordPerfect will locate subsequent occurrences of **conf** until it reaches the end of the document. When that happens, *** Not found *** will be displayed in the status line (you may have to look carefully; it flashes by quickly).
[F2] [F2]	Tries to find the next occurrence of **conf**. This is in the word **conference** at location **Ln 2.67" Pos 5.2"**.
[F2] [F2]	Tries to find the next occurrence of **conf**. No more are found and so the message *** Not found *** flashes on the status line and the cursor remains at location **Ln 2.67" Pos 5.2"**.

You may find the following tricks helpful when using the *Search* feature:

- To locate a complete word (e.g., **the**) rather than a part of a word (e.g., **the**se) you should insert blank spaces before and after the word you are looking for. This works because WordPerfect considers blank spaces to be characters just like letters and digits.

- Lowercase letters will match both uppercase and lowercase characters (i.e., the search is case insensitive when you use lowercase letters in the search string). Thus, searching for **yes** will locate **yes**, **YES**, and **Yes**. However, uppercase characters will match only uppercase characters. Thus, searching for **Yes** will locate **Yes** and **YES** but not **yes**.
- Use **[Shift-F2]** instead of **[F2]** to do a *backward* search. This searches the document from the cursor to the beginning of the document. In this case the message **<- Srch:** appears on the status line. The **<-** indicates that the search will be performed to the left (i.e., toward the beginning of the document).
- Use **[up arrow]** or **[down arrow]** after the **Srch** message has been displayed to change the direction of the search. For example, if **-> Srch:** is displayed (indicating a forward search) and you press the **[up arrow]** key, the search direction will change to **<- Srch:** (indicating a backward search).
- Unless you tell it differently, WordPerfect will only search the displayed text of a document. To do an *extended* search that includes headers, footers, footnotes, endnotes, graphics box captions, and text boxes you must press **[Home]** just before pressing **[F2]**.
- As is true with most WordPerfect operations, **[F1]** serves as a cancel key. Thus, pressing **[F1]** during a search will cancel it.

As a further illustration, search for a **[Tab]** code by doing the following:

Keystroke	*Action Resulting from Keystroke*
[arrow]	If it is not already there, use the **[arrow]** keys or mouse to move the cursor to the word **conference** (location **Ln 2.67" Pos 5.2"**).
[Shift-F2]	Begins a backwards search and displays **<- Srch:** on the status line. WordPerfect will institute the search from the current cursor position (it should be at location **Ln 2.67" Pos 5.2"**) toward the top of the document.
[Tab]	Pressing this key will display the WordPerfect code for tab. The status line will look as follows:
	`<- Srch: [Tab]_`
[F2]	Locates the first occurrence of the code **[Tab]** toward the beginning of the document. This should be at the first word of the paragraph, **We**, at location **Ln 2.67" Pos 2.5"**.

Continued . . .

Keystroke	Action Resulting from Keystroke
[Alt-F3]	Selects the *Reveal Codes* feature and displays the following:

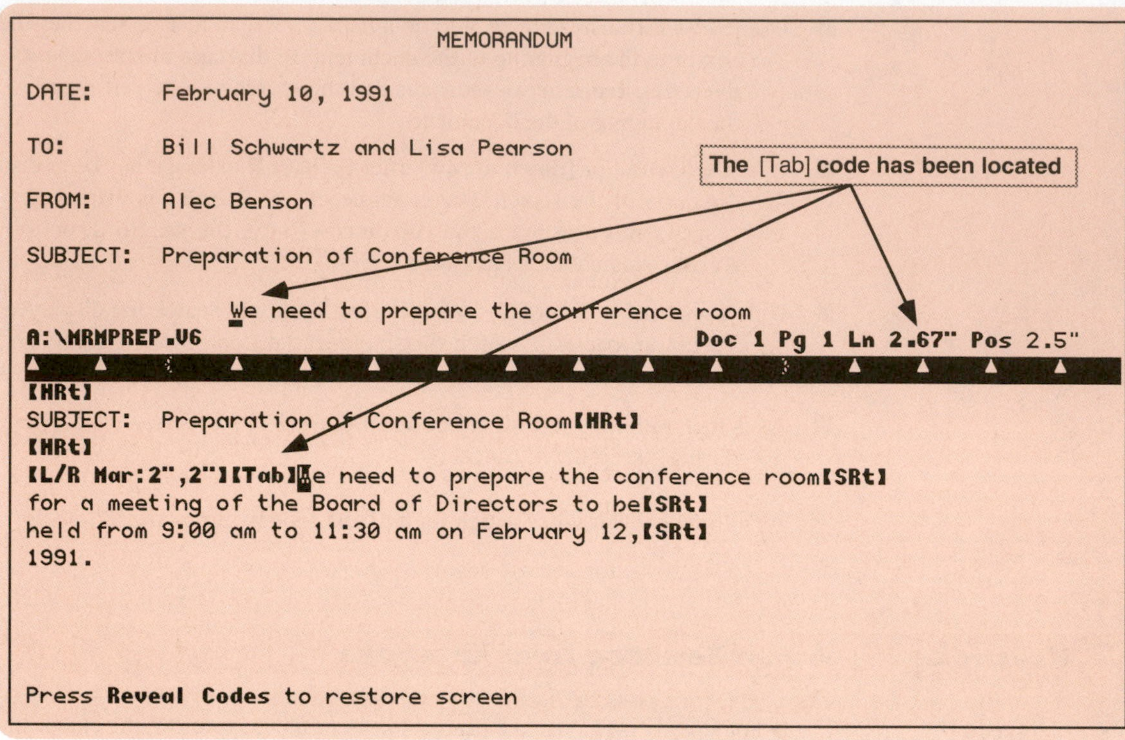

[Alt-F3]	Cancels *Reveal Codes* and returns to the normal display.

Global Search and Replacement

In addition to searching for strings and codes, WordPerfect can replace all or selected occurrences of those strings and codes. This process is sometimes called a *global search and replace*. For example, in the memo **MRMPREP.V6**, replace the word **conference** with **executive conference** by doing the following:

Keystroke	Action Resulting from Keystroke
[Home] [Home] ↑	Moves the cursor to the top of the document. This is important because *Replace* only works forward through a document.
[Alt-F2]	Invokes the *Replace* feature and displays **w/Confirm? No (Yes)** on the status line. WordPerfect is asking if you want to confirm each replacement before it is done. If you say **Yes**, each time a string is located you will be asked if it should be replaced or not. If you say **No**, then all occurrences of the string will be replaced in one sweep of the document.
Y	Specifies that **Y**es, each replacement is to be confirmed. This takes more time but it may prevent you from making a serious mistake. After pressing **Y**, WordPerfect will display the search definition as before: **-> Srch:**. In fact, if you have not exited the document since searching for **[Tab]** in the last section, it also will be displayed.

Continued . . .

Keystroke	Action Resulting from Keystroke
conference	Specifies the string to be searched for. Be careful when using *Replace*. If you are lazy and only enter a part of a string, WordPerfect will replace only that part (e.g., if you specify that you want to replace **conf** with **executive conf**, then WordPerfect will replace not only **conference** with **executive conference**, but also **confirm** with **executive confirm** and **confuse** with **executive confuse** and so on).
[F2]	Displays **Replace with:** on the status line. Whatever you type next will act as the replacement text.
executive conference	Specifies the replacement text.
[F2]	Begins the search process. When the word **conference** is found, WordPerfect will display **Confirm? No (Yes)**. Typing **Y** will replace the text, typing **N** will skip the text.
Y	Performs the replacement. Note that because **Conference** was capitalized in the document its replacement, **Executive conference**, is capitalized. However, the second word, **conference**, is not capitalized. You will have to do that later. WordPerfect then automatically searches for the next occurrence of **conference**. The next occurrence is found in the first line of the first paragraph.
Y	Confirms that the replacement should take place, replaces **conference** with **executive conference**, and searches for the next occurrence of **conference**. If you want to stop the process at any time, press **[F1]**.

When all occurrences of **conference** have been found, WordPerfect will return to the editing screen. At this point, the memo should appear as follows:

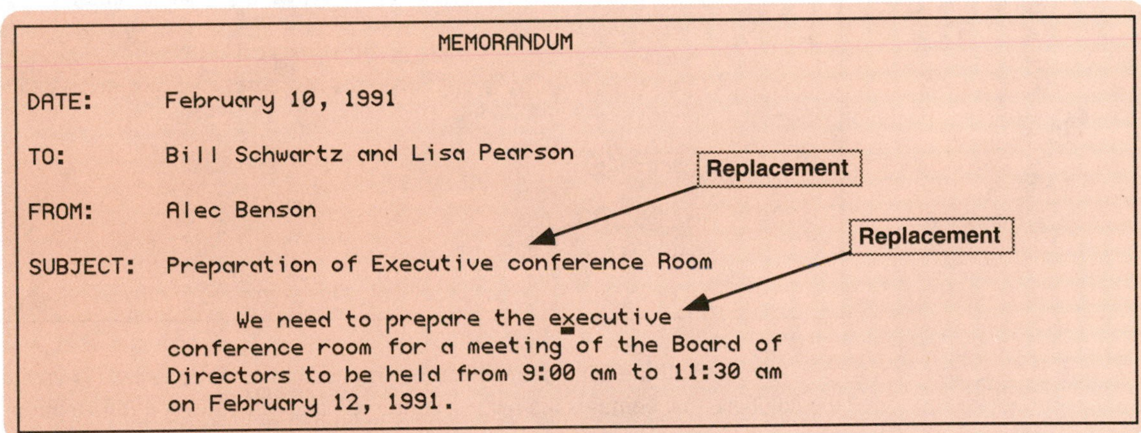

[F10]	Saves the document. Use **A:MRMPREP.V9** ↵ for the file specification.
[F7]	Exits the current document.
N	Specifies that you do not want to save the document.
N	Specifies that you do not want to exit WordPerfect and displays a blank WordPerfect screen.

Search and *Replace* can also be used to save time when creating a new document. For example, suppose you want to write a term paper about the effects of microcomputers on privacy in our modern society. The word *microcomputers* would have to be typed many times throughout that paper. However, instead of typing the 14 letters of *microcomputers* each time you want to use the word, you could use a code word such as *m1* at each location where *microcomputers* is to appear. Then, after the paper has been typed, you could use global *Search* and *Replace* to replace each occurrence of **m1** with **microcomputers**. In a long paper, that could save you a considerable amount of typing.

TO TAKE A BREAK Press **[F7]**, type **N**, type **Y**, remove diskette(s). To resume (hard disk): Insert *Data* diskette, type **A:** ↵, type **C:\WP51\WP A:MRMPREP.V9** ↵. To resume (two drive): Insert diskettes, type **A:** ↵, type **B:WP A:MRMPREP.V9** ↵.

Merging Data into Documents

The **Merge** feature allows users to merge data from one document (e.g., a name and address database) into another document (e.g., a form letter). The result is a series of documents (e.g., personalized letters) that contain much of the same information but are individualized in some way. This process is usually called mail merge because it can be used to create many individualized letters.

For example, let's say that the chairperson of a charity wants to send out thank you letters to people who have sent in contributions to the organization. Each letter should have the same message but a different name, address, title, and amount contributed. A typical letter would look like the following:

```
Save the Children Fund
1344 South Fourth Street
Minneapolis, MN  55455
February 15, 1991

Colette Brietkritez
1401 NE Elm Street
Boston, MA 09801

Dear Ms. Brietkritez:

Thank  you for your generous contribution of $100 to our fund.
Your gift will bring much happiness to many needy children and
their families.

If you have any questions concerning our organization,  please
call me at 624-1102.

Sincerely,

Terry Lamb, DDS
Honorary Chairperson
```

To create all the personalized letters, you need to do three tasks: (1) create a secondary file (this is the database that contains the names, addresses, and other needed information of selected contributors); (2) create a primary file (this is a standard form letter that contains the basic information each person should receive and special codes to indicate where personalized data are to be inserted); (3) use the *Merge* feature to insert the information from the database into the form letter. We will do each of these in turn.

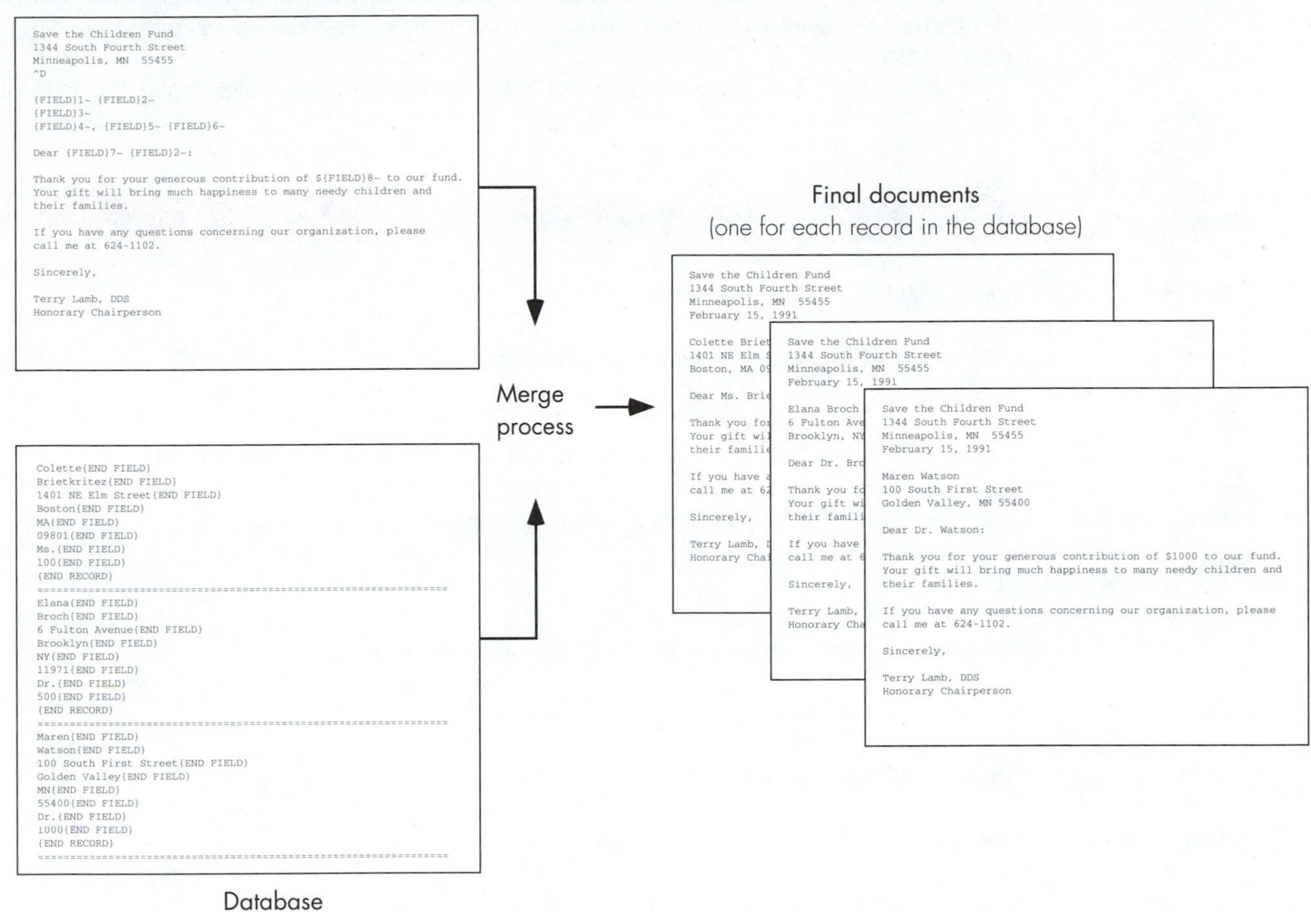

Form letter
(contains fixed text and merge codes)
Save the Children Fund
1344 South Fourth Street
Minneapolis, MN 55455
^D
{FIELD}1~ {FIELD}2~
{FIELD}3~
{FIELD}4~, {FIELD}5~ {FIELD}6~
Dear {FIELD}7~ {FIELD}2~:
Thank you for your generous contribution of ${FIELD}8~ to our fund. Your gift will bring much happiness to many needy children and their families.
If you have any questions concerning our organization, please call me at 624-1102.
Sincerely,
Terry Lamb, DDS
Honorary Chairperson
Merge process
Final documents
(one for each record in the database)
Save the Children Fund
1344 South Fourth Street
Minneapolis, MN 55455
February 15, 1991
Maren Watson
100 South First Street
Golden Valley, MN 55400
Dear Dr. Watson:
Thank you for your generous contribution of $1000 to our fund. Your gift will bring much happiness to many needy children and their families.
If you have any questions concerning our organization, please call me at 624-1102.
Sincerely,
Terry Lamb, DDS
Honorary Chairperson
Colette{END FIELD}
Brietkritez{END FIELD}
1401 NE Elm Street{END FIELD}
Boston{END FIELD}
MA{END FIELD}
09801{END FIELD}
Ms.{END FIELD}
100{END FIELD}
{END RECORD}
Elana{END FIELD}
Broch{END FIELD}
6 Fulton Avenue{END FIELD}
Brooklyn{END FIELD}
NY{END FIELD}
11971{END FIELD}
Dr.{END FIELD}
500{END FIELD}
{END RECORD}
Maren{END FIELD}
Watson{END FIELD}
100 South First Street{END FIELD}
Golden Valley{END FIELD}
MN{END FIELD}
55400{END FIELD}
Dr.{END FIELD}
1000{END FIELD}
{END RECORD}
Database
(contains data to be placed into form letter)

• *Creating a Secondary File (Database)* •

You have to provide WordPerfect with a secondary file that contains some information about each contributor. This is referred to as a **database** file. Each different type of information (e.g., last name, first name, street address) is called a field (for more information on databases and fields, see Part III, Chapter 1). In this instance, the following information is needed:

Field Number	***Meaning***	***Example***
1	First name	Colette
2	Last name	Brietkritez
3	Street address	1401 NE Elm Street
4	City	Boston
5	State of residence	MA
6	Postal zipcode	08001
7	Title	Ms.
8	Number of dollars contributed	100

To provide this information on each contributor, enter the data listed on the next two pages into a WordPerfect document and save it under the name **CONTRIB**. Each field (piece of data) must be entered on its own line. When the cursor gets to the end of a line, do not press **[Enter]**. Instead, press **[F9]**, thereby inserting a special code (called an *end-of-field marker*). This code is needed by WordPerfect to complete the merge process. End-of-field markers are indicated by the code **{END FIELD}**.

The information for the first person would be entered as follows (begin from a blank WordPerfect screen):

Keystroke	*Action Resulting from Keystroke*
Colette	Specifies the first name of the first contributor.
[F9]	Displays **{END FIELD}** (an *end-of-field* marker) and automatically wraps the cursor around to the next line.
	USERS OF VERSION 5.0 The code **^R** is displayed instead of **{END FIELD}**.
Brietkritez [F9]	Specifies the last name and inserts an end-of-field marker.
1401 NE Elm Street [F9]	Specifies the street address and inserts an end-of-field marker.
Boston [F9]	Specifies the city and inserts an end-of-field marker.
MA [F9]	Specifies the state and inserts an end-of-field marker.
09801 [F9]	Specifies the zipcode and inserts an end-of-field marker.
Ms. [F9]	Specifies the title and inserts an end-of-field marker.
100 [F9]	Specifies the amount contributed and inserts an end-of-field marker.
	Now you must tell WordPerfect that this is the end of the data for this person by inserting an *end-of-record* marker (this appears as **{END RECORD}** on the screen).
[Shift-F9]	Displays the following menu on the status line:
	`1 Field; 2 End Record; 3 Input; 4 Page Off; 5 Next Record; 6 More: 0`
	USERS OF VERSION 5.0 Version 5.0 displays a list of merge codes rather than the above menu.
E	Selects **2 End Record** (or **^E** if you are using version 5.0). This inserts an end-of-record code **{END RECORD}** (or **^E** if you are using version 5.0) and a hard page break (indicated by a line of equal signs) into the file. This completes the record for **Colette**. The screen should look like the following:

Continued . . .

Keystroke	Action Resulting from Keystroke

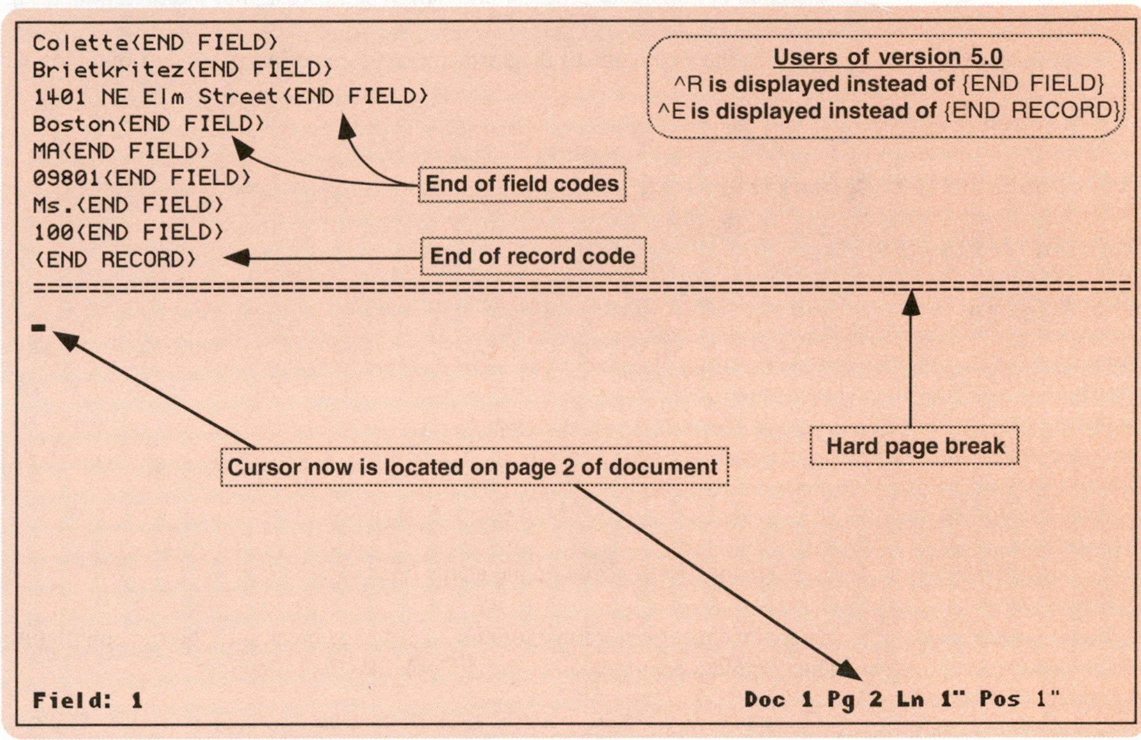

Follow the same procedure for the next two people:

Keystroke	Action Resulting from Keystroke
Elana [F9]	Specifies the first name of the second contributor and inserts an end-of-field marker.
Broch [F9]	
6 Fulton Avenue [F9]	
Brooklyn [F9]	
NY [F9]	
11971 [F9]	
Dr. [F9]	
500 [F9]	Enters the last piece of information for this person.
[Shift-F9]	Displays the *Merge* menu on the status line.

Continued . . .

Keystroke	Action Resulting from Keystroke
E	Inserts an end-of-record marker and a hard page break into the file completing the record for **Elana**.
Maren [F9]	Specifies the first name of the third contributor and inserts an end-of-field marker.
Watson [F9]	
100 South First Street [F9]	
Golden Valley [F9]	
MN [F9]	
55400 [F9]	
Dr. [F9]	
1000 [F9]	
[Shift-F9]	Displays the *Merge* menu on the status line.
E	Inserts an end-of-record marker and a hard page break into the file completing the record for **Maren**. The complete document now should look like the following:

```
Colette<END FIELD>
Brietkritez<END FIELD>
1401 NE Elm Street<END FIELD>
Boston<END FIELD>
MA<END FIELD>
09801<END FIELD>
Ms.<END FIELD>
100<END FIELD>
<END RECORD>
================================================================================
Elana<END FIELD>
Broch<END FIELD>
6 Fulton Avenue<END FIELD>
Brooklyn<END FIELD>
NY<END FIELD>
11971<END FIELD>
Dr.<END FIELD>
500<END FIELD>
<END RECORD>
================================================================================
Maren<END FIELD>
Watson<END FIELD>
100 South First Street<END FIELD>
Golden Valley<END FIELD>
MN<END FIELD>
55400<END FIELD>
Dr.<END FIELD>
1000<END FIELD>
<END RECORD>
================================================================================
```

Keystroke	Action Resulting from Keystroke
	If you see any errors, go back and correct them using the standard editing techniques.
[F10]	Saves the document. Use the name **A:CONTRIB**.

Continued . . .

Keystroke	Action Resulting from Keystroke
[F7]	Exits this document.
N	Specifies that the file is not to be saved.
N	Specifies that you do not want to exit WordPerfect.

• *Creating a Form Letter* •

Now type the form letter to be used with the data. The letter should be typed as usual except that, at every location where you want a particular piece of information to be inserted from the **CONTRIB** data file, you must insert a special WordPerfect code indicating a field number by pressing **[Shift-F9]**, typing the letter **F**, and then typing the number of the field to be used.

Begin with a blank WordPerfect screen and type the top three lines of the letter:

```
Save the Children Fund
1344 South Fourth Street
Minneapolis, MN  55415
▬
```

The fourth line of the letter is to contain the current date. You can have WordPerfect enter this for you by using the special date code:

Keystroke	Action Resulting from Keystroke
[Ctrl-D]	Inserts the date code, **^D**.
	USERS OF VERSION 5.0 You may insert the date code by pressing **[Shift-F9]** (to display the codes menu) and then pressing **D**. The date code **^D** will be displayed at the cursor.
↵ ↵	Pressing **[Enter]** twice inserts a blank line.

The sixth line is to contain the first and last names of the contributor. Those values will be merged from the data file **CONTRIB**. To indicate this, type in the following, beginning at location **Ln 1.83" Pos 1"**:

Keystroke	Action Resulting from Keystroke
[Shift-F9]	Specifies that a piece of data is to be merged at this location and displays the *Merge* menu on the status line.
	USERS OF VERSION 5.0 The *Merge* menu will be different but you can still use the following keystrokes.
F	Specifies that text is to be merged from a given **F**ield into the current document. WordPerfect then displays the following on the status line:

```
Enter Field: ▬
```

Continued . . .

Keystroke	Action Resulting from Keystroke
	This is asking for a field identification name or number. We will use identification numbers. WordPerfect keeps track of the fields by numbering them sequentially from the first field to the last. Thus, field 1 is the person's first name, field 2 is the person's last name, and so on. Field 8 is the amount of the contribution.
1 ↵	Specifies that data from field **1** (the contributor's first name) is to be used. WordPerfect will insert the characters **{FIELD}1~** at the cursor.
	USERS OF VERSION 5.0 The code **^F1^** will be displayed instead of **{FIELD}1~**.
[Spacebar]	Inserts a blank space.
[Shift-F9]	Indicates the next location for a merge.
F	Specifies that a piece of data is to be inserted here.
2 ↵	Specifies that a piece of data from field **2** is to be used here. WordPerfect will insert the characters **{FIELD}2~** at the cursor.
	Continue typing the letter in the same manner. Whenever you are to insert data from the data file **CONTRIB**, press **[Shift-F9]**, type **F**, type the number of the field to be inserted, and finally press **[Enter]**. The final document should look like the following:

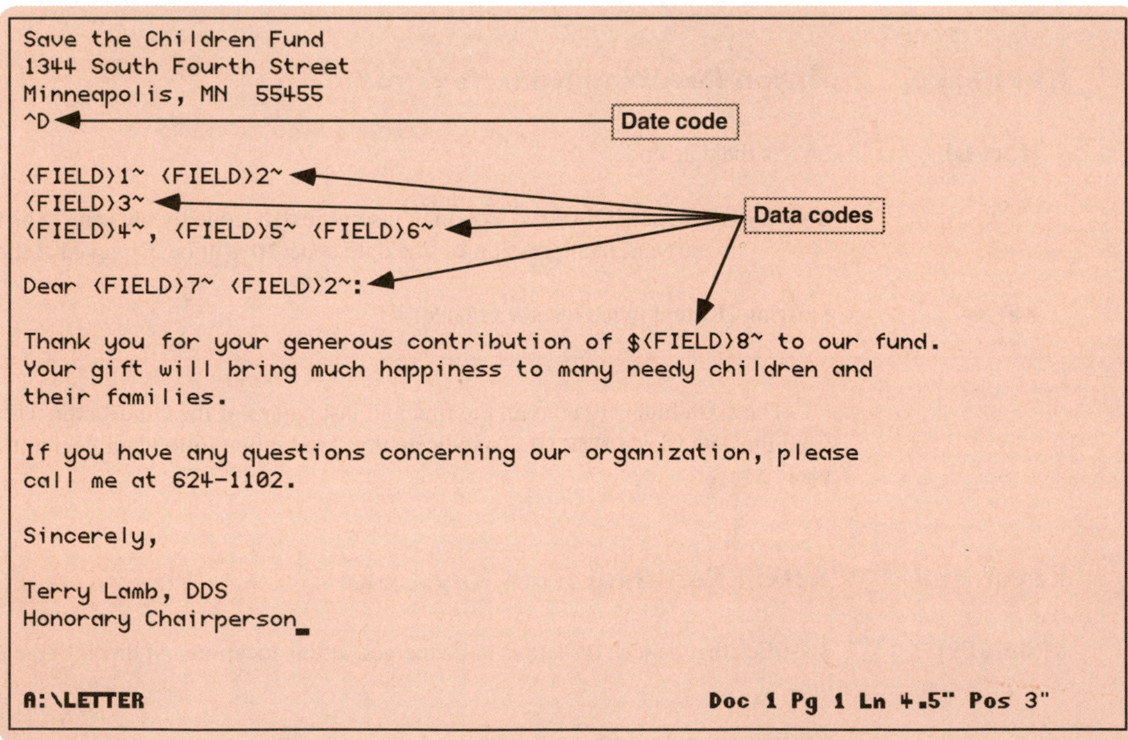

```
Save the Children Fund
1344 South Fourth Street
Minneapolis, MN  55455
^D

<FIELD>1~ <FIELD>2~
<FIELD>3~
<FIELD>4~, <FIELD>5~ <FIELD>6~

Dear <FIELD>7~ <FIELD>2~:

Thank you for your generous contribution of $<FIELD>8~ to our fund.
Your gift will bring much happiness to many needy children and
their families.

If you have any questions concerning our organization, please
call me at 624-1102.

Sincerely,

Terry Lamb, DDS
Honorary Chairperson

A:\LETTER                                  Doc 1 Pg 1 Ln 4.5" Pos 3"
```


Keystroke	Action Resulting from Keystroke
[F10]	Saves the document. Use the name **A:LETTER**.
[Shift-F3]	Switches to a new (blank) document. Running mail merge while a document is displayed may cause the personalized letters created in the process to be inserted into the displayed document (that is not what you want).

• *Merging Data into a Form Letter* •

The personalized letters now can be created on the screen by doing the following:

Keystroke	Action Resulting from Keystroke
[Ctrl-F9]	Selects the *Merge* feature and displays the following on the status line:

```
1 Merge; 2 Sort; 3 Convert Old Merge Codes: 0
```

1 **Merge** allows you to merge data from the secondary file (the file containing the data) into the primary file (the file that has the form letter).

2 **Sort** allows you to sort the contents of a specified file using techniques similar to those discussed on page W120 for sorting lines of data. The type of sort would be **Merge sort** because you are sorting a file that contains merge commands.

3 **Convert Old Merge Codes** allows you to convert merge codes created in version 5.0 of WordPerfect into version 5.1 codes.

USERS OF VERSION 5.0 In place of the third option is **Sort Order**. This allows you to change the order in which the sort is carried out.

Keystroke	Action Resulting from Keystroke
M (or **1**)	Selects **1 Merge** and requests the **Primary file**. This is the form letter called **LETTER**.
A:LETTER ↵	Provides the primary file specification and requests the **Secondary file**. The secondary file is the data file, **CONTRIB**.
A:CONTRIB ↵	Provides the secondary file specification and begins the merging process. The word *** Merging *** appears briefly on the status line. Finally, a document that contains the letters is displayed on the screen.

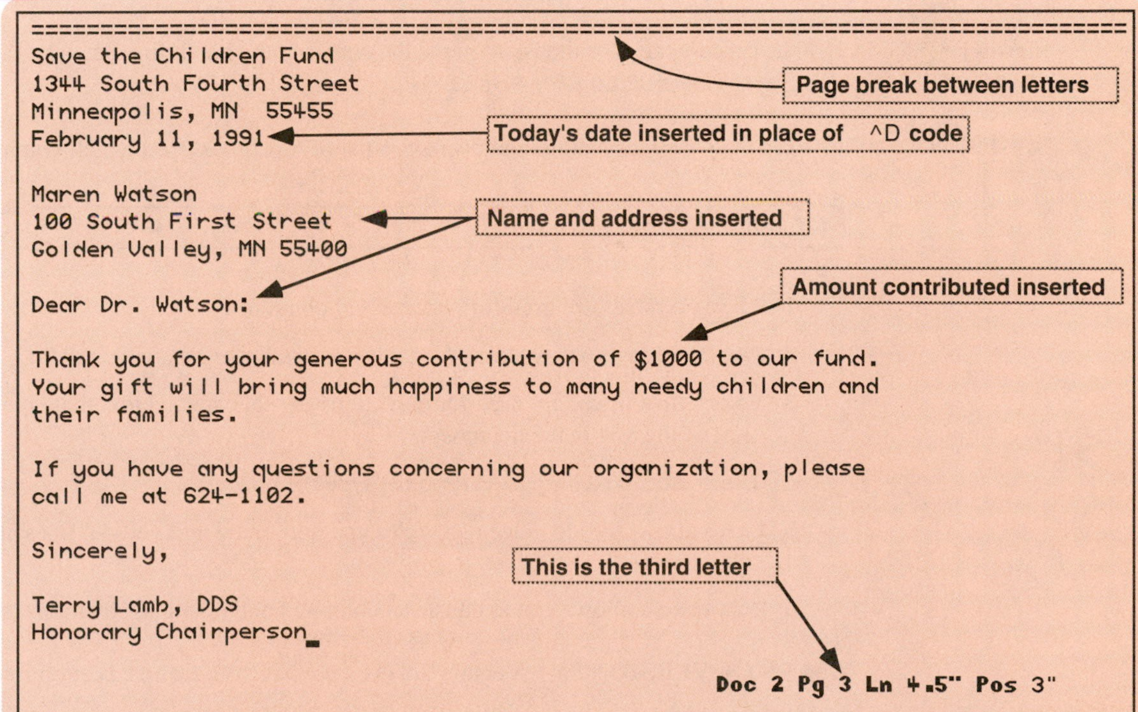

Save the Children Fund
1344 South Fourth Street
Minneapolis, MN 55455
February 11, 1991
Maren Watson
100 South First Street
Golden Valley, MN 55400
Dear Dr. Watson:
Thank you for your generous contribution of $1000 to our fund. Your gift will bring much happiness to many needy children and their families.
If you have any questions concerning our organization, please call me at 624-1102.
Sincerely,
Terry Lamb, DDS
Honorary Chairperson
Doc 2 Pg 3 Ln 4.5" Pos 3"
Page break between letters
Today's date inserted in place of ^D code
Name and address inserted
Amount contributed inserted
This is the third letter

Continued . . .

Keystroke	Action Resulting from Keystroke
	You can scroll through, edit, and print the document in the usual ways. Recall that the line of equal signs represents a hard page break (see pp. W91–92), which causes the letters to be printed on separate sheets of paper.
[F7]	Exits this document (the mail merged letters).
`N`	Specifies that this document is not to be saved.
`Y`	Specifies that document 2 is to be exited.
[F7]	Exits this document (the form letter).
`N`	Specifies that this document is not to be saved.
`N`	Specifies that you do not want to exit WordPerfect and presents you with a blank WordPerfect screen.

Graphics

The WordPerfect **Graphics** feature allows you to insert pictures, charts, and tables into your documents. The graphics can be created from scratch using so-called painting programs or they can be created by optically scanning actual drawings or photographs (this takes special equipment). You can also buy files that contain pictures (called *clip art*) created by others; in fact, the WordPerfect *Fonts/Graphics* diskette contains 30 such images.

Let's see how to insert a picture into a document by doing the following:

Keystroke	Action Resulting from Keystroke
[Shift-F10]	Retrieves a file.
`A:MEMO3` ↵	Provides the file specification and loads the file into the blank WordPerfect screen.
[arrow]	Use the **[arrow]** keys or mouse to move the cursor to the blank line between the first and second paragraphs (location **`Ln 2" Pos 1"`**).
[Alt-F9]	Invokes the *Graphics* feature and displays a list of box types from which you may choose:

```
1 Figure; 2 Table Box; 3 Text Box; 4 User Box; 5 Line; 6 Equation: 0
```

1 **`Figure`** boxes are used for pictures and diagrams.

2 **`Table Box`** boxes are used for tables of numbers or statistical data.

3 **`Text Box`** boxes are used for quotations or other special text that is to be set off from the rest of the text in the document.

4 **`User Box`** boxes are used for other types of images.

5 **`Line`** allows you to place rectangles and horizontal and vertical lines at different locations on the page.

6 **`Equation`** allows you to construct complex mathematical equations (see pp. W139–48).

USERS OF VERSION 5.0 Version 5.0 does not have the **`Equation`** option.

Continued . . .

Keystroke	Action Resulting from Keystroke

F (or **1**) Selects **1 Figure** and displays the following menu:

```
Figure: 1 Create; 2 Edit; 3 New Number; 4 Options: 0
```

1 **Create** allows you to create (import) a figure.

2 **Edit** allows you to modify an already existing figure.

3 **New Number** allows you to renumber figures.

4 **Options** allows you to change many parts of a figure including its border style and spacing, the method used for numbering, and shading.

C (or **1**) Selects **1 Create** and displays the following definition menu:

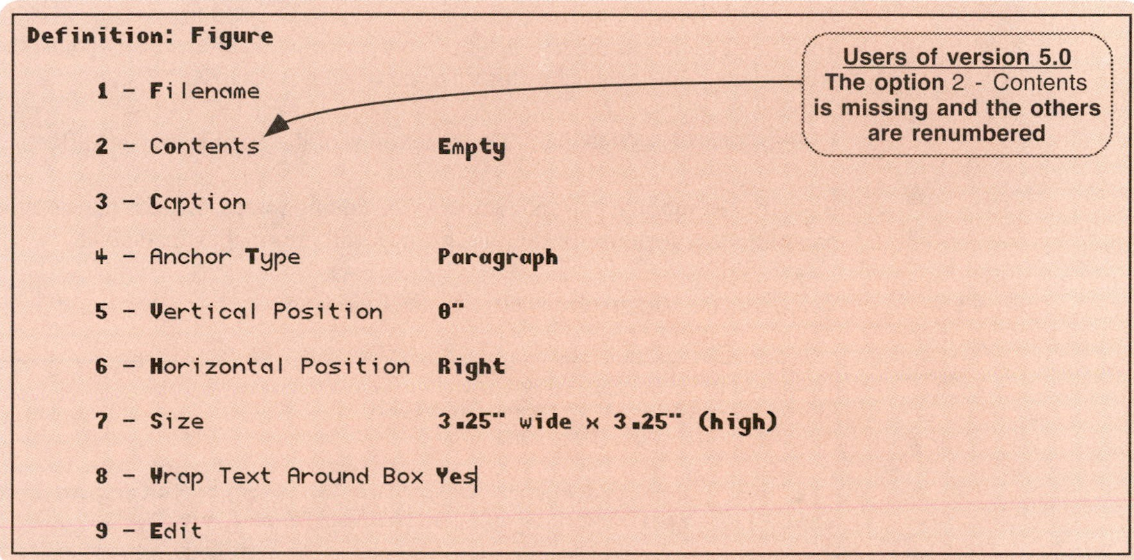

Definition: Figure
1 - Filename
2 - Contents Empty
3 - Caption
4 - Anchor Type Paragraph
5 - Vertical Position 0"
6 - Horizontal Position Right
7 - Size 3.25" wide x 3.25" (high)
8 - Wrap Text Around Box Yes
9 - Edit
Users of version 5.0
The option 2 - Contents is missing and the others are renumbered

F (or **1**) Selects **1 - Filename**. This is the name of the file that contains the picture to be used (be sure to provide the full file specification).

Hard-disk system

IF YOU ARE USING A HARD-DISK SYSTEM: The graphics files probably are already installed in the WordPerfect subdirectory. If they are not, see your instructor for help.

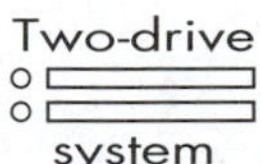

IF YOU ARE USING A TWO-DRIVE SYSTEM: Replace the *WordPerfect Data* diskette in drive A: with the *Fonts/Graphics* diskette.

The file you want contains a picture of an IBM PC and is called **PC-1.WPG** (the extension **WPG** stands for WordPerfect Graphic).

USERS OF VERSION 5.0 The name of the file that contains the picture is **PC.WPG**.

Hard-disk system

IF YOU ARE USING A HARD-DISK SYSTEM: Type **C:\WP51\ PC-1.WPG ↵**.

Two-drive system

IF YOU ARE USING A TWO-DRIVE SYSTEM: Type **A:PC.WPG.↵**.

Continued . . .

Notice that the size of the picture is given as **3.25" wide x 2.35" (high)**. The picture is a little too big for the current memo so change the width to 2 inches by doing the following:

USERS OF VERSION 5.0 The size option is number **6** in version 5.0, not number 7.

S (or **7**) — Selects **7 - Size** and displays the following on the status line:

```
1 Set Width/Auto Height; 2 Set Height/Auto Width; 3 Set Both; 4 Auto Both: 0
```

USERS OF VERSION 5.0 The menu labels are slightly different and option **4 Auto Both** is missing.

H (or **2**) — Selects **2 Set Height/Auto Width** and displays the current height of the picture.

2 ↵ — Specifies 2 inches as the new height. WordPerfect will automatically adjust the width to keep the same proportions as the original picture. The new width is set to **2.76"**.

USERS OF VERSION 5.0 The dimensions of the graphic may be different.

[F7] — Exits the definition menu and returns to the editing screen. It looks like nothing has changed, but pressing the **[down arrow]** key a few times will reformat the paragraph.

↓ ↓ — Reformats the paragraph and displays the following:

```
Memo to:  All Employees
Memo from:  Matt Wilson, PRESIDENT
Date:  February 10, 1991

We have purchased enough wonderful IBM microcomputers so that
each employee can have one on his/her desk.
                                   FIG 1
Please pick up your machine at the
loading dock as soon as possible.

Also, please see the receptionist
to sign up for a training session
on how to use your new machine.

cc:
Smith,   Jim,       555-2132
Benson,  Geri,      553-3224
Perez,   Juan,      545-8912
Daniels, Matt,      555-6672
Wheeler, Vanessa,   505-6540



A:\MEMO3                          Doc 1 Pg 1 Ln 2.33" Pos 1"
```

The printed version of the document will appear as follows:

Continued . . .

Keystroke	Action Resulting from Keystroke

```
Memo to:  All Employees
Memo from:  Matt Wilson, PRESIDENT
Date:  February 10, 1991

We have purchased enough wonderful IBM microcomputers so that each
employee can have one on his/her desk.

Please pick up your machine at the loading dock
as soon as possible.

Also, please see the receptionist to sign up for
a training  session  on  how  to  use  your  new
machine.

cc:
Smith,    Jim,       555-2132
Benson,   Geri,      553-3224
Perez,    Juan,      545-8912
Daniels,  Matt,      555-6672
Wheeler,  Vanessa,   505-6540
```

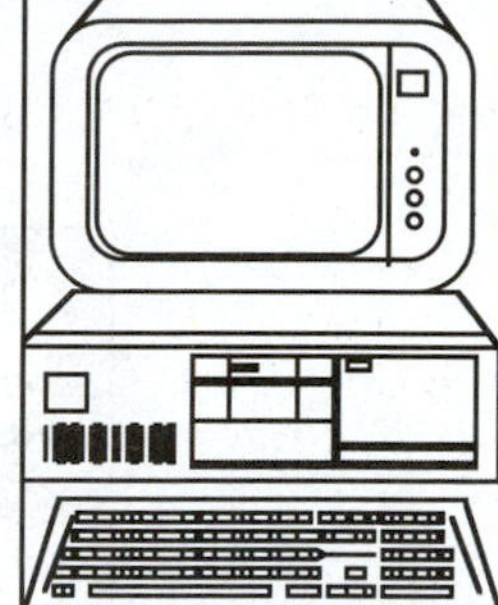

You may either view or print the final document using the *Print* feature (use the **[Shift-F7]** key). Be aware, however, that not all monitors are able to display graphics and not all printers are able to print graphics. If you have difficulty with this, ask your instructor for help.

Two-drive system

IF YOU ARE USING A TWO-DRIVE SYSTEM: Be sure to replace the *Fonts/Graphics* diskette in drive A: with your *WordPerfect Data/Boot* diskette.

[F10] Saves the document. Use the name **A:MEMO3.FIG**.

[F7] Exits this document.

N Specifies that the file is not to be saved.

N Specifies that you do not want to exit WordPerfect and presents you with a blank WordPerfect screen.

TO TAKE A BREAK Press **[F7]**, type **N**, type **Y**, remove diskette(s). To resume (hard disk): Insert *Data* diskette, type **A:** ↵, type **C:\WP51\WP** ↵. To resume (two drive): Insert diskettes, type **A:** ↵, type **B:WP** ↵.

Creating Technical Equations

Using a word processor to write technical memos or papers has always been difficult because of the special symbols needed in scientific and mathematical formulas. To create simple mathematical or scientific expressions with superscripts (e.g., terms with exponents such as X^2) or subscripts (e.g., H_2O), WordPerfect uses the *Font* feature. For more complex expressions, WordPerfect provides an easy-to-use equation editor that treats the expressions as graphics. Using this feature, you can insert complex equations into any WordPerfect document.

To illustrate how subscripts, superscripts, and the equation editor work, let's create a short document that contains two formulas:

1. When natural gas (methane) burns, it produces carbon dioxide (which contributes to global warming), water, and heat according to the following reaction:

$$CH_4 + 2\,O_2 \rightarrow CO_2 + 2\,H_2O$$

2. The solution to a quadratic equation of the form $aX^2 + bX + c = 0$ is given by the following:

$$X_{1,2} = \frac{-b \pm \sqrt{b^2 - 4ac}}{2a}$$

Begin from a blank WordPerfect document and type the following:

```
Creating Equations

When natural gas (CH4) burns, it produces carbon dioxide (CO2),
water (H2O), and heat according to the following reaction:

                                          Leave three blank lines here

The solution to a quadratic equation of the form aX2 + bX + c = 0
can be written as follows:

_
```

Keystroke	Action Resulting from Keystroke
[F10]	Specifies that the document is to be saved.
A:EQ-V1 ↵	Specifies the name for the document and returns to the editing screen.
[arrow]	Use the **[arrow]** keys or mouse to move the cursor to the **4** in the chemical formula for methane (**Ln 1.33" Pos 3"**).
	REMEMBER . . . you can use your mouse to select the block and then skip the next two steps. In this case, using the keyboard is probably easier.
[Alt-F4]	Turns on the *Block* feature.
[right-arrow]	Press the **[right-arrow]** key once to highlight the **4**.
[Ctrl-F8]	Selects the *Font* feature and displays the following menu:

```
Attribute: 1 Size; 2 Appearance: 0
```

Keystroke	Action Resulting from Keystroke
S (or **1**)	Selects **1 Size** and displays its menu.

```
1 Suprscpt; 2 Subscpt; 3 Fine; 4 Small; 5 Large; 6 Vry Large; 7 Ext Large: 0
```

Keystroke	Action Resulting from Keystroke
B (or **2**)	Selects **2 Subscpt** and returns to the editing screen. WordPerfect has inserted a subscript code on either side of the **4**. When printed, the **4** will be a subscript.

Continued . . .

Keystroke	Action Resulting from Keystroke
[Alt-F3]	Reveals the codes.

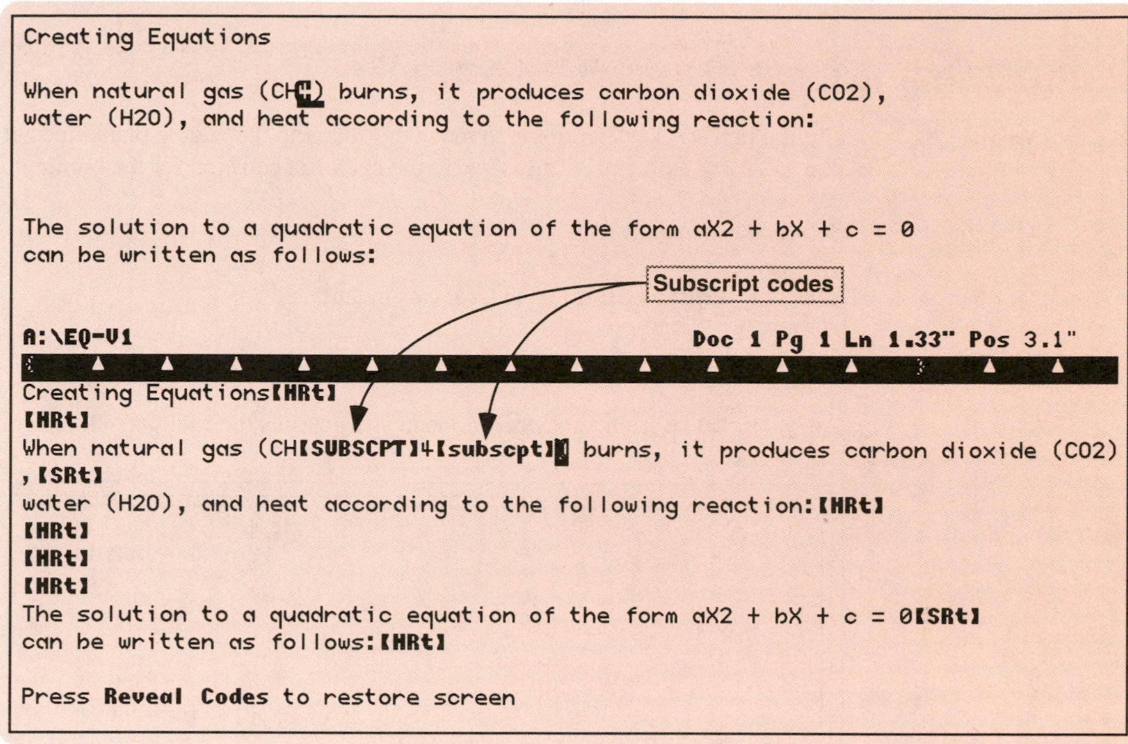
Creating Equations
When natural gas (CH4) burns, it produces carbon dioxide (CO2),
water (H2O), and heat according to the following reaction:
The solution to a quadratic equation of the form aX2 + bX + c = 0
can be written as follows:
Subscript codes
A:\EQ-V1
Doc 1 Pg 1 Ln 1.33" Pos 3.1"
Creating Equations[HRt]
[HRt]
When natural gas (CH[SUBSCPT]4[subscpt]) burns, it produces carbon dioxide (CO2)
,[SRt]
water (H2O), and heat according to the following reaction:[HRt]
[HRt]
[HRt]
[HRt]
The solution to a quadratic equation of the form aX2 + bX + c = 0[SRt]
can be written as follows:[HRt]
Press Reveal Codes to restore screen

Keystroke	Action Resulting from Keystroke
[Alt-F3]	Hides the codes. Repeat the procedure for the **2** in **CO2** and **H2O** so that they are subscripts.

A similar procedure is used to make superscripts. For example, make the **2** in **aX2** a superscript (i.e., an exponent) by doing the following:

Keystroke	Action Resulting from Keystroke
[arrow]	Use the **[arrow]** keys or mouse to move the cursor to the **2** in the quadratic equation (**Ln 2.17" Pos 6.1"**). **REMEMBER . . .** you can use your mouse to select the block and then skip the next two steps. In this case, using the keyboard is probably easier.
[Alt-F4]	Turns on the *Block* feature.
[right-arrow]	Press the **[right-arrow]** key once to highlight the **2**.
[Ctrl-F8]	Selects the *Font* feature and displays its menu.
S (or **1**)	Selects **1 Size** and displays its menu.
P (or **1**)	Selects **1 Suprscpt** and returns to the editing screen. WordPerfect has inserted a superscript code on either side of the **2**. When printed, the **2** will be an exponent.

To construct the actual equations, you must use the equation editor.

USERS OF VERSION 5.0 The equation editor is not available in version 5.0. You will not be able to complete the rest of this section.

Keystroke	Action Resulting from Keystroke
[arrow]	Use the **[arrow]** keys or mouse to move the cursor to the middle blank line between the two paragraphs (**`Ln 1.83" Pos 1"`**). This is where the chemical equation for the burning of methane will be placed.
[Alt-F9]	Selects the *Graphics* feature.
`E` (or **6**)	Selects **6 `Equation`** from the *Graphics* menu.
`C` (or **1**)	Selects **1 `Create`** from the **`Equation`** menu.
`E` (or **9**)	Selects **9 `Edit`** from the **`Create`** menu and presents the equation editor screen:

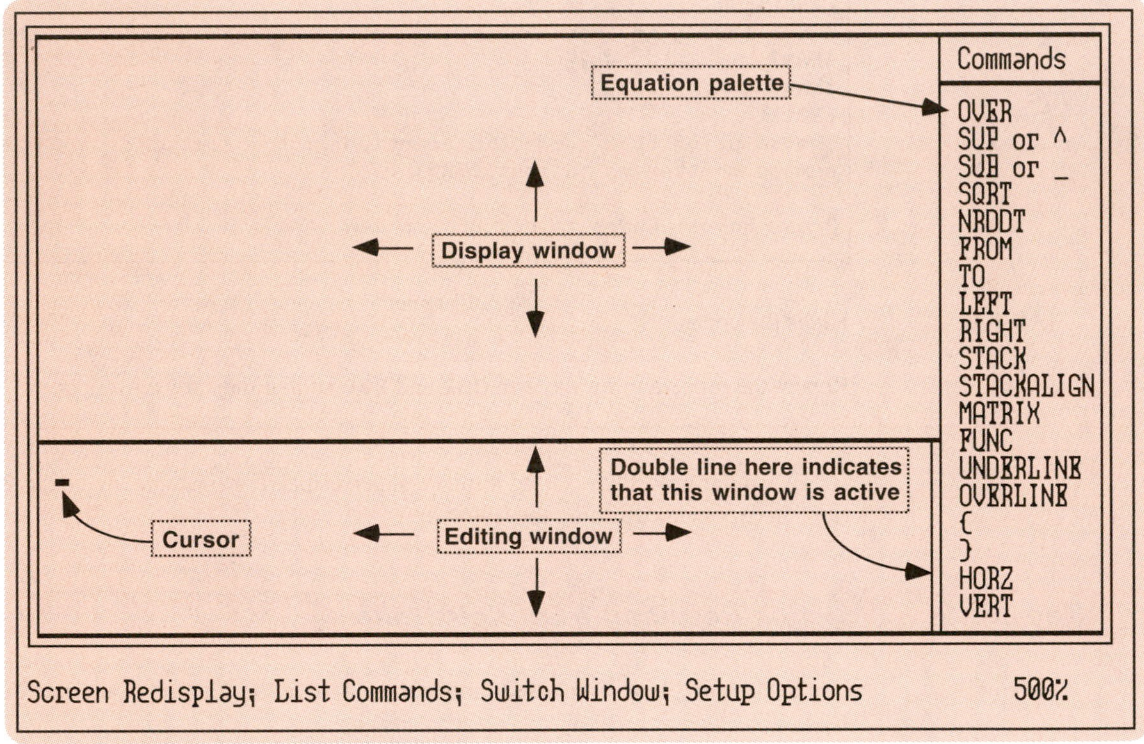

Editing window is where the codes for the equation will be entered and edited.

Display window is used to show the formula as it will appear when the document is viewed or printed. Notice the **`500%`** in the lower right-hand corner of the screen. This indicates that the view in the display window is magnified five times (500%). The printed version, however, will be normal size.

Continued . . .

Keystroke	Action Resulting from Keystroke
	Equation palette provides a list of commands and symbols that can be used in the equation. For example: **OVER** is used for fractions as in **A OVER B**, which would produce $\frac{A}{B}$. **SUP** or ^ is used for superscripts as in **X SUP 2**, which would produce X^2. **SUB** or _ is used for subscripts as in **X SUB 2**, which would produce X_2. **SQRT** is used for square roots as in **SQRT{X}**, which would produce $\sqrt{X}$.

The editing window is currently active (it contains the cursor and shows a double vertical line on its right-hand side). As a quick, first example, code the mixed number one and three-fourths (i.e., $1\frac{3}{4}$) by typing the following:

Keystroke	Action Resulting from Keystroke
1 3 OVER 4	Codes the fraction $1\frac{3}{4}$. The whole-number part of the fraction is simply typed as it normally would be. Then a space is inserted to separate the whole number from the fraction. Notice that the fraction is formed using the keyword **OVER** in the form "numerator over denominator." To see how the fraction will look in the final printed version of the document, use the *Screen* feature to make the display window active.
[Ctrl-F3]	Displays the coded fraction as it will appear in its final form.

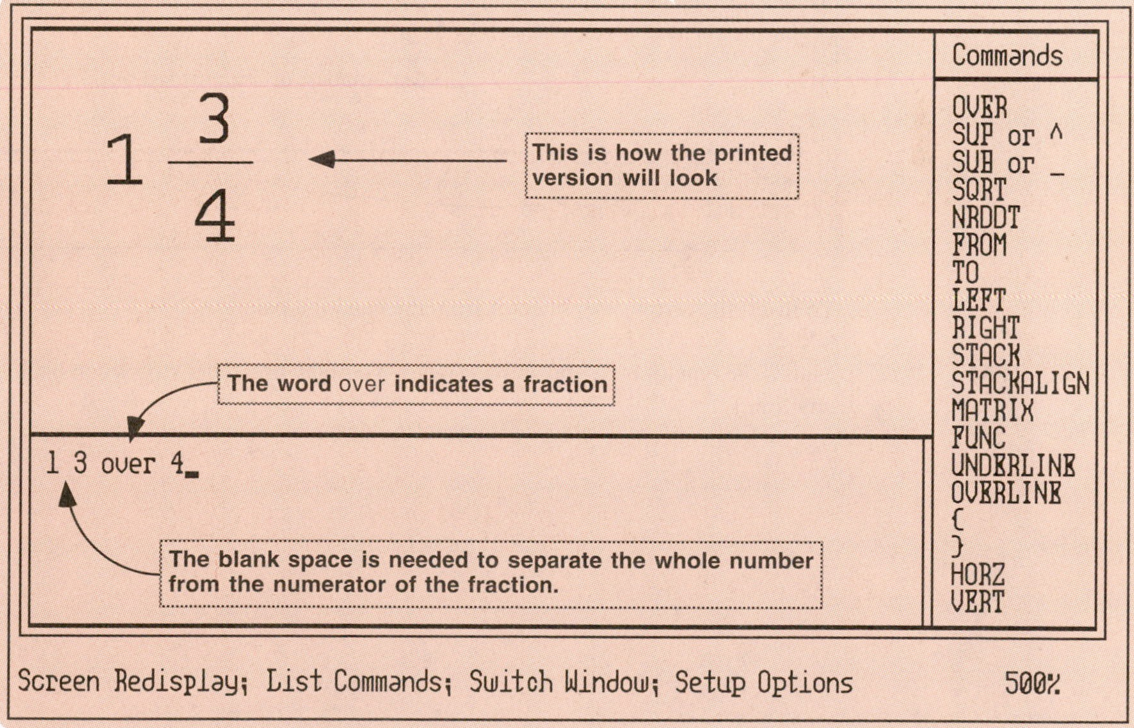

To view the other symbols in the equation palette, use the *List Files* feature to make the equation palette active and then the **[arrow]**, **[PageDown]**, and **[PageUp]** keys to select different palettes. To return to the editing window, use **[F7]**. We will need to do this during the creation of the natural gas equation:

$$CH_4 + 2\ O_2 \rightarrow CO_2 + 2\ H_2O$$

Keystroke	Action Resulting from Keystroke
[Backspace]	Use the **[Backspace]** key to delete the mixed number in the editing window. Then, type the first part of the equation as follows:

`CH SUB 4 + 2 O SUB 2`

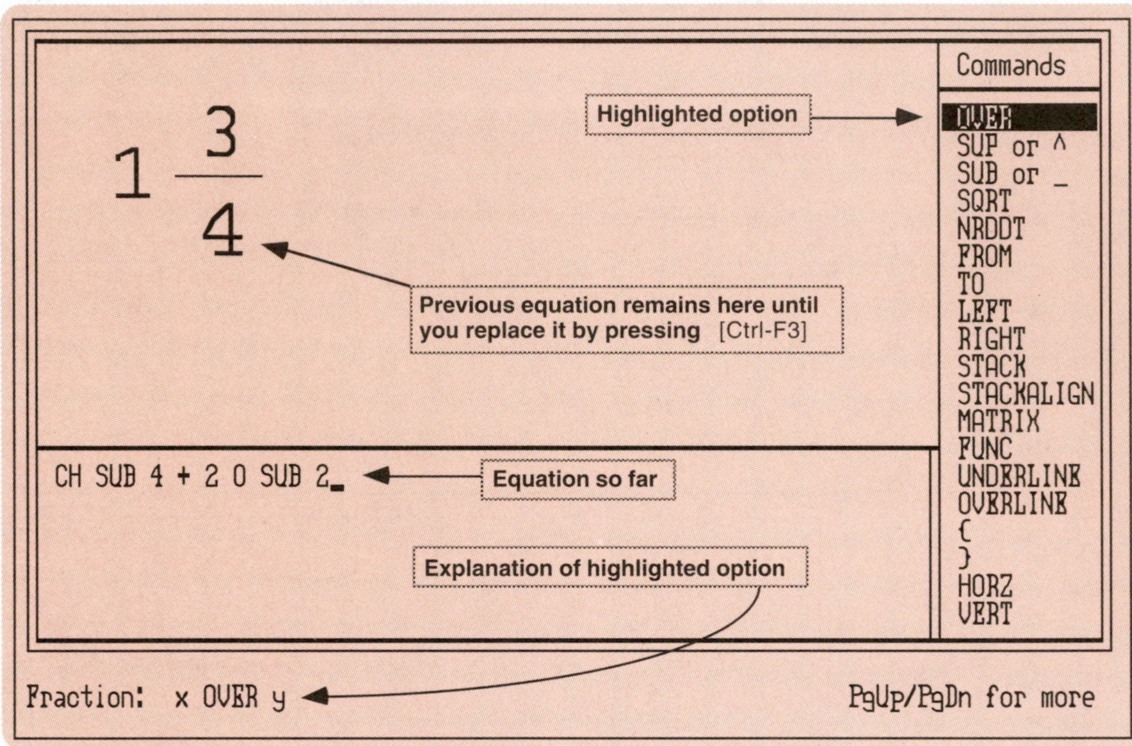

To insert the arrow, →, select it from the equation palette.

Keystroke	Action Resulting from Keystroke
[F5]	Makes the equation palette active. (Note: You may press **[F7]** to switch back to the editing window at any time).

Continued . . .

Keystroke	Action Resulting from Keystroke
[PageDown] [PageDown] [PageDown] [PageDown]	Pressing **[PageDown]** four times scrolls through some of the different symbol palettes until the arrows palette is displayed. 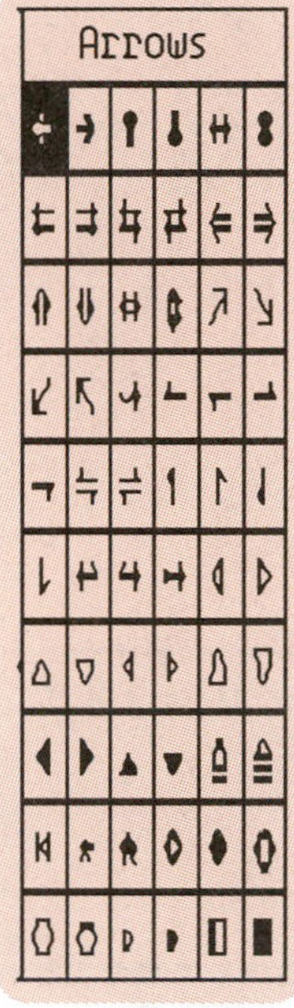 To select a particular symbol from the palette, use the **[arrow]** keys or mouse to highlight it and then press **[Enter]**.
[arrow]	Use the **[arrow]** keys or mouse to highlight the right-pointing arrow from the palette (first row, second column). The word **`Right Arrow`** should appear on the lower left-hand side of the screen.
[Enter]	Inserts the highlighted symbol into the equation at the cursor and makes the editing window active again. CH SUB 4 + 2 O SUB 2 → _ Now, complete the equation so that it looks as follows: **`CH SUB 4 + 2 O SUB 2 → CO SUB 2 + 2 H SUB 2 O`**

Continued . . .

Keystroke	Action Resulting from Keystroke
[Ctrl-F3]	Displays the equation as it will look when printed:

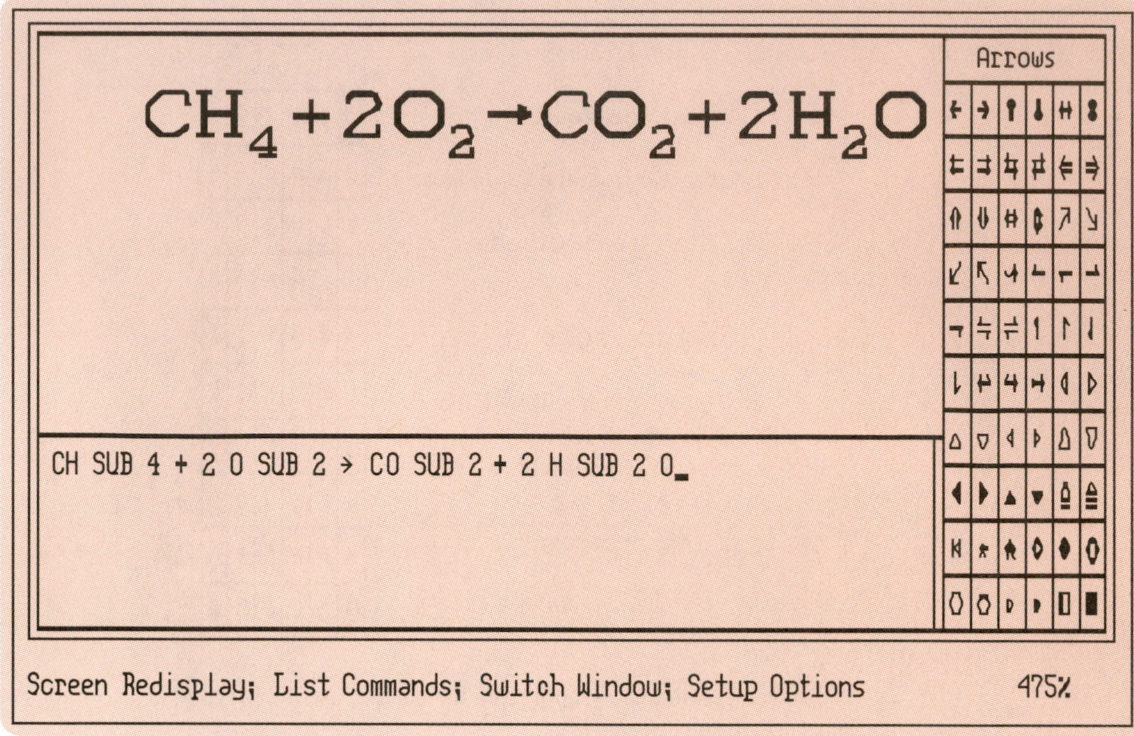

This equation is complete so you now can return to the editing screen by using the *Exit* key.

Keystroke	Action Resulting from Keystroke
[F7] [F7]	Exits the equation editor and returns to the editing screen. Notice that a graphic marker has been inserted into the document showing where the equation will be placed.

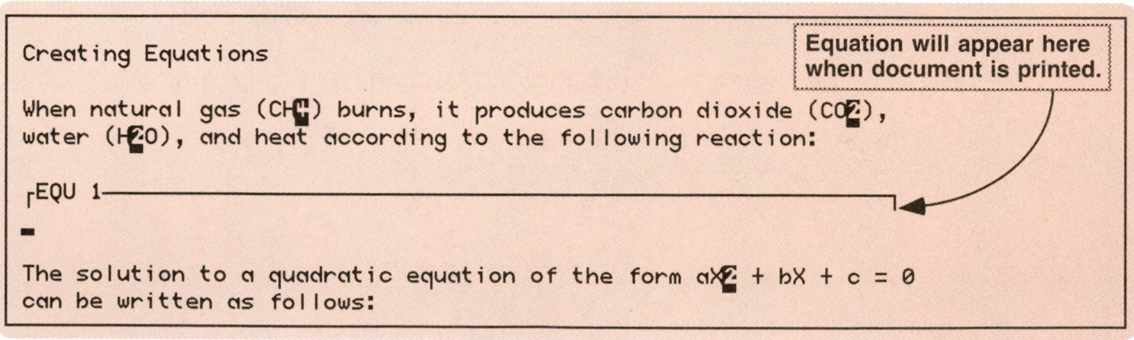

Now, insert the quadratic formula in the space just below the second paragraph.

Keystroke	Action Resulting from Keystroke
[arrow]	Use the [arrow] keys or mouse to move the cursor to the blank line after the last paragraph (**`Ln 3.17" Pos 1"`**).
[Alt-F9]	Selects the *Graphics* feature.
`E` (or **`6`**)	Selects **`6 Equation`** from the *Graphics* menu.
`C` (or **`1`**)	Selects **`1 Create`** from the **`Equation`** menu.
`E` (or **`9`**)	Selects **`9 Edit`** from the **`Create`** menu and presents the equation editor screen. Type the following equation:

```
X SUB 1 , SUB 2 = {-b PLUSMINUS SQRT {b SUP 2 - 4ac}} OVER {2a}
```

To see what the equation will look like, use the *Screen* feature.

[Ctrl-F3]	Displays the equation as it will appear when printed.

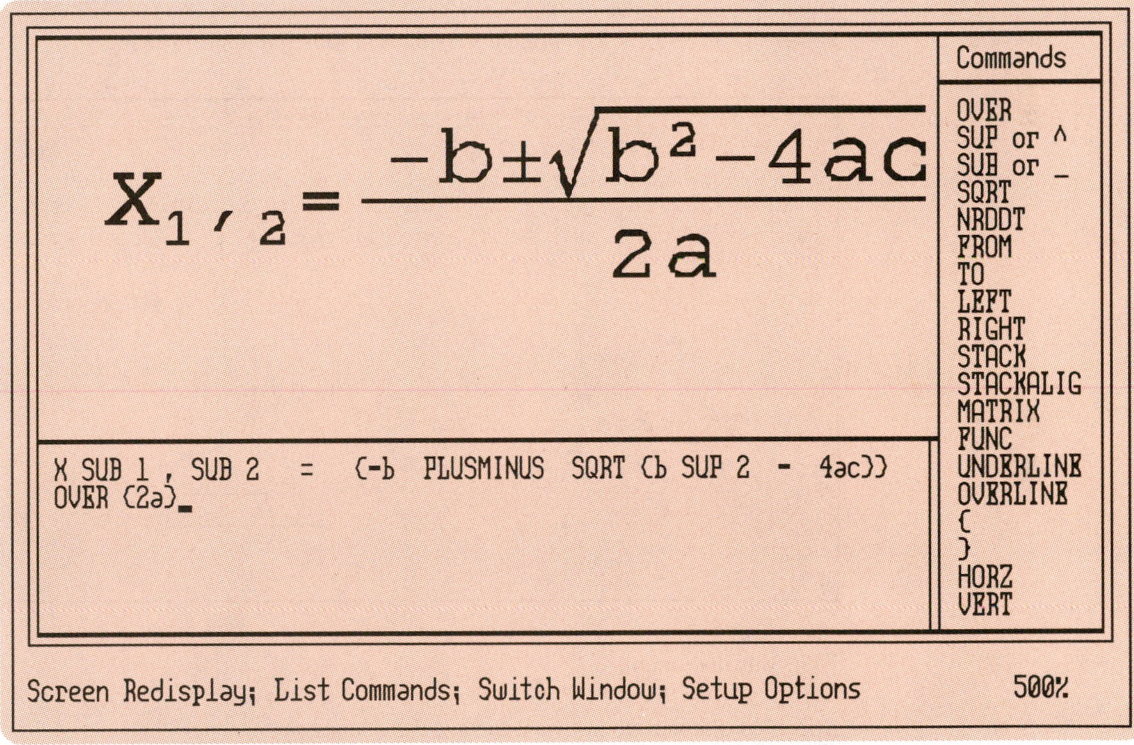

Continued . . .

Keystroke	Action Resulting from Keystroke
[F7] [F7]	Exits the equation editor and returns to the editing screen.

```
Creating Equations

When natural gas (CH4) burns, it produces carbon dioxide (CO2),
water (H2O), and heat according to the following reaction:

EQU 1

The solution to a quadratic equation of the form aX2 + bX + c = 0
can be written as follows:

EQU 2
```

Keystroke	Action Resulting from Keystroke
[F10]	Saves the document. Use the name **A:EQ-V2**.
[Shift-F7]	Displays the *Print* menu.
F (or **1**)	Prints the document. The printed version will look like the following:

Creating Equations

When natural gas (CH_4) burns, it produces carbon dioxide (CO_2), water (H_20), and heat according to the following reaction:

$$CH_4+2O_2 \rightarrow CO_2+2H_2O$$

The solution to a quadratic equation of the form $aX^2 + bX + c = 0$ can be written as follows:

$$X_{1,2} = \frac{-b\pm\sqrt{b^2-4ac}}{2a}$$

Keystroke	Action Resulting from Keystroke
[F7]	Exits this document.
N	Specifies that you do not want to save the document.
N	Specifies that you do not want to exit WordPerfect and presents you with a blank WordPerfect screen.

Macros

A **macro** is a program (a set of instructions) that tells an application to do something. In their simplest form, WordPerfect macros are sets of keystrokes (including text and special WordPerfect keys) that the user has told WordPerfect to memorize. This set of keystrokes is given a name and saved as a file with the extension **WPM** (**W**ord**P**erfect **M**acro) on the disk. For the advanced user, WordPerfect offers a *macro language* that is very much like a specialized programming language. Using this language, the user can customize the entire WordPerfect environment to fit a particular office setting or situation.

Unless you tell it differently, WordPerfect will store your macros in the subdirectory that contains the WordPerfect program (e.g., **C:\WP51**). If you are using someone else's computer, you should inform WordPerfect to store your macros on your *WordPerfect Data* diskette by doing the following:

Keystroke	Action Resulting from Keystroke
[Shift-F1]	Selects the *Setup* feature and displays its menu.
L (or **6**)	Selects **6 - Location of Files** and displays its menu.

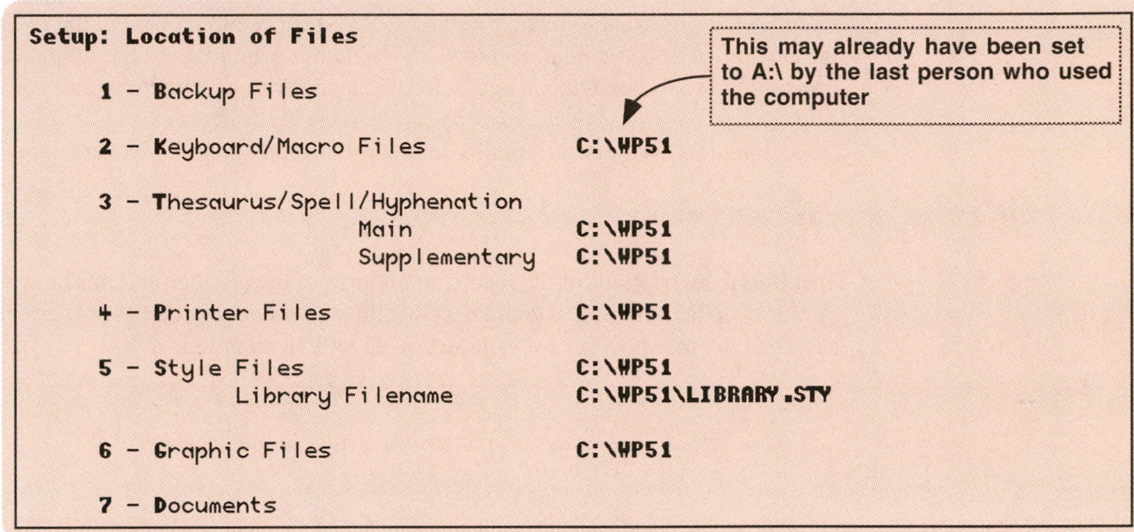

Keystroke	Action Resulting from Keystroke
K (or **2**)	Selects **Keyboard/Macro Files** and places the cursor under the drive specification.
A:\\ ↵	Specifies that the keyboard and macro files are to be stored in the root directory of the diskette in drive A:. Keyboard files are macros that you can create to change the definition of different keys (e.g., you could change the function of the **[F8]** key from underline to italic if you wished).
[F7]	Exits *Setup* and returns to the editing screen.

• A Macro to Set Margins and Tabs •

Let's create a macro that will allow you to change the margins and tabs in a ruler with a single keystroke. The ruler is to be set so that the left-hand and right-hand margins are at 2 inches and there is a single tab at position 2.5 inches. Before you begin, be sure that a blank WordPerfect screen is displayed (use **[F7]** to exit your current document if necessary). You do not have to define a macro from a blank document, but this acts as a safety feature in case you make a major mistake.

Keystroke	Action Resulting from Keystroke
[Ctrl-F10]	Begins the definition of the macro and displays the words **Define Macro** on the status line. The first part of the definition is the name of the macro. A macro can be named in one of three ways: ■ A one to eight character word (such as **RULER**). To run a macro that has been named in this way, press **[Alt-F10]** and then type the name of the macro. The number of these macros is only limited by the room on your disk to store them.

Continued . . .

Keystroke	Action Resulting from Keystroke
	■ A single letter, **A** through **Z**, in conjunction with the **[Alt]** key (e.g., **[Alt-R]**). To run a macro that has been named in this way, simply hold down **[Alt]** and tap the letter used to define the macro. You are limited to 26 macros of this type (one for each letter of the alphabet).
	■ Press **[Enter]** without typing any other characters (this creates a temporary macro that will be erased when you exit WordPerfect).
[Alt-R]	Specifies a name for the macro (R for Ruler) and requests that you enter a **Description** of the macro on the status line. If a macro with this name already exists, WordPerfect will display a message stating so and ask if you want to replace or edit it. If you choose to replace it, the old macro will be erased and the new one will be saved in its place. If you do not want to erase the old macro, cancel the operation by pressing **[F1]** and begin the macro definition again with a different name.
	Now, enter the macro description. The description can be up to 39 characters in length.
Ruler LM 2" RM 2" Tab 2.5" ↵	
	Specifies a description for the macro and returns to the editing screen. The words **Macro Def** begin blinking on the left-hand side of the status line to remind you that WordPerfect is now memorizing your keystrokes. From now on, everything you do will be recorded.

Now, let's set the margins and tabs for a ruler in the usual way.

Keystroke	Action Resulting from Keystroke
[Shift-F8]	Selects the *Format* feature and displays its menu.
L (or **1**)	Selects **1 - Line** and displays its menu.
M (or **7**)	Selects **7 - Margins** and places the blinking cursor under the indicator for the left margin.
2	Specifies that the new left margin is to be **2** inches from the left-hand side of the page.
↓	Moves the cursor down one line so that it is blinking under the right margin indicator.
2	Specifies that the new right margin is to be **2** inches from the right-hand side of the page.
[F7]	Exits the **Margins** option.
T (or **8**)	Selects **8 - Tab Set** and displays the tabs ruler at the bottom of the screen.

```
L....L....L....L....L....L....L....L....L....L....L....L....L....L....L....L....L...
|    ^    |    ^    |    ^    |    ^    |    ^    |    ^    |    ^    |    ^
-1"       0"        +1"       +2"       +3"       +4"       +5"       +6"
Delete EOL (clear tabs); Enter Number (set tab); Del (clear tab);
Type; Left; Center; Right; Decimal; .= Dot Leader; Press Exit when done.
```

Continued . . .

Keystroke	Action Resulting from Keystroke
	USERS OF VERSION 5.0 Because version 5.0 does not have different tab types (it only supports absolute tabs), skip the next two steps.
T	Selects **Type** and displays its menu.
A (or **1**)	Selects **1 Absolute** and returns to the tabs ruler screen.
0 ↵	Moves the cursor to the far left-hand side of the tabs ruler and inserts a tab stop.
[Ctrl-End]	Clears all the tab stops at and to the right of the cursor.
2.5 ↵	Inserts a left tab 2.5 inches from the left-hand side of the page.
[F7]	Saves the changes to the ruler, exits **Tab Set**, and returns to the *Format* **Line** menu.
[F7]	Exits the *Format* **Line** menu and returns to the editing screen. Notice that **Macro Def** is still blinking on the status line.
[Ctrl-F10]	Ends the macro definition and saves the keystrokes just given in a file called **ALTR.WPM (ALT** for **[Alt]** key, **R** for **[R]** key, and **.WPM** for **W**ord**P**erfect **M**acro) on the diskette in drive A: (or in the **C:\WP51** subdirectory if you did not change the location of the macro files using the *Setup* feature). If you want to see the file name in the directory, you can use the *List Files* feature by pressing **[F5]**.

Try running the macro on the document **MEMO2** by doing the following:

Keystroke	Action Resulting from Keystroke
[F7]	Exits the current document. You may think that this is not necessary because the screen looks blank. However, you have just inserted WordPerfect codes that can only be seen using **[Alt-F3]**. We do not want these codes in the next document.
N	Specifies that you do not want to save the document. The macro has already been written to disk so not saving the document will not affect it.
N	Specifies that you do not want to exit WordPerfect.
[Shift-F10]	Invokes the *Retrieve* feature.
A:MEMO2 ↵	Specifies the name of the file to be retrieved. The margins and tab stops are set to their default values (left and right margins at 1 inch and tab stops every .5 inch).
[arrow]	Use the **[arrow]** keys or mouse to move the cursor to the first letter of the second paragraph (location **Ln 2.17" Pos 1"**).
[Tab]	Moves the first letter of the paragraph to the next tab stop to the right.

Continued . . .

Keystroke	Action Resulting from Keystroke
[Home] ←	Moves the cursor to the left-hand edge of the line. The top of the screen now should look like the following:

```
Memo to:  All Employees
Memo from:  Matt Wilson, PRESIDENT
Date:  February 10, 1991

We have purchased enough wonderful IBM microcomputers so that
each employee can have one on his/her desk.

_    Please pick up your machine at the loading dock as soon as
possible.

Also, please see the receptionist to sign up for a training
session on how to use your new machine.
```

Keystroke	Action Resulting from Keystroke
[Alt-R]	Runs the macro. While the macro is running the message `* Please wait *` will appear on the status line. The screen now should look as follows:

```
Memo to:  All Employees
Memo from:  Matt Wilson, PRESIDENT
Date:  February 10, 1991

We have purchased enough wonderful IBM microcomputers so that
each employee can have one on his/her desk.

                    Please pick up your machine at the
               loading dock as soon as possible.

               Also, please see the receptionist to sign up
               for a training session on how to use your new
               machine.
```

New tab stop and margins begin at the second paragraph and are in effect from then on

Notice that all the paragraphs from the cursor on down have been reformatted using the new margins and tab stop. Remember, when WordPerfect makes a change to margins or tabs, the change is in effect until the end of the document or until another margin set or tab set code is encountered.

• A Macro to Enter Blocks of Text •

Macros can also be created to enter often-used blocks of text. For example, suppose you want to set up a macro that will insert your name and address into a document. Then, whenever you need to enter that information, all you would have to do is run the macro.

Keystroke	Action Resulting from Keystroke
[F7]	Exits the current document.
N	Specifies that you do not want to save the document.
N	Specifies that you do not want to exit WordPerfect and displays a blank WordPerfect screen.

Continued . . .

Keystroke	Action Resulting from Keystroke
[Ctrl-F10]	Begins the definition of the macro and displays the words **Define Macro** on the status line. We could use a letter to define the macro (as we did in the last example). This time, however, let's give the macro a descriptive name.
NAME-ADD ↵	Specifies a name for the macro and requests a description.
Name and Address ↵	Specifies a description for the macro and returns to the editing screen. The words **Macro Def** begin to blink. At this point you may type the information to be saved. For example (use your own name and address):

```
Douglas F. Robertson
128 Pleasant Street SE
Minneapolis, MN  55455
▬
```

Keystroke	Action Resulting from Keystroke
[Ctrl-F10]	Ends the macro definition. The keystrokes just given will be saved in a file called **NAME-ADD.WPM**.

From now on, whenever you need your name and address entered into a document all you need to do is run the macro. Just for practice, run the macro two times by doing the following:

Keystroke	Action Resulting from Keystroke
[Alt-F10]	Requests the name of the macro to be run.
NAME-ADD ↵	Specifies the name of the macro and runs it.
	Run the macro again by repeating the keystrokes. Notice how fast the macro runs.
[Alt-F10]	Requests the name of the macro to be run.
NAME-ADD ↵	Specifies the name of the macro and runs it. The top of the screen now should look as follows:

```
Douglas F. Robertson    )
128 Pleasant Street SE  )  Original macro definition
Minneapolis, MN  55455  )
Douglas F. Robertson    )
128 Pleasant Street SE  )  First run of macro
Minneapolis, MN  55455  )
Douglas F. Robertson    )
128 Pleasant Street SE  )  Second run of macro
Minneapolis, MN  55455  )
```

You may view the details of WordPerfect macros and make changes to them by using the *Macro* **Edit** option. We will not discuss this feature in detail, but just to give you an idea of how to use it, change the zipcode from **55455** to **55101** by doing the following:

Keystroke	Action Resulting from Keystroke

[Ctrl-F10] — Begins the definition of a macro and displays the words **Define Macro** on the status line.

NAME-ADD ↵ — Specifies a name for the macro to define or edit and displays the following on the status line:

NAME-ADD.WPM Already Exists: 1 Replace; 2 Edit; 3 Description: 0

1 Replace allows you to replace the macro **HOME-ADD** with a new one.

2 Edit allows you to view the details of the macro and make changes to it.

3 Description allows you to change the description of the macro.

USERS OF VERSION 5.0 The third option, **3 Description**, is not available in this menu but is an option in the **2 Edit** screen.

E (or **2**) — Selects **2 Edit** and displays the following:

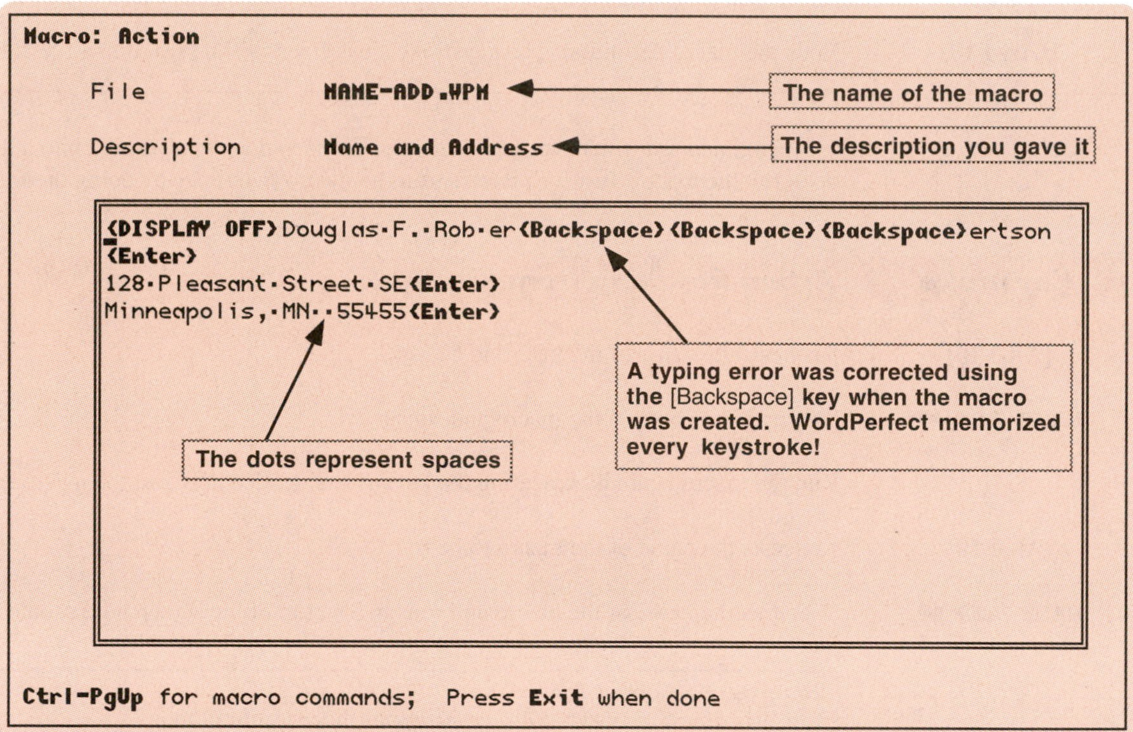

The macro description is contained inside the double-lined box. The cursor is located at the upper left-hand corner of the box. You may move the cursor using the **[arrow]** keys or the mouse.

USERS OF VERSION 5.0 Before doing the following, press **A** (or **2**) to select **2 - Action** from the menu at the top of the **Edit** screen.

[arrow] — Use the **[arrow]** keys or mouse to move the cursor to the bottom of the display, just below **Minneapolis**.

Notice the code **{DISPLAY OFF}**. This was automatically inserted by WordPerfect at the beginning of the macro definition. It prevents the macro commands from being displayed as the macro is being run (this allows the macro to run faster). To make the commands visible while the macro is being run you would change this to **{DISPLAY ON}**.

Continued . . .

Keystroke	Action Resulting from Keystroke
	You can display a list of codes, such as **{DISPLAY OFF}**, by pressing **[Ctrl-PageUp]** (this option is not available in version 5.0).
	USERS OF VERSION 5.0 You cannot display the list of codes so skip the next three steps on ringing the bell and go directly to changing the zipcode.
[Ctrl-PageUp]	Displays a list of codes in the upper right-hand corner of the screen.

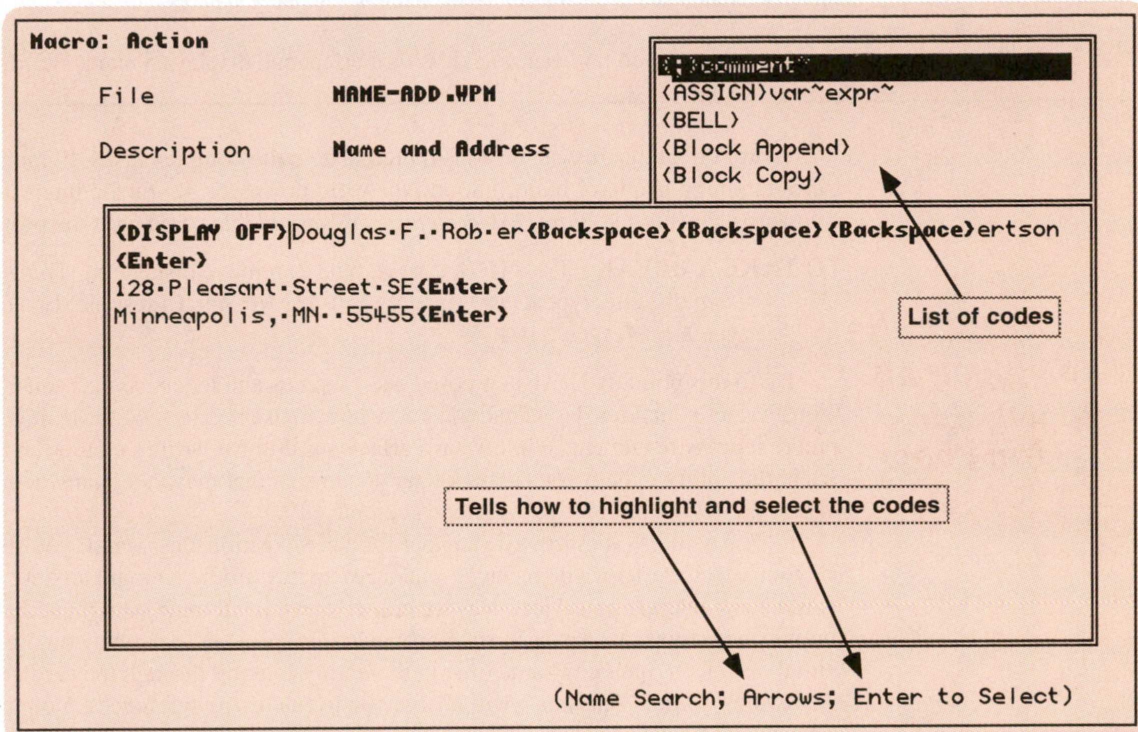

Keystroke	Action Resulting from Keystroke
	Just for fun, let's insert the **{BELL}** code at the end of the macro (this will cause the speaker to beep at the end of the macro).
[arrow]	Use the **[arrow]** keys or mouse to highlight **{BELL}**.
↵	Selects the **{BELL}** command and returns control to the edit window.
	Now, let's change the zipcode.
[arrow]	Use the **[arrow]** keys or mouse to move the cursor to the first character of the zipcode **55455**.
55101	Use the standard editing techniques to change **55455** to **55101**.
	USERS OF VERSION 5.0 Press **[F7]** to return to the *Macro* **Edit** screen.
[F7]	Exits the *Macro* **Edit** option and returns to the editing screen.

Run the new macro to see how it works.

Keystroke	Action Resulting from Keystroke
[Alt-F10]	Requests the name of the macro to be run.
NAME-ADD ↵	Specifies the name of the macro and runs it. The speaker should beep and the name and address should be inserted at the cursor (the zipcode should be **55101** rather than **55455**).
[F7]	Exits the current document.
N	Specifies that you do not want to save the document.
N	Specifies that you do not want to exit WordPerfect and displays a blank WordPerfect screen.

WordPerfect macros can be constructed to do quite complex tasks. In fact, they are very much like a programming language built right into the word processor. If you are interested in more information on macros, consult the *WordPerfect Reference Manual* that came with the program.

TO TAKE A BREAK Press **[F7]**, type **N**, type **Y**, remove diskette(s). To resume (hard disk): Insert *Data* diskette, type **A:** ↵, type **C:\WP51\WP** ↵. To resume (two drive): Insert diskettes, type **A:** ↵, type **B:WP** ↵.

Putting It All Together in a Term Paper

Up to this point, we have composed short memos and letters so that you could practice using WordPerfect's features. Now that you know how to use a variety of these, it is time to practice creating a more lengthy document. While WordPerfect is useful for writing memos and letters, its real strength lies in the ability to help you create longer documents that may take many hours to research, outline, write, and rewrite until a final version is completed.

Let's say that you must write a paper for a composition class. First, you should decide upon a topic for your paper. Perhaps you recently read a newspaper article on math anxiety and you decide that this would be an interesting subject. Having chosen the general topic, you must then find numerous sources (books, magazines, newspapers, scholarly journals, speeches, personal communications, etc.) that deal with the subject. Spending some time in the library looking through the card catalog and the *Readers' Guide to Periodical Literature* will enable you to find many references. You may even be able to use a computerized database such as the Knowledge Index to help you search for references.

As you locate and read references related to your topic, you will need to take notes (3 x 5-inch index cards are good for this) and to clearly document all the sources of ideas and direct quotations. This will help you to gain a basic understanding of the topic and will be a source of notes and references that can be used later when you begin to outline and then to write your paper. As you collect more information, you may begin to develop some ideas as to what you want to say about the subject. Are you going to simply report on what you have read or will you make comments on and evaluations of the material? What will be the central idea or thesis of your paper? How can you organize the information you have collected and synthesize the parts you feel are important and of interest to your readers?

• Developing an Outline •

Let's say that you have decided upon the following thesis statement:

```
Math anxiety is a problem for many adults, but intervention programs,
such as the one at the University of Minnesota, can help students
overcome their anxiety and learn mathematics.
```

The next step is to develop an outline for the paper. The outline shows the overall organization of the paper and the relationships of the ideas to each other. It also shows which ideas are most important (the major headings) and which are of lesser importance.

Let's say that you have developed the following outline for the paper:

```
I.     General comments
       A.    Definition
       B.    Symptoms
```

II. Cyclic nature of math anxiety
    A. Past experiences
    B. Avoidance
    C. Poor preparation
    D. Poor performance
III. The math anxiety program at the University of Minnesota
    A. Genesis
        1. History of department offering program
        2. Development of program
    B. Clientele served
    C. Description of current program
IV. Conclusion

• *Writing the First Draft* •

Using the outline as a guide, you then write the text of the paper. Do not expect to be able to write a good paper from start to finish in a smooth and easy fashion. Writing is difficult for most people and just about everyone has to make revisions to their writing. It is not unusual to make five or six drafts of a paper before you get it the way you want it.

Let's say that you have written a draft of the paper based on the above outline. At this point, you should not worry about the way the paper looks but only about what it says. Later, you can add underlining, boldfacing, footnotes, and other formatting.

A draft of the paper is given on the next three pages[1]. (Note: Your instructor may make the text of the paper available to you on disk so that you do not have to type it yourself). To save time when typing the paper, the code **m1** was used in place of the word **mathematics**. When the paper is edited, the codes can be changed to the correct word using WordPerfect's *Search* and *Replace* features.

Math anxiety is a term popularized during the mid-seventies to describe the feelings of mental disorganization, fear, or even panic that prevent some people from effectively learning or working with m1 (Tobias, 1980). Many people, including some m1 teachers, have felt anxiety toward m1 at one time or another, but each person's experience is uniquely his or her own. While the causes of math anxiety are varied they usually occur before adulthood and so by the time many students reach college age they exhibit the symptoms of math anxiety and the problem interferes with their performances in situations where m1 is required.

Some people are able to channel the feelings of anxiety into interest and excitement and the anxiety is not a serious problem. However, for the severely math-anxious person, the excitement crosses over into panic and the anxiety becomes debilitating. Emotions take over control of the mind and body and productive work grinds to a halt.

The symptoms exhibited by the math anxious may lead to a vicious cycle of math avoidance characterized by the following (Kogelman & Warren 1978):

Phase 1. Intense emotional negative reactions to situations where numbers are required. This may be caused by unpleasant experiences with m1 in the past. These feelings lead to ...

Phase 2. Avoidance of situations in which m1 is a part. People who dislike working with numbers will naturally try to avoid situations where numbers must be used. This avoidance leads to ...

Phase 3. Poor preparation in m1. Obviously, if a person avoids m1, she or he will not get much practice or try to learn new m1.

[1]This term paper is based on "A Program for the Math Anxious at the University of Minnesota" by Douglas F. Robertson, *The AMATYC Review*, Fall, 1991.

This lack of preparation leads to ...
Phase 4. Poor performance in ml. As with any other physical or cognitive process, people who rarely work with ml will not be able to do it when they have to. This lack of ability to perform, of course, leads to ...
Phase 1. Intense emotional negative reactions...and so on.

This cycle is often repeated over and over until the math anxious person completely adjusts his or her life so that ml is avoided no matter what the cost. By the time adulthood is reached, the math anxious person may be convinced (with good evidence) that he or she cannot do ml. Without intervention, the cycle is rarely broken (Mathison & Robertson 1980).

The Math Anxiety Program of the University of Minnesota

The Math Anxiety Program of the University of Minnesota was designed to help math anxious adults learn basic ml. The program is offered in the evenings through the department of Continuing Education for Women (CEW). This department was created in 1960 for the purpose of relating higher education to the changing needs of women. Its original objective was to identify the educational needs of women and to provide the resources that would assist them in developing their abilities to the fullest. Today, CEW serves the educational needs of approximately 6,000 women and men each year. CEW is typical of the many specialized departments and colleges housed within the University whose purpose is to provide services to students with widely varying academic abilities and backgrounds. Indeed, through the General College, one of the fifteen colleges that comprise the University, arithmetic, elementary, and intermediate algebra are taught in noncredit courses to approximately 2,700 students per year.

The CEW Math Anxiety Program had its beginnings in 1975 when an accounting professor and an economics professor came to CEW to discuss the academic problems being experienced by some of the women in their classes. These women were highly intelligent and motivated. Many had earned college degrees or had successfully completed some college work, but were having difficulty coping with the quantitative aspects of the accounting and economics courses. The students spoke of blocking out numbers, avoiding situations requiring the use of ml, not remembering how to do simple computations, and developing tension when faced with computations and testing.

The CEW staff investigated the situation by talking to the students and the course instructors, and by examining the available literature on the problems women have with ml. This research led to the development of the Math Anxiety Program in 1976 (Hendel 1977). Since then, over 5,000 students (80% of whom are women) ranging in age from 14 to 73 (average 28) have taken ml courses offered through the program (Lindoo, 1988). Approximately 82% of the current program participants are working full- or part-time, 14% are regular students (at the University or at other two-year or four-year colleges), and 14% classify themselves as homemakers. Currently the program offers courses in arithmetic, elementary and intermediate algebra, and introductory statistics. The CEW department supports the small administrative costs required to run the program and student tuition covers the cost of instruction.

Conclusion

Math anxiety is a serious problem for some adults. The Department of Continuing Education for Women at the University of Minnesota has developed a comprehensive program to help adult students who suffer from math anxiety understand their problems and learn basic ml. The three components of the program, a diagnostic clinic, individualized tutoring, and content courses, are designed to analyze student needs, both mathematical and emotional, and to address those needs in a sensitive and humanistic manner. While developing such a program is time consuming, it is not difficult and, once the program is implemented, it is self-supporting.

Typing the References Finally, you may type the references you cited in the paper. The two most commonly used reference forms are from the Modern Language Association's *MLA Handbook for Writers of Research Papers* (used mainly in the humanities) and from the American Psychological Association's (APA) *Publication Manual of the American Psychological Association* (used mainly in the social sciences). The following references follow the APA form:

Works Cited

Hendel, D. D. (1977). The Math Anxiety Program: its genesis and evaluation in Continuing Education for Women. Minneapolis: University of Minnesota, Measurement Services Center.

Kogelman, S. & Warren, J. (1978). Mind over math. New York: Dial Press.

Lindoo, S. (1988). Report of a survey of the CEW Math Anxiety Program. Minneapolis: University of Minnesota, Department of Continuing Education for Women.

Mathison, M. A. & Robertson, D. F. (1980, August). Interventions in math anxiety for adults. Paper presented at the Fourth International Congress on Mathematical Education, Berkeley, CA.

Tobias, S. (1980). Overcoming math anxiety. Boston: Houghton Mifflin.

• Preparing the Final Draft •

The difficult part now is complete. All that is left to do is to adjust the text so that it follows a form that is acceptable for a term paper. There are many such forms so be sure that the one you choose is acceptable to the journal or professor for whom you are writing the paper.

Title Page Begin from a blank WordPerfect screen (if necessary, use **[F7]** to exit an existing document) and type the following title page (use your own name, of course). Do not worry about formatting—you will do that after the paper has been typed.

```
A Program for the Math Anxious
at the University of Minnesota

by
Dennis Adams

Professor Gidmark
GC 1421
```

To enter the date you may either type it by hand or use the WordPerfect *Date* feature. Let's do the latter:

Keystroke	Action Resulting from Keystroke
[Shift-F5]	Selects the *Date/Outline* feature.

```
1 Date Text; 2 Date Code; 3 Date Format; 4 Outline; 5 Para Num; 6 Define: 0
```

1 Date Text inserts the current date at the cursor as a piece of text (just as if you had typed it yourself).

2 Date Code inserts a date code at the cursor that will be updated each time the document is retrieved or printed.

3 Date Format allows you to change the way the date is displayed.

4 Outline allows you to create outlines quickly and easily (you will do that in just a minute).

5 Para Num allows you to number paragraphs.

6 Define allows you to define the way the paragraph numbering and outlining will be displayed.

Keystroke	Action Resulting from Keystroke
T (or **1**)	Selects **Date Text** and inserts the current date at the cursor. Note that the date inserted is that which is on the computer's clock. If the clock has the wrong date you may drop to DOS by pressing **[Ctrl-F1]** and then **2**, then set the date by typing **DATE MM-DD-YY ↵**, and return to WordPerfect by tapping any key.

Typing the Outline Type the top portion of the outline page.

Keystroke	Action Resulting from Keystroke
[Ctrl-Enter]	Inserts a page break between the title page and the outline page.

Type the title of the paper again (or copy it from the top of the document) and then the thesis statement. After this is done the top of the screen should look like the following:

```
A Program for the Math Anxious
at the University of Minnesota

by
Dennis Adams

Professor Gidmark
GC 1421
February 11, 1991
==========================================================================
A Program for the Math Anxious
at the University of Minnesota

THESIS:  Math anxiety is a problem for many adults, but
intervention programs, such as the one at the University of
Minnesota, can help students overcome their anxiety and learn
mathematics.

_
```

Page break is inserted by pressing [Ctrl-Enter]

Continued . . .

Keystroke	Action Resulting from Keystroke
[F10]	Requests that the document be saved.
A:\ANXIETY1 ↵	Provides the file specification for this draft of the document and returns to the editing screen.

Type the outline itself. WordPerfect has a special *Outline* feature that makes the construction of formal outlines quite easy. This feature numbers your paragraphs using outline notation and automatically renumbers the entries as you move, add, or delete items. The outline numbering begins at the left-hand margin and uses each tab stop for the next level in the outline. To move to a lower outline level, press **[Tab]**; to move to a higher outline level, press **[Shift-Tab]**; to move to a new line, press **[Enter]**.

Keystroke	Action Resulting from Keystroke
[Shift-F5]	Selects the *Date/Outline* feature.
O (or **4**)	Selects **4 Outline** and displays the outline menu.
	USERS OF VERSION 5.0 The menu is different for version 5.0. The word **Outline** will appear immediately on the screen. You should skip the next step.
O (or **1**)	Selects **1 On**. The word **Outline** appears in the lower left-hand corner of the screen.
↵	Inserts the first number (**I.**) in the outline.
[Shift-F4]	Indents to the next tab stop where the typing will begin. You should not use the **[Tab]** key here because pressing it will move the cursor to the next level of the outline. If you want to use the regular tabs instead of indent you must press **[Spacebar]** (to insert one blank space) and then the **[Tab]** key will function normally.
	Type the first entry of the outline (**General comments** ↵):

```
A Program for the Math Anxious
at the University of Minnesota

by
Dennis Adams

Professor Gidmark
GC 1421
February 11, 1991
================================================================================
A Program for the Math Anxious
at the University of Minnesota

THESIS:  Math anxiety is a problem for many adults, but
intervention programs, such as the one at the University of
Minnesota, can help students overcome their anxiety and learn
mathematics.

I.   General comments
II._

Outline                                         Doc 1 Pg 2 Ln 2.5" Pos 1.3"
```

Pressing [Enter] moves the cursor to the next line and automatically displays the next outline number.

Continued . . .

Keystroke	Action Resulting from Keystroke
[Tab]	Moves to the next lower outline level (i.e., the second level) and displays **A**.

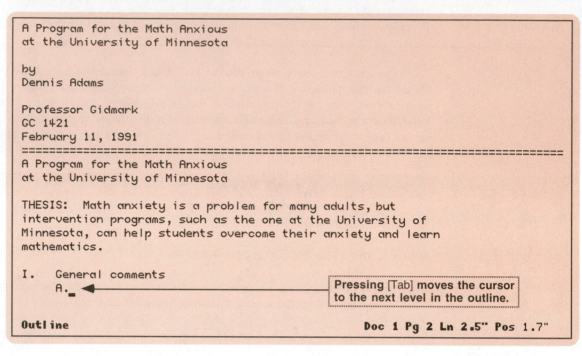

```
A Program for the Math Anxious
at the University of Minnesota

by
Dennis Adams

Professor Gidmark
GC 1421
February 11, 1991
=================================================================================
A Program for the Math Anxious
at the University of Minnesota

THESIS:  Math anxiety is a problem for many adults, but
intervention programs, such as the one at the University of
Minnesota, can help students overcome their anxiety and learn
mathematics.

I.   General comments
     A._

Outline                                    Doc 1 Pg 2 Ln 2.5" Pos 1.7"
```

Pressing [Tab] moves the cursor to the next level in the outline.

[Shift-F4] Indents to the next tab stop where you can type the second entry of the outline (**Definition ↵**).

USERS OF VERSION 5.0 When you press **[Enter]**, WordPerfect will display **II**. on the next line rather than **B**. Press **[Tab]** to change the **II**. into **B**.

[Shift-F4] Indents to the next tab stop where you can type the third entry in the outline (**Symptoms ↵**).

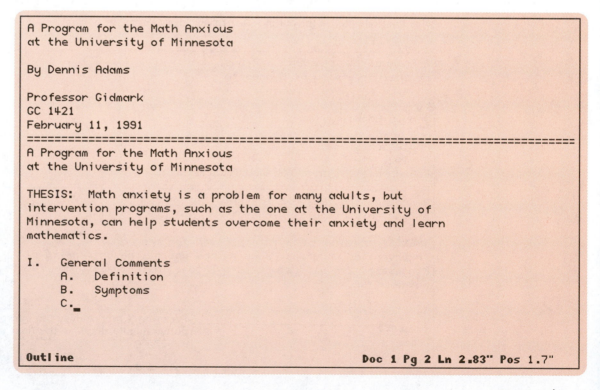

```
A Program for the Math Anxious
at the University of Minnesota

By Dennis Adams

Professor Gidmark
GC 1421
February 11, 1991
=================================================================================
A Program for the Math Anxious
at the University of Minnesota

THESIS:  Math anxiety is a problem for many adults, but
intervention programs, such as the one at the University of
Minnesota, can help students overcome their anxiety and learn
mathematics.

I.   General Comments
     A.   Definition
     B.   Symptoms
     C._

Outline                                    Doc 1 Pg 2 Ln 2.83" Pos 1.7"
```

Continued . . .

Keystroke	Action Resulting from Keystroke
	USERS OF VERSION 5.0 When you press **[Enter]**, WordPerfect will display **`II.`** on the next line rather than **`C`**. Thus, you may skip the next step.
[Shift-Tab]	Moves to the next higher outline level and displays **`II.`**
[Shift-F4]	Indents to the next tab stop where you can type the fourth entry in the outline (**`Cyclic nature of math anxiety ↵`**).
	Continue typing the outline in a like manner. Each time you want to move to a lower outline level, press **[Tab]**; each time you want to move to a higher outline level, press **[Shift-Tab]**; each time you want to go to a new line, press **[Enter]**. When you have finished, your outline should look like the following:

```
I.    General Comments
      A.    Definition
      B.    Symptoms
II.   Cyclic nature of math anxiety
      A.    Past experiences
      B.    Avoidance
      C.    Poor preparation
      D.    Poor performance
III.  The math anxiety program at the University of Minnesota
      A.    Genesis
            1.    History of department offering
                  program
            2.    Development of program
      B.    Clientele served
      C.    Description of current program
IV.   Conclusion
```

When you have finished the outline, do the following to exit the *Outline* feature.

Keystroke	Action Resulting from Keystroke
[Shift-F5]	Selects the *Date/Outline* feature.
`O` (or **4**)	Selects **`4 Outline`** and displays the outline menu.
	USERS OF VERSION 5.0 The menu is different for version 5.0. The word **`Outline`** will disappear from the screen. You should skip the next step.
`F` (or **2**)	Selects **`2 Off`**. The word **`Outline`** disappears from the lower left-hand corner of the screen.
[F10]	Requests that the document be saved.

Continued . . .

Keystroke	Action Resulting from Keystroke
A:\ANXIETY2 ↵	Provides the file specification for this draft of the document and returns to the editing screen. The entire document so far should look like the following:

```
A Program for the Math Anxious
at the University of Minnesota

By Dennis Adams

Professor Gidmark
GC 1421
February 11, 1991
=================================================================================
A Program for the Math Anxious
at the University of Minnesota

THESIS:  Math anxiety is a problem for many adults, but
intervention programs, such as the one at the University of
Minnesota, can help students overcome their anxiety and learn
mathematics.

I.   General Comments
     A.   Definition
     B.   Symptoms
II.  Cyclic nature of math anxiety
     A.   Past experiences
     B.   Avoidance
     C.   Poor preparation
     D.   Poor performance
III. The math anxiety program at the University of Minnesota
     A.   Genesis
          1.   History of department offering
               program
          2.   Development of program
     B.   Clientele served
     C.   Description of current program
IV.  Conclusion

_
A:\ANXIETY2                                    Doc 1 Pg 2 Ln 5" Pos 1"
```

WordPerfect inserts codes rather than text when you use **[Tab]** to display the outline numbers. This means that if you decide to rearrange some parts of the outline the numbers are automatically adjusted to fit the new arrangement. You can use *Reveal Codes* to display them:

Keystroke	Action Resulting from Keystroke
[Alt-F3]	Reveals the hidden codes.

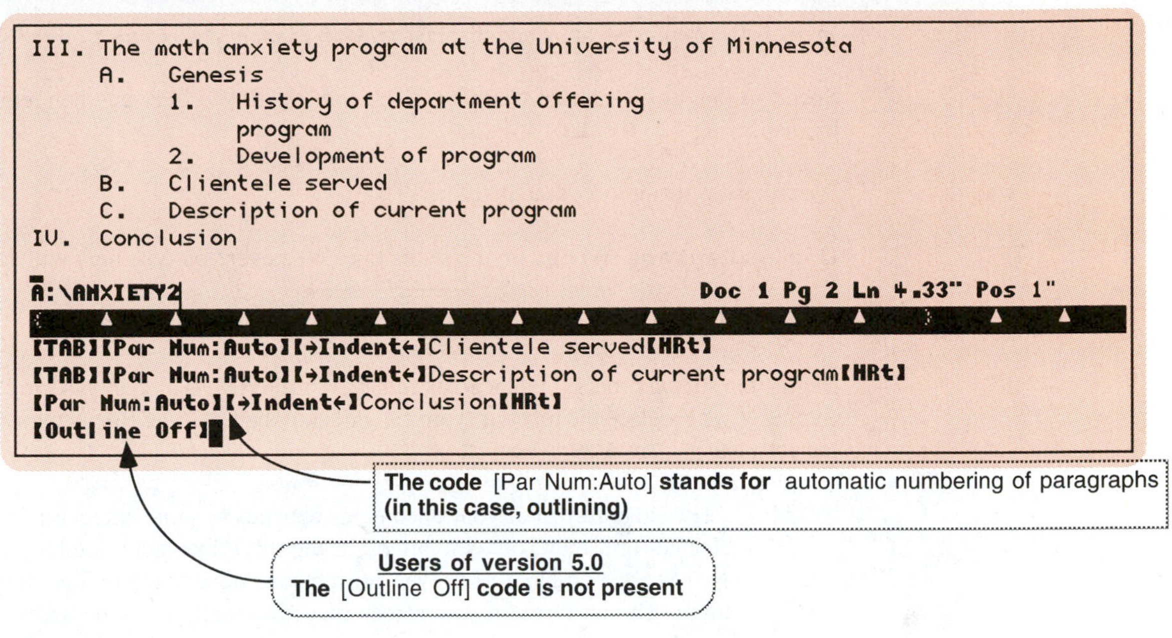

III. The math anxiety program at the University of Minnesota
A. Genesis
1. History of department offering program
2. Development of program
B. Clientele served
C. Description of current program
IV. Conclusion
A:\ANXIETY2
Doc 1 Pg 2 Ln 4.33" Pos 1"
[TAB][Par Num:Auto][→Indent←]Clientele served[HRt]
[TAB][Par Num:Auto][→Indent←]Description of current program[HRt]
[Par Num:Auto][→Indent←]Conclusion[HRt]
[Outline Off]
The code [Par Num:Auto] stands for automatic numbering of paragraphs (in this case, outlining)
Users of version 5.0
The [Outline Off] code is not present

Keystroke	Action Resulting from Keystroke
[Alt-F3]	Hides the codes again.

Typing the Body of the Paper The body of the paper shown on pp. W157–59 now can be inserted. To save you time, your instructor may have stored a copy of the paper on disk under the name **TERMPAP** so that you can simply retrieve it into the current document. If that is not the case, you will have to type it yourself.

Keystroke	Action Resulting from Keystroke
[arrow]	Use the **[arrow]** keys, if necessary, to move the cursor to the bottom of the document (location **Pg 2 Ln 5" Pos 1"**).
[Ctrl-Enter]	Inserts a page break between the outline page and the body of the paper.
[Shift-F10]	Specifies that you want to retrieve a WordPerfect file and requests the name.

C:\WP51\WPDOCS\TERMPAP ↵

Specifies the name of the file to be retrieved and inserts it at the cursor. Note that your instructor may have saved the file in a different subdirectory. In that case, replace **C:\WP51\WPDOCS** with the correct path specification.

Using the Search and Replace Features As was mentioned earlier, the code **m1** was used in place of the word **mathematics** when the draft of the paper was typed. This saved a considerable amount of typing because the word **mathematics** appears 18 times in the paper and each time **m1** was typed in place of **mathematics**, nine keystrokes were saved. This means that a total of 9 x 18 = 162 keystrokes were saved by using the code. The code can be converted to the proper word using the *Search* and *Replace* features.

Keystroke	Action Resulting from Keystroke
[Home] [Home] ↑	Moves the cursor to the top of the document.
[Alt-F2]	Invokes the *Replace* feature and displays **w/Confirm? No (Yes)** on the status line.
Y	Specifies that **Y**es, each replacement is to be confirmed. WordPerfect then requests the search definition by displaying **-> Srch:**
m1	Specifies the string to be searched for.
[F2]	Displays **Replace with:** on the status line. Whatever you type next will act as the replacement text.
mathematics	Specifies the replacement text.
[F2]	Begins the search process. When **m1** is found, WordPerfect will display **Confirm? No (Yes)**. Typing **Y** will replace the text but typing **N** will skip the text. The first occurrence of **m1** should be at location **Pg 3 Ln 1.5" Pos 2.4"**. **NOTE . . .** The exact format of your documents depends to some extent on the printer that has been selected for use by your computer. For the short documents we have created so far this probably was not a problem. However, for this long document you may find that the location of the cursor (**Ln** and **Pos**) on your screen may not exactly coincide with the location we describe. This does not necessarily mean that you are doing something wrong. It may mean simply that your computer system (both hardware and software) is configured differently from ours.
Y	Performs the replacement and automatically searches for the next occurrence of **m1**.

Continue replacing all occurrences of **m1** with **mathematics** until the end of the document has been reached.

Formatting the Paper Set up the general format of the paper. Term papers usually are double-spaced with 1-inch margins:

Keystroke	Action Resulting from Keystroke
[Home] [Home] ↑	Moves the cursor to the top of the document.
[Shift-F8]	Selects the *Format* feature and displays its menu.
L (or **1**)	Selects **Line** and displays its menu.
S (or **6**)	Selects **Line Spacing** and highlights the current setting (it should be **1**).
2 ↵	Specifies that double-spacing is to be used throughout the document.
M (or **7**)	Selects **Margins** and highlights the current left margin setting.
1 ↵	Specifies a 1-inch left margin and highlights the right margin setting.
1 ↵	Specifies a 1-inch right margin.
↵	Exits the *Format* **Line** menu and returns to the *Format* menu.

Continued . . .

Keystroke	Action Resulting from Keystroke
P (or 2)	Selects **Page** and displays its menu.
M (or 5)	Selects **Margins** and highlights the top margin setting.
1 ↵	Specifies a 1-inch top margin and highlights the bottom margin setting.
1 ↵	Specifies a 1-inch bottom margin.
[F7]	Exits the *Format* **Page** menu and returns to the document.
[F10]	Requests that the document be saved.
A:\ANXIETY3 ↵	Provides the file specification for this draft of the document and returns to the editing screen.

Formatting the Title Page The title and your name should be centered about four inches from the top of the page. If this paper is for a class, the teacher's name, course number, and the date should appear right justified in the lower right-hand corner of the page.

Keystroke	Action Resulting from Keystroke
[Home] [Home] ↑	Moves the cursor to the top of the document (if necessary).
↵	Press **[Enter]** nine times to move the first line of the title page (the title of the paper) down 3 inches. The location of the cursor should be **Pg 1 Ln 4" Pos 1"**.
	REMEMBER . . . you can use your mouse to select the block and then skip the next two steps.
[Alt-F4]	Turns on the *Block* feature.
[arrow]	Use the **[arrow]** keys or mouse to move the cursor to the last character in your name (location **Pg 1 Ln 5.33" Pos 2.2"**).
[Shift-F6] Y	Selects the *Center* feature and centers the blocked text.
[arrow]	Use the **[arrow]** keys or mouse to move the cursor to the first character in the line containing the professor's name (location **Pg 1 Ln 6" Pos 1"**).
↵	Press **[Enter]** nine times to move the next part of the title page (the name of the professor) down 3 inches. The location of the cursor should be **Pg 1 Ln 9" Pos 1"**.
[Alt-F4]	Turns on the *Block* feature.
[arrow]	Use the **[arrow]** keys or mouse to move the cursor to the last character in the date (location **Pg 1 Ln 9.67" Pos 2.7"**).
[Alt-F6] Y	Right justifies the blocked text.
[F10]	Requests that the document be saved.
A:\ANXIETY4 ↵	Provides the file specification for this draft of the document and returns to the editing screen.

At this point, the title page of the document should look like the following:

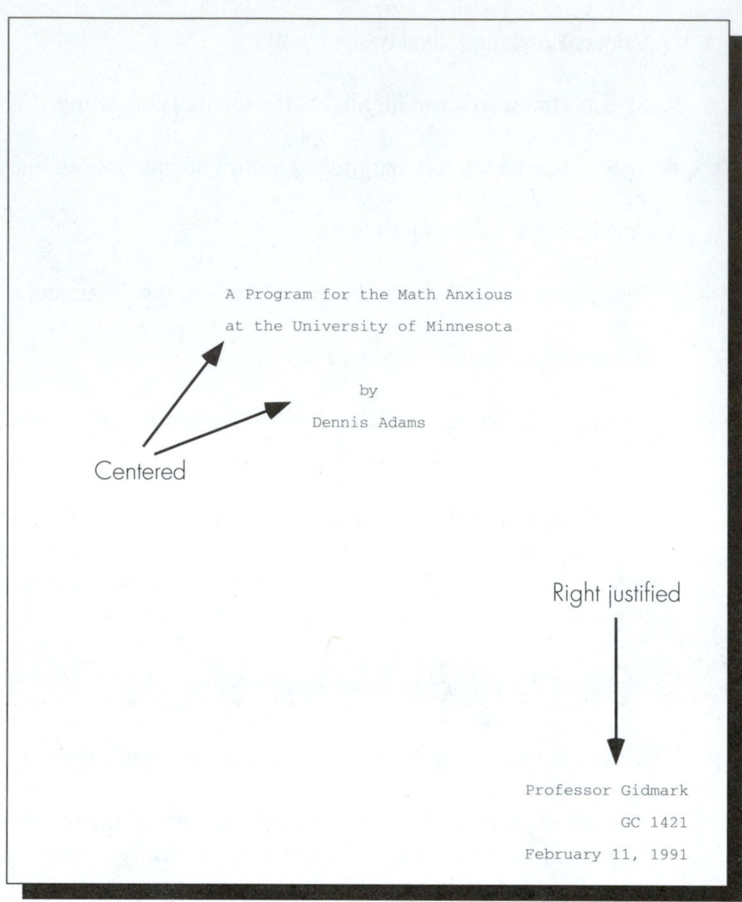

A Program for the Math Anxious
at the University of Minnesota
by
Dennis Adams
Centered
Right justified
Professor Gidmark
GC 1421
February 11, 1991

Formatting the Outline Page The title should be centered and the thesis statement should be indented.

Keystroke	Action Resulting from Keystroke
[arrow]	Use the **[arrow]** keys or mouse to move the cursor to the first character on the outline page (location **`Pg 2 Ln 1" Pos 1"`**). Pressing **[PageDown]** will also do this.
	REMEMBER . . . you can use your mouse to select the block and then skip the next two steps.
[Alt-F4]	Turns on the *Block* feature.
[arrow]	Use the **[arrow]** keys or mouse to move the cursor to the last character in the title (location **`Pg 2 Ln 1.33" Pos 4"`**).
[Shift-F6] `Y`	Centers the blocked text.
[arrow]	Use the **[arrow]** keys or mouse to move the cursor to the first character in the word **`THESIS`** (location **`Pg 2 Ln 2" Pos 1"`**).
[Alt-F4]	Turns on the *Block* feature.
[arrow]	Use the **[arrow]** keys or mouse to move the cursor to the colon just to the right of the word **`THESIS`** (location **`Pg 2 Ln 2" Pos 1.6"`**).

Continued . . .

Keystroke	Action Resulting from Keystroke
[F8]	Underlines the selected block.
[arrow]	Use the **[arrow]** keys or mouse to move the cursor to the first character in the thesis statement (the **`M`** in **`Math`** at **`Pg 2 Ln 2" Pos 1.9"`**).
[Shift-F4]	Indents the thesis statement.
[arrow]	Use the **[arrow]** keys or mouse to move the cursor to the last character in the thesis statement (location **`Pg 2 Ln 3" Pos 6.5"`**). This will reformat the paragraph.
[F10]	Requests that the document be saved.
`A:\ANXIETY5` ↵	Provides the file specification for this draft of the document and returns to the editing screen.

The outline page of the printed document should look like the following:

```
                    A Program for the Math Anxious
                    at the University of Minnesota

THESIS:   Math anxiety is a problem for many adults, but
          intervention programs, such as the one at the
          University of Minnesota, can help students
          overcome their anxiety and learn mathematics.

I.   General comments
     A.   Definition
     B.   Symptoms
II.  Cyclic nature of math anxiety
     A.   Past experiences
     B.   Avoidance
     C.   Poor preparation
     D.   Poor performance
III. The math anxiety program at the University of Minnesota
     A.   Genesis
          1.   History of department offering
               program
          2.   Development of program
     B.   Clientele served
     C.   Description of current program
IV.  Conclusion
```

Repeating the Title The title should again appear at the top of the third page. To save time, let's simply copy the centered title from the first page of the document.

Keystroke	Action Resulting from Keystroke
[Ctrl-Home]	Displays the words **`Go to`** on the status line. This is the quick way of moving to a specific page in a long document. You simply type the number of the page you want to go to. Of course, you can always use the **[arrow]** keys, **[PageUp]**, and/or **[PageDown]** instead.
2 ↵	Specifies the page number. The cursor moves to the top of page 2 (the outline page).
	Be sure the cursor is at the left edge of the screen (**`Pg 2 Ln 1" Pos 1"`**). If it is not, use the **[arrow]** keys to place it there. When you copy the text, you want to be sure to copy the centering codes.
	REMEMBER . . . you can use your mouse to select the block and then skip the next two steps.
[Alt-F4]	Turns on the *Block* feature.
↓ ↓ ↓	Moves the cursor down three lines (this blocks the title and the blank line just below it).
[Ctrl-F4]	Selects the *Move* feature.
B (or **1**)	Specifies that a **B**lock of text is to be operated upon.
C (or **2**)	Specifies that the block is to be **C**opied.
[PageDown]	Moves the cursor to the top of the next page (the first page of text).
[Enter]	Inserts the copied block at the cursor.

```
                 A Program for the Math Anxious

                 at the University of Minnesota



     Math anxiety is a term popularized during the mid-seventies

to describe the feelings of mental disorganization, fear, or even

panic that prevent some people from effectively learning or

working with mathematics (Tobias, 1980).  Many people, including

some mathematics teachers, have felt anxiety toward mathematics

at one time or another, but each person's experience is uniquely

his or her own.  While the causes of math anxiety are varied they

usually occur before adulthood and so by the time many students

reach college age they exhibit the symptoms of math anxiety and

A:\ANXIETY5                                  Doc 1 Pg 3 Ln 1" Pos 1"
```

Creating Headers Create a header for the rest of the paper by doing the following:

Keystroke	Action Resulting from Keystroke
[arrow]	Use the **[arrow]** keys, if necessary, to move the cursor to the first character on page 3 where the body of the paper begins (location **`Pg 3 Ln 1" Pos 1"`**).
[Shift-F8]	Selects the *Format* feature and displays its menu.
`P` (or **`2`**)	Selects **`Page`** and displays its menu.
`N` (or **`6`**)	Selects **`6 - Page Numbering`** so that you may change the number of the first page of text to 1 (i.e., the title and outline pages should not be counted in the page numbering).
	USERS OF VERSION 5.0 Pressing **`N`** (or **`6`**) will select **`New Page Number`** from the menu. Then press **`1`** followed by **[Enter]** to set the new page number to 1. Skip the next three steps.
`N` (or **`1`**)	Selects **`New Page Number`** and deletes the current page number.
`1` ↵	Specifies that the page number should begin at **`1`**.
[Enter]	Exits from the **`Page Numbering`** menu and returns to the *Format* **`Page`** menu.
`H` (or **`3`**)	Selects **`Headers`** and asks if you want to define **`Header A`** or **`Header B`**.
`A` (or **`1`**)	Selects **`Header A`**.
`P` (or **`2`**)	Selects **`Every Page`** and displays a blank header screen.
[Alt-F6]	Right justifies the line about to be entered.
	Type in the following header (use your own name, of course):
	`Dennis Adams, page`
[Ctrl-B] ↵	Recall that pressing **[Ctrl-B]** will display the code **`^B`**, which instructs WordPerfect to insert the current page number at that location in the header.
[F7]	Exits the header definition.
[F7]	Exits the *Format* feature and returns to the editing screen. Note that the page number on the status line has changed from **`Pg 3`** to **`Pg 1`** to reflect the renumbering. Also note that the line position has changed from **`Ln 1" to Ln 1.5"`** to accommodate the header you just installed.
[F10]	Requests that the document be saved.
`A:\ANXIETY6` ↵	Provides the file specification for this draft of the document and returns to the editing screen.

Inserting Footnotes A footnote needs to be inserted after the words **`Math anxiety`** in the first sentence of the body of the paper. Footnotes and endnotes are used to make comments without interrupting the flow of the text in the document. *Footnotes* are placed at the bottom (foot) of the page on which they are referenced while *endnotes* are gathered together and placed at the back (end) of the document.

WordPerfect allows you to have both footnotes and endnotes in the same document. The notes are automatically numbered and placed either at the bottom of the page (footnotes) or in a location of your choice in the document (endnotes).

Keystroke	Action Resulting from Keystroke
[arrow]	Use the [arrow] keys or mouse to move the cursor to the space after the words **Math anxiety** (location **Pg 1 Ln 2.5" Pos 2.7"**).
[Ctrl-F7]	Selects the *Footnote/Endnote* feature and displays its menu.
F (or **1**)	Selects **Footnote** and displays its menu.
C (or **1**)	Selects **Create** and displays an almost-blank screen with the number **1** in the upper left-hand corner. Type the following footnote:

```
     1The term mathaphobia is used in place of math anxiety by
many mathematics educators._
```

Keystroke	Action Resulting from Keystroke
[F7]	Exits the **Footnote** option and returns to the editing screen.

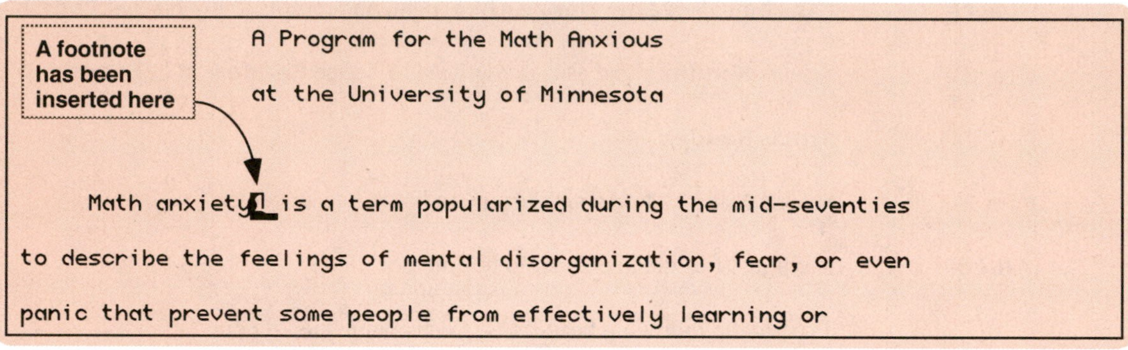

Keystroke	Action Resulting from Keystroke
[F10]	Requests that the document be saved.
A:\ANXIETY7 ↵	Provides the file specification for this draft of the document and returns to the editing screen.

Creating Hanging Paragraphs The paragraphs beginning with the word **Phase** need to be changed into hanging paragraphs.

Keystroke	Action Resulting from Keystroke
[arrow]	Use the [arrow] keys or mouse to move the cursor to the first letter of the word **Phase** (location **Pg 1 Ln 9.17" Pos 1"**). **USERS OF VERSION 5.0** Because of slight differences in the way version 5.0 formats documents, the location of the word **Phase** will be **Pg 2 Ln 1.5" Pos 1"**. The rest of the positions given in this section may be slightly off also.
[F4] [F4]	Indents the paragraph two tab stops to the right of the cursor.

Continued . . .

Keystroke	Action Resulting from Keystroke
[Shift-Tab]	Moves the first line back (to the left) one tab stop. This creates the hanging part of the paragraph.
[arrow]	Use the [arrow] keys or mouse to move the cursor to the first letter of the next occurrence of the word **Phase** (location **Pg 2 Ln 2.5" Pos 1"**). This will reformat the paragraph:

```
     Phase 1.  Intense emotional negative reactions to situations
--------------------------------------------------------------------------------
          where numbers are required.  This may be caused by
          unpleasant experiences with mathematics in the past.
          These feelings lead to ...
Phase 2.  Avoidance of situations in which mathematics is a part.
People who dislike working with numbers will naturally try to
avoid situations where numbers must be used.  This avoidance
leads to ...
Phase 3.  Poor preparation in mathematics.  Obviously, if a
person avoids mathematics, she or he will not get much practice
or try to learn new mathematics.  This lack of preparation leads
to ...
A:\ANXIETY7                                   Doc 1 Pg 2 Ln 2.5" Pos 1"
```

Page-break marker

Repeat this procedure for each paragraph beginning with the word **Phase** (at lines **Ln 2.5, Ln 3.83, Ln 5.17, and Ln 6.83**).

Centering and Boldfacing Section Titles Center and boldface the title of the second section of the paper (**The Math Anxiety Program of the University of Minnesota**).

Keystroke	Action Resulting from Keystroke
[arrow]	Use the [arrow] keys or mouse to move the cursor to the first letter of the word **The** (location **Pg 2 Ln 9.83" Pos 1"**).
	REMEMBER . . . you can use your mouse to select the block and then skip the next two steps. In this case, using the keyboard is probably easier.
[Alt-F4]	Selects the *Block* feature.

Continued . . .

Keystroke	Action Resulting from Keystroke
[End]	Moves the cursor to the last character in the section title (location **Pg 2 Ln 9.83" Pos 6.5"**).
[Shift-F6] Y	Selects the *Center* feature and centers the title.
[arrow]	Use the **[arrow]** keys or mouse to again move the cursor to the first letter of the word **The** (location **Pg 2 Ln 9.83" Pos 1.45"**).
[Alt-F4]	Selects the *Block* feature.
[End]	Moves the cursor to the last character in the section title (location **Pg 2 Ln 9.83" Pos 7.05"**).
[F6]	Selects the *Bold* feature and makes the title bold.
↓	Reformats the line.

```
        course, leads to ...

     Phase 1.  Intense emotional negative reactions...and so on.

     This cycle is often repeated over and over until the math

anxious person completely adjusts his or her life so that

mathematics is avoided no matter what the cost.  By the time

adulthood is reached, the math anxious person may be convinced

(with good evidence) that he or she cannot do mathematics.

Without intervention, the cycle is rarely broken (Mathison &

Robertson 1980).
                                                    Page-break marker

    The Math Anxiety Program of the University of Minnesota _
-------------------------------------------------------------------------
     The Math Anxiety Program of the University of Minnesota was
A:\ANXIETY7                                Doc 1 Pg 2 Ln 9.83" Pos 7.05"
```

Follow the same procedure to center, boldface, and properly space the titles of the sections **Conclusion** (location **Pg 4 Ln 7.5" Pos 1"**) and **Works Cited** (location **Pg 5 Ln 3.5" Pos 1"**).

[F10]	Requests that the document be saved.
A:\ANXIETY8 ↵	Provides the file specification for this draft of the document and returns to the editing screen.

Formatting the References Section The references in the **`Works Cited`** section need to be set up as hanging paragraphs.

Keystroke	*Action Resulting from Keystroke*
[arrow]	Use the **[arrow]** keys or mouse to move the cursor to the first letter of the word **`Hendel`** (location **`Pg 5 Ln 4.17" Pos 1"`**) in the **`Works Cited`** section.
[F4]	Indents the paragraph one tab stop to the right of the cursor.
[Shift-Tab]	Moves the first line back (to the left) one tab stop. This creates the hanging part of the reference.
[arrow]	Use the **[arrow]** keys or mouse to move the cursor to the first letter of the next reference (**`Kogleman`** at **`Pg 5 Ln 5.5" Pos 1"`**). This will reformat the paragraph:

```
                          Works Cited

Hendel, D. D. (1977).  The Math Anxiety Program: its genesis and
     evaluation in Continuing Education for Women.  Minneapolis:
     University of Minnesota, Measurement Services Center.

Kogelman, S. & Warren, J. (1978).  Mind over math.  New York:
Dial Press.

Lindoo, S. (1988).  Report of a survey of the CEW Math Anxiety
Program.  Minneapolis:  University of Minnesota, Department of
Continuing Education for Women.
A:\ANXIETY8                             Doc 1 Pg 5 Ln 5.5" Pos 1"
```

Repeat the process for each of the references listed.

The names of the books and reports listed in the **`Works Cited`** section must be underlined.

Keystroke	*Action Resulting from Keystroke*
[arrow]	Use the **[arrow]** keys or mouse to move the cursor to the first letter of the title of the first reference (**`The Math Anxiety Program`** located at **`Pg 5 Ln 4.17" Pos 3.3"`**) in the **`Works Cited`** section.

Continued . . .

Keystroke	Action Resulting from Keystroke
	REMEMBER . . . you can use your mouse to select the block and then skip the next two steps.
[Alt-F4]	Selects *Block* feature.
[arrow]	Use the **[arrow]** keys or mouse to move the cursor to the last character in the title (location **`Pg 5 Ln 4.16" Pos 5.9"`**).
[F8]	Underlines the title. Repeat the process for each of the references listed and then save the document.
[F10]	Requests that the document be saved.
`A:\ANXIETY9` ↵	Provides the file specification for this draft of the document and returns to the editing screen.

Paginating the Document Finally, check that the pagination of the document makes sense by scrolling through it and noting where the page breaks occur. You may want to make some final adjustments by adding some blank lines and deleting others. Save the final document using the name **`ANXIETY.FIN`**.

Reviewing the Final Document The final document should look like that shown below. Remember, your document might look slightly different because of the printer you are using and how you fine tuned the formatting.

```
A Program for the Math Anxious

at the University of Minnesota


by

Dennis Adams



                    Professor Gidmark
```

```
        A Program for the Math Anxious

        at the University of Minnesota

THESIS:  Math anxiety is a problem for many adults, but
         intervention programs, such as the one at the
         University of Minnesota, can help students
         overcome their anxiety and learn mathematics.

I.   General comments
     A.  Definition
     B.  Symptoms
II.  Cyclic nature of math anxiety
     A.  Past experiences
     B.  Avoidance
     C.  Poor preparation
     D.  Poor performance
III. The math anxiety program at the University of Minnesota
     A.  Genesis
         1.  History of department offering
             program
         2.  Development of program
     B.  Clientele served
     C.  Description of current program
IV.  Conclusion
```

Dennis Adams, page 1

A Program for the Math Anxious
at the University of Minnesota

Math anxiety[1] is a term popularized during the mid-seventies to describe the feelings of mental disorganization, fear, or even panic that prevent some people from effectively learning or working with mathematics (Tobias, 1980). Many people, including some mathematics teachers, have felt anxiety toward mathematics at one time or another, but each person's experience is uniquely his or her own. While the causes of math anxiety are varied they usually occur before adulthood and so by the time many students reach college age they exhibit the symptoms of math anxiety and the problem interferes with their performances in situations where mathematics is required.

Some people are able to channel the feelings of anxiety into interest and excitement and the anxiety is not a serious problem. However, for the severely math anxious person, the excitement crosses over into panic and the anxiety becomes debilitating. Emotions take over control of the mind and body and productive work grinds to a halt.

The symptoms exhibited by the math anxious may lead to a vicious cycle of math avoidance characterized by the following (Kogelman & Warren 1978):

[1]The term mathaphobia is used in place of math anxiety by many mathematics educators.

Dennis Adams, page 2

Phase 1. Intense emotional negative reactions to situations where numbers are required. This may be caused by unpleasant experiences with mathematics in the past. These feelings lead to ...

Phase 2. Avoidance of situations in which mathematics is a part. People who dislike working with numbers will naturally try to avoid situations where numbers must be used. This avoidance leads to ...

Phase 3. Poor preparation in mathematics. Obviously, if a person avoids mathematics, she or he will not get much practice or try to learn new mathematics. This lack of preparation leads to ...

Phase 4. Poor performance in mathematics. As with any other physical or cognitive process, people who rarely work with mathematics will not be able to do it when they have to. This lack of ability to perform, of course, leads to ...

Phase 1. Intense emotional negative reactions...and so on.

This cycle is often repeated over and over until the math anxious person completely adjusts his or her life so that mathematics is avoided no matter what the cost. By the time adulthood is reached, the math anxious person may be convinced (with good evidence) that he or she cannot do mathematics. Without intervention, the cycle is rarely broken (Mathison & Robertson 1980).

Dennis Adams, page 3

The Math Anxiety Program of the University of Minnesota

The Math Anxiety Program of the University of Minnesota was designed to help math anxious adults learn basic mathematics. The program is offered in the evenings through the department of Continuing Education for Women (CEW). This department was created in 1960 for the purpose of relating higher education to the changing needs of women. Its original objective was to identify the educational needs of women and to provide the resources that would assist them in developing their abilities to the fullest. Today, CEW serves the educational needs of approximately 6,000 women and men each year. CEW is typical of the many specialized departments and colleges housed within the University whose purpose is to provide services to students with widely varying academic abilities and backgrounds. Indeed, through the General College, one of the fifteen colleges that comprise the University, arithmetic, elementary, and intermediate algebra are taught in noncredit courses to approximately 2,700 students per year.

The CEW Math Anxiety Program had its beginnings in 1975 when an accounting professor and an economics professor came to CEW to discuss the academic problems being experienced by some of the women in their classes. These women were highly intelligent and motivated. Many had earned college degrees or had successfully completed some college work, but were having difficulty coping with the quantitative aspects of the accounting and economics

Dennis Adams, page 4

courses. The students spoke of blocking out numbers, avoiding situations requiring the use of mathematics, not remembering how to do simple computations, and developing tension when faced with computations and testing.

The CEW staff investigated the situation by talking to the students and the course instructors, and by examining the available literature on the problems women have with mathematics. This research led to the development of the Math Anxiety Program in 1976 (Hendel 1977). Since then, over 5,000 students (80% of whom are women) ranging in age from 14 to 73 (average 28) have taken mathematics courses offered through the program (Lindoo, 1988). Approximately 82% of the current program participants are working full- or part-time, 14% are regular students (at the University or at other two-year or four-year colleges), and 14% classify themselves as homemakers. Currently the program offers courses in arithmetic, elementary and intermediate algebra, and introductory statistics. The CEW department supports the small administrative costs required to run the program and student tuition covers the cost of instruction.

Conclusion

Math anxiety is a serious problem for some adults. The Department of Continuing Education for Women at the University of Minnesota has developed a comprehensive program to help adult students who suffer from math anxiety understand their problems and learn basic mathematics. The three components of the program,

Dennis Adams, page 5

a diagnostic clinic, individualized tutoring, and content courses, are designed to analyze student needs, both mathematical and emotional, and to address those needs in a sensitive and humanistic manner. While developing such a program is time consuming, it is not difficult and, once the program is implemented, it is self-supporting.

Works Cited

Hendel, D. D. (1977). The Math Anxiety Program: its genesis and evaluation in Continuing Education for Women. Minneapolis: University of Minnesota, Measurement Services Center.

Kogelman, S. & Warren, J. (1978). Mind over math. New York: Dial Press.

Lindoo, S. (1988). Report of a survey of the CEW Math Anxiety Program. Minneapolis: University of Minnesota, Department of Continuing Education for Women.

Mathison, M. A. & Robertson, D. F. (1980, August). Interventions in math anxiety for adults. Paper presented at the Fourth International Congress on Mathematical Education, Berkeley, CA.

Tobias, S. (1980). Overcoming math anxiety. Boston: Houghton Mifflin.

Generating a Table of Contents and Index

For long or complex documents, a table of contents (sometimes referred to as TOC) and an index make finding particular items easier for the reader who does not have the time, desire, or need to read the entire document. A table of contents is a listing of the major topics with corresponding page numbers and usually is located at the beginning of the document. An index provides a detailed list of the entire contents with page references and is usually located at the end of the document.

The term paper developed in the previous section is really too short to have a table of contents or an index but let's generate both just to see how it is done in WordPerfect.

There are three general steps in the process:

1. Mark the text to be included in the table of contents or index using the *Mark Text* feature.
2. Specify the location for the table of contents or index and define its form (if desired).
3. Generate the table or index.

• Creating a Table of Contents •

First, let's generate the table of contents and place it just after the thesis statement (just before the first page of text in the document) and include the three section headings **The Math Anxiety Program of the University of Minnesota**, **Conclusion**, and **Works Cited**.

Begin the process with the document **ANXIETY.FIN** displayed on the WordPerfect screen.

Mark the Text Mark the text to be included in the table of contents.

Keystroke	Action Resulting from Keystroke
[arrow]	Use the **[arrow]** keys or mouse to move the cursor to the first letter of the section heading **`The Math Anxiety Program of the University of Minnesota`** (location **`Pg 3 Ln 1.5" Pos 1.45"`**).

Be careful when you position the cursor. Recall that we inserted a page numbering code to renumber the pages so that the body of the paper begins on page 1. If you start at the top of the document and press **[PageDown]** twice, the cursor will be placed at the top of the third page (which is actually page 1 of the body of the document). The status line may show this as **`Pg 3`** because the cursor is directly on the page renumbering code and so it has not yet taken effect. This is not the "page 3" you want!

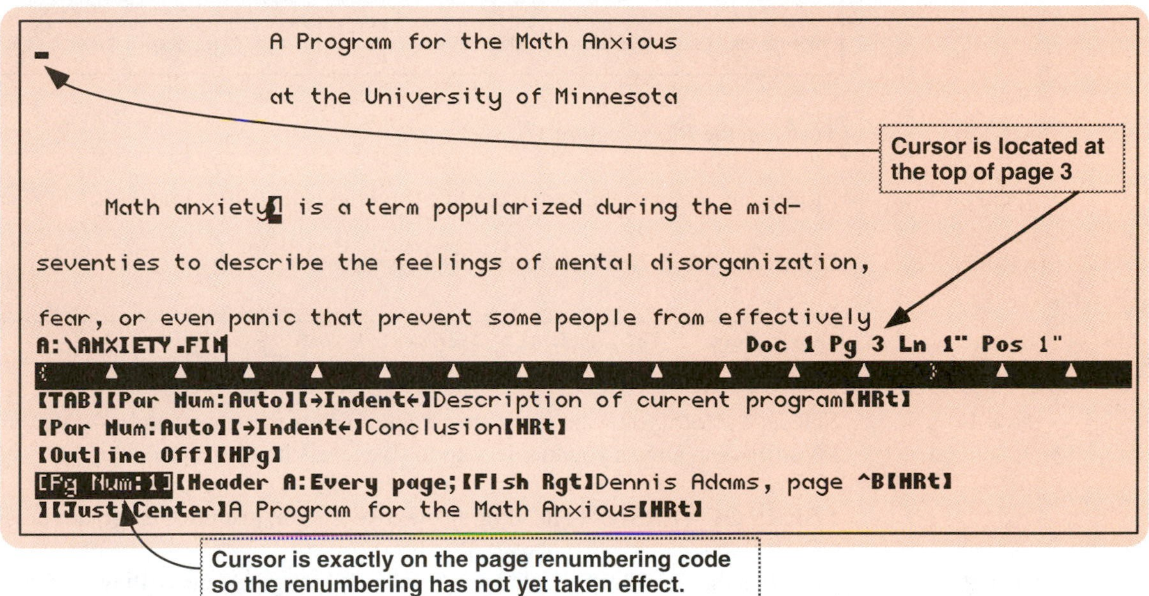

If you press the **[right arrow]** key once, the cursor in the text window remains where it is but the cursor in the *Reveal Codes* window moves one code to the right. Now the **`Pg`** indicator on the status line shows that you are on page 1 because the page renumbering has taken effect.

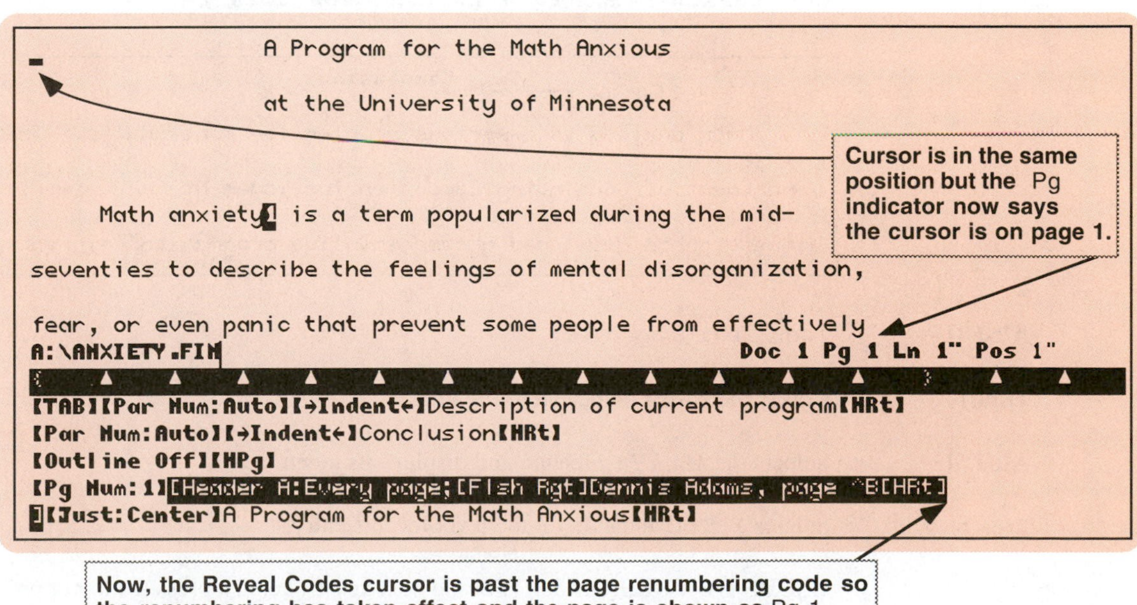

Continued . . .

Keystroke	Action Resulting from Keystroke
	Thus, be sure you are at the correct position in the document (**Pg 3 Ln 1.5" Pos 1.45"**) before you mark the text. The cursor should be located as shown below:

Cursor

```
The Math Anxiety Program of the University of Minnesota
     The Math Anxiety Program of the University of Minnesota was
designed to help math anxious adults learn basic mathematics. The
program is offered in the evenings through the department of
```

Keystroke	Action Resulting from Keystroke
[Alt-F4]	Turns on the *Block* feature.
[End]	Moves the cursor to the end of the line (highlights the entire line).
[Alt-F5]	Selects the *Mark Text* feature and displays its menu.

```
Mark for: 1 ToC; 2 List; 3 Index; 4 ToA: 0
```

Keystroke	Action Resulting from Keystroke
C (or **1**)	Selects **1 ToC** (you want to define a **T**able **o**f **C**ontents entry) and asks you for the level for this entry (WordPerfect allows you to select up to five levels in a table of contents).
	USERS OF VERSION 5.0 For the next keystroke, just press **1** (do not press **[Enter]**).
1 ↵	Specifies that this entry should be in level 1 and returns to the editing screen.
	The other two table of contents entries can be selected using the same procedure.
[arrow]	Use the **[arrow]** keys or mouse to move the cursor to the first letter of the section heading **Conclusion** (location **Pg 4 Ln 7.5" Pos 3.75"**).

Cursor

```
          Conclusion
     Math anxiety is a serious problem for some adults.  The
Department of Continuing Education for Women at the University of
Minnesota has developed a comprehensive program to help adult
```

Keystroke	Action Resulting from Keystroke
[Alt-F4]	Turns on the *Block* feature.
[End]	Moves the cursor to the end of the line.
[Alt-F5]	Selects the *Mark Text* feature and displays its menu.
C (or **1**)	Selects **1 ToC** and asks for the level for this entry.
	USERS OF VERSION 5.0 For the next keystroke, just press **1** (do not press **[Enter]**).
1 ↵	Specifies the level and returns to the editing screen.

Continued . . .

Keystroke	Action Resulting from Keystroke
[arrow]	Use the **[arrow]** keys or mouse to move the cursor to the first letter of the section heading **`Works Cited`** (location **`Pg 5 Ln 2.83" Pos 3.7"`**).

```
          Cursor ——►  Works Cited
Hendel, D. D. (1977).  The Math Anxiety Program: its genesis and
     evaluation in Continuing Education for Women.  Minneapolis:
     University of Minnesota, Measurement Services Center.
```

Keystroke	Action Resulting from Keystroke
[Alt-F4]	Turns on the *Block* feature.
[End]	Moves the cursor to the end of the line.
[Alt-F5]	Selects the *Mark Text* feature and displays its menu.
C (or **1**)	Selects **`1 ToC`** and asks for the level for this entry.
	USERS OF VERSION 5.0 For the next keystroke, just press **1** (do not press **[Enter]**).
1 ↵	Specifies the level and returns to the editing screen.
	The three entries now have been selected.

Specify the Location Specify the location for the table of contents and define its form (if desired).

Keystroke	Action Resulting from Keystroke
[Home] [Home] ↑	Moves the cursor to the top of the document.
[PageDown] [PageDown]	Moves the cursor to the top of the third page of the document (after the title page and the outline page).
[Ctrl-Enter]	Inserts a hard page break (so that the table of contents appears on its own page).
↑	Moves the cursor up to the newly inserted blank page.
`Table of Contents` ↵	
	Specifies the title for this page. The screen should look like the following:

Continued . . .

Keystroke	Action Resulting from Keystroke

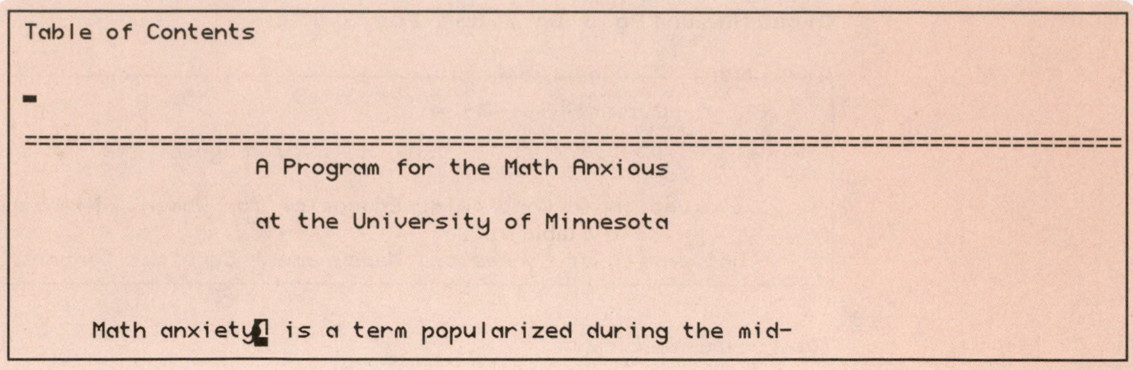

```
Table of Contents

▬
==========================================================================
                    A Program for the Math Anxious

                    at the University of Minnesota


      Math anxiety1 is a term popularized during the mid-
```

At this point you need to tell WordPerfect to insert a **ToC** marker (so that it knows where to put the **T**able **o**f **C**ontents); you also may change some of the default settings for the form of the table of contents.

Keystroke	Action Resulting from Keystroke
[Alt-F5]	Selects the *Mark Text* feature and displays its menu.
D (or **5**)	Selects **5 Define** and displays its menu.
C (or **1**)	Selects **1 - Define Table of Contents** and displays its menu.

```
Table of Contents Definition

      1 - Number of Levels               1

      2 - Display Last Level in          No
            Wrapped Format

      3 - Page Numbering - Level 1       Flush right with leader
                           Level 2
                           Level 3
                           Level 4
                           Level 5
```

For this simple example, we will use the default settings, which specify one level in the table, no wrapping of the last level, and page numbering that is flush right with a leader. These items may be changed as desired (for more information, see the *WordPerfect Reference Manual*).

[F7]	Exits the menu and returns to the editing screen. WordPerfect inserts a hidden code **[Def Mark:ToC,1:5]** to show where the table of contents will be placed after it is generated.

Generate the Table of Contents

Keystroke	Action Resulting from Keystroke
[Alt-F5]	Selects the *Mark Text* feature and displays its menu.
G (or **6**)	Selects **6 Generate** and displays its menu.
G (or **5**)	Selects **5 - Generate Tables, Indexes, Cross-References, etc**, which specifies that you want to generate a table and reminds you that any preexisting tables will be replaced. Typing **Y** for **Y**es will generate a new table while typing **N** for **N**o will return to the editing screen.
Y	Specifies that you want to generate a new table.

WordPerfect will display a **Generation in progress** message on the status line and in a few seconds will return to the editing screen.

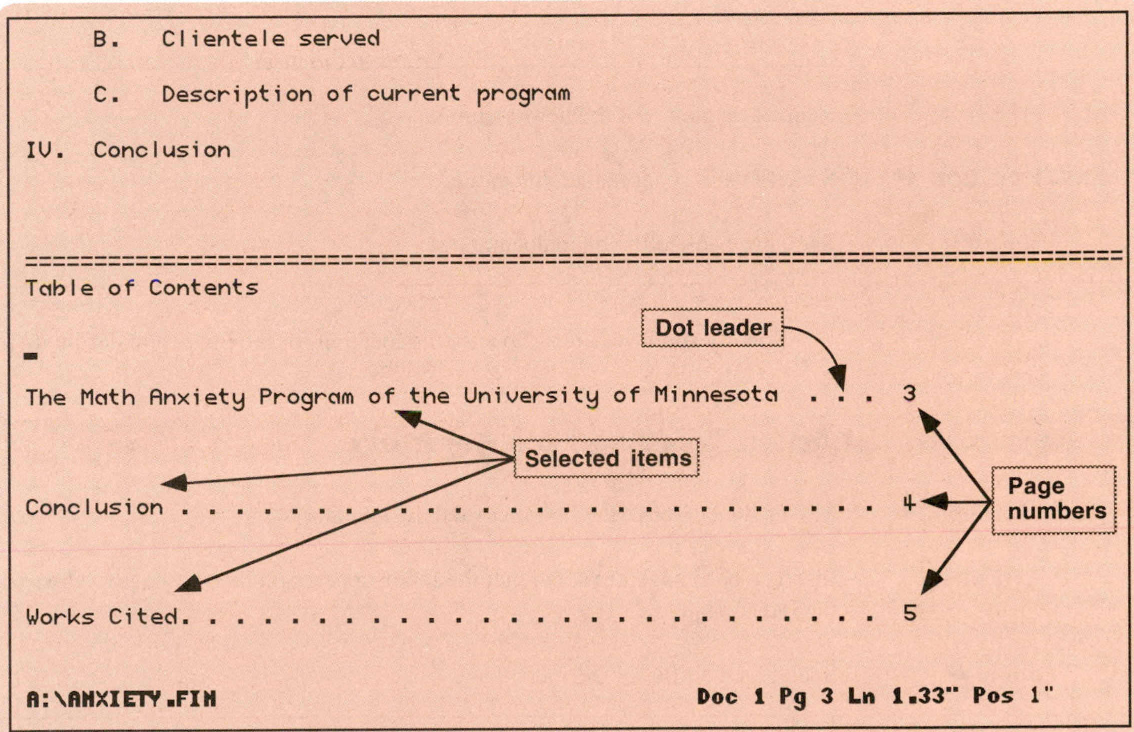

Depending on whether or not you included the various formatting codes (e.g., for bold) when you selected the entries for the table of contents, you may have to clean up the table a bit. That can be done using *Reveal Codes* (press the **[Alt-F3]** keys) and the standard editing techniques to remove the unwanted codes.

Press **[F10]** and save the document under the name **ANXIETY.TOC**.

• Creating an Index •

Now let's generate an index and place it at the end of the document. Normally, an index would include many references, but for this example let's just include occurrences of **anxiety**, **symptom**, and **University of Minnesota** from the body of the paper.

Mark the Text Mark the text to be included in the index. This can be done as with the table of contents by blocking each entry and then using the *Mark Text* feature (use the **[Alt-F5]** keys). One minor difference is that if the entry is a single word, you do not have to block it before marking. Simply place the cursor anywhere in the word to be marked and press **[Alt-F5]**, then **I** (or **3**) to select **Index**, and then press **[Enter]** twice.

Index entries may also be indicated through the use of a *concordance file*, which is basically another WordPerfect document that already contains all the index entries. You then ask WordPerfect to index all words in the main document that also occur in the concordance file.

While both individual indexing and concordance file indexing can be mixed within a single document, we will use the latter method to create the index for the term paper.

Keystroke	Action Resulting from Keystroke
[Shift-F3]	Switches to a blank WordPerfect screen. Type the three index entries, one per line, and then save the file. For large concordance files, if you type the entries in alphabetical order (or sort the file after you have finished typing all the entries), the indexing process will go much faster.

Type the following three entries:

```
anxiety
symptoms
University of Minnesota
```

Keystroke	Action Resulting from Keystroke
[F10]	Requests a name for the new document.
ANXIETY.CON ↵	Specifies the concordance file name.
[Shift-F3]	Switches back to the main document.

Specify the Location Specify the location for the index and define its form (if desired).

Keystroke	Action Resulting from Keystroke
[Home] [Home] ↓	Moves the cursor to the bottom of the document.
[Ctrl-Enter]	Inserts a hard page break (so that the index appears on its own page). Now, you may type the title for the index page.
Index ↵	Specifies the title for the index page.

As was the case with the table of contents, at this point you may modify the default definition of the form of the index. For this simple example, we will use the default settings. These items may be changed as desired (for more information, see the *WordPerfect Reference Manual*).

Keystroke	Action Resulting from Keystroke
[Alt-F5]	Selects the *Mark Text* feature and displays its menu.
D (or **5**)	Selects **5 Define** and displays its menu.
I (or **3**)	Selects **3 - Define Index** and asks for the name of the concordance file.
A:ANXIETY.CON ↵	Specifies the name of the concordance file.
2	Specifies the type of numbering to be used (**Page numbers to follow entries**) and returns to the editing screen.

Pagination We need to make one minor adjustment before we generate the index. Recall that because we wanted to begin the numbering of the body of the text with page 1 we had to insert a code that told WordPerfect to begin renumbering the pages just before the body of the text began. This means that there are two *page 1s* (the title page and the first page of the body of the text), two *page 2s* (the outline page and the second page of the body of the text), and two *page 3s* (the table of contents and the third page of the body of the text). If we generate the index with the current page numbering system, WordPerfect will not consider each *page 1* (or *2* or *3*) separately and the result will look like the following:

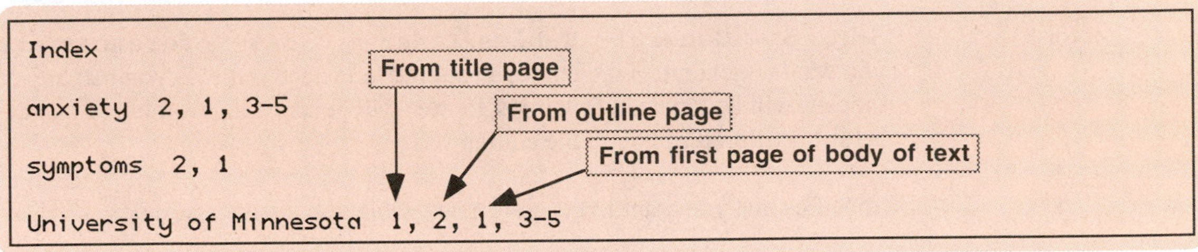

Look at the entry for **`University of Minnesota`**. It appears on both *page 1*s and makes the entry look strange. A simple way to fix this problem is to insert a WordPerfect code at the beginning of the document that says to use Roman numerals (i, ii, iii) for the first set of page numbers and Arabic numerals (1, 2, 3) for the second set of page numbers.

Keystroke	Action Resulting from Keystroke
[Home] [Home] ↑	Moves the cursor to the top of the document.
[Shift-F8]	Selects the *Format* feature and displays its menu.
`P` (or **`2`**)	Selects **`2 - Page`** and displays its menu.
`N` (or **`6`**)	Selects **`6 - Page Numbering`** and displays its menu.
	USERS OF VERSION 5.0 The cursor will be under the **`1`** just to the right of **`6 - New Page Number`**. Skip the next step.
`N` (or **`1`**)	Selects **`1 - New Page Number`**, blanks the number indicated, and moves the cursor to that position.

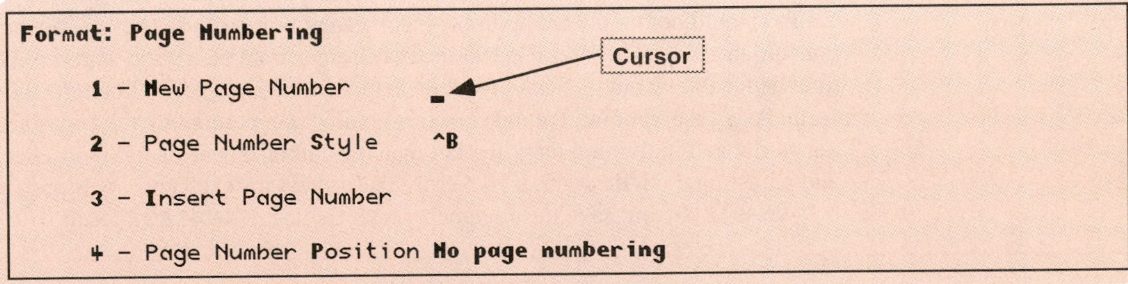

Keystroke	Action Resulting from Keystroke
`i` ↵	Specifies that the page numbering is to begin with **`i`** (i.e., page one using Roman numerals).
[F7]	Exits the *Format* feature and returns to the editing screen.

The code **`[Pg Num:i]`** has been inserted into the document indicating that page numbering is to begin at **`i`** (i.e., Roman numeral one). Now, when the index is created, the entries on the first three pages will have numbers **`i`**, **`ii`**, and **`iii`** while the numbers after that will have Arabic numbers.

Generate the Index Now let's generate the index by doing the following:

Keystroke	Action Resulting from Keystroke
[Alt-F5]	Selects the *Mark Text* feature and displays its menu.
G (or **6**)	Selects **6 Generate** and displays its menu.
G (or **5**)	Selects **5 - Generate Tables**, **Indexes**, **Cross-References**, **etc**, which specifies that you want to generate a table of contents and index and reminds you that any preexisting tables or indexes will be replaced. Typing **Y** for **Y**es will generate a new table of contents and index while typing **N** for **N**o will return you to the editing screen.
Y	Specifies that you want to generate a new table of contents and index.

WordPerfect will display **Generation in progress** on the status line and in a few seconds will return to the editing screen.

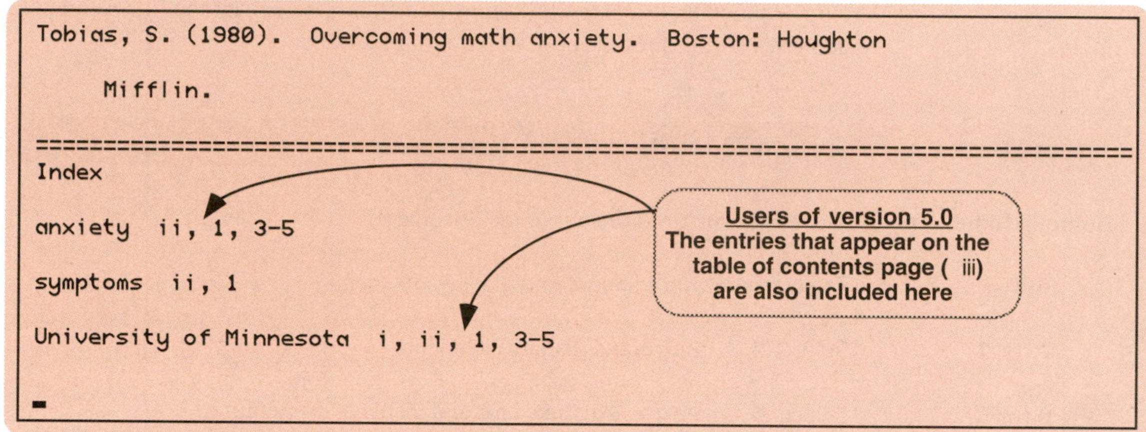

As was the case with the table of contents, you may want to edit the index. For example, you may not want the entries from the title and thesis pages included in the index. Also, the pages **3-5** for the **anxiety** entry imply that the anxiety topic begins on page 3 and goes through page 5. This may not be the case (i.e., the word may simply appear on page 3 and then again, in another context, on page 4 and then again on page 5). Thus, you may want to go back to check the context for each index entry to see if the index reflects what you want. In addition, different forms of the word (e.g., **anxieties** or **anxious**) would not be picked up in the index generation because they are not specifically included in the concordance file. The WordPerfect index feature gives you a good start but it takes a human who is knowledgeable about the contents of the paper and the subject to fine tune the index into a more useful form. As a case in point, the index of this book was generated by the computer using both a concordance file and individual marking, but then the authors spent many hours checking out the references and adjusting the index entries to be sure the context for each entry was properly stated.

Press **[F10]** and save the document under the name **ANXIETY.NDX**.

TO TAKE A BREAK Press **[F7]**, type **N**, type **Y**, remove diskette(s). To resume (hard disk): Insert *Data* diskette, type **A: ↵**, type **C:\WP51\WP ↵**. To resume (two drive): Insert diskettes, type **A: ↵**, type **B:WP ↵**.

Homework Exercises

① Use the **Word Search** option of the *List Files* feature (use the **[F5]** key) to search your *WordPerfect Data* diskette for the names of all documents that contain your name. When the search is completed, do a screen dump of the *List Files* screen.

---

② Create a WordPerfect document that contains the names, companies, phone numbers, and sales totals of some of your business contacts. Set up the document so that the name begins in column 1 (**Pos 1"**), the company in column 20 (**Pos 2.9"**), the phone number in column 35 (**Pos 4.4"**), and the total sales in column 45 (**Pos 5.4"**). The document should look like the following:

Column 1 (Pos 1")	Column 20 (Pos 2.9")	Column 35 (Pos 4.4")	Column 45 (Pos 5.4")
Bliss Bill,	NSP,	555-2311,	15221.00
Wheeler Katie,	Land O'Lakes,	555-2213,	25111.00
Moony Hal,	Geosyncronics,	555-0054,	15455.00
Bast Peg,	UNISYS,	555-6672,	12110.00

Save the document as a regular WordPerfect file (use the **[F10]** key) under the name **HWW3-02R** and then print it. Also, save the document as a text (ASCII) file (use the **[Ctrl-F5]** key to do this) under the name **HWW3-02T**.

---

③ Write a memo to one of your subordinates complimenting his or her outstanding performance over the last six months. List the things you are particularly pleased with (this may include things such as efficiency, hard work, cheerful disposition, dedication to the job, creativity, intelligence, and productivity). Save the document under the name **HWW3-03** and then print it.

---

④ Modify the memo from Exercise 3 by inserting, at the bottom of the memo, data from the file **HWW3-02T**, which you created in Exercise 2. Do this by moving to the bottom of the memo and typing **Below are listed the sales totals for the other top employees:**. Next, use *Text In/Out* to load the file **HWW3-02T** into the bottom of the memo. Save the document under the name **HWW3-04** and then print it.

---

⑤ Retrieve the document **HWW2-09**, which you created for Exercise 9 in Chapter 2 (word processing tutor advertisement), and type the following at the bottom: **Satisfied customers include:**. Then, use the cutting and pasting technique described in this chapter to copy the middle two lines from the file **HWW3-02R** (data for Katie and Hal) and paste them at the bottom of the document. Save the document as **HWW3-05** and then print it.

Continued . . .

⑥ Sort, in ascending order by last name, the data in the document **HWW3-02R**, which you created in Exercise 2. Save the document as **HWW3-06** and then print it.

---

⑦ Use string search to locate all occurrences of the string **555** in the document **HWW3-02R** from Exercise 2. Replace each **555** with **999**. Save the document as **HWW3-07** and then print it.

---

⑧ Use the *Merge* feature to create a personal letter to each of the following people:

First name	***Last name***	***Company***
Sandy	Loken	Happy Tooth Dental Supply, Inc.
Anita	Leggott	Fiddle Fine Frames, Inc.
Juan	Morales	Sunset Oil Company

Use the following form letter:

```
  Memo to:  (FIELD)1~  (FIELD)2~
Memo from:  Lea Wiger

     We are interested in talking to the employees of (FIELD)3~
     about our child care services.  I will be calling you
     soon to make arrangements for our presentation.
```

USERS OF VERSION 5.0 The field codes will look different than those shown above.

Save the database as **HWW3-08D** and then print it. Save the form letter as **HWW3-08L** and then print it. Finally, use the *Merge* feature to create the individual letters and print them.

---

⑨ Write a short essay on a subject of your choice (e.g., the beauty of the butterfly) and insert a graphic somewhere in the document. Select one of the graphics files (i.e., those with the extension **WPG** such as **BUTTRFLY.WPG**) from the ones that came with the WordPerfect program. Save the document as **HWW3-09** and then print it.

---

⑩ Create the document displayed below, save it as **HWW3-10**, and then print it. You will have to use the equation editor to create the equation.

For a right triangle, the length of the hypotenuse is given by the following formula:

$$C=\sqrt{A^2+B^2}$$

where C = the length of the hypotenuse
A = the length of one side
B = the length of the third side

USERS OF VERSION 5.0 Because version 5.0 does not have an equation editor you cannot do this exercise.

CHAPTER THREE

⑪ Create a macro that can be run by pressing **[Alt-H]** and save it on your *WordPerfect Data* diskette. The macro should set up a ruler with the left-hand margin set to 1 inch, the right-hand margin set to 3 inches, and a single tab set at 1.5 inches. To show that the macro has been saved, use the *Edit Macro* feature to display the macro codes, and do a screen dump.

---

⑫ Create a macro using the name **HW-TOP** and save it on your *WordPerfect Data* diskette. The macro should display a one-line header for your homework assignments for an English course with your name in the upper left-hand corner, the course number in the center, and the date in the upper right-hand corner of the display. To show that the macro has been saved, use the Edit Macro feature to display the macro codes and do a screen dump.

---

⑬ Use the *Outline* feature to create an outline for a paper on a topic of your choice. The outline should include at least three major headings (i.e., **I.**, **II.**, and **III.**), one of which should contain at least two subheadings (i.e., **A.** and **B.**). Save the document as **HWW3-13** and then print it.

---

⑭ Write a paper that is at least three pages long on a topic of your choice. The paper should follow the model described in this chapter including a title page, outline page, table of contents, header (with your name and the page number), and an index (with at least three entries) at the end. Save the document as **HWW3-14** and then print it.

---

⑮ Use the *Index* feature to create an index for one of your previously saved documents. The index should include at least three entries generated by a concordance file. Save concordance file as **HWW3-15C** and then print it. Save the final indexed document as **HWW3-15** and then print it.

Advanced DOS

Objectives *After you have completed this chapter, you should be able to*

- Define common terms associated with DOS.
- Explain the difference between internal and external DOS files.
- Use **DISKCOPY** and **DISKCOMP** to copy and compare entire diskettes.
- Use **COPY CON** to create text files from within the DOS environment.
- Use **TYPE** and **PRINT** to display and print the contents of files.
- Use **COPY** and **COMP** to copy and compare files or groups of files.
- Use **COPY** to merge files.
- Use global characters ***** and **?** with various DOS commands.
- Use **RENAME** to change the names of files.

CHAPTER 4

- Use **DELETE** to erase files or groups of files.
- Use **DIR** to display an entire directory or a selected part of a directory.
- Use **SORT** to produce a sorted directory.
- Use pipes to link DOS commands.
- Use **MORE** to display output one screen at a time.
- Use miscellaneous commands including **TIME**, **DATE**, **VOL**, **VER**, **CLS**, **LABEL**, and **PROMPT**.
- Use **PATH** to create an extended search path.
- Create an **AUTOEXEC.BAT** file.

Introduction

DOS is an acronym for the **D**isk **O**perating **S**ystem of the microcomputer. DOS tells the computer how to perform such operations as inputting data, storing data on disks, sending information to the screen or printer, and processing numerical data. If you are using an IBM PC, the DOS used by your computer is referred to as PC-DOS. If you are using an IBM-compatible computer (such as a Zenith or a Tandy), the DOS is called MS-DOS. MS-DOS was developed by Microsoft Corporation and is, for all practical purposes, identical to PC-DOS. We will refer to the disk operating system simply as DOS.

In this chapter we will examine the details of a number of DOS commands that enable us to create, modify, and get information about individual files and groups of files stored on a disk. Examples of such files are the commands, such as **FORMAT**, and the WordPerfect application and associated documents. In addition to commands like **DIR**, which were discussed briefly in previous chapters, we will discuss new commands designed to help the user better control the functioning of the computer to meet specific needs.

Definitions

Before reading this chapter, you should familiarize yourself with some of the terms frequently encountered when talking about DOS:

Command . . . (W193)An instruction given to the computer (e.g., **DIR**). *Internal* DOS commands are the ones most commonly used and so are built into DOS and stored in a file called **COMMAND.COM**. *External* DOS commands are stored in separate files whose names are listed in the DOS directory and whose contents must be read from the disk into RAM in order to operate (e.g., **FORMAT**). Files with the extensions **COM**, **EXE**, or **BAT** are external commands.

Directory . . . (W198) A listing of the names of files stored on a disk.

Disk Operating System (DOS) . . . (W192) A set of programs stored on disk that act as the interface between the user and the computer hardware.

File . . . . (W194) A collection of related information that is stored as a logical unit in the memory of the computer (e.g., a letter written in WordPerfect or the **FORMAT.COM** file in the DOS subdirectory).

Filter . . . (W200) A program or command that reads data from a file or input device (e.g., the keyboard), modifies the data (e.g., alphabetizes it), and then sends the modified data to another file or output device (e.g., the monitor).

Global character . . . (W199) A character (**?** or *****) that can take the place of one or more other characters in a command. These are sometimes referred to as *wild-card* characters.

Pipe . . . (W200) The chaining of DOS programs or commands so that the output from one program or command (e.g., **DIR**) can be used as the input of another program or command (e.g., **SORT**). The symbol **|**, called a pipe, is used to chain the two commands (e.g., **DIR | SORT** sorts the directory before displaying it).

Redirection . . . Instructing a program or command to receive its input from (or send its output to) some device other than the keyboard (for input) or the monitor (for output). The symbol **<** redirects input. The symbol **>** redirects output (e.g., **DIR > PRN** redirects the listing of the directory from the monitor to the printer).

Switch . . . (W201) An option in a DOS command that indicates how the command is to be carried out. Switches are always preceded by a **/**.

User Interface . . . The point of meeting between the computer and the computer user.

Disk Operating System (DOS)

Computer scientists are continually making refinements and adding features to computer systems. As new technology and ideas emerge, the operating system of the computer must be updated to work correctly with the new hardware and software. Thus, different versions of DOS appear from time to time and are given identifying decimal numbers such as 4.0. The first digit, 4, indicates that a major revision has been made to the operating system. The digit to the right of the decimal point, 0, refers to the number of minor revisions that have been made to the major revision. The first version of DOS appeared in 1980 and was labeled 1.0. When hard-disk drives became available DOS had to be modified (version 2.0) to work properly with them. Version 2.1 was needed to accommodate half-height disk drives and then version 3.0 was developed so that high capacity $5\frac{1}{4}$-inch floppy drives could be used. Version 3.1 addressed the needs of computer networks while version 3.2 allowed the use of $3\frac{1}{2}$-inch disk drives. Version 3.3 enabled the computer to use high density $3\frac{1}{2}$-inch disk drives and hard drives with a capacity of greater than 32 megabytes. Version 4.0 introduced the DOS shell (a simplified user interface) and the ability to run multiple programs simultaneously, while version 5.0 features on-line help and improved memory management.

This book uses version 4.0 of DOS. Most of the features we discuss will be found in DOS versions 2.0 or higher so even if your version of DOS is different from 4.0 you will probably not experience any major difficulties.

The DOS diskettes that come bundled with the microcomputer have many different commands, each of which carries out a different function. For example, the **DIR** command causes a listing of the names of all the files stored on the default directory to be displayed on the screen, while the **FORMAT** command prepares a blank diskette so that it can be used in an IBM microcomputer.

There are two types of DOS commands: internal and external. Internal DOS commands are the most commonly used commands and so are built into DOS and stored in a file called **COMMAND.COM**. When the computer is booted this file is loaded into the main memory. The directory command, **DIR**, is an example of an internal command. Its name does not appear in the DOS directory because it is a part of the file **COMMAND.COM**. In this chapter we will discuss the following internal DOS commands:

CLS	**COPY**	**DATE**	**DEL**	**DIR**	**PATH**
PROMPT	**RENAME**	**TIME**	**TYPE**	**VER**	**VOL**

External DOS commands are stored in separate files whose names are listed in the DOS directory and whose contents must be read from the disk in order to operate. Commands with the extensions **COM**, **EXE**, or **BAT** are external commands. **FORMAT** is an example of an external command; its name appears in the DOS directory as **FORMAT.COM**. The extension of an external command, such as **COM** in **FORMAT.COM**, is not needed when invoking the command.

Other types of file extensions include **SYS**, which tells the computer to perform certain actions important to the operating system; **DOC** or **TXT**, which indicate that a file is a text file; **BAS**, which indicates that a file was created using the programming language BASIC; and **BAT**, which says a file contains a series of commands that can be given to the computer in a batch (one right after the other).

There are many external commands and, in fact, the user may create and store his or her own external commands. We will discuss the following external commands in this chapter:

COMP DISKCOMP DISKCOPY FORMAT LABEL MORE PRINT SORT

Booting the Computer

Begin your work in this chapter by setting up the computer as follows:

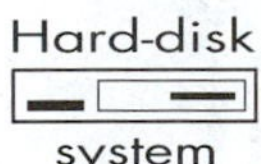

IF YOU ARE USING A HARD-DISK SYSTEM: Be sure the floppy disk drive is empty and then turn on the machine. The DOS files should be in a subdirectory called **\DOS** on the C: drive (if they are not, see your instructor for directions). Type **CD\DOS** ↵ to make the DOS subdirectory the default directory. The system prompt, **C:\DOS>**, should be displayed on the screen.

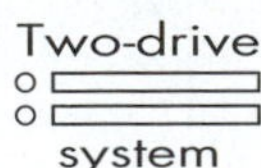

IF YOU ARE USING A TWO-DRIVE SYSTEM: Insert the DOS diskette into the A: drive and then turn on the machine. Enter the date and time if requested to do so. Then, move the DOS diskette to the B: drive and type **B:** ↵ to make B: the default drive. The system prompt, **B:\>**, should be displayed on the screen.

Have your *WordPerfect Data* diskette and a blank diskette handy—you will need to use both in the exercises that follow.

Commands for Entire Disks

You have already used the **FORMAT** command to prepare a blank diskette so that it could be used by an IBM microcomputer. This is an example of a command that acts on an entire disk at one time. Be careful! Commands that work on an entire disk at one time can have the effect of erasing or otherwise altering all of the files on the disk. If, for example, you tell the computer to format a disk that already contains files, all those files will be erased.

Remember, if you want to clear the contents of the screen, you may type **CLS** ↵. This will not affect information stored in the main memory or on any of the disks. Also, pressing **[Ctrl-C]** will abort most operations before they finish executing.

• Disk Copy Command •

The disk copy command (**DISKCOPY**) is an external command that makes a copy of an entire diskette at one time. Because this is an external command the DOS directory should be the default before executing this command.

A command such as **DISKCOPY A: B:** would copy the contents of the diskette in drive A: (called the *source* diskette) to the diskette in drive B: (called the *target* diskette). If the diskette in drive B: has not been formatted, then **DISKCOPY** will display the message **Formatting while copying** and format the target disk before writing to it. When **[Enter]** is pressed, the computer will request that the diskette to be copied be placed in the A: drive and that the blank diskette be placed in the B: drive. Once this is done, pressing any key will begin the copy process. Note that any information that might have been saved on the diskette in the B: drive is written over (erased) in much the same way as a tape recorder will record over previously recorded material. Also note that the diskettes in drives A: and B: must be the same size and capacity (e.g., if your computer has a $3\frac{1}{2}$-inch A: drive and a $5\frac{1}{4}$-inch B: drive then you cannot use both drives with **DISKCOPY**—in that case, use the **DISKCOPY A: A:** command given below).

If you have a one-floppy-drive system, you would use **DISKCOPY A: A:** to copy an entire diskette. This command tells the computer to use the same disk drive (A:) for both the source and the target diskette. The computer will prompt you to eject one diskette and insert the other at the proper times (this may force you to swap diskettes many times and therefore may take several minutes to complete).

When the copy process has finished, the computer will ask **Copy another diskette (Y/N)?** Typing **Y** (**Y**es) will cause the process to begin again. Typing **N** (**N**o) will return control to DOS and display the system prompt.

Try the **DISKCOPY** command by doing the following:

1. Write protect your *WordPerfect Data* diskette. If you are using a $5\frac{1}{4}$-inch diskette, place a write-protect tab (a piece of tape) over the write-enable notch in the upper right-hand corner; if you are using a $3\frac{1}{2}$-inch diskette, move the button in the upper right-hand corner so that the window is open.

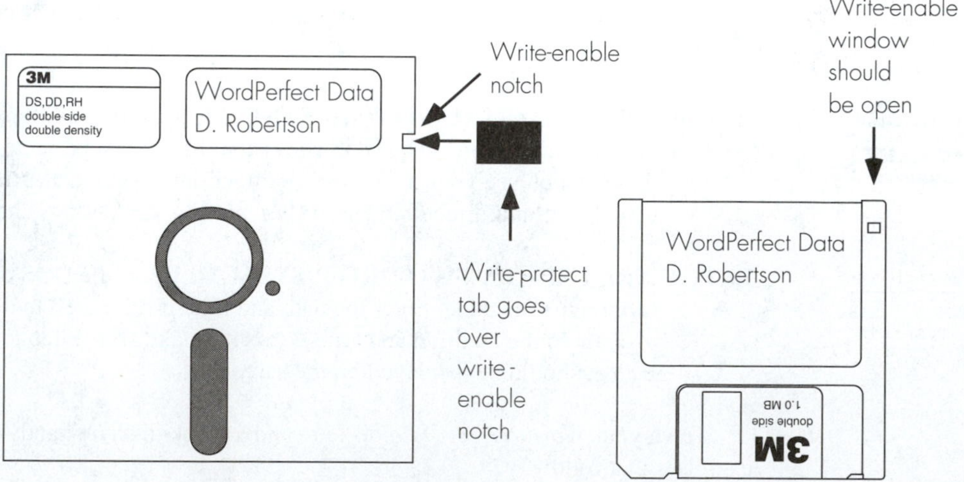

When a diskette is *write protected*, the computer is denied permission to write any information onto the diskette. This is important when using **DISKCOPY** because if you get mixed up and insert the *target* (blank) diskette into the drive when the computer asks for the *source* (master) diskette, the computer will copy the blank diskette onto the master diskette. In effect, the computer will make a copy of the blank diskette and you will end up with two blank diskettes rather than two copies of the master diskette. Remember, the computer always does what you tell it to do rather than what you mean for it to do.Write protection is a precaution against accidental loss of data. If you mix up the **DISKCOPY** command or the diskettes the write protection will stop the *WordPerfect Data* diskette from being erased.

2. Write *WPD-BU* (for WordPerfect data backup) on a diskette label and place the label on a blank diskette.

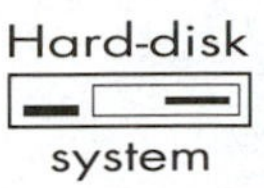

IF YOU ARE USING A HARD-DISK SYSTEM:

Keystroke	Action Resulting from Keystroke
DISKCOPY A: A: ↵	
	Begins the copy process. The computer will ask you to **Insert the SOURCE diskette in drive A:**. At this point, insert your write-protected *WordPerfect Data* diskette into the A: drive.
[Enter]	Continues the copy process. The computer will copy as much of the diskette as it can to main memory. It then will ask you to **Insert TARGET diskette in drive A:**. At this point, remove the the *WordPerfect Data* diskette and insert the blank diskette into the A: drive.
[Enter]	Continues the copy process. The computer will write the information from its main memory to the diskette. It then will ask you to **Insert the SOURCE diskette in drive A:** again. This process will continue until the disk has been copied.
N ↵	Specifies that you do not want to copy more diskettes and returns control to DOS.

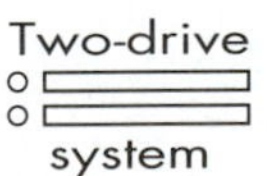

IF YOU ARE USING A TWO-DRIVE SYSTEM:

Keystroke	Action Resulting from Keystroke
DISKCOPY A: B: ↵	
	Begins the copy process. The computer will ask you to **Insert the SOURCE diskette in drive A:** and **Insert TARGET diskette in drive B:**. Remember, this only works if the A: and B: diskettes are the same size and capacity. If they are not, use **DISKCOPY A: A:**. At this point, insert the write-protected *WordPerfect Data/Boot* diskette into the A: drive and the blank diskette into the B: drive.
[Enter]	Continues the copy process. The computer will make the copy.
N ↵	Specifies that you do not want to copy more diskettes and returns control to DOS.
	Place the DOS diskette in the B: drive.

The entire process would look like the following for copying a high density diskette (1440K) on a hard-disk system with one floppy disk drive:

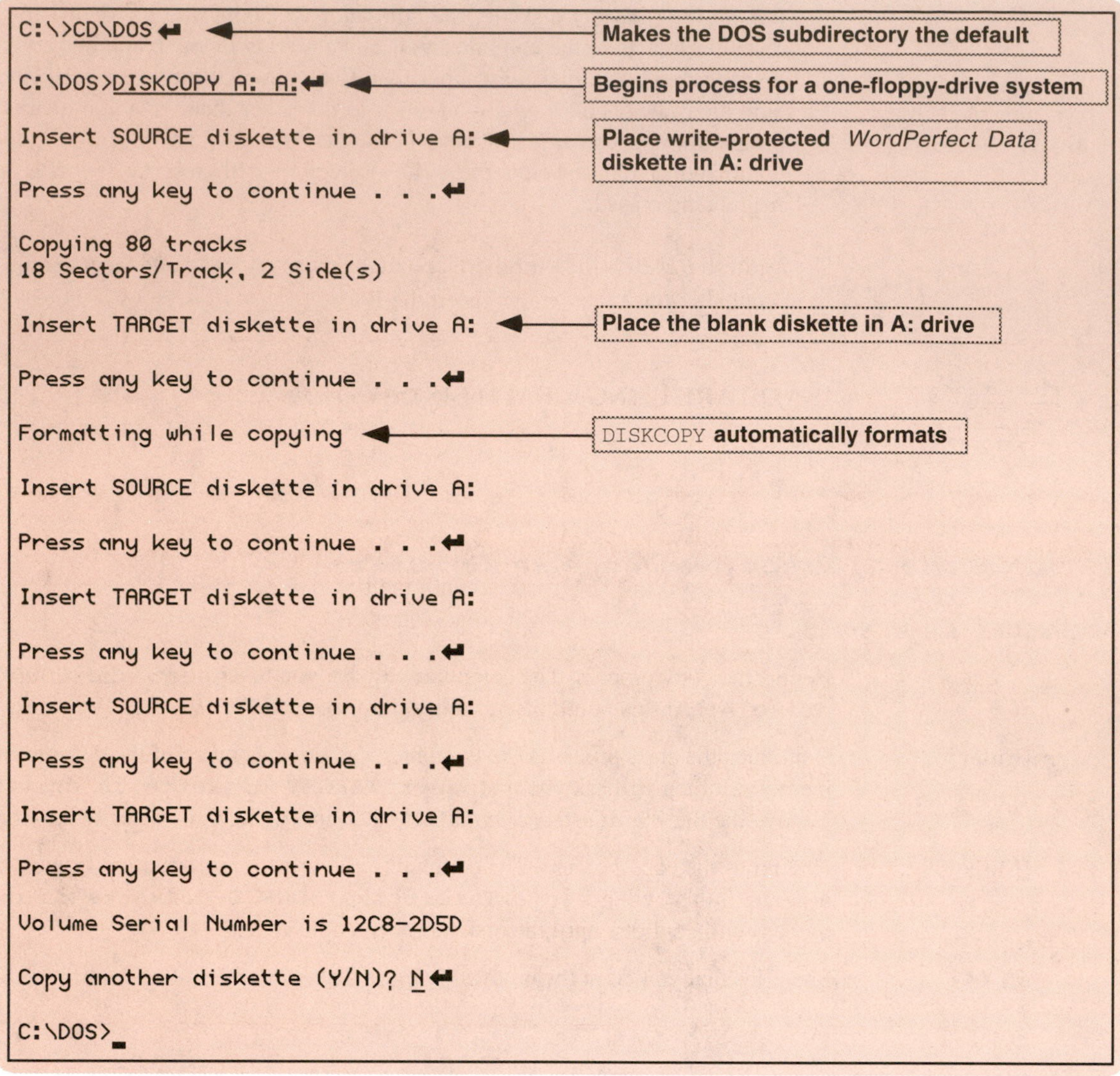

C:\>CD\DOS
Makes the DOS subdirectory the default
C:\DOS>DISKCOPY A: A:
Begins process for a one-floppy-drive system
Insert SOURCE diskette in drive A:
Place write-protected WordPerfect Data diskette in A: drive
Press any key to continue . . .
Copying 80 tracks
18 Sectors/Track, 2 Side(s)
Insert TARGET diskette in drive A:
Place the blank diskette in A: drive
Press any key to continue . . .
Formatting while copying
DISKCOPY automatically formats
Insert SOURCE diskette in drive A:
Press any key to continue . . .
Insert TARGET diskette in drive A:
Press any key to continue . . .
Insert SOURCE diskette in drive A:
Press any key to continue . . .
Insert TARGET diskette in drive A:
Press any key to continue . . .
Volume Serial Number is 12C8-2D5D
Copy another diskette (Y/N)? N
C:\DOS>

• *Disk Comparison Command* •

The disk comparison command (**DISKCOMP**) is an external command that compares the contents of two diskettes to see whether they are identical. This command may be used right after a **DISKCOPY** command to see if any errors were made in the copy process. If the diskettes are identical, the message **Diskettes compare OK** is issued. If **DISKCOMP** detects any differences, then the **DISKCOPY** process should be repeated.

The command **DISKCOMP A: B:** compares the contents of the diskette in drive A: to the contents of the diskette in drive B:. If you have a one-floppy-drive system, the command **DISKCOMP A: A:** should be used. It is similar to the above command except that the same drive (**A:**) is used for both the first and the second diskette.

Try the **DISKCOMP** command by doing the following:

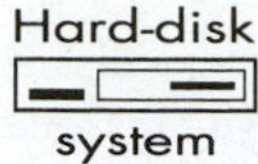

IF YOU ARE USING A HARD-DISK SYSTEM: Be sure the DOS directory is the default (if not, type **CD\DOS** ↵).

Keystroke	Action Resulting from Keystroke
DISKCOMP A: A: ↵	
	Begins the comparison process. The computer will ask you to **Insert the FIRST diskette in drive A:**. At this point, insert the *WordPerfect Data* diskette into the A: drive.
[Enter]	Continues the comparison process. The computer will copy as much of the diskette as it can into its main memory. It then will ask you to **Insert SECOND diskette in drive A:**. At this point, remove the *WordPerfect Data* diskette and insert the backup diskette (*WPD-BU*) into the A: drive.
[Enter]	Continues the comparison process. The computer will compare the information in its main memory to that on the diskette. It then will ask you to **Insert the FIRST diskette in drive A:** again. This process will continue until the two diskettes have been compared. If the diskettes are identical, the computer will respond with **Compare OK** and then ask if you want to **Compare another diskette (Y/N) ?**.
N ↵	Specifies that you to not want to compare more diskettes and returns control to DOS.
	Place the *WPD-BU* diskette in the A: drive and place the *WordPerfect Data* diskette in a safe place.

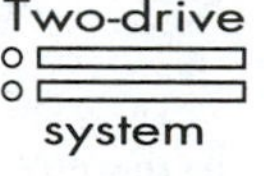

IF YOU ARE USING A TWO-DRIVE SYSTEM: Be sure the DOS diskette is in the B: drive and that B: is the default drive (if not, type **B:** ↵).

Keystroke	Action Resulting from Keystroke
DISKCOMP A: B: ↵	
	Begins the comparison process. The computer will ask you to **Insert the FIRST diskette in drive A:** and **Insert the SECOND diskette in drive B:**. At this point, insert the backup diskette (*WPD-BU*) into the A: drive and the *WordPerfect Data/Boot* diskette into the B: drive.
[Enter]	Continues the comparison process. The computer will compare the contents of the two diskettes. If the diskettes are identical, the computer will respond with **Compare OK** and then ask if you want to **Compare another diskette (Y/N) ?**.
N ↵	Specifies that you to not want to compare more diskettes and returns control to DOS.
	Place the DOS diskette in the B: drive (keep the *WPD-BU* in the A: drive) and place the *WordPerfect Data/Boot* in a safe place.

• Formatting Command •

The formatting command (**FORMAT**) is an external command that initializes (prepares) a disk so that it can be used by an IBM or IBM-compatible microcomputer. To format a high-density diskette located in the A: drive, the command **FORMAT A:/S/V/F:1440** could be used, where

A: is a parameter that specifies the drive that contains the diskette to be formatted.

/S is an optional switch (option) that has the effect of transferring the system file, **COMMAND.COM**, to the newly formatted diskette. This enables the new diskette to boot the computer without the aid of the DOS diskette or without having DOS on the hard drive.

/V is an optional switch that allows the user to specify a volume label (a name such as **ROBERTSON**) for the diskette. The label can be from one to eleven characters in length.

/F:1440 is an optional switch that formats the diskette in high-density (1440K of memory) mode. Note that in order to use the 1440 designation you must have a high-density diskette (it will say HD on it) and a high-density drive (the button on the drive may display a label something like 1.44). Be sure to check diskette and drive compatibility before formatting a diskette. Depending on the diskette and drive, the 1440 can be replaced with 160, 180, 320, 360, 720, or 1200. If you leave off the **/F:size** switch, the computer will format the diskette using the default size (which is different for different drives).

REMEMBER . . . pressing **[Ctrl-C]** will abort most DOS commands, including the formatting process. For example:

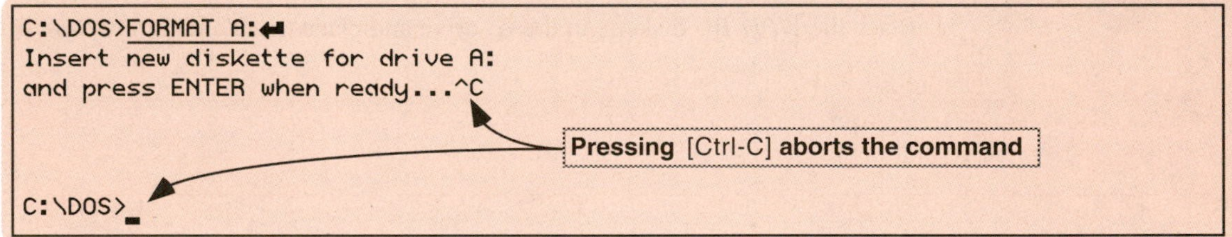

C:\DOS>FORMAT A:
Insert new diskette for drive A:
and press ENTER when ready...^C
Pressing [Ctrl-C] aborts the command
C:\DOS>_

Commands for Displaying Information

A number of commands enable users to display information about specific files and to display the contents of the files. For the examples that follow, the default directory should be DOS (**C:\DOS**) or, if you are using a two-drive system, the drive that holds the DOS diskette (**B:**). The *WPD-BU* diskette should be in drive A:. The actual files that you have on your *WPD-BU* diskette may be different from the ones listed below.

• Directory Command •

The directory command (**DIR**) is an internal command that displays information about the files saved on a disk. This command has a number of different forms:

DIR displays the names of all the files in the default directory (in this case, **C:\DOS** or **B:**). The file names are not displayed in alphabetical order but usually in the order in which they were saved (but not always). Later, we will see how to get an alphabetical listing of the file names.

DIR A: displays the names of all the files on the diskette in the A: drive. This would list all the files on the *WPD-BU* diskette since that diskette is currently in the A: drive.

DIR /P displays the default directory one screen (page) at a time. Pressing any key will continue the display process until the screen is filled once again or until all the file names have been listed.

DIR /W displays the default directory in **W**ide format (across the screen rather than down the screen).

DIR A:MEMO1 displays the directory listing for the file **MEMO1**, which resides on the diskette in the A: drive.

```
C:\DOS>DIR A:MEMO1↵

 Volume in drive A is ROBERTSON
 Directory of  A:\

MEMO1                931 02-10-91   8:10a
        1 File(s)    1281024 bytes free

C:\DOS>_
```

To display the names of selected files, **global characters** can be used. These are characters that can take the place of one or more other characters in a command.

- The global character ***** can be used to take the place of any group of characters.
- The global character **?** can be used to take the place of any one character.

DIR A:MEMO*.* Displays the directory listing only for those files on A: that begin with **MEMO**, regardless of what the rest of the file name or extension is.

```
C:\DOS>DIR A:MEMO*.*↵

 Volume in drive A is ROBERTSON
 Directory of  A:\

MEMO1                931 02-10-91   8:10a
MEMO2                921 02-10-91   9:03a
MEMO2    BU          921 02-10-91   9:03a
MEMO3               1066 02-11-91   2:16p
MEMO4               1067 02-11-91   2:49p
MEMO3    FIG        5501 02-11-91   3:06a
        6 File(s)    1281024 bytes free

C:\DOS>_
```

DIR A:MEMO??. (The period after the second question mark is a part of the command.) Displays the directory listing only for those files that begin with the four letters **MEMO**, have exactly two characters after the four letters, and have no extension (notice in the following screen dump that the file **MEMO3.FIG** is not displayed because it has an extension **.FIG**):

```
C:\DOS>DIR A:MEMO??.↵

 Volume in drive A is ROBERTSON
 Directory of  A:\

MEMO1                931 02-10-91   8:10a
MEMO2                921 02-10-91   9:03a
MEMO3               1066 02-11-91   2:16p
MEMO4               1067 02-11-91   2:49p
        4 File(s)    1281024 bytes free

C:\DOS>_
```

Try the **DIR** command by doing the following:

Keystroke	Action Resulting from Keystroke
DIR A:*.WPM ↵	Displays a listing of the files in the diskette in drive A: which have any name (indicated by the *) but which have the extension **WPM** (these are WordPerfect macros).

• Sort Command •

The sort command (**SORT**) is an external command that loads and executes a filter called **SORT.EXE**. A **filter** is a special type of command that processes information in order to change it in some way (much like the air filter on an automobile engine changes the air sent to the engine by removing some of the dust). The **SORT** command takes input from either the keyboard or a file and arranges it in alphabetical order. For example, **SORT** can be used to produce an alphabetized listing of the directory of a disk. To do this, the computer must be given two commands that are linked. First, the **DIR** command must be issued so that the computer will produce a listing of the directory. Then, the output from the **DIR** command needs to be sent to the **SORT** filter which will arrange the directory information alphabetically. The computer can be given two separate commands at the same time if they are linked using a character called a **pipe**. The pipe, |, is used to capture the output from one DOS command and make it available as the input for another DOS command. Try the **SORT** command by doing the following:

Keystroke	Action Resulting from Keystroke
DIR A: | C:\DOS\SORT ↵	Displays the directory of the diskette in the A: drive sorted by file name (for a two-drive system with the DOS diskette in the B: drive, the command is **DIR A: | B:\SORT**). The **DIR A:** says to display the directory of the diskette in the A: drive. The pipe, |, says to take the listing of the directory and, instead of actually displaying it on the screen, to send it to the next command after the |. The **C:\DOS\SORT** says to find the program called **SORT** on the diskette in the **DOS** directory in drive C: and then to run that program using the listing of the directory from the **DIR A:** command as input. Note that if the default directory is **C:\DOS**, that part of the command can be omitted (i.e., you could type **DIR A: | SORT** instead).

```
C:\DOS>DIR A:  | C:\DOS\SORT↵


       60 File(s)    1280512 bytes free
 Directory of  A:\
 Volume in drive A is ROBERTSON
ALTR      WPM       129 02-11-91   3:25a
ANXIETY   CON       588 02-11-91   5:13p
ANXIETY   FIN      9914 02-11-91   4:56p
ANXIETY   NDX     10533 02-11-91   5:32p
ANXIETY   TOC     10234 02-11-91   5:06p
ANXIETY1            980 02-11-91   3:56p
ANXIETY2           1827 02-11-91   3:57p
ANXIETY3           8749 02-11-91   4:01p
ANXIETY4           8951 02-11-91   4:10p
ANXIETY5           9036 02-11-91   4:21p
ANXIETY6           9225 02-11-91   4:30p
ANXIETY7           9365 02-11-91   4:38p
```

Continued . . .

Keystroke	Action Resulting from Keystroke

```
NAME-ADD WPM        233 02-11-91   3:40a
PHONETXT            146 02-11-91   1:41p
PHONEWP             455 02-11-91   1:54p
SPELL1              924 02-10-91  12:45p
TERMPAP            6940 09-11-90   1:18p
THESAU1             920 02-10-91  12:56p

C:\DOS>_
```

Depending on the system you are using, there may be a couple of file names such as **0F16273E** and **0F162827** added to the top of the list. These are called *scratch* files because they are created by the computer to store temporary data during the sorting process (like using scratch paper to do a math problem). They are emptied at the end of the sort process and can be ignored.

By default, **SORT** arranges the records based on the characters beginning in column 1. If you want to sort by data in a different column you would add **/+n** to the end of the **SORT** command, where **n** is the column number where you want the sort to begin. For example, the following command would sort the entries in the directory by size (which begins in column 14) rather than by name: **DIR A: | SORT /+14**.

• Display More Command •

The display more command (**MORE**) is an external command that loads and executes a program called **MORE.COM**. This program acts as a filter that reads data from an input device or file and sends the data to an output device or file one screen at a time. For example, **DIR A: | C:\DOS\MORE** lists the directory of the diskette in the A: drive one screen at a time. The **DIR A:** says to display the directory of the diskette in the A: drive. The pipe, **|** , says to take the listing of the directory and, instead of actually displaying it on the screen, to send it to the next command after the **|** . The **C:\DOS\MORE** says to find the program called **MORE** on the DOS subdirectory and to run that program using the listing of the directory from the **DIR A:** command as input. After 24 lines of output have been displayed, the computer stops displaying new lines and the message **-- More --** appears at the bottom of the screen. Pressing any key will continue the output display. The effect of this command is similar to **DIR A: /P**. Try the **MORE** command by doing the following:

Keystroke	Action Resulting from Keystroke
DIR A: | SORT | MORE ↵	Displays a sorted listing of the directory of the diskette in the A: drive, one screen at a time.

TO TAKE A BREAK Remove diskette(s). To resume (hard disk): Type **CD\DOS ↵**, insert *WPD-BU* diskette. To resume (two drive): Insert the DOS diskette in the B: drive and the *WPD-BU* diskette in the A: drive and type **B: ↵**.

Commands for Files

There are a number of commands that act on individual files or, in some instances, groups of files. For example, the **COPY** command makes a backup copy of a single file or a group of files.

• Copy from the Console Command •

The copy from the console command (**COPY CON**) is an internal command that allows the user to create a file while in the DOS environment by typing the information on the keyboard. This command is used to create small text files without having to access a word processor. For example, **COPY CON PHONES** creates a new file called **PHONES** and stores whatever is typed next on the keyboard as data for that file. To terminate the data entry process, the **[F6]** and then **[Enter]** keys must be pressed.

On page W114 you used WordPerfect to create a file called **PHONETXT**, which contained the names and phone numbers of five friends. The file looked like the following:

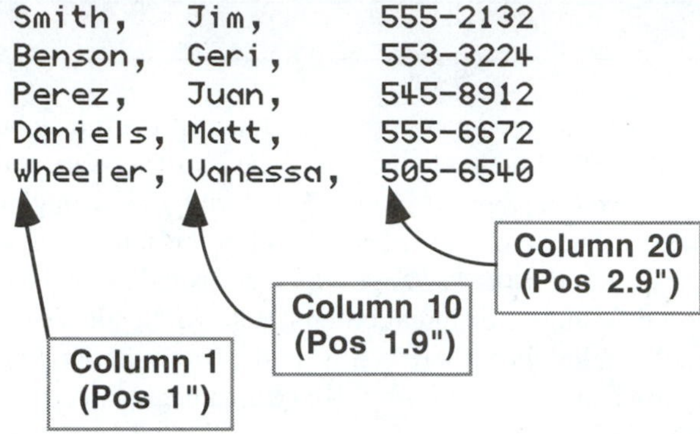

Smith, Jim, 555-2132
Benson, Geri, 553-3224
Perez, Juan, 545-8912
Daniels, Matt, 555-6672
Wheeler, Vanessa, 505-6540
Column 20 (Pos 2.9")
Column 10 (Pos 1.9")
Column 1 (Pos 1")

Each line of this file is called a *record.* For each record, the last name begins in column 1, the first name begins in column 10, and the phone number begins in column 20. The spacing of the entries is accomplished by using the space bar and counting (e.g., **Smith,** has 6 characters and, therefore, 3 blank spaces are needed between **Smith,** and **Jim** to make **Jim** start at column 10). Try the **COPY CON** command by doing the following:

Keystroke	Action Resulting from Keystroke
COPY CON A:PHONES ↵	Begins the copy process. The computer will not respond at all but will wait for you to type in the contents of the file.
	Type the names and phone numbers listed above. Be careful! Once you have pressed **[Enter]** at the end of a line you cannot go back and modify that line (as you could with the word processor). Before you press **[Enter]**, check the line to be sure it is correct and use **[Backspace]**, if needed, to correct errors. If you do make a mistake, you can retype the entire file or load the file into the word processor and edit it.
	After you have finished typing the five records you must tell the computer to exit **COPY CON** mode.
[F6] ↵	Terminates the **COPY CON** command. The whole process should look like the following:

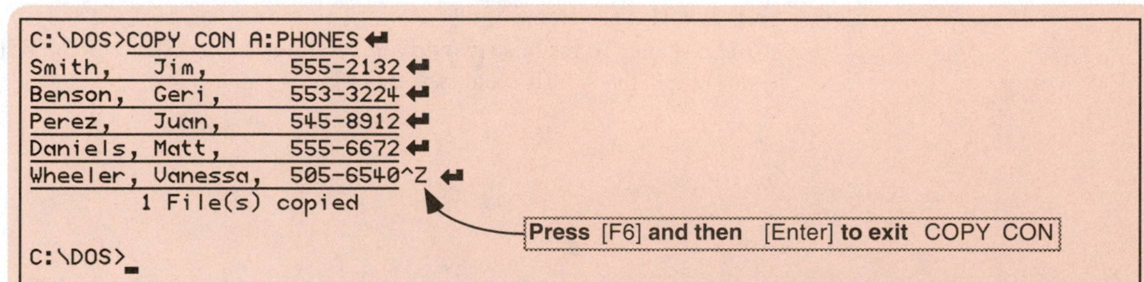

C:\DOS>COPY CON A:PHONES ↵
Smith, Jim, 555-2132 ↵
Benson, Geri, 553-3224 ↵
Perez, Juan, 545-8912 ↵
Daniels, Matt, 555-6672 ↵
Wheeler, Vanessa, 505-6540^Z ↵
1 File(s) copied
Press [F6] and then [Enter] to exit COPY CON
C:\DOS>_

Data may not be added to an existing file using **COPY CON**. If you want to add another name to the **PHONES** file, you will have to use the word processor to modify the file or create a new file with the additional names and then merge the two files (merging files will be discussed later). If you were to type **COPY CON PHONES** again and then type more names, the original names would be erased and only the new names would be saved.

Files created with the **COPY CON** command are like the DOS text file you created with WordPerfect. These files are also known as ASCII (American Standard Code for Information Interchange) files and may be read by other programs. For example, if you wanted to use the data in the **PHONES** file in a letter created by WordPerfect, you could do so using the *Text In/Out* feature.

• Type Command •

The type command (**TYPE**) is an internal command that displays the contents of a file. For example, **TYPE A:PHONES** displays the contents of the file **PHONES**, which is located on the diskette in the A: drive. Try the **TYPE** command by doing the following:

Keystroke	Action Resulting from Keystroke
TYPE A:PHONES ↵	Displays the contents of the file **PHONES**.

```
C:\DOS>TYPE A:PHONES ↵
Smith,   Jim,       555-2132
Benson,  Geri,      553-3224
Perez,   Juan,      545-8912
Daniels, Matt,      555-6672
Wheeler, Vanessa,   505-6540
C:\DOS>_
```

The **TYPE** and **SORT** commands may be combined using a pipe. For example, display the contents of the file **PHONES** in alphabetical order by doing the following:

Keystroke	Action Resulting from Keystroke
TYPE A:PHONES | SORT ↵	Displays the contents of the file **PHONES** in alphabetical order. The **TYPE** command says to display the file on the screen but the pipe, **|** , says to send the output to the **SORT** program first.

```
C:\DOS>TYPE A:PHONES | SORT ↵
Benson,  Geri,      553-3224
Daniels, Matt,      555-6672
Perez,   Juan,      545-8912
Smith,   Jim,       555-2132
Wheeler, Vanessa,   505-6540

C:\DOS>_
```

Continued . . .

Keystroke	Action Resulting from Keystroke
	The data can be sorted by first name by telling the computer to look at the characters beginning in column 10 when arranging the names.
TYPE A:PHONES | SORT /+10 ↵	Displays the contents of the file **PHONES** in alphabetical order but by first name (i.e., by the characters beginning in column 10).

```
C:\DOS>TYPE A:PHONES | SORT /+10↵
Benson,  Geri,      553-3224
Smith,   Jim,       555-2132
Perez,   Juan,      545-8912
Daniels, Matt,      555-6672
Wheeler, Vanessa,   505-6540X

C:\DOS>_
```

• Print Command •

The print command (**PRINT**) is an external command that is analogous to the **TYPE** command, except that the output is sent to the printer rather than to the screen. For example, **PRINT A:PHONES** prints the contents of the file **PHONES**, which is on the diskette in the A: drive. As with all external commands, the computer must know where to find the file called **PRINT**. If it cannot, the error message **Bad command or file name** will be displayed and the file will not be printed. Changing the command to **C:\DOS\PRINT A:PHONES** would fix this problem.

Try the **PRINT** command by doing the following (be sure that a printer is attached to your computer and that the printer is turned on and loaded with paper):

Keystroke	Action Resulting from Keystroke
PRINT A:PHONES ↵	Sends the contents of the file **PHONES** to the printer. The first time you use **PRINT** during a session the computer may issue the message **Name of list device [PRN]:**. The message is asking which print device (printer) should receive the output. In most cases, **PRN** will be the device (the computer assumes this as the default value so you only need to press **[Enter]**). Other possible devices include **LPT1**, **LPT2**, **COM1**, **COM2**, and **AUX**.

```
C:\DOS>PRINT A:PHONES↵
Name of list device [PRN]:↵     <---- You may or may not get this message
Resident part of PRINT installed

  A:\PHONES is currently being printed

C:\DOS>
```

If you want to print more than one file at a time, you can do so by typing a list of file specifications (**drive:filename.extension**). For example, typing **PRINT A:PHONES A:PHONETXT** would print the files **PHONES** and **PHONETXT**, both of which reside on the diskette in the A: drive. Do not use **PRINT** to print your WordPerfect documents unless they have been saved as ASCII text files. WordPerfect stores documents in a coded format that will make your printer go crazy if you try to use **PRINT**.

• Copy Command •

The copy command (**COPY**) is an internal command that makes a copy of a file (or a group of files). The copy of the file may have either the same name as the original or a different name, and it may reside on a different disk.

COPY A:PHONES C: copies the file **PHONES**, which is on the diskette in drive A:, to the root directory in drive C:. An exact copy of the file is made and stored in drive C: under the same name, **PHONES**.

COPY A:PHONES C:\PHONES2 copies the file **PHONES**, which is on the diskette in drive A:, to the root directory of drive C: and saves it under the new name, **PHONES2**.

COPY PHONES PHONES2.TXT copies the file **PHONES**, which is on the disk in the default drive, and saves it under the new name, **PHONES2.TXT**, but in the same directory as the original.

Try the **COPY** command by doing the following:

Keystroke	Action Resulting from Keystroke
COPY A:PHONES A:PHONES2 ↵	Makes a copy of **PHONES** under a new name, **PHONES2**, on the diskette in the A: drive.
DIR A:PHONES* ↵	Displays the names of all files on the diskette in drive A: that begin with **PHONES**. The name of the new file should be listed.

```
C:\DOS>COPY A:PHONES A:PHONES2↵
        1 File(s) copied

C:\DOS>DIR A:PHONES*↵

 Volume in drive A is ROBERTSON
 Directory of  A:\

PHONES               143 02-11-91   6:20p
PHONES2              143 02-11-91   6:20p
        2 File(s)    1279488 bytes free

C:\DOS>_
```

To copy more than one file at a time, global characters can be used as they are in the **DIR** command.

- The global character ***** can be used to take the place of any group of characters.
- The global character **?** can be used to take the place of any one character.
- **COPY A:*.WPM C:** copies from the diskette in drive A: to the root directory of drive C: all files with any name (indicated by the asterisk, *****) but with the extension **.WPM**. The files **ALTR.WPM**, **NAME-ADD.WPM**, **ALTH.WPM**, and **HW-TOP.WPM** all would be copied.
- **COPY A:MEM??.* C:** copies from the diskette in drive A: to the root directory of drive C: all files with names that have exactly five characters and that begin with **MEM**. The files may have any extension. The files **MEMO1**, **MEMO2**, **MEMO2.BU**, **MEMO3**, **MEMO3.FIG**, and **MEMO4** would be copied.
- **COPY A:*.* B:** copies all files (any name, *****, and any extension, **.***) from drive A: to the diskette in the B: drive. This will work on a one-floppy-drive system, but the computer will ask you to swap diskettes every so often (as was the case with **DISKCOPY**).

Try the **COPY** command by doing the following:

Keystroke	Action Resulting from Keystroke
COPY A:MEMO? A:MEMO?BU ↵	Makes copies of **MEMO1**, **MEMO2**, **MEMO3**, and **MEMO4** and saves them under the new names **MEMO1BU**, **MEMO2BU**, **MEMO3BU**, and **MEMO4BU**. Because no extension is specified the computer will not copy files **MEMO2.BU** and **MEMO3.FIG**.
DIR A:MEMO*.* ↵	Displays a listing of the files whose names begin with **MEMO**. The screen should look like the following:

```
C:\DOS>COPY A:MEMO? A:MEMO?BU↵
A:MEMO1
A:MEMO2
A:MEMO3
A:MEMO4
        4 File(s) copied

C:\DOS>DIR A:MEMO*.*↵

 Volume in drive A is ROBERTSON
 Directory of  A:\

MEMO1                931 02-10-91   8:10a
MEMO2                921 02-10-91   9:03a
MEMO2    BU          921 02-10-91   9:03a
MEMO3               1066 02-11-91   2:16p
MEMO4               1067 02-11-91   2:49p
MEMO3    FIG        5501 02-11-91   3:06a
MEMO1BU              931 02-10-91   8:10a
MEMO2BU              921 02-10-91   9:03a
MEMO3BU             1066 02-11-91   2:16p
MEMO4BU             1067 02-11-91   2:49p
       10 File(s)    1274368 bytes free

C:\DOS>_
```

The copy command also can be used to combine files by listing the file names to be combined with the plus sign (+) between the names. For example, suppose you wanted to combine the contents of files **PHONES** and **PHONES2** into a third file called **ALLPHONE**. The command **COPY A:PHONES + A:PHONES2 A:ALLPHONE** combines the files **PHONES** and **PHONES2** and stores the new file under the name **ALLPHONE** on the diskette in the A: drive. Note that the files **PHONES** and **PHONES2** remain unchanged.

• *Compare Files Command* •

The compare files command (**COMP**) is an external command that compares the contents of two files. This command is useful after a **COPY** command has been executed to see whether the new copy of the file is identical to the original file (i.e., to see whether there have been any errors during the copying process). **COMP** is an external command and, therefore, the DOS subdirectory or diskette is needed to execute it.

Keystroke	Action Resulting from Keystroke

COMP A:MEMO1 A:MEMO1BU ↵

Compares file **MEMO1** and file **MEMO1BU**. If the files are identical, the message **Files compare OK** is issued. Sometimes the message **Eof mark not found** is issued. **Eof** stands for **E**nd **of** **f**ile marker, which is a special code found at the very end of a file. You can ignore this message.

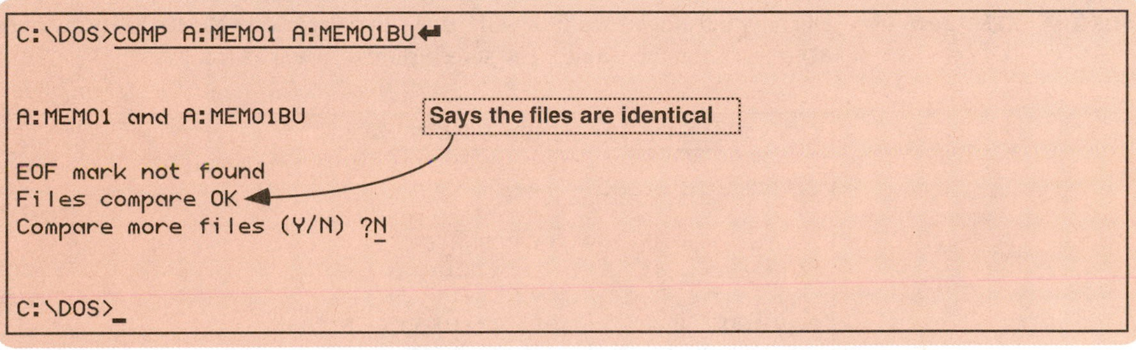
C:\DOS>COMP A:MEMO1 A:MEMO1BU
A:MEMO1 and A:MEMO1BU
Says the files are identical
EOF mark not found
Files compare OK
Compare more files (Y/N) ?N
C:\DOS>_

If the two files to be compared are on different diskettes, you may simply enter **COMP** ↵. In this case, the computer will ask you to **Enter primary filename** and wait for you to type the file specification of one of the files. When you press **[Enter]**, the computer will ask for the file specification of the other file. When you press **[Enter]** you will be prompted to insert the proper diskettes at the proper times.

• *Rename Command* •

The rename command (**RENAME**) is an internal command that changes file names. For example, **RENAME A:MEMO1BU BEANS** changes the name of the file **MEMO1BU** to **BEANS**. Notice that the **A:** is not needed (or allowed) on the second file name. This is because you cannot move the file to a different diskette using the **RENAME** command (to do that you would use the **COPY** command).

Keystroke	*Action Resulting from Keystroke*
RENAME A:MEMO?BU DOCU?BU ↵	Changes the names of all files on the A: drive that begin with the characters **MEMO**, have any one character next (represented by the **?**), and end with **BU**, into new files with names beginning with **DOCU**.
DIR A:DOCU*.* ↵	Displays a listing of the files with names that begin with **DOCU**.
DIR A:MEMO?BU ↵	Displays a listing of the files with names that begin with **MEMO**, have any one character next, and end in **BU** (there should be none). The screen should appear as follows:

```
C:\DOS>RENAME A:MEMO?BU DOCU?BU↵

C:\DOS>DIR A:DOCU*.*↵

 Volume in drive A is ROBERTSON
 Directory of  A:\

DOCU1BU              931 02-10-91    8:10a
DOCU2BU              921 02-10-91    9:03a
DOCU3BU             1066 02-11-91    2:16p
DOCU4BU             1067 02-11-91    2:49p
        4 File(s)     1274368 bytes free

C:\DOS>DIR A:MEMO?BU↵

 Volume in drive A is ROBERTSON
 Directory of  A:\

File not found

C:\DOS>_
```

• Delete Command •

The delete command (**DEL**) is an internal command that erases a file, or group of files, from the disk. Be careful! Once a file is deleted using the **DEL** command it usually cannot be restored at a later time (it is sometimes possible for computer experts to restore deleted files, but this takes special skills and software to accomplish). For example, **DEL A:BEANS** deletes the file **BEANS** from the root directory of the diskette in drive A:.

Try the **DEL** command by doing the following:

Keystroke	Action Resulting from Keystroke
DEL A:DOCU* ↵	Deletes all files on drive A: that begin with **DOCU** and have any other characters. This will delete the files **DOCU1BU**, **DOCU2BU**, **DOCU3BU**, and **DOCU4BU**.
DIR A:DOCU*.* ↵	Displays a list of files whose names begin with **DOCU** (there should be none).

```
C:\DOS>DEL A:DOCU*↵

C:\DOS>DIR A:DOCU*↵

 Volume in drive A is ROBERTSON
 Directory of  A:\

File not found

C:\DOS>_
```

Miscellaneous Commands

DOS has many other commands that make using the computer more efficient and enable users to perform specific tasks that might be needed by some applications programs. If you are interested in these commands, consult the *DOS Reference Manual* that came with your computer. A few of these commands are listed here. Do not try to learn all the commands at one time; there are too many and you probably will need to memorize only a few.

Time Command This internal command (**TIME**) displays the time of day in the form *hours: minutes:seconds.hundredths of seconds* as recorded by the computer's clock. This command gives the user the opportunity to make a correction to the time if needed. If no correction is necessary, simply press **[Enter]**.

```
C:\DOS>TIME ↵
Current time is 11:36:01.71a
Enter new time: 13:24 ↵

C:\DOS>_
```

Date Command Similar to the **TIME** command, this internal (**DATE**) command displays the current date in the form *month-day-year* and allows the user to change the date. For example, **DATE** displays the current date and requests a new one while **DATE 2-11-91** sets the new date to February 11, 1991 without displaying the date currently on the computer's clock.

Volume Command This internal command (**VOL**) displays the volume name of a disk. For example, **VOL A:** displays the name of the volume (disk) in the A: drive.

Change Volume Label Command This external command (**LABEL**) allows the user to change the label (name) of a volume. For example, **LABEL A:** displays the current label of the diskette in the A: drive and requests a new one.

Version Command This internal command (**VER**) displays the version number of DOS the system is currently using. This may be important because some applications may not work on early versions of DOS.

Clear Screen Command This internal command (**CLS**) erases the screen, except for the system prompt, and places the cursor at the upper left-hand side of the screen.

Change System Prompt Command This internal command (**PROMPT**) allows the user to change the system prompt. The default prompt consists of the default drive name and the *greater than* symbol (e.g., **C>**). However, the system prompt can be displayed in a number of different ways by executing the **PROMPT** command. For example, try each of the following:

Keystroke	Action Resulting from Keystroke
PROMPT $V ↵	Displays the DOS **V**ersion number as the system prompt instead of the drive name.
PROMPT $T ↵	Displays the current **T**ime as the system prompt.
PROMPT $P ↵	Displays the directory **P**ath of the default drive as the system prompt.
PROMPT $G ↵	Displays the is **G**reater than (**>**) character as the system prompt.
PROMPT Time is $T and directory is PG ↵	Combines the previous three prompts.
PROMPT ↵	Displays the default prompt.
PROMPT PG ↵	Displays the path and the **>** character (this is usually a good choice).

The last three examples are shown in the following screen dump:

```
C:\DOS>PROMPT Time is $T and directory is $P$G ↵

Time is 13:34:34.79 and directory is C:\DOS>PROMPT ↵

C>PROMPT $P$G ↵

C:\DOS>_
```

Set Command Search Path This internal command (**PATH**) sets the command search path (i.e., it tells the computer where to look for an executable file if the file is not found in the current directory). The **PATH** command only works for files that can be executed (usually, these are files that have the extension **COM**, **EXE**, or **BAT**). Thus, **PATH** cannot be used to find files created by applications (such as word-processing documents). For example, **PATH** displays the current search path setting. If no path has yet been set, the words **No Path** are displayed. In this case, if an application is requested, only the current directory will be searched for the file that contains the application. For example, suppose the *WPD-BU* diskette is in drive A:, and the system prompt **A:\>** is displayed (this means A: is the default drive). If you type **DIR | SORT ↵**, the message **Bad command or file name** will be displayed because you have not told DOS to search any directory other than the current one for the **SORT** filter.

The command **PATH C:\DOS** tells the computer to search the DOS subdirectory when a command is given. For example, if you type **PATH C:\DOS ↵** and then type **DIR | SORT ↵**, DOS will search the DOS subdirectory for the sorting program. The result will be that the program will be found and executed (a sorted listing of the directory of the diskette in drive A: will be displayed).

The word **PATH** followed by a semicolon (i.e., **PATH;**) tells the computer that you do not want a command search path. In this case, the computer will search only the current directory when you ask it to access an executable file.

Try the **PATH** command by doing the following:

Keystroke	*Action Resulting from Keystroke*
PATH ↵	Displays the current search path.
PATH; ↵	Tells DOS to search only the current directory for executable commands.
A: ↵	Makes A: the default directory.
DIR *.WPM | SORT ↵	This is intended to display a list of all WordPerfect macros in alphabetical order. However, it should produce an error message because there is no search path setting.
PATH C:\DOS ↵	Creates a command search path so that DOS will search the DOS subdirectory on the C: drive when a command is given.
DIR *.WPM | SORT ↵	Displays a sorted directory of the default drive. This time there should be no error message because the computer knows to search the DOS subdirectory for the file called **SORT**.

Continued . . .

Keystroke **Action Resulting from Keystroke**

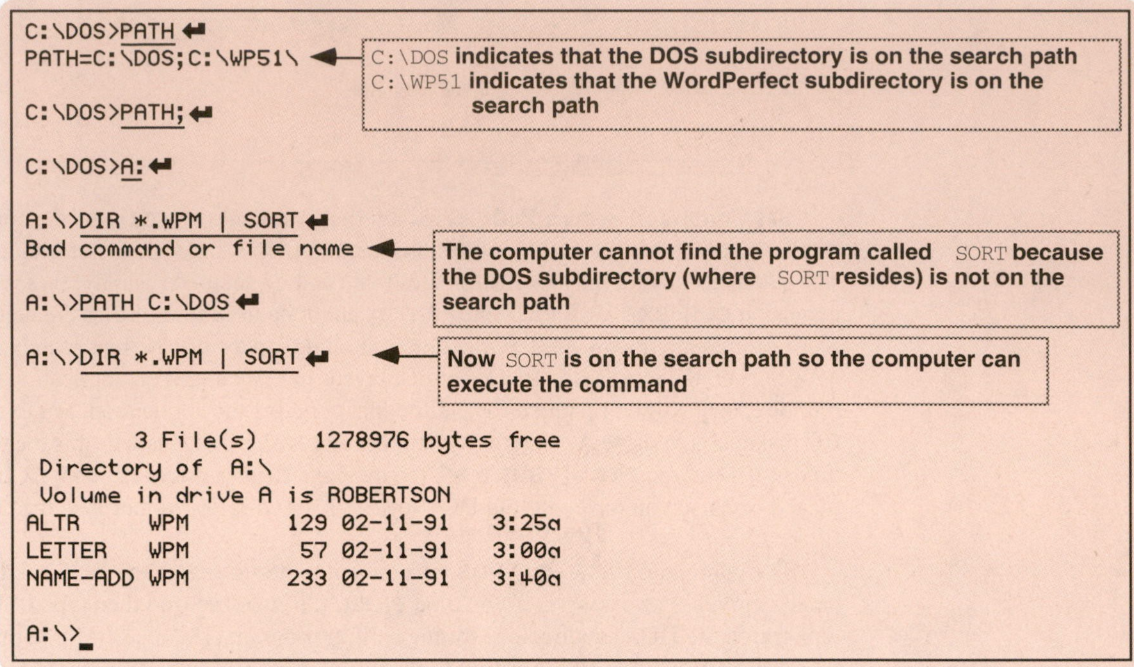

C:\DOS>PATH
PATH=C:\DOS;C:\WP51\
C:\DOS indicates that the DOS subdirectory is on the search path
C:\WP51 indicates that the WordPerfect subdirectory is on the search path
C:\DOS>PATH;
C:\DOS>A:
A:\>DIR *.WPM | SORT
Bad command or file name
The computer cannot find the program called SORT because the DOS subdirectory (where SORT resides) is not on the search path
A:\>PATH C:\DOS
A:\>DIR *.WPM | SORT
Now SORT is on the search path so the computer can execute the command
3 File(s) 1278976 bytes free
Directory of A:\
Volume in drive A is ROBERTSON
ALTR WPM 129 02-11-91 3:25a
LETTER WPM 57 02-11-91 3:00a
NAME-ADD WPM 233 02-11-91 3:40a
A:\>_

To restore the original command search path, reboot the computer by doing the following:

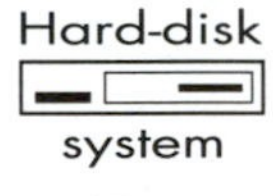

IF YOU ARE USING A HARD-DISK SYSTEM: Remove the diskette from drive A: and then press **[Ctrl-Alt-Del]**. This will reboot the computer and restore the original command search path.

IF YOU ARE USING A TWO-DRIVE SYSTEM: Remove the diskettes, place the DOS diskette in drive A:, and then press **[Ctrl-Alt-Del]**. This will reboot the computer and restore the original command search path.

Automatic Execution of a Batch File This file is created by the user to automatically execute a set (batch) of commands when the computer is booted. It is useful when you want to execute the same set of commands each time the computer is started. For example, you can use the **`COPY CON`** command to create an **`AUTOEXEC.BAT`** file that will do the following every time the computer is booted:

- Ask the user to enter the current date (this is not necessary if your computer has a battery-operated clock).
- Ask the user to enter the current time (this is not necessary if your computer has a battery-operated clock).
- Set the search path so that the DOS subdirectory is in the path.
- Set the system prompt to display the working subdirectory and **>** as the system prompt.

The process of creating such a file would look like the following (do not do this unless you have consulted your instructor or are using your own computer or you may destroy an already existing **AUTOEXEC.BAT** file). With this file stored in the root directory of C: (or on your boot diskette if you are using a two-drive system) the computer will execute each of the commands at startup.

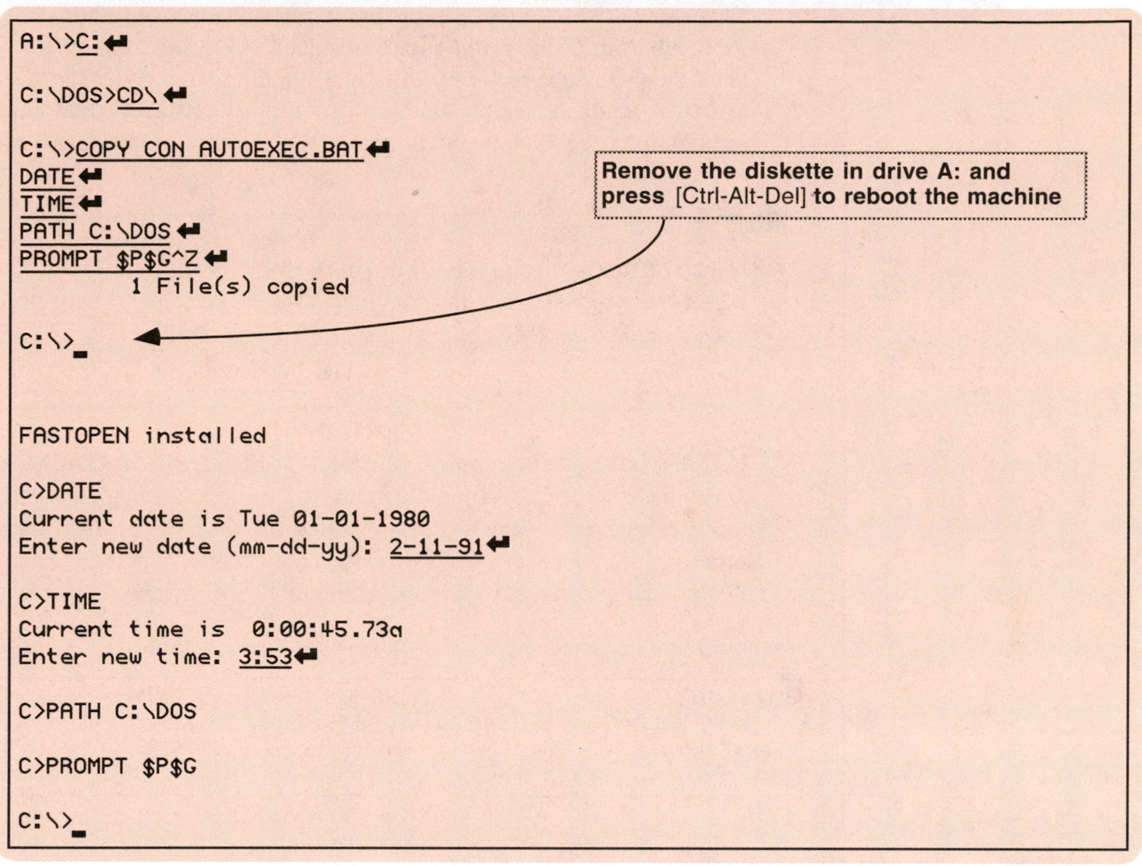

```
A:\>C:
C:\DOS>CD\
C:\>COPY CON AUTOEXEC.BAT
DATE
TIME
PATH C:\DOS
PROMPT $P$G^Z
        1 File(s) copied

C:\>_

FASTOPEN installed

C>DATE
Current date is Tue 01-01-1980
Enter new date (mm-dd-yy): 2-11-91

C>TIME
Current time is  0:00:45.73a
Enter new time: 3:53

C>PATH C:\DOS

C>PROMPT $P$G

C:\>_
```

Remove the diskette in drive A: and press [Ctrl-Alt-Del] to reboot the machine

TO TAKE A BREAK Remove diskette(s). To resume (hard disk): Type **CD\DOS** ↵. To resume (two drive): Insert DOS diskette.

Homework Exercises

These exercises will give you practice in using a number of different commands. Remember, to use *external* commands such as **DISKCOPY**, **COMP**, and **SORT**, you must have the DOS subdirectory (or diskette) on the search path. The *internal* commands such as **COPY**, **RENAME**, and **DIR** are resident in the **COMMAND.COM** file in your root directory or boot diskette so you do not need the DOS diskette when using those commands.

---

① Use **DISKCOPY** to make a backup copy of your *WordPerfect Data* diskette. Use **DISKCOMP** to check that the copying was done correctly. Use **[Ctrl-PrintScreen]** to produce a hard copy of the entire process.

---

② Use the **COPY CON** command to create a file called **CONTACTS** on your *WordPerfect Data* diskette. The file should contain the names, companies, phone numbers, and sales totals of business contacts. After entering the data, do a screen dump to show the entire process. Use the data given below (the name begins in column 1, the company in column 20, the phone number in column 35, and total sales for the person in column 45).

```
Column 1           Column 20      Column 35 Column 45
↓                  ↓              ↓         ↓
Bliss Bill,        NSP,           555-2311, 15221.00
Wheeler Katie,     Land O'Lakes,  555-2213, 25111.00
Moony Hal,         Geosyncronics, 555-0054, 15455.00
Bast Peg,          UNISYS,        555-6672, 12110.00
```

---

③ Use the **TYPE** command to display the contents of the file **CONTACTS**, which you created in Exercise 2. Do a screen dump to show the process.

---

④ Use the **PRINT** command to print the contents of the file **CONTACTS**, which you created in Exercise 2. Do a screen dump to show the process.

---

⑤ Use the **COPY** command to make a backup copy of the file **CONTACTS**, which you created in Exercise 2. The original file should be on the *WordPerfect Data* diskette and the copy should be written to the *WPD-BU* diskette that you created in this chapter. Call the backup file **CONTACTS.BAK**. Do a screen dump to show the process.

---

⑥ Use the **COMP** command to see whether the files **CONTACTS** and **CONTACTS.BAK**, from Exercise 5, are identical. Depending on the number of disk drives your computer has, you may have to use **COMP** without any parameters to accomplish this task. Do a screen dump to show the process.

⑦ Use **RENAME** to change the name of the file **CONTACTS.BAK**, from Exercise 5, to **CONTACTS.BK2**. Do a screen dump to show the process.

---

⑧ Use **DIR** to display a listing of only those files on your *WordPerfect Data* diskette whose names begin with **HW**. Do a screen dump to show the process.

---

⑨ Use the **DIR** and **SORT** commands to display the directory of your *WordPerfect Data* diskette with the files listed in alphabetical order. Use **[Ctrl-PrintScreen]** to produce a hard copy of the entire process.

---

⑩ Use **TYPE** and **SORT** to display the records (lines) of the file **CONTACTS**, which you created in Exercise 2, in alphabetical order, by last name. Do a screen dump to show the process.

---

⑪ Use the following internal commands and do a screen dump to show the process:

a. **TIME** to display the current time
b. **DATE** to display the current date
c. **VOL** to display the volume name of the diskette in drive A:
d. **VER** to display the version of DOS you are using

---

⑫ Create an **AUTOEXEC.BAT** file on your *WPD-BU* diskette that will do the following when the computer is booted and do a screen dump to show the process:

a. ask the user to enter the date and time
b. set a command search path so that the DOS subdirectory in drive C: (or B: if you are using a two-drive system) is searched when a command is given
c. clear the screen
d. display the directory of the diskette in the A: drive

Use **TYPE** to display the contents of your **AUTOEXEC.BAT** file and then do a screen dump.

APPENDIX:
Summary of Selected DOS and WordPerfect Features

DOS • Using Subdirectories •

A subdirectory is a file that contains the names of other files you have chosen to group together under one heading. Subdirectories are especially important if you are using a hard disk where hundreds or even thousands of separate files may be stored. For example, you might want to group all the WordPerfect files under one subdirectory and all the dBASE files in another. This would enable you and the computer to find individual files faster than if the files were stored in one big directory.

For the purposes of illustration, let's say you want to set up directories as follows:

Name	Function
DOS	Contains all DOS files.
WP51 (or **WP50**)	Contains all WordPerfect version 5.1 (or version 5.0) files. Within this subdirectory will be three other subdirectories named as follows:
COURSE	Contains WordPerfect files associated with a computer course (e.g., homework assignments).
BUSINESS	Contains WordPerfect files associated with your business (e.g., correspondence with customers).
PERSONAL	Contains WordPerfect files associated with your personal life (e.g., letters to friends).
123	Contains all Lotus 1-2-3 files.
DB	Contains all dBASE files.
BA	Contains all BASIC files.

The subdirectories and their relationship to each other are portrayed in the following diagram:

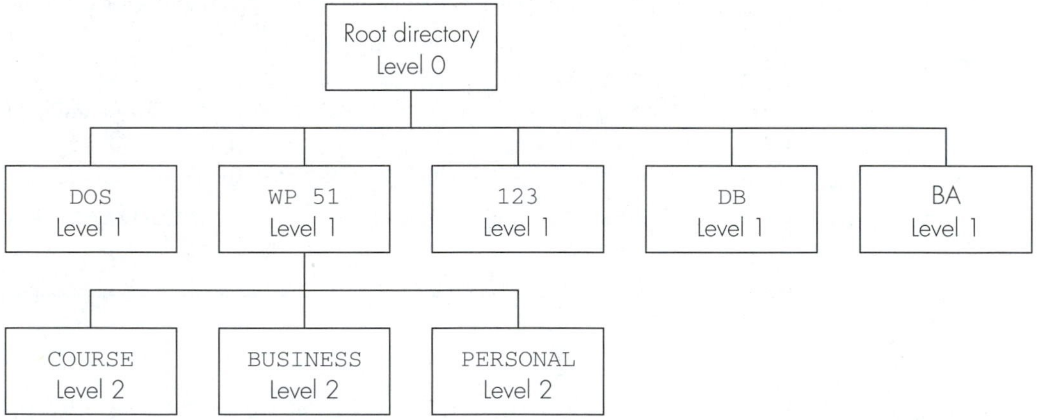

Note how the above illustration looks like a family tree. The top level is the *root* directory (or main directory) and is the one that is usually entered when the computer is booted. The directories in the next level (1) are called *children* of the root directory and they are also called the *parents* of bottom level (2) directories, and so on.

To work effectively with subdirectories, you will need to know how to do the following:

Create Subdirectories The **MD** (**M**ake **D**irectory) command is used to create (make) subdirectories. For example, to create the level 1 subdirectories previously listed, enter the following commands:

Keystroke	Action Resulting from Keystroke
MD\DOS ↵	Creates a subdirectory called **DOS**. The letters **MD** stand for **M**ake **D**irectory and **DOS** is the name of the subdirectory to be created. The back slash **** refers to the root directory and, in this instance, means that the subdirectory **DOS** is to be a child of the root directory. To create the other level 1 subdirectories, type in the following:
MD\WP51 ↵	Creates a subdirectory called **WP51**.
MD\123 ↵	Creates a subdirectory called **123**.
MD\DB ↵	Creates a subdirectory called **DB**.
MD\BA ↵	Creates a subdirectory called **BA**.

To create the level 2 subdirectories for **WP51**, do the following:

Keystroke	Action Resulting from Keystroke
MD\WP51\COURSE ↵	Creates a subdirectory called **COURSE** (which is a child of subdirectory **WP51**, which is a child of the root subdirectory).
MD\WP51\BUSINESS ↵	Creates a subdirectory called **BUSINESS**.
MD\WP51\PERSONAL ↵	Creates a subdirectory called **PERSONAL**.

Changing Subdirectories The **CD** (**C**hange **D**irectory) command is used to switch (change) from one subdirectory to another. For example:

Keystroke	Action Resulting from Keystroke
CD\WP51 ↵	Changes to the **WP51** subdirectory from any other subdirectory.
CD\WP51\BUSINESS ↵	Changes to the **BUSINESS** subdirectory from any other subdirectory.
	**** says go to the root directory
	WP51 says go to the **WP51** subdirectory
	BUSINESS says go to the **BUSINESS** subdirectory

There are three special symbols that can be used to speed up the **CD** command:

**** (backslash) is the symbol for the root directory.

. (single period) is the symbol for the current subdirectory.

.. (double period) is the symbol for the parent subdirectory.

For example:

Keystroke	Action Resulting from Keystroke
CD .. ↵	Transfers to the **WP51** subdirectory *if* you are currently in the **COURSE**, **BUSINESS**, or **PERSONAL** subdirectory (i.e., transfers to the parent of the current subdirectory).
CD ↵	Transfers to the root directory from any subdirectory.

Displaying the Active Directory The **CD** (**C**hange **D**irectory) command can be used to display the active subdirectory. For example, if you are currently in the **COURSE** subdirectory in drive C:, typing **CD** will display the following:

C:\WP51\COURSE

Displaying the Structure of the Directory The external command **TREE** is used to display the structure of the entire directory. Because **TREE** is an external command, a file called **TREE.COM** must be on the search path before the file can be executed. For example, to display the structure of the directories in the C: drive you would type the following:

Keystroke	Action Resulting from Keystroke
CD C:	Switches to the root directory of the C: drive.
C:\DOS\TREE ↵	Displays the subdirectory structure of the C: drive.

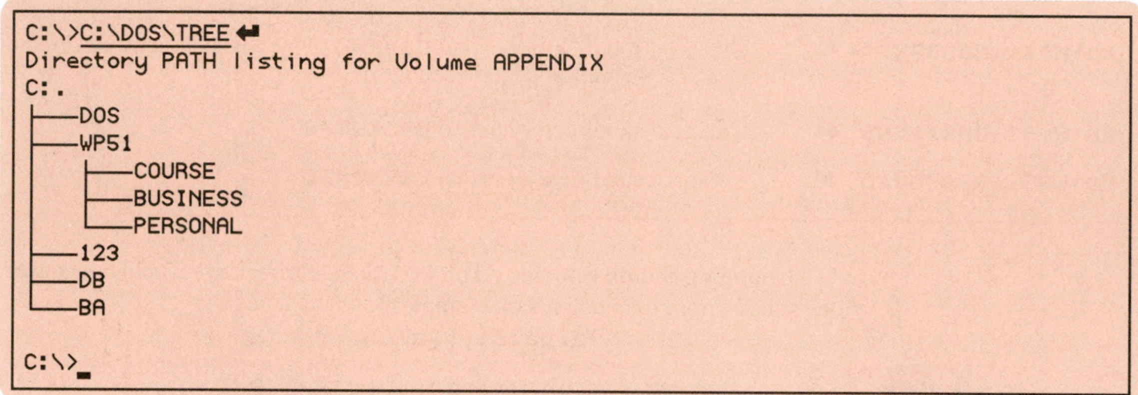

```
C:\>C:\DOS\TREE ↵
Directory PATH listing for Volume APPENDIX
C:.
├───DOS
├───WP51
│   ├───COURSE
│   ├───BUSINESS
│   └───PERSONAL
├───123
├───DB
└───BA

C:\>_
```

If you type **C:\DOS\TREE/F ↵**, the names of all the files (as well as the subdirectories) will be listed. For a hard disk, this may be quite a long list. If you type **:\DOS\TREE/F | MORE ↵**, the output will be listed one screen at a time. To abort the command, press **[Ctrl-C]**.

Removing Subdirectories The **RD** (**R**emove **D**irectory) command is used to delete (remove) a subdirectory. A subdirectory must be empty before it can be removed. For example, suppose you wanted to remove the level 2 subdirectory **PERSONAL**:

Keystroke	Action Resulting from Keystroke
CD\WP51\PERSONAL ↵	Switches to the **PERSONAL** subdirectory.
DEL *.* ↵	Deletes all files in the subdirectory.
Y ↵	Confirms that you want to delete all files.
CD .. ↵	Switches to the parent of **PERSONAL**.
RD PERSONAL ↵	Deletes (removes) the **PERSONAL** subdirectory.

Moving Files between Subdirectories The regular DOS **COPY** command (see pp. W205–207) can be used to copy files from one subdirectory to another. You must be sure to give the complete path for the files (the path includes the subdirectory names—see p. W211). For example, let's say there is a file called **HWW2-01** in the **COURSE** subdirectory that you want to move into the **DB** subdirectory. First, you would copy the file from **COURSE** to **DB** and then delete it from **COURSE**:

Keystroke	Action Resulting from Keystroke
COPY\WP51\COURSE\HWW2-01 \DB ↵	
	Copies the file **HWW2-01** from the subdirectory **COURSE** to the subdirectory **DB**.
DEL \WP51\COURSE\HWW2-01 ↵	
	Deletes the file **HWW2-01** from the subdirectory **COURSE**.

• Summary of Selected Commands •

The following is a brief listing of DOS commands with reference to pages in the text. If the topic was not covered in the text, N/C is listed instead of a page number. Optional parameters (such as **drive** or **path**) are enclosed in square brackets **[ ]**. The word **filespec** refers to a **file spec**ification including the drive, file name, and extension (e.g., **A:HOMEINV1.DBF**).

Note that **external commands** are those that are contained in files in the DOS subdirectory. In order to execute those commands the directory path to the file must be given. For example, if the file for the external command **CHKDSK** is in the DOS subdirectory of the C: drive and the **A>** prompt is showing, then typing **CHKDSK A: ↵** will produce the error message **Bad command or file name** (unless the extended search path has been set to include the DOS subdirectory). Typing **C:\DOS\CHKDSK A: ↵** will produce the desired output.

Page	Type	Command	Explanation
N/C	External:	**APPEND**	Sets the search path for data files (for executable files, see **PATH**).
	Form:	**APPEND [drive:path1];[drive:path2]...**	
	Example:	**APPEND A:**	Searches the A: drive when data files are accessed.
N/C	Internal:	**BREAK**	Sets the status of the break key **[Ctrl-C]**
	Form:	**BREAK ON** or **BREAK OFF**	
	Example:	**BREAK ON**	Tells DOS to check to see if **[Ctrl-C]** is pressed during functions other than keyboard, screen, or printer activity (such as disk reads or writes).
W217	Internal:	**CD**	**C**hanges from one sub**D**irectory to another.
	Form:	**CD [path]**	
	Example:	**CD \WP51**	Changes from current subdirectory to subdirectory **WP51**, which is located in the root directory of the default drive.
C45	External:	**CHKDSK**	Checks files and directories on a disk and produces a report on the status of the disk and RAM memory.
	Form:	**CHKDSK [drive:path] [/V]**	
	Example:	**CHKDSK A:**	Produces a status report of the diskette in the A: drive.
C36	Internal:	**CLS**	Clears the display and leaves only the system prompt.
	Form:	**CLS**	
	Example:	**CLS**	
D82	Internal:	**COMMAND**	Begins a secondary command processor (used when dropping to DOS from within an application — to return to the application, type **EXIT**).
	Form:	**COMMAND**	
	Example:	**COMMAND**	
W207	External:	**COMP**	Compares the contents of two files.
	Form:	**COMP [filespec1] [filespec2]**	

Continued . . .

Page	Type	Command	Explanation
	Example:	**COMP F1 F2**	Compares the files **F1** and **F2**. If they are identical, displays **Files compare OK**. To compare diskettes, use **DISKCOMP**.
W205	Internal:	**COPY**	Copies one or more files.
	Form:	**COPY filespec1 filespec2**	
	Example:	**COPY A:F1.* C:**	Copies files from drive A: that have the name **F1** and any extension. Copies have the same names and are written to drive C:.
W210	Internal:	**DATE**	Displays the date and allows the user to change it.
	Form:	**DATE [mm-dd-yy]**	
	Example:	**DATE [06-10-91]**	Changes the date on the computer's clock to 10 June 1991.
W209	Internal:	**DEL**	Deletes the specified files from the disk.
	Form:	**DEL filespec [/P]**	
	Example:	**DEL A:D1.***	Deletes all files from the diskette in the A: drive that have the filename **D1** and any extension.
W198	Internal:	**DIR**	Displays the directory of a specified disk.
	Form:	**DIR [filespec] [/P] [/W]**	
	Example:	**DIR /P**	Displays the directory of the default drive and pauses as the screen fills.
W196	External:	**DISKCOMP**	Compares the contents of two diskettes.
	Form:	**DISKCOMP drive1: drive2:**	
	Example:	**DISKCOMP A: A:**	Compares two diskettes using same drive A: (a message will be issued when the diskettes must be exchanged). If the diskettes are identical, the message **Disks compare OK** is issued. To compare files, use **COMP**.
W194	External:	**DISKCOPY**	Copies the contents of an entire diskette onto another diskette.
	Form:	**DISKCOPY drive1: drive2:**	
	Example:	**DISKCOPY A: A:**	Copies the contents of one diskette (the source) onto another diskette (the target) using the same drive A: (a message will be issued when the diskettes must be exchanged). Note that any information on the target diskette will be lost.
W68	External:	**EXIT**	Exits the **COMMAND.COM** program.
	Form:	**EXIT**	
	Example:	**EXIT**	
W41	External:	**FORMAT**	Initializes a diskette so that it can be used by a particular type of computer.
	Form:	**FORMAT [drive:][/S][/V][/F:size]**	
	Example:	**FORMAT A:/V/F:1440**	Formats the diskette in the A: drive as a high density diskette and asks for a volume name for the diskette.
L109	External:	**GRAPHICS**	Allows printing a graphics screen using **[PrintScreen]**
	Form:	**GRAPHICS**	
	Example:	**GRAPHICS**	
W210	External:	**LABEL**	Allows the user to modify the volume name of a disk.
	Form:	**LABEL [drive:] [label]**	
	Example:	**LABEL A:**	Allows the user to modify the volume name of the diskette in the A: drive.

Continued . . .

Page	Type	Command	Explanation
W217	Internal:	MD	Creates (**M**akes) a sub**D**irectory.
	Form:	MD [drive:][path]	
	Example:	MD C:\WP51	Creates a subdirectory called **WP51** on the C: drive.
W201	External:	MORE	Sends data to the output device one screen at a time.
	Form:	source | MORE	
	Example:	DIR A: | C:\DOS\MORE	Displays the directory of the diskette in the A: drive one screen at a time. The file **MORE** is located on the C: drive in subdirectory **DOS**.
W211	Internal:	PATH	Sets the search directory path.
	Form:	PATH [drive1:][path];[drive2:][path];...	
	Example:	PATH C:\DOS	Sets the search path so that the DOS subdirectory on drive C: will be searched when a command is given.
W204	External:	PRINT	Prints the contents of a specified file.
	Form:	PRINT [filespec]	
	Example:	PRINT F1	Prints the contents of the file **F1**.
W210	Internal:	PROMPT	Changes the system prompt.
	Form:	PROMPT [text] [code]	
	Example:	PROMPT PG	Displays the working directory of the default drive and the **>** character as the prompt .
W208	Internal:	RENAME	Renames a file or list of files.
	Form:	RENAME filespec1 filespec2	
	Example:	RENAME F1.* F1BU.*	Renames all the files with the name **F1** and any extension so that the new names will be **F1BU** with the same extensions.
W218	Internal:	RD	**R**emoves a sub**D**irectory.
	Form:	RD [drive:] path	
	Example:	RD C:\WP51\COURSE	Removes subdirectory **COURSE** from the C: drive.
W200	External:	SORT	Sorts data.
	Form:	SORT[/R][/+n]	
	Example:	C:\DOS\SORT /R /+20 <PHONES	Sorts the data input from the file **PHONES** in reverse order, with the sort beginning with column **20**. The **SORT** file is on the DOS subdirectory.
W209	Internal:	TIME	Displays the time of day and allows the user to change it.
	Form:	TIME [hours:minutes:seconds]	
	Example:	TIME 16:30	Resets the system clock to 4:30 pm.
W218	External:	TREE	Displays subdirectory paths.
	Form:	TREE [path] [/f]	
	Example:	TREE C: /F	Displays the directories and file names of the C: drive.
W203	Internal:	TYPE	Displays the contents of a specified file.
	Form:	TYPE [filespec]	
	Example:	TYPE F1	Displays the contents of file **F1** on the screen.
W210	Internal:	VER	Displays the version of DOS currently running.
	Form:	VER	
	Example:	VER	
W210	Internal:	VOL	Displays the volume label of the specified disk.
	Form:	VOL [drive:]	
	Example:	VOL A:	Displays the volume label of the diskette in the A: drive.

The default screen colors may be changed by doing the following:

Keystroke	Action Resulting from Keystroke
[Shift-F1]	Selects the *Setup* feature and displays its menu.

```
Setup

     1 - Mouse

     2 - Display

     3 - Environment

     4 - Initial Settings

     5 - Keyboard Layout

     6 - Location of Files
```

Keystroke	Action Resulting from Keystroke
D (or 2)	Selects **2 - Display** and displays its menu.

```
Setup: Display

     1 - Colors/Fonts/Attributes

     2 - Graphics Screen Type        CGA 640X200 2 color

     3 - Text Screen Type            Auto Selected

     4 - Menu Options

     5 - View Document Options

     6 - Edit-Screen Options
```

Keystroke	Action Resulting from Keystroke
C (or 1)	Selects **1 - Colors** and displays its menu.

```
Setup: Colors

     1 - Screen Colors

     2 - Fast Text                                   Yes
           (may cause snow on screen)
```

Keystroke	Action Resulting from Keystroke
S (or 1)	Selects **1 - Screen Colors** and displays its menu.

Continued . . .

```
Setup: Colors                 A B C D E F G H I J K L M N O P
                                B C D E F G H I J K L M N O P
Attribute                     Foreground  Background  Sample
Normal                             E           A       Sample
Blocked                            A           H       Sample
Underline                          E           A       Sample
Strikeout                          I           A       Sample
Bold                               I           A       Sample
Double Underline                   I           A       Sample
Redline                            I           A       Sample
Shadow                             I           A       Sample
Italics                            I           A       Sample
Small Caps                         I           A       Sample
Outline                            I           A       Sample
Subscript                          I           H       Sample
Superscript                        I           H       Sample
Fine Print                         I           A       Sample
Small Print                        I           A       Sample
Large Print                        E           A       Sample
Very Large Print                   E           A       Sample
Extra Large Print                  E           A       Sample
Bold & Underline                   P           H       Sample
Other Combinations                 I           A       Sample

Switch documents; Move to copy settings      Doc 1
```

[arrow]	Use the **[arrow]** keys to select the **Foreground** color code of the attribute whose color you want to change. Then, type the letter of the color you want.
[arrow]	Use the **[arrow]** keys to select the **Background** color code of the attribute whose color you want to change. Then, type the letter of the color you want.
	Continue in this manner until you have selected all the colors you want.
[F7]	Exits the color menu and returns to normal mode.

• *The Mouse and Cursor Control* •

In most instances, you may position the cursor by using the mouse instead of the **[arrow]** keys. As a general rule, if you want to move the cursor up or down a few lines or left or right a few characters, it is faster to use the **[arrow]** keys. However, for larger movements across the screen, the mouse may be a better choice. As you become more familiar with the mouse you will find out by trial and error the method that is best for you.

For practice, try moving around the document **MEMO1** using the mouse by doing the following (begin with **MEMO1** displayed on the screen—see pp. W32–35 for help in loading a document):

1. Move the cursor to the top of the screen by pressing **[Home] Home] ↑**. The location on the status line should read **Ln 1" Pos 1"**.
2. Move the mouse until the first letter in the second sentence (the **P** in **Please pick up your**...) is highlighted by the mouse cursor (remember, the mouse cursor is a black or orange rectangle while the regular cursor is a blinking underline):

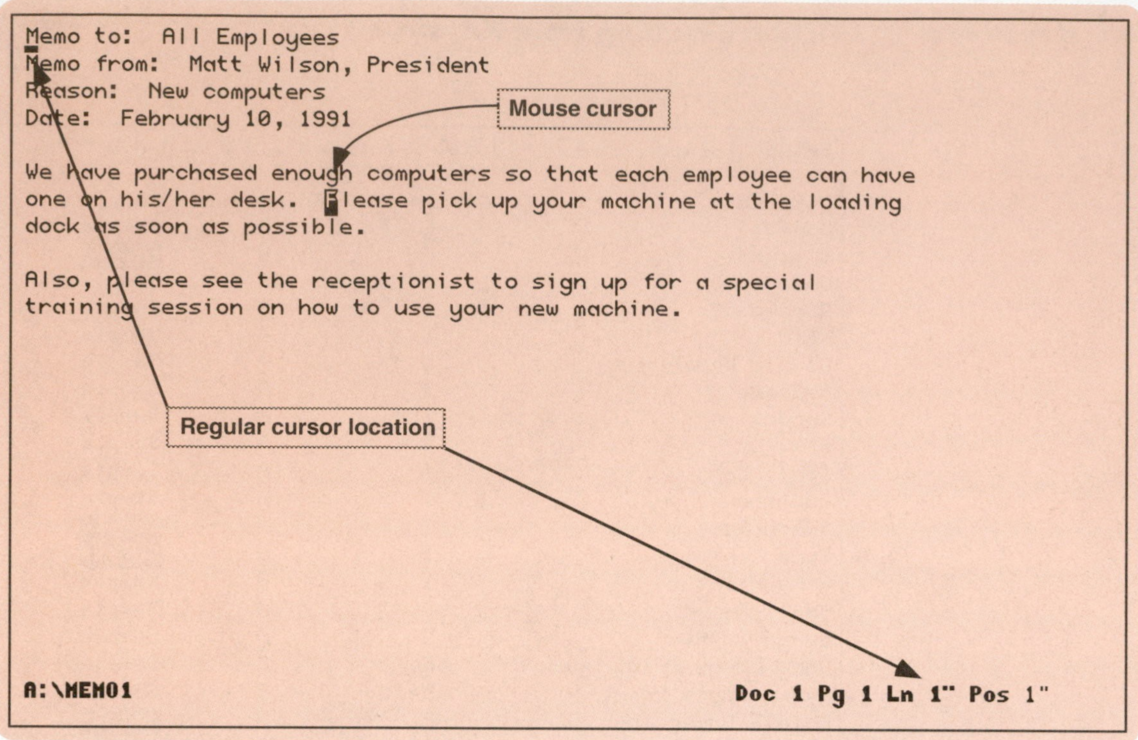

Memo to: All Employees
Memo from: Matt Wilson, President
Reason: New computers
Date: February 10, 1991
Mouse cursor
We have purchased enough computers so that each employee can have
one on his/her desk. Please pick up your machine at the loading
dock as soon as possible.
Also, please see the receptionist to sign up for a special
training session on how to use your new machine.
Regular cursor location
A:\MEMO1
Doc 1 Pg 1 Ln 1" Pos 1"

3. While holding the mouse perfectly still, click the *left* mouse button. The cursor will move to the location of the mouse cursor and the status line will display the location as **`Ln 2" Pos 3.2"`**.

4. Press **[End]**. This will move the cursor to the end of the line (location **`Ln 2" Pos 7.4"`**) and the mouse cursor will disappear. To make the mouse cursor reappear, move the mouse very slightly (actually, if you just touch the mouse the cursor will probably reappear—it is very sensitive).

5. Use the **[F7]** key to exit the document.

• *The Mouse and Blocking* •

For practice, load the document **`MRMPREP.V2`** and try using the mouse to select the first sentence of the first paragraph as a block by doing the following:

1. Move the cursor to the top of the screen by pressing **[Home] Home]** 🡅. The location on the status line should read **`Ln 1" Pos 1"`**.

2. Move the mouse until the first letter in the first paragraph (the **`W`** in **`We need to prepare`**...) is highlighted by the mouse cursor.

3. While holding the mouse perfectly still, click the *left* mouse button. The cursor will move to the location of the mouse cursor and the status line will display the location as **`Ln 2.67" Pos 2.5"`**.

4. Hold down the *left* mouse button and slide the mouse (this is called a *drag*) until the mouse cursor is at the end of the sentence (the space just past the period), and then let up on the button. As soon as you begin to slide the mouse (with the *left* button held down), the words **`Block on`** begin flashing on the status line. As you continue to slide the mouse, the block is selected. When you stop moving the mouse and let up the button, the block will remain selected just as if you had used the **[Alt-F4]** and **[arrow]** keys.

MEMORANDUM

DATE: February 10, 1991

TO: Bill Schwartz and Lisa Pearson

FROM: Alec Benson

SUBJECT: Preparation of Conference Room

We need to prepare the conference room for a meeting of the Board of Directors to be held from 9:00 am to 11:30 am on February 12, 1991. The following have to be taken care of by that time:

1. The room needs to be cleaned (call Quick Klean Company?).

2. An overhead projector and a screen have to be rented (call Readi Rents?) and set up at the front of the room.

3. Name tags for the twenty participants need to be prepared. See Jim Wilson for the list of names.

Block on **Doc 1 Pg 1 Ln 3.17" Pos** 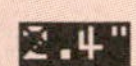

Note that the mouse cursor is not a part of the selected block. You now may do any operation on the block (e.g., copy, move, delete).

5. To unselect the block, click the *left* mouse button. To select another block, follow the exact same procedure.

• Some Mouse Tips •

As you become more familiar with your mouse, the following tips may be of some interest to you.

1. This is the most important tip of all: You do not have to use the mouse when working with WordPerfect. In fact, you may find it easier to do some operations using the keyboard instead of the mouse. As you become more familiar with the mouse, you will be able to decide when to use it and when not to. If it gets in your way, do not use it.
2. Holding down either button and then clicking the other button is the same as tapping the **[F1]** key (i.e., this cancels an operation). If you have a three-button mouse, clicking the middle button has the same effect.
3. Clicking the *right* mouse button when a menu is displayed is the same as tapping the **[F7]** key (i.e., it exits the menu).
4. If you hold down the *right* mouse button and then drag the mouse so that the mouse cursor moves off the screen (top, bottom, left, or right), the text will automatically scroll with the mouse cursor (of course this assumes that there is text to scroll to).
5. When in *List Files*, if you highlight a subdirectory, click the *left* button twice, and then click the *right* button once, the files from that subdirectory will be displayed.
6. You can customize the operation of your mouse by using the *Setup* feature. To do this, press **[Shift-F1]** to select *Setup* and then press **[1]** to select **1 - Mouse** (or use the mouse to select **Mouse** from the **Setup** menu under the **File** menu). This will present you with a list of options for your mouse. See the *WordPerfect Reference Manual* for more details.
7. Keep your mouse environment as clean as possible. The little ball on the bottom can easily pick up dust, dirt, and bread crumbs which can cause problems. You should periodically

clean your mouse to keep it in good operating condition (see the cleaning instructions that came with your mouse).

8. A major problem with using a mouse is that it is in a new location after each use. This makes it necessary to take your eyes off your work to find the little rodent when you need to use it and that slows you down. Also, because you must move the mouse to operate it, you need some clear space on your desk top (a big problem for messy writers with small offices). One solution to this problem is to replace your mouse with a *track ball.* A track ball is basically a mouse turned upside down so that the roller ball is facing up. With a track ball, you roll your fingers over the ball without moving the device itself. Some people love track balls (e.g., one of the authors of this book) while others hate them (the other author). You might try one out to see if you like it.

• Summary of Selected Features •

The following is a brief description of many of the WordPerfect version 5.1/5.0 commands and features with reference to pages in the text. Items with N/C in place of a page number were not specifically covered in the text but are provided for your information. Consult the *WordPerfect Reference Manual* for more details.

Quick Review

Page	Keystrokes	Description
W7	WP ↵	Access WordPerfect from the DOS environment.
W32	[F7] N N	Clear the screen (without saving the current document).
W18–19	[F7] N Y	Exit WordPerfect (without saving current document) and return to DOS.
W15	[Shift-F7]	Print a document.
W33	[F5] ↵ R	Retrieve a document (use **[arrow]** keys to select file from list).
W93	[Shift-F10]	Retrieve a document (type file specification).
W14	[F10]	Save a document.

Cursor Control

Page	Keystrokes	Description
W49	←	Move the cursor one character **left**.
W49	→	Move the cursor one character **right**.
W49	↑	Move the cursor one line **up**
W49	↓	Move the cursor one line **dwn**.
W49	↵	Move the cursor down and to the left (add a line).
W49	[Ctrl ←]	Move to the **previous** word on the line.
W49	[Ctrl →]	Move to the **next** word on the line.
W49	[Home] ←	Move the cursor to the **left** end of text.
W49	[Home] →	Move the cursor to the **right** end of text.
W49	[Home] ↑	Move the cursor to the **top** of screen.
W49	[Home] ↓	Move the cursor to the **bottom** of screen.

Continued . . .

Page	Keystrokes	Description
W50	**[Home] [Home] ↑**	Move the cursor to the **top** of the document.
W50	**[Home] [Home] ↓**	Move the cursor to the **bottom** of the document.
W50	**[PageDown]**	Move the cursor to the first line of the **next** page.
W50	**[PageUp]**	Move the cursor to the first line of the **previous** page.
W50	**Numeric keypad +**	Move the cursor to the last line on the screen.
W50	**Numeric keypad –**	Move the cursor to the first line on the screen.
W50	**[Tab]**	Move the cursor **right** to the next tab stop.
W50	**[Shift-Tab]**	Move the cursor **left** to the previous tab stop.
W50	**[End]**	Move the cursor to the end of the current line.

Modifying Lines

Page	Keystrokes	Description
W12	**[Backspace]**	Delete the character to the left of the cursor (i.e., backspace over the previous character).
N/C	**[Ctrl-Backspace]**	Delete the word at the cursor.
W30	**[Ctrl-End]**	Delete from the cursor to the end of the line.
W30	**[Delete]**	Delete the character at the cursor.
W28	**[Insert]**	Toggle between insert and typeover modes.
W49	**↵**	Insert a new line.
N/C	**[Ctrl-PageDown]**	Delete to the end of the page.

Features

Page	Keystrokes	Description
W71	**[Alt-F4]**	Block—turn on or off.
W85	**[F6]**	Boldface a selected block of text.
W12	**[F1]**	Cancel an operation.
W84	**[Shift-F3]**	Case conversion (switch)—change uppercase letters into lowercase letters and vice versa of a selected block.
W83	**[Shift-F6]**	Center a selected block of text.
N/C	**[Shift-F8]** `P C`	Center the page between top and bottom.
W51	**[Alt-F3]**	Codes, reveal (show WordPerfect codes for indents, margins, returns, tabs, etc.).
W110–11	**[F5] ↵** `C`	Copy a file.
W71–75	**[Ctrl-F4]**	Copy or cut sentences, paragraphs, pages, or selected blocks of text.

Continued . . .

Page	Keystrokes	Description
W48	[Shift-F5] T	Date, insert current date at cursor.
N/C	[F5] ↵ D	Delete a file from within *List Files* feature.
W30	[Ctrl-End]	Delete from the cursor to the end of the line.
W30	[Delete]	Delete the character at the cursor.
N/C	[Ctrl-Backspace]	Delete the word at the cursor.
N/C	[Ctrl-PageDown]	Delete to the end of the page.
W69	[Shift-F8] L S 2 ↵	Double space text.
W68	[Ctrl-F1] G	Drop to DOS (execute DOS commands without leaving WordPerfect). To return to WordPerfect, type **EXIT** ↵.
W18–19	[F7]	Exit a document and/or WordPerfect.
W136–37	[Alt-F9] F	Figure (graphics).
W89	[Alt-F6]	Flush right (align selected block on the right-hand margin).
W87–89	[Shift-F8] P F	Footers, create and edit.
W172	[Ctrl-F7] F	Footnote, create and edit.
W53	[Shift-F8]	Format lines (justification, numbering, spacing, margins, tabs), pages (center, footers, headers, numbering) or the entire document.
W136–37	[Alt-F9] F	Graphics (figure).
W91	[Ctrl-Enter]	Hard page break.
W52	[Enter]	Hard return.
W87–88	[Shift-F8] P H	Headers, create and edit.
W10–12	[F3]	Help screens.
W62	[F4]	Indent from the left.
W62	[Shift-F4]	Indent from the left and right.
W116	[Ctrl-F5] T R	Insert text from a file into the current file.
W79	[Shift-F8] L J	Justify (line up) lines of text.
W79	[Shift-F8] L N	Line numbering, set.
W69	[Shift-F8] L S	Line spacing, adjust.
W106–12	[F5] ↵	List files.
W109	[F5] ↵ L	Look at (examine) a file.
W148	[Ctrl-F10]	Macro define.
W153	[Alt-F10]	Macro execute.
W130	[Shift-F9]	Mail merge, insert codes.
W135	[Ctrl-F9] M	Mail merge, carry out process.
W52	[Shift-Tab]	Margin release (tab to the left).
W58	[Shift-F8] L M	Margin set (left and right).
N/C	[Shift-F8] P M	Margin set (top and bottom).
W130	[Shift-F9]	Merge, insert codes.

Continued . . .

Page	Keystrokes	Description
W135	**[Ctrl-F9]** `M`	Merge, carry out process.
N/C	**[Ctrl-F4]** `A M`	Move page which contains cursor.
W74	**[Ctrl-F4]** `P M`	Move paragraph which contains cursor.
W71–72	**[Ctrl-F4]** `B`	Move selected block (use **[Alt-F4]** to select first).
W75–76	**[Ctrl-F4]** `S M`	Move sentence which contains cursor.
W79	**[Shift-F8]** `L N`	Numbering—line.
W161	**[Shift-F5]** `O`	Outline.
W87	**[Shift-F8]** `P`	Page format (numbering, centering, length, headers, footers).
N/C	**[F5]** ↵ `P`	Print a document (select from a list).
W15	**[Shift-F7]**	Print the current document.
W126	**[Alt-F2]**	Replace (search for and replace specific characters).
W33	**[F5]** ↵ `R`	Retrieve a document (use **[arrow]** keys to select the file name from list).
W93	**[Shift-F10]**	Retrieve a document (type file specification).
W51	**[Alt-F3]**	Reveal codes (show WordPerfect codes for indents, margins, returns, tabs, etc.).
W14	**[F10]**	Save a file.
W124	**[F2]**	Search for specific characters or codes beginning at the cursor and searching toward the **bottom** of the document.
W125	**[Shift-F2]**	Search for specific characters or codes beginning at the cursor and searching toward **top** of the document.
W68	**[Ctrl-F1]** `G`	Shell (execute DOS commands without leaving WordPerfect). To return, type **`EXIT`** ↵.
W121	**[Ctrl-F9]**	Sort lines, paragraphs or merge codes.
W69	**[Shift-F8]** `L S`	Spacing—line.
W93	**[Ctrl-F2]**	Spell—check the spelling of a document.
N/C	**[Ctrl-F3]** `W`	Split the screen into two windows.
W118	**[Shift-F3]**	Switch between documents.
W53–55	**[Shift-F8]** `L T`	Tab, set.
W116	**[Ctrl-F5]** `T R`	Text in (insert text from a file you specify into the current file).
W96	**[Alt-F1]**	Thesaurus.
W28	**[Insert]**	Typeover (toggles between insert and typeover mode).
W85	**[F8]**	Underline selected block.
W17	**[Shift-F7]** `V`	View a document (print preview).

Selected Codes The following codes can be made visible by pressing **[Alt-F3]**. They may be deleted by using the **[arrow]** keys to highlight them and then pressing **[Delete]**. Some of the codes will have extra information displayed inside the square brackets. For example, **`[L/R Mar:1",2"]`** means that the left margin is set to one inch while the right margin is set to two inches.

Page	Keystroke that produces code	Code	Description
W71	[Alt-F4]	`[block]`	Beginning of a selected block of text.
W85	[F6]	`[BOLD][bold]`	Bold (begin and end).
W83	[Shift-F6]	`[Center]`	Center one line of text between left and right margins. Compare with `[Just:Center]` which centers several lines of text.
N/C	[Shift-F8] **P C**	`[Center Pg]`	Center page between top and bottom margins.
W48	[Shift-F5] **T**	`[Date]`	Date feature.
W184	[Alt-F5] **D I**	`[Def Mark:Index]`	Index definition.
W182	[Alt-F5] **D C**	`[Def Mark:ToC]`	Table of contents definition.
N/C		`[End Def]`	End definition for index, list or table of contents.
W142	[Alt-F9] **E C**	`[Equ Box]`	Equation box.
W136–37	[Alt-F9] **F C**	`[Fig Box]`	Figure (graphic) box.
W89	[Alt-F6]	`[Flsh Rt]`	Flush right (right justify) text.
W87–89	[Shift-F8] **P F**	`[Footer]`	Footer definition.
W87–89	[Shift-F8] **P H**	`[Header]`	Header definition.
W91	[Ctrl-Enter]	`[HPg]`	Hard page.
W52	[Enter]	`[HRt]`	Hard return.
W62	[F4]	`[->Indent]`	Indent from the left.
W62	[Shift-F4]	`[->Indent<-]`	Indent from the left and right.
N/C	[Alt-F5] **I**	`[Index]`	Index entry.
W78	[Shift-F8] **L J C**	`[Just:Center]`	Center justification (different code in version 5.0).
W78	[Shift-F8] **L J F**	`[Just:Full]`	Full justification (different code in version 5.0).
W78	[Shift-F8] **L J L**	`[Just:Left]`	Left justification (different code in version 5.0).
W78	[Shift-F8] **L J R**	`[Just:Right]`	Right justification (different code in version 5.0).
W58	[Shift-F8] **L M**	`[L/R Mar]`	Margin setting.
W79	[Shift-F8] **L N**	`[Ln Num]`	Line numbering.
W69	[Shift-F8] **L S**	`[Ln Spacing]`	Line spacing.
W52	[Shift-Tab]	`[<-Mar Rel]`	Left margin release.
W180	[Alt-F5] **C**	`[Mark:ToC]`	Table of contents entry.
W185	[Shift-F8] **P N**	`[Pg Num]`	New page number, begin.
W52		`[SRt]`	Soft return (word wrap was employed).

Continued . . .

Page	Keystroke that produces code	Code	Description
W140	[Ctrl-F8] **S B**	**[SUBSCRPT][subscrpt]**	Subscript (begin and end)
W141	[Ctrl-F8] **S P**	**[SUPRSCRPT][suprscrpt]**	Superscript (begin and end)
W50	[Tab]	**[Tab]**	Left tab.
W53–55	[Shift-F8] **L T**	**[Tab Set]**	Tab setting.
W85	[F8]	**[UND][und]**	Underline (begin and end).

Pull-Down Menu Organization For your reference, the next two pages contain charts showing the organization of the WordPerfect pull-down menus.

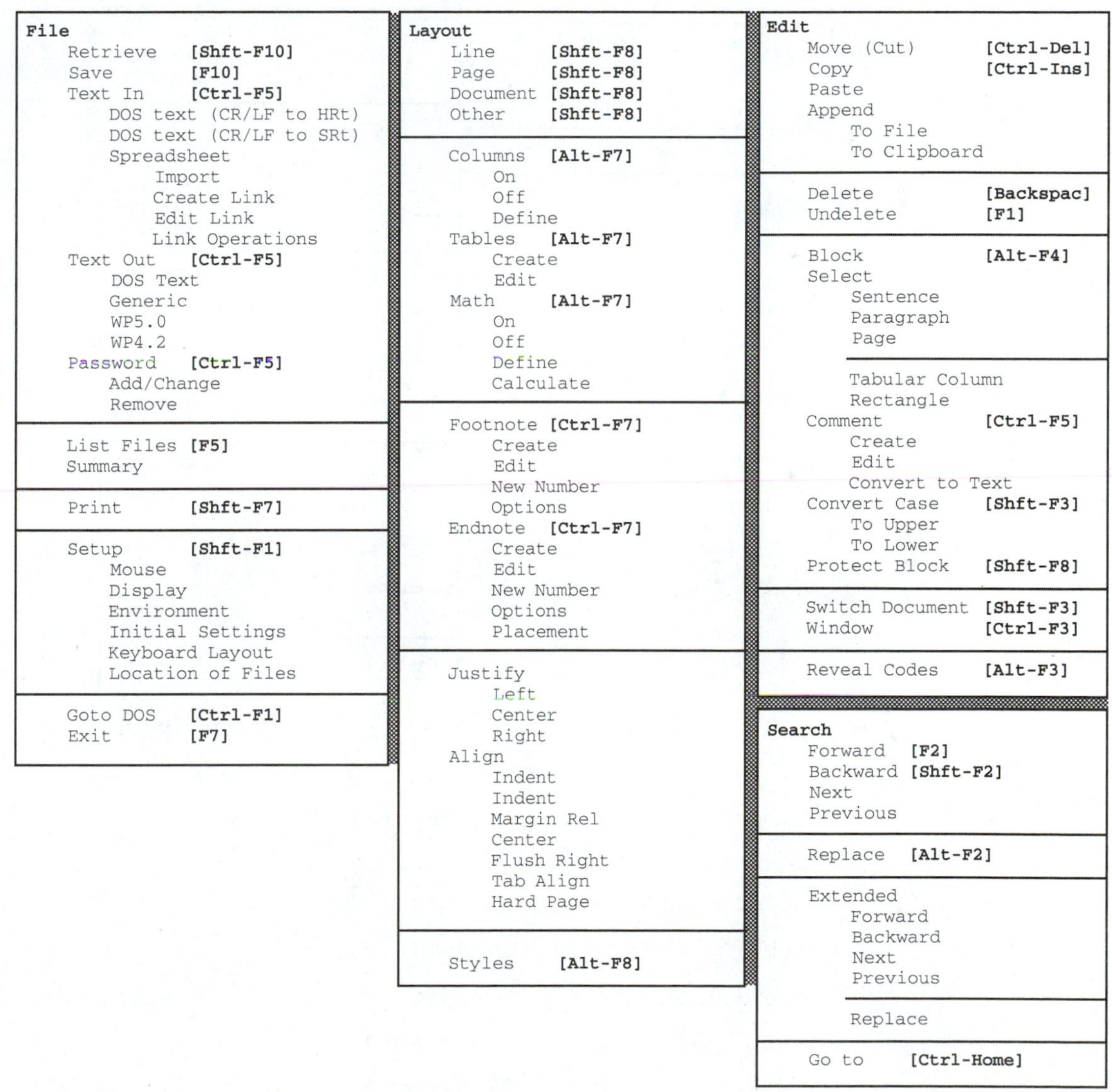

```
File
    Retrieve     [Shft-F10]
    Save         [F10]
    Text In      [Ctrl-F5]
        DOS text (CR/LF to HRt)
        DOS text (CR/LF to SRt)
        Spreadsheet
            Import
            Create Link
            Edit Link
            Link Operations
    Text Out     [Ctrl-F5]
        DOS Text
        Generic
        WP5.0
        WP4.2
    Password     [Ctrl-F5]
        Add/Change
        Remove
    -----------------------
    List Files [F5]
    Summary
    -----------------------
    Print        [Shft-F7]
    -----------------------
    Setup        [Shft-F1]
        Mouse
        Display
        Environment
        Initial Settings
        Keyboard Layout
        Location of Files
    -----------------------
    Goto DOS     [Ctrl-F1]
    Exit         [F7]
```

```
Layout
    Line      [Shft-F8]
    Page      [Shft-F8]
    Document  [Shft-F8]
    Other     [Shft-F8]
    -----------------------
    Columns   [Alt-F7]
        On
        Off
        Define
    Tables    [Alt-F7]
        Create
        Edit
    Math      [Alt-F7]
        On
        Off
        Define
        Calculate
    -----------------------
    Footnote  [Ctrl-F7]
        Create
        Edit
        New Number
        Options
    Endnote   [Ctrl-F7]
        Create
        Edit
        New Number
        Options
        Placement
    -----------------------
    Justify
        Left
        Center
        Right
    Align
        Indent
        Indent
        Margin Rel
        Center
        Flush Right
        Tab Align
        Hard Page
    -----------------------
    Styles     [Alt-F8]
```

```
Edit
    Move (Cut)           [Ctrl-Del]
    Copy                 [Ctrl-Ins]
    Paste
    Append
        To File
        To Clipboard
    -----------------------
    Delete               [Backspac]
    Undelete             [F1]
    -----------------------
    Block                [Alt-F4]
    Select
        Sentence
        Paragraph
        Page
        ---------------
        Tabular Column
        Rectangle
    Comment              [Ctrl-F5]
        Create
        Edit
        Convert to Text
    Convert Case         [Shft-F3]
        To Upper
        To Lower
    Protect Block        [Shft-F8]
    -----------------------
    Switch Document      [Shft-F3]
    Window               [Ctrl-F3]
    -----------------------
    Reveal Codes         [Alt-F3]
```

```
Search
    Forward   [F2]
    Backward  [Shft-F2]
    Next
    Previous
    -----------------------
    Replace   [Alt-F2]
    -----------------------
    Extended
        Forward
        Backward
        Next
        Previous
        ---------------
        Replace
    -----------------------
    Go to     [Ctrl-Home]
```

Graphics

- Figure [Alt-F9]
  - Create
  - Edit
  - New Number
  - Options
- Table Box [Alt-F9]
  - Create
  - Edit
  - New Number
  - Options
- Text Box [Alt-F9]
  - Create
  - Edit
  - New Number
  - Options
- User Box [Alt-F9]
  - Create
  - Edit
  - New Number
  - Options
- Equation [Alt-F9]
  - Create
  - Edit
  - New Number
  - Options

- Line [Alt-F9]
  - Create Horizontal
  - Create Vertical
  - Edit Horizontal

- Edit Vertical

Font

- Base Font [Ctrl-F8]

- Normal [Ctrl-F8]
- Appearance [Ctrl-F8]
  - Bold
  - Underline
  - Double Underline
  - Italics
  - Outline
  - Shadow
  - Small Cap
  - Redline
  - Strikeout
- Superscript
- Subscript
- Fine
- Small
- Large
- Very Large
- Extra Large

- Print Color [Ctrl-F8]

- Characters [Ctrl-V]

Tools

- Spell [Ctrl-F2]
- Thesaurus [Alt-F1]

- Macro
  - Define
  - Execute
- Date Text [Shft-F5]
- Date Code [Shft-F5]
- Date [Format [Shft-F5]

- Outline [Shft-F5]
  - On
  - Off
  - Move Family
  - Copy Family
  - Delete Family
- Paragraph Number [Shft-F5]
- Define [Shft-F5]

- Merge Codes [Shft-F9]
  - Field
  - End Record
  - Input
  - Page Off
  - Next Record
  - More
- Merge [Ctrl-F9]

- Sort [Ctrl-F9]

- Line Draw [Ctrl-F3]

Mark

- Index [Alt-F5]
- Table of Contents
- List
- Cross-Reference [Alt-F5]
  - Reference
  - Target
  - Both
- Table of Authorities
  - Mark Short
  - Mark Full
  - Edit Full

- Define
  - Index
  - Table of Contents
  - List
  - Table of Authorities

- Generate

- Master Documents
  - Expand
  - Condense
- Subdocument [Alt-F5]

- Document Compare
  - Add Markings

Help

- Help [F3]
- Index
- Template

PART II

Lotus 1-2-3 Release 2.2

Introduction to Spreadsheets

Objectives *After you have completed this chapter, you should be able to*

- Define commonly used terms associated with spreadsheet programs.
- Access the Lotus 1-2-3 spreadsheet program.
- Identify the different parts of the Lotus 1-2-3 screen.
- Access on-line help from a spreadsheet program.
- Access and use Lotus 1-2-3 menus to perform various tasks.
- Exit the Lotus 1-2-3 environment and return to the DOS environment.
- Enter labels, numeric data, and formulas into a worksheet.
- Format, save, retrieve, and print a worksheet.
- Drop to DOS (i.e., execute DOS commands without exiting Lotus 1-2-3).

CHAPTER 1

- Insert and delete rows of a worksheet.
- Employ predefined spreadsheet functions such as **@AVG** and **@SUM**.
- Use the *Undo* feature to cancel the effect of a command.
- Mark and name cell ranges.
- Sort worksheet data using different criteria.
- Set global defaults for a worksheet.
- Switch between manual and automatic recalculation.
- Select various printing options including headers, footers, and numbering.

Introduction

A **spreadsheet** is a ledger or table used for mathematical calculations and for the recording of transactions. An electronic spreadsheet is a computer-based spreadsheet that uses columns and rows to store, compute, rearrange, and display information of a numeric, alphanumeric, or graphical type.

Spreadsheets are used to help make business decisions by keeping easily retrievable records and by allowing the user to monitor the effects of changes in specific financial strategies. Individuals may also do this in their personal finances. For example, let's say that you enter your tax return for this year on a spreadsheet. You can enter what you think you will earn and what you expect for deductions. The spreadsheet can be programmed to compute your estimated tax. Of course, if the tax laws change before next year, the projections will be in error, but you still can get a very good idea of what your tax will probably be. Next, you can change your deductions (e.g., increase charitable contributions) and the spreadsheet will instantly show the effect on your final tax. The more complex your tax situation, the more options you have, and the more information you can get from the spreadsheet analysis.

Spreadsheets also can be used to keep track of inventory, accounts, names and addresses, or anything else that involves numbers or other types of information.

In this book, we will focus on the Lotus 1-2-3 Release 2.2 spreadsheet program. This program was introduced in 1983 and has since become the industry standard for spreadsheets. The program is actually three programs integrated into a single package (hence the name 1-2-3). With it you can perform traditional spreadsheet operations, but you also can create and manipulate databases and graphs.

Definitions

Before beginning a specific example, you should familiarize yourself with the definitions of some terms frequently encountered when talking about spreadsheets. As you read through the definitions, refer to the following figure:

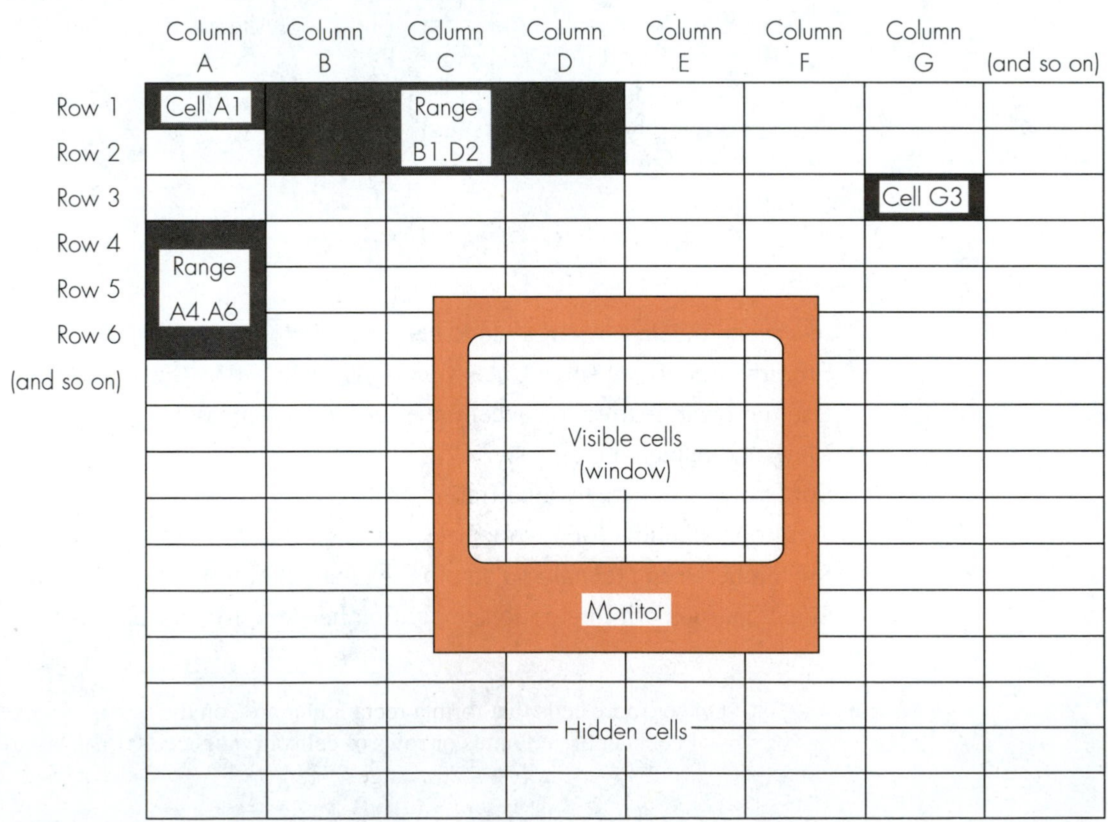

Active cell . . . (L12) The cell currently being worked on. The active cell can be changed using the **[F5]** (**Go To**) key, the movement keys such as **[Home]** and **[End]**, and the **[arrow]** keys in much the same way that the cursor was moved in WordPerfect.

Automatic recalculation . . . (L66) The feature that automatically recalculates all formulas and functions whenever a cell value is changed.

Cell . . . (L12) A location within a spreadsheet used to store a single piece of information. Cells may contain numbers, text (also called labels or titles), or formulas. They are similar to the variables used in computer languages such as BASIC. A cell is one column wide and one row high.

Cell format . . . (L23) The way the contents of a cell are to appear on the screen. For example, cells can be formatted so that values are displayed with a specified number of decimal places, commas, the dollar sign, or the percent sign. Cells also can be formatted so that their contents are hidden (i.e., do not appear on the screen at all) or labels are right-, center-, or left-justified. A cell format does not affect the contents of the cell, only the way the contents appear on the screen.

Cell pointer . . . (L13) A rectangular block on the screen, usually in reverse video (black on white rather than white on black), that indicates which cell is currently active.

Cell width . . . (L22) The number of characters a cell can display.

Coordinates . . . (L39) The location of a cell within a spreadsheet. The column component of the cell coordinate is usually written first and designated with a letter while the row component is usually designated with a number. For example, the coordinates **G3** would refer to column **G** (the seventh column from the left) and row **3** (the third row from the top).

Function . . . (L46) A shorthand formula for a predetermined operation. For example, **@AVG(A1.A5)** will find the average of all the numbers in cells **A1**, **A2**, **A3**, **A4**, and **A5**. With such functions, you do not have to figure out the actual formula needed. A list of many of the functions available in Lotus 1-2-3 is in the Appendix.

Label . . . (L18) Text information used to describe some aspect of the spreadsheet (e.g., a column heading). This is also referred to as a title.

Mathematical operators . . . (L33) The symbols used to indicate mathematical operations. Lotus 1-2-3 uses the standard computer notation for the mathematical operations:

addition (+), such as	**6 + 2**
subtraction (–), such as	**6 – 2**
multiplication (*), such as	**6*2**
division (/), such as	**6/2**
exponentiation (^), such as	**6^2**

Numeric Formula . . . (L34) A mathematical expression within the spreadsheet. This can include both numbers and cell coordinates. For example, **B3/100 + C3** means that the contents of cell **B3** will be divided by **100**, then the quotient will be added to the contents of cell **C3** and then the result will be displayed in the active cell.

Range . . . (L30) One or more cells that form a rectangular area on the screen. Ranges can be specific rectangular groups of cells, entire columns or rows of cells, or single cells. Ranges are identified using the coordinates of two opposite corners of the range separated by one or two periods (Lotus 1-2-3 always stores the ranges with two periods even if you only type one).

B1.D2 is a range that includes cells **B1**, **B2**, **C1**, **C2**, **D1**, and **D2**. Notice that the range is defined by the cell coordinates of two opposite corners of the rectangle, separated by a period:

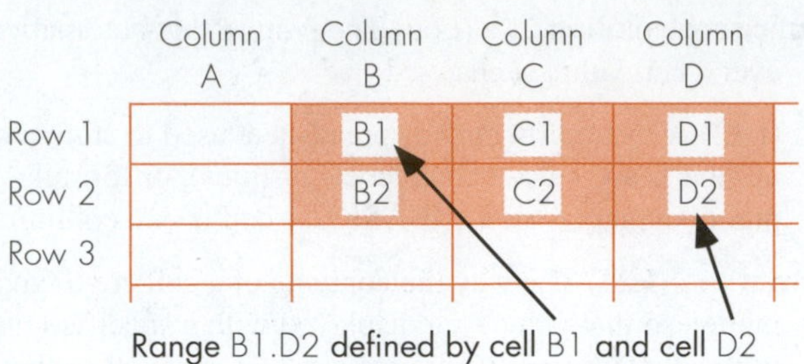

Range B1.D2 defined by cell B1 and cell D2

The order in which you write the cell coordinates makes no difference, nor do the corners you pick (as long as they are opposite corners). Also, you may insert one or two periods between the cell coordinates. Thus, the above range could be identified in any of the following ways:

Range	Comment
B1.D2	Uses the upper-left and lower-right corners with one period.
D2.B1	Uses the upper-left and lower-right corners but in reverse order, with one period.
B1..D2	Uses the upper-left and lower-right corners with two periods.
D2..B1	Uses the upper-left and lower-right corners but in reverse order, with two periods.
B2.D1	Uses the lower-left and upper-right corners with one period.
D1.B2	Uses the lower-left and upper-right corners but in reverse order, with one period.
B2..D1	Uses the lower-left and upper-right corners with two periods.
D1..B2	Uses the lower-left and upper-right corners but in reverse order, with two periods.

For consistency in this book, we will describe ranges using the upper-left and lower-right corners with one period (e.g., **B1.D2**).

A1.A1 is a range that includes only cell **A1**:

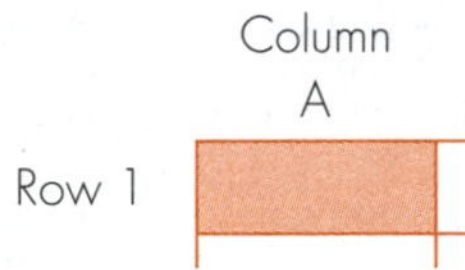

G1.G31 is a range that includes all cells in column **G** from row **1** through row **31** (i.e., cells **G1**, **G2**, **G3**, ... **G31**):

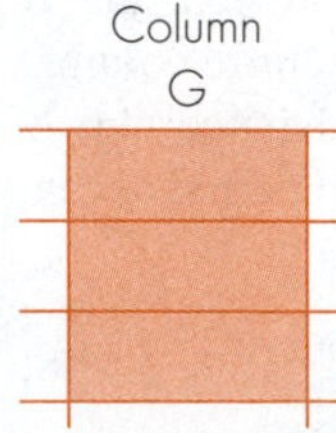

A3.D3 is a range that includes all cells in row **3** from column **A** through column **D** (i.e., cells **A3**, **B3**, **C3**, and **D3**):

	Column A	Column B	Column C	Column D
Row 1				
Row 2				
Row 3				

Window . . . (L13) The cells of the worksheet that can be seen on the computer display at one time. This is usually only a small part of the entire worksheet.

Worksheet . . . (L12) The matrix of rows and columns, including any data that have been entered, displayed by a spreadsheet program. Synonymous with *spreadsheet*.

System Requirements

The full Lotus 1-2-3 package distributed by Lotus Development Corporation contains twelve diskettes, a 400-page *Lotus 1-2-3 Set-Up Guide,* and a 600-page *Lotus 1-2-3 Reference Manual.* In order to work with Lotus 1-2-3 you must have an IBM or IBM-compatible computer system that has two floppy disk drives (or a hard disk) and at least 320K of RAM. Note that Lotus 1-2-3 supports up to 640K of conventional memory and 4mb of expanded memory.

For your information and reference, a summary of selected Lotus 1-2-3 Release 2.2 features appears in the Appendix. In addition, a keyboard template that contains a summary of many program features is located at the end of this book. If your keyboard has twelve function keys along the top, cut out the two halves of the template, tape the ends together, and place the template around the function keys. If your keyboard has ten function keys along the left-hand side, you still may use the top of the template, but the bottom must be cut off.

Lotus 1-2-3 can be run on many different computer systems that have different monitors, printers, keyboards, and microprocessors. Before you use the program you must first install it so that it knows specifically which hardware you will be using. The installation process is accomplished in three steps. First, you must run an initialization program to record your name and the name of your company (if appropriate) on the *Lotus 1-2-3 System* diskette. This uniquely identifies you as the owner of the program (remember, like WordPerfect and most other programs, Lotus 1-2-3 is copyrighted and it is illegal, and unethical, to give copies to others). The second step in the installation process is to make copies of the Lotus 1-2-3 master diskettes either on your hard disk or on other floppy diskettes. The last step is to run the install program in order to specify the particular type of hardware (e.g., monitor, printer) you will be using.

For the purposes of this book, we will assume that Lotus 1-2-3 has already been properly installed on your computer system. If it has not, the installation process is described in detail in the *Lotus 1-2-3 Set-Up Guide.*

Lotus 1-2-3 is a large program that is designed to be operated on a hard-disk system. In this book, we will assume that you are working on such a system and that the Lotus 1-2-3 software has been installed on the hard disk in a subdirectory with path **C:\123**. However, we will also provide pertinent information for those of you working on a two-drive system. In either case, your course instructor may give you different directions for accessing the program and for saving data files for the particular computer system available to you in your school's computer lab.

Formatting a Data Diskette

Before turning on the computer, be sure you have the proper diskettes handy.

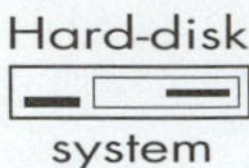

IF YOU ARE USING A HARD-DISK SYSTEM, you need a blank diskette that will serve as your *Lotus Data* diskette. You will use this diskette for storing the Lotus 1-2-3 worksheets that you create. If you are using your own computer, you do not need this diskette (you will want to save files directly to your hard disk).

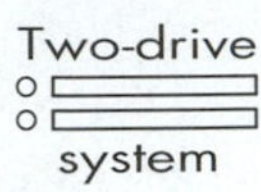

IF YOU ARE USING A TWO-DRIVE SYSTEM, you need the DOS diskette, a backup copy of the *Lotus System* diskette (one of the twelve diskettes that came with the full Lotus 1-2-3 package), and a blank diskette that will serve as your *Lotus Data/Boot* diskette (you will store your worksheets on this diskette).

Start up your computer and then format a blank diskette to serve as the *Lotus Data* diskette by doing the following:

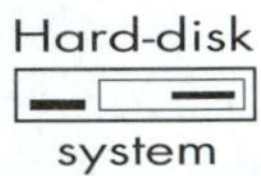

IF YOU ARE USING A HARD-DISK SYSTEM, do the following:

- Write *Lotus Data/Boot* and your name on a diskette label, attach the label to a new diskette, and insert the diskette into the A: drive.
- Type **FORMAT A:/V/F:*size*** (***size*** is diskette capacity — 360, 720, 1200, or 1440) and press **[Enter]**.
- When asked to enter a label, type your last name and press **[Enter]**.
- When asked **Format another (Y/N)?**, type **N** and press **[Enter]**. The system prompt **C:\>** will then be displayed.

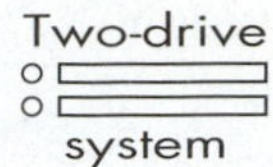

IF YOU ARE USING A TWO-DRIVE SYSTEM, do the following:

- Write *Lotus Data/Boot* and your name on a diskette label, attach the label to a new diskette, and insert the diskette into the B: drive (the DOS diskette should still be in drive A:).
- Type **FORMAT B:/S/V/F:*size*** (***size*** is diskette capacity — 360, 720, 1200, or 1440) and press **[Enter]**.
- When asked to enter a label, type your last name and press **[Enter]**.
- When asked **Format another (Y/N)?**, type **N** and press **[Enter]**. The system prompt **A>** will then be displayed.
- In Chapter 7 you will need to use an external DOS command called **GRAPHICS** in order to do screen dumps of graphs displayed by Lotus 1-2-3. Copy the necessary file from the DOS diskette to your *Lotus Data/Boot* diskette by typing: **COPY A:GRAPHICS.COM B: ↵**.
- Replace the DOS diskette in drive A: with the newly created *Lotus Data/Boot* diskette.
- Insert the *Lotus System* diskette into the B: drive. If you do not have a *Lotus System* diskette, see the installation instructions in the *Lotus 1-2-3 Set-Up Guide*. The *Lotus System* diskette contains the programs needed to do everything except print graphs (for that you need the *PrintGraph* diskette), access on-line help (for that you need the *Help* diskette), and transfer data to and from other applications such as dBASE (for that you need the *Translate* diskette).

Accessing Lotus 1-2-3

To load the Lotus 1-2-3 program into the main memory of the computer, do the following:

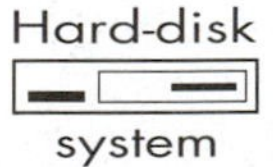

IF YOU ARE USING A HARD-DISK SYSTEM, be sure the *Lotus Data* diskette is in the A: drive and then type the following:

Keystroke	Action Resulting from Keystroke
C: ↵	Makes C: the default drive.
CD\123 ↵	Changes to the **123** subdirectory. The system prompt should look like **C:\123\>**. If the Lotus 1-2-3 files are in a subdirectory with a name other than **123**, use that name in place of **123**.
LOTUS ↵	Loads the program into the main memory of the computer and displays the 1-2-3 Access System screen.

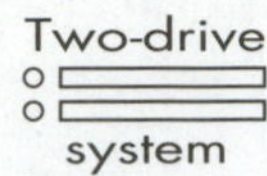

IF YOU ARE USING A TWO-DRIVE SYSTEM, be sure the *Lotus Data/Boot* diskette is in drive A: and the *Lotus System* diskette is in drive B: and then type the following:

Keystroke	Action Resulting from Keystroke
B: ↵	Makes B: the default drive.
LOTUS ↵	Loads the program into the main memory of the computer and displays the 1-2-3 Access System screen.

In a few seconds, the following will appear on the screen:

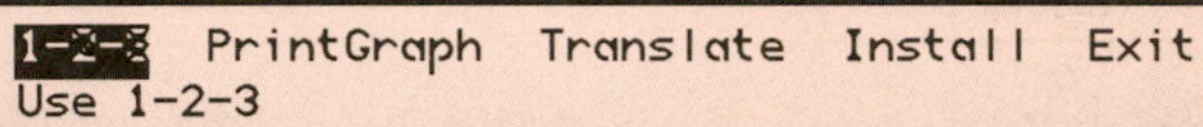

```
1-2-3  PrintGraph  Translate  Install  Exit
Use 1-2-3

                    1-2-3 Access System
                   Copyright  1986, 1989
               Lotus Development Corporation
                    All Rights Reserved
                        Release 2.2

The Access system lets you choose 1-2-3, PrintGraph, the Translate utility,
and the Install program, from the menu at the top of this screen.  If
you're using a two-diskette system, the Access system may prompt you to
change disks.  Follow the instructions below to start a program.

o  Use → or ← to move the menu pointer (the highlighted rectangle
   at the top of the screen) to the program you want to use.

o  Press ENTER to start the program.

You can also start a program by typing the first character of its name.

Press HELP (F1) for more information.
```

The screen is divided into two parts. The first line of the top section displays a menu of five options. An option can be selected by using the **[arrow]** keys and then pressing **[Enter]** or by typing the first character of the desired option.

```
1-2-3  PrintGraph  Translate  Install  Exit
```

1-2-3 allows you to enter the main spreadsheet/graphics/database program. This is the choice you will normally select. In fact, if you type **123** instead of **LOTUS** while in DOS, the Access system will be skipped and the main program will be loaded directly.

PrintGraph allows you to print graphs with a number of enhancements such as different fonts, colors, legends, and sizes.

Translate allows you to import data created by other programs and to export data for use by other programs.

Install allows you to configure the program to match your hardware or to make changes in the current installation.

Exit quits the Access System and returns control to DOS.

The second line of the top section gives a short description of the option highlighted. For example, use the **[arrow]** keys to highlight the **Translate** option:

```
1-2-3  PrintGraph  Translate  Install  Exit
Transfer data between 1-2-3 and other programs
```

The bottom of the screen provides information on how to use the 1-2-3 Access System. Note that the bottom line of the screen tells you to press **[F1]** if you need more information (i.e., *Help*) on the 1-2-3 Access System.

To access the main program, type **1** (or, if you prefer, use the **[arrow]** keys to highlight **1-2-3** and then press the **[Enter]** key). The following copyright screen will be displayed for a few seconds while the program loads into the computer's main memory.

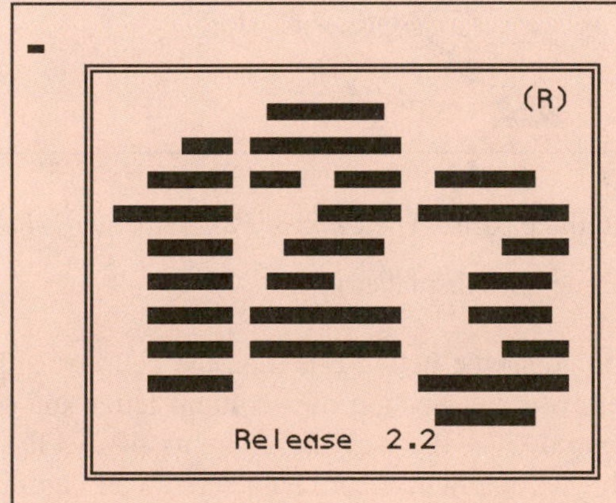


```
Copyright  1985, 1989
Lotus Development Corporation
All Rights Reserved
2W00213-8813343

Licensing Information:

   User Name: Douglas Robertson
Company Name: University of Minnesota

          Use, duplication, or sale of this software, except as
          described in the Lotus License Agreement, is strictly
          prohibited.  Violators may be prosecuted.
```

Notice the copyright statement. It says that the program is copyrighted and, therefore, may not be copied by you to give to others. However, if you are the licensed owner of the program you may make backup copies for your own use. In a few seconds an empty worksheet will be displayed.

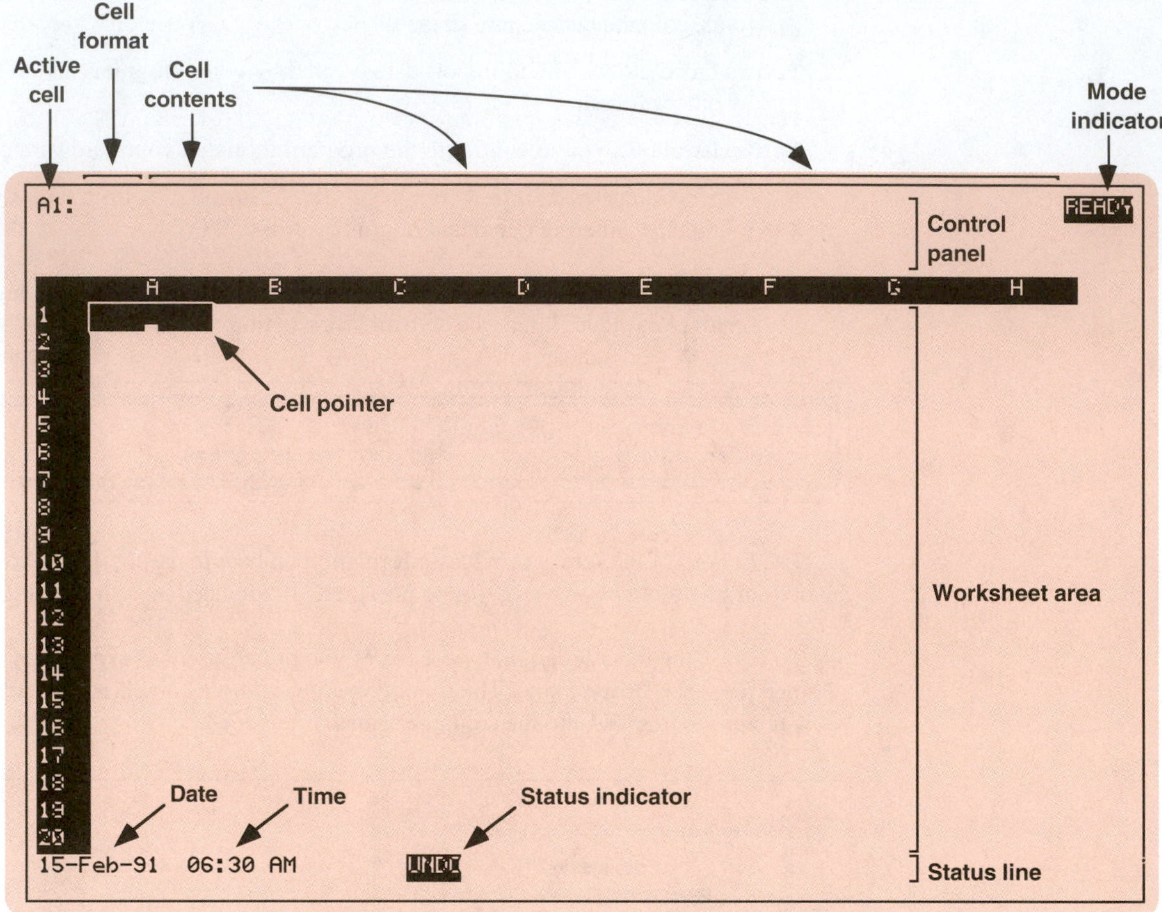

The screen is broken up into three parts: The *Control Panel*, the *worksheet area*, and the *status line*.

Control Panel (the first three lines displayed).

- Line 1 contains information about the **active cell** (i.e., the cell currently being worked on) such as the cell address (the intersection of a column letter and row number—in this case, **A1**), the **cell format** (i.e., the way the contents of a cell are displayed on the screen), the **cell width** (i.e., the number of characters a cell can display), the **cell contents** (currently, the cell is empty), whether or not the cell is protected from being modified, and the **mode indicator** (the word READY means that the program is waiting for your next command or data entry).
- Line 2 will display menu choices after you tell Lotus 1-2-3 to display the main menu.
- Line 3 will display options of menu choices or explanations of highlighted options.

Worksheet Area (the next 20 lines displayed). This is where Lotus 1-2-3 will display the data, formulas, and labels you enter. In this visible part of the spreadsheet, the rows are **labeled** using numbers **1** through **20** and the columns are labeled with the letters **A** through **H**. The intersection of a row and a column is called a **cell**. Because 20 rows and 8 columns are displayed, there are $20 \times 8 = 160$ cells visible on the screen. Even though you can only see 160 cells at a time, Lotus 1-2-3 allows you to have worksheets that contain millions of cells (although they all may not be able to fit into the computer's memory at one time). You can even link worksheets so that data from one worksheet can be used by other worksheets.

The highlighted rectangle in the upper left-hand corner of the screen where column **A** intersects with row **1** (this location is called **A1**) is called the **cell pointer**. It indicates the active cell. This is where data and formulas you type will be placed when **[Enter]** is pressed. The different parts of the screen will be discussed in more detail later.

Status Line (the bottom line of the display). The status line displays the date and time, or the current file name, error messages, and status indicators such as:

CAPS, which indicates that the **[Caps Lock]** key has been pressed and all letters will be in uppercase.

NUM, which indicates that the **[Num Lock]** key has been pressed and the numeric keypad can be used for entering numbers.

OVR, which indicates that the **[Insert]** key has been pressed placing you in **OV**e**R**type mode—this is what WordPerfect called *Typeover* mode.

SCROLL, which indicates that the **[Scroll Lock]** key has been pressed—pressing an **[arrow]** key will move the entire window in the direction of the arrow instead of moving the cell pointer.

UNDO, which indicates that you may undo your last operation using the **[Alt-F4]** key.

Moving around the Lotus 1-2-3 Screen

You can change the active cell by using the **[arrow]** keys in much the same way you move the cursor around in a word-processing program. In addition, if you want to move to a cell that is not displayed on the screen, you can move to the edge of the screen and simply keep pressing the **[arrow]** key. In that case, the screen will scroll (shift) so that you can view the active cell. For example, to make cell **C2** active you would press the **[right arrow]** key twice and the **[down arrow]** key once. As you press the **[arrow]** keys, Lotus 1-2-3 adjusts the screen so that the active cell is always displayed. In addition, you can go to a specific cell by using the **[F5]** key. For example, make cell **J57** active by doing the following:

Keystroke	Action Resulting from Keystroke
[arrow]	Use the **[arrow]** keys to make cell **C2** active. Notice that the location of the cell pointer, **C2**, is indicated on the left-hand side of the top line of the screen.
[F5]	Specifies that you want to move the cell pointer (go to) and displays the following message in the control panel:

```
Enter address to go to: C2
```

Notice that the current position of the cell pointer, **C2**, is displayed. As soon as you begin to enter the destination cell, **J57**, the current cell pointer position disappears and is replaced by that which you type. When you press **[Enter]**, the cell pointer will be moved to that location.

J57 ↵	Moves the cell pointer to **J57**. Notice the change in the column letters and row numbers displayed on the screen:

Continued . . .

Keystroke	Action Resulting from Keystroke

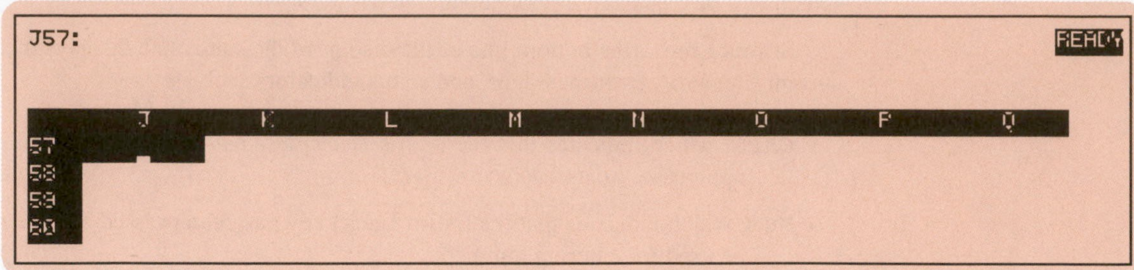

Currently, columns **J** through **Q** and rows **57** through **76** are displayed.

Just to see how it works, enter a piece of data into cell **J57** by typing the following:

Keystroke	Action Resulting from Keystroke
1.2 ↵	Enters the value **1.2** into the active cell. Notice how the value appears in the first line of the screen as well as in the cell **J57**.
[F5]	Specifies that you want to move the cell pointer and displays **Enter address to go to: J57** in the Control Panel.
A1 ↵	Moves the cell pointer to **A1**. Now columns **A** through **H** and rows **1** through **20** are displayed.

The following special keys enable you to move around the spreadsheet screen:

Keystroke	Action Resulting from Keystroke
[Tab]	Moves the cell pointer one screen to the right (**I1** now should be the active cell).
[Ctrl →]	Like **[Tab]**, moves the cell pointer one screen to the right (**Q1** now should be the active cell).
[Shift-Tab]	Moves the cell pointer one screen to the left (**I1** now should be the active cell).
[Ctrl ←]	Like **[Shift-Tab]**, moves the cell pointer one screen to the left (**A1** now should be the active cell).
[PageDown]	Scrolls one screen (20 rows) toward the end of the spreadsheet (**A21** now should be the active cell).
[PageUp]	Scrolls one screen (20 rows) toward the beginning of the spreadsheet (**A1** now should be the active cell).
[End] [Home]	Moves the cell pointer to the bottom of the active area (**J57** now should be the active cell). The *active area* is that part of the worksheet that contains values or formulas or that has been formatted. In this case, a value had been entered into cell **J57** and so the active area is defined as the rectangle between **A1** and **J57**.
[End] ↑	Moves the cell pointer in the direction of the **[arrow]** key to the next cell that contains an entry or to the edge of the worksheet. Cell **J1** now should be active.
[End] ↓	Makes cell **J57** active.
[End] →	Makes cell **IV57** active.

Continued . . .

Keystroke	Action Resulting from Keystroke
[End] ←	Makes cell **J57** active.
[Home]	Moves the cell pointer to the upper left-hand corner of the worksheet (usually cell **A1**).

Getting On-Line Help from Lotus 1-2-3

Lotus 1-2-3 has an extensive on-line *Help* feature. Practice using this feature by doing the following (if you are using a two-drive system, replace the *Lotus System* diskette in drive B: with the *Help* diskette):

Keystroke	Action Resulting from Keystroke
[F1]	Invokes the *Help* feature and displays the following screen:

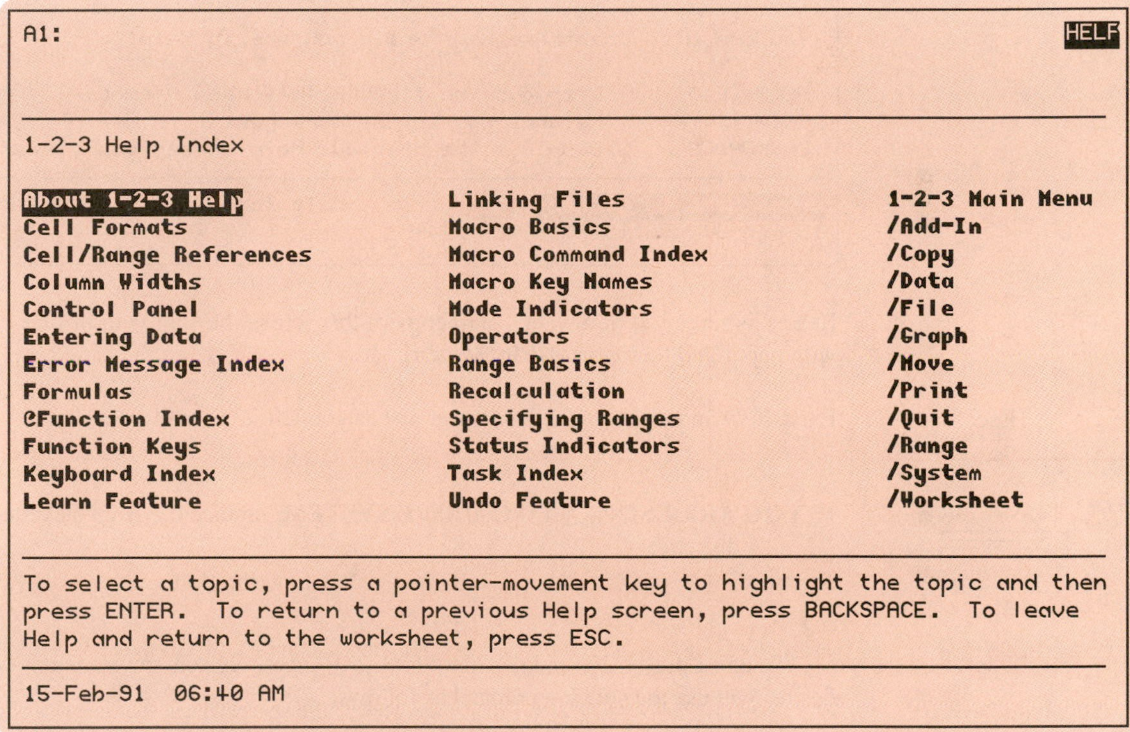

This screen provides an index of the *Help* options as well as information on using the *Help* feature. To display a particular *Help* screen, use the **[arrow]** keys to select the item you want and then press **[Enter]**. For example, to display more information on using the *Help* feature, do the following:

[arrow]	If necessary, use the **[arrow]** keys to highlight **About 1-2-3 Help**.
[Enter]	Displays a screen giving more information on using the *Help* feature.

Continued . . .

Keystroke	Action Resulting from Keystroke

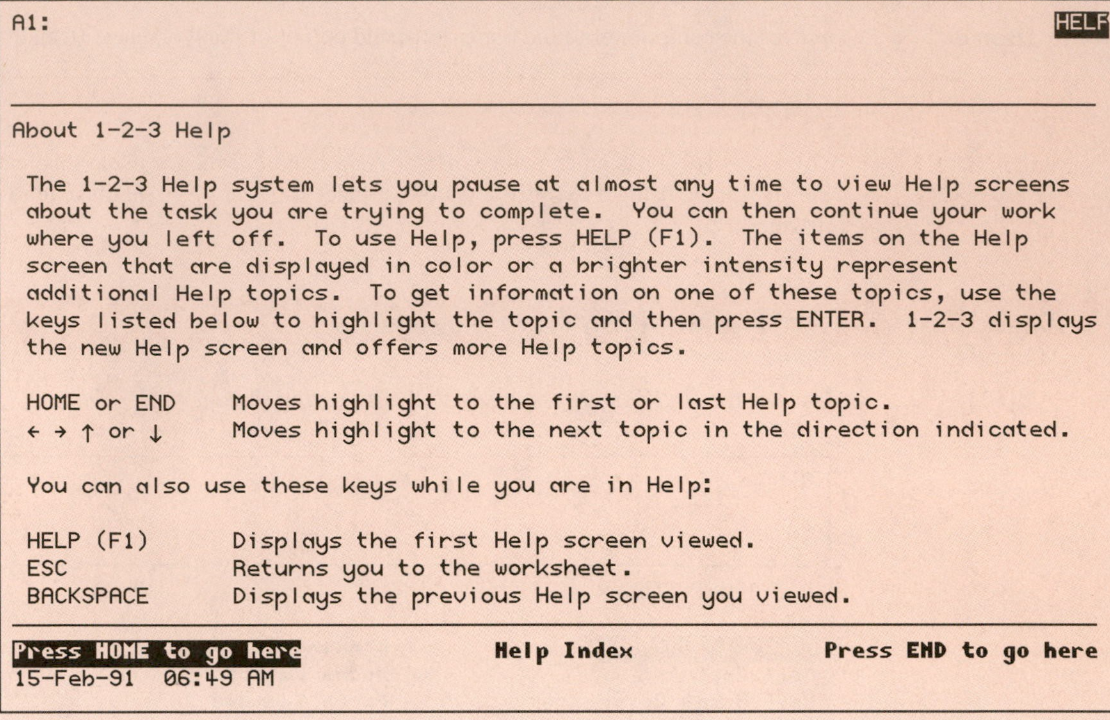
A1: HELP

About 1-2-3 Help

The 1-2-3 Help system lets you pause at almost any time to view Help screens about the task you are trying to complete. You can then continue your work where you left off. To use Help, press HELP (F1). The items on the Help screen that are displayed in color or a brighter intensity represent additional Help topics. To get information on one of these topics, use the keys listed below to highlight the topic and then press ENTER. 1-2-3 displays the new Help screen and offers more Help topics.

HOME or END	Moves highlight to the first or last Help topic.
← → ↑ or ↓	Moves highlight to the next topic in the direction indicated.

You can also use these keys while you are in Help:

HELP (F1)	Displays the first Help screen viewed.
ESC	Returns you to the worksheet.
BACKSPACE	Displays the previous Help screen you viewed.

Press HOME to go here Help Index Press END to go here
15-Feb-91 06:49 AM

Read this screen. If you want a hard copy of this screen, be sure your printer is turned on and loaded with paper and then press **[PrintScreen]**.

[Esc] Exits *Help* and displays the worksheet just as you left it.

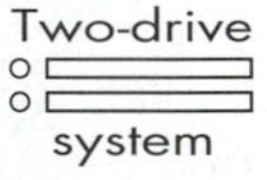

IF YOU ARE USING A TWO-DRIVE SYSTEM, replace the *Help* diskette with the *Lotus System* diskette.

Exiting Lotus 1-2-3

To exit Lotus 1-2-3 and return to the 1-2-3 Access System environment (and then to DOS if you so desire) you use the **Quit** command as follows:

Keystroke	Action Resulting from Keystroke
/	Alerts Lotus 1-2-3 that a special command is about to be entered and displays the main menu on the second line of the control panel:

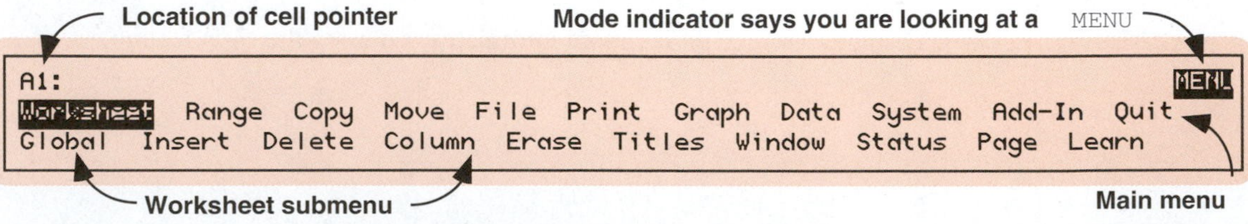

Continued . . .

Keystroke	Action Resulting from Keystroke
	Notice that the first item of the menu, **Worksheet**, is highlighted. The submenu for **Worksheet** appears in the third line of the control panel:

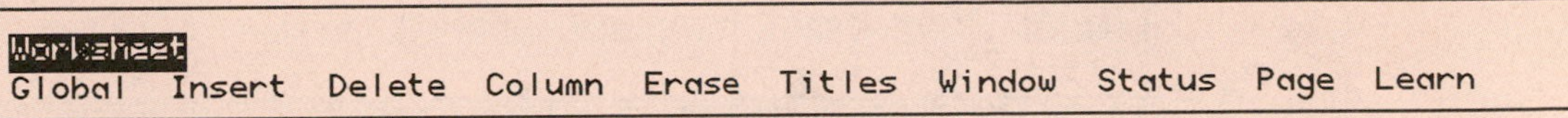

The main menu lists ten command options. Many of these will be discussed in some detail later. For now, you are only interested in quitting the program so you should select **Quit** either by typing the letter **Q** or by using the **[arrow]** keys to highlight **Quit** and then pressing **[Enter]**. Let's use the **[arrow]** keys this time:

[arrow] Use the **[arrow]** keys to highlight the word **Quit**. Notice that as the highlighting moves to the right across the screen the third line of the control panel changes to display a submenu or a brief explanation of the highlighted command. When **Quit** has been selected, the control panel will appear as follows:

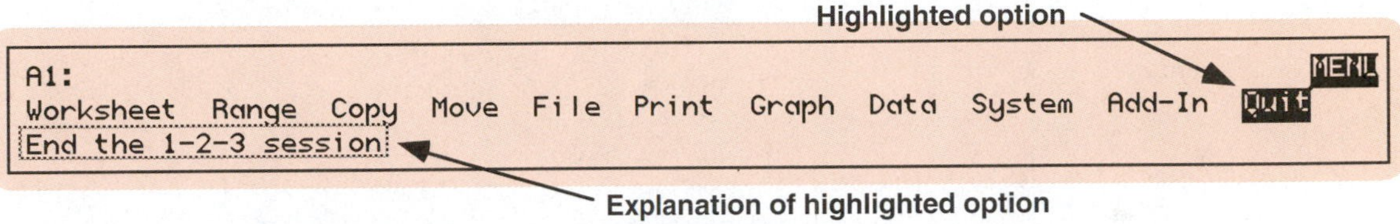

[Enter] Selects the highlighted option and provides you with two choices:

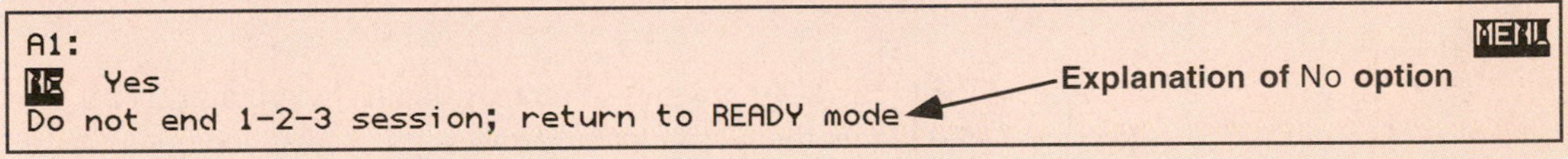

No means you do not want to quit the program and returns you to **READY** mode (i.e., returns you to the worksheet).

Yes means you want to quit the program and return to the 1-2-3 Access System environment.

Y Selects **Yes** from the two options listed (you also could have used the **[arrow]** keys to select **Yes** and then pressed the **[Enter]** key). The program will beep at you, display a message reminding you that you have not saved the current worksheet, and give you two choices again:

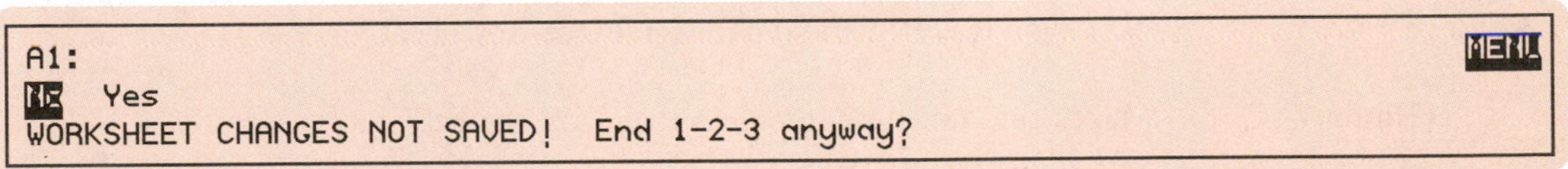

No means you do not want to quit the program and returns you to **READY** mode (i.e., returns you to the worksheet).

Yes means you want to quit the program without saving the current worksheet and return to the 1-2-3 Access System environment. For this example, you do not want to save the worksheet so **Yes** is the option you should select.

Continued . . .

Keystroke	Action Resulting from Keystroke
Y	Selects **Yes** and returns control to the 1-2-3 Access System.

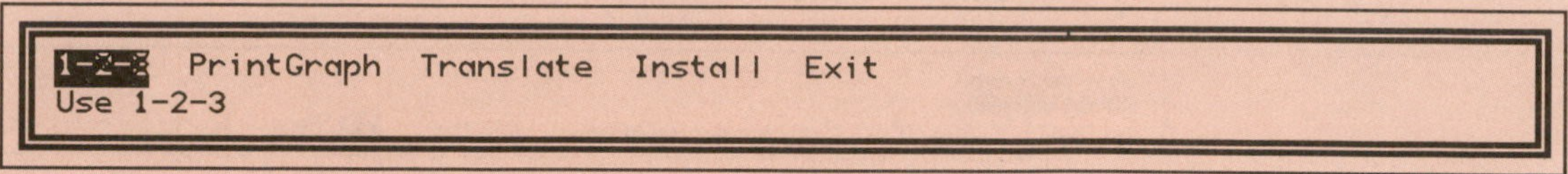

At this point you may select one of the five options again. To return to DOS, you would select **Exit**.

E	Selects **Exit** and returns to the DOS environment.

Simple Payroll Worksheet

To see how useful Lotus 1-2-3 can be, let's construct a simple payroll worksheet that produces the output displayed below:

Employee	Pay Rate	Hours	Total Pay
--------	--------	-----	---------
Roberts Matt	$4.00	30.0	$120.00
Simm Keisha	$3.00	50.0	$150.00
Tech Sara	$6.00	21.0	$126.00
Well Vanessa	$5.00	40.0	$200.00

Access the Lotus 1-2-3 program. You may do this by typing **LOTUS ↵** as you did before and then selecting **1-2-3** from the Access menu. However, if you are not going to use the other programs (**PrintGraph**, **Translate**, and **Install**) you may bypass the the 1-2-3 Access System and load the spreadsheet program directly by simply typing **123 ↵**. This is a faster and more memory efficient way of accessing the spreadsheet program.

Keystroke	Action Resulting from Keystroke
123 ↵	Loads the Lotus 1-2-3 program directly and presents a blank worksheet screen.

Now, you may begin to type data into the worksheet.

[Home]	Makes cell **A1** active (it probably already was active).
Employee	Enters the label **Employee** into the first line of the control panel. If you make a mistake while typing (and before pressing the **[Enter]** key), you can use the **[Backspace]** key to correct the error. Notice the following as you type:

- The word you are typing is not entered directly into cell **A1**. Instead, the blinking cursor disappears from cell **A1** and reappears on the left-hand side of the second line of the control panel as you type. This location is referred to as the *input line* because it is where values that are input appear before being entered into the appropriate cell.
- The word **UNDO** disappears from the status line. This means that the undo key (i.e., the **[Alt-F4]** key) will not work while you are entering data.
- The word **LABEL** appears in the mode indicator box in the control panel.

Continued . . .

Keystroke	Action Resulting from Keystroke

Mode indicator
Cursor
A1:
Employee_ ← Input line →
LABEL

To actually enter the word **Employee** into cell **A1**, press **[Enter]** or an **[arrow]** key. Pressing **[Enter]** will insert **Employee** into cell **A1** and leave that cell active. Pressing **[down-arrow]** will also insert **Employee** into cell **A1** but will make cell **A2** active. Likewise, pressing **[right-arrow]** will insert **Employee** and make cell **B1** active.

Keystroke	Action Resulting from Keystroke
↵	Enters the label **Employee** into the active cell.

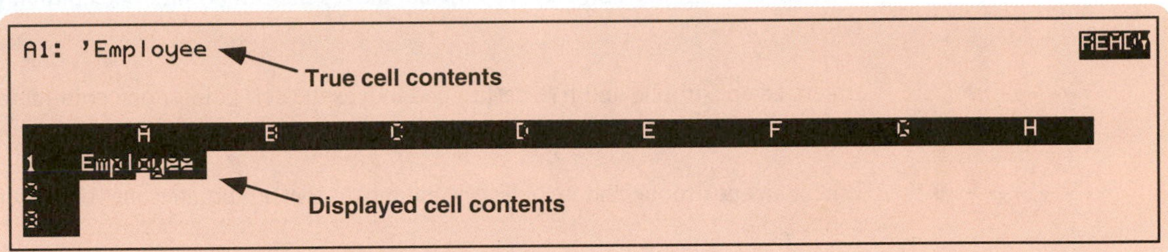

'Employee appears on the input line to show the true contents of the active cell; the apostrophe, **'**, is automatically inserted by Lotus 1-2-3 to indicate that the information in the cell is a label (text) and that the label is to be *left justified* (i.e., lined up on the left-hand side of the cell). Left-justification is the default. If you wanted to have the label *right justified* (i.e., lined up on the right-hand side of the cell), you would type a quotation mark (") as the first character in the label (e.g., **"Employee**). The quotation mark would not appear in the cell, but it would appear on the input line. If you wanted the label to be centered in the cell, you would type a circumflex (^) as the first character (e.g., **^Employee**).

READY appears in the mode indicator box.

Keystroke	Action Resulting from Keystroke
→	Moves the cell pointer one column to the right (cell **B1** becomes active).
Pay Rate →	Enters the label **Pay Rate** and moves the cell pointer one column to the right (cell **C1** becomes active).
Hours →	Enters the label **Hours** and moves the cell pointer one column to the right (cell **D1** becomes active).
Total Pay ↓	Enters the label **Total Pay** and moves the cell pointer one row down (cell **D2** becomes active).
[End] ←	Moves the cell pointer to the left-hand edge of the worksheet (cell **A2** becomes active).
'-------- ↵	Enters an apostrophe and eight dashes, which are used to separate the column heading from the data.

Continued . . .

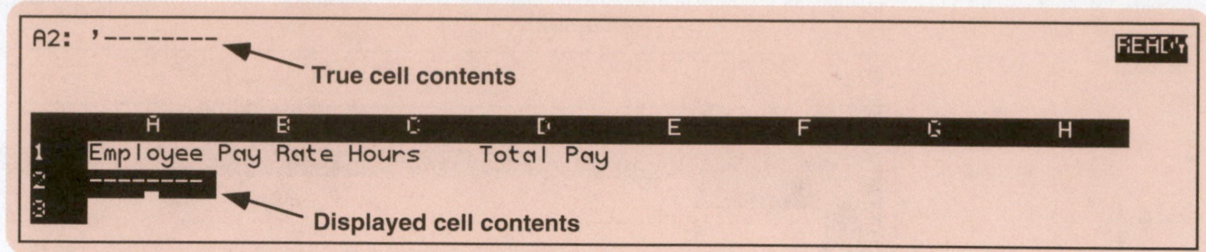

The apostrophe tells Lotus 1-2-3 that what follows is a label (text) rather than a number (such as **-2**) or a formula. If you try to type eight dashes without the leading apostrophe, Lotus 1-2-3 assumes that the dashes are negative signs for a number and beeps at you when you press **[Enter]**. In that case, it will keep you in **EDIT** mode until you correct the error or press **[Esc]**.

Keystroke	Action Resulting from Keystroke
→	Moves the cell pointer one column to the right (cell **B2** becomes active).
'-------- →	Enters an apostrophe and eight dashes and moves the cell pointer one column to the right (cell **C2** becomes active).
'----- →	Enters an apostrophe and five dashes and moves the cell pointer one column to the right (cell **D2** becomes active).
'--------- ↓	Enters an apostrophe and nine dashes and moves the cell pointer one row down (cell **D3** becomes active).
[End] ←	Moves the cell pointer to the left-hand edge of the worksheet (cell **A3** becomes active).
Roberts Matt ↵	Enters the name of the first person. Notice that the name **Roberts Matt** has twelve characters (including the space) but that each of the columns **A** through **H** is only nine characters wide. As long as there is no entry in cell **B3**, the entry from cell **A3** will spill over into the space reserved for cell **B3**.

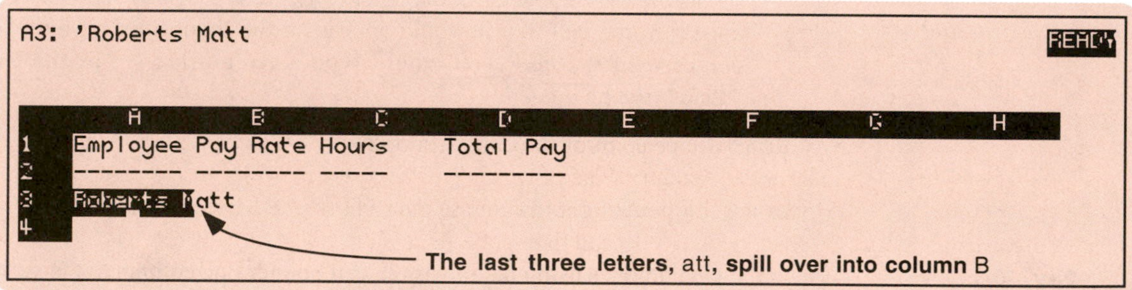

When you enter data into cell **B3** (e.g., Matt's rate of pay), the last three characters in his name will be cut off and only **Roberts M** will be displayed. Don't worry about this now; it will be fixed later (see p. L24).

Keystroke	Action Resulting from Keystroke
→	Moves the cell pointer one column to the right (cell **B3** becomes active).
4 →	Enters the value **4** and moves the cell pointer one column to the right (cell **C3** becomes active). Notice that you do not enter the dollar sign. The cells will be formatted later with the dollar sign and the proper number of decimal places displayed.

Continued . . .

Keystroke	Action Resulting from Keystroke
30 ↓	Enters the value **30** and moves the cell pointer one row down (cell **C4** becomes active). Notice that the column heading, **Hours**, and the value in the column, **30**, are not lined up. This is because labels are automatically left-justified while numbers are automatically right-justified. We will make this look better later.
[End] ←	Moves the cell pointer to the left-hand edge of the worksheet (cell **A4** becomes active).

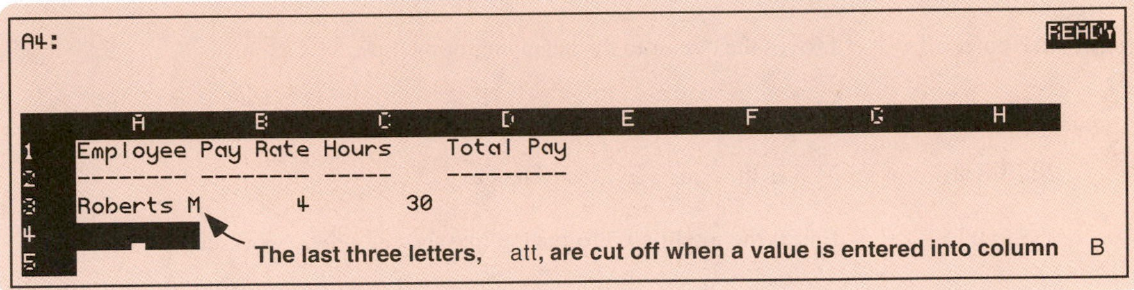

Continue to type the entries until all the raw data have been entered. Remember — do not type the dollar signs (**$**); they will be entered later by the program. Also, values for **Total Pay** need not be entered; they will be calculated by the program.

When you have finished entering all the raw data, the top of the screen should look as follows:

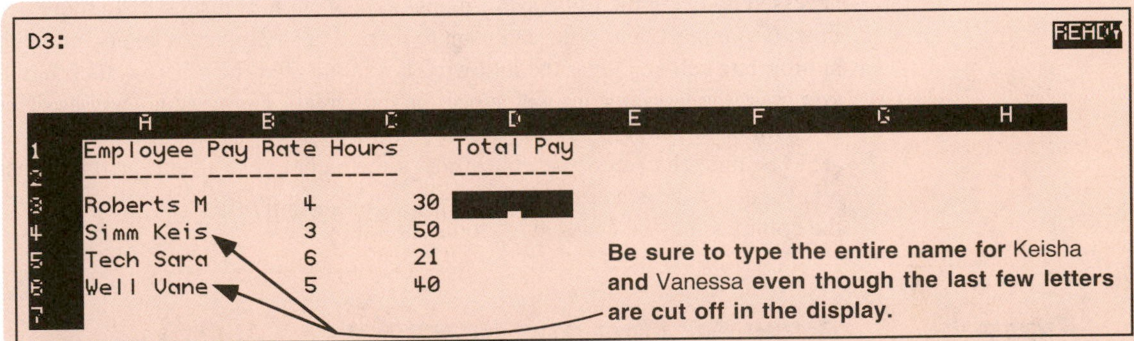

If you notice an error in your typing after you have pressed **[Enter]**, you may go back to that cell and retype the entry. The old entry will be replaced with the new one. You also may change the contents of a cell by editing it rather than completely replacing it. To edit a cell, move the cell pointer to the cell you want to edit and then press **[F2]**. This switches to **EDIT** mode, and you can employ the standard editing techniques using the **[arrow]**, **[Backspace]**, **[Delete]**, and **[Insert]** keys to make changes to the line without retyping the entire line. Below is a list of some special editing features that you can use while in **EDIT** mode:

Keystroke	Action Resulting from Keystroke
→	Moves the cursor one character to the right (as in WordPerfect).
←	Moves the cursor one character to the left (as in WordPerfect).
↑	Completes the modification and moves the cell pointer up one cell.
↓	Completes the modification and moves the cell pointer down one cell.

Continued . . .

Keystroke	Action Resulting from Keystroke
[Insert]	Toggles between insert and overtype (as in WordPerfect).
[Delete]	Deletes the character at the cursor (as in WordPerfect).
[Backspace]	Deletes the character to the left of the cursor (as in WordPerfect).
[End]	Moves the cursor to the end of the line (as in WordPerfect).
[Home]	Moves the cursor to the beginning of the line.
[Tab]	Moves the cursor five characters to the right.
[Shift-Tab]	Moves the cursor five characters to the left.
[Enter]	Enters the modified information into the cell on the worksheet.
[Esc]	Clears the edit line. If you press **[Enter]** when the edit line is empty (clear), the original entry will be preserved. To completely erase the contents of a cell you must use *Range Erase* (see below).
[Esc] [Esc]	Ignores any changes (keeps the original data in the cell).

Note that in order to completely erase a cell you must use the *Range Erase* feature, which is accessed by using the Lotus 1-2-3 menus. This feature is discussed in more detail on page L49. For now, if you make a mistake and want to make a cell completely blank, move the cell pointer to the appropriate cell and press the following keys, one after the other: **/**, then **R**, then **E**, then **[Enter]**. As you press the keys, menus will appear on the screen. These menus will be discussed later.

Notice how the right sides of some of the names are cut off because all columns are automatically set to be nine characters wide but some of the names are longer than this. When a column is too narrow, text is cut off (truncated) while numbers appear as asterisks rather than their true values. The widths of the columns may be changed by doing the following:

Keystroke	Action Resulting from Keystroke
/	Alerts Lotus 1-2-3 that a special command is about to be entered and displays the main menu on the second line of the Control Panel at the top of the screen.

```
D3:                                                                 MENU
Worksheet  Range  Copy  Move  File  Print  Graph  Data  System  Add-In  Quit
Global  Insert  Delete  Column  Erase  Titles  Window  Status  Page  Learn
```

Because you are going to do something that affects the entire worksheet, you may choose **Worksheet** by doing *one* of the following:

- Use the **[arrow]** keys, if necessary, to highlight **Worksheet** and then press **[Enter]**.
- Press the first letter of the word **Worksheet**. We will use this method because it is faster. However, when you press the letter key be sure to say (to yourself or out loud) the name of the command you are executing. This is very important because it will help you remember the command name and make what you are doing more meaningful.

Continued . . .

Keystroke	Action Resulting from Keystroke

W Selects **Worksheet**, and displays its submenu.

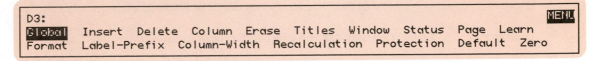

```
D3:                                                                     MENU
Global  Insert  Delete  Column  Erase  Titles  Window  Status  Page  Learn
Format  Label-Prefix  Column-Width  Recalculation  Protection  Default  Zero
```

If you wanted only to change the width of column **A**, you could type **C** to select the **Column** option and then **S** to select **Set-Width**. However, for this exercise, you should change the width of all the columns. Making a change to the entire worksheet is called a **global change.** Hence, you want to select **Global** from the menu.

G Selects **Global** and displays its submenu along with the current global settings for the worksheet:

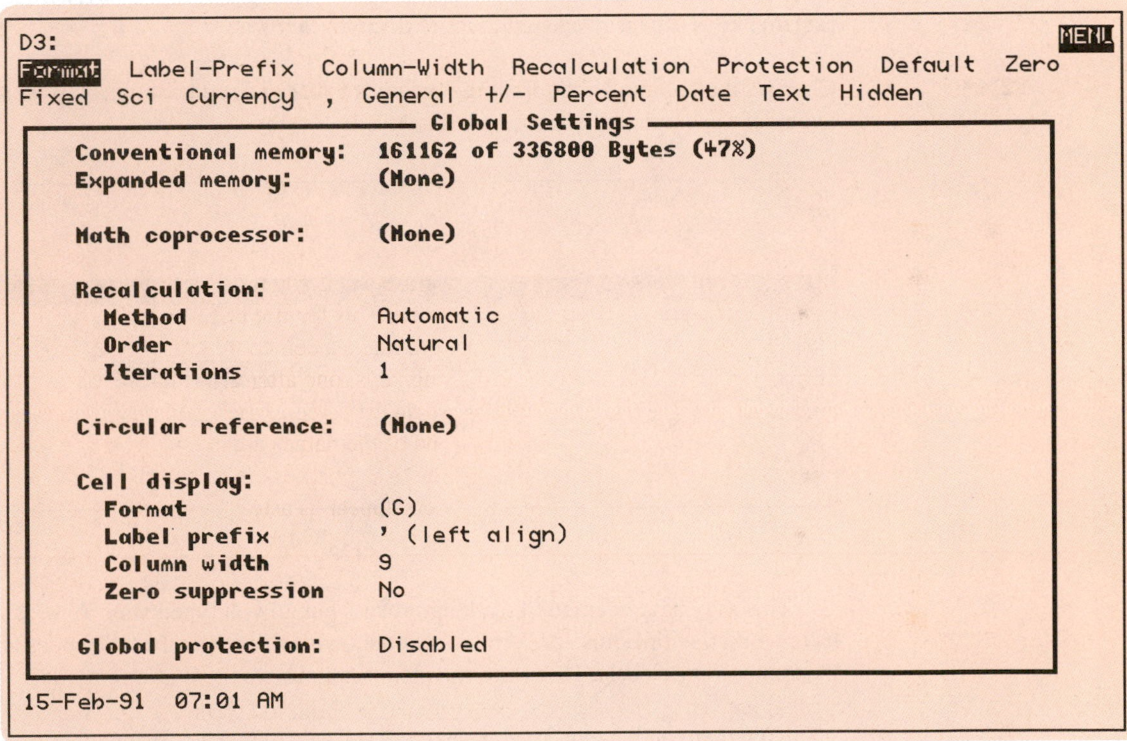

Many of the settings will be discussed later. For now, look at the section labeled **Cell Display**:

Format (G) means that the format for each cell has been set to the default global settings. This means that numbers are right justified with a single space on the right-hand side of the number (this space is reserved for the percent sign or for a right parenthesis). Labels may be left justified, right justified, or centered, depending on the label prefix used.

Label prefix ' (left align) means that labels will be left justified. This can be changed by typing the slash and the first letter of each word in the following commands (don't do this): **/** **W**(orksheet) **G**(lobal) **L**(abel-Prefix).

Column width 9 means that the default width for columns is 9 characters wide. This is what we want to change.

Continued . . .

Keystroke	Action Resulting from Keystroke

Zero suppression No means that zeros are displayed where appropriate. You may choose to display blanks or other characters for zero values by typing the following command (don't do this): **/ W**(orksheet) **G**(lobal) **Z**(ero).

C — Selects **Column-Width** and asks for the desired column width.

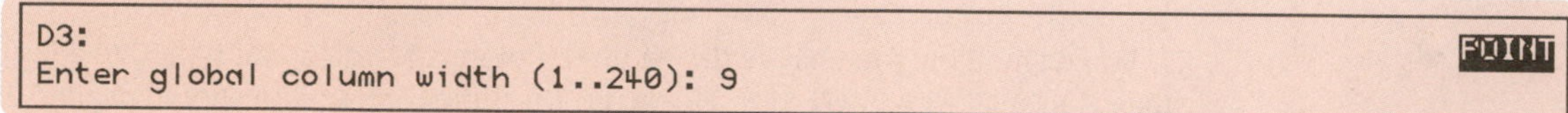

Notice that the current value, **9**, already is displayed.

Notice the word **POINT** in the upper-right corner of the control panel. This means you are in **POINT** mode and may select the column width either by typing a new one (we will do this) or by using the **[arrow]** keys (this is discussed in more detail on p. L88).

12 ↵ — Changes the column width of all the columns to **12** and returns control to **READY** mode. Now, all the letters of the employee's names are displayed.

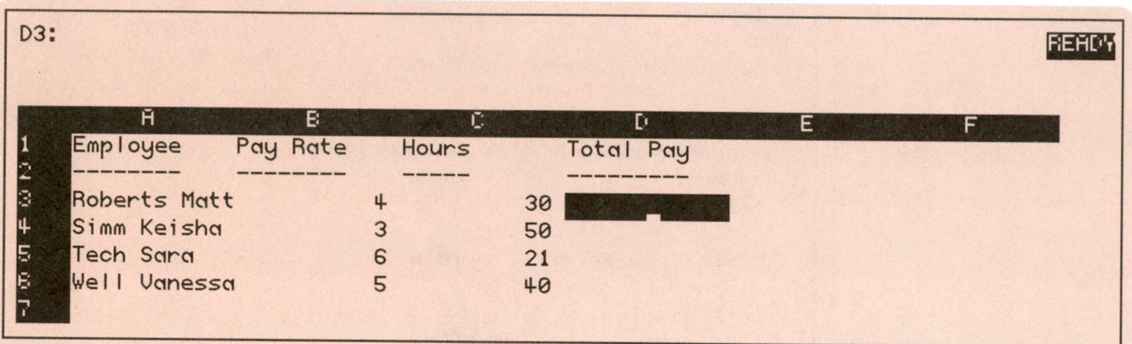

This may have seemed like a long process but all you typed was: **/ W G C 12 ↵**. Once you have worked with Lotus 1-2-3 for a few hours, you will remember the codes and will not have to read the menus very closely. However, the menus are always there as a reminder.

Saving a Worksheet

Now that you have had a chance to enter data and make a format change, it would be a good idea to save the worksheet before continuing. Frequent saving of files is insurance against accidental loss of data.

Keystroke	Action Resulting from Keystroke
/	Displays the main menu.
F	Selects **File** and displays its menu.

```
D3:                                                                  MENU
Retrieve  Save  Combine  Xtract  Erase  List  Import  Directory  Admin
Erase the current worksheet from memory and display the selected worksheet
```

Continued . . .

Keystroke	Action Resulting from Keystroke

S Selects **Save** and displays the following in the control panel:

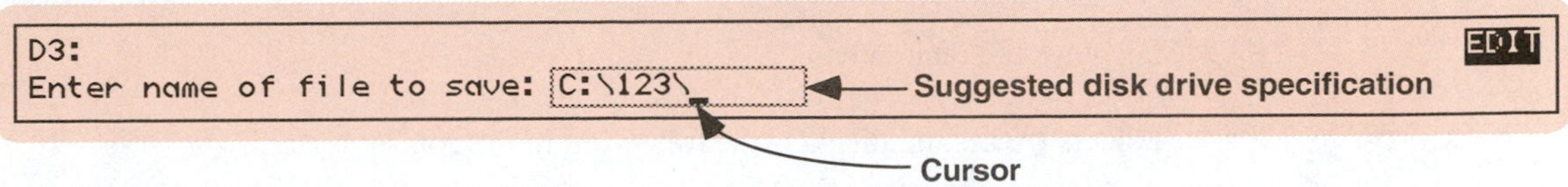

If you are using a hard-disk system, Lotus 1-2-3 displays **C:\123** as the suggested drive specification because it assumes that the file is to be stored on the **C:** drive in the subdirectory called **123**. If you are using a two-drive system the suggested drive may be **B:**. In either case, you should save the file on your *Lotus Data* diskette in drive A: by doing the following:

[Esc] Erases the suggested drive designation. (Note: In some instances, Lotus 1-2-3 may suggest a new drive designation such as **B:**. If that happens, press **[Esc]** again to erase that designation.)

Now, you must provide the file specification.

- The drive designator should be A:.
- The name can be any allowable file name (i.e., it must be from one to eight characters long and may contain only letters, digits, and a few special characters including the hyphen **-** and the underscore _, but spaces are not allowed). Use the name **PAY-V1** (for **PAY**roll worksheet, **V**ersion **1**). You will be saving many different versions of the worksheet (**PAY-V1**, **PAY-V2**, **PAY-V3**, etc.) for two reasons: (1) we will refer back to different versions in order to illustrate different Lotus 1-2-3 features and (2) saving multiple versions of a file enables you to go back to a previous version if you totally mess up the current version (that sometimes happens, even to the best of us). When you are sure that you no longer need a past version of a file you can delete it from the data diskette or hard disk.
- If you choose not to specify a file name extension, Lotus 1-2-3 will automatically use the extension **WK1**.

A:PAY-V1 ↵ Provides the file specification, saves the file to the diskette in drive A:, and returns control to **READY** mode.

If a file called **A:PAY-V1.WK1** is already saved on your *Lotus Data* diskette, Lotus 1-2-3 will display the following three options in the control panel:

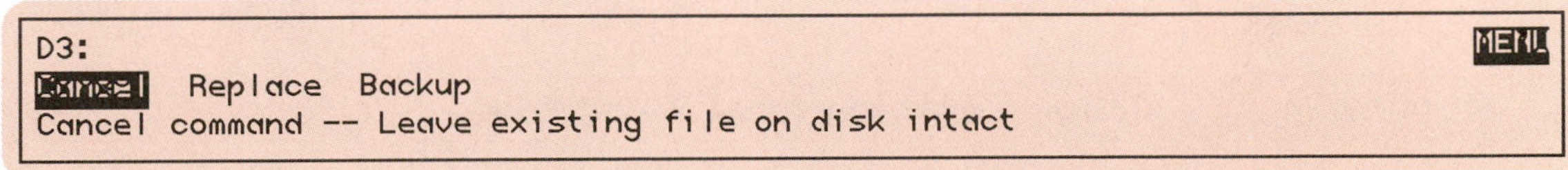

Cancel means that you want to cancel the save operation and return to **READY** mode.

Replace means that you want to replace the existing file with the current worksheet. If you are working on someone else's computer (e.g., at work or at school) it is not a good idea to choose this option because you may mistakenly erase a file belonging to someone else. Unless you are absolutely sure that you want to erase the original file, do not choose this option.

Backup means that you want to save the file with the given name but with a **.BAK** extension. This probably is your best choice if you see this message.

You now may use the quit command to exit Lotus 1-2-3.

Keystroke	Action Resulting from Keystroke
/	Displays the main menu.
Q	Selects **Quit** and displays the following in the control panel:

```
D3:                                                             MENU
No  Yes
Do not end 1-2-3 session; return to READY mode
```

Pressing **Y** will return control to DOS. Pressing **N** will return to **READY** mode.

Keystroke	Action Resulting from Keystroke
Y	Specifies that **Y**es, you are sure that you want to quit the spreadsheet program and returns control to DOS. Note that if you have made changes since the last time the document was saved, instead of exiting the program the computer will beep and display the following message:

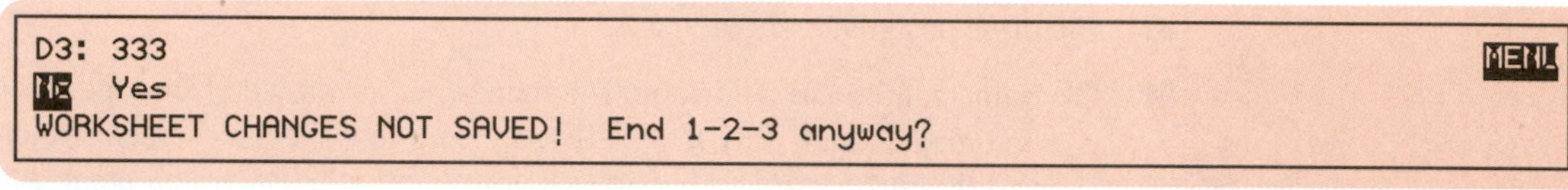

This is a reminder that if you quit the worksheet, any changes you made since the last save will be lost. To save the document, press **N** and then go through the save procedure by typing **/** (to bring up the main menu), **F** (to select **F**ile), **S** (to select **S**ave), and then type the file specification. To return to the DOS environment press **Y** again.

TO TAKE A BREAK Remove diskette(s).To resume (hard disk): Insert *Data* diskette, type **C:** ↵, **CD\123** ↵. To resume (two drive): Insert diskettes, type **B:** ↵.

Setting Global Defaults

A *global setting* is one that affects an entire worksheet or the Lotus 1-2-3 program as a whole. A *global default* is the setting that the program assumes unless you tell it differently. For example, if you are using a hard-disk system, Lotus 1-2-3 probably will assume that you want to save files to, and retrieve files from, the **123** subdirectory on the hard disk (i.e., the default directory will be **C:\123**). However, you probably are saving all your files on the *Lotus Data* diskette in drive A:. Therefore, changing the default directory to A: will make file saving and retrieval easier.

Access the Lotus 1-2-3 program and then change the default directory by doing the following:

Keystroke	Action Resulting from Keystroke
123 ↵	Loads the program into the main memory of the computer and displays a blank worksheet.
/	Displays the main menu.
W	Selects **Worksheet** and displays its menu.
G	Selects **Global** and displays its menu.

Continued . . .

Keystroke	Action Resulting from Keystroke
D	Selects **`Default`** and displays its menu.

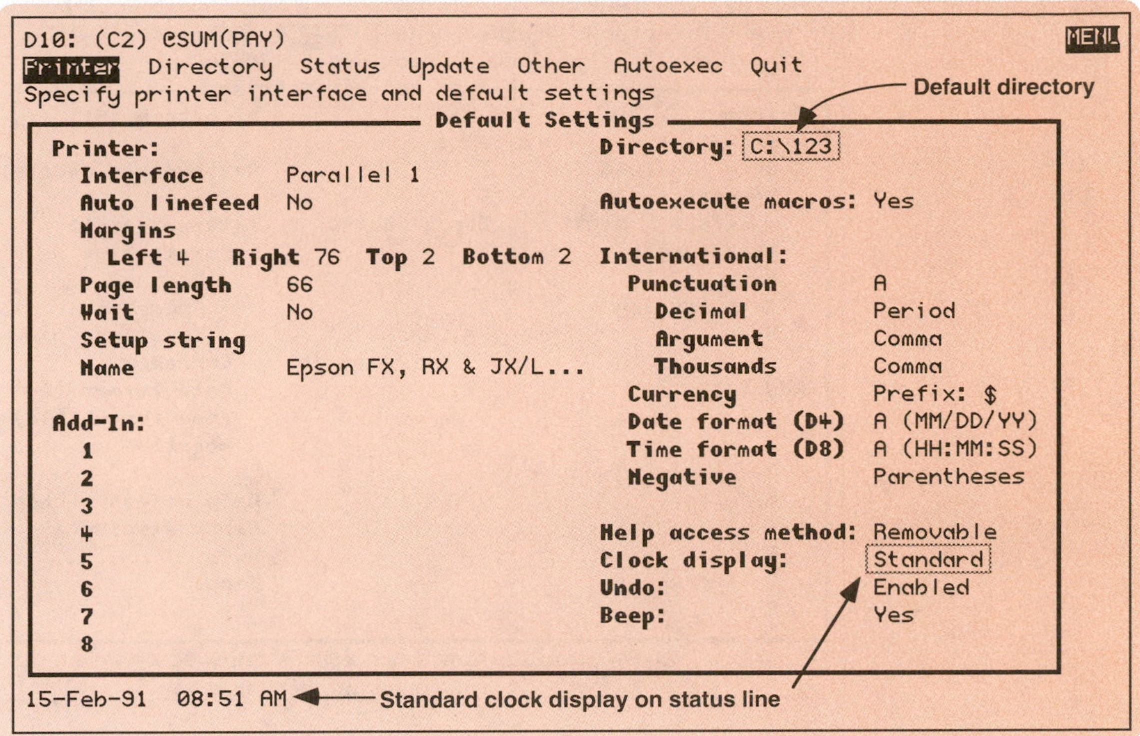

Most of the defaults listed can be changed from within the program, but some, such as the type of monitor you are using, must be changed from within the Install program (this is a program supplied by Lotus that copies the needed files from the master diskettes to your hard drive or backup diskettes and sets up various default settings such as what type of monitor and printer you are using). The defaults were chosen by the program developers because they felt that these settings would be the ones most people would use most of the time. For our purposes, changing the directory default to A: would make it more convenient when saving and retrieving files. This can be accomplished by doing the following:

Keystroke	Action Resulting from Keystroke
D	Selects **`Directory`** and asks you to **`Enter default directory`**. First, you must use **[Esc]** to erase the current setting.
[Esc]	Erases the current default directory setting.
A: ↵	Specifies the new default setting and displays it in the **`default settings`** window.

We also can change the default so that the file name of the current worksheet is displayed in place of the date and time on the status line:

Keystroke	Action Resulting from Keystroke
O	Selects **`Other`** and displays its menu.
C	Selects **`Clock`** and displays its menu.
F	Selects **`Filename`**.

Continued . . .

Keystroke	Action Resulting from Keystroke

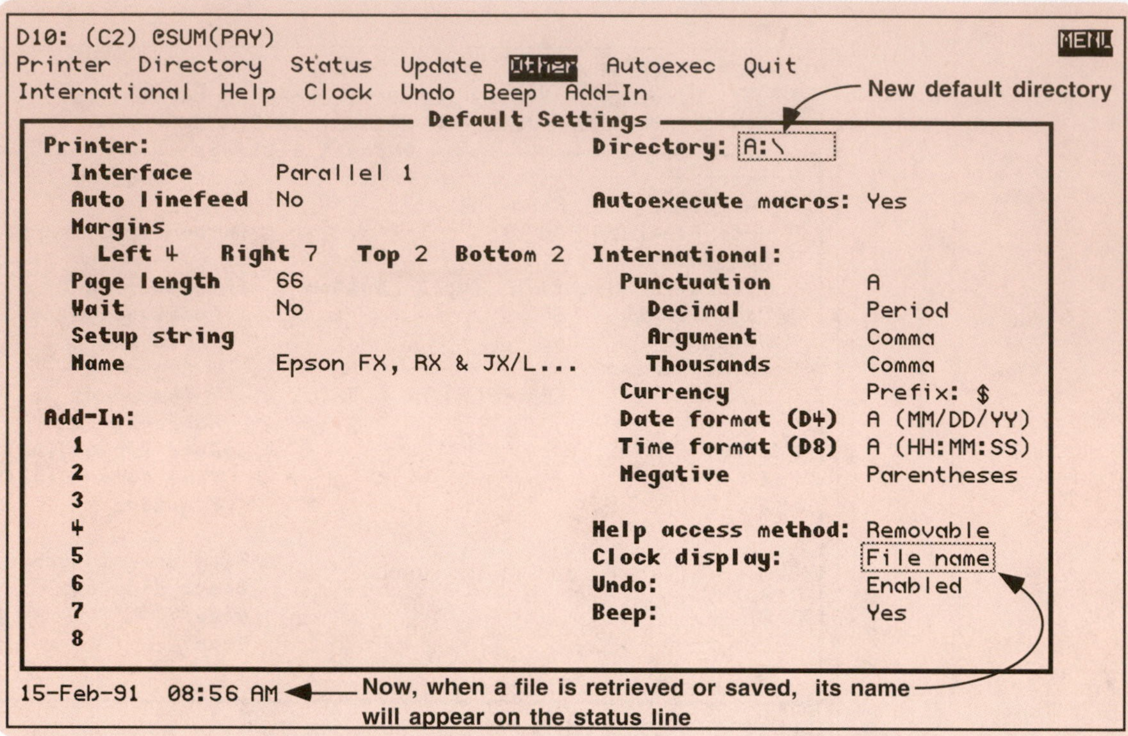

From now on, whenever a file is saved or retrieved, its name will be displayed on the status line in place of the date and time. Note that if the active worksheet has not been saved (and therefore does not yet have a file name) the date and time will be displayed.

These settings will remain in effect only until you exit the Lotus 1-2-3 program. The next time you use the program, the default settings will be reinstated unless you use the **Update** option.

U	Selects **Update** and writes the current settings to a configuration file called **123.CNF**. Now, for all future sessions, the default directory will be A: and the file name will be displayed in the status line.
Q	Selects **Quit** and returns to **READY** mode.

Now, whenever you want to save or retrieve a file, Lotus 1-2-3 will present you with a list of files that reside on the default (A:) drive, and after the file has been retrieved its name will appear on the status line.

Retrieving and Modifying a Worksheet

Now, let's retrieve the worksheet you just saved and make modifications to it by formatting the display so that it looks nicer and then adding formulas to calculate the total pay for each employee.

Step 1 Retrieve the worksheet **PAY-V1** by doing the following:

Keystroke	Action Resulting from Keystroke
/	Displays the main menu.
F	Selects **File** and displays its menu.
R	Selects **Retrieve** and requests the name of the file to be retrieved.

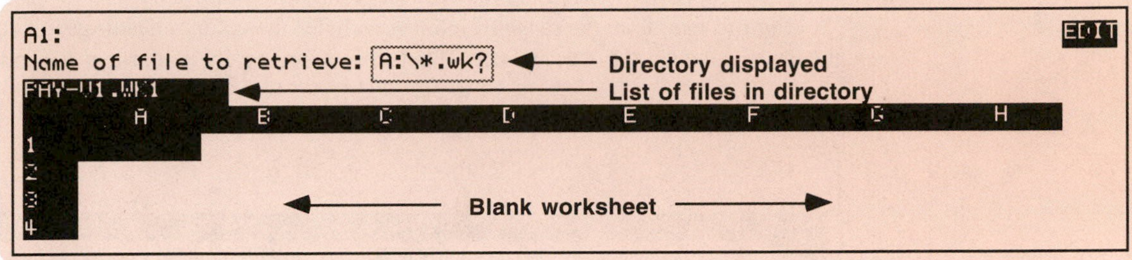

Notice the second line of the display: **A:*.wk?**. This specifies which file names will be listed in line three of the display:

A: says to list the names of files stored on the diskette in drive A:.

\ says to look in the root directory of that drive (because the diskette in drive A: has no subdirectories, this has no effect).

* is a global character that can stand for any number of characters (see pp. W192 and W199). The effect is that files with any names will be displayed.

.wk? specifies the file name extension. Recall that the **?** is a global character that can take the place of a single character. The effect of this extension is to list only files with three-character extensions where the first two characters must be **wk** (recall that Lotus 1-2-3 automatically saves files with the extension **WK1**).

The effect of this file specification is to display the names of all files with **wk** as the first two characters of the file name extension residing in the root directory of the diskette in drive A:. Because you have saved only one worksheet so far, only the name **PAY-V1.WK1** is listed.

Keystroke	Action Resulting from Keystroke
[arrow]	Use the **[arrow]** keys, if necessary, to highlight the file name **PAY-V1.WK1**.
[Enter]	Retrieves the highlighted file and returns to **READY** mode. The worksheet should appear exactly as you left it:

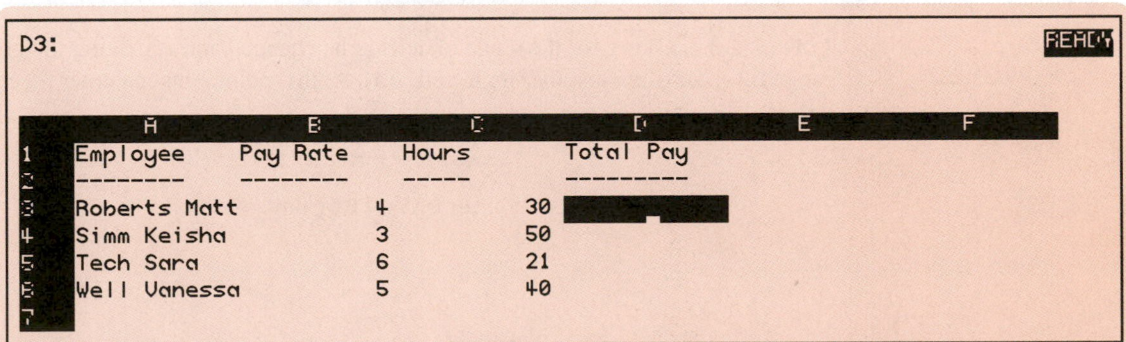

Step 2 Notice that the column headings of the worksheet are not lined up with the numeric entries. This is because the standard alignment used by Lotus 1-2-3 is left justification for text (the employee names and the column headings) and right justification for numbers (the values for pay rates and hours). You can make the display look better by right justifying the column headings for columns **B**, **C**, and **D**.

When you want to work with only a part of the worksheet you must select a **range** of cells. Recall from page L5 that a range is one or more cells that form a rectangular area on the screen. This is similar to blocks of text defined in word-processing applications except that a range of cells in Lotus 1-2-3 must be rectangular whereas a block of text could have other shapes.

For this example, the range of interest includes the column headings in cells **B1**, **C1**, and **D1** and the dashes in cells **B2**, **C2**, and **D2**. This forms a rectangle with corners **B1** and **D2**.

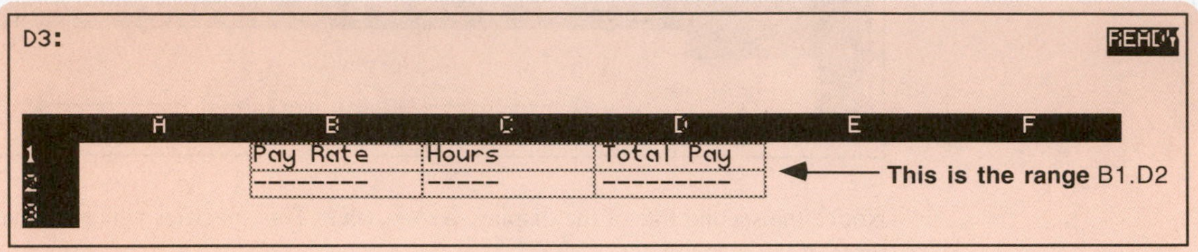

A range is designated by stating the cell coordinates of two opposing corners separated by one or two periods. Thus, this range could be designated as **B1.D2** (or **B1..D2**. or **D2.B1** or **D2..B1** or **B2.D1** or **B2..D1** or **D1.B2** or **D1..B2**). To right justify the column headings, do the following:

Keystroke	***Action Resulting from Keystroke***
/	Displays main menu.
R	Selects **Range** and displays its menu. You need to change the justification of the labels (text), so you must select the **Label** submenu.
L	Selects **Label** and displays its menu. You need to right justify the labels, so you must select the **Right** submenu.
R	Selects **Right** and displays the following in the input line:

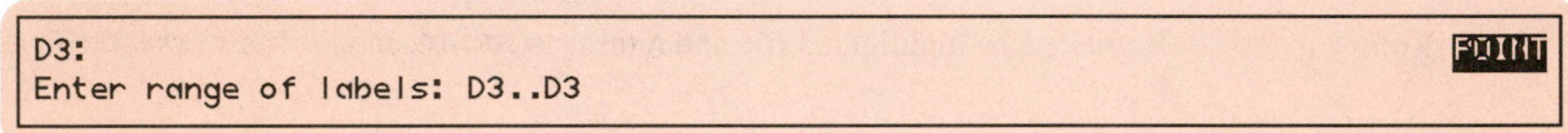

Lotus 1-2-3 is asking for the range of cells to be changed and is making the guess that it will be the range **D3..D3** (i.e., just the single cell, **D3**). At this point, you can enter the range of cells you want to define.

Continued . . .

Keystroke	Action Resulting from Keystroke
B1.D2 ↵	Specifies the range of cells, adjusts the cells, and returns to **READY** mode. Notice that all entries in the specified range now are right justified (lined up on the right-hand side of the column).

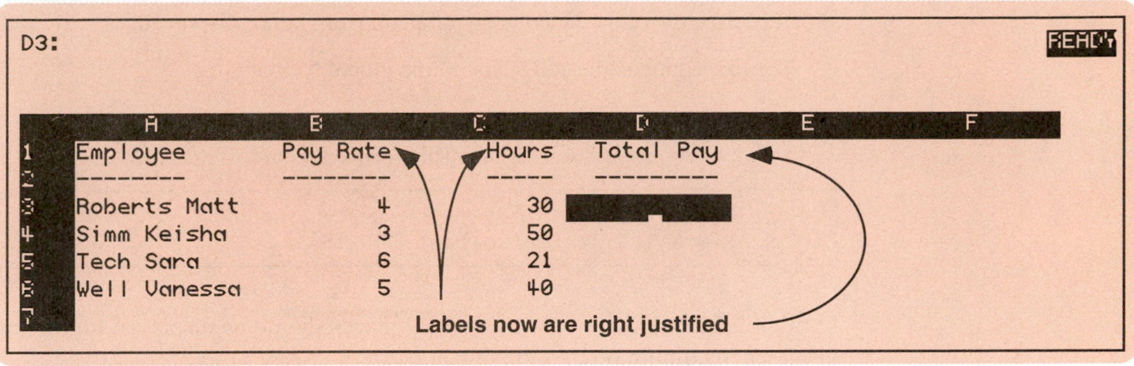

Step 3 The number of decimal places displayed in any cell can be changed by using the **Format** option. Display the hours worked (column **C**) using one decimal place by doing the following:

Keystroke	Action Resulting from Keystroke
/	Displays the main menu.
R	Selects **Range** and displays its menu.

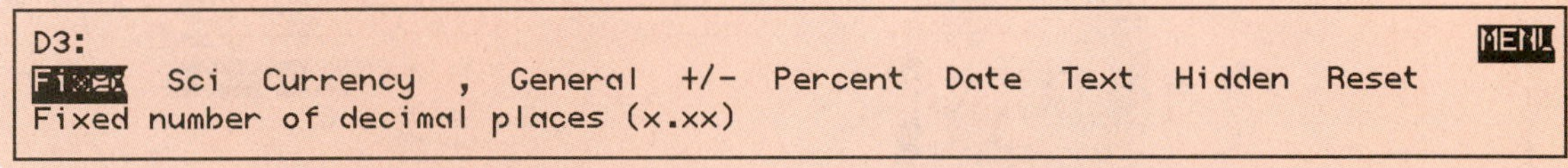

Keystroke	Action Resulting from Keystroke
F	Selects **Format** and displays its menu.

Fixed displays numbers rounded to a specified number of decimal places (e.g., if two decimal places were specified, the number **2.448** would be displayed as **2.45**).

Sci displays numbers using scientific (sometimes called exponential) notation to a specified number of decimal places (e.g., if one decimal place was specified, the number **28000** would be displayed as **2.8E+4**).

Currency displays numbers with the dollar sign, commas as separators, and a specified number of decimal places (e.g., if two decimal places were specified, the number **28000.448** would be displayed as **$28,000.45**).

, (comma) displays the same way as **Currency** but without the dollar sign.

General displays numbers using standard notation unless they are too large or too small to fit into a cell.

+/- displays a horizontal bar graph of plus or minus signs.

Percent displays numbers as percentages (i.e., multiplied by 100 and with a percent symbol).

Continued . . .

Keystroke	Action Resulting from Keystroke
	`Date` allows you to select the format for dates and times.
	`Text` displays formulas instead of values.
	`Hidden` prevents the contents of a cell from being displayed.
	`Reset` changes the cells back to the global format.
F	Selects **`Fixed`** and displays the following:

```
D3:                                                          EDIT
Enter number of decimal places (0..15): 2
```

Lotus 1-2-3 is asking how many decimal places should be displayed for numeric values (you may display a maximum of 15 decimal places).

Keystroke	Action Resulting from Keystroke
1 ↵	Specifies that one decimal place is to be displayed and requests the range. For this example, the numbers in column **C** are to be selected.
`C1.C20 ↵`	Selects all the cells from **`C1`** through **`C20`**, changes the number of decimal places displayed in this range, and returns to **READY** mode. Note that even though there are no values in cells below **`C6`**, the formatting will take care of future additions to the worksheet.

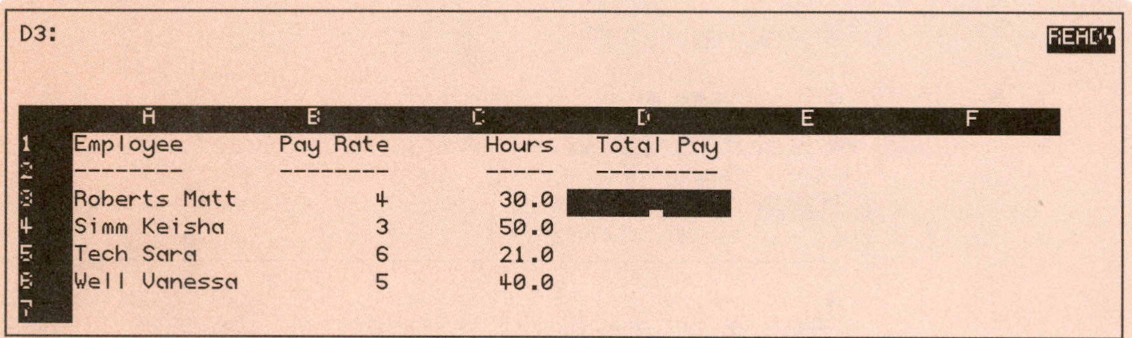

Step 4 Numeric values can be changed so that they look like they represent currency (money) by displaying two decimal places and inserting the dollar sign to the left of the numbers. Try this for the values in columns **B** and **D** by doing the following:

Keystroke	Action Resulting from Keystroke
/	Displays the main menu.
R	Selects **`Range`** and displays its menu.
F	Selects **`Format`** and displays its menu.
C	Selects **`Currency`** and asks for the number of decimal places to be displayed.
2 ↵	Specifies that two decimal places are to be displayed and requests the range. For this example, the numbers in column **B** are to be selected. The numbers in column **D** will be selected later.

Continued . . .

Keystroke	Action Resulting from Keystroke
B1.B20 ↵	Selects all the cells from **B1** through **B20**, changes the number of decimal places displayed in this range, and returns to **READY** mode.

You may follow the same procedure to change the display of numbers in column **D** to a currency format. To do that, type the following command: **/** **R**(ange) **F**(ormat) **C**(urrency) **2** ↵ **D1.D20** ↵. The screen should look as follows:

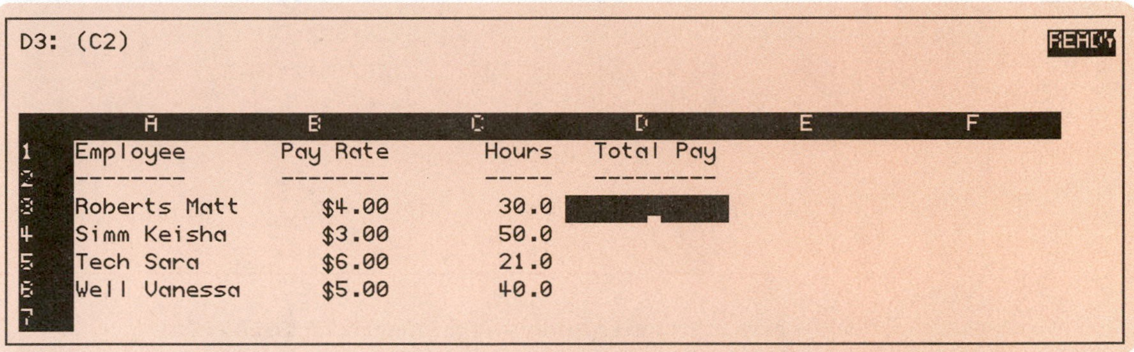

In the above screen, notice the **D3: (C2)** on the left-hand side of the top line. The **D3** identifies the active cell. The **C** means that the value in cell **D3** has been formatted as **C**urrency and the **2** means that two decimal places are to be displayed.

Step 5 The cells under **Total Pay** are to contain information that must be calculated by a formula using data from other cells. In algebra, you would use variables such as *x* and *y* in formulas to represent such values. In programming languages, such as BASIC, you would use variable names such as *rate* and *hours* in formulas. Lotus 1-2-3 uses cell locations instead of variable names. For example, to calculate the total pay for Roberts, you would multiply his rate of pay (from cell **B3**) by his hours worked (from cell **C3**) and display the result in cell **D3**.

Before actually performing the keystrokes to calculate the **Total Pay** for Roberts, a quick review of **mathematical notation** and order of operations might be beneficial. Lotus 1-2-3 uses the following notation for mathematical operations:

Symbol	Operation	Example
^	exponent	**5^2**, which means **5**^{2} or **5** times **5**
*	multiplication	**2*3**, which means **2** times **3**
/	division	**6/2**, which means **6** divided by **2**
+	addition	**5 + 3**, which means **5** plus **3**
-	subtraction	**5 - 2**, which means **5** minus **2**

Lotus 1-2-3 uses the standard order of precedence when doing mathematical calculations:

1. All work inside parentheses is done first. If the parentheses are nested (i.e., one set inside another set), the calculation inside the innermost parentheses is done first.
2. Exponents are done next.
3. Multiplication and division are done next, working left to right.
4. Addition and subtraction are done last, working left to right.

To be sure that you understand the order of operations, work out the answers to the following arithmetic problems (the answers are given below):

	Problem	**Problem using Lotus 1-2-3 notation**
1.	$2 + 3 \times 4$	**2+3*4**
2.	$2 + 36 \div 3 \times 4$	**2+36/3*4**
3.	$2 + 36 \div (3 \times 4)$	**2+36/(3*4)**
4.	$2 + 36 \div 3^2$	**2+36/3^2**
5.	$2 + 36 \div (3 + 2 \times (8 - 5))$	**2+36/(3+2*(8-5))**
6.	$2 + \dfrac{(8+2)}{(6-4)}$	**2+(8+2)/(6-4)**

Answers: [1] **14**, [2] **50**, [3] **5**, [4] **6**, [5] **6**, [6] **7**

Now, enter the keystrokes for the formula for **Total Pay**:

Keystroke	Action Resulting from Keystroke
[arrow]	Use the **[arrow]** keys, if necessary, to make cell **D3** active (or, you could press **[F5]** and then type **D3** ↵).
+	Indicates that the item in the active cell is to be a numeric expression (the mode indicator in the upper right-hand corner of the screen shows this by displaying **VALUE**). If you do not enter **+** as the first character, Lotus 1-2-3 will assume the entry is to be text and display the formula (**B3*C3**) instead of evaluating it and displaying the answer (**$120.00**). Lotus 1-2-3 assumes that entries are labels unless they begin with **0 1 2 3 4 5 6 7 8 9 – + . (@ #** or **$**.
B3*C3 ↵	Calculates the product of the numbers in cells **B3** and **C3** and displays the answer in the active cell (**D3**). You should check the answer using a calculator to be sure that it is correct. It is very easy to make a typographical mistake. For example, if you typed **B4*C3**, Lotus 1-2-3 would display the wrong answer (**$90.00**). Always check the answers.

After pressing **[Enter]**, the product of **B3** and **C3** is displayed in cell **D3** and the top of the screen looks as follows (note that cell **D3** is still active):

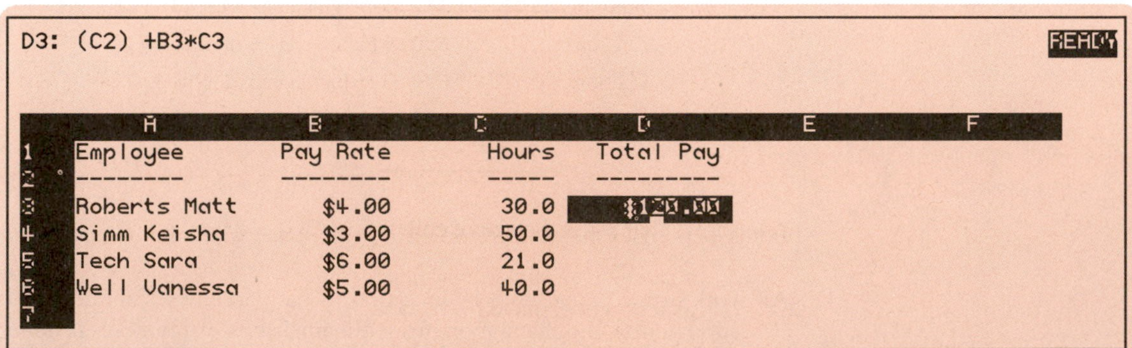

Continued . . .

Keystroke	Action Resulting from Keystroke

Notice the top line of the control panel:

```
D3: (C2) +B3*C3                                                    READY
```

D3 shows that **D3** is the active cell.

(C2) indicates that numeric entries for this cell are formatted for **C**urrency (i.e., the dollar sign is displayed) and that **2** decimal places are displayed.

+ indicates that the entry is a numeric expression.

B3*C3 shows the formula used to calculate the value displayed in the cell.

Remember, to enter a numeric expression that begins with a cell reference, you must precede the expression with a plus sign. To see what happens if you forget to use the plus sign, try the following:

Keystroke	Action Resulting from Keystroke
[arrow]	Use the **[arrow]** keys to make cell **D4** active.
B4*C4	Before you press **[Enter]**, the mode indicator will display **LABEL** indicating that Lotus 1-2-3 thinks you are entering a label (i.e., text) rather than a formula.
↵	Enters the expression into cell **D4**. Because Lotus 1-2-3 thinks you are entering a label, **B4*C4** is displayed in cell **D4** rather than the product of the values in cells **B4** and **C4**.

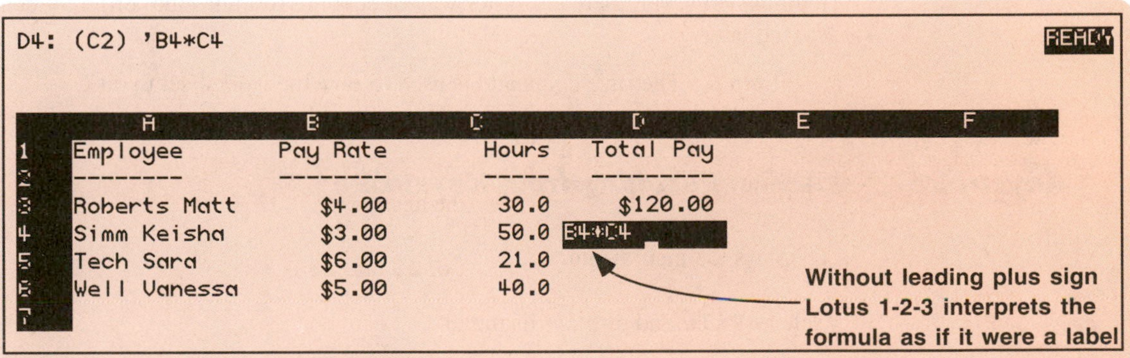

Notice the top line of the control panel:

```
D4: (C2) 'B4*C4                                                    READY
```

D4 shows that **D4** is the active cell

(C2) indicates that numeric entries for this cell are formatted for **C**urrency and that **2** decimal places are displayed

' indicates that the entry is a label (text)

B4*C4 shows the text entered into the cell

Continued . . .

Keystroke	Action Resulting from Keystroke
	Because the contents of this cell are in error, you should replace the cell contents with the correct formula by retyping it with the plus sign as follows:
+B4*C4 ⬇	Calculates the product of the numbers in cells **B4** and **C4**, displays the answer in the active cell (**D4**), and moves the cell pointer down one cell.
+B5*C5 ⬇	Calculates the product of the numbers in cells **B5** and **C5**, displays the answer in the active cell (**D5**), and moves the cell pointer down one cell.
+B6*C6 ↵	Calculates the product of the numbers in cells **B6** and **C6** and displays the answer in the active cell (**D6**). Note that because you used **[Enter]** rather than **[down-arrow]**, **D6** remained the active cell.

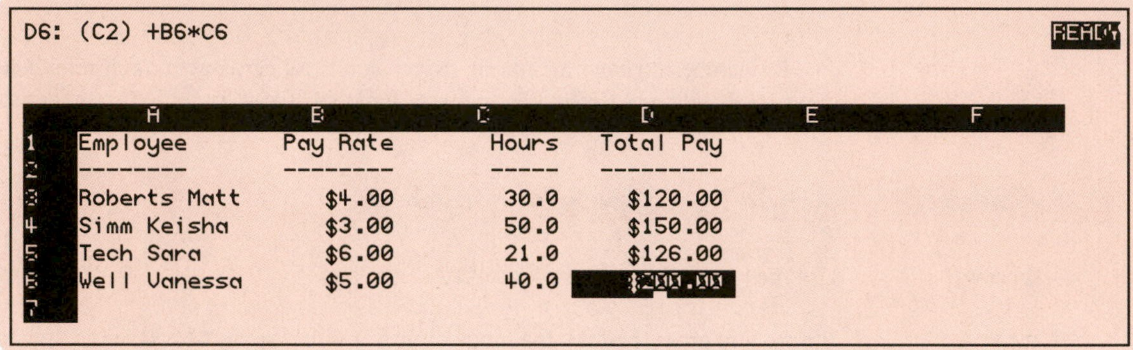

Check the values for **Total Pay** using a calculator to be sure they are correct.

If there were 100 names on the list, the process of typing a formula for each person would be very tedious. However, there is a faster way of copying formulas into different cells. This process is discussed later.

Step 6 The save command is used to save the worksheet to disk.

Keystroke	Action Resulting from Keystroke
/	Displays the main menu.
F	Selects **File** and displays its menu.
S	Selects **Save** and requests the file specification.

Depending on how you first accessed the worksheet, the suggested file specification shown on your screen may be different. If you want to save the modified worksheet using the suggested specification you would press **[Enter]**. However, for this second example, you should use the file specification: **A:PAY-V2.WK1**.

Continued . . .

Keystroke	Action Resulting from Keystroke

REMEMBER . . . We will give new names to different versions of the same file as insurance against major, difficult to fix, errors and because earlier versions may be used later to illustrate new Lotus 1-2-3 features. After you have finished this entire book you may want to go back and delete some or all of the earlier versions of your files.

PAY-V2 ↵ Provides the file specification, saves the file to the diskette in drive A:, and returns to **READY** mode. As was discussed on page L25, you may get the following displayed in the control panel:

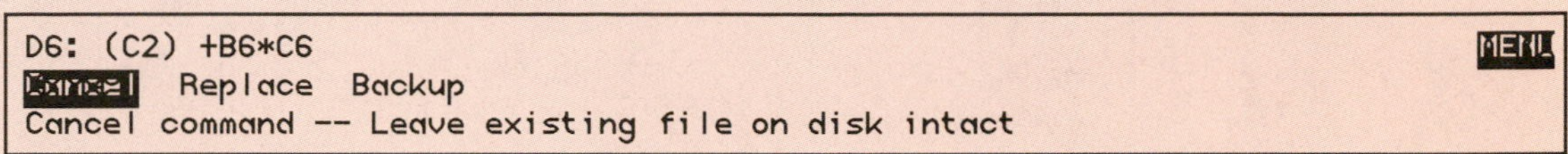

This means that a file has already been saved using the specification **A:PAY-V2.WK1**. You will have to decide whether to cancel the operation and use a different name (press **C**), replace the existing file (press **R**), or make a backup copy (press **B**):

Printing a Worksheet

To get a hard copy of the worksheet you could use **[PrintScreen]**. This will print the contents of the screen (the worksheet entries plus the control panel and the row and column headings). However, if the worksheet is larger than one screen or if you want the hard copy to look nicer or if you want to incorporate it into a WordPerfect document, you must use the print command.

Keystroke	Action Resulting from Keystroke
/	Displays the main menu.
P	Selects **Print** and displays its menu.

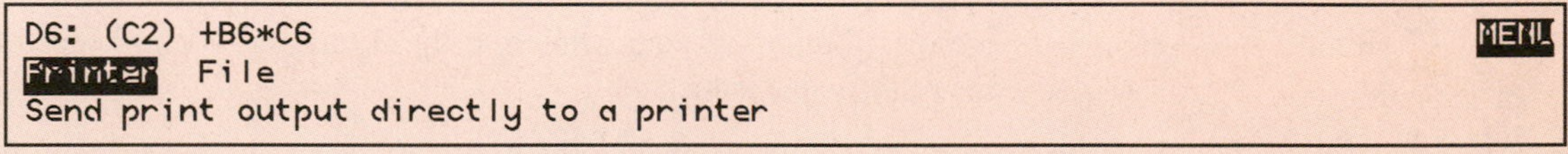

Printer sends the output directly to a printer.

File sends a copy of the output to a file that you can print from later or incorporate into documents created by other programs such as WordPerfect.

Continued . . .

Keystroke	Action Resulting from Keystroke
P	Selects **Printer** and displays its menu.

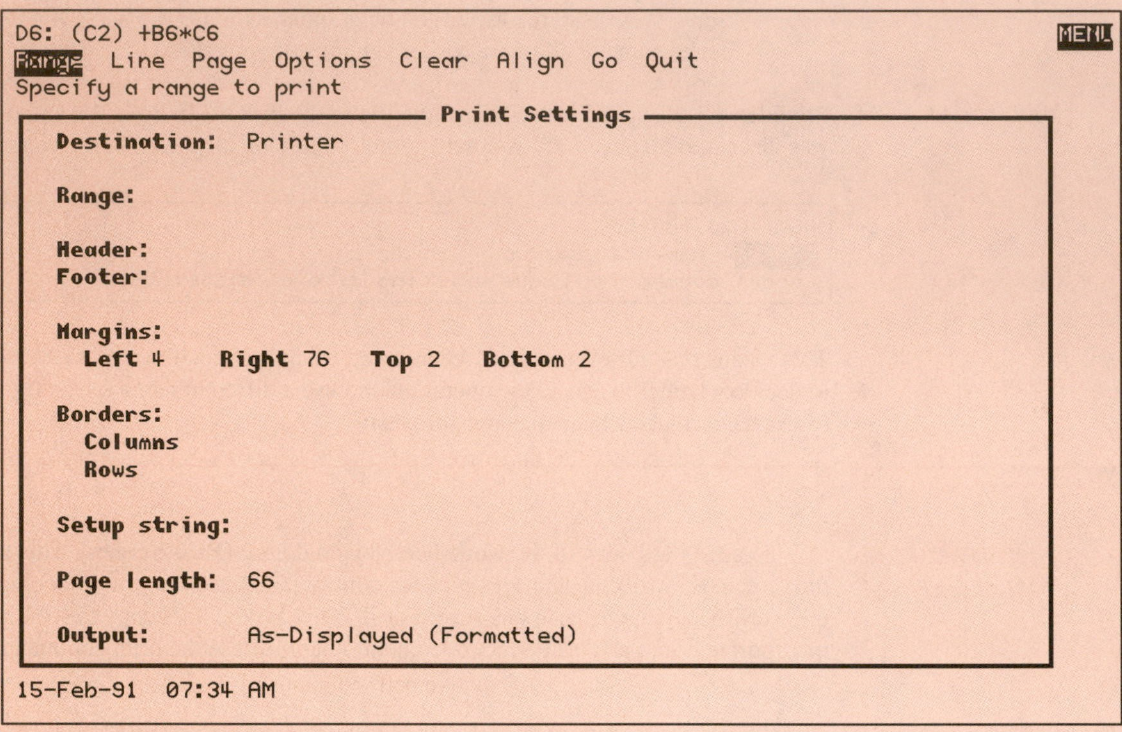

Range allows you to print the entire worksheet or just a part of it. If you have not printed this worksheet before, the default range will be blank. Otherwise, the previous range will be displayed.

Line allows you to advance the printer's paper one line at a time.

Page allows you to advance the printer's paper one page at a time. Use this instead of the page eject button on your printer so that Lotus 1-2-3 can keep track of where the top edge of the paper is located.

Options allows you to change the print settings including headers, footers, margins, borders, and page length.

Clear allows you to erase previously entered settings.

Align specifies that the paper is adjusted to begin printing at the top of the page and resets the page numbering to 1. Selecting **Align** before printing will ensure that headers (see p. L68), footers, and page breaks will be in their proper places.

Go begins the printing process.

Quit returns control to **READY** mode.

Many of the above options will be discussed later. For now, use the **Range** option to select the entire worksheet and then print it using the other default options.

Continued . . .

Keystroke	Action Resulting from Keystroke

R — Selects **Range**, switches to **POINT** mode, and displays the worksheet.

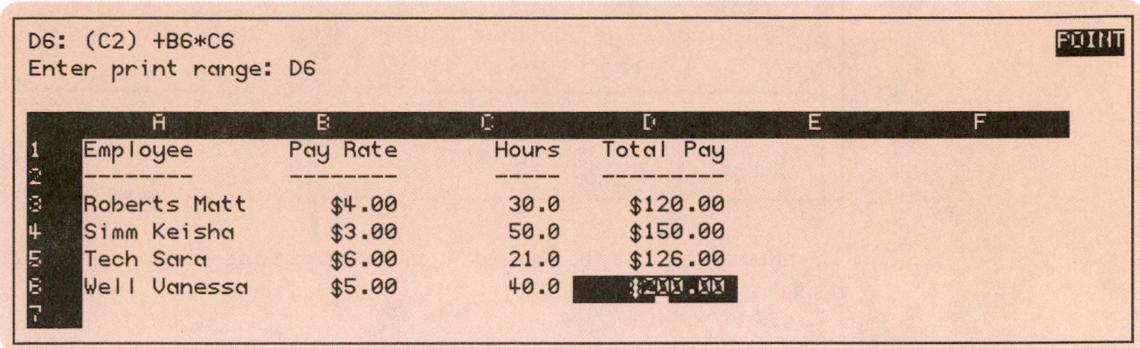

While in **POINT** mode you may select the range as you did before by typing the **coordinates** of two opposite corners of the range separated by one or two periods (you would type **A1.D6** ↵ to select all the entries in this worksheet). However, Lotus 1-2-3 offers a more graphic way of selecting ranges using the **[arrow]** keys. Try defining the range by doing the following:

[Home] — Makes cell **A1** active. This cell will be the upper left-hand corner of the range rectangle. You could just as easily have used the **[arrow]** keys to make cell **D6** active to define the lower right-hand corner of the cell.

(period) — Pressing the period *anchors* the active cell (**A1**) and displays **A1..A1** in the control panel. An anchored cell is one that remains fixed (selected) while you use the **[arrow]** keys to move the cell pointer to a different location.

[arrow] — Use the **[arrow]** keys to move the cell pointer to cell **D6**. As you press the **[arrow]** keys all the cells between the anchor cell (**A1**) and the active cell are selected. When you have finished, cells **A1** through **D6** will be selected and the screen will look as follows:

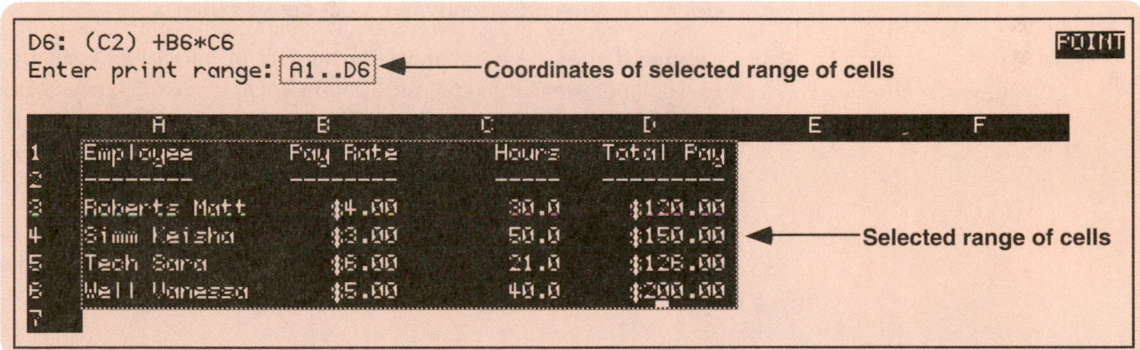

[Enter] — Defines the selected range and returns to the print settings screen. Notice that the seventh line from the top specifies the range as **A1..D6**.

Continued . . .

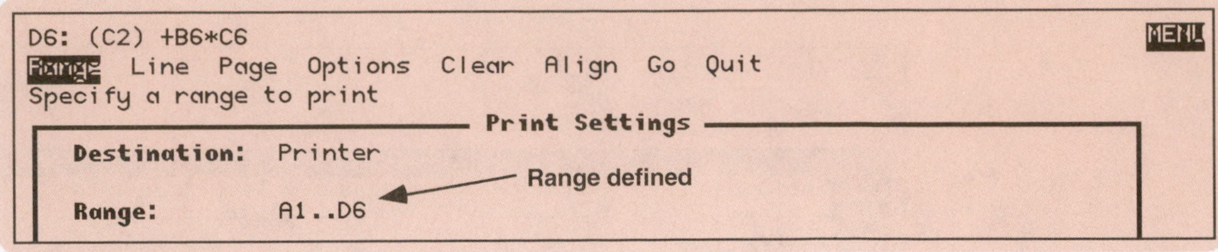
```
D6: (C2) +B6*C6                                              MENU
Range  Line  Page  Options  Clear  Align  Go  Quit
Specify a range to print
                        Print Settings
  Destination:  Printer
  Range:        A1..D6
```


The other settings may be changed by selecting **Options**. For now, use the default printing options displayed:

Header is something that is printed at the top of each page of output. Even though no header is indicated, Lotus 1-2-3 reserves three lines for a header.

Footer is something that is printed at the bottom of each page of output. Even though no footer is indicated, Lotus 1-2-3 reserves three lines for a footer.

Margins:

Left 4 Right 76: The left and right margins can be set anywhere from 0 to 240 characters. The default is 4 and 76 (for standard 10-pitch text, this corresponds to a $\frac{4}{10}$-inch margin on both sides of the page). This means that up to 72 characters can be printed across a page.

Top 2 Bottom 2: The top and bottom margins can be set anywhere from 0 to 32 lines. The default is 2 lines (for standard text, this corresponds to a $\frac{1}{3}$-inch margin at the top and bottom of the page).

Borders Allows you to print headings on rows and/or columns to improve the readability of the printed output. Currently, no borders are indicated.

Setup string allows you to change the size or style of type printed by sending certain codes to the printer. Currently, no codes are specified.

Page length allows you to change the number of lines of text printed per page to be from 1 to 100. For standard type, an $8\frac{1}{2} \times 11$-inch sheet of paper corresponds to 66 lines. Recall that three lines are reserved for a header, three lines are reserved for a footer, two lines are reserved for the top margin, and two lines are reserved for the bottom margin. This leaves 66 –3 –3 –2 –2 = 56 lines of output per page.

Output allows you to print the output of the worksheet as it appears on the screen (this is the default) or you may print the cell formulas or include the headers, footers and page breaks.

The default then, is a 66-line page with five blank lines at the top and bottom, $\frac{4}{10}$-inch margins on the sides, and the output printed exactly as it is displayed.

Before doing the next step, be sure your printer is connected to the computer, turned on, loaded with paper, and the paper is properly aligned in the printer.

A Selects **Align**. This tells Lotus 1-2-3 that the paper is properly positioned in the printer.

Continued . . .

Keystroke	Action Resulting from Keystroke

G Selects **Go** and begins the printing process. The word **WAIT** appears in the mode box as the file is being printed. The printed version of the file appears exactly as it does on the screen. If necessary, you may use **[Ctrl-Break]** to abort the printing process before it is completed. This will display the message **Printer error** at the bottom of the screen and the mode indicator box will blink the word **ERROR** on and off. If this happens, press **[Enter]** to return to **READY** mode, then fix the printer (e.g., turn on the printer) and try printing again.

The printed output should look like the following:

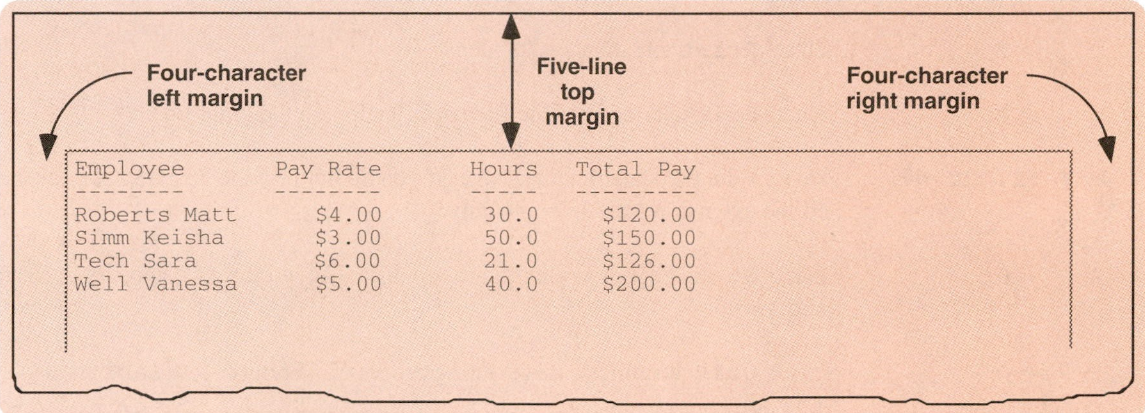

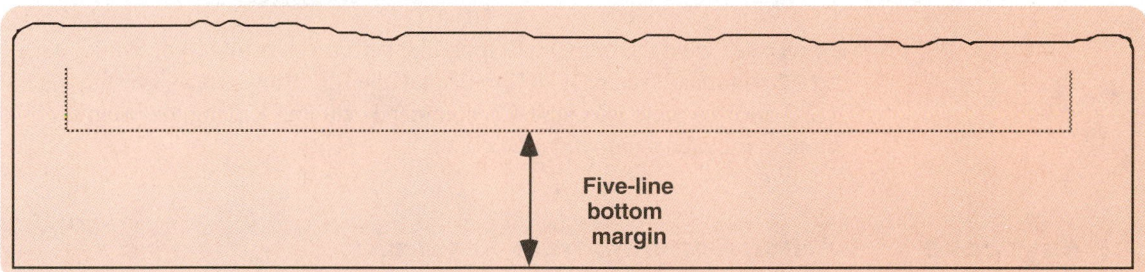

Note that if you press **G** again the printing will begin exactly where it left off (on the same page and without five lines for the top margin and header). To print another copy beginning on a new page, select **Page** first (this will eject the paper to the top of the next sheet), then **Align**, and then **Go**.

P Selects **Page** and ejects the sheet of paper currently in the printer.

A Selects **Align** to inform Lotus 1-2-3 that the paper is properly aligned in the printer (this gets you or someone else ready to print again).

Q Selects **Quit** and returns to **READY** mode.

It is sometimes useful to send the output to a file rather than to the printer. You may want to do this if there is no printer attached to the computer but you still want to see how the output will look. Or, you may want to incorporate the output into another document, such as a letter you wrote using WordPerfect. You may even want to send a copy of the output to another computer over a telephone line.

Save the output on a file called **PAY-V2.TXT** by doing the following:

Keystroke	Action Resulting from Keystroke
/	Displays the main menu.
P	Selects **Print** and displays its menu.
F	Selects **File** and requests the file specification on the input line.
PAY-V2.TXT ↵	Provides the file specification. Note: If you do not provide an extension for the file, Lotus 1-2-3 will add the extension **PRN** automatically.
G	Selects **Go** and begins writing the file to disk. The word **WAIT** appears in the mode box as the file is being saved.
Q	Selects **Quit**, terminates this printing process, and returns to **READY** mode.

Dropping to DOS

To see what the output will look like before you print it, you could exit Lotus 1-2-3 and use the **TYPE** command (see p. W203) to display the file. However, as was the case with WordPerfect, Lotus 1-2-3 allows you to execute DOS commands without leaving the program by doing the following (this process is called *dropping to DOS*):

Keystroke	Action Resulting from Keystroke
/	Displays the main menu.
S	Selects **System** and suspends operation of Lotus 1-2-3. The following is displayed:

```
(Type EXIT and press ENTER to return to 1-2-3)


Microsoft(R) MS-DOS(R) Version 4.01
             (C)Copyright Microsoft Corp 1981-1988

C:\123>_
```

Continued . . .

Keystroke	Action Resulting from Keystroke
TYPE A:PAY-V2.TXT ↵	Displays the contents of the file as follows:

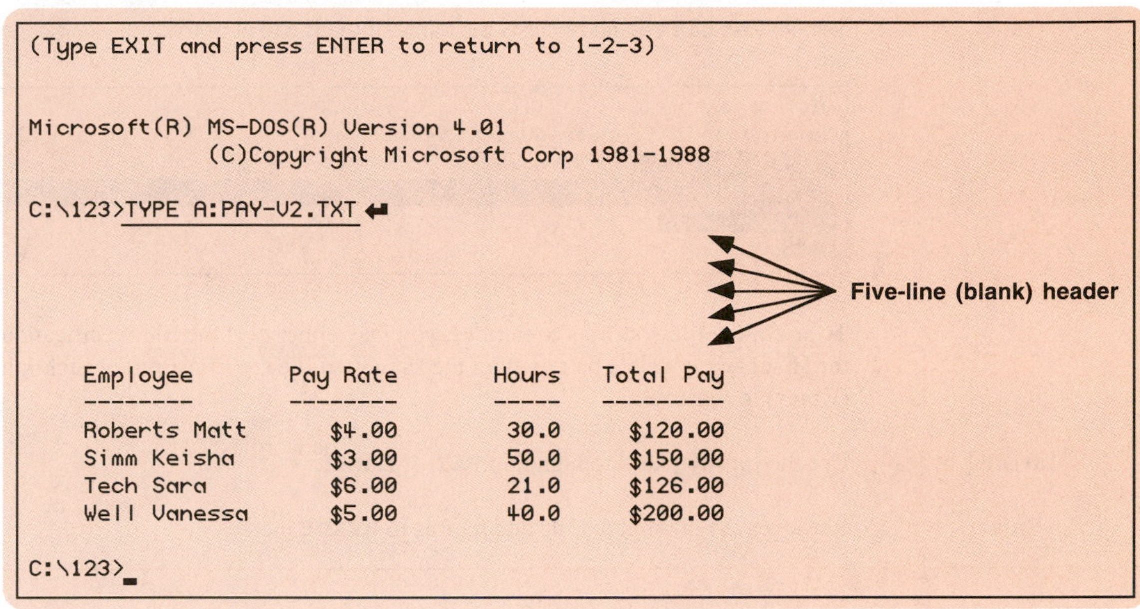
```
(Type EXIT and press ENTER to return to 1-2-3)


Microsoft(R) MS-DOS(R) Version 4.01
             (C)Copyright Microsoft Corp 1981-1988

C:\123>TYPE A:PAY-V2.TXT ↵






    Employee        Pay Rate       Hours    Total Pay
    --------        --------       -----    ---------
    Roberts Matt       $4.00        30.0      $120.00
    Simm Keisha        $3.00        50.0      $150.00
    Tech Sara          $6.00        21.0      $126.00
    Well Vanessa       $5.00        40.0      $200.00

C:\123>_
```


Keystroke	Action Resulting from Keystroke
EXIT ↵	Returns control to Lotus 1-2-3.

This ends the instruction on printing. Quit the spreadsheet program and return to DOS by doing the following.

Keystroke	Action Resulting from Keystroke
/	Displays the main menu.
Q	Selects **Quit** and asks if you are sure that you want to quit.
Y	Specifies that **Y**es, you want to quit and returns control to the DOS environment.

TO TAKE A BREAK Remove diskette(s). To resume (hard disk): Insert *Data* diskette, type **C: ↵**, **CD\123 ↵**. To resume (two drive): Insert diskettes, type **B: ↵**.

Adding More Data to a Worksheet

Data for more employees can be added to the worksheet just completed by doing the following:

Step 1 Access the Lotus 1-2-3 program and load the worksheet **PAY-V2** by doing the following:

Keystroke	Action Resulting from Keystroke
123 ↵	Loads the Lotus 1-2-3 program directly and presents a blank worksheet on the screen.

Continued . . .

Keystroke	Action Resulting from Keystroke
/	Displays the main menu.
F	Selects **File** and displays its menu.
R	Selects **Retrieve** and requests the name of the file to be retrieved.

```
A1:                                                              FILES
Name of file to retrieve: A:\*.wk?
PAY-V1.WK1          PAY-V2.WK1
        A           B          C          D          E          F          G          H
1
2
```

To select the file you want to retrieve, you may either type the file specification (you may have to use the **[Esc]** key to delete part or all of the suggested file specification) or highlight its name and press **[Enter]** to retrieve it.

[arrow]	Use the [arrow] keys to highlight **PAY-V2.WK1**.
[Enter]	Retrieves the highlighted file and returns to **READY** mode.

Step 2 Extend the worksheet by adding data in columns **A**, **B**, and **C** for two more people by typing the following:

Cell	Type this	Comment
	[arrow]	Use the **[arrow]** keys to make cell **A7** active.
A7	**Taylor David** ➡	Pressing **[right-arrow]** enters the name and makes active the cell immediately to the right.
B7	**4** ➡	Displays **$4.00** and moves one cell to the right. Lotus 1-2-3 automatically enters the **$** and the **.00** because the cell has already been formatted to display numbers as currency with two decimal places (see p. L32).
C7	**35** ⬇ ⬅ ⬅	Displays **35.0** and moves one cell down and two cells to the left (to cell **A8**). Lotus 1-2-3 automatically enters the **.0** because the cell has already been formatted to display numbers with one decimal place (see p. L31).
A8	**Garcia Rosa** ➡	Enters the name and moves one cell to the right.
B8	**4** ➡	Displays **$4.00** and moves one cell to the right.
C8	**50** ↵	Displays **50.0** and keeps cell **C8** active.

After doing this, the screen should look like the following:

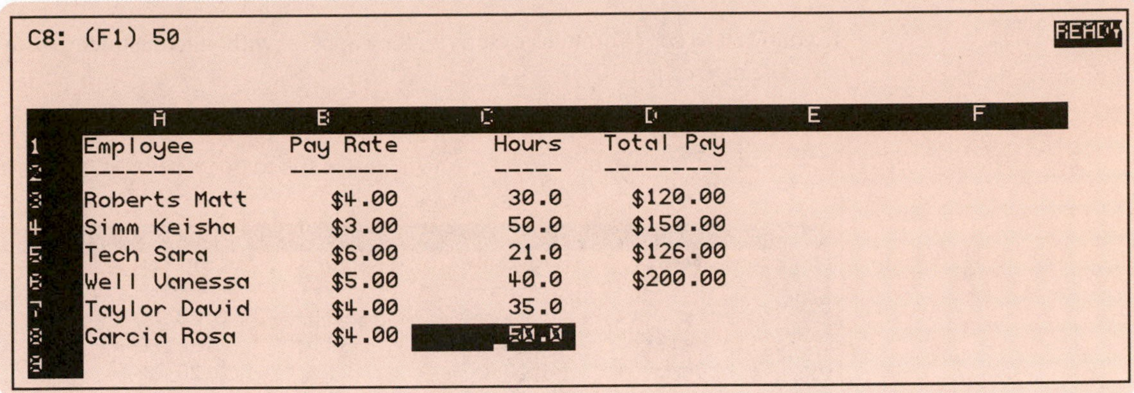
C8: (F1) 50 READY

	A	B	C	D	E	F
1	Employee	Pay Rate	Hours	Total Pay		
2	---------	---------	-----	---------		
3	Roberts Matt	$4.00	30.0	$120.00		
4	Simm Keisha	$3.00	50.0	$150.00		
5	Tech Sara	$6.00	21.0	$126.00		
6	Well Vanessa	$5.00	40.0	$200.00		
7	Taylor David	$4.00	35.0			
8	Garcia Rosa	$4.00	50.0			
9						

In the above screen dump, notice the **C8: (F1)** in the upper left-hand corner of the screen. The **C8** identifies the active cell. The **F** means that the value in cell **C8** has been formatted as a **F**ixed decimal number and the **1** means that one decimal place is to be displayed.

Step 3 The formulas for the total pay have to be entered. You could type them as you did in the last section, but Lotus 1-2-3 provides an easy way to copy information from one cell to another.

Keystroke	Action Resulting from Keystroke
/	Displays the main menu.
C	Selects **Copy** and displays the following in the control panel:

```
C8: (F1) 50                                          POINT
Enter range to copy FROM: C8..C8
```

In this case, you want to copy the formula for the total pay *from* cell **D3** (or cell **D4** or **D5** or **D6**, it makes no difference).

D3 ↵ Specifies that the formula from cell **D3** is to be copied and displays the following in the control panel:

```
C8: (F1) 50                                          POINT
Enter range to copy TO: C8
```

You want to copy the formula *to* the cells for the total pay of the two new people (Taylor's total pay should go in cell **D7** and Garcia's total pay should go in cell **D8**). Therefore, the range of cells to copy to is **D7.D8**.

D7.D8 ↵ Specifies the destination for the copy and pastes the formula from cell **D3** into cells **D7** and **D8**. It would not make sense to copy the formula *exactly* as it appears in cell **D3** (i.e., **B3*C3**). This would mean that the formula for the total pay of Taylor would be calculated using the data from cells **B3** and **C3**, which are the values for Roberts. When Lotus 1-2-3 copies a formula, unless you tell it not to, it does so in a *relative* way. This means that if you are copying a formula into a certain row, then all row references will be made to that new row, even if they were not made to that row in the original formula. Thus, **B3*C3** becomes **B7*C7** when pasted into row **7** and **B3*C3** becomes **B8*C8** when pasted into row **8**.

Continued . . .

Keystroke	Action Resulting from Keystroke

If you want to copy formulas exactly as they appear (without adjustment), you will have to use absolute referencing (see p. L107).

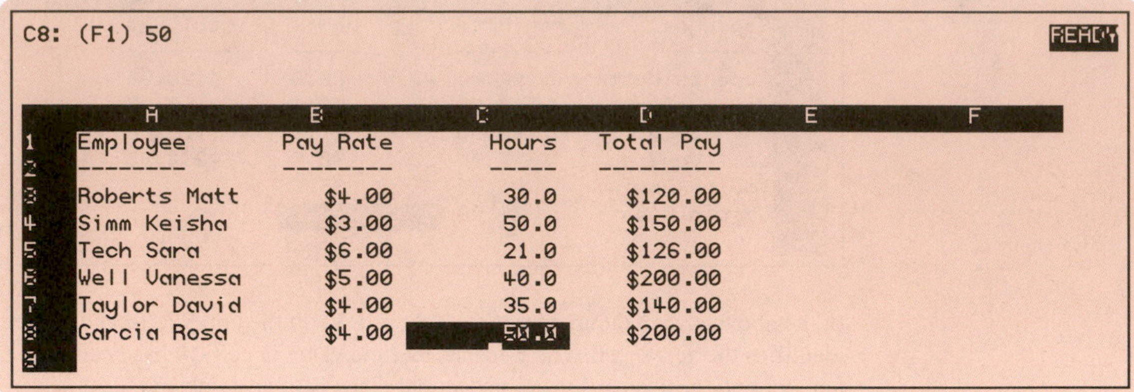
C8: (F1) 50 READY

	A	B	C	D	E	F
1	Employee	Pay Rate	Hours	Total Pay		
2	---------	---------	-----	---------		
3	Roberts Matt	$4.00	30.0	$120.00		
4	Simm Keisha	$3.00	50.0	$150.00		
5	Tech Sara	$6.00	21.0	$126.00		
6	Well Vanessa	$5.00	40.0	$200.00		
7	Taylor David	$4.00	35.0	$140.00		
8	Garcia Rosa	$4.00	50.0	$200.00		
9						

Use a calculator to check the values in cells **D7** and **D8**. Always check the answers.

Step 4 Save the worksheet on a file called **PAY-V3** by doing the following:

Keystroke	Action Resulting from Keystroke
/	Displays the main menu.
F	Selects **File** and displays its menu.
S	Selects **Save** and requests a name for the file. The suggested file specification probably will be **A:\PAY-V2.WK1** (i.e., the specification of the currently active file). You may have to use **[Esc]** to delete those parts of the suggested specification that you do not want to use.
PAY-V3 ↵	Provides the new file specification, saves the worksheet to the diskette in drive A:, and returns to **READY** mode.

Computing Totals and Averages

Lotus 1-2-3 has a number of special functions that will do specified computations quickly and easily. For example, suppose you wanted to find the sum and the average of the hours worked and total pay earned for each person listed in the wages worksheet, **PAY-V3**. You could type individual formulas for these. The formula for the sum of the total pay earned for all the employees would be **+D3+D4+D5+D6+D7+D8** while the average would be **+(D3+D4+D5+D6+D7+D8)/6**. However, you can find these values more easily using the sum function (**@SUM**) and the average (**@AVG**) function.

Keystroke	Action Resulting from Keystroke
[arrow]	Use the **[arrow]** keys to make cell **A10** active.
Totals ↓	Enters the label for the row that will contain the totals for the columns and moves the cell pointer down one row (cell **A11** becomes active).

Continued . . .

Keystroke	Action Resulting from Keystroke
Averages → → →	Enters the label for the row that will contain the averages for the columns and moves the cell pointer three columns to the right (cell **D11** becomes active).
@AVG(D3.D8) ↵	Calculates the average of the values in the range **D3** through **D8** and displays the answer in the active cell. Notice that while the answer is displayed in the active cell the formula is displayed in the control panel. Carefully examine the parts of the formula:

@ Indicates that this is a special Lotus 1-2-3 function.

AVG is the name of the function (**AV**era**G**e). Be sure you type **AVG** and not **AVE**!

(**D3.D8**) is the range that the function is to operate on. Remember, even if you type one period (**D3.D8**) Lotus 1-2-3 will store and display two periods (**D3..D8**). This means that the function will find the average of the values in cells **D3**, **D4**, **D5**, **D6**, **D7**, and **D8**.

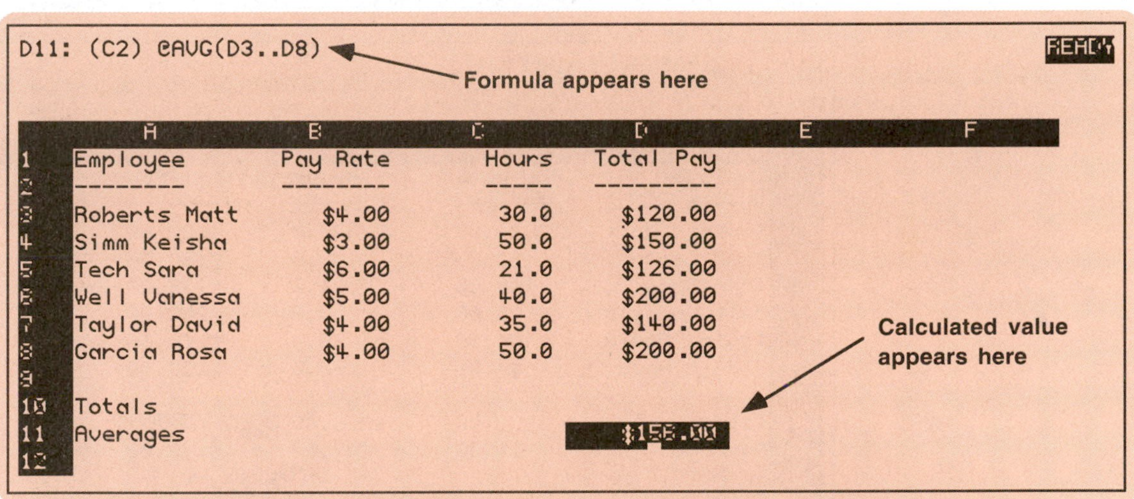

Use a calculator to check the value in cell **D11**. Always check the answers. Now, enter the formula for the sum of the values in column **D**.

Keystroke	Action Resulting from Keystroke
↑	Makes cell **D10** active.
@SUM(D3.D8) ↵	Calculates the sum of the values in the range **D3** through **D8** and displays the result in the active cell. Use a calculator to check the value in cell **D10**. Always check the answers.

Care must be taken when entering ranges. For example, if you were to mistakenly enter **@SUM(D3.D10)** in cell **D10**, the computer would calculate the sum by including the sum itself as a part of the calculation (this is referred to as a *circular reference*). Each time Lotus 1-2-3 recalculates the values in the worksheet the value in cell **D10** would erroneously get bigger and bigger (there are times when this is necessary but we will not discuss them in this book). You can tell if you have a circular reference because Lotus 1-2-3 will display the word **CIRC** on the status line indicating that you have a **CIRC**ular reference (i.e., a formula that depends on its own value). If that happens, look carefully at your formulas to find where you have made an error in the cell references.

The formulas for sum and average can be copied into cells **B10** through **C11** using the copy command as follows:

Keystroke	Action Resulting from Keystroke
/	Displays the main menu.
C	Selects **Copy** and asks you to **Enter range to copy FROM**.
D10.D11 ↵	Specifies that the formulas from cells **D10** and **D11** are to be copied. Note that you can specify these cells using the **POINT** technique described on page L39 (i.e., make cell **D10** active, press **[.]**, use the **[arrow]** keys to make cell **D11** active, and then press **[Enter]**. You then are asked to **Enter range to copy TO**.
B10.C11 ↵	Specifies the destination for the copy and copies the formulas as follows: ▮ The formula in cell **D10** is copied (with proper adjustments) into cells **B10** and **C10**. ▮ The formula in cell **D11** is copied (with proper adjustments) into cells **B11** and **C11**.

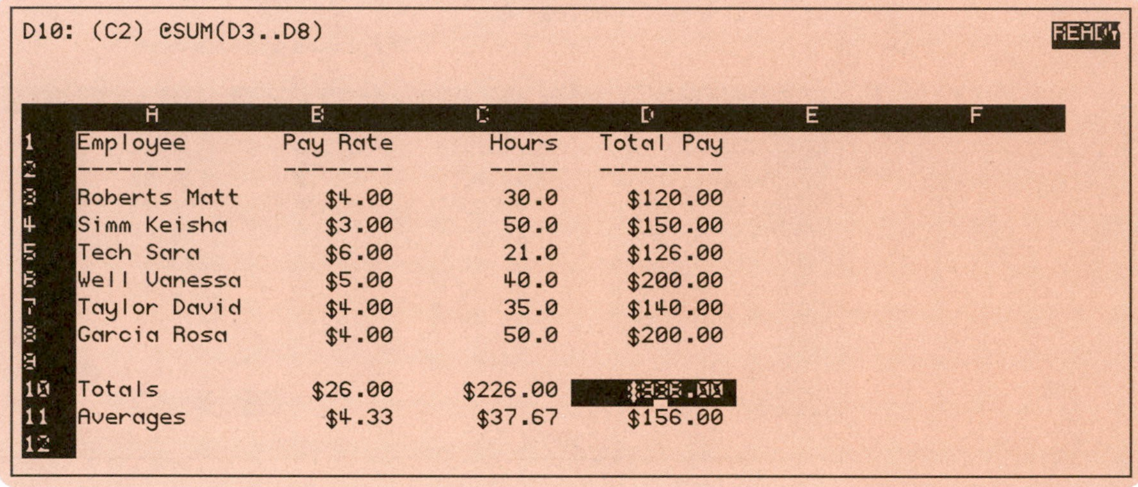

D10: (C2) @SUM(D3..D8)   READY

	A	B	C	D	E	F
1	Employee	Pay Rate	Hours	Total Pay		
2	--------	--------	-----	---------		
3	Roberts Matt	$4.00	30.0	$120.00		
4	Simm Keisha	$3.00	50.0	$150.00		
5	Tech Sara	$6.00	21.0	$126.00		
6	Well Vanessa	$5.00	40.0	$200.00		
7	Taylor David	$4.00	35.0	$140.00		
8	Garcia Rosa	$4.00	50.0	$200.00		
9						
10	Totals	$26.00	$226.00	[illegible]		
11	Averages	$4.33	$37.67	$156.00		
12						

Use a calculator to check the values in cells **B10** through **C11**. Always check the answers.

There are two problems here. First, when Lotus 1-2-3 copies a formula, it also copies the formatting from the cell that contains the formula. In this example, this causes the sum and average in cells **C10** and **C11** (for hours) to be formatted as if they were dollar values (with the dollar sign and two decimal places displayed). Thus, you have to reformat those cells.

Keystroke	Action Resulting from Keystroke
/	Displays the main menu.
R	Selects **Range** and displays its menu.
F	Selects **Format** and displays its menu.
F	Selects **Fixed** and asks you to **Enter number of decimal places**.
1 ↵	Specifies that one decimal place is to be displayed and asks you to **Enter range to format**.
C10.C11 ↵	Selects cells **C10** and **C11**, changes the number of decimal places displayed in this range, removes the dollar sign, and returns to **READY** mode.

The second problem is that the sum of the rates of pay in cell **B10** really makes no sense. That cell should be erased using the *Range Erase* feature.

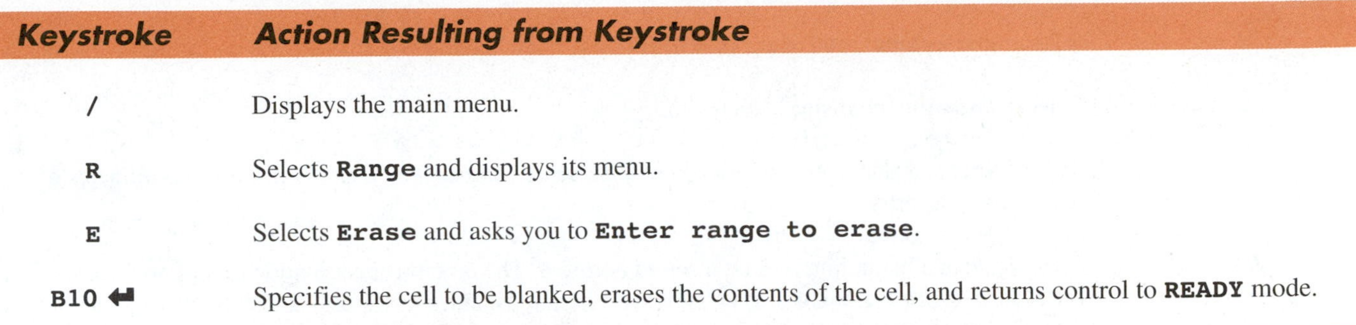

Keystroke	Action Resulting from Keystroke
/	Displays the main menu.
R	Selects **Range** and displays its menu.
E	Selects **Erase** and asks you to **Enter range to erase**.
B10 ↵	Specifies the cell to be blanked, erases the contents of the cell, and returns control to **READY** mode.

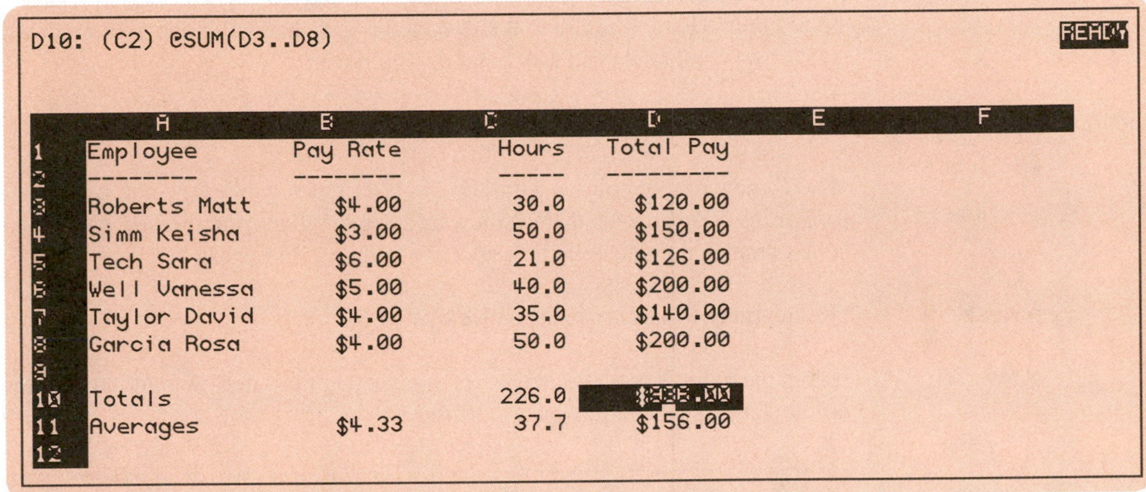

D10: (C2) @SUM(D3..D8) READY

	A	B	C	D	E	F
1	Employee	Pay Rate	Hours	Total Pay		
2	--------	--------	-----	---------		
3	Roberts Matt	$4.00	30.0	$120.00		
4	Simm Keisha	$3.00	50.0	$150.00		
5	Tech Sara	$6.00	21.0	$126.00		
6	Well Vanessa	$5.00	40.0	$200.00		
7	Taylor David	$4.00	35.0	$140.00		
8	Garcia Rosa	$4.00	50.0	$200.00		
9						
10	Totals		226.0	$936.00		
11	Averages	$4.33	37.7	$156.00		
12						

Save the worksheet on a file called **PAY-V4** by doing the following:

Keystroke	Action Resulting from Keystroke
/	Displays the main menu.
F	Selects **File** and displays its menu.
S	Selects **Save** and requests a name for the file.
PAY-V4 ↵	Provides the new file specification, saves the worksheet to the diskette in drive A:, and returns to **READY** mode. Be sure that you have the proper file specification before you press **[Enter]**.

The **@SUM** and **@AVG** functions are quick, easy to use, and quite flexible. For example, if you were to insert a new row of data, say at row **4**, the **@SUM** and **@AVG** functions would be changed automatically to reflect this modification. Try this by doing the following:

Keystroke	Action Resulting from Keystroke
/	Displays the main menu.
W	Selects **Worksheet** and displays its menu.
I	Selects **Insert** and displays its menu.
R	Selects **Row** and asks you to **Enter row insert range**. You are to enter the coordinates of the row(s) to be inserted.
A4	Specifies that a blank line is to be inserted at row **4**. The column specification makes no difference (you could have typed **B4** or **C4** or **D4**). However, if you just enter **4**, Lotus 1-2-3 will tell you that you have specified an **Invalid cell or range address** when **[Enter]** is pressed. In that case, you should press **[Esc]** to return to **READY** mode. You then will have to re-enter the **W**(orksheet), **I**(nsert), and **R**(ow) commands and then enter a valid range.
↵	When **[Enter]** is pressed, notice how all the rows below row **4** are moved down one row.

When a new row or column is inserted, it is completely blank (i.e., it has no values, formulas, labels, or formatting). This means that if you want to enter values into the new row, you must also format those cells to match the others in the respective columns. For example:

[arrow]	Use the **[arrow]** keys to make cell **B4** active.
8 ↵	Enters the value **8** into the active cell. Notice that the value entered into the active cell does not have the dollar sign or two decimal places displayed.

B4: 8 READY

No formatting is indicated for this cell so only the raw number is displayed

	A	B	C	D	E	F
1	Employee	Pay Rate	Hours	Total Pay		
2	--------	--------	-----	---------		
3	Roberts Matt	$4.00	30.0	$120.00		
4		8				
5	Simm Keisha	$3.00	50.0	$150.00		
6	Tech Sara	$6.00	21.0	$126.00		
7	Well Vanessa	$5.00	40.0	$200.00		
8	Taylor David	$4.00	35.0	$140.00		
9	Garcia Rosa	$4.00	50.0	$200.00		
10						
11	Totals		226.0	$936.00		
12	Averages	$4.86	37.7	$156.00		

You would have to use the *Format* feature to format this cell for currency and two decimal places (see p. L32).

[arrow]	Use the **[arrow]** keys to make cell **D11** active. Notice how the formula has changed from **@SUM(D3.D8)** to **@SUM (D3.D9)**. In other words, if you were to add data to row **4**, the sums and averages in rows **11** and **12** would be correctly calculated.

Continued . . .

Keystroke	Action Resulting from Keystroke

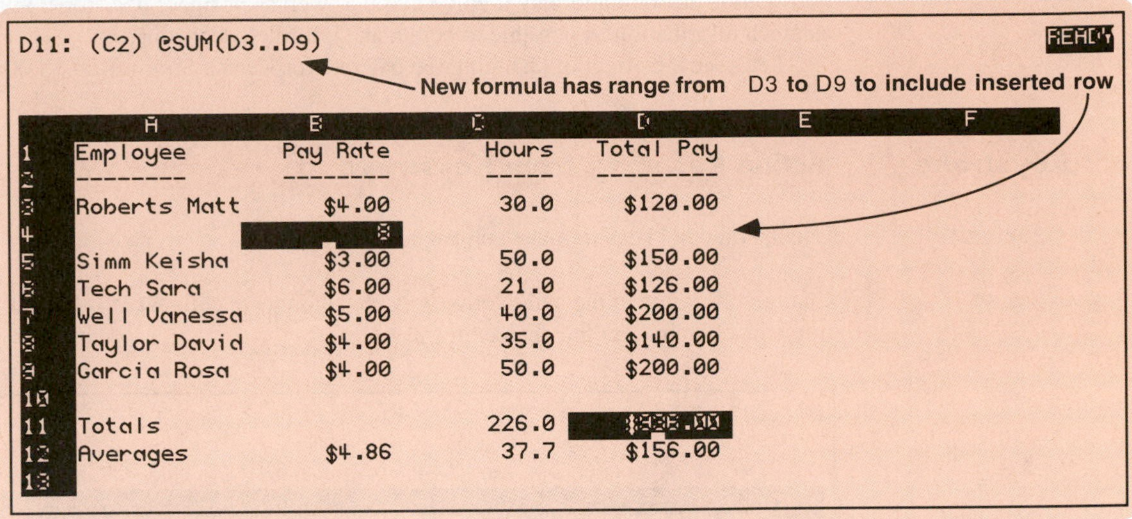

D11: (C2) @SUM(D3..D9)
READY
New formula has range from D3 to D9 to include inserted row
Employee Pay Rate Hours Total Pay
Roberts Matt $4.00 30.0 $120.00
Simm Keisha $3.00 50.0 $150.00
Tech Sara $6.00 21.0 $126.00
Well Vanessa $5.00 40.0 $200.00
Taylor David $4.00 35.0 $140.00
Garcia Rosa $4.00 50.0 $200.00
Totals 226.0
Averages $4.86 37.7 $156.00

You must be somewhat careful when inserting rows or columns. If you insert a row (or column) that is outside the original range of the function, that row (or column) will not be included in the range specified in the function. For example, if you insert a new row at row **10**, the formula for the sum will not be updated to **@SUM(D3.D10)** but will remain **@SUM(D3.D9)**.

Delete the new row by doing the following (the steps are almost identical to those given for inserting a row):

Keystroke	Action Resulting from Keystroke
/	Displays the main menu.
W	Selects **Worksheet** and displays its menu.
D	Selects **Delete** and displays its menu.
R	Selects **Row** and requests the range to be deleted.
A4 ↵	Deletes row **4** and returns control to **READY** mode. The worksheet now should look like it did when you saved it as **PAY.V4**.

What-If Analysis

The ability of a spreadsheet program to accept new or modified data and then to perform calculations quickly on that data enables users to answer *what-if* questions. For example, in relation to the worksheet you just completed, you might ask, *What* happens to the total cost for labor *if* the minimum wage is raised to $5.00 per hour? Using the worksheet, you can change the pay rates of Matt, Keisha, David, and Rosa to $5.00 and immediately see the change in the total labor costs (pay) for the company. Then, you can think about what the effect will be on your company's profits. Being able to make changes to data, and then immediately to see the effects of those changes, helps the user make decisions about the best course of action to take under different circumstances.

For example, if the budget remains the same (i.e., if the company cannot pay out more money for labor), how many workers will have to be laid off because of increased costs? Or, can the higher costs be absorbed by reducing the hours worked for all workers by ten percent? Finding the answers to such questions is difficult and may involve moral as well as business decisions. In any case, a manager needs as much information as possible to help make informed decisions.

Let's see the effect of changing the pay rate for Keisha Simm from $3.00 to $5.00.

Keystroke	Action Resulting from Keystroke
[arrow]	Use the **[arrow]** keys to make cell **B4** active.
5 ↵	Changes the value in the cell. Notice how the amounts in cells **B11**, **D4**, **D10**, and **D11** change immediately to reflect the change in cell **B4**.

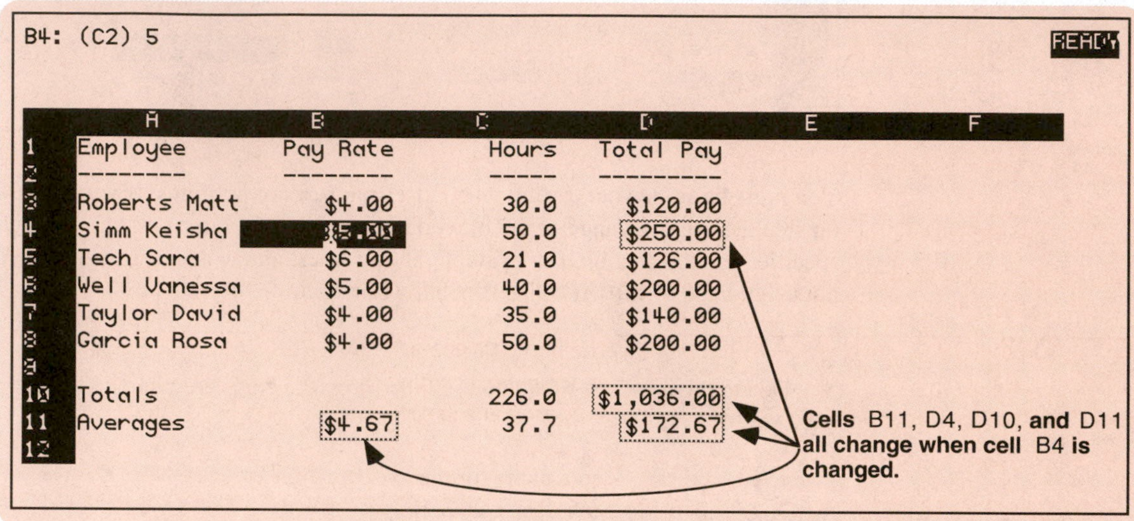
B4: (C2) 5 READY

	A	B	C	D	E	F
1	Employee	Pay Rate	Hours	Total Pay		
2	--------	--------	-----	---------		
3	Roberts Matt	$4.00	30.0	$120.00		
4	Simm Keisha	$5.00	50.0	$250.00		
5	Tech Sara	$6.00	21.0	$126.00		
6	Well Vanessa	$5.00	40.0	$200.00		
7	Taylor David	$4.00	35.0	$140.00		
8	Garcia Rosa	$4.00	50.0	$200.00		
9						
10	Totals		226.0	$1,036.00		
11	Averages	$4.67	37.7	$172.67		
12						

Recall that the *Undo* feature allows you to cancel the effect of the last command or value entered. This is useful if you make an error or if you want to cancel the effect of the last modification. Just for practice, try using the *Undo* feature to undo the last value change.

Keystroke	Action Resulting from Keystroke
[Alt-F4]	Invokes the *Undo* feature and cancels the effect of the last modification. Keisha's pay rate in cell **B4** goes back to $3.00 and the values in cells **B11**, **D4**, **D10**, and **D11** return to their previous values. If you press **[Alt-F4]** again, you will undo the undo and Keisha's pay will change to $5.00 again. *Undo* undoes the previous command even if it was an *Undo* command!

Marking and Naming Ranges

Lotus 1-2-3 allows the user to mark ranges using the **[arrow]** keys and to give names to ranges so that they are easier to remember. To illustrate this, let's mark the range of cells **D3** through **D8** and give it the name **PAY** by doing the following (begin from the worksheet called **PAY-V4**):

Keystroke	Action Resulting from Keystroke
[arrow]	Use the **[arrow]** keys to make cell **D3** active.
/	Displays the main menu.
R	Selects **Range** and displays its menu.
N	Selects **Name** and displays its menu.

```
D3: (C2) +B3*C3                                                    MENU
Create  Delete  Labels  Reset  Table
Create or modify a range name
```

Create allows you to create or modify a range name.

Delete allows you to delete a range name.

Labels allows you to create range names from a range of labels.

Reset allows you to delete all the range names.

Table allows you to create a table of range names.

Keystroke	Action Resulting from Keystroke
C	Selects **Create** and asks for the name of the range you wish to define.
PAY ↵	Specifies the name of the new range. Names of ranges can have from 1 to 15 characters including letters, digits and the underscore. The name should begin with a letter and should not include spaces, punctuation marks, cell coordinates (such as **B2**) or formulas (such as **@SUM**). After you have provided a name for the range, Lotus 1-2-3 anchors the active cell and requests the range definition. You can define the range either by typing the range specification (e.g., **D3.D8**) or by using the **[arrow]** keys as follows:
↓ ↓ ↓ ↓ ↓	Press the **[down-arrow]** key five times to move the cell pointer to **D8**. As **[down-arrow]** is pressed, the cells **D3** through **D8** are selected, and the words on the input line change to **Enter range: D3..D8**.

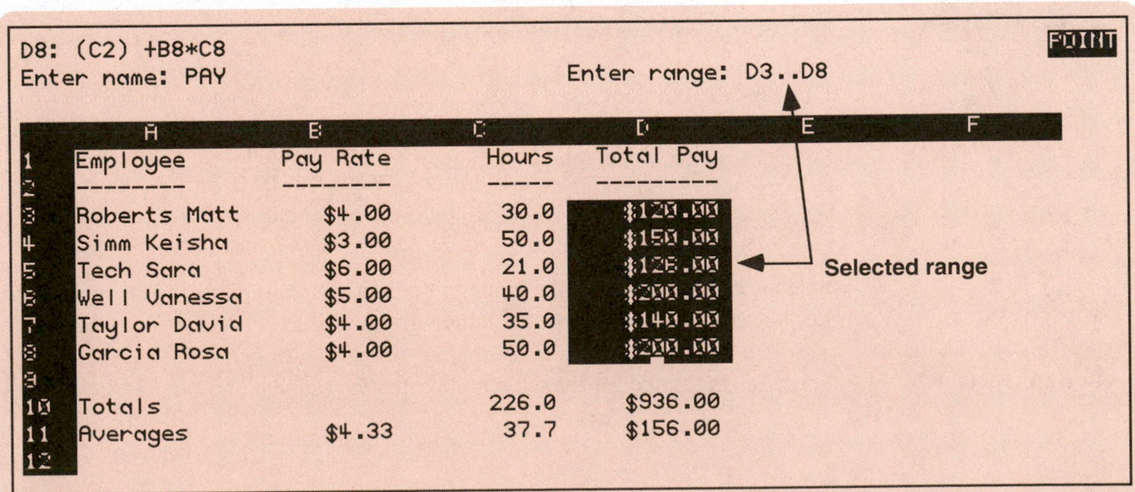

Continued . . .

Keystroke	Action Resulting from Keystroke
↵	Saves the range of cells selected (**D3** through **D8**) under the name **PAY**. From now on, whenever you want to refer to the range of cells **D3** through **D8**, you need only specify the range name, **PAY**. For example, the formula in cell **D10** now could be written as **@SUM(PAY)** rather than **@SUM(D3.D8)**, and the formula in cell **D11** could be written as **@AVG(PAY)** rather than **@AVG(D3.D8)**. If you insert rows, the named range will be redefined accordingly (e.g., inserting a new row 4 will redefine the range **PAY** to be from **D3** through **D9**). Also, previously defined uses of the range will now contain the new name.

Define one more range by doing the following:

Keystroke	Action Resulting from Keystroke
/	Displays the main menu.
R	Selects **Range** and displays its menu.
N	Selects **Name** and displays its menu.
C	Selects **Create** and asks for the name of the range you wish to define.
HOURS ↵	Specifies the name of the new range and requests the range specification.
C3.C8 ↵	Specifies the range, saves the named range, and returns to **READY** mode (you could use the **[arrow]** keys to specify the range as in the previous example).

If you want to get a list of the named ranges for the active worksheet, you would use the *Table* feature. This feature allows you to create a two-column table that alphabetically lists the defined range names and their corresponding addresses.

Keystroke	Action Resulting from Keystroke
/	Displays the main menu.
R	Selects **Range** and displays its menu.
N	Selects **Name** and displays its menu.
T	Selects **Table**, asks for the range of cells in which to place the table (this can be any blank range). Let's use **A13.B20** so that the table will be visible.
A13.B20 ↵	Specifies the range for the table and writes the range names and addresses in the table.

Continued . . .

Keystroke	Action Resulting from Keystroke

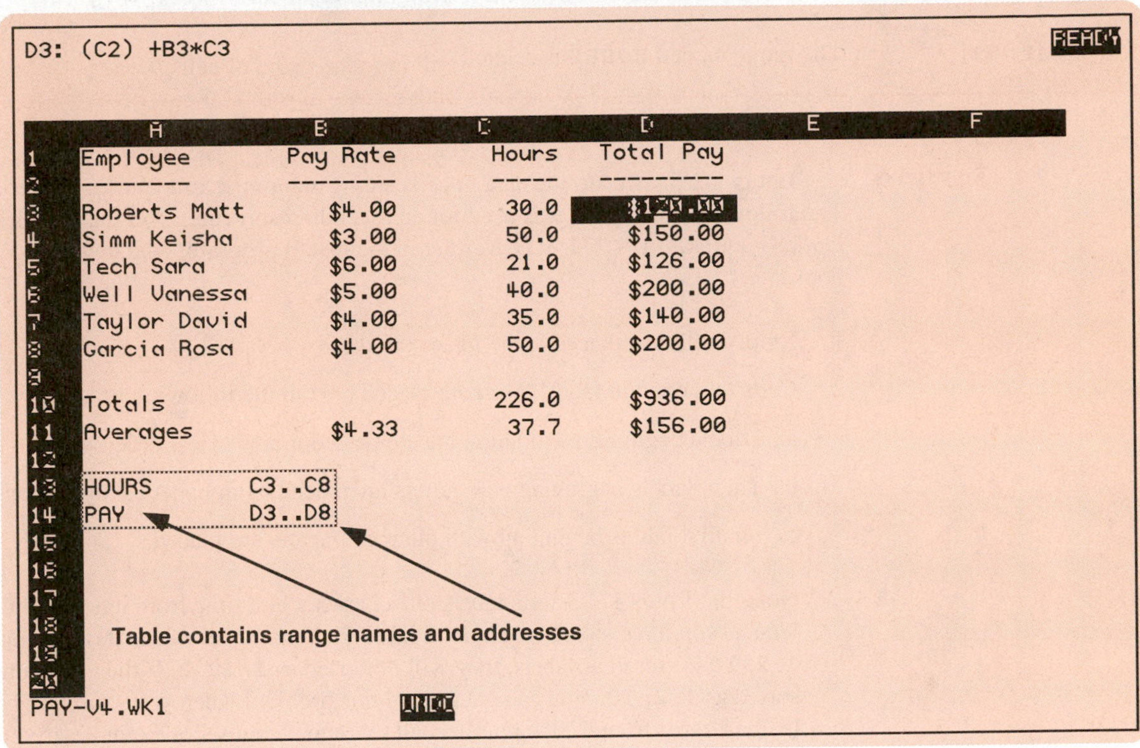

D3: (C2) +B3*C3
READY
A B C D E F
1 Employee Pay Rate Hours Total Pay
2 --------- --------- ----- ---------
3 Roberts Matt $4.00 30.0 $120.00
4 Simm Keisha $3.00 50.0 $150.00
5 Tech Sara $6.00 21.0 $126.00
6 Well Vanessa $5.00 40.0 $200.00
7 Taylor David $4.00 35.0 $140.00
8 Garcia Rosa $4.00 50.0 $200.00
10 Totals 226.0 $936.00
11 Averages $4.33 37.7 $156.00
13 HOURS C3..C8
14 PAY D3..D8
Table contains range names and addresses
PAY-V4.WK1
UNDO

Save the worksheet as **PAY-V5** by typing the following command: **/ F**(ile) **S**(ave) **PAY-V5** ↵.

If, at some later time, you would like to delete a named range you may use the *Range Delete* command. For example, delete the range **HOURS** by doing the following:

Keystroke	Action Resulting from Keystroke
/	Displays the main menu.
R	Selects **Range** and displays its menu.
N	Selects **Name** and displays its menu.
D	Selects **Delete**, asks for the name of the range you wish to delete, and displays a listing of range names in the control panel.

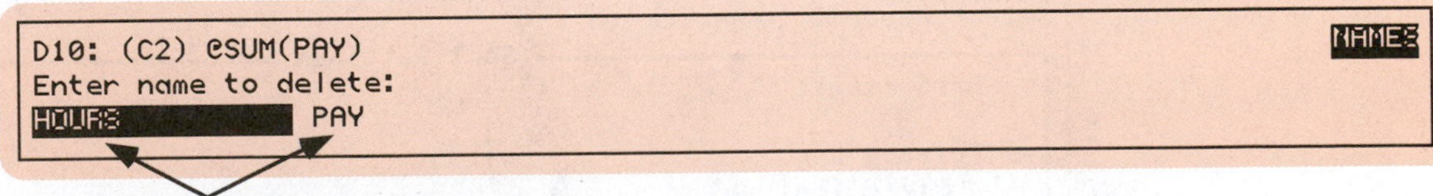

Two ranges have been named so far

You may either type the name of the range to be deleted or use the **[arrow]** keys to highlight the name in the list given.

Continued . . .

Keystroke	Action Resulting from Keystroke
[arrow]	Use the [arrow] keys, if necessary, to highlight **HOURS**.
[Enter]	The range named **HOURS** is deleted.

Sorting

Lotus 1-2-3 will sort the data in cells in any column or row in either ascending or descending order. The following sorting order is used for an ascending sort (the order may be changed using *Advanced Options* and *Modify Current Driver Set* in the Install program, which will not be discussed in this book):

1. Empty cells are placed at the top of the list.
2. Cells that contain labels (text) are placed next in the following order:
   a. Labels beginning with numbers are placed in numerical order.
   b. Then, labels beginning with letters are placed in alphabetical order, regardless of case.
   c. Finally, labels beginning with other characters are placed.

   Note that Lotus 1-2-3 sorts labels one character at a time from left to right. This can cause problems if you have stored numbers as labels rather than as values. For example, if the list of numbers **1**, **2**, **10** is stored as labels, they will be sorted as **1**, **10**, **2**. If they are stored as values, they will be sorted as **1**, **2**, **10**. You can get around this problem when you store numbers as labels by using leading zeros to make the numbers all the same length. For example, if you store **1** as **01** and **2** as **02**, the list of three numbers will be sorted correctly as **01**, **02**, **10**.
3. Cells that contain values are placed last, in numerical order.

For example, suppose you want the data in the payroll worksheet listed in alphabetical order by employee name.

Keystroke	Action Resulting from Keystroke
/	Displays the main menu.
D	Selects **Data** and displays its menu.
S	Selects **Sort** and displays its menu:

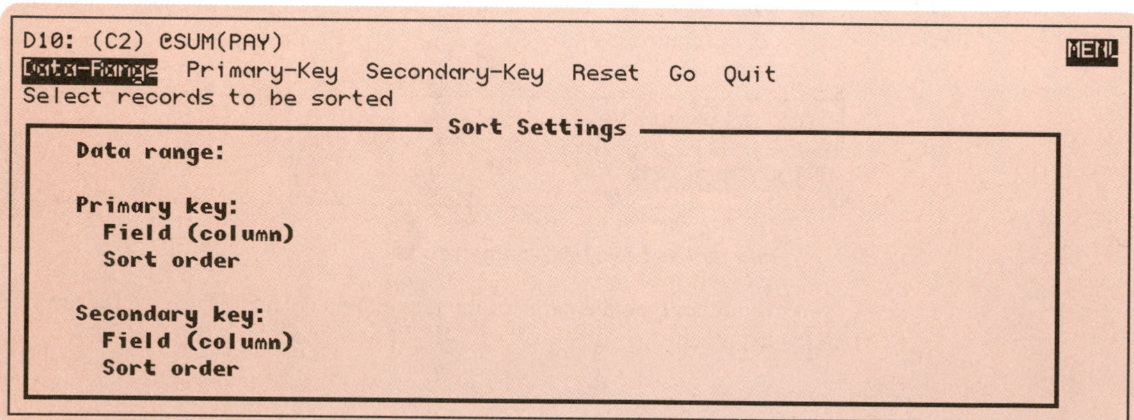

Continued . . .

Data-Range allows you to select the range of cells to be sorted.

Primary-Key allows you to select a range of cells to act as the primary sort key (the entire range of cells will be sorted based on the entries in the primary key).

Secondary-Key allows you to select a range of cells to act as a secondary sort key. This would be used to sort those items that have the same value in their primary key. For example, the primary key might be last name and the secondary key might be first name. The secondary key would be used to sort data for people with the same last name (e.g., Doug Smith, Bill Smith, and Mary Smith).

Reset allows you to clear the settings in the data range and sort keys so that you can do a different sort.

Go actually carries out the sort process and then returns to **READY** mode.

Quit returns to **READY** mode without sorting.

Keystroke	Action Resulting from Keystroke
D	Selects **Data-Range** and requests the range for the cells you want sorted.
A3.D8 ↵	Specifies the range of cells to be sorted. Note that the range includes all the data to be sorted and not just the names. You want the names (column **A**) and their respective pay rates (column **B**), hours (column **C**), and totals (column **D**) to be kept together during the sort. You do not want the labels (rows **1** and **2**) and the totals and averages (rows **10** and **11**) included in the sort. After pressing **[Enter]**, the sort menu is displayed again. Now, you must tell Lotus 1-2-3 how the sort is to be done.
P	Selects **Primary-Key** and asks for the **Primary sort key**. The primary key is the cell range upon which the sort is to be based. For this example, the sort is to be done by employee name (cells **A3** through **A8**).
A3.A8 ↵	Specifies that the sort is to be based on the values in cells **A3** through **A8** (i.e., employee names) and asks for the sort order (ascending, A through Z, or descending, Z through A).
A ↵	Specifies that the sort is to be done in **A**scending order and displays the sort menu again.

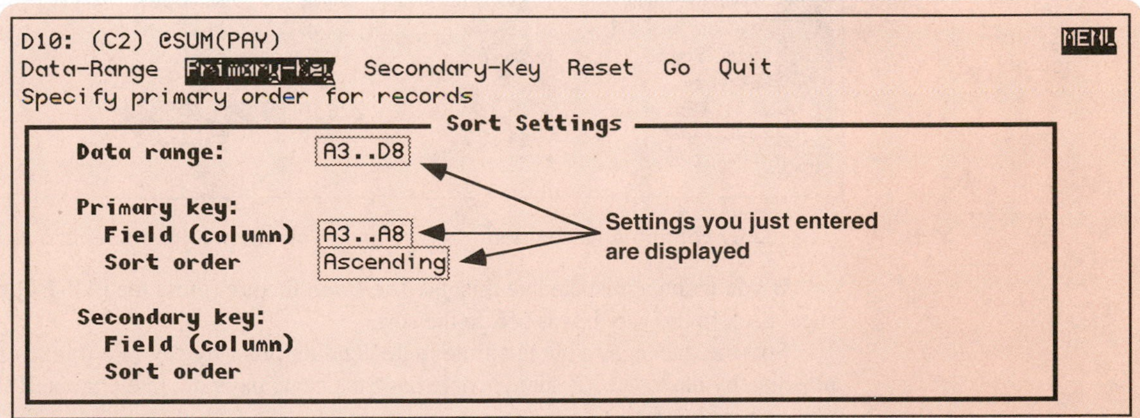

If you wanted to sort on a second criterion, you could specify it by selecting **Secondary-Key**. For this example, you will use only a single sort key. Therefore, tell Lotus 1-2-3 to go ahead and do the sort by pressing the letter **G** (for **G**o).

Continued . . .

G Tells Lotus 1-2-3 to **G**o ahead and sort the data in the selected range. The list now should be in alphabetical order:

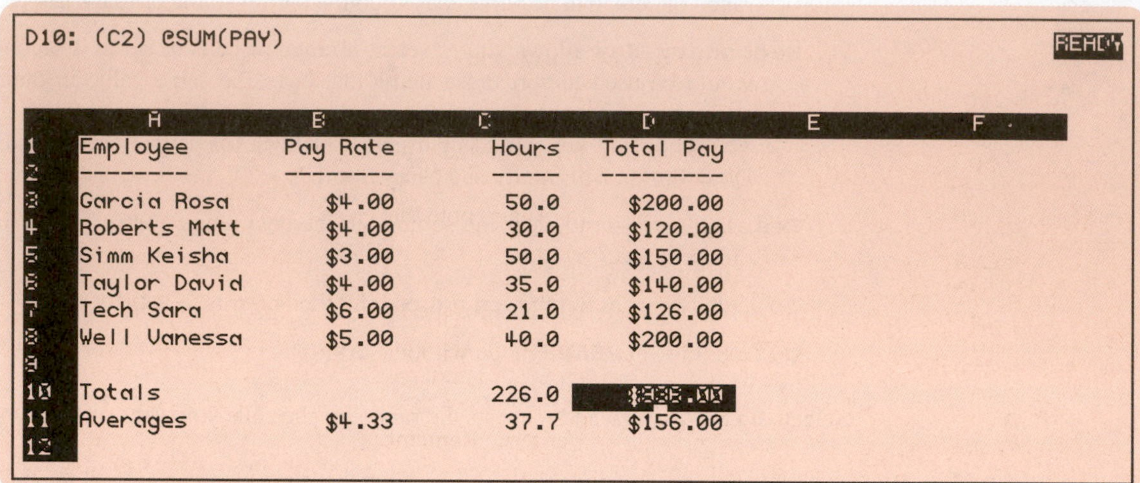

D10: (C2) @SUM(PAY) READY

	A	B	C	D	E	F
1	Employee	Pay Rate	Hours	Total Pay		
2	--------	--------	-----	---------		
3	Garcia Rosa	$4.00	50.0	$200.00		
4	Roberts Matt	$4.00	30.0	$120.00		
5	Simm Keisha	$3.00	50.0	$150.00		
6	Taylor David	$4.00	35.0	$140.00		
7	Tech Sara	$6.00	21.0	$126.00		
8	Well Vanessa	$5.00	40.0	$200.00		
9						
10	Totals		226.0	$936.00		
11	Averages	$4.33	37.7	$156.00		
12						

As was mentioned, the range to be sorted must be carefully defined. If you were to specify the sort range as only column **A** (the names) by entering **A1.A11** rather than **A3.D8** (don't do this!), the labels (names, column heading, and other labels) in column **A** would be rearranged but the data in the rest of the columns would remain in their original positions. The result would be chaos.

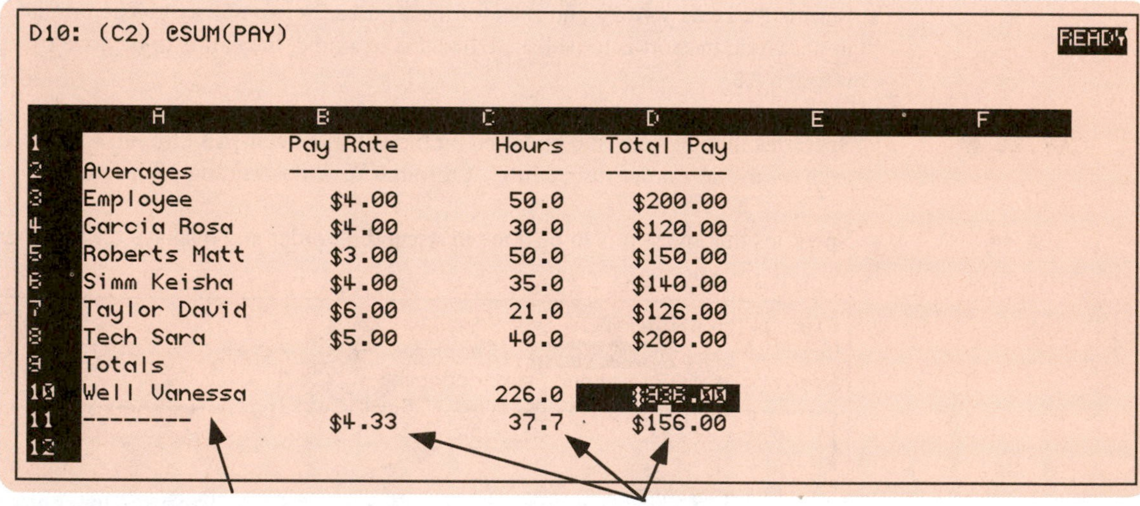

D10: (C2) @SUM(PAY) READY

	A	B	C	D	E	F
1		Pay Rate	Hours	Total Pay		
2	Averages	--------	-----	---------		
3	Employee	$4.00	50.0	$200.00		
4	Garcia Rosa	$4.00	30.0	$120.00		
5	Roberts Matt	$3.00	50.0	$150.00		
6	Simm Keisha	$4.00	35.0	$140.00		
7	Taylor David	$6.00	21.0	$126.00		
8	Tech Sara	$5.00	40.0	$200.00		
9	Totals					
10	Well Vanessa		226.0	$936.00		
11	--------	$4.33	37.7	$156.00		
12						

Only column A was sorted **The other columns remain as they were**

If you make a mistake like this, use the *Undo* feature (press the **[Alt-F4]** key) to change the worksheet back to the way it was before the sort.

Sort the data again, but this time in descending order by pay rate (highest pay rate first) and within pay rate, by name (i.e., if some people have the same pay rate, like Garcia, Roberts, and Taylor, they will be listed alphabetically).

Keystroke	Action Resulting from Keystroke
/	Displays the main menu.
D	Selects **Data** and displays its menu.
S	Selects **Sort** and displays its menu.
D	Selects **Data-Range** and requests the range for the cells you want sorted. If you have not changed the range since the last sort, the suggested range will still be **A3.D8**.
A3.D8 ↵	Specifies cells to be sorted. Again, note that the range includes all the data to be sorted and not just the pay rates and names.
P	Selects **Primary-Key** and asks for the **Primary sort key**. If you have not changed the setting since the last sort, the suggested range will still be **A3.A8**. For this example, the sort is to be done first by pay rate (cells **B3** through **B8**) and then by employee (cells **A3** through **A8**).
B3.B8 ↵	Specifies the primary sort criteria. Remember, you can use **POINT** to select the range by using the **[arrow]** keys to make **B3** active, pressing **[.]**, using the **[arrow]** keys to make **B8** active, and pressing **[Enter]**.
D ↵	Specifies that the sort is to be done in descending order.
S	Selects **Secondary-Key** and requests the **Secondary sort key**. The secondary key tells Lotus 1-2-3 what to sort on if there are two values of the primary key that are the same. For this example, you want the names listed alphabetically if the pay rates are identical. Therefore, the secondary sort key would be the data in column **A**.
A3.A8 ↵	Specifies the secondary sort criteria.
A ↵	Specifies that the sort is to be done in ascending order.

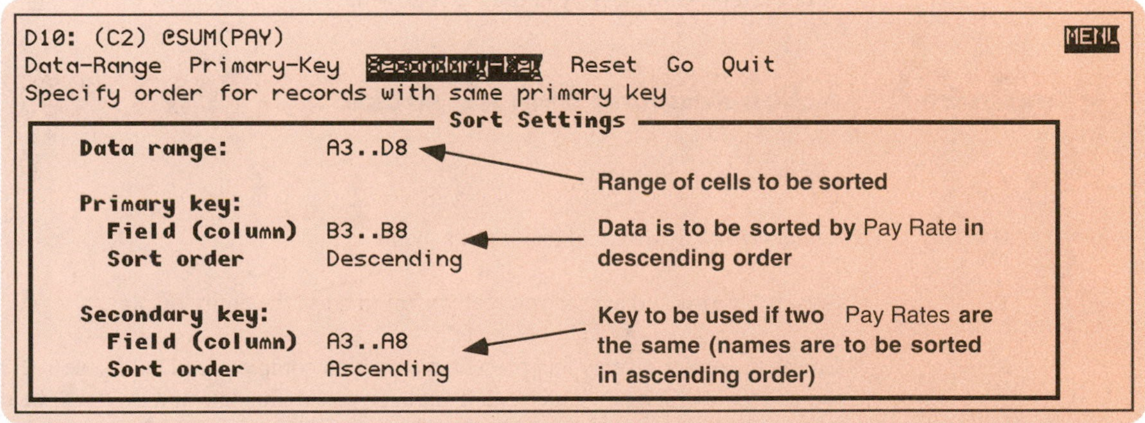

G	Tells Lotus 1-2-3 to **G**o ahead and sort the data in the selected range. The list now should be sorted as follows:

Continued . . .

Keystroke	Action Resulting from Keystroke

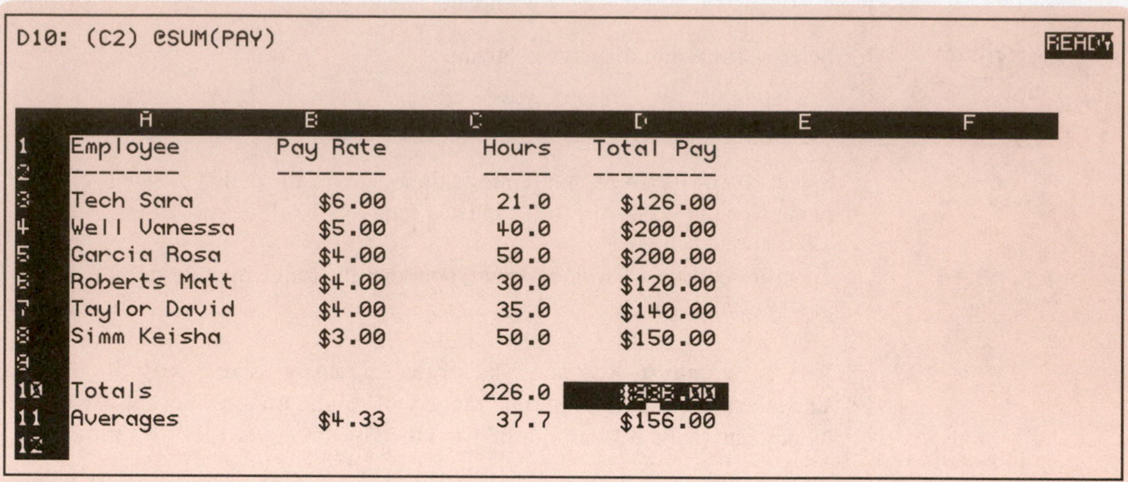
D10: (C2) @SUM(PAY) READY

	A	B	C	D	E	F
1	Employee	Pay Rate	Hours	Total Pay		
2	--------	---------	-----	---------		
3	Tech Sara	$6.00	21.0	$126.00		
4	Well Vanessa	$5.00	40.0	$200.00		
5	Garcia Rosa	$4.00	50.0	$200.00		
6	Roberts Matt	$4.00	30.0	$120.00		
7	Taylor David	$4.00	35.0	$140.00		
8	Simm Keisha	$3.00	50.0	$150.00		
9						
10	Totals		226.0	[illegible]		
11	Averages	$4.33	37.7	$156.00		
12						

Note that if you change a rate of pay and then want to sort the data again, you do not have to reset the sort parameters. All you would have to do is type the following command: **/** **D**(ata) **S**(ort) **G**(o) and the sort would be performed using the previous settings.

Save the sorted worksheet as **PAY-V6** by typing the following command: **/** **F**(ile) **S**(ave) **PAY-V6** ↵.

Erasing the Screen

If you are working on one worksheet and would like to switch to another, simply save the current worksheet by typing **/** **F**(ile) **S**(ave) and then retrieve the new worksheet by typing **/** **F**(ile) **R**(etrieve). Lotus 1-2-3 does not retrieve one worksheet into another (unless you specifically ask it to do that).

If you want to begin with a completely blank Lotus 1-2-3 screen, you may either quit the program by typing **/** **Q**(uit) **Y**(es) and then access it again by typing **123** ↵ or simply erase all the cells of your current worksheet by doing the following:

Keystroke	Action Resulting from Keystroke
/	Displays the main menu.
W	Selects **Worksheet** and displays its menu.
E	Selects **Erase** and asks if you really want to erase the entire display.
Y	Erases the entire display and presents you with a completely blank Lotus 1-2-3 worksheet. Because the worksheet is brand new and has not yet been saved, the date and time will be displayed on the status line. As soon as you save the file, the file name will replace the date and time on the status line.

TO TAKE A BREAK Type **/** **Q**(uit) **Y**(es), remove diskette(s). To resume (hard disk): Insert *Data* diskette, type **C:** ↵, **CD\123** ↵, **123** ↵. To resume (two drive): Insert diskettes, type **B:** ↵, **123** ↵.

A Gradebook Worksheet

To illustrate some additional features of Lotus 1-2-3, let's develop a worksheet that will keep track of the grades in a computer class called *GC 1571 Introduction to Microcomputer Applications*. The gradebook should list the students and all their scores on homework, quizzes, and tests, and determine the final total points for each student. The total points are to be calculated using 20 percent for quizzes, 15 percent for homework, 30 percent for the midterm exam, and 35 percent for the final exam. Later, in the next chapter, you will modify the worksheet so that it also determines the letter grade for each student and graphs the results.

This worksheet will be too big to be displayed completely on the screen at one time. Therefore, you will have to scroll left and right using **[Tab]** and **[Shift-Tab]**. The complete final worksheet is shown below for illustration only; not all of it will fit on the screen at one time.

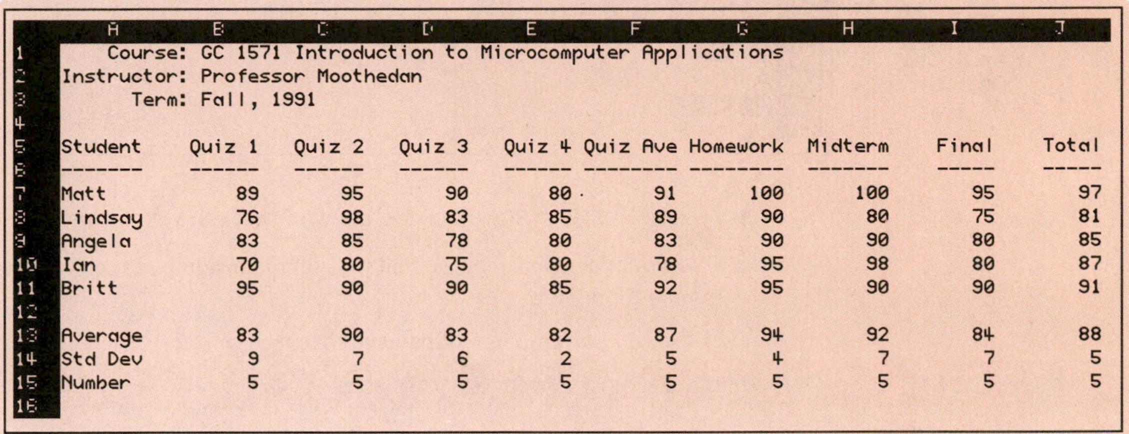

	A	B	C	D	E	F	G	H	I	J
1	Course: GC 1571 Introduction to Microcomputer Applications									
2	Instructor: Professor Moothedan									
3	Term: Fall, 1991									
4										
5	Student	Quiz 1	Quiz 2	Quiz 3	Quiz 4	Quiz Ave	Homework	Midterm	Final	Total
6	-------	------	------	------	------	--------	--------	-------	-----	-----
7	Matt	89	95	90	80	91	100	100	95	97
8	Lindsay	76	98	83	85	89	90	80	75	81
9	Angela	83	85	78	80	83	90	90	80	85
10	Ian	70	80	75	80	78	95	98	80	87
11	Britt	95	90	90	85	92	95	90	90	91
12										
13	Average	83	90	83	82	87	94	92	84	88
14	Std Dev	9	7	6	2	5	4	7	7	5
15	Number	5	5	5	5	5	5	5	5	5
16										

Step 1 Begin from a completely blank worksheet screen and type the text information in rows **1** through **6** and the raw data in columns **A** through **J** (for columns **F** and **J**, just type the heading in cells **F5** and **F6** and **J5** and **J6**; you will enter the proper formulas later).

To make the text look nicer, the colons in rows **1**, **2**, and **3** were lined up. To do this, four spaces must be inserted to the left of the word **Course** and six spaces to the left of **Term**. The spaces may be inserted to the left of the text by preceding the spaces with an apostrophe, **'**. Recall from page L19 that the apostrophe is used to indicate a label that is to be left justified. Thus, the entry in cell **A1** looks like the following:

```
Course: GC 1571 Introduction to Microcomputer Applications
```

Notice that cell **A1** is only nine characters wide but the text in that cell is much longer. Recall that Lotus 1-2-3 will display and print all the text in a cell as long as there is nothing in the cells immediately to the right (cells **B1** through **G1**). A similar situation occurs in cells **A2** and **A3**.

Also, recall that in order to enter the dashes in line **6**, you must begin each cell with an apostrophe, otherwise Lotus 1-2-3 will think that the dashes are multiple negative signs rather than labels. For example, the entry for cell **A6** would be **'-------**.

After entering the data, the worksheet should look like the following (again, it will not all fit on the screen at one time):

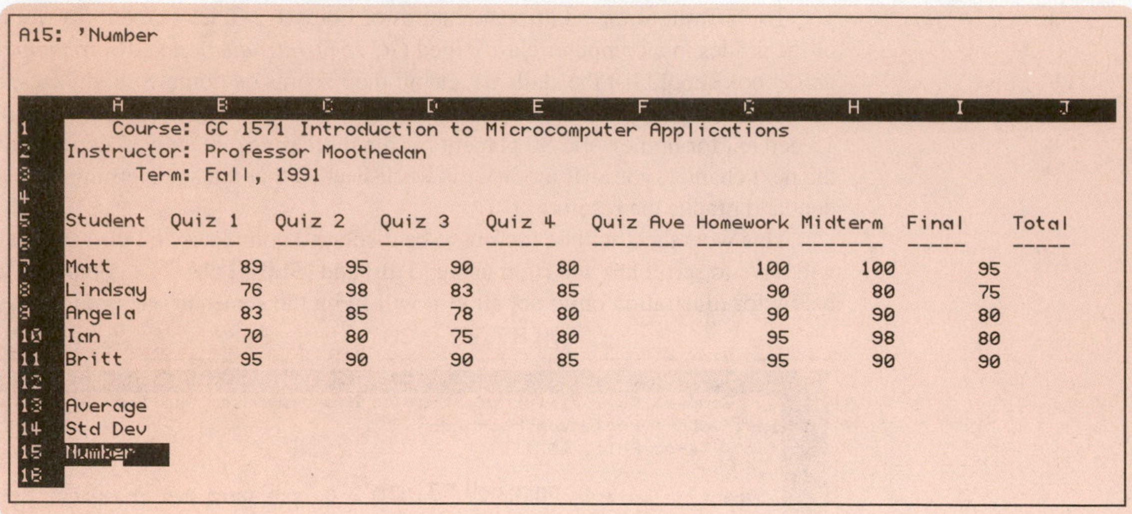

A15: 'Number

	A	B	C	D	E	F	G	H	I	J
1	Course: GC 1571 Introduction to Microcomputer Applications									
2	Instructor: Professor Moothedan									
3	Term: Fall, 1991									
4										
5	Student	Quiz 1	Quiz 2	Quiz 3	Quiz 4	Quiz Ave	Homework	Midterm	Final	Total
6	-------	------	------	------	------	--------	--------	-------	-----	-----
7	Matt	89	95	90	80		100	100	95	
8	Lindsay	76	98	83	85		90	80	75	
9	Angela	83	85	78	80		90	90	80	
10	Ian	70	80	75	80		95	98	80	
11	Britt	95	90	90	85		95	90	90	
12										
13	Average									
14	Std Dev									
15	Number									
16										

Step 2 Use **/** **F**(ile) **S**(ave) to save the worksheet on your *Lotus Data* diskette as **GRADE-V1**.

Step 3 Format the worksheet so that the column headings in cells **B5** through **J6** are right justified by doing the following:

Keystroke	Action Resulting from Keystroke
/	Displays the main menu.
R	Selects **Range** (a range of cells is to be operated on).
L	Selects **Label** (the cells contain labels).
R	Selects **Right** (the cells are to be right justified).
B5.J6 ↵	Specifies the cell range, right justifies the cells, and returns to **READY** mode.

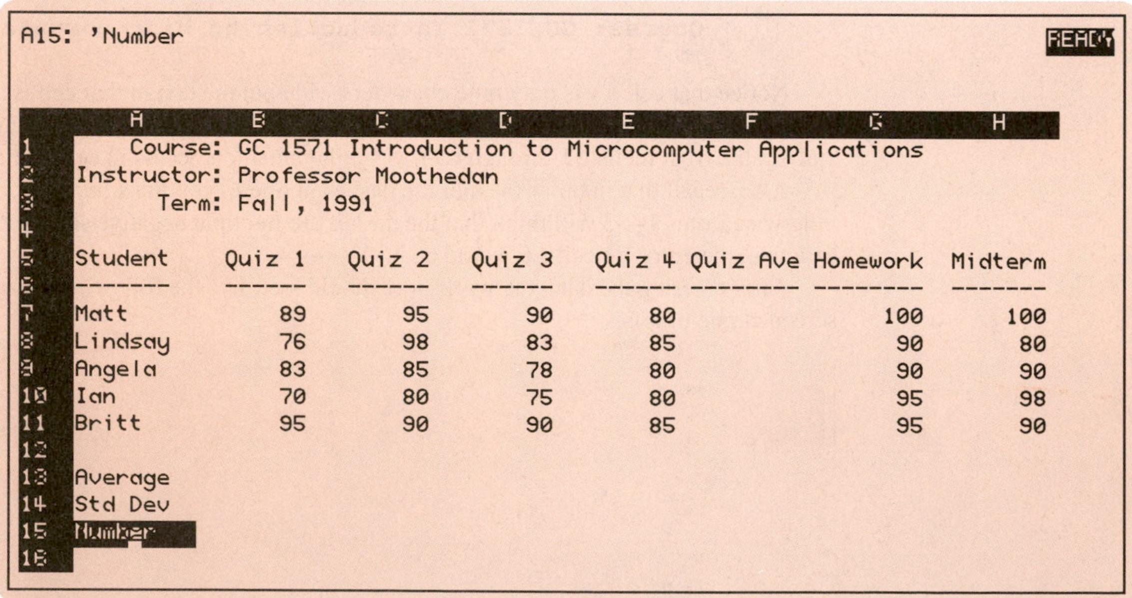

A15: 'Number READY

	A	B	C	D	E	F	G	H
1	Course: GC 1571 Introduction to Microcomputer Applications							
2	Instructor: Professor Moothedan							
3	Term: Fall, 1991							
4								
5	Student	Quiz 1	Quiz 2	Quiz 3	Quiz 4	Quiz Ave	Homework	Midterm
6	-------	------	------	------	------	--------	--------	-------
7	Matt	89	95	90	80		100	100
8	Lindsay	76	98	83	85		90	80
9	Angela	83	85	78	80		90	90
10	Ian	70	80	75	80		95	98
11	Britt	95	90	90	85		95	90
12								
13	Average							
14	Std Dev							
15	Number							
16								

Step 4 Enter the formula for Matt's quiz average in cell **F7**. The instructor for the course has decided to drop the lowest quiz score before calculating the average and, therefore, you cannot simply

use the **@AVG** function. The formula needed for each student is the following:

$$\frac{\text{(Sum of all quizzes for this student) – (Lowest quiz for this student)}}{\text{(Number of quizzes for this student) – 1}}$$

You may use the **@SUM** function (to find the **SUM** of all quizzes), the **@MIN** function (to find the **MIN**imum or lowest quiz score), and the **@COUNT** function (to **COUNT** the number of quizzes the student has taken). The formula that should be typed into cell **F7** (for Matt) would look like the following (note the use of parentheses for the numerator and denominator of the fraction):

Numerator **Denominator**

```
(@SUM(B7.E7)-@MIN(B7.E7))/(@COUNT(B7.E7)-1)
```

Keystroke	Action Resulting from Keystroke
[arrow]	Use the **[arrow]** keys to make cell **F7** active.
(@SUM(B7.E7)-@MIN(B7.E7))/(@COUNT(B7.E7)-1) ↵	Specifies the formula for the quiz average for Matt (do not use spaces in the formula) and displays the value (**91.33333**) in the active cell. If you make a typing mistake, Lotus 1-2-3 may beep at you and place you into **EDIT** mode. In that case, look carefully at what you typed to see if you can spot the error. If you cannot, try retyping the entire formula again.
	Copy this formula for the other students by doing the following:
/	Displays the main menu.
C	Selects **Copy** and requests the range to copy from.
F7 ↵	Specifies the cell to be copied and requests the range to be copied to.
F8.F11 ↵	Specifies the destination cells, copies the formula from cell **F7** into cells **F8** through **F11**, and returns to **READY** mode.

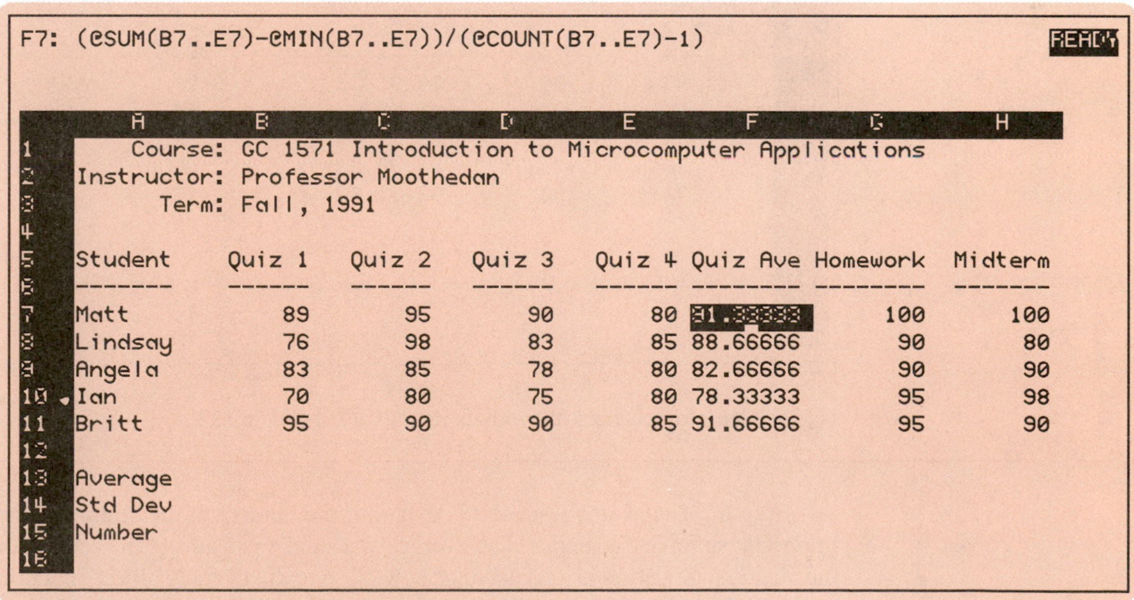

F7: (@SUM(B7..E7)-@MIN(B7..E7))/(@COUNT(B7..E7)-1) READY

	A	B	C	D	E	F	G	H
1	Course: GC 1571 Introduction to Microcomputer Applications							
2	Instructor: Professor Moothedan							
3	Term: Fall, 1991							
4								
5	Student	Quiz 1	Quiz 2	Quiz 3	Quiz 4	Quiz Ave	Homework	Midterm
6	--------	------	------	------	------	--------	--------	-------
7	Matt	89	95	90	80	91.33333	100	100
8	Lindsay	76	98	83	85	88.66666	90	80
9	Angela	83	85	78	80	82.66666	90	90
10	Ian	70	80	75	80	78.33333	95	98
11	Britt	95	90	90	85	91.66666	95	90
12								
13	Average							
14	Std Dev							
15	Number							
16								

Use a calculator to check the values in cells **F7** through **F11**.

Step 5 Enter the formula for the total in cell **J7**. The total points are to be calculated using 20 percent for quizzes, 15 percent for homework, 30 percent for the midterm exam, and 35 percent for the final exam. The corresponding formula is:

.20*Quiz average + .15*Homework + .30* Midterm + .35*Final exam

Keystroke	Action Resulting from Keystroke
[arrow]	Use the [arrow] keys to make cell **J7** active.
.2*F7+.15*G7+.30*H7+.35*I7 ↵	Specifies the formula for the total for Matt (do not use spaces in the formula) and displays the value (**96.51666**) in the active cell.
	Copy this formula for the other students by doing the following:
/	Displays the main menu.
C	Selects **Copy** and requests the range to copy from.
J7 ↵	Specifies the cell to be copied and requests the range to be copied to.
J8.J11 ↵	Specifies the destination cells, copies the formula from cell **J7** into cells **J8** through **J11**, and returns to **READY** mode.

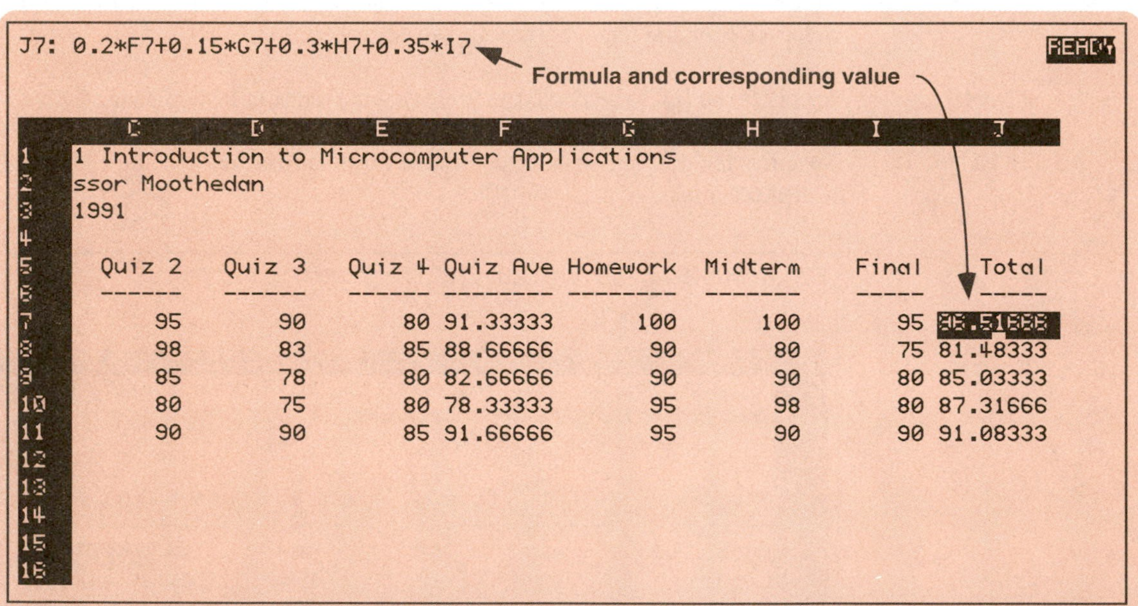

	C	D	E	F	G	H	I	J
1	1 Introduction to Microcomputer Applications							
2	ssor Moothedan							
3	1991							
4								
5	Quiz 2	Quiz 3	Quiz 4	Quiz Ave	Homework	Midterm	Final	Total
6	------	------	------	--------	--------	-------	-----	-----
7	95	90	80	91.33333	100	100	95	96.51666
8	98	83	85	88.66666	90	80	75	81.48333
9	85	78	80	82.66666	90	90	80	85.03333
10	80	75	80	78.33333	95	98	80	87.31666
11	90	90	85	91.66666	95	90	90	91.08333
12								
13								
14								
15								
16								

Use a calculator to check the values in cells **J7** through **J11**.

Step 6 The average, standard deviation, and number at the bottom of the worksheet provide important summary statistics. The average is a single measure of the scores considered as a group while the standard deviation is a measure of how close to the average all the individual scores are. A large standard deviation means that the scores are widely dispersed about the average while a small standard deviation indicates that the scores are bunched closely about the average.

Enter the formulas for the average, standard deviation, and number in rows **13**, **14**, and **15**, respectively. You can use the standard Lotus 1-2-3 functions to do this for column **B**, and then copy the formulas to all other columns:

1. Type the following formula in cell **B13**: **@AVG(B7.B11)**
2. Type the following formula in cell **B14**: **@STD(B7.B11)**
3. Type the following formula in cell **B15**: **@COUNT(B7.B11)**

Copy the above formulas to the other cells in rows **13**, **14**, and **15** by doing the following:

Keystroke	Action Resulting from Keystroke
/	Displays the main menu.
C	Selects **Copy** and requests the range to copy from.
B13.B15 ↵	Specifies the range to be copied from and requests the range to be copied to.
C13.J15 ↵	Specifies the destination cells, copies the formulas from cells **B13**, **B14**, and **B15** into cells **C13** through **J15**, respectively, and returns to **READY** mode.

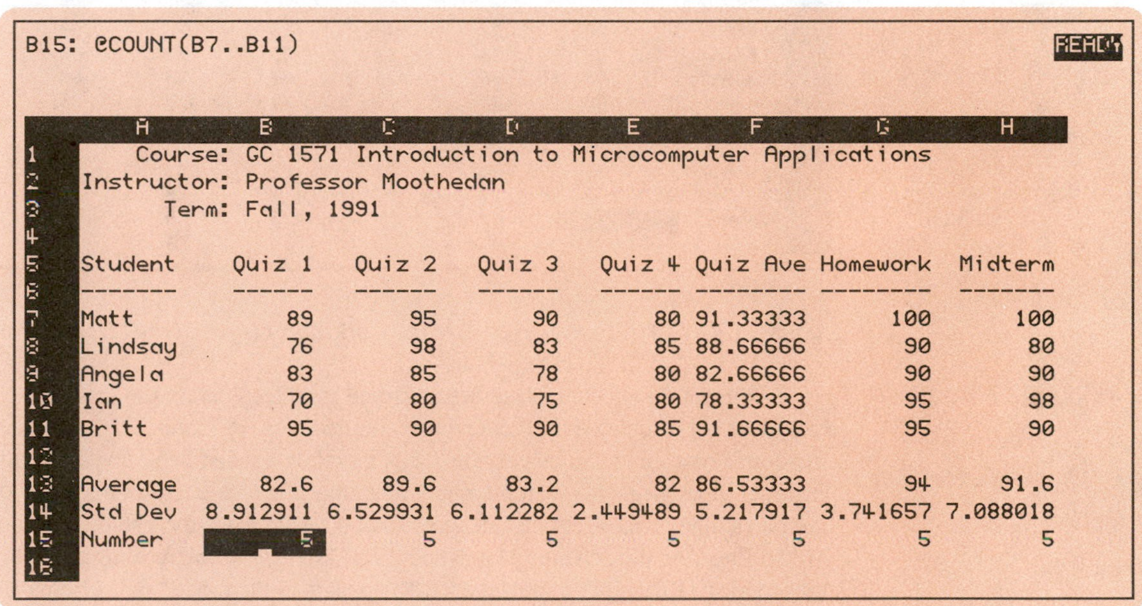

B15: @COUNT(B7..B11) READY

	A	B	C	D	E	F	G	H
1	Course: GC 1571 Introduction to Microcomputer Applications							
2	Instructor: Professor Moothedan							
3	Term: Fall, 1991							
4								
5	Student	Quiz 1	Quiz 2	Quiz 3	Quiz 4	Quiz Ave	Homework	Midterm
6	--------	------	------	------	------	--------	--------	-------
7	Matt	89	95	90	80	91.33333	100	100
8	Lindsay	76	98	83	85	88.66666	90	80
9	Angela	83	85	78	80	82.66666	90	90
10	Ian	70	80	75	80	78.33333	95	98
11	Britt	95	90	90	85	91.66666	95	90
12								
13	Average	82.6	89.6	83.2	82	86.53333	94	91.6
14	Std Dev	8.912911	6.529931	6.112282	2.449489	5.217917	3.741657	7.088018
15	Number	5	5	5	5	5	5	5
16								

Step 7 The last thing to do for this worksheet is to format all the values so that they are rounded off to whole numbers.

Keystroke	Action Resulting from Keystroke
/	Displays the main menu.
W	Selects **Worksheet** (you are going to do an operation on the entire worksheet).

Continued . . .

Keystroke	Action Resulting from Keystroke
G	Selects **Global** (you are going to do the operation to all the entries in the worksheet).
F	Selects **Format** (you are going to change the format of the cells).
F	Selects **Fixed** (you want to format the values so that they display a fixed number of decimal places).
0 ↵	Specifies the number of decimal places to be displayed, rounds all the values to that number of decimal places, and returns to **READY** mode.

The final worksheet should look like the following (again, the entire worksheet will not appear on the screen all at the same time):

```
B15: @COUNT(B7..B11)

        A          B         C         D         E         F         G         H         I         J
1        Course: GC 1571 Introduction to Microcomputer Applications
2   Instructor: Professor Moothedan
3          Term: Fall, 1991
4
5   Student     Quiz 1    Quiz 2    Quiz 3    Quiz 4  Quiz Ave Homework  Midterm    Final     Total
6   --------    ------    ------    ------    ------  -------- --------  -------    -----     -----
7   Matt            89        95        90        80        91      100      100       95        97
8   Lindsay         76        98        83        85        89       90       80       75        81
9   Angela          83        85        78        80        83       90       90       80        85
10  Ian             70        80        75        80        78       95       98       80        87
11  Britt           95        90        90        85        92       95       90       90        91
12
13  Average         83        90        83        82        87       94       92       84        88
14  Std Dev          9         7         6         2         5        4        7        7         5
15  Number           5         5         5         5         5        5        5        5         5
16
```

Step 8 Use **/** **F**(ile) **S**(ave) to save the worksheet on your *Lotus Data* diskette as **GRADE-V2**.

Manual versus Automatic Recalculation

As the data in the worksheet are modified to reflect changes in scores, the effects on the entire worksheet are calculated (or recalculated) immediately by Lotus 1-2-3. This is called **automatic recalculation**. For a small worksheet, this takes less than a second and does not cause a problem. However, for larger worksheets that contain many formulas, the recalculation may take quite a bit of time because when a change is made to one cell, Lotus 1-2-3 recalculates the values for all cells affected.

To illustrate this, change Matt's score on Quiz 1 to 90 by moving the cell pointer to **B7**, typing **90**, and pressing **[Enter]**. The message **WAIT** appears in the mode box as Lotus 1-2-3 recalculates all the formulas. (Depending on your machine, **WAIT** may be displayed for up to three seconds; if you have a fast machine, it may flash by so fast that you do not even see it).

To save time when entering or changing data, you can instruct Lotus 1-2-3 to not recalculate the formulas every time a new value is typed into any one cell. This means that as the data are changed, the computed values (**Quiz Ave**, **Total**, **Average**, **Std Dev**, and **Number** in this example) will remain the same until you specifically instruct the computer to recalculate those values. To have the computer do the recalculation, you must press **[F9]**.

To illustrate this, turn off automatic recalculation by doing the following:

Keystroke	Action Resulting from Keystroke
/	Displays the main menu.
G	Selects **Global**.
W	Selects **Worksheet**.
R	Selects **Recalculation**.
M	Selects **Manual**. This means that Lotus 1-2-3 will not recalculate formulas as you change values in the different cells. The next time you change a cell value, the word **CALC** will appear on the status line at the bottom of the display, but no recalculation will be done.
[arrow]	Use the **[arrow]** keys to make cell **B7** active.
20 ↵	Changes the score for Quiz 1 for Matt. Note that as soon as **[Enter]** is pressed, the word **CALC** appears at the bottom of the screen, but the quiz average for Matt (cell **F7**) and the values for the summary data in rows **13**, **14**, and **15** are not changed.
[F9]	Says to recalculate the formulas. After this key has been pressed, **CALC** disappears from the status line and the correct values of the formulas are displayed.

Turn automatic recalculation back on by doing the following:

Keystroke	Action Resulting from Keystroke
/	Displays the main menu.
W	Selects **Worksheet**.
G	Selects **Global**.
R	Selects **Recalculation**.
A	Selects **Automatic**. This means that Lotus 1-2-3 now will automatically recalculate any formulas as values are changed in the cells that affect those formulas.
89 ↵	Changes the score in cell **B7** back to **89** and automatically recalculates all the formulas.

Printing Options

Lotus 1-2-3 offers many options that can be used to enhance the printed version of a worksheet. For example, headers and footers can be added, the margins can be changed, borders can be set to print on every page of output, the page length can be adjusted to match the size of the paper used by the printer, formulas can be printed instead of values, and others.

To illustrate some of the options, use the print command to do the following to the **GRADE-V2** worksheet:

- Print the data from columns **A** and **B** only.
- Include a header that contains your name left justified, the course number centered, and the date right justified.
- Include a footer that contains the page number centered.
- Print the contents of the cells, one per line, rather than the values displayed (e.g., for cell **B13**, print the formula **@AVG(B7.B11)** instead of the value **83**).

Keystroke	Action Resulting from Keystroke
/	Displays the main menu.
P	Selects **Print** and displays its menu.
P	Selects **Printer** and displays its menu.
R	Selects **Range** and requests the range to be printed. For this example, the data of interest are in columns **A** and **B**.
A1.B15 ↵	Specifies the range to be printed and returns to the **Printer** menu.
O	Selects **Options** and displays its menu.

```
Header  Footer  Margins  Borders  Setup  Pg-Length  Other  Quit
Create a header
```

H	Selects **Header** and requests the header to be placed at the top of each page of output. You may use the following special characters within headers and footers:

- **#** prints the page number.
- **@** prints the date.
- **|** justifies the text to the right of the symbol. If no **|** is present, text is left justified. The first occurrence of **|** centers text following it and the second occurrence of **|** right justifies text following it.

Douglas Robertson |GC 1571 |@ ↵

Specifies the header and returns to the **Options** menu. **Douglas Robertson** will be left justified, **GC 1571** will be centered, and the date (represented by the **@** symbol) will be right justified.

F	Selects **Footer** and requests the footer to be placed at the bottom of each page of output.
|page # ↵	Specifies the footer and returns to the **Options** menu.
O	Selects **Other** and displays its menu

```
As-Displayed  Cell-Formulas  Formatted  Unformatted
Print range as displayed
```

Data may be printed either **As-Displayed** or using **Cell-Formulas**:

As-Displayed prints the worksheet as it appears on the screen. This is the default setting.

Cell-Formulas prints the contents of nonblank cells, one per line, as they are actually stored (e.g., for cell **B13**, the formula **@AVG(B7..B11)** will be printed instead of the value **83**).

In addition, printing may be either **Formatted** or **Unformatted** :

Continued . . .

Formatted prints headers, footers, and page breaks. This option is used to restore standard printing after **Unformatted** has been selected.

Unformatted does not print headers, footers, page breaks, and top and bottom margins. This is useful if you are writing the data to a file and want only the body of the worksheet copied.

C Selects **Cell-Formulas** and returns to the **Options** menu.

O Selects **Other** and displays its menu

F Selects **Formatted** and returns to the **Options** menu. The **Print Settings** now should look as follows:

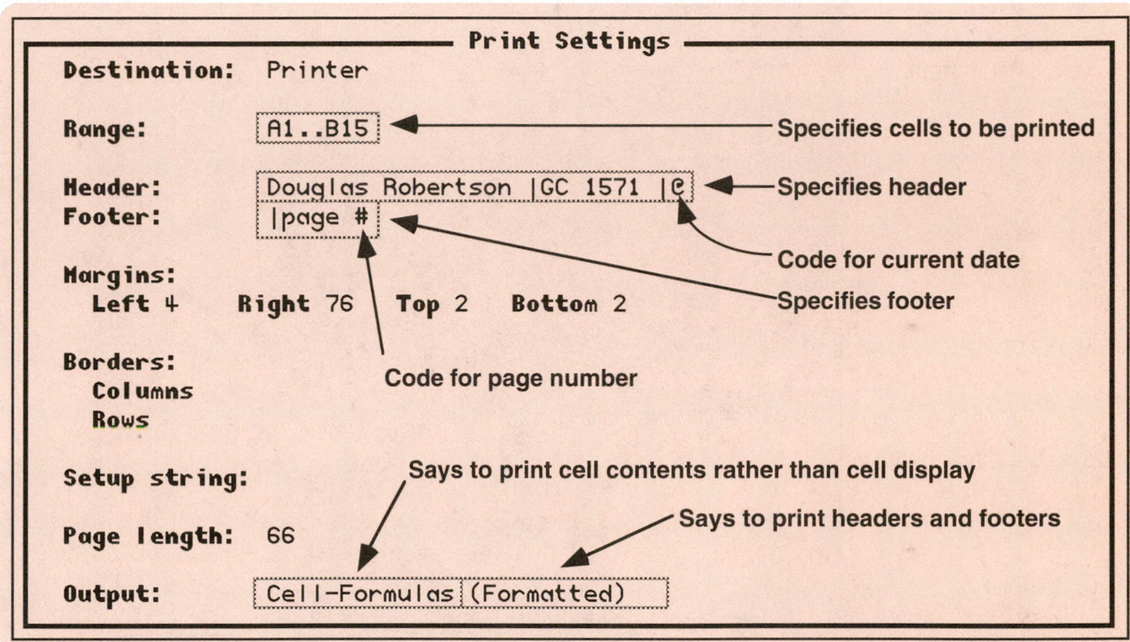

[Esc] Returns to the **Print** menu.

Before doing the next step, be sure your printer is connected to the computer, turned on, loaded with paper, and the paper is properly aligned in the printer.

A Selects **Align**. This tells Lotus 1-2-3 that the paper is properly positioned in the printer.

G Selects **Go** and begins the printing process. The word **WAIT** appears in the mode box as the file is being printed.

P Selects **Page** and ejects the sheet of paper currently in the printer. Note that the footer is not printed until **Page** has been selected.

A Selects **Align** to inform Lotus 1-2-3 that the paper is properly aligned in the printer (this gets you ready to print again).

Continued . . .

Keystroke	Action Resulting from Keystroke
Q	Selects **Quit** and returns to **READY** mode.
	The printed output should look like the following:

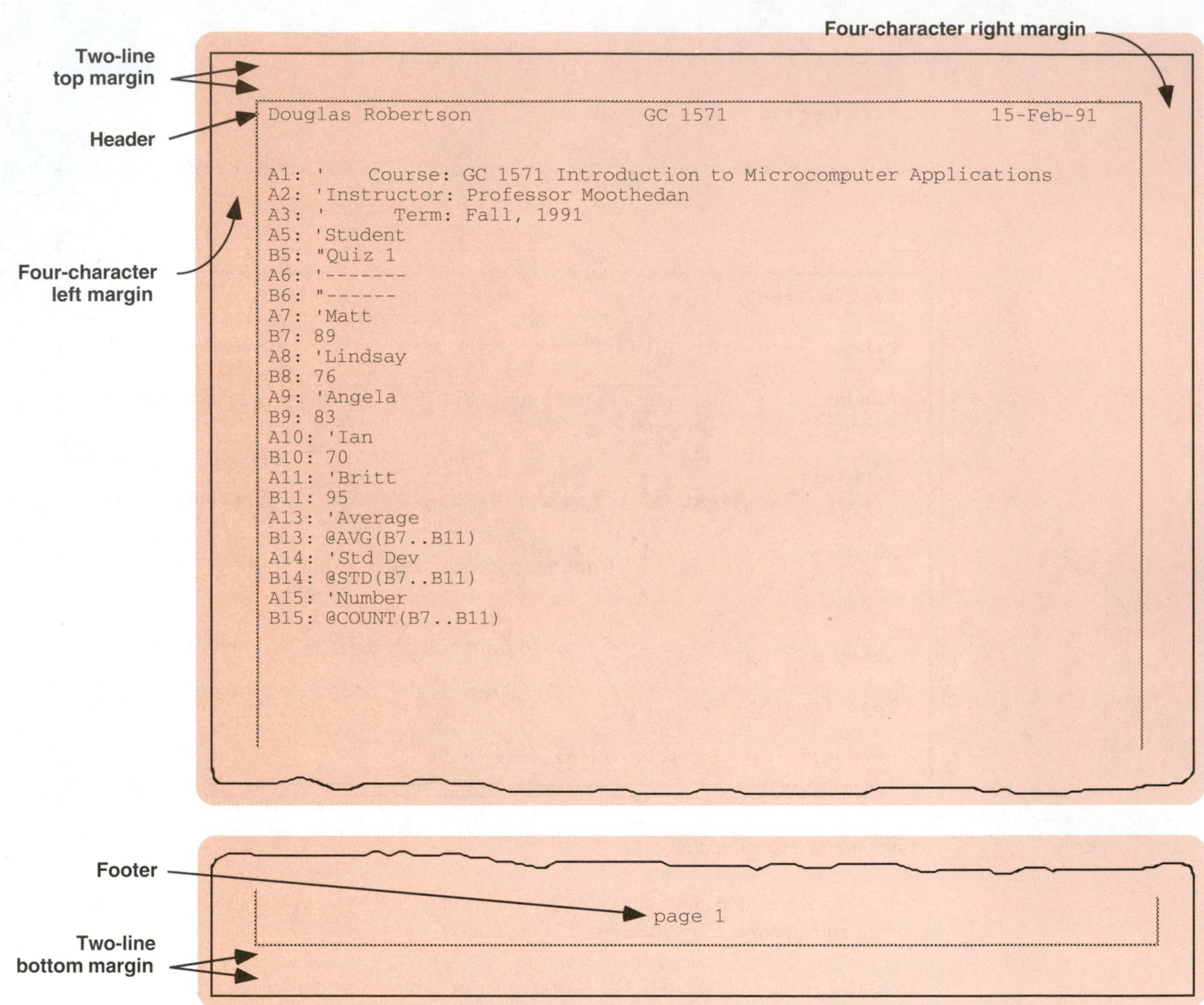


```
Douglas Robertson              GC 1571                        15-Feb-91

A1: '    Course: GC 1571 Introduction to Microcomputer Applications
A2: 'Instructor: Professor Moothedan
A3: '      Term: Fall, 1991
A5: 'Student
B5: "Quiz 1
A6: '-------
B6: "------
A7: 'Matt
B7: 89
A8: 'Lindsay
B8: 76
A9: 'Angela
B9: 83
A10: 'Ian
B10: 70
A11: 'Britt
B11: 95
A13: 'Average
B13: @AVG(B7..B11)
A14: 'Std Dev
B14: @STD(B7..B11)
A15: 'Number
B15: @COUNT(B7..B11)

                                page 1
```

Use **/** **F**(ile) **S**(ave) to save the worksheet on your *Lotus Data* diskette as **GRADE-V3** and use **/** **Q**(uit) **Y**(es) to exit the program and return to DOS.

The Allways Spreadsheet Publisher

Allways is a program that is packaged along with Lotus 1-2-3 Release 2.2. Once installed, it can run in concert with the spreadsheet program to provide you with the ability to produce presentation-quality output directly from Lotus 1-2-3. In order to use Allways, you must have a hard-disk system with at least 1,100K of free space and at least 512K of RAM memory available.

The Allways system allows you to

- Create output that contains up to eight different fonts.
- Underline and boldface text and values.
- Change the height of rows and the width of columns.
- Add shading to selected parts of the worksheet.
- Incorporate vertical and horizontal lines into the output.
- Enclose ranges or individual cells in boxes.
- Include graphs in worksheet output.
- Use a color printer to create impressive output.

So that you can see the difference between printing using the regular Lotus 1-2-3 print feature and the Allways Spreadsheet Publisher, two samples of printed output from the worksheet **PAY-V6** are shown in Figures 6-1 and 6-2.

Figure 6-1

Printed output using the regular print command.

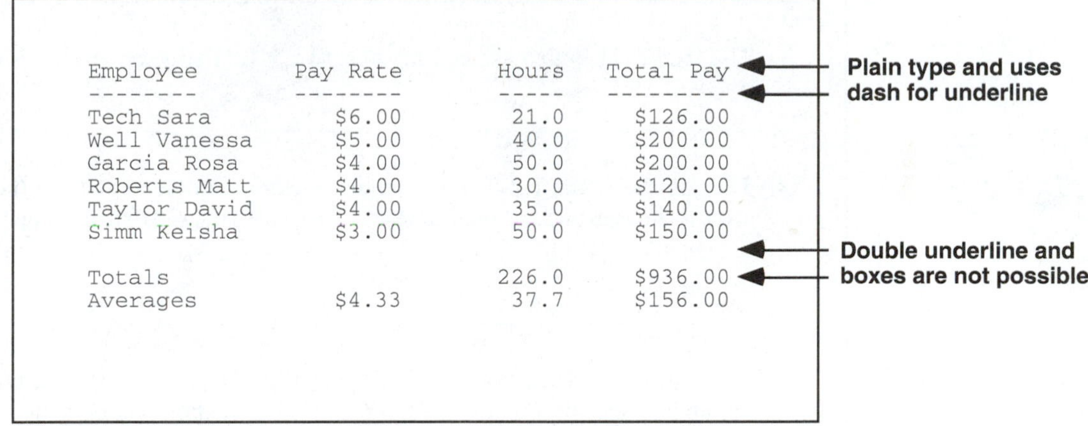

Employee	Pay Rate	Hours	Total Pay
--------	--------	-----	---------
Tech Sara	$6.00	21.0	$126.00
Well Vanessa	$5.00	40.0	$200.00
Garcia Rosa	$4.00	50.0	$200.00
Roberts Matt	$4.00	30.0	$120.00
Taylor David	$4.00	35.0	$140.00
Simm Keisha	$3.00	50.0	$150.00
Totals		226.0	$936.00
Averages	$4.33	37.7	$156.00

Figure 6-2

Printed output using the Allways Spreadsheet Publisher.

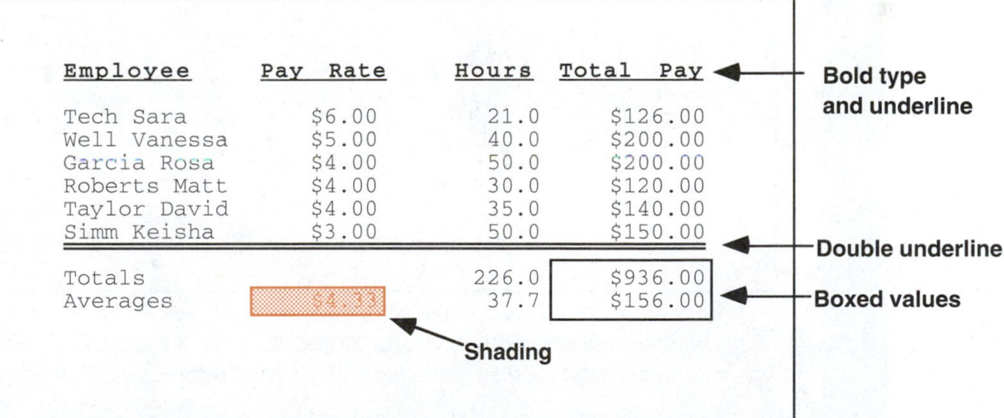

Employee	**Pay Rate**	**Hours**	**Total Pay**
Tech Sara	$6.00	21.0	$126.00
Well Vanessa	$5.00	40.0	$200.00
Garcia Rosa	$4.00	50.0	$200.00
Roberts Matt	$4.00	30.0	$120.00
Taylor David	$4.00	35.0	$140.00
Simm Keisha	$3.00	50.0	$150.00
Totals		226.0	$936.00
Averages	$4.33	37.7	$156.00

Because Allways only changes the way the final printed output of a worksheet looks, we will not discuss it in detail. If you are interested in learning more about this program, consult the *Lotus 1-2-3 Release 2.2 Reference Manual.*

TO TAKE A BREAK Remove diskette(s). To resume (hard disk): Insert *Data* diskette, type **C:** ↵, **CD\123** ↵, **123** ↵. To resume (two drive): Insert diskettes, type **B:** ↵, **123** ↵.

Homework Exercises

In the exercises that follow, be sure to check the answers to formulas with a calculator. It is very easy to make a typing mistake when entering formulas and very difficult to find such errors without checking the calculations by hand. As you work on these exercises, you should save multiple versions of your worksheets just in case you make a major error and have to start over from scratch.

① Use the **[F5]** key to make cell **X200** active. Use **[PrintScreen]** to show the result.

② Display the Lotus 1-2-3 *Help* screen for label alignments (access the *Help* feature, select **Cell Formats**, and then **Label Formats**). Use **[PrintScreen]** to show the resulting screen.

③ Molly wants to keep track of the checks she writes for budgeting purposes. She wants to set up a spreadsheet that will display information about her personal checks and categorize them as food, clothes, school, entertainment, and miscellaneous. Use Lotus 1-2-3 to create a worksheet that will display and print out the information listed below.

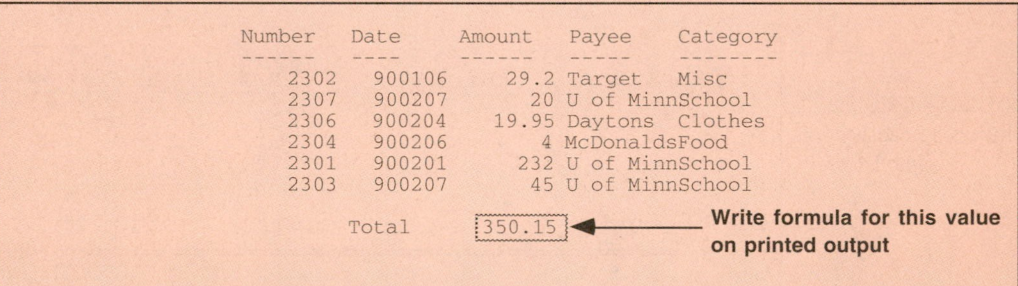

Number	Date	Amount	Payee	Category
------	----	------	-----	--------
2302	900106	29.2	Target	Misc
2307	900207	20	U of Minn	School
2306	900204	19.95	Daytons	Clothes
2304	900206	4	McDonalds	Food
2301	900201	232	U of Minn	School
2303	900207	45	U of Minn	School
	Total	350.15		

Write formula for this value on printed output

The dates are entered in the form **YYMMDD** where **YY** represents the year, **MM** represents the month and **DD** represents the day (e.g., **910106** represents January 6, 1991.

For this exercise, enter the data exactly as it appears above. Don't worry about formatting the worksheet (you will do that in Exercise 4). Note that the boxed value **350.15** at the bottom of the output is the sum of the values in the **Amount** column. That number should be calculated by Lotus 1-2-3 using the **@SUM** function. To show that you have used the correct function, handwrite the formula for that cell on the printed output. Save the worksheet under the name **HWL1-03** and then print it.

CHAPTER ONE

④ Format the worksheet you created in Exercise 3 so that it looks nicer. All the cells should be right justified and have a column width of 12; the values in the column labeled **Amount** should display two decimal places and a dollar sign. The printed output should look like the following:

```
  Number        Date      Amount       Payee    Category
  ------        ----      ------       -----    --------
    2302      900106      $29.20      Target        Misc
    2307      900207      $20.00   U of Minn      School
    2306      900204      $19.95     Daytons     Clothes
    2304      900206       $4.00  McDonalds        Food
    2301      900201     $232.00   U of Minn      School
    2303      900207      $45.00   U of Minn      School

               Total     $350.15
```

Save the worksheet under the name **HWL1-04** and then print it.

---

⑤ Sort the data in the worksheet from Exercise 4 by **Category** in ascending order and, within **Category**, by **Amount** in descending order. Save the worksheet under the name **HWL1-05** and then print it. The printed output should look like the following:

```
  Number        Date      Amount       Payee    Category
  ------        ----      ------       -----    --------
    2306      900204      $19.95     Daytons     Clothes
    2304      900206       $4.00  McDonalds        Food
    2302      900106      $29.20      Target        Misc
    2301      900201     $232.00   U of Minn      School
    2303      900207      $45.00   U of Minn      School
    2307      900207      $20.00   U of Minn      School

               Total     $350.15
```

---

⑥ Kris wants to compute her grade-point average (GPA) for the courses she has completed in her first term of college. One way to compute a GPA is to carry out the following steps:

a. Assign a value to each course grade. An A is worth 4 points, a B is worth 3, a C is worth 2, a D is worth 1, and an F is worth 0.
b. For each course, multiply the value of the grade from step a by the number of credits for that course.
c. Add up the results from step b.
d. Divide the answer from step c by the total number of credits for all courses.

Use Lotus 1-2-3 to create a worksheet that will compute Kris's GPA, rounded off to one decimal place. Use the data supplied below to make the printed output look like the following:

Continued . . .

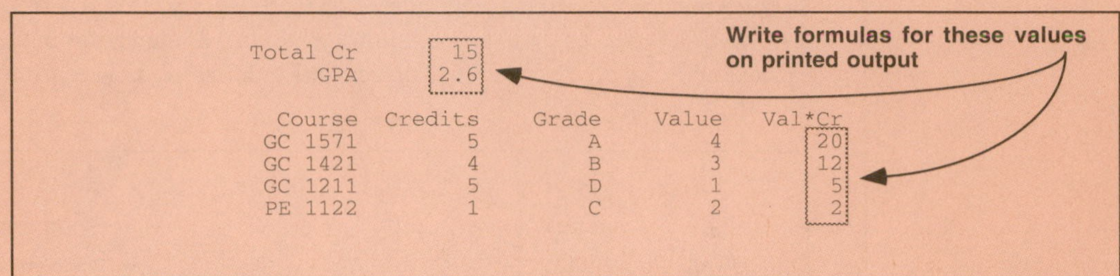

The boxed values should be calculated by Lotus 1-2-3. Write the actual formulas on the printed output next to the appropriate numbers. For those formulas that are identical except for cell locations (e.g., cells **E5**, **E6**, **E7**, and **E8**), you need only write the formula for one cell. Save the worksheet under the name **HWL1-06** and then print it.

---

⑦ Modify the worksheet you produced in Exercise 6 so that it includes the following extra data:

Course	**Credits**	**Grade**
GC 1422	4	A
GC 1172	5	B

Be sure to check the formulas so that the new worksheet correctly computes the total credits earned and the GPA for all six courses. Save the worksheet under the name **HWL1-07** and then print it.

---

⑧ The diving team was in a recent competition where four judges evaluated the divers' performances. To make the judging fair, the score for each dive was calculated by throwing out the highest and lowest scores and then calculating the average of the remaining scores.

Construct a worksheet that displays each diver's name and scores from the judges and calculates the average score for each diver. In the sample output displayed below, the formula for the **Score** for each person should be constructed as follows:

a. The sum of the judges' scores for a person is calculated first.
b. Then the lowest score (use the **@MIN(range)** function) is subtracted from that sum.
c. Then the highest score (use the **@MAX(range)** function) is subtracted from that value.
d. Finally, the value is divided by the number of scores used. This is similar to the **Quiz Ave** score in the Gradebook worksheet discussed on page L61.

The output should look like the following:

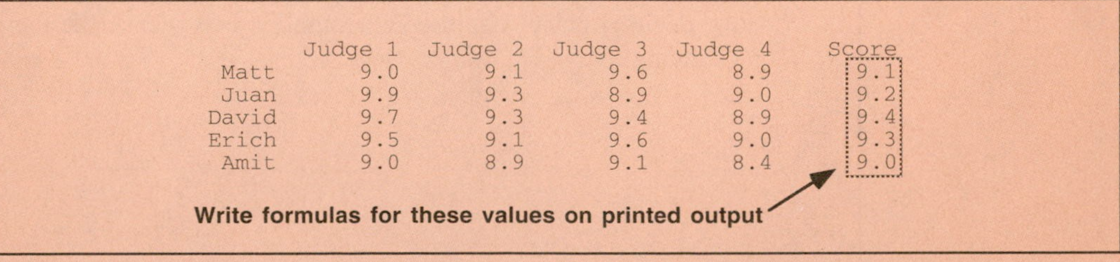

CHAPTER ONE

Remember that in order to display numbers such as **9.0** you must format the cells for one digit to the right of the decimal point (if you do not format the cell and type **9.0**, Lotus 1-2-3 will display it as **9**). If you enter **9.0** as a label, Lotus 1-2-3 will assign it a value of zero and this will cause an error in the average score.

The boxed values should be calculated by Lotus 1-2-3. Write the actual formulas on the printed output next to the appropriate numbers. For those formulas that are identical except for cell locations you need only write the formula for one cell. Save the worksheet under the name **HWL1-08** and then print it.

---

⑨ Print the worksheet from Exercise 8 with a header that includes your name in the upper left-hand corner, the date centered, and the page number in the upper right-hand corner.

---

⑩ For the worksheet from Exercise 8, print the contents of the cells, one per line, rather than the values displayed.

---

⑪ Micro Stuff, Inc. is a company that sells microcomputer software. Its employees are paid a monthly salary of $1000 plus a 7% commission on everything they sell. Construct a worksheet that displays the sales summary chart given below and save it under the name **HWL1-11**.

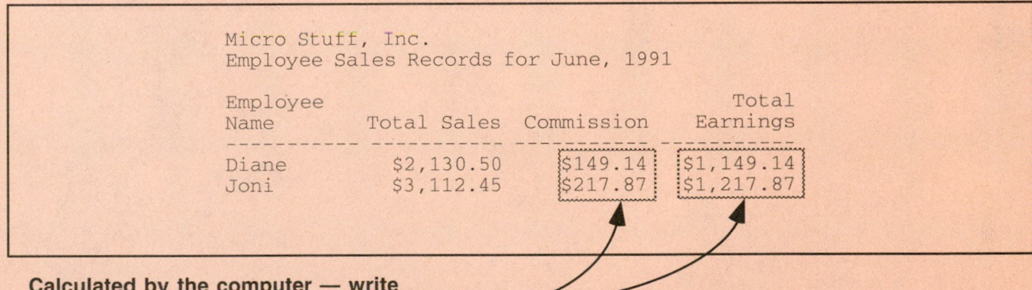

```
Micro Stuff, Inc.
Employee Sales Records for June, 1991

Employee                                          Total
Name          Total Sales  Commission          Earnings
-----------  -----------  -----------  -----------
Diane          $2,130.50      $149.14     $1,149.14
Joni           $3,112.45      $217.87     $1,217.87
```

Calculated by the computer — write formulas for these values on printed output

Note that the numbers are formatted as currency with the dollar sign, a comma to separate the hundreds and thousands place, and two digits to the right of the decimal point. You must enter the numbers without the dollar sign and commas (e.g., type **2130.5** for Diane's total sales). If you type the number with the dollar sign and commas (e.g., **$2,130.50**), Lotus 1-2-3 will beep at you when you press **[Enter]** and place you directly into **EDIT** mode. In that case, press **[Esc]** to exit or use the regular editing techniques to remove the dollar sign and comma and then press **[Enter]**.

The boxed values should be calculated by Lotus 1-2-3. Write the actual formulas on the printed output next to the appropriate numbers. For those formulas that are identical except for cell locations you need only write the formula for one cell.

More Spreadsheets

Objectives *After you have completed this chapter, you should be able to*

- Split the Lotus 1-2-3 screen horizontally or vertically.
- Synchronize split screens.
- Freeze titles so that they are always displayed.
- Insert new rows and columns into an existing worksheet.
- Use pre-programmed functions to display the date and time.
- Use the **`FILL`** function to place sequential values into cells.
- Instruct Lotus 1-2-3 to make simple selections using IF/THEN/ELSE statements.

CHAPTER 2

- Instruct Lotus 1-2-3 to make complex selections using nested IF/THEN/ELSE statements.
- Use **@VLOOKUP** and **@HLOOKUP** to look up values from a table.
- Use the **@NA** function to identify missing or unknown values.
- Create bar graphs, line graphs, and pie graphs.
- Print graphs using the PrintGraph program.
- Import graphs into WordPerfect documents.
- Create, execute, and modify macros.

Introduction

In this chapter we will discuss a number of features that make Lotus 1-2-3 a powerful spreadsheet program. Among the most important are the ability to make decisions using IF/THEN/ELSE statements, much like those used in programming languages such as BASIC, and the ability to graph information contained in a worksheet.

Definitions

Before beginning a specific example, you should familiarize yourself with some terms frequently encountered when talking about word processing:

Absolute reference . . . (L107) A cell or range reference that always remains the same, even if it is copied to another cell location. These references are indicated using a dollar sign to the left of the column letter and/or row number. For example, if a certain formula contains **A3** and that formula is copied to a different cell, the **A3** will not be adjusted to fit the new location. Compare this with relative reference.

Logical formula . . . (L94) One of three types of formulas recognized by Lotus 1-2-3. Logical formulas evaluate a condition and determine if it is true or false. These formulas use logical operators and/or special functions (e.g., **@SUM**).

Logical operator . . . (L94) Symbol used in logical formulas to make comparisons or to create complex formulas that combine two or more formulas into one. The logical operators include **=**, **<**, **>**, **<=**, **>=**, **<>**, **#AND#**, **#OR#**, and **#NOT#**.

Macro . . . (L131) A set of keystrokes and instructions that can be used to automate a particular task. The keystrokes are stored as labels (text) in a cell or range of cells of a worksheet so that they can be executed at any time, usually by pressing just two keys.

Relative reference . . . (L107) A cell or range that is interpreted relative to the current cell location. For example, if a certain formula contains **A3** and that formula is copied to a different cell, the **A3** will be adjusted to fit the new location.

String formula . . . One of three types of formulas recognized by Lotus 1-2-3. A string formula works on groups of characters (e.g., text and punctuation) using the string operator **&** (ampersand) and/or special functions. For example, if cell **A3** contains the label **Harlan**, then the string formula **+"Dear Ms. "&A3** would display **Dear Ms. Harlan**. String formulas are not discussed in this book.

Window . . . (L79) A portion of the screen that is dedicated to a specific purpose.

Splitting the Screen

On page L66, you saved a worksheet, **GRADE-V2**, that contained the grades of a class of five students. As you recall, the worksheet was too large to completely fit on the screen at one time and, therefore, you had to scroll between parts of the worksheet using **[Tab]** (scroll right) and **[Shift-Tab]** (scroll left). This becomes inconvenient when working on larger spreadsheets because you may have to scroll through three or four screens to find the place you want. Also, you may want to see at the same time two parts of the worksheet that are far apart (e.g., columns **A** and **Z**).

Lotus 1-2-3 has a feature that allows you to split the screen so that you can simultaneously view two different parts of the worksheet. For example, suppose, in worksheet **GRADE-V2**, you want to view the name, score on quiz 1, and total score for each student at the same time. It is possible to have Lotus 1-2-3 split the screen so that columns **A**, **B**, **C**, and **J** are displayed simultaneously. To do this, follow the directions given below:

Step 1 Boot your computer, place your *Lotus Data* diskette in drive A:, and access the Lotus 1-2-3 program. Then, use **/ F**(ile) **R**(etrieve) to load the worksheet **GRADE-V2**.

Step 2 Before the screen can be split, you must show Lotus 1-2-3 where the split is to occur:

Keystroke	Action Resulting from Keystroke
[arrow]	Use the **[arrow]** keys to make cell **D1** active. When the screen is split, the active cell (**D1**) will become the upper left-hand cell in the new screen.

Continued . . .

Keystroke	Action Resulting from Keystroke
`/`	Displays the main menu.
`W`	Selects **Worksheet**.
`W`	Selects **Window**. A **window** is a part of the screen that is dedicated to a particular purpose. When the screen is split, there will be two windows, each one showing a part of the active worksheet. The window menu appears as follows:

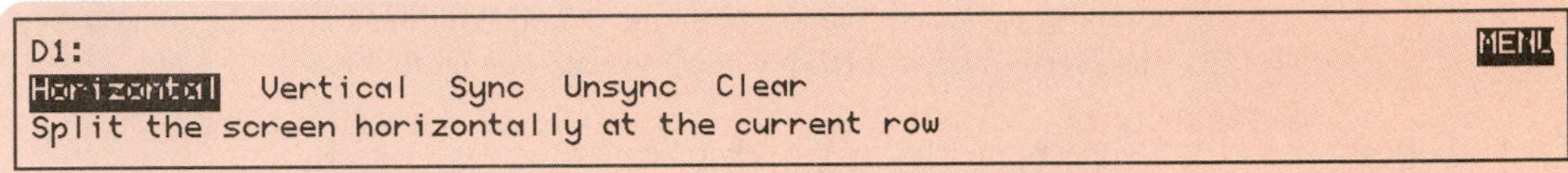

Horizontal splits the screen at the current row into a top window and a bottom window.

Vertical splits the screen at the current column into a left window and a right window.

Sync synchronizes scrolling in the two windows so that both windows scroll together.

Unsync removes the synchronization so that one window remains stationary while the other scrolls.

Clear unsplits the screen so that only one screen is displayed.

To split the screen vertically into left-hand and right-hand windows, select **Vertical**.

Keystroke	Action Resulting from Keystroke
`V`	Selects **Vertical**, splits the screen vertically into two parts, and returns control to **READY** mode. Columns **A**, **B**, and **C** are displayed in the left-hand screen and columns **D** through **H** are displayed in the right-hand screen. Notice that the row numbers are displayed on each screen and that **C1** becomes the active cell:

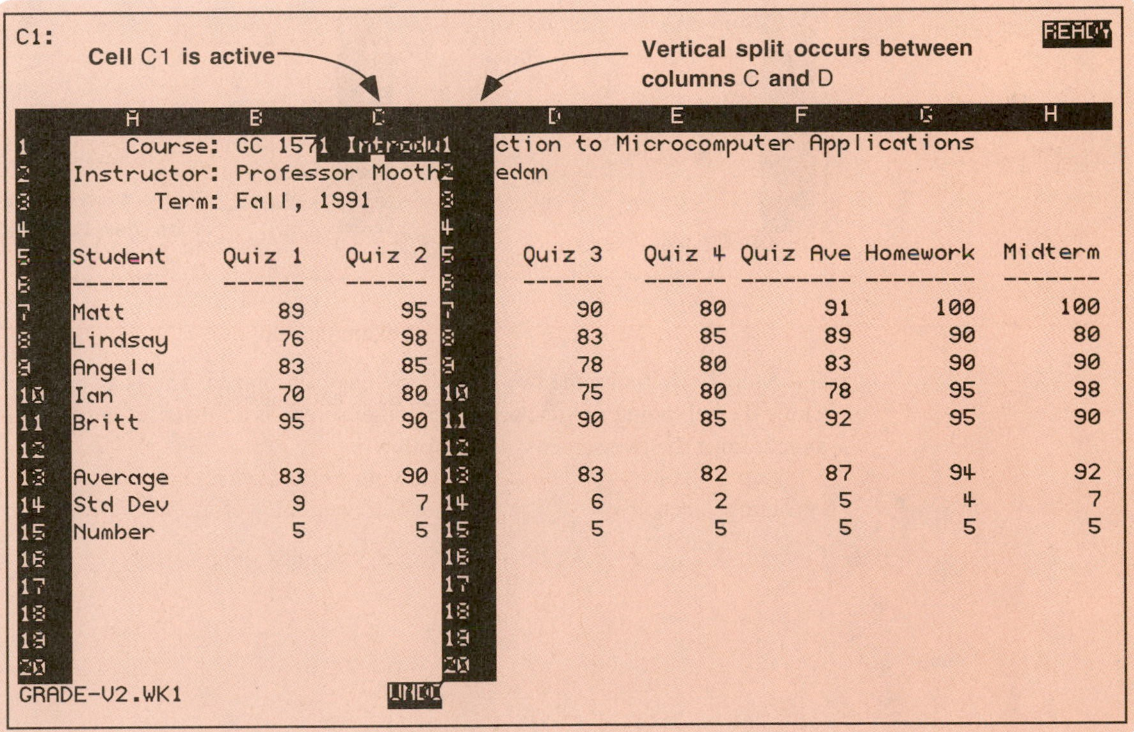

Step 3 The left-hand screen is the active one and **C1** is the active cell. The **[arrow]** keys may be used to change the active cell, as usual, in the left-hand screen, but the right-hand screen will remain constant (this means that the screens are *unsynchronized*). To make the right-hand screen active you would use the **[F6]** key:

Keystroke	Action Resulting from Keystroke
[F6]	Switches the active screen. Now, the right-hand screen is active and cell **D1** is the active cell.
	If you want to see columns **A**, **B**, and **C** and, at the same time, column **J** (total points), you would use the **[arrow]** keys or **[F5]** to move the cell pointer to **J1**:
[F5]	Requests the name of the cell to be made active.
J1 ↵	Makes cell **J1** active.

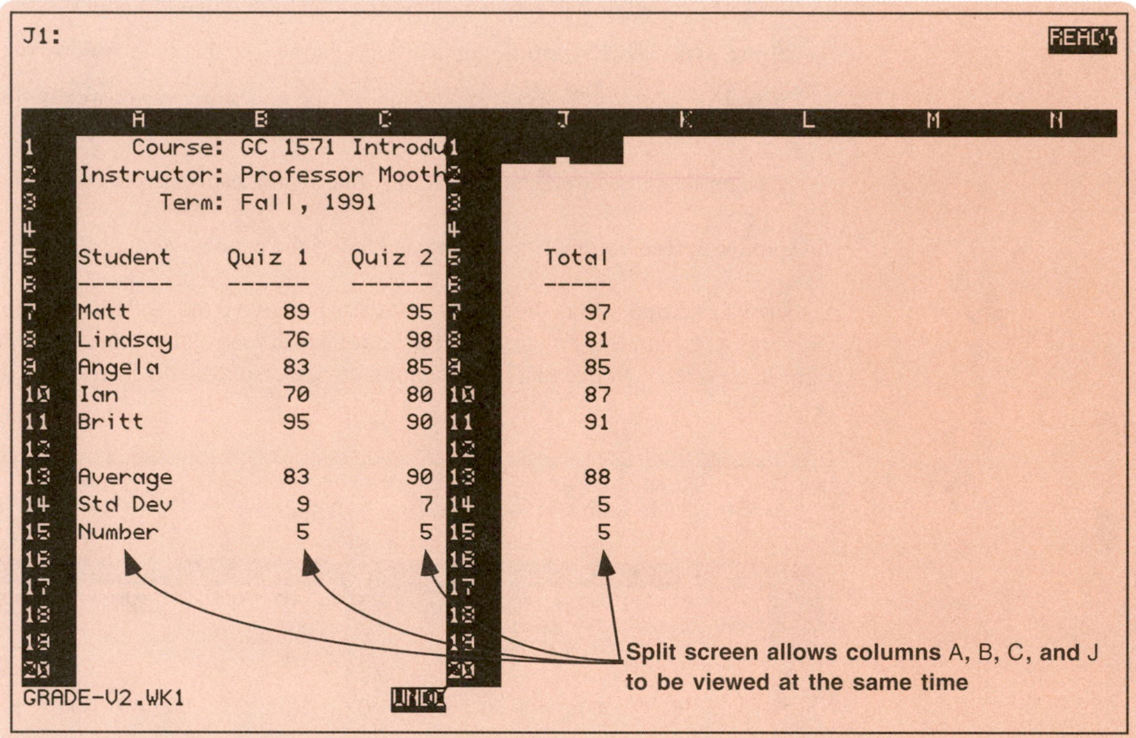

Step 4 Initially, the two screens are unsynchronized. They can be synchronized so that when you move the cell pointer in one screen the other screen is adjusted (if necessary) to keep things lined up. To synchronize the two screens, do the following:

Keystroke	Action Resulting from Keystroke
/	Displays the main menu.
W	Selects **Worksheet**.
W	Selects **Window**.
S	Selects **Sync** (**Sync**hronize the screens).
↓	Use the **[down arrow]** key to make cell **J21** active. Notice that as the cell pointer moves from cell **J20** to cell **J21** the rows remain lined up (i.e., Matt's total stays with his name and other data).
↓	Use the **[down arrow]** key to make cell **J30** active and notice how the left-hand screen adjusts to keep the rows lined up.

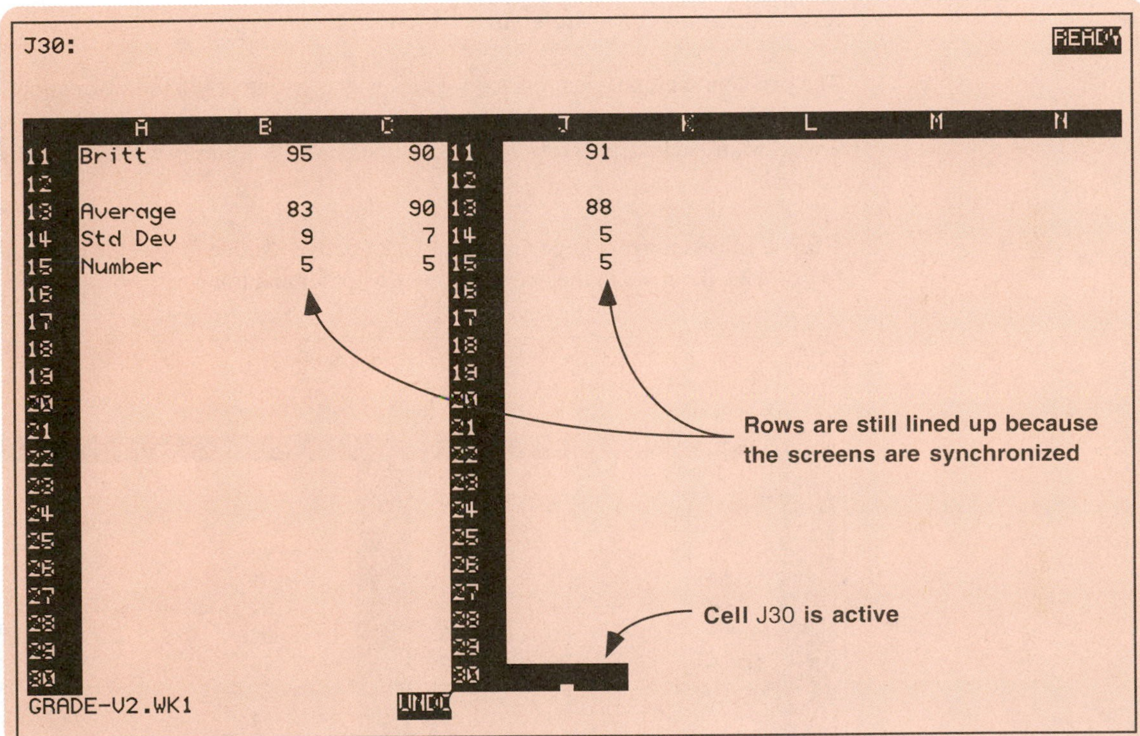

Use the **[arrow]** keys to move around the screen some more and notice how both screens move at the same time when you move vertically (but not when you move horizontally).

[F5]	Requests the name of the cell to be made active.
X200 ↵	Makes cell **X200** active. Notice that columns **A**, **B**, and **C** in the inactive window (i.e., the left-hand window) have remained stationary while the active window (i.e., the right-hand window) has scrolled to column **X**. The row numbers for both windows have changed to **200**.

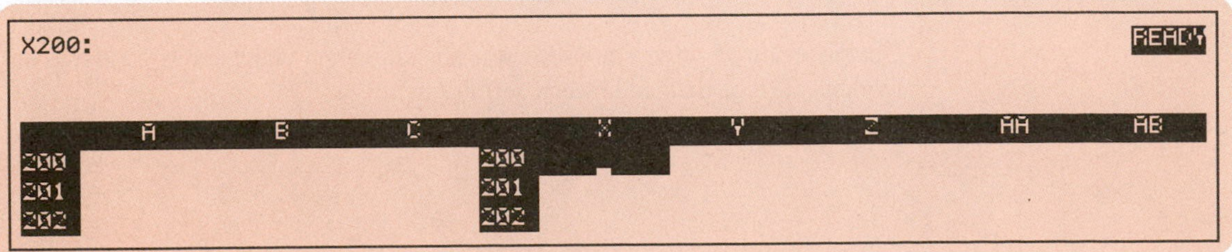

Step 5 To unsynchronize the windows so that one remains stationary while the other scrolls, do the following:

Keystroke	Action Resulting from Keystroke
[F5]	Requests the name of the cell to be made active.
J1 ↵	Makes cell **J1** active again.
/	Displays the main menu.
W	Selects **Worksheet**.
W	Selects **Window**.
U	Selects **Unsync** (**Unsync**hronize the screens).

The problem with unsynchronized screens is that, eventually, the information in the rows or columns may not line up properly. For example, if you press the **[down-arrow]** key repeatedly until cell **J21** is active, Matt's data (from row **7**) become lined up with Lindsay's total score (in row **8**). This can lead to confusion.

↓ Use the **[down arrow]** key to make cell **J21** active. Notice that as the cell pointer moves from cell **J20** to cell **J21** the rows in the two windows do not remain lined up.

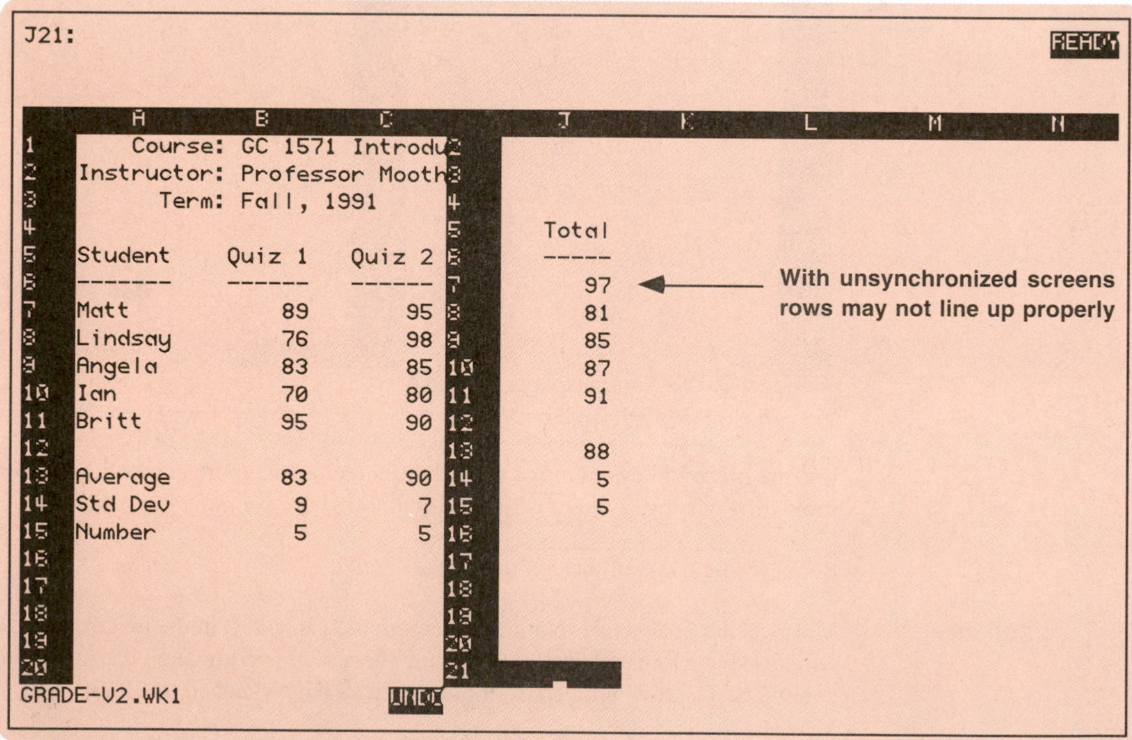

Unsynchronized screens are sometimes useful when you want to view two unrelated parts of a worksheet (e.g., data and macro definitions).

Step 6 To unsplit the screens (i.e., to return to regular, one screen, mode) use the clear command:

Keystroke	Action Resulting from Keystroke
/	Displays the main menu.
W	Selects **Worksheet**.
W	Selects **Window**.
C	Selects **Clear**, unsplits the screens, and returns control to **READY** mode.

The screens may also be split horizontally by selecting **Horizontal** from the **Window** menu. However, screens cannot be split horizontally and vertically at the same time.

Freezing (Locking) Titles

Sometimes you may want to view a part of a worksheet that is off the screen but you want to view the column and/or row headings at the same time. For example, let's say that you want to look at the final scores for students, but you want the column headings in rows **1** through **6** to be displayed (so you can see what the numbers represent) and you want to see the student names in column **A** as well (so you can tell who scored what). You can do this by freezing the titles in rows **1** through **6** and the names in column **A**:

Keystroke	Action Resulting from Keystroke
[Home]	Moves the cursor to cell **A1**.
[arrow]	Use the [arrow] keys to move the cell pointer to **B7**. This is the first score of the first student in the worksheet. When the titles are frozen, all rows above this row (rows **1** through **6**) and all columns to the left of this column (only column **A**) will be frozen.
/	Displays the main menu.
W	Selects **Worksheet**.
T	Selects **Titles** and displays its menu.

```
B7: 89                                                        MENU
Both  Horizontal  Vertical  Clear
Freeze all rows and columns above and to the left of the cell pointer
```

Both freezes all rows above the cell pointer and all columns to the left of the cell pointer.

Horizontal freezes only rows above the cell pointer.

Vertical freezes only columns to the left of the cell pointer.

Clear unfreezes all columns and rows.

Continued . . .

Keystroke	Action Resulting from Keystroke
B	Selects **Both**, freezes the selected rows and columns, and returns control to **READY** mode.
[arrow]	Use the **[arrow]** keys to move the cell pointer to cell **N7**. Notice how column **A** remains on the screen no matter how far to the right you scroll. Similarly, if you use the **[arrow]** keys to move down the screen, rows **1** through **6** remain on the screen no matter how far down you move.
[arrow]	Use the **[arrow]** keys to move the cell pointer to cell **N22**. Notice how rows **1** through **6** remain on the screen.

```
N22:                                                        READY

        A          H          I          J        K        L        M        N
1     Cours
2  Instructo
3       Ter
4
5  Student     Midterm     Final     Total
6  -------     -------     -----     -----
9  Angela           90        80        85
10 Ian              98        80        87
11 Britt            90        90        91
12
13 Average          92        84        88
14 Std Dev           7         7         5
15 Number            5         5         5
16
17
18
19
20
21
22
GRADE-V2.WK1                UNDO
```

Frozen titles (rows 1 through 6 and column A)

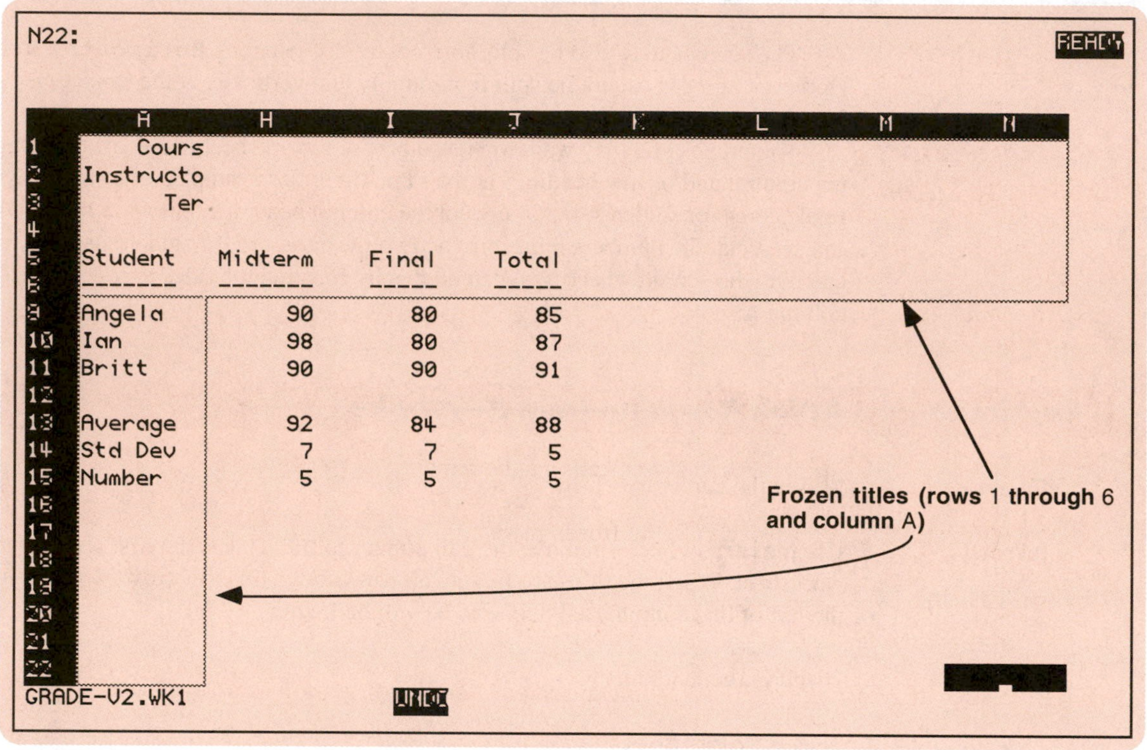

Strange things will happen if you try to make a frozen cell active. Lotus 1-2-3 will display a second set of frozen rows and/or columns right next to the original set. For example, make cell **A1** active by using the **[F5]** key:

Keystroke	Action Resulting from Keystroke
[F5]	Requests the name of the cell to be made active.
A1 ↵	Makes cell **A1** active and displays a second set of frozen cells.

Continued . . .

Keystroke	Action Resulting from Keystroke

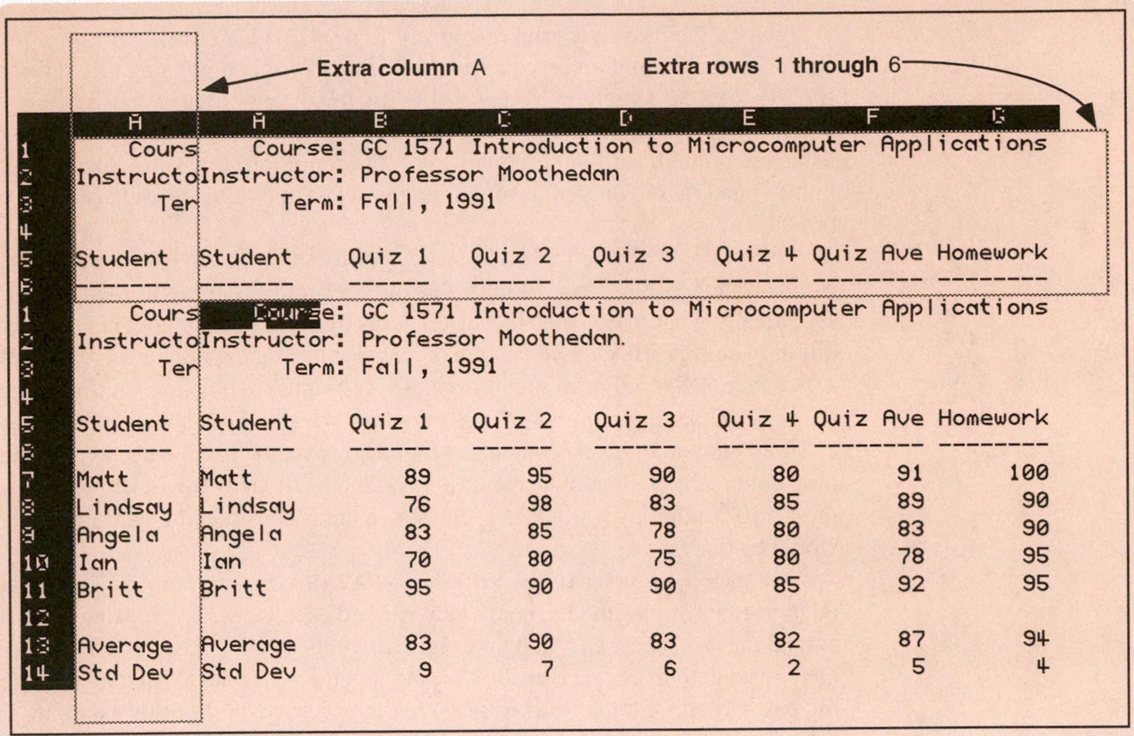

The extra set of frozen cells can be removed by doing the following:

[PageDown] [PageUp]	Clears the extra set of frozen rows.
[Ctrl →] [Ctrl ←]	Clears the extra set of frozen columns. Cell **B7** now should be active.

Because column **A** and rows **1** through **6** are frozen, when you press **[Home]** the cell pointer moves to cell **B7** (where the titles were frozen), rather than to **A1**.

Cells can be unfrozen by doing the following:

Keystroke	Action Resulting from Keystroke
[Home]	Moves the cell pointer to cell **B7** (it probably was already there).
/	Displays the main menu.
W	Selects **Worksheet**.
T	Selects **Titles**.
C	Selects **Clear**, unfreezes the titles, and returns control to **READY** mode. Now, pressing **[Home]** will move the cell pointer to **A1**.
[Home]	Moves the cell pointer to cell **A1**.

TO TAKE A BREAK Remove diskette(s). To resume (hard disk): Insert *Data* diskette, type **`C:`** ↵, **`CD\123`** ↵, **`123`** ↵. To resume (two drive): Insert diskettes, type **`B:`** ↵, **`123`** ↵.

Making Simple Decisions

One of the most powerful features of Lotus 1-2-3 is its ability to carry out alternative actions based on the evaluation of certain conditions. One way of accomplishing this is through the use of an IF/THEN/ELSE structure. You probably use this type of logic every day. For example, you might say that IF it is raining outside THEN I will take my umbrella with me ELSE (i.e., if it is not raining) I will leave my umbrella at home. You evaluate the condition (i.e., you look out the window to see if it is raining) and, based on your evaluation, you select one of the two alternatives (carry the umbrella or not).

When computers are asked to make decisions they usually must be given a clear-cut condition to evaluate such as X > 2 (i.e., if the value of the variable X is larger than 2) and then they must be told specifically what to do when the statement is true and what to do when the statement is false. The condition in an IF/THEN/ELSE statement may use the logical operators **=**, **<**, **>**, **<=**, **>=**, **<>**, **`#AND#`**, **`#OR#`**, and **`#NOT#`**. For example, suppose we wanted to display an error message if a pay rate were under $2.00 per hour or over $10.00 per hour. We could use a decision logic such as IF the contents of cell **`A2`** is under 2 OR the contents of cell **`A2`** is over 10 THEN display **`Error in Rate`** ELSE display nothing. The compound condition could be written as **`A2 < 2 #OR# A2 > 10`**. If either one of these two conditions is true, the entire statement is considered true and the message **`Error in Rate`** would be displayed.

On page L49, you saved a worksheet, **`PAY-V4`**, that computed the pay earned by employees based on their rates of pay and the hours they worked each week. As an example of a simple decision, let's extend the worksheet so that it takes into account overtime pay as well as regular pay. Regular pay is the pay an employee receives for working less than or equal to 40 hours in one week. Overtime pay is the pay earned for hours worked per week in excess of 40. For this example, assume that the rate of pay for overtime hours is 1.5 times the rate for regular hours (e.g., if a person normally earns $4.00 per hour, that person would earn 1.5*4, or $6.00, per hour for overtime work).

The final worksheet should look like the following:

```
G7: (C2) [W9] +E7+F7                                                        READY

      A         B                 C             D        E         F         G
1  Puter Pals, Inc., Payroll Summary
2        Date:     15-Feb-91
3        Time:       10:29 AM
4
5              Num Employee          Pay Rate     Hours  Reg Pay    OT Pay  Total Pay
6              --- ------------      --------     -----  -------    ------  ---------
7                1 Roberts Matt         $4.00      30.0  $120.00     $0.00    $120.00
8                2 Simm Keisha          $3.00      50.0  $120.00    $45.00    $165.00
9                3 Tech Sara            $6.00      21.0  $126.00     $0.00    $126.00
10               4 Well Vanessa         $5.00      40.0  $200.00     $0.00    $200.00
11               5 Taylor David         $4.00      35.0  $140.00     $0.00    $140.00
12               6 Garcia Rosa          $4.00      50.0  $160.00    $60.00    $220.00
13             --- ------------      --------     -----  -------    ------  ---------
14                 Totals                         226.0  $866.00   $105.00    $971.00
15                 Averages             $4.33      37.7  $144.33    $17.50    $161.83
16
17
```

Begin by accessing Lotus 1-2-3 and then use **/** **F**(ile) **R**(etrieve) to load the worksheet **PAY-V4**.

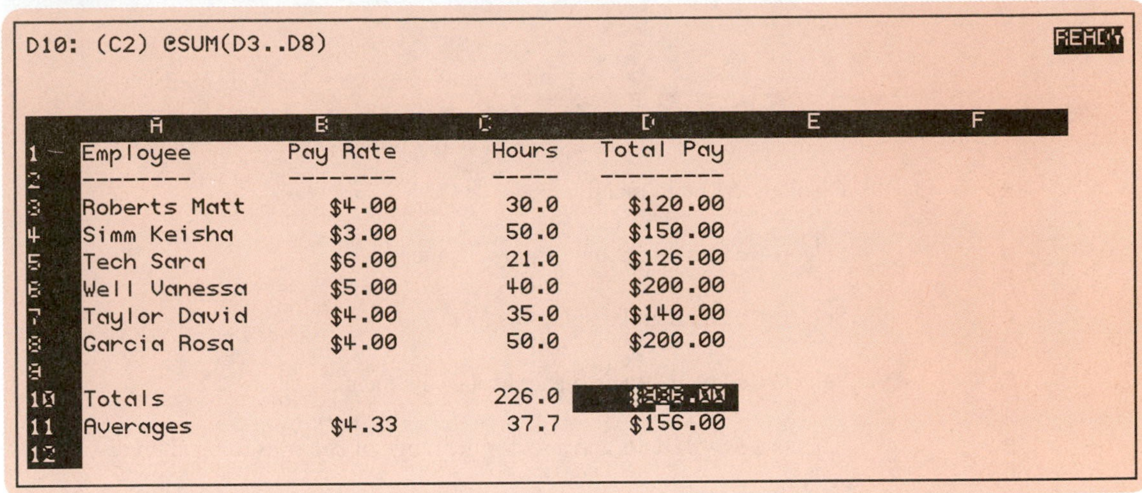

D10: (C2) @SUM(D3..D8)
READY
A B C D E F
Employee Pay Rate Hours Total Pay
Roberts Matt $4.00 30.0 $120.00
Simm Keisha $3.00 50.0 $150.00
Tech Sara $6.00 21.0 $126.00
Well Vanessa $5.00 40.0 $200.00
Taylor David $4.00 35.0 $140.00
Garcia Rosa $4.00 50.0 $200.00
Totals 226.0
Averages $4.33 37.7 $156.00

Insert new columns for **Num** (the employee number that will be entered into a new column **A**), **Reg Pay** (the regular pay earned that will be entered into a new column **E**), and **OT Pay** (the overtime pay earned that will be entered into a new column **F**). You must use the **Insert** command to do this:

Keystroke	Action Resulting from Keystroke
[Home]	Makes cell **A1** active.
/	Displays the main menu.
W	Selects **Worksheet** and displays its menu.
I	Selects **Insert** and displays its menu. You may insert either columns or rows.
C	Selects **Column** and asks you to specify a range of columns to insert. New columns will be inserted to the left of the specified column letters. For example, typing **A1** inserts a new column to the left of the current column **A**, which will shift right to become column **B**.
A1 ↵	Inserts a column to the left of column **A**. You must use a valid single-cell reference (like **A1**) or a valid cell range (such as **A1.A1**) or the message **Invalid range or cell address** will appear.
	Now, insert columns for **Reg Pay** (new column **E**) and **OT Pay** (new column **F**) by doing the following:
/	Displays the main menu.
W	Selects **Worksheet** and displays its menu.
I	Selects **Insert** and displays its menu.
C	Selects **Column** and asks you to specify a range of columns to insert.
E1.F1 ↵	Inserts a new column **E** and a new column **F** to the left of the **Tot Pay** column. Note that the entire worksheet no longer fits on the screen. To see the **Tot Pay** column, you can use the [arrow] keys or press [Tab].

It would be a good idea to reduce the widths of columns **D** through **G** so that you can see the entire worksheet without having to scroll back and forth. To change the widths of the columns, do the following:

Keystroke	Action Resulting from Keystroke
/	Displays the main menu.
W	Selects **Worksheet** and displays its menu.
C	Selects **Column** and displays its menu.
C	Selects **Column-Range** and displays its menu.
S	Selects **Set-Width** and asks for the range of columns to be altered.
D1.G1 ↵	Specifies that columns **D** through **G** are to be altered and requests the new width. If you know exactly how wide you want the columns, you could enter that number here. Unfortunately, we do not really know if the column widths should be 11 or 10 or 9, etc. We could enter 11 and then see if column **G** appears on the screen. If it does not, we could try 10 and then 9 and so on. However, the word **POINT** in the mode box indicates that you may also use the **[arrow]** keys to change the width. Pressing **[right-arrow]** will increase the column width by one character (e.g., from 12 to 13). Likewise, pressing **[left-arrow]** will decrease the column width by one character. Changing the column width using the **[arrow]** keys is a bit slower than simply typing a number, but you can see what happens at each step of the way. To illustrate this, use the **[left-arrow]** key to reduce the widths of the selected columns one character at a time.
[left-arrow]	Reduces the widths of the columns to 11 and shows the columns with their new widths on the screen.
[left-arrow]	Reduces the widths of the columns to 10.
[left-arrow]	Reduces the widths of the columns to 9. Notice how column **G** suddenly appears on the screen. This is as far as you need to go.

Continued . . .

Keystroke	Action Resulting from Keystroke
[Enter]	Confirms the new widths and returns to **READY** mode.

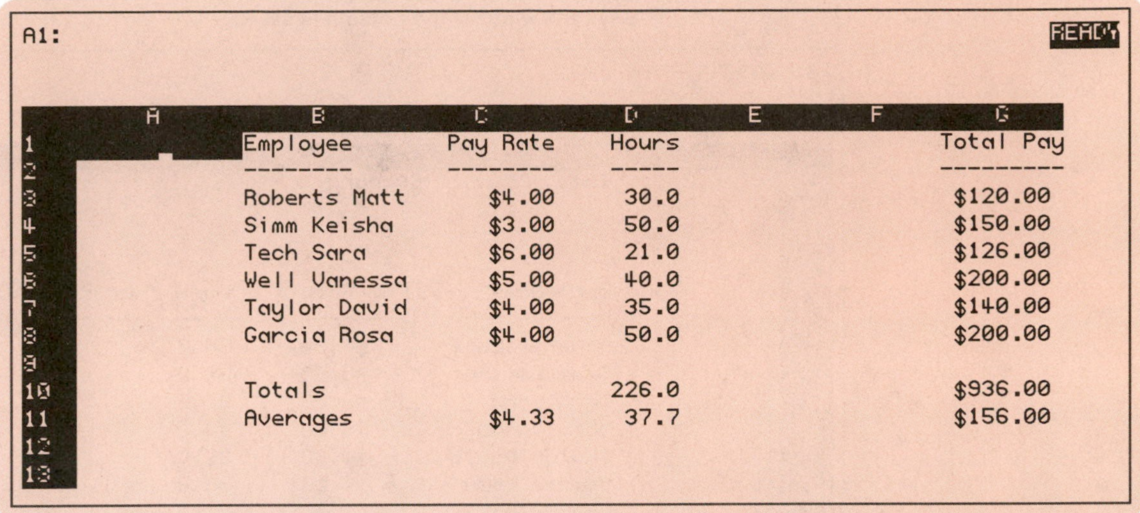

A1: READY

	A	B	C	D	E	F	G
1		Employee	Pay Rate	Hours			Total Pay
2		--------	--------	-----			---------
3		Roberts Matt	$4.00	30.0			$120.00
4		Simm Keisha	$3.00	50.0			$150.00
5		Tech Sara	$6.00	21.0			$126.00
6		Well Vanessa	$5.00	40.0			$200.00
7		Taylor David	$4.00	35.0			$140.00
8		Garcia Rosa	$4.00	50.0			$200.00
9							
10		Totals		226.0			$936.00
11		Averages	$4.33	37.7			$156.00
12							
13							

Four new rows need to be inserted at the top of the worksheet.

Keystroke	Action Resulting from Keystroke
/	Displays the main menu.
W	Selects **Worksheet** and displays its menu.
I	Selects **Insert** and displays its menu.
R	Selects **Row** and asks you to specify the range of rows to insert.
A1.A4 ↵	Inserts four blank rows above row **1**. The old row **1** now becomes row **5**.

Enter the labels in rows **1** through **6** so that the display looks like that shown below. To right justify the labels in rows **2**, **3**, **5**, and **6**, type a quotation mark (**"**) as the first character in the cell. As was mentioned on page L19, this is a special code that instructs Lotus 1-2-3 to right justify a label. In contrast, typing an apostrophe (**'**) will left justify the label and typing a circumflex (**^**) will center the label.

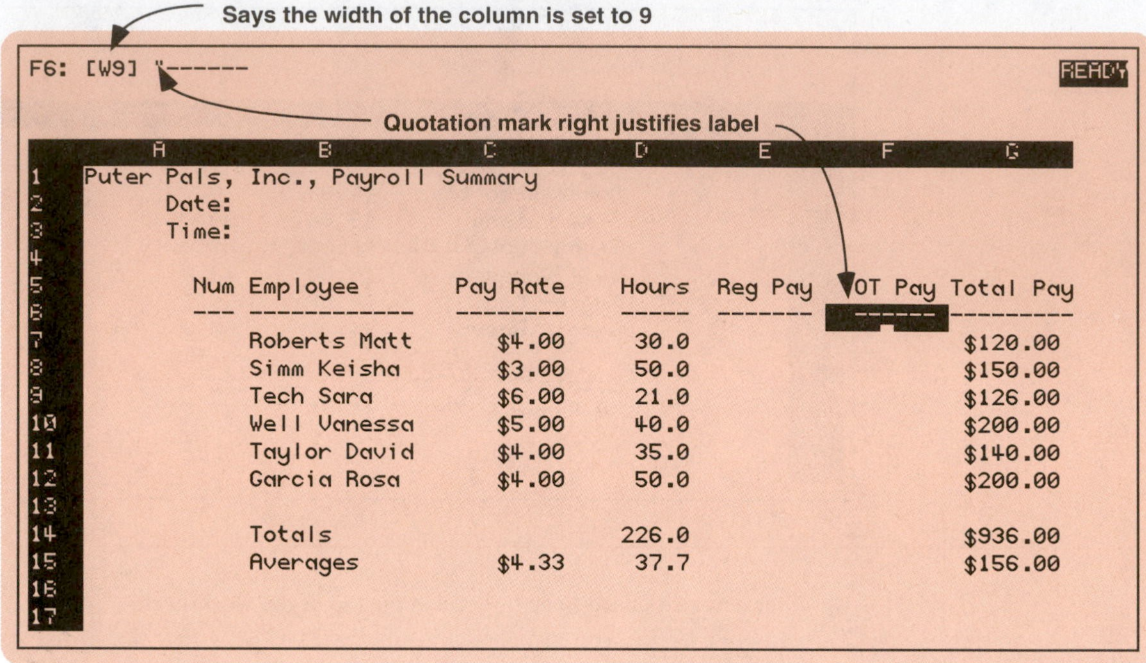

The dashes may be added to line **13** by typing them individually or by copying line **6** onto line **13**. The command used to do the copying would be **/ C**(opy) **A6.G6 ↵ A13.G13 ↵** (see p. L45 for more information on copying).

You can display the current date in cell **B2** by using the **@NOW** function Actually, this function accesses the current date and time (from the computer's clock) and returns a decimal number. The digits to the left of the decimal point represent the date while the digits to the right of the decimal point represent the time. For example, if today's date is February 15, 1991 and the time is 9:32 a.m., the **@NOW** function would display **33284.39726**. The value **33284** is the number of days since January 1, 1900 and the **.39726** represents the time since midnight (each second is represented by the number .0000115741).

This type of time representation is useful if you need to do arithmetic on dates (e.g., have the spreadsheet calculate the number of days before New Year's day). Usually, you simply want the computer to display the current date in a standard format. To do that, you must format the cell that will hold the date, in this case, cell **B2**:

Keystroke	*Action Resulting from Keystroke*
[arrow]	Use the **[arrow]** keys to make cell **B2** active.
@NOW ↵	Displays today's date and time in the default format (i.e., the number of days since January 1, 1900 and the elapsed time since midnight). Depending on the date you do this, the value should be between **33000** and **34000**.
/	Displays the main menu.
R	Selects **Range** and displays its menu.
F	Selects **Format** and displays its menu.

Continued . . .

Keystroke	Action Resulting from Keystroke
D	Selects **Date** and displays its menu:

```
B2: @NOW                                                                    MENU
1 (DD-MMM-YY)  2 (DD-MMM)  3 (MMM-YY)  4 (Long Intn'l)  5 (Short Intn'l)  Time
Lotus standard long form
```

Keystroke	Action Resulting from Keystroke
1	Selects **1 (DD-MMM-YY)** to display **D**ay, then **M**onth, then **Y**ear and requests the range to be formatted.
B2 ↵	Specifies the cell to be formatted. Cell **B2** now should contain the current date in a form such as **15-Feb-91**.

A similar procedure may be followed to display the current time in cell **B3**, except that the cell must be formatted for time display.

Keystroke	Action Resulting from Keystroke
[arrow]	Use the **[arrow]** keys to make cell **B3** active.
@NOW ↵	Displays the time of day in the default format. The number in the cell should be something like **33284.40009**. To format the time so that it appears with hours first and then minutes enter the following command:

/ R(ange) **F**(ormat) **D**(ate) **T**(ime) **2 B3** ↵

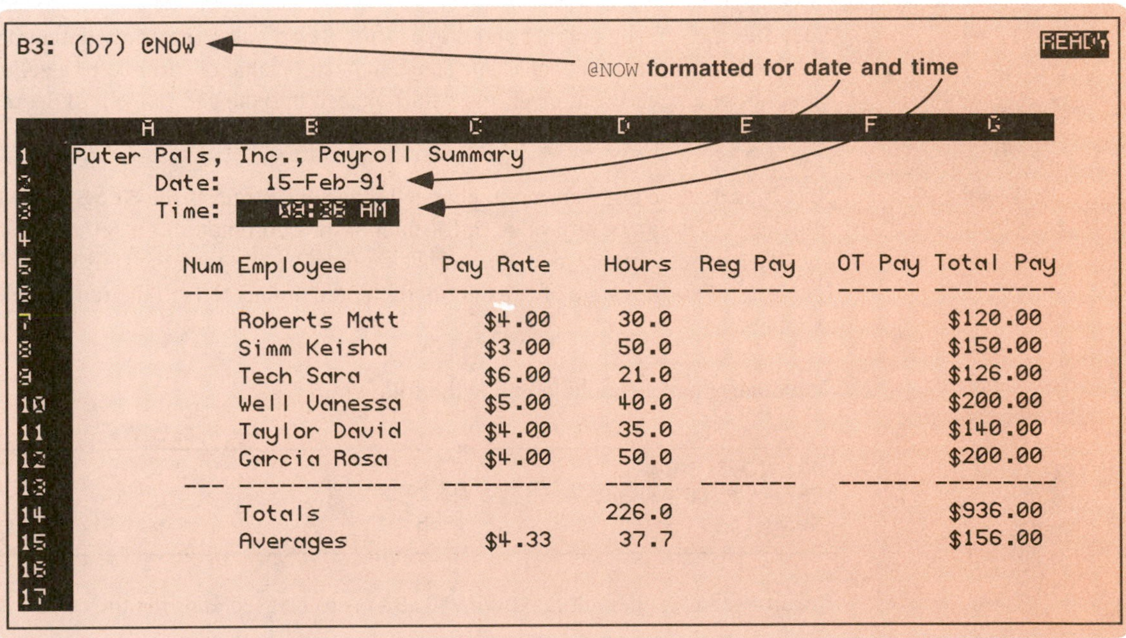

	A	B	C	D	E	F	G
1	Puter Pals, Inc., Payroll Summary						
2	Date:	15-Feb-91					
3	Time:	09:36 AM					
4							
5	Num	Employee	Pay Rate	Hours	Reg Pay	OT Pay	Total Pay
6	---	------------	--------	-----	-------	------	---------
7		Roberts Matt	$4.00	30.0			$120.00
8		Simm Keisha	$3.00	50.0			$150.00
9		Tech Sara	$6.00	21.0			$126.00
10		Well Vanessa	$5.00	40.0			$200.00
11		Taylor David	$4.00	35.0			$140.00
12		Garcia Rosa	$4.00	50.0			$200.00
13	---	------------	--------	-----	-------	------	---------
14		Totals		226.0			$936.00
15		Averages	$4.33	37.7			$156.00
16							
17							

Notice that the time displayed in cell **B3** is **9:36 AM** and that it does not change as time goes by. This is because the time in cell **B3** is changed only when the formulas in the worksheet are recalculated. If you press **[F9]** to recalculate the formulas, the time in cell **B3** will be updated.

It is possible to enter the numbers in cells **A7** through **A12** in three different ways:

- You could simply type **1** in cell **A7**, **2** in cell **A8**, and so on. This is easy for a small set of data but inconvenient for larger sets.
- A more efficient way is to type the formula **+A6+1** into cell **A7**. Because cell **A6** contains text, Lotus 1-2-3 will assume a value of **0** when the contents of that cell is used in a computation. Thus, the number **1** (the result of **0+1**) will be entered into cell **A7**. Then, you could copy the formula from cell **A7** into cells **A8** through **A12**.
- The fastest way is to use the Lotus 1-2-3 *Fill* feature. This feature allows you to *fill* a range of cells with values. You tell Lotus 1-2-3 what number to begin with, what increment to use, and when to stop, and it does the rest. In the present example, you want to begin with **1** in cell **A7** and count by ones until cell **A12** is reached.

Keystroke	Action Resulting from Keystroke
/	Displays the main menu.
D	Selects **Data** and displays its menu:

```
B3: (D7) @NOW                                                              MENU
Fill  Table  Sort  Query  Distribution  Matrix  Regression  Parse
Fill a range with a sequence of values
```

Keystroke	Action Resulting from Keystroke
F	Selects **Fill** and asks for the range of cells to be filled.
A7.A12 ↵	Specifies the range to be filled and requests the **Start** value. This can be any value or formula or a cell that contains a value.
1 ↵	Specifies the starting number and requests the **Step** value (i.e., how the numbers will change as Lotus 1-2-3 moves from cell to cell). The step can be any value or formula or a cell that contains a value. If you choose a negative number, the values placed into the cell range will decrease rather than increase by this amount.
1 ↵	Specifies that the numbers are to change by one and requests the **Stop** value (i.e., the maximum value allowed). This can be any value or formula or the coordinates of a cell that contains a value. If you specify a negative step value, the stop value must be less than the start value. If the stop value is reached before the range of cells is filled, the remaining cells in the range are erased but not filled with numbers.

The control panel should look like the following:

```
B3: (D7) @NOW                                                              EDIT
Enter fill range: a7.a12
Start: 1                    Step: 1                    Stop: 8191
```

Keystroke	Action Resulting from Keystroke
↵	Specifies that the default maximum (**8191**) is to be used and fills the cells with the numbers.

Continued . . .

Keystroke	Action Resulting from Keystroke

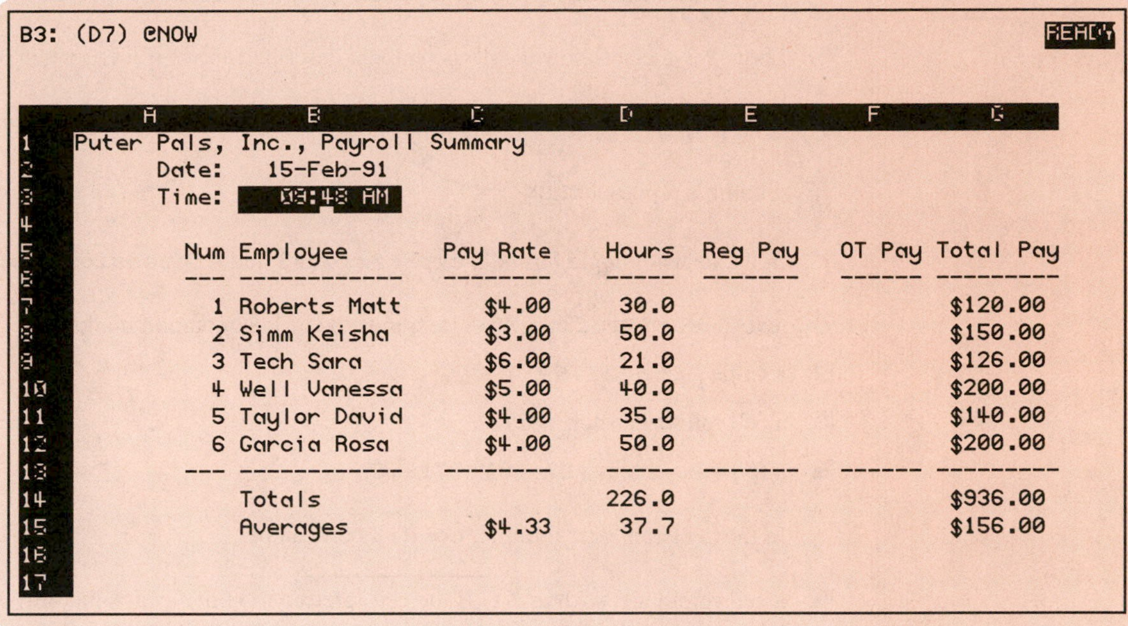

B3: (D7) @NOW   READY

	A	B	C	D	E	F	G
1	Puter Pals, Inc., Payroll Summary						
2		Date: 15-Feb-91					
3		Time: 08:48 AM					
4							
5	Num	Employee	Pay Rate	Hours	Reg Pay	OT Pay	Total Pay
6	---	------------	--------	-----	-------	------	---------
7	1	Roberts Matt	$4.00	30.0			$120.00
8	2	Simm Keisha	$3.00	50.0			$150.00
9	3	Tech Sara	$6.00	21.0			$126.00
10	4	Well Vanessa	$5.00	40.0			$200.00
11	5	Taylor David	$4.00	35.0			$140.00
12	6	Garcia Rosa	$4.00	50.0			$200.00
13	---	------------	--------	-----	-------	------	---------
14		Totals		226.0			$936.00
15		Averages	$4.33	37.7			$156.00
16							
17							

As a precaution against loss of data, use **/** **F**(ile) **S**(ave) to save the worksheet under the name **PAY-V9**.

To calculate the regular pay in column **E**, you need to have the program examine the hours worked to see if they are more than 40. The decision logic to compute regular pay can be broken down into two parts, depending on whether or not the person has worked more than 40 hours:

- If the person has worked 40 or less hours, then his or her regular pay is computed using the regular formula (i.e., hours*rate).
- However, if the person has worked over 40 hours, then his or her regular pay is computed using the same formula but with the hours set to 40 (i.e., the maximum number of regular hours a person can work is 40).

The decision logic for regular pay could be written as follows using an IF/THEN/ELSE format.

IF HOURS <= 40

THEN calculate regular pay using REG PAY = HOURS*RATE

ELSE calculate regular pay using REG PAY = 40*RATE

Similarly, the decision logic to compute overtime pay could be described as follows:

- If the person has worked 40 or less hours, then his or her overtime pay is zero (i.e., the person has not worked overtime).
- However, if the person has worked over 40 hours, then his or her overtime pay is computed by multiplying the overtime hours (this would be the total hours minus the 40 regular hours) by the overtime rate of pay (this would be 1.5 times the regular rate).

The decision logic for overtime pay could be written as follows using an IF/THEN/ELSE format:

IF HOURS <= 40

THEN calculate overtime pay using OVERTIME PAY = 0

ELSE calculate overtime pay using OVERTIME PAY = (HOURS – 40)*RATE*1.5

Lotus 1-2-3 can follow the decision logic described above if it is written in the following form:

@IF(condition,expression#1,expression#2)

First comma replaces **THEN** — Second comma replaces **ELSE**

In the decision logic formula, **expression#1** and **expression#2** can be:

- text such as **"Profits Up"** (text must be inside quotation marks).
- a value such as **23.6**.
- a cell reference such as **C7**.
- a formula such as **(D7-40)*C7*1.5**.

In the decision logic formula, **condition** can be:

- a cell reference, such as **A1**. If the cell referred to contains a value of 0 or text, the condition is considered false and **expression#2** will be processed and its value displayed. If the cell referred to contains any value other than 0, the condition is considered true and **expression#1** will be processed and its value displayed. For example, the statement **@IF(A1,"True","False")** would display **False** if cell **A1** contains the value 0 or text, and **True** if cell **A1** contains a value other than 0.

Note that instead of variable names, such as **HOURS**, you must use cell locations, such as **D7**. Lotus 1-2-3 cells are really just addresses (storage locations) for particular values or formulas and in that sense are similar to variables in algebra.

- a logical formula such as **B2*B3**. If the value of the formula is 0, the condition is considered false and **expression#2** will be processed and its value displayed. If the value of the formula is anything other than 0, the condition is considered true and **expression#1** will be processed and its value displayed. For example, the statement **@IF(B2*B3,"True","False")** would display **False** if the product of the values in cells **B2** and **B3** is 0, and **True** if the product of the values in cells **B2** and **B3** is not 0.
- an equation or inequality such as **G7>5**, or **A2="Date"**. If the equation or inequality is false, **expression#2** will be processed and its value displayed; if the equation or inequality is true, **expression#1** will be processed and its value displayed. Both logical and relational operators can be used in a condition. Allowable **logical operators** for the equation or inequality are:

These three operators are sometimes called *Boolean* or *complex* operators:

#OR# means *or*, as in **B3=5 #OR# B3=6** (if either condition is true, the entire condition is considered true).

#AND# means *and*, as in **B3=5 #AND# B3=6** (both conditions must be true for the entire condition to be considered true).

#NOT# means *not*, as in **#NOT#B3**.

Allowable relational operators are:

= equal to

<> not equal to

> greater than

< less than

>= greater than or equal to

<= less than or equal to

Relational operators are also known as comparison operators.

For the present problem, to calculate the pay earned by Matt Roberts for working regular hours, the following logic would be used:

IF HOURS <= 40

THEN calculate regular pay using REG PAY = HOURS*RATE

ELSE calculate regular pay using REG PAY = 40*RATE

The formula for this statement is

```
 IF HOURS <= 40 THEN REG PAY = HOURS*RATE ELSE REG PAY = 40*RATE
@IF(   D7   <= 40    ,               D7*C7      ,           40*C7)
```

Enter this formula into cell **E7** by doing the following:

Keystroke	Action Resulting from Keystroke
[arrow]	Use the **[arrow]** keys to make cell **E7** active.
@IF(D7<=40,D7*C7,40*C7) ↵	Specifies the formulas to be used to compute the pay for regular hours worked by Matt. This says that if the contents of cell **D7** (i.e., the hours for Matt) is less than or equal to 40, then the formula for cell **E7** is **D7*C7** (i.e., Matt's hours times his rate of pay). Otherwise, the formula for cell **E7** is **40*C7** (i.e., Matt's regular hours, which must be 40 if he worked overtime, times his rate of pay).

You can enter a similar formula for overtime pay, which is to be displayed in cell **F7**:

IF HOURS <= 40

THEN calculate overtime pay using OVERTIME PAY = 0

ELSE calculate overtime pay using OVERTIME PAY = (HOURS – 40)*RATE*1.5

```
 IF HOURS <= 40 THEN OT PAY = 0 ELSE OT PAY = (HOURS-40)*RATE*1.5
@IF(  D7   <= 40    ,          0   ,            ( D7   -40)* C7 *1.5)
```

Enter this formula into cell **F7** by doing the following:

Keystroke	Action Resulting from Keystroke
[arrow]	Use the **[arrow]** keys to make cell **F7** active.
@IF(D7<=40,0,(D7-40)*C7*1.5) ↵	Specifies the formulas to be used to compute the pay for overtime hours worked by Matt. This says that if the contents of cell **D7** (i.e., the hours for Matt) is less than or equal to 40, then the entry for cell **F7** is **0** (i.e., Matt has not worked overtime so his overtime pay is zero). Otherwise, the formula for cell **F7** is **(D7-40)*C7*1.5** (i.e., Matt's overtime hours × his rate of pay × 1.5 for time and a half).

Finish row **7** by entering the new formula for the total pay (the sum of the regular and overtime pay).

Keystroke	Action Resulting from Keystroke
[arrow]	Use the **[arrow]** keys to make cell **G7** active.
+E7+F7 ↵	Enters the formula to compute the total pay for Matt. Remember, an entry that begins with a letter (even a cell reference) is considered text. Therefore, be sure to begin a formula with a **+** so that Lotus 1-2-3 knows the cell contains a formula.

The formulas for cells **E8** through **G12** (for the five other employees) are the same as those for **E7** through **G7** (for Matt), except that the values in the formulas need to be adjusted to use data from the proper rows. You can use the copy command to enter the formulas:

Keystroke	Action Resulting from Keystroke
/	Displays the main menu.
C	Selects **Copy** and requests the range to copy from.
E7.G7 ↵	Specifies cells **E7**, **F7**, and **G7** are to be copied and requests the range to copy to.
E8.G12 ↵	Specifies the destination range, copies the formulas into the range, and returns control to **READY** mode. Remember, the formulas are automatically adjusted so that the correct data are used.

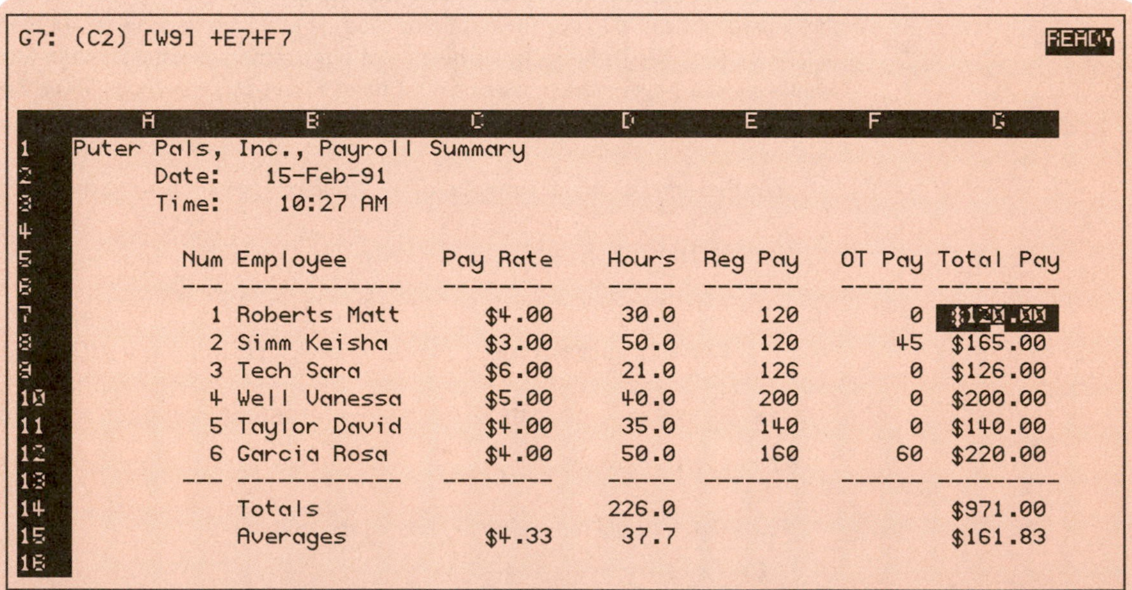

G7: (C2) [W9] +E7+F7 READY

	A	B	C	D	E	F	G
1	Puter Pals, Inc., Payroll Summary						
2		Date: 15-Feb-91					
3		Time: 10:27 AM					
4							
5	Num	Employee	Pay Rate	Hours	Reg Pay	OT Pay	Total Pay
6	---	-------------	---------	-----	-------	------	---------
7	1	Roberts Matt	$4.00	30.0	120	0	$120.00
8	2	Simm Keisha	$3.00	50.0	120	45	$165.00
9	3	Tech Sara	$6.00	21.0	126	0	$126.00
10	4	Well Vanessa	$5.00	40.0	200	0	$200.00
11	5	Taylor David	$4.00	35.0	140	0	$140.00
12	6	Garcia Rosa	$4.00	50.0	160	60	$220.00
13	---	-------------	---------	-----	-------	------	---------
14		Totals		226.0			$971.00
15		Averages	$4.33	37.7			$161.83
16							

Copy the formulas for totals and averages into cells **E14** through **F15** using the following copy command: **/** **C**(opy) **G14.G15** ↵ **E14.F15** ↵.

Format the cells in columns **E** and **F** for currency by entering the following command: **/** **R**(ange) **F**(ormat) **C**(urrency) **2** ↵ **E7.F15** ↵.

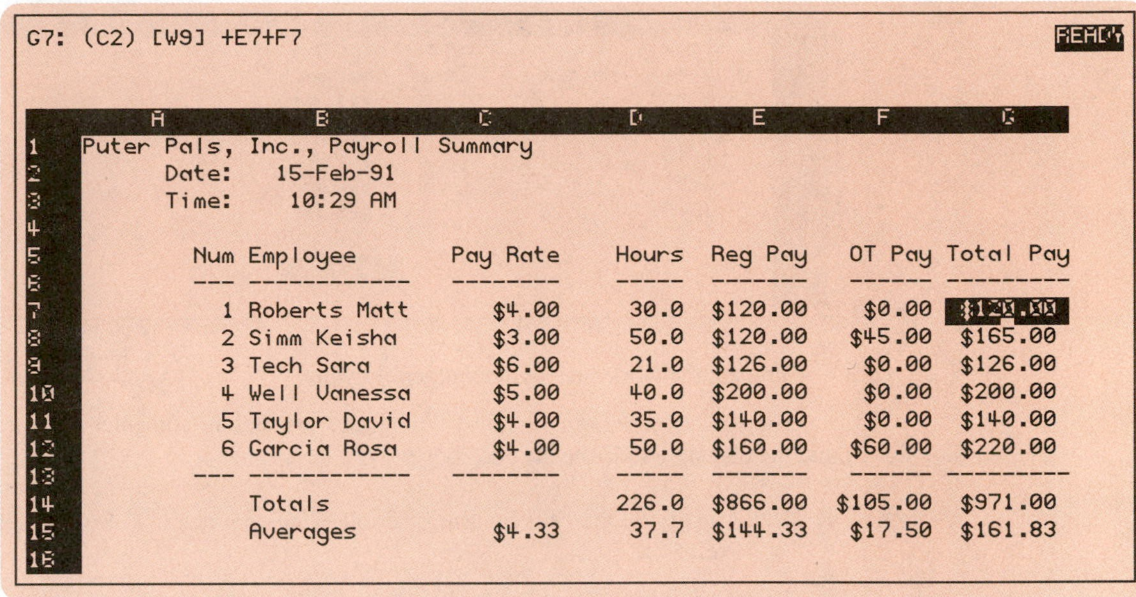

G7: (C2) [W9] +E7+F7 READY

	A	B	C	D	E	F	G
1	Puter Pals, Inc., Payroll Summary						
2		Date: 15-Feb-91					
3		Time: 10:29 AM					
4							
5	Num	Employee	Pay Rate	Hours	Reg Pay	OT Pay	Total Pay
6	---	-------------	---------	-----	--------	------	---------
7	1	Roberts Matt	$4.00	30.0	$120.00	$0.00	$120.00
8	2	Simm Keisha	$3.00	50.0	$120.00	$45.00	$165.00
9	3	Tech Sara	$6.00	21.0	$126.00	$0.00	$126.00
10	4	Well Vanessa	$5.00	40.0	$200.00	$0.00	$200.00
11	5	Taylor David	$4.00	35.0	$140.00	$0.00	$140.00
12	6	Garcia Rosa	$4.00	50.0	$160.00	$60.00	$220.00
13	---	-------------	---------	-----	--------	------	---------
14		Totals		226.0	$866.00	$105.00	$971.00
15		Averages	$4.33	37.7	$144.33	$17.50	$161.83
16							

Use **/** **F**(ile) **S**(ave) to save the worksheet under the name **PAY-V10**. Then quit the program and return to DOS.

TO TAKE A BREAK Remove diskette(s). To resume (hard disk): Insert *Data* diskette, type **C:** ↵, **CD\123** ↵. To resume (two drive): Insert diskettes, type **B:** ↵.

Making Complex Decisions

Let's set up a worksheet that uses a more complex **@IF** structure. In this example, you will create a worksheet that calculates the shipping charges for items mailed out from Turkey Feather Electronics, a computer software company located in Oakville, Washington. The shipping charges are based on the weight of the item and the postal zone. The postal zone, which is based on zipcodes, is a number between 1 and 8 that tells how far the item must be shipped from its originating address. The following rules apply:

Weight (in pounds)	***Shipping charges (in dollars)***		
Under 5	5	+	(weight) * (postal zone)
5 to 10	10	+	(weight in excess of 5 pounds) * (postal zone)
over 10	15	+	(weight in excess of 10 pounds) * (postal zone)

The final worksheet should look like the following:

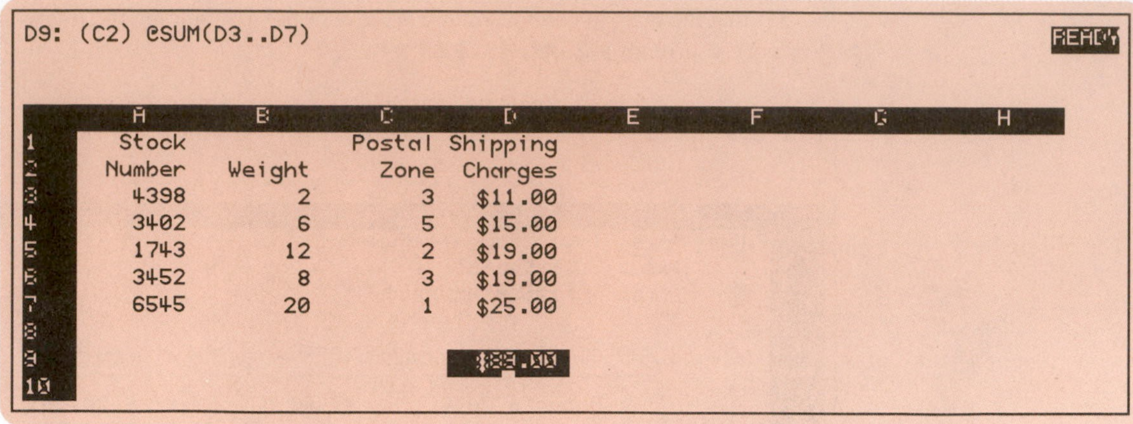

D9: (C2) @SUM(D3..D7) READY

	A	B	C	D	E	F	G	H
1	Stock		Postal	Shipping				
2	Number	Weight	Zone	Charges				
3	4398	2	3	$11.00				
4	3402	6	5	$15.00				
5	1743	12	2	$19.00				
6	3452	8	3	$19.00				
7	6545	20	1	$25.00				
8								
9				$89.00				
10								

Prepare the worksheet by doing the following:

Step 1 Access Lotus 1-2-3 by typing **123** ↵. Before you enter any data, format the worksheet so that the display looks like the one above:

- Right justify all the cells by using the following command: **/** **W**(orksheet) **G**(lobal) **L**(abel-Prefix) **R**(ight).
- For the numbers in column **D**, display the dollar sign and round the values off to two decimal places by using the following command: **/** **R**(ange) **F**(ormat) **C**(urrency) **2** ↵ **D1.D21** ↵.

Step 2 Enter the raw data and labels in the usual way. After this is done, the screen will look as follows:

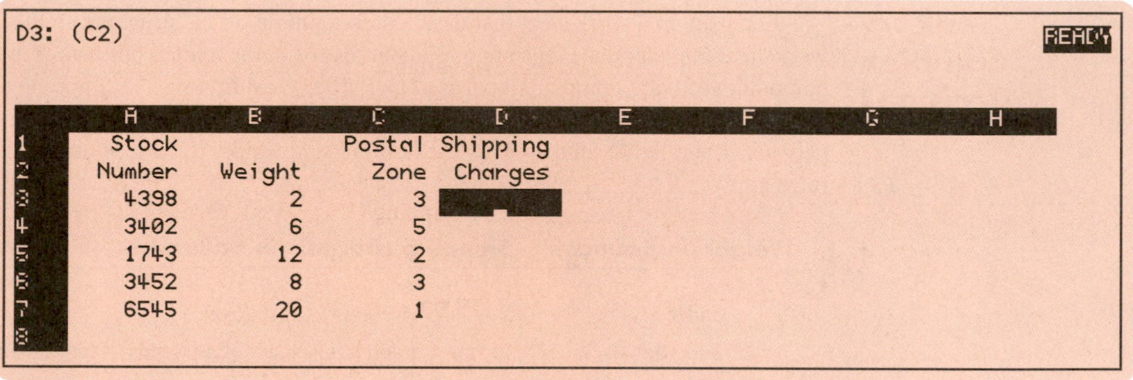

D3: (C2) READY

	A	B	C	D	E	F	G	H
1	Stock		Postal	Shipping				
2	Number	Weight	Zone	Charges				
3	4398	2	3					
4	3402	6	5					
5	1743	12	2					
6	3452	8	3					
7	6545	20	1					
8								

Step 3 Enter the formula for computing the shipping charges in column **D**. The shipping charges are computed using the same **@IF** function that you used in the last example.

@IF(condition,expression#1,expression#2)

This function says that **IF** the **condition** is true, then the result of **expression#1** is displayed in the active cell but **IF** the **condition** is false, then the result of **expression#2** is displayed. Recall that the commas take the place of the words THEN and ELSE in the actual Lotus 1-2-3 statement.

For this problem, the **@IF** expression must check the weight of each item and then select one of three formulas, depending on the value for the weight. One version of the decision logic is given below:

IF weight < 5

THEN shipping charge = 5 + (weight) * (postal zone)

ELSE

IF weight <= 10

THEN shipping charge = 10 + (weight –5) * (postal zone)

ELSE shipping charge = 15 + (weight –10) * (postal zone)

Notice that one **@IF** statement is nested inside (contained within) another. This is necessary because there are three choices and each **@IF** can only select between two alternatives.

- If the weight is under 5 pounds, the shipping charge is computed using 5 + (weight) * (postal zone).
- If the weight is 5 or more pounds, you need to check to see whether it is under 10 pounds. If it is, the shipping charge is computed using 10 + (weight – 5) * (postal zone). Note that (weight – 5) provides the weight in excess of 5 pounds. This is similar to the payroll formula for calculating overtime hours where you had to find the hours in excess of 40 to multiply by the overtime rate of pay.
- If the weight is not 10 pounds or less, then the shipping charge is computed using 15 + (weight – 10) * (postal zone). Again, note that (weight – 10) provides the weight in excess of 10 pounds.

Using Lotus 1-2-3 notation, each of the variable names (weight and postal zone) must be replaced with cell locations. Thus, for the first item (#4398 in row **3**), cell location **B3** would be entered in place of weight (because the weight of the item is located in cell **B3**). Likewise, in place of postal zone, cell location **C3** would be entered.

Using cell locations in place of variable names, the decision logic for the formula to be entered in cell **D3** (for item #4398) becomes the following:

IF **B3** < 5

THEN shipping charge = 5+**B3*C3**

ELSE

IF **B3** <= 10

THEN shipping charge = 10+(**B3**-5)***C3**

ELSE shipping charge = 15+(**B3**-10)***C3**

The corresponding Lotus 1-2-3 formula that should be entered into cell **D3** would look like the following:

```
@IF(B3<5,5+B3*C3,@IF(B3<=10,10+(B3-5)*C3,15+(B3-10)*C3))
```

Note the correspondence between the decision logic and the Lotus 1-2-3 statement:

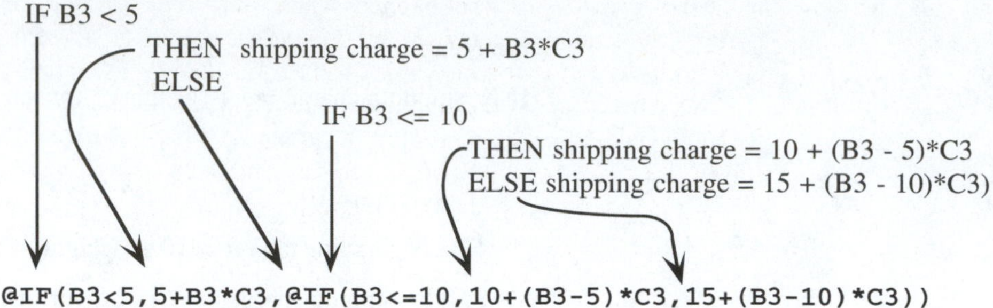

Study the structure of the above Lotus 1-2-3 statement. The following diagram may help:

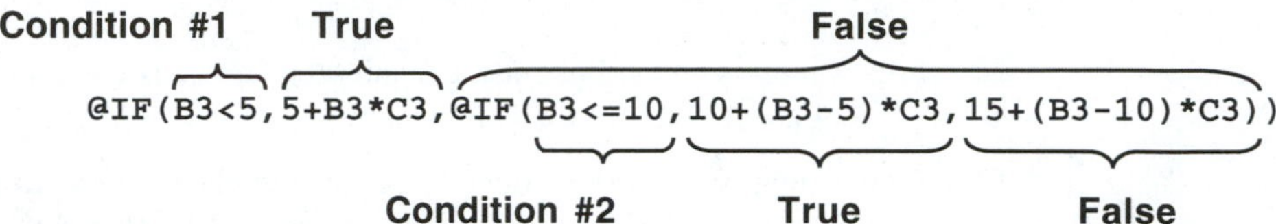

The above expression is not as complicated as it first appears. However, you may have to study it for a while to fully understand it.

After the formula is entered into cell **D3** and **[Enter]** is pressed, the screen will look as follows:

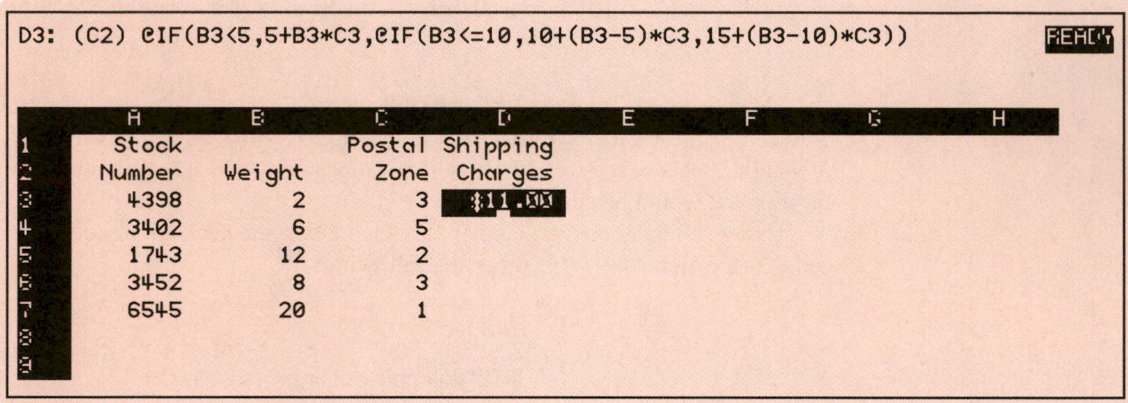

D3: (C2) @IF(B3<5,5+B3*C3,@IF(B3<=10,10+(B3-5)*C3,15+(B3-10)*C3)) READY

	A	B	C	D	E	F	G	H
1	Stock		Postal	Shipping				
2	Number	Weight	Zone	Charges				
3	4398	2	3	$11.00				
4	3402	6	5					
5	1743	12	2					
6	3452	8	3					
7	6545	20	1					
8								
9								

Step 4 The formulas for cells **D4** through **D7** can be copied from cell **D3** by using the following command: **/ C**(opy) **D3 ↵ D4.D7 ↵**.

Step 5 The total in cell **D9** can be calculated using the formula **@SUM(D3.D7) ↵**.

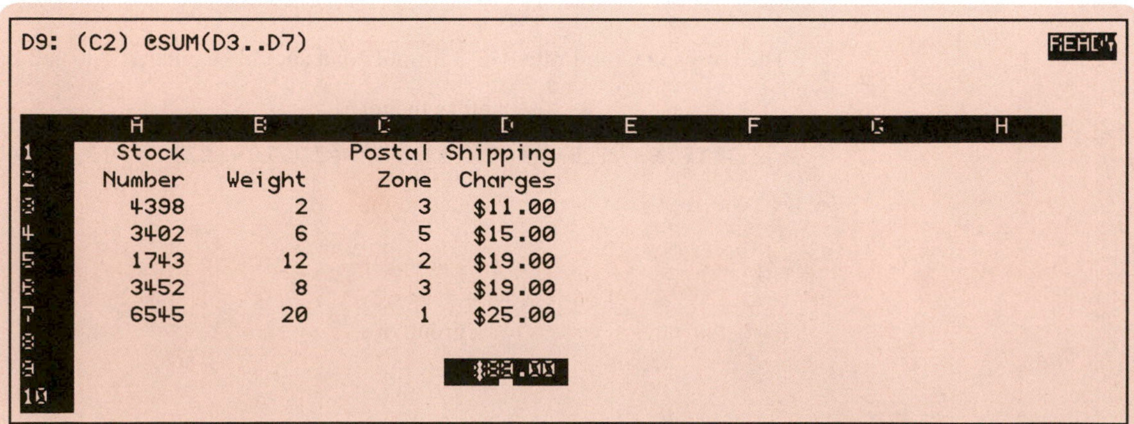

D9: (C2) @SUM(D3..D7) READY

	A	B	C	D	E	F	G	H
1	Stock		Postal	Shipping				
2	Number	Weight	Zone	Charges				
3	4398	2	3	$11.00				
4	3402	6	5	$15.00				
5	1743	12	2	$19.00				
6	3452	8	3	$19.00				
7	6545	20	1	$25.00				
8								
9				$89.00				
10								

Step 6 Use **/** **F**(ile) **S**(ave) to save the worksheet using the name **SHIP-V1**.

Step 7 Let's see what happens when some of the data are changed. For example, change the postal zone in cell **C5** to **8** and then press **[Enter]**. Notice how the value for the shipping charges changes to **$31.00** and the value for the total changes to **$101.00** as soon as **[Enter]** is pressed.

What happens to the computed values if there is a piece of data missing? Change cell **C5** again, but this time make it blank by pressing **/** **R**(ange) **E**(rase) **C5** ↵. The value for the shipping charges in cell **D5** is changed to **$15.00** and the total in cell **D9** is changed to **$85.00**. Because cell **C5** is blank, its value was assumed to be **0** by the formula in cell **D5**. Therefore, the value for the shipping charges was set to **$15.00** (because the postal zone in cell **C5** was assumed to be **0**, multiplying **0** times the weight resulted in **0** for the extra charge).

What should happen if a value is missing? Should it be set to zero or should the computer not do any calculations that involve the missing value? Usually, it is best to instruct the computer not to do the calculations. However, if you change the value in cell **C5** from blank to **Unknown**, to indicate that you do not know the postal zone, you get the same value, **$15.00**, for the shipping charges. This is because Lotus 1-2-3 considers the value of labels (text) to be zero. To deal with this problem, Lotus 1-2-3 has a special function, **@NA**, to indicate that a value is **N**ot **A**vailable. If you type **@NA** into cell **C5** and press **[Enter]**, Lotus 1-2-3 will display **NA** and will not do any calculations that involve the **NA** value. The screen will look as follows:

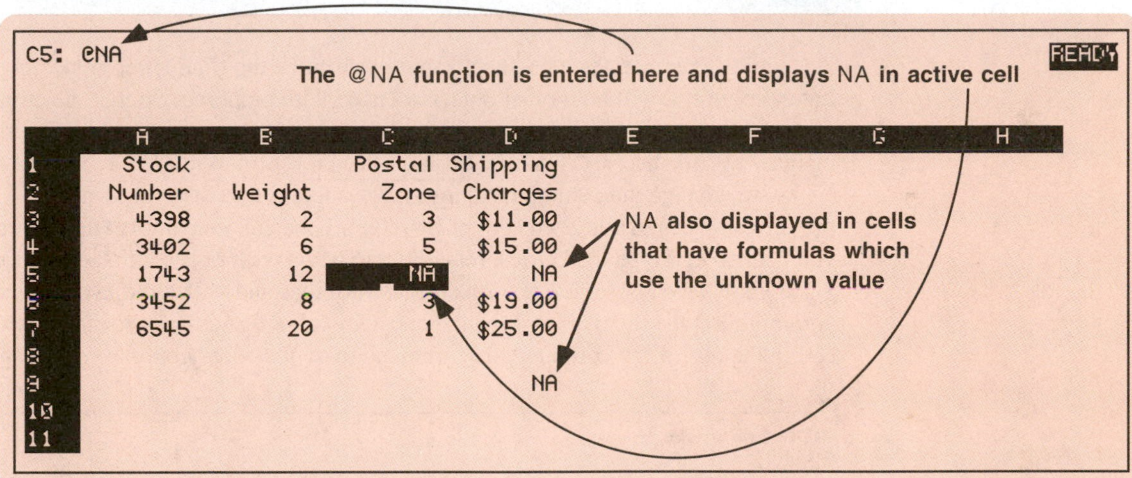

NA appears in cell **D5** because the formula in that cell uses a value from cell **C5**, but cell **C5** contains **@NA** and so the formula cannot be computed. Similarly, cell **D9** has a formula that uses information from cell **D5** and so cannot be computed. Be careful. If you type **NA** into a cell (i.e., if you leave off the **@**), Lotus 1-2-3 will consider it text and assign a value of zero to it. You must type **@NA** for the value to be considered **N**ot **A**vailable.

Now that the general format of the worksheet has been completed, you can use it to calculate the shipping charges of any of the items listed. In fact, you could do some What-If analysis, as you did with the payroll worksheet on page L51. For example, you could quickly determine what the new cost of shipping all the items would be if item number 1743 were shipped to Postal Zone 6 rather than 2. To do this, simply make cell **C5** active and type **6** ↵. The change in shipping charges would be displayed immediately for that item as well as the total for all items. Using a similar process, you could find the answers to many questions relating to shipping charges (both for individual items and total items) such as, What if the weight of an item increases or decreases? What if an item is shipped to another postal zone? What if more items are added to the list?

Extending the Gradebook Worksheet

As another example of **@IF** statements, let's extend the Gradebook worksheet, **GRADE-V2**, that you saved on page L66, so that it displays a final letter grade for each student. As you recall, that worksheet displayed the records for a group of students in a computer class and calculated the total points earned by all students.

Use / F(ile) R(etrieve) to retrieve the worksheet **GRADE-V2**.

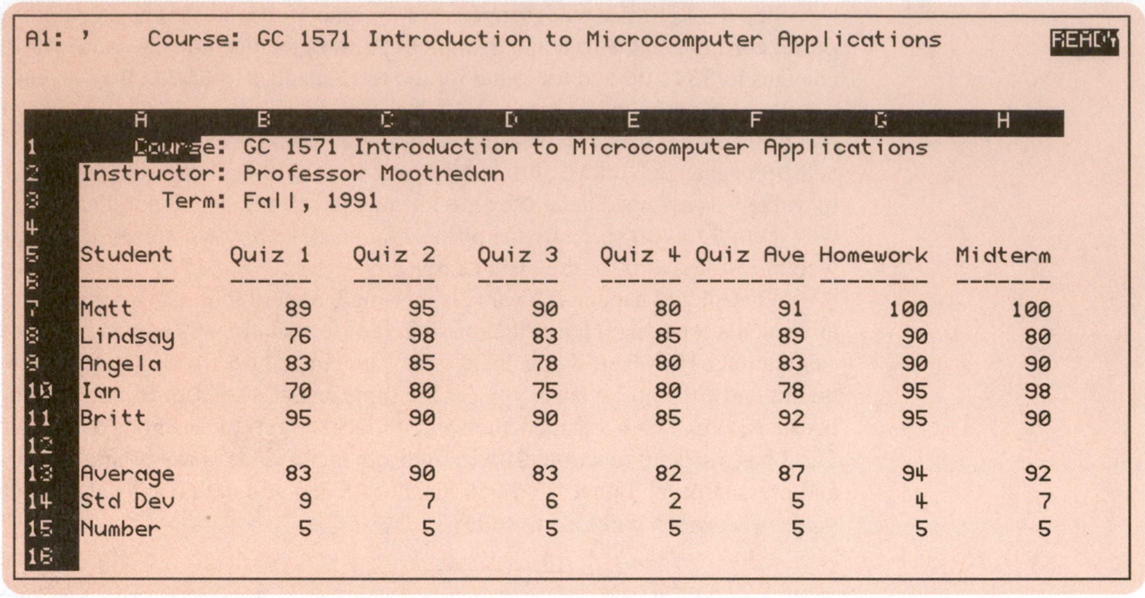

```
A1: '     Course: GC 1571 Introduction to Microcomputer Applications          READY

            A          B          C          D          E          F          G          H
1          Course: GC 1571 Introduction to Microcomputer Applications
2    Instructor: Professor Moothedan
3          Term: Fall, 1991
4
5    Student       Quiz 1     Quiz 2     Quiz 3     Quiz 4  Quiz Ave  Homework   Midterm
6    -------       ------     ------     ------     ------  --------  --------   -------
7    Matt              89         95         90         80        91       100       100
8    Lindsay           76         98         83         85        89        90        80
9    Angela            83         85         78         80        83        90        90
10   Ian               70         80         75         80        78        95        98
11   Britt             95         90         90         85        92        95        90
12
13   Average           83         90         83         82        87        94        92
14   Std Dev            9          7          6          2         5         4         7
15   Number             5          5          5          5         5         5         5
16
```

In this example, the worksheet should determine the final letter grade and display it in column **K**. Later, column **L** will hold other data associated with graphing. So that the entire worksheet will fit on the screen at one time, change the width of columns **B** through **L** to **6** by entering the following command: / **W**(orksheet) **C**(olumn) **C**(olumn-Range) **S**(et-Width) **B1.L1** ↵ **6** ↵.

Also, change the column headings in rows **5** and **6** to those shown below. You can do this by using the edit key **[F2]** to edit each cell, or by retyping the entries entirely (this is probably easier to do). If you choose to retype the entries, remember to begin each entry with a quotation mark, ", so that Lotus 1-2-3 knows the entries are text rather than formulas and will right justify them. To enter the dashes, you might retype them all, or type the entry for cell **K6** and then use the copy command to replicate this cell in the rest of the columns (the command to do the copy would be / **C**(opy) **K6** ↵ **B6.J6** ↵.

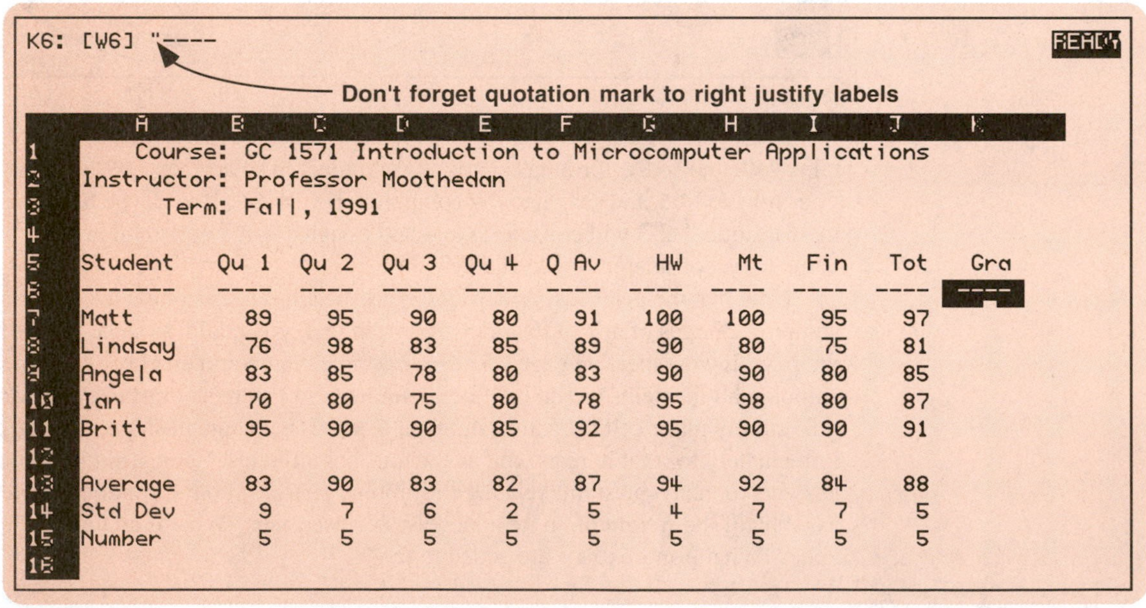

```
K6: [W6] "----                                                               READY
       Don't forget quotation mark to right justify labels

            A       B     C     D     E     F     G     H     I     J     K
1          Course: GC 1571 Introduction to Microcomputer Applications
2    Instructor: Professor Moothedan
3          Term: Fall, 1991
4
5    Student      Qu 1  Qu 2  Qu 3  Qu 4  Q Av    HW    Mt   Fin   Tot   Gra
6    -------      ----  ----  ----  ----  ----  ----  ----  ----  ----  ----
7    Matt           89    95    90    80    91   100   100    95    97
8    Lindsay        76    98    83    85    89    90    80    75    81
9    Angela         83    85    78    80    83    90    90    80    85
10   Ian            70    80    75    80    78    95    98    80    87
11   Britt          95    90    90    85    92    95    90    90    91
12
13   Average        83    90    83    82    87    94    92    84    88
14   Std Dev         9     7     6     2     5     4     7     7     5
15   Number          5     5     5     5     5     5     5     5     5
16
```

For this example, we will assume the following grading curve:

Total points	***Letter grade***
90 – 100	A
80 – 89	B
70 – 79	C
65 – 69	D
0 – 64	F

The decision logic for selecting the proper grade would be

IF Total >= 90
THEN Grade = A
ELSE
    IF Total >= 80
    THEN Grade = B
    ELSE
        IF Total >= 70
        THEN Grade = C
        ELSE
            IF Total >= 65
            THEN Grade = D
            ELSE Grade = F

To change this into the proper Lotus 1-2-3 form, you would have to enter the following into cell **K7**:

```
@IF(J7>=90,"   @IF(J7>=90,"   A",@IF(J7>=80,"   B",@IF(J7>=70,"
C",@IF(J7>=65,"   D","   F"))))
```

Study this formula very carefully to be sure you understand how the **@IF** statements have been nested as the decision logic requires. Also, be careful when you type this formula.

- You must have the **@** to the left of each **IF**.
- You must have the **(** to the right of each **IF**.
- In order to have the letter grades centered in their respective cells, three blank spaces were inserted inside the quotation marks for each grade.
- Each letter grade must be enclosed in quotation marks (e.g., **"   A"**).
- The number of right and left parentheses must match (hence the need for the four right-parentheses at the end of the statement).

If you make an error, use the standard editing techniques to modify the formula. If you see an error after the formula has been entered into a cell, you can use the *Edit* feature (press the **[F2]** key).

After you have correctly entered the formula into cell **K7**, you must copy it into cells **K8** through **K11** by using the copy command: **/ C**(opy) **K7 ↵ K8.K11 ↵**

```
K7: [W6] @IF(J7>=90,"    A",@IF(J7>=80,"    B",@IF(J7>=70,"    C",@IF(J7>=65,"READY

      A           B       C       D       E       F       G       H       I       J       K
1       Course: GC 1571 Introduction to Microcomputer Applications
2  Instructor: Professor Moothedan
3         Term: Fall, 1991
4
5  Student       Qu 1    Qu 2    Qu 3    Qu 4    Q Av     HW      Mt     Fin     Tot     Gra
6  -------       ----    ----    ----    ----    ----    ----    ----    ----    ----    ----
7  Matt            89      95      90      80      91     100     100      95      97       A
8  Lindsay         76      98      83      85      89      90      80      75      81       B
9  Angela          83      85      78      80      83      90      90      80      85       B
10 Ian             70      80      75      80      78      95      98      80      87       B
11 Britt           95      90      90      85      92      95      90      90      91       A
12
13 Average         83      90      83      82      87      94      92      84      88
14 Std Dev          9       7       6       2       5       4       7       7       5
15 Number           5       5       5       5       5       5       5       5       5
16
17
```

Use **/** **F**(ile) **S**(ave) to save the worksheet under the name **GRADE-V4**.

Looking up Values in a Table

In the gradebook problem, we used IF/THEN/ELSE statements to assign letter grades to students by comparing their total points to a predetermined grading curve. The curve is displayed in the following table:

Total points	*Letter grade*
90 – 100	A
80 – 89	B
70 – 79	C
65 – 69	D
0 – 64	F

The IF/THEN/ELSE statements compared the total points of a particular student with values on the above table and then selected the letter grade assigned to those values. In essence, the IF/THEN/ELSE statements were designed to *look up* the proper letter grade on the table. Lotus 1-2-3 has a pair of special *lookup* functions, **@VLOOKUP** and **@HLOOKUP**, that are designed to do the same task. Both of these functions work the same way except that **@VLOOKUP** looks up values on a **V**ertical table while **@HLOOKUP** looks up values on a **H**orizontal table.

To see how these functions work, let's modify the worksheet **GRADE-V4** so that it uses a lookup table rather than IF/THEN/ELSE statements to select a letter grade for each student. This will be a two-step process: (1) the grading curve table will be entered into the worksheet and (2) the lookup formulas will be entered into the proper cells in column **K**.

Step 1 Create the lookup table by entering into the worksheet the values given in the following screen dump. Notice that the body of the table (excluding the column headings, which are for reference only) is located in the range **M7.O11**. Also notice that the table has been rearranged so that the grade of **F** is at top and the grade of **A** is at the bottom. This is necessary because tables used with the lookup functions must be written with the first column in ascending order.

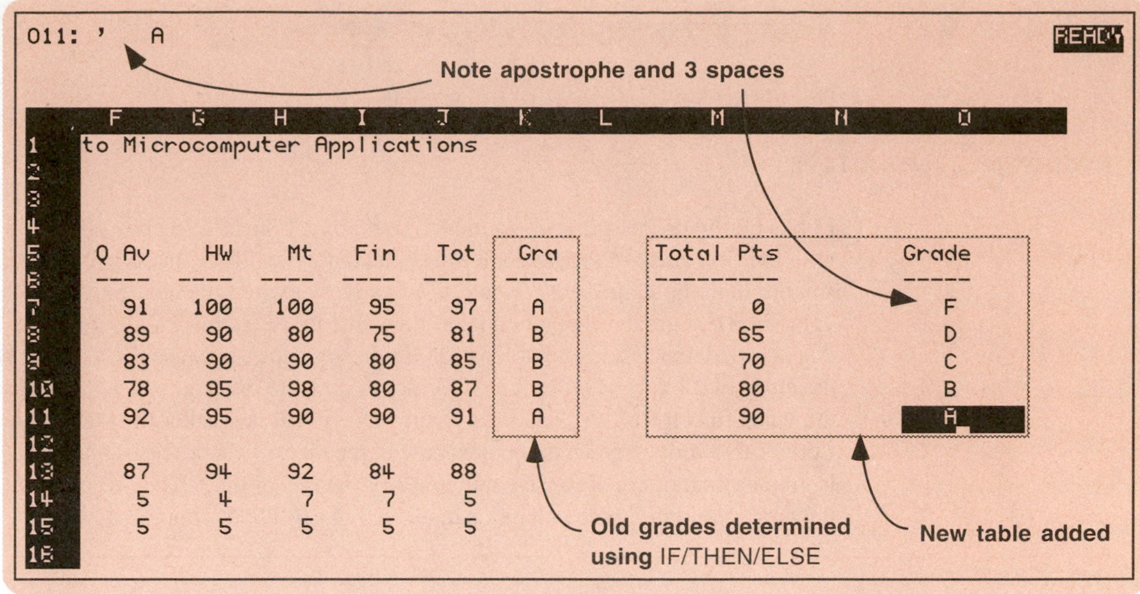

Step 2 Now, we need to modify the formula in cell **K7** so that it looks up the grade for Matt in the grading curve table rather than selecting the grade with an IF/THEN/ELSE statement. To do this, we will use the vertical lookup function **@VLOOKUP**. This function has the following form:

@VLOOKUP(x,range,column-offset)

x is the key that is to be compared to the values in the first column of the table. In this example, **x** would be the cell address, **J7**, of the total points for Matt. In general, **x** can be any value greater than or equal to the first value in the table. If it is too small (in this case, less than 0), an error message (**ERR**) will be displayed; if it is too large (in this case, over 90), the last value in the appropriate column will be displayed.

range is the location of the table in the worksheet. In this example, the body of the table (i.e., the part not including the column headings) is located in the range **M7.O11**. In general, the range can be any range name or address. The values in the first column of the range must be in ascending order.

column-offset is the number of columns to the right of the first column that the sought-after label or value resides (i.e., the column that contains the letter grades). The first column is numbered 0 (e.g., column **M**, which contains the total points, is considered column 0); the second column is numbered 1 (e.g., the blank column **N**); the third column is numbered 2 (e.g., the column **O**, which contains the actual letter grades, is considered column 2).

The entry for cell **K7** (the letter grade for Matt) would be **@VLOOKUP(J7,M7.O11,2)**.

J7 is the cell address that contains the key (total points) that will be used to select a letter grade from the table.

M7.O11 is the range that contains the body of the table.

2 is the number of columns to the right of the first column in the table where the letter grades reside.

Keystroke	Action Resulting from Keystroke
[arrow]	Use the [arrow] keys to make cell **K7** active.

@VLOOKUP(J7,M7.O11,2) ↵

Looks up the proper grade in the table. To do this, Lotus 1-2-3 compares the value in cell **J7** (i.e., **97**) with the first entry in the first column of the table (i.e., the value **0** in cell **M7**). If the value in **M7** is smaller than the value in **J7**, Lotus 1-2-3 moves down to the next row in the table. However, if the value in **M7** is greater than or equal to the value in **J7**, Lotus 1-2-3 will move **2** columns to the right and display the letter grade at that location. In this example, because the value in **M7** (i.e., **0**) is smaller than the entry in **J7** (i.e., **97**), Lotus 1-2-3 moves down to the next row and compares the value in **J7** with the value in cell **M8** (i.e., **65**). Again, the value in **M8** is smaller than the value in **J7** (i.e., **65** < **97**) so Lotus 1-2-3 moves down to the next row in the table. This process continues until the value in column **M** is greater than or equal to the value in **J7** or the end of the table is reached. In either case the label in the corresponding grade column is displayed in cell **K7** (it should be **A**).

After you have correctly entered the formula into cell **K7**, you should copy it into cells **K8** through **K11** by using the copy command: **/ C**(opy) **K7** ↵ **K8.K11** ↵.

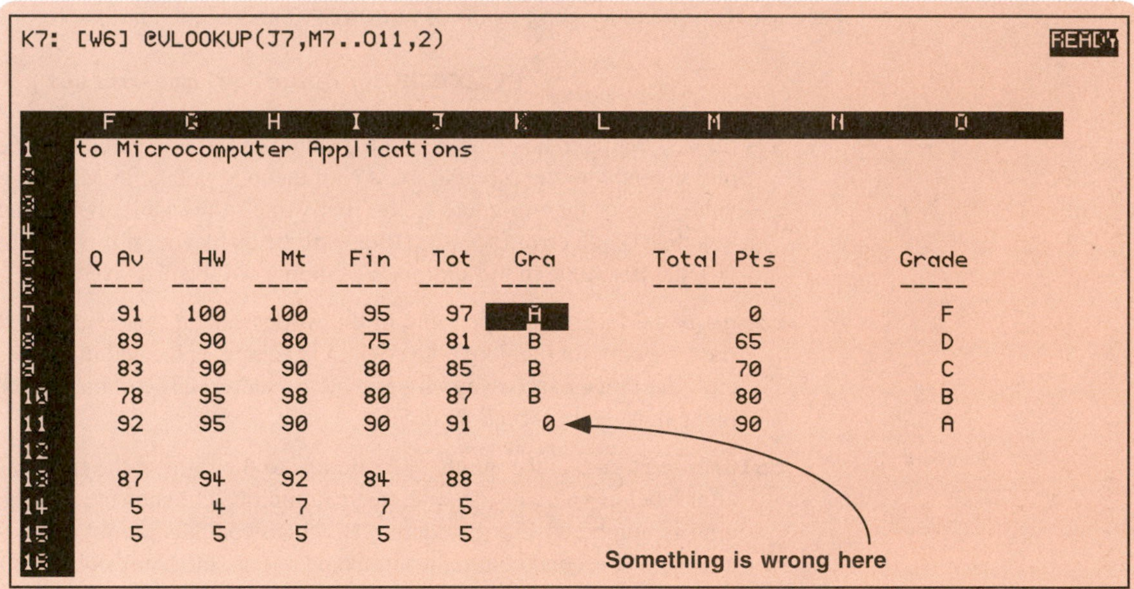

Notice that the letter grade in cell **K11** is not correct. To check the formula in cell **K11**, use the **[arrow]** keys to make that cell active.

```
K11: [W6] @VLOOKUP(J11,M11..O15,2)                                    READY

      F      G      H      I      J      K      L      M      N      O
 1  to Microcomputer Applications
 2
 3
 4
 5   Q Av    HW     Mt    Fin    Tot    Gra         Total Pts         Grade
 6   ----   ----   ----   ----   ----   ----        ---------         -----
 7     91    100    100     95     97   A                   0           F
 8     89     90     80     75     81   B                  65           D
 9     83     90     90     80     85   B                  70           C
10     78     95     98     80     87   B                  80           B
11     92     95     90     90     91      0               90           A
12
13     87     94     92     84     88
14      5      4      7      7      5
15      5      5      5      5      5
16
```

The formula is not correct

Notice that the table range in cell **K11** is not correct. The formula lists the range as **M11.O15** rather than **M7.O11**. Recall from page L45 that when Lotus 1-2-3 copies a formula it adjusts the formula to fit the new range of cells. Thus, when the formula from cell **K7** was copied into cell **K11** all the references were adjusted accordingly (i.e., the row numbers were increased by 4). Thus, **J7** was converted to **J11**, **M7** was converted to **M11**, and **O11** was converted to **O15**.

Most of the time, this type of adjustment makes sense. However, in this case, we want the range that identifies the lookup table to remain the same no matter where the lookup formula is located. We accomplish this by using what is called **absolute referencing.** This type of referencing tells Lotus 1-2-3 *not* to adjust the cell references when it copies a formula. To change from **relative referencing** (where the formulas are automatically adjusted) to absolute referencing (where the formulas are not adjusted) you simply place a dollar sign (**$**) in front of the row number or column letter in the original formula. Thus,

@VLOOKUP(J7,M7.O11,2) is changed into **@VLOOKUP(J7,M7.O11,2)**.

Notice that dollar signs are not used in cell reference **J7**. That is because we want the cell references for the key (i.e., column **J**) to be adjusted during the copy (i.e., we want **J7** to become **J11** when the formula is copied but we want **M7.O11** to remain the same).

Keystroke	Action Resulting from Keystroke
[arrow]	Use the **[arrow]** keys to make cell **K7** active again. You may either edit the cell (press the **[F2]** key) or retype it as follows:
@VLOOKUP(J7,M7.O11,2) ↵	Looks up the proper grade in the table.

After you have fixed the formula in cell **K7**, copy it into cells **K8** through **K11** by using the copy command: **/ C**(opy) **K7** ↵ **K8.K11** ↵. If you then use the **[arrow]** keys to make cell **K11** active, the screen will look as follows:

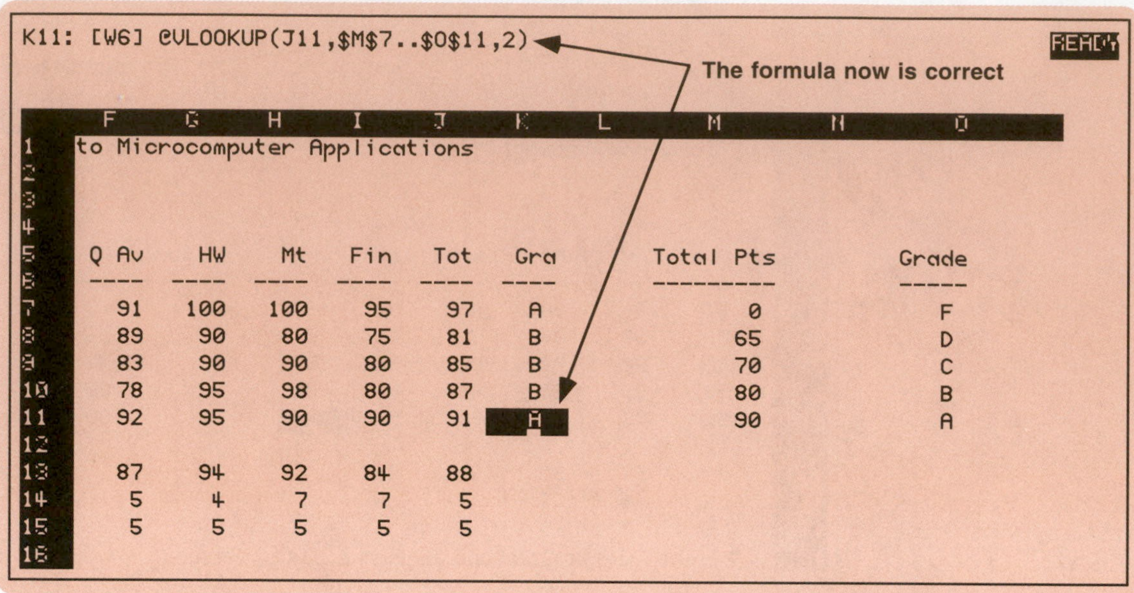

Notice that cell **J7** was correctly adjusted to **J11** but that cells **M7.O11** were not adjusted because of the dollar signs.

Use **/ F**(ile) **S**(ave) to save the worksheet under the name **GRADE-V5**.

Finally, use **/ Q**(uit) **Y**(es) to quit the program. This will return control to the DOS environment.

TO TAKE A BREAK Remove diskette(s). To resume (hard disk): Insert *Data* diskette, type **C:** ↵, **CD\123** ↵. To resume (two drive): Insert diskettes, type **B:** ↵.

Creating Graphs

To visually represent data entered on a worksheet, Lotus 1-2-3 can create graphs in the following forms:

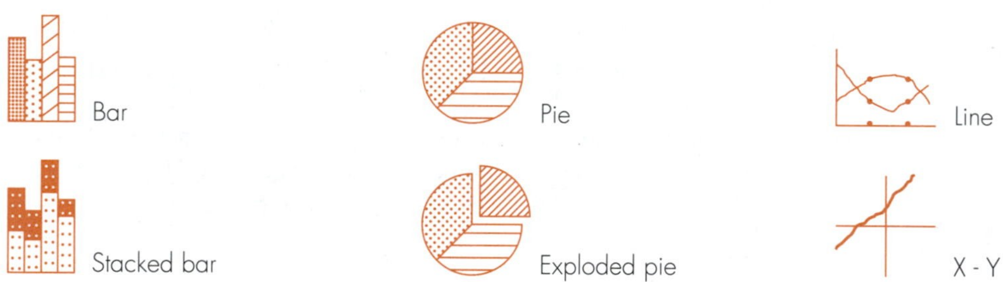

The Lotus 1-2-3 *Graphics* feature is used to create and view the graphs (to actually view a graph, your monitor must have a graphics display adapter attached). To print a graph you may use the **[PrintScreen]** key to dump a graph displayed on the monitor to the printer or the PrintGraph program that came with Lotus 1-2-3 program. To print a graph you must have a graphics printer.

Let's create a bar graph using the data from the payroll worksheet, **PAY-V10**, that you saved on page L97. First, a number of different graphs will be constructed and displayed on the screen. The last graph will be printed using the **[PrintScreen]** key and then it will be printed using the PrintGraph program.

In order to use **[PrintScreen]** to print a graph you must execute the DOS **GRAPHICS** command before accessing Lotus 1-2-3. This command allows you to do screen dumps of graphic material.

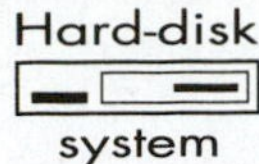

IF YOU ARE USING A HARD-DISK SYSTEM, do the following (it is assumed that there is a subdirectory called DOS on your hard disk that contains all the DOS files:

Keystroke	Action Resulting from Keystroke
`C:\DOS\GRAPHICS` ↵	
	Executes the external DOS command called **GRAPHICS**.
`CD\123` ↵	Switches to the **123** subdirectory, if necessary.
`LOTUS` ↵	Loads the 1-2-3 Access System program and displays its menu.
`1`	Loads the Lotus 1-2-3 program and displays a blank worksheet.

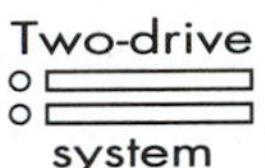

IF YOU ARE USING A TWO- DRIVE SYSTEM, If you followed the directions on page L8 for formatting your *Lotus Data/Boot* diskette and copied the **GRAPHICS.COM** program to that diskette, you do not need the DOS diskette to do the following. However, if you did not copy the **GRAPHICS.COM** program, replace your *Lotus Data/Boot* diskette in drive A: with the DOS diskette before doing the following:

Keystroke	Action Resulting from Keystroke
`A:GRAPHICS` ↵	Executes the external DOS command called **GRAPHICS**. If necessary, replace the DOS diskette in drive A: with your *Lotus Data/Boot* diskette.
`B:` ↵	Switches to the B: drive.
`LOTUS` ↵	Loads the 1-2-3 Access System program and displays its menu.
`1`	Loads the Lotus 1-2-3 program and displays a blank worksheet.

Now, you are ready to begin creating, displaying, and printing graphs.

Keystroke	Action Resulting from Keystroke
`/`	Displays the main menu.
`F`	Selects **File**.
`R`	Selects **Retrieve**.

Continued . . .

Keystroke	Action Resulting from Keystroke
PAY-V10 ↵	Loads the worksheet **PAY-V10** into the program.

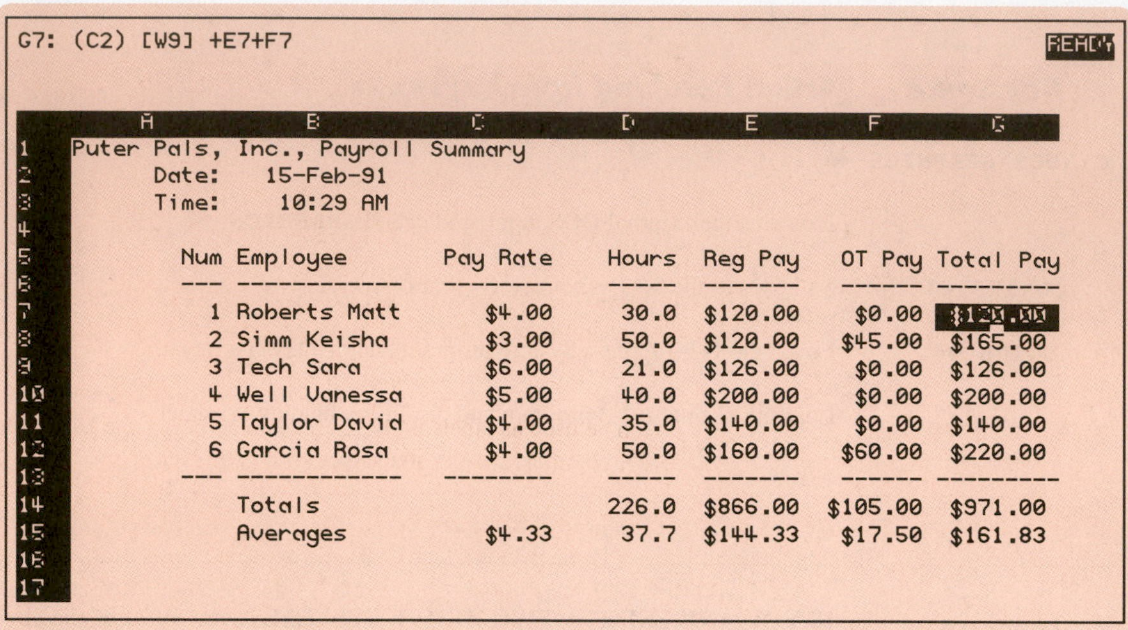

Keystroke	Action Resulting from Keystroke
[arrow]	Use the **[arrow]** keys to make cell **A17** active. This is not really necessary, but moving the cursor to a blank cell will make the control panel a little easier to read.
/	Displays the main menu.
G	Selects **Graph** and displays its menu and the graph settings window:

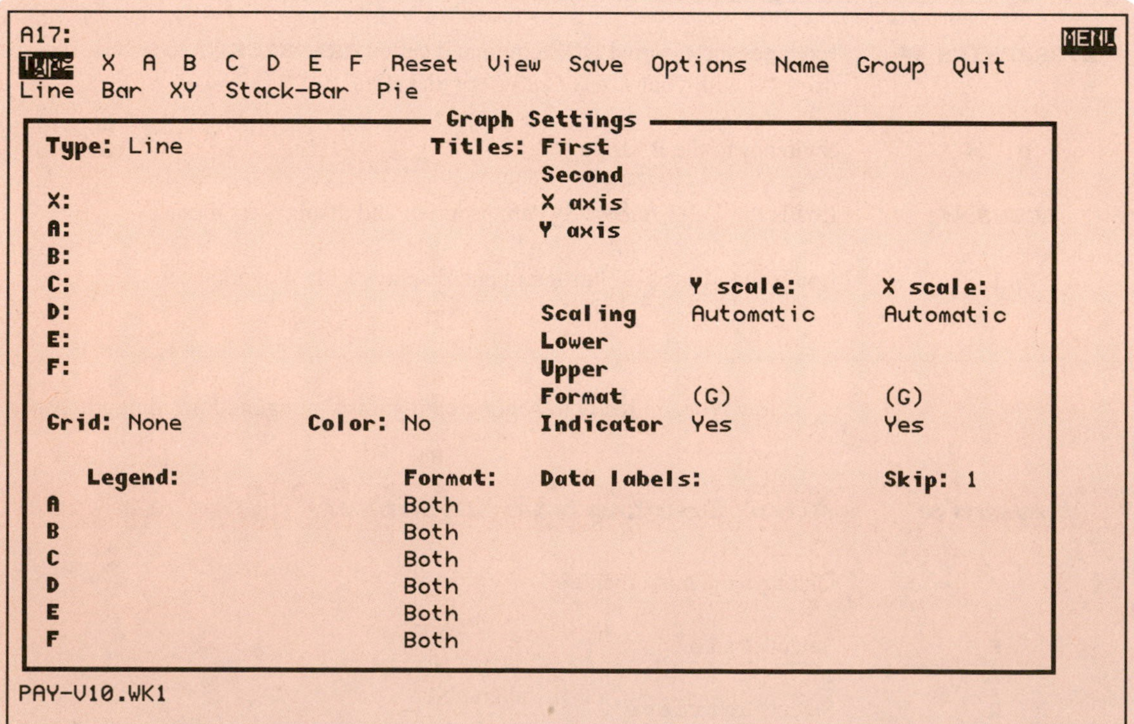

Continued . . .

Keystroke	Action Resulting from Keystroke
T	Selects **Type** and displays its menu.
B	Selects **Bar** and returns to the **Graph** menu. At this point, Lotus 1-2-3 knows what type of graph to create (a **Bar** graph), but it does not know what data to graph.
	Lotus 1-2-3 allows you to graph six different ranges of data simultaneously; these are selected by using the letters **A**, **B**, **C**, **D**, **E**, and **F** in the menu. For this first example, you will graph only one range. Later, you can add other ranges to make the graph more extensive.
	You also may select a range for the labels to be used in the graph.
X	Specifies that you want to define a range for the graph labels and asks you to **Enter x-axis range**. You may select the range either by typing the range or by using the **POINT** method with the **[arrow]** keys (see p. L39).
B7.B12 ↵	Specifies the cells to be used as labels in the graph (the names of the employees) and returns to the **Graph** menu. Now, you must specify the values to be graphed.
A	Specifies that you want to define a range of values to be graphed and asks you to **Enter first data range**. This is the list of values to be graphed.
G7.G12 ↵	Specifies the range of values to be graphed and returns to the **Graph** menu. At this point, each of the entries you have made is listed in the graph settings window:

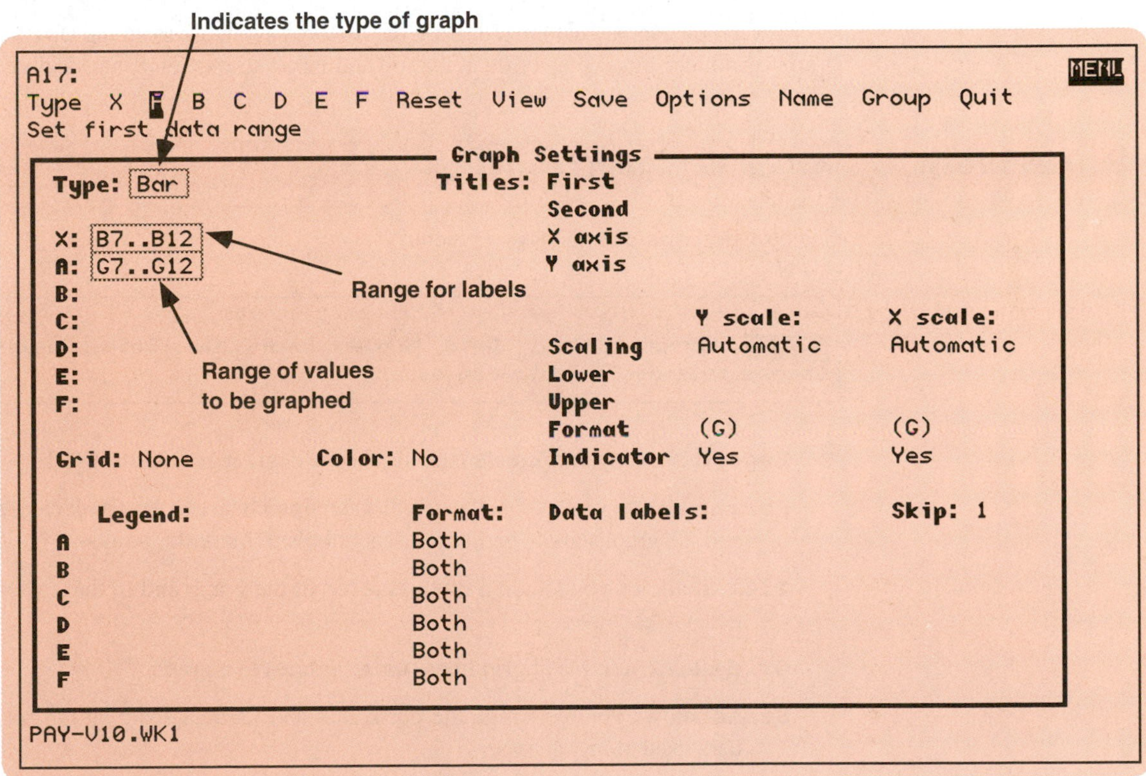

Keystroke	Action Resulting from Keystroke
	To see the graph on the screen, select **View**.
V	Selects **View** and displays the graph on the screen.

Continued . . .

Keystroke	Action Resulting from Keystroke

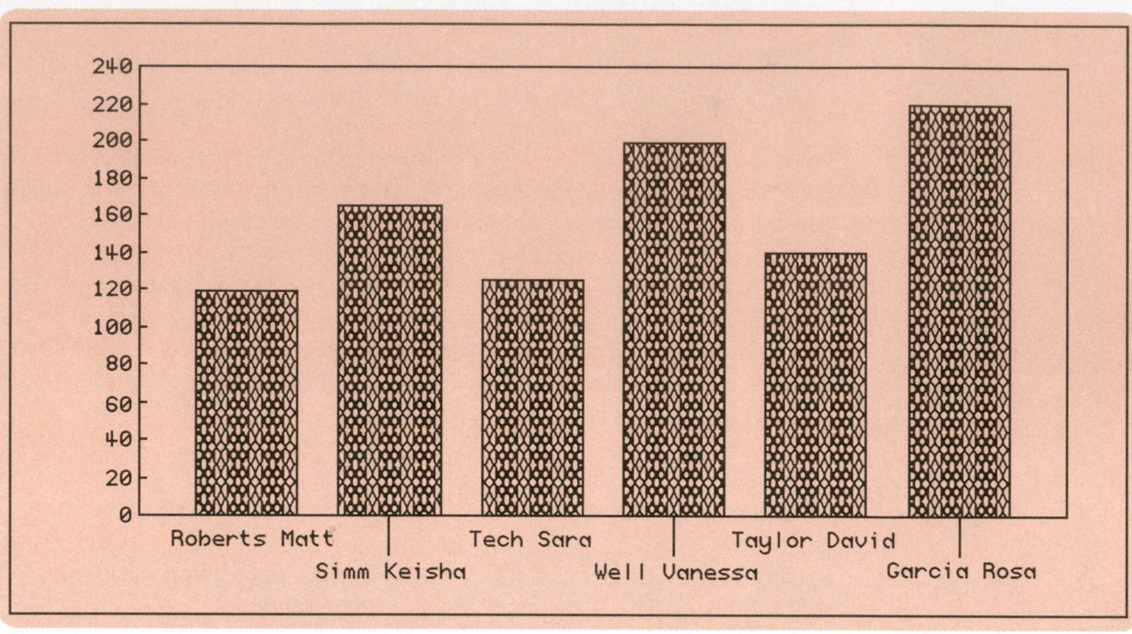

Keystroke	Action Resulting from Keystroke
[Esc]	Exits from view mode (the graph disappears from the screen) and displays the **Graph** menu.

The graph can be customized using the features available from the **Options** menu. Let's make the graph a bit nicer by adding a title at the top and labels to the horizontal and vertical axes.

Keystroke	Action Resulting from Keystroke
O	Selects **Options** and displays its menu:

Legend allows you to create legends for the data ranges, A through F.

Format allows you to specify whether data points are to be connected when producing line and *XY* graphs and whether to use symbols to mark the points.

Titles allows you to add a title to the top of the graph and to the *X* (horizontal) and *Y* (vertical) axes.

Grid allows you to add grid lines (for reference) to a graph.

Scale allows you to change the horizontal and vertical scale and to set the format of numbers used along an axis.

Continued . . .

Keystroke	Action Resulting from Keystroke
	Color allows you to display graphs in color (you must have a color monitor). **B&W** turns off color and displays graphs in black and white. **Data-Labels** allows you to use the contents of a range as labels for bars or points in a graph.
T	Selects **Titles** and displays its menu:

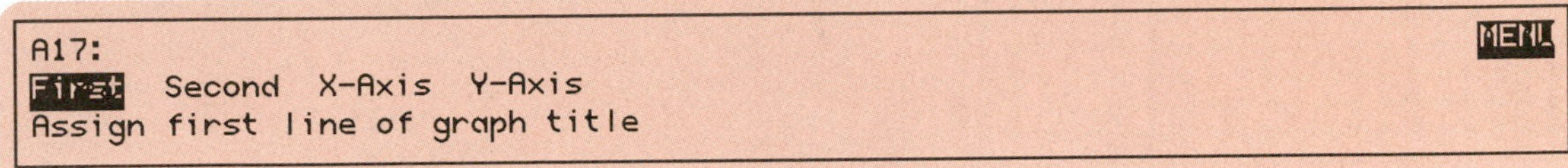

Keystroke	Action Resulting from Keystroke
	First allows you to assign a title to the first line of the graph. **Second** allows you to assign a title to the second line of the graph. **X-Axis** allows you to assign a title to the *X* axis. **Y-Axis** allows you to assign a title to the *Y* axis.
F	Selects **First** and asks you to **Enter first line of graph title**.
Puter Pals, Inc. Payroll ↵	
	Specifies the title. Notice that, after **[Enter]** is pressed, the title is displayed next to **Titles: First** in the upper right-hand corner of the graph settings window. Control is returned to the **Options** menu.
T	Selects **Titles** and displays its menu.
S	Selects **Second** and asks you to **Enter second line of graph title**.
Week of 9 Sep 91 ↵	
	Specifies the title. Notice that this second title is displayed next to **Second**.
T	Selects **Titles** and displays its menu.
X	Selects **X-axis** and asks you to **Enter x-axis title**.
Employee Names ↵	Specifies the title for the *X* axis.
T	Selects **Titles** and displays its menu.
Y	Selects **Y-axis** and asks you to **Enter y-axis title**.
Total Pay ↵	Specifies the title for the *Y* axis. At this point, the graph settings should look like the following:

Continued . . .

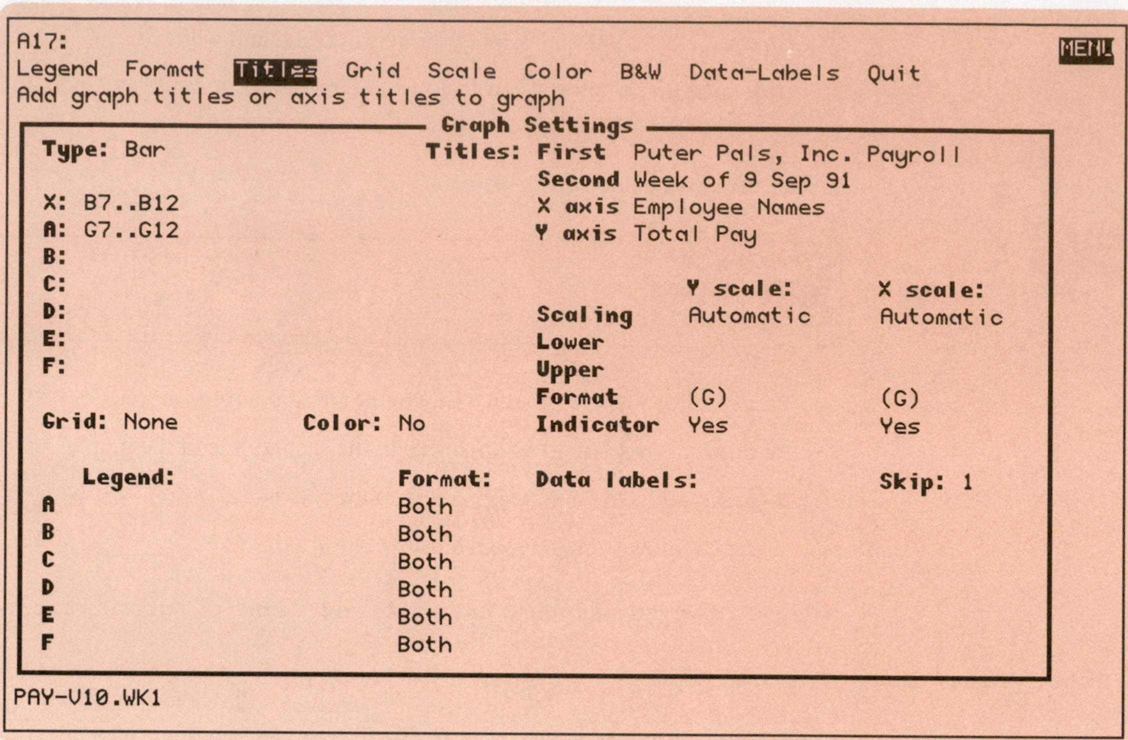

If you have made a mistake and want to change one of the options, you may do so by selecting the option again and typing the new value.

To view the graph, you first must leave the **`Options`** menu.

[Esc] Exits the **`Options`** menu and displays the **`Graph`** menu again.

`V` Selects **`View`** and displays the graph on the screen.

Continued . . .

Keystroke	Action Resulting from Keystroke

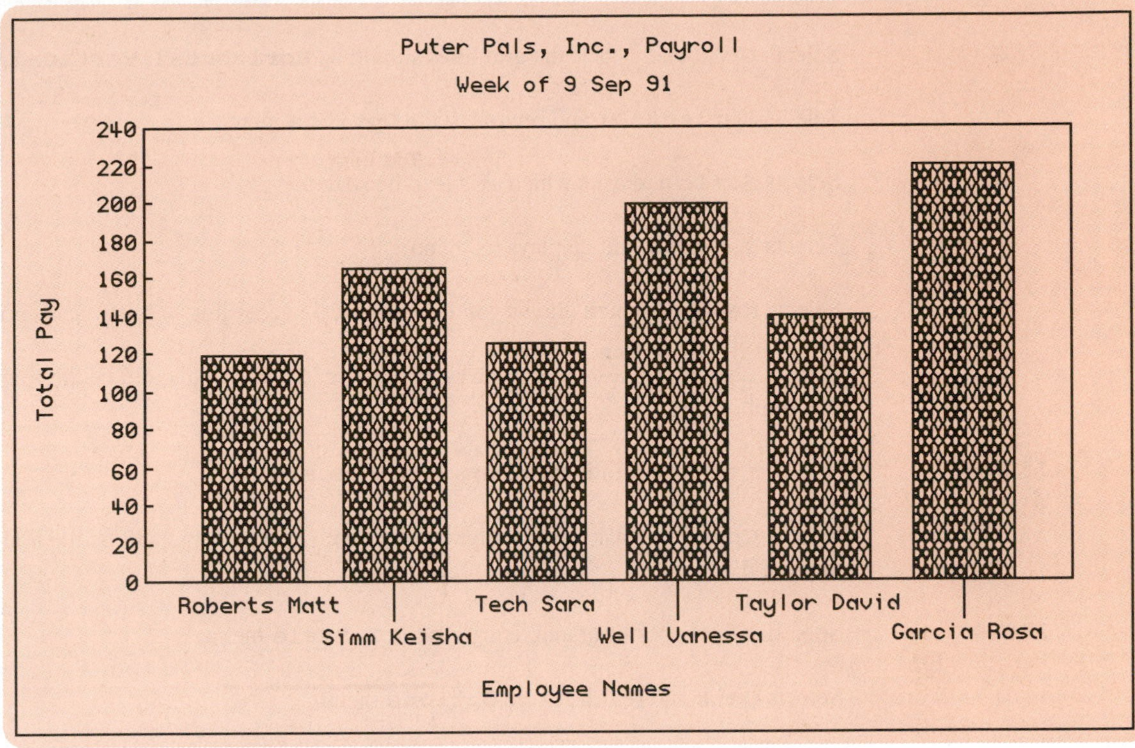

Keystroke	Action Resulting from Keystroke
[Esc]	Exits **View** and displays the **Graph** menu again.

The data may be displayed in a line graph or pie graph by selecting the appropriate graph type from the **Type** menu. Let's produce a line graph of the data and use the **Options** menu to change the scale of the *Y* axis and to add horizontal grid lines and data labels.

Keystroke	Action Resulting from Keystroke
T	Selects **Type** and displays its menu.
L	Selects **Line** and returns to the **Graph** menu.

Continued . . .

Keystroke	Action Resulting from Keystroke
O	Selects **Options** and displays its menu.
G	Selects **Grid** and asks if the grid lines should be **Horizontal**, **Vertical**, or **Both**.
H	Selects **Horizontal** and returns to the **Options** menu.
S	Selects **Scale** and asks which axis is to be scaled.
Y	Selects **Y-Scale** and displays its menu.
M	Selects **Manual**, which allows you to set the scale according to lower and upper limits you specify.
L	Selects **Lower** and asks you to **Enter lower limit**. This will be the lowest value displayed on the graph.
110 ↵	Specifies the lower limit and returns to the **Y-Scale** menu.
U	Selects **Upper** and asks you to **Enter upper limit**. This will be the highest value displayed on the graph.
230 ↵	Specifies the upper limit and returns to the **Y-Scale** menu.
Q	Selects **Quit** and returns to the **Options** menu.
D	Selects **Data-Labels** and displays its menu. This option allows you to use the contents of a range of cells as labels for the points displayed on the graph. In this example, we will use the total sales for each employee.
A	Selects **A** and requests the range to be used.
G7.G12 ↵	Specifies the range and asks where the label is to be placed on the graph in relation to the data point.
A	Selects **Above** and returns to the **Data-Labels** menu.
Q	Selects **Quit** and returns to the **Options** menu.
Q	Selects **Quit** and returns to the **Graph** menu.
	Notice how all of the information is displayed in the graph settings window for reference.
V	Selects **View** and displays the graph.

Continued . . .

Keystroke	Action Resulting from Keystroke

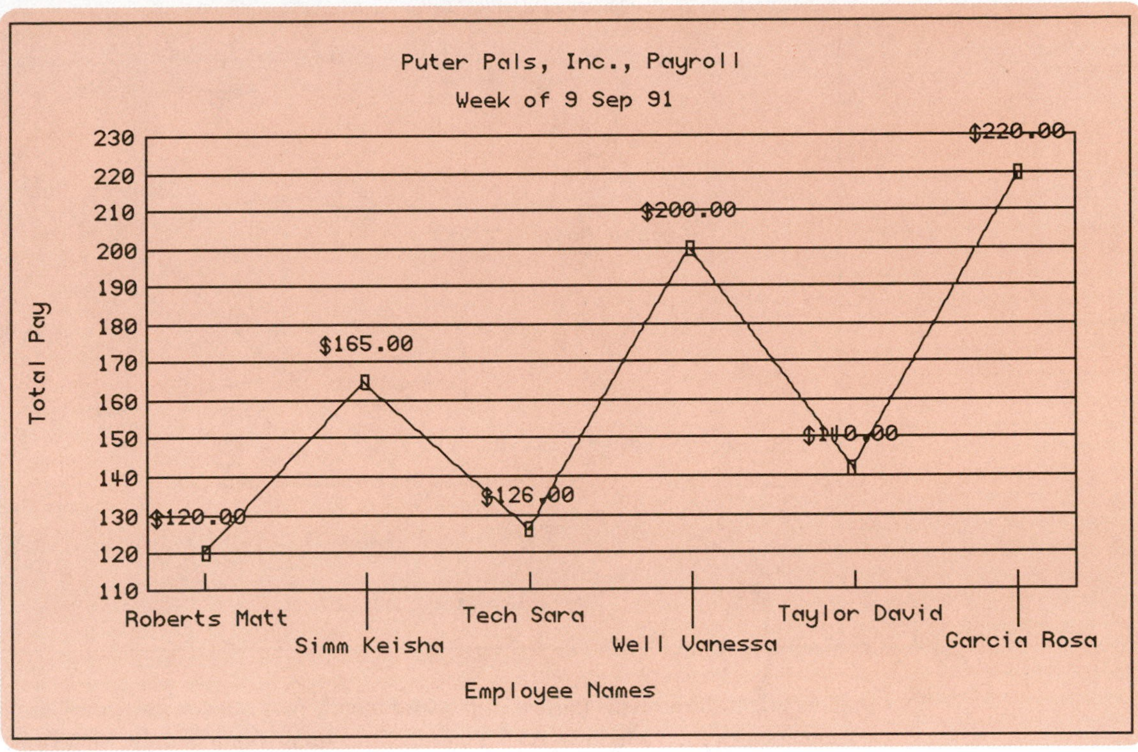

Keystroke	Action Resulting from Keystroke
[Esc]	Exits view and returns control to the **`Graph`** menu.

To construct a pie graph, simply select **`Pie`** from the **`Type`** menu. Lotus 1-2-3 will use the **`X`** range (employee names) as pie wedge labels, the **`A`** range (total pay) to calculate the sizes of the wedges, and the **`B`** range to specify the shadings or colors for each pie wedge (see below).

Keystroke	Action Resulting from Keystroke
`T`	Selects **`Type`** and displays its menu.
`P`	Selects **`Pie`** and returns control to the **`Graph`** menu.
`V`	Selects **`View`** and displays the graph on the screen.

Continued . . .

Keystroke	Action Resulting from Keystroke

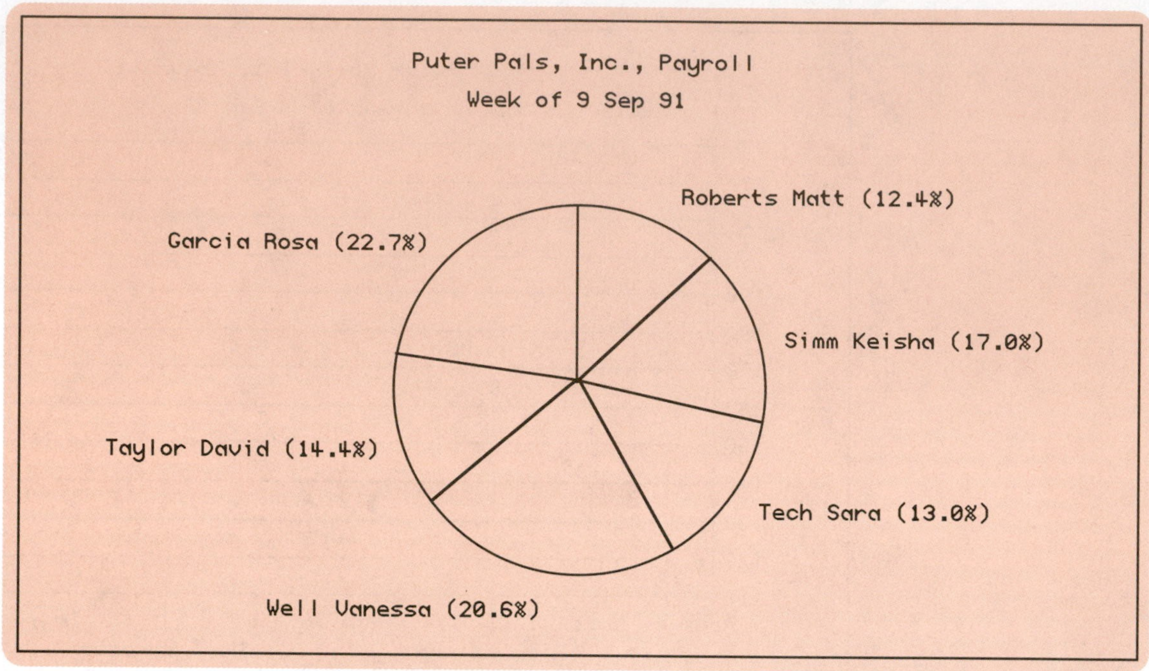

This graph shows what portion of the total money paid out was earned by each employee as well as the percentage of the whole for each section of the graph. For example, Matt Roberts's pay of $120 accounts for 12.4% of the total pay earned by the six employees (120/971 = 12.4%). The percentages are automatically calculated and displayed and cannot be suppressed.

[Esc]	Exits **`View`** and returns to the **`Graph`** menu.
[Esc]	Exits **`Graph`** and returns to the main menu.
[Esc]	Exits the main menu and returns control to **`READY`** mode.

Fancy Pie Graphs

You can make the pie graph more interesting by adding shading or color or by exploding (emphasizing) one or more of the pie wedges. Lotus 1-2-3 offers eight different shading patterns (coded 0 through 7) for monochrome monitors and up to eight colors for systems with an EGA color display and video card. We will only discuss different shading patterns.

To produce a graph with different shading patterns, you first create a range of data in your worksheet that lists the codes of the shading patterns you want to use. Then, you tell Lotus 1-2-3 to use those patterns when it creates the graph.

To illustrate this, let's make a pie chart of the total pay in worksheet **`PAY-V10`** that uses different shading codes for the pie wedges (begin from **`READY`** mode in worksheet **`PAY-V10`**).

Keystroke	Action Resulting from Keystroke
[arrow]	Use the **[arrow]** keys to make cell **`H7`** active.
	You need to enter the shading codes into cells **`H7`** through **`H12`** (one code for each employee). For this example, it really does not matter which pattern is associated with which employee, so you could just enter the numbers **`1`** through **`6`** in the cells.
	You could enter the codes manually, or you could use a formula, or you could use the *Fill* feature (see p. L92). For these data, the *Fill* feature takes about as much time as it would to enter the numbers by hand. However, for larger data sets, the *Fill* feature can save a lot of time. Just for practice, use the *Fill* feature:

Continued . . .

Keystroke	Action Resulting from Keystroke
/	Displays the main menu.
D	Selects **Data** and displays its menu.
F	Selects *Fill* and asks for the range of cells to be filled.
H7.H12 ↵	Specifies the range to be filled and requests the starting number.
1 ↵	Specifies the starting number and requests the step (i.e., how the numbers will change as Lotus 1-2-3 moves from cell to cell).
1 ↵	Specifies that the numbers are to change by one, and requests the maximum value allowed.
↵	Specifies that the default maximum (**8191**) is to be used and fills the cells with the numbers:

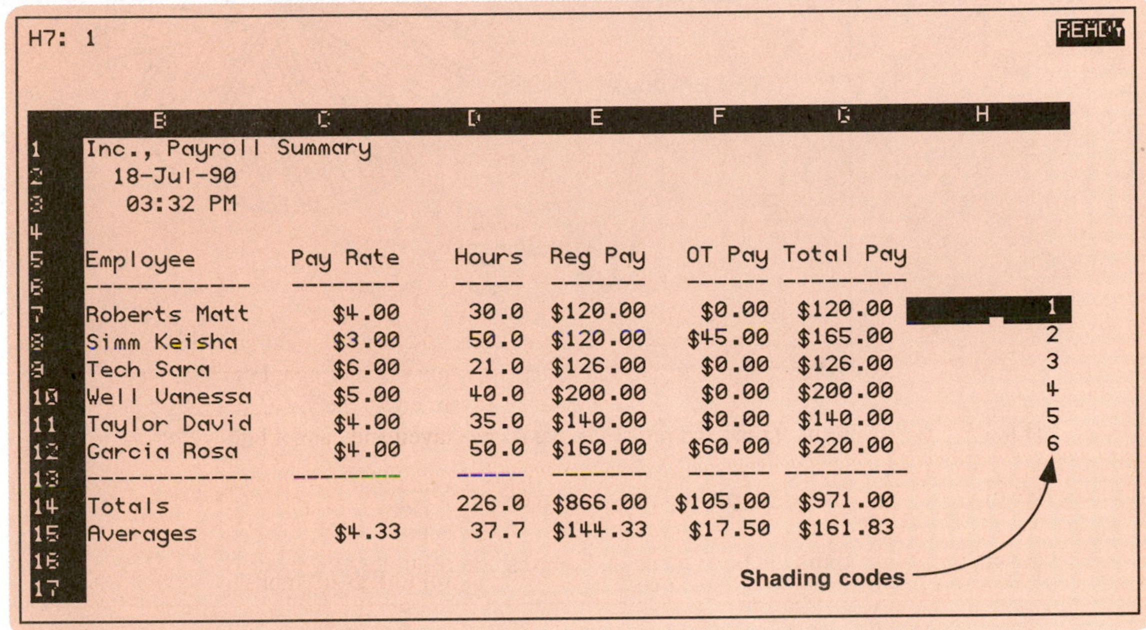

H7: 1 READY

	B	C	D	E	F	G	H
1	Inc., Payroll Summary						
2	18-Jul-90						
3	03:32 PM						
4							
5	Employee	Pay Rate	Hours	Reg Pay	OT Pay	Total Pay	
6	------------	--------	-----	-------	------	---------	
7	Roberts Matt	$4.00	30.0	$120.00	$0.00	$120.00	1
8	Simm Keisha	$3.00	50.0	$120.00	$45.00	$165.00	2
9	Tech Sara	$6.00	21.0	$126.00	$0.00	$126.00	3
10	Well Vanessa	$5.00	40.0	$200.00	$0.00	$200.00	4
11	Taylor David	$4.00	35.0	$140.00	$0.00	$140.00	5
12	Garcia Rosa	$4.00	50.0	$160.00	$60.00	$220.00	6
13	------------	--------	-----	-------	------	---------	
14	Totals		226.0	$866.00	$105.00	$971.00	
15	Averages	$4.33	37.7	$144.33	$17.50	$161.83	
16							
17							

As a backup precaution, use **/ F**(ile) **S**(ave) to save the worksheet under the name **PAY-V11**.

Now that the shading codes have been entered, tell Lotus 1-2-3 to create the graph once again. This time, however, you will have to specify two ranges of values to be used in the graph. The first range, **A**, will be the names of the students. The second range, **B**, will be the shading codes you just entered.

Keystroke	Action Resulting from Keystroke
/	Displays the main menu.
G	Selects **Graph** and displays its menu.
T	Selects **Type** and displays its menu.
P	Selects **Pie** and returns to the **Type** menu. The values for **X** (the labels) and **A** (the names) already have been entered. All you have to enter are the shading codes.
B	Specifies that a second range is to be graphed and requests the range specification.
H7.H12 ↵	Specifies that the values in cells **H7** through **H12** are to be used and returns to the **Graph** menu.
V	Selects **View** and displays the graph on the screen.

Continued . . .

Keystroke	Action Resulting from Keystroke

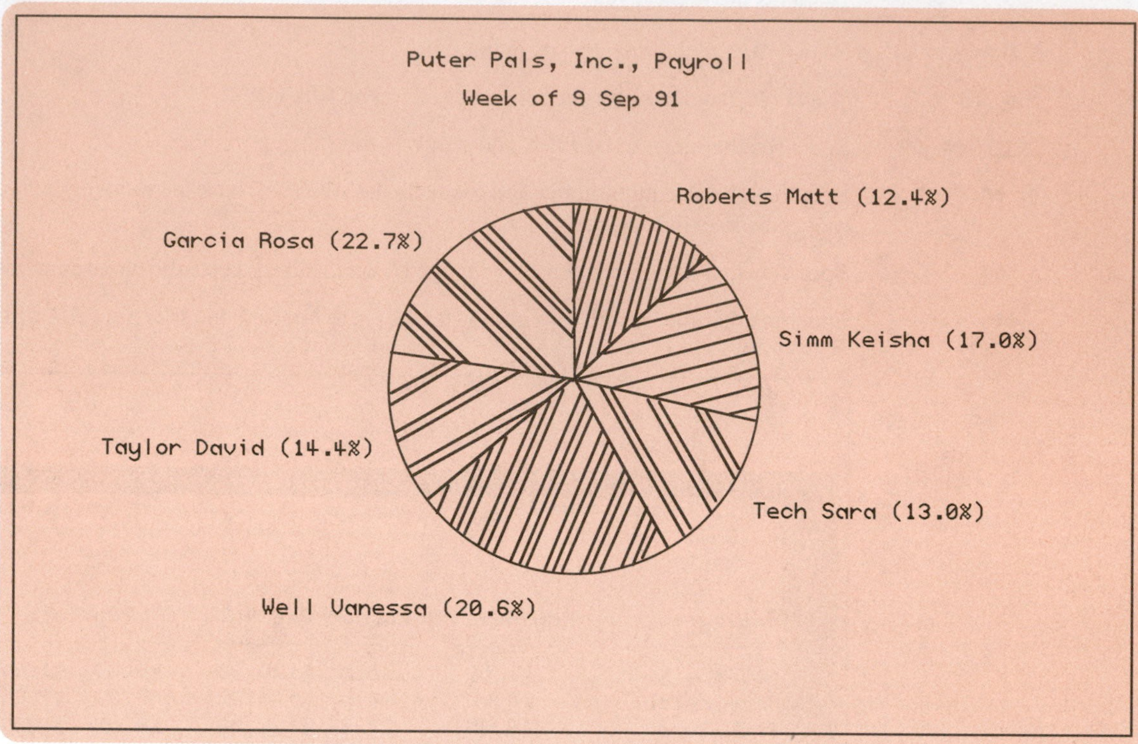

[Esc]	Exits **View** and returns to the **Graph** menu.
[Esc]	Exits **Graph** and returns to the main menu.
[Esc]	Exits the main menu and returns control to **READY** mode.

Exploding a pie chart is also easy to do. An exploded pie chart has a portion that is set apart from the rest to make it stand out:

To make an exploded pie chart, you simply add 100 to the shading code of the section you want emphasized (e.g., code **6** in cell **H12** would become code **106**). To make the graph more interesting, you could emphasize the largest total pay (for Rosa Garcia) by exploding that value.

Keystroke	Action Resulting from Keystroke
[arrow]	Use the **[arrow]** keys to make cell **H12** active. This cell contains the shading code for Rosa Garcia. To explode this part of the graph, add 100 to the code.
106 ↵	Changes the code from shading only to shading and exploding the wedge. When the graph is viewed, the pie wedge for Rosa Garcia will be set apart from the others. Note that you could use the **@IF** and **@MAX** functions to have Lotus 1-2-3 automatically add 100 to the shading code of the person with the largest total pay. To view the graph you may enter **/ G**(raph) **V**(iew) or use the *Display Graph* feature key (i.e., the **[F10]** key).

Continued . . .

Keystroke	Action Resulting from Keystroke
/	Displays the main menu.
G	Selects **Graph** and displays its menu.
V	Selects **View** and displays the graph on the screen.

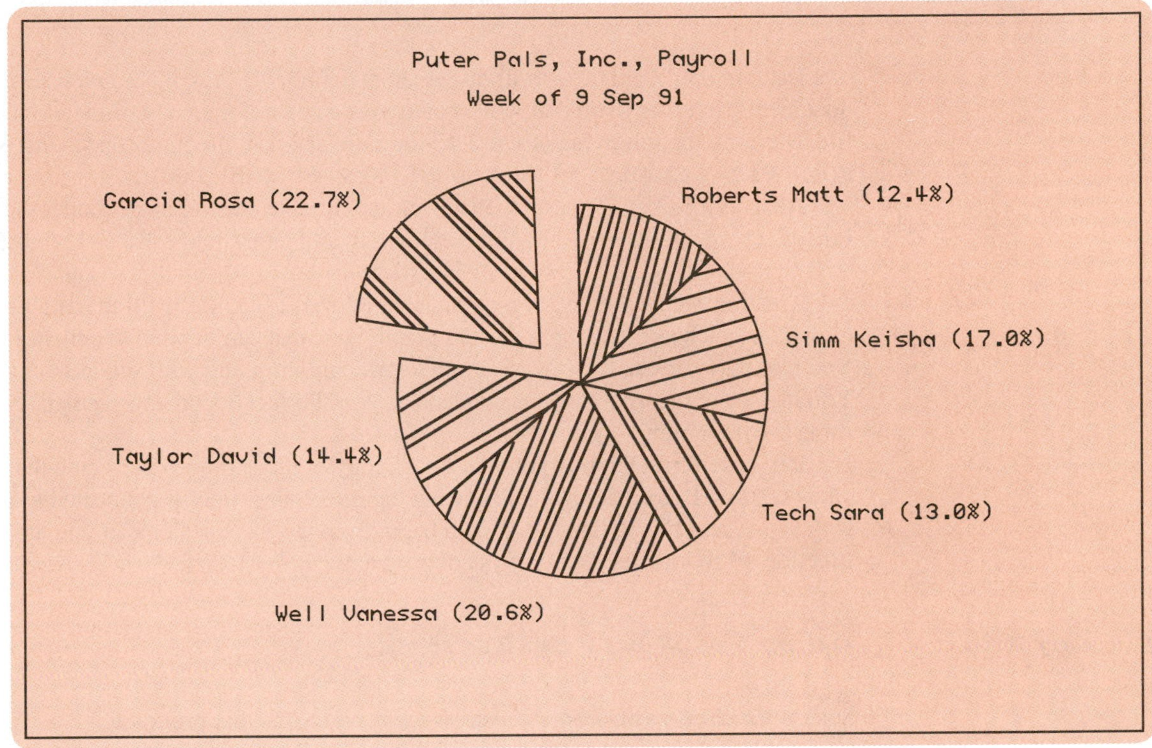

To produce a hard copy of the graph, you may use the **[PrintScreen]** key to send a screen dump of the graph displayed in **VIEW** mode to your printer (you must have a graphics printer!) or you may exit the Lotus 1-2-3 program and use the PrintGraph program (see the next section).

First, try using the **[PrintScreen]** key. Be sure your printer is connected to the computer, loaded with paper, and turned on. Also, you should have executed the DOS **GRAPHICS** command (see pp. L108–109) before trying to do the screen dump.

Keystroke	Action Resulting from Keystroke
[PrintScreen]	Sends the contents of the screen to the printer. The graph should appear exactly as it does on the screen.
[Esc]	Exits **View** and returns to the **Graph** menu.

In order to print the graph using another program, you must first save an image of the graph in a special graphics file. You use the **Save** command to do this.

Keystroke	Action Resulting from Keystroke
S	Selects **Save** and saves the current graph in a file so that it can be used by other programs such as PrintGraph, Allways, or WordPerfect.

Continued . . .

Keystroke	Action Resulting from Keystroke
PAY-V12.PIC ↵	Provides the file specification for the graph file. The **.PIC** extension indicates that the file is a **PIC**ture (graph) file.
[Esc]	Exits **Graph** and returns control to the main menu.
[Esc]	Exits the main menu and returns control to **READY** mode.

Later in this chapter, we will discuss how to import Lotus 1-2-3 graphs and data into WordPerfect documents. In order to do that, you should save a copy of the body of the worksheet in a text (ASCII) file by typing the following (see p. L42 for more detailed directions on saving ASCII files): **/ P**(rint) **F**(ile) **PAY-V12.TXT** ↵ **R**(ange) **B5.G15** ↵ **G**(o) **Q**(uit).

Also, as a precaution, use **/ F**(ile) **S**(ave) to save the worksheet under the name **PAY-V12**. Finally, use **/ Q**(uit) **Y**(es) to quit the program and return to the 1-2-3 Access System.

Using PrintGraph

Creating a screen dump of a graph is quick and easy, but the PrintGraph program offers a number of options, such as changing fonts and graph sizes, that can be used to enhance the final printed copy. You also may use the Allways program to print graphs along with actual worksheet cells and other text. You may even incorporate your graphs into WordPerfect documents (see pp. W136–39) and print them using that program.

Let's use PrintGraph to produce a hard copy of the exploded pie graph that you created in the previous section. Before doing the following, be sure your printer is connected to the computer, loaded with paper, and turned on. You should begin from the Access menu (if you are currently in DOS, type **LOTUS** ↵ to load the Access System program).

Keystroke	Action Resulting from Keystroke
P	Selects **PrintGraph** from the Access menu and loads that program.

IF YOU ARE USING A TWO-DRIVE SYSTEM, you will be asked to **Insert the PrintGraph Disk into your diskette drive**. Find this diskette, insert it into the B: drive in place of the *Lotus 1-2-3 System* diskette, and press **[Enter]**.

A startup screen will appear and then, in a few seconds, the following screen will be displayed:

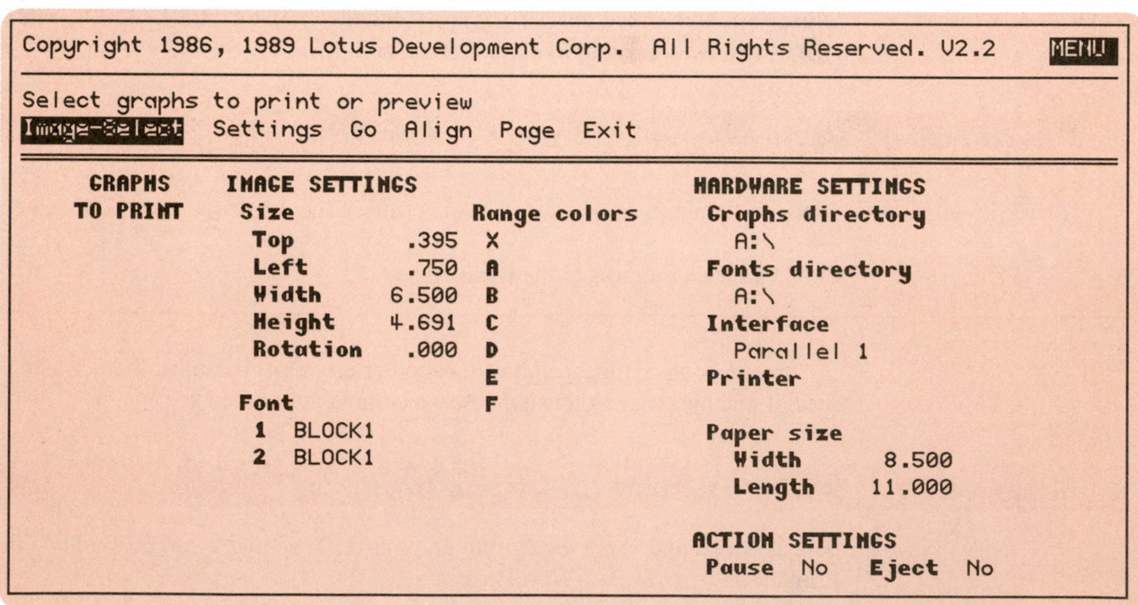

For this example, let's print the graph using two different fonts (recall that a font is a set of type styles and sizes). Before you can print the graph, you must check and adjust, if necessary, the printer settings. Look at the right-hand column labeled **HARDWARE SETTINGS**:

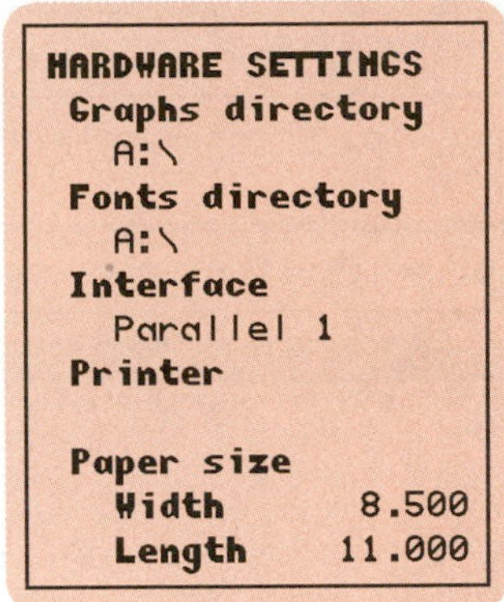

The settings indicate that the file containing the graph is on the diskette in drive A:; the files containing the fonts are on the diskette in drive A:; the printer interface is through the first parallel port; no printer has been selected; the paper size is $8\frac{1}{2}$ by 11 inches. You may have to change some or all of these settings.

Step 1 Select a printer by doing the following:

Keystroke	Action Resulting from Keystroke
S	Selects **Settings** and displays its menu.

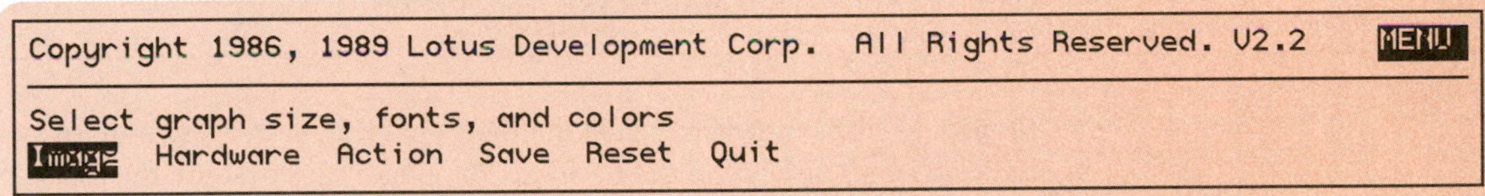

Keystroke	Action Resulting from Keystroke
H	Selects **Hardware** and displays its menu.

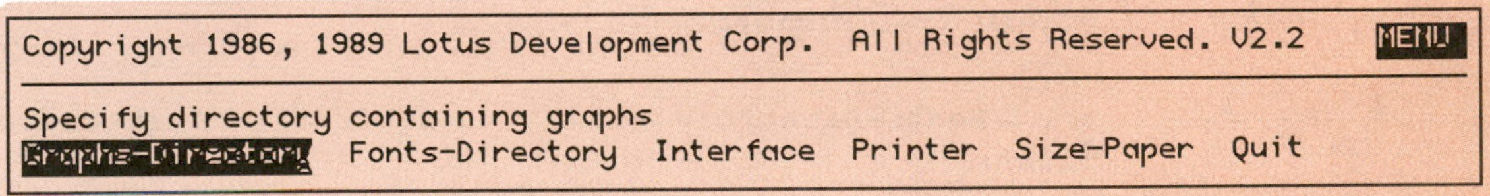

Keystroke	Action Resulting from Keystroke
P	Selects **Printer** and displays a list of the printers that are available to your system.

Continued . . .

Keystroke	Action Resulting from Keystroke
	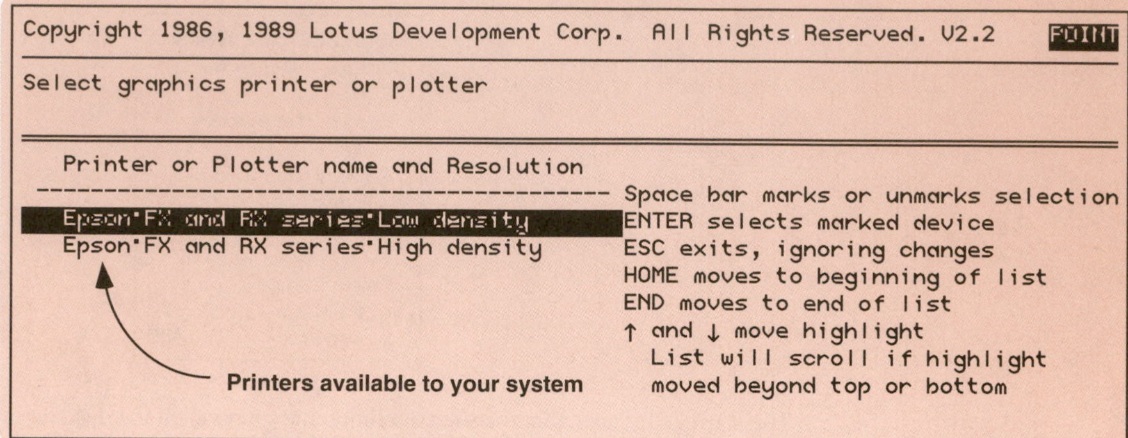
	It is a good idea to select the low-density mode for your printer because the final graph will print much faster than using high density (although the graph will not look quite as nice).
[arrow]	Use the **[arrow]** keys, if necessary, to highlight the appropriate printer (e.g., **`Epson'FX and RX series'Low density`**).
[Spacebar]	Marks the printer with a **#** to the left of its name.
[Enter]	Selects the marked printer and returns to the **`Hardware`** menu. The printer name should appear under the word **`Printer`** in the **`HARDWARE SETTINGS`**.

Step 2 Tell the program where the fonts are located. For a two-drive system, the fonts should be on the *PrintGraph* diskette in the B: drive. For a hard-disk system, the fonts should be located in the **`123`** subdirectory.

Keystroke	Action Resulting from Keystroke
F	Selects **`Fonts-Directory`** and asks you to **`Enter directory containing font (.FNT) files`**.
[Esc]	Erases the default drive specification.
C:\123 ↵	Changes the directory to the subdirectory called **`123`** on the **`C:`** drive.
Two-drive system	**IF YOU ARE USING A TWO-DRIVE SYSTEM,** type **`B:`** ↵ instead.

Continued . . .

Keystroke	Action Resulting from Keystroke
	The name of the proper directory should appear under **Fonts directory** in the **HARDWARE SETTINGS**.
[Esc]	Exits **Hardware** and returns to the PrintGraph menu.

For this example, the graph directory is properly set to A: (i.e., the graph file is located on your *Lotus Data* diskette in drive A:). If your graph file is in a different directory (e.g., C:\), you will have to change the directory by using the **Settings** option. In that case, type **[Esc]** **S**(ettings) **H**(ardware) **G**(raphs-Directory) **[Esc]** **C:** ↵ **[Esc]**.

Step 3 Specify the name of the file that contains the graph.

Keystroke	Action Resulting from Keystroke
I	Selects **Image-Select** and displays a listing of the graphics (**PIC**) files saved on the diskette in drive A: (there probably will be only one such file).

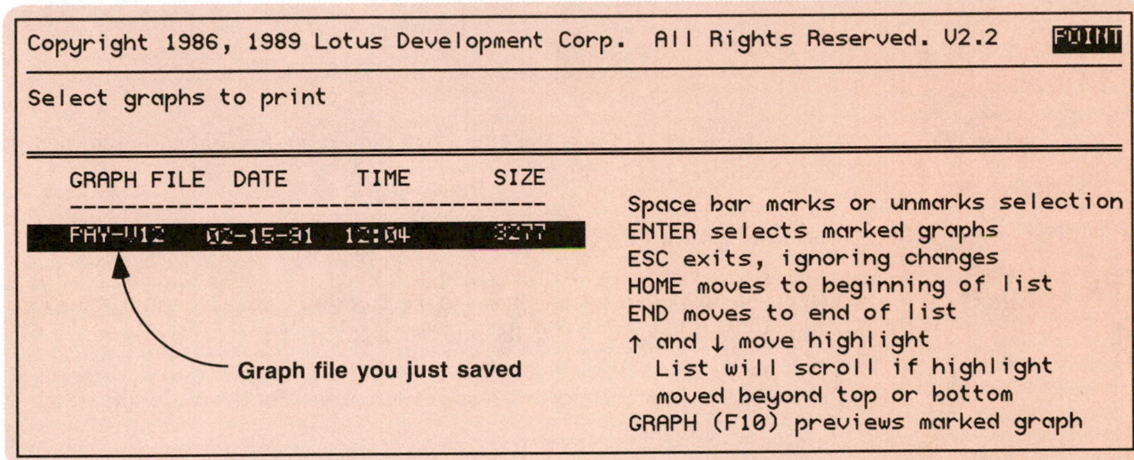

Keystroke	Action Resulting from Keystroke
[arrow]	Use the **[arrow]** keys, if necessary, to highlight the file called **PAY-V12**.
[Spacebar]	Marks the file with a # to the left of its name.
[Enter]	Selects the marked file and returns to the PrintGraph menu. The file name **PAY-V12** should appear in the column labeled **GRAPHS TO PRINT**.

Step 4 Specify which fonts will be used for the graph.

Keystroke	Action Resulting from Keystroke
S	Selects **Settings** and displays its menu.
I	Selects **Image** and displays its menu.

Continued . . .

Keystroke	Action Resulting from Keystroke
F	Selects **Font** and displays a **1** and a **2**. The **1** refers to the first line (i.e., the title) of the graph while the **2** refers to the rest of the text (e.g., labels, names of axes).
1	Selects **1** and provides a list of available fonts for the first line of the graph.

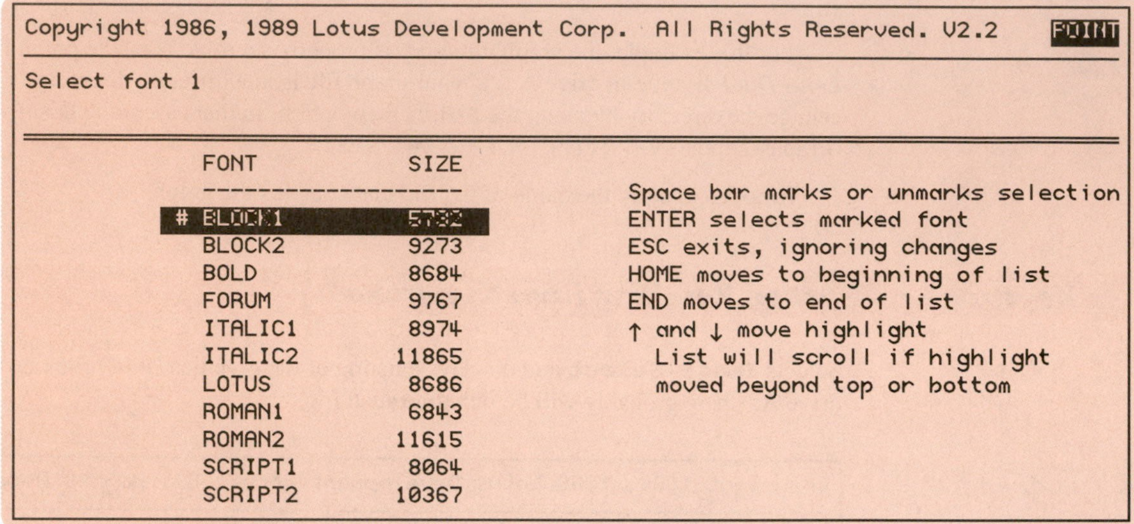

Keystroke	Action Resulting from Keystroke
[arrow]	Use the **[arrow]** keys to select **ITALIC2**. Selecting this font will print the first line of the graph in a heavy italic print (***like this***).
[Spacebar]	Marks the font with a **#** to the left of its name.
[Enter]	Selects the marked font and returns to the **Image** menu. The font name **ITALIC2** should appear in the column labeled **Font** next to the number **1**.
	Follow the same procedure to select a different font for the rest of the text.
F	Selects **Font** and displays a **1** and a **2**.
2	Selects **2** and provides a list of available fonts for the rest of the text.
[arrow]	Use the **[arrow]** keys to select **ROMAN2**.
[Spacebar]	Marks the font with a **#** to the left of its name.
[Enter]	Selects the marked font and returns to the **Image** menu. The font name **ROMAN2** should appear in the column labeled **Font** next to the number **2**.
[Esc]	Exits the **Image** menu and returns to the **Settings** menu.
[Esc]	Exits the **Settings** menu and returns to the main menu.
	Notice that all your selections are displayed on the screen.

Continued . . .

Keystroke	Action Resulting from Keystroke

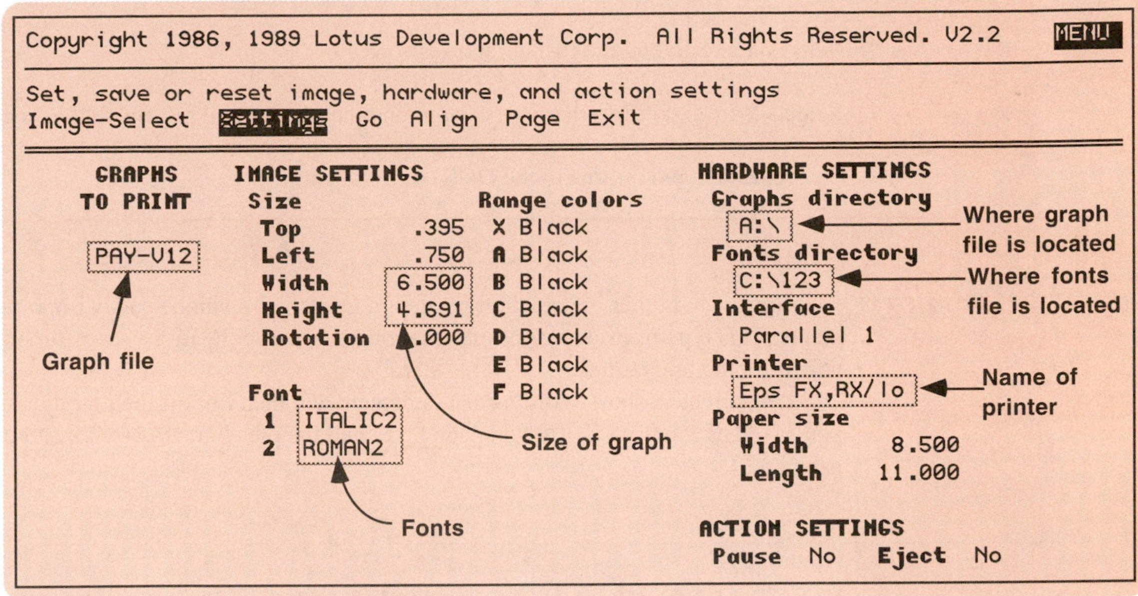

Step 5 Print the graph. Be sure the paper is properly positioned in the printer before doing the following:

Keystroke	Action Resulting from Keystroke
A	Selects **Align** to tell the program that the paper is properly positioned in the printer.
G	Selects **Go** and prints the graph.

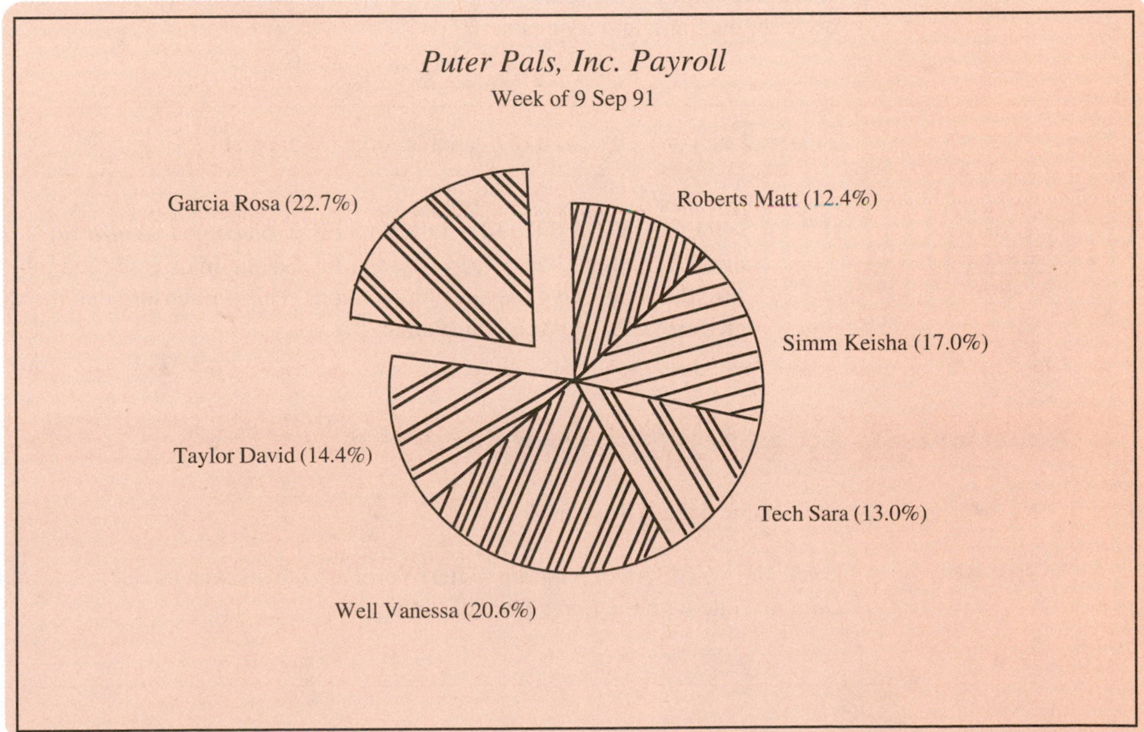

Continued . . .

Keystroke	Action Resulting from Keystroke
P	Selects **Page** to eject the sheet to the top of the next page.
E	Selects **Exit** to end the PrintGraph session.
Y	Selects **Yes** to confirm that you want to end the session and returns to the Access menu.
E	Selects **Exit** and returns to the DOS environment.

Importing Lotus 1-2-3 Output into WordPerfect Documents

Graphs and other information created in Lotus 1-2-3 can be easily imported into WordPerfect documents. This type of exchange of information between applications saves time and increases the usefulness of both applications.

Let's create a short WordPerfect document and then import the output from the worksheet that you saved as **PAY-V12.TXT** on page L122 and the pie chart **PAY-V12.PIC** that you saved on page L122.

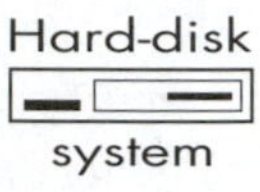

IF YOU ARE USING A HARD-DISK SYSTEM, the following assumes that there is a subdirectory called **WP51** (or **WP50** if you are using version 5.0) on your hard disk that contains all the WordPerfect files.

Keystroke	Action Resulting from Keystroke
A: ↵	Defines the default drive as A:.
C:\WP51\WP ↵	Loads the WordPerfect program. If you get a message saying that there is insufficient memory to load the program, remove the diskette in drive A:, reboot the computer (use the **[Ctrl-Alt-Del]** key combination), and try again.

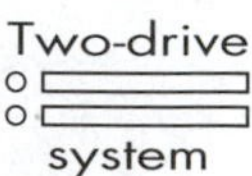

IF YOU ARE USING A TWO-DRIVE SYSTEM, place your *WordPerfect Data* diskette in drive A: and the *WordPerfect System #1* diskette in drive B: and reboot the computer (use the **[Ctrl-Alt-Del]** key combination). This will ensure that the **CONFIG.SYS** file is properly executed for WordPerfect.

Keystroke	Action Resulting from Keystroke
A: ↵	Defines the default drive as A:.
B:WP ↵	Loads the WordPerfect program. After WordPerfect has been loaded, replace the *WordPerfect Data* diskette with the *Lotus Data* diskette.

After WordPerfect has been accessed, type the following memo (use your own name in the **Memo from** line):

```
  Memo to:  Kathy Riley
Memo from:  Bobby McGee
     Date:  15 September 1991

We have completed the summary of employee earnings for the week
of 9 September 1991.  The raw data are listed below.

The following graph should help to give you a better idea of the
relative amounts earned by individual employees:

If you have any questions, give me a call (373-9836)._
```

Save the file and then import the file **PAY-V12.TXT** by doing the following:

Keystroke	Action Resulting from Keystroke
[F10]	Selects the *Save Files* feature and requests a name for the file to be saved.
A:IMPORT1 ↵	Provides the file specification.
[arrow]	Use the **[arrow]** keys to move the cursor to the blank line between the first and second paragraphs (location **Ln 2" Pos 1"**).
[Shift-F10]	Selects the *Retrieve Files* feature and requests the name of the file to be retrieved.
A:PAY-V12.TXT ↵	Provides the file specification and inserts the file into the WordPerfect document at the location of the cursor.

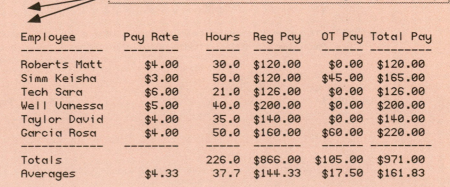

```
  Memo to:  Kathy Riley
Memo from:  Bobby McGee
     Date:  15 September 1991

We have completed the summary of employee earnings for the week
of 9 September 1991.  The raw data are listed below.
_
```

Delete four of these five blank lines using the [Delete] key

```
    Employee        Pay Rate    Hours  Reg Pay    OT Pay Total Pay
    ------------    --------    -----  -------    ------ ---------
    Roberts Matt       $4.00     30.0  $120.00     $0.00   $120.00
    Simm Keisha        $3.00     50.0  $120.00    $45.00   $165.00
    Tech Sara          $6.00     21.0  $126.00     $0.00   $126.00
    Well Vanessa       $5.00     40.0  $200.00     $0.00   $200.00
    Taylor David       $4.00     35.0  $140.00     $0.00   $140.00
    Garcia Rosa        $4.00     50.0  $160.00    $60.00   $220.00
    ------------    --------    -----  -------    ------ ---------
    Totals                      226.0  $866.00   $105.00   $971.00
    Averages           $4.33     37.7  $144.33    $17.50   $161.83

The following graph should help to give you a better idea of the
A:\IMPORT1                                Doc 1 Pg 1 Ln 2" Pos 1"
```

Continued . . .

Keystroke	Action Resulting from Keystroke
[Delete]	Use the **[Delete]** key to delete four of the blank lines in the imported text (these are caused by Lotus 1-2-3 inserting a blank header). Also, if your default margins are smaller than the width of the imported table there may be other blank lines or wrapped text. In that case, adjust the margins so that the table looks like that shown above.
[arrow]	Use the **[arrow]** keys to move the cursor to the blank line just above the last paragraph (location **`Ln 4.5" Pos 1"`**).
[Alt-F9]	Invokes the *Graphics* feature and displays its menu.
`F` (or **1**)	Selects **`1 Figure`** and displays a list of options.
`C` (or **1**)	Selects **`1 Create`** and displays the definition menu.
`F` (or **1**)	Selects **`1 - Filename`** and requests the name of the file that contains the picture to be used.
`A:PAY-V12.PIC` ↵	Provides the file specification and loads the graphic into the current document.
[F7]	Exits the definition menu and returns to text entry mode. Pressing the **[down arrow]** key will reformat the paragraph.
↓ ↓	Reformats the paragraph and displays the following:

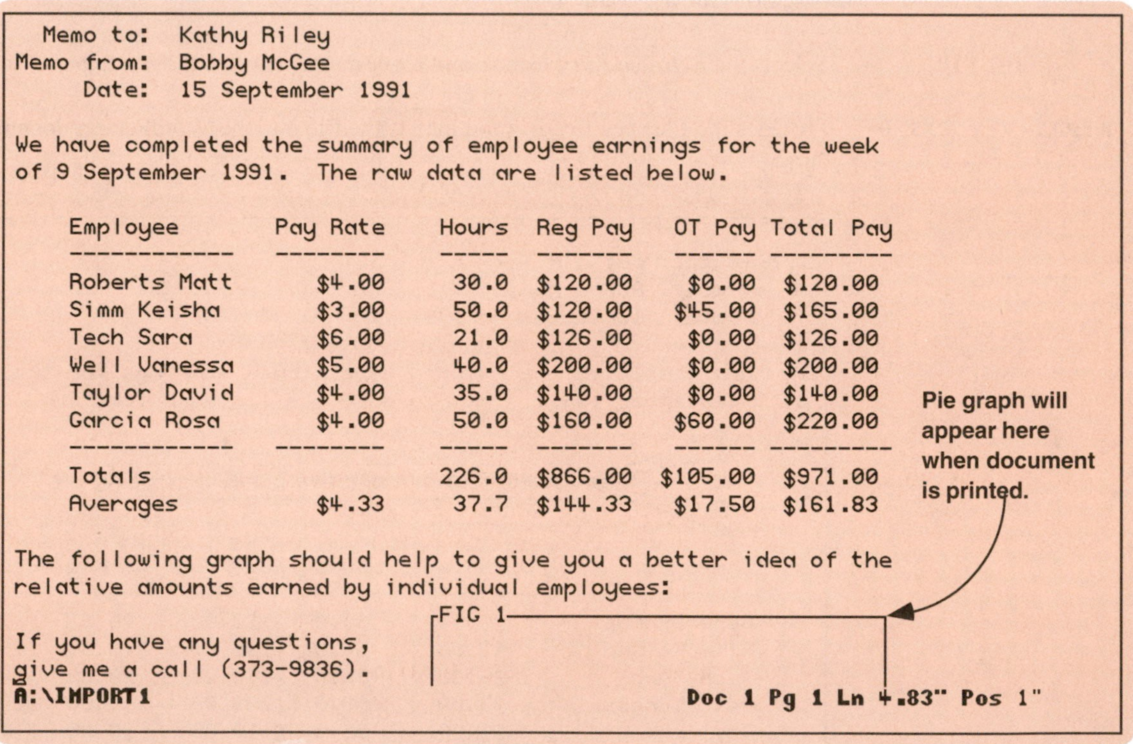

```
  Memo to:   Kathy Riley
Memo from:   Bobby McGee
     Date:   15 September 1991

We have completed the summary of employee earnings for the week
of 9 September 1991.  The raw data are listed below.

    Employee        Pay Rate     Hours  Reg Pay    OT Pay  Total Pay
    ------------    --------     -----  -------    ------  ---------
    Roberts Matt       $4.00      30.0  $120.00     $0.00   $120.00
    Simm Keisha        $3.00      50.0  $120.00    $45.00   $165.00
    Tech Sara          $6.00      21.0  $126.00     $0.00   $126.00
    Well Vanessa       $5.00      40.0  $200.00     $0.00   $200.00
    Taylor David       $4.00      35.0  $140.00     $0.00   $140.00
    Garcia Rosa        $4.00      50.0  $160.00    $60.00   $220.00
    ------------    --------     -----  -------    ------  ---------
    Totals                       226.0  $866.00   $105.00   $971.00
    Averages           $4.33      37.7  $144.33    $17.50   $161.83

The following graph should help to give you a better idea of the
relative amounts earned by individual employees:
                                   FIG 1
If you have any questions,
give me a call (373-9836).
A:\IMPORT1                                  Doc 1 Pg 1 Ln 4.83" Pos 1"
```


To see the document as it will appear in printed form, use the *Print* **`View`** feature.

Keystroke	Action Resulting from Keystroke
[Shift-F7]	Invokes the *Print* feature.
V (or **6**)	Selects **6 View** and displays the document as it will appear when printed. Notice the table of data and the graph, both of which were created by Lotus 1-2-3.
3	Selects **Full Page**.

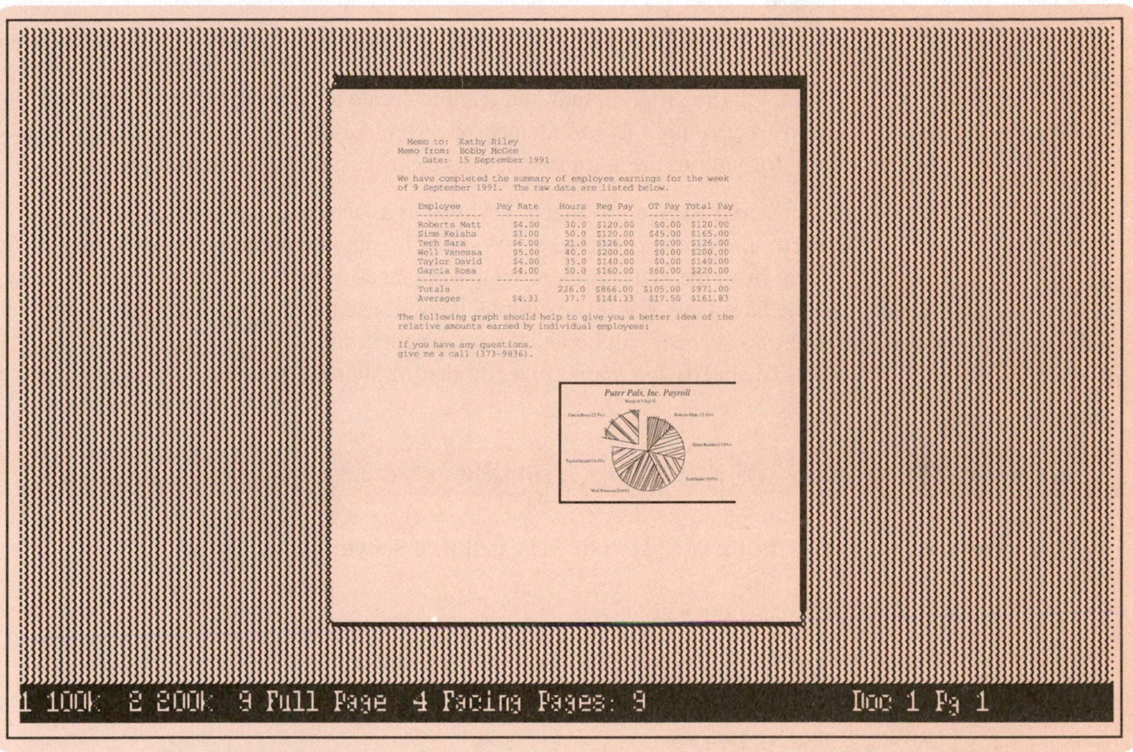

Memo to: Kathy Riley
Memo from: Bobby McGee
Date: 15 September 1991

We have completed the summary of employee earnings for the week of 9 September 1991. The raw data are listed below.

Employee	Pay Rate	Hours	Reg Pay	OT Pay	Total Pay
Roberts Matt	$4.00	30.0	$120.00	$0.00	$120.00
Simm Keisha	$3.00	50.0	$120.00	$45.00	$165.00
Tech Sara	$6.00	21.0	$126.00	$0.00	$126.00
Well Vanessa	$5.00	40.0	$200.00	$0.00	$200.00
Taylor David	$4.00	35.0	$140.00	$0.00	$140.00
Garcia Rosa	$4.00	50.0	$160.00	$60.00	$220.00
Totals		226.0	$866.00	$105.00	$971.00
Averages	$4.33	37.7	$144.33	$17.50	$161.83

The following graph should help to give you a better idea of the relative amounts earned by individual employees:

If you have any questions, give me a call (373-9836).

Keystroke	Action Resulting from Keystroke
[F7]	Exits *View*.
[F7]	Exits the document and asks if you want to save it.
Y	Selects **Yes** and suggests a name.
A:IMPORT2 ↵	Provides the file specification and asks if you want to exit WordPerfect.
Y	Specifies that you want to exit WordPerfect and returns to the DOS environment.

Creating Macros Using Learn

A **macro** is a set of keystrokes and/or instructions that can be used to automate a particular task. The keystrokes are stored as labels (text) in a cell or range of cells of a worksheet so that they can be executed at any time, usually by pressing just two keys. Recall that on pages W148–56 you created a macro in WordPerfect to do a repetitive task. Lotus 1-2-3 macros are created and function in a manner similar to those found in WordPerfect.

Lotus 1-2-3 macros are actually special text cells saved with your worksheets or other special macro worksheets. To illustrate how macros can be defined and used, create a macro that will format a range of cells for currency (i.e., so that the values in the specified range display a dollar sign and two decimal places).

First, access Lotus 1-2-3 and then use **/ F**(ile) **R**(etrieve) to retrieve the worksheet **PAY-V1**. We will use this simple worksheet to illustrate how to create, save, and run a macro.

```
D3:                                                                    READY

       A            B           C            D            E           F
1  Employee     Pay Rate    Hours        Total Pay
2  --------     --------    -----        ---------
3  Roberts Matt        4           30
4  Simm Keisha         3           50
5  Tech Sara           6           21
6  Well Vanessa        5           40
7
```

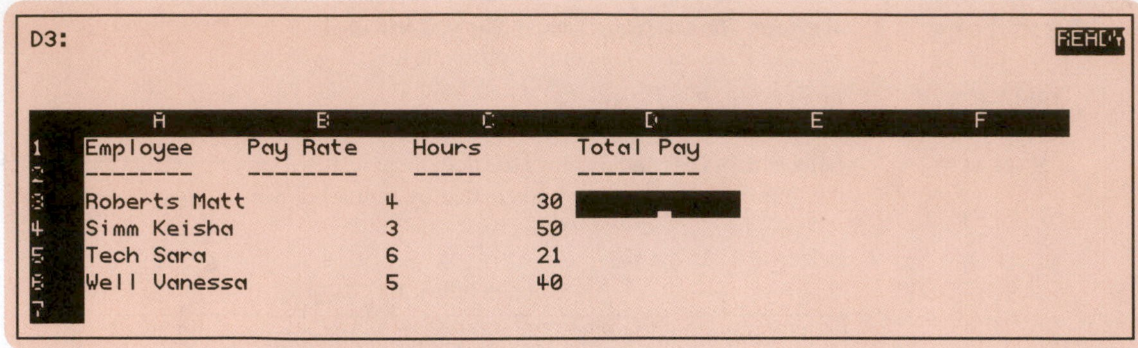

Next, tell the program that you want to create a macro using the *Learn* feature. This feature allows you to instruct Lotus 1-2-3 to memorize certain keystrokes. To use Learn, you need to provide three pieces of information: the learn range, the keystrokes, and the macro name.

Learn Range A macro is saved as a label in a specified cell or group of cells. These cells are referred to as the *learn range*. You can use any blank range of cells, but be sure that it is far enough away from the active area of your worksheet so that it will not be accidentally erased or overwritten at some later date. For this example, we will use the single cell **B10** so that the macro and the active part of the worksheet will be visible at the same time.

To specify the learn range, do the following:

Keystroke	Action Resulting from Keystroke
[arrow]	Use the **[arrow]** keys to make cell **B10** active.
/	Displays the main menu.
W	Selects **Worksheet**.
L	Selects **Learn**.

```
B10:                                                                    MENU
Range   Cancel   Erase
Specify a learn range in which to store keystrokes
```

Range allows you to specify a range in which to store your keystrokes.

Cancel allows you to cancel the currently specified range.

Erase allows you to erase the contents of the currently specified range.

Keystroke	Action Resulting from Keystroke
R	Selects **Range** and asks you to **Enter learn range**. Lotus 1-2-3 stores macros in single cells or in a single column of cells. A single cell can hold up to 240 characters while a column can hold virtually any number of commands. For this example, use cell **B10** to store the keystrokes.
B10 ↵	Specifies the learn range and returns to **READY** mode.

Keystrokes To create the macro, use the **[Alt-F5]** key to tell Lotus 1-2-3 to begin memorizing your keystrokes. Then, simply press the keys as you normally would to carry out the process. For this example, the keystrokes will be **/ R**(ange) **F**(ormat) **C**(urrency) **2 [Enter]**.

To specify the keystrokes, do the following:

Keystroke	***Action Resulting from Keystroke***
[Alt-F5]	Turns on the *Learn* feature and displays **LEARN** on the status line at the bottom of the screen. From now on, Lotus 1-2-3 will memorize your keystrokes.
/	Displays the main menu.
R	Selects **Range**.
F	Selects **Format**.
C	Selects **Currency**.
2 ↵	Specifies the number of decimal places to be displayed and requests the range to format. At this point, you should turn off the *Learn* feature because you will want to specify a different range each time you run the macro.
[Alt-F5]	Turns off the *Learn* feature and **LEARN** disappears from the status line. As soon as you begin typing the cell range, cell **B10** will display the macro keystrokes **/rfc2~**. The tilde (~) shows where the **[Enter]** key was pressed.
D3.D6 ↵	Specifies the range of cells to be formatted for currency and returns to **READY** mode.

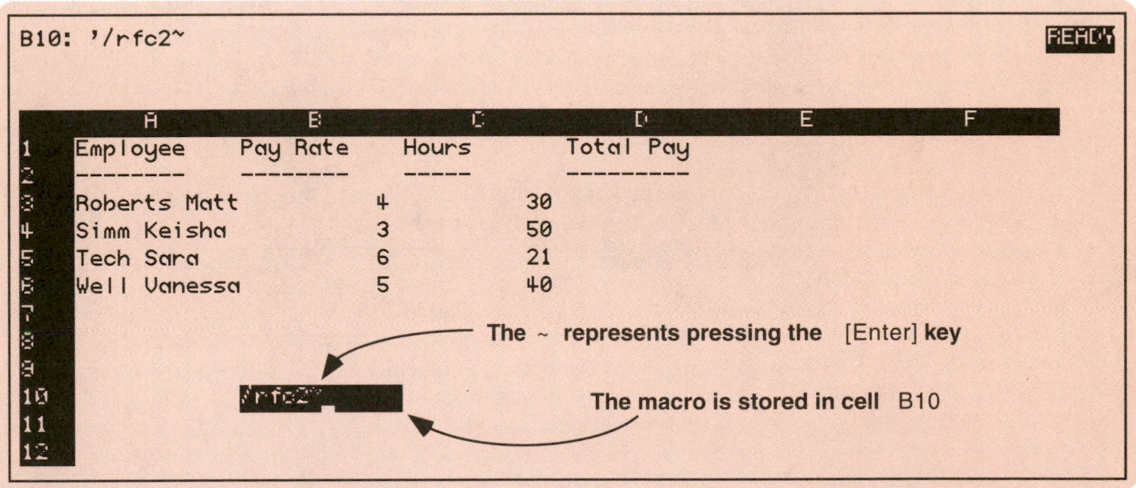

Name Naming a macro is just like naming a range (see pp. L52–54). Like range names, macro names can consist of up to 15 letters, digits, and special characters (*not* including spaces, commas, semicolons, and periods). Also, do not use names that could be interpreted as cell locations (e.g., **B12**) or functions (e.g., **@SUM**).

Macros also can be named using a backslash and a single letter (e.g., **\M**). In that case, the macro can be run using the **[Alt]** key in conjunction with the letter key (e.g., pressing **[Alt-M]** would run the macro whose name is **\M**). This type of naming is discussed on pages L136–37.

For this example, let's use the name **MONEY**.

Keystroke	Action Resulting from Keystroke
/	Displays the main menu.
R	Selects **Range**.
N	Selects **Name**.
C	Selects **Create** and asks you to **Enter name**.
MONEY ↵	Specifies the name of the macro and requests the range.
B10 ↵	Specifies the range to be named and returns to **READY** mode.

It is a good idea to document your macros so that the names and functions will be obvious to you at a later date. You can do this by entering the name of the macro in cell **A10** and a brief description of what it does in cell **C10**. For example:

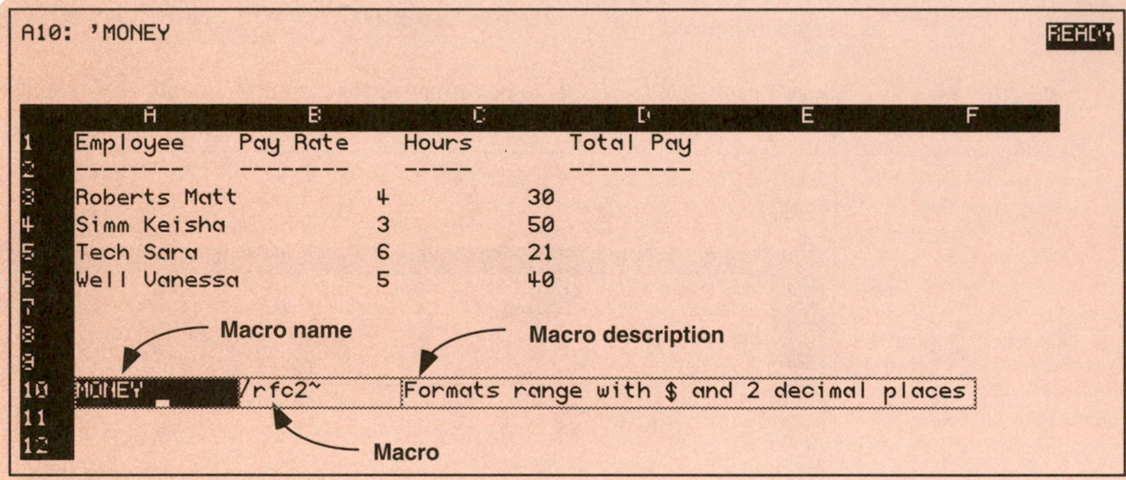

Running Macros

To run the macro just created, use the **[Alt-F3]** key:

Keystroke	Action Resulting from Keystroke
[Alt-F3]	Specifies that a macro is to be run and displays a list of currently saved macros (there is only one — **MONEY**):

```
A10: 'MONEY                                                    NAMES
Select the macro to run:
MONEY
```

Keystroke	Action Resulting from Keystroke
[arrow]	Use the **[arrow]** keys, if necessary, to select the macro called **MONEY** (or simply type the word **MONEY**).
↵	Runs the macro (executes the stored keystrokes) and requests the range to format. Notice how quickly the keystrokes are executed.
B3.B6 ↵	Specifies the range to format, formats the cells, and returns to **READY** mode.

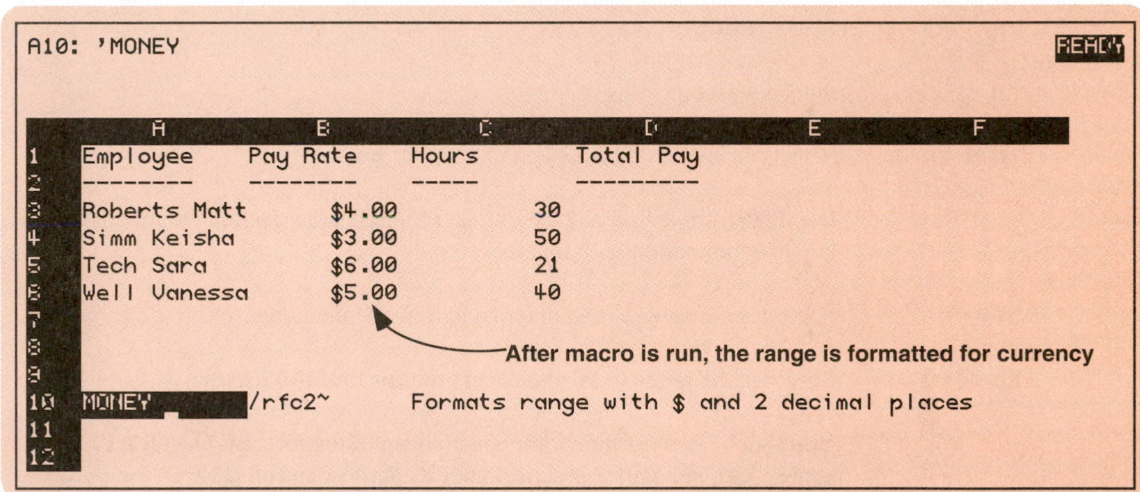

A10: 'MONEY
READY
A B C D E F
1 Employee Pay Rate Hours Total Pay
2 -------- -------- ----- ---------
3 Roberts Matt $4.00 30
4 Simm Keisha $3.00 50
5 Tech Sara $6.00 21
6 Well Vanessa $5.00 40
After macro is run, the range is formatted for currency
10 MONEY /rfc2~ Formats range with $ and 2 decimal places
11
12

Creating Macros by Entering Labels

Macros can be stored in a single cell (up to a maximum of 240 characters) or in a column of consecutive cells. When a macro is run, the execution begins at the first cell in the range and continues through adjacent cells in the same column until a blank cell is reached. If you have more than one macro in a worksheet, be sure to separate them with at least one blank cell or Lotus 1-2-3 will think they are all a single macro and execute them one after the other.

Let's create a second macro that will automate the process of saving a worksheet to the diskette in drive A:. You could use the same procedure as you did when you created the last macro. However, even though using the *Learn* feature to create macros is easy, it is generally faster to define a macro by simply typing the proper keystrokes into a specific cell. Let's use this method to create a second macro.

Keystroke	Action Resulting from Keystroke
[arrow]	Use the **[arrow]** keys to make cell **B12** active. This cell will hold the new macro.

Continued . . .

Keystroke	Action Resulting from Keystroke
	Next, type in the keystrokes needed to save a file. By now, you probably have done this so many times that you know the keystrokes by heart (they are **/** to bring up the main menu, **F** to select **File**, and **S** to select **Save**).
	Be careful when you type the keystrokes. You must tell Lotus 1-2-3 that the keystrokes are labels and that they are to be entered into the active cell rather than executed. To do that, you must type a label prefix such as a single apostrophe, **'**, as the first character in the label. If you do not do this, the keystrokes will be considered commands and they will be executed rather than entered into the active cell.
/fs ↵	Specifies the keystrokes for the macro and enters them into the active cell.

Now, the macro must be given a name by doing the following:

Keystroke	Action Resulting from Keystroke
/	Displays the main menu.
R	Selects **Range**.
N	Selects **Name**.
C	Selects **Create** and asks you to **Enter name**.
	For this example, use a backslash and a single letter so that the macro can be executed with the **[Alt]** key in combination with that letter.
\S ↵	Specifies the name of the macro and requests the range.
B12 ↵	Specifies the range to be named and returns to **READY** mode.
	You should also document the macro by entering its name in cell **A12** (be sure to type **'\S** and not simply **\S**) and a brief description of its purpose in cell **C12**.

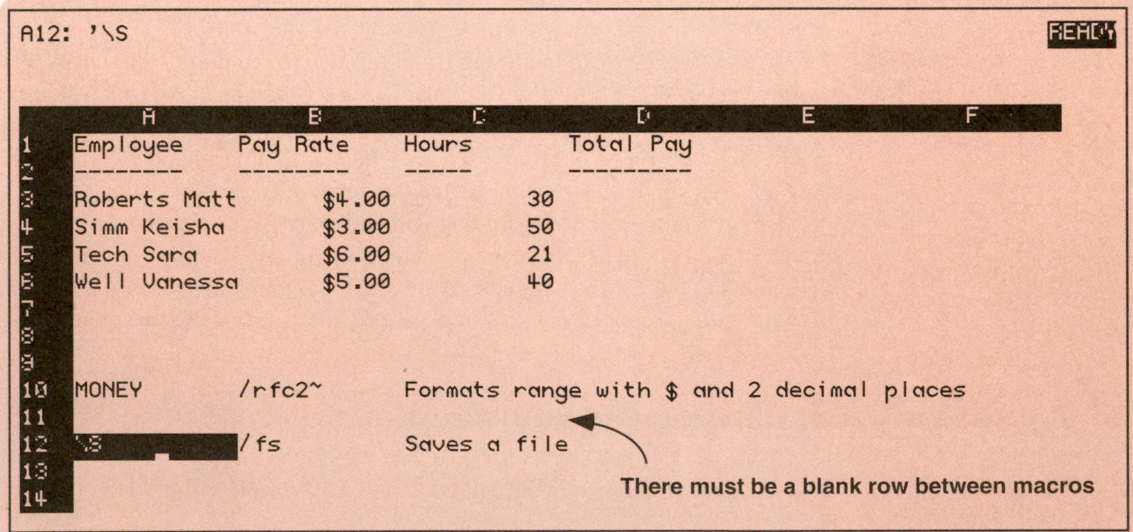

Continued . . .

Keystroke	Action Resulting from Keystroke
	From now on, to save this worksheet all you have to do is press **[Alt-S]** and then type a name for the file.
[Alt-S]	Executes the *Save* macro and requests a name for the file to be saved.
PAY-MAC1 ↵	Specifies the file name, saves the current worksheet using that name, and returns to **READY** mode.

In the above example, note that cell **A12** contains **'\S** (as is shown in the control panel) but only **\S** is displayed at location **A12**. Recall that the apostrophe (**'**) is a special code that informs Lotus 1-2-3 that the cell contains text (in this case, the characters **\S**). If you were to type **\S** (without the apostrophe) in a cell, Lotus 1-2-3 would assume that it was a command rather than text and invoke its *Repeat* feature. *Repeat* allows you to quickly enter repeating text by preceding it with a back slash (\). For example, if you were to type **\S** in cell **A14**, the cell would fill with **S**'s; if you were to type **\Love** into cell **A15** the cell would fill with **Love**:

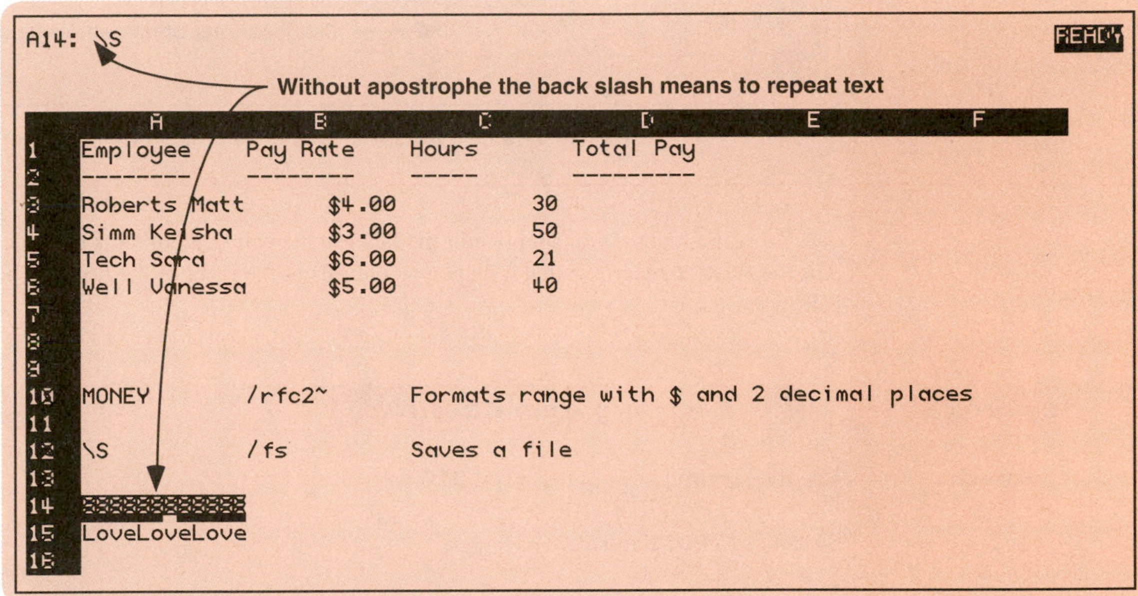

Listing and Editing Macros

You can get a listing of the names of macros by using the *Table* feature. This is useful if your macros are not visible on the screen and you have forgotten where they were stored.

Keystroke	Action Resulting from Keystroke
/	Displays the main menu.
R	Selects **Range** and displays its menu.
N	Selects **Name** and displays its menu.
T	Selects **Table**, asks for the range of cells in which to place the table (this can be any blank range). Let's use **A14.B20** so that the table will be visible.
A14.B20 ↵	Specifies the range for the table and writes the range names and addresses in the table.

Continued . . .

Keystroke	Action Resulting from Keystroke

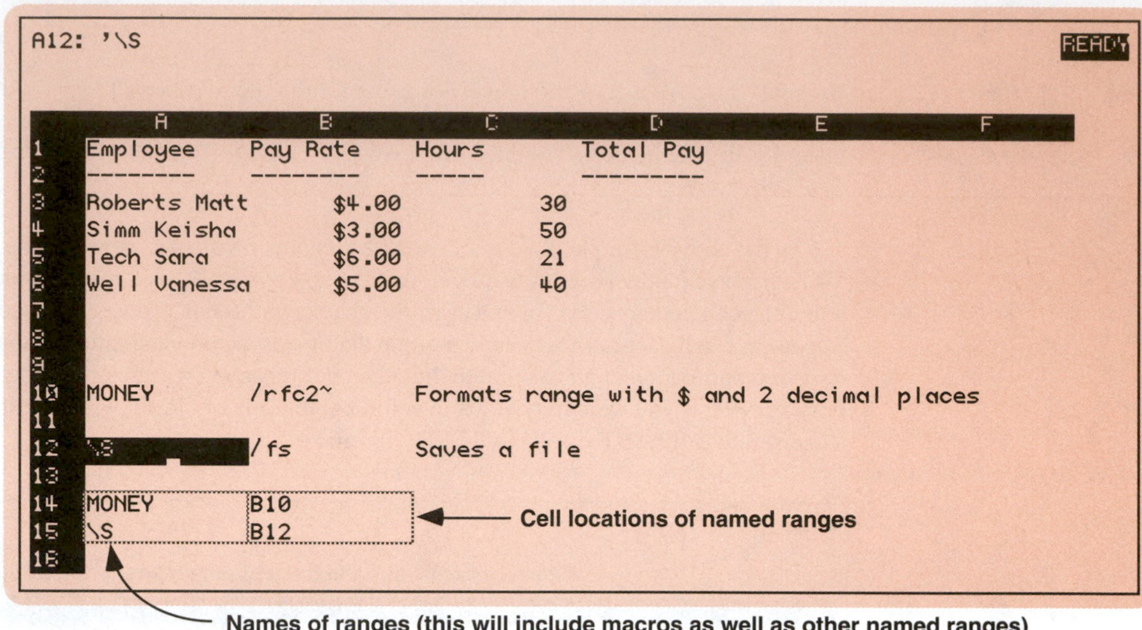

Names of ranges (this will include macros as well as other named ranges)

To edit a macro, you simply edit the label in the cell that contains the macro. For example, to edit the **MONEY** macro so that it displays no digits to the right of the decimal point, you would do the following:

Keystroke	Action Resulting from Keystroke
[arrow]	Use the **[arrow]** keys to make cell **B10** active.
[F2]	Switches to **EDIT** mode.
	Use the standard editing techniques to change the **2** in **'/rfc2~** into a **0**.
↵	Enters the modified label into cell **B10**.

Now, execute the **MONEY** macro by doing the following:

Keystroke	Action Resulting from Keystroke
[Alt-F3]	Specifies that a macro is to be run and displays a list of currently saved macros.
MONEY ↵	Runs the macro called **MONEY** and requests the range to format.
B3.B6 ↵	Specifies the range to format, formats the cells, and returns to **READY** mode.

Continued . . .

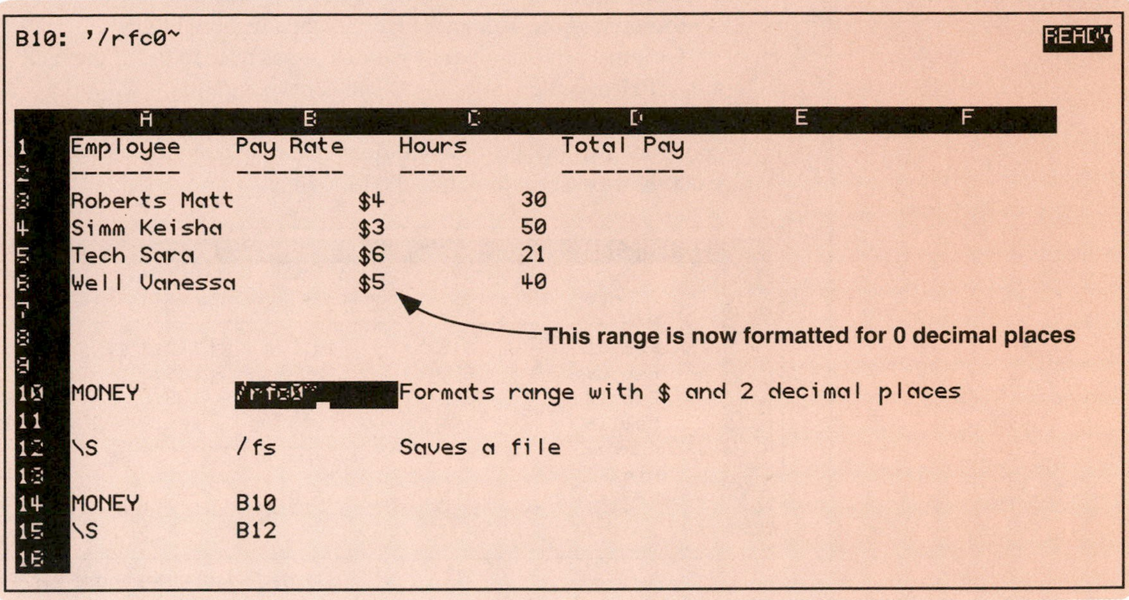

Use your *Save* macro to save the worksheet as **PAY-MAC2** by pressing **[Alt-S]** and then typing **PAY-MAC2 ↵**. Then, use **/ Q**(uit) **Y**(es) to exit the program.

As you can see, macros are very easy to create, run, and modify. If you think you will have to do a set of keystrokes more than once in a worksheet (e.g., changing numeric values to currency, saving different versions of a worksheet, or printing a worksheet), you might as well create a macro to do the task.

Macros created in one worksheet are not directly available to other worksheets. However, Lotus 1-2-3 does allow you to copy macros (and other cell ranges) from one worksheet to another, and it does have a program add-in called *Macro Library Manager* that allows you to create libraries of macros that can be accessed by other worksheets. For more information, consult the *Lotus 1-2-3 Reference Manual.*

TO TAKE A BREAK Remove diskette(s). To resume (hard disk): Insert *Data* diskette, type **C: ↵**, **CD\123 ↵**, **123 ↵**. To resume (two drive): Insert diskettes, type **B: ↵**, **123 ↵**.

Homework Exercises

① Alberto Contino wanted to find out what kind of gas mileage his new car was getting, so he collected the following data:

Date	*Odometer*	*Gallons*	*Price*
Feb 01	315	10.2	110.9
Feb 06	670	13.4	109.9
Feb 12	896	8.8	109.9
Feb 16	1194	11.3	109.9

Continued . . .

where

Date is the date he filled up the tank with gas
Odometer is the odometer reading when he bought gas
Gallons is the number of gallons of gas needed to fill the tank
Price is the cost of the gas in cents per gallon

Construct a worksheet that will display the information given and use proper formatting to make the worksheet look like the following:

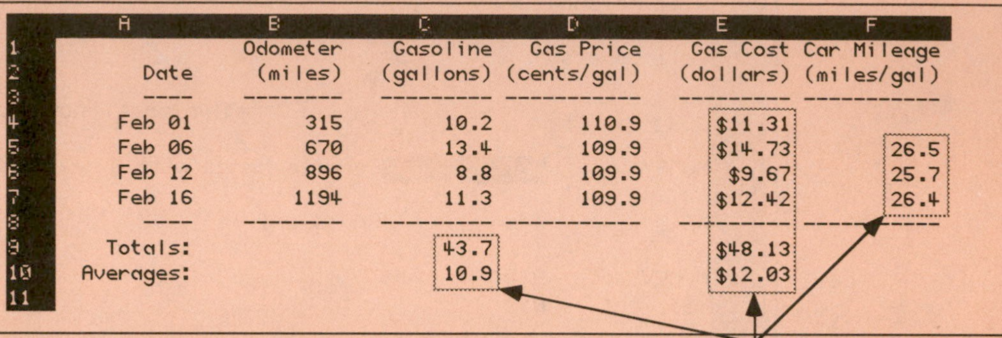

	A	B	C	D	E	F
1		Odometer	Gasoline	Gas Price	Gas Cost	Car Mileage
2	Date	(miles)	(gallons)	(cents/gal)	(dollars)	(miles/gal)
3	----	--------	---------	-----------	---------	-----------
4	Feb 01	315	10.2	110.9	$11.31	
5	Feb 06	670	13.4	109.9	$14.73	26.5
6	Feb 12	896	8.8	109.9	$9.67	25.7
7	Feb 16	1194	11.3	109.9	$12.42	26.4
8	----	--------	---------	-----------	---------	-----------
9	Totals:		43.7		$48.13	
10	Averages:		10.9		$12.03	
11						

Write formulas for these values on printed output.

The boxed values should be calculated by Lotus 1-2-3. Write the actual formulas on the printed output next to the appropriate numbers. For those formulas that are identical except for cell locations (e.g., cells **F5** and **F6**), you need only write the formula for one cell. Save the worksheet as **HWL2-01** and then print it.

---

② For the worksheet from Exercise 1, split the screen vertically between columns **C** and **D** and arrange the two screens so that they appear as shown below:

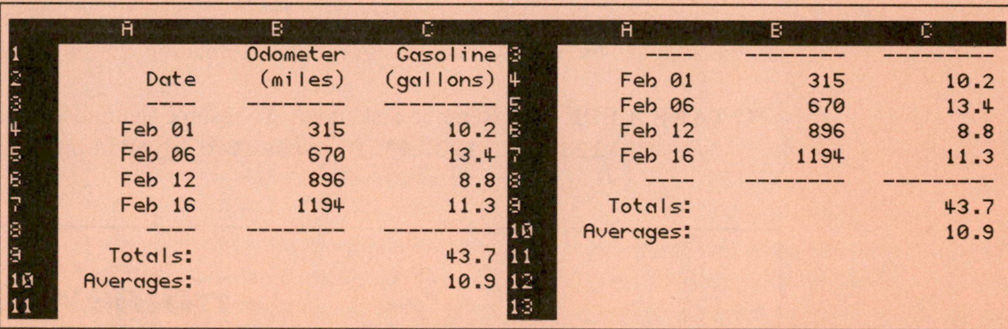

	A	B	C
1		Odometer	Gasoline
2	Date	(miles)	(gallons)
3	----	--------	---------
4	Feb 01	315	10.2
5	Feb 06	670	13.4
6	Feb 12	896	8.8
7	Feb 16	1194	11.3
8	----	--------	---------
9	Totals:		43.7
10	Averages:		10.9
11			

	A	B	C
3	----	--------	---------
4	Feb 01	315	10.2
5	Feb 06	670	13.4
6	Feb 12	896	8.8
7	Feb 16	1194	11.3
8	----	--------	---------
9	Totals:		43.7
10	Averages:		10.9
11			
12			
13			

Do a screen dump of the result. Then, unsplit the screen.

---

③ For the worksheet from Exercise 1, lock the titles in rows **1**, **2**, and **3** and column **A**. Use the **[arrow]** keys so that column **E** appears next to column **A** and row **7** appears next to row **3** as follows:

```
     A          E          F           G          H
1           Gas Cost  Car Mileage
2     Date  (dollars) (miles/gal)
3     ----  --------- -----------
7   Feb 16     $12.42        26.4
8     ----  --------- -----------
9   Totals:    $48.13
10 Averages:   $12.03
```

Do a screen dump of the result and then unlock the titles.

---

④ Use row insertion to insert two new rows at the top of the worksheet you created in Exercise 1. Then, insert the label **`Date:`** in cell **`A1`** and use the **`@NOW`** function to display the current date in cell **`B1`**. Format cell **`B1`** so that the date is displayed in the form **`DD-MMM-YY`**. Finally, insert the following two new sets of data into rows **`10`** and **`11`** of the worksheet:

Date	*Odometer*	*Gallons*	*Price*
Feb 21	1380	6.7	111.9
Feb 28	1690	11.0	111.9

Be sure to adjust the formulas, if needed, to take the new data into account in the totals and averages. You may notice that the sum displayed in cell **`E13`** is off by one cent. This is because the values in column **`E`** are calculated to 14 decimal places but you have displayed them rounded off to 2 decimal places. Lotus 1-2-3 does its calculations on the actual values and not the rounded off values.

The final worksheet should look like the following:

```
      A          B           C           D           E          F
1    Date:    15-Feb-91
2
3            Odometer    Gasoline   Gas Price    Gas Cost  Car Mileage
4     Date    (miles)   (gallons) (cents/gal)   (dollars) (miles/gal)
5     ----   --------   --------- -----------   --------- -----------
6   Feb 01        315        10.2       110.9     $11.31
7   Feb 06        670        13.4       109.9     $14.73        26.5
8   Feb 12        896         8.8       109.9      $9.67        25.7
9   Feb 16       1194        11.3       109.9     $12.42        26.4
10  Feb 21       1380         6.7       111.9      $7.50        27.8
11  Feb 28       1690        11.0       111.9     $12.31        28.2
12    ----   --------   --------- -----------   --------- -----------
13  Totals:                  61.4                 $67.93
14 Averages:                 10.2                 $11.32
15
```

Save this worksheet using the name **`HWL2-04`** and then print it.

---

⑤ Modify the worksheet from Exercise 4 so that it uses **`@VLOOKUP`** to look up comments in a table and then displays the comments in column **`G`**. The selection criteria for the comments is as follows.

Continued . . .

Comment	***Gas Mileage (from column F)***
None	Blank (as from cell **G6**)
Poor	20.0 through 25.9
Fair	26.0 through 26.9
Good	27.0 through 27.9
Excellent	28.0 and over

Save the worksheet using the name **HWL2-05** and then print it. Write on the printed output the formula you use for the **@VLOOKUP** command for one of the cells in column **G**.

---

⑥ Sharon Long, the owner of MicroMania Computers, Inc., a computer retail store, wants to keep a record of her employees' sales performances.

Use the data given below and proper formatting to construct a worksheet that displays the number, name, hardware sales, software sales, and total sales of all employees. Display the current date and time as recorded on the computer's clock using the **@NOW** function.

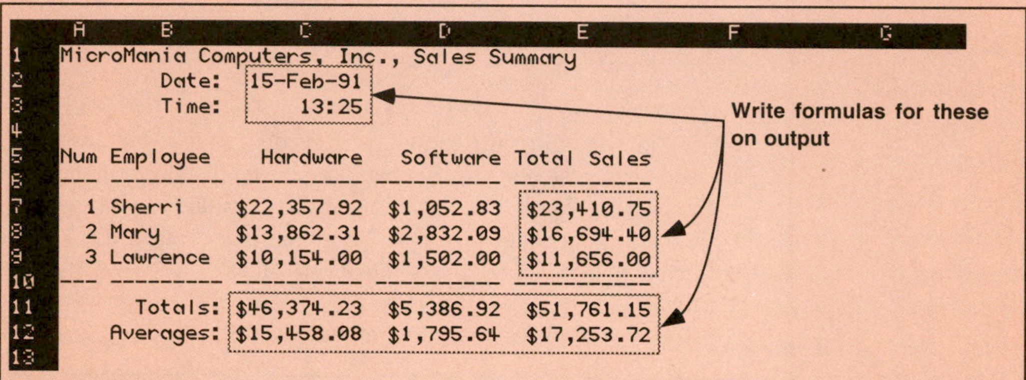

The boxed values should be calculated by Lotus 1-2-3. Write the actual formulas on the printed output next to the appropriate numbers. For those formulas that are identical except for cell locations, you need only write the formula for one cell. Save the worksheet using the name **HWL2-06** and then print it.

---

⑦ Construct a bar chart of the data from Exercise 6. Use the employee names as the independent variable (i.e., the labels) and the total sales as the dependent variable (i.e., the values to be graphed) and include appropriate headings. The graph should look like the following:

CHAPTER TWO

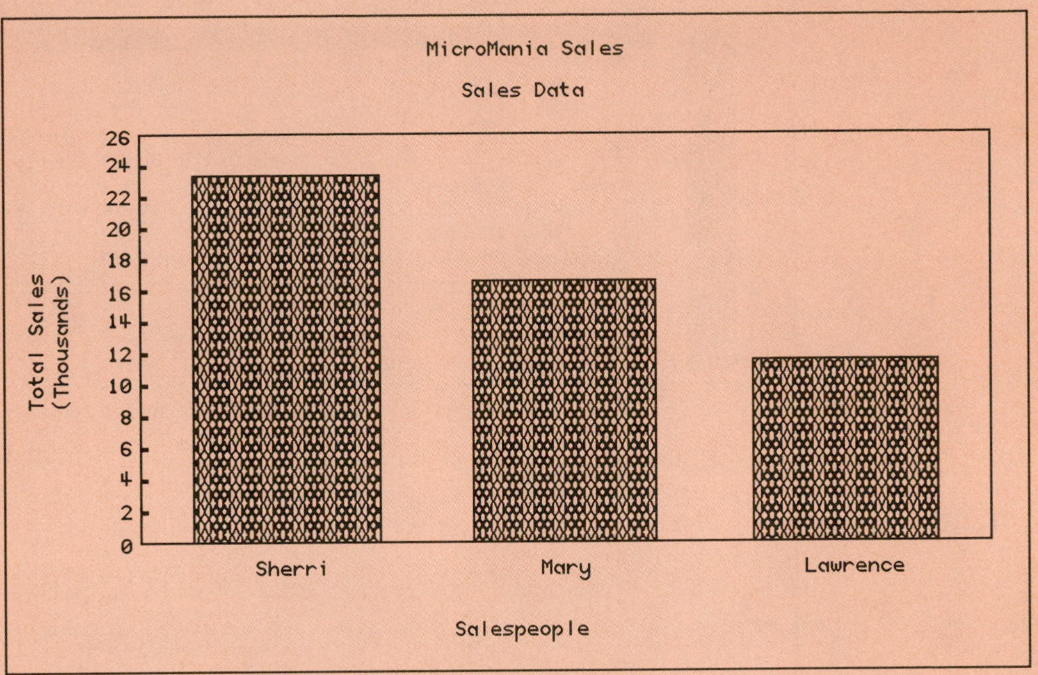

Save the worksheet with the graph definition as **HWL2-07** and then print the graph using **[PrintScreen]**. Also, save the graph image as **HWL2-07.PIC** (this file will be used in Exercise 11).

---

⑧ Construct and print an exploded pie chart of the data from Exercise 6. Use the employee names as the independent variable (i.e., the labels) and the hardware sales as the dependent variable (i.e., the values to be graphed) and include appropriate headings. Explode the wedge representing Sherri.

Save the worksheet with the graph definition as **HWL2-08** and use **[PrintScreen]** to print the graph.

---

⑨ Extend the worksheet from Exercise 6 by computing the earnings of the employees. Employees earn a base salary of $10,000 per year plus a commission on items they sell. The commissions are computed as follows:

Hardware sales—employee earns a 10% commission on hardware sales up to the first $20,000 worth of equipment sold, and then 12% on all hardware sales over $20,000.

Software sales—employee earns 8% on all sales.

Be sure to carefully think through and write out the IF/THEN/ELSE decision logic before you begin to enter the formula into the worksheet. The time you spend thinking about what you have to do will save you a lot of time in the long run.

Use proper formatting to make the worksheet look like the following:

Continued . . .

CHAPTER TWO

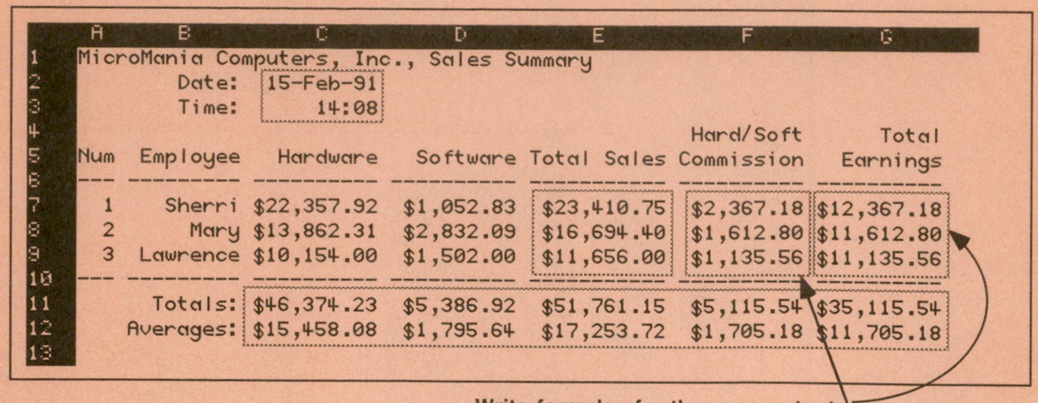

MicroMania Computers, Inc., Sales Summary

Date: 15-Feb-91
Time: 14:08

Num	Employee	Hardware	Software	Total Sales	Hard/Soft Commission	Total Earnings
1	Sherri	$22,357.92	$1,052.83	$23,410.75	$2,367.18	$12,367.18
2	Mary	$13,862.31	$2,832.09	$16,694.40	$1,612.80	$11,612.80
3	Lawrence	$10,154.00	$1,502.00	$11,656.00	$1,135.56	$11,135.56
	Totals:	$46,374.23	$5,386.92	$51,761.15	$5,115.54	$35,115.54
	Averages:	$15,458.08	$1,795.64	$17,253.72	$1,705.18	$11,705.18

Write formulas for these on output

The boxed values should be calculated by Lotus 1-2-3. Write the actual formulas on the printed output next to the appropriate numbers. For those formulas that are identical except for cell locations (e.g., cells **F7** and **F8**), you need only write the formula for one cell.

Save the worksheet under the name **HWL2-09** and then print it.

---

⑩ Save the printed version of the worksheet you created in Exercise 6 to a file called **HWL2-10.PRN**. Drop to DOS and use the DOS **TYPE** command to display the contents of the file. Do a screen dump of the display.

---

⑪ Create a memo using WordPerfect and then import the file you saved in Exercise 10 and the graph you saved in Exercise 7. Save the final letter as **HWL2-11** and print it. The final document should look like the following:

Memo to: Dave Giese
Memo from: Sharon Long
Date: 15 February 1991

Below is a summary of the employee earnings for our department for the month of January.

Num	Employee	Hardware	Software	Total Sales
1	Sherri	$22,357.92	$1,052.83	$23,410.75
2	Mary	$13,862.31	$2,832.09	$16,694.40
3	Lawrence	$10,154.00	$1,502.00	$11,656.00
	Totals:	$46,374.23	$5,386.92	$51,761.15
	Averages:	$15,458.08	$1,795.64	$17,253.72

As you can see from the bar chart below, Sherri should receive the bonus for this month.

I will make travel arrangements with her for her all-expenses paid trip to Hawaii.

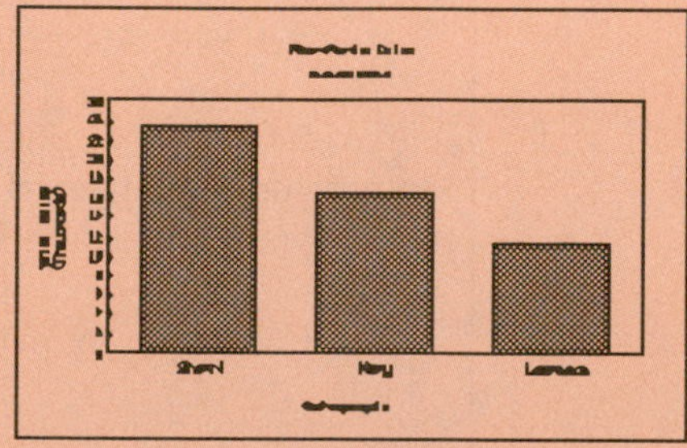

CHAPTER TWO

⑫ Create a macro that can be run by pressing **[Alt-D]** which will format a cell containing the **@NOW** function to display the date in the form **DD-MMM-YY**. Store the macro name in cell **A16**, the keystrokes in cell **B16**, and a description of what the macro does in cell **C16**. Save the worksheet using the name **HWL2-12** and then do a screen dump showing cells **A16**, **B16**, and **C16**.

APPENDIX: Summary of Selected Lotus 1-2-3 Features

The following is a brief description of many of the Lotus 1-2-3 Release 2.2 commands and features with reference to pages in the text. Items with N/C in place of a page number were not specifically covered in the text but are provided for your information. Consult the *Lotus 1-2-3 Reference Manual* for more details.

Quick Review

Page	Keystrokes	Description
L18	`123` ↵	Access Lotus 1-2-3 from the DOS environment.
L16	**[ESC]**	Cancel a command or close a menu.
L60	`/ W E Y`	Clear the screen (without saving the current worksheet). Use **[Alt-F4]** to undo.
L49	`/ R E...`	Erase a range of cells (specify range).
L16	`/ Q Y Y`	Exit Lotus 1-2-3 (without saving the current worksheet) and return to DOS.
L37	`/ P P...`	Print a worksheet.
L29	`/ F R...`	Retrieve a worksheet (specify name).
L24	`/ F S...`	Save a worksheet (specify name).

Cursor Control in `READY` and `POINT` Modes

Page	Keystrokes	Description
L18	↵	Enter a label, value, or formula into a cell and leave that cell active.
L13	←	Move the cell pointer 1 cell **left**.
L13	→	Move the cell pointer 1 cell **right**.
L13	↑	Move the cell pointer 1 cell **up**.
L13	↓	Move the cell pointer 1 cell **down**.
L14	**[Ctrl →]** or **[Tab]**	Move **right** one screen.
L14	**[Ctrl ←]** or **[Shift-Tab]**	Move **left** one screen.
L14	**[End]** plus **[arrow]**	Move the cell pointer in the direction of the arrow to the next cell containing an entry.
L15	**[Home]**	Move the cell pointer to cell **`A1`**.
L14	**[End] [Home]**	Move the cell pointer to the lower right corner of the active area.
L14	**[PageUp]**	Move the cell pointer **up** one screen.
L14	**[PageDown]**	Move the cell pointer **down** one screen.
L13	**[F5]** . . . (GoTo)	Move the cell pointer to a specific cell (specify cell).
L80	**[F6]** (Window)	Move the cell pointer to the next window (use only when the screen has been split).

Cursor Control in **EDIT** Mode

Page	Keystrokes	Description
L22	↵	Complete editing and leave the cell pointer at the current cell.
L21	←	Move the cursor 1 character **left**.
L21	→	Move the cursor 1 character **right**.
L21	↑	Complete editing and move the cell pointer 1 cell **up**.
L21	↓	Complete editing and move the cell pointer 1 cell **down**.
L22	**[Ctrl →]** or **[Tab]**	Move the cursor **right** 5 characters.
L22	**[Ctrl ←]** or **[Shift-Tab]**	Move the cursor **left** 5 characters.
L22	**[End]**	Move the cursor to the **last** character of the line.
L22	**[Home]**	Move the cursor to the **first** character of the line.
L22	**[Backspace]**	Delete 1 character to the left of the cursor.
L22	**[Delete]**	Delete 1 character at the cursor.
L22	**[Esc]**	Delete all characters on the line.
L22	**[Insert]**	Toggle between insert (**INS**) and typeover (**OVR**) modes.

Cell Entry Prefixes

Page	Prefix	Description
L19	'	Align labels on the left-hand side of the cell.
L19	"	Align labels on the right-hand side of the cell.
L19	^	Center labels in the cell.
L34	+	Indicates a formula (e.g., **+B3*B4** finds the product of the values in cells **B3** and **B4**).
L47	@	Indicates a special Lotus 1-2-3 function (e.g., **@SUM(B3.B9)**).
L137	\	Causes text to repeat (e.g., **\R** will fill the cell with **R**'s).

Features

Page	Keystrokes	Description
L18	**123** ↵	Access Lotus 1-2-3 from the DOS environment.
N/C	**[F4]**	Address, change range address amongst relative, absolute, and mixed while in **EDIT** mode.
L66	**[F9]**	Calculate, recalculates the worksheet formulas.
L16	**[Esc]**	Cancel a command or close a menu.
L60	**/ W E Y**	Clear the screen (without saving the current worksheet). Use **[Alt-F4]** to undo.

Continued . . .

Page	Keystrokes	Description
L45	/ C...	Copy a range of cells (specify range).
L94	@IF(condition,true,false)	Decision making.
L42	/ S	Drop to DOS (execute DOS commands without leaving Lotus 1-2-3). To return, type **EXIT** ↵.
L21	[F2]	Edit the contents of the active cell.
N/C	/ F E...	Erase a file from the disk (specify name).
L49	/ R E...	Erase a range of cells (specify range).
L60	/ W E Y	Erase the worksheet from the screen.
L16	/ Q Y Y	Exit Lotus 1-2-3 (without saving the current worksheet) and return to DOS.
L92	/ D F...	Fill a range of cells with numbers (specify range and values).
L31	/ R F...	Format a range of cells (specify format).
L13	[F5]...	Go to a specified cell.
L110	/ G...	Graph data (specify type, range, etc.).
L15	[F1]	Help screen.
L87	/ W I C...	Insert a range of columns (specify range).
L50	/ W I R...	Insert a range of rows (specify range).
L30	/ R L...	Justify a range of cells (specify left, right or center).
L133	[Alt-F5]	Macro define (turns on macro learn function). Specify learn range first.
L135	[Alt-F3]	Macro execute (specify macro name).
L16	/	Main menu display.
L13	[F5]...	Move the cell pointer to the specified cell location.
N/C	/ M...	Move data from one cell range to another (specify ranges).
L52	/ R N...	Name a range of cells (specify range and name).
L54	/ R N T...	Names, display a list of defined range names.
L68	/ P P O...	Page format (header, footer, margins, borders). Specify desired options.
L122	LOTUS ↵ P...	Print a graph using the *PrintGraph* program (begin from DOS or the Access menu). Graph must have already been saved using **/ G S...**
L37	/ P P...	Print a worksheet.
L66	[F9]	Recalculate all worksheet formulas.
L29	/ F R...	Retrieve a worksheet (specify name).
L24	/ F S...	Save a worksheet (specify name).
L42	/ S	Shell (execute DOS commands without leaving Lotus 1-2-3). To return, type **EXIT** ↵.

Continued . . .

Page	Keystrokes	Description
L56	/ D S...	Sort a range of cells (specify range and sort keys).
L79	/ W W...	Split the screen into two windows (specify how).
L80	[F6]	Switch windows (i.e., move the cell pointer to the next window).
L52	[Alt-F4]	Undo the last operation.
L22–24	/ W C C S...	Width of columns (define or change). Specify range and width.
L80	[F6]	Window, move the cell pointer to the next window.

Relational Operators

Page	Operator	Description
L94	=	Equal to.
L94	<>	Not equal to.
L95	>	Greater than.
L95	<	Less than.
L95	>=	Greater than or equal to.
L95	<=	Less than or equal to.

Mathematical Operators

Page	Operator	Description
L33	+	Addition.
L33	-	Subtraction.
L33	*	Multiplication.
L33	/	Division.
L33	^	Exponentiation (e.g., 5^2 is written as **5^2**).
L33	( )	Parentheses (for grouping or to change the order in which mathematical operations are to be performed).

Logical Operators

Page	Operator	Description
L94	**#AND#**	Boolean *and* (used to connect two conditions, both of which must be true for the entire condition to be true).
L94	**#OR#**	Boolean *or* (used to connect two conditions, either one of which may be true for the entire condition to be true).
L94	**#NOT#**	Boolean *not* (reverses a condition—false becomes true and vice versa).

Selected Mathematical and Statistical Functions

Page	Operator	Description
N/C	**@ABS(X)**	Calculates the absolute value of **X**.
L47	**@AVG** (range)	Calculates the average of the cells in the specified range.
L63	**@COUNT** (range)	Counts the number of nonblank cells in the specified range.
N/C	**@LN(X)**	Calculates the natural log of **X**.
L74	**@MAX** (range)	Finds the maximum value in the specified range.
L63	**@MIN** (range)	Finds the minimum value in the specified range.
L101	**@NA**	Indicates the value is not available.
N/C	**@SQRT(X)**	Calculates the square root of **X**.
L65	**@STD** (range)	Calculates the *population* standard deviation.
L47	**@SUM** (range)	Calculates the sum of the cells in the specified range.

Menu Organization For your reference, the next two pages contain charts showing the organization of many of the commands available through the Lotus 1-2-3 menus.

```
Worksheet
    Global
        Format
            Fixed
            Sci
            Currency
            ,
            General
            +/-
            Percent
            Date
            Text
            Hidden
        Label-Prefix
            Left
            Right
            Center
        Column-Width
        Recalculation
            Natural
            Automatic
            Manual
            Iteration
        Protection
        Default
            Printer
            Directory
            Status
            Update
        Zero
    Insert
        Column
        Row
    Delete
        Column
        Row
    Column
        Set-Width
        Reset-Width
        Hide
        Display
        Column-Range
            Set-Width
            Reset-Width
    Erase
    Titles
        Both
        Horizontal
        Vertical
        Clear
    Window
        Horizontal
        Vertical
        Sync
        Unsync
        Clear
    Status
    Page
    Learn
        Range
        Cancel
        Erase
```

```
Range
    Format
        Fixed
        Sci
        Currency
        ,
        General
        +/-
        Percen
        Date
        Text
        Hidden
        Reset
    Label
        Left
        Right
        Center
    Erase
    Name
        Create
        Delete
        Labels
        Reset
        Table
    Justify
    Prot
    Unprot
    Input
    Value
    Trans
    Search
        Formulas
        Labels
        Both
```

```
Copy
    Enter range to copy FROM
    Enter range to copy TO
```

```
Move
    Enter range to move FROM
    Enter range to move TO
```

```
File
    Retrieve
    Save
        Cancel
        Replace
        Backup
    Combine
        Copy
        Add
        Subtract
    Xtract
        Formulas
        Values
    Erase
        Worksheet
        Print
        Graph
        Other
    List
        Worksheet
        Print
        Graph
        Other
        Linked
    Import
        Text
        Numbers
    Directory
    Admin
```

Print
- Printer
  - Range
  - Line
  - Page
  - Options
    - Header
    - Footer
    - Margins
    - Borders
    - Setup
    - Pg-Length
    - Other
      - As-Displayed
      - Cell-Formulas
      - Formatted
      - Unformatted
    - Quit
- File
  - Range
  - Line
  - Page
  - Options
    - Header
    - Footer
    - Margins
    - Borders
    - Setup
    - Pg-Length
    - Other
      - As-Displayed
      - Cell-Formulas
      - Formatted
      - Unformatted
    - Quit

Graph
- Type
  - Line
  - Bar
  - XY
  - Stack-Bar
  - Pie
- X
- A
- B
- C
- D
- E
- F
- Reset
- View
- Save
- Options
  - Legend
  - Format
  - Titles
  - Grid
  - Scale
  - Color
  - B&W
  - Data-Labels
  - Quit
- Name
  - Use
  - Create
  - Delete
  - Reset
  - Table
- Group
  - Columnwise
  - Rowwise
- Quit

PrintGraph
- Image-Select
- Settings
  - Image
  - Hardware
    - Graphs-Directory
    - Fonts-Directory
    - Interface
    - Printer
    - Size-Paper
    - Quit
  - Action
  - Save
  - Reset
  - Quit
- Go
- Align
- Page
- Exit

Data
- Fill
- Table
- Sort
  - Data-Range
  - Primary-Key
  - Secondary-Key
  - Rest
  - Go
  - Quit
- Query
- Distribution
- Matrix
- Regression
- Parse

System
- (Temporarily return control to DOS)

Add-In
- Attach
- Detach
- Invoke
- Clear
- Quit

Quit
- Yes
- No

PART III

dBASE IV

Introduction to Database Management

Objectives *After you have completed this chapter, you should be able to*

- Explain the basic concepts and terms related to databases and database management systems.
- Access the dBASE IV program.
- Identify the different parts of the dBASE IV screen.
- Explain the differences between using the Control Center and the dot prompt.
- Access on-line help from dBASE IV.
- Create a database structure that can be used by dBASE IV.

CHAPTER 1

- Enter data into a database.
- Display data of a database.
- Create view queries to display selected database information.
- Locate records in a database using complex searching strategies.
- Modify and delete selected records in a database.
- Create and modify reports on selected records of a database using a variety of formats.

Introduction

A **database** is a collection of related information stored in the memory of a computer or on a disk. A *database management system (DBMS)* is a set of computer programs whose purpose is to make it easy and efficient for users to record, store, modify, and retrieve individual pieces or groups of data. Computerized databases take the place of the traditional file folders and index files used to keep track of related information. Most database management systems are able to do the following tasks: add or delete information, search for information based on some attribute of the data, modify (update) information, arrange the data according to some specified criteria, and print reports in different formats.

Database management programs are useful in both business and the home. For example, a business may create a database for payroll to keep track of employee names, social security numbers, addresses, salaries, and numbers of deductions and use that information to print paychecks and to keep records for the IRS. The same business may have another database for personnel that includes information on names, social security numbers, salaries, job titles, addresses, employment histories, educational backgrounds, and training. In the home, a database management system can, for example, be used to create an inventory of household goods, important papers, financial holdings (bank accounts, stocks, bonds), a grocery list, a Christmas card list, or a record of items bought (for budgeting or tax purposes).

For the purposes of illustration, let's assume that you have set up a small home inventory database that contains the following information on 15 items in your house:

Category of item:	A general classification (e.g., furniture, appliance).
Name of item:	A descriptive name (e.g., recliner, dishwasher).
Manufacturer:	The name of the manufacturer (e.g., La-Z-Boy, Kitchen Aid).
Serial number:	The manufacturer's serial number used to identify the item.
Date of purchase:	The year, month, and day the item was purchased.
Value:	The purchase price. Some insurance policies will give you the full purchase price of an item that was destroyed or stolen, while others will prorate the purchase price based on the item's age.

The database can be visualized as being made up of a rectangular grid of rows and columns in much the same way as a spreadsheet. Each row in the database is called a **record** and contains all the information for a single item. Each column is called a **field** and contains the specific information about the records. In this example, the fields will be category, name, manufacturer, serial number, date of purchase, and value, and the records will be the specific data on each item. A single field must be the same width (size) for each record just as in a spreadsheet all cells in the same column must be the same width. This width is called the *field width*. You can picture the database for this example as follows:

	Field	Field	Field	Field	Field	Field
Field width →	1234567890	123456789012345	123456789012	1234567890	12345678	12345678
Field name →	CATEGORY	NAME	MANUFACT	SERIAL_NUM	DATE	VALUE
Record #1 →	Electronic	Computer	IBM	F3827122	02/10/90	1200.00
Record #2 →	Electronic	Pro Printer	IBM	03483	02/10/90	450.00
Record #3 →	Electronic	External drive	IBM	F392281	02/10/90	356.00
Record #4 →	Appliance	Microwave oven	Sears	2339112	01/22/89	450.00
Record #5 →	Appliance	Color TV	RCA	2338442	05/25/89	360.00
Record #6 →	Electronic	Stereo	Fischer	34562	03/12/89	412.00
Record #7 →	Furniture	Sofa	Wilder	---	11/21/84	450.00
Record #8 →	Furniture	Recliner	La-Z-Boy	---	03/23/87	350.00
Record #9 →	Furniture	Dry sink	Hand made	---	04/12/87	500.00
Record #10 →	Appliance	Refrigerator	Wards	493323	03/22/87	450.00
Record #11 →	Appliance	Stove	Wards	533282	03/22/87	350.00
Record #12 →	Appliance	Dishwasher	Kitchen Aid	04322344	09/23/81	550.00
Record #13 →	Furniture	Bed, mattress	Simmons	---	09/03/87	100.00
Record #14 →	Furniture	Bed, spring	Simmons	---	09/03/87	100.00
Record #15 →	Furniture	Bed, frame	Simmons	---	09/03/87	100.00

Once all the data have been entered into the database, you will be able to produce reports of various kinds, based on the stored information, or export the information to applications such as WordPerfect or Lotus 1-2-3. The data may also be accessed by computer programs written in languages such as BASIC,

Pascal, or C. In addition, you will be able to quickly and easily find, add, delete, or modify any item in the database.

As you can see, there are similarities between database management programs and spreadsheet programs. Spreadsheet programs tend to be more flexible than database management programs because they can store both formulas and raw data and because they are more powerful in doing mathematical calculations. However, database management programs are better suited for storing large sets of data, and they are more flexible in the way they generate reports. These differences and limitations are important but the line between database programs and spreadsheet programs is becoming blurred as new versions of the programs become available. Also, as you shall see, data can be easily transferred between the two types of programs.

Definitions

Before you begin to work with dBASE IV, you should familiarize yourself with the definitions of terms frequently encountered when talking about database management programs. Examples used here refer to the home inventory database discussed in the previous section.

Data . . . (D4): The facts and figures that, when correctly processed and interpreted, become information. The word *data* technically is a plural (as in *these data are correct*); the singular version is datum. However, most people ignore this distinction. *Numeric* data consists of values (numbers) that can be used in arithmetic computations. The cost (350) of the recliner is a piece of numeric data. *Alphanumeric* data consists of text (letters), digits, punctuation, and other special characters that can be stored, but which are not used in arithmetic computations. The name of the manufacturer of the recliner (La-Z-Boy) is a piece of alphanumeric data.

Database . . . (D4): A large collection of data that is organized in such a way that it can be easily accessed and modified. The complete set of data on the home inventory is a database.

Database management program . . . (D4): A computer program that is designed to create, organize, and provide access to databases. dBASE IV is a database management program.

Dot prompt . . . (D16): One of two modes of operation of dBASE IV (compare with the menu system). The user controls the dBASE IV program directly by typing commands available through the dBASE IV command language. Advanced users employ this method of giving dBASE IV instructions because it is fast and powerful.

Field . . . (D4): A group of characters that are meaningful. Fields are used to describe characteristics or attributes of sets of data. The values of all the items in the home inventory database is an example of a field (we would refer to it as the value field).

Menu system . . . (D9): One of two modes of operation of dBASE IV (compare with the dot prompt). The menu system provides a series of screens, menus, and prompts to help guide the user through the dBASE IV command structure.

Query . . . (D56): A query is a set of dBASE IV instructions that dictates which fields and records are to be displayed, printed, or edited. For example, you might want to display or print selected information on all the items in the home inventory database that have a value of over $400. If you ask the same type of question many times, you may want to set up a *query form,* which is like a questionnaire that requests specific information from you (e.g., the minimum value of the items you want listed).

Record . . . (D4): A group of fields that are related in some way. Each record of a database contains the same fields. All of the information on the recliner (category, name, manufacturer, serial number, date of purchase, and value) is considered one record of the home inventory database.

Record pointer . . . (D30): A number that is used by dBASE IV to keep track of the active record in the database. For example, if recliner is the eighth record in the database, then the record pointer for recliner would be 8.

User interface . . . (D9): The features of a program that control how the human user interacts with the program. dBASE IV has two main user interfaces: The Control Center, a menu-driven interface that allows users to select commands from pull-down menus, and the dot prompt, a command-driven interface that requires users to type commands using the correct words and syntax (rules of grammar).

Database Organizational Models

There are three common organizational models of database management programs: hierarchical, network, and relational.

• Hierarchical Database Model •

In the hierarchical model, data are organized in a manner similar to that of a family tree. Records may be thought of as *parents* of records just below them and as *children* of records just above them. A record can have only one parent but can have many children. For example, you might organize the inventory of your home in a hierarchical fashion as follows:

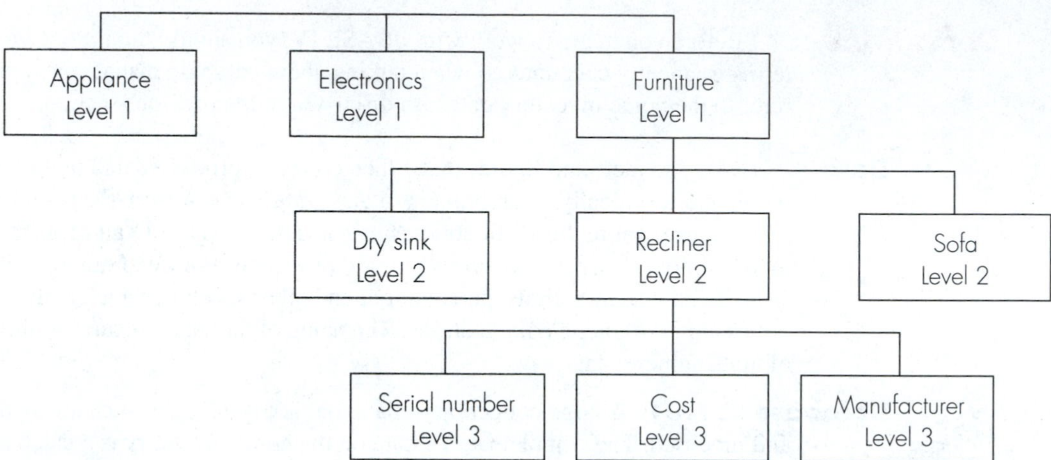

Recliner is the child of furniture and the parent of serial number, cost, and manufacturer. Note that to move from level 3 to level 1 you must go through level 2.

The advantage of this type of model is that data can be easily entered and retrieved. The disadvantage is that, because items in the lower levels are not directly linked, it is difficult to relate one piece of data to another, making such a system more complex than other types of systems.

• Network Database Model •

In the *network model*, the data are set up in a hierarchy, but paths between items are not restricted as in the *hierarchy model*. This allows one record to be linked directly to another even if the records do not have a parent-child relationship. The result is that each record can have many children and many parents. For example, the inventory of your home might look as follows in a network model:

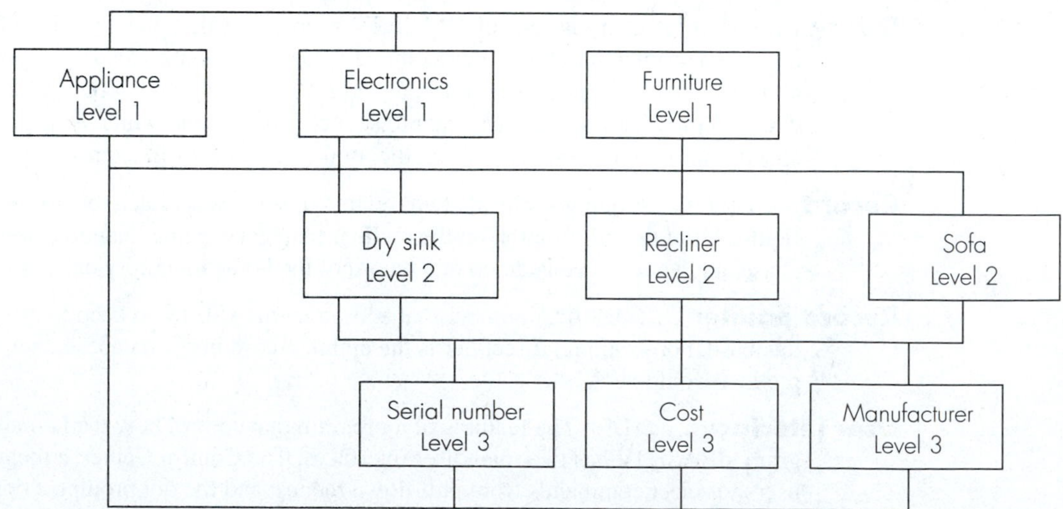

The advantage of the network database model is that many relationships are possible between entries. However, data can only be retrieved using the defined connections between the entries, and once the data structure has been defined it is difficult and costly to change.

• Relational Database Model •

In the *relational model*, the data are set up in two-dimensional tables that describe the relationships among the entries. The columns of the tables (referred to as *attributes*) contain characteristics of the data while the rows (referred to as *tuples*) contain the values of those attributes. For example, a home inventory might look as follows in a relational database:

Item name/Serial number pairs	
NAME	SERIAL_NUM
Dry sink	FSN3411
Recliner	3211
Sofa	8A332
...	...

Serial number/Value pairs	
SERIAL_NUM	VALUE
FSN3411	500
3211	350
8A332	450
...	...

Serial number/Manufacturer pairs	
SERIAL_NUM	MANUFACT
FSN3411	Hand made
3211	La-Z-Boy
8A332	Wilder
...	...

Relational databases are more flexible than hierarchical or network databases and are easier to use. However, relational databases tend to be slower, especially with large sets of data. dBASE IV is an example of a relational database.

System Requirements

The dBASE IV package distributed by the software publisher Ashton-Tate Corporation contains five $3\frac{1}{2}$-inch diskettes, a 780-page *Language Reference Manual*, and eleven smaller reference books and pamphlets. In order to work with dBASE IV you must have an IBM or IBM-compatible computer system that has a hard disk or is connected to a network and at least 640K of RAM.

For your information and reference, a summary of selected dBASE IV features appears on pages D204–16 of the Appendix. In addition, a keyboard template that contains a summary of many program features is located at the end of this book. If your keyboard has 12 function keys along the top, cut out the two halves of the template, tape the ends together, and place the template around the function keys. If your keyboard has 10 function keys along the left-hand side, you still may use the top of the template, but the bottom must be cut off.

dBASE IV must be installed on your computer system before running it. If it has not yet been installed, follow the installation process described in the manual *Getting Started with dBASE IV* that came with the program when you purchased it.

As was the case with WordPerfect and Lotus 1-2-3 we will assume that you are working on a hard-disk system and that the dBASE IV software has been installed on the hard disk in a subdirectory with path **C:\DBIV**. However, because dBASE IV is too large to run on a two-drive system, we will not provide information for such a system. Your course instructor may give you different directions for starting the program and for saving data files for the particular computer system available in your school's computer lab.

Formatting a Data Diskette

You need a blank diskette that will serve as your *dBASE Data* diskette. You will use this diskette for storing the dBASE IV files that you create. If you are using your own computer, you do not need this diskette because you will want to save files directly to your hard disk. If you so desire, and if there is room, you may use your *WordPerfect Data* or *Lotus Data* diskette to store your dBASE IV files. If you do that, it would be a good idea to create a subdirectory to separate the dBASE IV files from the WordPerfect or Lotus 1-2-3 files.

Boot your computer and then format a blank diskette to serve as the *dBASE Data* diskette by doing the following:

- Write *dBASE Data* and your name on a diskette label, attach the label to a new diskette, and insert the diskette into the A: drive.
- Type **FORMAT A:/V/F:*size*** (where ***size*** is diskette capacity—360, 720, 1200, or 1440) and tap **[Enter]**. Be sure your new diskette is in drive A: and then tap **[Enter]** again.

- When asked to enter a label, type your last name and tap **[Enter]**.
- When asked **Format another (Y/N)?**, type **N** and tap **[Enter]**. The system prompt **C:\>** will then be displayed.

Accessing dBASE IV

To load the dBASE IV program into the main memory of the computer, be sure your data diskette is in drive A: and then do the following:

Keystroke	Action Resulting from Keystroke
A: ↵	Makes **A:** the default drive.
C:\DBIV\DBASE ↵	Loads the program into the main memory of the computer and displays an animation showing the program name. If the dBASE IV files on your computer are in a subdirectory with a name other than **DBIV**, use that name in place of **DBIV** in the command **C:\DBIV\DBASE**.

After the animation, a license agreement is displayed. Read the agreement. After a few seconds, the license agreement will disappear and the Control Center screen will be displayed. The screen now should look as follows:

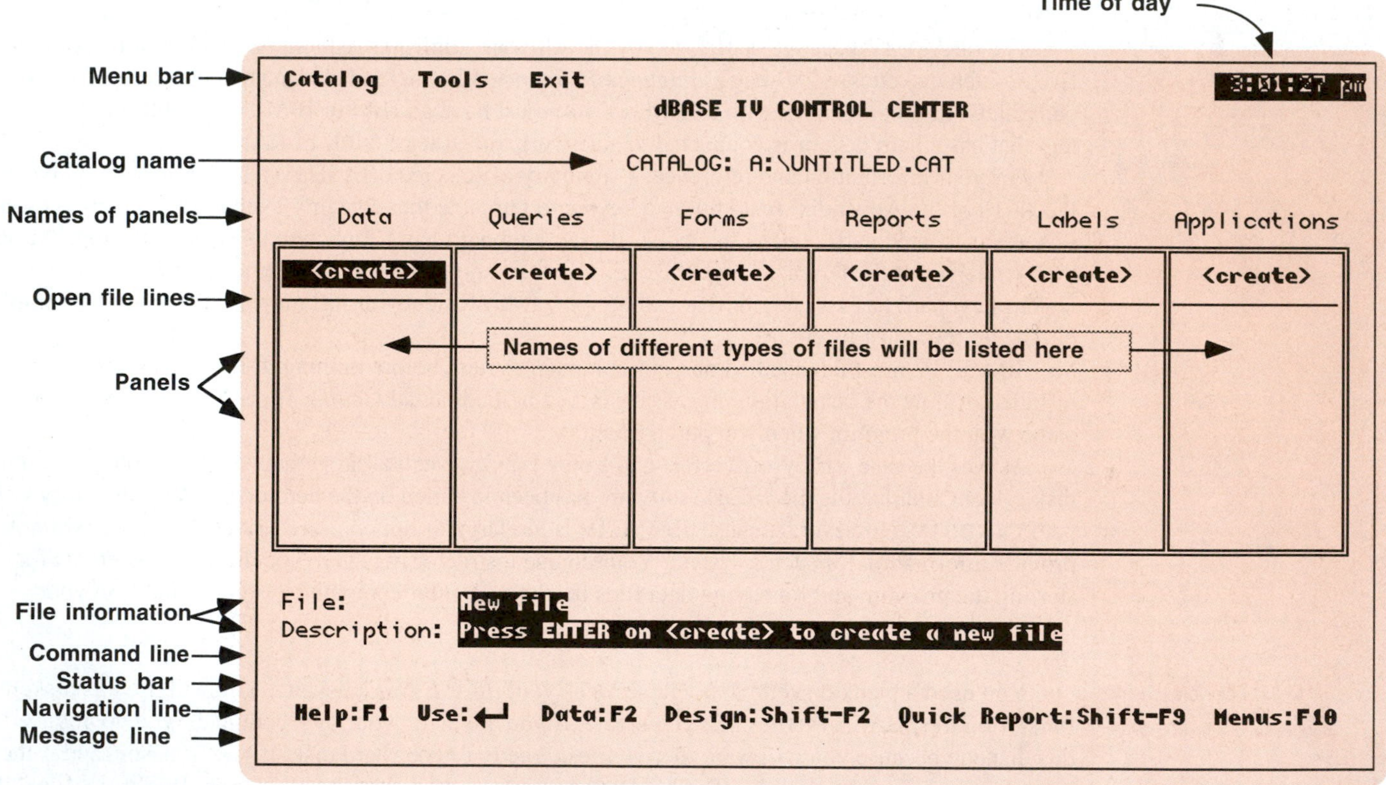

The dBASE IV Screen

dBASE IV has two main **user interfaces:** A menu-driven interface called the **menu system**, which is accessed through the Control Center shown in the above screen dump, and a command-driven interface called the dot prompt where you control the program by typing commands selected from the dBASE IV command language. The Control Center is designed for beginners who have not yet memorized the dBASE IV commands, while the dot prompt is for more advanced users. It allows them to bypass the menus, to give more sophisticated commands, and to write powerful programs in the dBASE IV programming language. Using the dot prompt is difficult at first because you must memorize the proper command in its exact format, including all punctuation, and then type it in without any errors. However, typing a command and its corresponding options is much faster than selecting them from multiple menus. In this chapter, we will use the menu system and the Control Center. Later, as you become more comfortable with the program, we will use the dot prompt.

• The Menu Bar •

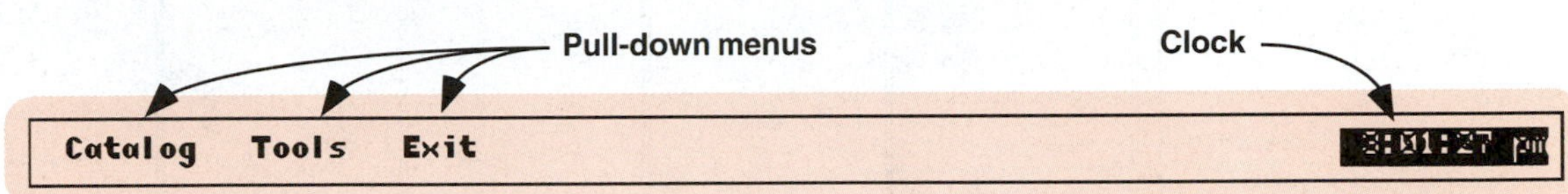

The Control Center menu bar displays the names of three pull-down menus that are used to help you remember dBASE IV commands:

`Catalog` contains options you may use to create, modify, and navigate between catalogs. As used by dBASE IV, a catalog is a group of files that are logically related in some way. For example, you may create a catalog called **`PERSONAL`** to hold dBASE IV files related to your personal life and another catalog called **`BUSINESS`** to hold files related to your business. Catalogs are similar to DOS subdirectories, but there are important differences, which we will discuss later.

`Tools` contains options you may use to help with the manipulation of files including DOS file operations, creating and running macros, importing and exporting data, protecting data from being altered, and changing the appearance of the screen (e.g., colors, highlights) and system defaults.

`Exit` contains one option that allows you to switch to the dot prompt and another that allows you to quit the program and return to DOS.

To open a menu you may either hold down the **[Alt]** key and then tap the key with the first letter of the menu you want to access (e.g., to select **`Exit`** you would tap **[Alt-E]**), or you can make the menu bar active by tapping **[F10]** and then use the **[arrow]** keys to move to and open the desired menu. To select an option from a menu either tap the first letter of the desired option (e.g., to select the **`Quit to DOS`** option tap **`Q`**) or use the **[arrow]** keys to highlight the option and then tap **[Enter]** to select it. To see how the pull-down menus work, follow the directions given below.

Keystroke	Action Resulting from Keystroke
[F10]	Makes the menu bar active and opens the **`Catalog`** menu.

Continued . . .

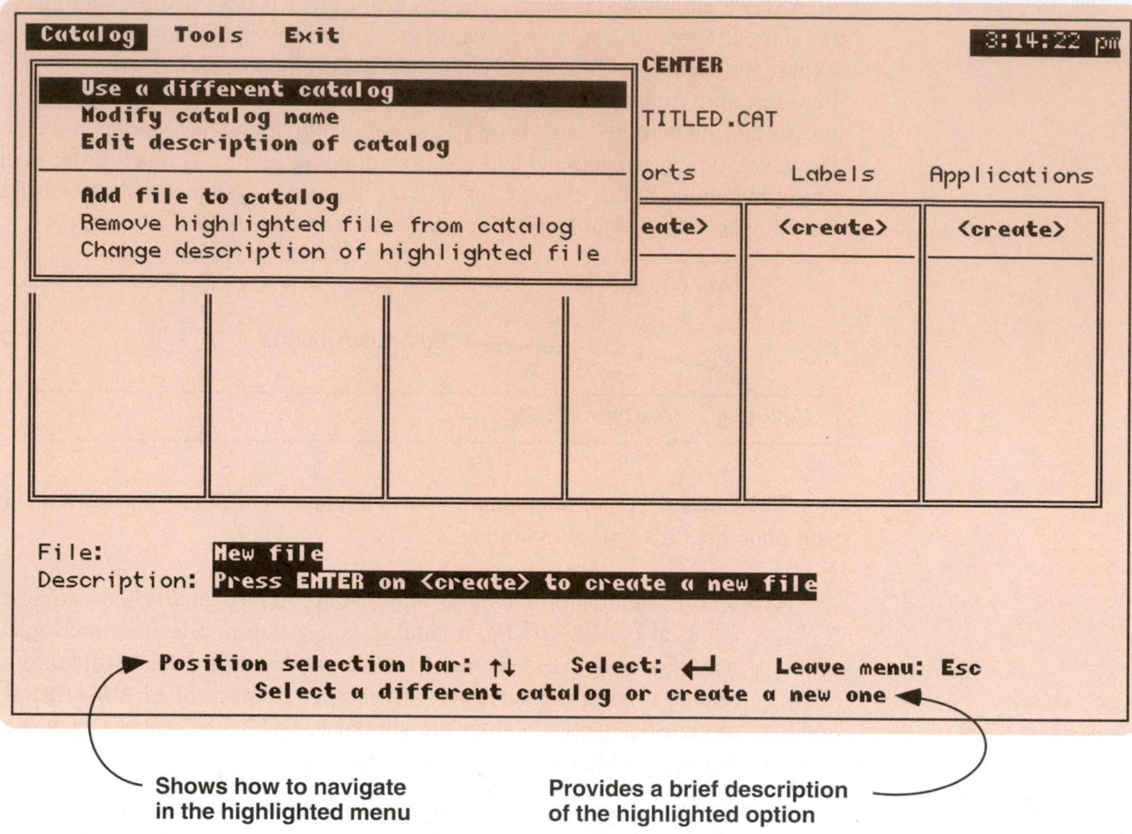

To move along the menu bar you may either use the **[arrow]** keys or hold down the **[Alt]** key and tap the first letter of the menu you wish to access.

[arrow] Use the **[arrow]** keys to move to the **`Exit`** menu.

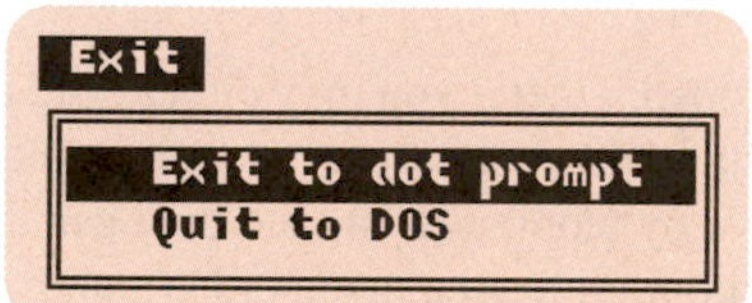

If you want to close (deactivate) the menu and leave the menu bar you can tap the **[Esc]** key.

[Esc] Closes the **`Exit`** menu, leaves the menu bar, and highlights **`<create>`** in the **`Data`** panel again.

[F10] Moves back to the menu bar but this time the **`Exit`** menu is opened. dBASE IV remembers which menu you last selected and opens that menu when you return to the menu bar by tapping **[F10]**.

[Esc] Closes the **`Exit`** menu, leaves the menu bar, and highlights **`<create>`** in the **`Data`** panel again.

Now, let's open a menu and select an option using the keystroke shortcuts.

[Alt-E] Pulls down the **`Exit`** menu.

[Q] Selects the **`Quit to DOS`** and returns to the DOS environment. Remember, when you are in a menu you need only tap the first letter of the option you want—you do not use the **[Alt]** key to select an option. The system prompt now should be displayed.

Continued . . .

Keystroke	Action Resulting from Keystroke
	*** END RUN dBASE IV A:\>_
	To get back into dBASE IV, type the following:
C:\DBIV\DBASE ↵	Starts the program. If the dBASE IV files on your computer are in a subdirectory with a name other than **DBIV**, use that name in place of **DBIV**.
[Enter]	Accepts the license agreement and displays the Control Center again.

Note that if you tap **[Enter]** after the license agreement disappears, dBASE IV will display the Data design screen (this screen will be discussed below). If that happens, tap **[Alt-E]** to open the **Exit** menu of the Data design screen and then tap **A** to select **Abandon changes and exit** to return to the Control Center.

• Catalog Name •

```
CATALOG: A:\UNTITLED.CAT
```

A catalog groups related files together for ease of handling and accessing. The default catalog is called **UNTITLED.CAT** and resides in the root directory (designated by the \) of the drive that was the default when you started dBASE IV (drive **A:**). The names of files that are currently assigned to the active catalog are displayed in the panels in the center of the screen (no file names are currently displayed because you have not added any files to the catalog).

• Panels •

Data	Queries	Forms	Reports	Labels	Applications
<create>	<create>	<create>	<create>	<create>	<create>

The panels contain the names of six different types of files that you can create:

Data lists database files that contain the raw data you wish to manipulate. Files with the extension **DBF** are included in this panel.

Queries lists files that contain information for viewing and selecting data. Files with the extension **QBE** and **UPD** are included in this panel.

Forms lists files that contain designs that enable you to customize dBASE IV screens to make data entry, editing, and viewing easier. Files with the extension **SCR** are included in this panel.

Reports lists files you will use to create reports on the database records. Files with the extension **FRM** are included in this panel.

Labels lists files you will use to create customized mailing labels based on the database records. Files with the extension **LBL** are included in this panel.

Applications lists files that are actually dBASE IV programs (i.e., lists of instructions used to accomplish a specific task). Files with the extension **APP** and **PRG** are included in this panel.

You may use the **[arrow]** keys to highlight the name of a file you want to open or to highlight **<create>**, which will allow you to create a new file of the type specified.

• Open-file Line •

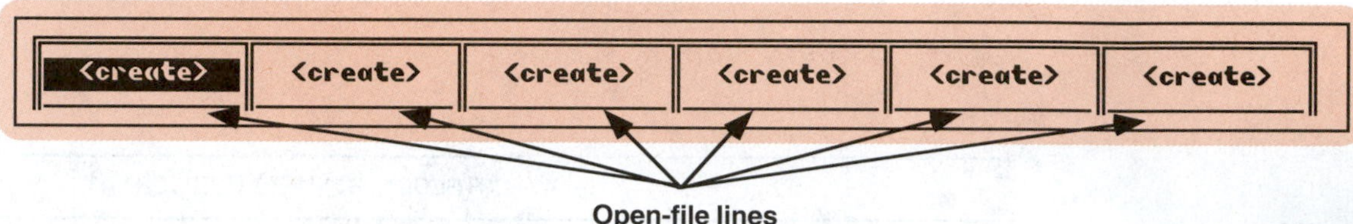

Files whose names are displayed above the open-file line are considered open (i.e., they are available to the memory of the computer). Currently, only **<create>** appears above the line in each panel because no files are open.

• File Information •

```
File:         New file
Description:  Press ENTER on <create> to create a new file
```

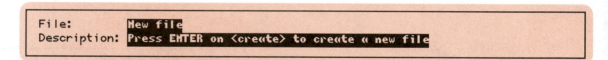

This line provides information on the currently highlighted file including its name and an optional one-line description of the file. Because you have not yet selected or created a database, **New file** is displayed and the **Description** line informs you as to how to create a new file.

• Command Line •

Because the Control Center is displayed, the command line is empty. This line is used to display the dot prompt and the commands you issue directly to dBASE IV through its command language.

• Status Bar •

The status bar provides information about the operation you are currently doing including the type of screen being displayed and the specification of the active file. The status bar is not displayed in the Control Center but a blank line is reserved for it anyway.

• Navigation Line •

```
Help:F1  Use:↵  Data:F2  Design:Shift-F2  Quick Report:Shift-F9  Menus:F10
```

The navigation line provides information on some of the common keystrokes you may want to use on the screen currently being displayed. For example, **`Help:F1`** means that if you tap the **[F1]** key a help screen will be displayed. **`Menus:F10`** means that if you tap **[F10]** the menu bar will be highlighted.

• *Message Line* •

The message line provides a brief description of a highlighted menu option, other information connected with the current screen, or a prompt that asks you to do something. The message line currently is blank.

Getting On-line Help from dBASE IV

dBASE IV has an extensive on-line *Help* feature that is accessed by tapping **[F1]**. The help screens are *context sensitive* meaning that the information displayed is dependent upon the location of the cursor in the Control Center or the contents of the command line when **[F1]** is tapped.

Practice using the *Help* feature by doing the following (begin from the Control Center with the word **`<create>`** highlighted in the **`Data`** panel):

Keystroke	*Action Resulting from Keystroke*
[F1]	Invokes the *Help* feature and displays the following screen:

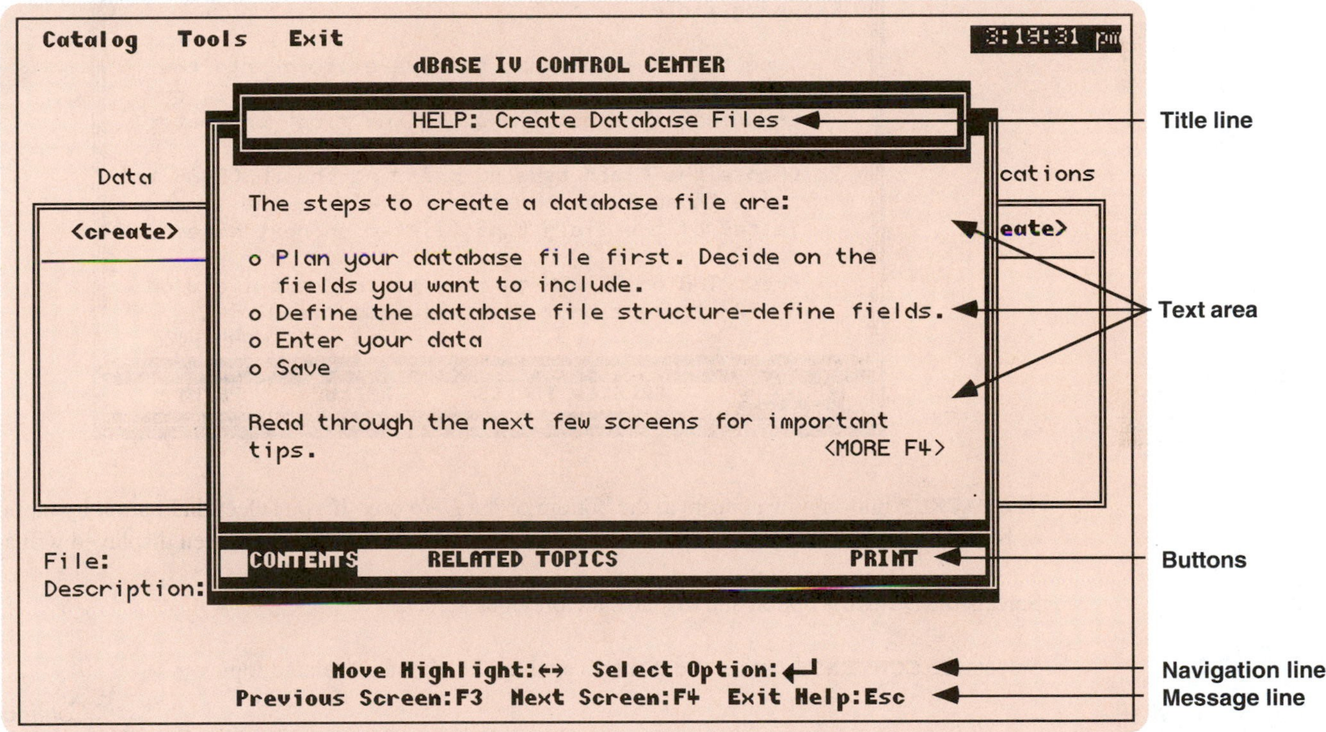

The screen that was displayed before you tapped **[F1]** (i.e., the Control Center) remains visible with the help box superimposed on top. This makes the entire screen a bit cluttered but helps you remember the context in which the help is given. The *Help* box has three main parts:

- *Title line* gives a brief description of the topic covered.
- *Text area* gives the explanation of the topic. Some topics have more information than can fit into a single box. In those cases you will see **`<MORE F4>`** displayed in the lower-right corner of the text area. This means that more information about the topic will be displayed if the **[F4]** key is tapped (the **[F4]** key is called the *next* key). If you tap **[F3]** the previous text area will be displayed (the **[F3]** key is called the *previous* key).

▮ *Buttons* provide the following additional *Help* options:

CONTENTS displays the table of contents for this particular part of the *Help* feature.

RELATED TOPICS displays a brief description of topics related to the current topic.

BACKUP (not currently displayed) allows you to retrace your steps through the *Help* screens. That button is not currently displayed because you have just entered *Help*. As soon as you move to another *Help* screen, the button will appear at the bottom of the *Help* box.

PRINT sends a copy of the *Help* information to the printer.

To *press* a button (i.e., select its option) you tap the key of the first letter of the button name or use the **[arrow]** keys to highlight the button and then tap **[Enter]**.

Keystroke	Action Resulting from Keystroke
[F4]	Displays more information on creating database files.

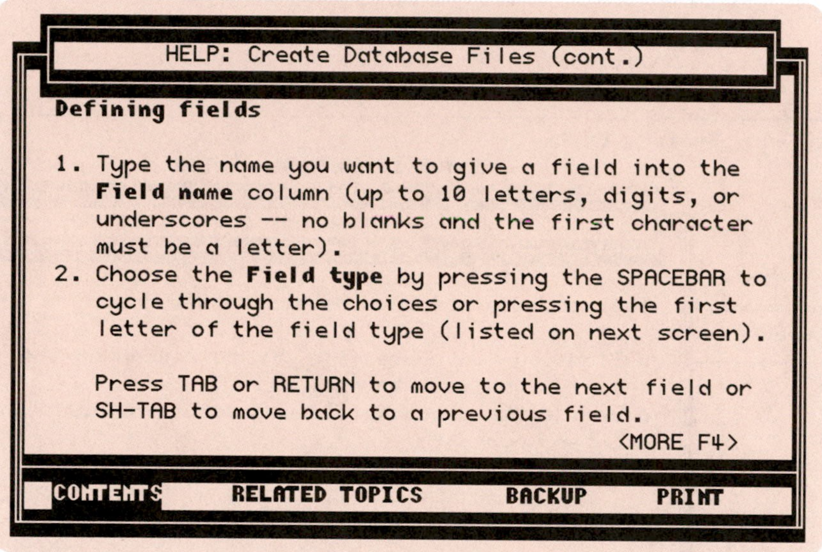

The **BACKUP** button now appears at the bottom of the *Help* box. If you select that button by tapping **B** or by using the **[arrow]** keys to select it and then tapping **[Enter]**, the last screen displayed will appear.

Keystroke	Action Resulting from Keystroke
B	Selects the **BACKUP** option and displays the previous screen.
C	Selects the **CONTENTS** option and displays a table of contents of related topics.

Continued . . .

Keystroke	Action Resulting from Keystroke

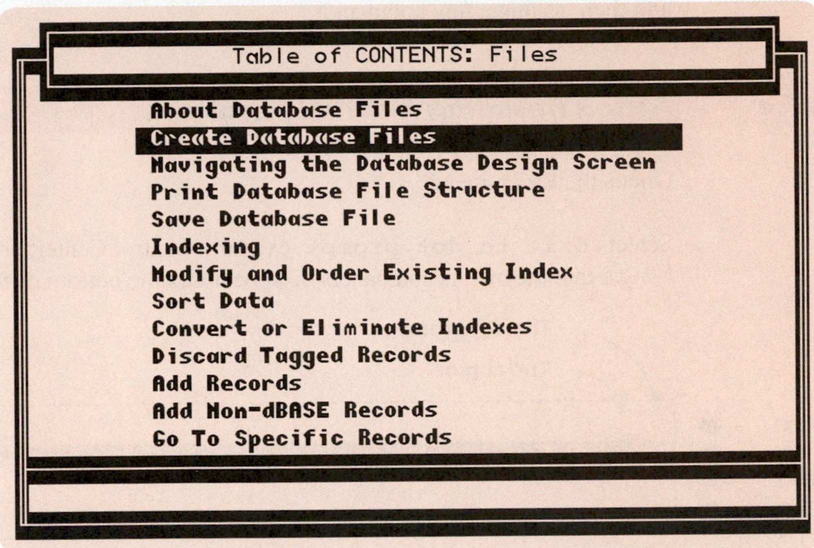

If you tap **[F3]** you will get a listing of more general topics. If you tap **[F4]** you will get a listing of more specific topics.

[F3] Displays a new table of contents with more general information about the Control Center.

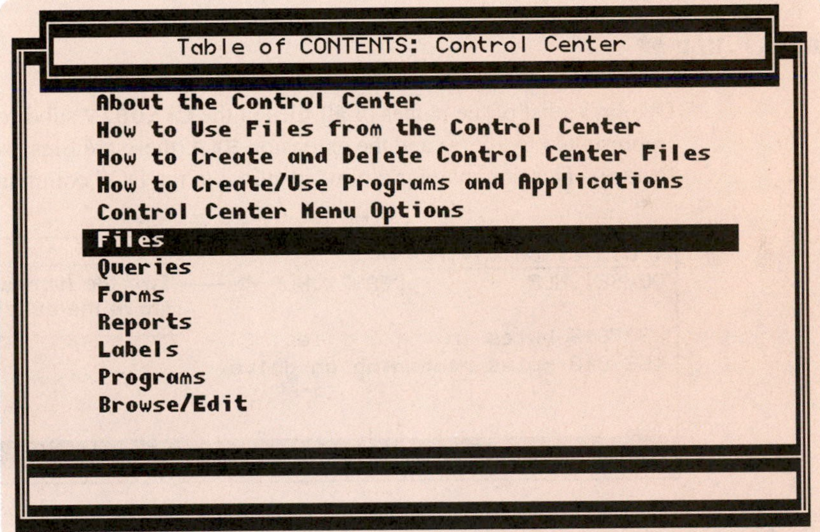

[Esc] Exits *Help* and displays the Control Center again.

The Dot Prompt

While the menu-oriented Control Center is convenient for beginners, as you gain experience you will want to use the command-oriented dot prompt to do much of your work. We will discuss the dot prompt in detail in the next chapter, but for now let's see how the dot prompt works by switching to it and then issuing a few commands.

Keystroke	Action Resulting from Keystroke
[Alt-E]	Opens the **Exit** menu.
E	Selects **Exit to dot prompt**, exits the Control Center, and places the cursor at the dot prompt. Notice that the menus and panels disappear and the bottom of the screen displays the following:

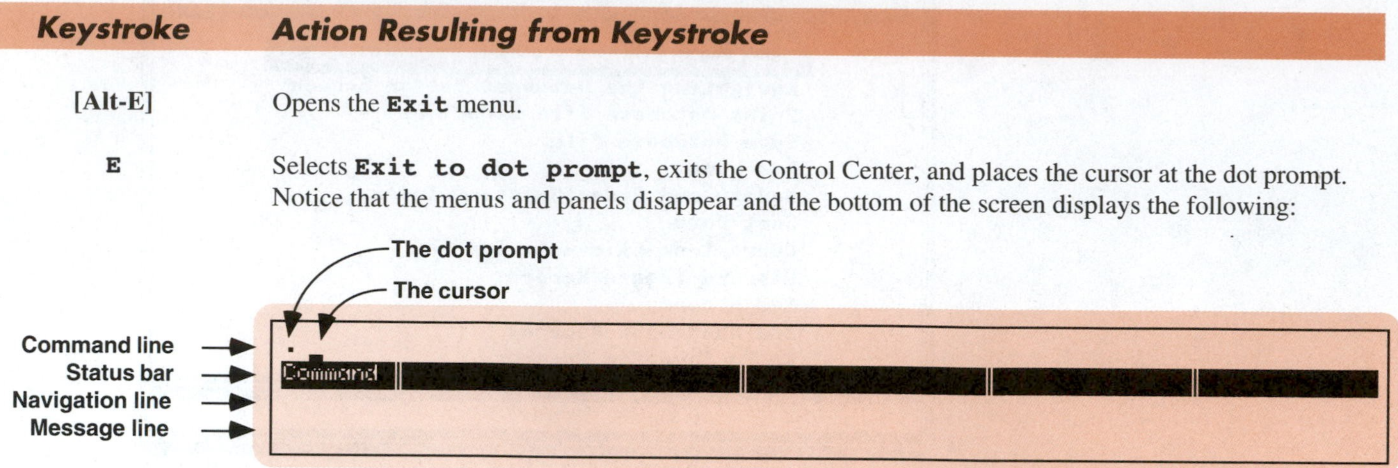

dBASE IV is waiting for you to type a command. Once you are an experienced user and have memorized many of the commands, using the dot prompt will be faster and easier than using the Control Center.

Now, try a few dot prompt commands:

DIR C:\DBIV*.HLP ↵

Displays a list of the names of all files in the **C:\DBIV** subdirectory that have any file name (represented by the *****) and the extension **HLP** (these are files associated with the dBASE IV *Help* feature). This command is almost identical to the DOS command **DIR C:\DBIV*.HLP/W**.

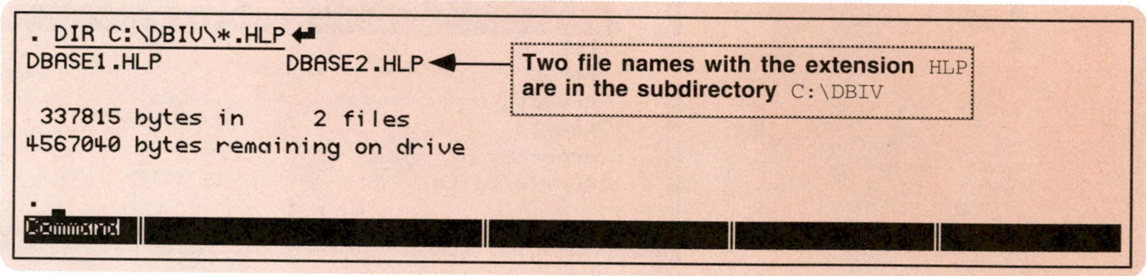

HELP DIR ↵ — Displays a *Help* screen explaining the **DIR** command. You may get help on any dot prompt command by typing **HELP** followed by the name of the command.

Continued . . .

Keystroke	**Action Resulting from Keystroke**
	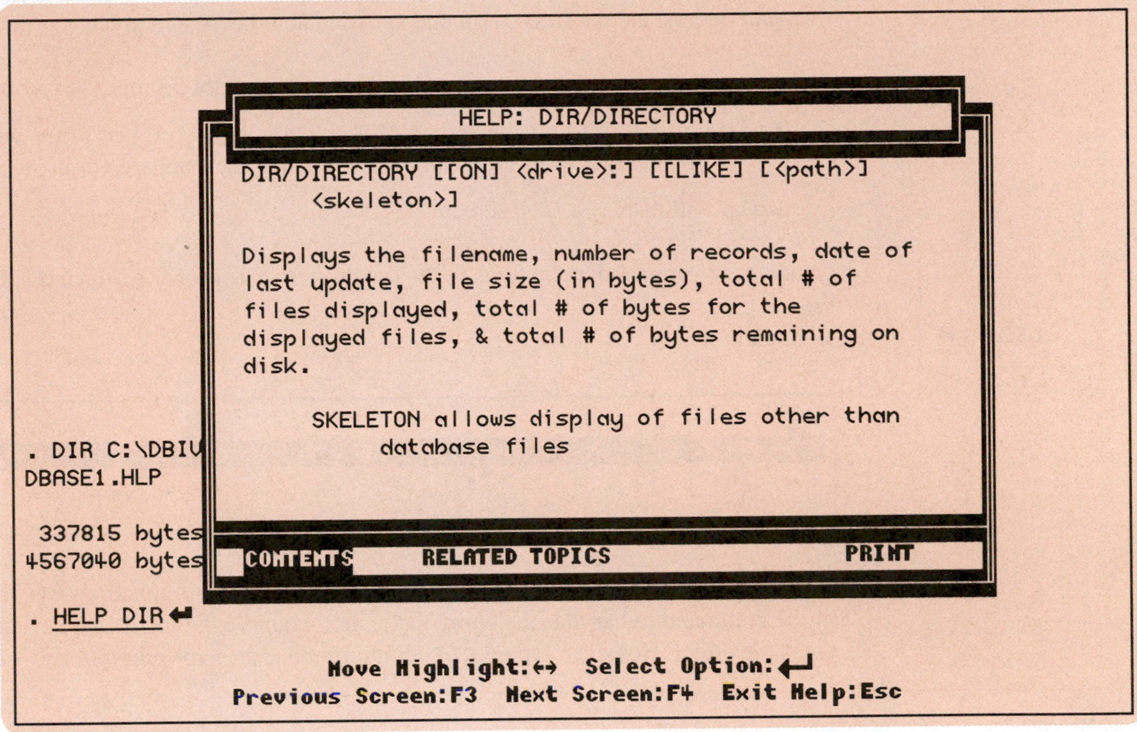
[Esc]	Exits *Help* and returns to the dot prompt.

The screen looks somewhat messy because dBASE IV did not erase the previous dot prompt commands but simply superimposed the *Help* screen over the already-existing screen. Let's clear the screen by doing the following:

Keystroke	**Action Resulting from Keystroke**
CLS ↵	The intent here is to clear the screen by using the DOS **CLS** command, but dBASE IV does not understand the **CLS** command and so displays the following error prompt box:

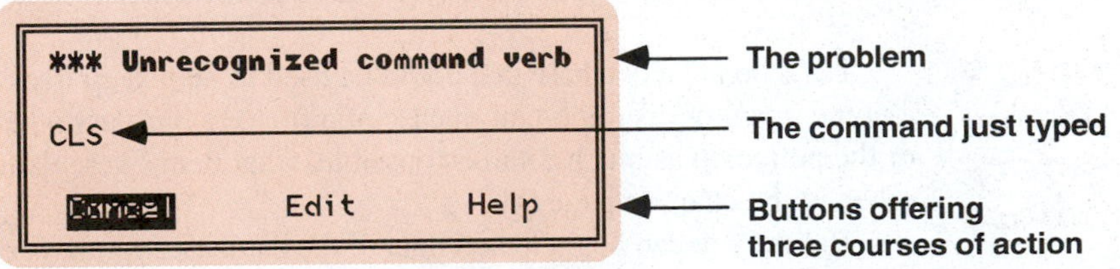

Continued . . .

Keystroke	Action Resulting from Keystroke
	The *command verb* is the part of a command that tells dBASE IV what action it is to take. dBASE IV does not understand the **CLS** command verb and so it beeps and gives you three courses of action. **Cancel** will cancel the command and return to the dot prompt with a blank command line. **Edit** will return to the dot prompt, but the command you just typed will be entered on the command line where you can modify it using the standard editing techniques. **Help** will display a *Help* screen.
C	Cancels the command and returns to the dot prompt. The proper command is **CLEAR**.
CLEAR ↵	Clears the screen.

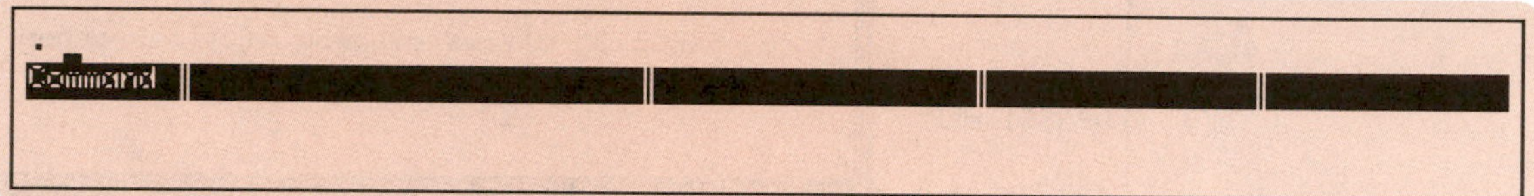

Note that you can abbreviate many dBASE IV commands and functions by typing the first four letters of the command rather than the entire name. For example, typing **CLEA** instead of **CLEAR** would have the same effect. However, typing **CLE** would produce an error prompt box.

Now that you have had a chance to see how the dot prompt commands work, let's return to the Control Center and create a database. Later, we will return to the dot prompt to manipulate the database and produce complex reports of its contents.

Keystroke	Action Resulting from Keystroke
ASSIST ↵	Switches from the dot prompt to the Control Center. The word **ASSIST** is a hold-over from previous versions of dBASE where the menu-driven mode of operation was called the *Assistant*. In dBASE IV, the Assistant has been replaced by a new menu system that is accessed through the Control Center. Note that instead of typing the word **ASSIST** and then tapping **[Enter]** you could have simply tapped the **[F2]** key. At the dot prompt, the **[F2]** key is assigned to issue the **ASSIST** command.

Defining a Home Inventory Database

Let's create a database that could be used to help keep track of items in a house or apartment. Such a home inventory is important in case of a fire or a burglary where you must tell an insurance company or the police, in as much detail as possible, what items were damaged or stolen. We will use the data given in the chart on page D4.

Before you can begin to add data to the database, you have to tell dBASE IV what the structure of the database will be. The structure is the *scaffolding* upon which dBASE IV will hang the data. It includes the names you will give to each data field (e.g., **NAME**, **VALUE**, **DATE**), the type of data (e.g., numeric, character, chronological), and the size of each piece of data (e.g., 15 characters for the **NAME**, 8 characters (sign, digits, and a decimal point) for the **VALUE**, 8 characters for the **DATE**). Planning the structure is important because once it is set and the data are entered, changing the structure is time consuming and expensive.

First, we will define the structure of the database, and then we will enter the data. Begin your work from the Control Center.

Keystroke	Action Resulting from Keystroke
[arrow]	If necessary, use the **[arrow]** keys to highlight **<create>** in the **Data** panel of the Control Center.

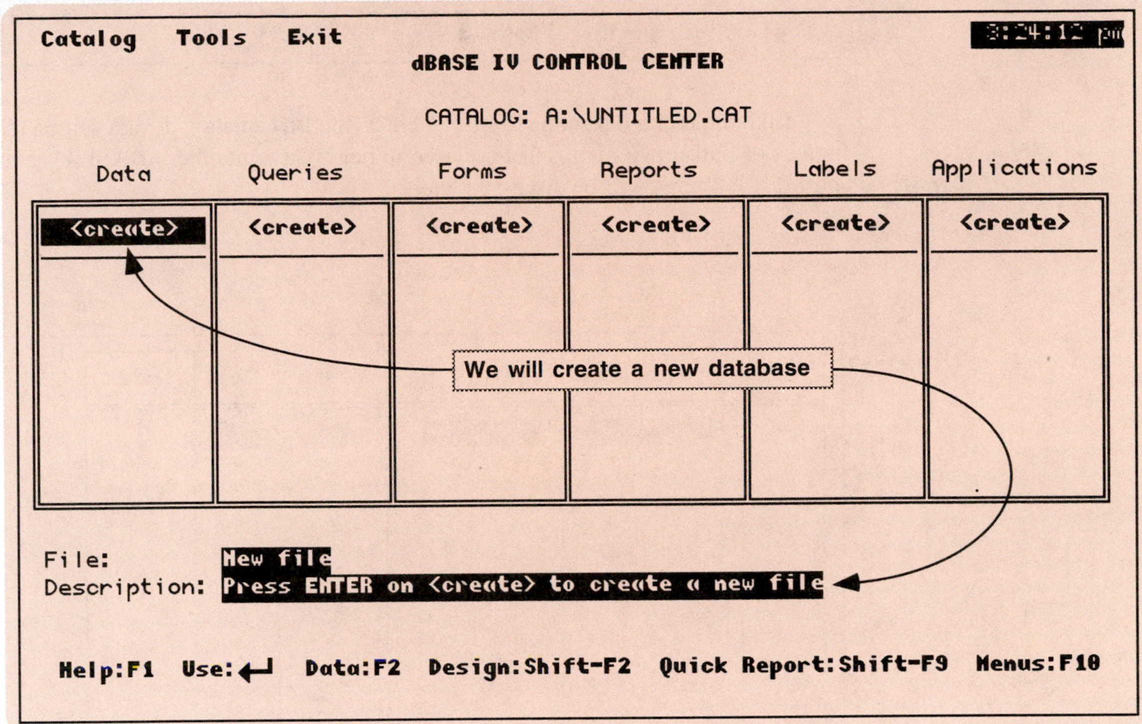

Keystroke	Action Resulting from Keystroke
[Enter]	Selects the **<create>** option and displays the **Database** design screen:

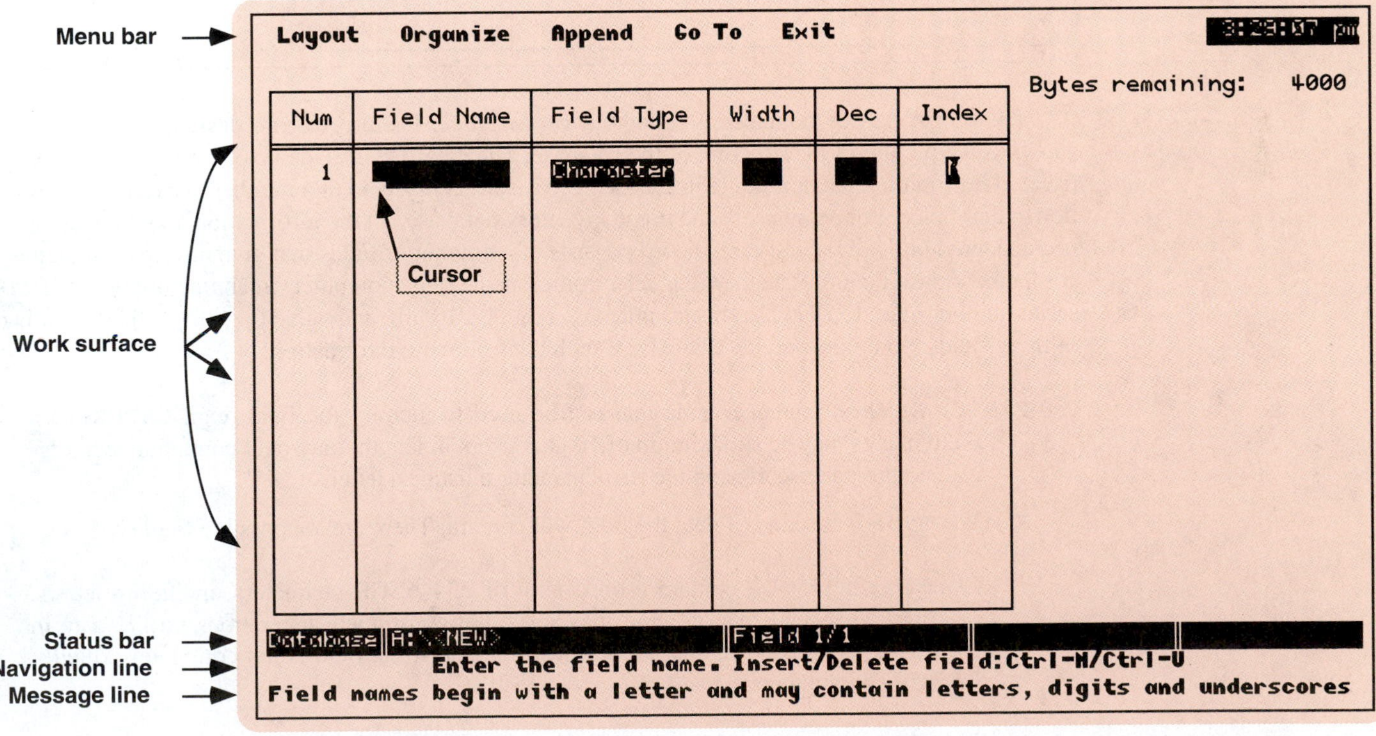

Let's examine the parts of this screen:

• *Menu Bar* •

```
Layout   Organize   Append   Go To   Exit
```

Like the menu bar in the Control Center, the **Database** design screen menu bar displays the names of pull-down menus that are used to help you remember dBASE IV commands. Many of the pull-down menus will be discussed later.

• *Work Surface* •

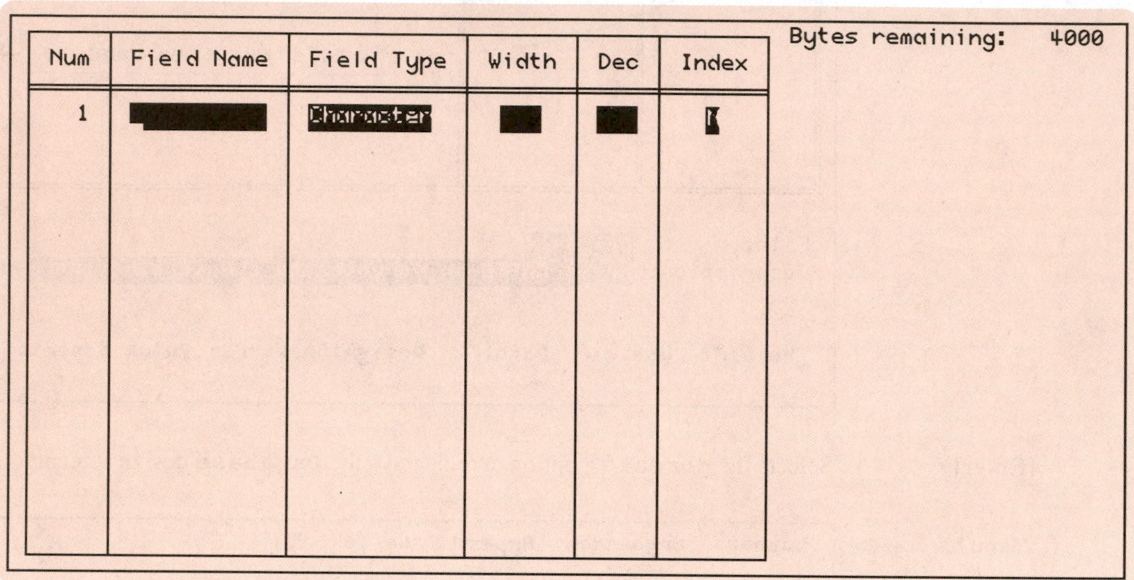

The central part of the screen is called the *work surface*. The **Database** design work surface shows you a picture of the structure of the database. The database is made up of a number of records (related information about a single item) and each record is made up of a number of pieces of information called fields. For example, in the home inventory database, all the information about the computer is considered one *record* and each record consists of a number of fields that give information on the computer's classification category (e.g., electronic), name (e.g., computer), manufacturer (e.g., IBM), serial number (e.g., F3827122), date of purchase (e.g., 02/10/90), and value (e.g., $1,200.00). For each of these fields, you must provide dBASE IV with the following information:

Field Name is a unique name that can be used to identify the field (e.g., **CATEGORY**). Field names may be a maximum of 10 characters in length, may only contain letters, digits, and the underscore, and the first character must be a letter.

Field Type is the kind of data the field will contain. There are six possible field types:

Character fields may contain a maximum of 254 ASCII characters, including letters, digits, and punctuation. You may not do any arithmetic operations on the data in character fields. The data are left justified and if the field is not completely filled it will contain trailing blanks.

Numeric fields can contain up to 20 characters, but only digits, a decimal point, and a sign (+ or –) are allowed. You may do arithmetic operations on the data in these fields. When you define a numeric field, you must specify the number of decimal places to be displayed for all records in that field. This will be entered under the column labeled **Dec** (see below). The numbers are right justified and, because all values in a given field will display the same number of decimal places, the decimal points will automatically be lined up.

Float fields are similar to numeric fields but the results of calculations involving this type of numbers are stored in the memory of the computer to a precision equal to that allowed by the computer. Float fields are used in place of numeric fields for applications where very large or very small numbers are needed.

Date fields are for dates in the form **MM/DD/YY** where **MM** is month, **DD** is day, and **YY** is year (e.g., **07/01/49** means July 1, 1949). You can do simple date arithmetic on data of this type (e.g., you could have dBASE IV add 30 days to today's date).

Logical fields can contain a true (**T**) or false (**F**) response or a yes (**Y**) or no (**N**) response.

Memo fields may contain up to 10 characters but may be used to record free-form text of just about any length. The memo field actually points to a file stored on your disk that is separate from the database file. These fields cannot be selected or sorted like other fields, but they are useful if you want to make notes about particular records. For example, you might want to note that the handmade dry sink in the home inventory database was constructed by Donald Lamb in 1974 as a wedding gift for his daughter Terry.

Width defines the maximum number of characters that a field can contain. A character field may contain a maximum of 254 characters while numeric fields may contain up to 20 characters (digits, sign, and decimal point).

Dec specifies the number of decimal places to be displayed for numeric and float fields.

Index allows you to create an index file that will arrange the records of the database according to a specified field. For example, a **Y** in the **Index** column of a field called **NAME** would allow you to arrange the records of the database in alphabetical order by the entries in that field. Indexing and sorting are discussed on pages D147–59.

• Status Bar •

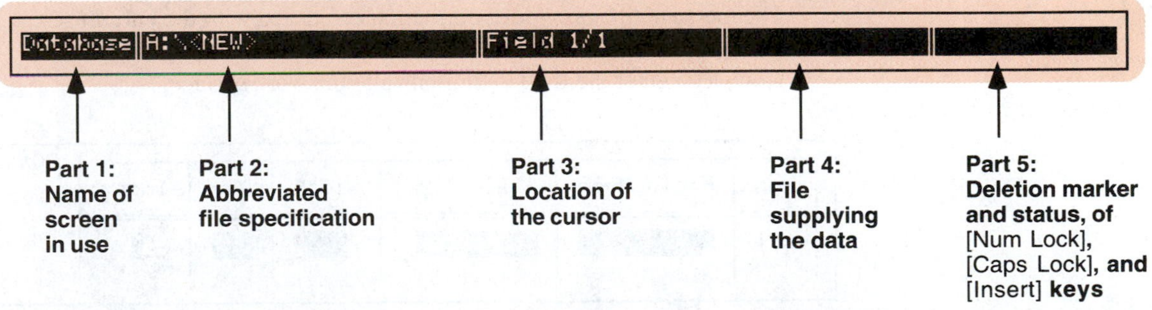

Part 1: Name of screen in use

Part 2: Abbreviated file specification

Part 3: Location of the cursor

Part 4: File supplying the data

Part 5: Deletion marker and status, of [Num Lock], [Caps Lock], and [Insert] keys

The status bar provides the following information about the current database operation:

Part 1 identifies the screen displayed by its function. The word **Database** is shown because the data design screen is presently being displayed.

Part 2 indicates the file you currently are working with. The file resides on drive **A:**, within the root directory \, and is a **<NEW>** file (i.e., you have not yet given it a name).

Part 3 indicates the location of the cursor. It is currently in **Field** number **1** of a total of **1** fields. If the cursor were located in field 3 of a database that had 5 fields, the indication would be **Field 3/5**. This part of the status bar shows different information depending on the type of screen you are using. For example, if you are in a Report screen, **Field x/y** would be replaced with **Line: xx Col: yy** to indicate that the cursor is at column **yy** of row **xx** (this will be discussed later).

Part 4 indicates the database file or view that is supplying the data for this operation. Currently, that part is empty because no database file has yet been assigned.

Part 5 indicates the status of the **[Num Lock]**, **[Caps Lock]**, and **[Insert]** keys. For example, if num lock is turned on (by tapping the **[Num Lock]** key), then **Num** will appear in this box. If caps lock is turned on (by tapping the **[Caps Lock]** key), then **Caps** will appear in this box. Currently, neither key is turned on. In other screens (e.g., **Browse** and **Edit**) this part also shows if the current record has been marked for deletion (see p. D44).

• Navigation Line •

```
Enter the field name. Insert/Delete field:Ctrl-N/Ctrl-U
```

The navigation line provides information on some of the operations you may want to perform on this screen.

Enter the field name means that you should begin typing the name of the first field.

Insert/Delete field:Ctrl-N/Ctrl-U means that you may insert a new field just above the cursor by tapping **[Ctrl-N]**, and you may delete the field at the cursor by tapping **[Ctrl-U]**.

• Message Line •

```
Field names begin with a letter and may contain letters, digits and underscores
```

The message line provides information connected with the current screen and selection. In this case, it is reminding you of the rules that govern the naming of fields.

Now, let's enter the field definitions into the work surface.

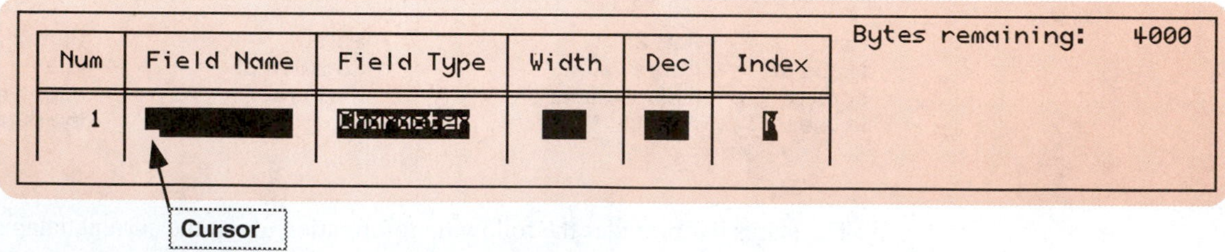

For the home inventory example, the fields will be defined as follows:

Field name	Field type	Field width	Decimals displayed
Category	Character	10	
Name	Character	15	
Manufact	Character	12	
Serial_Num	Character	10	
Date	Date	8	
Value	Numeric	8	2

Enter the information for the first field by doing the following:

Keystroke	Action Resulting from Keystroke
CATEGORY ↵	Specifies the name of the first field (this field contains the classification of the item, such as *furniture* or *appliance*). Notice how all letters are converted to uppercase even if you type them in lowercase. Tapping **[Enter]** sends the cursor to the next column to the right.
C	The default field type is **Character** and, therefore, dBASE IV displays that for you. Tapping **C** confirms that the type should be character and sends the cursor to the next column to the right.
10 ↵	Specifies the width of the first field. Notice that tapping **[Enter]** sends the cursor to the last column (**Index**) rather than to the **Dec** column. This is because the field type is **Character**, and it would not make sense to indicate a number of decimal places for a character field. **Dec** is used for numeric fields.
N	Specifies that the database is not to be indexed on this field and moves the cursor to the next line so that you can enter data on the second field. Indexing provides a way of arranging the database records in a specific order (e.g., alphabetically). Indexing is discussed on pages D147–57.

After entering the above values, the screen should look as follows:

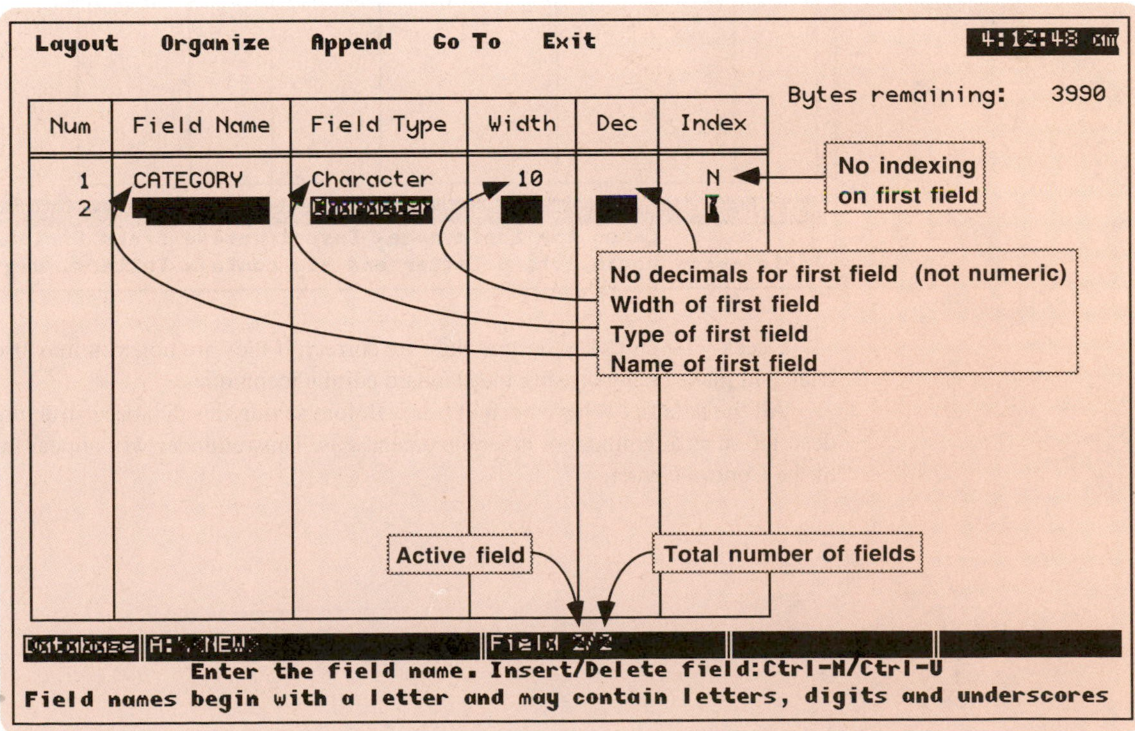

Enter the information for the rest of the fields in the same way.

- If you make a mistake, you may edit the entry in the usual way using the **[arrow]**, **[Backspace]**, **[Delete]**, and **[Insert]** keys.
- If you want to move back to a previous field tap **[up-arrow]**.
- If you want to move down to a field tap **[down-arrow]**.
- When you enter the field name **SERIAL_NUM**, dBASE IV will beep when you type the last letter (**M**) because you have reached the maximum number of characters allowable in a field name. When this happens, the cursor automatically moves to the next column.
- When you enter the field type for field 5 (**DATE**), you need only enter the first letter (**D** for date). dBASE IV will automatically fill in the rest of the word as well as the width (**8**).
- Similarly, when you enter the field type for field 6 (**VALUE**), you need only enter the first letter (**N** for numeric). When you enter the width and tap **[Enter]**, dBASE IV will automatically move the cursor over to the **Dec** column to enable you to enter the number of decimal places for that field.

When you have finished entering the information the screen should look like the following:

```
Layout   Organize   Append   Go To   Exit                          4:15:08 pm

                                                    Bytes remaining:   3937
 Num  Field Name   Field Type   Width  Dec  Index

  1   CATEGORY     Character     10          N
  2   NAME         Character     15          N
  3   MANUFACT     Character     12          N
  4   SERIAL_NUM   Character     10          N
  5   DATE         Date           8          N
  6   VALUE        Numeric        8     2    N
  7                Character

Database A:\<NEW>            Field 7/7
         Enter the field name. Insert/Delete field:Ctrl-N/Ctrl-U
Field names begin with a letter and may contain letters, digits and underscores
```

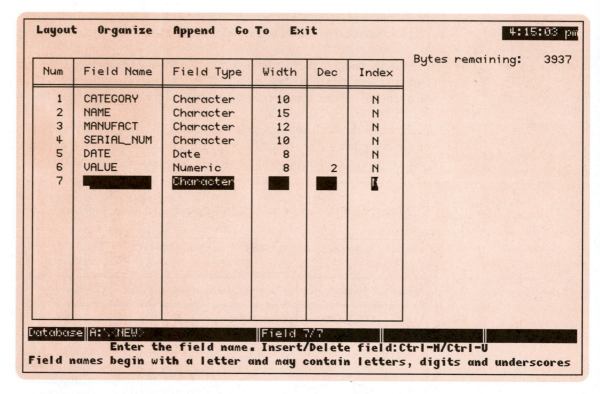

Check your entries to be sure they are correct. If they are not, you may use the **[arrow]** keys to go back and make changes using the standard editing techniques.

All the data fields have been defined. Before saving this database structure, let's add a one-line description as a reminder of what the database is. This reminder will appear in the file information part of the Control Center.

Keystroke	Action Resulting from Keystroke
[Alt-L]	Opens the **Layout** menu.
E	Selects the **Edit database description** option.

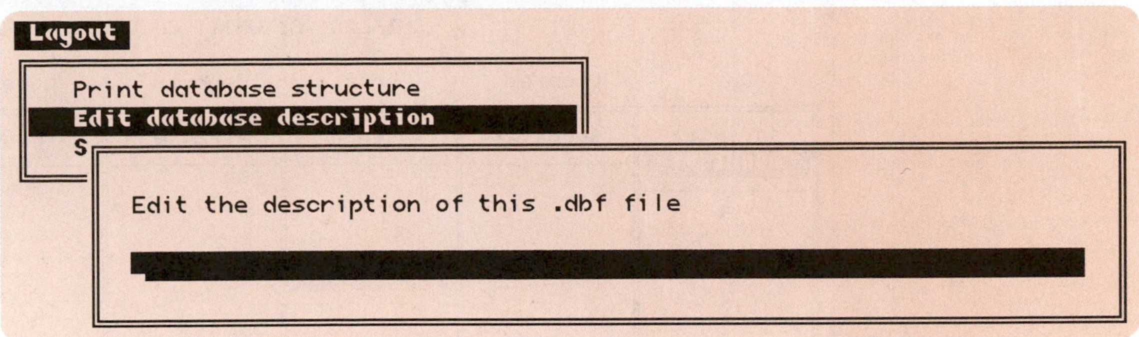

Type the following description for the database:

Sample home inventory database

Keystroke	Action Resulting from Keystroke
[Enter]	Accepts the description and returns to the Database design screen.
	To exit from the Database design screen do the following:
[Alt-E]	Opens the **Exit** menu.
S	Selects **Save changes and exit** and asks for a file specification for the database.

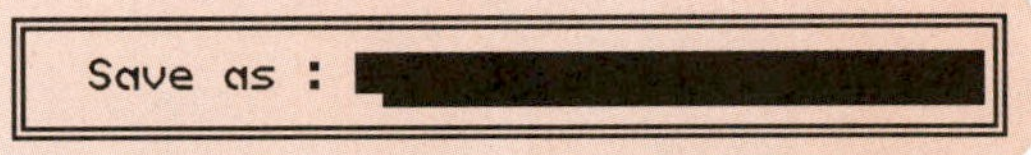

dBASE IV follows the same file name conventions as does DOS (i.e., from one to eight alphanumeric characters or special symbols and an optional one-, two-, or three-character extension). Because dBASE IV will automatically add the extension **DBF** to the file name, you need not type one. If you make a mistake while typing, use **[Backspace]** to correct it.

Keystroke	Action Resulting from Keystroke
A:\HOMEINV1 ↵	Provides the file specification for the database and saves it to disk. Note that if you want the database saved to a subdirectory on your hard drive you should replace the **A:** with the path to that subdirectory (e.g., replace **A:** with **C:\DBIV\DBDOCS**).

Continued . . .

Keystroke	Action Resulting from Keystroke

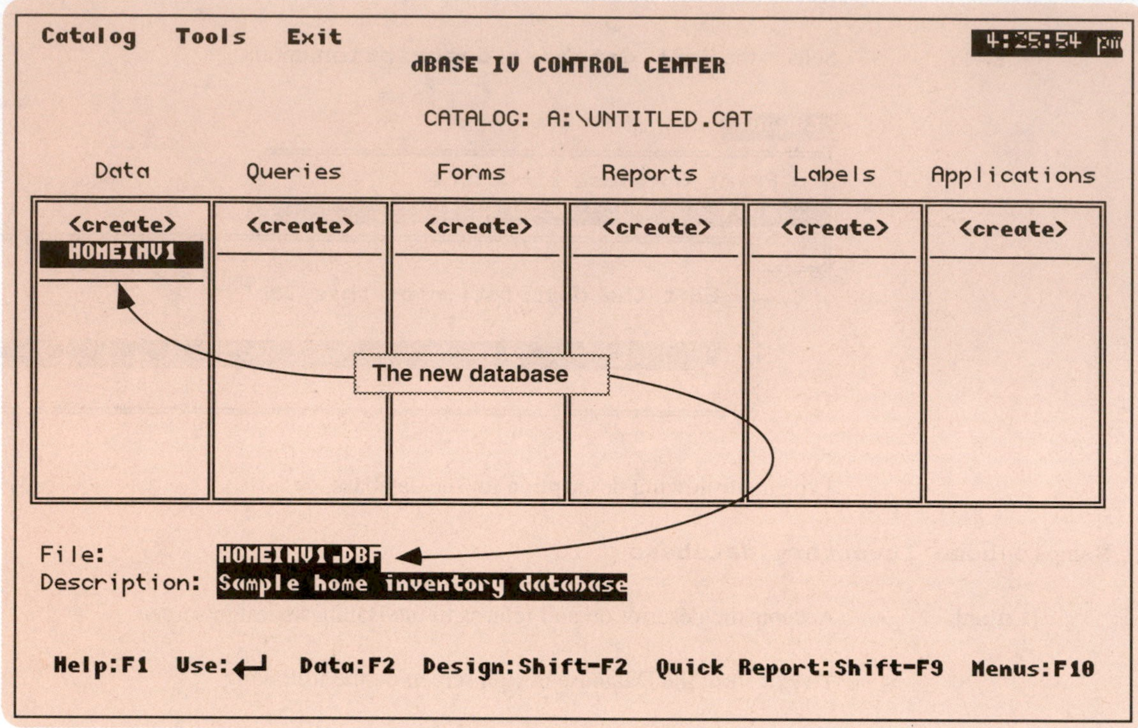

Notice that **HOMEINV1** appears above the open-file line. This means that the file is currently open and so it is available to the memory of the computer. If other database files are on your diskette, their names may appear below the open-file line.

Keystroke	Action Resulting from Keystroke
[Atl-E]	Opens the **Exit** menu.
Q	Selects **Quit to DOS** and returns to the DOS environment.

TO TAKE A BREAK Remove data diskette. To resume: Insert data diskette, type **A:** ↵.

Entering the Data

The structure of the database has been defined and now it is time to enter the data:

Keystroke	Action Resulting from Keystroke
C:\DBIV\DBASE ↵	Starts the program and displays the Control Center. When you start dBASE IV it selects as the active catalog the one you used just before you quit the program at the end of your last work session. Thus, the active catalog should be **A:\UNTITLED.CAT**. If it is not, you should switch to that catalog by tapping **[Alt-C]** to open the **Catalog** menu, then tap **U** to select the **Use a different catalog** option, then use the **[arrow]** keys to highlight **UNTITLED.CAT**, and then tap **[Enter]**. The name **HOMEINV1** should be displayed below the open-file line in the **Data** panel.

Continued . . .

Keystroke	Action Resulting from Keystroke

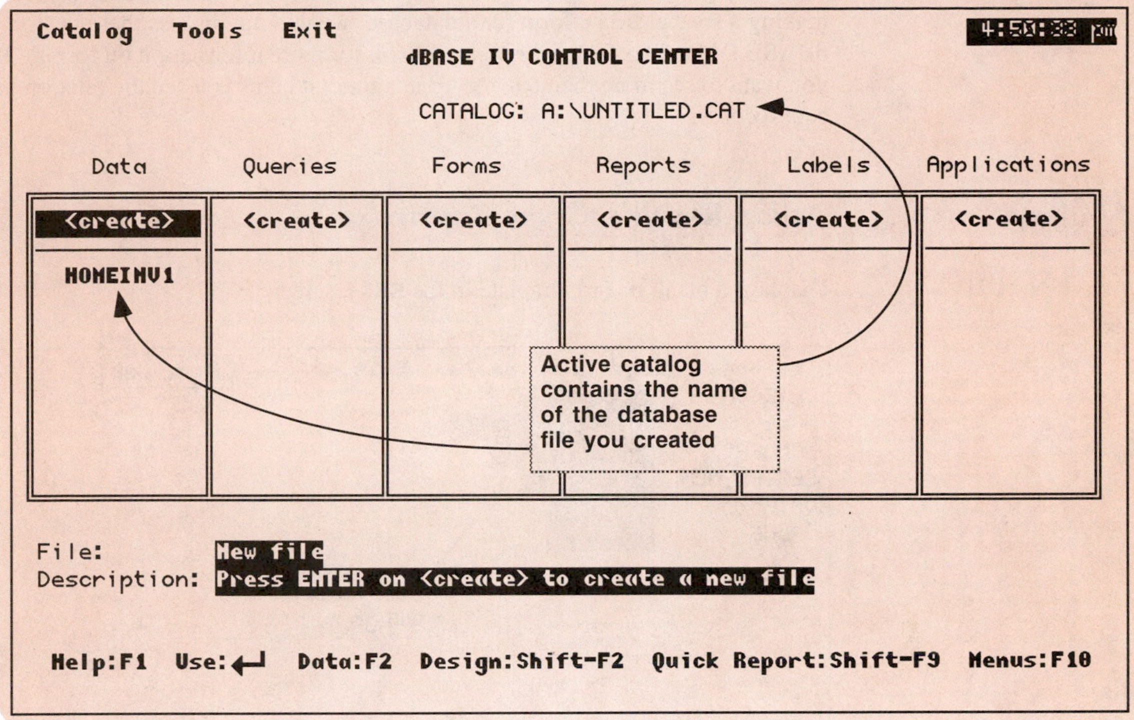

[arrow] Use the **[arrow]** keys to highlight **HOMEINV1** in the **Data** panel. To use that database, tap **[Enter]** after the file name has been selected (notice the reminder of this fact on the navigation line at the bottom of the screen).

[Enter] Selects the highlighted file and presents the following prompt box:

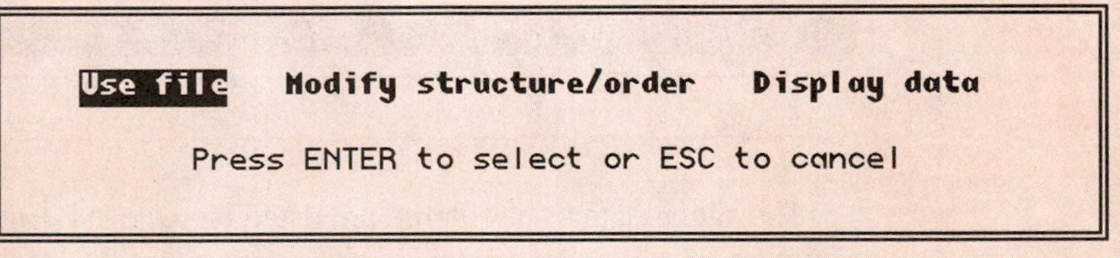

Use file opens the selected file and allows you to work on it.

Modify structure/order allows you to change the structure of the file (e.g., add or delete fields, change field lengths, types, or order).

Display data allows you to display the data in the file.

U Selects **Use file** and returns to the Control Center. The name of the chosen file, **HOMEINV1**, is displayed above the open-file line and on the line marked **File:** just below the panels. The description of the file is displayed on the line marked **Description:**.

Now, the data can be entered into the database. If you look at the navigation line at the bottom of the screen you will see **Data:F2**, which reminds you that the **[F2]** key is called the *data* key. Tapping this key will display either the **Edit** screen or the **Browse** screen. In the **Edit** screen all the data from a single record are displayed, one field per line. In the **Browse** screen, data from many records are displayed with all the data from each record on one line (if all the data from a record do not fit on one line, you will only see part of the data for each record). **Edit** and **Browse** provide essentially the same information but in a different format. **Edit** is useful for focusing on the data of one record and for entering new data. In fact, you can create customized **Edit** screens to suit your particular needs by making a special **Edit** form for a database (we will not discuss these customized forms—see the dBASE IV booklet *Using the Menu System* for more information on forms). **Browse** is useful when you want to see more than one record at a time; it helps you see the relation between the data in adjacent records.

Keystroke	Action Resulting from Keystroke
[F2]	Displays a blank record template in the **Edit** screen.

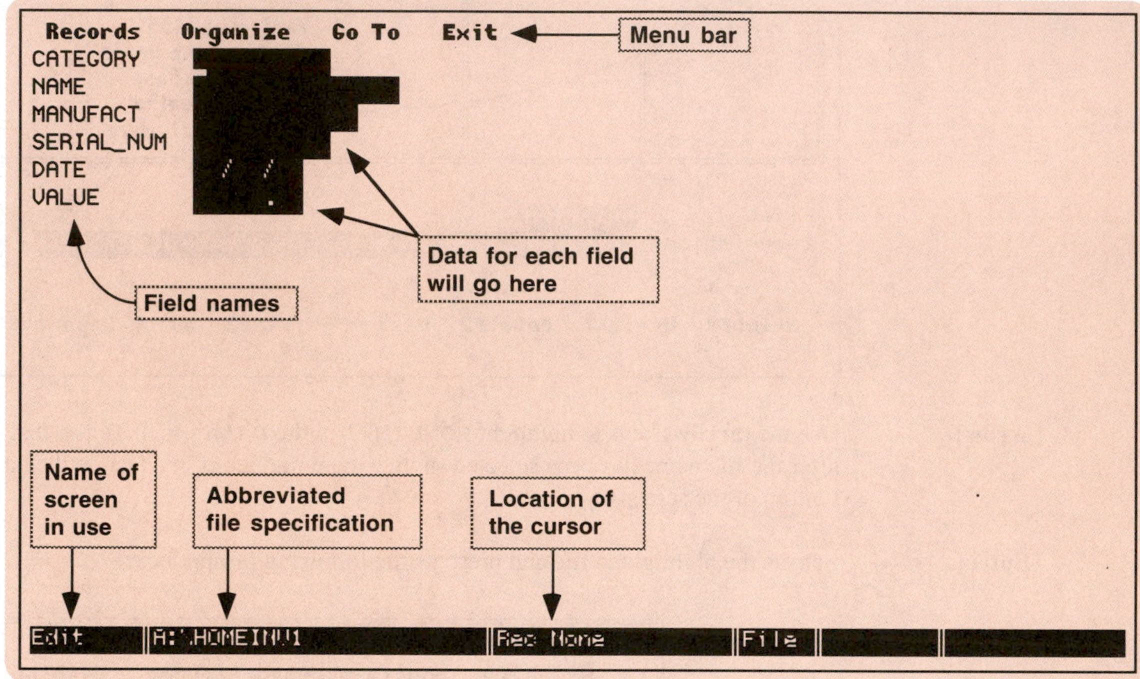

The actual data to be entered are listed on page D4. Enter the data for the first record by typing the following (if you make a mistake while typing, use the standard editing techniques to make corrections):

Keystroke	Action Resulting from Keystroke
Electronic	Specifies the entry for the field **CATEGORY**. Because this entry is exactly the same size as the field width, when you type the last letter of **Electronic**, dBASE IV will beep and then automatically move the cursor to the next field.
Computer ↵	Specifies the entry for the field **NAME** and moves the cursor to the next field.
IBM ↵	Specifies the entry for the field **MANUFACT** and moves the cursor to the next field.
F3827122 ↵	Specifies the entry for the field **SERIAL_NUM** and moves the cursor to the next field.

Continued . . .

Keystroke	Action Resulting from Keystroke

021090 Specifies the entry for the field **DATE**. As soon as you type the last **0**, dBASE IV will move the cursor to the next field. When you enter a date field, you may type the slashes to show dBASE IV where to separate the month, day, and year or you may enter leading zeros if the month, day, or year have only one digit. For example, the date July 1, 1949 could be entered by typing **070149** or **7/1/49**. If you have a date that is not in the twentieth century (e.g., July 4, 1776), you can use the **Century** command to have dBASE IV display four digits for the year instead of two.

At this point, before the last field (**Value**) has been entered, the screen will look like the following:

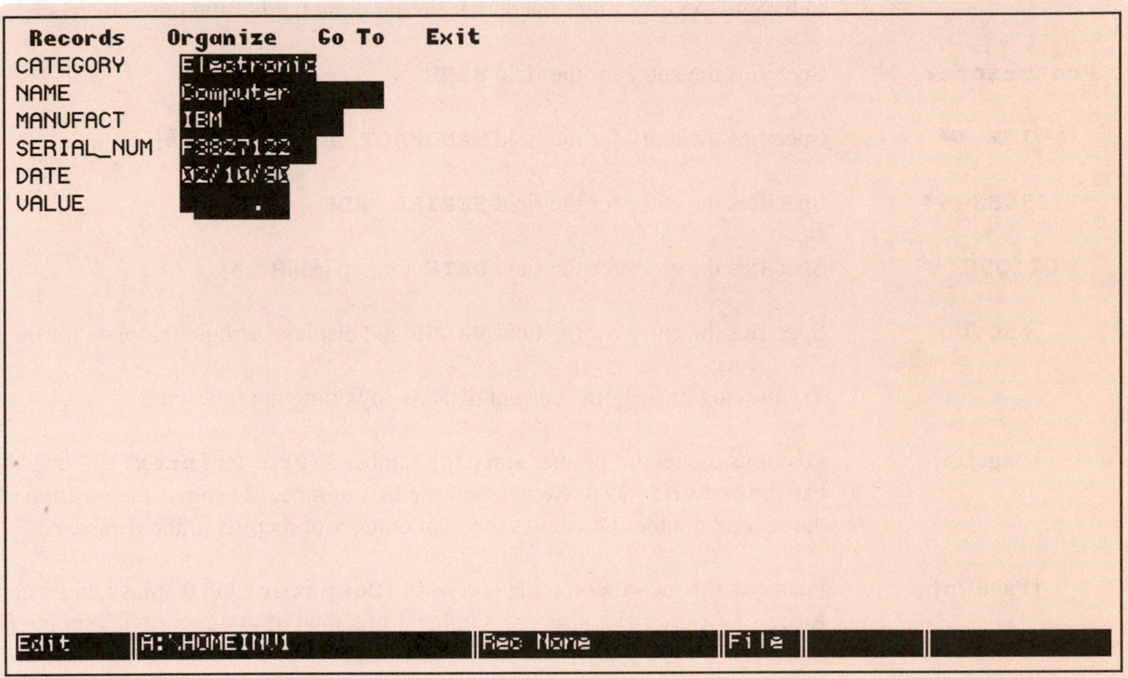

Now, type in the last entry for this record.

1200.00 Specifies the entry for the field **VALUE**. Notice that as soon as you type the last **0** on the right, a blank record template is displayed automatically and the status bar shows **Rec: EOF/1**

EOF means **E**nd **O**f **F**ile (this is the last record of the file).

/1 means that currently one record is in the file (you are working on the second record, but it has not yet been saved).

You may use **[PageUp]** to see the first record you entered.

[PageUp] Displays the previous record (i.e., record 1). The status bar will show **Rec: 1/1** to indicate that record 1 of a total of 1 records is being displayed.

To move down to the second (blank) record, tap **[PageDown]**.

[PageDown] Displays the message **===> Add new records? (Y/N)** on the navigation line. You want to add a new record so tap **Y** for **Y**es.

Y Displays a blank record template and waits for you to enter data.

Enter the second record by typing its data. As a shortcut to data entry, you may use the **[Shift-F8]** key. This is called the *ditto* key because if you tap it while in **Edit**, it will enter in the current record the data from the corresponding field of the previous record. For example, the **CATEGORY** field of the second record should contain **Electronic**, which is the same as the **CATEGORY** of the first record. When the cursor is in the **CATEGORY** field for record number 2 you may either type **Electronic** or tap **[Shift-F8]** and dBASE IV will enter **Electronic** for you.

Keystroke	Action Resulting from Keystroke
Electronic	Specifies the entry for the field **CATEGORY**. Instead of typing **Electronic**, you could tap **[Shift-F8]** to have dBASE IV enter the data from the same field of the previous record.
Pro Printer ↵	Specifies the entry for the field **NAME**.
IBM ↵	Specifies the entry for the field **MANUFACT**. Or, tap **[Shift-F8]**.
03483 ↵	Specifies the entry for the field **SERIAL_NUM**.
021090 ↵	Specifies the entry for the field **DATE**. Or, tap **[Shift-F8]**.
450.00	Specifies the entry for the field **VALUE** and displays a blank template for the next record.
	Try moving through the current database by doing the following:
[PageUp]	Positions the record pointer at record number 2 (**Pro Printer**) and displays that record. The status bar shows **Rec: 2/2**. Remember, the first number (**2**) shows the position of the record pointer, and the second number (**2**) shows the total number of records in the database.
[PageUp]	Positions the record pointer at record #1 (**Computer**) and displays that record. The status bar shows **Rec: 1/2** (you are at record number 1 of a total of two records). Tapping **[PageUp]** again will have no effect.
[PageDown]	Displays record number 2 (**Pro Printer**) again.
[PageDown]	Asks if you want to add new records.
N	Specifies that you do not want to add new records at this time (we will add more data later).
[Alt-E]	Opens the **Exit** menu.
E	Selects **Exit** and returns to the Control Center.

Saving Database Records to Disk

Frequent saving of the database as you enter records will provide some insurance against accidental loss in the event of a power failure or a hardware or software problem. When you enter data as in the previous section the data are not necessarily written to the disk but rather are written to a part of temporary memory called a buffer. The data are written to disk when the buffer becomes full or when you close the database either by selecting it in the Control Center and then selecting **Close file** or by selecting **Quit to DOS** from the **Exit** menu. What this means is that if you were to simply turn off the power to the computer right now, the data you just entered would be lost. It may look like dBASE IV has saved the data to disk but it has only been saved to the temporary buffer.

To save the database in its present form (i.e., with only two records entered), you may either quit the program or do the following (begin from the Control Center with **HOMEINV1** highlighted in the **Data** panel):

Keystroke	Action Resulting from Keystroke
[Enter]	Displays a prompt box similar to the one displayed when you opened **HOMEINV1**. The only change to the prompt box is that the first option is **Close file** rather than **Use file**.

```
Close file   Modify structure/order   Display data

      Press ENTER to select or ESC to cancel
```

Closing the file will write the data to disk.

Keystroke	Action Resulting from Keystroke
C	Selects **Close file**, writes the data to disk, and displays the Control Center again. Note that the active catalog is still **A:\UNTITLED.CAT** but the current file is listed as **New file** rather than **HOMEINV1** (because you have just closed that file).

At this point, you have actually saved the data to the disk. If a power failure occurs or if you simply turn off the computer, your data will be safe.

Note that you can instruct dBASE IV to save modifications to disk each time you make changes by typing **SET AUTOSAVE ON** from the dot prompt or by placing the command **AUTOSAVE=ON** in the **CONFIG.DB** file (for more information on this, see p. D111).

Appending New Records to the Database

Enter the rest of the data in the home inventory database by doing the following:

Keystroke	Action Resulting from Keystroke
[arrow]	Use the [arrow] keys to highlight **HOMEINV1** in the **Data** panel.
[Enter]	Selects the highlighted file and presents the following prompt box:

```
Use file   Modify structure/order   Display data

     Press ENTER to select or ESC to cancel
```

Keystroke	Action Resulting from Keystroke
U	Selects **Use file** and returns to the Control Center.
[F2]	Displays the last record you were working on (probably record number 1) in the **Edit** screen. Look at the entries on the menu bar:

```
Records   Organize   Go To   Exit
```

Continued . . .

Keystroke	Action Resulting from Keystroke
	Records allows you to add, blank, mark for deletion, and undo changes to specific records.
	Organize allows you to arrange the records according to a specified scheme (e.g., alphabetize them by name), and unmark or delete marked records.
	Go To allows you to display (go to) a specific record.
	Exit allows you to exit to the Control Center or transfer to another screen.
[Alt-R]	Opens the **Records** menu.
A	Selects **Add new records** and displays a blank record template.

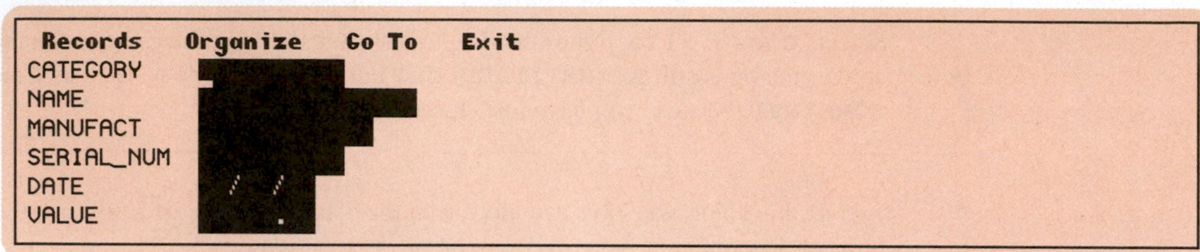

Enter the rest of the data as listed below. Remember, to speed up the process, you may use the **[Shift-F8]** key to copy data from the same field of the previous record into a new record.

	CATEGORY	NAME	MANUFACT	SERIAL_NUM	DATE	VALUE
Field width →	1234567890	123456789012345	123456789012	1234567890	12345678	12345678
Record # 1 →	← You have already entered the first and second records →					
Record # 2 →						
Record # 3 →	Electronic	External drive	IBM	F392281	02/10/90	356.00
Record # 4 →	Appliance	Microwave oven	Sears	2339112	01/22/89	450.00
Record # 5 →	Appliance	Color TV	RCA	2338442	05/25/89	360.00
Record # 6 →	Electronic	Stereo	Fischer	34562	03/12/89	412.00
Record # 7 →	Furniture	Sofa	Wilder	---	11/21/84	450.00
Record # 8 →	Furniture	Recliner	La-Z-Boy	---	03/23/87	350.00
Record # 9 →	Furniture	Dry sink	Hand made	---	04/12/87	500.00
Record # 10 →	Appliance	Refrigerator	Wards	493323	03/22/87	450.00
Record # 11 →	Appliance	Stove	Wards	533282	03/22/87	350.00
Record # 12 →	Appliance	Dishwasher	Kitchen Aid	04322344	09/23/81	550.00
Record # 13 →	Furniture	Bed, mattress	Simmons	---	09/03/87	100.00
Record # 14 →	Furniture	Bed, spring	Simmons	---	09/03/87	100.00
Record # 15 →	Furniture	Bed, frame	Simmons	---	09/03/87	100.00

After you have finished entering all the records you may use **Browse** to display up to 18 records in the database at one time (all the records for this small database). Recall that the **[F2]** is called the *data* key and may be used to switch between **Edit** and **Browse**.

Keystroke	Action Resulting from Keystroke
[F2]	Switches to **Browse**. Most of the screen will be blank and only the last record will be displayed. **Browse** is discussed in detail on page D36–56.
[PageUp]	Scrolls up one screen to reveal the rest of the records.

Continued . . .

Keystroke	Action Resulting from Keystroke

```
Records    Organize    Fields    Go To    Exit
```

CATEGORY	NAME	MANUFACT	SERIAL_NUM	DATE	VALUE
Electronic	Computer	IBM	F3827122	02/10/90	1200.00
Electronic	Pro Printer	IBM	03483	02/10/90	450.00
Electronic	External drive	IBM	F392281	02/10/90	356.00
Appliance	Microwave oven	Sears	2339112	01/22/89	450.00
Appliance	Color TV	RCA	2338442	05/25/89	360.00
Electronic	Stereo	Fischer	34562	03/12/89	412.00
Furniture	Sofa	Wilder	---	11/21/84	450.00
Furniture	Recliner	La-Z-Boy	---	03/23/87	350.00
Furniture	Dry sink	Hand made	---	04/12/87	500.00
Appliance	Refrigerator	Wards	493323	03/22/87	450.00
Appliance	Stove	Wards	533282	03/22/87	350.00
Appliance	Dishwasher	Kitchen Aid	04322344	09/23/81	550.00
Furniture	Bed, mattress	Simmons	---	09/03/87	100.00
Furniture	Bed, spring	Simmons	---	09/03/87	100.00
Furniture	Bed, frame	Simmons	---	09/03/87	100.00

```
Browse  A:\HOMEINV1  Rec 1/15  File
```

Look over the data carefully to be sure that they are correct. Use the normal editing techniques to correct any errors you may find (i.e., use the **[arrow]** keys to move to the error and then use **[Insert]**, **[Delete]**, and **[Backspace]** to make your changes).

Keystroke	Action Resulting from Keystroke
[Alt-E]	Opens the **Exit** menu.
E	Selects **Exit** and returns to the Control Center.

At this point, it would be a good idea to make a backup copy of the database as a precaution against accidental loss or corruption. There are a number of ways of doing this:

- Quit dBASE IV and then use the DOS **COPY** command (see p. W205).
- Suspend the dBASE IV program execution and drop to DOS (see p. D142) as we did with WordPerfect (see p. W68) and Lotus 1-2-3 (see p. L42).
- Select **Copy** from the **Operations** menu of the **DOS utilities** menu of the **Tools** menu of the Control Center (this is not as complicated as it sounds).
- Switch to the dot prompt and execute the **COPY TO** command. This command is specifically designed to copy all or part of a database file to a new database file.

Because it is quick and easy, we will use the **COPY TO** command at the dot prompt.

Keystroke	*Action Resulting from Keystroke*
[Alt-E]	Opens the **Exit** menu.
E	Selects **Exit to dot prompt**, exits the Control Center, and places the cursor at the dot prompt.

COPY TO A:\HOMEORG.DBF ↵

Copies the active database (**HOMEINV1.DBF**) to a new file called **HOMEORG.DBF**, which is to reside on the diskette in drive **A:**.

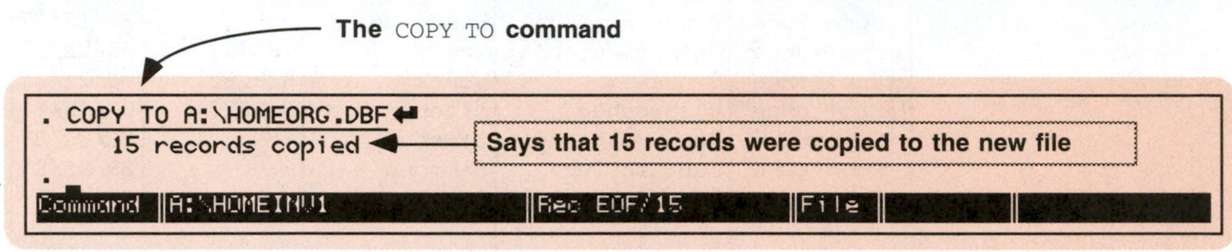

ASSIST ↵	Switches from the dot prompt back to the Control Center.

You may notice that the new file **HOMEORG** is not listed in the **Data** panel. You can add its name by selecting **Add file to catalog** from the **Catalog** menu.

Keystroke	*Action Resulting from Keystroke*
[Alt-C]	Opens the **Catalog** menu.
A	Selects **Add file to catalog** and opens a box showing the names of the different files you can add to the catalog. This type of box is called a *picklist* because it shows you a list of items you can pick from for the current operation.

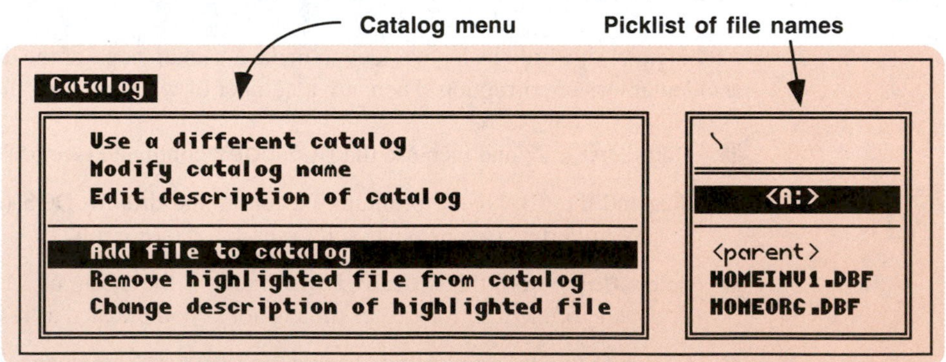

[arrow]	Use the **[arrow]** keys to highlight the file **HOMEORG.DBF**.
[Enter]	Selects the highlighted file and asks you for a description for the file. Type the following:

Backup file for home inventory example

Continued . . .

Keystroke	Action Resulting from Keystroke
[Enter]	Accepts the description and adds the name **HOMEORG** to the current catalog. The name now should be displayed in the **Data** panel.

Printing a Quick Report

To get a hard copy of the contents of the database we could display the entire database in **Browse** and then do a screen dump. That would be adequate for a small database like **HOMEINV1** but would not work for larger databases nor would it be helpful if we wanted to print a report using a specific format.

The usual way of getting hard copy of database information is to use a dBASE IV report form, which is a design for the display or printing of selected records or fields of the database. dBASE IV offers two kinds of reports: *quick reports*, which follow a standard format that is already programmed into the software, and *custom reports,* which can be designed to meet the specific needs of the user (these will be discussed in detail at the end of this chapter).

Let's use the dBASE IV *Quick Report* feature to produce a simple printed copy of the database. With quick reports, the data are printed exactly as they appear in the database. A page number and the date are included at the top of each page, the names of the fields are printed as column headers, and the totals of all numeric fields are printed at the bottom of the report.

Keystroke	Action Resulting from Keystroke
[Shift-F9]	Displays the *Quick Report* menu.

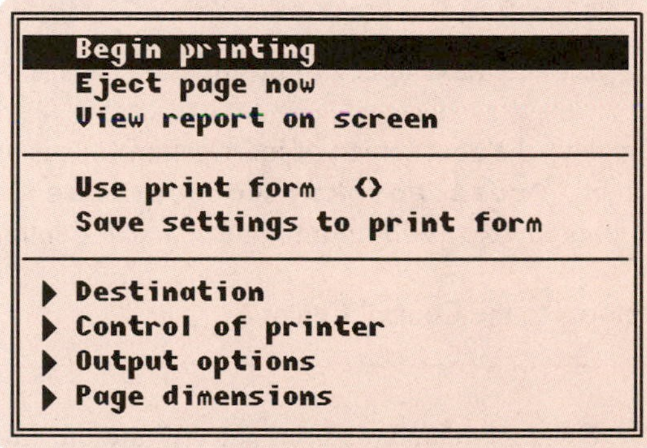

Options that can be selected when using *Quick Reports* include **Begin printing**, which starts the printing of the report using the current printer settings, and **View report on screen**, which displays the report on the screen, one screen at a time.

V	Selects **View report on screen**, constructs the report, and then displays it on the screen (this may take a few seconds).

Continued . . .

Keystroke	Action Resulting from Keystroke

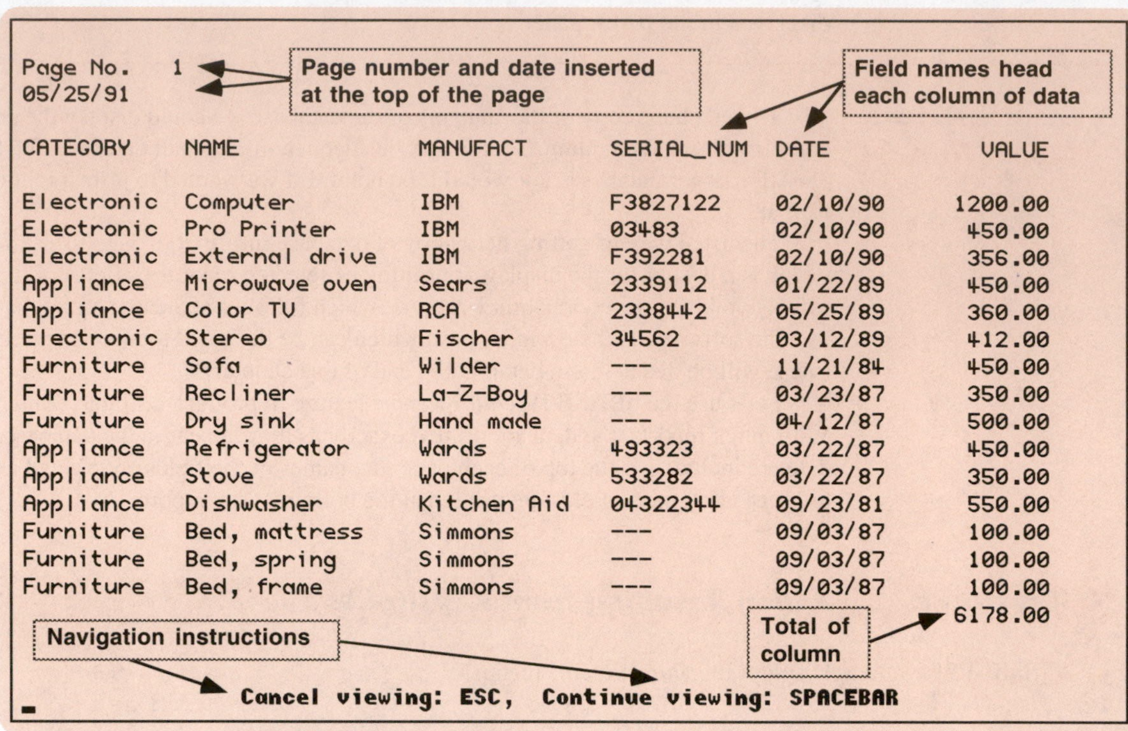

Page No. 1
05/25/91

CATEGORY	NAME	MANUFACT	SERIAL_NUM	DATE	VALUE
Electronic	Computer	IBM	F3827122	02/10/90	1200.00
Electronic	Pro Printer	IBM	03483	02/10/90	450.00
Electronic	External drive	IBM	F392281	02/10/90	356.00
Appliance	Microwave oven	Sears	2339112	01/22/89	450.00
Appliance	Color TV	RCA	2338442	05/25/89	360.00
Electronic	Stereo	Fischer	34562	03/12/89	412.00
Furniture	Sofa	Wilder	---	11/21/84	450.00
Furniture	Recliner	La-Z-Boy	---	03/23/87	350.00
Furniture	Dry sink	Hand made	---	04/12/87	500.00
Appliance	Refrigerator	Wards	493323	03/22/87	450.00
Appliance	Stove	Wards	533282	03/22/87	350.00
Appliance	Dishwasher	Kitchen Aid	04322344	09/23/81	550.00
Furniture	Bed, mattress	Simmons	---	09/03/87	100.00
Furniture	Bed, spring	Simmons	---	09/03/87	100.00
Furniture	Bed, frame	Simmons	---	09/03/87	100.00
					6178.00

Cancel viewing: ESC, Continue viewing: SPACEBAR

[Spacebar]	Displays the next screen of information (this is a blank screen because the active database is so small).
[Spacebar]	Displays the next screen of information (this is also a blank screen). The message at the bottom of the screen, **`Press any key to continue . . .`**, says that the display is complete and that tapping any key will return to the Control Center.
[Enter]	Returns to the Control Center.

Modifying the Database Using `Edit` and `Browse`

Once the data have been entered into the database, modifications can be made using **`Edit`** or **`Browse`**. For example, let's change the name of the item in record number 2 from **`Pro Printer`** to **`Impact Printer`**. To do this, we will access the **`Edit`** screen, move the record pointer to record number 2, and then use the standard editing techniques to make the required changes. Begin the following from the Control Center:

Keystroke	Action Resulting from Keystroke
[F2]	Displays the **`Browse`** or **`Edit`** screen (whichever you last accessed). If the **`Browse`** screen appears, tap **[F2]** again to switch to **`Edit`**.

Continued . . .

Keystroke	Action Resulting from Keystroke

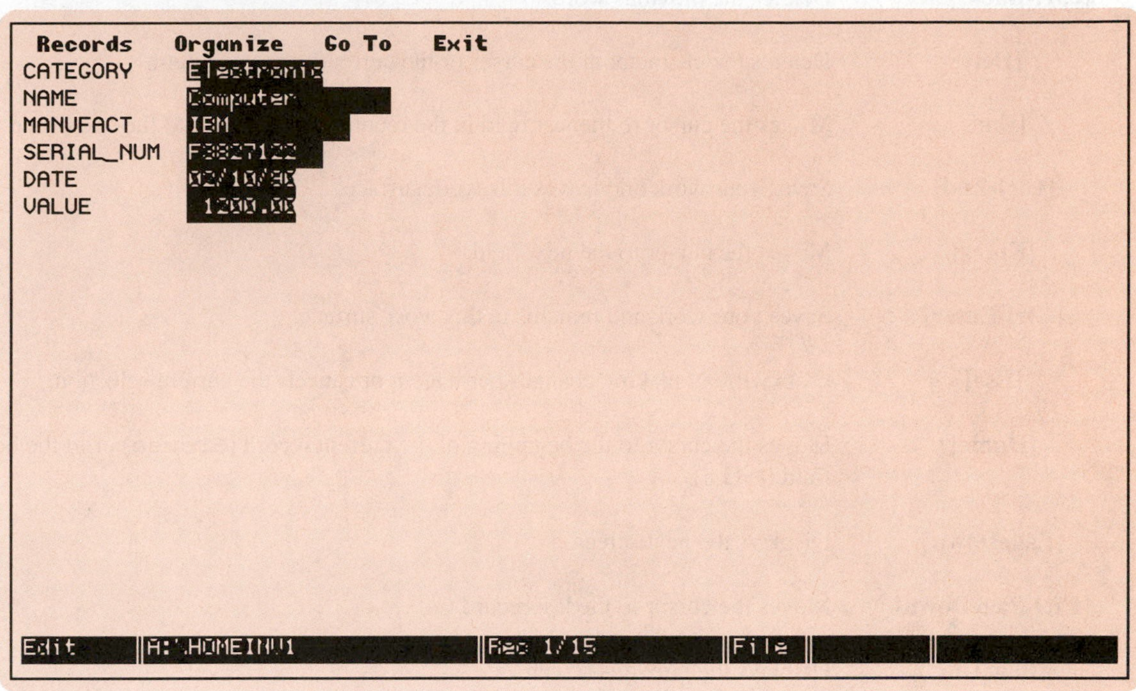

For your information and reference, the navigation keys that can be used while in either **Browse** or **Edit** are given below (do not try to memorize all of these—just keep them in mind as you work in **Edit** and **Browse** and refer back to this page when you need to):

Key	Comment
[Down arrow]	Moves the cursor to the next record (**Browse**) or field (**Edit**).
[Up arrow]	Moves the cursor to the previous record (**Browse**) or field (**Edit**).
[Left arrow]	Moves the cursor one character left.
[Ctrl-left arrow]	Moves the cursor to the beginning of the previous word.
[Right arrow]	Moves the cursor one character right.
[Ctrl-right arrow]	Moves the cursor to the beginning of the next word.
[Backspace]	Deletes the previous character.

Continued . . .

Key	Comment
[Ctrl-Backspace]	Deletes the previous word.
[Del]	Deletes the character at the cursor or the currently selected item.
[End]	Moves the cursor to the last field in the record (**Browse**) or to the end of the field (**Edit**).
[Ctrl-End]	Saves your work and leaves this work surface.
[Enter]	Moves the cursor to the next field.
[Ctrl-Enter]	Saves your work and remains in this work surface.
[Esc]	Exits without making changes permanent or cancels the current selection.
[Home]	Moves the cursor to the beginning of the current record (**Browse**) or to the beginning of the current field (**Edit**).
[PageDown]	Displays the next screen.
[Ctrl-PageDown]	Moves the cursor to the last record.
[PageUp]	Displays the previous screen.
[Ctrl-PageUp]	Moves the cursor to the first record.
[Shift-Tab]	Moves the cursor to the previous field.
[Tab]	Moves the cursor to the next field.
[Ctrl-U]	Marks the active record for deletion.
[Ctrl-Y]	Deletes text at and to the right of the cursor.
[F1]	Accesses the *Help* screens.
[F2]	Toggles between **Browse** and **Edit**.
[F3]	Moves the cursor to the previous field.
[F4]	Moves the cursor to the next field.
[F10]	Opens the menus on the menu bar.
[Shift-F2]	Transfers to design screen.
[Shift-F8]	Copies data from the corresponding field in the previous record.
[Shift-F9]	Creates a quick report.
[Shift-F10]	Accesses the macros menu.

Practice editing a record by going to record number 2 and changing **Pro Printer** to **Impact Printer** by doing the following:

Keystroke	Action Resulting from Keystroke
[Alt-G]	Opens the **Go To** menu.

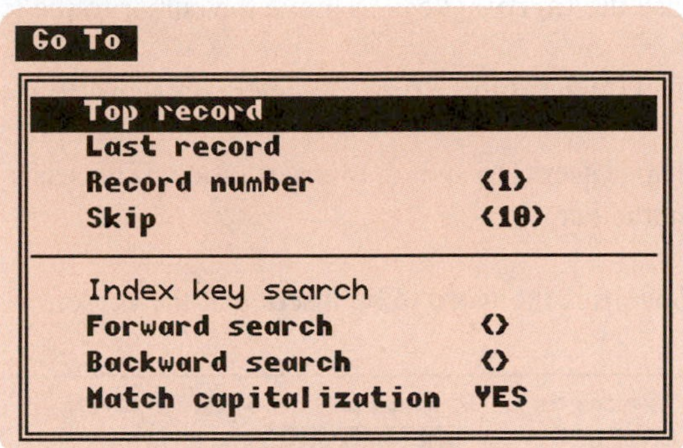

Top record allows you to move to the first record of the database (**[Ctrl-PageUp]** accomplishes the same thing when the menus are closed).

Last record allows you to move to the last record of the database (**[Ctrl-PageDown]** accomplishes the same thing when the menus are closed).

Record number allows you to move to a specific record number (you must specify the number).

Skip allows you to move a specified number of records toward the bottom of the database (if you enter a positive number at the prompt) or toward the top of the database (if you enter a negative number at the prompt).

Index key search saves processing time when searching on an indexed field (indexing is covered on pp. D147–57).

Forward search allows you to search for a record that contains a specific string (e.g., the word **Dishwasher** in the **NAME** field). The search begins at the current record and moves forward toward the bottom of the database.

Backward search is the same as **Forward search** but it progresses from the current record back toward the top of the database.

Match capitalization YES means that a string search is case sensitive (i.e., **dishwasher** is considered different from **Dishwasher**).

Keystroke	Action Resulting from Keystroke
R	Selects **Record number** and asks you to enter the number of the record you want to make active.

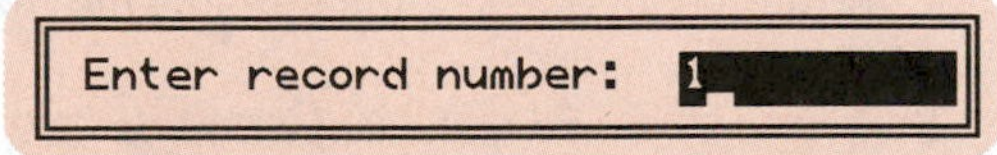

Be careful when you type the record number. dBASE IV does not erase the current record number when you enter a new one. Hence, if record number 1 is currently active and you type 2, record number 12 will be made active (i.e., the 2 you type will be appended to the end of the 1 already displayed to make 12).

Continued . . .

Keystroke	Action Resulting from Keystroke
[Backspace]	Deletes the displayed record number.
2 ↵	Specifies the new record number and makes that record active. You now may use the standard editing techniques to delete the word **Pro** and insert the word **Impact**.
[arrow]	Use the **[arrow]** keys to move the cursor to the first letter of the word **Pro**.
[Delete]	Tap **[Delete]** three times to delete the word **Pro**.
[Insert]	Tap **[Insert]** to switch to insert mode, if necessary. The letters **Ins** will appear on the right side of the status bar.
Impact	Specifies the word to be inserted at the cursor.

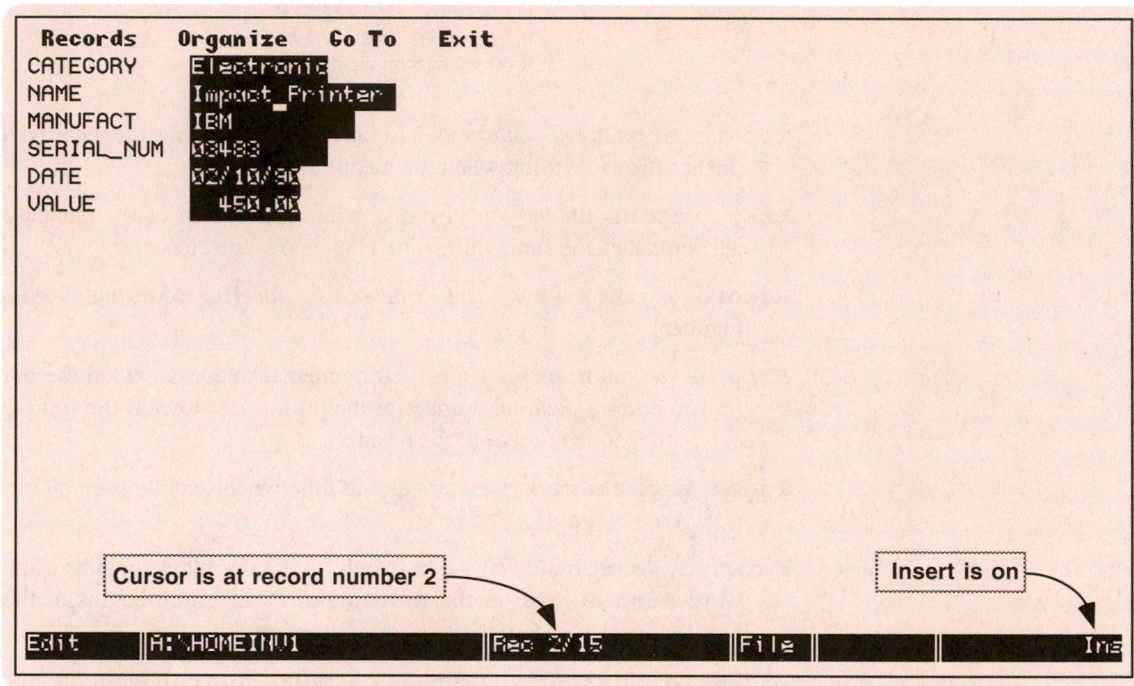

Modifications can also be made in the **Browse** screen. The process is similar to that used in **Edit**, but in **Browse** you can see more than one record at a time. However, if you have many fields or fields that are particularly wide, not all the fields for a given record may fit on the screen at one time. To remedy this, dBASE IV allows you to lock fields so that they remain displayed on the screen as others scroll off the screen (this is similar to locking titles in Lotus 1-2-3). Locking fields will be discussed on p. D42.

Switch to **Browse** and change **Color TV** to **19" Color TV** by doing the following:

Keystroke	Action Resulting from Keystroke
[F2]	Switches to the **Browse** screen from the **Edit** screen.

Continued . . .

Keystroke	*Action Resulting from Keystroke*

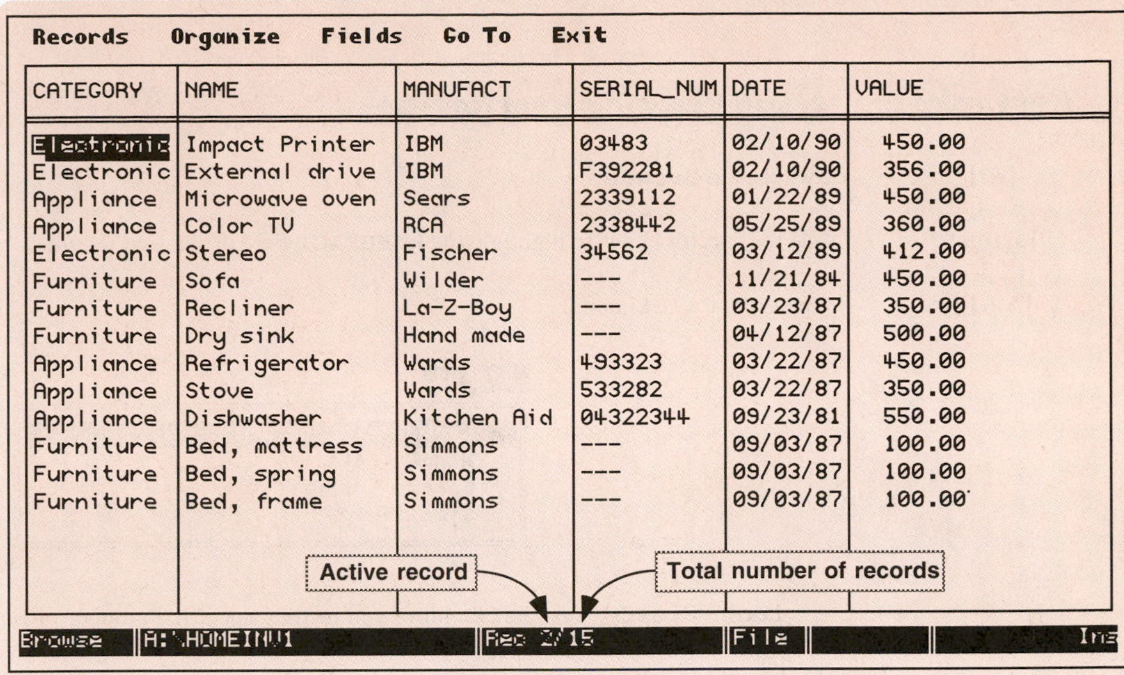

Records   Organize   Fields   Go To   Exit

CATEGORY	NAME	MANUFACT	SERIAL_NUM	DATE	VALUE
Electronic	Impact Printer	IBM	03483	02/10/90	450.00
Electronic	External drive	IBM	F392281	02/10/90	356.00
Appliance	Microwave oven	Sears	2339112	01/22/89	450.00
Appliance	Color TV	RCA	2338442	05/25/89	360.00
Electronic	Stereo	Fischer	34562	03/12/89	412.00
Furniture	Sofa	Wilder	---	11/21/84	450.00
Furniture	Recliner	La-Z-Boy	---	03/23/87	350.00
Furniture	Dry sink	Hand made	---	04/12/87	500.00
Appliance	Refrigerator	Wards	493323	03/22/87	450.00
Appliance	Stove	Wards	533282	03/22/87	350.00
Appliance	Dishwasher	Kitchen Aid	04322344	09/23/81	550.00
Furniture	Bed, mattress	Simmons	---	09/03/87	100.00
Furniture	Bed, spring	Simmons	---	09/03/87	100.00
Furniture	Bed, frame	Simmons	---	09/03/87	100.00

Notice that the active record (**Impact Printer**) is at the top of the list (record number 1 has scrolled off the top). To move the cursor to another location you may use the **[arrow]** keys or the options in the **Go To** menu. For this example it is easier to use the **[arrow]** keys, but if the desired record were not displayed on the screen then using the **Go To** menu might be faster.

[arrow]	Use the **[arrow]** keys to move the cursor to the first letter of the word **Color** in record number 5.
19"	Specifies the characters to be inserted at the cursor. Record number 5 now should look like the following:

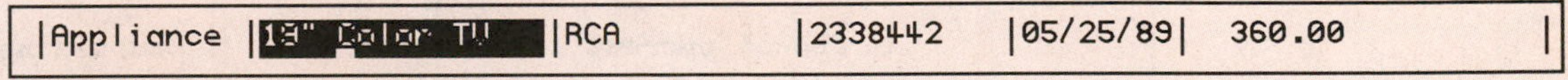

Appliance	19" Color TV	RCA	2338442	05/25/89	360.00

Note that if you modify a record and then change your mind and want to restore it to its original form, you can do so by selecting **Undo change to record** from the **Records** menu (tap **[Alt-R]** and then **U**). This is convenient but it only works if you have not yet moved the pointer from the record you want to restore. For example, if the pointer is still at record number 5 and you tap **[Alt-R]** and then **U**, the **NAME** field will be restored to **Color TV**. However, if you move the pointer to record number 6 and then back to record number 5 the undo change command will not work.

[Insert]	Tap **[Insert]** to switch back to typeover mode.
[Alt-E]	Opens the **Exit** menu.
E	Selects **Exit** and returns to the Control Center.

Altering the Browse Screen during Editing

If your database has many fields or if the widths of some fields are very wide, you may not be able to see all the fields as you edit. The **Fields** menu provides some options for temporarily changing the way the **Browse** screen looks. To see how this works, do the following (begin from the Control Center):

Keystroke	Action Resulting from Keystroke
[F2]	Switches to **Browse**.
[arrow]	Use the **[arrow]** keys to highlight the **MANUFACT** field of the first record.
[Alt-F]	Opens the **Files** menu.

```
Fields
 Lock fields on left  <0>
 Blank field
 Freeze field         <>
 Size field
```

Lock fields on left allows you to fix a specified number of fields on the left of the screen so that they do not move when you scroll to the right. This is similar to locking titles in Lotus 1-2-3 (see p. L83).

Blank field erases the contents of a field.

Freeze field limits editing to a specified field. This stops you from moving the cursor to any other field.

Size field allows you to change the number of characters displayed in a field.

Use this last option to increase the displayed size of the **MANUFACT** field by 28 by doing the following:

Keystroke	Action Resulting from Keystroke
S	Selects **Size field** and displays the following message at the bottom of the screen.

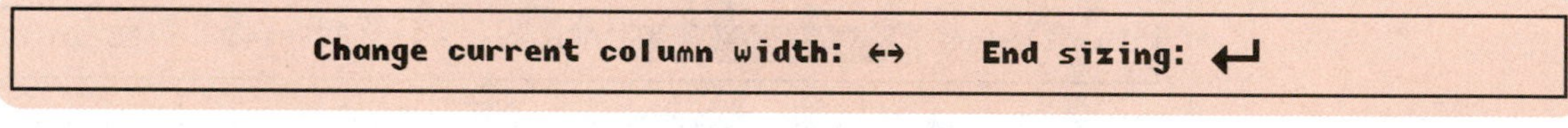

Use the **[right arrow]** key to increase the size of the column and the **[left arrow]** to decrease the size.

Keystroke	Action Resulting from Keystroke
[right arrow]	Tap the **[right arrow]** key 28 times to increase the width of the column.

Continued . . .

Keystroke	Action Resulting from Keystroke

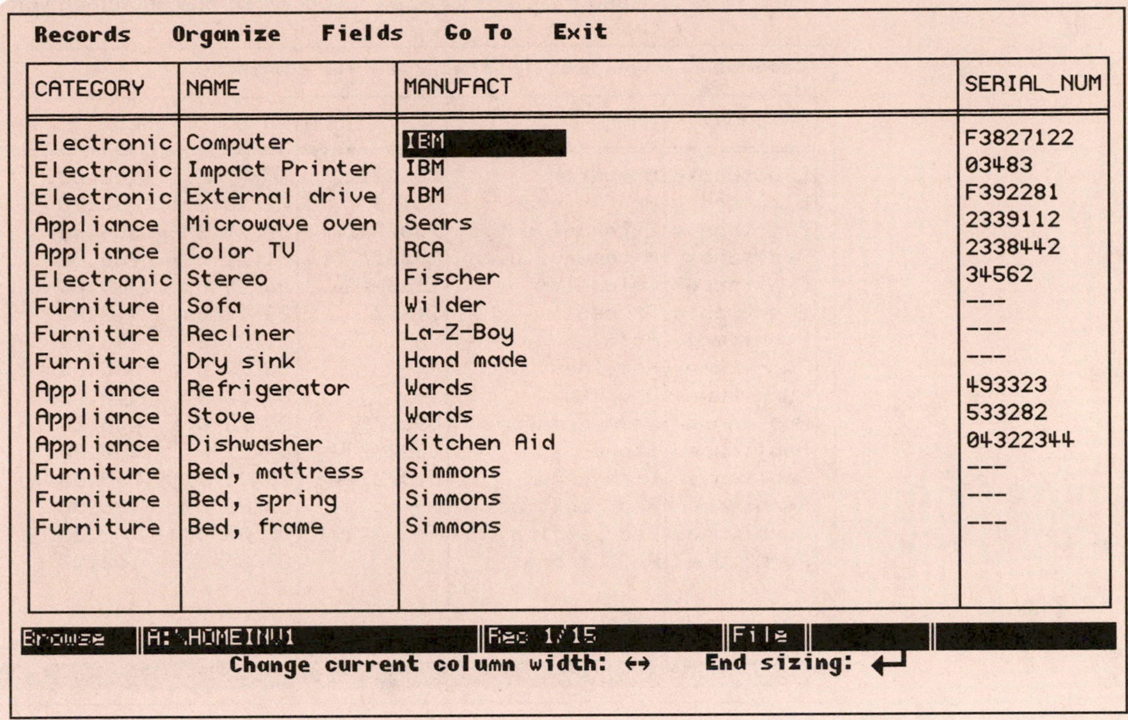

Records Organize Fields Go To Exit

CATEGORY	NAME	MANUFACT	SERIAL_NUM
Electronic	Computer	IBM	F3827122
Electronic	Impact Printer	IBM	03483
Electronic	External drive	IBM	F392281
Appliance	Microwave oven	Sears	2339112
Appliance	Color TV	RCA	2338442
Electronic	Stereo	Fischer	34562
Furniture	Sofa	Wilder	---
Furniture	Recliner	La-Z-Boy	---
Furniture	Dry sink	Hand made	---
Appliance	Refrigerator	Wards	493323
Appliance	Stove	Wards	533282
Appliance	Dishwasher	Kitchen Aid	04322344
Furniture	Bed, mattress	Simmons	---
Furniture	Bed, spring	Simmons	---
Furniture	Bed, frame	Simmons	---

Browse A:\HOMEINV1 Rec 1/15 File

Change current column width: ↔ End sizing: ↵

[Enter]	Fixes the displayed size and returns to **`Browse`**.

To lock a field so that it remains displayed on the screen while scrolling, you would select **`Lock fields on left`** from the **`Fields`** menu.

Keystroke	Action Resulting from Keystroke
[Alt-F]	Opens the **`Fields`** menu.
L	Selects **`Lock fields on left`** and asks for the number of fields on the left to remain stationary.
2	Specifies that the two left-most fields will remain stationary when scrolling.
[Tab] [Tab]	Pressing **[Tab]** two times moves the cursor to the **DATE** field. Notice that the **CATEGORY** and **NAME** fields remain stationary while the other fields scroll. The **MANUFACT** field is no longer visible.

Continued . . .

Keystroke	Action Resulting from Keystroke

CATEGORY and NAME are locked so MANUFACT scrolls off screen when more room is needed

```
Records  Organize  Fields  Go To  Exit

CATEGORY   NAME             SERIAL_NUM DATE      VALUE

Electronic Computer         F3827122   02/10/90  1200.00
Electronic Pro Printer      03483      02/10/90   450.00
Electronic External drive   F392281    02/10/90   356.00
Appliance  Microwave oven   2339112    01/22/89   450.00
Appliance  Color TV         2338442    05/25/89   360.00
Electronic Stereo           34562      03/12/89   412.00
Furniture  Sofa             ---        11/21/84   450.00
Furniture  Recliner         ---        03/23/87   350.00
Furniture  Dry sink         ---        04/12/87   500.00
Appliance  Refrigerator     493323     03/22/87   450.00
Appliance  Stove            533282     03/22/87   350.00
Appliance  Dishwasher       04322344   09/23/81   550.00
Furniture  Bed, mattress    ---        09/03/87   100.00
Furniture  Bed, spring      ---        09/03/87   100.00
Furniture  Bed, frame       ---        09/03/87   100.00

Browse  A:\HOMEINV1        Rec 1/15      File
```

[Alt-E]	Opens the **Exit** menu.
E	Selects **Exit** and returns to the Control Center.

The above changes were only temporary. The next time you switch to the **Browse** screen the fields will appear without the changes.

Deleting Records Using Edit and Browse

We can use **Browse** or **Edit** to delete records. Deleting records is a two-step process: First, you place a deletion marker on the records you wish erased and then you tell dBASE IV to actually erase the marked records from the database in what is called a *pack* operation. This two-step process is more efficient when you want to erase large numbers of records and it gives you a chance to change your mind about deleting specific records. As an analogy, you can think of marking the records for deletion as throwing some unwanted papers into a trash basket. You can change your mind (i.e., you can dig them out of the trash basket) at any time before the trash is hauled away by the trash collector (hauling the trash is like packing the database). Once the trash is in the garbage truck (i.e., once the database has been packed) the discarded items are gone for good. To illustrate this, let's delete record number 5 (the TV) by doing the following (begin from the Control Center):

Keystroke	Action Resulting from Keystroke
[F2]	Switches to **Browse** or **Edit**, depending on which you last used (probably **Browse**). If the **Edit** screen appears instead of the **Browse** screen, skip the next step.
[F2]	Switches to **Edit** from **Browse**. Record number 5 is probably displayed but if it is not, do the following:

Continued . . .

Keystroke	Action Resulting from Keystroke
[Alt-G]	Opens the **Go To** menu.
R	Selects the **Record number** option.
5 ↵	Provides the record number (remember, you may have to use **[Delete]** to remove the record number automatically displayed by dBASE IV).

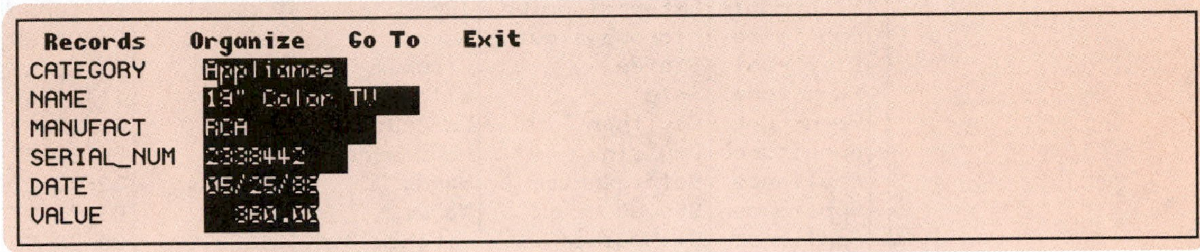

Keystroke	Action Resulting from Keystroke
[Alt-R]	Opens the **Records** menu.
M	Selects **Mark record for deletion**. Notice the word **Del** appears on the status bar to indicate that the active record has been marked for deletion but that the record still appears on the screen.

We can tell dBASE IV to actually erase the record (i.e., pack the database) by selecting **Erase marked records** from the **Organize** menu.

Keystroke	Action Resulting from Keystroke
[Alt-O]	Opens the **Organize** menu.
E	Selects **Erase marked records** and displays a prompt box asking you to confirm that all marked records should be erased.

Keystroke	Action Resulting from Keystroke
Y	Selects **Yes** and erases the marked record from the database. A box appears briefly in the middle of the screen indicating that the database is being packed. At the bottom of the box the message **14 records copied** flashes by (perhaps faster than you can see it). The **19" Color TV** record is gone and the status bar indicates that 14 (rather than 15) records are now in the database. If you switch to **Browse** you can see that records 1 through 4 have remained where they are but records 6 through 15 have become records 5 through 14 (there now are 14 records in the database).
[F2]	Switches to **Browse**.

Continued . . .

Keystroke	Action Resulting from Keystroke

```
Records   Organize   Fields   Go To   Exit

CATEGORY   NAME            MANUFACT     SERIAL_NUM  DATE      VALUE
Electronic Computer        IBM          F3827122    02/10/90  1200.00
Electronic Impact Printer  IBM          03483       02/10/90   450.00
Electronic External drive  IBM          F392281     02/10/90   356.00
Appliance  Microwave oven  Sears        2339112     01/22/89   450.00
Electronic Stereo          Fischer      34562       03/12/89   412.00
Furniture  Sofa            Wilder       ---         11/21/84   450.00
Furniture  Recliner        La-Z-Boy     ---         03/23/87   350.00
Furniture  Dry sink        Hand made    ---         04/12/87   500.00
Appliance  Refrigerator    Wards        493323      03/22/87   450.00
Appliance  Stove           Wards        533282      03/22/87   350.00
Appliance  Dishwasher      Kitchen Aid  04322344    09/23/81   550.00
Furniture  Bed, mattress   Simmons      ---         09/03/87   100.00
Furniture  Bed, spring     Simmons      ---         09/03/87   100.00
Furniture  Bed, frame      Simmons      ---         09/03/87   100.00

Browse  A:\HOMEINV1            Rec 1/14          File
```

You can mark for deletion and erase records from **Browse** as well as **Edit**. For example, let's mark for deletion the last three records (the bed mattress, spring, and frame):

Keystroke	Action Resulting from Keystroke
[arrow]	Use the **[arrow]** keys to move the pointer to record number 12 (**Bed, mattress**). You can mark this record for deletion by following the same procedure as before (open the **Records** menu and then select **Mark record for deletion**). A quicker way to mark a record for deletion is to use **[Ctrl-U]**.
[Ctrl-U]	Marks the active record for deletion. Notice the word **Del** on the status bar.
[arrow]	Use the **[arrow]** keys to move the pointer down one record (to record number 13).
[Ctrl-U]	Marks the active record for deletion (**Del** appears on the status bar).
[arrow]	Use the **[arrow]** keys to move the pointer down one record (to record number 14).
[Ctrl-U]	Marks the active record for deletion (**Del** appears on the status bar).

We really do not want these three records erased so let's unmark them. We can do this one at a time by making a record active and then selecting **Clear deletion mark** from the **Records** menu. Or, we can unmark all records at once by selecting **Unmark all records** from the **Organize** menu. We will do the latter.

Keystroke	Action Resulting from Keystroke
[Alt-O]	Opens the **Organize** menu.
U	Selects **Unmark all records** and asks you to confirm that you want to do that.
Y	Confirms that all records are to be unmarked. A box appears briefly in the middle of the screen indicating that all the marked records are being recalled. At the bottom of the box the message **3 records recalled** flashes by (perhaps faster than you can see it).
[Alt-E]	Opens the **Exit** menu.
E	Selects **Exit** and returns to the Control Center.

Records may also be marked for deletion through the use of the **DELETE** command at the dot prompt or by using update queries. A **query** is a set of instructions you give dBASE IV that tells it how to organize or change the data. An *update query* is used to make broad changes to the data. If the records you want deleted form a logical group (e.g., all records with **Furniture** in the **CATEGORY** field) you can use an update query to have dBASE IV mark them all for deletion at one time (i.e., you do not have to select and mark the records one by one). Queries are discussed on pages D56–74.

Arranging Records by Indexing

Records appear in the database file in the order in which they were originally entered. This lack of organization makes viewing the data difficult or inconvenient but it can be overcome by using the dBASE IV *Index* and *Sort* features. These two features provide easy ways to arrange records to suit your needs. Indexing a database only changes the way the records are displayed but does not change the physical arrangement of the records on the disk. Sorting actually rearranges the records on the disk. We will go through a brief example below and then return for a detailed discussion on pages D147–60.

Suppose you want to arrange the records in the database **HOMEINV1** so that they appear in alphabetical order by name. Displaying the records in this way would enable you to quickly find a particular item on the list. To arrange the records, we will create an index, which is a file that tells dBASE IV how the records are to be arranged when they are displayed or printed. To do this, follow the directions given below (begin from the Control Center with **HOMEINV1** as the active database):

Keystroke	Action Resulting from Keystroke
[F2]	Displays the **Browse** or **Edit** screen, whichever you last used. If **Edit** is displayed, press **[F2]** again to display **Browse**.
[Alt-O]	Opens the **Organize** menu.

Continued . . .

Keystroke	Action Resulting from Keystroke
C	Selects **Create new index** and displays its menu.

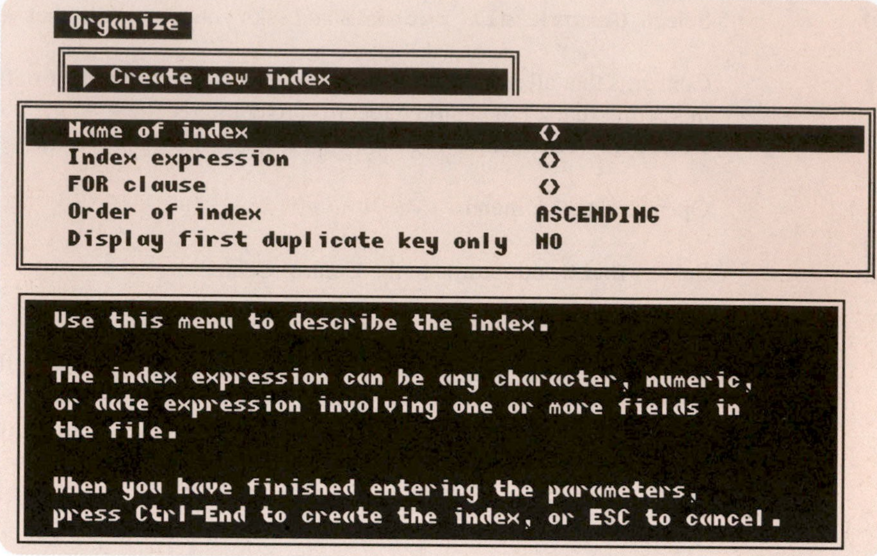

Name of index allows you to assign a name to the new index. Index names may be up to 10 characters long, must begin with a letter, and may contain letters, digits, and the underscore. The index names are referred to as *tags* and they are stored in a file with an **MDX** extension.

Index expression allows you to specify how the index is to work. The expression you enter can include field names (e.g., **NAME**), operators (e.g., +, –), and functions (e.g., **LOG**, **SIN**). If you wanted to arrange the records by **CATEGORY** and then, for those records with the same **CATEGORY**, arrange them by **NAME**, you would use **CATEGORY + NAME** for the index expression.

FOR clause allows you to select for indexing and display only those records that meet a specific condition (e.g., **VALUE > 400**).

Order of index allows you to arrange the records in ascending (A to Z) or in descending (Z to A) order. This is an ASCII ordering scheme, which means that all uppercase letters will be placed ahead of all lowercase letters. For example, **Zodda** would appear before **deMille** because uppercase **Z** comes before lowercase **d** in this type of ordering. Unless you tell it otherwise, dBASE IV will use the following order for indexing and sorting:

```
 !"#$%&'()*+,-./0123456789:;<=>?@
ABCDEFGHIJKLMNOPQRSTUVWXYZ[\]^_`
abcdefghijklmnopqrstuvwxyz{|}~
```

Continued . . .

Keystroke	Action Resulting from Keystroke

That is,

Blank space

Special characters: **!"#$%&'()*+,-./**

Digits: **0123456789**

Special characters: **:;<=>?@**

Uppercase letters: **ABCDEFGHIJKLMNOPQRSTUVWXYZ**

Special characters: **[\]^_`**

Lowercase letters: **abcdefghijklmnopqrstuvwxyz**

Special characters: **{|}~**

This ordering problem can be fixed by using the **UPPER** function in the index expression. **UPPER** converts all letters to uppercase while the indexing takes place. For example, the index expression **UPPER(NAME)** would arrange the records so that **deMille** comes before **Zodda**. Another fix for this problem would be to always use an uppercase letter at the beginning of a field (e.g., enter **Demille** instead of **deMille**). Be aware, however, that some people may be upset if they see their name represented differently from what they want or what is the norm for their culture.

Display first duplicate key only allows you to stop dBASE IV from displaying identical fields that are repeated. For example, if this option is set to **YES** and you were indexing on **CATEGORY**, then the word **Appliance** would appear only once for the first appliance record, and that field would be blank for the rest of the appliance records. The same would hold true for electronic goods and furniture.

N	Selects **Name of index** and waits for you to type the name of the index.
BYNAME ↵	Specifies the index tag (name).
I	Selects **Index expression** and waits for you to type the name of the field or fields you want to use for the index. For this example, the index should be based on the **NAME** field.
NAME ↵	Specifies the name of the field to serve as the basis for the index. Instead of typing this, you could press **[Shift-F1]** and select a name from a picklist of all available fields and operators.
[Ctrl-End]	Closes the **Create new index** menu, saves the index, and arranges the displayed records according to the index expression. Notice that the record indicator on the status bar indicates **Rec 14/14**, but the cursor is at the top of the display. This is because indexing does not change the record numbers, only the order in which the records appear. Hence, the **Bed, frame** is still record number 14 even though it appears first on the display.

Continued . . .

Keystroke	Action Resulting from Keystroke

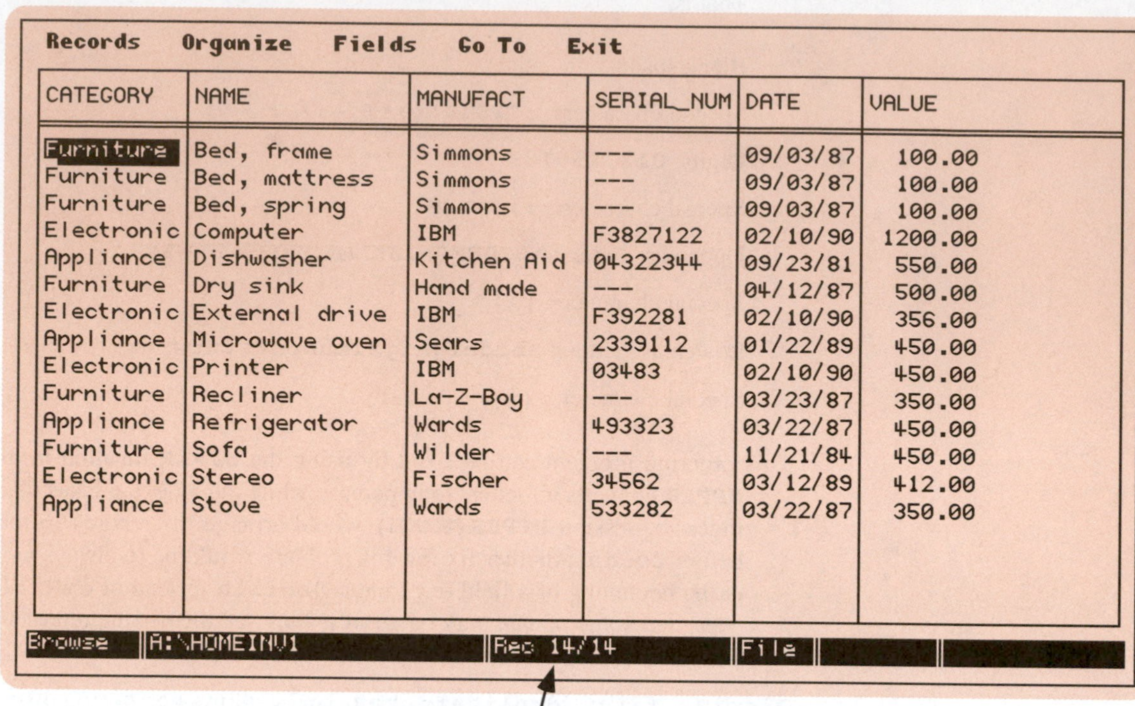

Records Organize Fields Go To Exit

CATEGORY	NAME	MANUFACT	SERIAL_NUM	DATE	VALUE
Furniture	Bed, frame	Simmons	---	09/03/87	100.00
Furniture	Bed, mattress	Simmons	---	09/03/87	100.00
Furniture	Bed, spring	Simmons	---	09/03/87	100.00
Electronic	Computer	IBM	F3827122	02/10/90	1200.00
Appliance	Dishwasher	Kitchen Aid	04322344	09/23/81	550.00
Furniture	Dry sink	Hand made	---	04/12/87	500.00
Electronic	External drive	IBM	F392281	02/10/90	356.00
Appliance	Microwave oven	Sears	2339112	01/22/89	450.00
Electronic	Printer	IBM	03483	02/10/90	450.00
Furniture	Recliner	La-Z-Boy	---	03/23/87	350.00
Appliance	Refrigerator	Wards	493323	03/22/87	450.00
Furniture	Sofa	Wilder	---	11/21/84	450.00
Electronic	Stereo	Fischer	34562	03/12/89	412.00
Appliance	Stove	Wards	533282	03/22/87	350.00

Browse A:\HOMEINV1 Rec 14/14 File

The cursor is at record number 14 **but that record now is first in the display because the records are indexed by** NAME

To create another index that arranges the records by **CATEGORY** and, within **CATEGORY**, by **NAME**, you would do the following:

Keystroke	Action Resulting from Keystroke
[Alt-O]	Opens the **Organize** menu.
C	Selects **Create new index** and displays its menu.
N	Selects **Name of index** and waits for you to type the name of the index.
BYCATNAM ↵	Specifies the index tag.
I	Selects **Index expression** and waits for you to type the name of the field or fields you want to use for the index.
CATEGORY + NAME ↵	Specifies the names of the fields to serve as the basis for the index.
[Ctrl-End]	Closes the **Create new index** menu, saves the index, and arranges the displayed records according to the index expression.

Continued . . .

Keystroke	Action Resulting from Keystroke

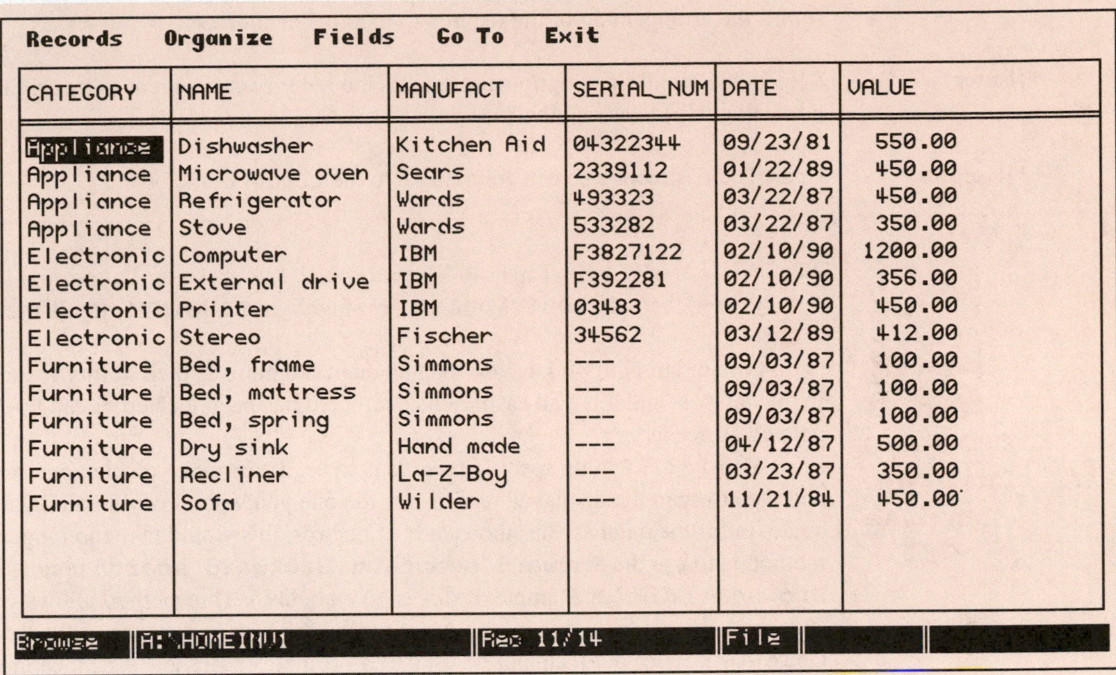

CATEGORY	NAME	MANUFACT	SERIAL_NUM	DATE	VALUE
Appliance	Dishwasher	Kitchen Aid	04322344	09/23/81	550.00
Appliance	Microwave oven	Sears	2339112	01/22/89	450.00
Appliance	Refrigerator	Wards	493323	03/22/87	450.00
Appliance	Stove	Wards	533282	03/22/87	350.00
Electronic	Computer	IBM	F3827122	02/10/90	1200.00
Electronic	External drive	IBM	F392281	02/10/90	356.00
Electronic	Printer	IBM	03483	02/10/90	450.00
Electronic	Stereo	Fischer	34562	03/12/89	412.00
Furniture	Bed, frame	Simmons	---	09/03/87	100.00
Furniture	Bed, mattress	Simmons	---	09/03/87	100.00
Furniture	Bed, spring	Simmons	---	09/03/87	100.00
Furniture	Dry sink	Hand made	---	04/12/87	500.00
Furniture	Recliner	La-Z-Boy	---	03/23/87	350.00
Furniture	Sofa	Wilder	---	11/21/84	450.00

Notice how the records are arranged by **CATEGORY** and, where records have the same **CATEGORY**, they are arranged by **NAME**.

You may select the appropriate index tag when you want to index the records of the database in a specific way by selecting **Order records by index** from the **Organize** menu. To return to the original ordering, you would select **Natural Order** from the **Order records by index** menu as follows:

Keystroke	Action Resulting from Keystroke
[Alt-O]	Opens the **Organize** menu.
O	Selects **Order records by index** and presents a picklist of available index tags.

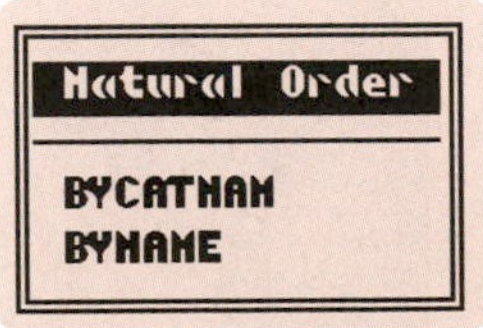

Keystroke	Action Resulting from Keystroke
[arrow]	Use the [arrow] keys to highlight **BYCATNAM**. The indexing expression appears in a box just to the left of the name to serve as a reminder of how the index arranges the records.

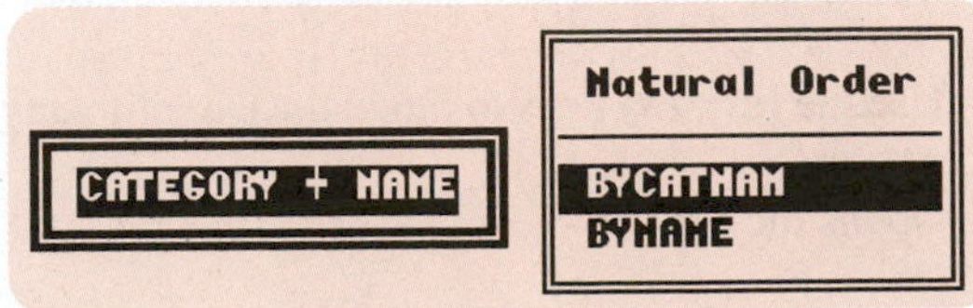

Continued . . .

Keystroke	Action Resulting from Keystroke
[arrow]	Use the [arrow] keys to highlight **Natural Order** at the top of the list. Selecting this option will return the arrangement of the records to their original order.
[Enter]	Selects the highlighted option and returns the record arrangement to its original order. You may have to do a [PageUp] to see all the records.
[Esc]	Cancels the **Browse** screen and returns to the Control Center.

TO TAKE A BREAK Tap [Alt-E]; **Q**. Remove data diskette. To resume: Insert data diskette; type **A:** ↵, then **C:\DBIV\DBASE** ↵; highlight **HOMEINV1**; tap [Enter], tap **U**.

Locating Specific Records in Edit and Browse

A major strength of database management programs is their ability to help the user locate records in the database quickly and easily. Once a record has been located, it can be displayed, modified, or deleted as needed.

One way of locating specific records is to use **Browse** to display one screen of records at a time and then to scan the displayed records for the one you want. For a small database this method is adequate, but if the database has thousands of records, this would take too long. An improvement on this method is to use the **Forward search** and **Backward search** options of the **Go To** menu in **Browse** or **Edit** (an example of this is given below). This method allows you to search for specific strings of characters (e.g., you can use it to find the first occurrence of the word **Furniture** in the **CATEGORY** field) but it cannot be used to do complex searches (e.g., it cannot be used to locate all items with a value over $400 that were purchased in 1989). A third method, which is quite powerful, is to use *queries* that enable you to provide dBASE IV with an example of the kind of information you want and then to have it scan the database and filter out all the records that do not match the conditions you specify. Queries are discussed on pages D56–72.

Let's do a simple search using the options available in **Browse** and **Edit**. We want to locate the record in the **HOMEINV1** database that contains the words **Dry sink** in the **NAME** field (begin from the Control Center with **HOMEINV1** selected).

Keystroke	Action Resulting from Keystroke
[F2]	Switches from the Control Center to **Browse**. If the **Edit** screen appears instead of **Browse**, skip the next step.
[F2]	Switches from **Browse** to **Edit**.

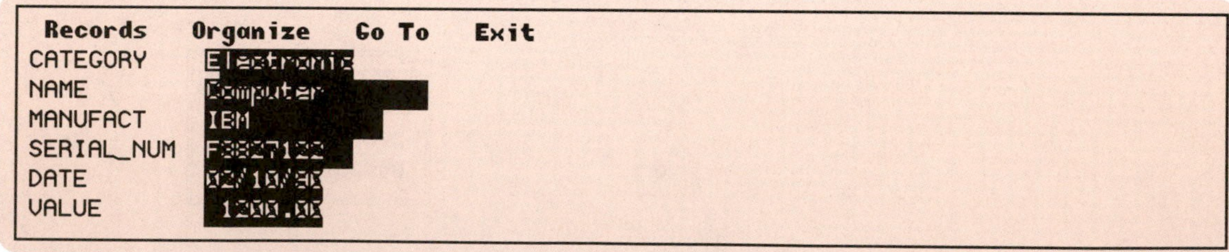

We want to locate the string **Dry sink** in the **NAME** field. Before opening the **Go To** menu we first must place the cursor in the **NAME** field so that dBASE IV knows which field to search.

Keystroke	Action Resulting from Keystroke
[arrow]	Use the [arrow] keys to move the cursor to any location in the **NAME** field.
[Alt-G]	Opens the **Go To** menu.

Continued . . .

Keystroke	Action Resulting from Keystroke

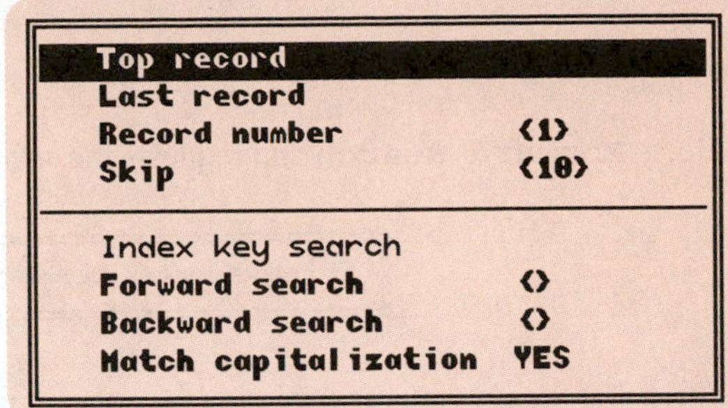

F — Selects **Forward search** and requests the string to search for.

Dry sink ↵ — Specifies the string to locate and displays the record that contains the string.

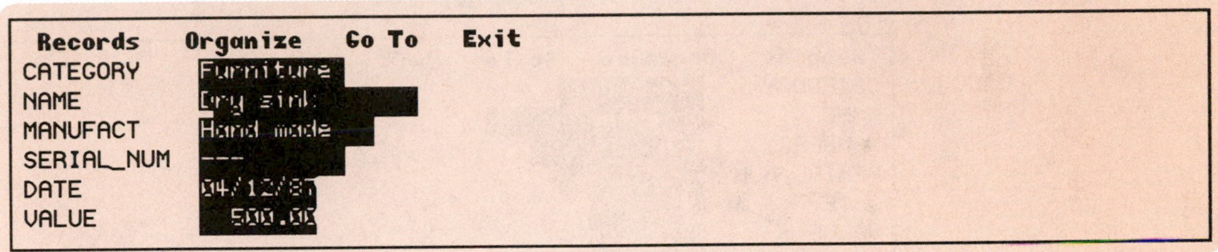

This type of searching has a few useful options.

Forward search means that the search will proceed from the current record toward the bottom of the database. If no matches are found when the bottom is reached, the search will begin at the top and continue to the current record.

Backward search means that the search will proceed from the current record back toward the top of the database. If no matches are found when the top is reached, the search will begin at the bottom and continue to the current record.

Match capitalization indicates whether or not the search will be case sensitive. Specifying **YES** for this option means that the string in the database must exactly match the string you specify, including the case of the letters (i.e., specifying **YES** would mean that **Dry sink** would not match **dry sink**). Tapping **M** to select this option toggles between **YES** to **NO**.

***** and **?** are wildcard characters can be used in the search specification. Wildcard characters in dBASE IV are similar to the DOS global characters discussed on page W199. The asterisk (*) can be used to take the place of any number of characters, whereas the question mark (?) can be used to take the place of only a single character. For example, suppose you want to locate records that were purchased in the month of February on any day and in any year. The specification for the search in the **DATE** field would be **02***. Follow the directions given below to carry out this search:

Keystroke	Action Resulting from Keystroke
[arrow]	Use the **[arrow]** keys to move the cursor to any location in the **DATE** field.
[Alt-G]	Opens the **Go To** menu.
F	Selects **Forward search** and requests the string to search for.

Notice that the previous search criterion appears in the prompt box. To erase it you could tap **[Backspace]** eight times or tap **[Home]** to move the cursor to the left edge of the field and then **[Ctrl-Y]** to erase all the characters at and to the right of the cursor. We will do the latter.

Keystroke	Action Resulting from Keystroke
[Home]	Moves the cursor to the left edge of the field.
[Ctrl-Y]	Erases all the characters at and to the right of the cursor.
02* ↵	Specifies the string to locate and displays the first record that contains the string.

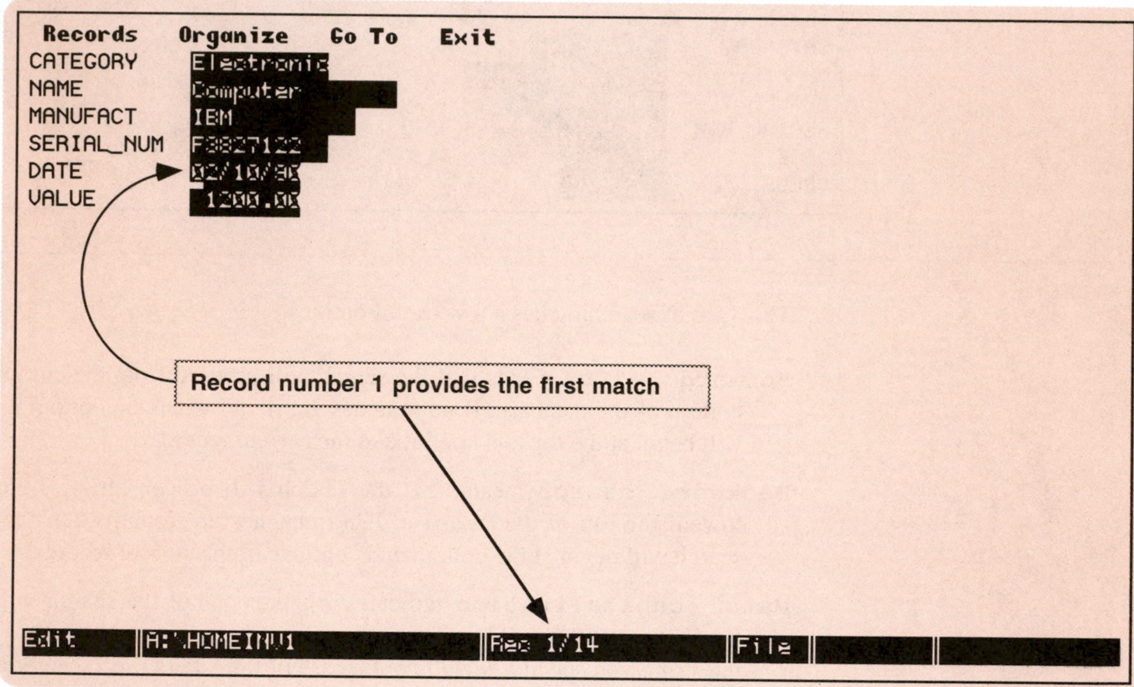

None of the records below **Dry sink** contained the proper string and so when dBASE IV reached the bottom of the file, it went to the top to continue the search.

To find the next occurrence of the string you could repeat the process or tap **[Shift-F4]** (this is called the *find next* key).

Continued . . .

Keystroke	Action Resulting from Keystroke
[Shift-F4]	Displays the next record that matches the search criterion.

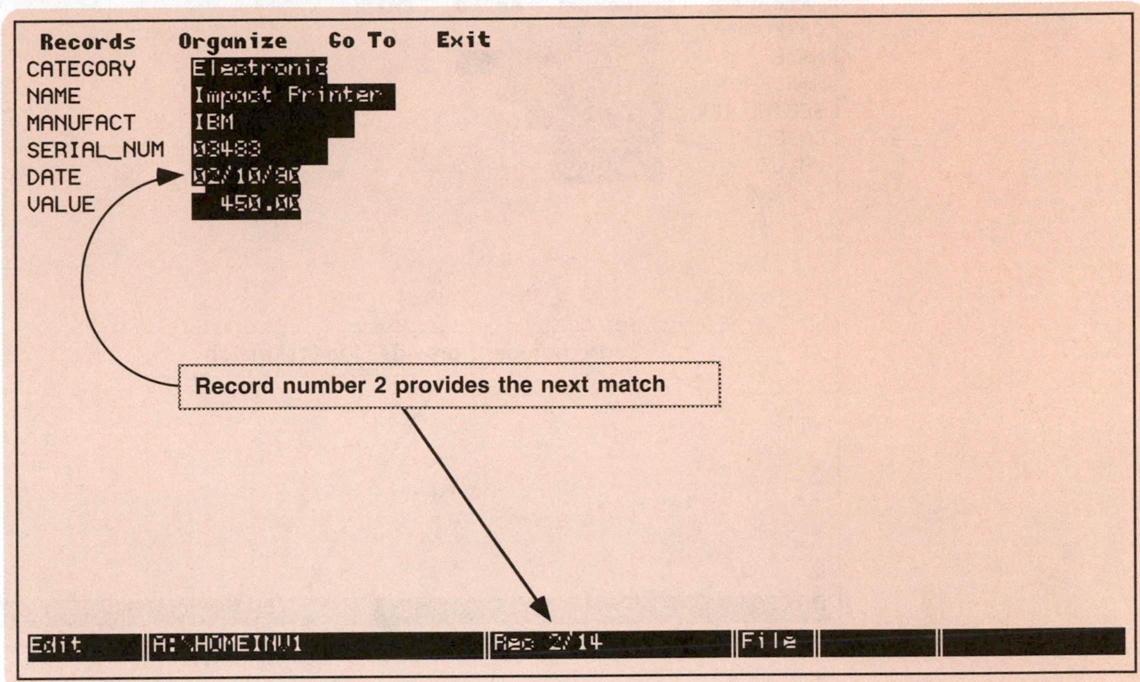

To locate records of items purchased in 1987, you could enter **`??/??/87`** as the search criterion. The first **`??`** means any month and the second **`??`** means any day.

Keystroke	Action Resulting from Keystroke
[Alt-G]	Opens the **`Go To`** menu.
`F`	Selects **`Forward search`** and requests the string to search for.
[Home]	Moves the cursor to the left edge of the field.
[Ctrl-Y]	Erases all the characters at and to the right of the cursor.
`??/??/87` ↵	Specifies the string to locate and displays the first record that contains the string.

Continued . . .

Keystroke	Action Resulting from Keystroke

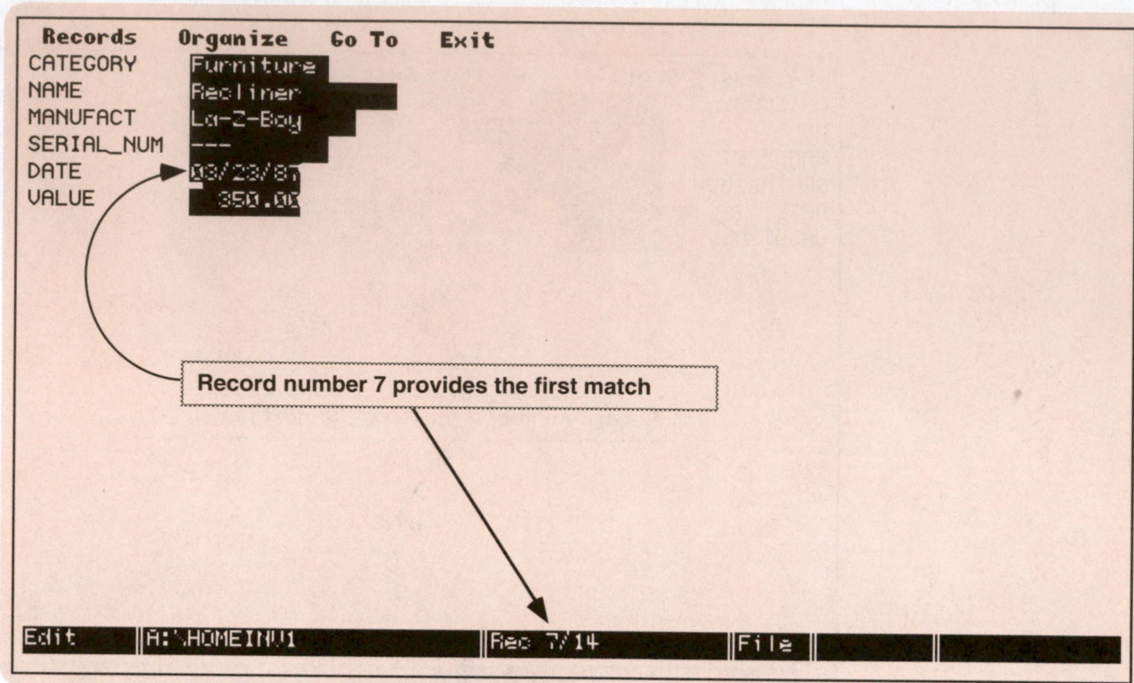

Note that entering **`*87`** in place of **`??/??/87`** would produce the same result.

[Alt-E]	Opens the **`Exit`** menu.
E	Selects **`Exit`** and returns to the Control Center.

The above methods are fine for simple searches. However, for complex searches or for searches that you do over and over again, queries must be used.

Queries

A *query* is a set of instructions you give dBASE IV that tells it how to organize, display, print, or change the data in your database. A *view query* shows you a picture (view) of selected data in your database. For example, in the home inventory database, you could set up a view query that would allow you to look at only the **`NAME`** and **`VALUE`** fields for those records purchased in 1989 whose value is over $200. An *update query* is used to make broad changes to the data. If the records you want deleted form a logical group (e.g., all records with **`Furniture`** in the **`CATEGORY`** field), you can use an update query to have dBASE IV mark them all for deletion at one time (i.e., you do not have to select and mark the records one by one). You could also use an update query to replace the word **`Furniture`** with **`Household`** in the **`CATEGORY`** field in all the records.

Let's set up a view query so that only the **`CATEGORY`**, **`NAME`**, **`DATE`**, and **`VALUE`** fields are displayed. Begin from the Control Center with the database **`HOMEINV1`** in use.

Keystroke	Action Resulting from Keystroke
[arrow]	Use the **[arrow]** keys to highlight **`<create>`** in the **`Queries`** panel.
[Enter]	Opens the **`Queries`** design screen. Tapping **[Shift-F2]** (this is called the *design* key) also opens this screen.

Continued . . .

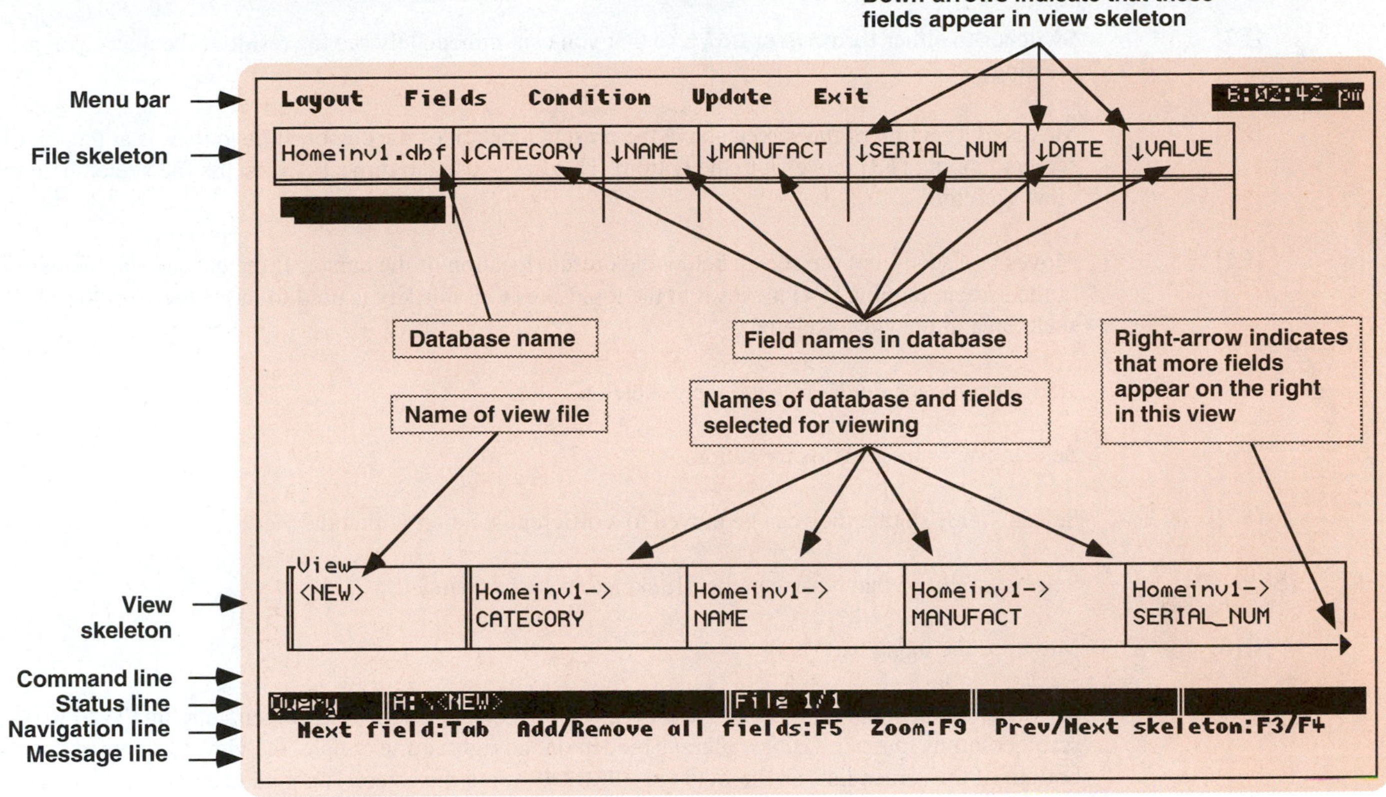

Menu bar contains the following menus:

`Layout` allows you to add or delete files from the active query, save database files in different forms, edit query descriptions, and save queries.

`Fields` allows you to add, remove, create, and sort on fields.

`Condition` allows you to add, remove, or show a condition box where you can give instructions that treat records as whole units rather than as groups of individual fields.

`Update` allows you to update queries.

`Exit` allows you to return to the Control Center.

File skeleton displays the field names of the selected database. Those field names with a downward-pointing arrow next to their names are included in the view skeleton (presently, all the field names have arrows next to them). You can have file skeletons that include more than one database at a time by selecting **`Add file to query`** from the **`Layout`** menu. That way you can select fields from different databases at the same time.

View skeleton shows the fields included in the current view. When you switch to **`Browse`** or **`Edit`**, only those fields that are in the view skeleton will be displayed.

Status bar shows the usual information on the query design you are creating or using.

Navigation line shows some of the keys you may use to move about the queries design screen. The functions of some of the special purpose keys are summarized in the following list:

Key	Comment
[F1]	Brings up the *Help* screen, just in case you need it.
[F2]	Switches to either **`Browse`** or **`Edit`** so that you can immediately see the result of the query you are creating.
[F3]	Moves to a section of the screen above the present location of the cursor. If the cursor is at the top of the screen, tapping **[F3]** moves it to the bottom. This key is used to move between the file skeleton and the view skeleton.
[F4]	Moves to a section of the screen below the present location of the cursor. If the cursor is at the bottom of the screen, tapping **[F4]** moves it to the top. Like **[F3]**, this key is used to move between the file skeleton and the view skeleton.
[F5]	Adds or removes fields from the view skeleton.
[F6]	Selects one or more fields for action.
[F7]	Selects fields so that they can be moved to a different location within the view.
[Shift-F7]	Selects a field so that its size in the file skeleton can be changed.
[F10]	Moves to the menu bar.
[Tab]	Moves to the next column. If there are more columns than can fit on the screen, tapping **[Tab]** will scroll columns to make visible columns hidden on the right. For example, the view skeleton at the bottom of the screen lists all the fields in **`HOMEINV1`**, but the screen is not wide enough to display the **`DATE`** and **`VALUE`** fields. To see those fields you can go to the view skeleton and then tab across the field names. When you reach **`SERIAL_NUM`** and tap **[Tab]**, the field names will scroll to the left to show you the next field on the right.
[Shift-Tab]	Moves to the previous column. If there are more columns than can fit on the screen, tapping **[Shift-Tab]** will scroll columns to make visible columns hidden on the left.
[Home]	Moves to the first column on the left.
[End]	Moves to the last column on the right.
[up arrow]	Moves up one row in a column.
[down arrow]	Moves down one row in a column.

Continue with the construction of the query by doing the following:

Keystroke	Action Resulting from Keystroke
[F4]	Moves to the view skeleton and highlights the first field (**`CATEGORY`**).

Continued . . .

Keystroke	Action Resulting from Keystroke

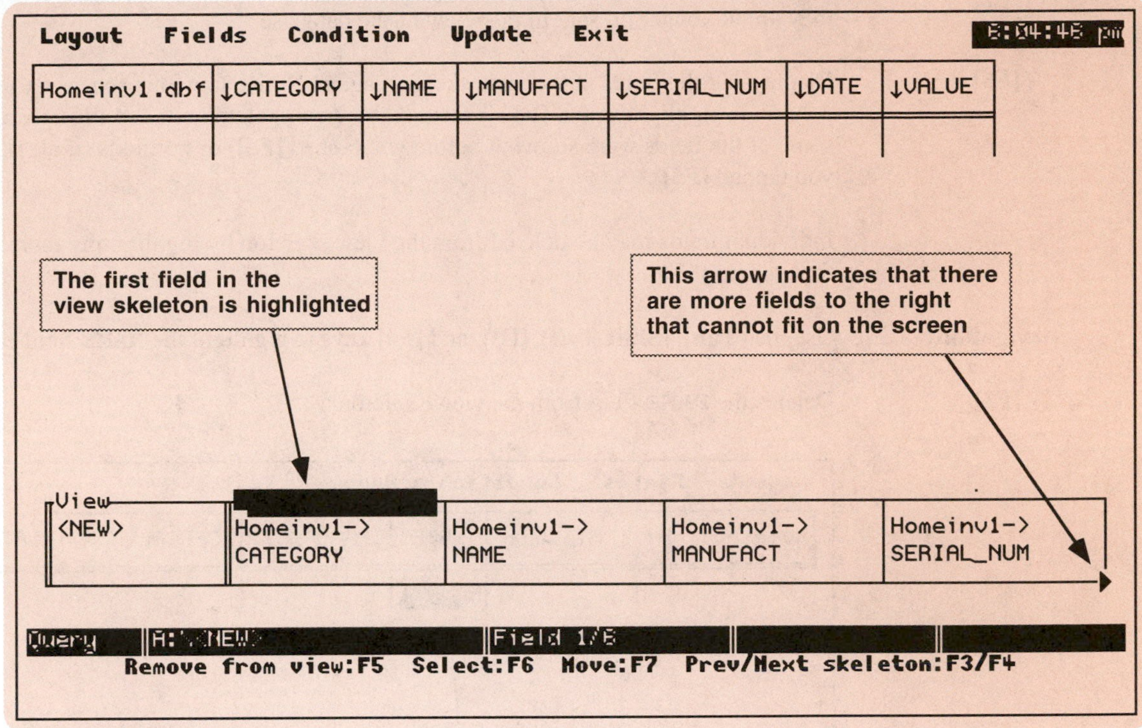

[Tab] Tap **[Tab]** five times to highlight the **VALUE** field. Notice how the **CATEGORY** and **NAME** fields scroll off the left side of the screen in order to make room for the **DATE** and **VALUE** fields.

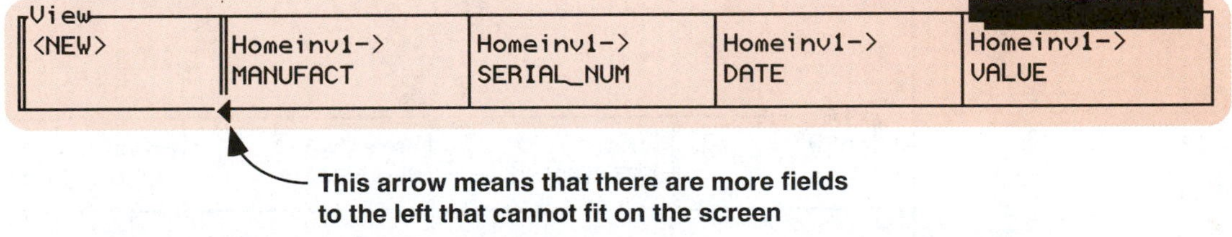

[Shift-Tab] Tap **[Shift-Tab]** five times to highlight the **CATEGORY** field again.

[F3] Moves back to the file skeleton.

Fields may be added to or deleted from the view skeleton by using **[F5]** (this is called the *field* key).

Keystroke	Action Resulting from Keystroke
[navigation]	Use the **[Tab]**, **[Shift-Tab]**, **[F3]**, and **[F4]** keys, if necessary, to highlight the database column of the file skeleton.

Homeinv1.dbf	↓CATEGORY	↓NAME	↓MANUFACT	↓SERIAL_NUM	↓DATE	↓VALUE

Continued . . .

Keystroke	Action Resulting from Keystroke
[F5]	Deletes all the fields displayed in the view skeleton. Of course, the fields are still in the database but they are no longer present in this view of the database.
[F5]	Displays all the fields in the view skeleton again. Notice how this acts as a toggle. If the database column is highlighted and **[F5]** is tapped, the view skeleton either will show all the fields (if none or some of the fields were showing before you tapped **[F5]**) or no fields (if all fields were showing before you tapped **[F5]**). Individual fields may be deleted from the view skeleton by highlighting them in the file skeleton and then tapping **[F5]**.
[navigation]	Use the **[Tab]**, **[Shift-Tab]**, **[F3]**, and **[F4]** keys to highlight the **NAME** field column of the file skeleton.
[F5]	Deletes the **NAME** field from the view skeleton.

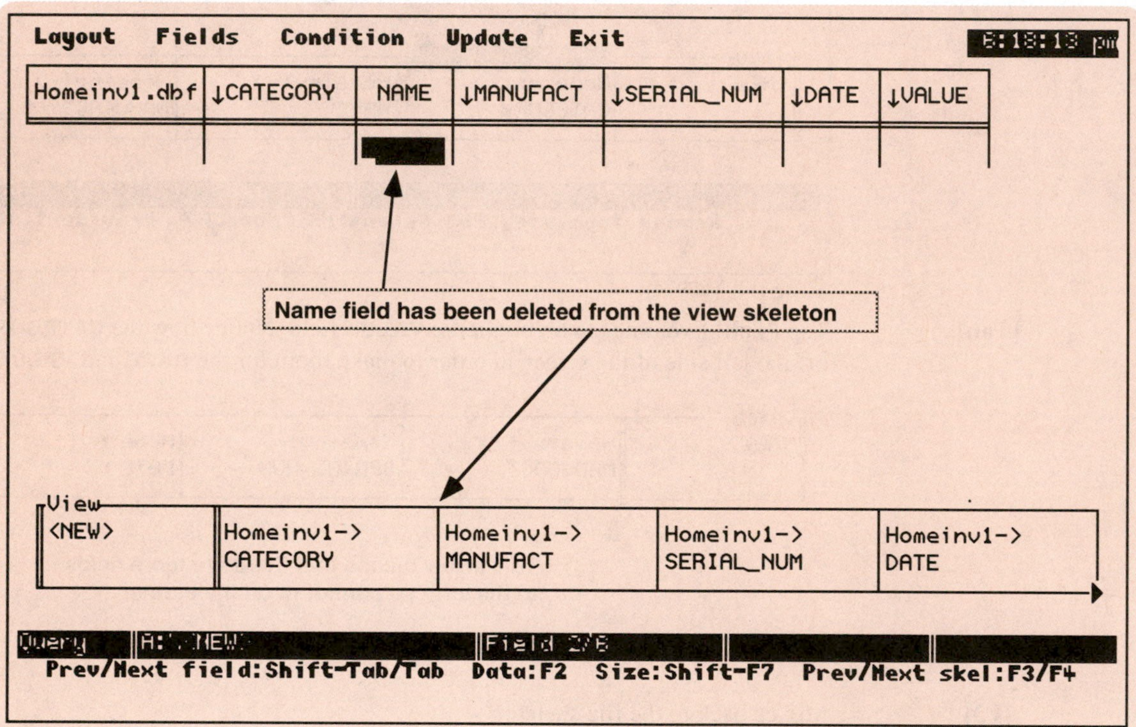

Keystroke	Action Resulting from Keystroke
[F5]	Inserts the **NAME** field from the view skeleton again but puts it on the right end of the view skeleton. To see it, switch to the view skeleton and move to the end.
[F4]	Moves to the view skeleton.
[End]	Moves to the right end of the view skeleton. Notice that the **NAME** field appears there.

Continued . . .

Keystroke	Action Resulting from Keystroke

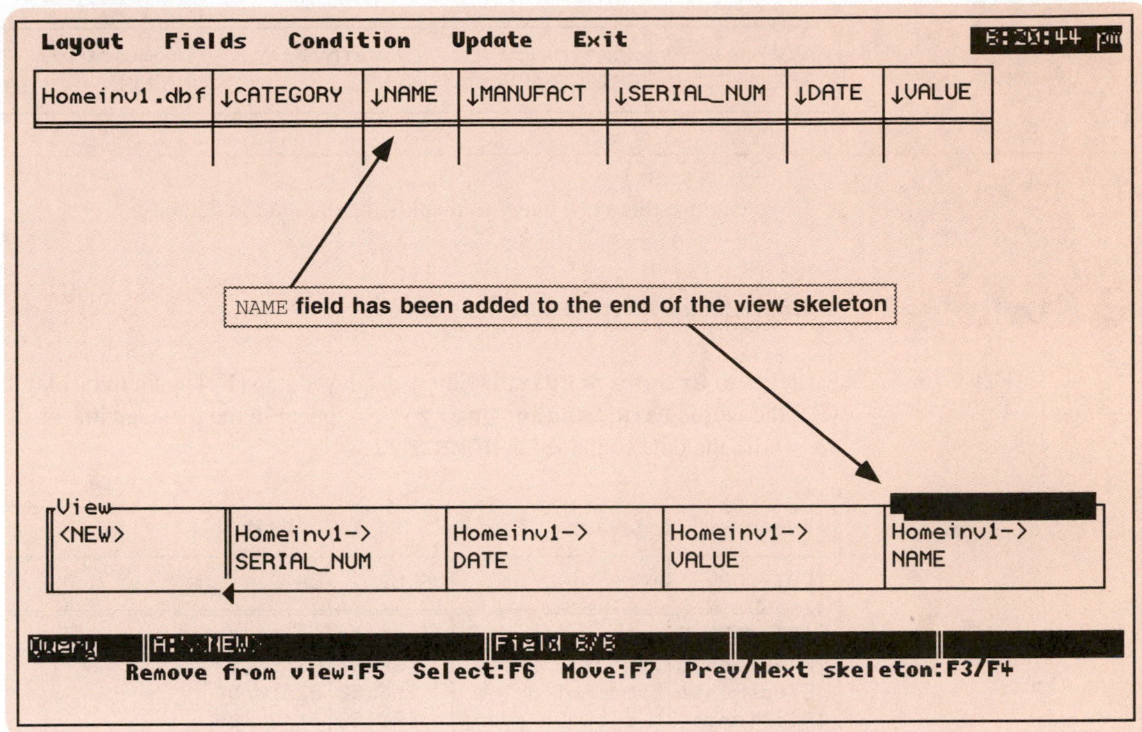

Set up a view query so that only the four fields **CATEGORY**, **NAME**, **DATE**, and **VALUE** are displayed, but reverse the positions of the last two fields so that **VALUE** precedes **DATE**.

Keystroke	Action Resulting from Keystroke
[navigation]	Use the **[Tab]**, **[Shift-Tab]**, **[F3]**, and **[F4]** keys to highlight the database column of the file skeleton.
[F5]	Deletes all the fields in the view skeleton. If they were not all deleted, tap **[F5]** again.
[Tab]	Use **[Tab]** to highlight the **CATEGORY** column.
[F5]	Selects the highlighted field and inserts it into the view skeleton.
[Tab]	Use **[Tab]** to highlight the **NAME** column.
[F5]	Selects the highlighted field and inserts it into the view skeleton.
[Tab]	Use **[Tab]** to highlight the **VALUE** column.
[F5]	Selects the highlighted field and inserts it into the view skeleton.
[Shift-Tab]	Use **[Shift-Tab]** to highlight the **DATE** column.
[F5]	Selects the highlighted field and inserts it into the view skeleton.

Continued . . .

Keystroke	Action Resulting from Keystroke

View <NEW>	Homeinv1-> CATEGORY	Homeinv1-> NAME	Homeinv1-> VALUE	Homeinv1-> DATE

We can use this view query to display the data in the database.

Keystroke	Action Resulting from Keystroke

[F2] Switches to **`Browse`** or **`Edit`**. If Edit is displayed, tap **[F2]** again to display **`Browse`**. After you tap **[F2]** the words **`Processing Query ...`** appear in the message line as dBASE IV constructs the view with the data contained in **`HOMEINV1`**.

Records Organize Fields Go To Exit

CATEGORY	NAME	VALUE	DATE
Electronic	Computer	1200.00	02/10/90
Electronic	Impact Printer	450.00	02/10/90
Electronic	External drive	356.00	02/10/90
Appliance	Microwave oven	450.00	01/22/89
Electronic	Stereo	412.00	03/12/89
Furniture	Sofa	450.00	11/21/84
Furniture	Recliner	350.00	03/23/87
Furniture	Dry sink	500.00	04/12/87
Appliance	Refrigerator	450.00	03/22/87
Appliance	Stove	350.00	03/22/87
Appliance	Dishwasher	550.00	09/23/81
Furniture	Bed, mattress	100.00	09/03/87
Furniture	Bed, spring	100.00	09/03/87
Furniture	Bed, frame	100.00	09/03/87

Only the four fields in this view are displayed

Browse | A:\<NEW> | Rec 1/14 | View

The view is also available in **`Edit`**.

[F2] Switches to **`Edit`** and displays the active record using the view skeleton.

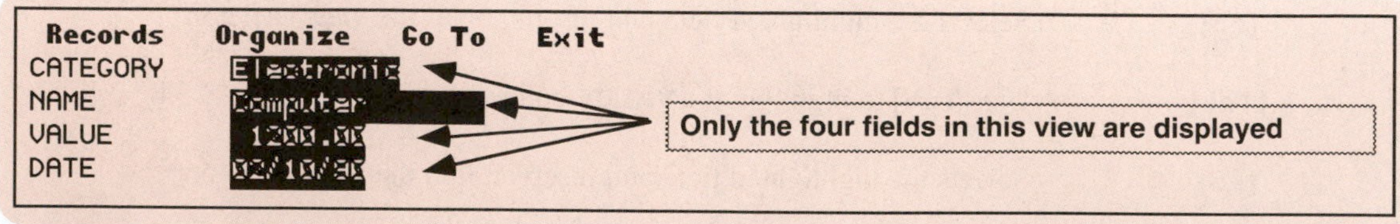

To return to the **`Query`** design screen you may tap **[Shift-F2]** or select **`Transfer to Query Design`** from the **`Exit`** menu.

[Shift-F2] Returns to the **`Query`** design screen.

We can save this query design by selecting **Save this query** from the **Layout** menu.

Keystroke	Action Resulting from Keystroke
[Alt-L]	Opens the **Layout** menu.
S	Selects **Save this query** and requests a file specification.
A:\QUE1 ↵	Provides the file specification and returns to the **Query** design screen. Notice the message **The query has been saved to disk** at the bottom of the screen.

Field positions in the view skeleton can be changed by using **[F6]** to select them and then using **[F7]** and **[Tab]** to move them to new locations. For example, move the **VALUE** field so that it is to the right of the **DATE** field by doing the following:

Keystroke	Action Resulting from Keystroke
[navigation]	Use the **[Tab]**, **[Shift-Tab]**, **[F3]**, and **[F4]** keys to highlight the **VALUE** column of the view skeleton.
[F6]	Selects the **VALUE** field.

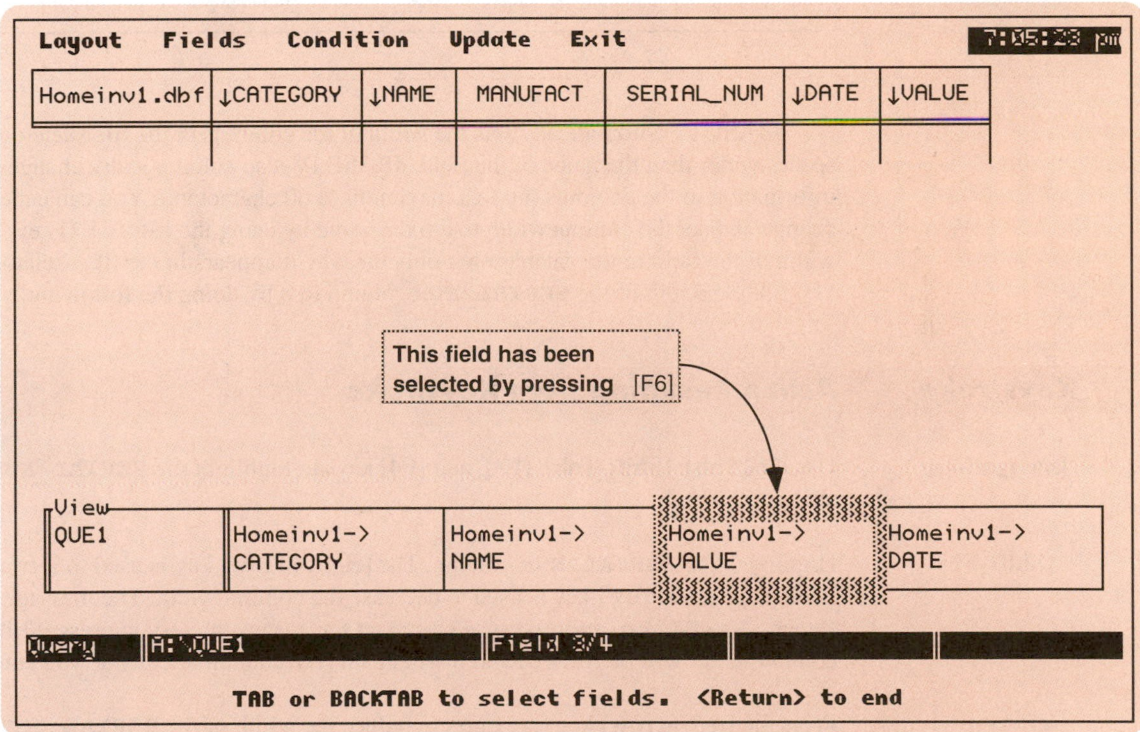

Keystroke	Action Resulting from Keystroke
[F7]	Begins the move operation.
[Tab]	Tap **[Tab]** once to move the selected field one column to the right. **[Shift-Tab]** is used to move to the left.
[Enter]	Confirms the move.

Continued . . .

Keystroke	Action Resulting from Keystroke

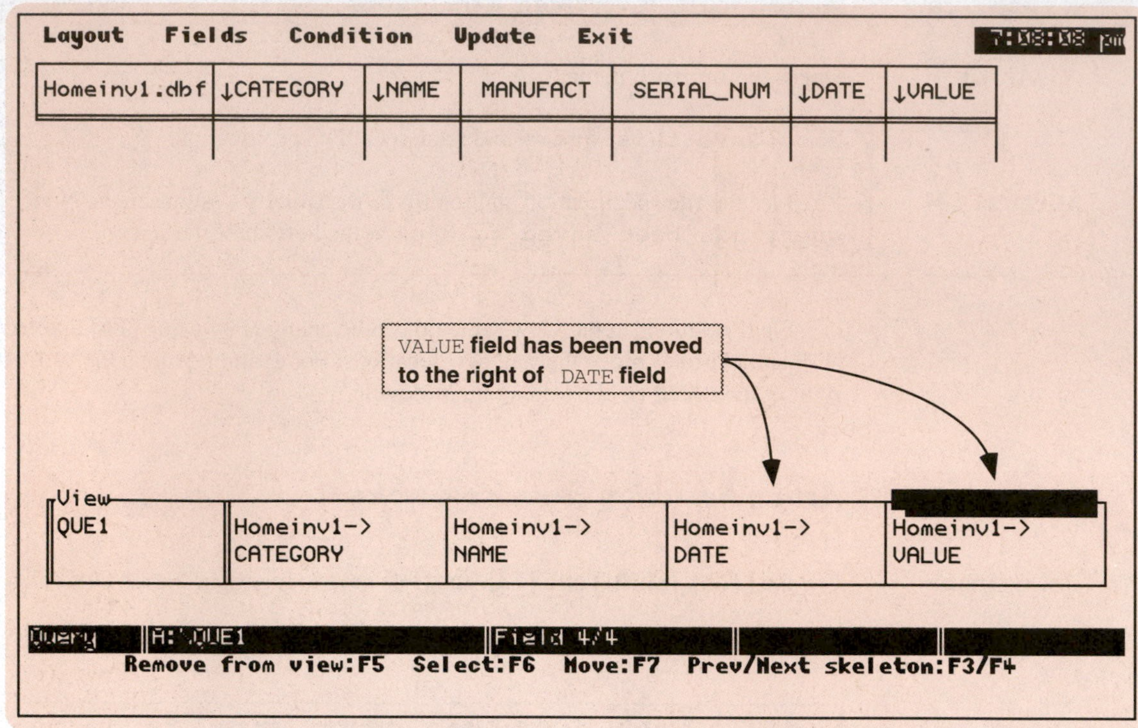

dBASE IV automatically sets the width of the columns in the file skeleton so that they are two spaces wider than the name of the field. dBASE IV also automatically changes this width as you add information to the columns (up to a maximum of 60 characters). You can cancel this automatic width change and set the column width to a fixed value by using the **[Shift-F7]** key. This does not affect the width of the field in the database but only the way it appears in the file skeleton of the **Query** screen.

Fix the width of the **SERIAL_NUM** column to 8 by doing the following:

Keystroke	Action Resulting from Keystroke
[navigation]	Use the **[Tab]**, **[Shift-Tab]**, **[F3]**, and **[F4]** keys to highlight the **SERIAL_NUM** column of the view skeleton.
[Shift-F7]	Highlights the **SERIAL_NUM** column. The **[right-arrow]** key is used to increase the column width while the **[left-arrow]** key is used to decrease the column width. The message at the bottom of the screen, **Sh-F7 to restore elasticity**, means that if you press **[Shift-F7]** again, the default column width will be restored and it will again resize automatically as you enter information.
[left-arrow]	Press the **[left-arrow]** key five times to reduce the width of the **SERIAL_NUM** column to 8. This provides more room for the other columns that will be needed later.
[Enter]	Confirms the change.

Return to the Control Center by doing the following:

Keystroke	Action Resulting from Keystroke
[Alt-E]	Opens the **Exit** menu.
S	Selects **Save changes and exit**, saves the modifications to the **Query** design screen, and returns to the Control Center. The name **QUE1** should be displayed in the **Queries** panel. If it is not, tap **[Alt-C]** to open the **Catalog** menu, tap **A** to select **Add file to catalog**, and then select **QUE1** from the picklist.

Using Queries to Filter Data

The power of a database management program is that it can store thousands of pieces of data in an organized fashion and can respond to questions asked about the data. For example, let's say that you remember buying an item for $450 but you can't remember what the item is. If the data are entered into the database, dBASE IV can locate the proper record (or records) for you by using a *filter* in a query. Recall from page W200 that a DOS filter is a special type of command (e.g., **SORT**) that processes information in order to change it in some way (much like the air filter on an automobile engine changes the air sent to the engine by removing some of the dust). A dBASE IV filter is a set of instructions (i.e., a command) that is used to select specific parts of the database (other parts are filtered out) so that they can be displayed or modified. To see how a filter works from within a query, do the following (begin from the Control Center with **HOMEINV1** in use).

Keystroke	Action Resulting from Keystroke
[arrow]	Use the **[arrow]** keys to highlight **QUE1** in the Control Center.
[Enter]	Selects the highlighted file and presents a prompt box.
M	Selects **Modify query** and displays the **Query** design screen with **CATEGORY**, **NAME**, **DATE**, and **VALUE** displayed in the view skeleton.

View QUE1	Homeinv1-> CATEGORY	Homeinv1-> NAME	Homeinv1-> DATE	Homeinv1-> VALUE

To have dBASE IV locate a record, or group of records, with certain characteristics, you simply enter the selection criteria into the file skeleton at the proper location. For the present example, we want to locate all records that have **450** in the **VALUE** field.

Keystroke	Action Resulting from Keystroke
[navigation]	Use the **[Tab]**, **[Shift-Tab]**, **[F3]**, and **[F4]** keys to highlight the **VALUE** column of the file skeleton.
=450 ↵	Specifies the search criterion for the **VALUE** field.

Homeinv1.dbf	↓CATEGORY	↓NAME	MANUFACT	SERIAL	↓DATE	↓VALUE
						=450

Continued . . .

Keystroke	Action Resulting from Keystroke
	If you would like to see the result of the query with this single condition, tap the Data key **[F2]**.
[F2]	Displays the message **`Processing query...`** at the bottom of the screen while dBASE IV does the search and then switches to **`Edit`** or **`Browse`**, whichever you last accessed. If **`Edit`** is displayed, tap **[F2]** again to display **`Browse`**.

```
Records   Organize   Fields   Go To   Exit

CATEGORY   | NAME            | DATE     | VALUE
Electronic | Impact Printer  | 02/10/90 |  450.00
Appliance  | Microwave oven  | 01/22/89 |  450.00
Furniture  | Sofa            | 11/21/84 |  450.00
Appliance  | Refrigerator    | 03/22/87 |  450.00
```

Keystroke	Action Resulting from Keystroke
	These are all the records with **`450`** in the **`VALUE`** field. If you want to edit a record, you could do so with the usual editing techniques. For example, modify record number 2 by changing **`Impact Printer`** to **`Printer`**.
[edit]	Use the normal editing techniques to delete the word **`Impact`** from record number 2. Remember, record number 2 is not the second record on the screen but the second record in the database. In the above screen dump, record number 2 is the active record.
	To switch back to the **`Query`** design, tap the design key **[Shift-F2]** or select **`Transfer to Query Design`** from the **`Exit`** menu.
[Shift-F2]	Switches back to the **`Query`** design.

We can further refine the search by adding more conditions. For example, suppose you want to see the records with **`450`** in the **`VALUE`** field and also **`02/10/90`** (i.e., February 10, 1990) in the **`DATE`** field. To do this you would leave the **`VALUE`** criterion alone and enter a date specification in the column under **`DATE`**.

Keystroke	Action Resulting from Keystroke
[navigation]	Use the **[Tab]**, **[Shift-Tab]**, **[F3]**, and **[F4]** keys to highlight the **`DATE`** column of the view skeleton.
`={02/10/90}` ↵	Specifies the search criterion for the **`DATE`** field. Notice that dates are enclosed in braces **`{ }`** and are written in the form **`MM/DD/YY`** (i.e., month, day, year). Also notice that as you enter the date, the width of the **`DATE`** column automatically increases to accommodate the size of the condition.

```
Homeinv1.dbf | ↓CATEGORY | ↓NAME | MANUFACT | SERIAL | ↓DATE        | ↓VALUE
             |           |       |          |        | ={02/10/90}  | =450
```

Keystroke	Action Resulting from Keystroke
[F2]	Switches to **`Browse`** and displays the result of the query. Only record number 2 fits both criteria.

Continued . . .

Keystroke	Action Resulting from Keystroke
	Records Organize Fields Go To Exit CATEGORY | NAME | DATE | VALUE Electronic | Printer | 02/10/90 | 450.00
[Shift-F2]	Switches back to the **Query** design.

The above search uses two conditions, both of which must be true for a record to be selected. This is called an AND condition because the only records displayed are those that match the first criterion (**VALUE** is **450**) AND the second criterion (date is February 10, 1990). To tell dBASE IV that you want an AND condition you must place the selection criteria in the same row in the file skeleton.

The opposite of an AND condition is an OR condition where only one of the criteria needs to be true for the statement to be considered true. If we wanted to look for records where the **VALUE** is **450** OR the **DATE** is **02/10/90**, we would use the same conditions as before but place them in different rows.

Keystroke	Action Resulting from Keystroke
[navigation]	Use the **[Tab]**, **[Shift-Tab]**, **[F3]**, and **[F4]** keys, if necessary, to highlight the **DATE** column of the view skeleton.
[Ctrl-Y]	Deletes the entry **={02/10/90}**.
[down arrow]	Moves to the next row in the **DATE** column.
={02/10/90} ↵	Specifies the search criterion for the **DATE** field. Because the two criteria are on separate rows, dBASE IV processes them as an OR rather than as an AND condition.

Homeinv1.dbf	↓CATEGORY	↓NAME	MANUFACT	SERIAL	↓DATE	↓VALUE
						=450
					={02/10/90}	

Keystroke	Action Resulting from Keystroke
[F2]	Switches to **Browse** and displays the result of the query.

Continued . . .

Records Organize Fields Go To Exit

CATEGORY	NAME	DATE	VALUE
Electronic	Computer	02/10/90	1200.00
Electronic	Printer	02/10/90	450.00
Electronic	External drive	02/10/90	356.00
Appliance	Microwave oven	01/22/89	450.00
Furniture	Sofa	11/21/84	450.00
Appliance	Refrigerator	03/22/87	450.00

These records are selected because they have a DATE of 02/10/90

These records are selected because they have a VALUE of 450

Browse A:\QUE1 Rec 1/14 View

The records displayed have either **02/10/90** in their **DATE** field or **450** in their **VALUE** field.

[Shift-F2] Switches back to the **Query** design.

Searches can be as simple or as complex as you need. In general, the following rules apply when working with filters:

Character fields such as **CATEGORY**, **NAME**, **MANUFACT**, and **SERIAL_NUM** must have condition values enclosed in quotation marks. For example, the following would select the records of items whose manufacturer is IBM:

Homeinv1.dbf	↓CATEGORY	↓NAME	MANUFACT	SERIAL	↓DATE	↓VALUE
			"IBM"			

The resulting **Browse** screen would be the following:

CATEGORY	NAME	DATE	VALUE
Electronic	Computer	02/10/90	1200.00
Electronic	Printer	02/10/90	450.00
Electronic	External drive	02/10/90	356.00

Notice that the selection can be made based on a field that is not included in the view. The view only specifies which fields are displayed and has nothing to do with which fields are available for processing.

Numeric fields, such as **VALUE**, may contain numbers or variables in the conditions. For example, the following would select the records of items whose **VALUE** is greater than or equal to **500**:

Homeinv1.dbf	↓CATEGORY	↓NAME	MANUFACT	SERIAL	↓DATE	↓VALUE
						>=500

The resulting **Browse** screen would be the following:

CATEGORY	NAME	DATE	VALUE
Electronic	Computer	02/10/90	1200.00
Furniture	Dry sink	04/12/87	500.00
Appliance	Dishwasher	09/23/81	550.00

Date fields, such as **DATE**, require values to be enclosed in braces **{ }** in the conditions. For example, the following would select the records of items that were purchased on or before March 22, 1987:

Homeinv1.dbf	↓CATEGORY	↓NAME	MANUFACT	SERIAL	↓DATE	↓VALUE
					<={03/22/87}	

The resulting **Browse** screen would be the following:

CATEGORY	NAME	DATE	VALUE
Furniture	Sofa	11/21/84	450.00
Appliance	Refrigerator	03/22/87	450.00
Appliance	Stove	03/22/87	350.00
Appliance	Dishwasher	09/23/81	550.00

Logical fields require values to be either **.T.** or **.F.** (the periods are required and tell dBASE IV that the **T** or **F** are logical values rather than the letters **T** or **F**). **HOMEINV1** has no logical fields.

As some of the above examples have shown, you can use relational operators (e.g., >, =) in conditions. These may be summarized as follows:

Operator	Comment
=	Equal to.
<> or #	Not equal to.
>	Greater than.
>= or =>	Greater than or equal to.
<	Less than.
<= or =<	Less than or equal to.
$	Contains—for example, **$"ard"** in the **MANUFACT** field of the file skeleton would display the two records that contain **Wards** in that field.

Homeinv1.dbf	↓CATEGORY	↓NAME	MANUFACT	SERIAL	↓DATE	↓VALUE
			$"ard"			

The resulting **Browse** screen would be the following:

CATEGORY	NAME	DATE	VALUE
Appliance	Refrigerator	03/22/87	450.00
Appliance	Stove	03/22/87	350.00

Like	A pattern match that allows you to use wildcard characters * and ? in character strings. For example, **Like "Bed*"** in the **NAME** field would display the three records that have the word **Bed** in that field.

Continued . . .

Operator	Comment

Homeinv1.dbf	↓CATEGORY	↓NAME	MANUFACT	SERIAL	↓DATE	↓VALUE
		Like "Bed*"				

The resulting **Browse** screen would be the following:

CATEGORY	NAME	DATE	VALUE
Furniture	Bed, mattress	09/03/87	100.00
Furniture	Bed, spring	09/03/87	100.00
Furniture	Bed, frame	09/03/87	100.00

Sounds like A Soundex match that allows you to enter strings that sound like the string you are searching for. This is useful when you are not sure of the exact spelling of an item. For example, **Sounds like "dri stink"** in the **NAME** field would locate the record containing **Dry sink**.

Homeinv1.dbf	↓CATEGORY	↓NAME	MANUFACT	SERIAL	↓DATE	↓VAL
		Sounds like "dri stink"				

The resulting **Browse** screen would be the following:

CATEGORY	NAME	DATE	VALUE
Furniture	Dry sink	04/12/87	500.00

Searches that meet multiple conditions can be made by placing values in different fields and in different rows within the file skeleton.

AND searches require that all conditions be met for the record to be selected. To specify an AND search, all conditions must be in the same row of the file skeleton. If the conditions are in the same field, then they must be separated by a comma. For example, the following condition would select records for appliances whose **VALUE** is over **400**:

Homeinv1.dbf	↓CATEGORY	↓NAME	MANUFACT	SERIAL	↓DATE	↓VALUE
	"Appliance"					>400

AND conditions in different fields must be on the same line

The resulting **Browse** screen would be the following:

CATEGORY	NAME	DATE	VALUE
Appliance	Microwave oven	01/22/89	450.00
Appliance	Refrigerator	03/22/87	450.00
Appliance	Dishwasher	09/23/81	550.00

The following condition would select records that were purchased in 1989 (i.e., the date has to be between January 1, 1989 and December 31, 1989, inclusive).

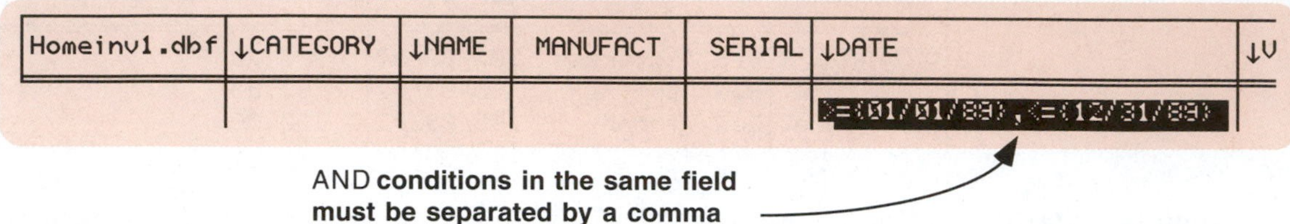

The resulting **Browse** screen would be the following:

CATEGORY	NAME	DATE	VALUE
Appliance	Microwave oven	01/22/89	450.00
Electronic	Stereo	03/12/89	412.00

The following condition would select records whose **VALUE** is over **400** that were purchased in 1989.

Homeinv1.dbf	↓NAME	MANUFACT	SERIAL	↓DATE	↓VALUE
				>=(01/01/89),<=(12/31/89)	>400

The resulting **Browse** screen would be the following:

CATEGORY	NAME	DATE	VALUE
Appliance	Microwave oven	01/22/89	450.00
Electronic	Stereo	03/12/89	412.00

OR searches require that any one condition be met for the record to be selected. To specify an OR search, the conditions must be on different rows of the file skeleton whether they are in the same field or different fields. For example, the following condition would select records for appliances or any other items whose **VALUE** is over **400**.

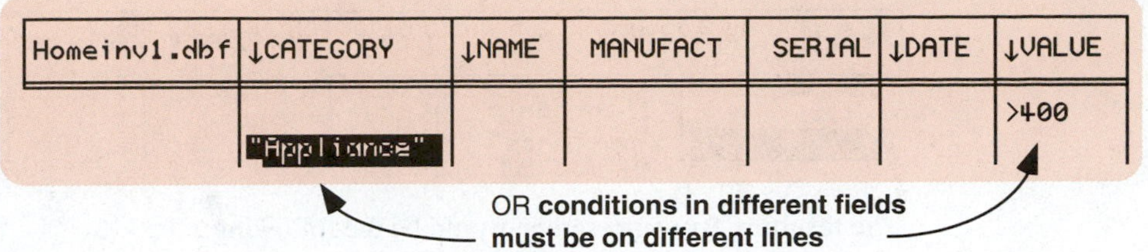

The resulting **Browse** screen would be the following:

CATEGORY	NAME	DATE	VALUE
Electronic	Computer	02/10/90	1200.00
Electronic	Printer	02/10/90	450.00
Appliance	Microwave oven	01/22/89	450.00
Electronic	Stereo	03/12/89	412.00
Furniture	Sofa	11/21/84	450.00
Furniture	Dry sink	04/12/87	500.00
Appliance	Refrigerator	03/22/87	450.00
Appliance	Stove	03/22/87	350.00
Appliance	Dishwasher	09/23/81	550.00

The following condition would select records for appliances or electronics.

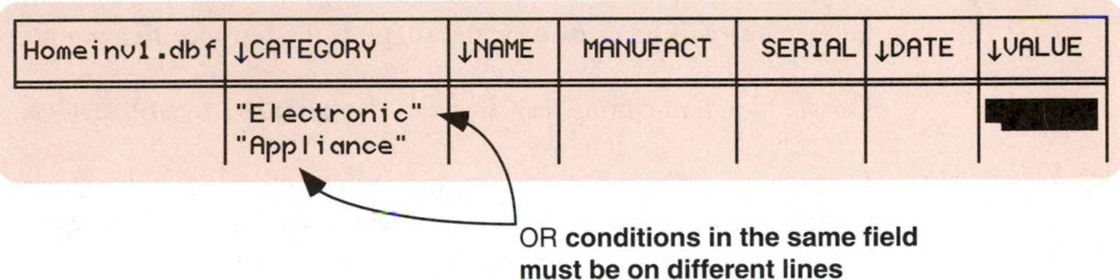

The resulting **Browse** screen would be the following:

CATEGORY	NAME	DATE	VALUE
Electronic	Computer	02/10/90	1200.00
Electronic	Printer	02/10/90	450.00
Electronic	External drive	02/10/90	356.00
Appliance	Microwave oven	01/22/89	450.00
Electronic	Stereo	03/12/89	412.00
Appliance	Refrigerator	03/22/87	450.00
Appliance	Stove	03/22/87	350.00
Appliance	Dishwasher	09/23/81	550.00

AND and OR conditions can be combined in one query. Each row is treated as an AND condition and is evaluated. Then the separate rows are evaluated as OR conditions. For example, you might want to select records of appliances or electronics that were purchased in 1989. The conditions **="Appliance"** and **="Electronic"** must appear on separate rows of the **CATEGORY** field. The date **>={01/01/89},<={12/31/89}** must be entered into each row of the **DATE** field. The condition is read as follows: Locate every record such that the **CATEGORY** is **Electronic** AND **DATE** is greater than or equal to **01/01/89** AND **DATE** is less than or equal to **12/31/89**, OR **CATEGORY** is **Appliance** AND **DATE** is greater than or equal to **01/01/89** AND **DATE** is less than or equal to **12/31/89**.

Homeinv1.dbf	↓CATEGORY	↓NAME	MANUFACT	SERIAL	↓DATE
	"Electronic"				>=<01/01/89>,<=<12/31/89>
	"Appliance"				>=<01/01/89>,<=<12/31/89>

The resulting **Browse** screen would be the following:

CATEGORY	NAME	DATE	VALUE
Appliance	Microwave oven	01/22/89	450.00
Electronic	Stereo	03/12/89	412.00

You can create queries with up to 12 rows of OR conditions, each of which can contain any number of AND conditions. As the above example shows, these can become quite confusing and must be thought through very carefully. Save the query under the name **AP&EL-89** by doing the following (begin from the **Query** design screen):

Keystroke	Action Resulting from Keystroke
[Alt-L]	Opens the **Layout** menu.
S	Selects **Save this query** and suggests the file specification **A:\QUE1.qbe**.
[edit]	Use the standard editing techniques to change **QUE1** to **AP&EL-89**.
[Enter]	Saves the query using new file specification and returns to the **Query** screen. Notice the message **The query has been saved to disk** at the bottom of the screen.
[Ctrl-End]	Exits the **Query** screen and returns to the Control Center. Instead of tapping **[Ctrl-End]** you could have selected **Save changes and exit** from the **Exit** menu.

TO TAKE A BREAK Tap **[Alt-E]**; **Q**. Remove data diskette. To resume: Insert data diskette; type **A:** ↵, then **C:\DBIV\DBASE** ↵; highlight **HOMEINV1**; tap **[Enter]**, tap **U**.

Creating Reports

Recall that there are two types of dBASE IV reports: quick reports, which use a standard format to produce hard copy of the data and custom reports, which can be designed to meet specific needs by producing information in specified formats on the screen, on a printer, or in a file on disk. Custom reports can also contain special calculated fields and graphic elements such as lines or boxes. Before you can produce a custom report, you must construct a report format, which is used by dBASE IV as a model for your report. The report format is saved as a file with the extension **FRM** and its name appears in the **Reports** panel of the Control Center.

Create a few report designs by doing the following (begin from the Control Center with **HOMEINV1** the active database):

Keystroke	Action Resulting from Keystroke
[arrow]	Use the **[arrow]** keys to highlight **<create>** in the **Reports** panel.
[Enter]	Selects **<create>** and displays the **Report** design screen with the **Layout** menu opened. We will discuss this menu later. For now, close the menu and study the design screen.

Continued . . .

Keystroke	Action Resulting from Keystroke
[Esc]	Closes the menu and presents the following design screen:

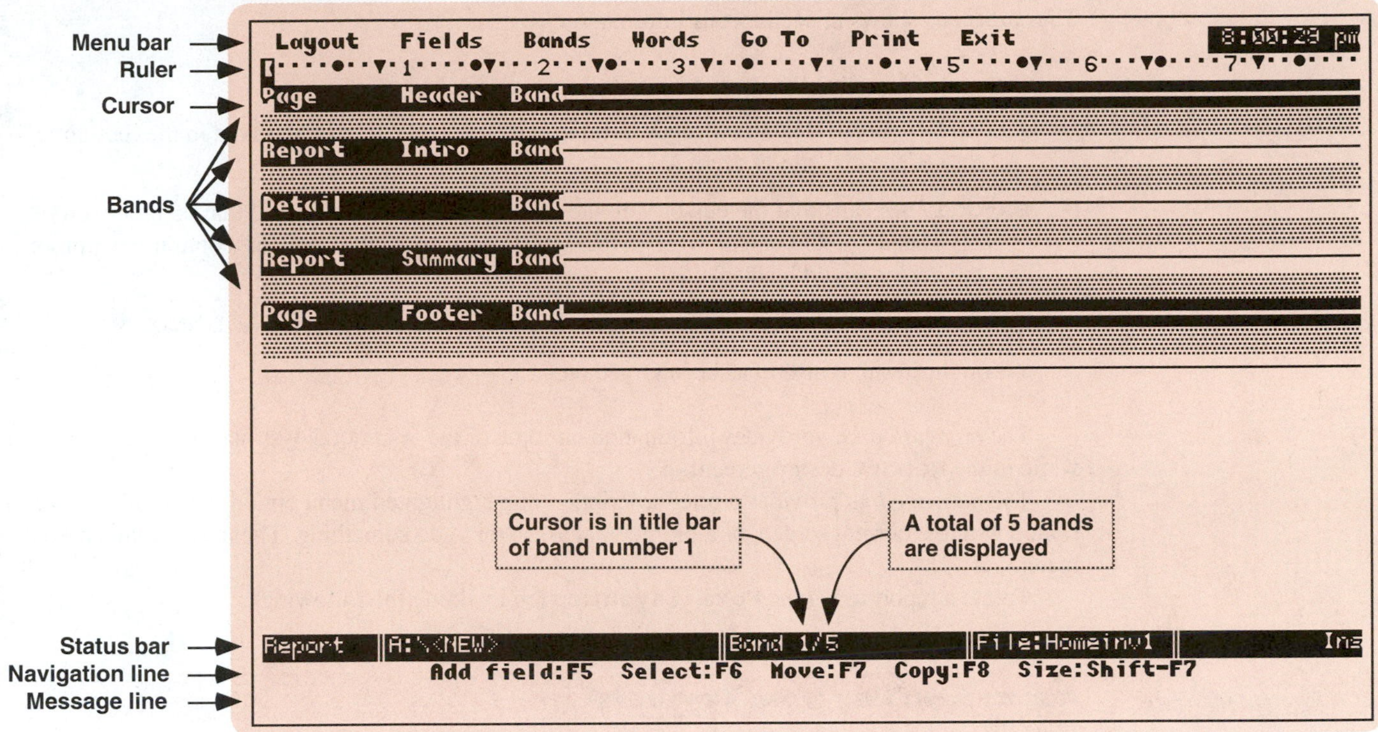

The *menu bar* contains many options connected with designing reports. As is the case with all other menu bars, it can be accessed by tapping **[F10]**. A particular menu can be opened by tapping **[Alt]** in conjunction with the first letter of the desired menu.

The *ruler* shows the horizontal location of the cursor and the locations of the margins (indicated by brackets) and tabs (indicated by inverted triangles). The numbers represent inches from the left margin. The ruler can be modified by choosing the **Modify ruler** option of the **Words** menu. When the cursor is in the ruler:

- A tab is inserted by tapping **!**.
- A tab is deleted by tapping **[Delete]**.
- The margins are changed by tapping [where you want the left margin and] where you want the right margin.
- Tapping **[Enter]** exits the ruler.

Bands are the five sections of the screen that show you a template for the report.

Page Header Band contains information that is printed at the top of each page. This usually contains information such as page numbers, the date the report was generated, and the names of the fields as column headers.

Report Intro Band contains information that is printed only on the first page of the report.

Detail Band contains information that is printed for each record selected from the database.

Report Summary Band contains information that is printed at the end of the report. This may be used to summarize information in the report.

Page Footer Band contains information that is printed at the bottom of each page.

The *status bar* shows miscellaneous information:

Report shows that the **Report** design screen is displayed.

A:\<NEW> means that a new report form is being created and will be saved in the root directory of the diskette in drive A:.

Band 1/5 means that the cursor is in the title bar of the first band and that there are a total of 5 bands. If the cursor were in the actual band itself, the row and column location of the cursor would be displayed.

File:Homeinv1 indicates that **HOMEINV1.DBF** is the currently active database.

Ins indicates that insert has been turned on.

The *navigation line* provides information on some of the common keystrokes you may want to use while in the **Report** design screen.

The *message line* provides a brief description of a highlighted menu option, other information connected with the current screen, or a prompt that asks you to do something. The message line currently is blank.

Create a report using the **Form layout** option by doing the following:

Keystroke	Action Resulting from Keystroke
[Alt-L]	Opens the **Layout** menu.
Q	Selects **Quick layouts** and displays its menu:

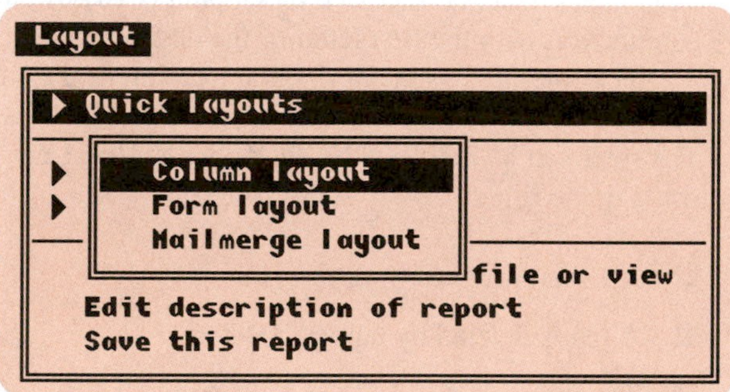

Column layout produces a report that looks like the **Browse** screen or a quick report where all the fields are laid out horizontally across the page, the field names appear as column headers, and the date and page number appear at the top of each page.

Form layout produces a report that looks like the **Edit** screen where the fields are laid out vertically down the page with one field per row and a blank line separates fields of adjacent records. The date and page number appear at the top of each page.

Mailmerge layout produces a report that is similar to the merge documents produced by WordPerfect.

Continued . . .

Keystroke	Action Resulting from Keystroke
F	Selects **Form layout** and displays its design screen (notice how similar it is to the **Edit** screen):

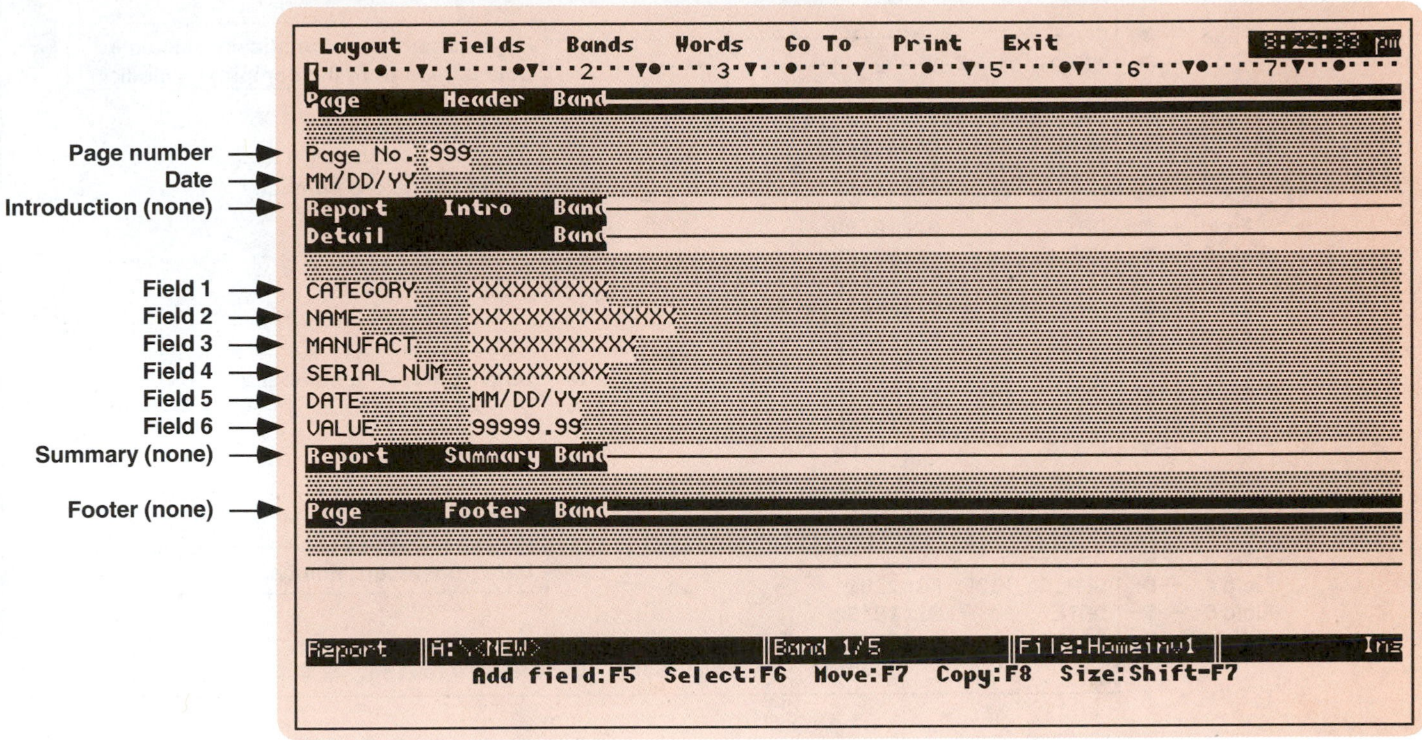

To see how a report using this layout will look in printed form we select **View report on screen** from the **Print** menu.

Keystroke	Action Resulting from Keystroke
[Alt-P]	Opens the **Print** menu.
V	Selects **View report** on screen and displays the report as it would appear in printed form (this may take a few seconds).

Continued . . .

Keystroke	Action Resulting from Keystroke

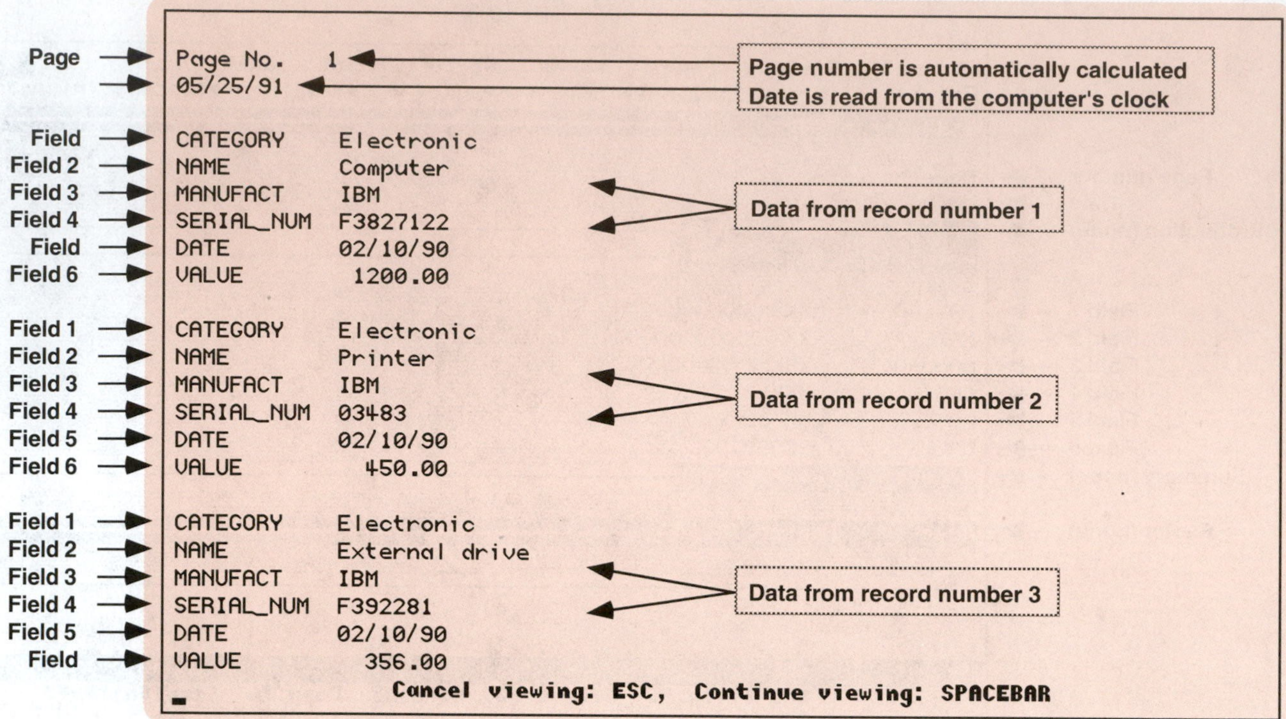

Notice how closely this output corresponds to the design screen shown in the previous screen dump.

To see the next screen full of data, tap **[Spacebar]**. To cancel viewing the output tap **[Esc]** and you will be returned to the **`Report`** design screen.

[Esc]	Cancels viewing the report and returns to the **`Report`** design screen.

To see how the report will look using the **`Column layout`** option, do the following:

Keystroke	Action Resulting from Keystroke
[Alt-L]	Opens the **`Layout`** menu.
Q	Selects **`Quick layouts`**.
C	Selects **`Column layout`** and displays its design screen. When the data are printed or displayed the output will look like the **`Browse`** screen display.

Continued . . .

Keystroke	Action Resulting from Keystroke

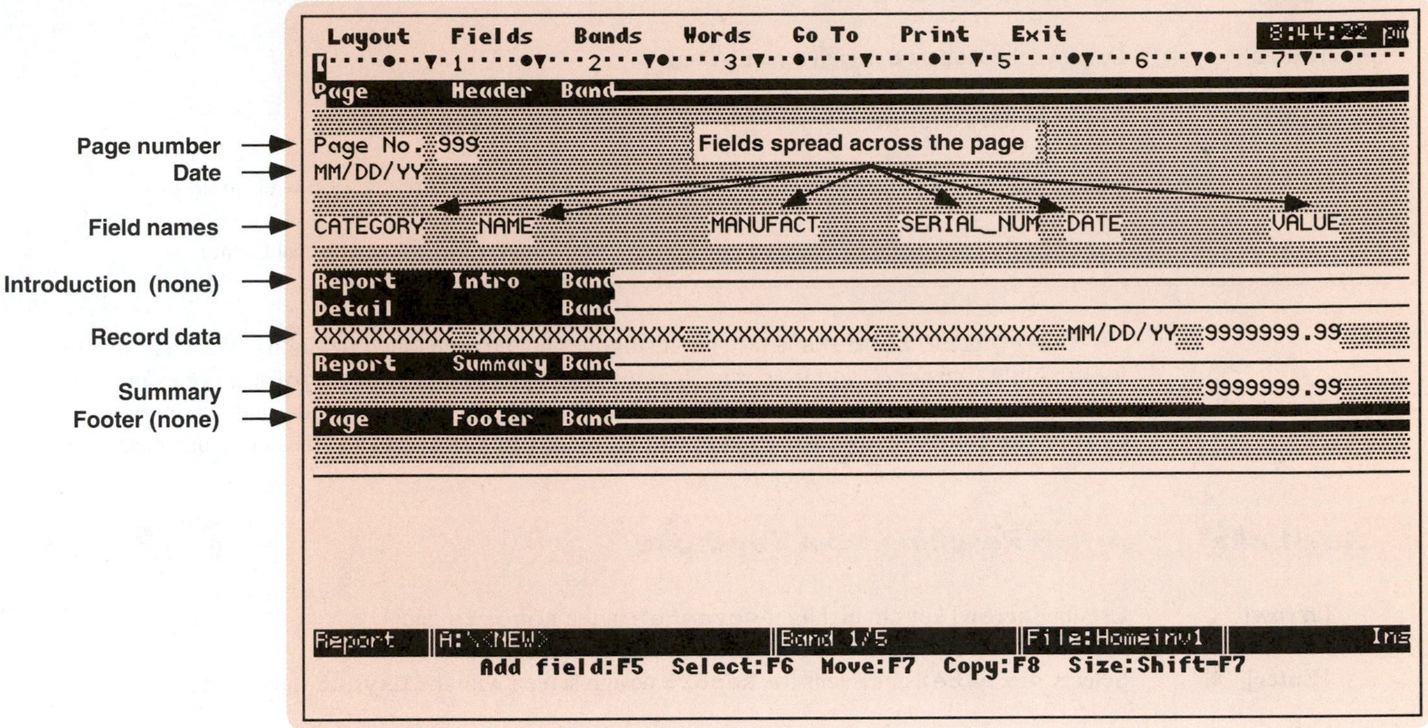

[Alt-P] Opens the **`Print`** menu.

V Selects **`View report on screen`** and displays the report as it would appear in printed form.

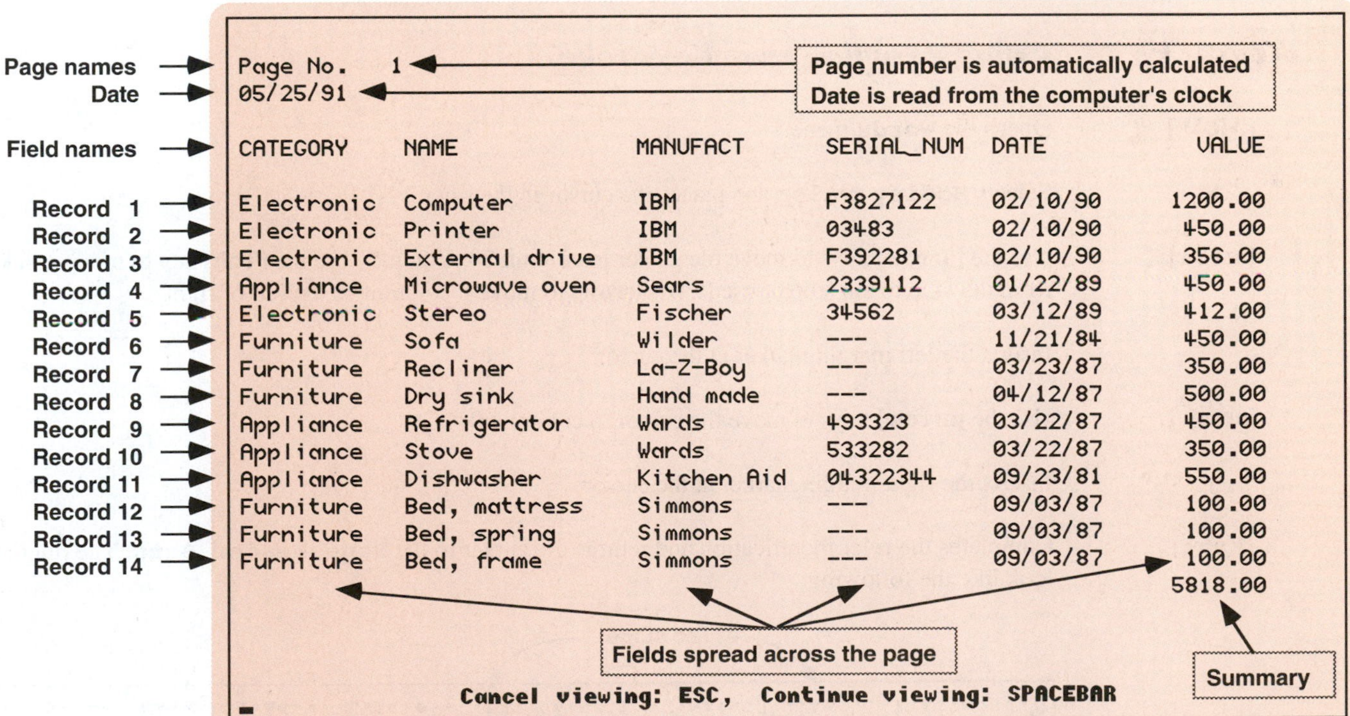

Notice how the report looks just like the quick report we generated on page D36.

Keystroke	Action Resulting from Keystroke
[Esc]	Cancels viewing the report.
[Enter]	Displays the **Report** design screen again.
[Alt-E]	Opens the **Exit** menu.
A	Selects **Abandon changes and exit** and asks if you are sure that you want to do this.
Y	Confirms that you want to abandon this report design and returns to the Control Center.

Using **Quick Layouts** is fast, but it still does not provide much flexibility. With a little effort we can build a custom report from scratch or modify one of the **Quick Layouts**. For example, let's create a custom report that includes an introduction, a page header, three fields, and summary statistics by doing the following (begin from the Control Center with **HOMEINV1** as the active database).

Keystroke	Action Resulting from Keystroke
[arrow]	Use the [arrow] keys to highlight **<create>** in the **Reports** panel.
[Enter]	Selects **<create>** and opens the **Report** design screen with the **Layout** menu opened.
[Esc]	Closes the menu and presents the design screen.

The default margins for text in a report are 0 and 254. We can change those by modifying the ruler.

Keystroke	Action Resulting from Keystroke
[Alt-W]	Opens the **Words** menu.
M	Selects **Modify ruler** and places the cursor in the ruler.
[arrow]	Use the [arrow] keys to move the cursor to column 20. You may use the [Tab] key to move quickly from tab stop to tab stop or use [Ctrl-arrow] to move 8 columns to the left or right.
[	Inserts the left margin marker at the cursor.
[arrow]	Use the [arrow] keys to move the cursor to column 60.
]	Inserts the right margin marker at the cursor.
[Enter]	Completes the ruler modification and returns the cursor to the **Page Header Band**. The ruler should look like the following:

Tab stops

```
[····●··▼·1·····●▼···[···▼●····3·▼··●·····▼·····●··▼·5·····●▼···]···▼●·····7·▼··●····
```

Left margin marker

Right margin marker

Continued . . .

Keystroke	Action Resulting from Keystroke
[arrow]	Use the **[arrow]** keys to move the cursor to column 20 in the gray area just below the **Page Header Band** bar. The status bar will display **Line:0 Col:20** indicating that the cursor is located at column 20 in line 0 of the **Page Header Band**.
	Type the header shown in the following screen dump:

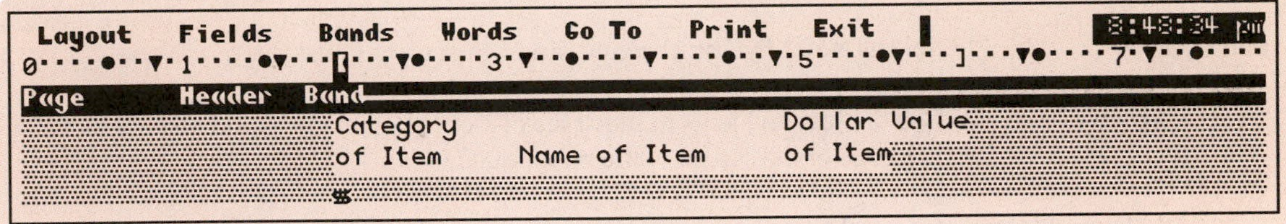

Draw a double line under the headings by doing the following:

Keystroke	Action Resulting from Keystroke
[Alt-L]	Opens the **Layout** menu.
L	Opens the **Line** menu.
D	Selects **Double line**.
[arrow]	Use the **[arrow]** keys, if necessary, to move the cursor so that it is just below the first column heading. When the cursor is in this position the middle of the status bar should read **Line:2 Col:20**. This refers to line 2 and column 20 in the **Page Header Band**.
[Enter]	Tells dBASE IV that the line is to begin at the cursor.
[arrow]	Use the **[arrow]** keys to move the cursor horizontally until it is at column 60. This draws the line.
[Enter]	Completes the line drawing.

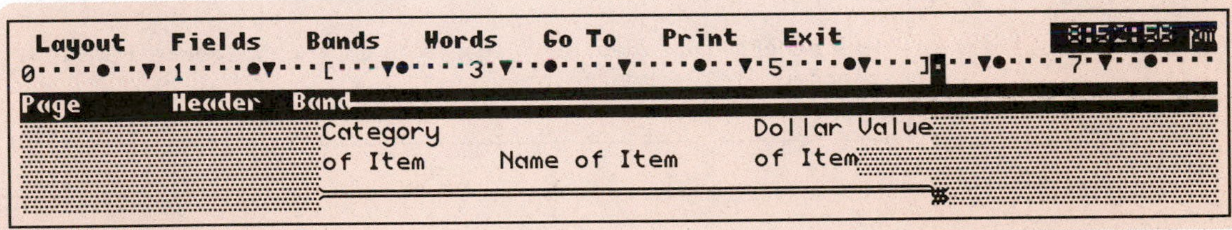

Most reports will include an introduction even if it is only a single line explaining the purpose of the report. However, the introduction can be quite long and detailed if you wish.

Keystroke	Action Resulting from Keystroke
[arrow]	Use the [arrow] keys to move the cursor to the line just under **Report Intro Band**. We want to use wider margins for the introduction and we want to enable word wrap so that long lines of text are adjusted to fit between the margins. This is similar to word wrap in WordPerfect.
[Alt-W]	Opens the **Words** menu.
M	Selects **Modify ruler** and places the cursor in the ruler.
[arrow]	Use the [arrow] keys to move the cursor to column 0. If you wish, you can use [Home] to move to the left edge of the screen while on the ruler.
[	Inserts the left margin marker at the cursor.
[arrow]	Use the [arrow] keys to move the cursor to column 75. If you wish, you can use [End] to move to the right edge of the screen while on the ruler.
]	Inserts the right margin marker at the cursor.
[Enter]	Completes the ruler modification and returns the cursor to the **Report Intro Band**.
[Alt-B]	Opens the **Bands** menu.
W	Changes **Word wrap band** from **NO** to **YES** and returns to the design screen. Notice that the gray background has disappeared from the **Report Intro Band**.

Type the introduction shown in the following screen dump:

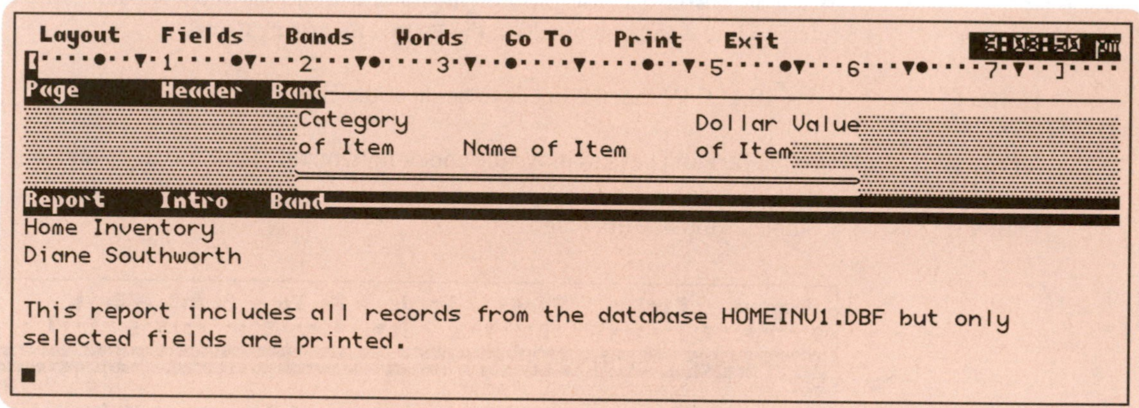

Unless we tell it otherwise, dBASE IV will print the page header at the top of the introductory page and it will begin printing the records right after the introduction. We can do the following to change this:

Keystroke	Action Resulting from Keystroke
[Alt-B]	Opens the **Bands** menu.
P	Changes **YES** to **NO** in **Page heading in report intro** and returns to the design screen. The introduction now appears above the **Page Header Band** to indicate that it will not contain the page header.
[arrow]	Use the **[arrow]** keys, if necessary, to move the cursor to the last line of the introduction (this should be a blank line and the status bar should show **Line:5 Col:0**).
[Alt-W]	Opens the **Words** menu.
I	Selects **Insert page break** and returns to the design screen. The page break is represented by the heavy dotted line at the bottom of the introduction section.

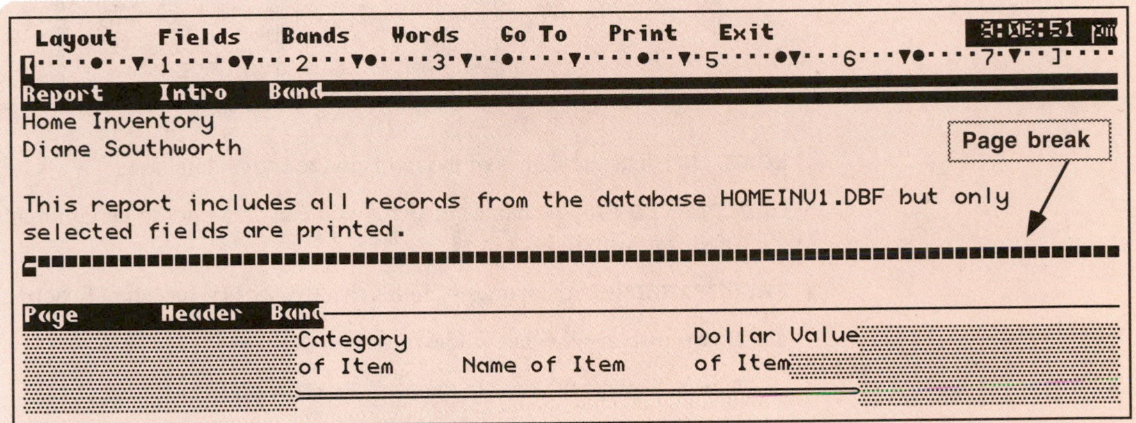

If you place the page break in the wrong location, move the cursor so that it is in the line with the page break and then tap **[Ctrl-Y]**. This will delete the entire line and you may try inserting the page break again.

We can indicate where the fields of each record will go by placing markers called *templates* into the **Detail Band**.

Keystroke	Action Resulting from Keystroke
[arrow]	Use the **[arrow]** keys to move the cursor to column 20 of the line just under **Detail Band**. This should line up with the heading of the first column.
[Alt-F]	Opens the **Fields** menu.
A	Selects **Add field** and opens a box showing the names of the different fields you can insert. This type of box is called a *picklist* because it shows you a list of items you can pick for the current operation.

Continued . . .

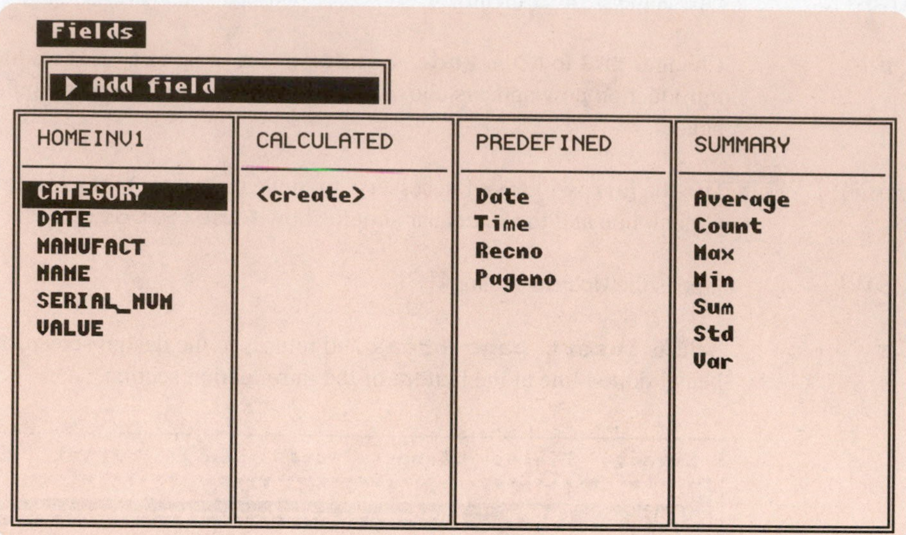

HOMEINV1 lists the names of the fields in the active database.

CALCULATED lists the names of fields you can create to do certain mathematical operations (none are listed).

PREDEFINED lists the names of fields that dBASE IV has already defined for you:

Date displays the date in the form **MM/DD/YY**.

Time displays the time in the form **HH:MM:SS**.

Recno displays the record number.

Pageno displays the page number.

SUMMARY lists the names of functions you can use to summarize data.

[arrow] Use the **[arrow]** keys, if necessary, to highlight the **CATEGORY** field.

[Enter] Selects the highlighted field and displays the attributes menu for the field.

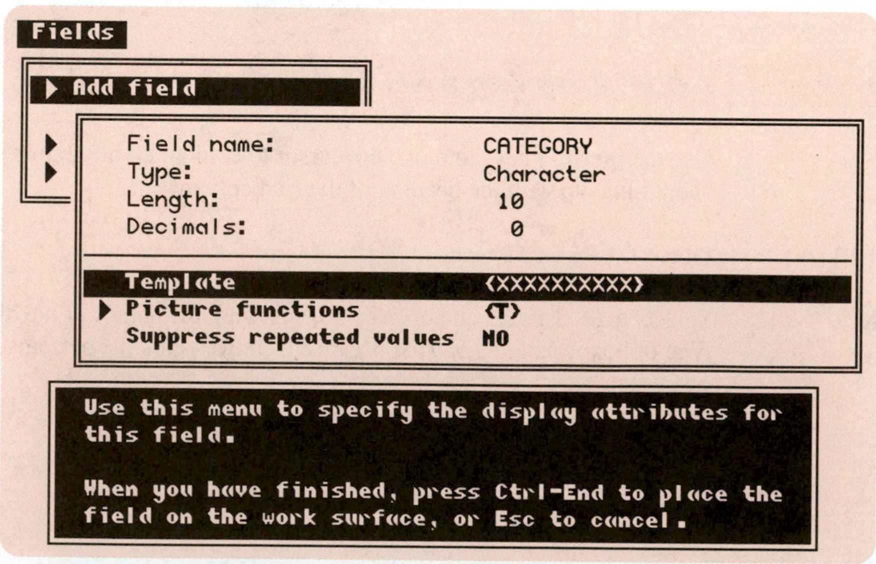

Continued . . .

Keystroke	Action Resulting from Keystroke

The first four lines give information on the selected field. The next three lines provide options:

Template shows the field type and the field width as it will appear in the report. Character fields appear as **X**s, numeric fields as **9**s, date fields as **MM/DD/YY**, and logical fields as **Y**s. The number of characters in the template indicates the number of characters that will be printed in the report. Thus, **{XXXXXXXXXX}** indicates a character field that will print 10 characters wide.

Picture functions provides a picklist of options that will alter the way the field will appear in the report such as displaying all letters in uppercase, aligning characters on the left or right, and displaying numbers with a dollar sign.

Suppress repeated values provides a way of not printing values in a field if the value of the previous record is identical to the value in the current record. For example, if the **CATEGORY** of records 1 and 2 is **Electronic**, then the word **Electronic** would appear only in record 1 of the report. This is useful for sorted lists because it reduces the amount of repetitive data displayed in the report.

[Ctrl-End] Accepts the attributes as they are and inserts the field template into the **Detail Band** of the report design.

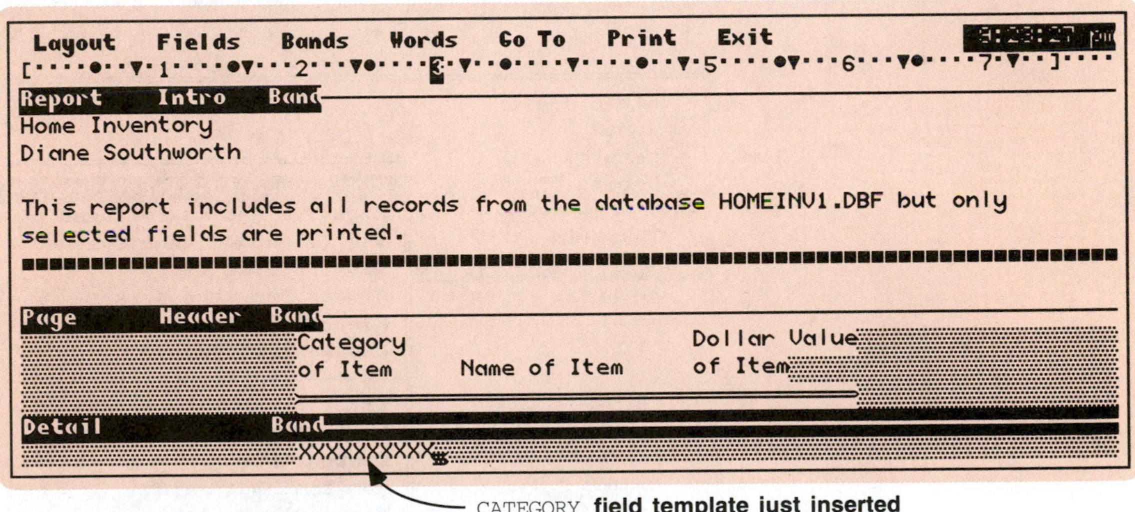

CATEGORY **field template just inserted**

We can follow a similar procedure to insert the other fields. Note that instead of using **[Alt-F]** and **A** to select **Add field** we can simply tap **[F5]** (this is called the *field* key).

[arrow] Use the **[arrow]** keys to move the cursor to column 32 of the line just under **Detail Band**. This should line up with the heading of the second column.

[F5] Selects **Add field** and opens a picklist showing the names of the different fields you can insert.

Continued . . .

Keystroke	Action Resulting from Keystroke
[arrow]	Use the **[arrow]** keys to highlight the **NAME** field.
[Enter]	Selects the highlighted field and displays the attributes menu.
[Ctrl-End]	Accepts the attributes as they are and inserts the field template into the **Detail Band** of the **Report** design.
[arrow]	Use the **[arrow]** keys to move the cursor to column 49 of the line just under **Detail Band**. This should line up with the heading of the third column.
[F5]	Selects **Add field** and opens a picklist showing the names of the different fields that can be inserted.
[arrow]	Use the **[arrow]** keys to highlight the **VALUE** field.
[Enter]	Selects the highlighted field and displays the attributes menu. We want to change the way the value is displayed so that a dollar sign is shown in front of the number.
P	Opens the **Picture functions** menu.

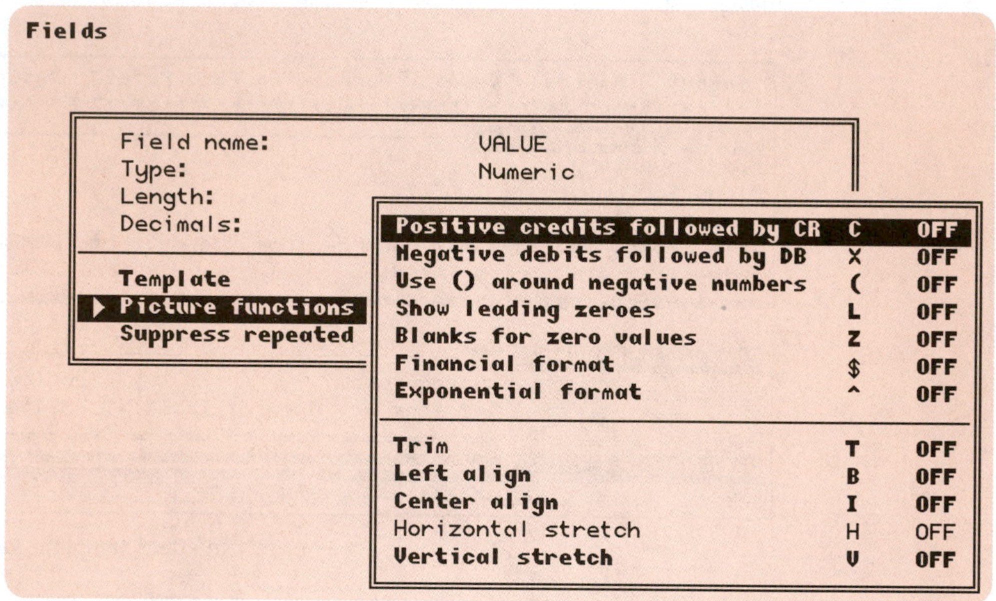

Keystroke	Action Resulting from Keystroke
F	Switches **Financial format** from **OFF** to **ON**. This will display the numbers in the **VALUE** field as currency (i.e., with a **$**).
[Ctrl-End]	Accepts the change and returns to the picklist.
[Ctrl-End]	Accepts the attributes and inserts the field template into the **Detail Band** of the **Report** design.

Continued . . .

Keystroke	Action Resulting from Keystroke

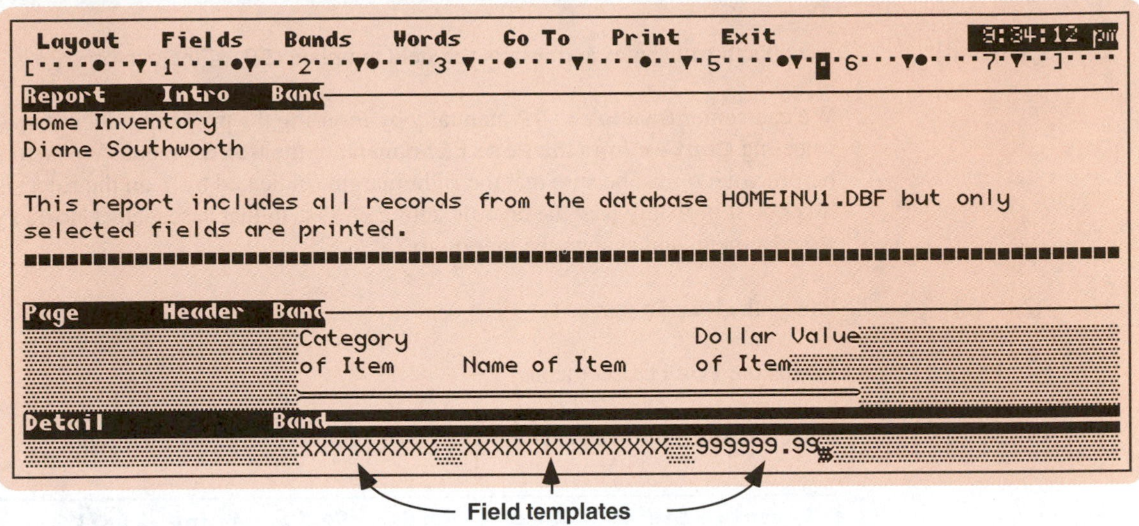

We will not add a footer to this report. However, we will add a summary that includes the number of items listed.

Keystroke	Action Resulting from Keystroke
[arrow]	Use the [arrow] keys to move the cursor to column 0 of the line just under **Report Summary Band**.
Number:	Provides a label for the number of items in the report.
[arrow]	Use the [arrow] keys to move the cursor to column 9 (two spaces to the right of **Number:**).
[F5]	Selects **Add field** and opens a picklist showing the names of the different fields you can insert.
[arrow]	Use the [arrow] keys to highlight **Count** in the **SUMMARY** picklist.
[Enter]	Selects the highlighted field and displays the attributes menu.
T	Opens the **Template** line and places the cursor just to the right of the number **9999999999**.
[Backspace]	Use the [Backspace] key to erase all but two of the **9**s. This means that we want to display only two digits for this field.

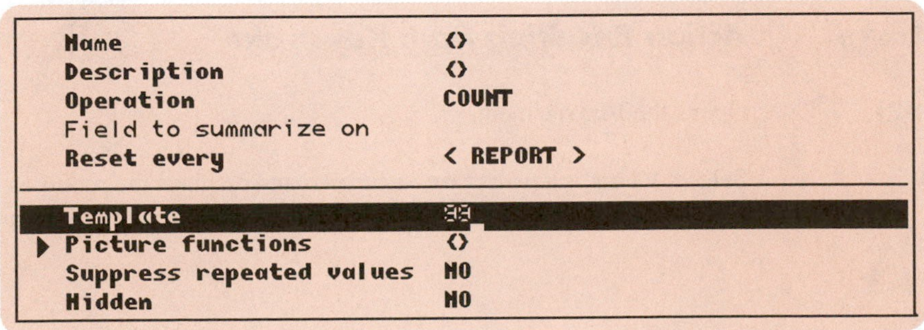

Continued . . .

Keystroke	Action Resulting from Keystroke
[Ctrl-End]	Accepts the template as modified.
[Ctrl-End]	Accepts the attributes and inserts the field template (**99**) at the cursor.
	We can center **Number: 99** manually by inserting the proper number of spaces to its left or by selecting **Center** from the **Position** menu of the **Words** menu. We will do the latter. However, before you do this, be sure that the right margin (indicated by **]** on the ruler) is visible at column 75. If it is not, it probably is at the default setting of 254. In that case, select **Modify ruler** from the **Words** menu and change the margin to 75.
[Alt-W]	Opens the **Words** menu.
P	Opens the **Position** menu.
C	Selects **Center** and centers the line in the summary section of the report.

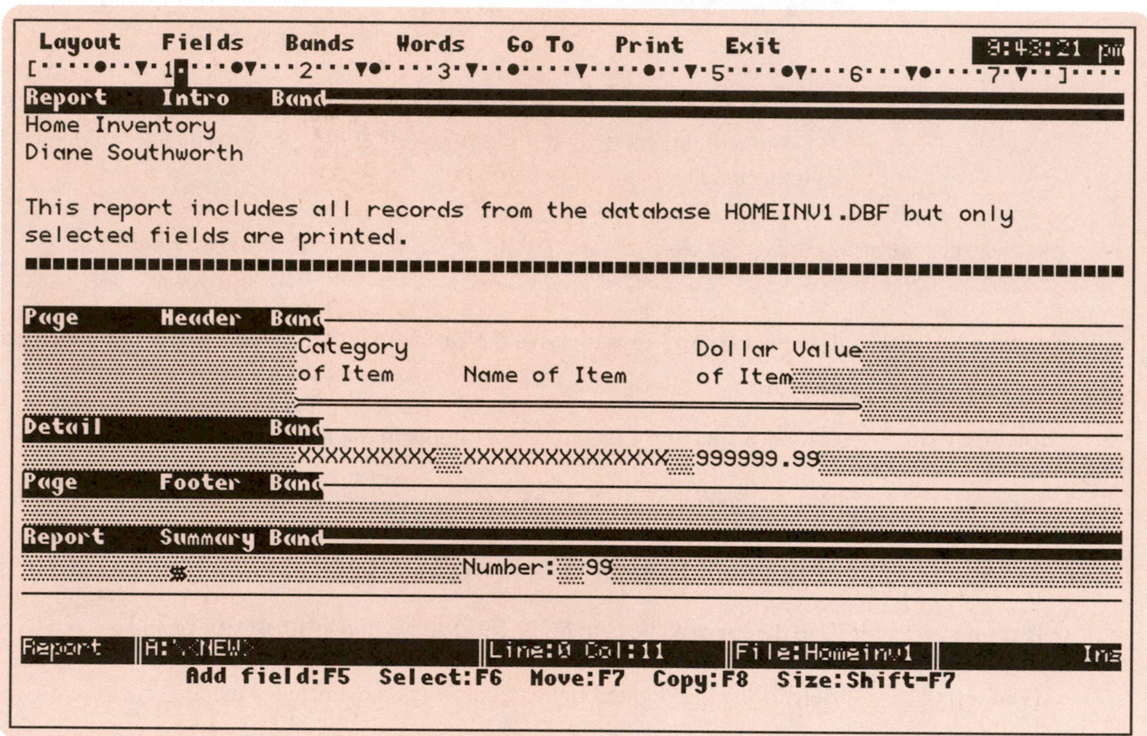

The report is complete. We can view it by doing the following:

Keystroke	Action Resulting from Keystroke
[Alt-P]	Opens the **Print** menu.
V	Selects **View report on screen** and displays the report as it would appear in printed form. The two printed pages that would be generated by this report design are shown below.

Continued . . .

Keystroke	Action Resulting from Keystroke

```
Home Inventory
Diane Southworth

This report includes all records from the database HOMEINV1.DBF but only
selected fields are printed.
```

Page 1 of the printed report

[Spacebar]	Use the **[Spacebar]** to view the different parts of the report.

```
Category                             Dollar Value
of Item      Name of Item            of Item

Electronic   Computer                  $1200.00
Electronic   Printer                    $450.00
Electronic   External drive             $356.00
Appliance    Microwave oven             $450.00
Electronic   Stereo                     $412.00
Furniture    Sofa                       $450.00
Furniture    Recliner                   $350.00
Furniture    Dry sink                   $500.00
Appliance    Refrigerator               $450.00
Appliance    Stove                      $350.00
Appliance    Dishwasher                 $550.00
Furniture    Bed, mattress              $100.00
Furniture    Bed, spring                $100.00
Furniture    Bed, frame                 $100.00
             Number:   14
```

Page 2 of the printed report

[Esc]	Cancels viewing the report and returns to the **`Report`** design screen.

The report form can be saved for future use by selecting **`Save this report`** from the **`Layout`** menu (this keeps the **`Report`** design screen active) or by selecting **`Save changes and exit`** from the **`Exit`** menu (this returns to the Control Center).

Keystroke	Action Resulting from Keystroke
[Alt-E]	Opens the **`Exit`** menu.
`S`	Selects **`Save changes and exit`**. dBASE IV will present a prompt box asking for a name for the file.
`A:\RPT1` ↵	Provides the file specification (dBASE IV automatically adds a file name extension **`FRM`**), saves the report file, and returns to the Control Center.

Modifying Reports

Once a report has been constructed it can be used as often as you wish in response to changes in the data or requests from various sources. Reports can be modified and saved under different names so that you may have a number of variations of the same report to suit different needs. For example, the report **RPT1.FRM** can be modified in the following ways:

- Add the page number and date to the header.
- Remove the double underline from the header.
- Delete the **CATEGORY** field.
- Add record numbers on the left of each record displayed.
- Insert text from a text (ASCII) file in the report summary.
- Save the new report design under the name **RPT2.FRM**.

To make the above modifications, begin from the Control Center with **HOMEINV1** as the active database and do the following:

Keystroke	Action Resulting from Keystroke
[arrow]	Use the **[arrow]** keys to highlight the file **RPT1** in the **Reports** panel.
[Enter]	Selects the highlighted file and presents the following prompt box:

```
Print report     Modify layout     Display data

      Press ENTER to select or ESC to cancel
```

Print report displays the **Print** menu and allows you to print or view the report.

Modify layout displays the **Report** design screen and allows you to change the design of the report.

Display data displays either the **Browse** or **Edit** screen, whichever was last displayed.

M	Selects **Modify layout** and displays the design screen for the report.

We want the new design screen to look like the following:

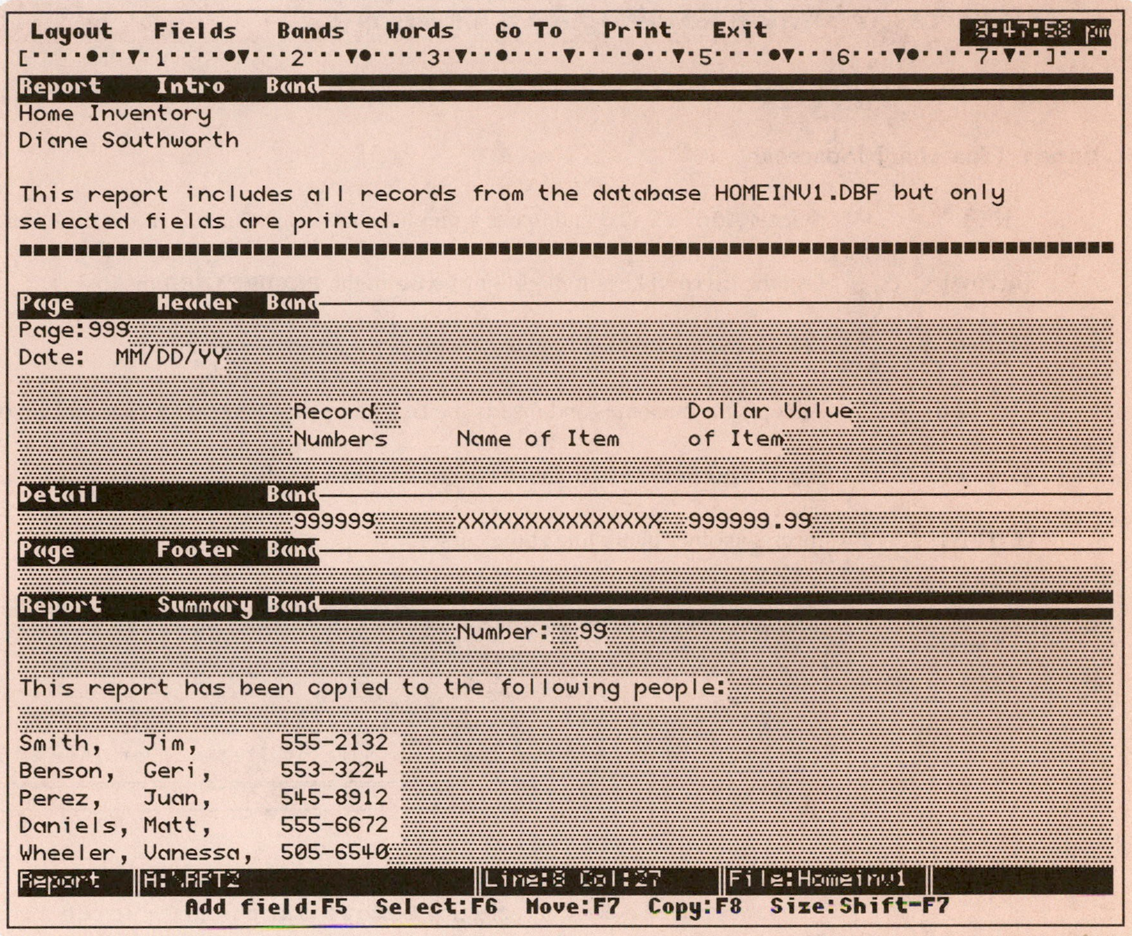

To insert the page number and date into the header band we will insert three new lines at the top of the band and then type the new entries.

Keystroke	Action Resulting from Keystroke
[arrow]	Use the **[arrow]** keys to move the cursor to the first column of the line just below **`Page Header Band`** (location **`Line:0 Col:0`** in that band). New lines can be inserted by selecting **`Add line`** from the **`Words`** menu, or by tapping **[Ctrl-N]**, or if insert is on (i.e., if **`Ins`** is displayed in the status bar) by tapping **[Enter]**.
[Ctrl-N]	Inserts a blank line at the cursor. Type the following:
`Page:`	
[F5]	Selects **`Add field`** and opens a picklist showing the names of the different fields you can insert. You could have tapped **[Alt-F]** and then **`F`** instead of tapping **[F5]**.
[arrow]	Use the **[arrow]** keys to highlight **`Pageno`** in the **`PREDEFINED`** picklist.
[Enter]	Selects the highlighted field and displays the attributes menu.
[Ctrl-End]	Accepts the attributes and inserts the field template (**`999`**) at the cursor.
[arrow]	Use the **[arrow]** keys to move the cursor down one line and to the left to location **`Line:1 Col:0`**.

Continued . . .

Keystroke	Action Resulting from Keystroke
[Ctrl-N]	Inserts another blank line at the cursor. Type **Date:** and then tap **[Spacebar]** twice:

Date: [Spacebar] [Spacebar]

Keystroke	Action Resulting from Keystroke
[F5]	Selects **Add field** and opens a picklist showing the names of the different fields you can insert.
[arrow]	Use the **[arrow]** keys to highlight **Date** in the **PREDEFINED** picklist.
[Enter]	Selects the highlighted field and displays the attributes menu.
[Ctrl-End]	Accepts the attributes and inserts the field template (**MM/DD/YY**) at the cursor.
[arrow]	Use the **[arrow]** keys to move the cursor down one line and to the left to location **Line:2 Col:0**.
[Ctrl-N]	Inserts another blank line at the cursor.

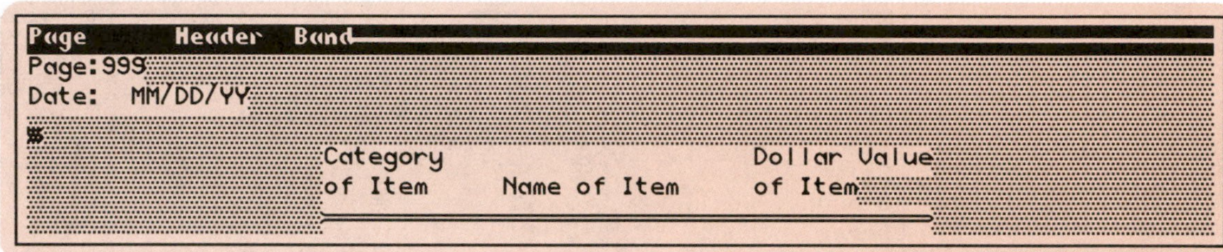

Lines can be deleted by selecting **Remove line** from the **Words** menu or by tapping **[Ctrl-Y]**. Delete the double underline from the report header by doing the following:

Keystroke	Action Resulting from Keystroke
[arrow]	Use the **[arrow]** keys to move the cursor to location **Line:5 Col:0** of the page header band (this is the line containing the double underline).
[Ctrl-Y]	Deletes the line containing the cursor.

Fields can be deleted by selecting **Remove field** from the **Fields** menu or by using the **[arrow]** keys to place the cursor at the field and tapping **[Delete]**. We can delete the **CATEGORY** field by doing the following:

Keystroke	Action Resulting from Keystroke
[Alt-F]	Opens the **Fields** menu.
R	Selects **Remove field** and presents a picklist of fields displayed in the report.

Continued . . .

Keystroke	Action Resulting from Keystroke

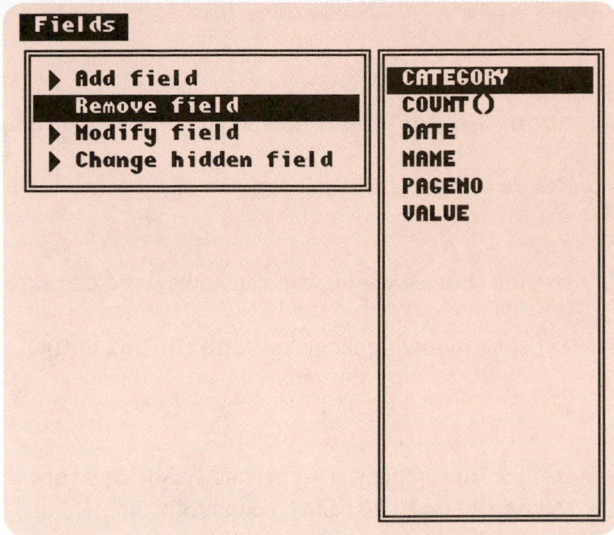

[arrow]	Use the **[arrow]** keys, if necessary, to highlight the field **`CATEGORY`**.
[Enter]	Deletes the field from the **`Detail Band`**. The other fields remain where they were.

Fields can be added by selecting **`Add field`** from the **`Fields`** menu. We will add a predefined field that will display the record number for each record by doing the following:

Keystroke	Action Resulting from Keystroke
[arrow]	Use the **[arrow]** keys to move the cursor to **`Line:0 Col:20`** of the **`Detail Band`**. This is the location where we want to insert the new field.
[F5]	Selects **`Add field`** and opens a picklist showing the names of the fields you can insert. You could have tapped **[Alt-F]** and then **`F`** instead of tapping **[F5]**.
[arrow]	Use the **[arrow]** keys to highlight **`Recno`** from the column labeled **`PREDEFINED`**.
[Enter]	Selects the highlighted field and displays the attributes menu.
[Ctrl-End]	Accepts the attributes and inserts the field template (**`999999`**) at the cursor.

```
Detail          Band
                    999999    XXXXXXXXXXXXXXX  999999.99
```

Change the header for this field by doing the following:

Keystroke	Action Resulting from Keystroke
[arrow]	Use the [arrow] keys to move the cursor to the space just to the right of the word **Category** in the **Page Header Band** (this should be location **Line:3 Col:28**).
	Before doing the next step, be sure that insert is turned off (i.e., be sure that **Ins** does not appear on the status bar).
[Backspace]	Use the [Backspace] key to delete the word **Category**.
	Type the following (begin at **Line:3 Col:20**):
Record	
[arrow]	Use the [arrow] keys to move the cursor down one line so that it is just below the **R** in **Record** (**Line:4 Col:20**) and type the following:
Numbers	

```
Page        Header  Band
Page:999
Date:  MM/DD/YY

                          Record                          Dollar Value
                          Numbers      Name of Item       of Item
```

As a precaution against loss of data, save the report design using the name **RPT2** by doing the following:

Keystroke	Action Resulting from Keystroke
[Alt-L]	Opens the **Layout** menu.
S	Selects **Save this report** and displays a **Save as** prompt box with the file specification **A:\RPT1.FRM**.
[Edit]	Use the standard editing techniques to change file specification to **A:\RPT2.FRM**.
[Enter]	Accepts the new file specification, saves the report format to disk, and returns to the design screen. The file path and name **A:\RPT2** should be displayed in the status bar.

Change the top of the report summary so that the sum of the **VALUE** field is displayed instead of the number of records listed. We have to change the label **Number:** (located at **Line:0 Col:32** of the **Summary Band**) and the field **COUNT** (located at **Line:0 Col:51** of the **Summary Band**).

Keystroke	Action Resulting from Keystroke
[arrow]	Use the [arrow] keys to move the cursor to the **Summary Band** and place it on the first letter of **Number:** (the location is **Line:0 Col:32**).
[edit]	Employ the usual editing techniques to change **Number:** to **Sum of values:**. The first letter of **Sum** should be at location **Line:0 Col:36**. Notice that as you insert more letters the **COUNT** field, represented by the **99**, moves to the right.
[arrow]	Use the [arrow] keys to move the cursor to the **COUNT** field, represented by the **99** at location **Line:0 Col:51**. The bottom of the screen should look like the following:

Keystroke	Action Resulting from Keystroke
[Delete]	Deletes the field **COUNT**.
[F5]	Selects **Add field** and opens a picklist showing the names of the different fields you can insert.
[arrow]	Use the [arrow] keys to highlight the **Sum** field in the **SUMMARY** column.
[Enter]	Selects the highlighted field and displays the attributes menu. We want to change the way the value is displayed so that a dollar sign is shown in front of the number.
P	Opens the **Picture functions** menu.
F	Switches **Financial format** from **OFF** to **ON**. This will display the numbers in the **VALUE** field as currency (i.e., with a **$**).
[Ctrl-End]	Accepts the change and returns to the picklist.
	We need to tell dBASE IV which field to sum.
F	Selects **Field to summarize on** and displays a picklist of field names.
[arrow]	Use the [arrow] keys to highlight the **VALUE** field.
[Enter]	Selects the highlighted field and displays the attributes menu again. Notice the field name **VALUE** in braces to the right of **Field to summarize on**.
T	Opens the **Template** line and places the cursor just to the right of the number **99999999.99**.
[Backspace]	Use the [Backspace] key to erase some of the **9**s so that the template reads **9999.99**.
[Ctrl-End]	Accepts the template as modified.
[Ctrl-End]	Accepts the attributes and inserts the field template (**9999.99**) at the cursor.

Continued . . .

Keystroke	Action Resulting from Keystroke

dBASE IV reports can be combined with documents from WordPerfect and worksheets from Lotus 1-2-3 to form a comprehensive dossier on a given topic. Also, like WordPerfect and Lotus 1-2-3, dBASE IV can import data from other sources so that the information does not have to be retyped. For example, we can insert data from a text (ASCII) file into the report summary by selecting **Write/read text file** from the **Words** menu. Let's see how this works by adding information from the file **PHONETXT** (which you saved as an ASCII file while working in WordPerfect on page W114). (If the file **PHONETXT** is not available, you may still do the following, but you will have to type the raw data yourself.)

Keystroke	Action Resulting from Keystroke
[arrow]	Use the **[arrow]** keys, if necessary, to move the cursor to the bottom of the **Summary Band** just to the right of **Sum of values: 9999.99** (the location is **Line:0 Col:58**).
[Enter] [Enter]	Moves the cursor down two lines. Type the following:

This report has been copied to the following people:

Keystroke	Action Resulting from Keystroke
[Enter] [Enter]	Moves the cursor down two lines.

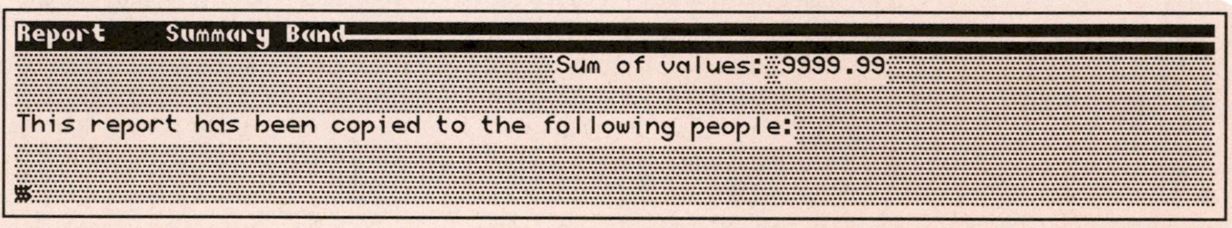

You now have two choices. You can type the names and phone numbers of the people to whom the report is to be sent or, if it is available, simply insert the data from the file **PHONETXT** that you created in WordPerfect. If **PHONETXT** is not available to you at this time, type the names and phone numbers yourself and then skip the first four keystrokes in the following table.

Keystroke	Action Resulting from Keystroke
[Alt-W]	Opens the **Words** menu.
W	Opens the **Write/read text file** menu.

Write selection to file allows you to make an ASCII file out of any text selected.

Read text from file allows you to insert at the cursor text from an ASCII file.

Continued . . .

Keystroke	Action Resulting from Keystroke
R	Selects **`Read text from file`** and asks for the name of the file.
	Remove your *dBASE data* diskette and insert your *WordPerfect Data* diskette into drive A:. If you do not have that diskette with you, see your instructor or tap **[Esc]** to cancel the operation. If the file **`PHONETXT`** is in a directory of your hard drive, use the proper directory path when you type the file specification.
`A:\PHONETXT.` ↵	Provides the file specification. The period at the end of **`PHONETXT.`** is needed because dBASE IV assumes the file name extension **`TXT`**, but **`PHONETXT.`** has no extension. The period indicates that the extension is blank.

```
Report    Summary Band
                                            Sum of values: 9999.99

This report has been copied to the following people:

Smith,    Jim,        555-2132
Benson,   Geri,       553-3224
Perez,    Juan,       545-8912
Daniels,  Matt,       555-6672
Wheeler,  Vanessa,    505-6540
```

Keystroke	Action Resulting from Keystroke
	If necessary, remove the *WordPerfect Data* diskette from drive A: and insert the *dBASE Data* diskette in its place.
	Save the new version of the report design under the name **`RPT2.FRM`** by doing the following:
[Alt-L]	Opens the **`Layout`** menu.
S	Selects **`Save this report`** and displays the file specification **`A:\RPT2.FRM`**.
[Enter]	Accepts the current file specification, saves the report format to disk and returns to the design screen.

To see how the new report will look, do the following:

Keystroke	Action Resulting from Keystroke
[Alt-P]	Opens the **`Print`** menu.
V	Selects **`View report on screen`** and displays the report as it would appear in printed form. The two printed pages that would be generated by this report design are shown below.

```
Home Inventory
Diane Southworth

This report includes all records from the database HOMEINV1.DBF but only
selected fields are printed.
```

Page 1 of the printed report

Continued . . .

```
Page:  1
Date:  05/25/91

                         Record                    Dollar Value
                         Numbers    Name of Item   of Item

                             1      Computer          $1200.00
                             2      Printer            $450.00
                             3      External drive     $356.00
                             4      Microwave oven     $450.00
                             5      Stereo             $412.00
                             6      Sofa               $450.00
                             7      Recliner           $350.00
                             8      Dry sink           $500.00
                             9      Refrigerator       $450.00
                            10      Stove              $350.00
                            11      Dishwasher         $550.00
                            12      Bed, mattress      $100.00
                            13      Bed, spring        $100.00
                            14      Bed, frame         $100.00
                                      Sum of values:  5818.00

This report has been copied to the following people:

Smith,   Jim,       555-2132
Benson,  Geri,      553-3224
Perez,   Juan,      545-8912
Daniels, Matt,      555-6672
Wheeler, Vanessa,   505-6540
```

Page 2 of the printed report

Keystroke	Action Resulting from Keystroke
[Esc]	Cancels viewing the report and returns to the **Report** design screen.
[Alt-E]	Opens the **Exit** menu.
A	Selects **Abandon changes and exit** and returns to the Control Center. Notice that two report forms, **RPT1** and **RPT2**, are displayed in the **Reports** panel.

Combining Queries and Reports

We can combine queries with reports to produce documents that look exactly as we wish and that contain only those records we specify. For example, let's use the report design **RPT2** with the query design **AP&EL-89** to produce a report that includes only appliances and electronic goods purchased in 1989 (begin from the Control Center).

Keystroke	Action Resulting from Keystroke
[arrow]	Use the [arrow] keys to highlight **AP&EL-89** in the **Queries** panel.
[Enter]	Selects the highlighted file and displays a prompt box asking how the file should be used.
U	Selects **Use view** and sets the view to match that described in **AP&EL-89** (the command **SET VIEW TO AP&EL-89.qbe** will flash across the screen). Recall that this query filtered out all records except for those appliances and electronic goods that were purchased in 1989.
[arrow]	Use the [arrow] keys to highlight **RPT2** in the **Reports** panel.
[Enter]	Selects the highlighted file and displays a prompt box asking how the file should be used.
P	Selects **Print report** and presents the following prompt box:

```
Current view            HOMEINV1.DBF

You may choose to use either the current database file
or view, or the database file or view usually
associated with the file you just selected.
```

Current view allows you to use the query view you just selected (**AP&EL-89**). Only records that match the filters in **AP&EL-89** will be selected for inclusion in the output.

HOMEINV1.DBF will use the normal view of the database (this means that all records will be selected for inclusion in the output).

C	Selects **Current view** and displays the **Print** menu, which allows you to choose how you want the file printed or displayed.
V	Selects **View report on screen**, processes the report, and displays it on the screen. The only difference between this report and the previous printing of it is that the records have been filtered so that only those appliances and electronic goods purchased in 1989 are displayed.

```
Home Inventory
Diane Southworth

This report includes all records from the database HOMEINV1.DBF but only
selected fields are printed.
```

Page 1 of the printed report using the RPT2 **report design and the** AP&EL-89 **query**

Continued . . .

```
Page:  1
Date:  05/25/91

                         Record                     Dollar Value
                         Numbers    Name of Item    of Item

                              4    Microwave oven     $450.00
                              5    Stereo             $412.00
                                       Sum of values: $862.00

This report has been copied to the following people:

Smith,   Jim,      555-2132
Benson,  Geri,     553-3224
Perez,   Juan,     545-8912
Daniels, Matt,     555-6672
Wheeler, Vanessa,  505-6540
```

Page 2 of the printed report using the RPT2 **report design and the** AP&EL-89 **query**

Keystroke	Action Resulting from Keystroke
[Esc]	Cancels viewing the report.
[Enter]	Returns to the Control Center.

File Types and Extensions

dBASE IV uses a number of different file types in order to accomplish different tasks in the most efficient manner possible. In the last section, for example, three separate files were created by dBASE IV when you generated a report using the **RPT2** report design:

- **RPT2.FRM** contains the report design information.
- **RPT2.FRG** contains the source code for the report (these are the actual program instructions created by dBASE IV).
- **RPT2.FRO** is a compiled version of the report form. This is a set of program instructions coded in a special way so that the instructions can be processed very quickly by the computer.

As you continue to work with dBASE IV you will notice more and more file names with different file name extensions appearing on your *dBASE Data* diskette. Some of the files are written in coded form to save disk space and increase processing speed. Others, like **RPT2.FRG**, are written in regular ASCII code and can be edited using any text editor (e.g., WordPerfect or the word processor built into dBASE IV). Sometimes experienced users edit these files to fine-tune various operations. Most users, however, just ignore the files and let dBASE IV handle them as it sees fit.

Below is a list of some of the file name extensions used by dBASE IV. A complete list can be found in the *dBASE IV Language Reference*.

File name extension	*Description*
BAK	Backup file (a copy of a file that was changed in some way).
CAT	File related to catalogs.
DB	Configuration file that contains dBASE IV startup defaults.
DBF	Database file.
DBT	Database memo file.
FRG	Report form source code file.
FRM	Report form file.
FRO	Compiled version of a report form file.
MDX	Multiple index file.
NDX	Single index file.
QBE	Query by example query file.
QBO	Compiled query file.
TXT	ASCII text output file.
UPD	Update query file.
VUE	View file.
WKS	Lotus 1-2-3 file generated by dBASE IV.

Aliases

An alias is an alternative name that dBASE IV allows you to assign to a database. During a particular work session, you may refer to the database using its alias instead of its real name, if you wish. This is helpful when you have written a procedure for one database and then want to use the procedure on another database without having to modify the procedure.

We will not discuss aliases but you may find the term popping up every once in a while as you access databases that you create in the Homework Exercises. This is because dBASE IV automatically assigns an alias to a database file whenever the file is opened. Usually, the alias assigned is the same as the regular name of the database and so you will not notice it at all. However, alias names may contain only letters, numbers, and underscores so if you use a name that contains another character (e.g., the dash –), dBASE will assign a different alias to that database. For example, when you use the database **`HWD1-02.DBF`**, which you will create in Homework Exercise 2, you may see a message similar to **`Default alias is A`** popping up. You can ignore the message and always use the regular name for the database.

TO TAKE A BREAK Tap **[Alt-E]**; **`Q`**. Remove data diskette. To resume: Insert data diskette; type **`A:`** ↵, then **`C:\DBIV\DBASE`** ↵.

Homework Exercises

Remember . . . when you modify a database the data are not necessarily written to the disk but rather are written to a part of temporary memory called a buffer. The data are written to disk when the buffer becomes full or when you close the database either by highlighting it in the Control Center, tapping **[Enter]**, and then selecting **`Close file`**, or by selecting **`Quit to DOS`** from the **`Exit`** menu. If you simply turn off the power to the computer before exiting dBASE IV and returning to DOS, you may lose data. It is a good idea to save your files often.

---

① Use the table of contents of the *Help* feature to display the on-line *Help* screen for relational operators used in **`Queries`**. Do a screen dump of the *Help* screen. It should look like the following:

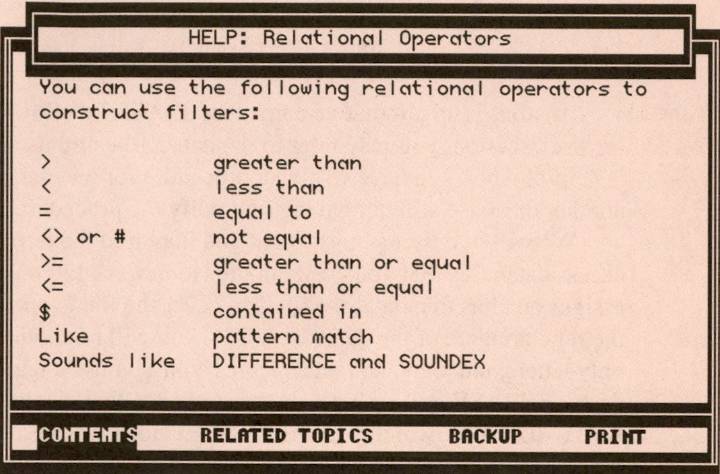

---

② Allen, the owner of the Katt Computer Company, has kept a record of all the money owed to him by his customers. The data are listed below:

NAME	BALANCE	PAST	STREET	CITY	STATE	ZIP
Janice	15	32	15 Softie Lane	Mpls	MN	55412
Jill	30	35	23 S Fourth St.	St. Paul	MN	55101
Sara	50	5	1 Perry Court	St. Paul	MN	55102
Jack	20	20	6 Bull Blvd.	Mpls	MN	55412
Keisha	34	0	12 First Ave.	Mpls	MN	55412

Create a dBASE IV database called **HWD1-02** and enter the above data using the field names, widths, and types listed below:

Name	**Type**	**Width**	**Decimals**	**Description**
NAME	character	6		name of client
BALANCE	numeric	7	2	number of dollars owed
PAST	numeric	2	0	number of days since last payment
STREET	character	15		street address
CITY	character	8		city of residence
STATE	character	2		state of residence
ZIP	character	5		postal ZIP code

Use **Browse** to display the entire database and do a screen dump of the display. It should look like the following:

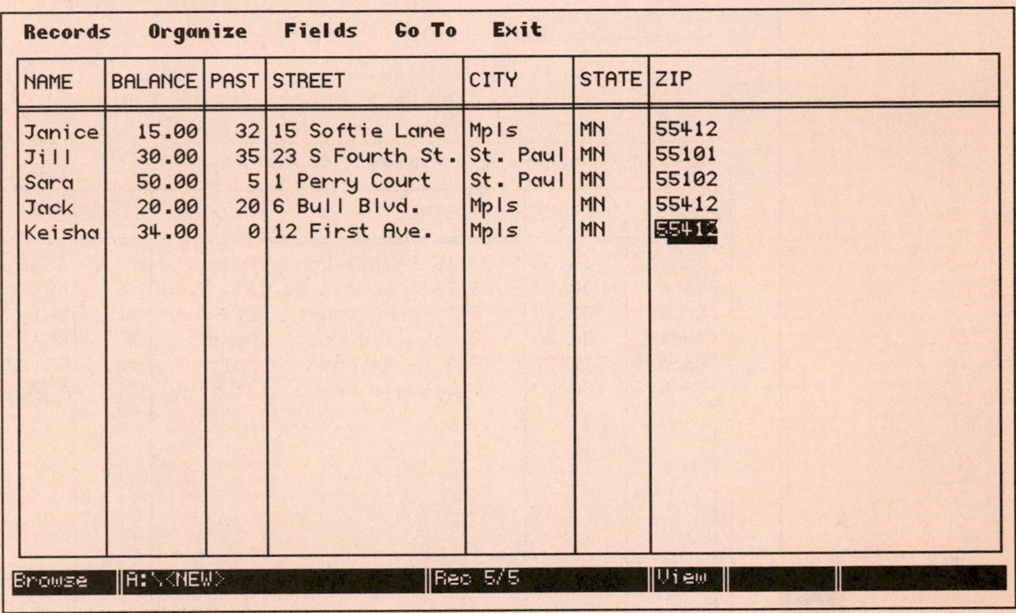

Records Organize Fields Go To Exit

NAME	BALANCE	PAST	STREET	CITY	STATE	ZIP
Janice	15.00	32	15 Softie Lane	Mpls	MN	55412
Jill	30.00	35	23 S Fourth St.	St. Paul	MN	55101
Sara	50.00	5	1 Perry Court	St. Paul	MN	55102
Jack	20.00	20	6 Bull Blvd.	Mpls	MN	55412
Keisha	34.00	0	12 First Ave.	Mpls	MN	55412

Browse A:\<NEW> Rec 5/5 View

---

③ Use the *Go To* feature in **Edit** to display the third record of the database **HWD1-02**. Do a screen dump of the result.

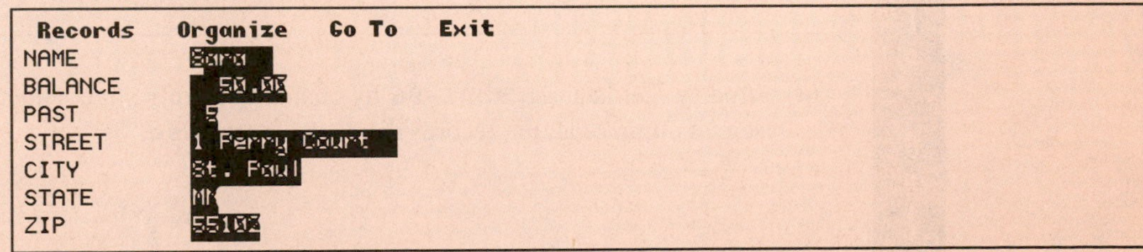

Records Organize Go To Exit
NAME Sara
BALANCE 50.00
PAST 5
STREET 1 Perry Court
CITY St. Paul
STATE MN
ZIP 55102

---

④ Print a Quick Report of the database, **HWD1-02**, created in Exercise 2.

Continued . . .

⑤ Use the dBASE IV searching techniques within **Browse** to locate the record of the customer in **HWD1-02** whose ZIP code is 55101. Do a screen dump of the result.

---

⑥ Make a backup copy of the database **HWD1-02**. Call the backup copy **HWD1-06**. Open the database and then do a screen dump of all the records displayed in **Browse**.

---

⑦ Modify the database **HWD1-06.DBF** by deleting Keisha's record from the list and adding the following data:

Name	***Balance***	***Past***	***Street***	***City***	***State***	***ZIP***
Rama	112	00	3 Renee Road	Mpls	MN	55412
Barb	100	04	5 Maple Drive	St. Paul	MN	55112

Do a screen dump of all the records displayed in **Browse**.

Records   Organize   Fields   Go To   Exit

NAME	BALANCE	PAST	STREET	CITY	STATE	ZIP
Janice	15.00	32	15 Softie Lane	Mpls	MN	55412
Jill	30.00	35	23 S Fourth St.	St. Paul	MN	55101
Sara	50.00	5	1 Perry Court	St. Paul	MN	55102
Jack	20.00	20	6 Bull Blvd.	Mpls	MN	55412
Rama	112.00	0	3 Renee Road	Mpls	MN	55412
Barb	100.00	4	5 Maple Drive	St. Paul	MN	55112

Browse ‖A:\HWD1-06 ‖Rec 6/6 ‖File ‖

---

⑧ Modify the database **HWD1-06** by changing Barb's street address to 625 First Ave. Do a screen dump of all the records displayed in **Browse**.

⑨ Create an index for the database **HWD1-06** so that the records are arranged by **CITY** and, within **CITY**, by **NAME**. Do a screen dump of all the records displayed in **Browse**. After you have done the screen dump, return the arrangement of the database records to their natural order.

---

⑩ Create a view query of **HWD1-06** that uses the following view skeleton:

View			
hwd1-10	Hwd1-06-> NAME	Hwd1-06-> PAST	Hwd1-06-> BALANCE

Do a screen dump of the **Query** design screen and then save the query as **HWD1-10**.

---

⑪ Display all the data of **HWD1-06** in **Browse** using the view query **HWD1-D10**.

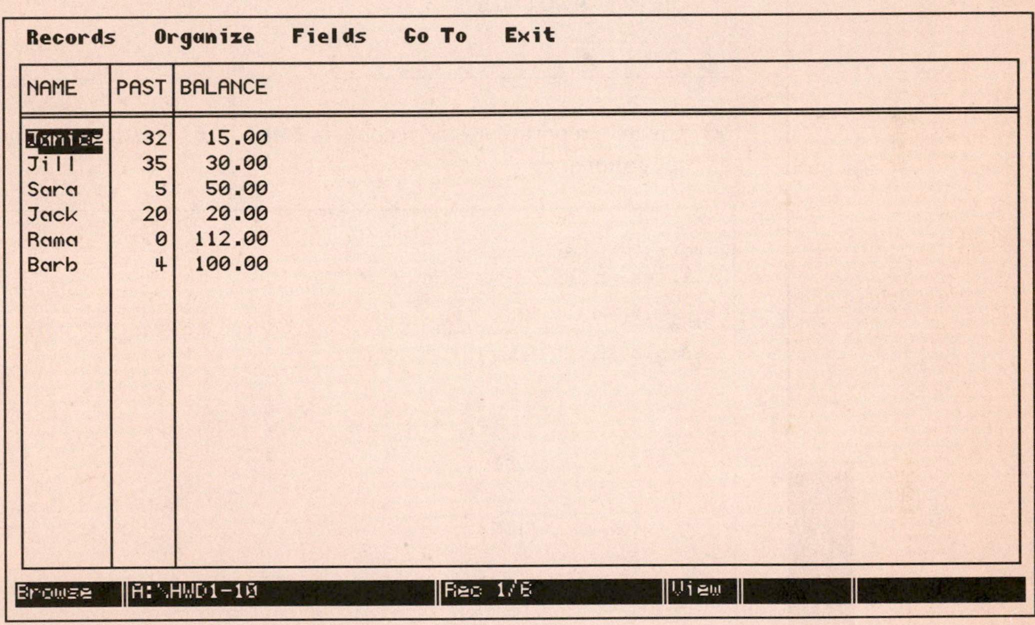

Records   Organize   Fields   Go To   Exit

NAME	PAST	BALANCE
Janice	32	15.00
Jill	35	30.00
Sara	5	50.00
Jack	20	20.00
Rama	0	112.00
Barb	4	100.00

Browse   A:\HWD1-10   Rec 1/6   View

---

⑫ Modify the query **HWD1-10.QBE** so that the **CITY** field is inserted between the **NAME** and **PAST** fields. The view skeleton should look like the following:

View				
hwd1-12	Hwd1-06-> NAME	Hwd1-06-> CITY	Hwd1-06-> PAST	Hwd1-06-> BALANCE

Save the query as **HWD1-12** and then do a screen dump of the **Query** design screen.

Continued . . .

⑬ Modify the query **HWD1-12** so that the only records of **HWD1-06** displayed are those of customers who live in Minneapolis (**Mpls**) and who have balances of $20 or more. Do a screen dump of the view query to show the file skeleton and then switch to **Browse** and do a screen dump of the records. Save the query as **HWD1-13**.

---

⑭ Modify the query **HWD1-13** so that the only records of database **HWD1-06** displayed are those of customers who live in Minneapolis or who have balances of $20 or more. Be sure to notice the difference between this exercise and Exercise 13. Do a screen dump of the view query and then switch to **Browse** and do a screen dump of the records. Save the query as **HWD1-14**.

---

⑮ Modify the query **HWD1-14** so that the only records of database **HWD1-06** displayed are those of customers who have balances between $18 and $40. Do a screen dump of the view query and then switch to **Browse** and do a screen dump of the records. Save the query as **HWD1-15**.

---

⑯ Create a report of all the records in **HWD1-06**. The output from the report should look like the following:

```
Katt Computer Company
Allen Johnson, President and CEO

The following is a report of all records to date of clients for whom we have
completed software projects.


                                                                  Page:  1
                                                              Date:  05/25/91

                                  Past
          Name      Balance   Due    Street              City      State  ZIP code

          Janice     $15.00    32    15 Softie Lane      Mpls        MN    55412
          Jill       $30.00    35    23 S Fourth St.     St. Paul    MN    55101
          Sara       $50.00     5    1 Perry Court       St. Paul    MN    55102
          Jack       $20.00    20    6 Bull Blvd.        Mpls        MN    55412
          Rama      $112.00     0    3 Renee Road        Mpls        MN    55412
          Barb      $100.00     4    625 First Ave.      St. Paul    MN    55112

          Number of clients listed:    6
Average number of days past due:  16
         Total amount owed us:  $327.00
```

Save the report form using the name **HWD1-16** and then print it.

CHAPTER ONE

⑰ Modify the report **HWD1-16** as shown below and then combine it with the query **HWD1-15** to produce a report that lists selected fields of the records for customers who have balances between $10 and $40. The output from the report should look like the following:

```
Katt Computer Company
Allen Johnson, President and CEO

The following is a report of all customers who have balances between $10 and
$40.

                                                      Page:  1
                                                      Date:  05/25/91

                                      Past
                  Name      Balance    Due    City
                  ==================================
                  Janice     $15.00    32     Mpls
                  Jill       $30.00    35     St. Paul
                  Jack       $20.00    20     Mpls

                Number of clients listed:          3
          Average number of days past due:        29
                     Total amount owed us:    $65.00
```

Save the report form using the name **HWD1-17** and then print it.

More Database Management

Objectives *After you have completed this chapter, you should be able to*

- Modify the **`CONFIG.DB`** file to customize the dBASE IV workspace.
- Create and modify dBASE IV catalogs.
- Issue dBASE IV commands from the dot prompt.
- Index the records of a database using the **`INDEX`** command.
- Use **`INDEX`** to create subtotals in reports.
- Sort the records of a database using the **`SORT`** command.
- Modify the structure of a database by deleting fields, reordering fields, changing the names of fields, changing field widths, and adding fields.

CHAPTER 2

- Clone databases to create new ones with the same or different structure and/or data.
- Create individualized form letters using *Mailmerge.*
- Create mailing labels from a database.
- Export selected records and fields of a database in a variety of file formats.
- Import data from a dBASE IV database into a Word Perfect document or a Lotus 1-2-3 worksheet.
- Import data from a Lotus 1-2-3 worksheet into a dBASE IV database.

Introduction

In this chapter we look at the dot prompt in detail and examine a number of advanced dBASE IV features including working with different catalogs, arranging data, modifying the structure of a database, and merging data into form letters. We will also work through examples where information is exchanged between dBASE IV, WordPerfect, and Lotus 1-2-3. This type of integration between computer programs is useful because it reduces the amount of data entry when the same information is to be used by different applications. In general, once data have been typed into the computer, they should never have to be typed again. If they are needed in a different form, you should be able to export the data from one file and import it into another file.

Customizing the dBASE IV Environment

dBASE IV stores many of its program defaults in a file called **CONFIG.DB**. To see the **CONFIG.DB** file on your system, do the following (begin from the DOS system prompt):

Keystroke	Action Resulting from Keystroke
A: ↵	Ensures that the default drive is A:.
TYPE C:\DBIV\CONFIG.DB ↵	
	Displays the contents of the dBASE IV configuration file. If the dBASE IV files on your computer are in a directory with a different name, use that name in place of **C:\DBIV**. A screen similar to the following will be displayed:

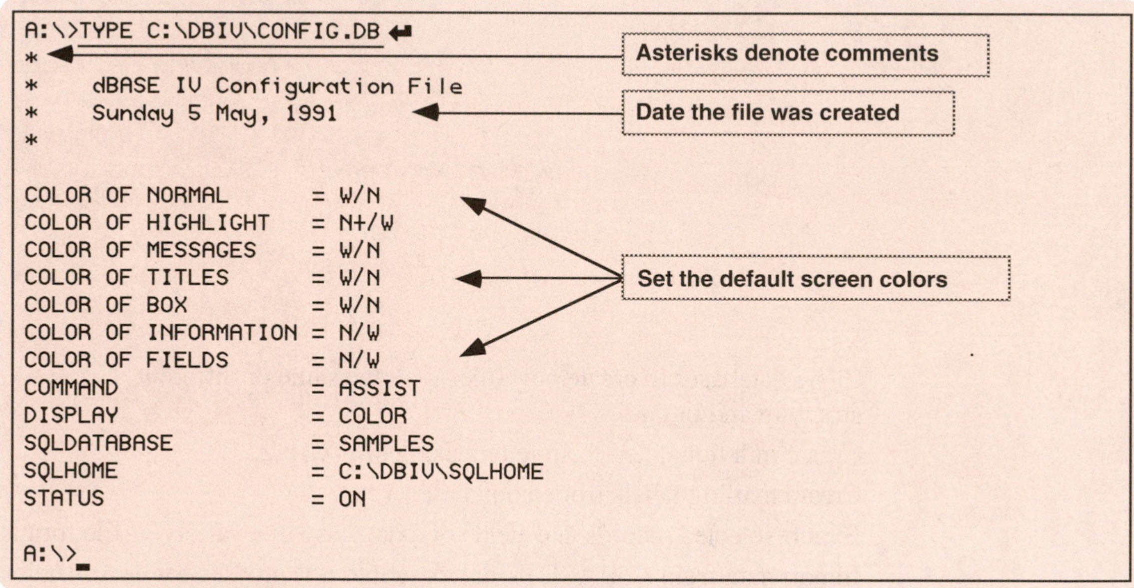

```
A:\>TYPE C:\DBIV\CONFIG.DB ↵
*
*     dBASE IV Configuration File
*     Sunday 5 May, 1991
*

COLOR OF NORMAL       = W/N
COLOR OF HIGHLIGHT    = N+/W
COLOR OF MESSAGES     = W/N
COLOR OF TITLES       = W/N
COLOR OF BOX          = W/N
COLOR OF INFORMATION  = N/W
COLOR OF FIELDS       = N/W
COMMAND               = ASSIST
DISPLAY               = COLOR
SQLDATABASE           = SAMPLES
SQLHOME               = C:\DBIV\SQLHOME
STATUS                = ON

A:\>_
```


In the above screen dump,

* (asterisks) denote comment lines. Any line beginning with an asterisk is considered a comment line and so is not processed. The comments are there to give the user extra information about the commands in the file.

COLOR OF NORMAL = W/N means that the color of normal text in the display will be white (**W**) on a black (**N**) background. The rest of the lines beginning with **COLOR OF** refer to the settings for the other parts of the screen. Note: In order to do the screen dumps for this book, the colors are all set to black (**N**) and white (**W**).

COMMAND = ASSIST means that the program will display the Control Center when it first starts (the word **ASSIST** refers to the name of the menu-driven interface of older versions of dBASE). Removing this command from the **CONFIG.DB** file will cause the dot prompt to appear when the program is started.

DISPLAY = COLOR means that a color monitor is being used.

SQLDATABASE = SAMPLES indicates the name of the SQL database that is activated when dBASE IV is started. SQL stands for *Structured Query Language,* which is an English-like data-handling language used to manipulate databases. SQL is beyond the scope of this book.

SQLHOME = C:\DBIV\SQLHOME indicates the directory path that contains the SQL database.

STATUS = ON means that the status bar usually will be displayed at the bottom of the screen. If you omit this command or if you change it to **STATUS = OFF**, the status bar will not be displayed while at the dot prompt.

There are many other commands that can be specified in the **CONFIG.DB** file. For more information, see the *dBASE IV Language Reference* for details or select the **Settings** option from the **Tools** menu and then tap **[F1]** to see help screens on the different settings. A brief explanation of some of the commands that you can include in a **CONFIG.DB** file is given below:

AUTOSAVE = ON specifies that changes to a record will be written to disk after each change is made rather than waiting until the record buffer is full or the database file is closed. For large databases, this slows down processing.

BELL = OFF specifies that no warning beep will sound when you enter an invalid data type or when you reach the end of an input area.

CATALOG = ADV_DBIV specifies that names of any files created or used will be added to the catalog called **ADV_DBIV**.

CENTURY = ON allows you to input four-digit numbers for years (e.g., 1776) when entering dates.

COLOR = OFF sets the display to monochrome. If you have a color monitor, the colors of the various parts of the screen can be set using special color codes. For example, **COLOR = GR+/R,W/R,GR+** would display regular text as yellow letters on a red background, highlighted text as white letters on a red background, and yellow for the border. For more information on setting colors, consult the *dBASE IV Language Reference*.

CLOCK = ON displays the clock while at the dot prompt.

DEFAULT = A sets the default disk drive to A:.

SHIFT-F2 = "Browse;" sets the **[Shift-F2]** key to execute the **Browse** command when it is pressed. If this command were in the **CONFIG.DB** file, tapping **[Shift-F2]** while at the dot prompt would type the word **Browse**, tap the equivalent of the **[Enter]** key (represented by the semicolon), and then display the **Browse** screen. You can use similar commands to change the definitions of **[F2]** through **[F10]**, **[Shift-F1]** through **[Shift-F9]**, and **[Ctrl-F1]** through **[Ctrl-F10]**. The **[F1]** key is reserved for *Help* and the **[Shift-F10]** and all the **[Alt]** key combinations are reserved for macros.

When you start dBASE IV it checks for a file called **CONFIG.DB** in the current directory (in all the examples we have used, this would be the **A:** directory). If it does not find such a file, it then looks for **CONFIG.DB** in the directory that contains the dBASE IV program (in all the examples we have used, this would be the **C:\DBIV** directory). If **CONFIG.DB** does not exist there, the program uses its internal default settings.

If you would like dBASE IV to use your own customized default settings each time it starts, you should create a **CONFIG.DB** file and store it on your *dBASE IV Data* diskette. That way, each time you start dBASE IV from the **A:\>** system prompt, it will use your **CONFIG.DB** file instead of the one on the hard drive.

Ways to make changes to the **CONFIG.DB** file include:

- Use **COPY CON** to create an entirely new **CONFIG.DB** file (see p. W202).
- Use WordPerfect to do the editing and then save the modified file as an ASCII file (use the *Text In/Out* feature—see p. W112–15).
- Use the program **DBSETUP** that came in the dBASE IV package.
- Use the **MODIFY COMMAND** command while at the dot prompt and edit the file.
- Use the *Edit* feature available from the **DOS Utilities** option of the **Tools** menu in the Control Center.

Set up a **CONFIG.DB** file on your *dBASE IV Data* diskette by doing the following (begin from DOS):

Keystroke	Action Resulting from Keystroke
A: ↵	Ensures that the default drive is A:.
C:\DBIV\DBASE ↵	Starts the dBASE IV program and displays the Control Center.
[Alt-T]	Opens the **Tools** menu.
D	Selects **DOS utilities** and displays its screen. The main part of the screen contains an alphabetical listing of the files on the diskette in drive A:. You may perform most DOS operations by selecting menu options or by typing a DOS command directly.

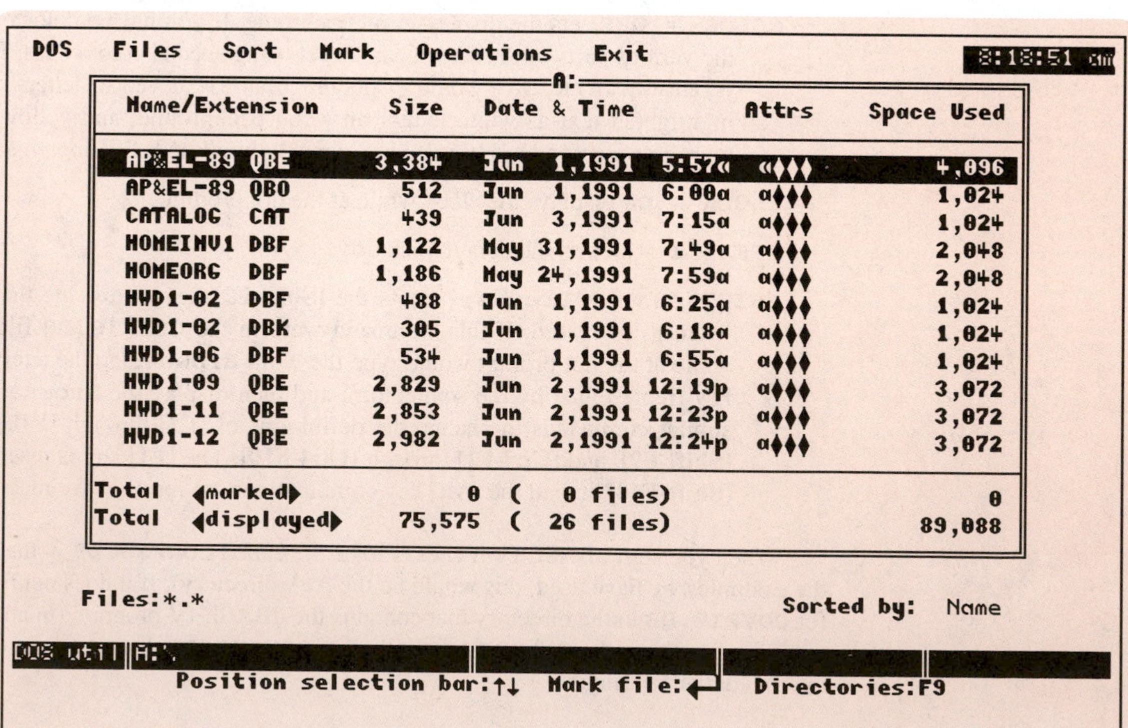

DOS Files Sort Mark Operations Exit 8:18:51 am
A:
Name/Extension Size Date & Time Attrs Space Used
AP&EL-89 QBE 3,384 Jun 1,1991 5:57a a♦♦♦ 4,096
AP&EL-89 QBO 512 Jun 1,1991 6:00a a♦♦♦ 1,024
CATALOG CAT 439 Jun 3,1991 7:15a a♦♦♦ 1,024
HOMEINV1 DBF 1,122 May 31,1991 7:49a a♦♦♦ 2,048
HOMEORG DBF 1,186 May 24,1991 7:59a a♦♦♦ 2,048
HWD1-02 DBF 488 Jun 1,1991 6:25a a♦♦♦ 1,024
HWD1-02 DBK 305 Jun 1,1991 6:18a a♦♦♦ 1,024
HWD1-06 DBF 534 Jun 1,1991 6:55a a♦♦♦ 1,024
HWD1-09 QBE 2,829 Jun 2,1991 12:19p a♦♦♦ 3,072
HWD1-11 QBE 2,853 Jun 2,1991 12:23p a♦♦♦ 3,072
HWD1-12 QBE 2,982 Jun 2,1991 12:24p a♦♦♦ 3,072
Total ◄marked► 0 (0 files) 0
Total ◄displayed► 75,575 (26 files) 89,088
Files:*.*
Sorted by: Name
DOS util A:\
Position selection bar:↑↓ Mark file:↵ Directories:F9

Continued . . .

Keystroke	Action Resulting from Keystroke
[Alt-D]	Selects **DOS** and displays its menu.

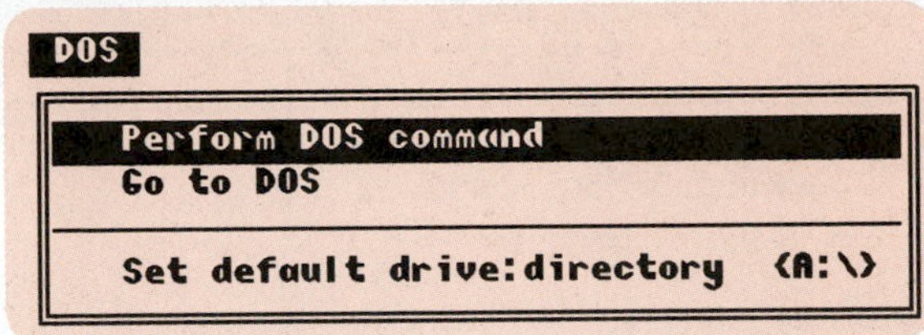

P Selects **`Perform DOS command`** and asks you to enter the DOS command you wish to execute.

`COPY C:\DBIV\CONFIG.DB A:` ↵

Copies the contents of the dBASE IV configuration file **`CONFIG.DB`** to the diskette in drive A:. If the dBASE IV files on your computer are in a directory with a different name, use that name in place of **`C:\DBIV`**.

[Enter] Displays the **`DOS utilities`** screen again.

[arrow] Use the **[arrow]** keys to highlight the file **`CONFIG.DB`** in the list of DOS files.

[Alt-O] Opens the **`Operations`** menu.

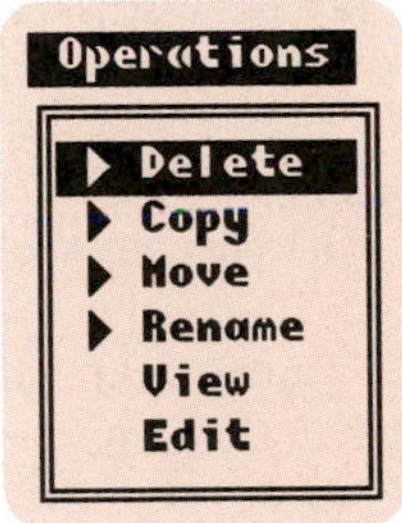

E Selects **`Edit`** and displays the highlighted file **`CONFIG.DB`** in the dBASE IV word processor so that it can be edited. The **`CONFIG.DB`** file on your computer is probably different from the one displayed below:

Continued . . .

Keystroke	Action Resulting from Keystroke

```
 Layout   Words   Go To   Print   Exit                                 8:22:38 am
*  <---------------------------------------- Cursor
*     dBASE IV Configuration File
*     Sunday 5 May, 1991
*

COLOR OF NORMAL        = W/N
COLOR OF HIGHLIGHT     = N+/W
COLOR OF MESSAGES      = W/N
COLOR OF TITLES        = W/N
COLOR OF BOX           = W/N
COLOR OF INFORMATION = N/W
COLOR OF FIELDS        = N/W
COMMAND                = ASSIST
DISPLAY                = COLOR
SQLDATABASE            = SAMPLES
SQLHOME                = C:\DBIV\SQLHOME
STATUS                 = ON

DOS util ||A:\CONFIG          ||Line:1 Col:1 ||          ||                Ins
```

Keystroke	Action Resulting from Keystroke
[arrow]	Use the [arrow] keys to move the cursor to the first column of the line that contains **COMMAND = ASSIST**. This tells dBASE IV to display the Control Center rather than the dot prompt when it starts up. Because we will concentrate on the dot prompt in this chapter we want to delete this line.
[Ctrl-Y]	Deletes the line. From now on, when you start dBASE IV from your *dBASE IV Data* diskette, it will go immediately to the dot prompt.
[arrow]	Use the [arrow] keys to move the cursor to the bottom of the file and then type the following:
CLOCK = ON ↵	Tells dBASE IV to display the clock in the upper right corner of the screen while at the dot prompt.
[Alt-E]	Opens the **Exit** menu.
S	Selects **Save changes and exit** and returns to the **DOS utilities** screen.
[Alt-E]	Opens the **Exit** menu of the **DOS utilities** screen.
E	Selects **Exit to Control Center**.
[Alt-E]	Opens the **Exit** menu of the Control Center.
Q	Selects **Quit to DOS**, exits dBASE IV, and returns to DOS.
DIR A:\CONFIG.* ↵	Displays the names of **CONFIG** files on the diskette in drive A:.

Continued . . .

Keystroke	Action Resulting from Keystroke

```
*** END RUN    dBASE IV

A:\>DIR A:\CONFIG.*↵

 Volume in drive A is ROBERTSON
 Volume Serial Number is 12E5-2041
 Directory of  A:\

CONFIG   DB        420 06-03-91    8:30a
CONFIG   BAK       424 06-03-91    8:30a
        2 File(s)     628736 bytes free

A:\>_
```

CONFIG.DB contains the new version of the file you just edited.

CONFIG.BAK contains the old version of the file (just in case you change your mind later).

TYPE CONFIG.DB ↵

Displays the contents of the newly modified **CONFIG.DB** file.

```
A:\>TYPE CONFIG.DB↵
*
*    dBASE IV Configuration File
*    Sunday 5 May, 1991
*

COLOR OF NORMAL        = W/N
COLOR OF HIGHLIGHT     = N+/W
COLOR OF MESSAGES      = W/N
COLOR OF TITLES        = W/N
COLOR OF BOX           = W/N
COLOR OF INFORMATION = N/W
COLOR OF FIELDS        = N/W
DISPLAY                = COLOR
SQLDATABASE            = SAMPLES
SQLHOME                = C:\DBIV\SQLHOME
STATUS                 = ON
CLOCK = ON

A:\>_
```

Because **COMMAND = ASSIST** is no longer in the file, when you start dBASE IV the dot prompt will be displayed instead of the Control Center. Also, because **CLOCK = ON** has been added to the file, the clock will appear in the upper right corner of the screen.

If you want to temporarily change one of the dBASE IV commands or functions, you can use the **Settings** option in the **Tools** menu of the Control Center or the **SET** command while at the dot prompt. For example:

- To change the default drive to B:, you would type **SET DEFAULT TO B ↵** at the dot prompt (don't do this now).

- To reassign the **[F2]** key so that tapping it switches you to the Browse screen, you would type **`SET FUNCTION F2 TO "Browse;"`** ↵ at the dot prompt (don't do this now).
- To open a catalog called ADV_DBIV so that when you use or create a new file its name is added to that catalog you would type **`SET CATALOG TO ADV_DBIV`** ↵ (don't do this now).

You may also use the **`SET`** command to display current configuration settings and to modify the settings by selecting options from menus. For example, if you type **`SET`** ↵ at the dot prompt (don't do this now), you will see the following screen:

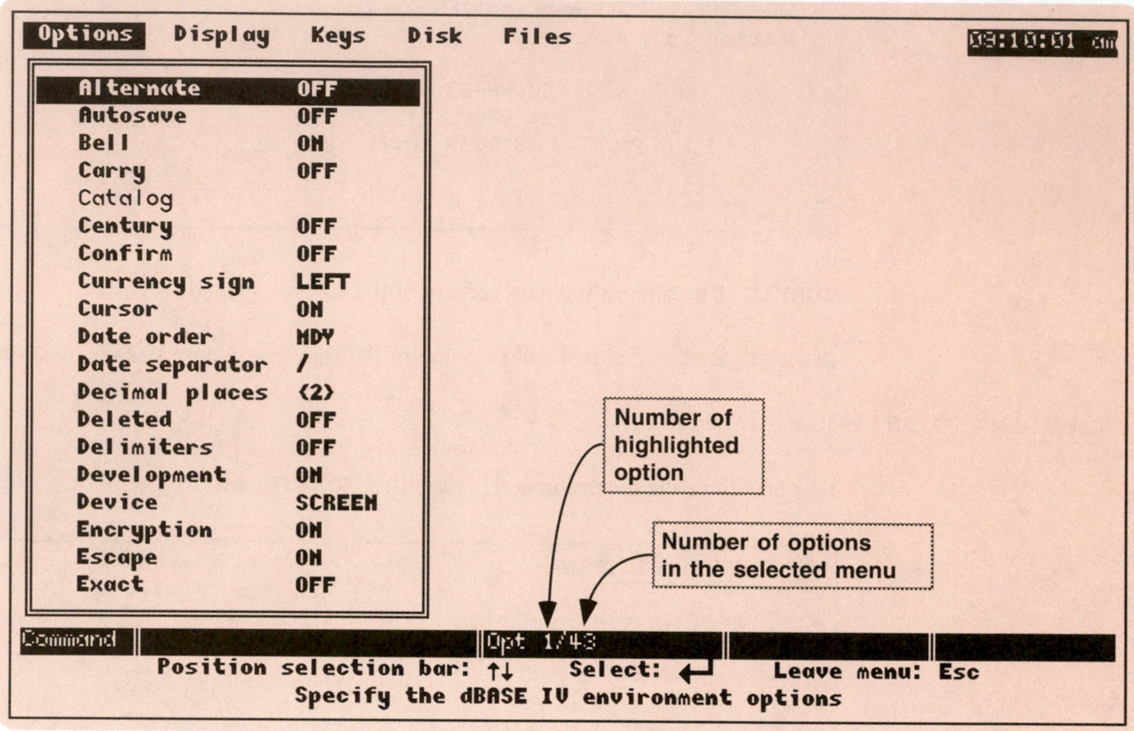

The five pull-down menus displayed along the top of the screen have the following functions:

`Options` allows you to change the dBASE IV environment in many ways. For example, the second item on the menu, **`Bell`** ... **`ON`** means that the bell option is turned on. To turn off that option, you would use the **[arrow keys]** to highlight it and then tap **[Enter]** to change **`ON`** to **`OFF`**. To turn it back on, you would tap **[Enter]** again. This is equivalent to **`BELL = ON`** in the **`CONFIG.DB`** file.

`Display` allows you to change the colors and highlights displayed on your monitor.

`Keys` allows you to reprogram the function keys. The **[F1]** key is reserved for the *Help* feature but the other nine keys can be programmed with commands that contain up to 33 characters each.

`Disk` allows you to define the default disk drive and the drive search path.

`Files` allows you to enter alternate file names for various operations such as printing, formatting, and indexing.

Be aware that changes you make using **`SET`** are in effect only until you **`QUIT`** dBASE IV or until you use a **`SET`** command to change them again. To fix the attributes so that they are set each time you access dBASE IV from DOS, you must enter the appropriate commands in the **`CONFIG.DB`** file.

Working with Catalogs

When the Control Center is displayed, only the names of those files that belong to the active catalog are shown in the panels. Catalogs function somewhat like DOS subdirectories in that they provide an easy method of organizing your files into logical groups. However, unlike DOS subdirectories, a catalog is simply a dBASE IV database that contains a list of file names and descriptions, it does not contain the data from the files. For this reason, file names may appear in as many different catalogs as you wish (but a file can reside in only one DOS subdirectory). Also, if you delete a file name from a catalog, the file whose name was deleted still remains on the disk (if you delete a file from a DOS subdirectory, the file itself, not just the name, is erased).

If you were working with a real home inventory database that contained information on all of your household goods, you might want to set up a catalog of files related to taxes (e.g., tax returns, accounting programs, correspondence with the IRS) and another related to insurance (e.g., insurance charges, correspondence with your insurance company). The home inventory database may be logically placed into both of these catalogs because some of the data may relate to both categories (e.g., your computer may be partially tax deductible because you use it in your business but it also may be insured against theft). dBASE IV would allow you to place the name of the home inventory database into both a tax and an insurance catalog so that when you are working on your taxes the database name would be visible in the **Data** panel and when you want to review your insurance portfolio the database name would be visible in that catalog. Note that if the name of the database is not in a catalog (and therefore not visible in the Control Center) you may still access it (we will do this later).

When you start dBASE IV and enter the Control Center, the last catalog you worked with is displayed as the active catalog. If you have not yet defined any catalogs, dBASE IV creates a catalog called **UNTITLED.CAT**. Through the **Catalog** menu of the Control Center you can switch to a different catalog, modify the name of a catalog, create or edit a one line description of a catalog, and add or delete a file name from a catalog. Because a catalog is simply a dBASE IV database with the file name extension **CAT** rather than **DBF**, you can delete a catalog simply by using the DOS **DEL** command to erase it as you would any other file.

You may have noticed how the panels in the Control Center are filling up with the names of the files you have created so far. You should have at least the following files listed:

CATALOG: A:\UNTITLED.CAT

Data	Queries	Forms	Reports	Labels	Applications
<create>	<create>	<create>	<create>	<create>	<create>
HOMEINV1	AP&EL-89		HWD1-16		
HOMEORG	HWD1-02		HWD1-17		
HWD1-02	HWD1-10		RPT1		
HWD1-06	HWD1-12		RPT2		
	HWD1-13				
	HWD1-14				
	HWD1-15				
	QUE1				

To help alleviate this name clutter, we will create two catalogs. The first, which we will call **BGN_DBIV.CAT**, will contain the names of all the files you created thus far. To create this catalog we will simply rename the catalog **UNTITLED.CAT**. The second catalog, which we will call **ADV_DBIV.CAT**, will contain the names of the files you create and use in this chapter on advanced dBASE IV features.

To create both catalogs, do the following (begin from DOS):

Keystroke	Action Resulting from Keystroke
A: ↵	Ensures that the A: drive is the default.
C:\DBIV\DBASE ↵	Starts the dBASE IV program and presents the dot prompt.

Continued . . .

Keystroke	Action Resulting from Keystroke
ASSIST ↵	Switches to the Control Center with the catalog **UNTITLED.CAT** in use.
[Alt-C]	Opens the **Catalog** menu.
M	Selects the **Modify catalog name** option, displays the name of the active catalog, and requests that you enter a name for the new catalog.

```
Catalog
  Use a different catalog
  Modify catalog name
  Enter new name for catalog: A:\UNTITLED.CAT
```

Keystroke	Action Resulting from Keystroke
[edit]	Employ the standard editing techniques to replace the current name **A:\UNTITLED.CAT** with the new name **A:\BGN_DBIV.CAT**.
[Enter]	Saves the new name for the catalog and returns to the Control Center. Notice that **A:\BGN_DBIV.CAT** is the active catalog and that all your files are listed in the panels.

Now, enter a one line description for the catalog.

Keystroke	Action Resulting from Keystroke
[Alt-C]	Opens the **Catalog** menu.
E	Selects the **Edit description of catalog** option and requests that you enter a one line description for the new catalog. Type the following description:

Files created while working through the first chapter on dBASE IV

Keystroke	Action Resulting from Keystroke
[Enter]	Accepts the description and returns to the Control Center. The description will be visible when if you select **Use a different catalog** from the **Catalog** menu and then highlight **\BGN_DBIV.CAT** in the picklist of catalog names (see below).

Create a new catalog for the files you will use and create in this chapter by doing the following:

Keystroke	Action Resulting from Keystroke
[Alt-C]	Opens the **Catalog** menu.
U	Selects the **Use a different catalog** option, and displays a picklist of catalog names on the right side of the screen.

Continued . . .

Keystroke	Action Resulting from Keystroke

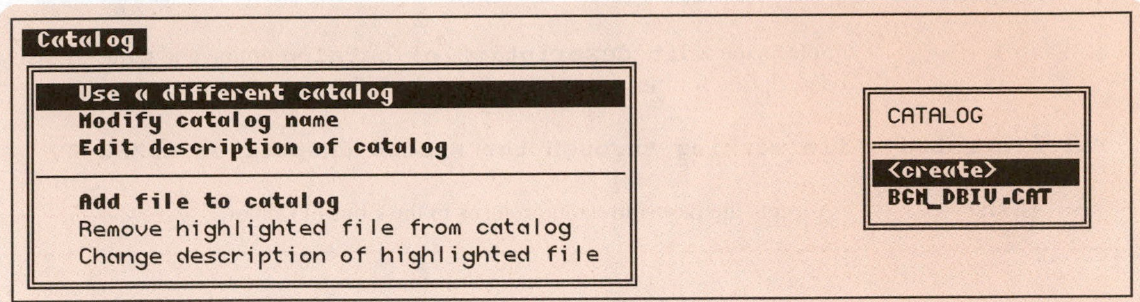

In the picklist on the right, the catalog you just created, **\BGN_DBIV.CAT**, is listed as well as **<create>** which will allow you to create a new catalog.

[arrow] Use the **[arrow]** keys, if necessary, to highlight **<create>**.

[Enter] Selects the highlighted option and asks for the name of the new catalog.

A:\ADV_DBIV.CAT

Specifies the name for the new catalog.

[Enter] Accepts the new name and returns to the Control Center. Notice that **A:\ADV_DBIV.CAT** now appears as the active catalog at the top of the screen but no files are listed in the panels because their names have not been added to the catalog.

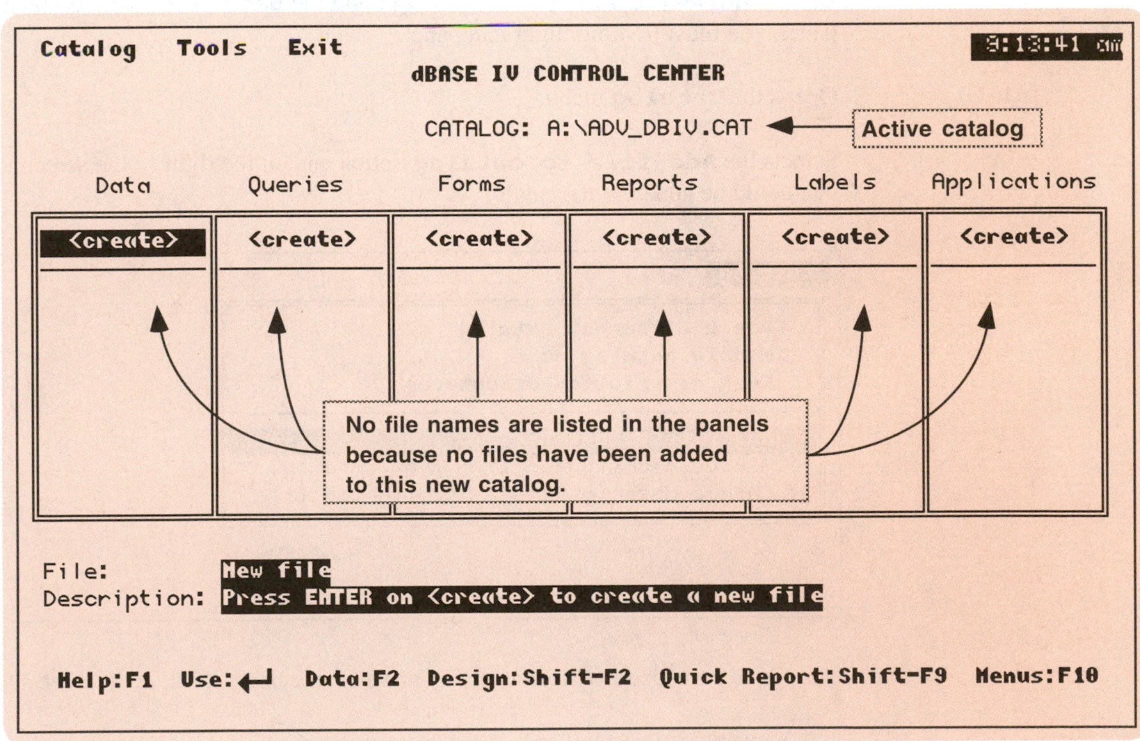

Enter a one line description for the catalog by doing the following:

Keystroke	Action Resulting from Keystroke
[Alt-C]	Opens the **Catalog** menu.
E	Selects the **Edit description of catalog** option and requests that you enter a one line description for the new catalog. Type the following:

Files created while working through the second chapter on dBASE IV

Keystroke	Action Resulting from Keystroke
[Enter]	Accepts the description and returns to the Control Center.

If you add **CATALOG = ADV_BGN** to the **CONFIG.DB** file, the names of files you use will always be automatically placed into the catalog **ADV_BGN**. If you want to have file names added to a different catalog you would select **Use a different catalog** from the **Catalog** menu and then highlight the one you want or enter **SET CATALOG TO <filename>** where **<filename>** is the name of the catalog you want to use. To stop adding names to the active catalog, enter **SET CATALOG OFF** at the dot prompt.

dBASE IV keeps track of the catalogs in a DOS file called **CATALOG.CAT**. If you do a directory listing of the file names with a **CAT** extension (e.g., **DIR *.CAT**), you will see the the catalog files just created as well as the catalog information file **CATALOG.CAT**.

Modifying Catalogs

The home inventory database will be needed for the work in this chapter. Add its name to the **ADV_DBIV** catalog by doing the following (begin from the Control Center):

Keystroke	Action Resulting from Keystroke
[arrow]	Use the **[arrow]** keys, if necessary, to highlight the **Data** panel. Before you can add a file name to a panel, you must first highlight that panel.
[Alt-C]	Opens the **Catalog** menu.
A	Selects the **Add file to catalog** option and, at the right of the screen, displays a picklist of files that could be added to the catalog.

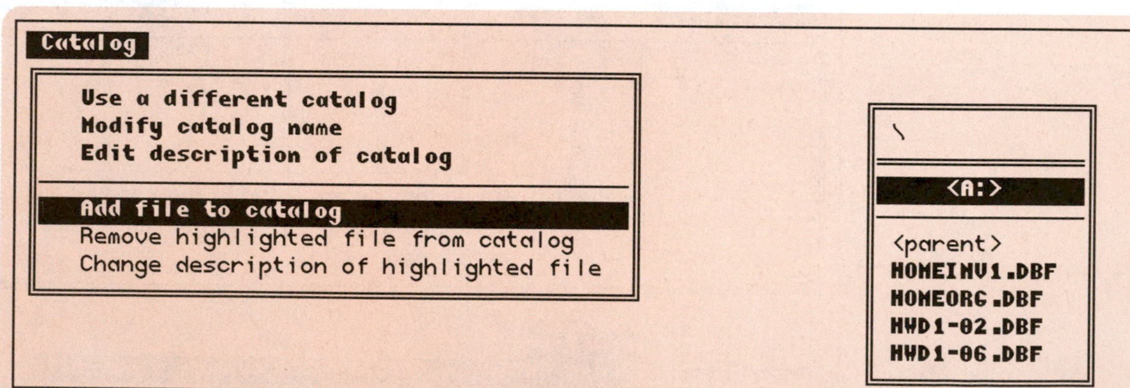

The file to be added may reside on any drive or directory. Look at the three sections of the display:

\ means you currently are in the root directory.

<A:> means you are looking at the diskette in drive A:. If you want to go to a different drive, highlight **<A:>** and tap **[Enter]**. A picklist of possible drives will be displayed so that you can select the one you want.

Continued . . .

Keystroke	Action Resulting from Keystroke
	<parent> allows you to move to the parent of the current subdirectory (you cannot do that now because you are in the root directory and that has no parent).
	HOMEINV1.DBF, **HOMEORG.DBF**, **HWD1-02.DBF**, and **HWD1-06.DBF** are the names of the database files in the current directory. You may pick for inclusion in the catalog any of the names listed.
[arrow]	Use the **[arrow]** keys to highlight **HOMEINV1.DBF**.
[Enter]	Selects the highlighted file and asks for a description for the file. Type the following:
Sample home inventory database ↵	
	Specifies the description and returns to the Control Center. Notice that the file **HOMEINV1** appears in the **Data** panel because it is now a part of the active catalog.

Remember that catalog files are simply standard dBASE IV database files with the file name extension **CAT** instead of **DBF**. They can be modified as shown above or by using the editing techniques we have described for other databases.

The Dot Prompt Revisited

You can accomplish many tasks using the menu-oriented Control Center but it does take a lot of time to navigate your way through menus and submenus. Experienced users prefer to use the command-oriented dot prompt where they can give instructions to the dBASE IV program directly using its own English-like language. At the dot prompt you may enter commands and accompanying options all at the same time.

To begin, exit the Control Center and access the dot prompt by doing the following:

Keystroke	Action Resulting from Keystroke
[Alt-E]	Opens the **Exit** menu.
E	Selects **Exit to dot prompt**, closes the Control Center, and displays the dot prompt and Status bar at the bottom of the screen (you can also access the dot prompt from the Control Center by tapping **[Esc]** and then **Y**). The Status bar is blank except for the word **Command** on the left side.

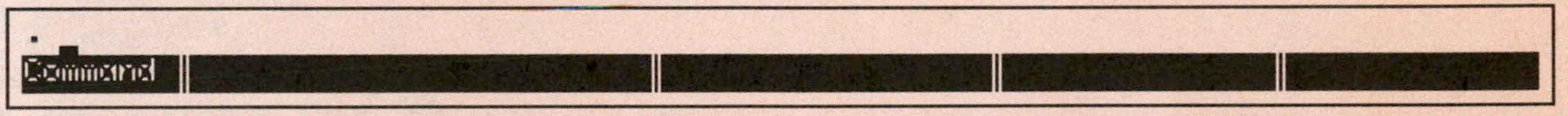

Before progressing further we should tell dBASE IV which database we want to use. We have done this before from the Control Center by highlighting the name of a database file, tapping **[Enter]**, and then **U** to indicate that we want to use the highlighted file. The equivalent dot prompt command is called **USE**. Tell dBASE IV that you want to use the database **HOMEINV1** by doing the following:

Keystroke	Action Resulting from Keystroke

USE A:\HOMEINV1.DBF ↵

Opens the database file **HOMEINV1** and makes its data available for processing. The path name **A:** is not needed if the file is located on the default drive and subdirectory and the extension **DBF** is only needed if the database name has an extension other than **DBF**. We include it just to be sure. The file specification appears on the Status bar along with the location of the record cursor in the file.

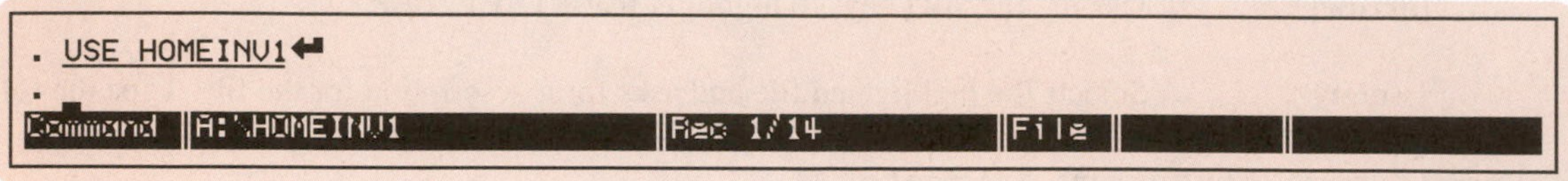

While at the dot prompt, the function keys are assigned the following tasks (these are completely different from the key assignments when a screen such as **Browse** is displayed):

[F1] Displays the main menu of the *Help* feature. Abbreviated directions for using *Help* are given at the bottom of the screen. *Help* is discussed in detail beginning on page D13.

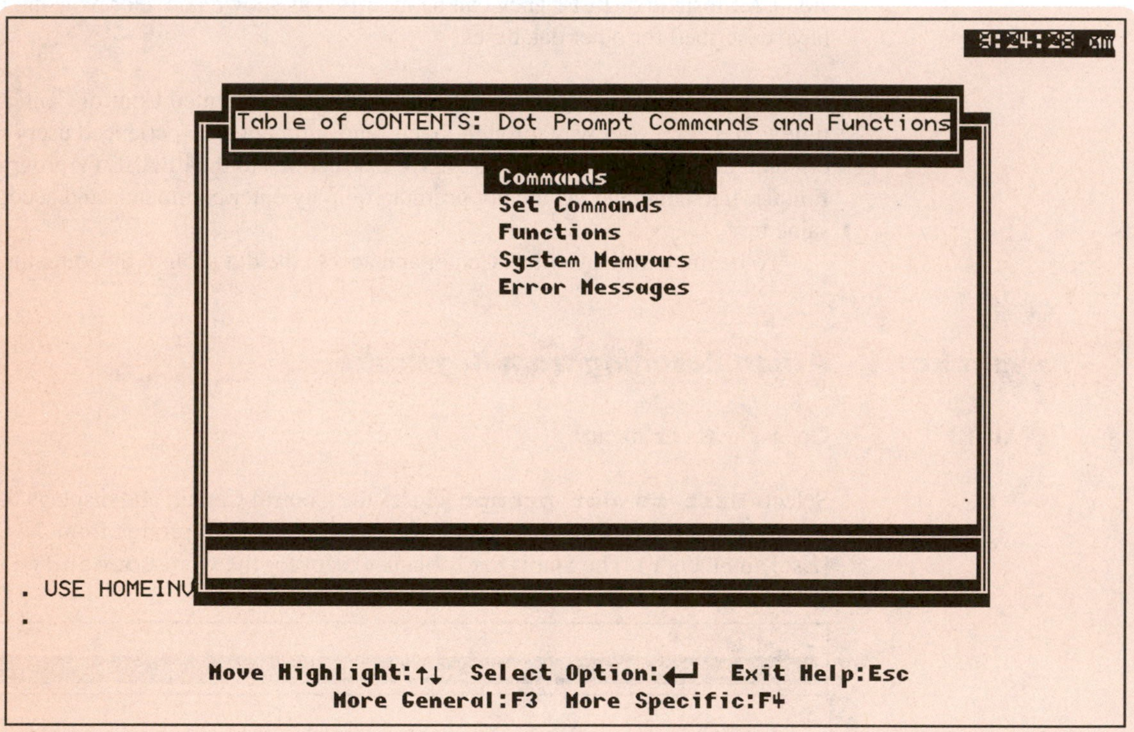

[Esc] Returns control to the dot prompt.

[F2] Types **assist** and switches to the Control Center. Notice that **HOMEINV1** is highlighted and appears above the open line in the **Data** panel.

Continued . . .

Keystroke	Action Resulting from Keystroke

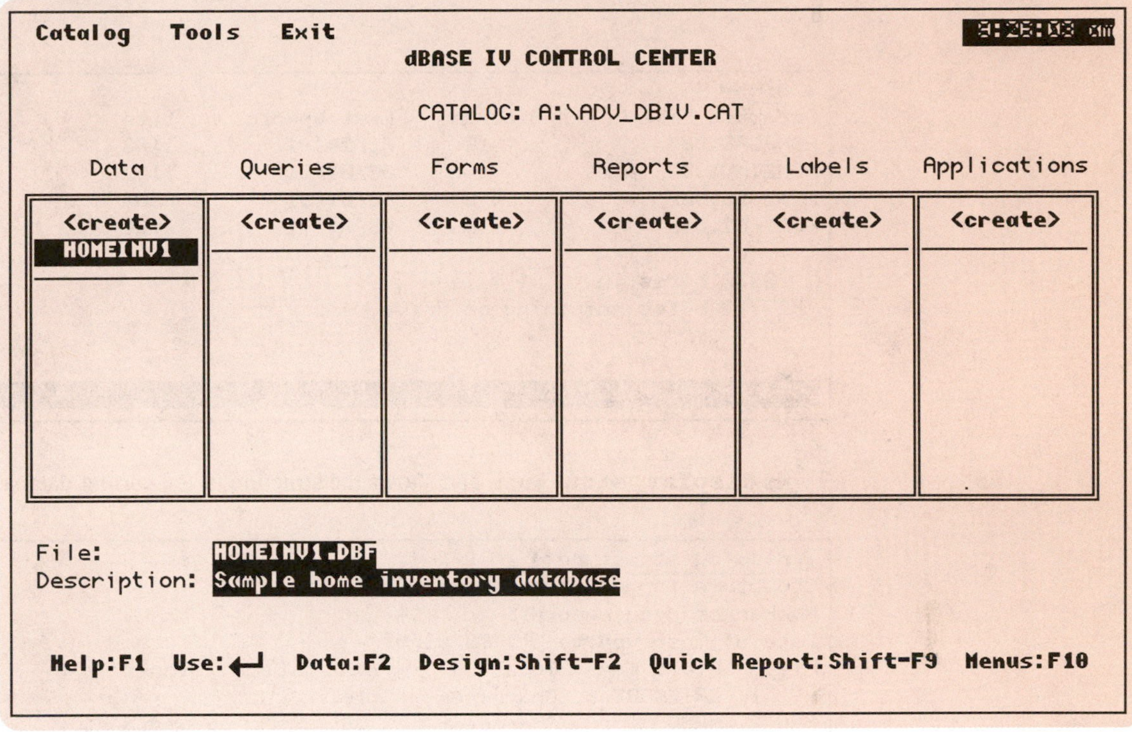

[Alt-E]	Opens the **`Exit`** menu.
`E`	Selects **`Exit to dot prompt`**, closes the Control Center, and displays the dot prompt and status bar at the bottom of the screen.
[F3]	Types **`list`** and displays a listing of all the records in the database. This command moves the record pointer to the end of the file (the Status bar displays the words **`Rec EOF/14`**).

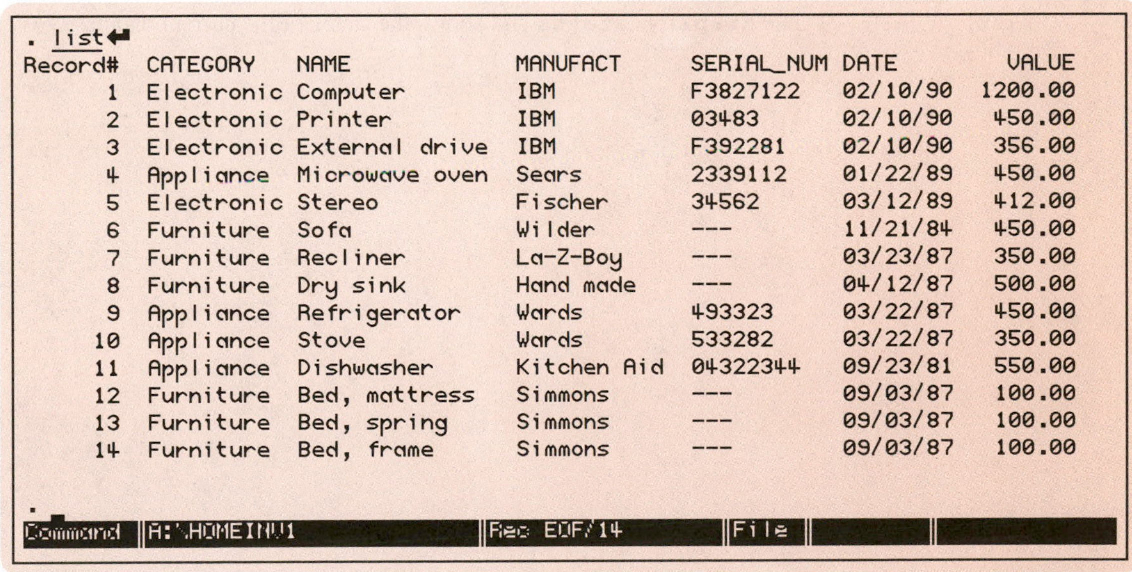

. list↵

Record#	CATEGORY	NAME	MANUFACT	SERIAL_NUM	DATE	VALUE
1	Electronic	Computer	IBM	F3827122	02/10/90	1200.00
2	Electronic	Printer	IBM	03483	02/10/90	450.00
3	Electronic	External drive	IBM	F392281	02/10/90	356.00
4	Appliance	Microwave oven	Sears	2339112	01/22/89	450.00
5	Electronic	Stereo	Fischer	34562	03/12/89	412.00
6	Furniture	Sofa	Wilder	---	11/21/84	450.00
7	Furniture	Recliner	La-Z-Boy	---	03/23/87	350.00
8	Furniture	Dry sink	Hand made	---	04/12/87	500.00
9	Appliance	Refrigerator	Wards	493323	03/22/87	450.00
10	Appliance	Stove	Wards	533282	03/22/87	350.00
11	Appliance	Dishwasher	Kitchen Aid	04322344	09/23/81	550.00
12	Furniture	Bed, mattress	Simmons	---	09/03/87	100.00
13	Furniture	Bed, spring	Simmons	---	09/03/87	100.00
14	Furniture	Bed, frame	Simmons	---	09/03/87	100.00

.

Command | A:\HOMEINV1 | Rec EOF/14 | File

Continued . . .

Keystroke	Action Resulting from Keystroke
[F4]	Types **dir** and displays a directory of database files (i.e., those with the extension **DBF**) on the default disk.

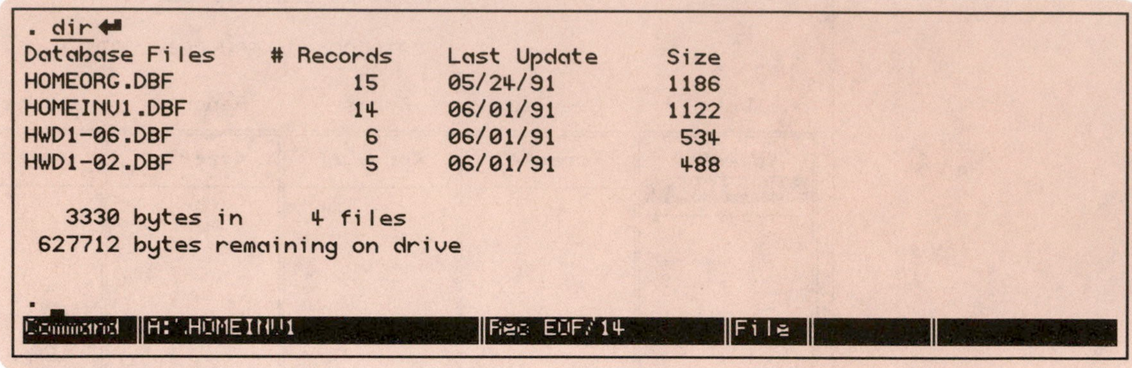

```
. dir
Database Files    # Records    Last Update     Size
HOMEORG.DBF             15     05/24/91        1186
HOMEINV1.DBF            14     06/01/91        1122
HWD1-06.DBF              6     06/01/91         534
HWD1-02.DBF              5     06/01/91         488

   3330 bytes in     4 files
 627712 bytes remaining on drive

.
Command  A:\HOMEINV1          Rec EOF/14        File
```

Keystroke	Action Resulting from Keystroke
[F5]	Types **display structure** and shows the structure of the current database.

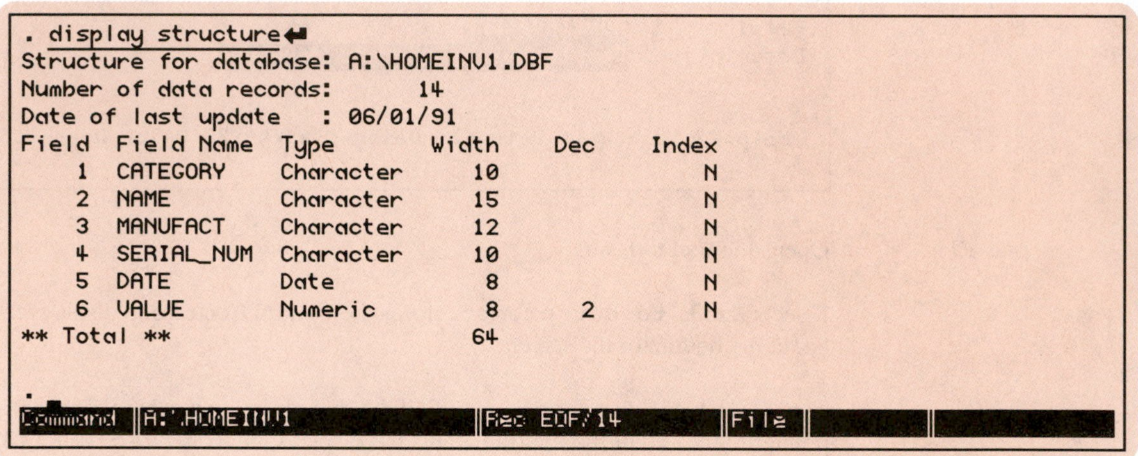

```
. display structure
Structure for database: A:\HOMEINV1.DBF
Number of data records:      14
Date of last update   : 06/01/91
Field  Field Name  Type       Width    Dec    Index
    1  CATEGORY    Character     10               N
    2  NAME        Character     15               N
    3  MANUFACT    Character     12               N
    4  SERIAL_NUM  Character     10               N
    5  DATE        Date           8               N
    6  VALUE       Numeric        8      2        N
** Total **                      64

.
Command  A:\HOMEINV1          Rec EOF/14        File
```

Keystroke	Action Resulting from Keystroke
[F6]	Types **display status** and shows the status of the current database.

Continued . . .

Keystroke | **Action Resulting from Keystroke**

```
                                                                  8:40:40 am
Currently Selected Database:
Select area:  1, Database in Use: A:\HOMEINV1.DBF   Alias: HOMEINV1

File search path:
OS Working drive/directory : A:\
Default disk drive: A:
Print destination:  PRN:
Margin =      0
Refresh count =     0
Reprocess count =    0
Number of files open =     3
Current work area =     1

ALTERNATE   - OFF  DELIMITERS - OFF  FULLPATH   - OFF  SAFETY     - ON
AUTOSAVE    - OFF  DESIGN     - ON   HEADING    - ON   SCOREBOARD - ON
BELL        - ON   DEVELOP    - ON   HELP       - ON   SPACE      - ON
CARRY       - OFF  DEVICE     - SCRN HISTORY    - ON   SQL        - OFF
CATALOG     - OFF  ECHO       - OFF  INSTRUCT   - ON   STATUS     - ON
CENTURY     - OFF  ENCRYPTION - ON   INTENSITY  - ON   STEP       - OFF
CONFIRM     - OFF  ESCAPE     - ON   LOCK       - ON   TALK       - ON
Press any key to continue...
Command  ║A:\HOMEINV1           ║Rec EOF/14      ║File ║
```

The display command shows information one screenful at a time. The words **`Press any key to continue...`** at the bottom of the screen mean that tapping a key will show the next screenful of information.

[Enter] Continues the display of the status of the current database.

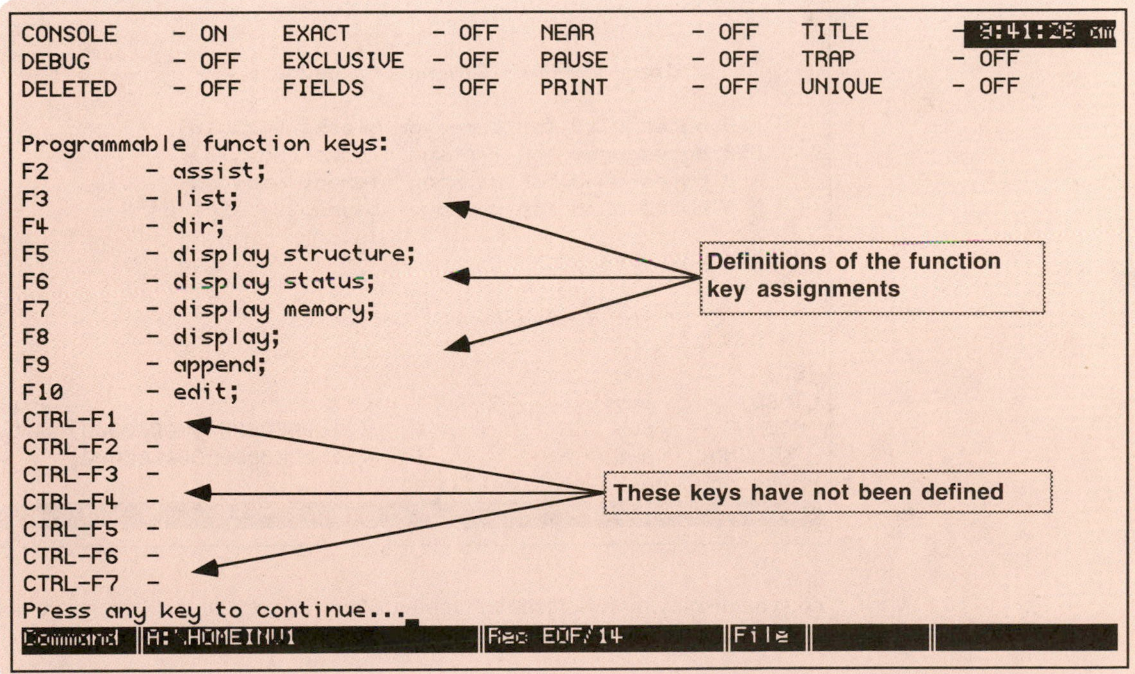

```
CONSOLE     - ON   EXACT      - OFF  NEAR       - OFF  TITLE      - 8:41:28 am
DEBUG       - OFF  EXCLUSIVE  - OFF  PAUSE      - OFF  TRAP       - OFF
DELETED     - OFF  FIELDS     - OFF  PRINT      - OFF  UNIQUE     - OFF

Programmable function keys:
F2         - assist;
F3         - list;
F4         - dir;
F5         - display structure;
F6         - display status;
F7         - display memory;
F8         - display;
F9         - append;
F10        - edit;
CTRL-F1  -
CTRL-F2  -
CTRL-F3  -
CTRL-F4  -
CTRL-F5  -
CTRL-F6  -
CTRL-F7  -
Press any key to continue...
Command  ║A:\HOMEINV1           ║Rec EOF/14      ║File ║
```

Definitions of the function key assignments
These keys have not been defined

[Enter] Continues the display of the status of the current database.

Continued . . .

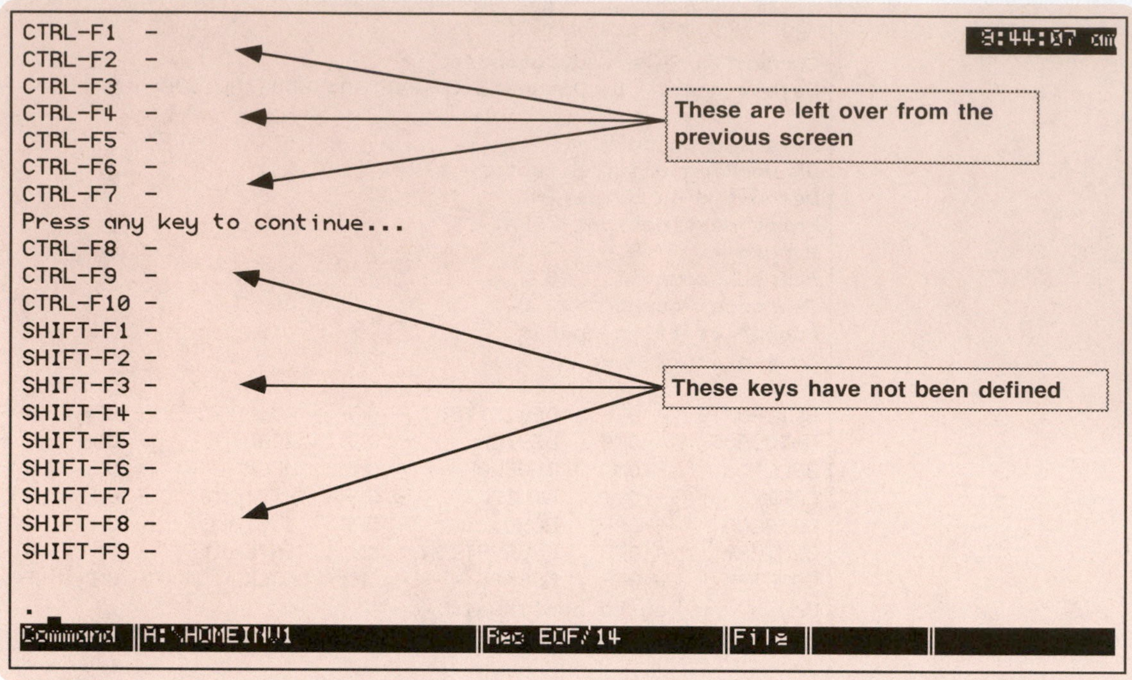

[F7] Types **display memory** and gives a status report on the computer's memory.

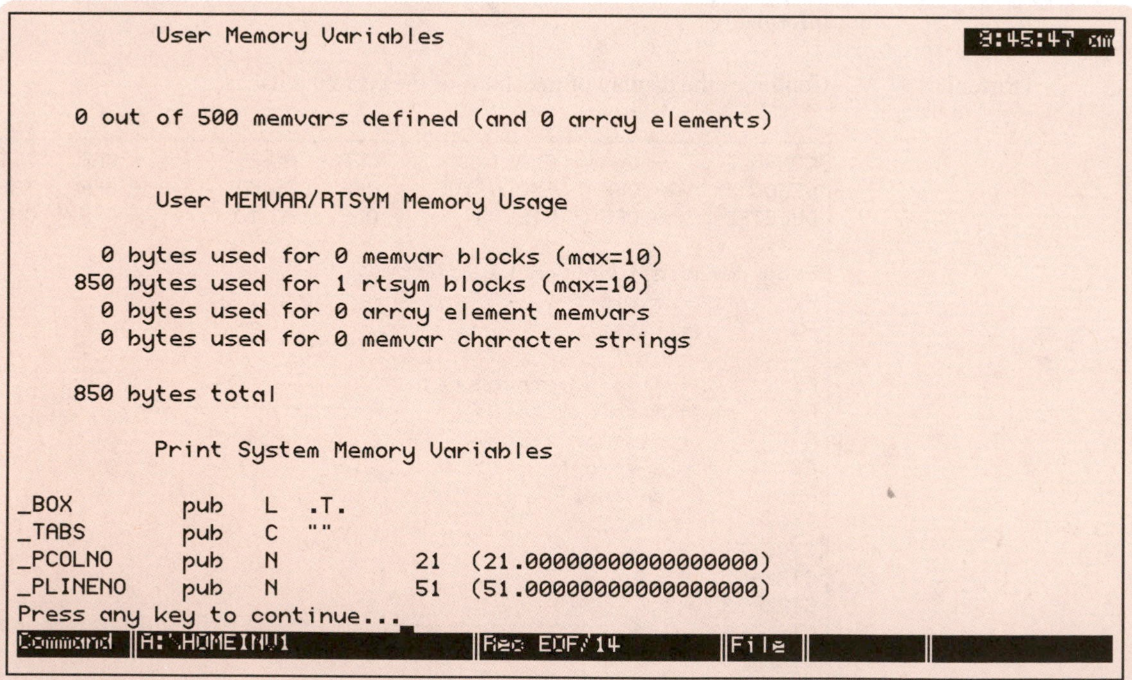

You can display more screens by tapping a key. The rest of the screens are not pertinent to our discussion so there is no need to display them. To abort the command, use the **[Esc]** key.

[Esc] Aborts the command and returns to the dot prompt.

Continued . . .

Keystroke	Action Resulting from Keystroke
	The record pointer is probably pointing at the end of the file. Move it to the first record in the file by using the **GOTO** command.
GOTO 1 ↵	Moves the pointer to the first record of the file.

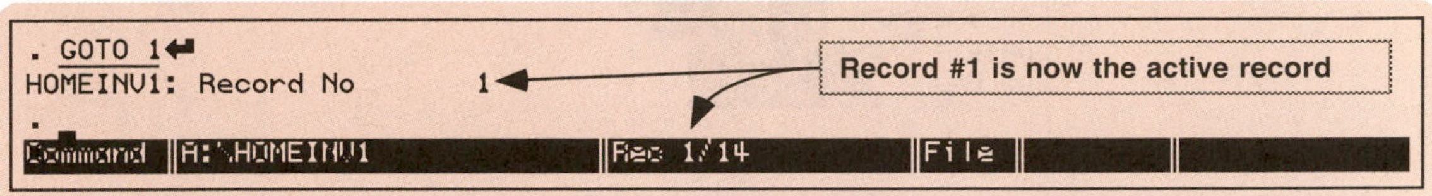

Keystroke	Action Resulting from Keystroke
[F8]	Types **display** and displays the contents of the active record. Because you just sent the pointer to the top of the file the display should look like the following:

Keystroke	Action Resulting from Keystroke
[F9]	Types **append** and displays the Edit screen with the record pointer at the end of the file. This allows you to append records to the end of the database.

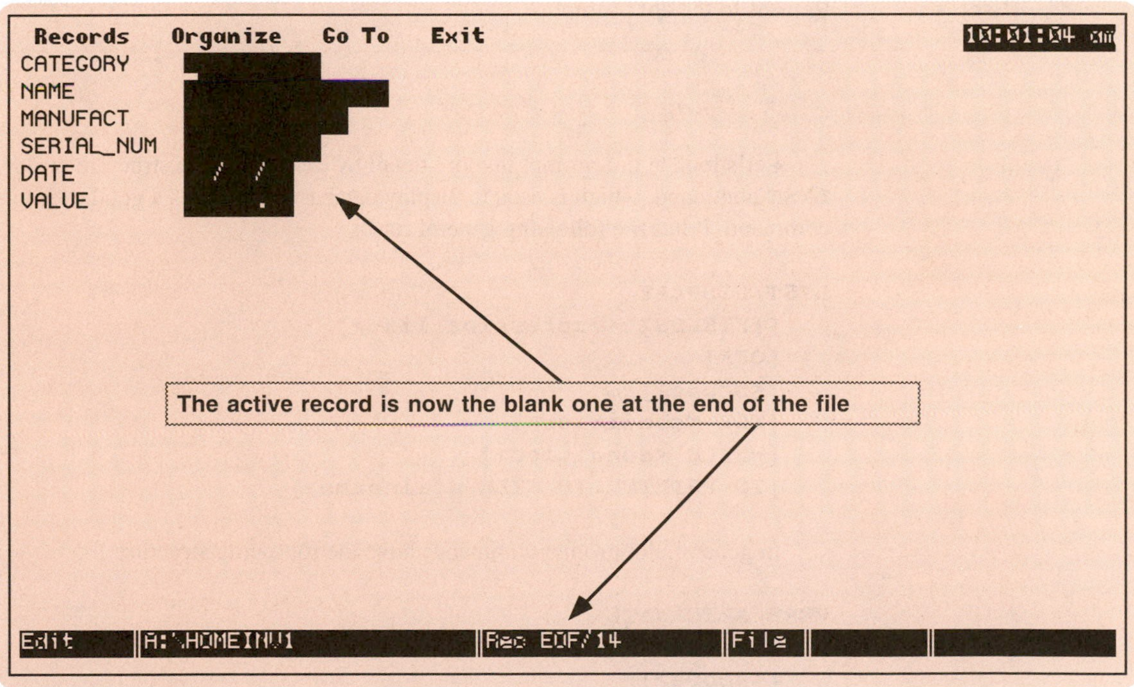

Keystroke	Action Resulting from Keystroke
[Esc]	Returns to the dot prompt.
[F10]	Types **edit** and displays the active record in the Edit screen. This should be the last record of the database. You now may edit the record as you wish.

Continued . . .

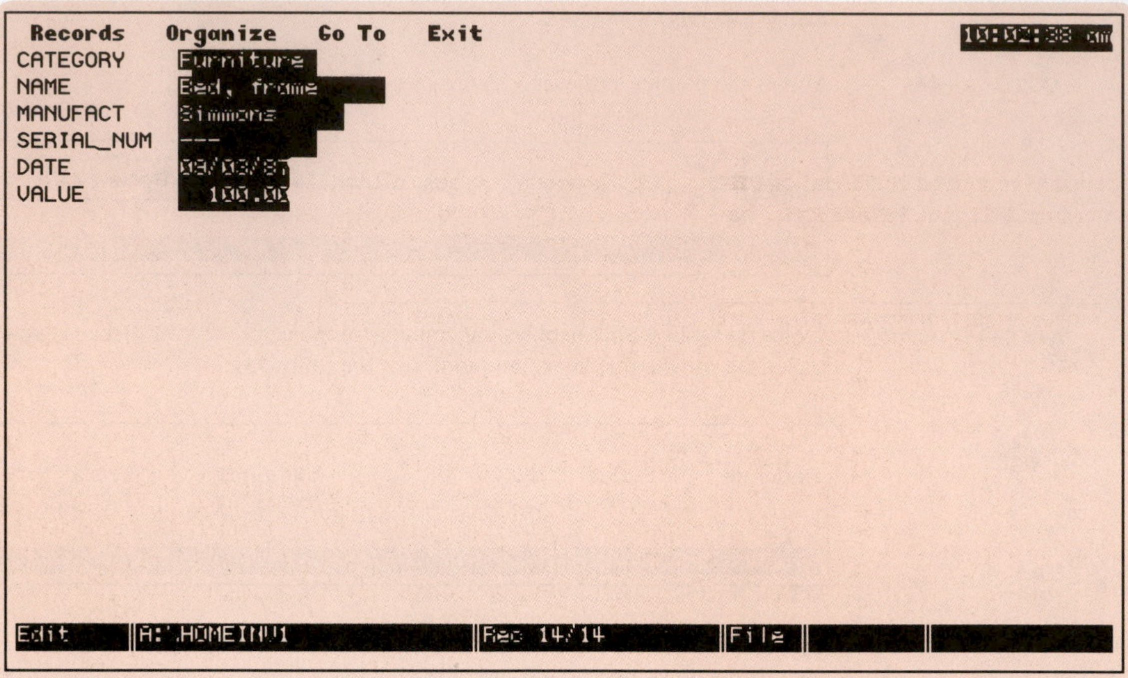

[Esc] Returns to the dot prompt.

• Using the Dot Prompt •

Let's look at dot prompt in more detail by examining the structure of dot prompt commands. The **LIST** command, which is used to display database records, is a good example of a typical dBASE IV command. It has the following general form:

```
LIST/DISPLAY
    [[FIELDS] <expression list>]
    [OFF]
    [<scope>]
    [FOR <condition>]
    [WHILE <condition>]
    [TO PRINTER/TO FILE <filename>]
```

In general, dot prompt commands have the following structure:

```
VERB/ALTERNATE
    [<expression list>]
    [<scope>]
    [FOR <condition>]
    [WHILE <condition>]
```

where

VERB is the actual command (like in English, the verb denotes the action that is to take place). For example, the word **LIST** is considered the verb in the **LIST** command.

/ separates choices for alternates. For example, **LIST/DISPLAY** means that you may use the verb **LIST** (to display records without pausing when the screen fills up) or **DISPLAY** (to display records one screen at a time).

[ ] indicates optional items—you may put them in or not as necessity dictates. For example, the **[OFF]** option will instruct dBASE IV to refrain from displaying record numbers when records are listed. Thus, **LIST** would display records with record numbers whereas **LIST OFF** would display records without record numbers.

< > indicates items that must be specified by you. For example, **<filename>** means that you must supply the name of a file. Thus, to list records to a file called **TEMP.TXT** you would enter **LIST TO FILE TEMP.TXT**.

? in the place of a required file name will cause dBASE IV to display a picklist of file names that may choose from (this is useful when you cannot remember the exact name of a file). This is not an option with the **LIST** command.

scope is an optional indicator that tells which records the command will affect. You may want to use scope when working with a large database where searching all the records might take a long time. There are four scope key words:

RECORD <n> specifies that the command is to affect a single record whose record number is **n**.

NEXT <n> specifies that the command is to affect the next **n** records.

ALL specifies that the command is to affect all records in the database.

REST specifies that the command is to affect all the records from the current one to the end of the file.

For example, **LIST NEXT 5** would list the next five records in the database.

expression list is usually a list of fields that are to be affected. For example, **LIST FIELDS NAME,DATE** would list data from the **NAME** and **DATE** fields only.

FOR allows the command to operate only on those records that meet a specified condition. For example, **LIST FOR CATEGORY = "Electronic"** would display only records that have **Electronic** in the **CATEGORY** field.

condition is an expression that limits the records affected by the command. These are like the Query conditions discussed on pages D65–72.

WHILE allows the command to operate while a particular condition is true. For example, **LIST WHILE RECNO() =< 10** would display records beginning at the current one and through record number 10 (i.e., it will display records while the record number is less than or equal to 10). **LIST WHILE CATEGORY = "Electronic"** would display records that have **Electronic** in the **CATEGORY** field while that condition is true. This is different from **FOR** because **FOR** will scan the entire database looking for the proper records but **WHILE** will stop scanning the database as soon as the condition becomes false.

To show the speed and ease of using the dot prompt, we will carry out some of the same operations that we did using the Control Center and the menus in Chapter 1 but this time we will use the equivalent dot prompt command. Begin the following from the dot prompt.

Close a File and Save Any Modifications to Disk

Keystroke	Action Resulting from Keystroke
CLOSE ALL ↵	Closes all open files and writes modifications to disk. The Status bar should be blank, except for the word **Command** on the left side and perhaps **Num** (the num lock toggle key indicator) and/or **Caps** (the caps lock toggle key indicator) and/or **Ins** (the insert toggle key indicator).

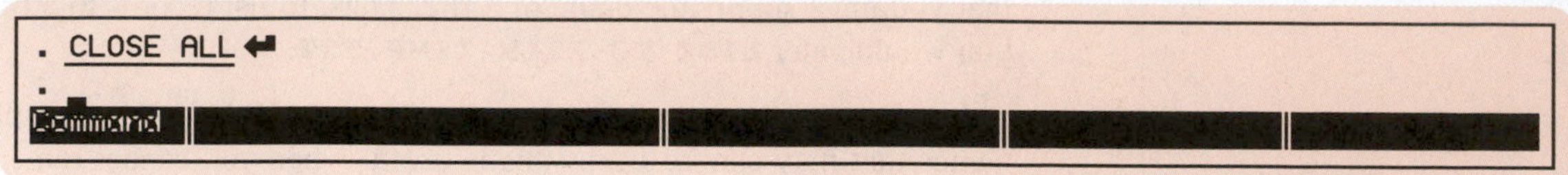

Open a File for Use

Keystroke	Action Resulting from Keystroke
USE ? ↵	Displays a picklist of database files that you can open.

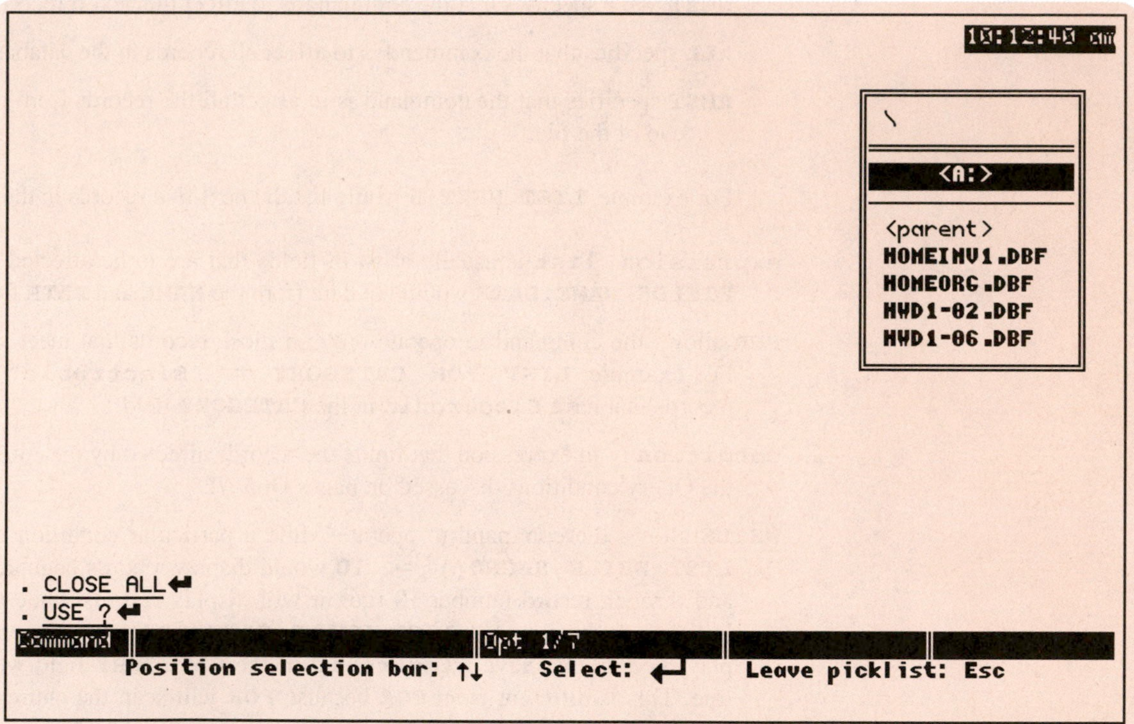

Keystroke	Action Resulting from Keystroke
[arrow]	Use the **[arrow]** keys to select **HOMEINV1.DBF**.
[Enter]	Opens the highlighted file and displays related information on the Status bar.

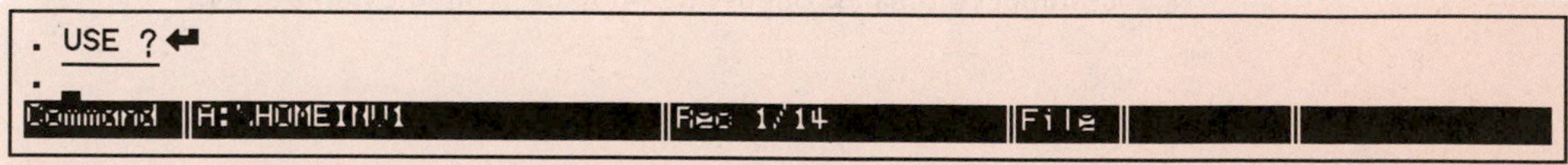

Note that you could have bypassed the picklist by typing **USE A:\HOMEINV1.DBF** instead of **USE ?**.

Append Records to the End of a Database

Keystroke	Action Resulting from Keystroke
APPEND ↵	Moves the record pointer to the end of the file and displays a blank **Edit** screen so that you can add new data.

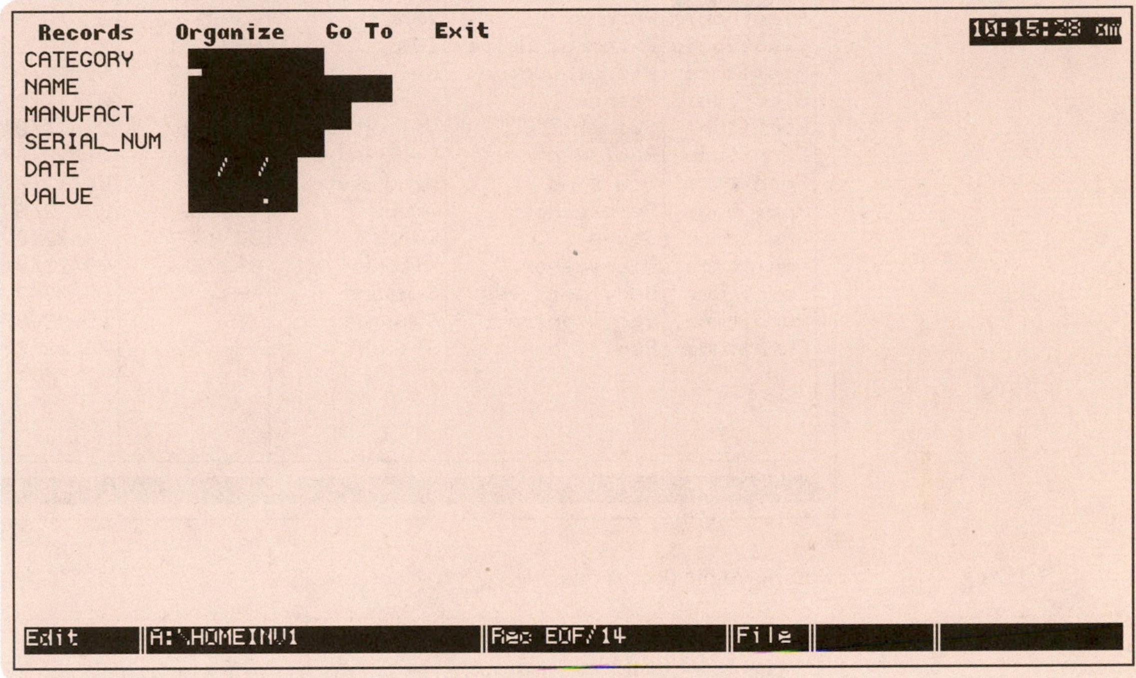

Keystroke	Action Resulting from Keystroke
[Esc]	Aborts the append process and returns to the dot prompt.

Switch to Browse to View, Edit, or Append Records

Keystroke	Action Resulting from Keystroke
BROWSE ↵	Switches to **Browse**.
[PageUp]	Moves the pointer to the top of the screen.

Continued . . .

Keystroke	Action Resulting from Keystroke

Records   Organize   Fields   Go To   Exit   10:18:34 am

CATEGORY	NAME	MANUFACT	SERIAL_NUM	DATE	VALUE
Electronic	Computer	IBM	F3827122	02/10/90	1200.00
Electronic	Printer	IBM	03483	02/10/90	450.00
Electronic	External drive	IBM	F392281	02/10/90	356.00
Appliance	Microwave oven	Sears	2339112	01/22/89	450.00
Electronic	Stereo	Fischer	34562	03/12/89	412.00
Furniture	Sofa	Wilder	---	11/21/84	450.00
Furniture	Recliner	La-Z-Boy	---	03/23/87	350.00
Furniture	Dry sink	Hand made	---	04/12/87	500.00
Appliance	Refrigerator	Wards	493323	03/22/87	450.00
Appliance	Stove	Wards	533282	03/22/87	350.00
Appliance	Dishwasher	Kitchen Aid	04322344	09/23/81	550.00
Furniture	Bed, mattress	Simmons	---	09/03/87	100.00
Furniture	Bed, spring	Simmons	---	09/03/87	100.00
Furniture	Bed, frame	Simmons	---	09/03/87	100.00

Browse | A:\HOMEINV1 | Rec 1/14 | File

[Esc] Returns to the dot prompt.

Display Specific Records We can use the **DISPLAY** or **LIST** command. The command **DISPLAY** without any options shows only the active record. **DISPLAY ALL** and **LIST** show all the records of the database except that **DISPLAY** shows them one screenful at a time whereas **LIST** does not pause when the screen fills up. If you add search conditions to the ends of the commands then only those records that match the conditions will be displayed.

Keystroke	Action Resulting from Keystroke
DISPLAY ↵	Displays the active record only.

```
. DISPLAY ↵
Record#  CATEGORY   NAME              MANUFACT     SERIAL_NUM DATE         VALUE
      1  Electronic Computer          IBM          F3827122   02/10/90   1200.00
.
Command | A:\HOMEINV1 | Rec 1/14 | File
```

DISPLAY ALL ↵ Displays all the records of the database.

LIST ↵ Displays all the records of the database. Because the **HOMEINV1** database has less than 22 records (the maximum number of records that can be displayed on the screen) **LIST** and **DISPLAY ALL** have the same effect.

LIST FOR NAME = "Dry sink" ↵

Displays all records that contain **Dry sink** in the **NAME** field.

Continued . . .

Keystroke	Action Resulting from Keystroke

LIST FOR DATE = {02/10/90} ↵

Displays all records that contain **02/10/90** in the **DATE** field (note that dates must be enclosed within braces **{ }** rather than quotation marks).

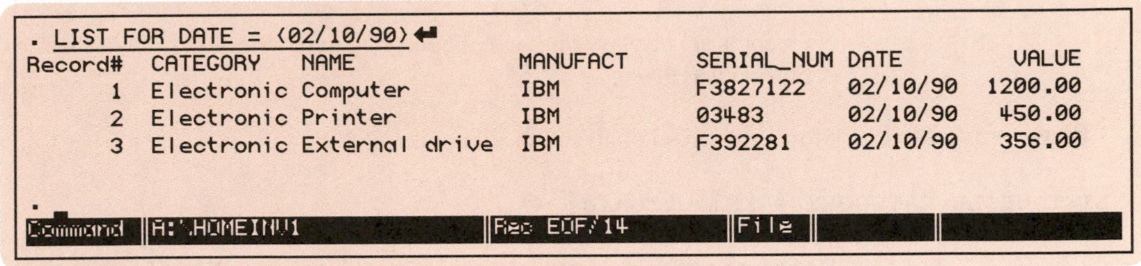

```
. LIST FOR DATE = {02/10/90}↵
Record#  CATEGORY   NAME            MANUFACT    SERIAL_NUM DATE         VALUE
      1  Electronic Computer        IBM         F3827122   02/10/90   1200.00
      2  Electronic Printer         IBM         03483      02/10/90    450.00
      3  Electronic External drive  IBM         F392281    02/10/90    356.00

.
Command ||A:\HOMEINV1          ||Rec EOF/14      ||File ||
```

GOTO 5 ↵ Makes record number 5 active.

LIST NEXT 5 ↵ Displays the next 5 records, beginning at the active record.

```
. GOTO 5↵
HOMEINV1: Record No       5
. LIST NEXT 5↵
Record#  CATEGORY   NAME            MANUFACT    SERIAL_NUM DATE         VALUE
      5  Electronic Stereo          Fischer     34562      03/12/89    412.00
      6  Furniture  Sofa            Wilder      ---        11/21/84    450.00
      7  Furniture  Recliner        La-Z-Boy    ---        03/23/87    350.00
      8  Furniture  Dry sink        Hand made   ---        04/12/87    500.00
      9  Appliance  Refrigerator    Wards       493323     03/22/87    450.00

.
Command ||A:\HOMEINV1          ||Rec 9/14        ||File ||
```

LIST FOR CATEGORY = "Electronic" ↵

Beginning at the active record displays only records that have **Electronic** in the **CATEGORY** field.

```
. LIST FOR CATEGORY = "Electronic"↵
Record#  CATEGORY   NAME            MANUFACT    SERIAL_NUM DATE         VALUE
      1  Electronic Computer        IBM         F3827122   02/10/90   1200.00
      2  Electronic Printer         IBM         03483      02/10/90    450.00
      3  Electronic External drive  IBM         F392281    02/10/90    356.00
      5  Electronic Stereo          Fischer     34562      03/12/89    412.00

.
Command ||A:\HOMEINV1          ||Rec EOF/14      ||File ||
```

LIST WHILE CATEGORY = "Electronic" ↵

Beginning at the active record, displays records that have **Electronic** in the **CATEGORY** field. Unlike **FOR**, however, as soon as a record is reached that does not have **Electronic** in the **CATEGORY** field, the list process stops.

Continued . . .

Keystroke	Action Resulting from Keystroke

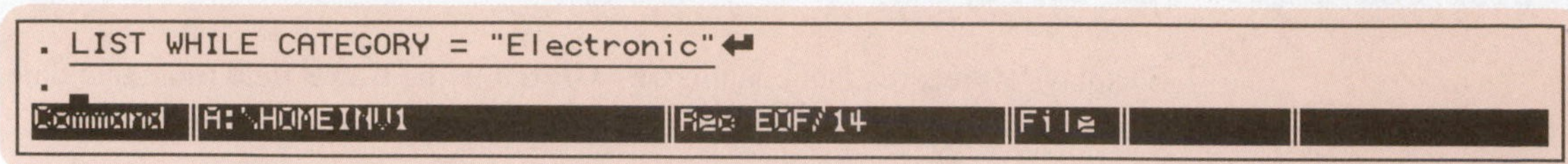
```
. LIST WHILE CATEGORY = "Electronic"
.
Command ║A:\HOMEINV1          ║Rec EOF/14      ║File ║
```

No records are displayed because the record pointer was at the end of the file (a blank record) when the command was given.

GOTO TOP ↵ Moves the record pointer to the top of the file.

LIST WHILE CATEGORY = "Electronic" ↵

Beginning at the active record, displays records that have **Electronic** in the **CATEGORY** field. As soon as a record is reached that does not have **Electronic** in the **CATEGORY** field, the list process stops.

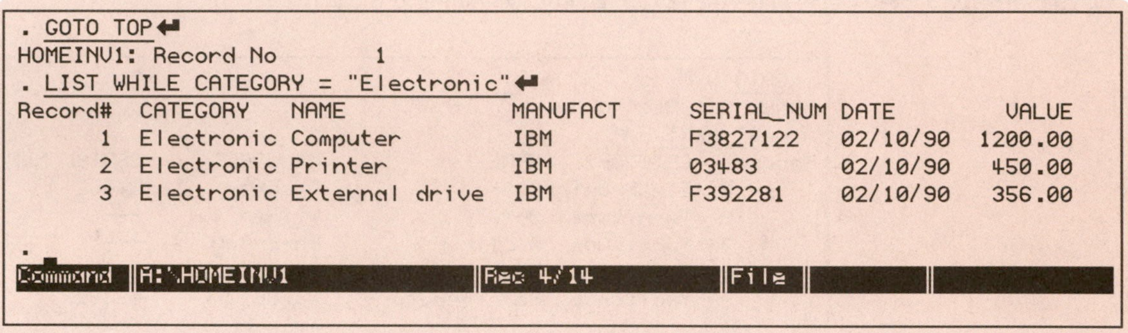
```
. GOTO TOP
HOMEINV1: Record No       1
. LIST WHILE CATEGORY = "Electronic"
Record#  CATEGORY   NAME               MANUFACT      SERIAL_NUM DATE        VALUE
      1  Electronic Computer           IBM           F3827122   02/10/90  1200.00
      2  Electronic Printer            IBM           03483      02/10/90   450.00
      3  Electronic External drive     IBM           F392281    02/10/90   356.00

.
Command ║A:\HOMEINV1          ║Rec 4/14        ║File ║
```

The first three records are listed because they have **Electronic** in the **CATEGORY** field. The listing stops when record 4 is checked because it does not have **Electronic** in the **CATEGORY** field. Compare this **LIST WHILE** command with the corresponding **LIST FOR** command.

Create a View Query

Keystroke	Action Resulting from Keystroke
CREATE VIEW TEMP ↵	Switches to the query design screen and creates a new query called **TEMP**.
[Esc]	Asks if you want to abandon the operation.
Y	Abandons the view query and returns to the dot prompt.

Modify a View Query

Keystroke	Action Resulting from Keystroke
MODIFY VIEW QUE1 ↵	
	Switches to the query design screen called **QUE1**.

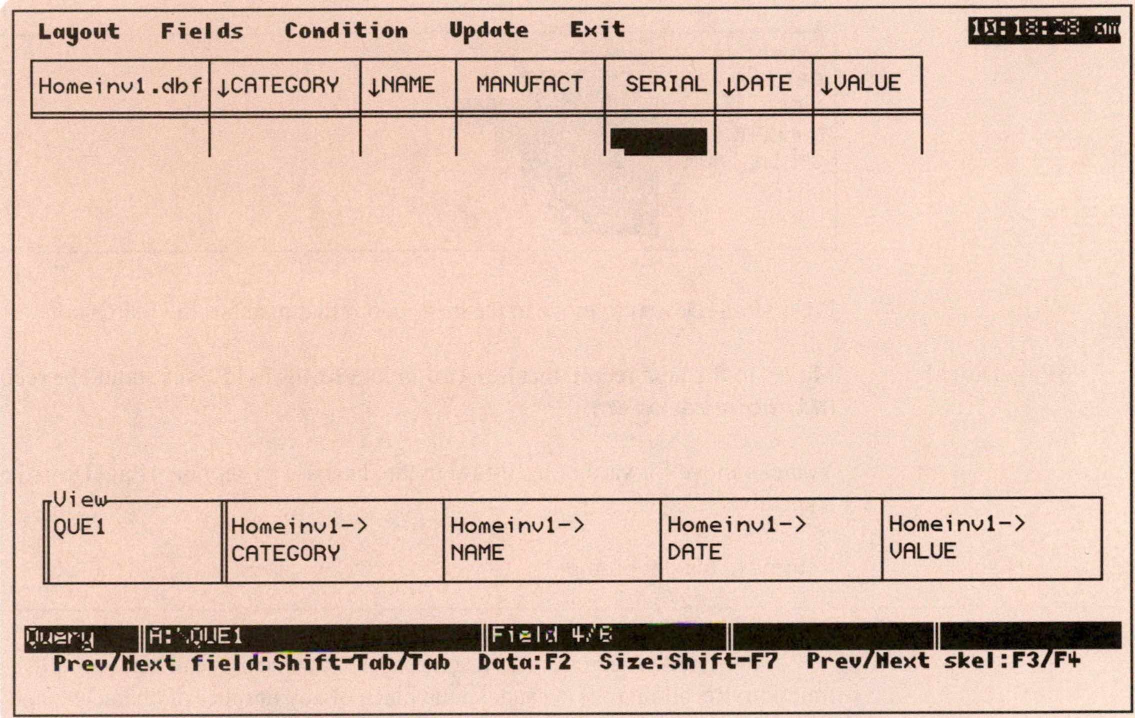

[Esc]	Asks if you want to abandon the operation.
Y	Abandons the view query and returns to the dot prompt.

Use Filters Use filters to select only those records that meet specific conditions so that they can be displayed, edited, or printed.

Keystroke	Action Resulting from Keystroke
LIST FOR VALUE = 450 ↵	
	Displays all records that have **450** in their **VALUE** field.

```
. LIST FOR VALUE = 450 ↵
Record#  CATEGORY    NAME            MANUFACT      SERIAL_NUM DATE        VALUE
      2  Electronic  Printer         IBM           03483      02/10/90   450.00
      4  Appliance   Microwave oven  Sears         2339112    01/22/89   450.00
      6  Furniture   Sofa            Wilder        ---        11/21/84   450.00
      9  Appliance   Refrigerator    Wards         493323     03/22/87   450.00

.
Command  A:\HOMEINV1             Rec EOF/14         File
```

LIST displays the records and then returns to the dot prompt. If you want to locate the records that match the search criteria and then edit them you would use the **EDIT** command.

Keystroke	Action Resulting from Keystroke

EDIT FOR VALUE = 450 ↵

Displays in the Edit screen the first record that has **450** in its **VALUE** field.

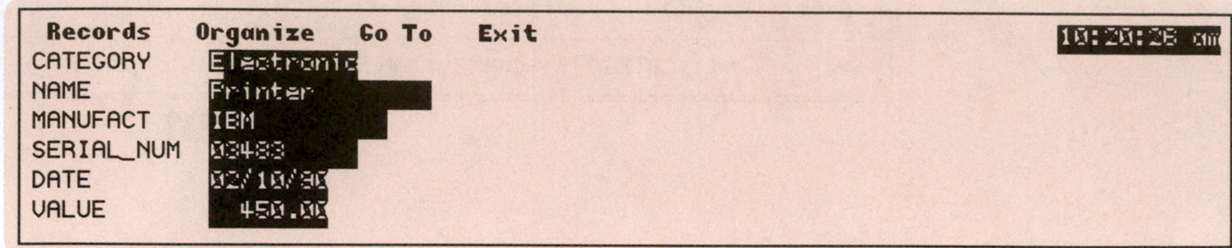

Press **[PageDown]** to move to the next record that matches the search condition.

[PageDown] Moves to the next record that has **450** in its **VALUE** field. This should be record number 4 (**Microwave oven**).

You can move forward or backward in the database by tapping **[PageDown]** and **[PageUp]**, respectively.

[Esc] Returns to the dot prompt.

Pattern match searches that use the ***** and **?** wildcards can be accomplished by using the **LIKE** function. Recall that the ***** can take the place of any number of characters and the **?** can take the place of a single character. The general form of this function is

LIKE (<pattern>,<expression>)

where

<pattern> is the string you want to search for (e.g., **Bed***).

<expression> is the field name or variable that you want to compare the pattern to (e.g., the field called **NAME**).

For example, the following would display all records that have the word **Bed** as the first three characters in the **NAME** field.

Keystroke	Action Resulting from Keystroke

LIST FOR LIKE("Bed*",NAME) ↵

Displays records that have **Bed** as the first three characters in the **NAME** field.

Continued . . .

Keystroke	Action Resulting from Keystroke

```
. LIST FOR LIKE("Bed*",NAME)↵
Record#  CATEGORY   NAME            MANUFACT     SERIAL_NUM DATE         VALUE
     12  Furniture  Bed, mattress   Simmons      ---        09/03/87    100.00
     13  Furniture  Bed, spring     Simmons      ---        09/03/87    100.00
     14  Furniture  Bed, frame      Simmons      ---        09/03/87    100.00

.
Command  A:\HOMEINV1               Rec EOF/14          File
```

This is exactly the same result as we had using Queries (see p. D71).

More complex search conditions can be specified by using multiple conditions. Recall that we created AND searches using Queries by placing multiple conditions on the same line in the File skeleton while the OR searches were indicated by placing the conditions on different lines. At the dot prompt, we can accomplish the same thing by using the **.AND.** and **.OR.** operators. For example, the following command will display the records for appliances that have a value over $400:

Keystroke	Action Resulting from Keystroke

LIST FOR CATEGORY = "Appliance" .AND. VALUE > 400 ↵

Displays all records that meet both conditions.

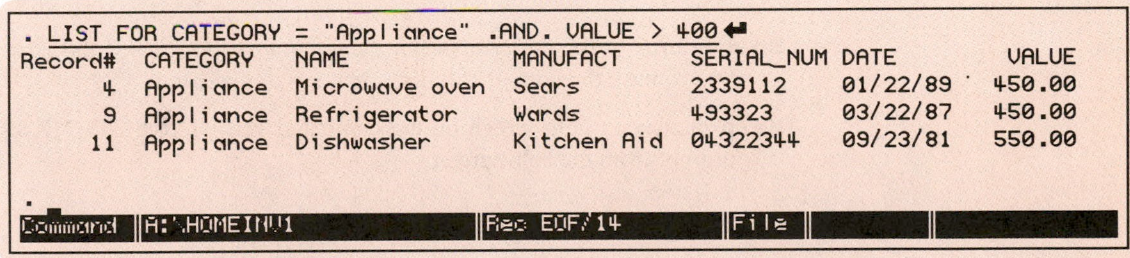

```
. LIST FOR CATEGORY = "Appliance" .AND. VALUE > 400↵
Record#  CATEGORY   NAME            MANUFACT     SERIAL_NUM DATE         VALUE
      4  Appliance  Microwave oven  Sears        2339112    01/22/89    450.00
      9  Appliance  Refrigerator    Wards        493323     03/22/87    450.00
     11  Appliance  Dishwasher      Kitchen Aid  04322344   09/23/81    550.00

.
Command  A:\HOMEINV1               Rec EOF/14          File
```

This is exactly the same result we obtained using Queries (see p. D70).

The following condition would select records that were purchased in 1989 (i.e., the date has to be between January 1, 1989 and December 31, 1989, inclusive).

Keystroke	Action Resulting from Keystroke

LIST FOR DATE >= {01/01/89} .AND. DATE <= {12/31/89}↵

Displays all records that meet both conditions.

Continued . . .

Keystroke	Action Resulting from Keystroke

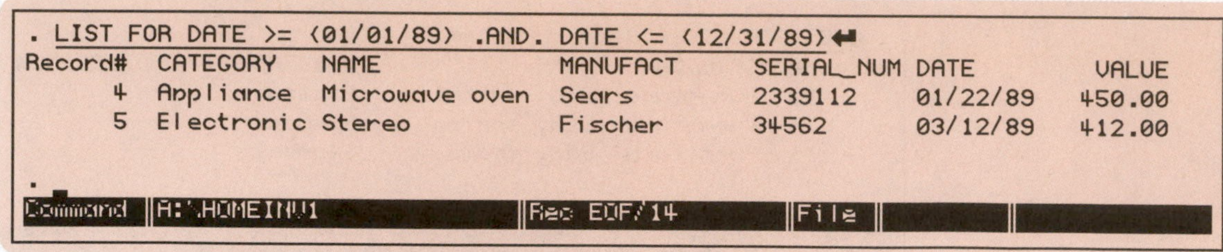

This is exactly the same result as we had using Queries (see p. D70).

Notice that each condition is complete. If you try to take a shortcut by omitting the second **DATE** in the command, an error message will appear.

LIST FOR DATE >= {01/01/89} .AND. <= {12/31/89} ↵

Causes a beep and an error message to appear.

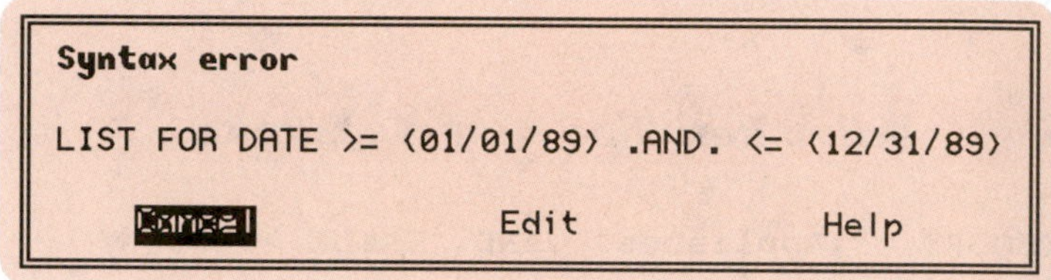

Cancel allows you to abort the command and return to the dot prompt with the command line blank.

Edit returns to the dot prompt but the command that caused the error is displayed so that you can use the normal editing techniques to modify it.

Help displays a help screen on the command verb (**LIST**). Tap **[Esc]** to return to the dot prompt from the help screen.

C Selects **Cancel** and returns to the dot prompt.

We can use an OR condition in a **LIST** command to select records for appliances or any other items whose value is over $400. This would be exactly the same command as with the previous AND condition but with the **.OR.** operator instead of the **.AND.** operator. You could retype the entire command or use the **[Up arrow]** key to cycle through your previous commands until you reach the one you want. Let's use this method.

Keystroke	Action Resulting from Keystroke
[Up arrow]	Displays the previous command at the dot prompt. This probably is the incorrect **LIST** command: **LIST FOR DATE >= {01/01/89} .AND. <= {12/31/89}**
[Up arrow]	Displays the next command in the buffer. This probably is the correct **LIST** command for finding 1989 records: **LIST FOR DATE >= {01/01/89} .AND. DATE <= {12/31/89}**
[Up arrow]	Displays the next command in the buffer. This probably is the **LIST** command for finding expensive appliances: **LIST FOR CATEGORY = "Appliance" .AND. VALUE > 400**

Continued . . .

Keystroke	Action Resulting from Keystroke
[Edit]	Use the normal editing techniques to change the word **AND** to **OR**.
[Enter]	Executes the command.

```
. LIST FOR CATEGORY = "Appliance" .OR. VALUE > 400
Record#  CATEGORY   NAME           MANUFACT     SERIAL_NUM DATE        VALUE
      1  Electronic Computer       IBM          F3827122   02/10/90  1200.00
      2  Electronic Printer        IBM          03483      02/10/90   450.00
      4  Appliance  Microwave oven Sears        2339112    01/22/89   450.00
      5  Electronic Stereo         Fischer      34562      03/12/89   412.00
      6  Furniture  Sofa           Wilder       ---        11/21/84   450.00
      8  Furniture  Dry sink       Hand made    ---        04/12/87   500.00
      9  Appliance  Refrigerator   Wards        493323     03/22/87   450.00
     10  Appliance  Stove          Wards        533282     03/22/87   350.00
     11  Appliance  Dishwasher     Kitchen Aid  04322344   09/23/81   550.00

.
Command ║A:\HOMEINV1            ║Rec EOF/14        ║File ║
```

This is the same result we obtained using Queries on page D71.

The AND and OR conditions can be combined to form complex conditions. For example, on page D72 we created a query called **AP&EL-89** to filter out all records except those of appliances or electronics that were purchased in 1989. To accomplish the same task at the dot prompt, you would instruct dBASE IV to **LIST** every record **FOR** which the **CATEGORY** is **Electronic AND** the **DATE** is greater than or equal to **01/01/89 AND** the **DATE** is less than or equal to **12/31/89**, **OR** the **CATEGORY** is **Appliance AND** the **DATE** is greater than or equal to **01/01/89 AND** the **DATE** is less than or equal to **12/31/89**. The command is displayed below. It is longer than will fit on one line of the screen and so as you type it some of the command will scroll off the left side of the command line. However, after you press **[Enter]** the entire command will be displayed. Be careful when you type this in, it is easy to make a typing error. If you make a mistake you can always edit it.

```
LIST FOR (CATEGORY = "Electronic" .AND. DATE >= {01/01/89} .AND. DATE <= {12/31/89})
.OR. (CATEGORY = "Appliance" .AND. DATE >= {01/01/89} .AND. DATE <= {12/31/89})
```

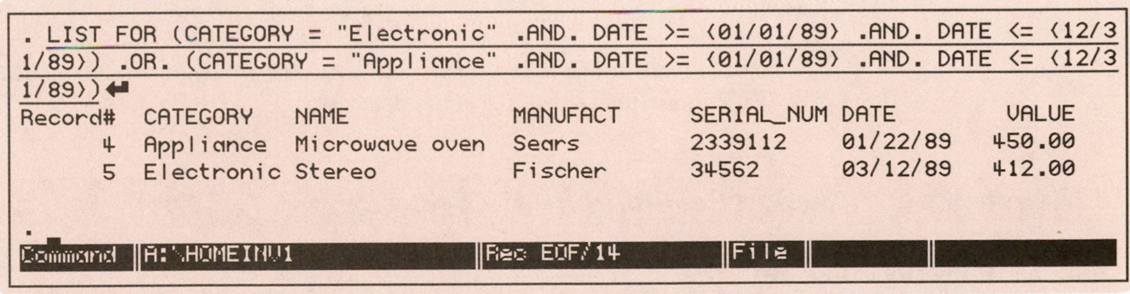

```
. LIST FOR (CATEGORY = "Electronic" .AND. DATE >= {01/01/89} .AND. DATE <= {12/3
1/89}) .OR. (CATEGORY = "Appliance" .AND. DATE >= {01/01/89} .AND. DATE <= {12/3
1/89})
Record#  CATEGORY   NAME           MANUFACT     SERIAL_NUM DATE        VALUE
      4  Appliance  Microwave oven Sears        2339112    01/22/89   450.00
      5  Electronic Stereo         Fischer      34562      03/12/89   412.00

.
Command ║A:\HOMEINV1            ║Rec EOF/14        ║File ║
```

Notice how the dBASE IV command closely matches the English version. The differences in syntax are the following:

- Parentheses enclose the two parts of the OR condition to indicate that those conditions are to be evaluated first and the OR condition is to be evaluated last. The structure should be as follows: **(...AND...) .OR. (...AND...)**. Actually, the command will work without the parentheses because dBASE IV normally evaluates AND before OR. However, using parentheses forces you to explicitly state the order in which you want the conditions evaluated. Page D212 of the Appendix gives a summary of the order of operations used by dBASE IV.
- Strings are enclosed in quotation marks (e.g., **"Electronic"**).
- The relational operators AND and OR are enclosed in periods (i.e., **.AND.** and **.OR.**).
- Dates are enclosed in braces (e.g., **{01/01/89}**).

Use predefined queries to display selected records The previous example displayed records using the same selection criteria that we set up in the query called **AP&EL-89**. Instead of reentering the selection criteria in a **LIST** command we could have instructed dBASE IV to use the view of the file defined by **AP&EL-89** and then told it to do a simple **LIST**. This is useful when you want to do the same type of search over and over again at different times.

Keystroke	Action Resulting from Keystroke
SET VIEW TO A:\AP&EL-89 ↵	Executes the query described by **AP&EL-89**. In the Status bar, the database name **HOMEINV1** has been replaced by the query name **AP&EL-89** and the word **File** has been replaced by the word **View**. The database records now will be filtered through the view described by **AP&EL-89**.
LIST ↵	Displays all the records using the view described by **AP&EL-89**.

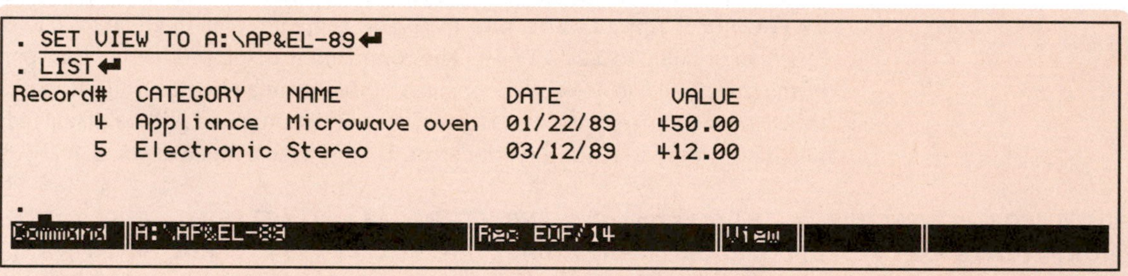

```
. SET VIEW TO A:\AP&EL-89↵
. LIST↵
Record#  CATEGORY   NAME            DATE      VALUE
      4  Appliance  Microwave oven  01/22/89  450.00
      5  Electronic Stereo          03/12/89  412.00

.
Command ║A:\AP&EL-89         ║Rec EOF/14      ║View║
```

To deactivate the view described by **AP&EL-89** you would issue the **USE** command to instruct dBASE IV to use the view of the entire database.

Keystroke	Action Resulting from Keystroke
USE A:\HOMEINV1.DBF ↵	Opens the specified database file for use (it restores the normal view of **HOMEINV1**).
LIST ↵	Displays all records in **HOMEINV1**.

Create Reports To access a blank Report design screen so that you can create a new report you would type **CREATE REPORT <filename>** and then press **[Enter]**. The **<filename>** is the name you wish to give the report.

Modify Reports If you want to modify an already-existing report, you would use **MODIFY REPORT <filename>** and then press **[Enter]**. The **<filename>** is the name of the report you wish to modify. If you cannot remember the exact name of the report, replace **<filename>** with a question mark (i.e., type **MODIFY REPORT ?** and then press **[Enter]**) and dBASE IV will display a picklist of reports saved on the disk. You then can use the **[arrow]** keys to select the report you want to modify.

Modify the report **RPT1** by doing the following:

Keystroke	Action Resulting from Keystroke
MODIFY REPORT A:\RPT1 ↵	
	Displays the design screen for report **RPT1**.
[edit]	Use the normal editing techniques to delete all the text in the **Report Intro Band**. The fastest way to do this is to locate the cursor at the first line of the **Report Intro Band** and then press **[Ctrl-Y]** seven times (once for each line to be deleted).

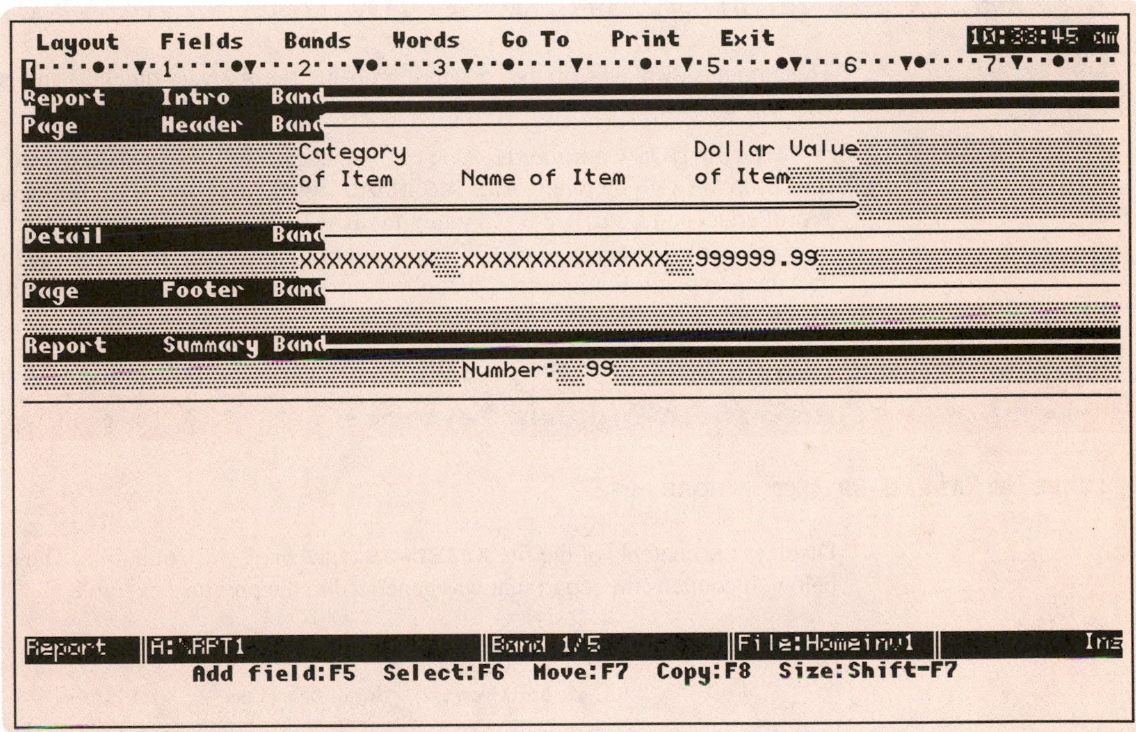

Keystroke	Action Resulting from Keystroke
[Alt-L]	Opens the **Layout** menu.
S	Selects **Save this report** and asks for a name for the report.
[edit]	Use the normal editing techniques to change the suggested name to **A:\RPTDOT.FRM**
[Enter]	Saves the report under the new name.
[Alt-E]	Opens the **Exit** menu.
A	Selects **Abandon changes and exit** and returns to the dot prompt.

Use Reports If you want to print or view a report you would use the **REPORT FORM** command. For example, to use the report design **RPTDOT** to print a report that includes only appliances and electronic goods purchased in 1989 you would type the following (do not do this now):

```
REPORT FORM A:\RPTDOT FOR (CATEGORY = "Electronic" .AND. DATE >= {01/01/89}
        .AND. DATE <= {12/31/89}) .OR. (CATEGORY = "Appliance"
    .AND. DATE >= {01/01/89} .AND. DATE <= {12/31/89}) TO PRINTER ↵
```

Notice how this command is identical to the previous **LIST** command except that the word **LIST** has been replaced with **REPORT FORM A:\RPTDOT** and the words **TO PRINTER** have been added to the end of the command to send the output to the printer.

If you want to send the output to an ASCII (text) file, you would give the same command but replace **TO PRINTER** with **TO FILE <filename>** where **<filename>** is the name of the file you want to store the output on. For example, the following command would send the output to a file called **AP&EL-89.TXT** (type this).

```
REPORT FORM A:\RPTDOT FOR (CATEGORY = "Electronic" .AND. DATE >= {01/01/89}
        .AND. DATE <= {12/31/89}) .OR. (CATEGORY = "Appliance"
.AND. DATE >= {01/01/89} .AND. DATE <= {12/31/89}) TO FILE A:\AP&EL-89.TXT ↵
```

The output is displayed on the screen (it probably flies by very quickly) and is also stored in the file **AP&EL-89.TXT**.

Execute DOS Commands You can suspend dBASE IV operations and execute DOS commands (i.e., drop to DOS) by typing **RUN COMMAND ↵**. This is similar to dropping to DOS from WordPerfect and Lotus 1-2-3. To return to dBASE IV, you would type **EXIT ↵**.

You can execute a single DOS command from the dot prompt by preceding the command with an exclamation point. For example, the following would display the contents of the file **AP&EL-89.TXT** which you just created in the previous example:

Keystroke	Action Resulting from Keystroke
!TYPE A:\AP&EL-89.TXT | MORE ↵	
	Displays the contents of the file **AP&EL-89.TXT** one screen at a time. The top of the screen is shown below. It contains the report that was generated in the previous example.

```
             Category                                Dollar Value
             of Item       Name of Item              of Item
             ===============================================
             Appliance     Microwave oven             $450.00
             Electronic    Stereo                     $412.00
                           Number:     2
```

[Enter]	Displays the next screen (it is blank).
[Enter]	Displays the next screen (it is blank) and returns to the dot prompt.

Modify Catalog Files Because catalog files are standard dBASE IV database files with the extension **CAT** in place of **DBF** they can be modified in the usual ways. To open the catalog **BGN_DBIV.CAT** and display its structure you would do the following:

Keystroke	Action Resulting from Keystroke

USE A:\BGN_DBIV.CAT ↵

Opens the specified database file for use.

LIST STRUCTURE ↵

Displays the structure of the active database.

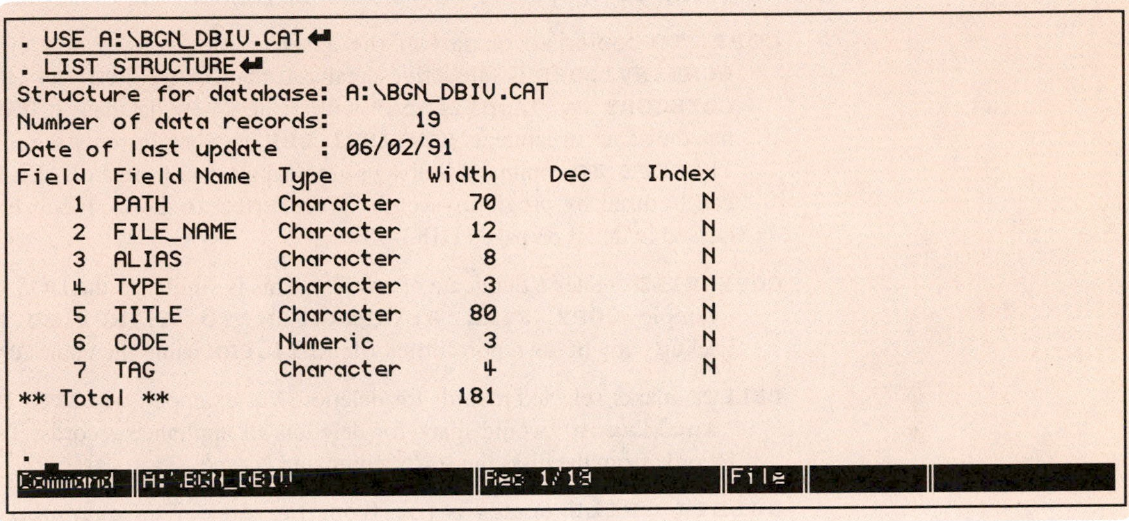

. USE A:\BGN_DBIV.CAT↵
. LIST STRUCTURE↵
Structure for database: A:\BGN_DBIV.CAT
Number of data records: 19
Date of last update : 06/02/91
Field Field Name Type Width Dec Index
1 PATH Character 70 N
2 FILE_NAME Character 12 N
3 ALIAS Character 8 N
4 TYPE Character 3 N
5 TITLE Character 80 N
6 CODE Numeric 3 N
7 TAG Character 4 N
** Total ** 181
Command
Rec 1/19
File

If you wanted to edit the contents of the file you would enter **Browse** or **Edit** and make the modifications in the usual ways.

To open the home inventory database again, do the following:

Keystroke	Action Resulting from Keystroke

USE A:\HOMEINV1.DBF ↵

Opens the specified database file for use.

Miscellaneous Dot Prompt Commands

dBASE IV has many other commands that are useful in different circumstances. Some simple examples are given below to give you an idea of the breadth of the available commands. For more information on any of the commands, consult the *dBASE IV Language Reference*.

AVERAGE calculates the average of numeric expressions or fields. For example, **AVERAGE FOR CATEGORY = "Appliance"** calculates the average of the numeric fields in the active database for those records whose **CATEGORY** is **Appliance**. Because the **HOMEINV1** database has one numeric field (**VALUE**) the average is calculated for that field only.

CALCULATE calculates financial and statistical functions on the data. For example, **CALCULATE FOR CATEGORY = "Appliance" AVG(VALUE), CNT(), MAX(VALUE), SUM(VALUE)** calculates the average, count, maximum, and sum of the **VALUE** field for those records whose **CATEGORY** is **Appliance**.

```
. CALCULATE FOR CATEGORY = "Appliance" AVG(VALUE), CNT(), MAX(VALUE), SUM(VALUE)

      4 records
AVG(VALUE)       CNT() MAX(VALUE) SUM(VALUE)
       450           4        550        1800

.
Command  ||A:\HOMEINV1          ||Rec EOF/14      ||File ||
```

CLOSE releases files from dBASE IV. For example, **CLOSE ALL** closes all types of dBASE IV files currently active while **CLOSE DATABASES** closes only active database files.

COPY TO copies all or part of the active database to a new file. For example, if **HOMEINV1.DBF** is the active database, then **COPY TO A:\HOMEBU.DBF FOR CATEGORY = "Appliance"** will create a new database called **HOMEBU.DBF** that has the same structure as **HOMEINV1.DBF** but contains only the records for appliances. The **COPY TO** command is also used to export data from a dBASE IV database so that it can be used by programs such as WordPerfect or Lotus 1-2-3. Exporting data is discussed in detail on pages D182–95.

COPY FILE creates a duplicate of any file. This is similar to the DOS **COPY** command. For example, **COPY FILE A:\RPT1.FRM TO A:\RPT1BU.FRM** would create a backup copy of the report format file **RPT1.FRM** using the name **RPT1BU.FRM**.

DELETE marks selected records for deletion. For example, **DELETE FOR CATEGORY = "Appliance"** would mark for deletion all appliance records. To actually delete the records from the disk, the **PACK** command is used.

DELETE FILE erases a file from the disk. For example, **DELETE FILE A:\RPT1BU.FRM** would delete the file **RPT1BU.FRM** from the current directory.

DIR displays a listing of the files in a directory similar to that displayed by the DOS **DIR** command. You can use the DOS global characters ***** and **?** to display the names of files that meet certain criteria. For example, **DIR *.FRM** would display the names of all report form files (i.e., those that have the extension **FRM**).

INDEX ON creates an index that can be used to arrange records alphabetically, chronologically, or numerically. Indexing is discussed in detail on pages D147–57.

PACK permanently removes records that have been marked for deletion.

QUIT closes all files, exits dBASE IV, and returns to DOS.

RECALL reinstates records that have been marked for deletion by the **DELETE** command. For example, **RECALL ALL** will remove deletion markers from all records in the database. Note that you cannot use **RECALL** to reinstate records of a database that has been packed or zapped (see below).

RENAME changes the name of a file. For example, **RENAME A:\HOMEBU.DBF TO BEANS** would change the name of **HOMEBU.DBF** to **BEANS**.

REPLACE replaces one value in a specified field with another value. For example, **REPLACE FOR MANUFACT ="IBM" MANUFACT WITH "IBM Corp"** would change the value in the field **MANUFACT** to **IBM Corp** for those records that have **IBM** in the **MANUFACT** field.

SKIP moves the record pointer a specified number of records forward or backward. For example, if the record pointer is currently at record number 5 and you enter **SKIP 5** the record pointer will be moved to record number 10.

SORT TO creates a new database in which the records are arranged alphabetically, chronologically, or numerically. Sorting is discussed in detail on pages D158–60.

ZAP removes all records from the active database file but keeps the structure intact. Note that you cannot use **RECALL** to reinstate records of a database that has been zapped.

For practice, use some of the above commands to do the following (begin from the dot prompt):

1. Open the database file **HOMEINV1**.
2. Make a backup copy of the file.
3. Display a directory of all database files.
4. Delete the records of all appliances.
5. Mark for deletion records for appliances.
6. Erase records marked for deletion.
7. Replace the manufacturer **IBM** with **IBM Corp**.
8. Delete all the records in the file.
9. Close the file.
10. Erase the file from the disk.

Keystroke	Action Resulting from Keystroke
USE A:\HOMEINV1.DBF ↵	Opens the specified database file for use.
COPY TO A:\HOMEBU.DBF ↵	Creates a new file called **HOMEBU.DBF** which is an exact copy of the active database file.
DIR A:*.DBF ↵	Lists the names of all database files on the diskette in drive A:.

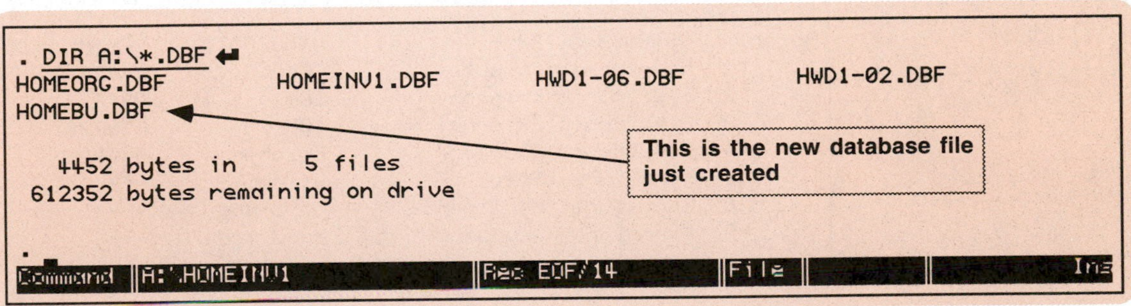

Keystroke	Action Resulting from Keystroke
USE A:\HOMEBU.DBF ↵	Opens the new database file.
DELETE FOR CATEGORY = "Appliance" ↵	Marks for deletion all appliance records. The records that will be deleted when the database is closed or packed are marked with asterisks.
LIST ↵	Displays all records of the database.

Continued . . .

Keystroke	Action Resulting from Keystroke
PACK ↵	Deletes marked records.

```
. USE HOMEBU ↵
. DELETE FOR CATEGORY = "Appliance" ↵
     4 records deleted
. LIST ↵
Record#  CATEGORY   NAME                MANUFACT      SERIAL_NUM DATE        VALUE
      1  Electronic Computer            IBM           F3827122   02/10/90  1200.00
      2  Electronic Printer             IBM           03483      02/10/90   450.00
      3  Electronic External drive      IBM           F392281    02/10/90   356.00
      4 *Appliance  Microwave oven      Sears         2339112    01/22/89   450.00
      5  Electronic Stereo              Fischer       34562      03/12/89   412.00
      6  Furniture  Sofa                Wilder        ---        11/21/84   450.00
      7  Furniture  Recliner            La-Z-Boy      ---        03/23/87   350.00
      8  Furniture  Dry sink            Hand made     ---        04/12/87   500.00
      9 *Appliance  Refrigerator        Wards         493323     03/22/87   450.00
     10 *Appliance  Stove               Wards         533282     03/22/87   350.00
     11 *Appliance  Dishwasher          Kitchen Aid   04322344   09/23/81   550.00
     12  Furniture  Bed, mattress       Simmons       ---        09/03/87   100.00
     13  Furniture  Bed, spring         Simmons       ---        09/03/87   100.00
     14  Furniture  Bed, frame          Simmons       ---        09/03/87   100.00
.
Command  ||A:\HOMEBU          ||Rec EOF/14     ||File ||        ||        Ins
```

Asterisk indicates records marked for deletion

Keystroke	Action Resulting from Keystroke
LIST ↵	Displays all records of the database. The records that were marked for deletion (i.e., appliances) now are gone.

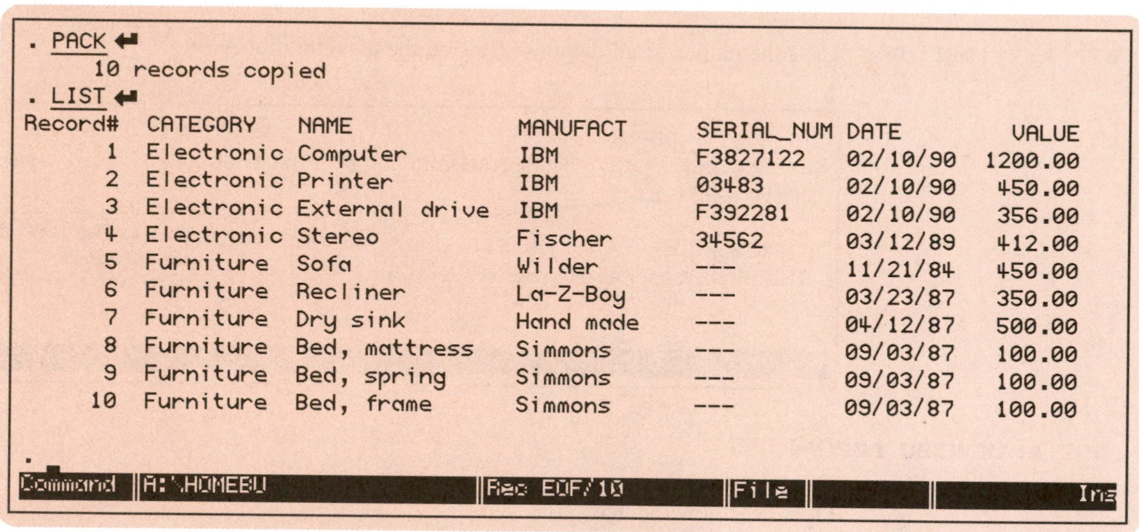

```
. PACK ↵
     10 records copied
. LIST ↵
Record#  CATEGORY   NAME                MANUFACT      SERIAL_NUM DATE        VALUE
      1  Electronic Computer            IBM           F3827122   02/10/90  1200.00
      2  Electronic Printer             IBM           03483      02/10/90   450.00
      3  Electronic External drive      IBM           F392281    02/10/90   356.00
      4  Electronic Stereo              Fischer       34562      03/12/89   412.00
      5  Furniture  Sofa                Wilder        ---        11/21/84   450.00
      6  Furniture  Recliner            La-Z-Boy      ---        03/23/87   350.00
      7  Furniture  Dry sink            Hand made     ---        04/12/87   500.00
      8  Furniture  Bed, mattress       Simmons       ---        09/03/87   100.00
      9  Furniture  Bed, spring         Simmons       ---        09/03/87   100.00
     10  Furniture  Bed, frame          Simmons       ---        09/03/87   100.00
.
Command  ||A:\HOMEBU          ||Rec EOF/10     ||File ||        ||        Ins
```

REPLACE FOR MANUFACT ="IBM" MANUFACT WITH "IBM Corp" ↵

Changes the manufacturer's name from **IBM** to **IBM Corp** for all records whose manufacturer is IBM.

LIST ↵	Displays all records of the database.

Continued . . .

Keystroke | **Action Resulting from Keystroke**

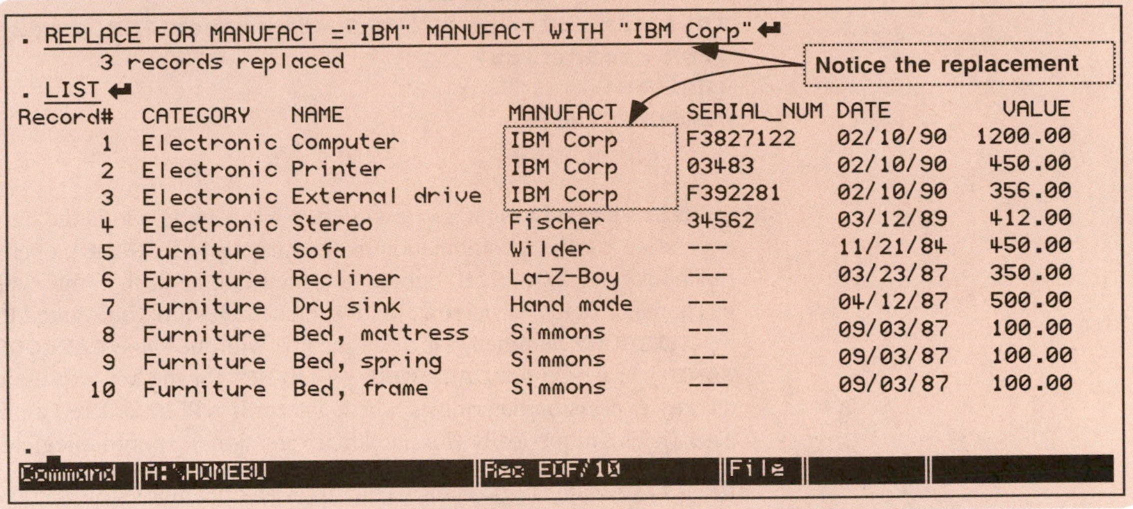

```
. REPLACE FOR MANUFACT ="IBM" MANUFACT WITH "IBM Corp"
     3 records replaced
. LIST
Record#  CATEGORY    NAME              MANUFACT    SERIAL_NUM DATE        VALUE
      1  Electronic Computer           IBM Corp    F3827122   02/10/90  1200.00
      2  Electronic Printer            IBM Corp    03483      02/10/90   450.00
      3  Electronic External drive     IBM Corp    F392281    02/10/90   356.00
      4  Electronic Stereo             Fischer     34562      03/12/89   412.00
      5  Furniture  Sofa               Wilder      ---        11/21/84   450.00
      6  Furniture  Recliner           La-Z-Boy    ---        03/23/87   350.00
      7  Furniture  Dry sink          Hand made   ---        04/12/87   500.00
      8  Furniture  Bed, mattress      Simmons     ---        09/03/87   100.00
      9  Furniture  Bed, spring        Simmons     ---        09/03/87   100.00
     10  Furniture  Bed, frame         Simmons     ---        09/03/87   100.00

.
Command  A:\HOMEBU                 Rec EOF/10          File
```


ZAP ↵ — Deletes all records in the database. The file structure remains intact.

Y — Confirms that all records should be deleted.

LIST ↵ — Displays all records of the database.

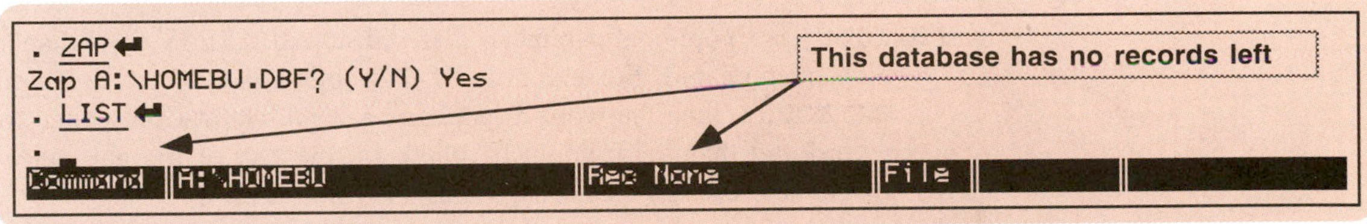

```
. ZAP
Zap A:\HOMEBU.DBF? (Y/N) Yes
. LIST
.
Command  A:\HOMEBU                 Rec None            File
```


CLOSE ALL ↵ — Closes all open files.

DELETE FILE A:\HOMEBU.DBF ↵

Erases the specified file from the disk.

Practice using these commands until you get a feeling for how they work. In most cases they are quite logical although the syntax is sometimes confusing.

TO TAKE A BREAK Type **QUIT** ↵. Remove data diskette. To resume: Insert data diskette; type **A:** ↵, then **C:\DBIV\DBASE** ↵.

Indexing a Database

On pages D47–52 we briefly discussed using indexes to arrange the way records of a database file are displayed or printed. In this section, we will discuss indexing in more detail and provide you with the opportunity to practice creating and using complex indexes initiated at the dot prompt.

Recall that indexing a database creates a set of instructions which tell dBASE IV how to display records, but indexing does not physically rearrange the records. This makes indexing fast and flexible because you may create many different indexes for the same set of data and then use those indexes when the need arises.

The **INDEX** command is used to create indexes at the dot prompt. It has the following general form:

```
INDEX ON <key expression>
   TO <.ndx filename> / TAG <tag name> [OF <.mdx filename>]
   [FOR <condition>
   [UNIQUE]
   [DESCENDING]
```

where

<key expression> is the expression that you want to use as the basis for the index. The expression can be a combination of field names (e.g., **NAME**), operators (e.g., +, -), and functions (e.g., **LOG**, **SIN**) but the fields must all be of the same type (e.g., they must all be character fields, or numeric fields, or date fields). If you wanted to arrange the records by **CATEGORY** and then, for those records with the same **CATEGORY**, arrange them by **NAME**, you would use **CATEGORY + NAME** for the key expression. The data type of the key expression determines whether records will be ordered alphabetically (for character fields), numerically (for numeric expressions), or chronological (for date fields).

<.ndx filename> is the name of the file where the index instructions will be stored.

TAG <tag name> [OF <.mdx filename>] is an alternative to using the **<.ndx filename>** where the index instructions are added to a multiple index file as index tags. We used tags when we did the indexing on pages D47–52.

[FOR <condition>] is an optional clause that allows you to select for indexing and display only those records that meet the search condition (e.g., **VALUE > 400**). These conditions can only be used with **mdx** tags and not with **ndx** files.

[UNIQUE] is an optional parameter that will stop dBASE IV from displaying identical fields that are repeated. For example, if this option is selected and you were indexing on **CATEGORY**, then the word **Appliance** would appear only once for the first appliance record and that field would be blank for the rest of the appliance records. The same would hold true for electronic goods and furniture.

[DESCENDING] is an optional parameter that indexes the records in descending order. This option can only be used with **mdx** tags and not with **ndx** files.

The index command may seem confusing at first, but it is quite logical. The following are some examples of **INDEX** that would be entered directly at the dot prompt (these are only examples; do not type them yet):

INDEX ON CATEGORY TO A:\HOMECAT creates a file that contains the indexing keys for all the records of the active database so that they are in alphabetical (ascending) order based on the field **CATEGORY**. The name of the new index file is **HOMECAT.NDX** (the extension **NDX** is automatically added by dBASE IV).

INDEX ON CATEGORY + NAME TO A:\HOMECANA is similar to the above **INDEX** command except that the records are arranged first on field **CATEGORY** and then, for records of the same **CATEGORY**, the arrangement is based on field **NAME**. The name of the new index file is **HOMECANA.NDX**.

INDEX ON STR(YEAR(DATE),4) + STR(MONTH(DATE),2) + STR(DAY(DATE),2) + NAME TO A:\HOMEDANA arranges all the records in the active database so that they are in chronological order (by **DATE**) and, for those with the same **DATE**, arranges the records alphabetically by **NAME**. The reason this expression appears so complicated is that whenever you create an index on more than one field, dBASE IV requires that all the fields be the same type (character, number, or date). In this example, the **DATE** field is of type date and the **NAME** field is of type character. To make the field types identical, the **DATE** field is broken up into three parts (**YEAR**, **MONTH**, and **DAY**), and then each of those parts must be converted into a character field by using the **STR** function:

YEAR(DATE) converts the year part of the field **DATE** into a four-digit number. For example, if the date is **02/10/90** then the year **90** is converted into **1990**.

MONTH(DATE) converts the month part of the field **DATE** into a one- or two-digit number. For example, if the date is **02/10/90** then the month **02** is converted into **2**.

DAY(DATE) converts the day part of the field **DATE** into a one- or two-digit number. For example, if the date is **02/10/90** then the day **10** is converted into **10**.

The **STR** function converts each of the numbers from the date into a character (string) type entry.

STR(YEAR(DATE),4) converts the number from the **YEAR(DATE)** function into a character representation (e.g., **1990** represented as a number is changed into the four-character string **1990** — to us they look the same, but to dBASE IV these are different!).

STR(MONTH(DATE),2) converts the number from the **MONTH(DATE)** function into a character representation (e.g., **2** represented as a number is changed into the two-character string **02**).

STR(DAY(DATE),2) converts the number from the **DAY(DATE)** function into a character representation (e.g., **10** represented as a number is changed into the two-character string **10**).

Notice that the order given for the indexing is **YEAR**, then **MONTH**, then **DAY**, then **NAME**. This is because we want all records of the same year to be grouped together and then, for those records with the same year, the grouping should be by month, then by day, and then, finally, by name.

Try the **INDEX** command by doing the following (begin at the dot prompt):

Keystroke	***Action Resulting from Keystroke***
USE A\:HOMEINV1.DBF ↵	
	Opens the specified database file for use.
LIST ↵	Lists the contents of the active database.

```
. USE A:\HOMEINV1.DBF ↵
. LIST ↵
Record#  CATEGORY    NAME              MANUFACT      SERIAL_NUM DATE         VALUE
      1  Electronic  Computer          IBM           F3827122   02/10/90   1200.00
      2  Electronic  Printer           IBM           03483      02/10/90    450.00
      3  Electronic  External drive    IBM           F392281    02/10/90    356.00
      4  Appliance   Microwave oven    Sears         2339112    01/22/89    450.00
      5  Electronic  Stereo            Fischer       34562      03/12/89    412.00
      6  Furniture   Sofa              Wilder        ---        11/21/84    450.00
      7  Furniture   Recliner          La-Z-Boy      ---        03/23/87    350.00
      8  Furniture   Dry sink          Hand made     ---        04/12/87    500.00
      9  Appliance   Refrigerator      Wards         493323     03/22/87    450.00
     10  Appliance   Stove             Wards         533282     03/22/87    350.00
     11  Appliance   Dishwasher        Kitchen Aid   04322344   09/23/81    550.00
     12  Furniture   Bed, mattress     Simmons       ---        09/03/87    100.00
     13  Furniture   Bed, spring       Simmons       ---        09/03/87    100.00
     14  Furniture   Bed, frame        Simmons       ---        09/03/87    100.00

.
Command ║A:\HOMEINV1        ║Rec EOF/14     ║File ║
```

Continued . . .

INDEX ON CATEGORY + NAME TO A:\HOMECANA ↵

Creates an index file called **HOMECANA.NDX** to arrange the records by **CATEGORY** and, within **CATEGORY**, by **NAME**.

LIST ↵ Lists the contents of the active database.

```
. INDEX ON CATEGORY + NAME TO A:\HOMECANA↵
  100% indexed          14 Records indexed
. LIST ↵
Record#  CATEGORY   NAME             MANUFACT     SERIAL_NUM DATE        VALUE
     11  Appliance  Dishwasher       Kitchen Aid  04322344   09/23/81   550.00
      4  Appliance  Microwave oven   Sears        2339112    01/22/89   450.00
      9  Appliance  Refrigerator     Wards        493323     03/22/87   450.00
     10  Appliance  Stove            Wards        533282     03/22/87   350.00
      1  Electronic Computer         IBM          F3827122   02/10/90  1200.00
      3  Electronic External drive   IBM          F392281    02/10/90   356.00
      2  Electronic Printer          IBM          03483      02/10/90   450.00
      5  Electronic Stereo           Fischer      34562      03/12/89   412.00
     14  Furniture  Bed, frame       Simmons      ---        09/03/87   100.00
     12  Furniture  Bed, mattress    Simmons      ---        09/03/87   100.00
     13  Furniture  Bed, spring      Simmons      ---        09/03/87   100.00
      8  Furniture  Dry sink         Hand made    ---        04/12/87   500.00
      7  Furniture  Recliner         La-Z-Boy     ---        03/23/87   350.00
      6  Furniture  Sofa             Wilder       ---        11/21/84   450.00

.
Command ||A:\HOMEINV1          ||Rec EOF/14     ||File ||
```

Notice that the records are displayed in the desired arrangement, but the record numbers have not been changed (hence, they are not in numerical order).

DISPLAY STATUS ↵

Displays information on the status of the current database and associated files. The top of the screen looks like the following:

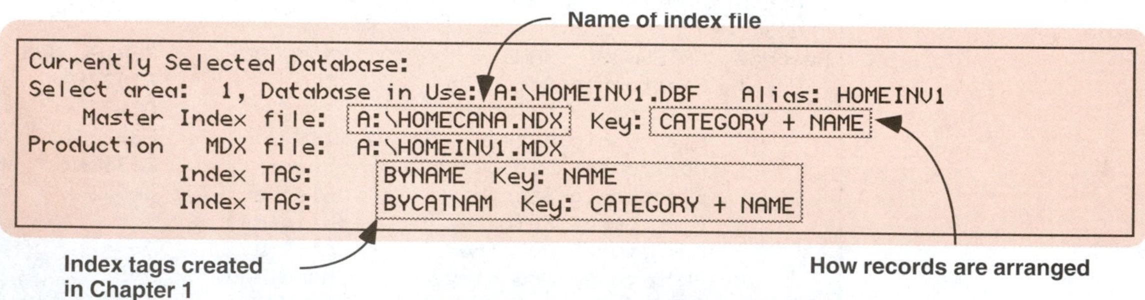

The third line in the above display lists **A:\HOMECANA.NDX** as the master index file and **CATEGORY + NAME** as the key. This means that the active database (**A:\HOMEINV1.DBF**) is currently being indexed by the file **HOMECANA.NDX**, and that the index key is **CATEGORY + NAME** (i.e., the file is arranged by **CATEGORY** and then, within **CATEGORY**, by **NAME**). The index tags **BYNAME** and **BYCATNAM**, which were created in Chapter 1, are also listed along with their key expressions.

[Esc] Cancels the rest of the file status display.

More than one index file can be created for a given database. For example, suppose you wanted to index the file again, but this time by value:

Keystroke	Action Resulting from Keystroke
INDEX ON VALUE TO A:\HOMEVAL ↵	
	Creates an index file called **HOMEVAL.NDX** which arranges the display of the active database so that records are in ascending order by the numbers in field **VALUE**.
LIST ↵	Lists the contents of the active database. Notice that the records are in order by **VALUE**.

```
. INDEX ON VALUE TO A:\HOMEVAL↵
  100% indexed          14 Records indexed
. LIST↵
Record#  CATEGORY    NAME             MANUFACT      SERIAL_NUM DATE       VALUE
     12  Furniture   Bed, mattress    Simmons       ---        09/03/87  100.00
     13  Furniture   Bed, spring      Simmons       ---        09/03/87  100.00
     14  Furniture   Bed, frame       Simmons       ---        09/03/87  100.00
      7  Furniture   Recliner         La-Z-Boy      ---        03/23/87  350.00
     10  Appliance   Stove            Wards         533282     03/22/87  350.00
      3  Electronic  External drive   IBM           F392281    02/10/90  356.00
      5  Electronic  Stereo           Fischer       34562      03/12/89  412.00
      2  Electronic  Printer          IBM           03483      02/10/90  450.00
      4  Appliance   Microwave oven   Sears         2339112    01/22/89  450.00
      6  Furniture   Sofa             Wilder        ---        11/21/84  450.00
      9  Appliance   Refrigerator     Wards         493323     03/22/87  450.00
      8  Furniture   Dry sink         Hand made     ---        04/12/87  500.00
     11  Appliance   Dishwasher       Kitchen Aid   04322344   09/23/81  550.00
      1  Electronic  Computer         IBM           F3827122   02/10/90 1200.00

.
Command  ||A:\HOMEINV1          ||Rec EOF/14      ||File ||
```

To change from one index file to another, use the **SET INDEX** command. For example, the currently active index file is **HOMEVAL.NDX**. To switch back to the index file **HOMECANA.NDX**, type the following:

Keystroke	Action Resulting from Keystroke
SET INDEX TO A:\HOMECANA.NDX ↵	
	Makes the file **HOMECANA.NDX** the current (master) index file.
LIST ↵	Displays the contents of the active database indexed according to **HOMECANA.NDX**.

The **SET ORDER** command is used to open an index tag (such as **BYNAME**, which we created on p. D49). For example:

Keystroke	Action Resulting from Keystroke
SET ORDER TO TAG BYNAME ↵	
	Uses the index tag **BYNAME** to arrange the display of the records.
LIST ↵	Displays the contents of the active database indexed according to **BYNAME**.

```
. SET ORDER TO TAG BYNAME↵
Master index: BYNAME
. LIST↵
Record#  CATEGORY    NAME              MANUFACT      SERIAL_NUM DATE        VALUE
     14  Furniture   Bed, frame        Simmons       ---        09/03/87   100.00
     12  Furniture   Bed, mattress     Simmons       ---        09/03/87   100.00
     13  Furniture   Bed, spring       Simmons       ---        09/03/87   100.00
      1  Electronic  Computer          IBM           F3827122   02/10/90  1200.00
     11  Appliance   Dishwasher        Kitchen Aid   04322344   09/23/81   550.00
      8  Furniture   Dry sink          Hand made     ---        04/12/87   500.00
      3  Electronic  External drive    IBM           F392281    02/10/90   356.00
      4  Appliance   Microwave oven    Sears         2339112    01/22/89   450.00
      2  Electronic  Printer           IBM           03483      02/10/90   450.00
      7  Furniture   Recliner          La-Z-Boy      ---        03/23/87   350.00
      9  Appliance   Refrigerator      Wards         493323     03/22/87   450.00
      6  Furniture   Sofa              Wilder        ---        11/21/84   450.00
      5  Electronic  Stereo            Fischer       34562      03/12/89   412.00
     10  Appliance   Stove             Wards         533282     03/22/87   350.00

.
Command  ║A:\HOMEINV1        ║Rec EOF/14      ║File ║
```

Finally, to display the database in its original, unindexed form, use the **SET ORDER TO** command without an argument:

Keystroke	Action Resulting from Keystroke
SET ORDER TO ↵	
	Restores the database to its natural order. When the database is listed, the records will be displayed in their original, unsorted order.
LIST ↵	Displays the contents of the active database.

Continued . . .

Keystroke	Action Resulting from Keystroke

```
. SET ORDER TO↵
Database is in natural order
. LIST↵
Record#  CATEGORY   NAME             MANUFACT      SERIAL_NUM DATE        VALUE
      1  Electronic Computer         IBM           F3827122   02/10/90  1200.00
      2  Electronic Printer          IBM           03483      02/10/90   450.00
      3  Electronic External drive   IBM           F392281    02/10/90   356.00
      4  Appliance  Microwave oven   Sears         2339112    01/22/89   450.00
      5  Electronic Stereo           Fischer       34562      03/12/89   412.00
      6  Furniture  Sofa             Wilder        ---        11/21/84   450.00
      7  Furniture  Recliner         La-Z-Boy      ---        03/23/87   350.00
      8  Furniture  Dry sink         Hand made     ---        04/12/87   500.00
      9  Appliance  Refrigerator     Wards         493323     03/22/87   450.00
     10  Appliance  Stove            Wards         533282     03/22/87   350.00
     11  Appliance  Dishwasher       Kitchen Aid   04322344   09/23/81   550.00
     12  Furniture  Bed, mattress    Simmons       ---        09/03/87   100.00
     13  Furniture  Bed, spring      Simmons       ---        09/03/87   100.00
     14  Furniture  Bed, frame       Simmons       ---        09/03/87   100.00

.
Command ||A:\HOMEINV1          ||Rec EOF/14        ||File ||      ||
```

Using INDEX to Create Groups in Reports

With very little effort, you can use indexing to help create reports that provide information on groups of records in addition to individual records. In this context, grouping means that records with the same value in a specified field are separated from other records by a blank line. For example, if the database is indexed by **CATEGORY**, you can have dBASE IV group the data so that the appliances, electronics, and furniture groups are separated by a blank line and you can produce summary statistics on the individual groups. This is useful, for example, if you are interested in determining the value of all of your electronic equipment.

As an example of this, follow the directions given below to create a report where the fields are arranged by **CATEGORY** and **NAME** and which displays subtotals for each different category (begin from the dot prompt).

Keystroke	Action Resulting from Keystroke

USE A:\HOMEINV1.DBF ↵

Opens the specified database file for use.

SET INDEX TO A:\HOMECANA.NDX ↵

Specifies the active index file.

COPY FILE A:\RPTDOT.FRM TO A:\HOMEGRP.FRM ↵

Makes a copy of the report design **RPTDOT** using the new name **HOMEGRP**. This will allow you to retain the original report form while creating a new, modified version of it for use in carrying out the current task.

MODIFY REPORT A:\HOMEGRP.FRM ↵

Specifies that the new report form **HOMEGRP** is to be modified. The report form screen is displayed.

Continued . . .

Keystroke	Action Resulting from Keystroke

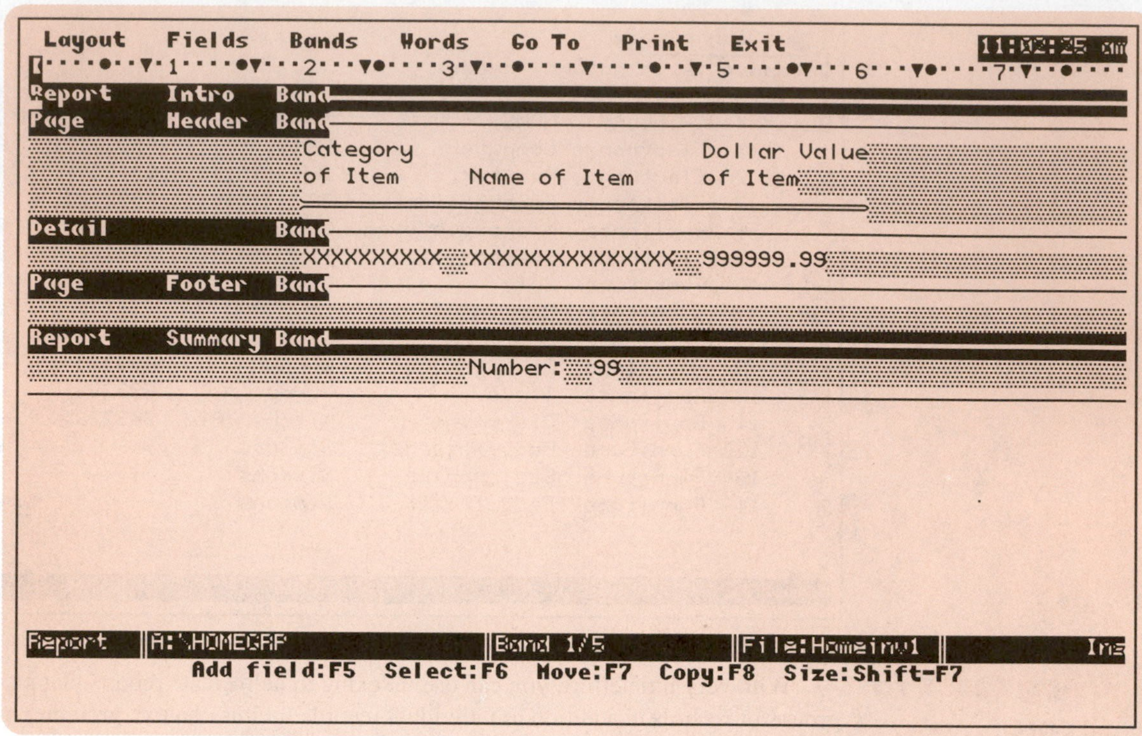

First we need to tell dBASE IV how to group the data.

Keystroke	Action Resulting from Keystroke
[Alt-B]	Opens the **Bands** menu.
A	Selects **Add a group band** and displays its menu.

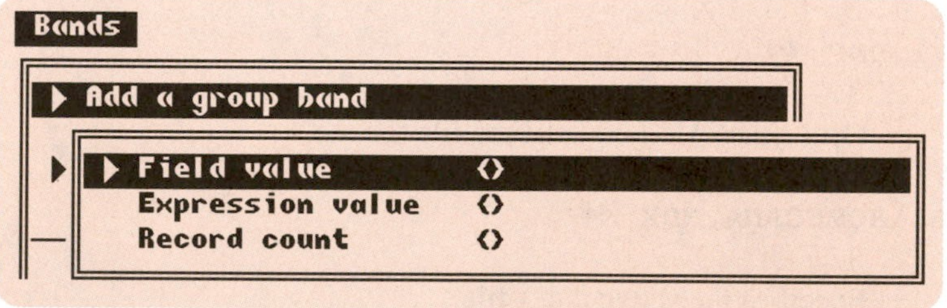

We need to tell dBASE IV which field to use when forming the groups.

F	Selects **Field value** and displays a picklist of field names.
[arrow]	Use the [arrow] keys, if necessary, to highlight the **CATEGORY** field.
[Enter]	Selects the highlighted field and returns to the Report design screen. Two new bands **Group 1 Intro Band** and **Group 1 Summary Band** have been added to the report design just above and below the **Detail Band**.

Continued . . .

Keystroke	Action Resulting from Keystroke

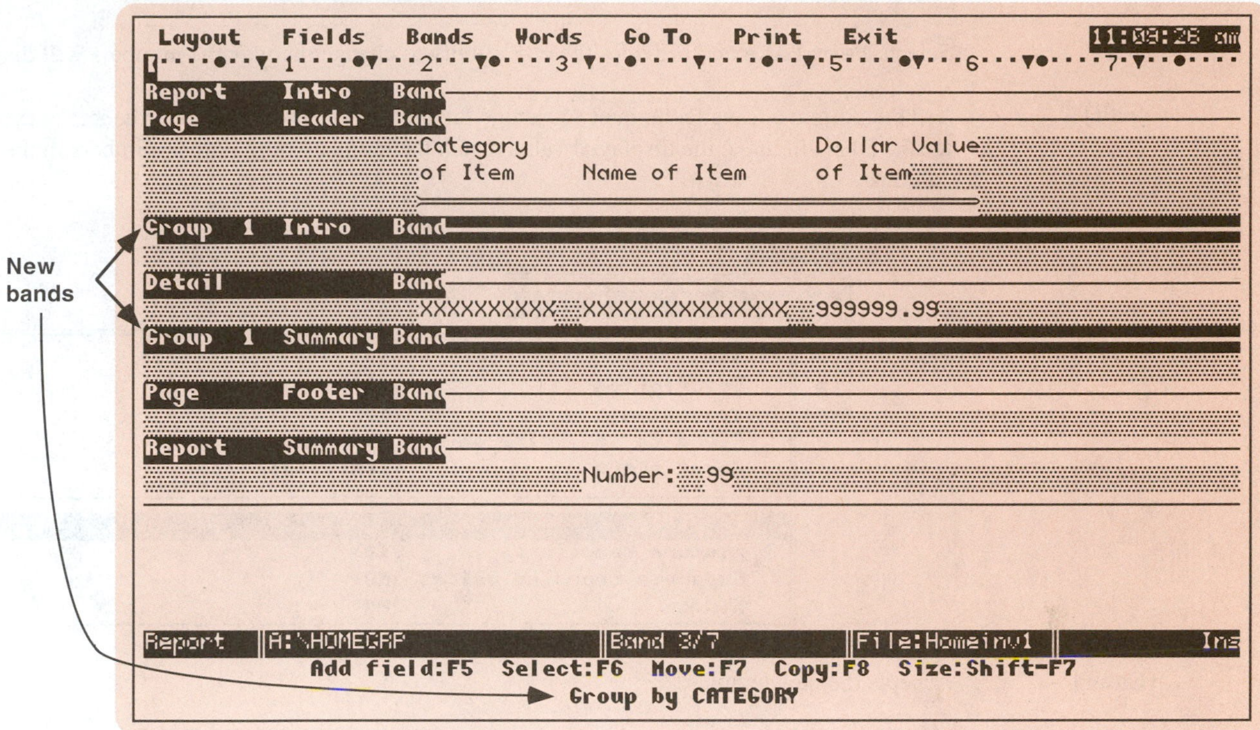

We can add a summary field to display the subtotals for each group.

Keystroke	Action Resulting from Keystroke
[arrow]	Use the [arrow] keys to move the cursor to the **`Group 1 Summary Band`** so that it is just under the value template **`999999.99`** (location **`Line:0 Col:49`**).
[Alt-F]	Opens the **`Fields`** menu.
A	Selects **`Add field`** and presents a picklist of items that can be added to the report design.
[arrow]	Use the [arrow] keys to highlight **`Sum`** in the **`SUMMARY`** column.
[Enter]	Selects the highlighted field and presents its attributes menu.
F	Selects **`Field to summarize on`** and presents a picklist of fields.
[arrow]	Use the [arrow] keys, if necessary, to highlight **`VALUE`**.
[Enter]	Selects the highlighted field and returns to the attributes menu.
P	Selects **`Picture functions`** and displays its menu.
F	Selects **`Financial format`** and changes **`OFF`** to **`ON`**. This will display the numbers as currency (i.e., with a dollar sign).

Continued . . .

Keystroke	Action Resulting from Keystroke
[Ctrl-End]	Accepts the picture functions attributes and returns to the attributes menu.
T	Selects **Template** and provides the opportunity to change the way the numbers will display.
[edit]	Use the normal editing techniques to change the number of **9**s displayed to the left of the decimal point to six. This will make the displayed value match the template of the other numbers in the **VALUE** column.

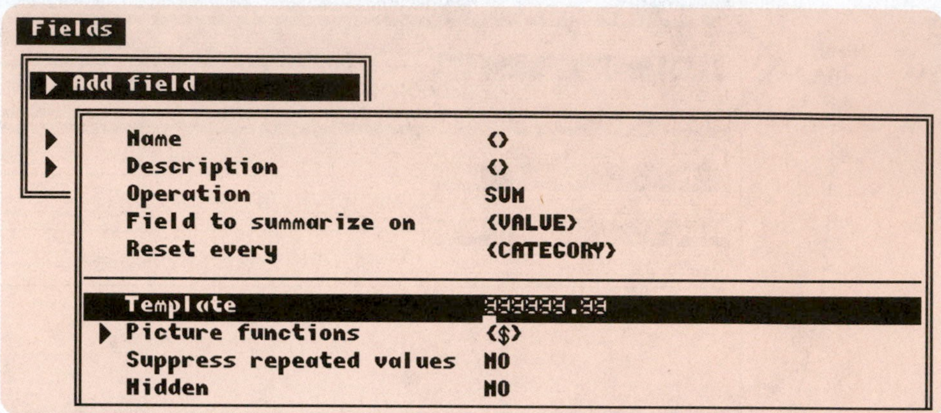

Keystroke	Action Resulting from Keystroke
[Enter]	Accepts the new template.
[Ctrl-End]	Accepts the attributes and returns to the Report design screen.
[Alt-P]	Opens the **Print** menu.
V	Selects **View report on screen** and displays the following:

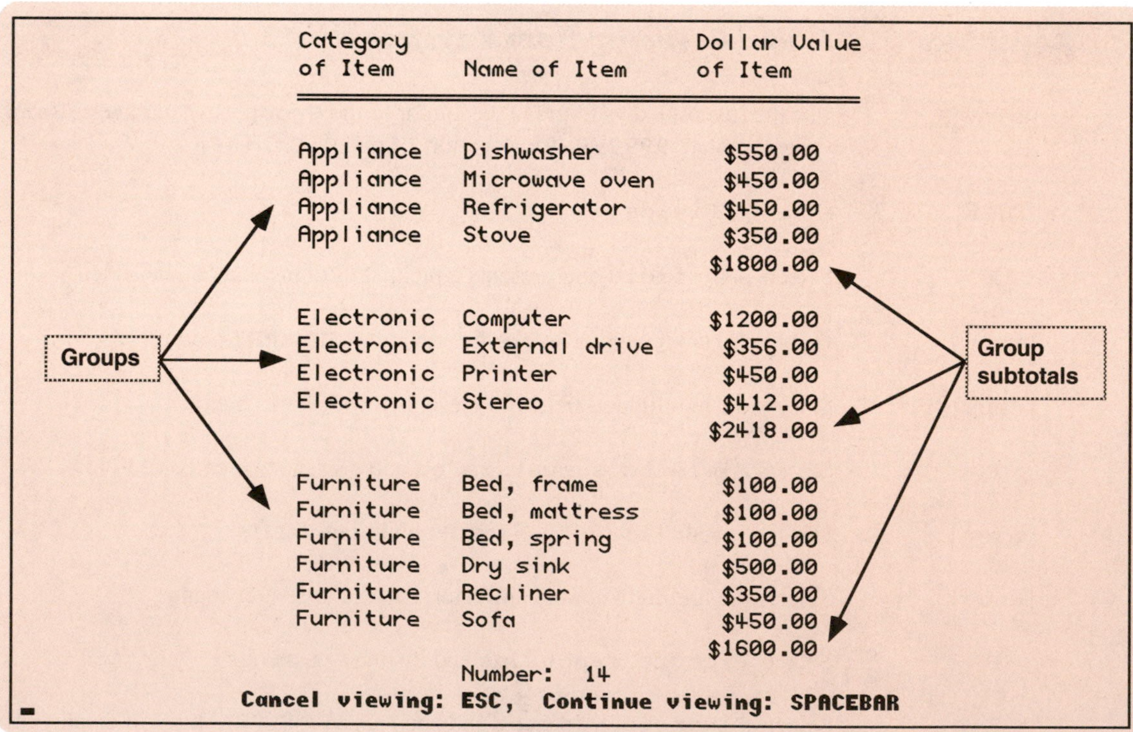

Continued . . .

Keystroke	Action Resulting from Keystroke
	Notice how the records are grouped by category and the sum of the values in each category is displayed.
[Esc]	Cancels the view process and returns to the Report design screen.
[Alt-E]	Opens the **Exit** menu.
S	Selects **Save changes and exit** and returns to the dot prompt.

It only makes sense to form groups when the database is indexed on the field you want to group on. For example, if the database were indexed on the **NAME** field and you form groups based on the **CATEGORY** field there will be more than one group for each value in the **CATEGORY** field. The output of such a report would look like the following (this is not very useful).

```
Category                      Dollar Value
of Item      Name of Item     of Item
==========================================

Furniture    Bed, frame          $100.00
Furniture    Bed, mattress       $100.00
Furniture    Bed, spring         $100.00
                                 $300.00

Electronic   Computer           $1200.00
                                $1200.00

Appliance    Dishwasher          $550.00
                                 $550.00

Furniture    Dry sink            $500.00
                                 $500.00

Electronic   External drive      $356.00
                                 $356.00

Appliance    Microwave oven      $450.00
                                 $450.00

Electronic   Printer             $450.00
                                 $450.00

Furniture    Recliner            $350.00
                                 $350.00

Appliance    Refrigerator        $450.00
                                 $450.00

Furniture    Sofa                $450.00
                                 $450.00

Electronic   Stereo              $412.00
                                 $412.00

Appliance    Stove               $350.00
                                 $350.00
             Number:  14
```

Sorting a Database

Sorting a database is similar to indexing in that it allows you to arrange the way the records appear on the screen and in reports. Unlike indexing, however, the **SORT** command creates a copy of the active database and physically arranges the records in the order prescribed by you. This has the advantage that the records are physically stored on disk in a logical arrangement rather than in the order in which they were entered. The result is that reports are generated faster from a sorted file. The disadvantages of using **SORT** instead of **INDEX** are numerous:

- For large databases, physically rearranging and copying the records may take a significant amount of processing time (minutes to hours) and, because a copy of the entire database is made, the sort process may take up a large amount of disk space.
- **SORT** changes the record numbers of most records and this may lead to confusion if you switch from the sorted to the original database.
- You must re-sort the entire database even if you add just one record.
- A file can only be sorted in one way at a time. If you want to produce a report that has items alphabetized by name and then, a few minutes later, one that is in order by date, you have to go through the entire sorting process all over again.
- **SORT** only works on individual fields and not on field expressions.

For the aforementioned reasons, **INDEX** is used much more often than **SORT**. However, there are times when **SORT** might be appropriate.

- **SORT** must be used when you want to arrange the data in descending order in one field and ascending order in another. For example, you might want the **HOMEINV1** records arranged chronologically with the latest purchase first and alphabetically by name for those records that were purchased in the same month or year.
- **SORT** must be used when you want to do a *dictionary* sort rather than an *ASCII* sort. In a dictionary sort, the uppercase letters are treated as equal to their lowercase equivalents (e.g., the arrangement would be AaBbCc, etc.) whereas in the ASCII sort all the uppercase letters are placed before the lowercase letters (e.g., ABC and then abc). (Recall from p. D49, however, that you can use the **UPPER** function to work around this problem using indexing).
- **SORT** allows you to make an organized backup copy of a database that should not change (e.g., a snapshot of the personnel records of your company for the year 1990). In that case, a sorted database would be adequate because records would never be added, deleted, or edited.

Sorting can be accomplished by selecting the **Sort database on field list** option from the **Organize** menus of the **Edit**, **Browse**, or **Database** design screens. Using the menus, you would enter the fields that are to serve as the sort keys and then indicate whether the sort on each field is to be ascending ASCII, descending ASCII, ascending dictionary, or descending dictionary. Pressing **[Ctrl-End]** saves the sort parameters and asks you for a file name to store the new, sorted, database.

You can also enter the commands at the dot prompt. The following examples of **SORT** are only examples, do not type them yet:

SORT TO A:\HOMECAT.DBF ON CATEGORY arranges all the records of the active database so that they are in ascending alphabetical order based on the field **CATEGORY**. The sorted records are written to a new file called **HOMECAT.DBF** (if you do not provide an extension, **DBF** is automatically added by dBASE IV). The original database file remains unchanged. Compare this command to the comparable **INDEX** command:

```
SORT TO A:\HOMECAT.DBF ON CATEGORY
INDEX ON CATEGORY TO A:\HOMECAT.NDX
```

SORT TO A:\HOMECANA.DBF ON CATEGORY,NAME is similar to the above command except that the records are sorted first on field **CATEGORY** and then, for records of the same **CATEGORY**, the sort is done on field **NAME**. Compare this command to the comparable **INDEX** command:

```
SORT TO A:\HOMECANA.DBF ON CATEGORY,NAME
INDEX ON CATEGORY+NAME TO A:\HOMECANA.NDX
```

Notice that the **SORT** command uses a comma to separate the field names (**CATEGORY, NAME**), whereas the **INDEX** command uses the **+** to separate the names (**CATEGORY + NAME**).

SORT TO A:\HOMECANA.DBF ON CATEGORY/D,NAME/AC is similar to the above command except that the records are sorted first on field **CATEGORY** in **D**escending order (hence the **/D**). Then, for records of the same **CATEGORY**, the sort is done on field **NAME** in **A**scending order, while ignoring the **C**ase of the characters (hence the **/AC**) The uppercase and lowercase characters are arranged in regular alphabetical order rather than with all uppercase characters first and then all lowercase characters. There is no comparable **INDEX** command

SORT TO A:\HOMEDANA.DBF ON DATE,NAME arranges all the records in the active database so that they are in chronological order (by **DATE**) and, for those with the same **DATE**, the records are arranged by **NAME**. Compare this command to the comparable **INDEX** command (the command should all be typed on one line):

```
SORT TO A:\HOMEDANA.DBF ON DATE,NAME
INDEX ON STR(YEAR(DATE),2) + STR(MONTH(DATE),2) +
STR(DAY(DATE),2) + NAME TO A:\HOMEDANA.NDX
```

Try the **SORT** command by doing the following (begin from the dot prompt):

Keystroke	Action Resulting from Keystroke
USE A:\HOMEINV1.DBF ↵	
	Opens the specified database file for use.
SORT TO A:\HOMECANA.DBF ON CATEGORY/D,NAME/AC ↵	
	Sorts the active database using the field **CATEGORY** as the main key (in descending order) and the field **NAME** as the second key (in ascending order, ignoring the case of the letters). The effect will be to sort the records in reverse alphabetical order by **CATEGORY** and then, for those records that have the same **CATEGORY**, to sort them by **NAME** in alphabetical order, ignoring the case of the letters. The active database does not change after a sort; the sorted database has been written to a different file called **HOMECANA.DBF**.
USE A:\HOMECANA.DBF ↵	
	Opens the specified database file for use.
LIST ↵	Lists the contents of the active database. This is the newly created, sorted file.

Continued . . .

```
. USE HOMEINV1←
. SORT TO A:\HOMECANA.DBF ON CATEGORY/D,NAME/AC←
  100% Sorted           14 Records sorted
. USE A:\HOMECANA.DBF←
. LIST←
Record#  CATEGORY    NAME               MANUFACT      SERIAL_NUM DATE          VALUE
      1  Furniture   Bed, frame         Simmons       ---        09/03/87     100.00
      2  Furniture   Bed, mattress      Simmons       ---        09/03/87     100.00
      3  Furniture   Bed, spring        Simmons       ---        09/03/87     100.00
      4  Furniture   Dry sink           Hand made     ---        04/12/87     500.00
      5  Furniture   Recliner           La-Z-Boy      ---        03/23/87     350.00
      6  Furniture   Sofa               Wilder        ---        11/21/84     450.00
      7  Electronic  Computer           IBM           F3827122   02/10/90    1200.00
      8  Electronic  External drive     IBM           F392281    02/10/90     356.00
      9  Electronic  Printer            IBM           03483      02/10/90     450.00
     10  Electronic  Stereo             Fischer       34562      03/12/89     412.00
     11  Appliance   Dishwasher         Kitchen Aid   04322344   09/23/81     550.00
     12  Appliance   Microwave oven     Sears         2339112    01/22/89     450.00
     13  Appliance   Refrigerator       Wards         493323     03/22/87     450.00
     14  Appliance   Stove              Wards         533282     03/22/87     350.00

.
Command ||A:\HOMECANA          ||Rec EOF/14      ||File ||     ||
```

Modifying the Database Structure

The structure of a database is the way in which you define the field names, field types, field lengths, number of decimal places (for numeric fields), and index tags. Because this is the scaffolding upon which the data will be placed, it is important to carefully plan the database structure before you actually create it in dBASE IV and enter the data. Careful planning will save you much time in the long run because you will not have to change structural components of your database even though the actual data probably will change. Planning is the most important part of any interaction with the computer but it is the part given the least attention by novice computer users. Planning a database is like making a blueprint of a building before beginning construction. The more carefully thought through and laid out the plans, the easier the construction and the less likely will be the need for changes at some later date. Making modifications are costly, time consuming, and many times are difficult to accomplish.

However, even the most carefully planned databases may need to be modified as the needs of the users change. The **DISPLAY STRUCTURE** command allows you to view the structure of a database while the **MODIFY STRUCTURE** command allows you to change the structure.

Changing the structure of a database that already contains data can cause problems if you are not careful. For example, if you change the names of two fields at the same time you must be sure that dBASE IV copies the proper data into the proper field. To guard against data loss (which is a pain because lost data have to be reentered) or data corruption (which is tragic because you may not know that the data are incorrect and keep on using them), please note the following when modifying the structure of a database:

- When you modify a structure, dBASE IV actually creates a new structure and then copies the data from the old database to the new. Be sure you have enough disk space to accomplish the task.
- The data are transferred from the old database structure to the new using the field names that are common to both structures. This means that you can delete as many fields as you wish at the same time without loss of data.
- If only one field is renamed, the data are transferred by position in the database and no data will be lost. However, if you change a field name and its width or type at the same time, the data for that field will be lost. If you need to change a field name and width, you

should change the name, then save the file, and then use **MODIFY STRUCTURE** again to change the field width and/or type. This will save you the trouble of reentering data for renamed fields.

- If more than one field is renamed, the data for those fields are not transferred to the new structure. This guarantees that there will be no mixups where data are placed into the wrong field. The problem is that you have to reenter the data into these fields. If you have to change the names of two or more fields, change the name of one field, then save the file, and then use **MODIFY STRUCTURE** again to change the name of the next field, and so on.

It is good practice to follow the procedure given below when modifying the structure of a database:

1. Use the **COPY TO** command to make a backup copy of the database before you modify its structure. If you make a major mistake, you can always go back to your copy. We followed this advice when we made modifications to files in WordPerfect and Lotus 1-2-3. When you use **MODIFY STRUCTURE**, dBASE IV creates a backup file of the database using the same name but with the extension **DBK**. However, the file is overwritten (replaced by) a new backup file the next time you use the **MODIFY STRUCTURE** command so your own backup is additional insurance against data loss. If you are using a large database you must be sure that your disk has enough room to make these copies.
2. Modify the structure of the backup copy of the database.
3. Use **DISPLAY STRUCTURE** and check the new structure to see if it is correct.
4. Use **DISPLAY ALL** to check the data to see if they are correct. For a large database, this would not be practical. But, you could check a sample of the data by entering **LIST NEXT 10** (displays the next 10 records in the database), **SKIP 100** (skips the next 100 records), **LIST NEXT 10**, etc.
5. Use **DELETE FILE** to delete the backup copy of the old database (or, you could keep the old copy if disk space permitted).

To illustrate modifying the structure of a database, change **HOMEINV1** in the following ways:

- Delete the fields **MANUFACT**, **SERIAL_NUM**, and **DATE**.
- Change the order of the fields by making **NAME** precede **CATEGORY** in the display.
- Select only the electronic items for inclusion in the new database.
- Change the name of the **VALUE** field to **COST**.
- Change the width of the **NAME** field to 20 columns.
- Add a new field called **COMMENT**. This will be a memo field that can be used to store comments about the individual records.

The first three changes will be accomplished using the **COPY TO** command to copy selected portions of the active database **HOMEINV1** onto a new file which we will call **HOMEMOD1**. The last four changes will be made to the new file **HOMEMOD1** using the **MODIFY STRUCTURE** command.

For reference, the structure of the old database, **HOMEINV1**, with two sample records, is given below:

Field width →	1234567890	123456789012345	123456789012	1234567890	12345678	12345678
Field name →	CATEGORY	NAME	MANUFACT	SERIAL_NUM	DATE	VALUE
Record #1 →	Electronic	Computer	IBM	F3827122	02/10/90	1200.00
Record #2 →	Electronic	Printer	IBM	03483	02/10/90	450.00

The structure of the new database, **HOMEMOD1**, with two sample records, is given below:

	NAME	CATEGORY	COST	COMMENT
Field width →	12345678901234567890	1234567890	12345678	1234567890
Field name →	NAME	CATEGORY	COST	COMMENT
Record #1 →	Computer	Electronic	1200.00	MEMO
Record #2 →	Printer	Electronic	450.00	memo

Follow the steps given below to accomplish this transformation (begin from the dot prompt with **HOMEINV1.DBF** in use).

Step 1: Copy the Database Because we want to have only selected fields and records in the new database, we will use **COPY TO** to create a new database called **HOMEMOD1.DBF** that contains only the desired data and fields from the old database. The fields to be copied are: **NAME**, **CATEGORY**, and **VALUE**. Copying only these fields will effectively delete the unwanted fields from the new database (i.e., they will not be copied). Copying the fields in this order will effectively rearrange them in the new database so that they are in the desired sequence. Also, the records to be copied are only those that have **CATEGORY = "Electronic"**.

In summary, we want to **COPY** from the current database **TO** a new database called **A:\HOMEMOD1.DBF** the **FIELDS NAME**, **CATEGORY**, and **VALUE FOR** only those records in which the **CATEGORY** is equal to (=) **Electronic**. The proper syntax for the command is as follows:

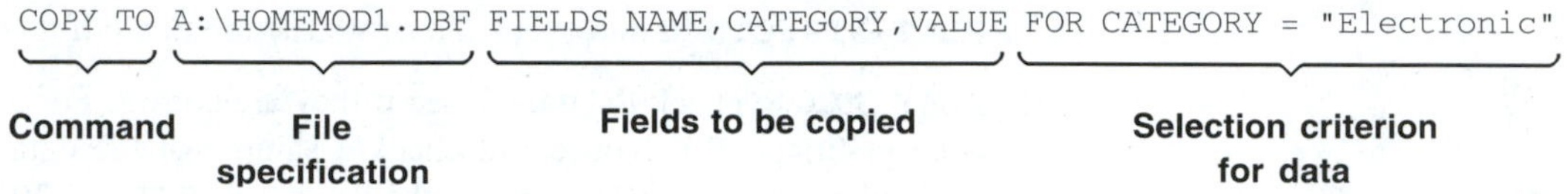
COPY TO A:\HOMEMOD1.DBF FIELDS NAME,CATEGORY,VALUE FOR CATEGORY = "Electronic"
Command
File specification
Fields to be copied
Selection criterion for data

Type this command and tap **[Enter]**. Be careful! The selection criterion is case sensitive (**Electronic** is not the same as **ELECTRONIC**). dBASE IV will copy the appropriate records and fields and display the message **4 records copied** (there are only four records whose type is **Electronic**).

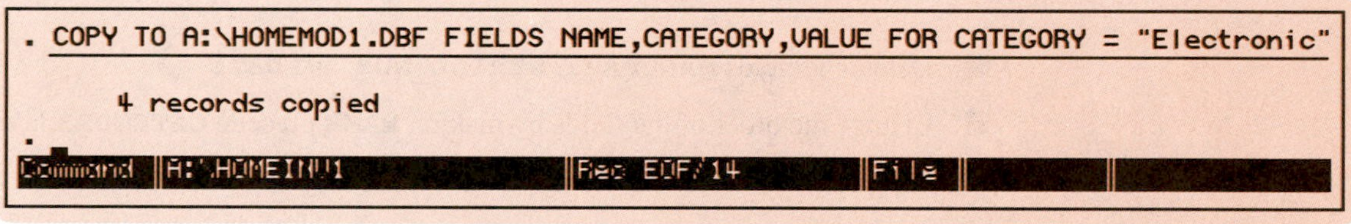
. COPY TO A:\HOMEMOD1.DBF FIELDS NAME,CATEGORY,VALUE FOR CATEGORY = "Electronic"
4 records copied
Command A:\HOMEINV1 Rec EOF/14 File

Step 2: Modify the Structure of the Backup Copy After the records have been copied to the new file, load that file into dBASE IV, and then list the contents (just to see what is there) by doing the following:

Keystroke	*Action Resulting from Keystroke*
USE A:HOMEMOD1.DBF ↵	Opens the specified database file for use.
LIST ↵	Displays the contents of the active database. The screen should look as follows:

Continued . . .

Keystroke	Action Resulting from Keystroke

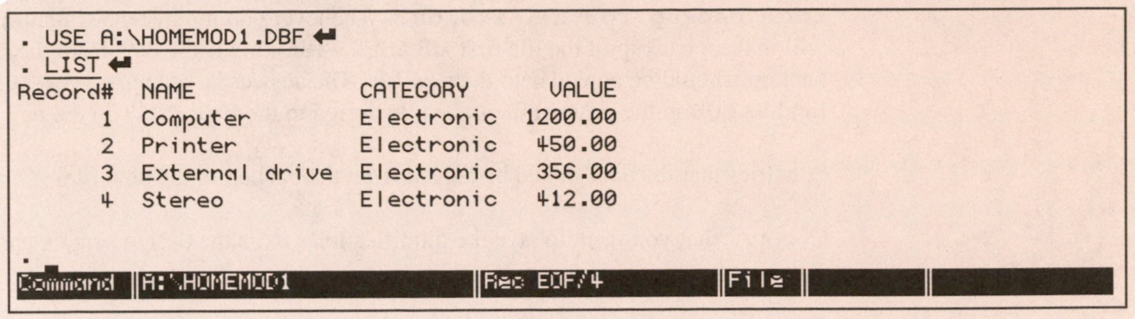

Use the **MODIFY STRUCTURE** command to display the Database design screen so that you can change field names, change field widths, and add fields.

Keystroke	Action Resulting from Keystroke
MODIFY STRUCTURE ↵	Displays the Database design screen of the active database and allows you to modify it as needed.

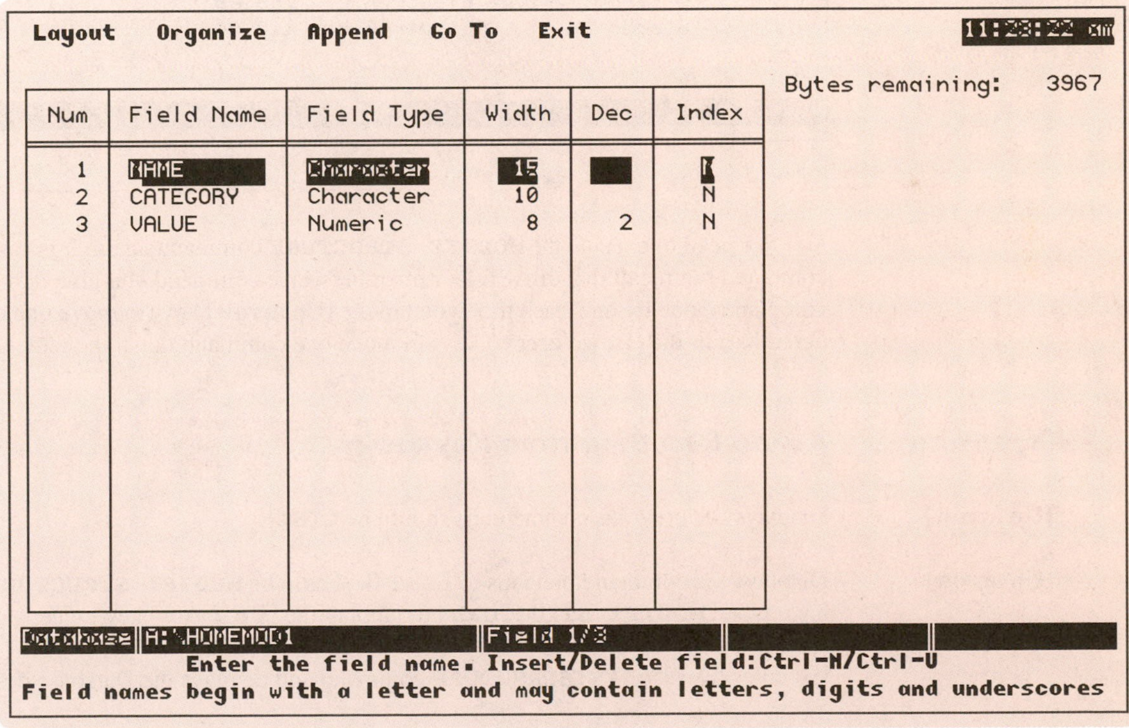

[edit]	Use the normal editing techniques to change the field name **VALUE** to **COST**.

Before making the next modification, you must exit the Database design screen to give dBASE IV a chance to make the above alteration. You will lose data if you insert or delete fields and, at the same time, change field names.

Keystroke	Action Resulting from Keystroke
[Ctrl-End]	Specifies that the modifications are to be saved. dBASE IV will ask **Should data be COPIED from backup for all fields?**. Whenever you modify the structure of a database, dBASE IV will make a backup of the file first. dBASE IV is asking if the data from the original file (now the backup) should be copied onto the new file. The answer is, of course, yes; you want the data from the field **VALUE** in the original file to be transferred to the field **COST** in the new file.
Y	Specifies that the data should be copied from the backup to the new file.
Y	Confirms that you want to save the modifications, exits the design screen, and returns to the dot prompt.

You can see the contents of the modified file by listing the file:

Keystroke	Action Resulting from Keystroke
LIST ↵	Lists the contents of the active database. The only change from the previous listing is the name of the last field (it now reads **COST**).

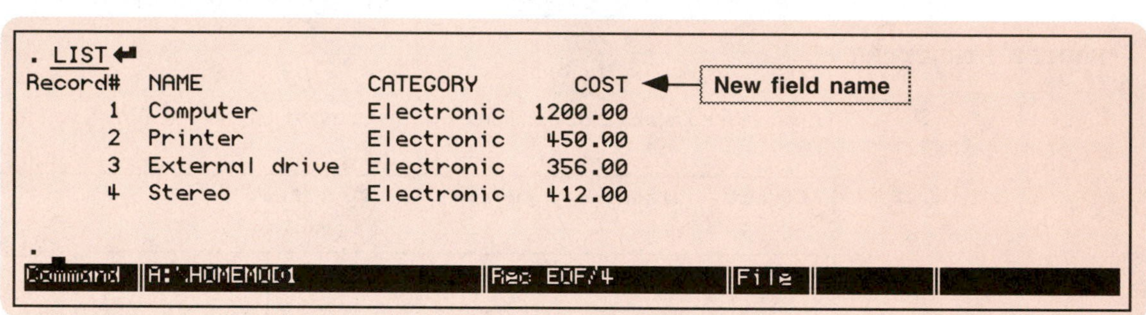

We need to execute the **MODIFY STRUCTURE** command again. It is easy enough to retype the command but recall that dBASE IV remembers each command you give it and will redisplay those commands, one by one, each time you tap the **[Up arrow]** key (to move one command up the remembered list) or the **[Down arrow]** key (to move one command down the remembered list).

Keystroke	Action Resulting from Keystroke
[Up arrow]	Displays the previous command (it should be **LIST**).
[Up arrow]	Displays the command previous to **LIST** (it should be **MODIFY STRUCTURE**). Of course, you could have typed **MODIFY STRUCTURE** but tapping the **[Up arrow]** key twice is much faster.
[Enter]	Executes the **MODIFY STRUCTURE** command and displays the Database design screen.
[edit]	Use the normal editing techniques to change the width of the **NAME** field from **15** to **20**.
[arrow]	Use the **[arrow]** keys to move down past the third field to create a fourth field.
COMMENT ↵	Specifies the name of the new field and moves the cursor to the **Field Type** option.

Continued . . .

Keystroke	Action Resulting from Keystroke
`M`	Specifies that the new field will be a memo field and moves the cursor to the next line. Memo fields are automatically given a width of 10 to hold a *memo marker* that will be used to indicate whether or not a memo exits for a particular record. The memos you create can be as long as you want.

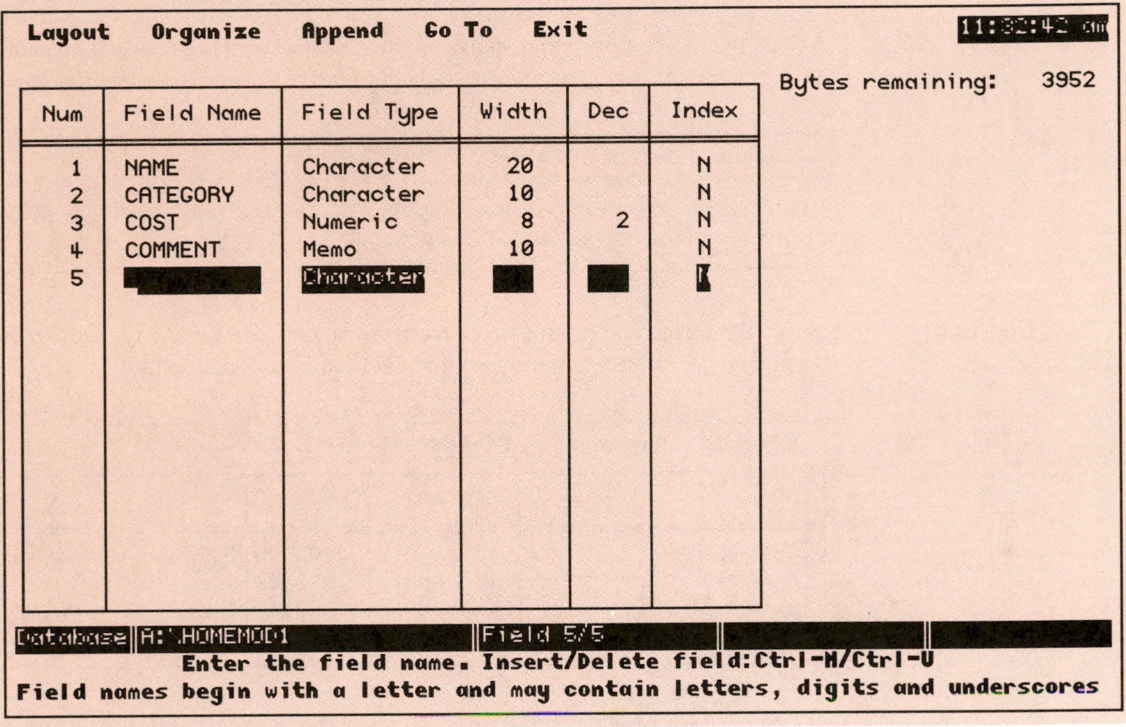

Keystroke	Action Resulting from Keystroke
[Ctrl-End]	Specifies that the modifications are to be saved.
`Y`	Confirms that you want to save the modifications, exits the design screen, and returns to the dot prompt.
`LIST ↵`	Lists the contents of the active database. Note that the **`COMMENT`** field contains the word **`memo`** indicating that this is a memo field. When you actually add a memo to a record the lowercase **`memo`** is changed to uppercase **`MEMO`** to indicate that a memo exists for that record.

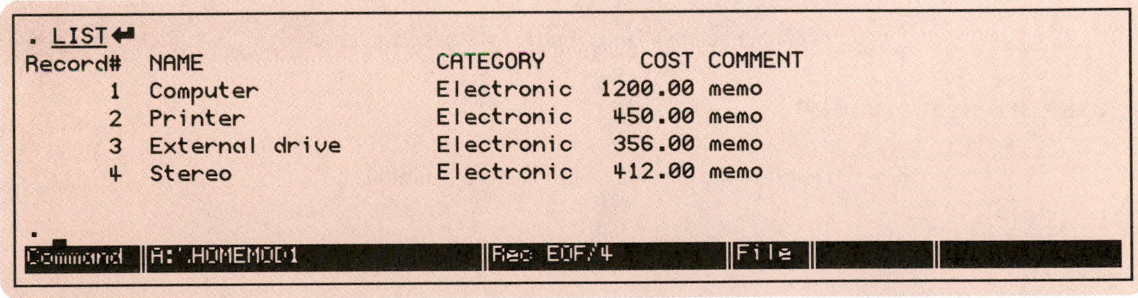

Now add a comment into the memo field for the first record.

Keystroke	Action Resulting from Keystroke
Browse ↵	Switches to **Browse**.
[arrow]	Use the **[arrow]** keys to highlight the word **memo** in the last column of the first record. You may open the memo field by tapping **[F9]** (zoom) or **[Ctrl-Home]**.
[F9]	Opens the memo field and displays the dBASE IV word processor. This word processor allows you to use the normal text entry and editing techniques. Enter the text shown below:

```
 Layout   Words   Go To   Print   Exit                                              12:00:48 pm
[···•···▼1····•·▼··2····▼····3·▼·•····4▼···•···▼5····•·▼··6····]····7··▼·•·····
This is my IBM 386-based computer.  It will be used for both my
business and my personal needs.
```

Keystroke	Action Resulting from Keystroke
[Ctrl-End]	Saves the memo and returns to the **Browse** screen. Notice that the word **memo** in the first record has been changed to **MEMO** to indicate that the field is no longer empty.

```
 Records   Organize   Fields   Go To   Exit                                   12:08:01 pm

 NAME                 CATEGORY     COST     COMMENT

 Computer             Electronic   1200.00  MEMO
 Printer              Electronic    450.00  memo
 External drive       Electronic    356.00  memo
 Stereo               Electronic    412.00  memo
```

If you need to erase a memo field, you can open it and delete all the text or highlight the field and then select **Blank field** from the **Fields** menu.

Keystroke	Action Resulting from Keystroke
[Esc]	Returns to the dot prompt.

Step 3: Check the Structure of the New Database Use the **DISPLAY STRUCTURE** command to show the structure of the new database. You should check to be sure that it is what you want.

Keystroke	Action Resulting from Keystroke
DISPLAY STRUCTURE ↵	
	Displays the structure of the active database.

Continued . . .

Keystroke	Action Resulting from Keystroke

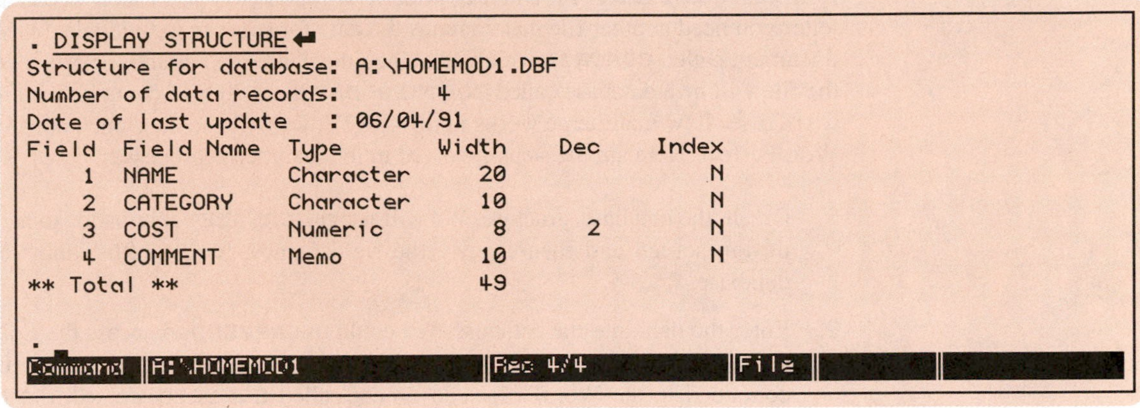

```
. DISPLAY STRUCTURE
Structure for database: A:\HOMEMOD1.DBF
Number of data records:       4
Date of last update   : 06/04/91
Field  Field Name  Type       Width    Dec    Index
    1  NAME        Character     20               N
    2  CATEGORY    Character     10               N
    3  COST        Numeric        8      2        N
    4  COMMENT     Memo          10               N
** Total **                      49

.
Command ║A:\HOMEMOD1          ║Rec 4/4          ║File ║
```

Step 4: Check the Data in the New Database Use the **LIST** command so that you can examine how the data were copied to the new database.

Keystroke	Action Resulting from Keystroke
LIST ↵	Displays the records of the active database.

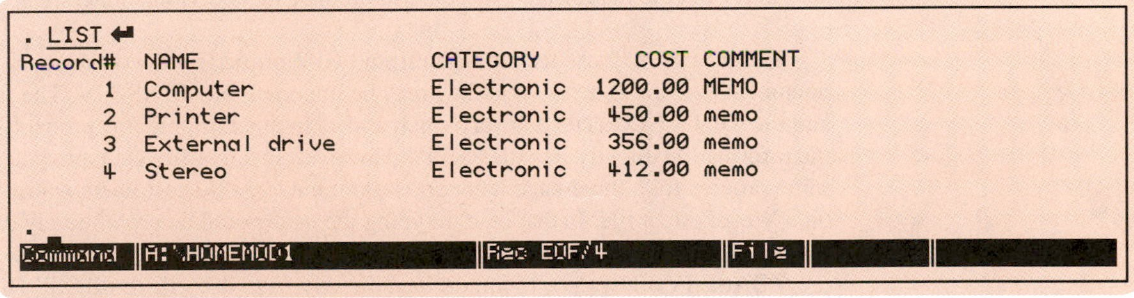

```
. LIST
Record#  NAME                  CATEGORY       COST  COMMENT
      1  Computer              Electronic  1200.00  MEMO
      2  Printer               Electronic   450.00  memo
      3  External drive        Electronic   356.00  memo
      4  Stereo                Electronic   412.00  memo

.
Command ║A:\HOMEMOD1          ║Rec EOF/4        ║File ║
```

Step 5: Delete or Archive the Old Database We want to keep the old database, **HOMEINV1.DBF** so we will not delete it at this time. dBASE IV has also created a backup file called **HOMEMOD1.DBK** which you may delete if you wish.

Exit dBASE IV by doing the following:

Keystroke	Action Resulting from Keystroke
QUIT ↵	Exits dBASE IV and returns to DOS.

TO TAKE A BREAK Remove data diskette. To resume: Insert data diskette.

Merging Data into Documents

On pages W128–36 we discussed using WordPerfect to produce form letters that were personalized with the names and addresses of the people to whom they were to be sent. dBASE IV can easily produce the same type of letters from a database of names and addresses using its *Mailmerge* feature. The concept of merging data into documents is the same in dBASE IV as it is in WordPerfect. In WordPerfect you created a form letter that contained text which was to appear in every letter sent out to contributors to the Save the Children Fund and variables to show where individualized data such as name and address were to be placed. In WordPerfect the form letter was a document called **LETTER** and the variables were merge codes such as **{FIELD}1**; in dBASE IV the form letter will be a report form called **LETTER.FRM** and the variables will be field names such as **CITY**. In addition to the form letter you need another file that contains the data for specific individuals. In WordPerfect the file was a document called **CONTRIB** which contained the names and addresses of the contributors; in dBASE IV the file will be a database called **CONTRIB.DBF** that will also contain the names and addresses.

To see how mailmerge works in dBASE IV, we will use the same data and form letter as we did for WordPerfect. Here are the steps involved in the mailmerge process:

1. Create the database structure. We will use the **CREATE** command to access the Database design screen and then specify the field names, field widths, and field types for the database.

2. Enter the data into the database. We could use **APPEND** to access the Edit screen and then type the records one by one. However, because we are using the same data as that which is contained in the WordPerfect document called **CONTRIB** we will not have to retype it. We will use the **APPEND FROM** command to insert the data into the database structure of **CONTRIB.DBF**.

3. Create the form letter. We will use the **CREATE REPORT** command to access the Report design screen and then enter the text for the letter in the detail band. In those places where we want to insert information from the database (e.g., the city where the addressee lives) we will insert a field marker (e.g., **CITY**) as we have done in previous reports. Because we will be using the same text that is in the WordPerfect document called **LETTER** we will not have to retype it—we will use the dBASE IV **Write/read text file** option to copy the text directly into the report from a document created by WordPerfect.

4. Carry out the mailmerge procedure to produce the individual letters.

Because we will use text and data from two WordPerfect documents, we first must convert those documents to ASCII text so that they may be imported into dBASE IV. The file **LETTER** is very short and the database **CONTRIB** is very small and so in this example it is probably faster to simply retype the information directly into dBASE IV. However, in a real-life example you may want to follow the same process for a three-page letter and send it out to 5,000 customers whose names and addresses are on a WordPerfect file. In that case, retyping the data would be prohibitively expensive. So, let's see how to import the data from WordPerfect.

dBASE IV allows you to import data directly from dBASE II, dBASE III, VisiCalc, Framework II, RapidFile, Multiplan, Lotus 1-2-3, and ASCII text files. If you want to import data from other types of files you must first convert them to one of the above formats. Importing is discussed in more detail on pages D186–92. For the present example, we will convert the WordPerfect files into ASCII text files (as we did on pp. W112–15) and then import the text into a Report design and a database.

If WordPerfect or the WordPerfect documents you created are no longer available to you, then skip the following conversion process. You will have to enter the letter and data by retyping it directly into dBASE IV. Begin the following from DOS.

Keystroke	Action Resulting from Keystroke
A: ↵	Ensures that the A: drive is the default.
C:\WP51\WP ↵	Starts WordPerfect and presents a blank document screen.
[Shift-F10]	Requests the name of a document to retrieve. Place the diskette that contains the file **LETTER** into drive A: and type the following:
A:LETTER ↵	Retrieves the document.

Continued . . .

Keystroke	Action Resulting from Keystroke

```
Save the Children Fund
1344 South Fourth Street
Minneapolis, MN  55415
<DATE>

<FIELD>1~ <FIELD>2~
<FIELD>3~
<FIELD>4~, <FIELD>5~ <FIELD>6~

Dear <FIELD>7~ <FIELD>2~:

Thank you for your generous contribution of $<FIELD>8~ to our fund.
Your gift will bring much happiness to many needy children and
their families.

If you have any questions concerning our organization, please
call me at 624-1102.

Sincerely,


Terry Lamb, D.D.S
Honorary Chairperson

A:\LETTER                                  Doc 1 Pg 1 Ln 1" Pos 1"
```

[Ctrl-F5] Accesses the *Text In/Out* feature and displays its menu.

```
1 DOS Text; 2 Password; 3 Save As; 4 Comment; 5 Spreadsheet: 0
```

T (or **1**) Selects **1 DOS Text** and displays its menu.

```
1 Save; 2 Retrieve (CR/LF to [HRt]); 3 Retrieve (CR/LF to [SRt] in HZone): 0
```

S (or **1**) Selects **1 Save** and requests a file name for the ASCII version of the document.

Place your *dBASE IV Data* diskette in drive A:

A:\LETTER.TXT ↵ Specifies the name for the file and returns to edit mode.

Place your *WordPerfect Data* diskette in drive A:

[F7] Exits this document.

N Specifies that the document is not to be saved.

N Specifies that you want to remain in WordPerfect and presents a blank WordPerfect screen.

[Shift-F10] Requests the name of a document to retrieve.

A:CONTRIB ↵ Retrieves the data document.

Continued . . .

Keystroke	Action Resulting from Keystroke

```
Colette{END FIELD}
Brietkritez{END FIELD}
1401 NE Elm Street{END FIELD}
Boston{END FIELD}
MA{END FIELD}
09801{END FIELD}
Ms.{END FIELD}
100{END FIELD}
{END RECORD}
================================================================================
Elana{END FIELD}
Broch{END FIELD}
6 Fulton Avenue{END FIELD}
Brooklyn{END FIELD}
NY{END FIELD}
11971{END FIELD}
Dr.{END FIELD}
500{END FIELD}
{END RECORD}
================================================================================
Maren{END FIELD}
Watson{END FIELD}
100 South First Street{END FIELD}
Golden Valley{END FIELD}
Field: 1                                          Doc 1 Pg 1 Ln 1" Pos 1"
```

We need to save this document as a text file also. However, this file will be read directly into a dBASE IV database structure and so it must be edited to ensure that all the data for one person appear on one line (this will be a single record in dBASE IV). In addition, all the elements that are not really data must be removed. This means that we need to change the **{END FIELD}** codes and the associated hard returns into a commas (to indicate separate fields in dBASE IV) and we must change the **{END RECORD}** codes and the associated hard page returns into hard returns (to indicate separate records in dBASE IV).

Keystroke	Action Resulting from Keystroke
[Shift-F8]	Accesses the *Format* feature and displays its menu.
L (or **1**)	Selects **1 - Line** and displays its menu.
M (or **7**)	Selects **7 - Margins** and moves the cursor to the left margin indicator.
0 ↵	Specifies the new left margin.
0 ↵	Specifies the new right margin.
[F7]	Exits the **Line** menu and returns to edit mode.
[Alt-F2]	Accesses the *Replace* feature and asks if you want the process with or without confirm.

Continued . . .

Keystroke	Action Resulting from Keystroke
N	Specifies that confirm is to be turned off and requests the item to be searched for. You want to search for the special code represented by **{END FIELD}** (produced by tapping the **[F9]** key) and the hidden code for the hard return (produced by tapping the **[Enter]** key).
[F9] [Enter]	Specifies the items to be searched for. Notice that the respective codes are displayed on the search line.

```
-> Srch: [Mrg:END FIELD][HRt]_
```

[Alt-F2]	Requests the replacement for the item. This will be a comma.
,	Specifies the replacement.
[Alt-F2]	Carries out the replacement process.
[Home] [Home] [Up arrow]	Moves the cursor to the top of the document.

```
Colette,Brietkritez,1401 NE Elm Street,Boston,MA,09801,Ms.,100,<END RECORD>
================================================================================
Elana,Broch,6 Fulton Avenue,Brooklyn,NY,11971,Dr.,500,<END RECORD>
================================================================================
Maren,Watson,100 South First Street,Golden Valley,MN,55400,Dr.,1000,<END RECORD>
================================================================================
```

[Alt-F2]	Accesses the *Replace* feature again and asks if you want the process with or without confirm.
N	Specifies that confirm is to be turned off and requests the items to be searched for.
, [Shift-F9] E [Ctrl-Enter]	Produces the codes of the items to be searched for. The respective codes are displayed on the search line.

```
-> Srch: ,[Mrg:END RECORD][HPg]_
```

[Alt-F2]	Requests the replacement for the items. This will be a hard return.
[Enter]	Specifies the replacement and inserts the hard return code **[HRt]** at the cursor.
[Alt-F2]	Carries out the replacement process.
[Home] [Home] [Up arrow]	Moves the cursor to the top of the document.

```
Colette,Brietkritez,1401 NE Elm Street,Boston,MA,09801,Ms.,100
Elana,Broch,6 Fulton Avenue,Brooklyn,NY,11971,Dr.,500
Maren,Watson,100 South First Street,Golden Valley,MN,55400,Dr.,1000
```

Continued . . .

Keystroke	Action Resulting from Keystroke
[Ctrl-F5]	Accesses the *Text In/Out* feature and displays its menu.
T (or **1**)	Selects **1 DOS Text** and displays its menu.
S (or **1**)	Selects **1 Save** and requests a file name for the ASCII version of the document.
	Place your *dBASE IV Data* diskette in drive A:
A:\CONTRIB.TXT ↵	Specifies the name for the file and returns to edit mode.
[F7]	Exits this document.
N	Specifies that the document is not to be saved.
Y	Specifies that you want to exit WordPerfect and return to DOS.

If you had to do this type of procedure often you could create a WordPerfect macro to accomplish the conversions for you. For the small documents we are working with, the above conversion process takes longer than retyping the data directly into dBASE IV. However, you now know how to do it for a set of data of any size. Also, note that the process is reversible. That is, if you have a dBASE IV database that contains names and addresses you could save it as an ASCII file and then add the codes in WordPerfect so that it could be used with the WordPerfect *Merge* feature.

Follow the steps given below to create the dBASE IV files needed to produce the mailmerge documents:

Step 1: Create the Database Structure Do the following to create the structure of the database that will contain the names and addresses of the contributors to the Save the Children Fund.

Keystroke	Action Resulting from Keystroke
A: ↵	Ensures that drive A: is the default.
C:\DBIV\DBASE ↵	Starts the dBASE IV program and displays the dot prompt.
CREATE A:\CONTRIB.DBF ↵	
	Accesses the Database design screen.
[edit]	Use the normal editing techniques to make the design screen look like the following:

Continued . . .

Keystroke	Action Resulting from Keystroke

```
Layout   Organize   Append   Go To   Exit                    9:14:35 am
                                                     Bytes remaining:   3937
 Num   Field Name   Field Type   Width   Dec   Index

  1    FIRST        Character       7            N
  2    LAST         Character      11            N
  3    STREET       Character      22            N
  4    CITY         Character      13            N
  5    ST           Character       2            N
  6    ZIP          Character       5            N
  7    TI           Character       3            N
  8    CONTRIB      Numeric         7      2     N

Database  A:\CONTRIB             Field 8/8
              Change option to index on this field:Spacebar
```

Keystroke	Action Resulting from Keystroke
E	Opens the **Exit** menu.
S	Selects **Save changes and exit**.
[Enter]	Confirms that you want to save the changes and exits to the dot prompt.

Step 2: Enter the Data into the Database If you did not create the file **CONTRIB.TXT** from the WordPerfect document **CONTRIB** you should type **APPEND** ↵ and enter the data for each record manually. If you did create the file **CONTRIB.TXT** you may use the **APPEND FROM** command to insert the data directly into the database.

Keystroke	Action Resulting from Keystroke
APPEND FROM A:\CONTRIB.TXT TYPE DELIMITED ↵	
	Inserts the data from file **CONTRIB.TXT** into the active database. The words **TYPE DELIMITED** mean that the file whose data are to be appended is an ASCII file with the fields for each record separated by commas and with records separated by hard returns.

Continued . . .

Keystroke	Action Resulting from Keystroke
BROWSE ↵	Switches to **Browse**.
[PageUp]	Moves to the top of the database and displays all the records.

FIRST	LAST	STREET	CITY	ST	ZIP	TI	CONTRIB
Colette	Brietkritez	1401 NE Elm Street	Boston	MA	09801	Ms.	100.00
Elana	Broch	6 Fulton Avenue	Brooklyn	NY	11971	Dr.	500.00
Maren	Watson	100 South First Street	Golden Valley	MN	55400	Dr.	1000.00

Keystroke	Action Resulting from Keystroke
[Esc]	Switches back to the dot prompt.

Step 3: Create the Form Letter Do the following to create a report form, insert the text file **LETTER.TXT**, and insert the field names where the personalized data are to go.

Keystroke	Action Resulting from Keystroke
CREATE REPORT A:\MAIL1 ↵	
	Accesses the Report design screen for the new report form **MAIL1**.
[Alt-L]	Opens the **Layout** menu.
Q	Selects **Quick layouts**.
M	Selects **Mailmerge layout** and displays its special design screen.

Continued . . .

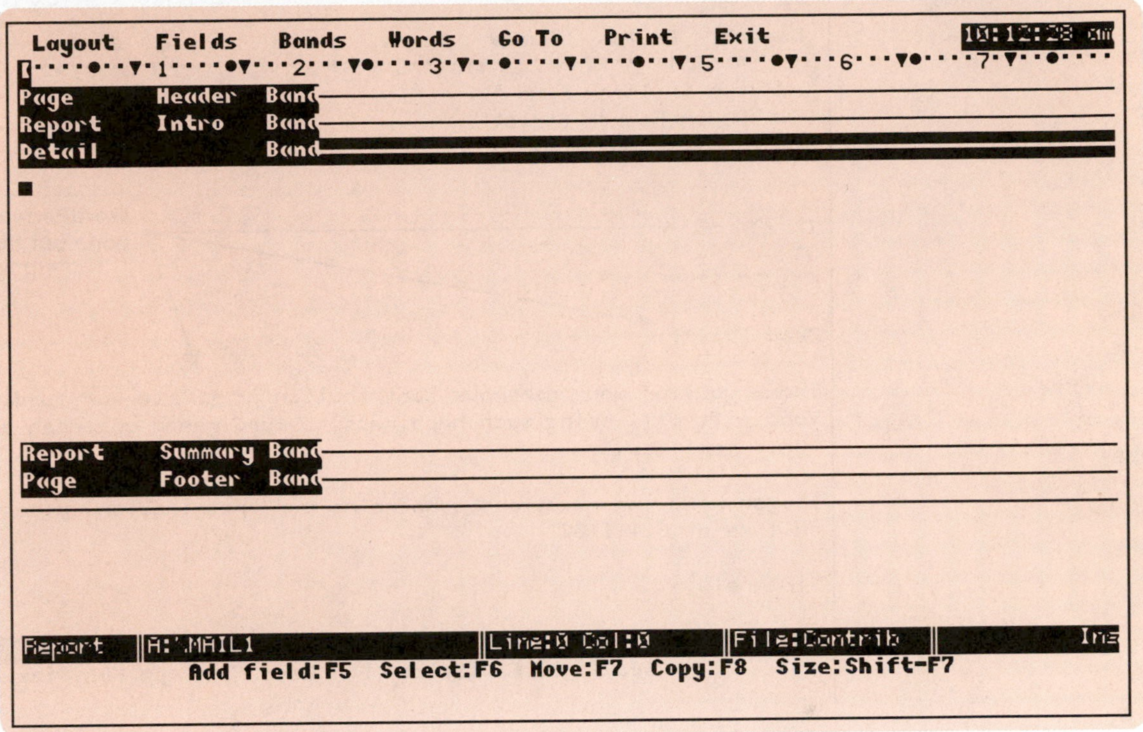

Keystroke	Action Resulting from Keystroke
[Alt-W]	Opens the **`Words`** menu.
`W`	Selects **`Write/read text file`**.
`R`	Selects **`Read text from file`** and asks for the name of the file to insert
`A:\LETTER.TXT` ↵	Specifies the name of the file and inserts the text at the cursor.
[Ctrl-PageUp]	Moves the cursor to the top of the band.

Continued . . .

Keystroke	Action Resulting from Keystroke

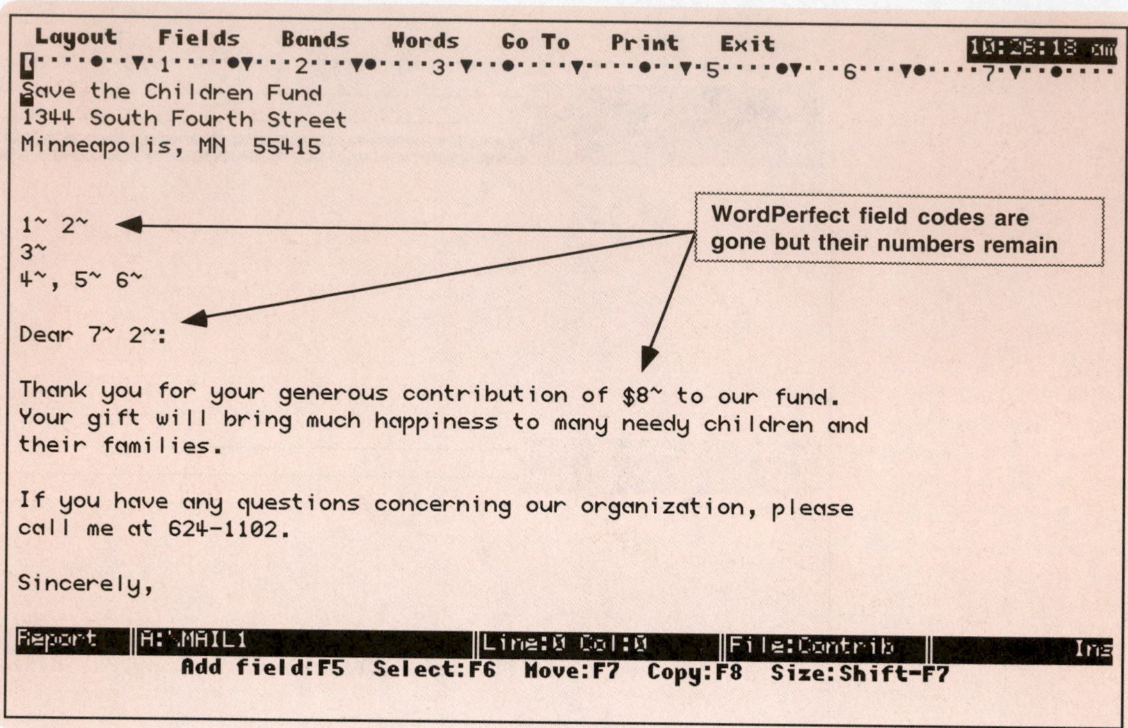

Layout Fields Bands Words Go To Print Exit 10:28:18 am
Save the Children Fund
1344 South Fourth Street
Minneapolis, MN 55415
1~ 2~
3~
4~, 5~ 6~
Dear 7~ 2~:
Thank you for your generous contribution of $8~ to our fund.
Your gift will bring much happiness to many needy children and
their families.
If you have any questions concerning our organization, please
call me at 624-1102.
Sincerely,
Report A:\MAIL1 Line:0 Col:0 File:Contrib Ins
Add field:F5 Select:F6 Move:F7 Copy:F8 Size:Shift-F7
WordPerfect field codes are gone but their numbers remain

The WordPerfect field codes have been deleted but the field numbers remain where they were in the original **LETTER** document. We need to replace the numbers with the proper dBASE IV field templates.

Keystroke	Action Resulting from Keystroke
[arrow]	Use the **[arrow]** keys to move the cursor to the blank line just below **Minneapolis** (location **Line:3 Col:0**). We will insert the current date at this location.
[F5]	Presents a picklist of fields that can be inserted at the cursor.
[arrow]	Use the **[arrow]** keys to highlight **Date** in the **PREDEFINED** column.
[Enter]	Selects the highlighted field and displays its attributes screen.
[Ctrl-End]	Accepts the attributes and returns to the Report design screen. Notice the field template **MM/DD/YY** at the cursor. When the letters are printed, the date on the computer's clock will be inserted at that location.
[arrow]	Use the **[arrow]** keys to move the cursor two lines down to the **1~** where the name of the addressee is to be inserted (location **Line:5 Col:0**).

Continued . . .

Keystroke	Action Resulting from Keystroke
[Delete]	Use the **[Delete]** key to delete the characters on that line.
[F5]	Presents a picklist of fields that can be inserted at the cursor.
[arrow]	Use the **[arrow]** keys to highlight **`TI`** in the **`CONTRIB`** column.
[Enter]	Selects the highlighted field and displays its attributes screen.

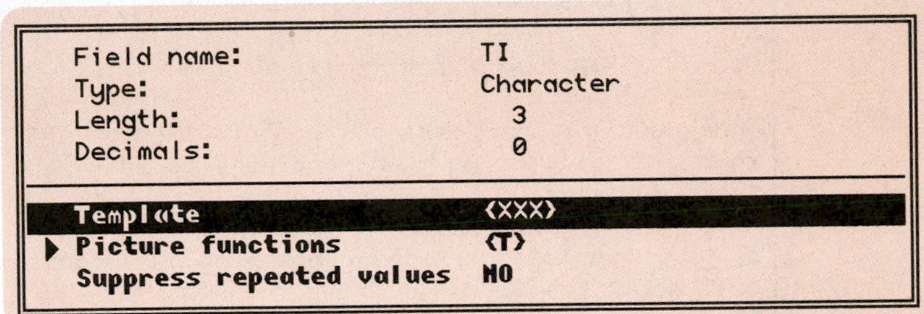

Notice that the **`Picture functions`** option has a **`{T}`** to its right. This means that any trailing blanks in the data will be trimmed (cut off) when the field is inserted. If this option were not selected, data that did not completely fill the field would have extra blank spaces on the right side which would make things look strange.

Keystroke	Action Resulting from Keystroke
[Ctrl-End]	Accepts the attributes and returns to the Report design screen. Notice the field template **`XXX`** at the cursor. When the letters are printed, the title of the addressee (from the **`TI`** field) will be inserted at that location.
[End]	Moves the cursor to the end of the line.
[Spacebar]	Inserts a blank space.
[F5]	Presents a picklist of fields that can be inserted at the cursor.
[arrow]	Use the **[arrow]** keys to highlight **`FIRST`** in the **`CONTRIB`** column.
[Enter]	Selects the highlighted field and displays its attributes screen.
[Ctrl-End]	Accepts the attributes and returns to the Report design screen. Notice the field template **`XXXXXXX`** at the cursor. When the letters are printed, the first name of the addressee (from the **`FIRST`** field) will be inserted at that location.

Continue inserting the field templates into the letter until it looks like the following:

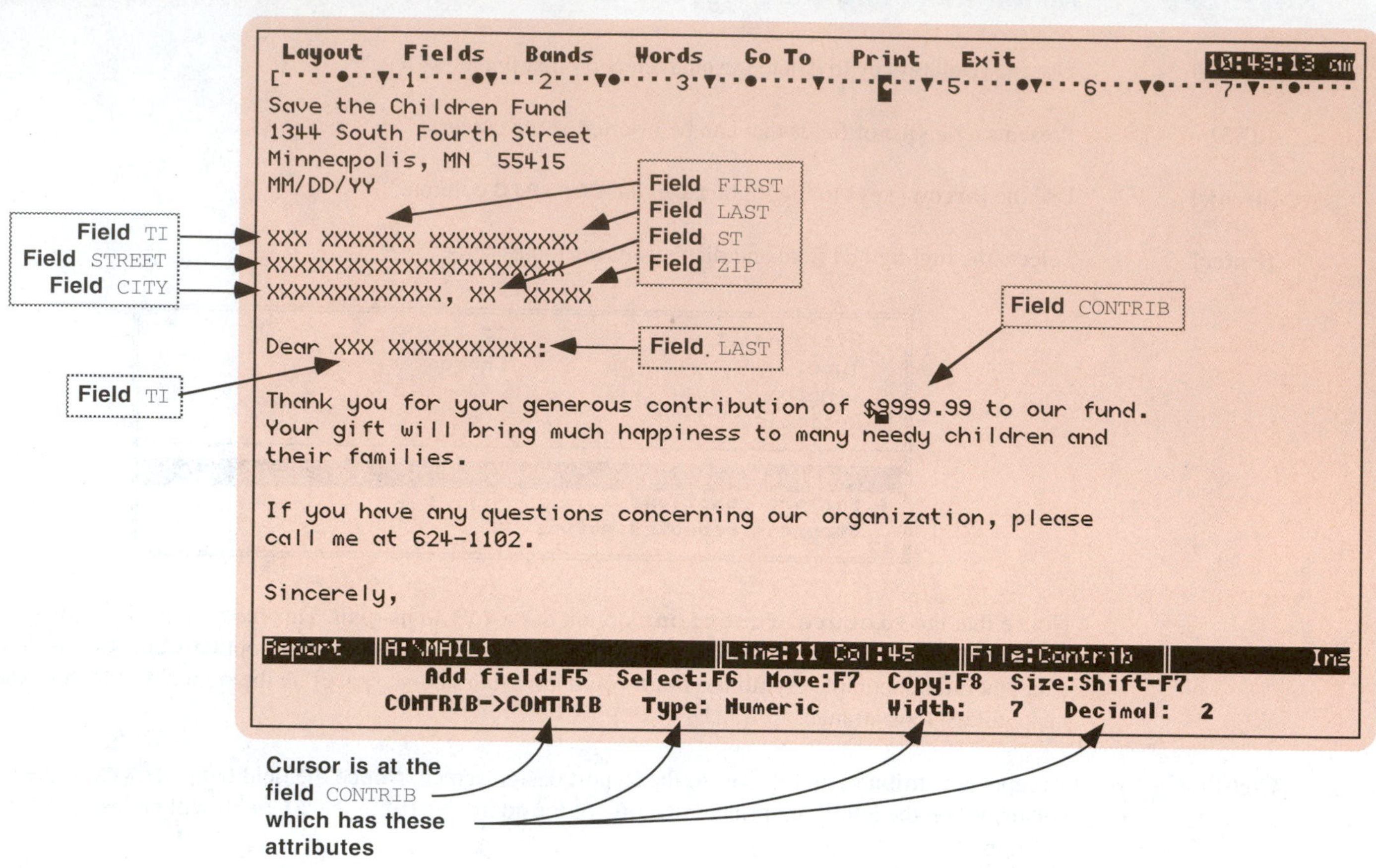

Keystroke	Action Resulting from Keystroke
[Alt-L]	Opens the **Layout** menu.
S	Selects **Save this report** and suggests the file specification **A:\MAIL1**.
[Enter]	Accepts the suggested file specification and saves the report.

Step 4: Produce the Individual Letters The final step is to produce the individual letters by printing the report form **MAIL1.FRM** (this is the form letter) using the data from the active database **CONTRIB.DBF**.

Keystroke	Action Resulting from Keystroke
[Alt-P]	Opens the **Print** menu.
V	Selects **View report on screen** and displays the first mailmerged letter. This letter is identical to the one produced by WordPerfect, except for the format of the date.

Continued . . .

Keystroke	Action Resulting from Keystroke

```
Save the Children Fund
1344 South Fourth Street
Minneapolis, MN  55415
06/08/91

Ms. Colette Brietkritez
1401 NE Elm Street
Boston, MA  09801

Dear Ms. Brietkritez:

Thank you for your generous contribution of $100.00 to our fund.
Your gift will bring much happiness to many needy children and
their families.

If you have any questions concerning our organization, please
call me at 624-1102.

Sincerely,


Terry Lamb, D.D.S
Honorary Chairperson
                    Cancel viewing: ESC,  Continue viewing: SPACEBAR
```

[Spacebar]	Use the **[Spacebar]** to view all the letters.
[Alt-E]	Opens the **`Exit`** menu.
S	Selects **`Save changes and exit`** and returns to the dot prompt.

Creating Mailing Labels

Creating mailing labels from a database of names and addresses is easily accomplished by using the Labels design screen. For example, we can produce mailing labels for the form letters created in the previous section by doing the following (begin from the dot prompt):

Keystroke	Action Resulting from Keystroke

`USE A:\CONTRIB.DBF` ↵

Makes the database **CONTRIB** active (it probably already was).

`CREATE LABEL A:\CONTRIB` ↵

Accesses the label design screen for a new label file called **CONTRIB** (dBASE IV will automatically add the extension **LBL**).

Continued . . .

Keystroke	Action Resulting from Keystroke

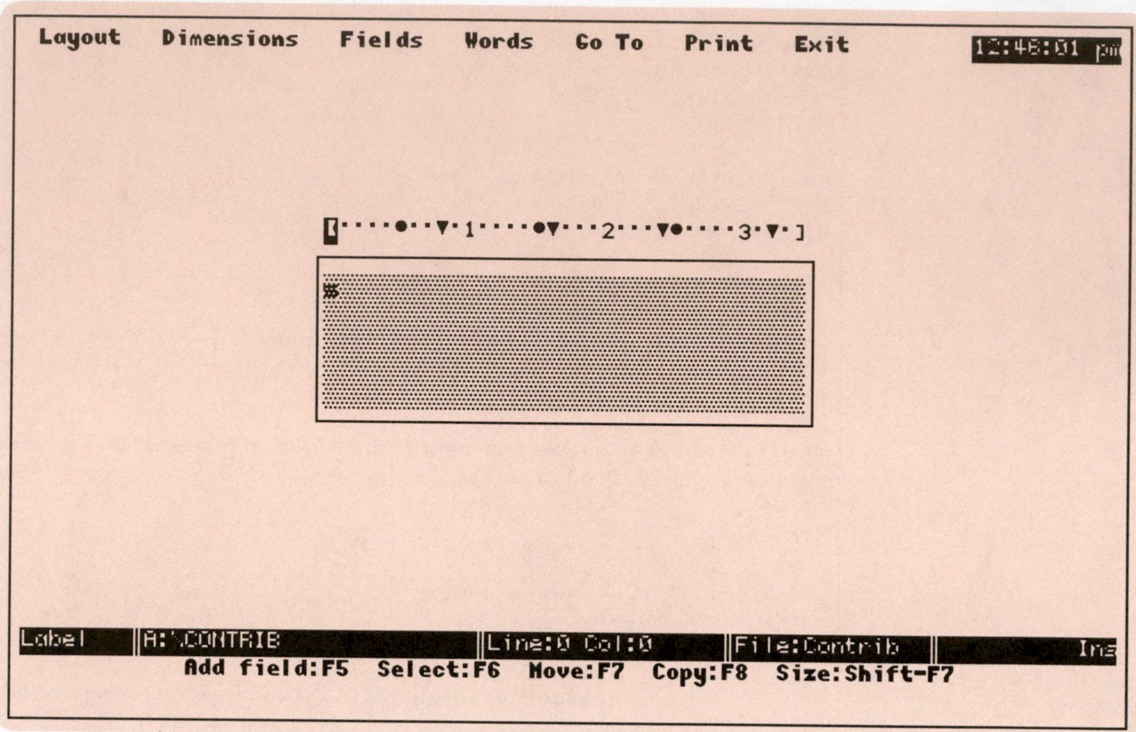

The menus included on the menu bar are ones we have seen before. The only new one is called **Dimensions**. That menu allows you to select the size of the label from a list of standard sizes or to create a size and organization of your own. We will use the predefined size displayed (15/16 inches high by 3 1/2 inches wide and one label across the page). This provides 5 lines for text.

You design the label using the same techniques as you do when designing a report. Use the **[arrow]** keys to move the cursor to any position inside the label and then type the desired text or select a field to be inserted at that location.

Keystroke	Action Resulting from Keystroke
[arrow]	Use the **[arrow]** keys to move the cursor to column 6 of the first line of the label (location **Line:0 Col:6**).
[F5]	Opens a picklist of the available fields. The first field will be the title of the person (e.g., Dr., Ms.)
[arrow]	Use the **[arrow]** keys to highlight **TI** in the **CONTRIB** column.
[Enter]	Selects the field **TI** and displays its attribute menu. We will just leave the attributes as they are for all the fields. Notice that the **Picture functions** attribute is again set to **{T}** to indicate that blank spaces will be trimmed off the right sides of the field when they occur.

Continued . . .

Keystroke	Action Resulting from Keystroke
[Ctrl-End]	Accepts the attributes, returns to the Label design screen, and inserts the template for the field **TI** at the cursor.

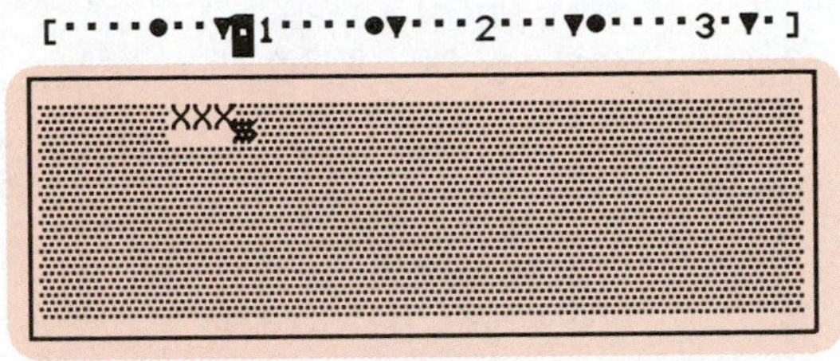

The rest of the fields and text can be entered following the same procedure. Be sure to use the **[Spacebar]** to insert blank spaces between fields rather than the **[arrow]** keys. This will ensure that dBASE IV will close up the empty space between fields whose data are not long enough to fill the field. Complete the label definition so that your screen looks like the following:

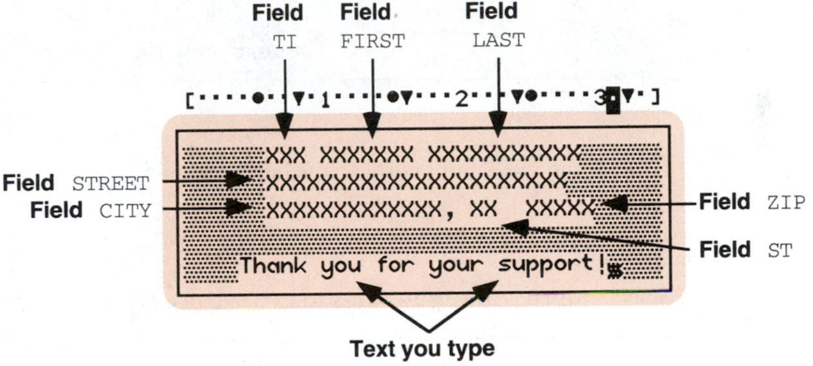

Save the label design and view the final labels by doing the following:

Keystroke	Action Resulting from Keystroke
[Alt-L]	Opens the **Layout** menu.
S	Selects **Save this report** and suggests the file specification **A:\CONTRIB.LBL**.
[Enter]	Accepts the suggested file specification and saves the label design.
[Alt-P]	Opens the **Print** menu. The third option, **Generate sample labels**, will print a sample label with Xs in place of the actual data. This is useful when trying to line up the paper labels in your printer. Select this option to print a single sample label, then adjust the labels in the printer, then print another sample label, then do another adjustment, and so on until the labels are properly aligned. For now, we will just view the labels on the screen.
V	Selects **View labels on screen**, generates the labels, and displays the following:

Continued . . .

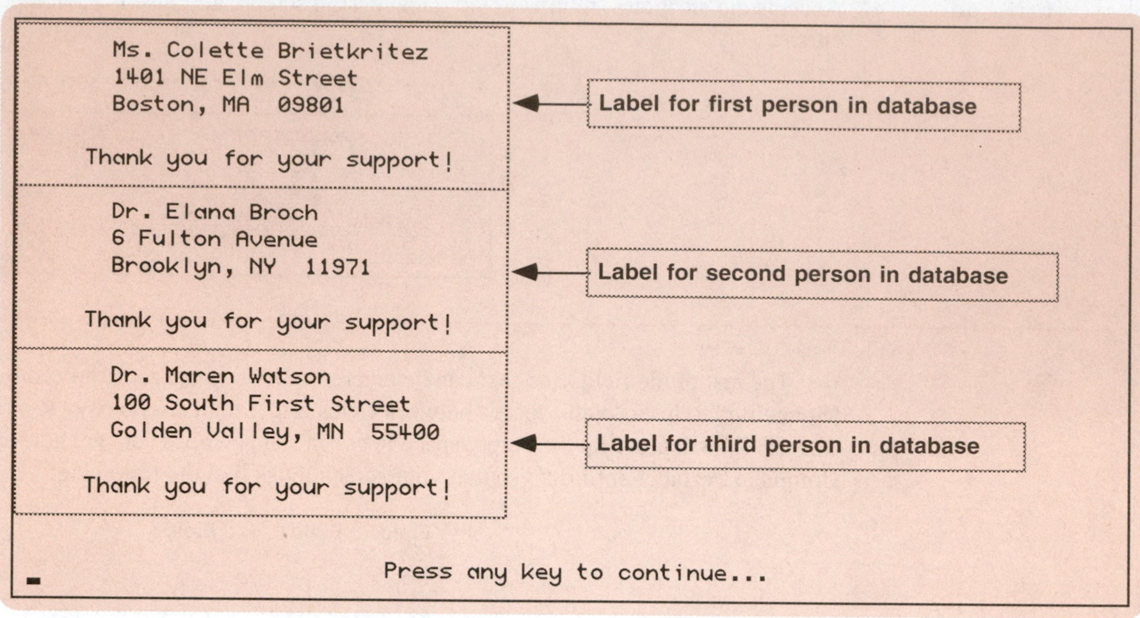

Keystroke	Action Resulting from Keystroke
[Esc]	Cancels the view and returns to the label design screen.
[Alt-E]	Opens the **`Exit`** menu.
`S`	Selects **`Save changes and exit`** and displays the dot prompt.

Moving Data between dBASE IV and Other Applications

As we have seen, sometimes information created by one software application is needed by another application. Like WordPerfect and Lotus 1-2-3, dBASE IV can export and import data in a number of different formats. For example, you might want to select a portion of a worksheet created in Lotus 1-2-3 and store and organize that information in a dBASE IV database. Or, you might want to insert information from a dBASE IV database into a letter written in WordPerfect, or use the data in a program written in a computer language such as BASIC or Pascal. If the information already exists somewhere on disk, you should be able to export it from one application and import it into another.

• Exporting dBASE IV Data •

Four dBASE IV commands that allow you to manipulate data from different types of files are **`APPEND FROM`**, **`COPY TO`**, **`EXPORT`**, and **`IMPORT`**.

`APPEND FROM` copies records from an existing file to the end of the active database. We used this command on page D173 to copy records from a text file into the database **`CONTRIB.DBF`**. The general form is:

```
APPEND FROM <filename>/?
    [[TYPE] <file type>]
    [FOR <condition>]
```

where

<filename> is the name of the file that contains the data you want to copy.

TYPE <file time> specifies the kind of file you are importing from. The supported file types are

DABASEII, which are dBASE II files. Note that dBASE IV can read dBASE III PLUS files directly and so you do not need to use a **TYPE** option to insert data from that type of file.

DELIMITED, which are ASCII files where the fields are separated by commas and the records are separated by carriage returns and line feeds.

DELIMITED WITH BLANK, which are like **DELIMITED** files except that fields are separated by blanks.

DELIMITED WITH <delimiter>, which are like **DELIMITED** files except that fields are separated by whatever character you supply in place of **<delimiter>**.

DIF, which are VisiCalc files.

FW2, which are Framework II files.

RPD, which are RapidFile files.

SDF, which are fixed length ASCII files. These are files where fields from record to record are the same length but are not delimited.

SYLK, which are Multiplan files.

WKS, which are Lotus 1-2-3 release 1A files. You should use the **IMPORT** command instead of **APPEND FROM** for Lotus 1-2-3 release 2.x files.

FOR <condition> allows you to select only those records that meet the specified condition.

COPY TO copies all or part of the active database to a new file. We used this command on page D34 to make a backup copy of **HOMEINV1.DBF** and again on page D162 to create a new database with a different structure. The general form is:

```
COPY TO <filename>
    [[TYPE] <file type>] / [PRODUCTION]
    [FIELDS <field list>]
    [FOR <condition>]
```

where

<filename> is the name of the new file you want to create.

TYPE <file time> specifies the kind of file you want to create. The supported file types are the same as for **APPEND FROM** with the addition of a type called **DBMEMO3** that converts the database into a format that can be read directly by dBASE III PLUS.

PRODUCTION allows you to copy the multiple index file associated with the database for dBASE IV type files.

FIELDS allows you to list the names of the fields you want to copy. Separate the field names with commas.

FOR <condition> allows you to select only those records that meet the specified condition.

EXPORT copies records from the active database to files usable by PFS:FILE, dBASE II, Framework II, or RapidFile.

IMPORT creates dBASE IV files from files using the PFS:FILE, dBASE II, Framework II, RapidFile, or Lotus 1-2-3 release 2.x formats.

Let's do a few examples of exporting information from a database. First, we will export the entire database **HOMEINV1.DBF** as an ASCII (text) type file so that the data can be used by other programs that do not support the dBASE IV format. This is easily accomplished by doing the following:

Keystroke	Action Resulting from Keystroke
USE A:\HOMEINV1.DBF ↵	
	Opens the specified database file for use.
COPY TO A:\HOMEINV1.TXT TYPE SDF ↵	
	Copies the active database in a fixed-length ASCII format (the fields from record to record are all the same length) to a file called **HOMEINV1.TXT**.

As a second example, suppose we want to send to an insurance company a letter that includes a listing of all electronic equipment in the home inventory database whose value is over $400. First, we will use the **COPY TO** command to create a text file called **EXPELECT** that contains only the required information. Next, we will import this file into a WordPerfect document.

Do the following to create the new file **EXPELECT**, which contains expensive electronic equipment (begin from the dot prompt):

Keystroke	Action Resulting from Keystroke
USE A:\HOMEINV1.DBF ↵	
	Opens the specified database file for use.
SET INDEX TO A:\HOMECANA.NDX ↵	
	Specifies the index file to be used (recall that this index sorts the records by **CATEGORY** and, within **CATEGORY**, by **NAME**).

To **COPY** records from the active database **TO** a new file called **EXPELECT**, and to list only the **FIELDS NAME**, **MANUFACT**, **SERIAL_NUM**, and **VALUE FOR** those records with **CATEGORY** equal to (=) **Electronic AND VALUE** greater than or equal to (>=) **400** and using a file **TYPE** where the data are in a standard text form (the official name is **S**ystem **D**ata **F**ormat ASCII form), type the following command (it should all be typed on one line):

```
COPY TO A:\EXPELECT.TXT  FIELDS NAME,MANUFACT,SERIAL_NUM,VALUE
    FOR CATEGORY = 'Electronic' .AND. VALUE >= 400 TYPE SDF
```

COPY TO duplicates the specified records.

A:EXPELECT.TXT is the specification of the file that will contain the copied records. If you do not include a file name extension, dBASE IV will add the extension **TXT** to indicate that the file is a text file.

FIELDS NAME,MANUFACT,SERIAL_NUM,VALUE is the list of the fields to be copied (if you leave off this part, all fields will be copied).

FOR CATEGORY = 'Electronic' .AND. VALUE >= 400 specifies that only those records that have the word **Electronic** in the **CATEGORY** field and a number greater than or equal to **400** in the **VALUE** field will be selected (if you leave this off, all records will be selected).

TYPE SDF specifies that the file will be created in **SDF** format. This means that the data are copied character by character and that corresponding fields in different records will be the same width. If you leave this off, the new file will be a dBASE IV type file (i.e., it will be written in coded form so that it could be read by dBASE IV but not by most other programs).

Type the above command at the dot prompt and then tap **[Enter]**. The screen will look like the following:

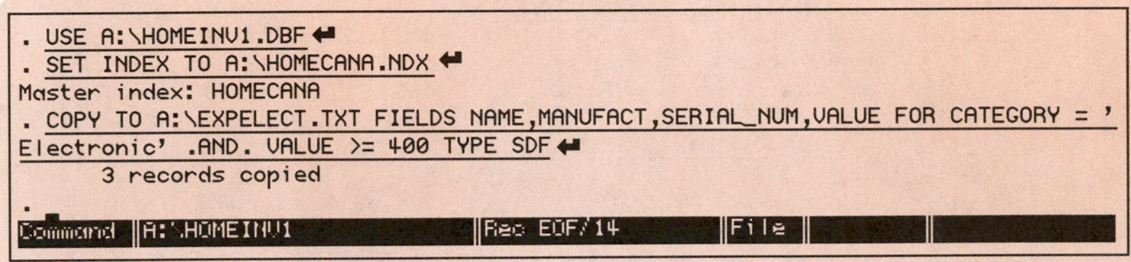

```
. USE A:\HOMEINV1.DBF ↵
. SET INDEX TO A:\HOMECANA.NDX ↵
Master index: HOMECANA
. COPY TO A:\EXPELECT.TXT FIELDS NAME,MANUFACT,SERIAL_NUM,VALUE FOR CATEGORY = '
Electronic' .AND. VALUE >= 400 TYPE SDF ↵
     3 records copied
.
Command ||A:\HOMEINV1 ||Rec EOF/14 ||File ||
```

Let's also save a version of the file **EXPELECT** that can be imported into a Lotus 1-2-3 worksheet. To create the new version of **EXPELECT** we need only change the file name extension and file **TYPE** to **WKS** to indicate that the file will be in a Lotus 1-2-3 format. The new command will look as follows (it should all be typed on one line):

```
COPY TO A:\EXPELECT.WKS FIELDS NAME,MANUFACT,SERIAL_NUM,VALUE
    FOR CATEGORY = 'Electronic' .AND. VALUE >= 400 TYPE WKS
```

Type this command (or edit the previous one) at the dot prompt and then tap **[Enter]**.

We will also save a version of the file **EXPELECT** that can be used as a data file by a programming application, such as BASIC, which uses commas to delimit (separate) data. Again, to create the new version of **EXPELECT** we need only change the **TYPE** of file to **DELIMITED** and the file name extension to **DEL** to indicate that this is a delimited file. The new command will look as follows (it should all be typed on one line):

```
COPY TO A:\EXPELECT.DEL FIELDS NAME,MANUFACT,SERIAL_NUM,VALUE
FOR CATEGORY = 'Electronic' .AND. VALUE >= 400 TYPE DELIMITED
```

Type this command (or modify your previous command) at the dot prompt and then tap **[Enter]**.

To see the files just created, exit to DOS and use the **TYPE** command:

Keystroke	Action Resulting from Keystroke
QUIT ↵	Exits dBASE IV and returns control to DOS.
TYPE A:\EXPELECT.TXT ↵	Displays the contents of the newly exported **SDF** file that we will use in WordPerfect.

Continued . . .

Keystroke	Action Resulting from Keystroke
TYPE A:\EXPELECT.WKS ↵	Displays the contents of the newly exported file that we will use in Lotus 1-2-3. This file is in coded form so it will look strange when displayed by DOS.
TYPE A:\EXPELECT.DEL ↵	Displays the contents of the newly exported **DELIMITED** file that can be used by a programming language such as BASIC.

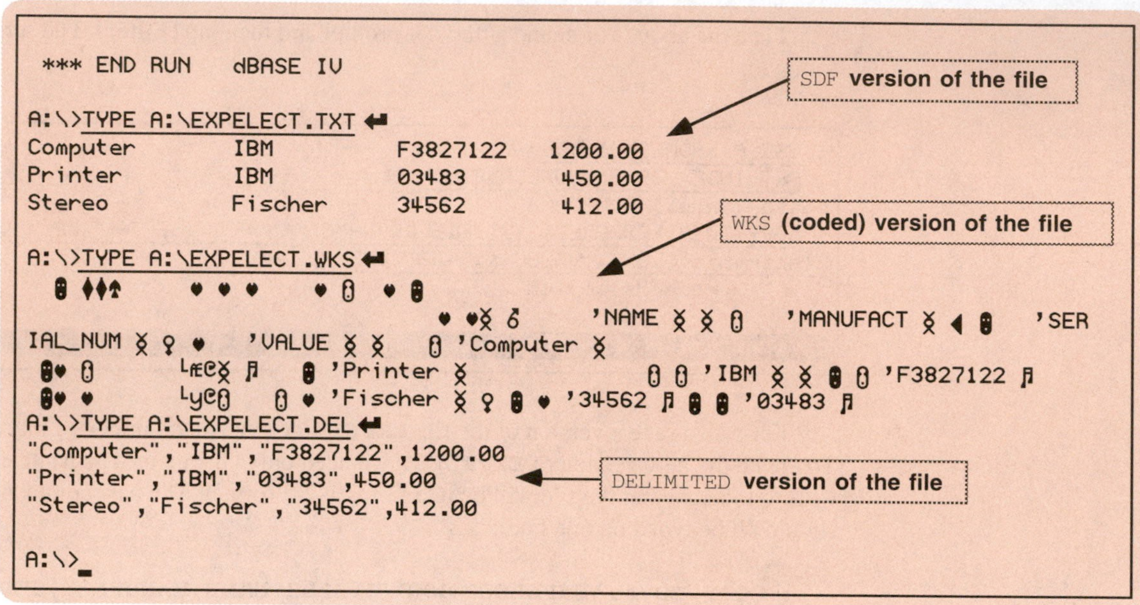

• Importing Data into WordPerfect •

The file **EXPELECT.TXT** can be imported into WordPerfect as a text file because it was saved in an ASCII format. Let's use WordPerfect to create a letter to an insurance company concerning the data in the file **EXPELECT.TXT** and then import the data directly into the document. To do this type the following:

Keystroke	Action Resulting from Keystroke
C:\WP51\WP ↵	Starts the WordPerfect program and presents a blank document screen.

Type the following letter and then save it on your *dBASE IV Data* diskette in drive A: by tapping **[F10]** and then typing **A:INSURE** ↵.

```
900 Wistful Lane
Minneapolis, MN 55414
16 February 1991

ABC Insurance Company
45 Park Avenue
New York, NY 11790

Dear Sir or Madam:

In response to your request of 10 February 1991, below is a list
of my electronics equipment valued at over $400.

If I can be of further help, please call me at (612) 555-2312.

Sincerely,


Sue Sherro_




A:\INSURE                                    Doc 1 Pg 1 Ln 4" POS 2"
```

Before you import the data into the WordPerfect document, you must tell WordPerfect where to put the information in the document. Place the cursor in the blank line right after the last sentence in the first paragraph (**Ln 3" Pos 1"**).

To import the data to WordPerfect:

Keystroke	Action Resulting from Keystroke
[Shift-F10]	Specifies that a file should be retrieved and its contents inserted at the cursor. WordPerfect will ask for the name of the **Document to be Retrieved:**
A:\EXPELECT.TXT ↵	Specifies the name of the file to be retrieved. The information from the file will be inserted at the location of the cursor.

Continued . . .

Keystroke	Action Resulting from Keystroke

```
900 Wistful Lane
Minneapolis, MN 55414
16 February 1991

ABC Insurance Company
45 Park Avenue
New York, NY 11790

Dear Sir or Madam:

In response to your request of 10 February 1991, below is a list
of my electronics equipment valued at over $400.
Computer        IBM         F3827122   1200.00
Printer         IBM         03483       450.00
Stereo          Fischer     34562       412.00

If I can be of further help, please call me at (612) 555-2312.

Sincerely,


Sue Sherro

A:\INSURE                                  Doc 1 Pg 1 Ln 3" POS 1"
```

You can use the WordPerfect editing techniques to make the document look nicer. For example,

Keystroke	Action Resulting from Keystroke
[Enter] [Enter]	Inserts two blank lines at the cursor.
[Up arrow]	Moves the cursor up to a blank line. Type the following column heading:

```
Name            Manufact     Serial #     Value
```

The final document should look like the following:

```
900 Wistful Lane
Minneapolis, MN 55414
16 February 1991

ABC Insurance Company
45 Park Avenue
New York, NY 11790

Dear Sir or Madam:

In response to your request of 10 February 1991, below is a list
of my electronics equipment valued at over $400.

Name            Manufact     Serial #      Value
Computer        IBM          F3827122    1200.00
Printer         IBM          03483        450.00
Stereo          Fischer      34562        412.00

If I can be of further help, please call me at (612) 555-2312.

Sincerely,


Sue Sherro
A:\INSURE                                 Doc 1 Pg 1 Ln 3.17" Pos 5.5"
```

Keystroke	Action Resulting from Keystroke
[F7]	Requests that the document be exited. WordPerfect will ask you if you want to save the document.
Y	Specifies that you want to save the document and requests a name for the file.
A:\INSURE2 ↵	Specifies the name of the document and asks if you want to exit WordPerfect.
Y	Specifies that you want to exit WordPerfect and returns to DOS.

• Importing Data into Lotus 1-2-3 •

The file **EXPELECT.WKS** can be imported directly into a Lotus 1-2-3 worksheet because it was saved in a Lotus format. To see how this works, do the following:

Keystroke	Action Resulting from Keystroke
C:\123\123 ↵	Starts the Lotus 1-2-3 program and presents a blank worksheet.
/ F(ile) R(etrieve)	Requests the name of the file to be retrieved. **EXPELECT.WKS** should appear in the list of file names. If it is not, type it in yourself.
[arrow]	Use the **[arrow]** keys to highlight **EXPELECT.WKS**.
[Enter]	Retrieves the specified file and returns to ready mode.

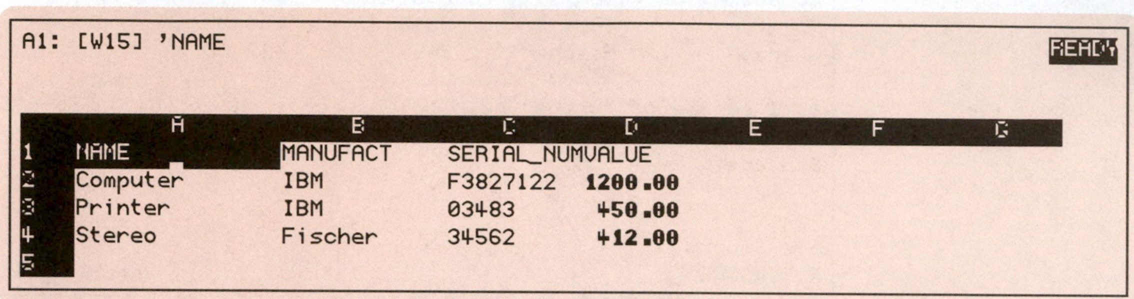

The data in the worksheet now can be manipulated as needed. Notice that the entries under **VALUE** in column **D** are highlighted (a different color on a color monitor or boldface on a monochrome monitor). This indicates that they are in an unprotected state, in other words they can be altered. This is also indicated by a **U** in the Control Center when one of the cells in column **D** is active. Lotus 1-2-3 allows you to protect the contents of specific cells from being changed through the use of its *Protect* feature. We did not discuss this feature so if you are interested, consult the *Lotus 1-2-3 Reference Manual*. This will not affect what we do next.

Lotus 1-2-3 can also import data directly from ASCII files such as **EXPELECT.TXT** and **EXPELECT.DEL** using the *File Import* feature. This is useful if the file was created by an application that does not support the **WKS** format. To see how this works, do the following:

Keystroke	Action Resulting from Keystroke
[arrow]	Use the **[arrow]** keys to make cell **A6** active.
/ F(ile) I(mport)	Opens the **Import** menu which presents two options: **Text** says that each line (record) of the file will be imported as if it were straight text. This means that all the fields of a single record are entered into a single cell. **Number** says that each line will be imported as if it contained numbers and text in quotation marks. This means that each record will have its own line and numbers and text within quotation marks will be entered into separate cells.
T	Selects **Text** and asks for the name of the file to be imported.

Continued . . .

Keystroke	Action Resulting from Keystroke

A:\EXPELECT.TXT ↵

Specifies the name of the file, loads the file, and returns control to **READY** mode. Because this is a straight text file, all the data for each record are placed into a single cell in column A (this is not what you want).

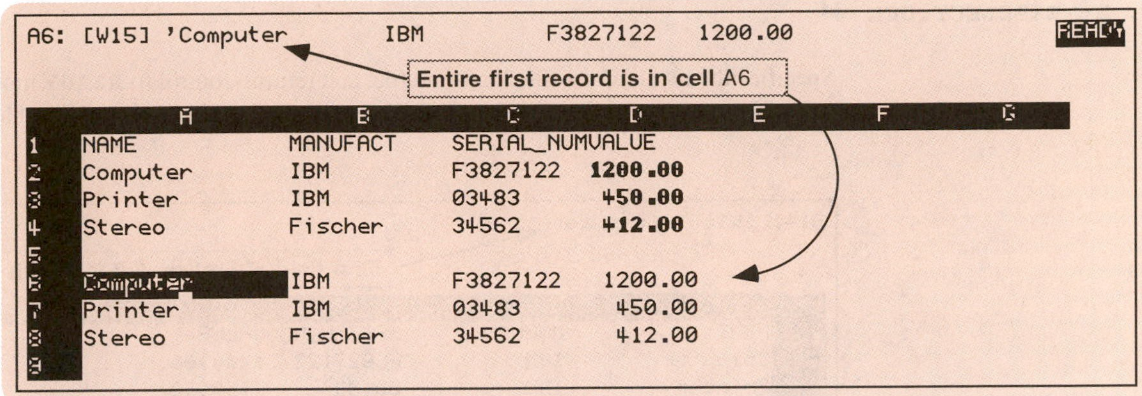

If you specify that the records are **Numbers**, then all the text will be ignored and each number will be placed into a separate cell (this is not what you want either but try it just to see what happens).

[arrow] Use the **[arrow]** keys to make cell **A10** active.

/ F(ile) I(mport) N(umbers)

Selects **Number** from the **Import** menu and asks for the name of the file to be imported.

A:\EXPELECT.TXT ↵

Specifies the name of the file, loads the file, and returns control to **READY** mode.

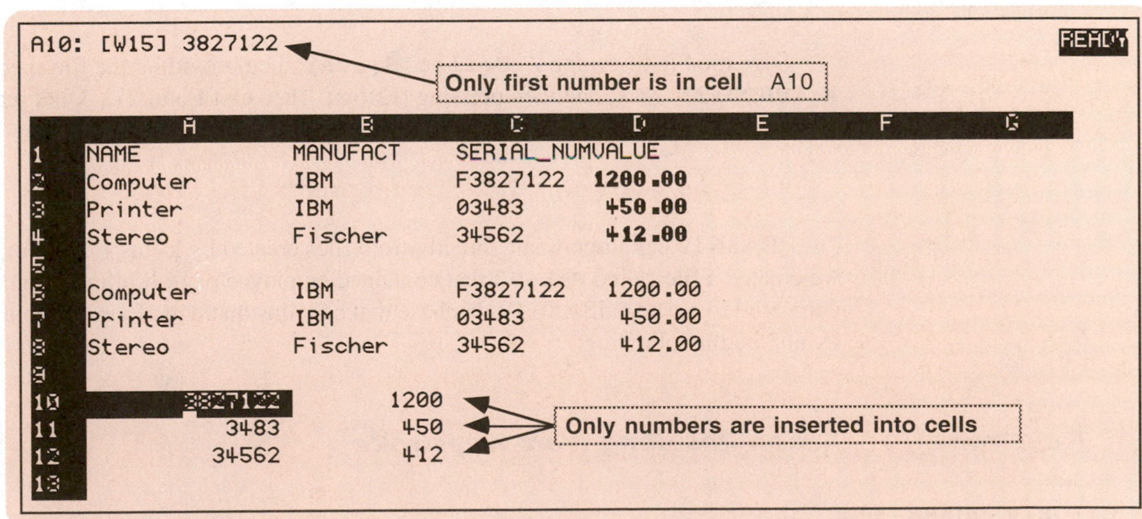

To insert the text and numbers into the proper cells you need to use the delimited file **EXPELECT.DEL**.

Keystroke	Action Resulting from Keystroke
[arrow]	Use the [arrow] keys to make cell **A14** active.

/ F(ile) I(mport) N(umbers)

Selects **Number** from the **Import** menu and asks for the name of the file to be imported.

A:\EXPELECT.DEL ↵

Specifies the name of the file, loads the file, and returns control to **READY** mode. Because this is a delimited text file the data from each field are entered into individual cells. This is what you want.

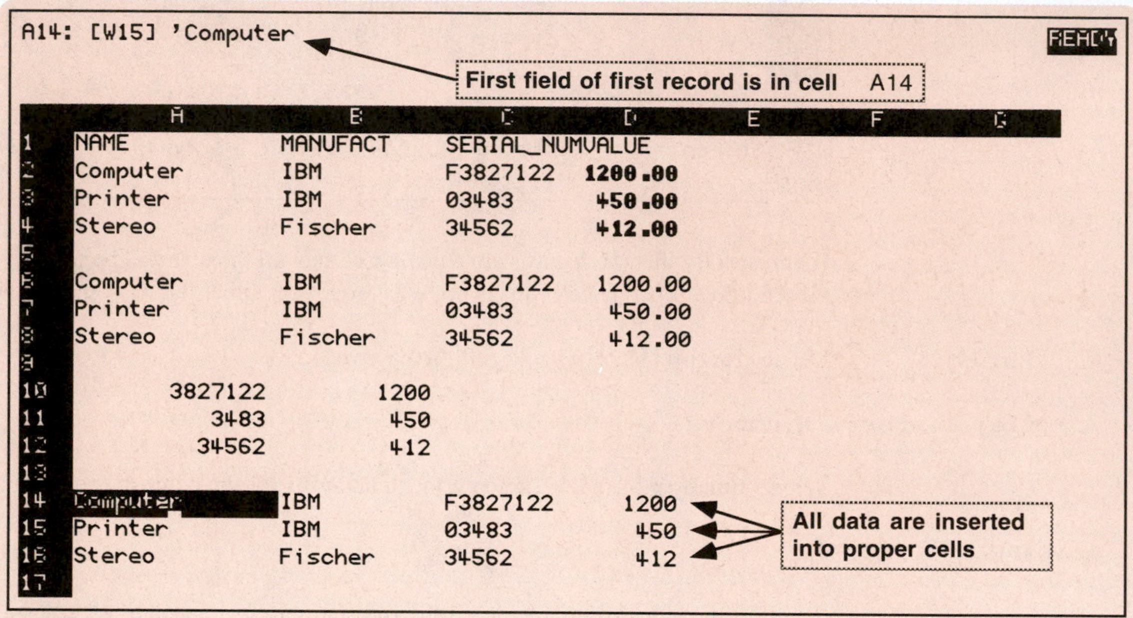

Save the file by typing **/ F(ile) S(ave)**, then providing the file specification **A:\DBTO123.WK1**, and then pressing **[Enter]**. Then exit Lotus 1-2-3 and return to DOS by typing **/ Q(uit) Y(es)**.

• Importing Lotus 1-2-3 Worksheets into dBASE IV •

dBASE IV can import data directly from files created by Lotus 1-2-3. For example, on page L46 we created a file called **PAY-V3** that contained employee payroll information. Let's use the **IMPORT** command to create a dBASE IV database that contains that data. Begin from the dot prompt in dBASE IV and do the following:

Keystroke	Action Resulting from Keystroke

C:\DBIV\DBASE ↵

Starts the dBASE IV program.

Place your *Lotus Data* diskette in drive A:

Continued . . .

Keystroke	Action Resulting from Keystroke

IMPORT FROM A:\PAY-V3.WK1 TYPE WK1 ↵

Creates a new dBASE IV database from the specified Lotus 1-2-3 worksheet. The new database file is automatically made active.

```
. IMPORT FROM A:\PAY-V3.WK1 TYPE WK1
    20 records added
Default alias is A
.
Command ║A:\PAY-V3          ║Rec 1/20        ║File
```

Place your *dBASE Data* diskette in drive A:

DISPLAY STRUCTURE ↵

Displays the structure of the new database.

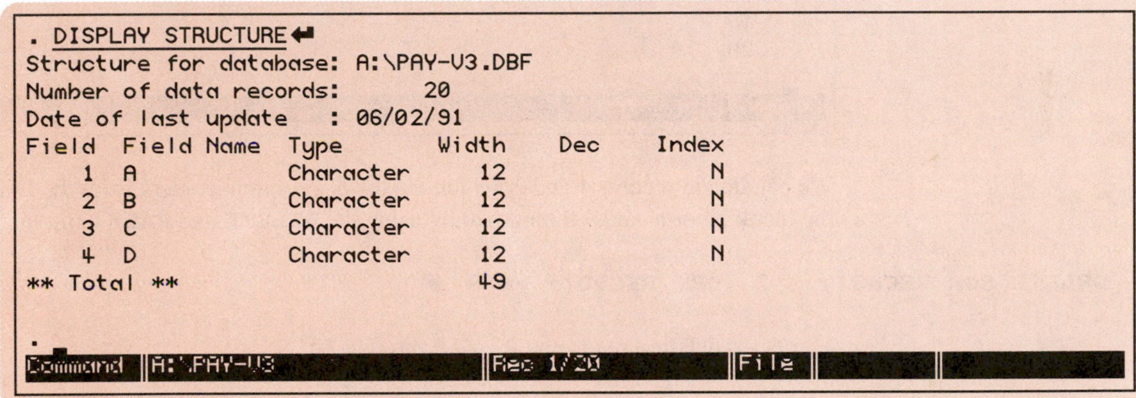

```
. DISPLAY STRUCTURE
Structure for database: A:\PAY-V3.DBF
Number of data records:      20
Date of last update   : 06/02/91
Field  Field Name  Type       Width    Dec    Index
    1  A           Character     12               N
    2  B           Character     12               N
    3  C           Character     12               N
    4  D           Character     12               N
** Total **                      49

.
Command ║A:\PAY-V3          ║Rec 1/20        ║File
```

There are 20 records in the new database because there is information in the first 20 rows of the Lotus 1-2-3 file. Rows 1 through 8 contain data while rows 9 through 20 contain formatting instructions and so are not completely blank as far as dBASE IV was concerned. The field names are defined as **A**, **B**, **C**, and **D** and correspond to the four columns of the original worksheet; each field is of type Character with a width equal to the width of the Lotus 1-2-3 column.

LIST ↵ Displays the contents of the new database.

Continued . . .

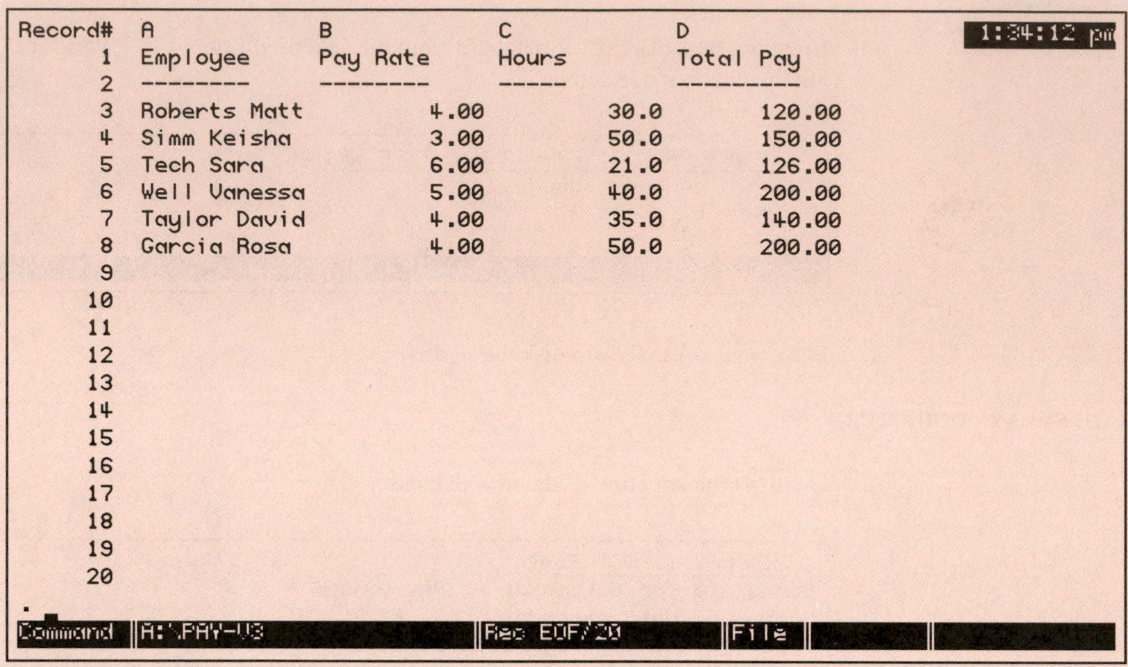

We can delete records 1 and 2, which are the old column headers from the Lotus 1-2-3 worksheet, and the blank records and 9 through 20 by using the **DELETE** and **PACK** commands.

DELETE FOR RECNO() <=2 .OR. RECNO() >= 9 ↵

Marks for deletion records 1, 2, and 9 through 20.

PACK ↵ Deletes the marked records.

LIST ↵ Displays the contents of the database.

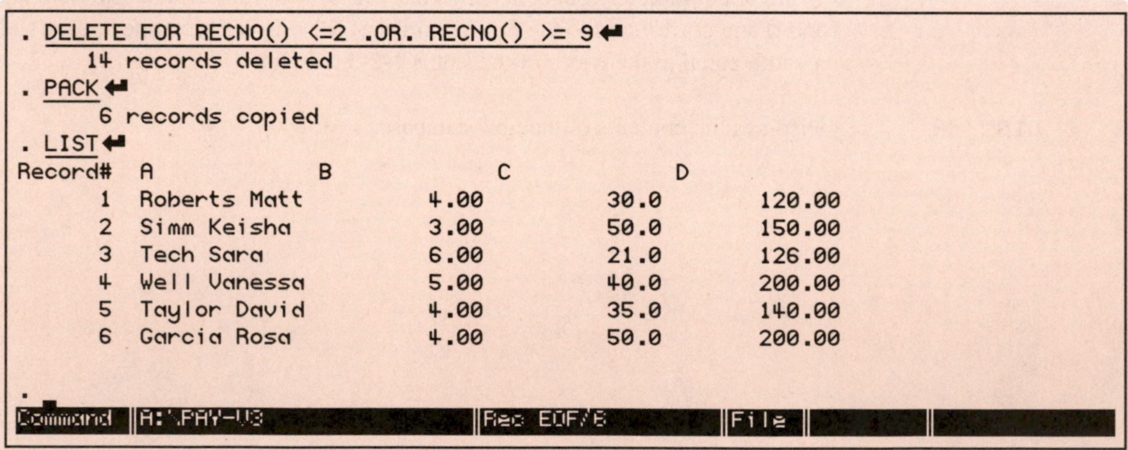

Continued . . .

Keystroke	Action Resulting from Keystroke
	The database can be further cleaned up changing the field names, widths, and types as needed (use **MODIFY STRUCTURE**). We will not bother to do that.
QUIT ↵	Exits dBASE IV and returns to DOS.

As you can see, applications can readily exchange data to suit the needs of the user. All the exporting and importing options may seem confusing at first but they give you complete control over the disposition of your data and are easy to use after a little practice.

TO TAKE A BREAK Remove data diskette. To resume: Insert data diskette; type **A:** ↵, then **C:\DBIV\DBASE** ↵.

Homework Exercises

REMEMBER . . . modifications made to the database are not written to the disk until you close the database file with the **CLOSE** command or by quitting the program and returning to DOS. If you simply turn off the power to the computer while dBASE IV is active, you may lose data.

① Modify the **CONFIG.DB** file on your *dBASE Data* diskette so that drive A: is the default drive whenever you start dBASE IV and tapping **[Ctrl-F2]** will switch to **Edit** from the dot prompt. Use the DOS **TYPE** command to display the contents of the new **CONFIG.DB** file and then do a screen dump.

② Create a new catalog called **HOMEWORK**, add the description **Chapter 2 homework exercise files**, and then add the database file **HOMEMOD1.DBF** to the catalog. Do a screen dump of the Control Center showing **HOMEWORK** as the active catalog.

Continued . . .

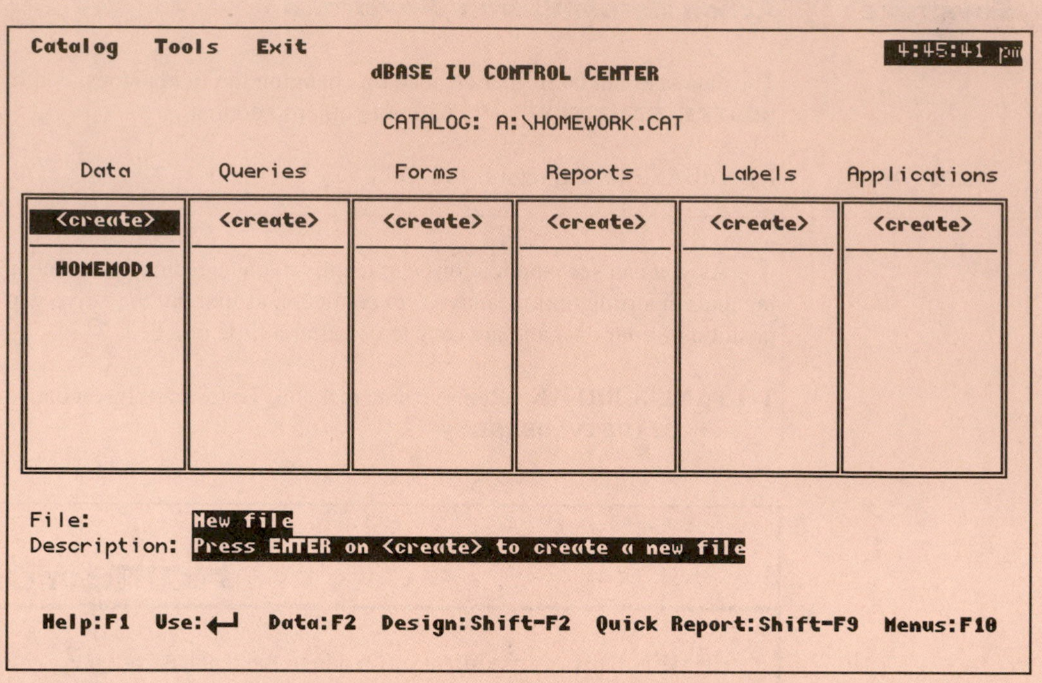

---

③ On page L73, you created a Lotus 1-2-3 worksheet **HWL1-04WK1**, that recorded information for Molly's checking account. Use **CREATE DATABASE** and/or **IMPORT FROM** to create a dBASE IV database called **HWD2-03.DBF** that contains the same information. After you have created the database, use **LIST STRUCTURE** and **LIST** to show the details of the database and do a screen dump. The screen dump should look like the following:

```
. LIST STRUCTURE ↵
Structure for database: A:\HWD2-03.DBF
Number of data records:       6
Date of last update   : 06/14/91
Field  Field Name  Type       Width    Dec    Index
    1  NUMBER      Character      6              N
    2  DATE        Date           8              N
    3  AMOUNT      Numeric        8      2       N
    4  PAYEE       Character     12              N
    5  CATEGORY    Character     12              N
** Total **                      47

. LIST ↵
Record#  NUMBER DATE       AMOUNT PAYEE        CATEGORY
      1    2302 01/06/90    29.20 Target       Misc
      2    2307 02/07/90    20.00 U of Minn    School
      3    2306 02/04/90    19.95 Daytons      Clothes
      4    2304 02/06/90     4.00 McDonalds    Food
      5    2301 02/01/90   232.00 U of Minn    School
      6    2303 02/07/90    45.00 U of Minn    School

.
Command  ||A:\HWD2-03          ||Rec EOF/6       ||File||
```

CHAPTER TWO

④ Use the **COPY TO** command to make a copy of the database **HWD2-03.DBF** which you created in Exercise 3. Call the new database **HWD2-04.DBF**. The new database should have the fields rearranged so that the field **PAYEE** is located directly to the right of the field **NUMBER**. After this is done, open the new database and then use **LIST** to show the details of the new database. Do a screen dump that shows the **COPY TO** command you used and the contents of the new database.

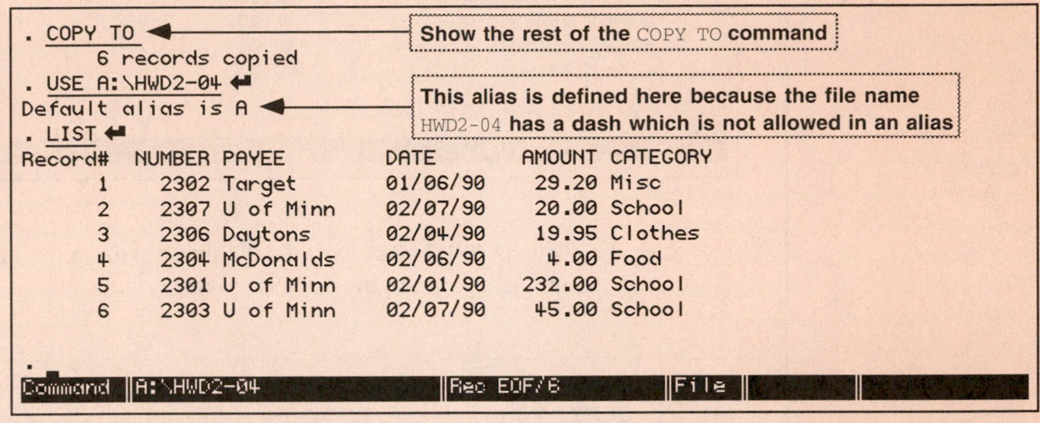

. COPY TO
6 records copied
. USE A:\HWD2-04
Default alias is A
. LIST
Record# NUMBER PAYEE DATE AMOUNT CATEGORY
1 2302 Target 01/06/90 29.20 Misc
2 2307 U of Minn 02/07/90 20.00 School
3 2306 Daytons 02/04/90 19.95 Clothes
4 2304 McDonalds 02/06/90 4.00 Food
5 2301 U of Minn 02/01/90 232.00 School
6 2303 U of Minn 02/07/90 45.00 School
Command A:\HWD2-04 Rec EOF/6 File
Show the rest of the COPY TO command
This alias is defined here because the file name HWD2-04 has a dash which is not allowed in an alias

---

⑤ Use the **LIST** command to display only those records in **HWD2-04.DBF** that have **School** in the **CATEGORY** field. Do a screen dump to show the command and the result.

---

⑥ Use the **LIST** command to display only those checks in **HWD2-04.DBF** that were written before February 2 or after February 6, 1990.

---

⑦ Use **Quick layout** to create a report for the database **HWD2-04.DBF** that will produce the output shown below. Save the report as **HWD2-07.FRM** and then use the **REPORT FORM** command to print the data for checks with a value over $21.00. Write the **REPORT FORM** command you used on the output. The printed output should look like the following:

```
Page No.    1
06/04/91

NUMBER   PAYEE          DATE          AMOUNT  CATEGORY

2302     Target         01/06/90       29.20  Misc
2301     U of Minn      02/01/90      232.00  School
2303     U of Minn      02/07/90       45.00  School
                                      306.20
```

Continued . . .

CHAPTER TWO

⑧ Create a view for the database **HWD2-04.DBF** that displays the data in the following way:

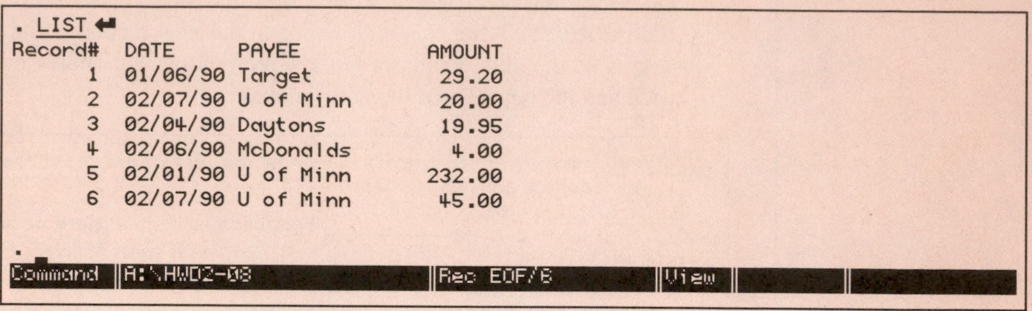

```
. LIST ↵
Record#  DATE      PAYEE            AMOUNT
      1  01/06/90  Target            29.20
      2  02/07/90  U of Minn         20.00
      3  02/04/90  Daytons           19.95
      4  02/06/90  McDonalds          4.00
      5  02/01/90  U of Minn        232.00
      6  02/07/90  U of Minn         45.00

.
Command  A:\HWD2-08          Rec EOF/6        View
```

Save the view as **HWD2-08**. Do a **LIST** that produces the above output and then do a screen dump. Finally, return the database to its normal view.

---

⑨ Use **COPY TO** to duplicate **HWD2-04.DBF** and call the new file **HWD2-09.DBF**. Use the **REPLACE** command on the new database **HWD2-09.DBF** to change the word **School** to **Educational** in the **CATEGORY** field. Then use **LIST** to show the result. Do a screen dump that shows the **REPLACE** command you used and the final listing of the modified records.

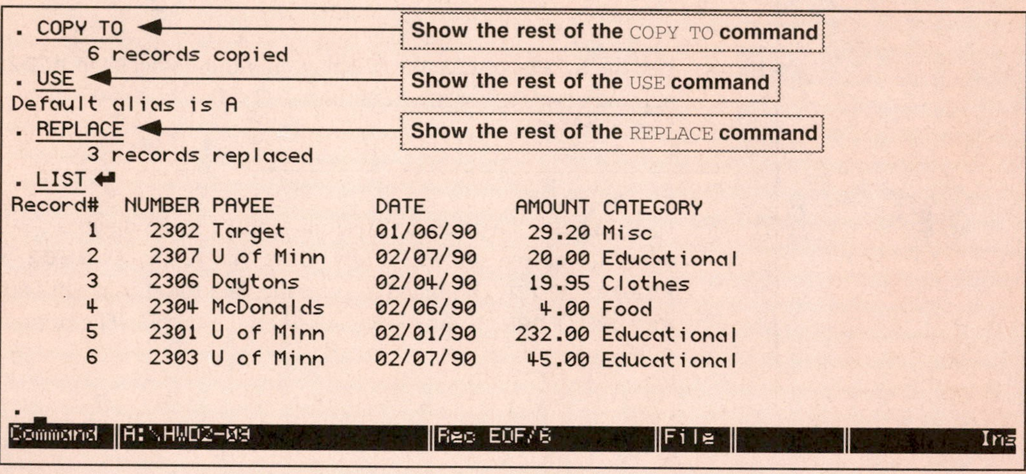

```
. COPY TO  ◄────  Show the rest of the COPY TO command
      6 records copied
. USE  ◄────  Show the rest of the USE command
Default alias is A
. REPLACE  ◄────  Show the rest of the REPLACE command
      3 records replaced
. LIST ↵
Record#  NUMBER PAYEE          DATE       AMOUNT CATEGORY
      1    2302 Target         01/06/90    29.20 Misc
      2    2307 U of Minn      02/07/90    20.00 Educational
      3    2306 Daytons        02/04/90    19.95 Clothes
      4    2304 McDonalds      02/06/90     4.00 Food
      5    2301 U of Minn      02/01/90   232.00 Educational
      6    2303 U of Minn      02/07/90    45.00 Educational

.
Command  A:\HWD2-09          Rec EOF/6        File                Ins
```

---

⑩ In database **HWD2-09.DBF**, mark for deletion records that represent checks with amounts under $21.00. Use **LIST** to display the data to show the deletion markers and then do a screen dump. Finally, use **RECALL** to reinstate the records marked for deletion.

CHAPTER TWO

⑪ Beginning with the database **HWD2-09.DBF**, make the following changes and save the modified database as **HWD2-11.DBF**:

a. Delete the field called **Category**.

b. Add a new character field called **TAX_DED** and define its field width as 2. This field will be used to indicate whether or not a record is tax deductible. Add data to the new field, **TAX_DED**, as follows:

D for records **2**, **3**, **5**, and **6**;
ND for records **1**, and **4**.

c. Change the name of the field called **Amount** to **Value**.

After this is done, use **LIST STRUCTURE** and **LIST** to show the details of the new database and do a screen dump.

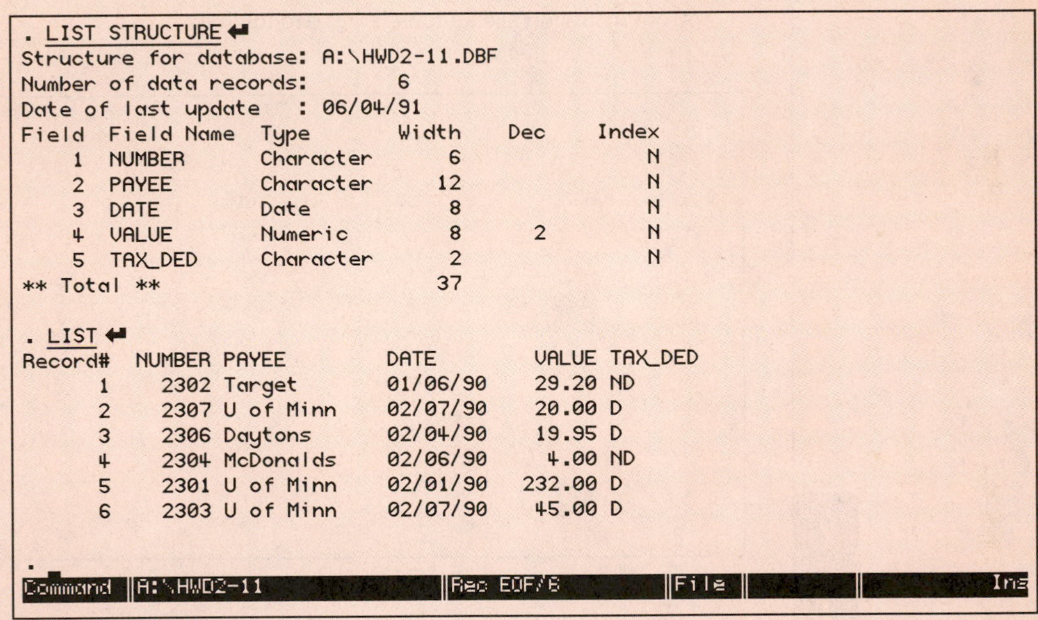

```
. LIST STRUCTURE ↵
Structure for database: A:\HWD2-11.DBF
Number of data records:       6
Date of last update   : 06/04/91
Field  Field Name  Type       Width    Dec    Index
    1  NUMBER      Character      6               N
    2  PAYEE       Character     12               N
    3  DATE        Date           8               N
    4  VALUE       Numeric        8      2        N
    5  TAX_DED     Character      2               N
** Total **                      37

. LIST ↵
Record#  NUMBER PAYEE        DATE        VALUE TAX_DED
      1    2302 Target       01/06/90    29.20 ND
      2    2307 U of Minn    02/07/90    20.00 D
      3    2306 Daytons      02/04/90    19.95 D
      4    2304 McDonalds    02/06/90     4.00 ND
      5    2301 U of Minn    02/01/90   232.00 D
      6    2303 U of Minn    02/07/90    45.00 D

.
Command ||A:\HWD2-11          ||Rec EOF/6       ||File ||      ||         Ins
```

⑫ Use **INDEX** to arrange the records in the database **HWD2-11.DBF** by **PAYEE** in ascending order. Use the name **HWD2-12.NDX** for the index file. Then use **LIST** to show the result. Do a screen dump that shows the **INDEX** command you used and the listing of the records.

Continued . . .

CHAPTER TWO

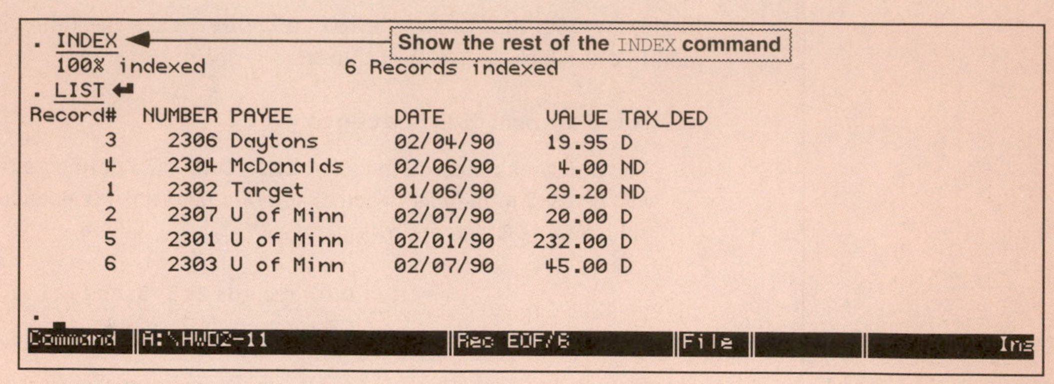

. INDEX
Show the rest of the INDEX command
100% indexed 6 Records indexed
. LIST
Record# NUMBER PAYEE DATE VALUE TAX_DED
3 2306 Daytons 02/04/90 19.95 D
4 2304 McDonalds 02/06/90 4.00 ND
1 2302 Target 01/06/90 29.20 ND
2 2307 U of Minn 02/07/90 20.00 D
5 2301 U of Minn 02/01/90 232.00 D
6 2303 U of Minn 02/07/90 45.00 D
Command A:\HWD2-11 Rec EOF/6 File Ins

---

⑬ Create a report called **HWD2-13** that displays the data in **HWD2-11.DBF** grouped on the **TAX_DED** field. The records should be alphabetized by **PAYEE** within each group and the sum of the **VALUE** column within each group should be displayed. The printed output from the report should look like the following:

```
Page No.    1
06/04/91

NUMBER   PAYEE          DATE            VALUE  TAX_DED

2306     Daytons        02/04/90        $19.95 D
2307     U of Minn      02/07/90        $20.00 D
2301     U of Minn      02/01/90       $232.00 D
2303     U of Minn      02/07/90        $45.00 D
                       Group total:    $316.95

2304     McDonalds      02/06/90         $4.00 ND
2302     Target         01/06/90        $29.20 ND
                       Group total:     $33.20

                      Report total:    $350.15
```

---

⑭ Use **SORT** to arrange the records in the database **HWD2-11.DBF** by **Payee** in ascending order and, within **Payee**, by **Value** in descending order. Save the sorted database in a file called **HWD2-14.DBF**. Do a screen dump that shows the **SORT** command you used and the listing of the new database.

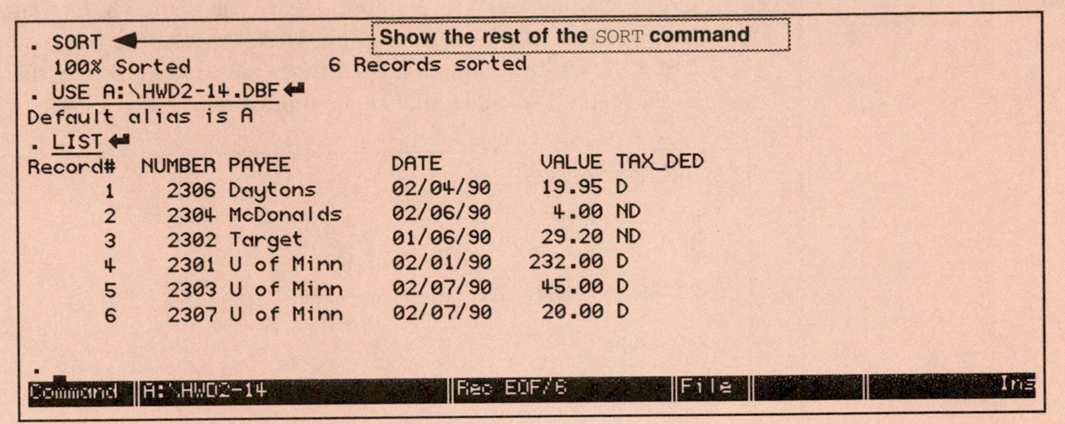

```
. SORT ◄──────────── Show the rest of the SORT command
  100% Sorted              6 Records sorted
. USE A:\HWD2-14.DBF↵
Default alias is A
. LIST↵
Record#  NUMBER PAYEE          DATE        VALUE TAX_DED
      1    2306 Daytons        02/04/90    19.95 D
      2    2304 McDonalds      02/06/90     4.00 ND
      3    2302 Target         01/06/90    29.20 ND
      4    2301 U of Minn      02/01/90   232.00 D
      5    2303 U of Minn      02/07/90    45.00 D
      6    2307 U of Minn      02/07/90    20.00 D

.
Command  A:\HWD2-14          Rec EOF/6      File           Ins
```

⑮ On page W214 you created a text file called **CONTACTS** that contained data on business associates. Use the dBASE IV *Mailmerge* feature to produce individualized form letters for those people on the list whose total sales are greater than $15,300. Print the letters as shown below:

```
  Memo to: Wheeler Katie
Memo from: Richard Bonacci
     Date: 06/04/91

     Congratulations on your yearly sales total of $25,111.00.  Your hard
work and dedication have helped us achieve our sales objectives.  As a small
token of our appreciation, a 10% bonus will be added to your next pay check.
```

```
  Memo to: Moony Hal
Memo from: Richard Bonacci
     Date: 06/04/91

     Congratulations on your yearly sales total of $15,455.00.  Your hard
work and dedication have helped us achieve our sales objectives.  As a small
token of our appreciation, a 10% bonus will be added to your next pay check.
```

Save the mailmerge report as **HWD2-15.FRM** and the database of contacts as **HWD2-15.DBF**. Do a screen dump of the report design screen for **HWD2-15.FRM** and then do a screen dump of a list of the database **HWD2-15DBF**.

Continued . . .

CHAPTER TWO

⑯ Create mailing labels for the form letters you printed in Exercise 15. Call the label design **HWD2-16.LBL**. Write the output from the **LABEL** command to a file called **HWD2-16.TXT** and then use the DOS **TYPE** command to display the labels. Do a screen dump of the result. It should look like the following:

```
A:\>TYPE HWD2-16.TXT
♀
       Wheeler Katie
       Land O'Lakes

CONCO consultants give good advice!


       Moony Hal
       Geosyncronics

CONCO consultants give good advice!


A:\>_
```

Do a screen dump of the label design screen for **HWD2-16.LBL**.

---

⑰ Create a Lotus 1-2-3 type file called **HWD2-17.WK1** from the data in **HWD2-11.DBF** for those records that are tax deductible and then load the file into Lotus 1-2-3. Do a screen dump of the worksheet. It should look like the following:

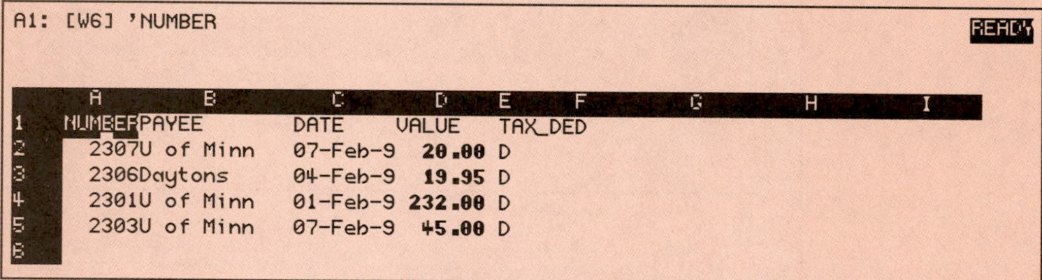

```
A1: [W6] 'NUMBER                                                    READY

      A     B           C         D       E       F       G       H       I
1  NUMBERPAYEE         DATE      VALUE   TAX_DED
2     2307U of Minn    07-Feb-9   20.00  D
3     2306Daytons      04-Feb-9   19.95  D
4     2301U of Minn    01-Feb-9  232.00  D
5     2303U of Minn    07-Feb-9   45.00  D
6
```

CHAPTER TWO

⑱ In Chapter 1, you created a database for the Katt Computer Company that contained data on its accounts. Export the data from the database **HWD1-06.DBF** for those persons whose accounts are over 30 days past due to a WordPerfect letter that asks a collection agency to collect the money. Save the letter as **HWD2-18.FIN**. The printed output should look like the following:

```
23 Hazel Lane
St. Paul, MN  55102
4 June, 1991

Quickie Collections
231 SE First Street
St. Paul, MN  55014

Dear Sir or Madam:

As per our standard agreement, please begin collection proceedings
for the following people whose accounts are past thirty days due.

Name     Balance  Past   Street               City      State  ZIP
Janice     15      32    15 Softie Lane       Mpls        MN   55412
Jill       30      35    23 S. Fourth St.     St. Paul    MN   55101

Thank you very much.

Sincerely,


Allen Johnson
President, Katt Computer Company
```

Appendix: Summary of Selected dBASE IV Features

The following is a brief description of many of the dBASE IV screens, commands, and features with reference to pages in the text. Items with N/C in place of a page number were not specifically covered in the text but are provided for your information. Consult the *dBASE IV Language Reference Manual* for more details.

Quick Review

Page	Command	Description
D8	**DBASE**	Access dBASE IV from the DOS environment.
D18, D172	**CREATE**	Create a new database structure.
D74, D174	**CREATE REPORT**	Create a report format.
D10, D144	**QUIT**	Exit dBASE IV and return to DOS.
D77, D142	**REPORT FORM filespec TO PRINT**	
		Print database information using the report form called **filespec**.
D27, D122	**USE filespec**	Retrieve a database called **filespec**.
D18, D122	**ASSIST**	Switch to the Control Center from the dot prompt.
D16	[Esc]	Switch to the dot prompt from the Control Center.
D32, D131	**BROWSE**	View, add, and/or edit records and fields.

The Control Center The Control Center provides access to the many screens and functions available in dBASE IV. To access a design screen in order to create or modify a file, use the **[arrow keys]** to highlight **<create>** or the name of the desired file in one of the panels and then press **[Enter]**.

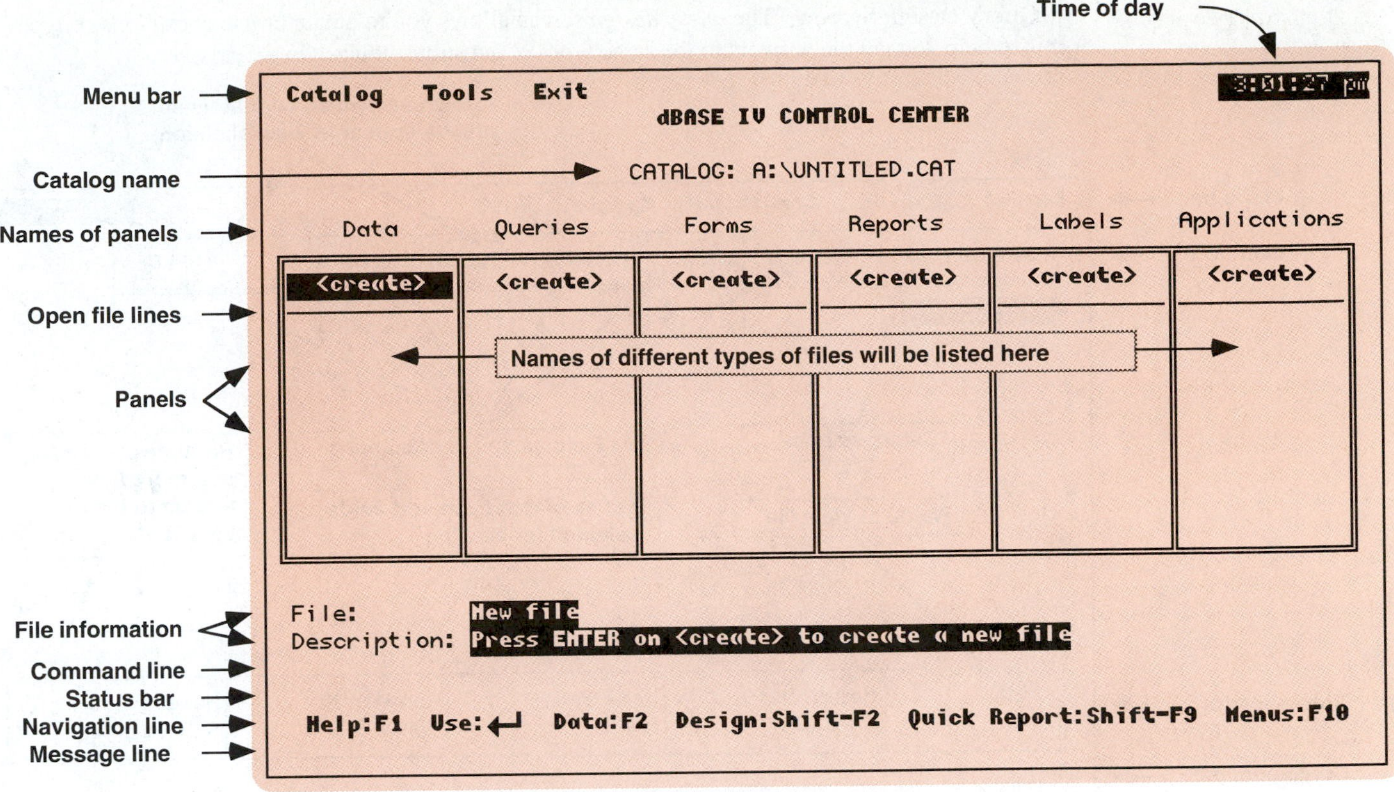

Database Design Screen The *database design* screen allows you to create a new database structure or modify an existing one. This screen may also be accessed by pressing **[Shift-F2]**.

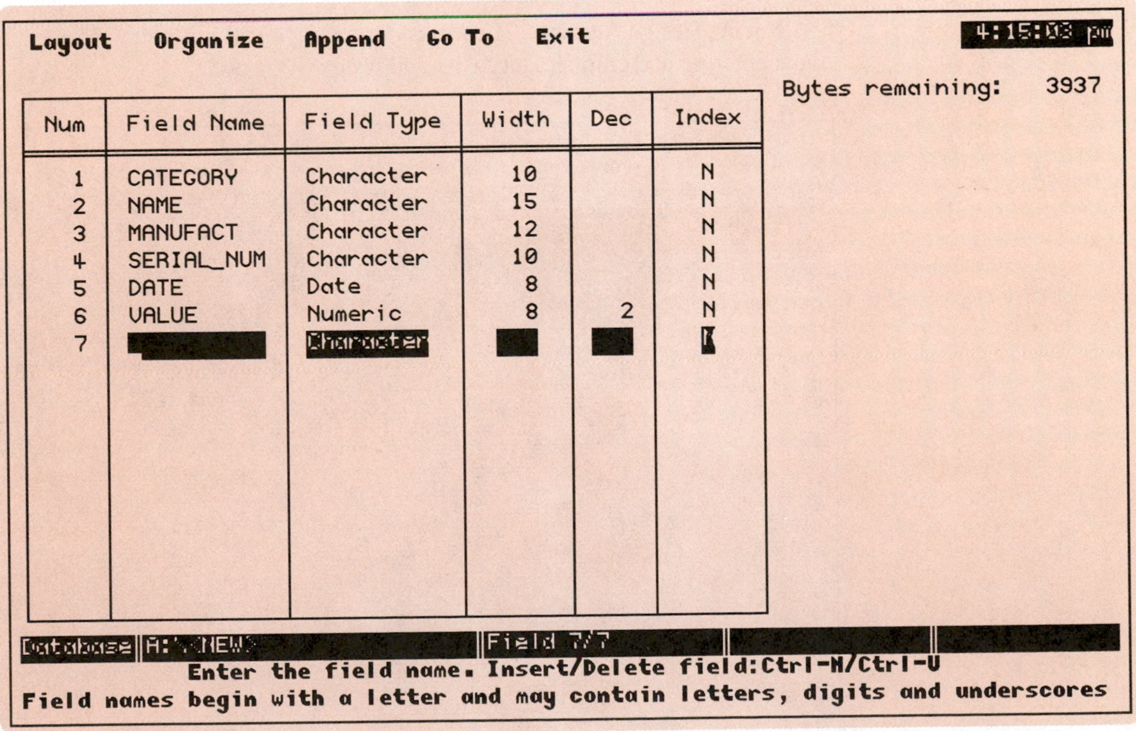

Query Design Screen The *query design* screen allows you to create or use questionnaire-type forms to help you get the answers to the same types of questions you ask over and over.

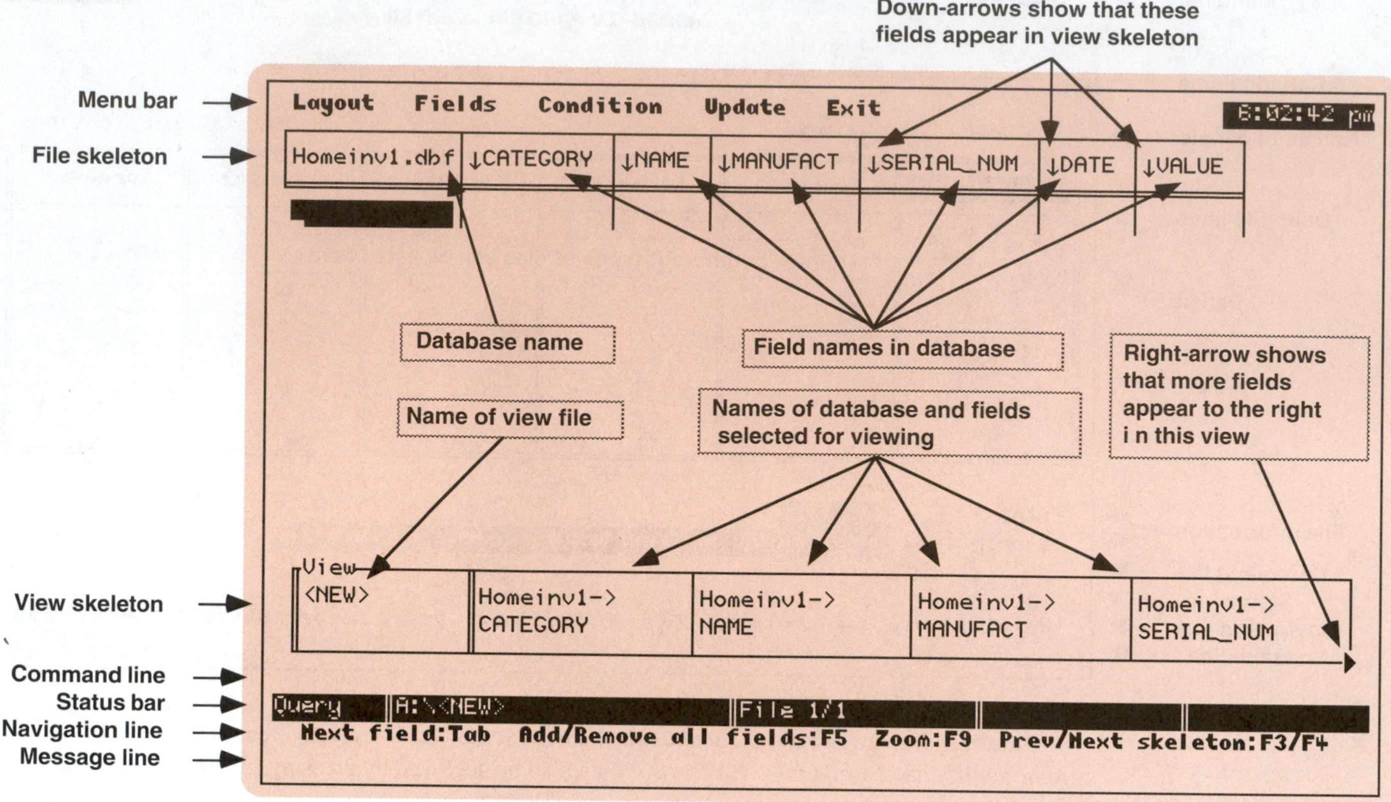

Forms Design Screen The *forms design* screen allows you to create customized forms that will make entering and editing data easier and faster.

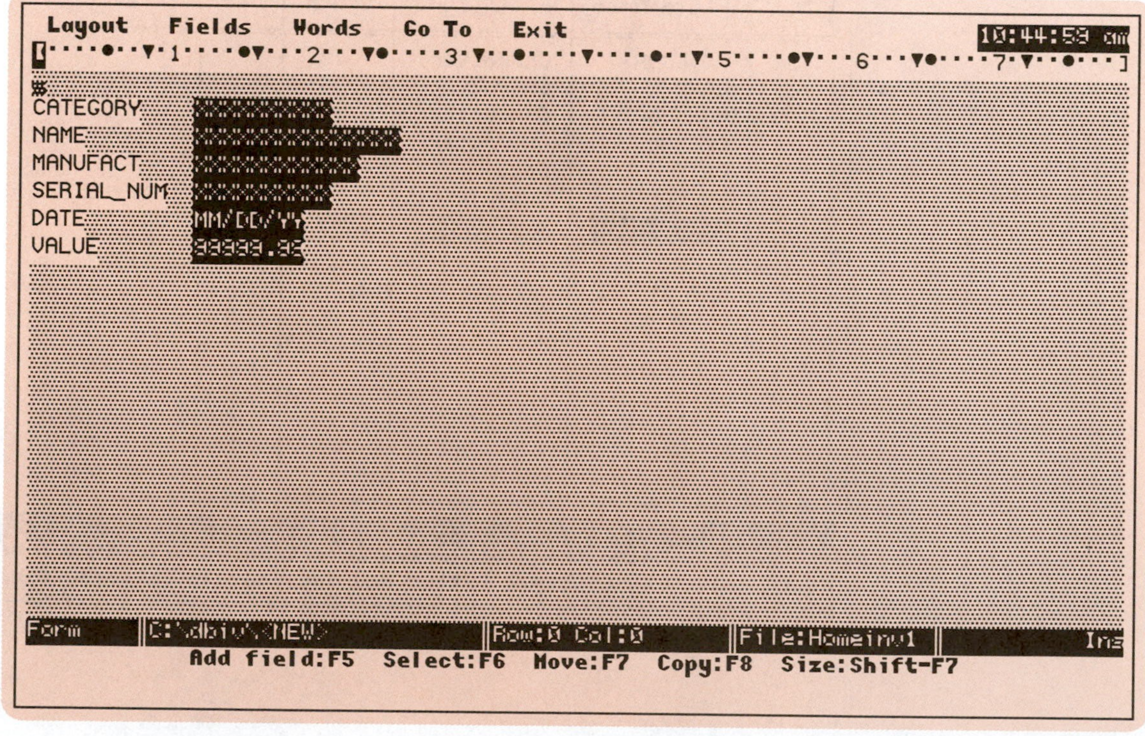

Report Design Screen The *report design* screen allows you to create reports of database information.

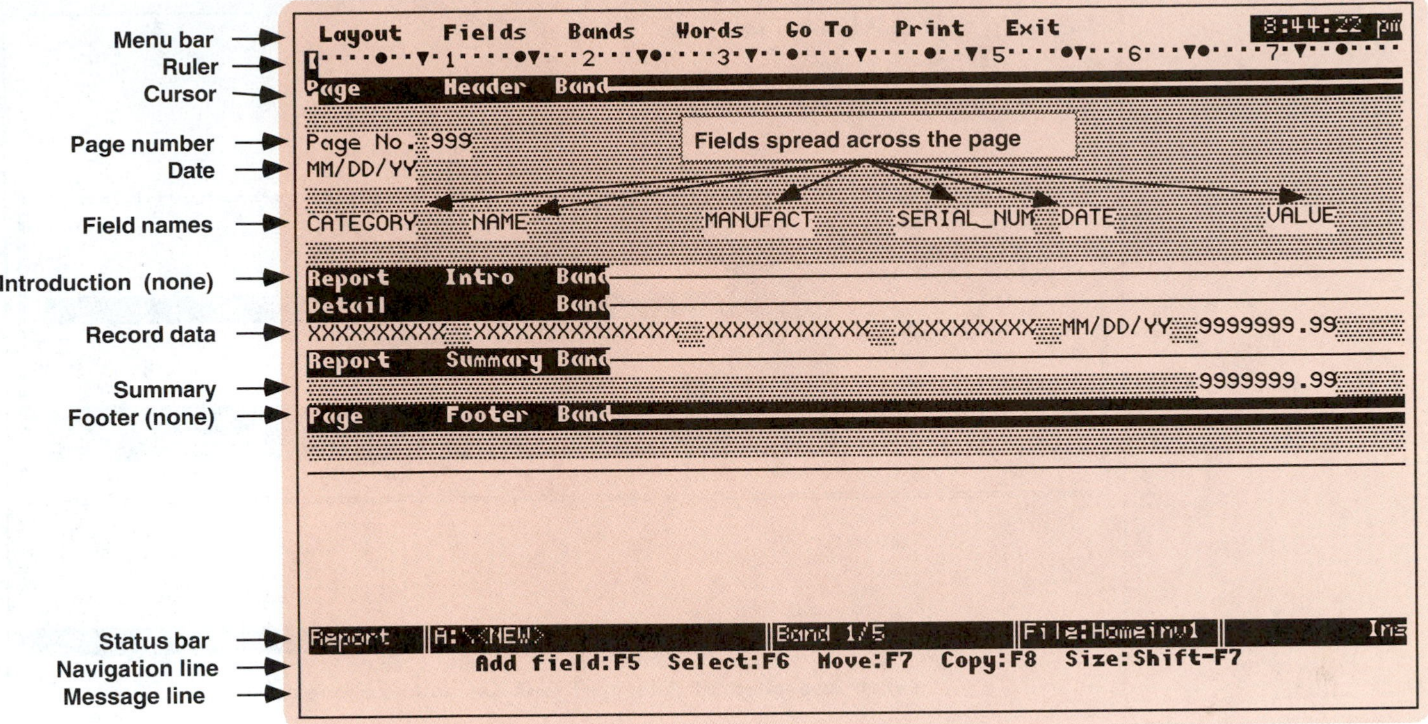

Label Design Screen The *label design* screen allows you to design mailing labels.

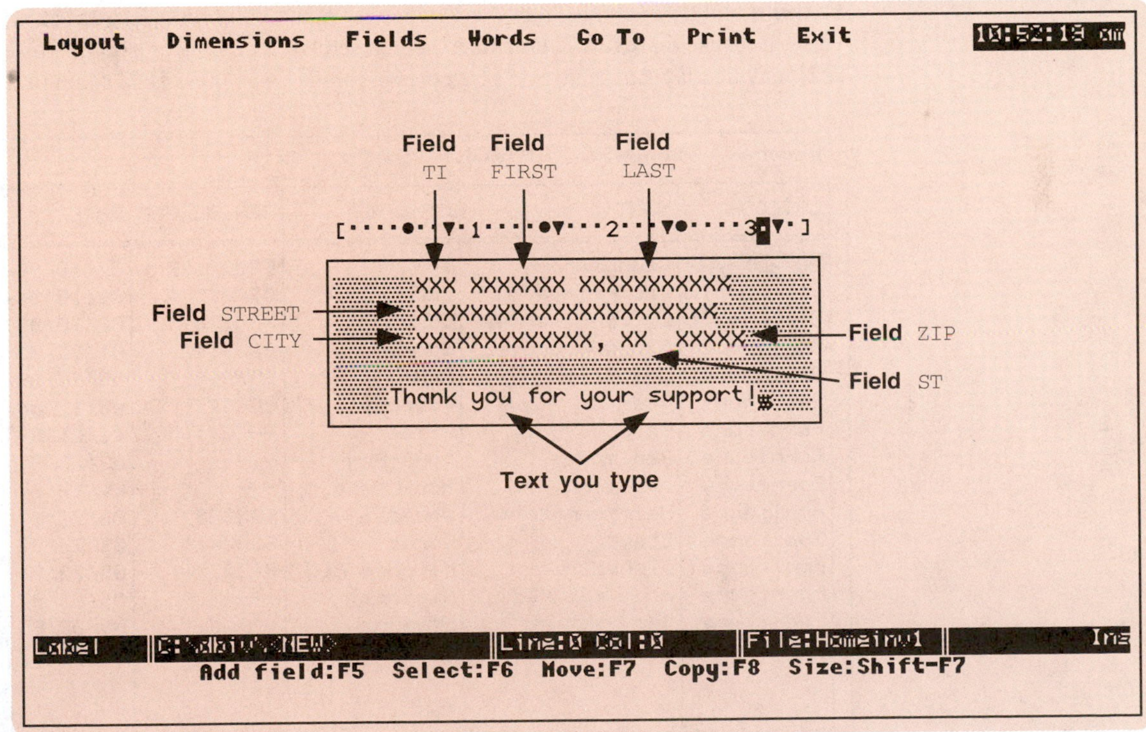

Applications Design Screen The *applications design* screen allows you to organize many program components into a single procedure that can be performed quickly and easily.

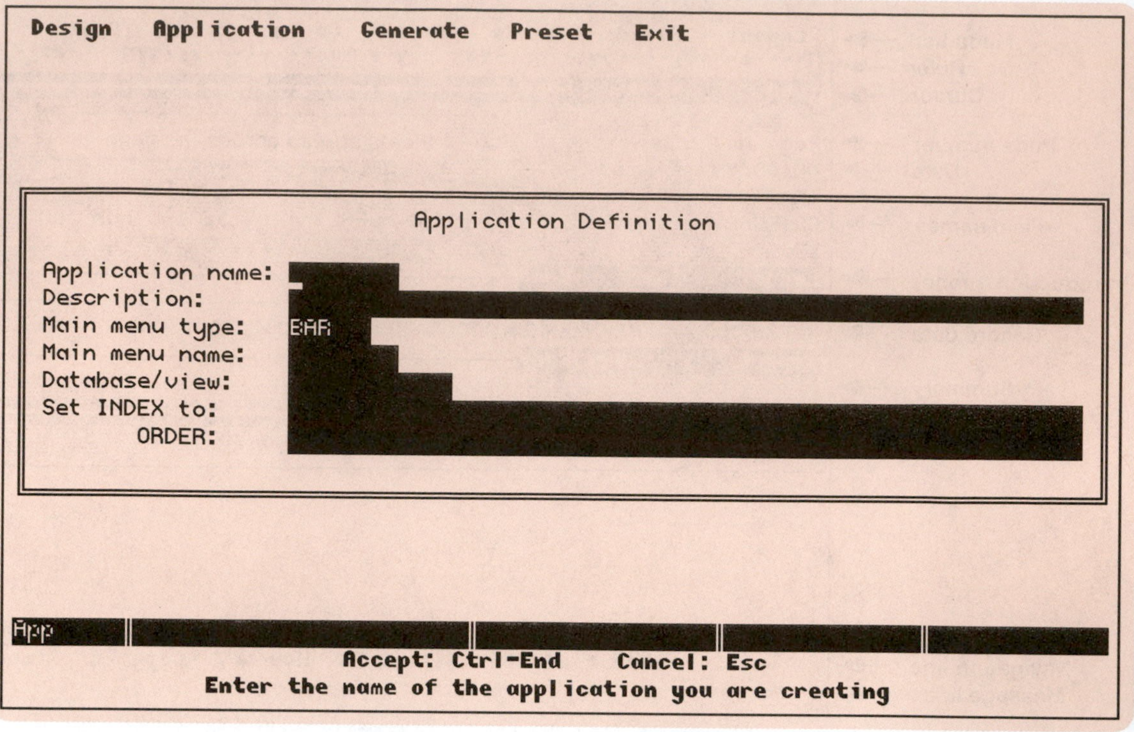

`Browse` Screen From the Control Center, press **[F2]** to access the **`Browse`** or **`Edit`** screen where you can examine and edit the contents of a database. The **[F2]** key is also used to switch between **`Browse`** and **`Edit`**. Thus, if you are in **`Browse`** and you press **[F2]**, **`Edit`** will be entered and vice versa. Because dBASE IV remembers which screen (**`Browse`** or **`Edit`**) was last displayed, pressing **[F2]** may display **`Edit`** instead of **`Browse`**. In that case, press **[F2]** again to display **`Browse`**.

Records Organize Fields Go To Exit

CATEGORY	NAME	MANUFACT	SERIAL_NUM	DATE	VALUE
Electronic	Computer	IBM	F3827122	02/10/90	1200.00
Electronic	Pro Printer	IBM	03483	02/10/90	450.00
Electronic	External drive	IBM	F392281	02/10/90	356.00
Appliance	Microwave oven	Sears	2339112	01/22/89	450.00
Appliance	Color TV	RCA	2338442	05/25/89	360.00
Electronic	Stereo	Fischer	34562	03/12/89	412.00
Furniture	Sofa	Wilder	---	11/21/84	450.00
Furniture	Recliner	La-Z-Boy	---	03/23/87	350.00
Furniture	Dry sink	Hand made	---	04/12/87	500.00
Appliance	Refrigerator	Wards	493323	03/22/87	450.00
Appliance	Stove	Wards	533282	03/22/87	350.00
Appliance	Dishwasher	Kitchen Aid	04322344	09/23/81	550.00
Furniture	Bed, mattress	Simmons	---	09/03/87	100.00
Furniture	Bed, spring	Simmons	---	09/03/87	100.00
Furniture	Bed, frame	Simmons	---	09/03/87	100.00

Browse A:\HOMEINV1 Rec 1/15 File

Edit Screen From the Control Center, press **[F2]** to access the **Browse** or **Edit** screen where you can examine and edit the contents of a database. The **[F2]** key is also used to switch between **Browse** and **Edit**. Thus, if you are in **Browse** and you press **[F2]**, **Edit** will be displayed and vice versa. Because dBASE IV remembers which screen (**Browse** or **Edit**) was last displayed, pressing **[F2]** may display **Edit** instead of **Browse**. In that case, press **[F2]** again to display **Browse**.

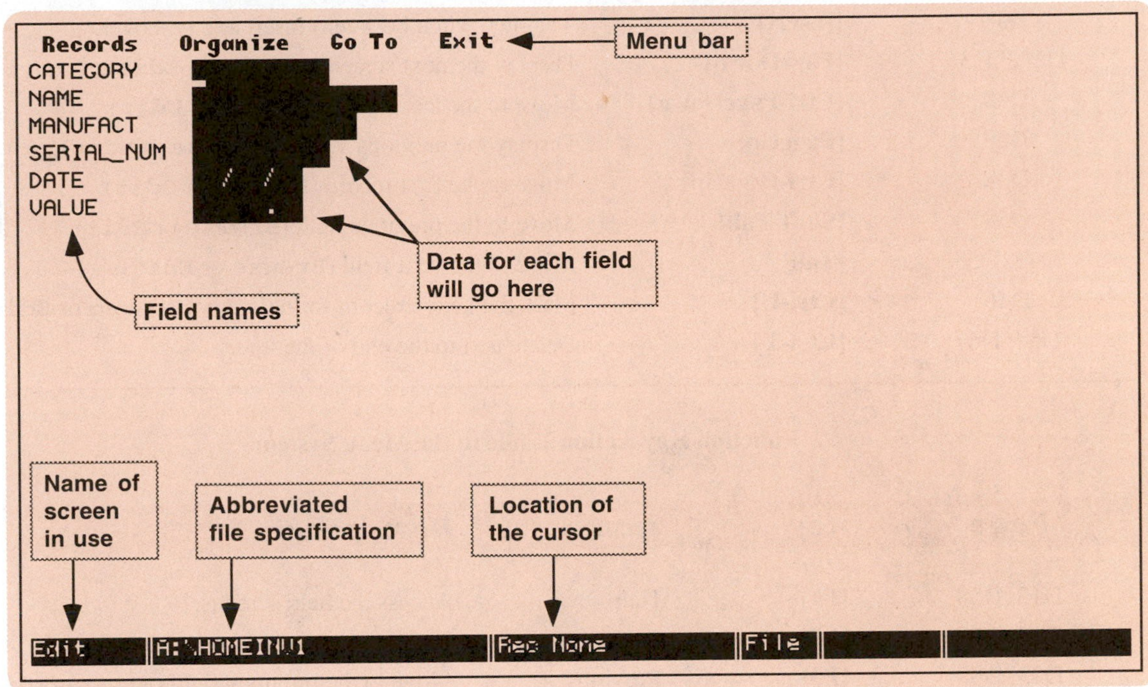

Special Keys Keys have different effects depending on which screen is displayed when they are pressed. For example, pressing **[F2]** from the Control Center will access either **Browse** or **Edit** while pressing **[F2]** at the dot prompt will switch to the Control Center.

Page	Key	Description
D24, D58	**[Down arrow]**	Move the cursor to the next record (**Browse**), field (**Edit**) or command (dot prompt).
D24, D138	**[Up arrow]**	Move the cursor to the previous record (**Browse**), field (**Edit**) or command (dot prompt).
D37	**[Left arrow]**	Move the cursor one character left.
D37	**[Ctrl-left arrow]**	Move to the beginning of the previous word.
D37	**[Right arrow]**	Move the cursor one character right.
D37	**[Ctrl-right arrow]**	Move to the beginning of the next word.
D37	**[Backspace]**	Delete the previous character.
D38	**[Ctrl-Backspace]**	Delete the previous word.
D38	**[Delete]**	Delete the character at the cursor or the currently selected item.
D38, D58	**[End]**	Move to the last field in the record (**Browse**) or to the end of the field (**Edit**).
D38, D49	**[Ctrl-End]**	Save your work and leave this work surface.
D38	**[Enter]**	Move the cursor to the next field (**Browse** or **Edit**).
D38	**[Ctrl-Enter]**	Save your work and remain in this work surface.

Continued . . .

Page	Key	Description
D10, D75	**[Esc]**	Exit without making changes permanent or cancel the current selection.
D38, D54	**[Home]**	Move to the beginning of current record (**Browse**) or move to the beginning of the current field (**Edit**).
D38	**[Insert]**	Toggle (switch between) insert and typeover.
D29, D136	**[PageDown]**	Display the next screen (**Browse** or **Edit**).
D38	**[Ctrl-PageDown]**	Move to the last record (**Browse** or **Edit**).
D29	**[PageUp]**	Display the previous screen (**Browse** or **Edit**).
D38	**[Ctrl-PageUp]**	Move to the first record (**Browse** or **Edit**).
D58	**[Shift-Tab]**	Move to the previous field (**Browse** or **Edit**).
D43, D58	**[Tab]**	Move to the next field (**Browse** or **Edit**).
D46	**[Ctrl-U]**	Mark the active record for deletion (**Browse** or **Edit**).
D54, D67	**[Ctrl-Y]**	Delete text to the end of the line.

Function Key Action While in the Menu System

Page	Key	Name	Description
D13, D58	**[F1]**	Help	Access the help screens.
D27, D58	**[F2]**	Data	Toggle between **Edit** and **Browse**.
D13, D58	**[F3]**	Previous	Move to the previous field (**Browse/Edit**), object (queries design), page (*Help*), or panel (Control Center).
D13, D58	**[F4]**	Next	Move to the next field (**Browse/Edit**), object (query design), page (*Help*), or panel (Control Center).
D58, D85	**[F5]**	Field	Add a field to a layout surface or view skeleton.
D58, D63	**[F6]**	Extend select	Select contiguous text and fields.
D58, D63	**[F7]**	Move	Move selected text and fields.
N/C	**[F8]**	Copy	Copy selected text and fields.
D166	**[F9]**	Zoom	Enlarge or shrink various objects.
D9, D58	**[F10]**	Menus	Move to the menu bar.
D49	**[Shift-F1]**	Pick	Display a list of items to pick from.
D56, D62	**[Shift-F2]**	Design	Transfer to design screen.
N/C	**[Shift-F3]**	Find previous	Find previous occurrence of search string.
D54	**[Shift-F4]**	Find next	Find next occurrence of search string.
N/C	**[Shift-F5]**	Find	Locate specified search string.
N/C	**[Shift-F6]**	Replace	Replace one string with another.
D58, D64	**[Shift-F7]**	Size	Change the size of design elements and column widths (**Browse**).
D30	**[Shift-F8]**	Ditto	Copy data from the corresponding field in the previous record.
D35	**[Shift-F9]**	Quick report	Print a report using the default settings.
D38, D111	**[Shift-F10]**	Macros	Access the macros menu.

Function Keys Action While at the Dot Prompt

Page	Key	Name	Description
D13, D122	**[F1]**	Help	Access the help screens.
D18, D122	**[F2]**	Assist	Switch to the Control Center.
D13, D123	**[F3]**	List	List the records of the active database.
D13, D124	**[F4]**	Dir	Display a list of database files in the current directory.
D124	**[F5]**	Display structure	Display field definitions of the active database.
D124	**[F6]**	Display status	Display information about the current work session.
D126	**[F7]**	Display memory	Display information on how dBASE IV is using the computer's memory.
D127	**[F8]**	Display	Display the contents of the current record.
D127	**[F9]**	Append	Add records to the end of the database.
D127	**[F10]**	Edit	Switch to the **Edit** screen for the current record.
N/C	**[Shift-F10]**	Macro menu	Display menu of macros.

Comparison Operators

Page	Operator	Description
D65, D132	=	Equal to.
D70	<>	Not equal to.
D70, D72	>	Greater than.
D70	<	Less than.
D73, D137	>=	Greater than or equal to.
D69, D137	<=	Less than or equal to.

Mathematical Operators

Page	Operator	Description
N/C	+	Addition.
N/C	-	Subtraction.
N/C	*	Multiplication.
N/C	/	Division.
N/C	^	Exponentiation (e.g., 5^2 is written as **5^2**).
N/C	**	Exponentiation (e.g., 5^2 is written as **5**2**).
N/C	( )	Parentheses (for grouping or to change the order in which mathematical operations are to be performed).

Logical Operators

Page	Operator	Description
D137	**.AND.**	Boolean *and* (used to connect two conditions, both of which must be true for the entire condition to be true).
D138	**.OR.**	Boolean *or* (used to connect two conditions, either one of which may be true for the entire condition to be true).
N/C	**.NOT.**	Boolean *not* (reverses a condition—false becomes true and vice versa).

Order in Which Operators Are Evaluated dBASE IV operators are evaluated in the order shown below. The order may be changed by using parentheses. For nested parentheses, the inner-most set is evaluated first.

Type	Operators	Order
Mathematical	**+,-,*,/,**,^,=**	Unary + and –, **, ^, * and /, + and –, from left to right.
String	**+, -**	From left to right.
Relational	**>, <, =, #, <>, >=, <=, $**	From left to right.
Logical	**.NOT., .AND., .OR.**	In the order **.NOT.**, **.AND.**, **.OR.**

Commands The following is a list of some of the commands available in dBASE IV, either through the dot prompt (you must type the command using the proper syntax) or through the Control Center (you may select commands, options, and parameters from menus). For the sake of simplicity, not all options are given—see the *dBASE IV Language Reference* manual for a complete list.

The syntax given for each command is for the dot prompt. Most commands consist of three major parts:

- A key word called a verb that describes what the command does. For example, the key word **LIST** instructs dBASE IV to list the contents of the active database.
- One or more options that give you a choice of things you may or may not want the command to do. For example, the option **TO FILE** in a **LIST** command instructs dBASE IV to send a list of the contents of the active database to a file (rather than to the screen or to the printer).
- One or more parameters that provide the specifics of exactly what you want done. For example, if you want to send a list of the contents of the active database to a file called **OUTLIST.TXT**, you must provide the proper file specification. In that case, you would use the command **LIST TO FILE A:\OUTLIST.TXT**. The file specification **A:\OUTLIST.TXT** is considered a parameter.

Study the following example of the **REPORT FORM** command, which is used to create a report from the active database using a report form file that was created by **CREATE REPORT** or **MODIFY REPORT**. The form of the command is the following:

```
REPORT FORM
     < report form filename >/?
     [PLAIN]
     [HEADING <character expression>]
     [NOEJECT]
     [SUMMARY]
     [<scope>]
     [FOR <condition>]
     [WHILE <condition>]
     [TO PRINTER/TO FILE <filename>]
```

The following symbols and abbreviations are used:

< > Angle brackets indicate required information (you must type it in but do not type the brackets). For example, **< report form filename >** means that you must supply the name of the report form when you give the command. For example, if you have created a report form called **HOMEALL.FRM**, then the **REPORT FORM** command might look like **REPORT FORM A:\HOMEALL.FRM**. This would create a report following the design given in the report form called **HOMEALL.FRM**.

? A question mark is referred to as a *query clause*. When you enter it in place of a file name, dBASE IV will present you with a list of file names from which to choose. Thus, if you cannot remember the exact name of the report file you want to use, you could type **REPORT FORM ?**, and dBASE IV would display a list of report forms that you could select from.

/ A slash indicates that you must select one of the options listed. For example, **<report form filename>/?** means that you may choose to type the name of the report form file, or you may type a question mark (which will display a list of the report form files in the current directory).

[ ] Square brackets indicate an optional item (i.e., you may use it or not, as you see fit). For example, **[FOR <condition>]** is an option that allows you to select for inclusion in the report only those records which match the condition specified. Thus, if you only want records whose **VALUE** field is more than $400, you could type **REPORT FORM A:\HOMEALL.FRM FOR VALUE > 400**.

Page	Command	Description
D127, D131	**APPEND [BLANK]**	Add records to the end of a database.
D173, D182	**APPEND FROM <filespec>/?** **[[TYPE] <filetype>]** **[FOR <condition>]**	Add (copy) records from another file to the end of the active database. Use **IMPORT** to copy Lotus 1-2-3 files.
D18, D122	**ASSIST**	Access the Control Center (switch from the dot prompt). Press **[Esc]** to switch back to the dot prompt.
D143	**AVERAGE [<num expr>]** **[<scope>]** **[FOR <condition>]** **[WHILE <condition>]**	Calculate the arithmetic mean (average) of numeric expressions.
D32, D131	**BROWSE**	Browse through, append, and edit records and fields. See also, **EDIT**.
D143	**CALCULATE [scope] <options>** **[FOR <condition>]** **[WHILE <condition>]**	Calculate financial and statistical functions. The option list includes **AVG**, **CNT**, **MAX**, **MIN**, **STD**, **SUM**, and **VAR**.
D18	**CLEAR**	Erase (clear) the screen.
D130, D144	**CLOSE ALL/ALTERNATE** **/DATABASES/FORMAT** **/INDEXES/PROCEDURE**	Close files. For databases, closing a file actually writes any modifications to disk.
D144, D153	**COPY FILE <file1> TO <file2>**	Copy the contents of one file into another.
N/C	**COPY STRUCTURE TO <filespec>** **[FIELDS <field list>]** **[[WITH] PRODUCTION]**	Copy the structure of the active database to another file without copying any records.

Continued . . .

Page	Command	Description
D144, D183	**COPY TO <filespec>** **[[TYPE] <file type>]** **/[[WITH] PRODUCTION]** **[FIELDS <field list>]** **[<scope>]** **[FOR <condition>]** **[WHILE <condition>]**	Copy the contents of one database into another dBASE IV database or other file type. You may specify the entire database or only selected records or fields, and you may specify the new file as type **DELIMITED**, **SDF**, **DBASEII**, **DEMEMO3**, **RPD**, **FW2**, **SYLK**, **DIF**, or **WKS**.
D179	**CREATE LABEL [<filespec>]**	Create a label form.
N/C	**CREATE QUERY [<filespec>]**	Create a query file.
D140, D174	**CREATE REPORT [<filespec>]**	Create a report format.
D118, D172	**CREATE [<filespec>]**	Create a structure for a new database.
D144, D194	**DELETE [<scope>]** **[FOR <condition>]** **[WHILE <condition>]**	Delete (mark for deletion) records. Use **PACK** to erase the records.
D144, D147	**DELETE FILE <filespec>/?**	Delete specified files (not records). Same as **ERASE**.
N/C	**DELETE TAG <tagname>** **[OF <filename.mdx>]**	Delete specified index tag contained in the multiple index file specified.
D114, D124	**DIRECTORY/DIR**	Directory (accepts DOS global characters to display the names of specific files).
D127, D132	**DISPLAY/LIST** **[[FIELDS] <expr list>]** **[OFF]** **[<scope>]** **[FOR <condition>]** **[WHILE <condition>]** **[TO PRINTER/TO FILE** **<filespec>]**	Display records and fields of the active database one screen at a time. **DISPLAY** shows only one record while **DISPLAY ALL** shows all records (this has the same effect as **LIST**).
D124, D150	**DISPLAY/LIST STATUS** **[TO PRINTER/TO FILE** **<filespec>]**	Display information about the current work session.
D166, D193	**DISPLAY/LIST STRUCTURE** **[TO PRINTER/TO FILE** **<filespec>]**	Display the field definitions of the active database.
D127, D136	**EDIT** **[<record number>]** **[FIELDS <field list>]** **[<scope>]** **[FOR <condition>]** **[WHILE <condition>]**	Edit a record and its associated fields. **EDIT** displays a single record in a vertical field arrangement while **BROWSE** displays multiple records in a tabular format.
D127, D136	**ERASE <filespec> / ?**	Erase specified files (not records). Same as **DELETE FILE**.
D127	**GO/GOTO** **[BOTTOM/TOP]** **[[RECORD] <rec num>]**	Position the pointer to the specified record number in the database.
D16	**HELP [dBASE IV keyword]**	Display information on dBASE IV commands, functions, and procedures.

Continued . . .

Page	Command	Description
D193	**IMPORT FROM <filespec>** **[TYPE] PFS/DBASEII/FW2** **/RPD/WK1**	Create dBASE IV files with data imported from PFS:FILE, dBASE II, Framework II, RapidFile, and Lotus 1-2-3.
D148, D158	**INDEX ON <key expr> TO** **<filename.ndx>** **/TAG <tagname>** **[OF <filename.mdx>]** **[FOR <condition>]** **[DESCENDING]**	Index (order) a database on the specified **key expr** and store the index on the file **filename.ndx** or in **tagname** of **filename.mdx**
N/C	**INSERT [BEFORE] [BLANK]**	Insert a new blank record at the current record location.
N/C	**LABEL FORM <label file> / ?** **[<scope>]** **[FOR <condition>]** **[WHILE <condition>]** **[SAMPLE]** **[TO PRINTER/TO FILE** **<filename>]**	Print information using the specified label format.
D128, D135	**LIST**	Same as **DISPLAY** but there is no pause when the screen fills up.
N/C	**LOCATE** **[FOR <condition>]** **[<scope>]** **[WHILE <condition>]**	Search the active database for a record that matches the specified condition.
D112	**MODIFY COMMAND/FILE <file>**	Access the dBASE IV editor and allows you to modify a command or file.
N/C	**MODIFY LABEL <filespec> / ?**	Modify a label form.
D141, D153	**MODIFY REPORT <filespec> / ?**	Modify a report format.
D163	**MODIFY STRUCTURE**	Modify the structure of a database.
D135	**MODIFY VIEW <filespec> / ?**	Modify a view file.
D144, D194	**PACK**	Pack the database by removing any records marked for deletion by the **DELETE** command.
D144	**QUIT**	Quit the dBASE IV program and return to DOS.
D144	**RECALL** **[<scope>]** **[FOR <condition>]** **[WHILE <condition>]**	Reinstate records marked for deletion.
D144	**RENAME <oldfile> TO <newfile>**	Rename a file.
D144, D146	**REPLACE <field> WITH <exp>** **[<scope>]** **[FOR <condition>]** **[WHILE <condition>]**	Replace the current contents of a field with the specified contents.
D142	**REPORT FORM <report file> / ?** **[PLAIN]** **[HEADING <char expr>]** **[NOEJECT]** **[SUMMARY]** **[<scope>]** **[FOR <condition>]** **[WHILE <condition>]** **[TO PRINTER/TO FILE <file>]**	Print information about a database using a report form file created using **CREATE REPORT**.

Continued . . .

Page	Command	Description
D142	**RUN/! <DOS command>**	Execute the specified DOS command. **RUN COMMAND** drops to DOS (suspends dBASE IV and allows you to run multiple DOS commands). Type **EXIT** ↵ to resume working in dBASE IV.
D115	**SET**	Display a menu for changing most dBASE IV **SET** commands.
D116	**SET CATALOG ON/OFF**	Create or open a catalog. **SET CATALOG TO** ↵ closes any open catalog.
D120	**SET CATALOG TO [<filespec>/?]**	**SET CATALOG OFF** ↵ Stops adding file names to open catalog.
N/C	**SET CLOCK ON/OFF** **SET CLOCK TO [<row>,<column>]**	Display or do not display the clock in the upper right hand corner of the screen or to the position indicated by **<row>,<column>**.
D115	**SET DEFAULT TO <drive>**	Set the default disk drive to **drive**.
N/C	**SET FILTER TO <condition>**	Allows the display of only those records that match **<condition>**. To turn off the filter enter **SET FILTER TO** ↵.
D151, D184	**SET INDEX TO <filespec> / ?** **[ORDER <filespec.ndx>** **/[TAG] <mdx tag>** **[OF <filespec.mdx>]]]**	Set the index so that it uses **filespec** or **mdx tag**. Entering **SET INDEX TO** ↵ closes the index files.
D151	**SET ORDER TO [TAG] <filespec>** **/<mdx tagname>** **[OF <filespec.mdx>]**	Set the specified tag of the open index file to the controlling index. Entering **SET ORDER TO** ↵ restores the records to their natural (record number) order.
D99, D140	**SET VIEW TO <query file> / ?**	Sets the view of the database so that it is filtered according to the specified query file. The **USE** command will return the view to normal.
D144, D161	**SKIP <number>**	Move the record pointer the specified number of records forward if **number** is positive or backward if **number** is negative.
D144, D158	**SORT TO <filespc> ON <field1>** **[/A] [/C] [/D]** **[, <field2>** **[/A] [/C] [/D]...]** **[ASCENDING]** **/[DESCENDING]** **[<scope>]** **[FOR <condition>]** **[WHILE <condition>]**	Create a new database and fill it with the sorted (alphabetized) records of the active database. **INDEX** usually is a better choice.
N/C	**SUM [<num expr>] [TO <var>]** **[<scope>]** **[FOR <condition>]** **[WHILE <condition>]**	Calculate the sum of numeric expressions.
N/C	**TYPE <file1>** **[TO PRINTER/TO FILE <file2>]**	Display the contents of a text file called **filespec1**.
D122, D130	**USE [<filespec> / ?]** **[[INDEX <.ndx/mdx files>]**	Retrieve a database called **filespec** and any specified index files.
D144, D147	**ZAP**	Remove all records from the active database file.

PART IV

Programming with BASIC

Introduction to BASIC

Objectives *After you have completed this chapter, you should be able to*

- Define commonly used terms associated with BASIC programming.
- Assess the BASIC interpreter from the DOS environment.
- Display the answers to numerical computations and strings using the **PRINT** statement.
- Save a BASIC program in compressed binary format or in ASCII format.
- Print program lists and output.

CHAPTER 1

- Determine when spaces are ignored and when they are not in BASIC programs.
- Modify programs by adding, deleting, and editing lines of BASIC code.
- Convert numbers written in exponential notation into regular decimal notation and vice versa.
- Exit the BASIC environment and return to the DOS environment.
- Locate and correct syntax errors in BASIC programs.

Introduction

In this part of the book, we will be working with BASIC programs instead of WordPerfect documents, Lotus 1-2-3 worksheets, or dBASE databases. A program is simply a set of instructions that you give the computer in order to have it accomplish a task. In one sense, you did this in DOS, WordPerfect, Lotus 1-2-3, and dBASE when you told the computer to print, calculate, edit, save, etc. The instructions you gave, other than entering straight text or numbers, were usually only a single keystroke (e.g., press **[F10]** to save a WordPerfect document) or sometimes a few key words (e.g., **`FORMAT A:/V/F:1440`** to format a diskette in DOS). The application you were using was programmed to do many (perhaps tens or hundreds) of very simple operations to accomplish the task you gave it through your command. In BASIC, we will have to be much more detailed with the commands because many have not been preprogrammed for us. As an analogy, telling Lotus 1-2-3 to use the **`@AVG`** function to calculate an average of a range of cells would be like a mother telling her son, "eat your beans." If the boy understands the command (i.e., he has been programmed by experience to know what to do when given the command), then he will carry out a large number of operations in order to accomplish the task (use his eyes to locate the beans, pick up his fork, scoop up the beans, move the fork full of beans to his mouth, open his mouth, put the bean-laden fork in his mouth, close his mouth, extract the fork while keeping the beans in his mouth, put the fork down, chew the beans, and swallow the beans). Likewise, the **`@AVG`** function has been preprogrammed to carry out a number of steps to find the average of the numbers. In BASIC, however, we have to tell the computer exactly what steps to follow in order to calculate an average.

In any situation where commands are given, the instructions must be clear and unambiguous, and they must be given in a way that is understandable to the object you want to control. For example, if you are in Mexico and say to a child *"Comate los frijoles"* you will get quite a different response than if you give the same instruction to a child in China. Similarly, you must be sure that the programming instructions you give to the computer are in a language that it understands. Remember though, that the computer speaks different languages depending on the active computer environment. For example, to erase a file called **`TEMP`** while in the DOS environment, you would enter **`DEL A:TEMP`**; to erase the file while in the dBASE environment, you would enter **`DELETE FILE A:TEMP`**; to erase the file while in the BASIC environment, you would enter **`KILL"A:TEMP"`**. The commands accomplish the same task but are written in different (although similar) languages. You must take care to give the command that matches the active computer environment.

The word **BASIC** is an acronym for **B**eginners **A**ll-purpose **S**ymbolic **I**nstruction **C**ode. This is a **high-level computer language** developed at Dartmouth College by John Kemeny and Thomas Kurtz in the early 1960s for the purpose of teaching students how to program computers. For a long time, BASIC was the only high-level language available on microcomputers. Even though BASIC was not intended to be used as a language for writing production programs (ones which would be run many times), it is the choice of many programmers because it is powerful and easy to use. In fact, today, BASIC is one of the most widely used computer languages in the world.

Computers do not speak BASIC. Computers only understand **machine language**, which consists of a series of 0s and 1s and is unintelligible to most humans. Translating from a high-level language such as BASIC into machine language is done by a program called an **interpreter** or a **compiler.** These programs serve as the intermediary between the human and the machine.

There are many different versions (dialects) of BASIC that have been designed to work on an IBM or compatible microcomputer including **IBM BASIC** (the version that is distributed by IBM on the DOS disk), **GW-BASIC** (from Microsoft, Inc.), **QuickBASIC** (also from Microsoft, Inc.), and **True BASIC** (from Kemeny and Kurtz). In this book, BASIC will be used to mean version 4.0 of IBM BASIC (this is virtually the same as GW-BASIC).

Definitions

Before beginning a specific example, you should familiarize yourself with the definitions of some terms frequently encountered when talking about BASIC programming.

BASIC . . . (B4) Acronym for **B**eginners **A**ll-purpose **S**ymbolic **I**nstruction **C**ode. A high-level computer language developed in the early 1960s by John Kemeny and Thomas Kurtz.

Code . . . (B19) BASIC code is another name for programming statements.

Compiler . . . (B4) A program that converts statements from a high-level computer language such as BASIC into a form that can be used directly by the computer. A compiler translates all the statements before it executes any of them (compare this with an interpreter).

Delimiter . . . (B12) A character used to separate two pieces of data. The comma is the usual delimiter in BASIC.

GW-BASIC . . . (B4) A version of BASIC developed by Microsoft Corporation (the *GW* stands for *Gee Whiz*).

High-level Language . . . (B4) A computer programming language such as BASIC or Pascal that allows users to write program code using simplified statements (such as **PRINT**) rather than machine-readable code.

IBM BASIC . . . (B4) A version of BASIC developed by IBM Corporation.

Interpreter . . . (B4) Similar to a compiler, an interpreter translates statements from a high-level computer language such as BASIC into a code that can be used directly by the computer. An interpreter executes a statement as soon as it translates it rather than translating all statements in a program and then executing them (compare this with a compiler).

Load . . . (B15) Retrieve a program from disk and place a copy of it into the RAM memory of the computer so that it can be interpreted and executed.

Machine Language . . . (B4) The fundamental language of a computer in which instructions can be directly carried out by the computer's central processing unit. Machine language, which consists of a series of 0s and 1s, is generally unreadable by humans.

Program . . . (B8) A set of instructions written in a computer language such as BASIC that tells the computer to carry out certain tasks.

Reserved word . . . (B12) A special word that the BASIC interpreter can recognize (e.g., **PRINT**); also referred to as **key word**.

RUN . . . (B10) Execute (follow the instructions given in) the statements in a program.

String . . . (B9) A sequence of characters that is treated as a single unit. In BASIC, strings usually are enclosed inside quotation marks.

Syntax . . . (B12) The grammar or set of rules that must be followed when writing in a programming language.

Syntax Errors . . . (B12) Errors in the structure of a BASIC statement (e.g., using a comma instead of a semicolon or omitting a needed quotation mark).

System Requirements

In order to work with the BASIC interpreter you must have an IBM or IBM-compatible computer system that has two floppy disk drives or a hard-disk drive and at least 256K of RAM.

For your information and reference, a summary of selected BASIC features appears on pages B274–88 of the Appendix. In addition, a keyboard template that contains a summary of many BASIC features is located at the end of this book. If your keyboard has 12 function keys along the top, cut out the two halves of the template, tape the ends together, and place the template around the function keys. If your keyboard has 10 function keys along the left-hand side, you still may use the top of the template, but the bottom must be cut off.

As was the case with the application programs, we will assume that you are working on a hard-disk system and that the BASIC interpreter (called **BASICA.COM** or **GWBASIC.COM**) has been installed on the hard disk in a subdirectory with path **C:\BA**. However, we will also provide pertinent information for those of you working on a two-drive system. In either case, your course instructor may give you different directions for accessing the interpreter and for saving data files for the particular computer system available to you in your school's computer lab.

Formatting a Data Diskette

Before turning on the computer, be sure you have the proper disks handy.

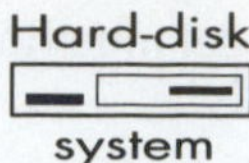

IF YOU ARE USING A HARD-DISK SYSTEM, you need a blank diskette that will serve as your *BASIC Data* diskette. You will use this diskette for storing the BASIC files that you create. If you are using your own computer, you do not need this diskette (you will want to save files directly to your hard disk). If you so desire and if there is room, you could use your *WordPerfect Data*, *Lotus Data*, or *dBASE Data* diskette to store your BASIC files.

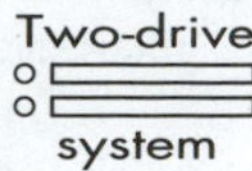

IF YOU ARE USING A TWO-DRIVE SYSTEM, you need the DOS diskette, a backup copy of the *BASIC Program* diskette, and a blank diskette that will serve as your *BASIC Data/Boot* diskette (you will store your files on this disk).

Boot the computer and then format a blank diskette to serve as the *BASIC Data* diskette by doing the following:

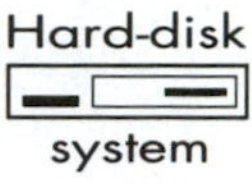

IF YOU ARE USING A HARD-DISK SYSTEM, do the following:

- Write *BASIC Data* and your name on a diskette label, attach the label to a new diskette, and insert the diskette into the A: drive.
- Type **`FORMAT A:/V/F:size`** (***`size`*** is the disk capacity — 360, 720, 1200, or 1440) and press **[Enter]**.
- When asked to enter a label, type your last name and press **[Enter]**.
- When asked **`Format another (Y/N)?`**, type **`N`** and press **[Enter]**. The system prompt **`C:\>`** will then be displayed.

IF YOU ARE USING A TWO-DRIVE SYSTEM, do the following:

- Write *BASIC Data/Boot* and your name on a diskette label, attach the label to a new diskette, and insert the diskette into the B: drive (the DOS diskette should still be in drive A:).
- Type **`FORMAT B:/S/V/F:size`** (***`size`*** is the disk capacity — 360, 720, 1200, or 1440) and press **[Enter]**.
- When asked to enter a label, type your last name and press **[Enter]**.
- When asked **`Format another (Y/N)?`**, type **`N`** and press **[Enter]**. The system prompt **`A>`** will then be displayed.
- Replace the DOS diskette in drive A: with the newly created *BASIC Data/Boot* diskette.
- Place the backup copy of the *BASIC Program* disk in drive B:.

Accessing BASIC

To load the BASIC interpreter into the main memory of the computer, do the following:

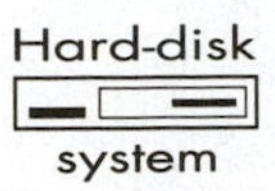

IF YOU ARE USING A HARD-DISK SYSTEM, be sure that the *BASIC Data* diskette is in the A: drive and then type the following:

Keystroke	Action Resulting from Keystroke
A: ↵	Makes A: the default drive.
C:\BA\BASICA ↵	Reads the BASIC interpreter called **BASICA** from the subdirectory called **BA** on the C: drive andloads it into the main memory of the computer. In a few seconds, the startup screen will be displayed. If the BASIC interpreter on your computer is in a subdirectory other than **BA**, use that name in place of **BA**. Also, if you are using a different version of BASIC (e.g., GW-BASIC), you may need to type a different command (e.g., **GWBASIC**) in place of **BASICA**.

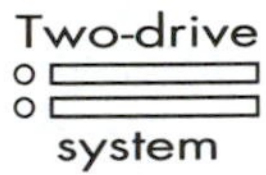

IF YOU ARE USING A TWO-DRIVE SYSTEM, be sure the *BASIC Data/Boot* diskette is in drive A: and a backup copy of the *BASIC Program* diskette is in drive B: and then type the following:

Keystroke	Action Resulting from Keystroke
A: ↵	Makes A: the default drive.
B:BASICA ↵	Reads the BASIC interpreter called **BASICA** from the diskette in the B: drive and loads it into the main memory of the computer. In a few seconds, the startup screen will be displayed. If you are using a different version of BASIC (e.g., GW-BASIC), you may need to type a different command (e.g., **GWBASIC**) in place of **BASICA**..

```
The IBM Basic
Version A4.00 Copyright IBM Corp. 1981, 1988
60655 Bytes free

Ok
_







1LIST  2RUN←  3LOAD"  4SAVE"  5CONT←  6,"LPT1  7TRON←  8TROFF←  9KEY  0SCREEN
```

Version A4.00 specifies the version of BASIC that is being used. The **A** stands for **A**dvanced BASIC and the **4.00** means that this version has undergone **4** major revisions since it was first introduced.

60655 Bytes specifies the amount of memory that is free to use for storage of programs and data. (Note: Your computer may indicate a different amount of memory).

Ok means that the BASIC interpreter is ready to process commands. This is equivalent to the DOS prompt, **C:\>**.

The bottom of the screen shows a menu that lists the function key numbers and a one-word reminder of what each does. The function keys do completely different things in BASIC than they did in the other application programs. Each key will be discussed in detail later.

A Simple BASIC Program

A **program** is a set of instructions written in a computer language like BASIC that tells the computer what to do. Your first program will instruct the computer to calculate and display the answers to two arithmetic problems and to display a string of characters.

Begin by typing the short program given below. If you make a typing mistake, you can use the **[Backspace]** key to make corrections while typing. Other editing procedures will be discussed in more detail later. In the following screen dumps, text that is typed by the computer user (i.e., you) is underlined and ↵ means the **[Enter]** key was tapped.

```
100 PRINT 2 + 3↵
200 PRINT 4 - 9↵
300 PRINT "That's all folks"↵

_
```

Each line of a BASIC program must have a line number that must be between **0** and **65529**. The line numbers can be incremented by any whole number, but steps of **50** or **100** are usually best. The line numbers indicate the order in which the BASIC statements are to be executed. The lines may be typed in any order, but the computer will automatically sort them into ascending numerical order. Let's look at what each line does:

Line Number	Comments
100	Instructs the computer to **PRINT** (actually, display on the screen) the answer to the problem **2 + 3**.
200	Instructs the computer to **PRINT** the answer to the problem **4 - 9**.
300	Instructs the computer to **PRINT** the characters inside the quotation marks exactly as they appear. The set of characters inside the quotation marks is called a **string.** A string is defined as a sequence of up to 255 characters (digits, letters, spaces, punctuation, special symbols) enclosed in quotation marks.

To have the computer execute the program (that is, actually carry out the instructions given in the program statements), type **RUN** and press **[Enter]**.

```
100 PRINT 2 + 3                  <- Program statements
200 PRINT 4 - 9                  <- Program statements
300 PRINT "That's all folks"     <- Program statements
RUN↵                             <- Executes the program
 5                               <- Program output from line 100
-5                               <- Program output from line 200
That's all folks                 <- Program output from line 300
Ok                               <- BASIC is ready for your next command
_                                <- Cursor
```

To add new lines, type them with the appropriate line numbers. In its memory, the computer will put the new lines wherever the line numbers say they belong. For example, to add a blank line to the output between lines **200** and **300** type a line number within that range and the word **PRINT** all by itself. The computer follows the instruction exactly: it prints nothing (i.e., a blank line).

```
250 PRINT↵
RUN↵
 5                     <- Line 100 executed first
-5                     <- Line 200 executed second
                       <- Line 250 executed third
That's all folks       <- Line 300 executed last
Ok
_
```

To delete an entire line from the program, simply type the line number and press **[Enter]**. For example, to remove lines **100** and **250** from the program, type the following:

```
100↵                   <- Line 100 is erased
250↵                   <- Line 250 is erased
RUN↵
-5                     <- Program output from line 200
That's all folks       <- Program output from line 300
Ok
_
```

The program has been modified a few times and you may have forgotten exactly what the entire program looks like. To display an exact listing of the program that the computer has in its memory, type **LIST** and press **[Enter]**:

```
LIST
200 PRINT 4 - 9
300 PRINT "That's all folks"
Ok

_
```

Saving a Program

At this point, it would be a good idea to save this program to the disk. To save a program, type **SAVE"** followed by the file specification for the program. Recall that the file specification begins with the disk drive designator (e.g., **A:**), followed by a one to eight character name (e.g., **PR1**), followed by an optional one to three character extension. If no extension is included, BASIC will automatically add the extension **.BAS** to the file name. Save the program to the disk in the A: drive using the name **PR1** by typing **SAVE"A:PR1** and tapping **[ENTER]**. When the process has been completed, **Ok** will appear on the screen.

The program is now saved on the disk in the A: drive under the name **PR1.BAS**. Because you accessed BASIC while A: was the default drive, the A: in the **SAVE** command is not needed (but should be used anyway just to be sure that you know where the program is being saved). You could have typed **SAVE"PR1** instead. If you had wanted to save the program to a disk in a subdirectory called **BASPROGS** that was a subdirectory of **BA** on the C: drive, you would have typed **SAVE"C:\BA\BASPROGS\PR1**.

Printing

Before actually printing the program and its output, the screen should be cleared of any unwanted characters. This may be done by typing **CLS** and then pressing **[Enter]**. **CLS** stands for **Cl**ear the **S**creen and has the effect of erasing the contents of the screen except for the word **Ok** in the upper left-hand corner and the menu of function keys at the bottom. An alternative to typing the **CLS** command is to press **[Ctrl-Home]**. The effect is the same except that the word **Ok** does not appear in the upper left-hand corner of the screen.

If you want to remove the menu of function keys from the bottom of the screen, type **KEY OFF** and press **[Enter]**. To display the function key menu at a later time, type **KEY ON** and press **[Enter]**.

There are many ways to produce a hard copy of the program and the output. Before attempting any of the following methods, be sure that a printer is attached to your computer, that the power to the printer is turned on, and that the printer is properly loaded with paper.

Method 1 Type **LIST** and press **[Enter]** to list the program on the screen and then type **RUN** and press **[Enter]** to display the output. Then, do a screen dump by pressing **[PrintScreen]** (or you may have to use the **[Shift-PrintScreen]** keys). This is the simplest way of getting a printed version of the **LIST** and **RUN** of a program. However, it only works for programs that can be completely displayed on the screen (24 or less lines in length) and have 24 or less lines of output.

Method 2 Before typing **LIST**, press **[Ctrl-PrintScreen]**. This sends a signal to the printer that instructs it to print everything as it is displayed on the screen. If you then type **LIST** and press **[Enter]**, the program listing will be displayed on the screen and printed on the printer at the same time. If you type **RUN** and press **[Enter]**, the program output will be displayed on the screen and printed on the printer at the same time. You can use this technique if you have a program whose list or run is longer than will fit on the screen at one time. To turn off this printing feature, press **[Ctrl-PrintScreen]** again. Turning the printer on and off in this fashion is known as *toggling* the printer.

Method 3 If a hard copy of only the output is desired, all the **PRINT** statements can be changed to **LPRINT** statements. The **L** in **LPRINT** stands for **L**ine printer and tells the computer to send the output to the printer rather than to the screen. Using **LPRINT** produces output *only* on the printer and not on the screen. This is somewhat inconvenient because to have the output displayed on the screen again you have to change all the **LPRINT**'s back into **PRINT**'s. However, there are situations where you may want information sent only to the printer and not displayed on the screen (e.g., printing out an invoice for a customer).

Method 4 If a hard copy of only the program listing is desired, typing **LLIST** and pressing **[Enter]** will instruct the computer to send a listing of the program to the printer rather than display it on the screen. Again, the first **L** in **LLIST** stands for **L**ine printer.

Method 5 If you type **`LIST,"LPT1:"`** or press **[F1]** and then **[F6]**, the computer will send a listing of the program to the printer.

Print a hard copy of the program, using Method 1, by doing the following:

Keystroke	Action Resulting from Keystroke
CLS ↵	Clears the screen.
LIST ↵	Displays a list of the program currently in memory.
RUN ↵	Executes the statements in the current program.
	Before doing the screen dump, be sure that a printer is attached to your computer, that the power to the printer is turned on, that the printer is properly loaded with paper, and that the *OnLine* status light (if your printer has one) is on. If your printer is shared with other computers, you may have to select other switches before using it. See your instructor if you need help.
[PrintScreen]	Prints the contents of the screen.

Spaces in BASIC

Spaces in BASIC statements are usually ignored. For example, replacing line **200** in program **PR1** with

```
20       0 PRINT 4          - 9
```

would instruct the computer to produce the same output as before. An exception to this rule is when spaces are included inside quotation marks. In that case the computer assumes that you want the spaces and will adjust the output accordingly. For example, changing line **300** to read

```
300 PRINT "Tha        t's all             folks"
```

will instruct the computer to display the extra spaces in the output:

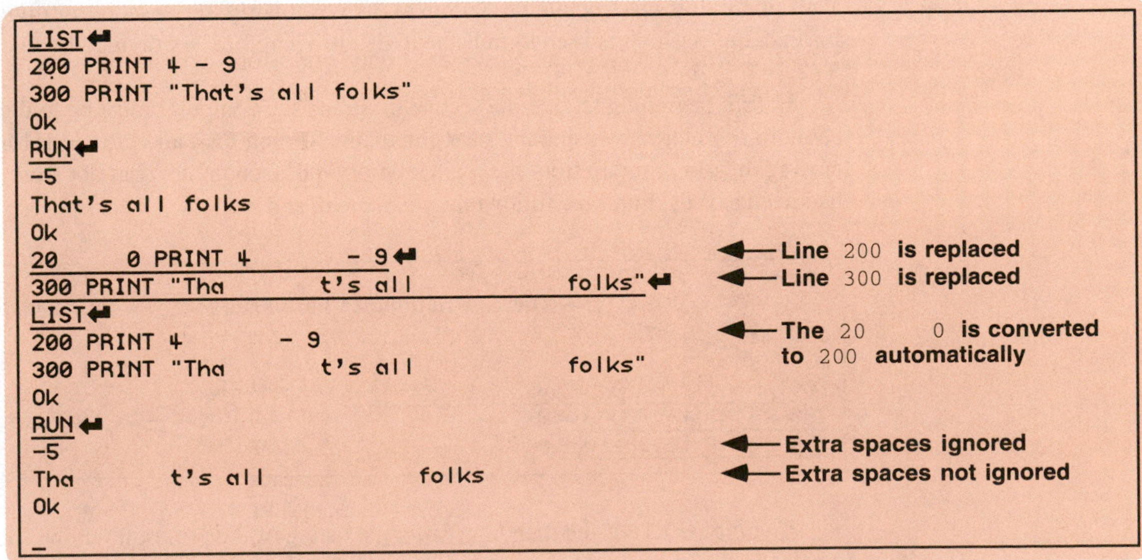
```
LIST↵
200 PRINT 4 - 9
300 PRINT "That's all folks"
Ok
RUN↵
-5
That's all folks
Ok
20      0 PRINT 4          - 9↵
300 PRINT "Tha        t's all             folks"↵
LIST↵
200 PRINT 4          - 9
300 PRINT "Tha        t's all             folks"
Ok
RUN↵
-5
Tha        t's all             folks
Ok
_
```


Spaces should be used to make the program statements more readable to a human. For example, **`200PRINT 4-9`** and **`200 PRINT 4 - 9`** produce the same output, but the latter statement is easier to read.

A second exception to the spaces rule is that spaces should not be used within a BASIC reserved word. A **reserved word** (sometimes called *keyword*) is one that has special meaning to the computer, like **PRINT**. If you type **PR   INT** instead of **PRINT**, the computer displays an error message because it interprets **PR** as a reserved word but **PR** has no meaning. For example:

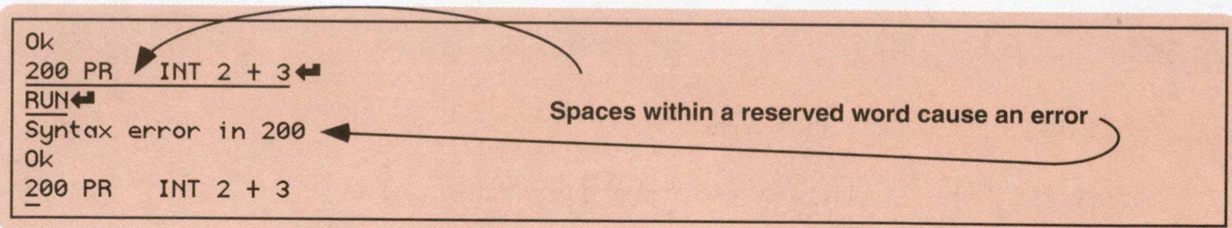

Ok
200 PR   INT 2 + 3
RUN
Syntax error in 200
Ok
200 PR   INT 2 + 3
Spaces within a reserved word cause an error

The phrase **Syntax error in 200** indicates that the BASIC interpreter cannot understand line **200**. The word **syntax** refers to the form in which the statement is written, like the grammar of an English sentence. The computer was not able to translate **PR   INT** properly. The incorrect line is displayed directly under the word **Ok** and the cursor is placed at the beginning of the line. This allows you to quickly make modifications to the offending BASIC statement using the **[arrow]**, **[Delete]**, and **[Insert]** keys.

Spaces are also used to **delimit** (separate) different parts of a BASIC statement. There must be at least one space between a reserved word and the rest of the statement. Thus, **200 PRINT4 - 9** would cause a syntax error as the following example shows:

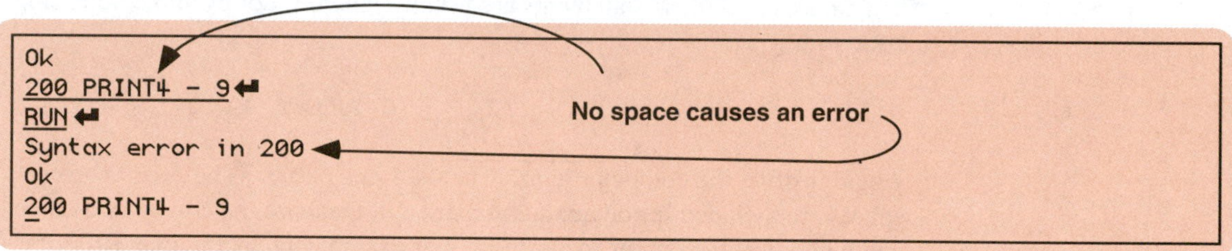

Ok
200 PRINT4 - 9
RUN
Syntax error in 200
Ok
200 PRINT4 - 9
No space causes an error

A Second BASIC Program

The next program illustrates how the computer does simple mathematical calculations. For adding and subtracting, the symbols **+** and **–** are used. However, as was the case with Lotus 1-2-3, the × and the dot are not used for multiplication because the × will be used as a variable (as in algebra) and the dot will represent the decimal point. In BASIC, the asterisk, *****, is used to represent multiplication. Thus, three times five would be written as **3*5**. Similarly, the symbol for division, ÷, is not used. Instead, the slash, **/**, is used to indicate division. Therefore, six divided by two would be written as **6/2**.

Before beginning to type the second program, the computer must be told that a new program is about to be entered by using the **NEW** command. Typing **NEW** and pressing **[Enter]** has the effect of erasing the old program from the main memory of the computer (but not from the disk, if the program had been saved). Enter the following:

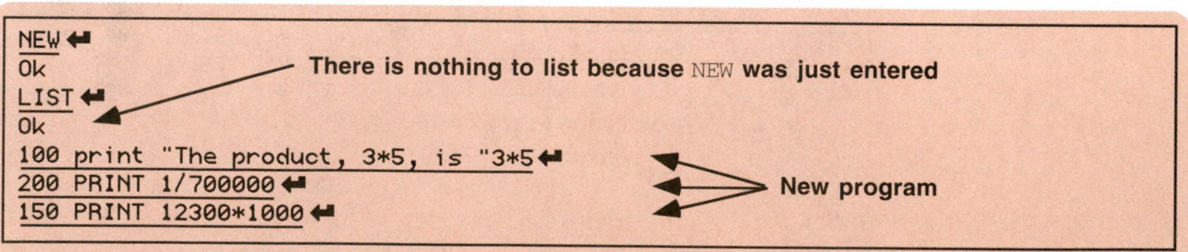

NEW
Ok
LIST
Ok
100 print "The product, 3*5, is "3*5
200 PRINT 1/700000
150 PRINT 12300*1000
There is nothing to list because NEW was just entered
New program

If you type **LIST** and then tap **[Enter]**, a listing of the program will be shown so that you can see what is in the computer's memory.

```
LIST ↵
100 PRINT "The product, 3*5, is "3*5
150 PRINT 12300*1000
200 PRINT 1/700000!
Ok
```

Computer automatically puts lines in numerical order

Notice that the lines were not typed in numerical order but the computer lists them that way. Also, the **PRINT** statement in line **100** was typed using lowercase letters (**print**), but the computer translated these into uppercase letters (**PRINT**). The computer does this for certain reserved words in BASIC. This is done so that the program is easier for humans to read.

Also, note that the computer added an exclamation point (**!**) to the end of **700000** in line **200**. This is because microcomputers usually store numbers in one of three ways:

- **Integers**, which are defined as whole numbers between -32768 and +32767, inclusive.
- **Single precision**, which are numbers that are not integers and have seven or fewer digits. The **!** indicates that **700000!** is a single precision number.
- **Double precision**, which are numbers that contain eight or more digits and are stored with seventeen digits of precision. Such numbers are indicated by a pound symbol (#) attached to the right-hand side of a number (e.g., **2.71828183#**). For the level of BASIC programming you will be doing, this distinction will be of little consequence. Therefore, if you discover that the computer has added an **!** or a **#** to the right-hand side of some of your numbers, you can ignore it.

Now, run the program:

```
LIST ↵
100 PRINT "The product, 3*5, is "3*5
150 PRINT 12300*1000
200 PRINT 1/700000!
Ok
RUN ↵
The product, 3*5, is  15
 1.23E+07
 1.428571E-06
Ok

_
```

The information inside the quotation marks in the first **PRINT** statement was displayed exactly as it appeared in the listing of the program (the multiplication problem, **3*5**, was displayed rather than the answer). The **3*5** that appears outside the quotation marks in line **100** was evaluated and the answer was displayed. Thus, to print both the answer and the problem itself, the problem must appear twice in the **PRINT** statement (once inside quotation marks and again outside quotation marks).

The computer printed out the answer to **1/700000** using **exponential notation.** The equivalent of **1.428571E-06** in regular decimal notation may be found by moving the decimal point six places in the negative (left) direction to get **.000001428571**. The computer output from line **150** is **1.23E+07**, which converts to **12300000** (the decimal point is moved seven places in the positive [right] direction).

Modify this program as shown below by adding a new line between lines **150** and **200**. The new line number shown is **160** but you could use any line number between **151** and **199**, inclusive.

```
160 PRINT "This is an added line", 8 + 1, 5 - 10
LIST
100 PRINT "The product, 3*5, is "3*5
150 PRINT 12300*1000
160 PRINT "This is an added line", 8 + 1, 5 - 10
200 PRINT 1/700000!
Ok
RUN
The product, 3*5, is  15
 1.23E+07
This is an added line          9             -5
 1.428571E-06
Ok
_
```

The statement in line **160** told the computer to display the string **This is an added line** and to calculate and display the answers to two arithmetic problems on the same line. The commas were used to delimit the three different parts of the output. If the commas had been left out, the computer would treat the string as one part and the numbers as one part. Thus, the two problems, **8 + 1** and **5 - 10**, would be treated as if they were one problem, **8 + 15 - 10**, and the answer would be 13.

Save the current program under the name **PR2** by typing **SAVE"A:PR2** and pressing **[Enter]**.

When BASIC saves a program, it does so in what is called **compressed binary** format. This is a special type of coding that uses less space on the disk than if the program were saved using normal text (ASCII) characters. For our purposes, the details of how the program is saved are not important. However, if you run across a situation where a BASIC program must be saved in ASCII characters (e.g., you want to insert a copy of the program into a WordPerfect document), simply attach **.TXT",A** to the end of the file name when saving the program. For example, save the file **PR2** in ASCII format under the name **PR2.TXT** by typing **SAVE"A:PR2.TXT",A** and pressing **[Enter]** (the **TXT** extension indicates that the file is a **TeXT** file rather than a coded BASIC file).

Returning to DOS

When you are through working in the BASIC environment and want to return to the DOS environment, type the word **SYSTEM** and press **[Enter]**. The **A:\>** then will be displayed. Remember, the DOS environment is completely different from the BASIC environment. Statements and commands which work fine in BASIC do not work in DOS and vice versa. You can think of it as travelling from one country to another. If you cross the border from China into Russia and continue to speak Chinese, you will not be understood.

For example, if you are in BASIC and type the DOS command **DIR** to list a copy of the disk directory, the error message **Syntax error** will be displayed. BASIC does not understand what **DIR** means even though DOS does. Similarly, if you exit BASIC using the **SYSTEM** command and then type the perfectly legal BASIC statement **100 PRINT 2 + 3** while in DOS, another error message is displayed.

```
DIR
Syntax error                 ◄— BASIC does not understand the DOS DIR command
Ok
SYSTEM

A:\>100 PRINT 2 + 3
Bad command or file name     ◄— DOS does not understand the BASIC PRINT statement

A:\>_
```

Just for fun, use the **TYPE** command to see the difference between the compressed binary and ASCII versions of the program **PR2**. As you recall, **TYPE** is a DOS command that displays the contents of any file on the disk. Look at the contents of the two files by typing **TYPE PR2.BAS** ↵ and then **TYPE PR2.TXT** ↵.

```
A:\>TYPE PR2.BAS ↵
Å↕d æ "The product, 3*5, is "¶δ■ ¥↕û æ ∟♀Θδ∟Φ♥ ╨↕á æ "This is an added line", ↓
 Θ ↕, ■ Ω ☓
        ╪↕╙ æ ↕∞↔ µ*ö
A:\>TYPE PR2.TXT ↵
100 PRINT "The product, 3*5, is "3*5
150 PRINT 12300*1000
160 PRINT "This is an added line", 8 + 1, 5 - 10
200 PRINT 1/700000!

A:\>_
```

BASIC coded version of program
ASCII version of program

As you can see, the first file is filled with strange characters and is generally unreadable. The second file looks exactly as you typed it because it was saved using ASCII characters.

Loading a BASIC Program

Access BASIC again and load the program **PR1** by typing **C:\BA\BASICA A:PR1** and pressing **[Enter]**. This will read the BASIC interpreter into RAM memory, load the program **PR1** into the BASIC interpreter, and then execute (**RUN**) the program. After this is done you should see a screen with the two lines of output from the program and **Ok** in the upper left-hand corner, but the function key menu along the bottom is not displayed. To display it, type **KEY ON** ↵.

To access a program when you are already in the BASIC environment you must use the **LOAD** command. For example, if you type **LOAD"A:PR2** and press **[Enter]**, the computer will erase the current program (**PR1**) from its RAM memory (but not from the disk!) and then load the program **PR2** from the disk in the A: drive into RAM memory. To see the contents of the program use the **LIST** command.

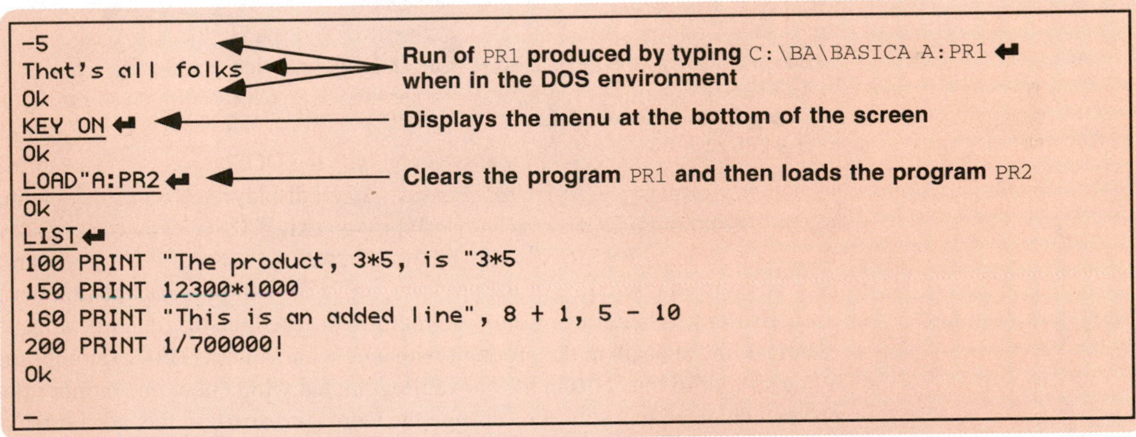

-5
That's all folks
Ok
KEY ON ↵
Ok
LOAD"A:PR2 ↵
Ok
LIST ↵
100 PRINT "The product, 3*5, is "3*5
150 PRINT 12300*1000
160 PRINT "This is an added line", 8 + 1, 5 - 10
200 PRINT 1/700000!
Ok
_
Run of PR1 produced by typing C:\BA\BASICA A:PR1 ↵ when in the DOS environment
Displays the menu at the bottom of the screen
Clears the program PR1 and then loads the program PR2

Editing a Program

You can make changes to a BASIC program using many of the same editing techniques that you used in WordPerfect using BASIC's *screen editor*. The functions of the **[arrow]**, **[Insert]**, and **[Delete]** keys are similar to those used by WordPerfect except that changes are not made in the main memory of the computer unless **[Enter]** is pressed before moving to the next line of the program. For example, suppose you want to insert the words **equal to** into line **100** of the above program so that it reads:

```
100 PRINT "The product, 3*5, is equal to "3*5
```

To do this, move the cursor to the space just after the word **is** in line **100** and press **[Insert]**. Unlike WordPerfect, BASIC is in typeover mode by default and must be changed to insert mode using the **[Insert]** key. When in insert mode, the cursor changes from a blinking line to a blinking box. Next, type the words **equal to** and observe how they are inserted into the line. If you move the cursor down a few lines using the **[arrow]** keys and then type **RUN** and press **[Enter]**, you will notice that the program output remains the same as it was before the change was made!

```
LIST ↵
100 PRINT "The product, 3*5, is equal to "3*5
150 PRINT 12300*1000
160 PRINT "This is an added line", 8 + 1, 5 - 10
200 PRINT 1/700000!
Ok
RUN ↵
The product, 3*5, is  15
 1.23E+07
This is an added line         9              -5
 1.428571E-06
Ok
_
```

Change made here does not appear in output here unless [Enter] **is pressed**

Unlike WordPerfect, in order to tell BASIC to enter into the computer's main memory the change you just made on the screen, you must press **[Enter]** before moving to the next line. In order to see how this works, repeat the editing process (insert the words **equal to**), but this time press **[Enter]** before moving to another line. When the program is run the correct output should be displayed.

```
LIST ↵
100 PRINT "The product, 3*5, is equal to "3*5 ↵
150 PRINT 12300*1000
160 PRINT "This is an added line", 8 + 1, 5 - 10
200 PRINT 1/700000!
Ok
RUN ↵
The product, 3*5, is equal to  15
 1.23E+07
This is an added line         9              -5
 1.428571E-06
Ok
_
```

When [Enter] **is pressed, change here does appear in output here**

To copy an entire line of the program, move the cursor to its line number, type a new number, and press **[Enter]**. When the program is either run or listed the original line appears where it was and the identical line appears in the program with a new line number. For example, suppose you want to include a line similar to line **100** in the above program but with a new line number (let's say **120**) and the product changed to a sum (i.e., change the word **product** to the word **sum** and change the * to +). To do this, move the cursor to line **100**, make the changes, and press **[Enter]**.

Changes made (120, sum, +)   Must tap [Enter] to have the changes take effect

```
120 PRINT "The sum, 3+5, is "3+5 ↵
150 PRINT 12300*1000
160 PRINT "This is an added line", 8 + 1, 5 - 10
200 PRINT 1/700000!
Ok
LIST ↵
100 PRINT "The product, 3*5, is "3*5  ◄— Old line 100 is untouched
120 PRINT "The sum, 3+5, is "3+5      ◄— New line 120 is added
150 PRINT 12300*1000
160 PRINT "This is an added line", 8 + 1, 5 - 10
200 PRINT 1/700000!
Ok

_
```

This version of the program can be saved under the same name, **PR2** by typing **SAVE"A:PR2** and pressing **[Enter]**. In this case, the old version is erased and replaced by the modified version. However, to save the program under a new name, say **PR3**, type **SAVE"A:PR3** and press **[Enter]**. In this case, both versions of the program are stored on the disk: the original version under the name **PR2** remains unchanged and the modified version is saved under the new name **PR3**. Unless the disk is filling up with many programs, it is a good idea to keep copies of multiple versions of the same program. You never know when you might want to go back to a previous version. Eventually, when you are sure that you have made all the changes you can think of, you can erase the old versions.

We have seen how lines can be deleted, one by one, by typing their line numbers and then pressing **[Enter]**. More than one line at a time can be deleted using the **DELETE** command. To delete lines **120** through **160**, type **DELETE 120-160** and press **[Enter]**. (The **DELETE** command is discussed in more detail on p. B50.)

```
LIST ↵
100 PRINT "The product, 3*5, is "3*5
120 PRINT "The sum, 3+5, is "3+5
150 PRINT 12300*1000
160 PRINT "This is an added line", 8 + 1, 5 - 10
200 PRINT 1/700000!
Ok
DELETE 120-160 ↵
Ok
LIST ↵
100 PRINT "The product, 3*5, is "3*5
200 PRINT 1/700000!
Ok

_
```

Save this version of the program under the name **PR4** by typing **SAVE"A:PR4** and pressing **[Enter]**.

Special Program Editor Keys

Below is a list of the special keys that can be used to help edit BASIC programs quickly and easily.

Keystroke	Action Resulting from Keystroke
←↑↓→	The **[arrow]** keys allow movement of the cursor as they did in WordPerfect.
[Ctrl →]	Moves the cursor to the next word (rather than the next character) to the right of its present location.
[Ctrl ←]	Moves the cursor to the next word (rather than the next character) to the left of its present location.
[Home]	Moves the cursor to the upper left-hand corner of the screen.
[Ctrl-Home]	Moves the cursor to the upper left-hand corner of the screen and erases the entire screen except for the function key menu at the bottom.
[Insert]	Toggles between typeover mode (the default) and insert mode. When in insert mode, as characters are inserted at the cursor, all characters to the right will move to the right.
[Delete]	Deletes the character at cursor (characters to the right move to the left but the cursor remains stationary).
[Backspace]	Deletes the character to the left of the cursor (characters to the right move to the left along with the cursor).
[End]	Moves the cursor to the end of the current line.
[Ctrl-End]	Erases all characters from the current cursor location to the end of the line.
[Esc]	Erases the line that contains the cursor (however, the line is still in the memory of the computer).

Errors in BASIC Programs

Consider the following program that illustrates some of the errors that can occur when using BASIC.

```
NEW↵
Ok
100 PRITN "Hours worked = " 40
200 PRINT Rate = $3.50
300 PRINT "Wages = $" 40*3.5
RUN↵
Syntax error in 100
Ok
100 PRITN "Hours worked = " 40
```

Before the computer can execute the instructions in a particular statement, it must first translate the instructions from BASIC, which humans can understand, into machine language, which computers can understand. In the above program, the computer tried to translate the instructions on line **100** but had difficulty because the word **PRINT** was misspelled. The computer knows how to translate **PRINT** but not **PRITN**. This error caused the computer to stop processing at line **100** and to display the message **Syntax error in 100**. The line with the error is displayed also, so that it can easily be fixed. Errors like misspelled words, as in line **100**, or forgetting to use quotation marks around a string, as in line **200**, are called **syntax errors.** They are errors in the *form* or *grammar* of the BASIC language. In English, such errors would include forgetting to capitalize the first letter of a sentence or putting a comma instead of a period at the end of a sentence.

When a syntax error occurs in BASIC, the BASIC interpreter does not understand the instruction. Of course, a human who speaks English could probably figure out that **PRITN** means **PRINT** from the context of the program. However, computers do not speak English. They are machines, which can only follow the instructions given to them. Therefore, programmers must be very careful when typing BASIC **code** (programming statements). It must be correct in every detail or the computer will not be able to process the instructions.

To fix this part of the program, either edit or retype line **100** so that **PRINT** is spelled correctly. Then, run the program.

```
100 PRINT "Hours worked = " 40
RUN
Hours worked =  40
Syntax error in 200
Ok
200 PRINT RATE = $3.5
```

Now the computer can translate and execute line **100**, but there is an error in line **200** (there should be quotation marks around **RATE = $3.5** because it is a string). Notice also that even though **Rate** was originally typed using both lowercase and uppercase letters, the computer changed all the letters to uppercase (**RATE**). That is because BASIC assumed that **Rate** was the name of a variable and it always changes variable names so that they are in uppercase letters. (Variables are discussed on p. B26.) Also note that the **$3.50** was changed to **$3.5**. BASIC will drop off trailing zeros of numbers unless you tell it specifically not to do so (this can be done with the **PRINT USING** statement, which is discussed on p. B35).

To fix the error, edit line **200** by inserting quotation marks around the string **Rate = $3.50**; then, run the program:

```
200 PRINT "Rate = $3.50"
RUN
Hours worked =  40
Rate = $3.50
Wages = $ 140
Ok
_
```

Another type of error can occur when you try to write large numbers using commas to separate the place values of hundreds and thousands, thousands and millions, etc. The computer uses commas to delimit different pieces of information and, thus, will not interpret the commas as we do in English. For example:

```
100 PRINT "One billion equals "1,000,000,000↵
200 PRINT "One billion equals "1000000000↵
300 PRINT "One billion equals "1E9↵
RUN↵
One billion equals  1         0              0              0
One billion equals  1000000000
One billion equals  1E+09
Ok
_
```

In English, large numbers are usually written with commas to make them easier to read. However, because the computer interprets the commas as delimiters in line **100**, the number **1,000,000,000** is treated as four separate numbers: **1** and **0** and **0** and **0**. The representation of one billion in line **200** is interpreted correctly by the computer. The representation of one billion in line **300**, which uses exponential notation, is also correctly interpreted by the computer.

When the program is listed, you can see how the computer interprets the numbers (in the display below, the **#** on the end of the number **1000000000#** is automatically placed there by the computer to indicate that the number is double precision—for all practical purposes you can ignore the **#**):

```
LIST↵
100 PRINT "One billion equals "1,0,0,0
200 PRINT "One billion equals "1000000000#
300 PRINT "One billion equals "1E+09
Ok
_
```

Long Lines

Long lines of characters written in a BASIC program wrap around to the next line just as they did in WordPerfect except that they are wrapped character by character rather than word by word. This means that the computer will break up words in the middle as the following example illustrates. The maximum number of characters that can be typed before pressing **[Enter]** is 255.

```
100 PRINT "This is a very long line of text.  In fact, it is longer than the scr
een is wide.  Notice how the computer automatically wraps the text around to the
 next line but does it character by character rather than word by word."↵
RUN↵
This is a very long line of text.  In fact, it is longer than the screen is wide
.  Notice how the computer automatically wraps the text around to the next line
but does it character by character rather than word by word.
Ok
_
```

Function Keys

As was the case with the other application programs, the function keys are used in BASIC for special purposes. The operations are outlined below for reference and most will be discussed in more detail in later chapters.

Menu Listing	Function
1LIST	Pressing **[F1]** displays the word **LIST**. If you then press **[Enter]**, a list of the program that is currently in memory will be displayed.
2RUN←	Pressing **[F2]** displays the word **RUN** and then executes the statements of the program that is currently in memory. The left arrow means that you do not have to tap **[Enter]** after tapping **[F2]**.
3LOAD"	Pressing **[F3]** displays **LOAD"**. If you then type a file specification such as **A:PR1** and press **[Enter]**, the computer will read the BASIC program from the disk in drive A: and place a copy of the program into the main memory of the computer.
4SAVE"	Pressing **[F4]** displays **SAVE"**. If you then type a file specification such as **A:PR1** and press **[Enter]**, the computer will write a copy of the program currently in memory to the default disk drive. This will replace any file that has the same name as the one you specified.
5CONT←	Pressing **[F5]** displays the word **CONT** and then continues the processing of a program that was suspended using **[Ctrl-Break]** (see p. B59).
6,"LPT1	Pressing **[F1]** (for **LIST**) followed by **[F6]** (for **,"LPT1:"**) sends a copy of the program that is currently in memory to the printer.
7TRON←	Pressing **[F7]** displays the word **TRON** and turns on the tracing function. When the trace is turned on, each time a program line is executed, the line number is displayed on the screen (see p. B51).
8TROFF←	Pressing **[F8]** displays the word **TROFF** and turns off the tracing function.
9KEY	Pressing **[F9]** displays the word **KEY** and permits you to change the function of any of the function keys. By default, it is set so that pressing **[F9]**, typing **OFF**, and pressing **[Enter]** will remove the function key menu from line 25 of the display. Pressing **[F9]**, typing **ON**, and pressing **[Enter]** will display the menu again.
0SCREEN	Pressing **[F10]** returns the program to character mode from graphics mode and turns off the color.

TO TAKE A BREAK Type **SYSTEM ↵**, remove diskette(s). To resume (hard disk): Insert *Data* diskette, type **A: ↵**, **C:\BA\BASICA↵**. To resume (two drive): Insert diskettes, type **A: ↵**, **B:\BASICA ↵**.

Homework Exercises

① Write a program that uses only **PRINT** statements to display the homework exercise number, the date, your name and address, and the number of seconds that you have lived as of your last birthday (multiply your age in years times 365 days per year times 24 hours per day times 3600 seconds per hour—ignore leap years). The output from your program should look like the following (the value in the box should be calculated by the computer):

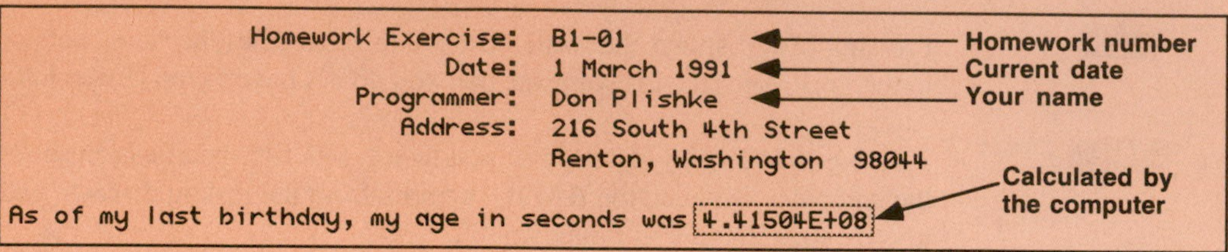

After you have typed the program and are sure that it works properly, do a **LIST** and a **RUN**, and save the program using the name **HWB1-01**. Use **[PrintScreen]** to get a hard copy of the **LIST** and **RUN**.

---

② Use the editing techniques described in this chapter to modify your program from Exercise 1 so that the output does not appear on the screen but goes directly to the printer (i.e., replace all the **PRINT**'s with **LPRINT**'s). Also, change the homework exercise number to **B1-02**. Save the program using the name **HWB1-02**. Run the program and then list it directly on the printer using the **LLIST** command.

---

③ In 1990, the federal debt was about $2,800,000,000,000.00 (i.e., 2.8 trillion dollars). If you laid 2.8 trillion one dollar bills (thickness .0043 inches) on top of each other, how high would the pile be, measured in inches, feet, and miles? Write a program that uses only **PRINT** statements to solve this problem. The output from your program should look like the following (the values in the boxes should be calculated by the computer):

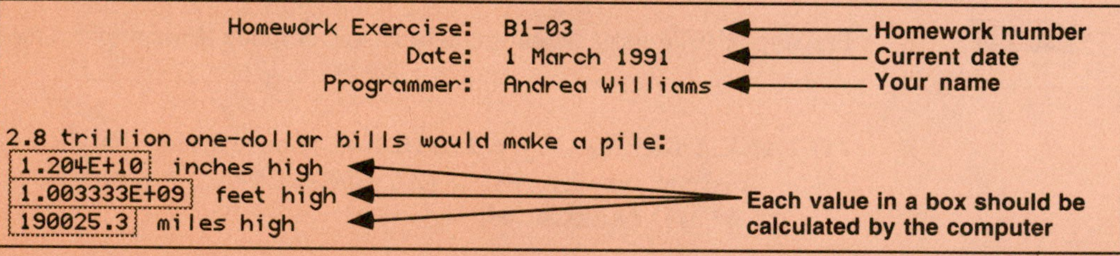

Be sure to think carefully about how you are going to solve the problem before you even consider writing the program. Once you know how to solve the problem, figure out the answer using a calculator and use this answer to check to see that the computer does the calculations correctly when you finally write and run the program.

Next, write the computer program that will solve the problem and produce the desired output. The program should contain the arithmetic needed to calculate the answer and not the answer itself. For example, if you wanted to find the number of inches in 2 feet, the BASIC statement would be:

CHAPTER ONE

```
10 PRINT 2*12 "= number of inches in 2 feet"
```

and not

```
10 PRINT 24 "= number of inches in 2 feet".
```

Save the program using the name **HWB1-03** and then produce a hard copy of both the **LIST** and **RUN** of the program.

---

④ Modify the program you wrote for Exercise 3 so that it calculates the yearly interest on the federal debt. Assume an annual rate of interest of 8%. To do the calculation, you must multiply 2.8 trillion by .08. The output from your program should look like that shown below (the value in the box should be calculated by the computer). Be aware that one of your **PRINT** statements will be longer than 80 characters and therefore will wrap around to the next line in both the **LIST** and **RUN** of the program.

```
                  Homework Exercise:  B1-04
                               Date:  1 March 1991
                         Programmer:  Willy Robertson

Assuming a rate of interest of 8% per year, the interest on 2.8 trillion dollars
 in one year would be [2.24E+11] dollars.
```

Calculated by the computer

Save the program using the name **HWB1-04** and then produce a hard copy of both the **LIST** and **RUN** of the program.

---

⑤ Modify the program you wrote for Exercise 4 so that it performs the calculations for interest rates of 1%, 2%, 3%, 4%, 5%, 6%, 7%, and 8%. To do this, you will have to add a new line of program code for each of the new interest rates. A quick way of adding the new lines would be to make seven copies of the program line that does the calculation for a rate of 8% (see p. B16 for more information on copying lines of code) and then to edit each line so that it has the correct interest rate in the calculation. The output from your program should look like the following (the values in the boxes should be calculated by the computer):

```
                  Homework Exercise:  B1-05
                               Date:  1 March 1991
                         Programmer:  Dao Truong

Assuming a rate of interest of 1% per year, the interest on 2.8 trillion dollars
 in one year would be [2.8E+10] dollars.
Assuming a rate of interest of 2% per year, the interest on 2.8 trillion dollars
 in one year would be [5.6E+10] dollars.
Assuming a rate of interest of 3% per year, the interest on 2.8 trillion dollars
 in one year would be [8.4E+10] dollars.
Assuming a rate of interest of 4% per year, the interest on 2.8 trillion dollars
 in one year would be [1.12E+11] dollars.
Assuming a rate of interest of 5% per year, the interest on 2.8 trillion dollars
 in one year would be [1.4E+11] dollars.
Assuming a rate of interest of 6% per year, the interest on 2.8 trillion dollars
 in one year would be [1.68E+11] dollars.
Assuming a rate of interest of 7% per year, the interest on 2.8 trillion dollars
 in one year would be [1.96E+11] dollars.
Assuming a rate of interest of 8% per year, the interest on 2.8 trillion dollars
 in one year would be [2.24E+11] dollars.
```

Save the program using the name **HWB1-05** and then produce a hard copy of both the **LIST** and **RUN** of the program.

Using BASIC Variables

Objectives *After you have completed this chapter, you should be able to*

- Discuss the differences between string and numeric variables.
- Use **LET** statements to assign values to variables.
- Use **PRINT** statements to display output from numbers, strings, numeric variables, and string variables.
- Explain the effects of commas and semicolons in **PRINT** statements.
- Use **TAB** and **SPC** in **PRINT** statements.

CHAPTER 2

- Use **PRINT USING** statements to format output.
- Translate arithmetic calculations into a format that can be used by BASIC.
- Use **AUTO** to display line numbers automatically.
- Use **REM** statements to properly document programs.
- Use various BASIC commands including **LIST**, **DELETE**, **LOAD**, **RUN**, **RENUM**, **TRACE**, **FILES**, **KILL**, **NEW**, and **SYSTEM**.

Introduction

Now that we have discussed writing simple programs with **PRINT** statements, let's explore a number of other BASIC statements that use variables to store data. Using variables greatly increases the flexibility of programs.

Variable Types

Similar to the variables used in algebra, BASIC variables are names that are used to represent certain values or expressions. In BASIC, variable names can be any length, but only the first 40 characters are considered by the computer (the remainder are ignored). Variable names can contain letters, digits, and a decimal point, but the first character must be a letter. Examples of allowable variables are: **X1**, **PAY.RATE**, and **TOTAL**.

There are a number of *reserved words* that cannot be used for variable names because they have special meanings for BASIC (such as **PRINT**). Some of the reserved words are listed below. A complete list is in the *IBM BASIC Reference Manual.*

AND	**AUTO**	**CALL**	**CIRCLE**	**CLOSE**	**COLOR**	**COMMON**	**DATA**
DRAW	**EDIT**	**ELSE**	**END**	**ERASE**	**ERROR**	**FIELD**	**FILES**
FOR	**GET**	**IF**	**INPUT**	**KEY**	**KILL**	**LET**	**LINE**
LIST	**LOCATE**	**MOTOR**	**NAME**	**NEW**	**NEXT**	**NOT**	**OFF**
OPEN	**OUT**	**PAINT**	**PLAY**	**PRINT**	**READ**	**REM**	**RETURN**
RUN	**SAVE**	**SOUND**	**STOP**	**THEN**	**TO**	**WAIT**	**WRITE**

Two different types of variables are used in BASIC: numeric and string. Numeric variables are those that represent numbers, or numeric expressions. String variables are those that represent strings of characters (letters, punctuation, or even digits that will not be used in arithmetic computations).

Both types of variables obey the same naming conventions except that string variables always end with a dollar sign to indicate that they represent strings. Examples of string variables are: **X1$**, **EMPLOYEE$**, and **SALES.23DEC$**. Also, the contents of a string variable is enclosed in quotation marks to indicate that it is a string rather than a number or numeric expression.

LET Statement

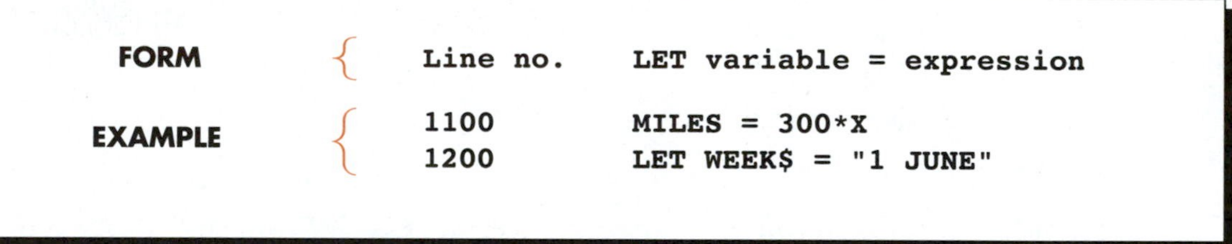

FORM	Line no.	LET variable = expression
EXAMPLE	1100	MILES = 300*X
	1200	LET WEEK$ = "1 JUNE"

The **LET** statement creates a storage location in the main memory of the computer, labels that location with the variable name, and stores the value of an expression at that location. The variable will have that value until it is changed by another statement. If a numeric variable is used, but it has not yet been defined, the computer assumes its value to be 0 (we say that the default value of a numeric variable is 0). If a string variable is used, but it has not yet been defined, the computer assumes its value to be the *null string* (a string that contains no characters). In most versions of BASIC, the word **LET** is optional and is rarely used. For example, **1100 LET A = 3** and **1100 A = 3** have the same meaning.

To illustrate the use of the **LET** statement, type the following program and save it under the name **LET-1**. **Please note:** To make the screen dumps that follow less cluttered and easier to read, the program lines that you type have not been underlined nor has the ↵ been added at the ends of the program lines. Only commands such as **NEW**, **RUN**, and **SAVE** have been underlined.

```
NEW
Ok
1100 A = 3
1200 B = 5
1300 PRINT A,B
1400 P$ = "Sara"
1500 A = 12
1600 PRINT "A="A,"B="B,"C="C,"P$="P$,"Q$="Q$
SAVE"A:LET1
Ok
RUN
 3             5
A= 12          B= 5          C= 0          P$=Sara          Q$=
Ok
```

Line Numbers	Comments
1100	Creates a storage location called **A** and assigns a value of **3** to that location.
1200	Creates a storage location called **B** and assigns a value of **5** to that location.
1300	Displays the values of **A** and **B** on the screen.
1400	Creates a storage location called **P$** and assigns a value of **Sara** to that location.
1500	Changes the value of **A** to **12**. The old value (i.e., 3) is erased and replaced with the new value (i.e., **12**).
1600	Displays the values of **A**, **B**, **C**, **P$**, and **Q$**. The value of **C** was never defined so the computer assumed a value of 0 (the *default* value of **C** is 0). Likewise, the value of **Q$** was never defined so the computer assumed an empty string for its value and so nothing was printed for **Q$** (the default value of **Q$** is the null, or empty, string).

The entire process of assigning values to variables may be illustrated graphically as follows:

***Memory Assignments for Program* LET-1**

Line no.	A	B	C	P$	Q$	
						Variable names
	0	0	0			Default values
1100	3					Assigned values
1200		5				Assigned values
1300	3	5				Output
1400				Sara		Assigned values
1500	12					Assigned values
1600	12	5	0	Sara		Output

The variable name must always be on the left-hand side of the equal sign. Even though **X = 4** and **4 = X** are equivalent in algebra, **4 = X** is an illegal BASIC statement. A simple way of remembering this is by saying to yourself:

The value on the right-hand side of the equal sign is stored at the location named on the left.

Or,

The value on the right-hand side of the equal sign is assigned to the variable named on the left.

In fact, the equal sign is misleading. A better way of indicating that the value **4** should be stored at location **X** would be to use an arrow pointing to the left, such as **X** ← **4**. Unfortunately, BASIC does not allow this type of notation.

Below is another program that illustrates assigning values to variables. Type it and then save it as **LET-2**:

```
NEW↵
Ok
1100 PERSON$ = "Matt"
1200 RATE = 5
1300 HOURS = 40
1400 PAY = RATE*HOURS
1500 PRINT "Employee","Pay Rate","Hours","Total Pay"
1600 PRINT PERSON$,RATE,HOURS,PAY
SAVE"A:LET2↵
Ok
RUN↵
Employee      Pay Rate      Hours       Total Pay
Matt           5             40          200
Ok
```

Line Numbers	Comments
1100	Creates a storage location called **PERSON$** and assigns the value **Matt** to that location.
1200	Creates a storage location called **RATE** and assigns the value **5** to that location.
1300	Creates a storage location called **HOURS** and assigns the value **40** to that location.
1400	Creates a storage location called **PAY** and assigns the product of the numbers stored in locations **RATE** and **HOURS** to that location (i.e., the value of **RATE** is multiplied by the value of **HOURS** and the result is assigned to location **PAY**).
1500	Displays the heading for the output.
1600	Displays the values of the variables.

Again, the entire process of assigning values to variables may be illustrated graphically as follows:

Memory Assignments for Program LET-2

Line no.	PERSON$	RATE	HOURS	PAY	
					Variable names
		0	0	0	Default values
1100	Matt				Assigned values
1200		5			Assigned values
1300			40		Assigned values
1400				5*40 (i.e., 200)	Calculation / Assigned values
1500					Displays string
1600	Matt	5	40	200	Output

Remember to use the proper type of variables in **LET** statements. For example, if line **1200** were changed to **1200 RATE$ = 5**, the error message **Type mismatch in 1200** would be displayed when the program is run. This means that you are trying to store a number (**5**) using a string variable (**RATE$**), but the BASIC interpreter will not allow that to happen. The screen would appear as follows (for the purpose of illustration, the statement that was changed in the following program is enclosed by a dotted box [see line **1200**]; the box does not actually appear on the computer display):

```
1100 PERSON$ = "Matt"
1200 RATE$ = 5                     <--- Wrong variable type causes an error
1300 HOURS = 40
1400 PAY = RATE*HOURS
1500 PRINT "Employee","Pay Rate","Hours","Total Pay"
1600 PRINT PERSON$,RATE,HOURS,PAY
RUN
Type mismatch in 1200
Ok
```

The type mismatch could be fixed by changing the **5** into a string by enclosing it in quotation marks. If this is done, the computer accepts the statement and does not display an error message. However, the values displayed for pay rate and total pay are not correct.

```
1100 PERSON$ = "Matt"
1200 RATE$ = "5"                   <--- Variable and value are the same type
1300 HOURS = 40                         so there is no syntax error. However,
1400 PAY = RATE*HOURS                   the answer is wrong.
1500 PRINT "Employee","Pay Rate","Hours","Total Pay"
1600 PRINT PERSON$,RATE,HOURS,PAY
RUN
Employee      Pay Rate      Hours         Total Pay
Matt           0             40            0
Ok
```

Line Numbers	Comments
1100	Creates a storage location called **PERSON$** and assigns the value **Matt** to that location.
1200	Creates a storage location called **RATE$** and assigns the value **5** to that location. Because the variable name has a dollar sign at the end, the computer stores the **5** as if it were just another character (like a letter) rather than the number **5**.
1300	Creates a storage location called **HOUR** and assigns the value **40** to that location.
1400	Creates a storage location called **PAY** and assigns the product of the values of the variables **HOUR** and **RATE** to that location. Because **RATE** has not been defined (remember, **RATE$** and **RATE** are two different variables), the value of **RATE** is assumed to be **0**. Thus, the value stored at location **PAY** is **0*40,** which is equal to **0**.
1600	Displays the values of the variables. Again, note that **RATE** was never defined so its value is **0**.

Remember to be careful not to use reserved words for variable names. For example, if you were to replace the variable **PERSON$** with **NAME$**, an error message would be displayed:

```
1100 NAME$ = "Matt"
1200 RATE$ = "5"
1300 HOURS = 40
1400 PAY = RATE*HOURS
1500 PRINT "Employee","Pay Rate","Hours","Total Pay"
1600 PRINT PERSON$,RATE,HOURS,PAY
RUN
Syntax error in 1100
Ok
1100 NAME$ = "Matt"
```

Using a reserved word as a variable causes a syntax error.

PRINT *Statement*

FORM	**Line no.**	**PRINT list**
EXAMPLE	**1100**	**PRINT "Week", "Miles", "Gallons"**
	1200	**PRINT WEEK$ TAB(16) MILES**
	1300	**PRINT 2 + 3**
	1400	**PRINT X*Y**
	1500	**PRINT "My name is "X$" and my age is "X+2**

As we have seen, the **PRINT** statement is used to display output on the monitor. It has many features that provide a good deal of control over the way the output is displayed.

• *Numbers* •

If arithmetic problems are placed in the **PRINT** statement, the answer to the problem is calculated and displayed. If the answer is positive, one blank space will be printed to the left of the number (in place of a plus sign). If the answer is negative, the negative sign will be printed. For example:

```
NEW↵
Ok
1100 PRINT 2 + 3
1200 PRINT 4 - 9
RUN↵
 5
-5
Ok
```

• *Strings* •

Characters enclosed in quotation marks (i.e., strings) in a **PRINT** statement will be displayed in the program output exactly as they appear in the **PRINT** statement (like quoting someone). This means that arithmetic problems that are placed inside quotation marks are displayed exactly as problems (no calculations are performed) when the program is run. Thus, if you want to display an arithmetic problem as well as its answer you must type the problem in two places in the **PRINT** statement: once inside quotation marks (to display the problem) and once outside the quotation marks (to display the answer).

```
NEW↵
Ok
1100 PRINT "This is a string"
1200 PRINT "2 + 3 =" 2 + 3
RUN↵
This is a string
2 + 3 = 5
Ok
```

This displays the answer

This displays the problem

• *Numeric Variables* •

If numeric variables are placed in a **PRINT** statement, the values of those variables are displayed. If the numeric variables are a part of a calculation, the answer is displayed.

```
NEW↵
Ok
1100 X = 5
1200 Y = 6
1300 PRINT X, Y, X*Y
Ok
RUN↵
 5             6             30
Ok
```

• *String Variables* •

If string variables are placed in a **PRINT** statement, the contents of those variables are displayed.

```
NEW↵
Ok
1100 X$ = "Hello"
1200 PRINT X$
RUN↵
Hello
Ok
```

• Commas •

Sections of output produced by a **PRINT** statement can be separated using either commas or semicolons. Commas have the effect of spreading the output across the screen by setting automatic tabs every 14 spaces. This means that items separated by commas in **PRINT** statements will begin printing at columns 1, 15, 29, 43, and 57. If you want to print a sixth item on the same line, it would have to begin printing at column 71 and the computer would try to reserve 14 spaces for that item. However, the computer screen will display a maximum of 80 characters on a line so the sixth item would wrap around to the next line.

```
NEW←
Ok
1100 PRINT "12345678901234567890123456789012345678901234567890123456789O"
1200 PRINT "*-Bgn at 1","*-Bgn at 15","*-Bgn at 29","*-Bgn at 43","*-Bgn at 57"
1300 PRINT -1,-2.34,-3,-4500,-5,-6
1400 PRINT 1,"This string has more than 14 spaces",3.2
SAVE"A:COMMA←
Ok
RUN←
123456789012345678901234567890123456789012345678901234567890
*-Bgn at 1    *-Bgn at 15   *-Bgn at 29   *-Bgn at 43   *-Bgn at 57
-1            -2.34         -3            -4500         -5
-6
 1            This string has more than 14 spaces       3.2
Ok

_
```

Automatic tabs

The -6 is here because it will not fit on the end of the previous line (this is similar to the word-wrap feature of WordPerfect)

Notice that the first five negative numbers produced by line **1300** begin printing at columns 1, 15, 29, 43, and 57 and that the sixth negative number (**-6**) is wrapped around to the next line. In line **1400**, the positive numbers appear to print one space to the right of the expected position. This is because BASIC will print a blank space instead of printing a plus sign for positive numbers. Note that the string **This string has more than 14 spaces** has more than 14 spaces so when the next number (**3.2**) is printed it begins at column 57 (essentially, the automatic tab positions at columns 29 and 43 are skipped because the string goes past column 43).

• Semicolons •

Like commas, semicolons are used to separate sections of the **PRINT** statement but they have the effect of displaying the output in a compact form. Each piece of output is printed directly after the piece to its left. However, numeric values are printed with a space directly to their right. For example:

```
NEW←
Ok
1100 X$ = "Pay"
1200 Y$ = "roll"
1300 PRINT 1;2;3;4;5;6
1400 PRINT -1;-2;-3;-4;-5;-6
1500 PRINT X$;Y$
SAVE"A:SEMI←
Ok
RUN←
 1  2  3  4  5  6
-1 -2 -3 -4 -5 -6
Payroll
Ok
```

If a semicolon or comma is placed at the end of a **PRINT** statement, the computer will not go to the next line in the output when it encounters the next **PRINT** statement — it will simply continue printing on the same line. For example, if you add a semicolon to the end of line **1300** in the previous program, the following will be displayed:

```
LIST ←
1100 X$ = "Pay"
1200 Y$ = "roll"
1300 PRINT 1;2;3;4;5;6;
1400 PRINT -1;-2;-3;-4;-5;-6
1500 PRINT X$;Y$
Ok
RUN ←
 1  2  3  4  5  6 -1 -2 -3 -4 -5 -6
Payroll
Ok
```

Semicolon here causes output from line 1400 to be printed on the end of the output from line 1300

Below is an example that illustrates the difference between commas and semicolons:

```
NEW ←
Ok
1100 A = 10
1200 B = -20
1300 PRINT A,B,"Output is spread out with commas"
1400 PRINT A;B;"Output is compact with semicolons"
1500 PRINT A;B;
1600 PRINT "A trailing ; causes printing to continue on same line"
1700 A$ = "Super"
1800 B$ = "man"
1900 PRINT A$,B$
2000 PRINT A$;B$
SAVE"A:COMSEMI ←
Ok
RUN ←
 10           -20           Output is spread out with commas   ← From line 1300
 10 -20 Output is compact with semicolons                      ← From line 1400
 10 -20 A trailing ; causes printing to continue on same line  ← From lines 1500 & 1600
Super         man                                              ← From line 1900
Superman                                                       ← From line 2000
Ok
```

Column 15 (-20) — Column 29 (Output is spread out with commas)

Line Numbers	Comments
1100	Creates a storage location called **A** and assigns the value **10** to that location.
1200	Creates a storage location called **B** and assigns the value **-20** to that location.
1300	Displays the values of **A** and **B** and the string inside the quotation marks. Because commas are used to separate the pieces of output (i.e., the two variables and the string), the automatic tabs are invoked causing the value of **B** to begin printing at column 15 and the string to begin printing at column 29.
1400	Also displays the values of **A** and **B** and the string inside the quotation marks. However, because semicolons are used to separate the pieces of output, the values of the numeric variables are displayed with a single space directly to their right.
1500	Displays the values of **A** and **B**. Because a semicolon is placed at the end of the line, the output from the next **PRINT** statement (i.e., line **1600**) will be displayed at the end of the output from line **1500**. Thus, the output from the two **PRINT** statements (lines **1500** and **1600**) is displayed on the same line.

Continued . . .

Line Numbers	Comments
1600	The output for this line is displayed on the end of the output from line **1500**.
1700	Creates a storage location **A$** and assigns the value **Super** to that location.
1800	Creates a storage location **B$** and assigns the value **man** to that location.
1900	Displays the values of the variables **A$** and **B$**. Because a comma is used to separate the variables, the value of **B$** begins printing at column 15.
2000	Also displays the values of the variables **A$** and **B$**. This time, however, because a semicolon is used to separate the variables, the value of **B$** begins printing right after the value of **A$**. With strings, there is no space inserted between the values as there is with numbers. Hence, printing **Super** followed by **man** displays **Superman**.

• TAB *Function* •

A BASIC *function* instructs the computer to perform a predetermined operation. The **TAB** function is an example of this. It is similar to the tab key on a typewriter in that it will move the cursor to any position to the right of its present position between columns 1 and 80. In the example below, **TAB(12)** in line **1500** causes the string **Pay Rate** to begin printing in column 12 (i.e., the **P** in **Pay** is displayed in column 12). Similarly, the **H** in **Hours** begins printing in column 24. Type the program and then save it under the name **TAB**.

```
NEW ↵
Ok
1100 PERSON$ = "Matt"
1200 RATE = 5
1300 HOURS = 40
1400 PAY = RATE*HOURS
1500 PRINT "Employee" TAB(12) "Pay Rate" TAB(24) "Hours" TAB(33) "Total Pay"
1600 PRINT PERSON$ TAB(15) RATE TAB(24) HOURS TAB(35) PAY
SAVE"A:TAB ↵
Ok
RUN ↵
Employee   Pay Rate    Hours    Total Pay
Matt           5        40          200
Ok
```

Column 12 Column 24 Column 33

The **TAB** function will only move the cursor to the right, never to the left. If the **TAB** function tells the computer to move the cursor to a position to its left, the computer will send the cursor to the next line and tab out to the proper position. In the example below, after the first string in line **100** has been displayed, the cursor is located at column 31. The **TAB(10)** says to go to column 10 but that would mean moving the cursor to the left. The result is that the computer goes to the next line and tabs out to column 10 to display the second string.

```
NEW ↵
Ok
100 PRINT "The TAB cannot move to the left" TAB(10) "As we can see"
RUN ↵
The TAB cannot move to the left
         As we can see
Ok
```

This should be printed on line above but TAB will not move to the left

• SPC *Function* •

The **SPC** function moves the cursor a specified number of spaces to the right from the present printing position. **SPC** moves the cursor a *relative* number of spaces whereas the **TAB** moves the cursor to an *absolute* position. Below is an example that shows the differences between **TAB** and **SPC**.

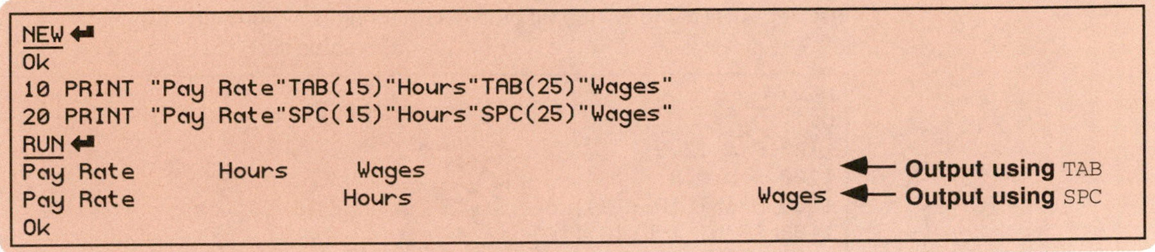

```
NEW ↵
Ok
10 PRINT "Pay Rate"TAB(15)"Hours"TAB(25)"Wages"
20 PRINT "Pay Rate"SPC(15)"Hours"SPC(25)"Wages"
RUN ↵
Pay Rate      Hours     Wages                              ← Output using TAB
Pay Rate               Hours                         Wages ← Output using SPC
Ok
```

The difference between the **TAB** and the **SPC** can be illustrated as follows:

Output using **TAB:**

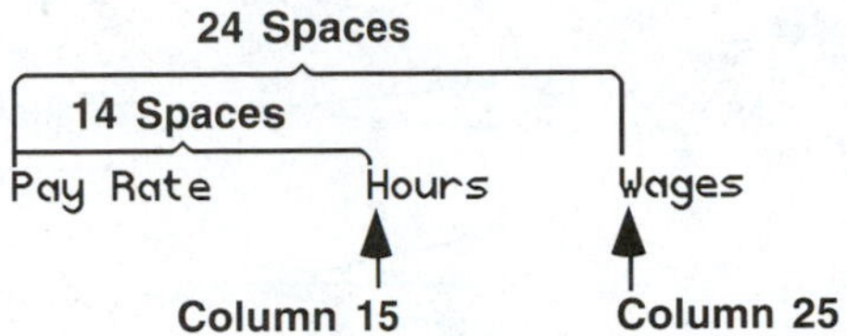

Output using **SPC:**

PRINT USING *Statement*

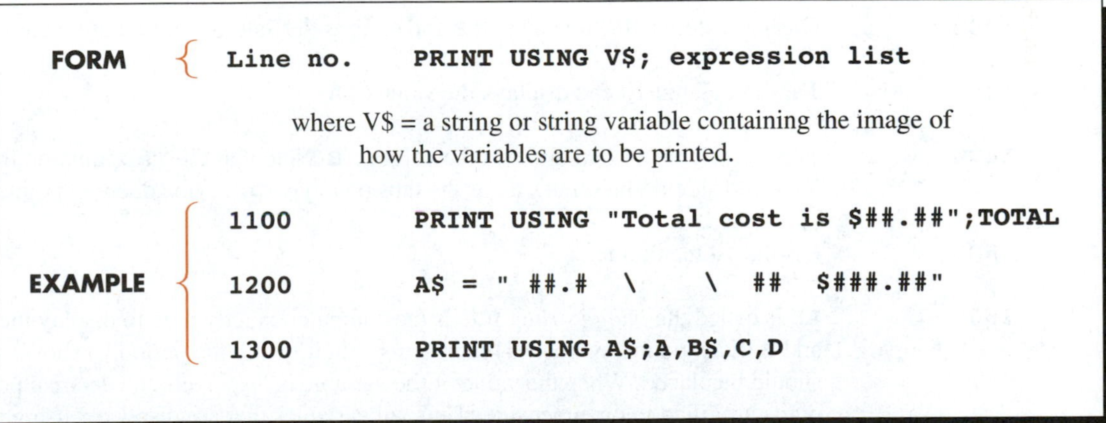

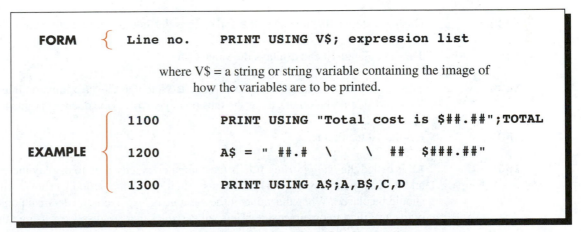

FORM { **Line no.** **PRINT USING V$; expression list**

where V$ = a string or string variable containing the image of how the variables are to be printed.

EXAMPLE

```
1100    PRINT USING "Total cost is $##.##";TOTAL
1200    A$ = " ##.#  \     \  ##   $###.##"
1300    PRINT USING A$;A,B$,C,D
```

Many times it is desirable to have output printed in a specific format. This is especially true when printing tables and charts where the decimal points must be lined up. This can be done by using the **PRINT USING** statement, which is simply an extension of the **PRINT** statement.

Below is an example of the difference between using **TAB** in a **PRINT** statement and **PRINT USING** to create similar output. The **TAB**s in lines **1300** and **1400** left justify the numbers **12.34** and **4.8**. The result is that the decimal points do not line up properly. Lines **1700** and **1800** employ **PRINT USING** to ensure that the decimal points are properly aligned.

```
NEW
Ok
1100 A = 12.34
1200 B = 4.8
1300 PRINT TAB(10); A
1400 PRINT TAB(10); B
1500 PRINT
1600 A$ = "            ##.##"
1700 PRINT USING A$; A
1800 PRINT USING A$; B
1900 PRINT USING "               ##.##"; B
SAVE"A:PRUSING1
Ok
RUN
          12.34   <-- TAB left justifies output (from lines 1300 and 1400)
          4.8     <--

          12.34   <--
           4.80   <-- PRINT USING lines up decimal points (from lines 1700 - 1900)
           4.80   <--
Ok
```

Line Numbers	Comments
1100	Creates a storage location called **A** and assigns the value **12.34** to that location.
1200	Creates a storage location called **B** and assigns the value **4.8** to that location.
1300	Tabs to column 10 and displays the value of **A**.
1400	Tabs to column 10 and displays the value of **B**. Note that the **TAB** function lines up the numbers on the left-hand side in the same way as the tabs on a typewriter (the decimal points are not lined up).
1500	Displays a blank line.
1600	**A$** is called the *image string*. It tells the computer exactly how to display the values of the variables **A** and **B**. Each pound symbol (#) represents a digit, while the period (.) shows where the decimal point should be placed. When the value of the variable is displayed, the decimal point is placed first, then the digits are filled in on either side. Thus, all variables that are displayed using this image will have their decimal points lined up.
1700	The **PRINT USING** statement tells the computer to display the value of variable **A** using the image contained in the string **A$**. Note that there must be a semicolon between the image string and the variable list.

Continued . . .

Line Numbers	Comments
1800	The **PRINT USING** statement says to display the value of variable **B** using the image contained in the string **A$**. Because the values of **A** and **B** are displayed using the same image string, their decimal points are lined up. Note also that the **PRINT USING** statement added a trailing **0** to **4.8** so that **4.80** was displayed.
1900	This has the same effect as line **1800**. Here, the image string is contained within the **PRINT USING** statement rather than on a separate line.

With **PRINT USING**, back slashes (\) must be used in the image string to indicate where the contents of string variables should be displayed and how many characters to display. For example:

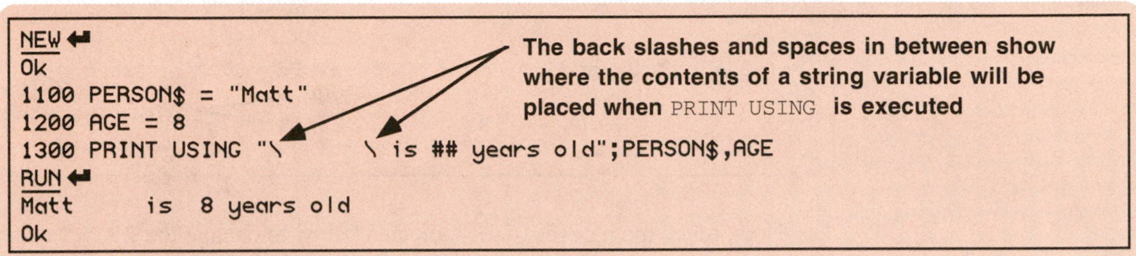

In line **1300**, the \   \ reserves 8 positions for the string **PERSON$** (each \ counts as a position and there are six blank spaces between the slashes reserving a total of 8 positions). The **##** reserves two positions for the value of **AGE**.

Be careful of the syntax of the **PRINT USING** statement. If you forget to include the semicolon between the image (or image variable) and the variable list, a syntax error will occur.

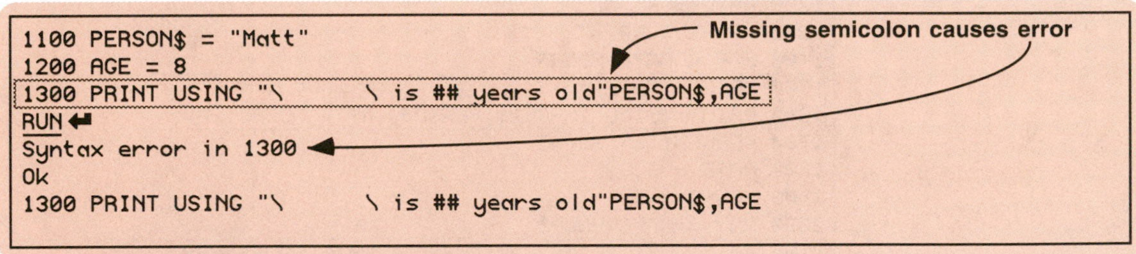

As another illustration of the **PRINT USING** statement, add more data to program **TAB** (from p. B34) and run it. Notice how the decimal points are not lined up in the output:

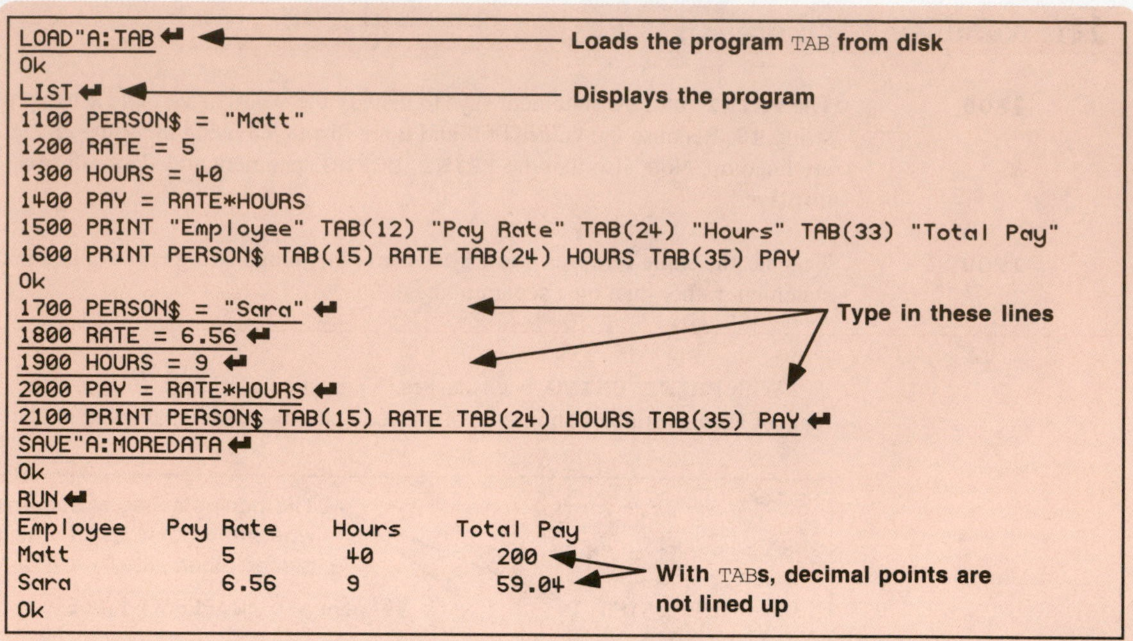

LOAD"A:TAB
Loads the program TAB from disk
Ok
LIST
Displays the program
1100 PERSON$ = "Matt"
1200 RATE = 5
1300 HOURS = 40
1400 PAY = RATE*HOURS
1500 PRINT "Employee" TAB(12) "Pay Rate" TAB(24) "Hours" TAB(33) "Total Pay"
1600 PRINT PERSON$ TAB(15) RATE TAB(24) HOURS TAB(35) PAY
Ok
1700 PERSON$ = "Sara"
1800 RATE = 6.56
1900 HOURS = 9
2000 PAY = RATE*HOURS
2100 PRINT PERSON$ TAB(15) RATE TAB(24) HOURS TAB(35) PAY
Type in these lines
SAVE"A:MOREDATA
Ok
RUN
Employee Pay Rate Hours Total Pay
Matt 5 40 200
Sara 6.56 9 59.04
Ok
With TABs, decimal points are not lined up

Now, make the modifications indicated below to change the **PRINT** statements into **PRINT USING** statements and notice how the decimal points are lined up when the program is run. Save the program as **PRUSING2**.

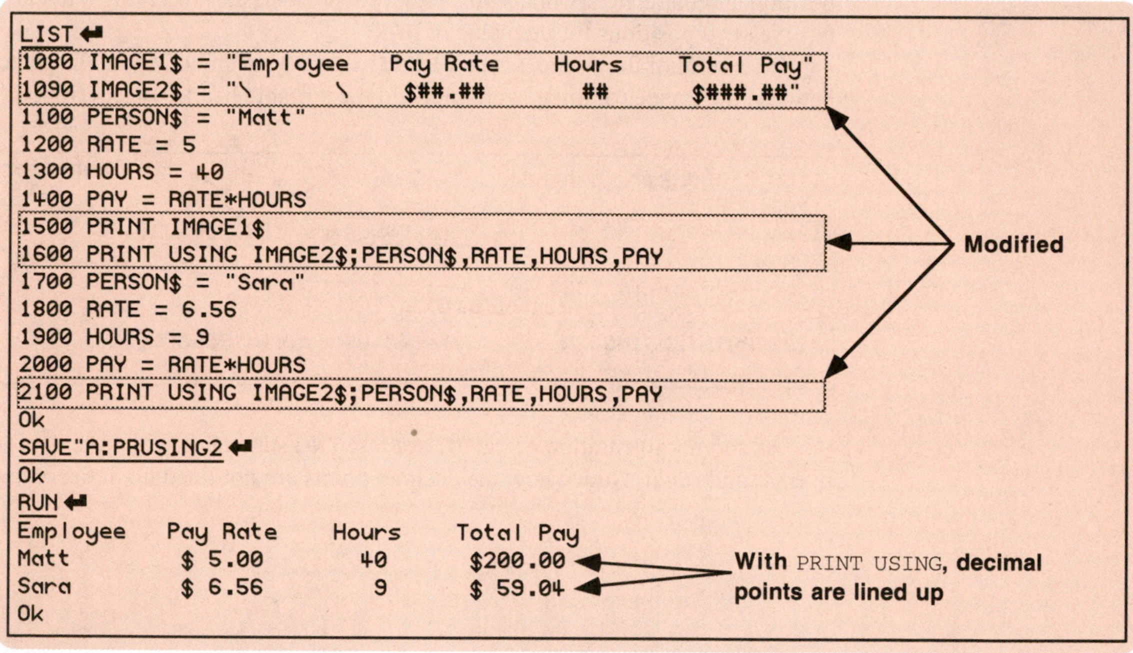

LIST
1080 IMAGE1$ = "Employee Pay Rate Hours Total Pay"
1090 IMAGE2$ = "\ \ $##.## ## $###.##"
1100 PERSON$ = "Matt"
1200 RATE = 5
1300 HOURS = 40
1400 PAY = RATE*HOURS
1500 PRINT IMAGE1$
1600 PRINT USING IMAGE2$;PERSON$,RATE,HOURS,PAY
1700 PERSON$ = "Sara"
1800 RATE = 6.56
1900 HOURS = 9
2000 PAY = RATE*HOURS
2100 PRINT USING IMAGE2$;PERSON$,RATE,HOURS,PAY
Ok
SAVE"A:PRUSING2
Ok
RUN
Employee Pay Rate Hours Total Pay
Matt $ 5.00 40 $200.00
Sara $ 6.56 9 $ 59.04
Ok
Modified
With PRINT USING, decimal points are lined up

What happens when the image string is either too large or too small for the variable being printed? Load the following program, **LIST** it, **SAVE** it to your *BASIC Data* diskette, and then **RUN** it as shown on the next page:

NOTE . . . We assume that many of the longer or difficult-to-type programs that follow have already been saved by your instructor on your computer's hard disk in a subdirectory with path **C:\BA** . If that is not the case, you should type the programs yourself and then save them on your *BASIC Data* diskette.

```
LOAD"C:\BA\PRUSING3 ⏎     ◄— Load the program from the hard drive or type it yourself
Ok
LIST ⏎
1100 BIGALPHA$    = "ABCDEFGHIJ"
1200 BIGNUMBER    = 1234567!
1300 SMALLALPHA$ = "ABC"
1400 SMALLNUMBER = 123
1500 PRINT USING            "\  \";BIGALPHA$
1600 PRINT USING "\          \";BIGALPHA$
1700 PRINT USING            "####";BIGNUMBER
1800 PRINT USING "###############";BIGNUMBER
1900 A = 34.59
2000 B = .02
2100 PRINT USING "##.#    "; A, B
2200 PRINT USING "**$##.##      "; 1.23, 123.45
2300 PRINT USING "######,.##"; 12345.6
2400 PRINT USING "The total cost is $$###.##  "; SMALLNUMBER
2500 PRINT USING "The total cost is $####.##  "; SMALLNUMBER
Ok
SAVE"A:PRUSING3 ⏎          ◄— Save the program to your BASIC Data diskette
Ok
RUN ⏎
ABCD                       ◄— Large string and small image causes truncation
ABCDEFGHIJ                 ◄— Small string and large image causes left justification
%1234567                   ◄— % means the image is too small for the number displayed
        1234567            ◄— Small number and large image causes right justification
34.6      0.0              ◄— The image automatically rounds off numbers to the specified
***$1.23     *$123.45          number of decimal places
 12,345.60
The total cost is  $123.00
The total cost is $ 123.00
Ok
```

Line Numbers	Comments
1100	Creates a storage location called **BIGALPHA$** and stores a ten-character string at that location.
1200	Creates a storage location called **BIGNUMBER** and stores a seven-digit number at that location.
1300	Creates a storage location called **SMALLALPHA$** and stores a three-character string at that location.
1400	Creates a storage location called **SMALLNUMBER** and stores a three-digit number at that location.
1500	Tries to display a *size 10* string (i.e., **ABCDEFGHIJ**) in a *size 4* image (i.e., **\ **). Because the image is too small for the value of the string variable, the string is truncated (cut off) and only the four left-most characters (**ABCD**) are displayed.
1600	Displays the entire string (the image is large enough to hold all the letters in the string). The characters are filled in from the left-hand side resulting in left justification. The rest of the space in the image that is not used is filled with blanks (this is called *blank fill*).
1700	Tries to display a *size 7* number (i.e., **1234567**) in a *size 4* image (i.e., **####**). Unlike the case with the strings, when the image is too small for the value of a numeric variable, a percent sign (**%**) is displayed on the left-hand side of the number and the entire number is displayed. Thus, if you see a **%** in front of a number it means that the image is too small to hold that number.

Continued . . .

Line Numbers	Comments
1800	Here the image is large enough to hold the entire number. The digits are filled in from the right-hand side (actually the decimal point) resulting in right justification. The space in the image to the left of the number that is not used is filled with blanks.
2100	The image contains enough pound symbols (**#**) for two digits to the left of the decimal point and one digit to the right. Because the value of **A** is **34.59**, the computer rounds off the value to **34.6** so that it will fit in the image. Similarly, the value of **B** is rounded off to one decimal place (i.e., **.02** is rounded off to **0.0**). Notice also that two variables are being displayed but only one set of pound symbols is in the image. The computer uses the same image for both variables and displays them on the same line.
2200	The asterisks are used for what is called *check protection*. When they are present in the image the computer will fill in the unused pound symbols with * instead of blanks. This makes it more difficult for someone to alter the number after it has been printed. This is used when checks are printed by computer to discourage people from tampering with the amount of the check.
2300	The single comma just to the left of the decimal point tells the computer to display commas in the correct positions for large numbers. Hence, the number **12345.6** is displayed with the comma between the hundreds and thousands place as **12,345.6**. This makes reading large numbers much easier.
2400	Two dollar signs on the left of a numeric image will cause a single dollar sign to be displayed directly to the left of a number as in **$123.00**.
2500	A single dollar sign on the left of a numeric image will cause a single dollar sign to be printed in the left-most position in the image as in **$ 123.00**.

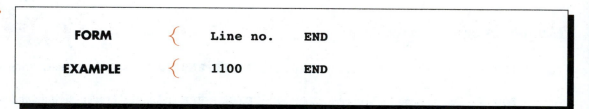

END *Statement*

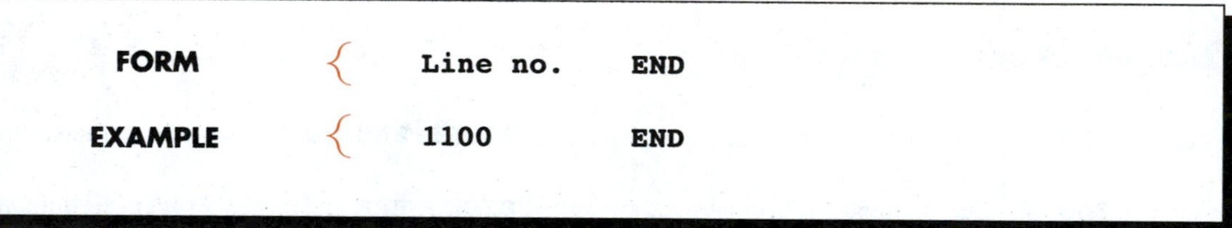

The **END** statement indicates the last line of the program. This statement is optional in most versions of BASIC.

TO TAKE A BREAK Type **SYSTEM ↵**, remove disk(s). To resume (hard disk): Insert *Data* disk, type **A: ↵**, **C:\BA\BASICA ↵**. To resume (two drive): Insert disks, type **A: ↵**, **B:\BASICA ↵**.

Multiple Statements on One Line

It is possible in BASIC to have more than one statement on a given line of code. This is done by separating the statements with a colon (:). For example, the following two programs produce the same output:

```
NEW ←
Ok
1100 A = 5
1200 B = 6
1300 PRINT A,B
RUN ←
 5             6
Ok


NEW ←
Ok
1100 A = 5 : B = 6 : PRINT A,B
RUN ←
 5             6
Ok
```

The advantage of doing this is that you can display more lines of code on the screen at one time and it sometimes makes the logic of a program more obvious.

Arithmetic Operations

As was discussed in the previous chapter, BASIC uses the normal mathematical symbols for addition (+) and subtraction (−) but uses an asterisk (*) to represent multiplication and a slash (/) to represent division. Exponents are represented using a circumflex (^) because there is no simple way to display superscripts in BASIC.

Below are examples of arithmetic problems written in both regular mathematical notation and BASIC notation:

Mathematical notation	***BASIC notation***
$2 + 3 \times 5$	2 + 3*5
$60 + 36 \div 2 \times 3$	60 + 36/2*3
$60 + 36 \div (2 \times 3)$	60 + 36/(2*3)
$60 + 36 \div (2 \times 3^2)$	60 + 36/(2*3^2)
$60 + 36 \div (2 \times 3)^2$	60 + 36/(2*3)^2
$60 + 2(3 - (3 - 5) + 7)$	60 + 2*(3 – (3 – 5) + 7)

BASIC also uses some special symbols when comparing two quantities or strings of characters. Below is a summary of the symbols and their meanings in BASIC.

Math symbol	***BASIC symbol***	***Meaning***	***Example***
$<$	<	less than	`A < B`
$>$	>	greater than	`A > 12`
$\leq$	<=	less than or equal to	`A <= X - 5`
$\geq$	>=	greater than or equal to	`T4 >= S + 1`
$=$	=	equal to	`A$ = B$`
$\neq$	<>	not equal to	`SEX$ <> "Male"`

Using the above symbols, any two quantities of the same variable type can be compared. This means that you can compare any two numbers or any two strings and determine which is *larger* or *smaller* or see if they have the same value. These symbols will be used in the next chapter.

BASIC carries out arithmetic operations using the same order as mathematicians do:

1. Operations within parentheses are done first. If the parentheses are *nested* (i.e., one set inside another), the work inside the innermost parentheses is done first.
2. Exponents and roots are evaluated next.
3. Multiplication and division are done next, working left to right. For example, in the problem 36/3*4 the 36/3 is done first and then the answer is multiplied by 4 to produce 48.
4. Addition and subtraction, working left to right, is done last.

To be sure that you remember how to apply the order of operations for mathematics problems, it would be a good idea to work out the solutions to the above arithmetic problems.

Below is a program that displays the solution to each of the above arithmetic problems. In order to display both the problem and the answer, each problem must be typed twice in the **PRINT** statement (once inside the quotation marks to display the problem and once outside the quotation marks to have the computer calculate and display the answer). **LOAD** the program, **LIST** it, **SAVE** it to your *BASIC Data* diskette, and then **RUN** it as shown below:

```
LOAD"C:\BA\ORDER ↵
Ok
LIST ↵
1100 PRINT "2 + 3*5 =" 2 + 3*5
1200 PRINT "60 + 36/2*3 =" 60 + 36/2*3
1300 PRINT "60 + 36/(2*3) =" 60 + 36/(2*3)
1400 PRINT "60 + 36/(2*3^2) =" 60 + 36/(2*3^2)
1500 PRINT "60 + 36/(2*3)^2 =" 60 + 36/(2*3)^2
1600 PRINT "60 + 2*(3 - (3 - 5) + 7) =" 60 + 2*(3 - (3 - 5) + 7)
Ok
SAVE"A:ORDER ↵
Ok
RUN ↵
2 + 3*5 = 17
60 + 36/2*3 = 114
60 + 36/(2*3) = 66
60 + 36/(2*3^2) = 62
60 + 36/(2*3)^2 = 61
60 + 2*(3 - (3 - 5) + 7) = 84
Ok
```

Be sure to follow the proper order of operations for all computations. For example, the following expression calculates the average of 6 and 10:

$$\frac{6 + 10}{2}$$

When this is translated into BASIC code the **/** symbol must be used to indicate division. If the problem is written as **6 + 10/2**, the following output results:

```
NEW ↵
Ok
1100 PRINT 6 + 10/2
RUN ↵
 11
Ok
```

The answer is wrong (the average of 6 and 10 could not possibly be 11). Did the computer make an error? No, the programmer did. According to the order of operations the computer is required to do division before addition so the computer first calculated 10/2 = 5, then added this result to 6, and finally displayed the answer, 11. Parentheses are needed to have the computer do the operations in the order that the programmer intended.

```
NEW ↵
Ok
1100 PRINT (6 + 10)/2
RUN ↵
 8
Ok
```

The above error was not a syntax error (i.e., the computer was able to interpret the instructions given to it) but it was an error of intent (the programmer did not intend to give the computer those instructions). This type of error is often difficult to detect because the programmer knows how to do the problem but tells the computer to do something else without realizing it (i.e., the computer does what the programmer says not what the programmer *means* to say). For that reason, you should always check by hand the answers calculated by the computer to be sure that they are correct. If the computer does 10,000 calculations for you so that it would not be practical for you to check all the answers, you should at least check some of them by hand to be sure that they are correct. If they are, you can be somewhat confident (but not 100% certain) that the other (unchecked) answers are correct. **Failure to check computer output for correctness can lead to disaster.**

Remember that the computer takes everything you write literally and that it does not understand English. This causes another unexpected result in the next program, which is supposed to display a phone number:

```
NEW ↵
Ok
1100 MY.PHONE = 373-4026
1200 PRINT MY.PHONE
RUN ↵
-3653
Ok
```

The reason the answer is not what we expect is that the dash in the phone number is interpreted as a subtraction symbol because **MY.PHONE** is a numeric variable (it has no dollar sign). Thus, the computer stores the difference between **373** and **4026**, which turns out to be **-3653**, at location **MY.PHONE**. To remedy this situation you could remove the dash from line **1100** so that it reads **1100 MY.PHONE = 3734026**. In this case the computer would automatically add an exclamation point **!** to the number when the program is listed indicating that it is a single-precision number (see p. B13). Because phone numbers are not normally used in arithmetic calculations, a better alternative would be to use a string variable and quotation marks such as **1300 MY.PHONE$ = "373-4026"**. Both situations are shown below:

```
NEW ↵
Ok
1100 MY.PHONE = 373-4026
1200 PRINT MY.PHONE
RUN ↵
-3653
Ok
1300 MY.PHONE$ = "373-4026" ↵
1400 PRINT MY.PHONE$ ↵
RUN ↵
-3653          ◄── Dash in 1100 interpreted as a subtraction
373-4026       ◄── Dash in 1300 interpreted correctly due to quotation marks
Ok
```

Round-off Errors

Most humans use what is referred to as a *base 10* number system to do mathematical calculations. This means that only the ten digits 0, 1, 2, 3, 4, 5, 6, 7, 8, and 9 are used. When numbers are written in base 10, both the values of the digits and their positions in the number are important. For example, in the number 111, there is a 1 in the hundreds place, a 1 in the tens place, and a 1 in the ones place. Thus, the value of the number is 1*100 + 1*10 + 1*1, which is 100 + 10 + 1, which adds up to one hundred eleven.

Microcomputers, on the other hand, do arithmetic operations using a base 2 number system and therefore only use the digits 0 and 1. In base 2, each place value differs from the next place value by a factor of 2. The number 111 in base 2 would be interpreted as having a 1 in the 4s place, a 1 in the 2s place, and a 1 in the 1s place. Thus, the value of the number is 1*4 + 1*2 + 1*1, which is 4 + 2 + 1, which adds up to 7.

The chart below compares the place values for base 10 and base 2 for a number with the digits ABCDE:

Place	**Value in Base 10**	**Value in Base 2**
A	10000	16
B	1000	8
C	100	4
D	10	2
E	1	1

When the computer does an arithmetic computation, it first converts the numbers from our base 10 system into its base 2 system. For integers, this works out just fine. For example:

Decimal	**Binary**	**Reason**
7	111	111 in binary means one 4 + one 2 + one 1
		which is 1*4 + 1*2 + 1*1
		which is 4 + 2 + 1
		which is 7
12	1100	1100 in binary means one 8 + one 4 + zero 2s + zero 1s
		which is 1*8 + 1*4 + 0*2 + 0*1
		which is 8 + 4 + 0 + 0
		which is 12

However, when converting numbers with decimal or fractional parts the computer sometimes has problems. For example, the number .1 (or 1/10) cannot be converted exactly into binary notation and thus must be rounded off at some point (much like the fraction 1/3 must be rounded off to .3 or .33 or .333, when being converted into a decimal in the base 10 number system). This round-off error may cause problems in some programs and on some computers. For example, consider the following program, which displays the answer to a simple subtraction problem:

```
NEW ↵
Ok
1100 A = 2.1
1200 B = 1.2
1300 PRINT A, B, A - B
RUN ↵
 2.1           1.2           .8999999
Ok
```

Incorrect answer due to round-off error

The answer should be .9 but, due to the problems with conversion to the base 2 number system, there is a round-off error. Because the round-off error is quite small, most of the time this will not adversely affect the output of the programs you write. However, if high precision is important in a particular application, you may have to be very careful that the answers the computer gives are the correct ones and you may have to use double-precision numbers (see p. B16). You can fix the way the output looks with a **PRINT USING** statement so that the value of **A - B** is rounded to one decimal place when it is displayed.

```
NEW ↵
Ok
1100 A = 2.1
1200 B = 1.2
1300 PRINT A, B, A - B
RUN ↵
 2.1           1.2           .8999999
Ok
1400 PRINT USING "##.#          ##.#          ##.#";A, B, A - B ↵
RUN ↵
 2.1           1.2           .8999999
 2.1           1.2           0.9  ←—— Answer appears correct
Ok                                    due to PRINT USING image
```

Auto Mode

The computer can be made to automatically type the line numbers when a program is being entered by invoking the **AUTO** command. It has the following form:

AUTO beginning line number,increment

For example, **AUTO 1100,100** instructs the computer to display line numbers beginning with **1100** and then to increment them in steps of **100** each time **[Enter]** is pressed. The result is that the computer types for you the line numbers **1100**, **1200**, **1300**, **1400**, etc. To exit from **AUTO**, press **[Ctrl-Break]** after a line number has been displayed by the computer.

In **AUTO** mode, an asterisk displayed next to a line number means there was a previous line with that number. That line will be replaced by the new one when **[Enter]** is pressed.

Below is an example of the use of the **AUTO** command. To begin, assume that a one line program is in memory:

```
NEW ↵
Ok
1200 PRINT 2 + 3 ↵         ←—— Original line 1200 in memory
AUTO 1100,100 ↵
1100 PRINT "Hello" ↵       ←—— The 1100 is displayed by the computer
1200*PRINT 5*3 ↵           ←—— The * to the right of 1200 means there already is a line 1200
1300 PRINT 8/2 ↵
1400 ←———————————————————— Tap [Ctrl-Break] to exit AUTO mode
Ok
LIST ↵
1100 PRINT "Hello"
1200 PRINT 5*3             ←—— Original line 1200 replaced by new line 1200
1300 PRINT 8/2
Ok
```

REM Statement

FORM {	**Line no. REM comment**
EXAMPLE {	**1100 REM Wages computed given rate and hours**

The **REM** statement allows the programmer to place *non-executable* **REM**arks into the program. Non-executable means that a statement is ignored by the computer when the program is executed (**RUN**). **REM** statements are used to document programs. For example, the first few lines of a program should have a short statement indicating what the program does. You will find that after writing 10 or 20 programs it is easy to forget what individual programs were designed to do. Stating the purpose of a program at the beginning serves as a reminder. Also, as the programs get more complicated, **REM** statements can be used to document how particular parts of the program work. It is also a good idea to include **REM** statements that state the programmer's name (to take the credit if the program is good or to take the heat if the program bombs) and the date the program was created and last modified (this makes it easier to tell which version of a program you are using).

REM statements should also be used to document the variables used and to insert any comments that might make the program easier to understand in the event that it must be modified later. Undocumented programs are very difficult and costly to modify because the new programmer must get the complete understanding of the logic used by the original programmer from reading the BASIC code. This may take a considerable amount of time. In addition, using **REM** statements to document program logic will force you to think more clearly about what it is you are doing. If you have difficulty writing down in English what you are trying to do, you probably have not thought it through enough to write proper BASIC code. This will be discussed in much more detail in Chapter 3.

To summarize, at the beginning of all programs it is good practice to list the following in **REM** statements:

- The purpose of the program.
- The name of the programmer.
- The dates the program was created and last modified.
- A list of the definitions of the variables used in the program.

To see how they work, let's add **REM** statements to the program **PRUSING2** (from p. B38). Below is a **LIST** and **RUN** of the original program:

```
LOAD"A:PRUSING2 ↵
Ok
LIST ↵
1080 IMAGE1$ = "Employee    Pay Rate     Hours     Total Pay"
1090 IMAGE2$ = "\        \   $##.##        ##       $###.##"
1100 PERSON$ = "Matt"
1200 RATE = 5
1300 HOURS = 40
1400 PAY = RATE*HOURS
1500 PRINT IMAGE1$
1600 PRINT USING IMAGE2$;PERSON$,RATE,HOURS,PAY
1700 PERSON$ = "Sara"
1800 RATE = 6.56
1900 HOURS = 9
2000 PAY = RATE*HOURS
2100 PRINT USING IMAGE2$;PERSON$,RATE,HOURS,PAY
Ok
RUN ↵
Employee    Pay Rate     Hours     Total Pay
Matt         $ 5.00        40       $200.00
Sara         $ 6.56         9       $ 59.04
Ok
```

This program may be modified to include **REM** statements by adding program lines and by editing existing lines using the standard editing techniques. In the following **LIST** of the modified program, called **WAGES1**, notice how the **REM** statements are used to document what the program does and who wrote it and to break up the program into separate blocks or modules, each of which does a specific task (define variables, define images, define values for variables, calculate pay, and display the final results). This modular design helps the programmer build a more logical program that is easier for humans to deal with. However, the changes made to this program are only cosmetic — the **REM** statements and extra spacing are ignored by the computer and, therefore, the output is exactly the same as the previous program. **LOAD** the new version of the program, **LIST** it, **SAVE** it to your *BASIC Data* diskette, and then **RUN** it as shown below:

```
LOAD"C:\BA\WAGES1
Ok
LIST
1010 REM Wages are computed given rate of pay and hours worked      } Purpose
1020 REM Douglas Robertson (373-4026), created 6 March 91           } Programmer & creation date
1030 REM Define variables:                                          }
1035 REM    PERSON$ = first name of employee                        }
1040 REM       RATE = rate of pay in dollars per hour               } Define variables
1045 REM      HOURS = number of hours worked during week            }
1050 REM        PAY = calculated wages in dollars                   }
1060 REM Define images for PRINT USING:                             }
1065    IMAGE1$ = "Employee    Pay Rate    Hours    Total Pay"     } Define images
1070    IMAGE2$ = "\        \    $##.##      ##      $###.##"      }
1080 REM Define values for first person:                            }
1100    PERSON$ = "Matt"                                            } Define data
1200    RATE = 5                                                    }
1300    HOURS = 40                                                  }
1350 REM Calculate pay for first person:                            } Calculate pay
1400    PAY = RATE*HOURS                                            }
1450 REM Display heading:                                           } Display heading
1500    PRINT IMAGE1$                                               }
1550 REM Display data and result for first person:                  } Display results
1600    PRINT USING IMAGE2$;PERSON$,RATE,HOURS,PAY                  }
1650 REM Define values for second person:                           }
1700    PERSON$ = "Sara"                                            } Define data
1800    RATE = 6.56                                                 }
1900    HOURS = 9                                                   }
1950 REM Calculate pay for second person:                           } Calculate pay
2000    PAY = RATE*HOURS                                            }
2050 REM Display data and result for second person:                 } Display results
2100    PRINT USING IMAGE2$;PERSON$,RATE,HOURS,PAY                  }
Ok
SAVE"A:WAGES1
Ok
RUN
Employee    Pay Rate    Hours    Total Pay   }
Matt         $ 5.00      40      $200.00     } Same output with REMs as without REMs
Sara         $ 6.56       9      $ 59.04     }
Ok
```

A non-executable remark may also be placed at the end of a line that has another statement on it by using a single quotation mark ('). For example, the following two statements have the same meaning in BASIC:

```
1400 PAY = RATE*HOURS
1400 PAY = RATE*HOURS    'Calculates pay
```

Everything after the single quotation mark is considered a remark and is ignored. (Note that the single quotation mark cannot be placed at the end of a **DATA** statement because the computer will interpret it as a piece of data rather than as a remark. **DATA** statements will be discussed in the next chapter.)

A Gas Mileage Program

To be sure that you understand the program statements discussed so far, another example is given below. Study the structure of the program and the extensive use of **REM** statements. Then, before looking at the **RUN** of the program, try to figure out for yourself what the output will be. If you can learn to *think* like the computer you will be better able to instruct it to do exactly what you want it to do. After you have tried to figure out the output yourself, **LOAD** the program, **LIST** it, **SAVE** it to your *BASIC Data* diskette, and then **RUN** it as shown below:

```
LOAD"C:\BA\GAS1 ↵
Ok
LIST ↵
1100 REM Calculates gas mileage given miles driven and gal of gas used
1200 REM Douglas Robertson (373-4026), created 6 Mar 91
1300 REM Define variables:
1400 REM   WEEK$ = week data were collected
1500 REM   MILES = miles driven that week
1600 REM     GAL = gallons of gas used that week
1700 REM   PRICE = price in cents per gallon of gas
1800 REM     MPG = computed value of miles per gallon of gas
1900 REM Define images for PRINT USING:
2000   IMAGE1$ = "    Week     Miles     Gallons     Price     Miles/Gallon"
2100   IMAGE2$ = "  ------    -----    -------     -----     ------------"
2200   IMAGE3$ = " \     \    ###.#      ##.#     $##.##         ##.#"
2300 REM Display column headings:
2400   PRINT IMAGE1$
2500   PRINT IMAGE2$
2600 REM Define values for variables:
2700   WEEK$ = "1 June"
2800   MILES = 300
2900   GAL = 15
3000   PRICE = 120
3100 REM Calculate gas mileage:
3200   MPG = MILES/GAL
3300 REM Display results
3400   PRINT USING IMAGE3$;WEEK$,MILES,GAL,PRICE/100,MPG
Ok
SAVE"A:GAS1 ↵
Ok
RUN ↵
    Week     Miles     Gallons     Price     Miles/Gallon
  ------    -----    -------     -----     ------------
  1 June    300.0      15.0     $ 1.20         20.0
Ok
```

Line Numbers	Comments
1100–1800	**REM** statements that describe what the program does, who wrote it, and how the variables are defined.
2000–2200	Images for the **PRINT USING** statements. Notice how the three images look almost exactly like the actual output.
2400–2500	Displays the column headings.
2700–3000	Assigns values to the variables. For example, line **2700** creates a storage location called **WEEK$** and assigns the value **1 June** to that location.
3200	Creates a storage location called **MPG** and assigns to that location the result (quotient) of dividing the value of **MILES** by the value of **GAL**.
3400	Displays the values of the variables. Note that the **PRICE** is divided by 100 because the price was entered in units of cents at line **3000** but it is displayed in units of dollars.

The whole process of assigning values to variables can be viewed graphically as follows (the images of the **PRINT USING** statements are not included):

Memory Assignments for Program GAS1

Line no.	WEEK$	MILES	GAL	PRICE	MPG	
						Variable names
		0	0	0	0	Default values
2700	1 June					Assigned value
2800		300				Assigned value
2900			15			Assigned value
3000				120		Assigned value
3200					300/15 (i.e., 20)	Calculation; Assigned value
3400	1 June	300	15	1.2	20	Output

Additional BASIC Commands

We have already discussed the **LIST**, **RUN**, **LOAD**, **NEW**, and **SAVE** commands. In this section, each of these commands is discussed in more detail and a number of new commands are introduced.

• *List Program Lines* (LIST) •

The **LIST** command displays the program lines on the screen. Programs more than 24 lines in length will not completely fit on the screen at one time and therefore entering **LIST** ↵ causes the screen to scroll quickly. This scrolling can be interrupted by pressing **[Pause]**. To continue the scrolling, press **[Enter]**. To stop the entire listing process, press **[Ctrl-Break]**.

Command	Description
LIST	Displays the entire program on the screen.
LIST,"LPT1:"	Lists the current program on the printer (**LPT1** stands for **L**ine **Pr**in**T**er — the colon is needed).
LIST 10	Displays only line **10** on the screen.
LIST 10-90	Displays all lines between **10** and **90**, inclusive.
LIST 10-90,"LPT1:"	Prints all lines between **10** and **90**, inclusive.
LIST 10-	Displays all lines from **10** to the end of the program.
LIST -90	Displays all lines from the first line through line **90**.

• *Delete Program Lines* (DELETE) •

The **DELETE** command deletes specified lines from the program in memory. To make the deletion permanent, the program must be saved using the **SAVE** command.

Command	Description
DELETE 10-90	Deletes all lines between **10** and **90**, inclusive.
DELETE 10-	Deletes all lines from line **10** to the end of the program.
DELETE -90	Deletes all lines from first line through line **90**.

• *Load a File from Disk* (LOAD) •

The **LOAD** command reads a program from the disk into the main memory of the computer.

Command	Description
LOAD"A:GAS1	Loads the program **GAS1** from the diskette in drive A: into the main memory of the computer.
LOAD"WAGES1	Loads the program **WAGES1** from the default drive (usually the A: drive) into the main memory of the computer.

• *Execute the Statements of a Program* (RUN) •

The **RUN** command directs the computer to execute (carry out) the instructions in a BASIC program.

Command	Description
RUN	Instructs the computer to follow the instructions given in the program, beginning execution with the first line of the program.
RUN 500	Instructs the computer to begin execution with the instructions at line **500** rather than at the first line of the program.

• *Change Program Line Numbers* (RENUM) •

The **RENUM** command allows the user to change the line numbers of a BASIC program.

Command	Description
RENUM	Renumbers the entire program. The first line is assigned the number **10**; the second line is assigned the number **20**, and so on in increments of **10**.

Continued . . .

Command	Description

```
NEW ↵
Ok
2 A = 4
67 B = 3
100 PRINT A, B
RENUM ↵          ◄— Renumbers program lines so that they begin at line number 10
Ok                  and change in increments of 10
LIST ↵
10 A = 4
20 B = 3
30 PRINT A, B
Ok
```

RENUM 300,,50 Renumbers a program so that the first line number is **300** and subsequent line numbers are incremented by **50**. The two commas between **300** and **50** are needed.

```
RENUM 300,,50 ↵  ◄— Renumbers program lines so that they begin at line number 300
Ok                  and change in increments of 50
LIST ↵
300 A = 4
350 B = 3
400 PRINT A, B
Ok
```

RENUM 500,350,50

Renumbers part of the program. The new numbering begins at line **350** rather than at the first line of the program. The new line numbers will begin at **500** and subsequent line numbers will be incremented by **50**.

```
300 A = 4
350 B = 3
400 PRINT A, B
Ok
RENUM 500,350,50 ↵  ◄— Renumbers program lines beginning at line 350 so that they begin
Ok                      at line number 500 and change in increments of 50
LIST ↵
300 A = 4           ◄— Line number 300 remains unchanged because renumbering began
500 B = 3               at line 350
550 PRINT A, B
Ok
```

• *Trace Program Execution* (TRACE) •

As programs become longer and more complex, it is sometimes useful to have the computer indicate which program statement is executing as the program runs. To accomplish this, **TRACE** can be turned on by typing **TRON** and pressing **[Enter]** or by just pressing **[F7]**. With **TRACE** turned on the computer will display, inside square brackets **[ ]**, the line number of each statement as it is executed.

```
LIST ↵
300 A = 4
500 B = 3
550 PRINT A, B
Ok
TRON ↵
Ok
RUN ↵
[300][500][550] 4             3
Ok
```

Turns on TRACE

Output from line 550

As each statement is executed, its line number is displayed inside brackets

To turn off the **TRACE** function, type **TROFF** and press **[Enter]** or just press **[F8]**.

• *Display Files Command* (FILES) •

The **FILES** command displays a listing of all or selected files saved on the disk. The file names are displayed across the screen along with any file name extensions. This is equivalent to the DOS command **DIR /W**. For example:

```
FILES"A: ↵
A:\
PR1      .BAS      PR2      .BAS      PR2      .TXT      PR3      .BAS
PR4      .BAS      HWB1-01  .BAS      HWB1-02  .BAS      HWB1-03  .BAS
HWB1-04  .BAS      LET1     .BAS      LET2     .BAS      COMMA    .BAS
SEMI     .BAS      COMSEMI  .BAS      TAB      .BAS      PRUSING1 .BAS
MOREDATA .BAS      PRUSING2 .BAS      PRUSING3 .BAS      ORDER    .BAS
WAGES1   .BAS      GAS1     .BAS
 338944 Bytes free

Ok
```

A more selective list may be displayed using the global characters * (asterisk) and **?** (question mark). As was the case in the DOS environment, the * may be used to take the place of any number of characters in a file name. For example, typing **FILES"*.BAS** ↵ will display the names of all files on the default disk that have the extension **BAS**, while typing **FILES"A:HW*.BAS** ↵ will list the names of only those files on the diskette in drive A: that begin with the letters **HW** and have the **BAS** extension.

```
FILES"A:HW*.BAS ↵
A:\
HWB1-01  .BAS      HWB1-02  .BAS      HWB1-03  .BAS      HWB1-04  .BAS
 338944 Bytes free

Ok
```

The **?** may be used to replace any one character and is therefore much more restrictive than the *. For example, typing **FILES"A:PR?.BAS** ↵ would display the names of all BASIC files on the diskette in drive A: that have the first two characters **PR** and any other character in the third position (where the **?** is located).

```
FILES"A:PR?.BAS ↵
A:\
PR1      .BAS      PR2      .BAS      PR3      .BAS      PR4      .BAS
 338944 Bytes free

Ok
```

What would happen if the **DIR** command were typed at this time? The error message **Syntax error** would be displayed. The **DIR** command is not a BASIC command, it is a DOS command. While you are in the BASIC environment you must use only BASIC commands.

• *Erase Files from the Disk* (KILL) •

The **KILL** command erases files from the disk in the same way as the DOS **DEL** command does.

Command	Description
KILL"A:PR1.BAS	Erases the file **PR1.BAS** from the diskette in drive A:. In order for this command to work properly, you must type the file name extension (e.g., **.BAS**) if the file has one. For example, typing **KILL"A:PR1** would result in the message **File not found** because the full file specification is **A:PR1.BAS**.

• *Clear RAM Memory in Preparation for a New Program* (NEW) •

The **NEW** command tells the computer that the programmer is ready to enter a new program. Any program in the main memory is erased when the **NEW** command is entered (but nothing is erased from the disk). Use **NEW** whenever you want to stop working on one program and begin working on another.

• *Return to DOS* (SYSTEM) •

The **SYSTEM** command returns control to DOS (i.e., this command will cause the computer to stop running BASIC and prepare itself to take commands directly from the disk operating system once again). After executing this command, the **A:\>** is displayed to signify that the computer is ready for a DOS command.

TO TAKE A BREAK Type **SYSTEM** ↵, remove diskette(s). To resume (hard disk): Insert *Data* diskette, type **A:** ↵, **C:\BA\BASICA**↵. To resume (two drive): Insert diskettes, type **A:** ↵, **B:\BASICA** ↵.

Homework Exercises

CHAPTER TWO

For each of the following homework exercises, write a BASIC program that will produce the output described. Each program should contain enough **REM** statements to clearly document the program. Unless instructed to do otherwise, produce a hard copy of a **LIST** and a **RUN** of each final working program. Also, save each program using a name such as **HWB2-01** for future reference.

① Write and run a program that uses **LET** statements to store your first name in a variable called **FIRST$**, your last name in a variable called **LAST$**, and your date of birth in a variable called **BORN$**. Use **PRINT** statements to display the values of the variables so that the output from your program looks like the following (use your own name and birthday, of course):

```
Homework B2-01                   Lauren Storla                    1 Mar 91

Storla, Lauren was born on 22 February, 1990
Lauren Storla was born on 22 February, 1990
```

Continued . . .

② Modify the program you wrote for Exercise 1 so that it uses **TAB**s to display the output beginning in columns 12, 25, and 40. The output from your program should look like the following:

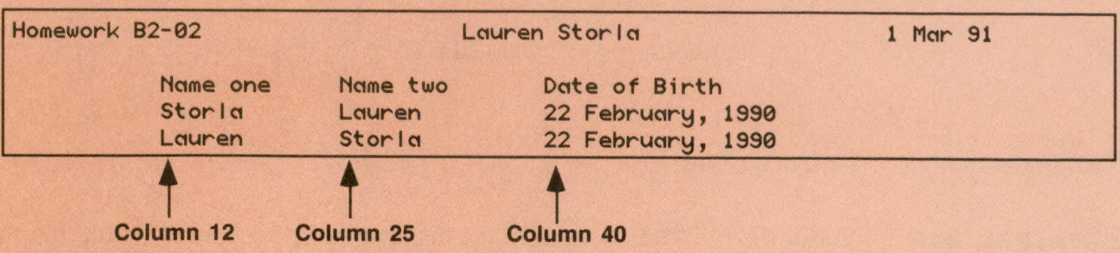

```
Homework B2-02                  Lauren Storla                 1 Mar 91

           Name one     Name two      Date of Birth
           Storla       Lauren        22 February, 1990
           Lauren       Storla        22 February, 1990
```


③ Modify the program you wrote for Exercise 2 so that it uses **PRINT USING** statements rather than **PRINT** statements to display the last three lines of output. The output should be identical to that of Exercise 2.

④ Write and run a program that uses **LET** statements to store the name of your favorite person in a variable called **FAV$**, and the number of years you have known that person in a variable called **YEAR**. Have the program convert the years into days. The output from your program should look like the following (the value in the box should be calculated by the computer):

```
Homework B2-04                  Carol Miller                  1 Mar 91

Haley is my favorite person.  I have known her for 1460 days
```

Calculated by the computer

⑤ Using a calculator, figure out the answers to the arithmetic problems given below. Next, write and run a program that uses **PRINT** statements to solve the problems. Have the computer print both the problems and the answers. Be sure to check to see if your answers are the same as those calculated by the computer. If there is a difference, make sure you find out where you made an error. The output from your program should look like the following (the values in the box should be calculated by the computer):

```
Homework B2-05                  Molly Collins                 1 Mar 91

Sample Calculations:

 40 = 16 + 36/3*2
 40 = 8^2*2/16*2*(3 + 2)^2/10
 29 = 32 - (15 - (8 - 2)*2)
-18 = -3^2 - (-3)^2
```

Calculated by the computer

⑥ Write a program that uses **PRINT** and **PRINT USING** statements to display the metric conversion chart given below. Recall that 2.54 centimeters equals one inch, and that there are 100 centimeters in a meter. The inches and centimeters should be rounded to one decimal place and meters should be rounded to two decimal places. The output from your program should look like the following (the values in the boxes should be calculated by the computer):

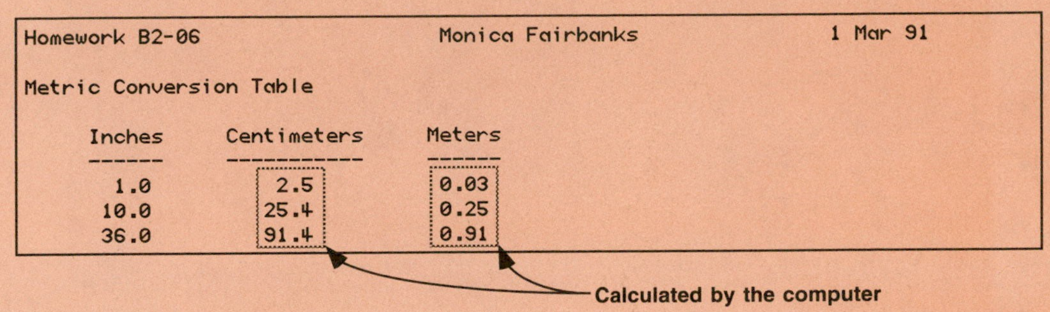

```
Homework B2-06                     Monica Fairbanks                 1 Mar 91

Metric Conversion Table

     Inches      Centimeters      Meters
     ------      -----------      ------
      1.0            2.5           0.03
     10.0           25.4           0.25
     36.0           91.4           0.91
```


---

⑦ Micro Stuff, Inc. is a company that sells microcomputer software. Its employees are paid a monthly salary of $1000 plus a 7% commission on everything they sell. Write and run a program that displays the sales summary chart given below. The program should include the following:

a. **LET** statements that assign values to variables for the employee name and the total sales.
b. The calculations of the commissions and the total earnings. The **LET** statements should provide the data and the computer should do the actual computations.
c. **REM** statements to properly document the program.
d. **PRINT USING** statements to round off the dollar values to the nearest cent and to display the results on the screen.
e. Use the following data for the names and total sales.

The output from your program should look like the following (the values in the boxes should be calculated by the computer):

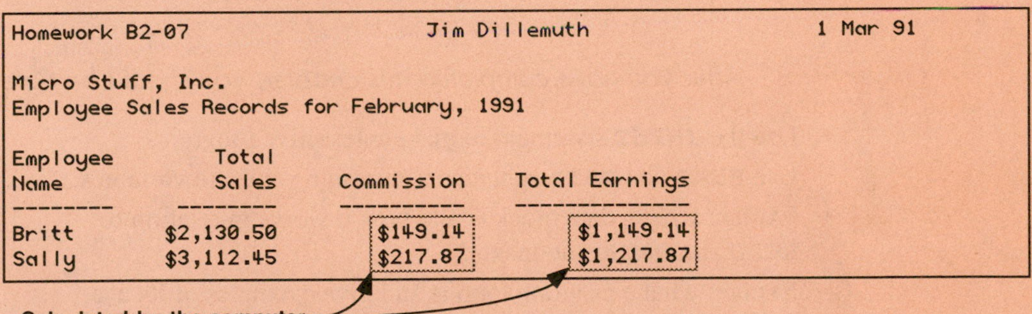

```
Homework B2-07                     Jim Dillemuth                     1 Mar 91

Micro Stuff, Inc.
Employee Sales Records for February, 1991

Employee          Total
Name              Sales       Commission     Total Earnings
--------        --------      ----------     --------------
Britt          $2,130.50       $149.14         $1,149.14
Sally          $3,112.45       $217.87         $1,217.87
```


Notice that the output from this program is identical to the Lotus 1-2-3 worksheet **HW1-11FIN** that you created in Part II, Chapter 1. Think back to when you did that homework exercise and compare it with this exercise. Which took you longer to do, the Lotus 1-2-3 worksheet or the BASIC program? Which was easier for you to do?

---

⑧ Use the **RENUM** command to change the line numbers of the program you wrote for Exercise 7 so that the first line number is **57** and the line numbers increase by threes (i.e., **57**, **60**, **63**, **66**, etc.). Print a **LIST** of the program.

---

⑨ Use the **LIST** command to list only the first six lines of the program that you wrote for Exercise 7. Do a screen dump to show the result.

---

⑩ Use the **FILES** command to display the names of only those files on your BASIC disk that begin with the letters **HW**. Do a screen dump to show the result.

Data, Loops, and Process

Objectives *After you have completed this chapter, you should be able to*

- Use the **INPUT** statement to make interactive programs.
- Use **READ** and **DATA** statements to assign values to variables.
- Explain what a data block is and how it works in relation to **READ** and **DATA** statements.
- Explain what a program loop is and give examples of its use.
- Use **FOR** and **NEXT** statements to form unconditional loops.
- Explain a structured procedure for writing programs.

CHAPTER 3

- Apply a structured procedure to the development of a program.
- Define pseudocode and explain its use.
- Develop the pseudocode for a given computer-based problem.
- Describe what a flowchart is and explain its use.
- Explain a process for debugging programs.
- Use WordPerfect to enter and edit programs.

Introduction

The **LET** statement was introduced in the previous chapter as a means of assigning values to variables. Using **LET** is convenient for small amounts of data or data that remain the same whenever the program is run, but it is not useful when data are to be input directly by the computer user during program execution or for large data sets. In this chapter two new data assignment statements (**INPUT** and **READ**) are introduced to overcome the limitations of the **LET** statement.

The **INPUT** and **READ** statements will enable you to write much more complex and useful programs. However, as you may have found, writing even simple programs takes some skill. To help you with the programming development process, a general procedure for writing BASIC programs will be discussed at the end of this chapter.

INPUT Statement

FORM
```
Line no.  INPUT "prompt"; variable1, variable2, ...
```

EXAMPLE
```
1000      INPUT "Type in week, miles"; WEEK$, MILES
1100      INPUT MONTH$, RATE
```

The **INPUT** statement enables the user to enter data into the main memory of the computer while the program is actually running. The program thus becomes *interactive* because it can ask the user questions and allow the user to respond to those questions by entering the appropriate data. The consequence of this is that the person who enters the data does not need to know how to write computer programs, only how to run them.

When the BASIC interpreter encounters an **INPUT** statement it displays a prompt and a question mark and then stops and waits for the user to enter the data requested. For example, the program below computes the sales tax on an item, given its price:

```
NEW
Ok
1100 INPUT "Enter the price";P
1200 PRINT "The 6% sales tax is ".06*P
RUN
Enter the price?    ←— Program execution pauses here and waits for user response
```

Line Numbers	Comments
1100	Displays the prompt **Enter the price** followed by a question mark. It then creates a storage location called **P**, and waits for the user to type a value for **P**. After the user types a value (e.g., **20**) and presses **[Enter]** the computer assigns this value to variable **P**.
1200	Computes the tax and displays the results. The entire run of the program will look like the following:

```
NEW
Ok
1100 INPUT "Enter the price";P
1200 PRINT "The 6% sales tax is ".06*P
RUN
Enter the price? 20    ←— Program execution continues after a value for P
The 6% sales tax is  1.2   has been typed and [Enter] has been tapped
Ok
```

What happens if the data entered are not understood by the BASIC interpreter? Run the program again but this time type **$20** instead of **20** when asked for the price.

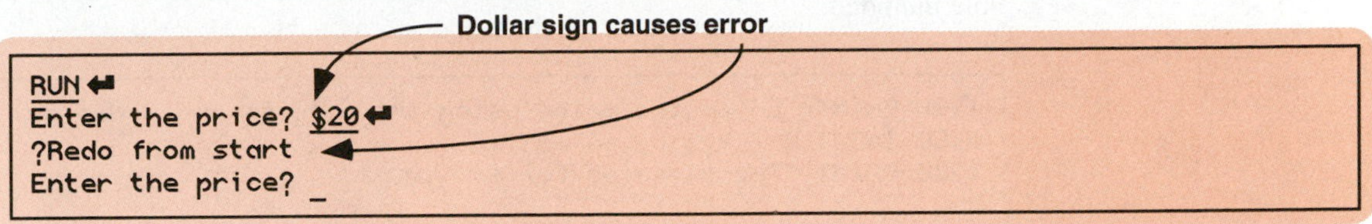

The user is requesting that the string **$20** be stored at a location labeled with the numeric variable **P**. BASIC will not allow this and so it displays the error message **?Redo from start** and then begins the program execution all over again. At this point the user may enter the value in the correct form (i.e., **20**), or abort the program by pressing **[Ctrl-Break].**

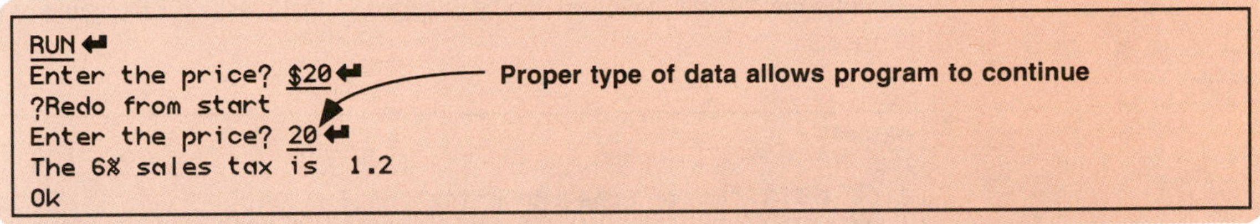

One of the nice things about using **INPUT** statements is that the person running the program does not have to know much about the program, or computers for that matter. The user simply responds to questions by supplying the requested data. However, as we have seen, the data must be in the right form or it will not be processed correctly. The program can be made a little more *user friendly* by including more instructions in the prompt on line **1100**, but errors can still occur.

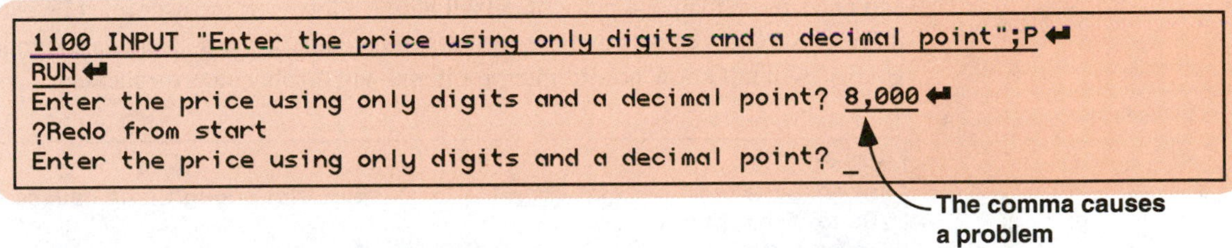

The new prompt provides clearer instructions, but this time an error is caused by the value **8,000**. Remember, numbers in BASIC are not written in the same way as we write numbers in English. BASIC uses the comma as a delimiter to separate pieces of data. Thus, BASIC interpreted **8,000** as two separate numbers: **8** and **000**. Because the **INPUT** statement had only one variable listed (the variable **P**), BASIC did not know what to do with the extra number and requested that the data be entered again.

If the program is run again but **8000** instead of **8,000** is entered at the prompt, the proper output is displayed.

```
?Redo from start
Enter the price using only digits and a decimal point? 8000
The 6% sales tax is  480
Ok
```

The prompt on the **INPUT** statement is optional. For example, line **1100** could have been broken up into a **PRINT** statement containing the prompt followed by an **INPUT** statement with just the variable included.

```
1100 PRINT "Enter the price using only digits and a decimal point";
1150 INPUT P
1200 PRINT "The 6% sales tax is ".06*P
Ok
RUN ↵
Enter the price using only digits and a decimal point? 8000↵
The 6% sales tax is  480
Ok
```

Values for more than one variable can be entered at one time using just one **INPUT** statement. For example, the **INPUT** statement can be changed so that it asks for the name of the item bought as well as its price.

```
NEW ↵
Ok
1100 INPUT "Enter name and price";N$,P
1200 PRINT "The 6% sales tax on "N$" is ".06*P
RUN ↵
Enter name and price? car,8000↵
The 6% sales tax on car is  480
Ok
```

Having more than one variable in an **INPUT** statement speeds up the processing because the user can enter more than one piece of data at a time. However, the user must be careful to enter the correct number of pieces of data and the correct type of data. If the user enters too much data or too little data, BASIC will not know how to interpret it and will display an error message.

```
RUN ↵
Enter name and price? car↵           ← Not enough data causes error
?Redo from start
Enter name and price? car,8,000↵     ← Too much data causes error
?Redo from start
Enter name and price? car,$8000↵     ← Wrong type of data causes error
?Redo from start
Enter name and price? car,8000↵      ← Correct type and quantity of data allows program
The 6% sales tax on car is  480        to continue processing
Ok
```

To see how a more complex program works, the gas mileage program **GAS1**, which you saved on page B48, can be revised by replacing the **LET** statements with an **INPUT** statement (see the dotted box in the display below). This new program is saved under the name **GAS2**. You should **LOAD** the new version of the program, **LIST** it, **SAVE** it to your *Basic Data* diskette, and then **RUN** it as shown on the next page:

```
LOAD"C:\BA\GAS2↵
Ok
LIST ↵3200
1100 REM Calculates gas mileage given miles driven and gal of gas used
1200 REM Douglas Robertson (373-4026), created 6 Mar 91
1300 REM Define variables:
1400 REM   WEEK$ = week data were collected
1500 REM   MILES = miles driven that week
1600 REM     GAL = gallons of gas used that week
1700 REM   PRICE = price in cents per gallon of gas
1800 REM     MPG = computed value of miles per gallon of gas
1900 REM Define images for PRINT USING:
2000   IMAGE1$ = "    Week     Miles     Gallons     Price    Miles/Gallon"
2100   IMAGE2$ = "  ------    -----    -------     -----    ------------"
2200   IMAGE3$ = "  \    \    ###.#      ##.#     $##.##        ##.#"
2210 REM Ask user for values of variables
2220 INPUT "Enter week, miles, gallons, price";WEEK$,MILES,GAL,PRICE
2300 REM Display column headings:
2400   PRINT IMAGE1$
2500   PRINT IMAGE2$
3100 REM Calculate gas mileage:
3200   MPG = MILES/GAL
3300 REM Display results
3400   PRINT USING IMAGE3$;WEEK$,MILES,GAL,PRICE/100,MPG
Ok
SAVE"A:GAS2↵
Ok
RUN ↵
Enter week, miles, gallons, price? 1 June,300,15,120↵
    Week     Miles     Gallons     Price    Miles/Gallon
  ------     -----     -------     -----    ------------
  1 June     300.0       15.0     $ 1.20        20.0
Ok
```

Modified lines

New line of output caused by `INPUT` at line `2220`

The output is almost the same as when **LET** statements were used except that the prompts (the questions asked by the program) also appear on the screen. The important difference is that the information was entered as the program was running rather than being a part of the program itself in **LET** statements.

Having the output contain both the request for data and the computed values makes the display somewhat confused. A more practical approach would be to clear the screen using the **CLS** statement just after the **INPUT** statement has been executed at line **2220**. In this case, the screen would appear as follows just after the data were typed and before **[Enter]** was pressed:

```
2230 CLS↵
RUN ↵
Enter week, miles, gallons, price? 1 June,300,15,120
```

After **[Enter]** is pressed, line **2230** is executed causing the screen to be cleared. The rest of the statements would then be executed causing the screen to look as follows:

```
    Week     Miles     Gallons     Price    Miles/Gallon
  ------     -----     -------     -----    ------------
  1 June     300.0       15.0     $ 1.20        20.0
Ok
```

Another way of separating the request for data and the table would be to have the request appear on the screen and the table appear only on the printer. That way you would get a hard copy of the table, which contains only the information you want. This would be easily accomplished in the above program by changing the **PRINT** statements in lines **2400**, **2500**, and **3400** into **LPRINT** statements (remember, **LPRINT** says to **PRINT** on the **L**ine printer).

READ *and* DATA *Statements*

FORM	Line no.	READ variable1, variable2, ...
	Line no.	DATA value1, value2, ...
EXAMPLE	1100	READ WEEK$, MILES, GAL, PRICE
	1200	DATA 1 July,300,15,120,8 July, 250,10,125

The **READ** and **DATA** statements assign values to variable names as do the **INPUT** and **LET** statements. The difference is that the **READ** and **DATA** statements separate the variable names from the data; the **READ** statements list the variables in one line (or lines) of code while the **DATA** statements list the values to be used for those variables in other lines of code. This way of assigning data to variables is useful when a large quantity of data are to be processed. The result is identical to using either **LET** or **INPUT** statements.

Below is an example of a simple program that uses **READ** and **DATA** statements:

```
NEW
Ok
10 READ A,B
20 DATA 1,2,3
30 PRINT A,B
40 DATA 4,5
50 READ A,C,D
60 PRINT A,B,C,D
SAVE"A:READ1
Ok
RUN
 1             2
 3             2             4             5
Ok
```

DATA statements, like **REM** statements, are considered non-executable. This means that the computer does not receive instructions from the **DATA** statements (as it does with most other BASIC statements) but only values for the variables. When **DATA** statements are contained in a program, the computer sets up a *data block* right after the **RUN** command is given. The data block is a continuous listing of all the values in all the **DATA** statements. The data are entered into the block in the order that they appear in the program. Then a *pointer* is set at the first piece of data in the block. For the program above, the data block would look like the following (the ellipses at the right of the data block indicate that the block goes on forever but the rest of the cells are empty):

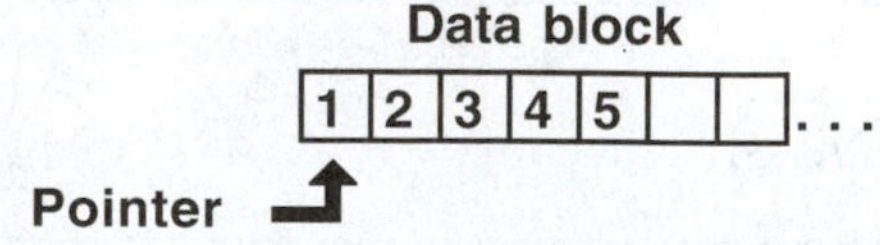

Because the **DATA** statements are non-executable, once this data block has been set up the **DATA** statements are no longer needed and so they are ignored during the rest of the processing.

When the **READ** statement in line **10** is executed, the computer creates a variable location called **A** and assigns the first value in the data block (**1**) to this location. The pointer then moves to the next position in the data block (the box with the **2** inside).

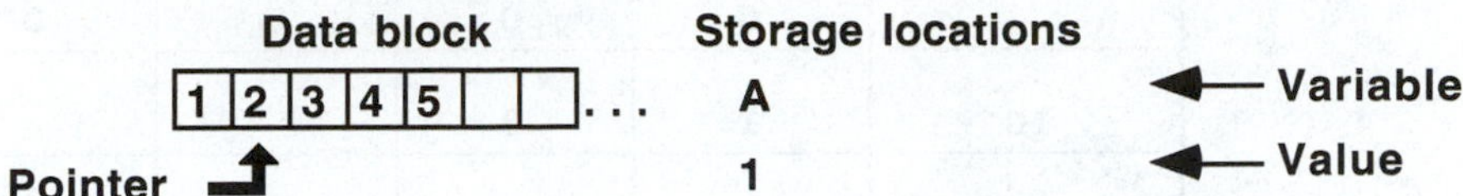

Still at line **10**, the computer creates a storage location called **B** and assigns the second value (**2**) to this variable. The pointer then moves to the next piece of data (**3**).

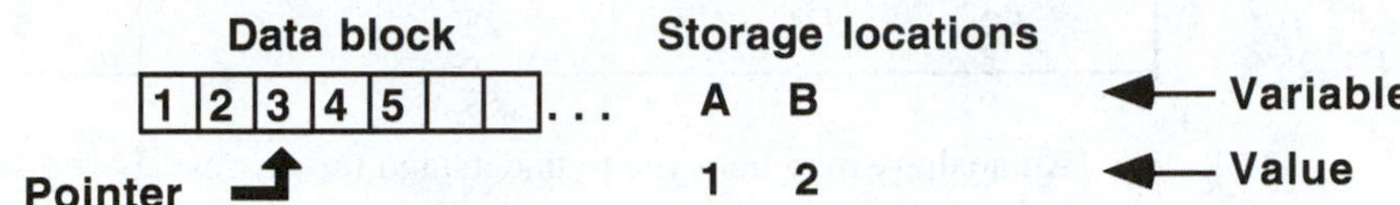

Control in the program then moves to line **20**, which contains a **DATA** statement. Because this statement is non-executable, control immediately goes to the next line (**30**). At line **30** the values of **A** and **B** are displayed.

Control then passes to line **40**, but because it contains a **DATA** statement, which is non-executable, control immediately goes to line **50**. At line **50** the computer assigns the value indicated by the pointer (**3**) to the variable **A**. The fact that **A** already had a value makes no difference; the computer simply replaces the current value of **A** with the new value and moves the data pointer to the next piece of data.

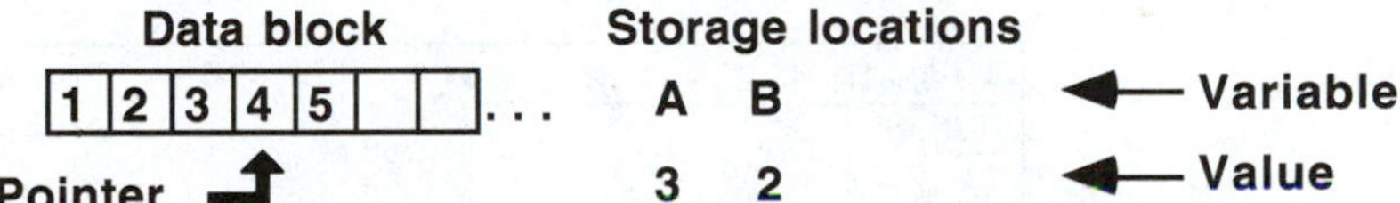

Still at line **50**, the computer creates a new storage location called **C** and assigns the number indicated by the pointer to this location. Thus, the value **4** is entered at location **C**. Likewise, the computer creates a storage location called **D** and assigns the value **5** to that location. Note that because the variable **B** did not appear in the **READ** statement at line **50**, the value of **B** was not changed.

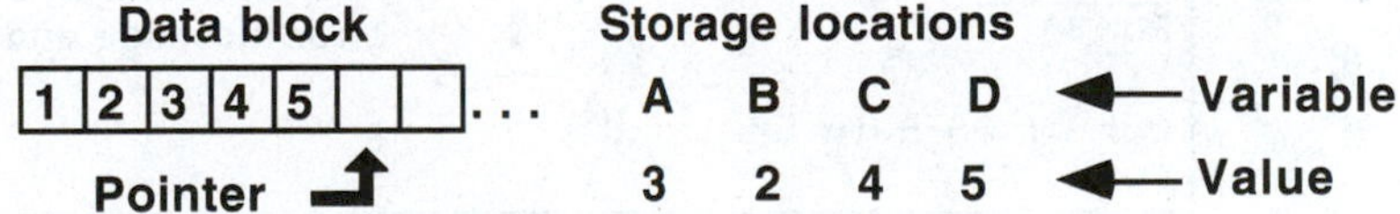

In summary, we see that the first two pieces of data were assigned to variables **A** and **B**, respectively, by the **READ** statement in line **10**. The next three pieces of data were assigned to variables **A**, **C**, and **D**, respectively, by the **READ** statement in line **50**. The following diagram may help you to visualize this:

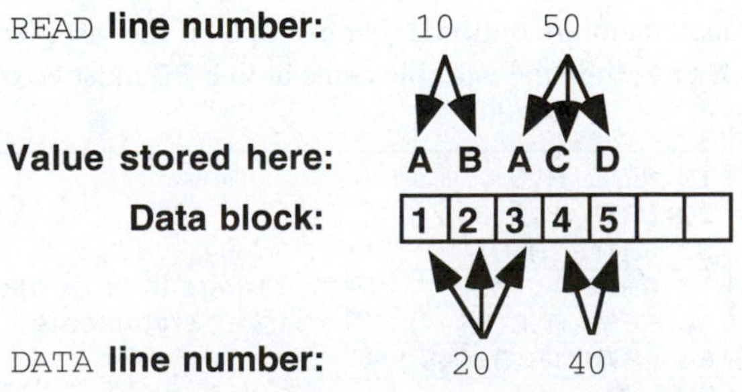

The whole process can be viewed as follows:

Memory Assignments for Program READ1

Line no.	A	B	C	D	
	0	0	0	0	Default values
10	1	2			Assigned value
30	1	2			Output
50	3		4	5	Assigned value
60	3	2	4	5	Output

(A, B, C, D: Variable names)

An analogy may help you to understand the process. If you wanted to read a number of different library books, you would first go to the library and check out all the books and bring them home. This is analogous to setting up the data block using all the **DATA** statements before any statements are executed. After you had all the books at home you could begin to read them, one by one. This is analogous to the **READ** statements taking values from the data block and assigning them to different variable locations as the statements are executed.

What happens if there are too many values in the **DATA** statements? Unlike the **INPUT** statement where the number of variables must exactly match the number of values, the extra values in a **DATA** statement are ignored. In the following example, line **40** is replaced with a new **DATA** statement that contains five extra pieces of data:

```
40 DATA 4,5,6,7,8,9,0
RUN
 1              2
 3              2              4              5
Ok
```

← Too much data in the DATA statement causes no problems (the extra data are ignored)

What happens if there are not enough values in the **DATA** statements?

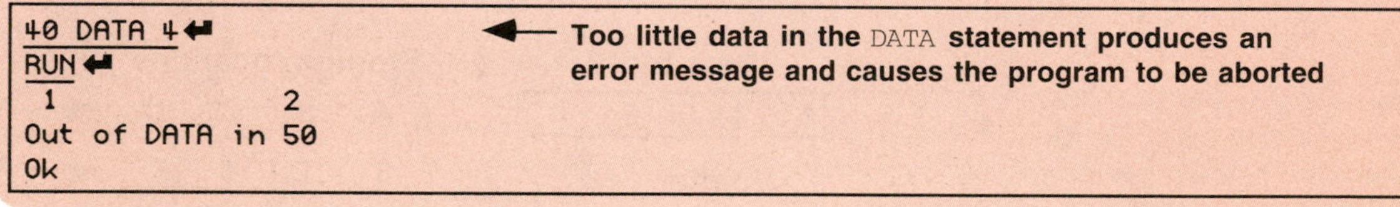

```
40 DATA 4
RUN
 1              2
Out of DATA in 50
Ok
```

← Too little data in the DATA statement produces an error message and causes the program to be aborted

At line **50** in the above example, the computer wants to assign a value to variable **D**, but there are no values left in the data list. Thus, an **Out of DATA** error message is displayed and program execution is halted.

If the **DATA** statements contain strings, the variables corresponding to those strings must have a dollar sign as their last character (i.e., they must be string variables). The quotation marks in a **DATA** statement are optional. For example, if the last piece of data (**5**) in line **40** is replaced with the string **Matt**, then the variable name at line **50** must be changed from **D** to **D$**:

```
10 READ A,B
20 DATA 1,2,3
30 PRINT A,B
40 DATA 4,"Matt"
50 READ A,C,D$
60 PRINT A,B,C,D,D$
RUN
 1              2
 3              2              4              0              Matt
Ok
```

← Strings in DATA statements must be read by string variables in READ statements

Line Numbers	Comments
10	Creates a storage location called **A** and assigns the first value (**1**) from the data list to that location. Also, creates a storage location called **B** and assigns the second value (**2**) from the data list to that location.
20	This is a non-executable statement and so control immediately passes to line **30**.
30	Displays the values of variables **A** and **B**.
40	This is a non-executable statement and so control immediately passes to line **50**.
50	Erases the value of **1** in storage location **A** and assigns the next value (**3**) from the data list to that location. Also, creates a storage location called **C** and assigns the next value (**4**) from the data list to that location. Also, creates a storage location called **D$** and assigns the next value (**Matt**) from the data list to that location.
60	Displays the values in storage locations **A**, **B**, **C**, **D**, and **D$**.

The storage locations may be summarized as follows:

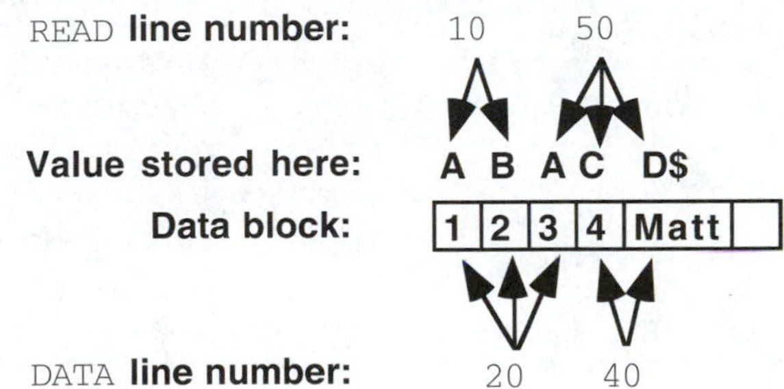

If the data type does not match the variable type (as in line **50** below), a syntax error is displayed and program execution is halted:

```
10 READ A,B
20 DATA 1,2,3
30 PRINT A,B
40 DATA 4,"Matt"
50 READ A,C,D          ◄— Variable D cannot be used to read string Matt
60 PRINT A,B,C,D,D$
Ok
RUN ↵
 1             2
Syntax error in 40
Ok
40 DATA 4,"Matt"       ◄— Computer assumes data are wrong rather than variable
```

At line **50**, the computer wants to assign the value **Matt** to the variable **D**. But because **Matt** is a string and **D** is a numeric variable, the computer does not know what to do and so it issues an error message and aborts the program. The error can be fixed by changing the **D** to **D$** in line **50**.

What happens if all the data are contained in a single **DATA** statement? In the next display, all the data from line **40** were added onto the end of line **20** and then line **40** was deleted:

```
10 READ A,B
20 DATA 1,2,3,4,"Matt"   <-- All data are in the same DATA statement
30 PRINT A,B
50 READ A,C,D$
60 PRINT A,B,C,D,D$
Ok
RUN
 1             2
 3             2             4             0             Matt
Ok
```

The output is the same as before. Because all the data are collected into a single block right at the beginning of execution of the program, it makes absolutely no difference whether the data are in a single **DATA** statement or in many different **DATA** statements as long as there is enough data overall to satisfy all the **READ** statements.

What happens if an arithmetic problem is entered into a **DATA** statement? For example, suppose line **20** is changed so that the number **4** is replaced with the sum **4+8**:

```
10 READ A,B
20 DATA 1,2,3,4+8,"Matt"   <-- Calculation in a DATA statement is not allowed
30 PRINT A,B
50 READ A,C,D$
60 PRINT A,B,C,D,D$
Ok
RUN
 1             2
Syntax error in 20
Ok
20 DATA 1,2,3,4+8,"Matt"
```

The first two pieces of data are correctly read on line **10** and the values are printed by line **30**. However, a problem occurs when line **50** is processed. Because **DATA** statements are not executable, they may not contain any arithmetic problems. The computer was expecting a single number from the **DATA** statement so that it could assign it to the variable **C** but it read something that was not a number (**4+8** is an arithmetic problem, not a number). BASIC interpreted **4+8** as a string and therefore could not assign it to the variable **C**. Thus, the message **Syntax error in 20** was issued and execution of the program halted.

To see how **READ** and **INPUT** differ, the gas mileage program **GAS2** can be modified so that it uses **READ** and **DATA** statements instead of **LET** or **INPUT** statements. **LOAD** the new version of the program, **LIST** it, **SAVE** it to your *BASIC Data* diskette, and then **RUN** it as shown on the next page:

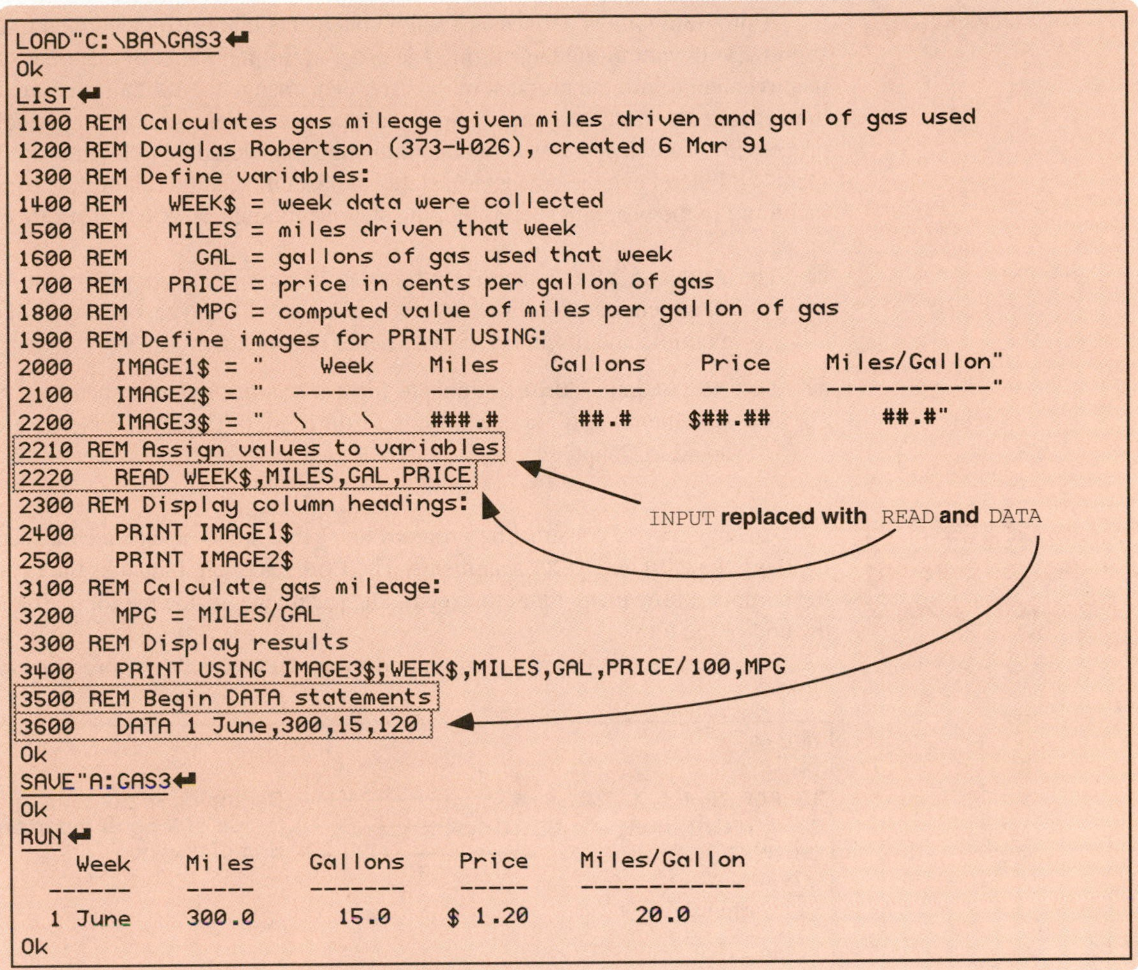
```
LOAD"C:\BA\GAS3
Ok
LIST
1100 REM Calculates gas mileage given miles driven and gal of gas used
1200 REM Douglas Robertson (373-4026), created 6 Mar 91
1300 REM Define variables:
1400 REM   WEEK$ = week data were collected
1500 REM   MILES = miles driven that week
1600 REM     GAL = gallons of gas used that week
1700 REM   PRICE = price in cents per gallon of gas
1800 REM     MPG = computed value of miles per gallon of gas
1900 REM Define images for PRINT USING:
2000   IMAGE1$ = "     Week     Miles     Gallons     Price     Miles/Gallon"
2100   IMAGE2$ = "   ------     -----     -------     -----     ------------"
2200   IMAGE3$ = "   \    \     ###.#        ##.#    $##.##             ##.#"
2210 REM Assign values to variables
2220   READ WEEK$,MILES,GAL,PRICE
2300 REM Display column headings:
2400   PRINT IMAGE1$
2500   PRINT IMAGE2$
3100 REM Calculate gas mileage:
3200   MPG = MILES/GAL
3300 REM Display results
3400   PRINT USING IMAGE3$;WEEK$,MILES,GAL,PRICE/100,MPG
3500 REM Begin DATA statements
3600   DATA 1 June,300,15,120
Ok
SAVE"A:GAS3
Ok
RUN
     Week     Miles     Gallons     Price     Miles/Gallon
   ------     -----     -------     -----     ------------
   1 June     300.0        15.0    $ 1.20             20.0
Ok
```


For the program above, the data block would look like this:

WEEK$	MILES	GAL	PRICE
1 June	300	15	120

At line **2220**, the computer creates the variable **WEEK$**, assigns the first piece of data (**1 June**) to that variable, and then moves the pointer to the next piece of data. Still at line **2220**, the computer creates a variable called **MILES** and assigns the value indicated by the pointer (**300**) to that variable. Next the variable **GAL** is created and assigned the value **15** and, finally, the variable **PRICE** is created and assigned the value **120**. Note that the **DATA** statement is located at the bottom of the program. This makes it easy to find. The rest of the program is the same as before.

Program Loops

A program *loop* is defined as a set of statements that is executed over and over again. For example, suppose you want to run the gas mileage program for a number of different sets of data. It would be inconvenient to run the program on one set, then change the **DATA** statement and run the program again, then change the **DATA** statement and run the program again, and so on until all the sets of data were processed. A much easier way of accomplishing this would be to include all the data in **DATA** statements and then have the computer process the data in a single run of the program. This can be done by including in the program special looping statements such as **FOR** and **NEXT** or **WHILE** and **WEND**.

- The **FOR** and **NEXT** statements form an *unconditional* loop because they execute a set of statements a prescribed number of times. This type of loop will be used in the next example and discussed in more detail in Chapter 5.
- The **WHILE** and **WEND** statements form a *conditional* loop because they execute a set of statements while a certain condition is met. These statements are discussed in more detail in Chapter 4.

Use of FOR *and* NEXT *to Form Program Loops*

An easy way of constructing program loops that are to be executed a specified number of times is by using the **FOR** and **NEXT** statements. The **FOR** statement indicates the beginning of a loop and tells the computer how many times to execute the statements inside the loop. The **NEXT** statement indicates the end of the loop.

For example, the following program displays **HELLO** exactly three times.

```
NEW ↵
Ok
10 FOR NUM = 1 TO 3          ◄──── Beginning of the loop
20    PRINT NUM; "  HELLO"   ◄──── Inside of loop is indented for easy reading
30 NEXT NUM                  ◄──── End of the loop
RUN ↵
 1    HELLO
 2    HELLO
 3    HELLO
Ok
```

Lines **10** and **30** of this program define the beginning and end of the loop. The variable **NUM** in line **10** is used by the **FOR** and **NEXT** statements to count the number of times the loop is executed. In this example, the **FOR** statement says to set the value of **NUM** to **1** (**FOR NUM = 1**) and keep executing the loop until the value of **NUM** exceeds **3** (**TO 3**). Each time the loop is executed the value of **NUM** is increased by **1**. The **PRINT** statement inside the loop is indented to make the loop obvious to the programmer. Of course, the computer does not care about the extra spaces between the line number and the word **PRINT**, but the indenting makes the program easier for humans to read.

Any legal numeric variable name can be used for the loop variable. For example, **NUM** could be replaced with **BEANS** and the output would be exactly the same:

```
10 FOR BEANS = 1 TO 3
20   PRINT BEANS; "   HELLO"
30 NEXT BEANS
RUN
 1   HELLO
 2   HELLO
 3   HELLO
Ok
```

As a second example of the use of **FOR** and **NEXT** statements, consider the following program, which reads the names of five people and displays those names in a numbered list. Notice that the statements inside the loop are indented to help the programmer see the loop better.

```
NEW
Ok
10 FOR X = 1 TO 5
20   READ N$
30   PRINT X;N$
40 NEXT X
50 DATA Matt,Sara,Keisha,Lisa,Brad
RUN
 1 Matt
 2 Sara
 3 Keisha
 4 Lisa
 5 Brad
Ok
```

A disadvantage of using **FOR** and **NEXT** statements for loops is that the programmer has to count the number of pieces of data and write that number in the **FOR** statement. In Chapter 4, the **WHILE** and **WEND** statements will be used to overcome this problem.

The **FOR** and **NEXT** statements can be used in the gas mileage program, **GAS3**, to tell the computer how many sets of data are to be processed. In the program listing on the next page, line **2700** was added to define the beginning of the loop and to indicate the number of times the loop is to be executed (three in this case). Note that the **READ** statement was moved to line **2900** so that it was inside the loop. However, lines **2400** and **2500**, the chart headings, are not inside the loop because if they were, every time the loop was executed the headings would appear (this would make the output rather cluttered). The statement **3450 NEXT ENTRY** defines the end of the loop. Also, two more sets of data were added to the bottom of the program and the lines inside the loop were indented to make it clear that they are a part of the loop. **LOAD** the new version of the program, **LIST** it, **SAVE** it to your *BASIC Data* diskette, and then **RUN** it as follows:

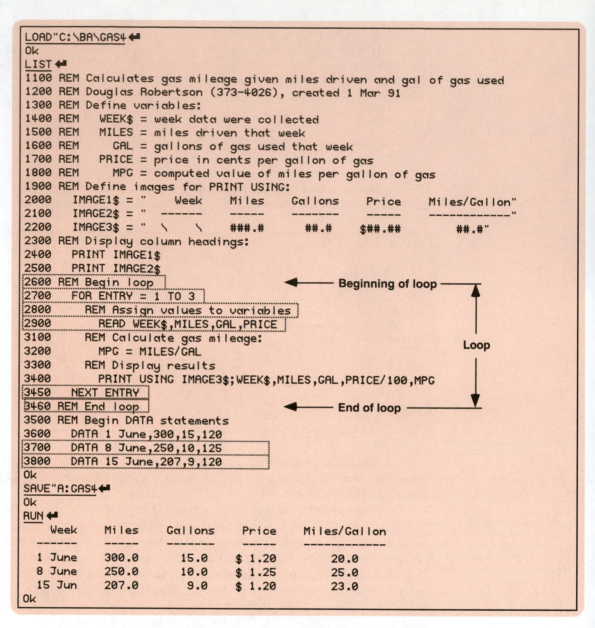

```
LOAD"C:\BA\GAS4
Ok
LIST
1100 REM Calculates gas mileage given miles driven and gal of gas used
1200 REM Douglas Robertson (373-4026), created 1 Mar 91
1300 REM Define variables:
1400 REM   WEEK$ = week data were collected
1500 REM   MILES = miles driven that week
1600 REM     GAL = gallons of gas used that week
1700 REM   PRICE = price in cents per gallon of gas
1800 REM     MPG = computed value of miles per gallon of gas
1900 REM Define images for PRINT USING:
2000   IMAGE1$ = "   Week      Miles     Gallons     Price     Miles/Gallon"
2100   IMAGE2$ = "  ------     -----     -------     -----     ------------"
2200   IMAGE3$ = "  \     \    ###.#       ##.#     $##.##          ##.#"
2300 REM Display column headings:
2400   PRINT IMAGE1$
2500   PRINT IMAGE2$
2600 REM Begin loop                          <—— Beginning of loop
2700   FOR ENTRY = 1 TO 3
2800     REM Assign values to variables
2900       READ WEEK$,MILES,GAL,PRICE
3100     REM Calculate gas mileage:              Loop
3200       MPG = MILES/GAL
3300     REM Display results
3400       PRINT USING IMAGE3$;WEEK$,MILES,GAL,PRICE/100,MPG
3450   NEXT ENTRY
3460 REM End loop                            <—— End of loop
3500 REM Begin DATA statements
3600   DATA 1 June,300,15,120
3700   DATA 8 June,250,10,125
3800   DATA 15 June,207,9,120
Ok
SAVE"A:GAS4
Ok
RUN
   Week      Miles     Gallons     Price     Miles/Gallon
  ------     -----     -------     -----     ------------
  1 June     300.0      15.0     $ 1.20          20.0
  8 June     250.0      10.0     $ 1.25          25.0
  15 Jun     207.0       9.0     $ 1.20          23.0
Ok
```

Notice what happens if the **PRINT** statements for the column headings were placed inside the loop (i.e., if the **FOR** statement was placed at line **2250** rather than at line **2700**):

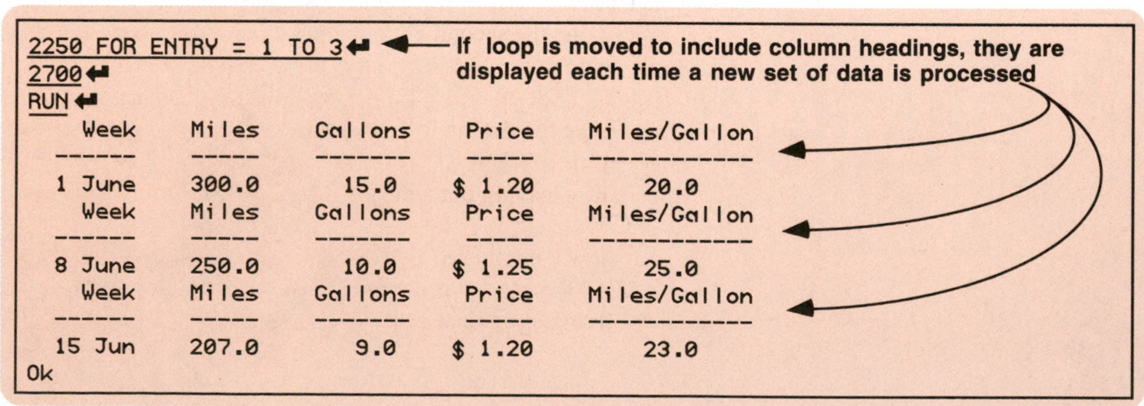

```
2250 FOR ENTRY = 1 TO 3
2700
RUN
   Week      Miles     Gallons     Price     Miles/Gallon
  ------     -----     -------     -----     ------------
  1 June     300.0      15.0     $ 1.20          20.0
   Week      Miles     Gallons     Price     Miles/Gallon
  ------     -----     -------     -----     ------------
  8 June     250.0      10.0     $ 1.25          25.0
   Week      Miles     Gallons     Price     Miles/Gallon
  ------     -----     -------     -----     ------------
  15 Jun     207.0       9.0     $ 1.20          23.0
Ok
```

If loop is moved to include column headings, they are displayed each time a new set of data is processed

A Temperature Conversion Program

The following program provides another example of the use of **FOR/NEXT** loops. The program reads temperatures in degrees Fahrenheit (at line **2300**) and converts them into degrees centigrade (at line **2400**). The program executes the loop exactly five times (i.e., until the last piece of data has been read and processed). Note that lines **2200** through **2600** are indented indicating that this is a loop and note the use of comments on the ends of lines **2100** through **2600**. **LOAD** the program, **LIST** it, **SAVE** it to your *BASIC Data* diskette, and then **RUN** it as shown below:

```
LOAD"C:\BA\TEMPCON1↵
Ok
LIST↵
1100 REM Converts degrees Fahrenheit into degrees centigrade
1200 REM Douglas Robertson (373-4026), created 1 Mar 91
1300 REM Define variables;
1400 REM  ENTRY = Loop variable
1500 REM    F = degrees Fahrenheit read from DATA list
1600 REM   C$ = comment on degrees Fahrenheit
1700 REM    C = calculated degrees centigrade
1800 REM Define images for PRINT USING:
1900   IMAGE1$ = "Degrees F   Degrees C    Comments"
2000   IMAGE2$ = "  ###.#        ###.#     \                    \
2100 PRINT IMAGE1$                            'Display heading
2200   FOR ENTRY = 1 TO 5                     'Begin loop
2300     READ F,C$                            'Assign values to variables
2400     C = 5/9*(F - 32)                     'Compute degrees centigrade
2500     PRINT USING IMAGE2$;F,C,C$           'Display results
2600   NEXT ENTRY                             'End loop
2700 REM Begin DATA statements
2800   DATA 212,Water boils
2900   DATA 98.6,Body temperature
3000   DATA 68,Room temperature
3100   DATA 32,Water freezes
3200   DATA -40,Really cold
Ok
SAVE"A:TEMPCON1↵
Ok
RUN↵
Degrees F   Degrees C    Comments
  212.0       100.0      Water boils
   98.6        37.0      Body temperature
   68.0        20.0      Room temperature
   32.0         0.0      Water freezes
  -40.0       -40.0      Really cold
Ok
```

Each set of data in the above program consisted of a pair of values—the first was the temperature in degrees Fahrenheit and the second was a comment about the temperature. Each set (pair) of data was placed on a separate line in the **DATA** statements in order to help the programmer clearly see the data. Of course, the computer does not care if all the data are on one line or on many lines, but it is usually easier for a human to see the data in logical sets rather than in one long line. Entering data in logical sets like this takes a little extra time (you have to type the word **DATA** more often) but it reduces the chances of inadvertently leaving out a piece of data.

Writing Programs

Now that you know a number of BASIC statements and can write simple programs, it is time to examine in more detail the general process of writing computer programs. We want to develop a general procedure for solving a problem using the computer.

Programmers have to be very careful when thinking about using the computer to solve problems. Sometimes it is easier and faster to solve problems by hand than it is to use the computer. Generally, if the problem does not involve a large amount of data or if the program will not be used over and over again, then using the computer to solve the problem will probably take more time than doing it by hand. Use the computer only when it is appropriate to do so.

Writing programs is both an art and a skill. There is no set procedure for doing it, but there are some general guidelines that can be followed to make the process more efficient. The key to writing good programs is to do a lot of thinking about the problem and planning what you are going to do before you sit down in front of the computer and begin typing. The procedure outlined in the next section can be used to help in that thought process.

General Procedure for Writing Programs

As an example of the process for writing computer programs, let's redo the wages program, **WAGES1** (see p. B47), but this time with loops so that the program will calculate the pay earned for any number of employees, given their hourly rates of pay and the number of hours they work in a week. As we go through the example, be sure to focus your attention on the process being used and not on "getting the answer." If you just wanted the answer you could do the problem by hand in about ten seconds. This programming procedure is one of the most important aspects of being able to use the computer to solve problems.

• The Task •

Write a program that will calculate the pay for each worker in a particular company and produce a table showing the name, pay rate, number of hours worked, and total pay of each worker.

• Step 1: Justify Using the Computer •

Decide if the computer is the proper tool to use to solve the problem. This may seem like an obvious step, but it is an important one. You want to be sure that using the computer to solve the problem is the right thing to do (i.e., will it save time, resources, and money?). It makes no sense to suggest an expensive high-tech solution to a problem that could be solved more quickly, easily, and cheaply using low-tech methods. In this example, if you just wanted to figure the pay for one person you would not use the computer; you would simply multiply on a calculator the hours a person has worked by his/her rate of pay and write down the answer. Writing a program to do this would be a waste of time and resources.

As a justification for using the computer for this problem, assume that you want to use the program every week to compute the pay for 500 employees. In that case, using the computer is appropriate.

• Step 2: Define the Problem •

Describe the problem in detail in terms of its desired output, the processing needed to produce the output, and the input needed in order to do the processing.

There are three basic parts in the definition of the problem:

- Output: What will the program instruct the computer to produce?
- Processing: How will the output be produced (what operations must be performed, and in what order, to produce the output)?
- Input: What data must be supplied to enable the computer to do the processing and generate the output?

Output Before you can begin to write the program, you need to have a specific goal in mind. That goal, of course, is the final output. It is important to decide right from the beginning exactly what it is that you wish to accomplish with the program.

Determining the exact nature of the output at the beginning of the programming procedure helps to organize your thoughts and to clarify the objective. If the program is being written for someone else, this step will help in the communication process between programmer and supervisor to make sure that the final program will perform according to the wishes of the person who wants the problem solved.

It is a good idea to include some real data along with the answers in the description of the output. For this problem, the output is to be the following chart:

```
Employee        Pay Rate        Hours    Total Pay
--------        --------        -----    ---------
Roberts Matt    $ 4.00          30.0     $120.00
Sim Keisha      $ 3.00          50.0     $150.00
Tech Sara       $ 6.00          21.0     $126.00
Well Vanessa    $ 5.00          40.0     $200.00

All data read, processing complete
```

Processing You must figure out how each piece of output will be generated. Remember, the computer is only a machine that cannot solve problems without being told exactly what to do. Think of the computer as a tool of the programmer in the same way that a hammer is a tool of a carpenter. The carpenter does not expect the hammer to build a house by itself. The carpenter builds the house and uses the hammer to make the job easier. Likewise, the programmer must already know how to solve the problem before she or he can use the computer as a tool in the problem solving process.

To get an idea of what information needs to be processed, we can look at the structure of the output and determine which parts are descriptive (e.g., column headings), which parts are supplied as data (e.g., names, rates of pay, and hours worked), and which parts are calculated (e.g., total pay). The output for this problem consists of six basic parts:

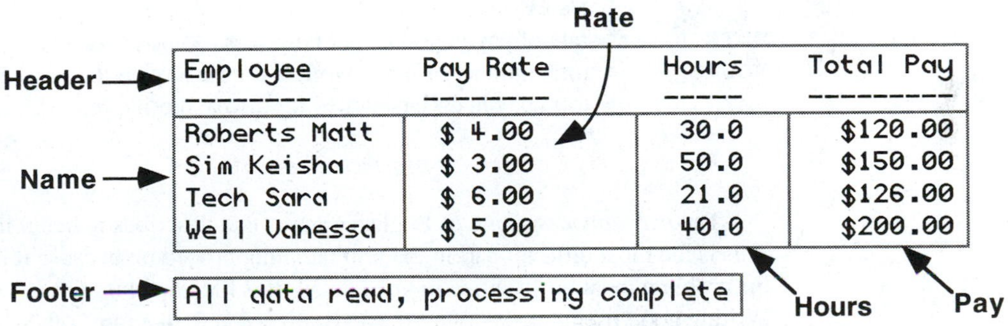

```
                                      Rate
Header --> Employee        Pay Rate          Hours    Total Pay
           --------        --------          -----    ---------
           Roberts Matt    $ 4.00  <--       30.0     $120.00
Name   --> Sim Keisha      $ 3.00            50.0     $150.00
           Tech Sara       $ 6.00            21.0     $126.00
           Well Vanessa    $ 5.00            40.0     $200.00
                                              ^          ^
Footer --> All data read, processing complete Hours      Pay
```

For each of these parts, do the following:

- Determine the origin of the information (where did the information come from? is it only descriptive? is it supplied as raw data? is it calculated?).
- Determine what other data are needed to produce it (e.g. the names are supplied by the **DATA** statements but the pay is calculated from the hours and rates).
- Determine where that data came from.

Each piece of information in the output for the wages program can be defined as follows:

Header: Descriptive information including the column headings.

Name: The names of the people in the form **Lastname** space **Firstname**. These are supplied by the **DATA** statements.

Rate: The rates of pay in dollars per hour. These are supplied by the **DATA** statements.

Hours: The hours worked in hours per week. These are supplied by the **DATA** statements.

Pay: The wages earned in dollars. These are calculated using **Pay = Rate*Hours**. If the problem were more complex, the number of calculations would be much greater and the types of calculations would be more complex. For example, you would need other formulas if the program were required to calculate federal, state, and social security withholding taxes.

Footer: Descriptive information indicating that all the data have been processed.

Input Now you must determine what input is needed in order to accomplish the processing outlined above and to produce the final output. For this simple problem, this has already been done because the data that must be input are listed in the chart. They are name of employee, rate of pay, and hours worked.

• Step 3: Define the Program Variables •

At this point, you know what you want to produce (the output), how it will be produced (the formulas needed for the computations), and what information is needed to do the computations (the input data). You can now define the variables to be used in the program.

Referring back to the table, it should be clear that the values that are read in as data (name, rate, and hours) or calculated from data (pay) should be assigned to variables. Along with the definition, an example of the information should be given so that it is clear what the structure of the data will be. For example:

EMPLOYEE$ = name of the employee in the form **Lastname** space **Firstname** (e.g., **Roberts Matt**)
RATE = rate of pay in dollars per hour (e.g., **3**)
HOURS = total number of hours worked for the pay period (e.g., **50**)
PAY = total pay in dollars earned for the pay period (e.g., **150**)

• Step 4: Construct the Pseudocode •

The *pseudocode* is a set of English phrases that describes in detail how the problem will be solved. This is the most difficult part in the programming procedure because it is where the logic used to solve the problem must be specified in great detail. It is like the blueprint in the construction of a house. Writing good pseudocode takes time and patience and, like most other forms of writing, many drafts before the final version is complete. Take your time and think through all the steps.

You may wonder why you don't just write the program in BASIC and be done with it. The reason is that English is probably the language you use most often to converse in and the one that you know best. You are used to thinking in English and communicating your thoughts to others in English. BASIC is similar to English, but it is very picky in its syntax (e.g., if a comma is inserted in place of a semicolon, the entire meaning of a statement may change). When you are trying to come up with the solution to a difficult problem you need to be able to concentrate on finding the solution to the problem and not on what type of punctuation to use. You need to focus on the logic of the problem-solving process rather than on the details of the language used to outline the solution to the problem.

For example, if this book were to be used in Mexico, it would have to be written in Spanish. However, our Spanish is not good enough to enable us to think of, or even communicate, all the ideas we want to present. Therefore, we would write the book in English where the vocabulary and grammar are easy for us and then translate it into Spanish. During that translation, we would have to constantly refer to a Spanish dictionary and grammar book to be sure that the way we were writing the ideas was correct for that language. Similarly, it will be easier for you to write your programs in English (which should be relatively easy for you) first and then translate them into BASIC (where you will have to worry about using the correct syntax and vocabulary).

Now, let's write the pseudocode. While constructing the pseudocode, it is helpful to look at the structure of the output as described in Step 2.

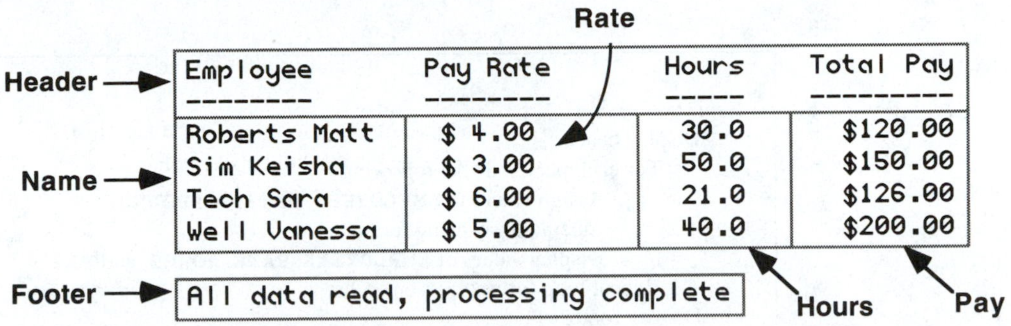

```
Employee          Pay Rate      Hours     Total Pay
--------          --------      -----     ---------
Roberts Matt      $ 4.00        30.0      $120.00
Sim Keisha        $ 3.00        50.0      $150.00
Tech Sara         $ 6.00        21.0      $126.00
Well Vanessa      $ 5.00        40.0      $200.00

All data read, processing complete
```

Thought Process	***Pseudocode***
Indicate the beginning of the program.	Begin processing
The output is produced from left to right and from top to bottom. The first part of the output is a column heading.	Display header
The next four lines of output contain the individual data for each person. The program must do a number of things for each person in the data list.	For each person do the following
For each individual, the raw data for **EMPLOYEE**, **RATE**, and **HOURS** must be supplied and assigned to memory cells.	Assign values to **EMPLOYEE$**, **RATE**, and **HOURS**
For each individual, the **PAY** is calculated from the input data. Thus, before the value can be displayed, it must be calculated.	Calculate pay using formula
The information for a single individual now is ready to be displayed.	Display values of **EMPLOYEE$**, **RATE**, **HOURS**, and **PAY**
With the exception of the document footer, all subsequent lines of output are the same as line three but with different data. This indicates that the end of a loop has been reached and that the same process must be repeated over and over until all the data have been used.	Repeat loop for next person on list

Continued . . .

Thought Process	Pseudocode
After all the data have been entered and processed, the program can display the document footer.	Display footer
The last piece of output has been displayed, so the program can end.	End processing

The pseudocode can be summarized as follows:

```
Begin processing
    Display header
        For each person do the following
            Assign values to EMPLOYEE$, RATE, and HOURS
            Calculate pay using formula
            Display values of EMPLOYEE$, RATE, HOURS, and PAY
        Repeat loop for next person on list
    Display footer
End processing
```

Read over the pseudocode to see if it accurately describes what the program is supposed to do. The program begins by displaying the column headings. Next, there is a loop where the data for each person are entered and the computations are carried out in the same fashion for every employee. The loop contains a series of sequences that are followed in order, one at a time. When it has finished processing the information for the first person, the computer goes back to the beginning of the loop and goes through the same process for the next person. This continues until the pay of every employee has been calculated and the results have been displayed. Finally, the document footer is displayed. This pseudocode will work whether we have 2 or 200 employees.

Some programmers like to use *flowcharts* in addition to, or in place of, a pseudocode. A flowchart is a visual representation of the logic of the program—it does in pictures what the pseudocode does in words. Using flowcharts allows you to see graphically how the logic of the program is structured and how the pieces fit together. A flowchart for the preceding program would look like the following (for more information on flowcharts, see p. B286–88 of the Appendix):

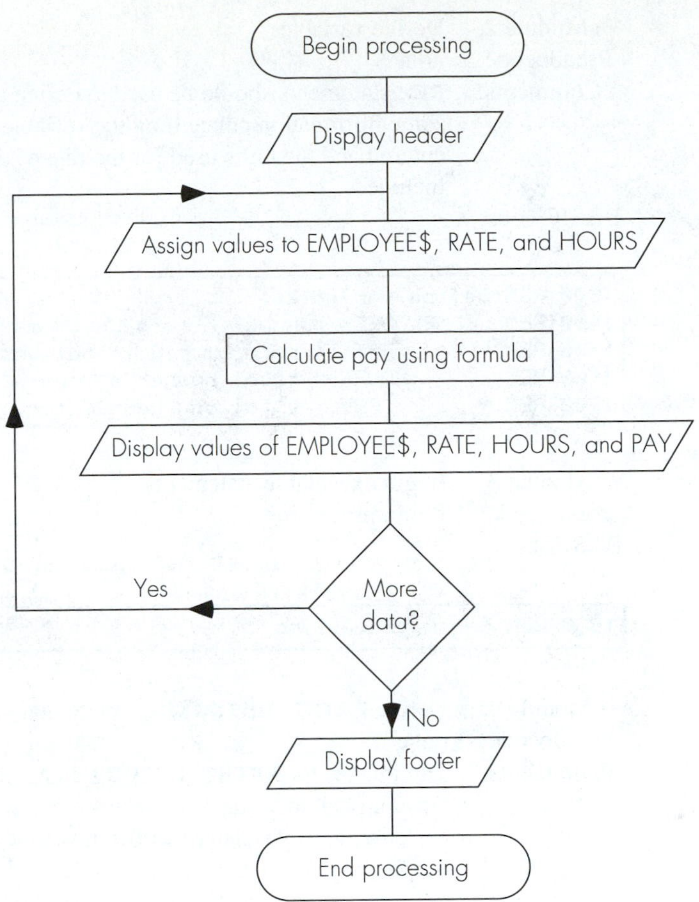

• *Step 5: Calculate the Answers* •

Using the pseudocode, check the answers on this small set of test data in order to gain some confidence that the logic outlined in the pseudocode is correct. The answers should be the same as those listed in the chart in Step 2.

• *Step 6: Translate the Pseudocode into BASIC* •

The translation into BASIC code is mostly just a rewrite of the pseudocode so that it follows the BASIC syntax. In many cases, a phrase in the pseudocode becomes a part of the BASIC code in the form of a **REM** statement. The translation process is done by thinking of the program as a set of modules, each of which has a specific function. Some of the modules are very short (one statement) while others are longer.

Module 1: Identify what the program does and who created it.
Pseudocode: none
BASIC code:

```
1100 REM Program to compute wages given total hours worked and pay rate
1200 REM Douglas Robertson (373-4026), created 1 Mar 91
```

Module 2: Define variables.
Pseudocode: none
Comments: **REM** statements should be used to define the variables used in the program. Note that some information concerning the variables (e.g., the way the employee name is to be entered and the units used for the rate of pay) is given and a set of sample data is included.
BASIC code:

```
1300 REM Define variables:
1400 REM   EMPLOYEE$ = name in form LastName Space First (e.g., Roberts Matt)
1500 REM        RATE = rate of pay in dollars per hour (e.g.,  3)
1600 REM       HOURS = total number of hours worked for pay period (e.g., 50)
1700 REM         PAY = total pay earned for pay period (e.g., 150)
```

Module 3: Begin executable statements.
Pseudocode: Begin processing.
BASIC code:

```
1800 REM Begin processing
```

Module 4: Define **PRINT USING** image statements.
Pseudocode: none
Comments: The images for **PRINT USING** statements should be defined in a single location. Grouping all the images together in this way makes lining up the columns in the chart easier to do. In fact, lines **2000** through **2300** look like an abbreviated version of the output.
BASIC code:

```
1900   REM Define PRINT USING images
2000     IMAGE1$ = "Employee          Pay Rate       Hours    Total Pay"
2100     IMAGE2$ = "--------          --------       -----    ---------"
2200     IMAGE3$ = "\               \  $##.##         ##.#      $###.##"
2300     IMAGE4$ = "All data read, processing complete"
```

Module 5: Display column heading.
Pseudocode: Display header
BASIC code:

```
2400   PRINT IMAGE1$                              'Display header
2500   PRINT IMAGE2$                              'Display header
```

Module 6: Mark beginning of the loop.
Pseudocode: For each person do the following
BASIC code:

```
2600     FOR NUM = 1 TO 4                         'For each person do the following
```

Module 7: Assign values to variables.
Pseudocode: Assign values to **EMPLOYEE$**, **RATE**, and **HOURS**
BASIC code:

```
2700         READ EMPLOYEE$,RATE,HOURS          'Assign values to name, rate, hours
```

Module 8: Compute pay.
Pseudocode: Calculate pay using formula
BASIC code:

```
2800         PAY = RATE*HOURS                   'Calculate pay using formula
```

Module 9: Display main body of table.
Pseudocode: Display values of **EMPLOYEE$**, **RATE**, **HOURS**, and **PAY**
BASIC code:

```
2900         PRINT USING IMAGE3$;EMPLOYEE$,RATE,HOURS,PAY
```

Module 10: Mark end of loop.
Pseudocode: Repeat loop for next person on list
BASIC code:

```
3000      NEXT NUM                              'Repeat loop for next person
```

Module 11: Display footer.
Pseudocode: Display footer
BASIC code:

```
3100   PRINT
3200   PRINT IMAGE4$                            'Display footer
```

Module 12: Mark the end of the executable statements.
Pseudocode: End processing
BASIC code:

```
3300 REM End processing
```

Module 13: List program data.
Pseudocode: none
Comment: Note that the structure of the data is outlined (as a reminder).
BASIC code:

```
3400 REM Define DATA list in form:
3500 REM DATA NAME           ,RATE,HOURS
3600     DATA Roberts Matt,   4,   30
3700     DATA Sim Keisha  ,   3,   50
3800     DATA Tech Sara   ,   6,   21
3900     DATA Well Vanessa,   5,   40
```

The program in its entirety is shown in Step 7.

• Step 7: Type the Program •

All that is left to do is to type the program into the computer, save it, and run it. Notice that the problem was solved and the program written before you came near the computer. If the steps up to this point have been carefully executed, the program should run correctly the first time without modification. **LOAD** the program, **LIST** it, and **SAVE** it to your *BASIC Data* diskette as follows:

```
LOAD"C:\BA\WAGES2↵
Ok
LIST↵
1100 REM Program to compute wages given total hours worked and pay rate
1200 REM Douglas Robertson (373-4026), created 1 Mar 91
1300 REM Define variables:
1400 REM   EMPLOYEE$ = name in form LastName Space First (e.g., Roberts Matt)
1500 REM        RATE = rate of pay in dollars per hour (e.g.,  3)
1600 REM       HOURS = total number of hours worked for pay period (e.g., 50)
1700 REM         PAY = total pay earned for pay period (e.g., 150)
1800 REM Begin processing
1900   REM Define PRINT USING images
2000     IMAGE1$ = "Employee       Pay Rate       Hours    Total Pay"
2100     IMAGE2$ = "--------       --------       -----    ---------"
2200     IMAGE3$ = "\            \  $##.##         ##.#      $####.##"
2300     IMAGE4$ = "All data read, processing complete"
2400   PRINT IMAGE1$                             'Display header
2500   PRINT IMAGE2$                             'Display header
2600     FOR NUM = 1 TO 4                        'For each person do the following
2700       READ EMPLOYEE$,RATE,HOURS             'Assign values to name, rate, hours
2800       PAY = RATE*HOURS                      'Calculate pay using formula
2900       PRINT USING IMAGE3$;EMPLOYEE$,RATE,HOURS,PAY
3000     NEXT NUM                                'Repeat loop for next person
3100   PRINT
3200   PRINT IMAGE4$                             'Display footer
3300 REM End processing
3400 REM Define DATA list in form:
3500 REM DATA NAME         ,RATE,HOURS
3600     DATA Roberts Matt,   4,   30
3700     DATA Sim Keisha  ,   3,   50
3800     DATA Tech Sara   ,   6,   21
3900     DATA Well Vanessa,   5,   40
Ok
SAVE"A:WAGES2↵
Ok
```

• Step 8: Run the Program •

```
RUN↵
Employee        Pay Rate       Hours    Total Pay
--------        --------       -----    ---------
Roberts Matt     $ 4.00         30.0     $120.00
Sim Keisha       $ 3.00         50.0     $150.00
Tech Sara        $ 6.00         21.0     $126.00
Well Vanessa     $ 5.00         40.0     $200.00

All data read, processing complete
Ok
```

• Step 9: Check the Computer's Results •

If the answers check, you can be somewhat confident that the program is correct. To gain more confidence, you could use another set of test data and compare the computer's answers with those calculated by hand. You might even try to put in some strange data (e.g., a pay rate of –2 or hours worked equal to 500) and see what the program does. We will discuss checking for the reasonableness of data and errors in data in Chapter 5 (p. B178–82). For now, we will assume the data are reasonable.

If the answers do not check, the program must be debugged (i.e., the errors must be located and corrected).

• Step 10: Debug the Program •

If the program aborts before completion or if the computer output does not match the hand calculations, you will have to spend some time debugging (fixing) the program.

The most common error for programs that do not run to completion are syntax errors such as the following:

- Spelling—for example, using **PRITN** rather than **PRINT**.
- Mismatched variable types—for example, using a numeric variable in a **READ** statement to input a string, as in:

```
2700 READ EMPLOYEE,RATE,HOURS
3600 DATA Roberts Matt,    4,    30
```

Or using a numeric variable to store a string, as in:

```
2000 IMAGE1 = "Employee"
```

- Leaving off the quotation marks around a string—for example:

```
2000 IMAGE1$ = Employee
```

- Missing or incorrect delimiters—for example, typing a decimal point (period) in place of a comma, as in:

```
3600 DATA Roberts Matt,    4.   30
```

- Incorrect syntax in statements—for example, using a comma rather than a semicolon just before the variable list in a **PRINT USING** statement, as in:

```
2900 PRINT USING IMAGE3$,EMPLOYEE$,RATE,HOURS,PAY
```

- Neglecting to write the word **REM** at the beginning of a remark statement—for example:

```
100 Program to compute wages.
```

If the program runs and gives you no error messages but the answers are not correct, check to see if the values in the **DATA** statements are correct (i.e., did you make a typographic error when entering the data?). Also, check the values of any other numbers that might be contained in **LET** or **PRINT** statements.

If you still cannot find the error, the problem may be in the logic of the program. This type of error is more serious because it implies a flaw in the design of the program structure itself. These errors are generally more difficult to find and correct, but you might try doing the following:

- Check the translation of the program from the pseudocode into BASIC code. Do the BASIC statements and the pseudocode say the same thing? You might want to turn on the **TRACE** function (press **[F7]**) to tell the computer to display each line number as it is executed. Are the line numbers executed in the proper order? Tracking the program execution in this way is time consuming but may prove fruitful. To turn **TRACE** off, press **[F8]**.
- If the translation seems correct, then check the pseudocode. It is human nature, especially when it comes to students writing computer programs, to want to spend time writing the BASIC code and watching it run rather than thinking about the logic of the program and writing the pseudocode. If you rushed through the planning stage, there is a good possibility that your final program will not do the job you intended. Check the pseudocode carefully and if you find errors, make the necessary corrections to the pseudocode and then to the BASIC code.

Remember, the computer always follows instructions to the letter. If there is a mistake, you told the program to instruct the computer to do something that was incorrect. Make any corrections that are necessary and run the program again.

Following the programming procedure described here may be difficult and time consuming for you at first. Typically, novice programmers are anxious to get to the machine and start typing BASIC code to see if a new program works. The exciting part of programming is typing **RUN** and watching the output appear on the screen. However, you must be patient. The time you spend thinking and planning will be returned to you tenfold in the end because your programs will contain few, if any, errors.

Think of writing a program as building a house. Before you invest a lot of time and money on materials and labor, you do a lot of planning. What should the house look like? What materials should be used? Where should the doors and windows be placed? Once the plan has been completely thought out, construction begins. If, after the house has been built, you decide to move a door or add a window, you can do it but it will be costly and time consuming. It would have been cheaper and easier to have made that change on the drawings before construction was started. The same is true for computer programs. The more planning you do before the program is coded into BASIC, the better will be the final product.

Using WordPerfect to Help Write BASIC Programs

You probably noticed that the programming process described in the previous section involves a lot of thinking and writing. The writing part, at least, can be made less tedious if you use WordPerfect as your basic writing tool. For example, let's use the first program presented in this chapter (the one that calculated sales tax) to illustrate how the variable definitions, pseudocode, and final program can be developed and edited in the WordPerfect environment and then loaded and run in the BASIC environment.

Exit BASIC and return to DOS by typing **SYSTEM ↵**. Then start the WordPerfect program by typing **C:\WP51\WP ↵** (for a hard-disk system) or **B:WP ↵** (for a two-drive system—of course, you must insert your *WordPerfect Program* diskette into drive B: before typing this).

After the blank WordPerfect screen appears, type the following variable definition and pseudocode:

```
Variable definitions:
  P = price in dollars (e.g., 8000)

Pseudocode:
Begin processing
  Ask user to enter item price
  Assign price to P
  Calculate tax
  Display tax
End processing
▬
```

To translate the variable definition and pseudocode into BASIC syntax requires editing in the form of adding lines of code, inserting line numbers, and inserting BASIC key words such as **`PRINT`**. Begin by typing the first two lines of the program:

```
Variable definitions:
  P = price in dollars (e.g., 8000)

Pseudocode:
Begin processing
  Ask user to enter item price
  Assign price to P
  Calculate tax
  Display tax
End processing

1100 REM Calculates sales tax
1200 REM Douglas Robertson (373-4026), created 1 Mar 91
▬
```

First two lines of the program

Make a copy of the variable definition and pseudocode and place it at the end of the program:

Keystroke	***Action Resulting from Keystroke***
[arrow]	Use the **[arrow]** keys (or use the mouse) to move the cursor to the first letter of the first word **`Variable`** (location **`Ln 1" Pos 1"`**).
[Alt-F4]	Specifies the beginning of the block.
[arrow]	Use the **[arrow]** keys to move the cursor to the end of the last phrase **`End processing`** (location **`Ln 2.5" Pos 2.4"`**).
[Ctrl-F4]	Specifies that the selected block is to be operated on.
`B` (or **`1`**)	Selects **`1 Block`**.

Continued . . .

Keystroke	Action Resulting from Keystroke
C (or **2**)	Selects **2 Copy**.
[arrow]	Use the **[arrow]** keys to move cursor so that it is just below the last line of the program (location **Ln 3.17" Pos 1"**).
[Enter]	Specifies that the block is to be moved and pastes it at the location of the cursor.

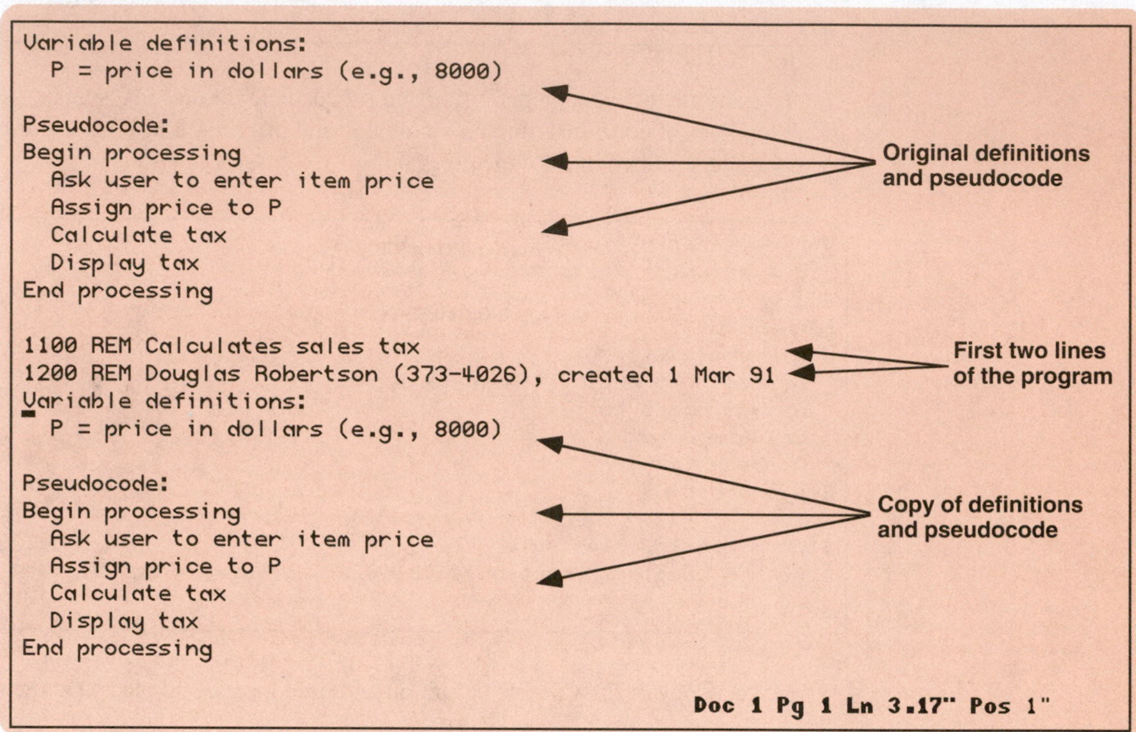

```
Variable definitions:
  P = price in dollars (e.g., 8000)

Pseudocode:
Begin processing
  Ask user to enter item price
  Assign price to P
  Calculate tax
  Display tax
End processing

1100 REM Calculates sales tax
1200 REM Douglas Robertson (373-4026), created 1 Mar 91
Variable definitions:
  P = price in dollars (e.g., 8000)

Pseudocode:
Begin processing
  Ask user to enter item price
  Assign price to P
  Calculate tax
  Display tax
End processing

                                   Doc 1 Pg 1 Ln 3.17" Pos 1"
```


Edit the copy of the variable definition and pseudocode so that it follows BASIC syntax (i.e., add line numbers, combine some of the pseudocode phrases into **REM** statements, insert **REM**, **INPUT**, and **PRINT** key words, and insert the mathematical calculation). When done, the program should look as follows (the added text is enclosed in dotted boxes):

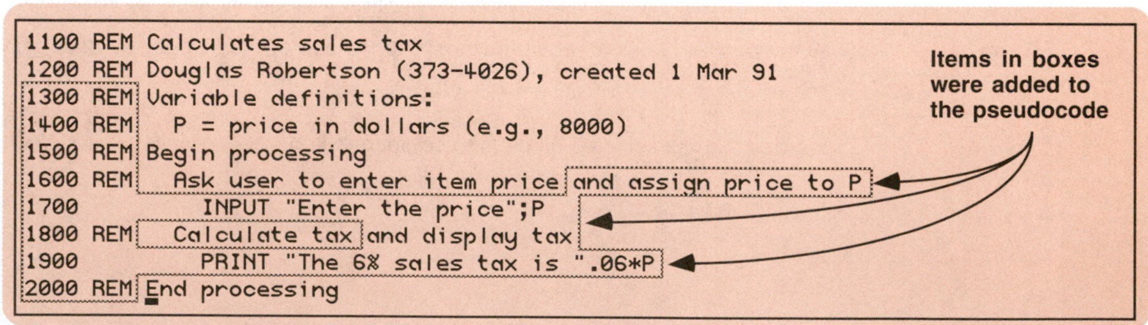

```
1100 REM Calculates sales tax
1200 REM Douglas Robertson (373-4026), created 1 Mar 91
1300 REM Variable definitions:
1400 REM   P = price in dollars (e.g., 8000)
1500 REM Begin processing
1600 REM   Ask user to enter item price and assign price to P
1700         INPUT "Enter the price";P
1800 REM   Calculate tax and display tax
1900         PRINT "The 6% sales tax is ".06*P
2000 REM End processing
```

To protect against accidental loss, save the WordPerfect document (use the **[F10]** key) using the name **A:TAX.WP**. The **WP** extension indicates that this is a WordPerfect file.

The program is complete. It now must be saved as an ASCII (text) file so that it can be accessed by BASIC. First, delete the text that is not part of the program and then save what is left (i.e., the program) as an ASCII file.

Keystroke	Action Resulting from Keystroke
[Home] [Home] ↵	Moves the cursor to the top of the document.
[Alt-F4]	Specifies the beginning of the block.
[arrow]	Use the **[arrow]** keys to move the cursor to the beginning of the program (the **1** in line number **1100** at location **Ln 2.83" Pos 1"**).
[Delete]	Specifies that the selected block is to be deleted.
Y	Confirms that the block is to be deleted. Now, only the program should remain.
[Ctrl-F5]	Selects the *Text In/Out* feature.
T (or **1**)	Specifies that the file is to be treated as a DOS text file.
S (or **1**)	Specifies that the file is to be saved.
A:TAX.BAS ↵	Specifies the name of the file and saves the program. The **BAS** extension indicates that the file will be used by BASIC.
[F7]	Exits this document.
N	Specifies that the file is not to be saved.
Y	Specifies that WordPerfect is to be exited and returns to DOS.

Now load and run the program in BASIC.

Keystroke	Action Resulting from Keystroke
C:\BA\BASICA ↵	Accesses BASIC from the hard drive (if you are using a two-drive system, place the *BASIC Program* diskette in drive B: and type **B:BASICA ↵**).
LOAD"A:TAX ↵	Loads the program **TAX.BAS** from the diskette in drive A:

Continued . . .

Keystroke	Action Resulting from Keystroke
LIST ↵	Lists the program.
RUN ↵	Runs the program.

```
LOAD"A:TAX ↵
Ok
LIST ↵
1100 REM Calculates sales tax
1200 REM Douglas Robertson (373-4026), created 1 Mar 91
1300 REM Variable definitions:
1400 REM   P = price in dollars (e.g., 8000)
1500 REM Begin processing
1600 REM   Ask user to enter item price and assign price to P
1700         INPUT "Enter the price";P
1800 REM   Calculate tax and display tax
1900         PRINT "The 6% sales tax is ".06*P
2000 REM End processing
Ok
RUN ↵
Enter the price? 20 ↵
The 6% sales tax is  1.2
Ok
```

Writing carefully thought-out and well-documented programs takes time and energy. However, using WordPerfect to help with the writing task will save you time in the long run, especially for the long and complex programs you will be writing in later chapters.

TO TAKE A BREAK Type **SYSTEM ↵**, remove diskette(s). To resume (hard disk): Insert *Data* diskette, type **A: ↵**, **C:\BA\BASICA ↵**. To resume (two drive): Insert diskettes; type **A: ↵**, **B:\BASICA ↵**.

Homework Exercises

For each of the following homework exercises, write a BASIC program that will produce the output described. Each program should contain enough **REM** statements to clearly document the program. Unless instructed to do otherwise, produce a hard copy of a **LIST** and a **RUN** of each of your final working programs. Also, save each program using a name such as **HWB3-01** for future reference. Your instructor may also ask you to hand in other materials related to the development of the programs such as the variable definitions and pseudocodes.

---

① For young adults, the approximate relation between height and weight is given by the formula:

$$W = 5.5(H - 40)$$

where

W= the person's weight in pounds

H= the person's height in inches

Use the programming procedure discussed in this chapter to develop an interactive program (using **INPUT** statements) that computes a person's ideal weight when his or her name and height in inches are entered.

Use the name **Matt** and a height of **50** inches to make the output look like that given below. The underlined parts are to be typed by the user via an **INPUT** statement and the value in the box should be calculated by the computer. The name **Matt** in the last line of output is to be printed by a **PRINT** statement using the same variable as was used in the **INPUT** statement.

```
Homework B3-01                  Joe Computer                  1 Mar 91

Enter your name and height in inches? Matt,50 ↵
Matt, your ideal weight is [55] pounds.
```

---

② Modify the program in Exercise 1 so that it reads the person's name and height from a **DATA** statement instead of an **INPUT** statement and produces output similar to that of the program in Exercise 1.

---

③ Modify the program in Exercise 2 so that it reads the person's name and height from a **DATA** statement and has a **FOR/NEXT** loop to produce output similar to that given below (use **50** inches for **Matt's** height, **65** inches for **Sara's** height and **51** inches for **Britt's** height). The values in the boxes are to be calculated by the computer:

Continued . . .

```
Homework B3-03                   Joe Computer                   1 Mar 91

Matt's height is 50  and his/her ideal weight is 55 pounds.
Sara's height is 65  and his/her ideal weight is 137.5 pounds.
Britt's height is 51  and his/her ideal weight is 60.5 pounds.
```

---

④ For a certain book, the relationship between the number of books printed and the cost of printing is given by **C = 30000 + 4*N** where **C** is the total cost of publishing the book and **N** is the total number of books published.

Use the programming procedure to develop a program that uses **READ** and **DATA** statements and **FOR** and **NEXT** statements to display the table given below. Use **PRINT USING** to display the number of copies as a whole number and to round the dollar values to the nearest cent. The values in the boxes are to be calculated by the computer:

```
Homework B3-04                   Joe Computer                   1 Mar 91

Number of
Copies         Total Cost         Cost per copy
---------      -----------        -------------
      1        $30004.00          $30004.00
    100        $30400.00          $  304.00
   1000        $34000.00          $   34.00
  10000        $70000.00          $    7.00
```

---

⑤ Modify the program you wrote for Exercise 7 in Chapter 2 so that it produces exactly the same output but uses **READ** and **DATA** statements in place of **LET** statements to assign data to variables and uses a **FOR/NEXT** loop to process the information for each employee. The output should look the same as before except for the homework number.

```
Homework B3-05                   Jim Dillemuth                   1 Mar 91

Micro Stuff, Inc.
Employee Sales Records for February, 1991

Employee        Total
Name            Sales     Commission    Total Earnings
--------     --------     ----------    --------------
Britt       $2,130.50       $149.14        $1,149.14
Sally       $3,112.45       $217.87        $1,217.87
```

---

⑥ From June through September, Northern States Power Company charges $.06192 per kilowatt hour (KWH) of electricity, no matter how much electricity a customer uses. It also charges a flat fee of $6.00 per month to help defray the costs of the power system, such as reading the electric meter and keeping accounts. Added to the bill is a city tax of 1.5% and a state tax of 6.0% on the cost of the electricity and the flat fee.

Use the programming procedure and the above information to develop a program that prints a table showing the total monthly electric bill for the three addresses listed below. The program should use **READ** and **DATA** statements to assign values to variables, **FOR** and **NEXT** statements for the loop, and **PRINT USING** statements to make the output look like the following (the values in the boxes are to be calculated by the computer):

```
Homework B3-06                    Joe Computer                    1 Mar 91

Electric Residential costs for June, 1990

                            Basic
                            Energy     Flat     City    State    Total
Address               KWH   Charge      Fee      Tax      Tax   Charge
----------------     ----  -------   ------   ------   ------  -------
5 Elm Street          305  $ 18.89   $ 6.00   $ 0.37   $ 1.49  $ 26.75
8 Perry Court        1902  $117.77   $ 6.00   $ 1.86   $ 7.43  $133.05
2 Adams Avenue       1001  $ 61.98   $ 6.00   $ 1.02   $ 4.08  $ 73.08
```

Decisions and Counting in BASIC

Objectives *After you have completed this chapter, you should be able to:*

- Use **IF/THEN/ELSE** to make simple selections.
- Use **AND** and **OR** to construct complex **IF/THEN/ELSE** conditions.
- Apply the programming procedure to develop a moderately complex program.
- Discuss the need for checking for errors in program data.
- Explain the difference between **FOR/NEXT** and **WHILE/WEND** loops.
- Create loops using **WHILE** and **WEND** statements.

CHAPTER 4

- Define and use data flags.
- Use counters to calculate the sum and average of a set of numbers.
- Define and use subroutines.
- Develop programs with multiple decision conditions.
- Define and use replacement statements.
- Find the largest and smallest number contained in a set of numbers.

Introduction

In this chapter we examine ways to instruct the computer to make decisions and to count and find sums of numbers. Keep in mind throughout all this that the computer is a machine which cannot really think or make decisions on its own. The programmer must think of every contingency and instruct the computer how to respond to every possible combination of events. As you will see, this is no simple task.

IF/THEN/ELSE Statements

FORM

```
Line no.  IF condition THEN Line# ELSE Line#
Line no.  IF condition THEN Statement ELSE Statement
```

EXAMPLE

```
1100      IF X = 2.3 THEN 500 ELSE 600
1200      IF COL$ = "GC" THEN PRINT "Gen Col"
          ELSE PRINT "Other"
1400      IF X + 3*Y < 5 THEN 1500
```

The **IF/THEN/ELSE** statement is called a *conditional transfer statement* because it tells the computer to transfer control to a specific line number (or execute a particular statement) if a certain condition is true and to transfer control to a different line number (or execute a particular statement) if the condition is false. If the **ELSE** part of the statement is omitted, control will automatically go to the next line in the program.

College Selection Program

As an example of the use of the **IF/THEN/ELSE** statement, suppose you were the Dean of the General College of the University of Minnesota and wanted a program that would access the university's student database and provide you with a list of General College students. To make this example easier, let's assume that there are only three students at the university (there actually are 48,000) and that there are only three colleges within the University: the General College (**GC**), the College of Liberal Arts (**CLA**), and the Institute of Technology (**IT**). The program listed below reads the names, colleges, and grade point averages of the students and selects and displays the names of only those students who are registered in the General College. **LOAD** the new version of the program, **LIST** it, **SAVE** it to your *BASIC Data* diskette, and then **RUN** it as shown below:

```
LOAD"C:\BA\SELECT1↵
Ok
LIST↵
1100 FOR N = 1 TO 3
1200    READ N$,C$,GPA         'N$ = name, C$ = college, GPA = Grade Point Average
1300    IF C$ = "GC" THEN PRINT N$
1400 NEXT N
1500    DATA Matt,GC,3.7
1600    DATA Keisha,IT,3.4
1700    DATA Sara,GC,2.8
Ok
SAVE"A:SELECT1↵
Ok
RUN↵
Matt  ◄——  Matt is selected because his college is GC
Sara  ◄——  Sara is selected because her college is GC
Ok
```

Line Numbers	Comments
1100	Marks the beginning of the loop. The loop will be processed exactly three times.
1200	Creates variable locations **N$**, **C$**, and **GPA** and assigns them the values of **Matt**, **GC**, and **3.7**, respectively.
1300	Checks the value of **C$** to see if it is exactly the same as the string **GC**. If it is (i.e., if **C$** contains exactly two characters, the first of which is the uppercase letter **G** and the second is the uppercase letter **C**), the value of **N$** is displayed. If **C$** is not exactly equal to the string **GC**, the **PRINT** statement is not executed and control is transferred to the next line (the **NEXT** statement at line number **1400**), and the next set of data is read.
1400	Marks the end of the loop. Control is transferred back to line **1100** and the process continues until the loop has been executed three times.

When the condition part of an **IF/THEN/ELSE** statement contains a string, care must be taken to ensure that the string is exactly correct. For example, if the data were changed so that the college for **Sara** is entered in lowercase letters (**gc**), she will not be selected and her name will not appear in the output.

```
LIST
1100 FOR N = 1 TO 3
1200   READ N$,C$,GPA       'N$ = name, C$ = college, GPA = Grade Point Average
1300   IF C$ = "GC" THEN PRINT N$
1400 NEXT N
1500   DATA Matt,GC,3.7
1600   DATA Keisha,IT,3.4
1700   DATA Sara,gc,2.8
Ok
RUN
Matt
Ok
```

Sara **is not selected because her college is** gc **(rather than** GC**)**

Matt **is selected because his college is** GC

The program can be modified so that it selects people based on other criteria. For example, the computer can be made to print the names of everyone whose grade point average is greater than 3.2. To do this only the condition in the **IF/THEN/ELSE** statement in line **1300** must be changed.

```
LIST
1100 FOR N = 1 TO 3
1200   READ N$,C$,GPA       'N$ = name, C$ = college, GPA = Grade Point Average
1300   IF GPA > 3.2 THEN PRINT N$
1400 NEXT N
1500   DATA Matt,GC,3.7
1600   DATA Keisha,IT,3.4
1700   DATA Sara,gc,2.8
Ok
RUN
Matt
Keisha
Ok
```

Condition is changed to check GPA

The value of GPA **for both** Matt **and** Keisha **is over** 3.2**, so both are selected**

We can make a selection based on two criteria at the same time by using the logical operator **AND** or the logical operator **OR** just as we did in dBASE. If the condition part of the **IF/THEN/ELSE** statement contains two conditions connected with an **AND**, then both conditions must be met for the statement to be true. For example, if the statement reads: **IF (C$ = "GC") AND (GPA > 3.2)** then, in order for the entire statement to be considered true, the person must be a GC student and he or she must also have a GPA greater than 3.2. The parentheses are used to make it clear that there are two conditions connected with the word **AND**.

```
LIST
1100 FOR N = 1 TO 3
1200   READ N$,C$,GPA        'N$ = name, C$ = college, GPA = Grade Point Average
1300   IF (C$ = "GC") AND (GPA > 3.2) THEN PRINT N$
1400 NEXT N
1500   DATA Matt,GC,3.7
1600   DATA Keisha,IT,3.4
1700   DATA Sara,gc,2.8
Ok
RUN
Matt
Ok
```

Condition is changed to check both college and grade point average

Only Matt is selected because he is the only person whose college is GC and whose GPA is greater than 3.2

If the **OR** connector is used, the entire condition is considered true if any part is true. For example, if you want to select those persons who are in **GC** and you want to be sure to include those whose college is listed as **GC** as well as **gc**, you would use **IF (C$ = "GC") OR (C$ = "gc")**. In this case, both **Sara** and **Matt** will be selected:

```
LIST
1100 FOR N = 1 TO 3
1200   READ N$,C$,GPA        'N$ = name, C$ = college, GPA = Grade Point Average
1300   IF (C$ = "GC") OR (C$ = "gc") THEN PRINT N$
1400 NEXT N
1500   DATA Matt,GC,3.7
1600   DATA Keisha,IT,3.4
1700   DATA Sara,gc,2.8
Ok
RUN
Matt
Sara
Ok
```

Condition is changed to check both uppercase and lowercase designation of college

Matt is selected because his college is GC

Sara is selected because her college is gc

To select all students who are in **GC** as well as those who have a **GPA** over 3.2 (regardless of their college), the following would be used:

```
1300 IF (C$ = "GC") OR (C$ = "gc") OR (GPA > 3.2) THEN PRINT N$
```

```
LIST
1100 FOR N = 1 TO 3
1200   READ N$,C$,GPA        'N$ = name, C$ = college, GPA = Grade Point Average
1300   IF (C$ = "GC") OR (C$ = "gc") OR GPA > 3.2 THEN PRINT N$
1400 NEXT N
1500   DATA Matt,GC,3.7
1600   DATA Keisha,IT,3.4
1700   DATA Sara,gc,2.8
Ok
RUN
Matt
Keisha
Sara
Ok
```

Condition is changed to check uppercase and lowercase designation of college and grade point average

Matt is selected because his college is GC

Keisha is selected because her grade point average is over 3.2

Sara is selected because her college is gc

To summarize the use of **AND** and **OR**:

True **AND** True is True	← Same →	True **OR** True is True
True **AND** False is False	← Different →	True **OR** False is True
False **AND** False is False	← Same →	False **OR** False is False

Determining an Insurance Premium

As another example, let's use **IF/THEN/ELSE** statements in an interactive program that computes the automobile insurance premium for a given individual based on age and number of accidents. If the person is age 20 or under, the base premium is $100. If the person is over 20, the base premium is $50. If the person has had no accidents, there is no additional premium. However, if the person has had one or more accidents, there is an additional premium of $60 plus $20 for each accident.

• *The Task* •

Write an interactive program that will determine the auto insurance premium based on the age and number of accidents of the applicant.

• *Step 1: Justify Using the Computer* •

This program will enable potential clients to quickly and accurately determine the premium the company would charge for an auto insurance policy.

• *Step 2: Define the Problem* •

Output For a 20-year-old person who has had no accidents, the output should look like the following:

```
RUN
                   What is your age? 20
How many accidents have you had? 0
                       Base premium: 100
                 Additional premium: 0
                      Total premium: 100
Ok
```

Processing Each piece of information in the output will be processed as follows:

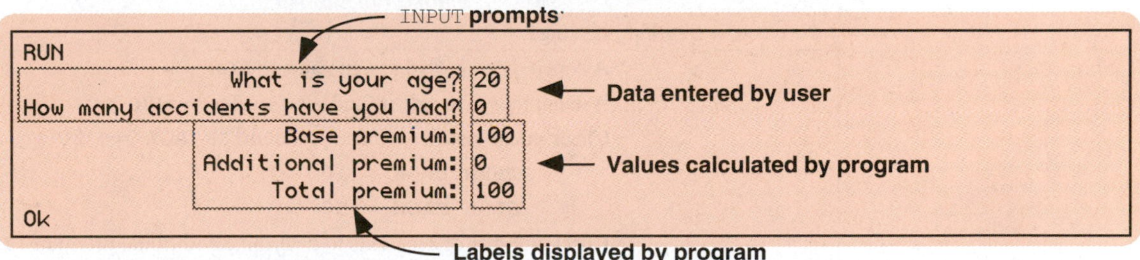

Each piece of information in the output can be defined as follows:

Input prompts: Questions asked so that the user can provide the necessary data to do the calculations.

Data entered by user: The age in years and number of accidents. These data are input by the user.

Labels displayed by program: Descriptive information on the values calculated by the computer.

Values calculated by program: Calculation of the base premium (based on age):

If age of person is 20 or less, base premium = 100

If age of person is over 20, base premium = 50

Calculation of the additional premium (based on the number of accidents):

If number of accidents is 0, additional premium = 0

If number of accidents is not 0, additional premium = 60 + 20*(number of accidents)

Calculation of the total premium (based on the base and additional premiums):

Total premium = Base premium + additional premium

Input Data needed for processing are the age of the person and the number of accidents he or she has had.

• *Step 3: Define the Program Variables* •

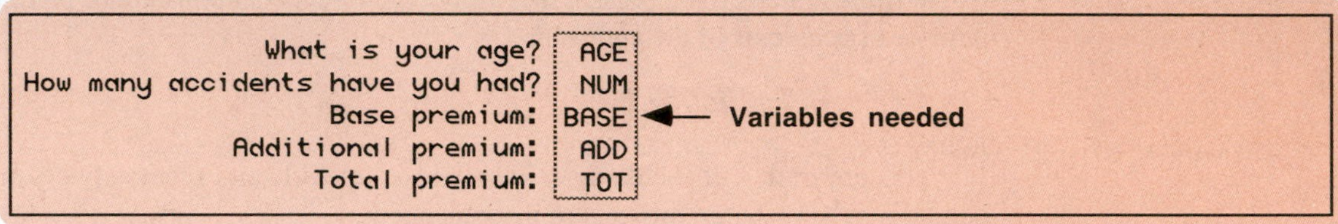

where,

AGE = person's age in years (input)
NUM = number of accidents person has had (input)
BASE = base premium (computed, based on age)
ADD = additional premium (computed, based on number of accidents)
TOT = total premium to be paid (computed, based on **BASE** and **ADD**)

• *Step 4: Construct the Pseudocode* •

Try constructing the pseudocode yourself. Then compare your pseudocode with that given below (your code may be different but just as correct).

```
Begin processing
        Ask person's age and assign value to AGE
        Ask number of accidents and assign value to NUM
        Check age to determine base premium. IF AGE =< 20
                THEN BASE = 100
                ELSE BASE = 50
        Check number of accidents to determine additional premium. IF NUM = 0
                THEN ADD = 0
                ELSE ADD = 60 + 20*NUM
        Compute total premium using TOT = BASE + ADD
        Display values of BASE, ADD, TOT
End processing
```

For your information, a flowchart of the program would look like the following:

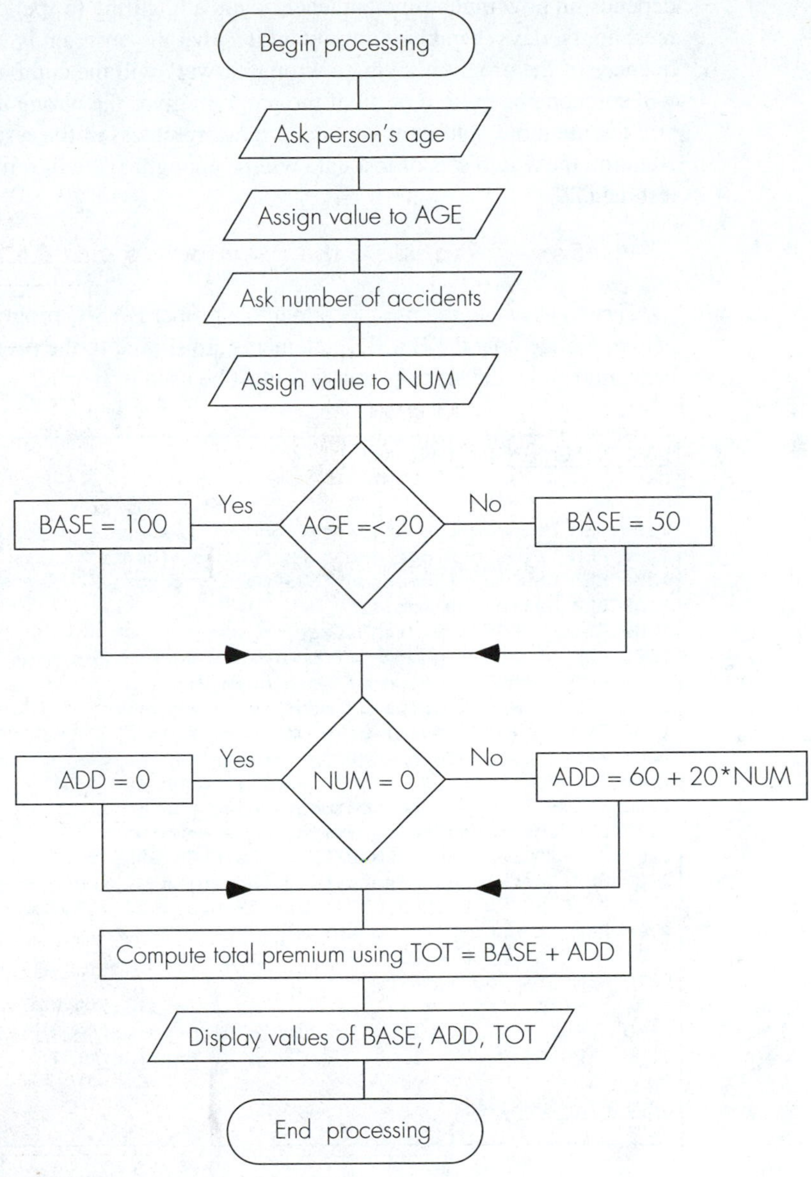

• *Step 5: Calculate the Answers* •

For the sample data given (a 20-year-old person with no accidents) the answers would be as follows:

BASE = 100 (because the person is not over 20)

ADD = 0 (because there are no accidents)

TOT = 100 + 0 = 100

For a 30-year-old person with two accidents the answers would be as follows:

BASE = 50 (because the person is over 20)

ADD = 60 + 2*20 = 100 ($60 plus $20 for each of 2 accidents)

TOT = 50 + 100 = 150

Should we do more sample calculations with more test data? Have all the possible combinations of age and number of accidents been taken care of? The decision as to how much test data you should use depends on how much time and energy you are willing to spend doing the calculations by hand (minutes, hours, days?) and how important it is that the program is working correctly (what are the consequences of the program giving a wrong answer? will the company lose money and if so, how much? will someone be injured or die if the program gives the wrong answer?). In general, the more testing you do, the more confident you are in the correctness of the results. For this program and the current situation these two sets of test data will be enough. We will return to this program later with more test data.

• Step 6: Translate the Pseudocode into BASIC •

Try to translate the pseudocode into a proper BASIC program before you look at the version given below. Notice how the BASIC statements are similar to the pseudocode except that they have line numbers and follow the strict syntax that must be used in BASIC:

```
LOAD"C:\BA\INSURE1
Ok
LIST
1100 REM Program computes semi-annual insurance premium given
1200 REM  person's age and number of accidents
1300 REM Douglas Robertson (373-4026), created 1 Mar 91
1400 REM Define variables:
1500 REM    AGE = person's age in years
1600 REM    NUM = number of accidents person has had
1700 REM   BASE = value of base premium
1800 REM    ADD = value of additional premium
1900 REM    TOT = total premium to be paid
2000 REM Input data on age and number of accidents
2100   INPUT "            What is your age";AGE
2200   INPUT "How many accidents have you had";NUM
2300 REM Check age to determine base premium.
2400   IF AGE =< 20 THEN BASE = 100 ELSE BASE = 50
2500 REM Check # accidents to determine additional premium.
2600   IF NUM = 0 THEN ADD = 0 ELSE ADD = 60 + 20*NUM
2700 REM Compute total premium
2800   TOT = BASE + ADD
2900 REM Display results
3000   PRINT "                   Base premium:"BASE
3100   PRINT "             Additional premium:"ADD
3200   PRINT "                  Total premium:"TOT
Ok
SAVE"A:INSURE1
Ok
```

Corresponding pseudocode statements
- Ask age and assign value to AGE (line 2100)
- Ask number of accidents and assign value to NUM (line 2200)
- Check age to determine base premium (line 2400)
- Check number of accidents to determine additional premium (line 2600)
- Compute total premium (line 2800)
- Display values of BASE, ADD, TOT (lines 3000–3200)

• Step 7: Type the Program •

Enter (or load) the above program and save it using the name **A:INSURE1**.

• Step 8: Run the Program •

Run this program for the two test cases. First, run it for a 20-year-old driver who has had no accidents.

```
RUN
              What is your age? 20
How many accidents have you had? 0
                    Base premium: 100
              Additional premium: 0
                   Total premium: 100
Ok
```

Next, run the program for a 30-year-old who has had two accidents:

```
RUN ←
                  What is your age? 30 ←
How many accidents have you had? 2 ←
                      Base premium: 50
                Additional premium: 100
                     Total premium: 150
Ok
```

• Step 9: Check the Computer's Results •

Check the output of the two test runs to see if the answers obtained by hand are the same as those provided by the computer. If they are, then you can be somewhat confident that the program is running correctly. Of course, you cannot be sure that the program is correct unless you check every calculation by hand but the more checking you do by hand the more confident you may be that the program is doing what you want it to do.

• Step 10: Debug the Program •

Because the answers check, debugging is not needed.

A word of caution is in order here. The program seems to work properly for the above set of test data and, in fact, is correct . . . sort of. Will the program provide the correct answers with all sets of data? Let's run the program one last time for a person who is 5 years old and who has had -8 accidents. Of course, these data are ridiculous. An insurance company would not issue auto insurance to a 5 year old (no driver's license), nor does it make any sense to have had negative eight accidents! Will the computer catch these obvious errors? Certainly not, unless the programmer has told the computer to check the age of the person to be sure it is 16 or higher and to check the number of accidents to be sure that it is zero or greater. The program does not make these checks but it does calculate a (ridiculous) premium for the person:

```
RUN ←
                  What is your age? 5 ←
How many accidents have you had? -8 ←
                      Base premium: 100
                Additional premium:-100
                     Total premium: 0
Ok
```

If this insurance company follows the recommendation of the computer, it will provide free auto insurance to a 5-year-old child. This could prove costly! We will discuss the important topic of checking data for errors in Chapter 6. For now, we will assume the data are always correct.

One final word about the development of this program. It took a lot of effort and time to go through the process of conceptualizing, writing, and testing the program. It would have been much quicker for me simply to write down the following program off the top of my head:

```
NEW ←
Ok
1 INPUT "Enter age & # accidents";A,N
2 IF A =< 20 THEN B = 100 ELSE B = 0
3 IF N = 0 THEN ADD = 0 ELSE ADD = 6+20*N
4 PRINT "Base ="B, "Additional ="ADD,"Total ="B + ADD
RUN ←
Enter age & # accidents? 20,0 ←
Base = 100    Additional = 0              Total = 100
Ok
```

The above program is what we call a *quick and dirty* solution. It gets the job done but has no beauty or finesse and could not easily serve as the basis for an expanded or modified version at a later time. Also, it completely lacks any instructional value or documentation. As you develop your programs, you will have to decide whether to do them quickly, just to get the job done, or to take more time and think about not only what you are doing but how you are doing it. Will your computer solutions be quick and dirty programs off the top of your head or will they be carefully crafted, well documented, computer works of art that are easily expanded and modified? There is a trade-off here and you have to decide which is best for you. Are you trying to get through this book with as little work and thinking as possible or are you trying to develop programming skills that will help you to use the computer as a problem-solving tool for the rest of your professional life? The important outcomes of your education are the processes that you experience and not necessarily the products that you create.

WHILE and WEND Statements

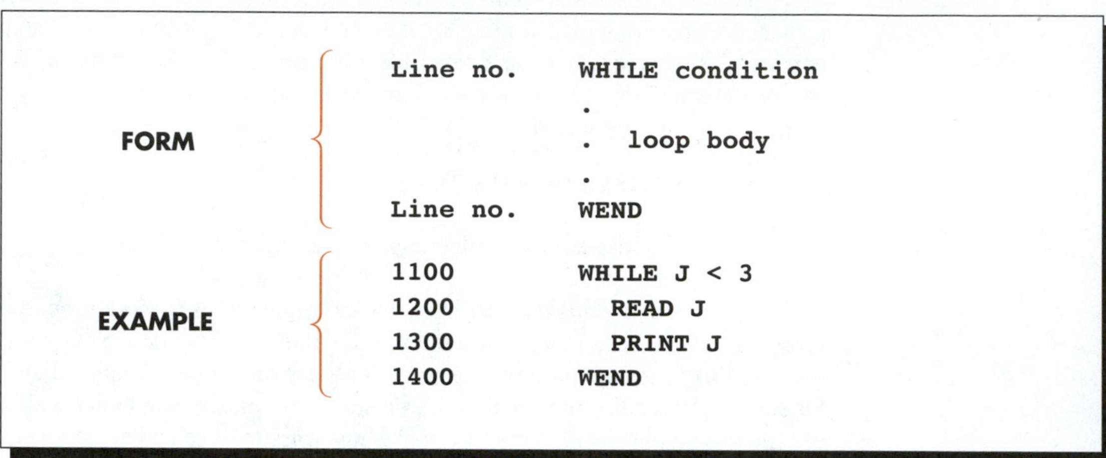

FORM

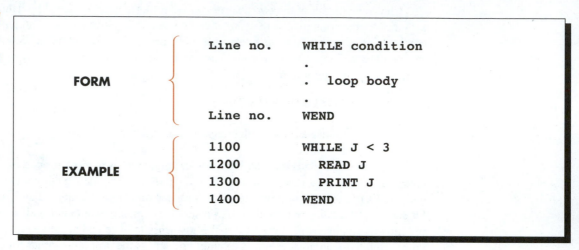

```
Line no.    WHILE condition
                 .
                 .  loop body
                 .
Line no.    WEND
```

EXAMPLE

```
1100        WHILE J < 3
1200          READ J
1300          PRINT J
1400        WEND
```

The **WHILE** and **WEND** statements allow the programmer to define a loop in much the same way as did the **FOR** and **NEXT** statements. However, rather than executing the statements inside the loop a specified number of times, the statements inside the **WHILE/WEND** loop are executed while a specified condition is satisfied. This condition is evaluated in much the same way as the condition of an **IF/THEN/ELSE** statement. In a **WHILE/WEND** loop, if the condition is true, the statements inside the loop are executed; if the condition is false, the loop is skipped and control passes to the statement just after the **WEND** statement. Study the following example:

```
NEW ↵
Ok
10 READ J
20 WHILE J < 3
30   PRINT J
40   READ J
50 WEND
60 PRINT "The loop has been exited.  The value of J is"J
70 DATA 1,2,3
Ok
RUN ↵
 1
 2
The loop has been exited.  The value of J is 3
Ok
```

Line Numbers	Comments
10	Creates a storage location called **J**, and assigns a value of **1** (the first entry on the data list) to that location.
20	Checks the value of **J** (which is **1**) to see if it is less than 3. If it is, the statements inside the loop (lines **30** and **40**) are executed. If it is not, control is transferred to the statement just after the **WEND** statement. Because the value of **J** (which is **1**) is less than 3, line **30** is executed next.
30	Displays the value of **J** (which is **1**).
40	Assigns the next number in the data list (which is **2**) to **J**.
50	Marks the end of the loop. Control is transferred back to the **WHILE** statement at line **20**.
20	Checks the value of **J** (which is **2**) to see if it is less than 3. Because it is, line **30** is executed next.
30	Displays the value of **J** (which is **2**).
40	Assigns the next number in the data list (which is **3**) to **J**.
50	Transfers control back to the **WHILE** statement at line **20**.
20	Checks the value of **J** (which is **3**) to see if it is less than 3. Because 3 is not less than 3, the loop is exited and control is transferred to the statement just after the **WEND** statement.
60	Displays the string and the value of **J** (which is **3**).

As another example, let's rewrite the college selection program, **SELECT1**, so that it uses **WHILE/WEND** rather than **FOR/NEXT** loops. The **FOR** statement in line **1100** is deleted, a **WHILE** statement is added at line **1250**, and the **NEXT** statement in line **1400** is replaced by a **WEND** statement. Also, another **READ** statement is added at line **1350** (**WHILE/WEND** loops typically have two **READ** statements—one just before the **WHILE** statement and one just before the **WEND** statement. This will be discussed in more detail later). **LOAD** the new version of the program, **LIST** it, **SAVE** it to your *BASIC Data* diskette, and then **RUN** it as shown below:

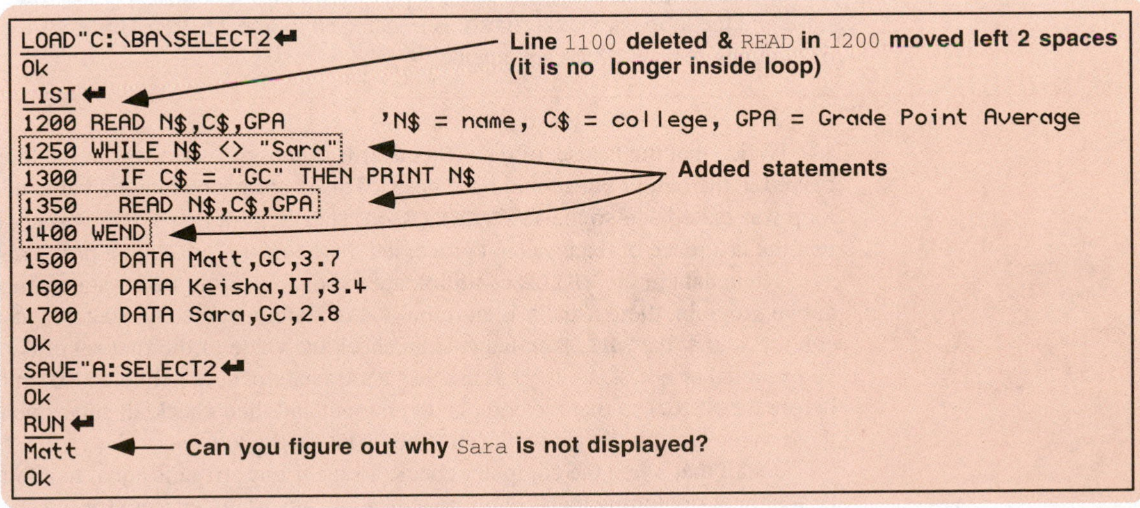

LOAD"C:\BA\SELECT2
Ok
LIST
1200 READ N$,C$,GPA
1250 WHILE N$ <> "Sara"
1300 IF C$ = "GC" THEN PRINT N$
1350 READ N$,C$,GPA
1400 WEND
1500 DATA Matt,GC,3.7
1600 DATA Keisha,IT,3.4
1700 DATA Sara,GC,2.8
Ok
SAVE"A:SELECT2
Ok
RUN
Matt
Ok
Line 1100 deleted & READ in 1200 moved left 2 spaces (it is no longer inside loop)
'N$ = name, C$ = college, GPA = Grade Point Average
Added statements
Can you figure out why Sara is not displayed?

Line Numbers	Comments
1200	Assigns the first set of data to the variables **N$**, **C$**, and **GPA**. Note that unlike the **FOR/NEXT** version of the program, this first **READ** statement is outside the loop. This is a typical arrangement for a **WHILE/WEND** loop.
1250	Defines the beginning of the loop. The value of **N$** (i.e., **Matt**) is compared with the string **Sara**. If they are not equal (**<>**), the condition is true and the statements inside the loop are executed. If they are equal, the condition is false, the loop is skipped, and control passes to the statement just after the **WEND** statement. Because **N$** has a value that is not **Sara**, the loop is executed. You could think of this statement as saying, "while the name is not **Sara**, do the following loop," or "do the following loop until the name is **Sara**."
1300	Checks the value of **C$** (i.e., **GC**) to see if it is exactly the same as the string **GC**. Because it is, the value of **N$** (i.e., **Matt**) is displayed.
1350	Assigns variable locations **N$**, **C$**, and **GPA** the values **Keisha**, **IT**, and **3.4**, respectively. Notice how the **READ** statement in the **WHILE/WEND** version of the program appears just before the loop begins (at line **1200**) and again at the end of the loop just before the **WEND** statement (at line **1350**). The **READ** in the **FOR/NEXT** version of the program appears only at the beginning of the loop, just after the **FOR** statement.
1400	Marks the end of the loop. Control is transferred back to line **1250** and the process is repeated. The computer continues to process the statements inside the loop while the condition in the **WHILE** statement is true. When it becomes false the loop is exited and the program ends.
1250	The value of **N$** (i.e., **Keisha**) is compared with the string **Sara**. Because they are not equal (**<>**) the condition is true and the statements inside the loop are executed.
1300	Checks the value of **C$** (i.e., **IT**) to see if it is exactly the same as the string **GC**. Because it is not, the value of **N$** (i.e., **Keisha**) is not displayed.
1350	Assigns variable locations **N$**, **C$**, and **GPA** the values **Sara**, **GC**, and **2.8**, respectively.
1400	Transfers control back to the beginning of the loop.
1250	The value of **N$** (i.e., **Sara**) is compared with the string **Sara**. Because they are equal, the condition is false and the loop is exited (control is transferred to line **1500**). This ends the program because the rest of the lines contain **DATA** statements.

Notice that the last set of data (**Sara**'s) was not processed within the loop (her name was not displayed in the output but should have been). This is because when the value of **N$** became **Sara**, the loop was exited and so the **IF/THEN/ELSE** statement in line **1300** was not executed. The effect is that the last piece of data was not processed. In the next section, that problem will be fixed.

When data in the **WHILE** condition are to be input using **READ** statements, as is the case in the above program, there usually is an initial **READ** statement (see line **1200**) just before the loop is entered so that the **WHILE** statement can check the value of the first set of data to see if the loop should be executed or not. Also, there is another **READ** statement (see line **1350**) at the end of the loop (just before the **WEND**) so that the computer can input and then check all subsequent values of the data before those values are processed by the statements inside the loop.

Recall that when the computer checks to see if one string is equal to another, the two strings must be identical (including the case of the letters and any blank spaces) for the statement to be true. Thus, the three strings **Sara**, **SARA**, and **sara** are not equal as far as the computer is concerned. However, when comparing numbers, the computer only compares their values and not the way they are written. Thus, the numbers **1E+15**, **1E15**, **1e15**, and **1.00e15** are all considered by the computer to have the same value. In fact, if **1.00e15** is entered into a program, the computer will automatically change it to **1E+15** when the program is listed (except if the number is in a **DATA** statement).

The structure of **WHILE/WEND** loops is different from the structure of **FOR/NEXT** loops in that **WHILE** and **WEND** are conditional looping statements whereas **FOR** and **NEXT** are unconditional looping statements. The **WHILE/WEND** loops may seem a little strange at first but, as you shall see, they are very useful.

TO TAKE A BREAK Type **SYSTEM ↵**, remove diskette(s). To resume (hard disk): Insert *Data* diskette, type **A: ↵**, **C:\BA\BASICA ↵**. To resume (two drive): Insert diskettes, type **A: ↵**, **B:\BASICA ↵**.

Data Flags

We have seen that program loops can be created using **FOR/NEXT** or **WHILE/WEND** to execute the same statements over and over again using different sets of data. This is a powerful technique, but it is usually inconvenient and sometimes impossible to count the number of pieces of data that are to be read and then insert this number in the **FOR** statement. Likewise, it is inconvenient and may lead to incorrect results to check the last piece of data and place that value in the **WHILE** condition (as in the previous program in line **1250**). In addition, in the last program, if there were two people with the name **Sara**, the loop would be exited when the first **Sara** was read and this would result in the rest of the data being skipped.

It would be better to put a *fake* piece of data at the end of the data list and then check to see when the computer has read that piece of data—when it has, the loop would be exited. Using a fake piece of data ensures that all the data will be processed before the loop is exited. A piece of fake data is commonly referred to as a *data flag* or a *dummy value* and it is usually placed at the end of a data list. A data flag, by definition, is a piece of data that could not possibly be a piece of data. We use this to signal (flag) the computer so that it knows that the end of the data list has been reached.

Let's modify the college selection program so that it uses a data flag in the **WHILE/WEND** condition. Use **1E+15** as the data flag for this program. We will assume that **1E+15** (this is the number *one quadrillion*) is a number that is so large that it could not possibly be a piece of real data. **LOAD** the new version of the program, **LIST** it, **SAVE** it to your *BASIC Data* diskette, and then **RUN** it as shown below:

```
LOAD"C:\BA\SELECT3↵
Ok
LIST↵
1200 READ N$,C$,GPA          'N$ = name, C$ = college, GPA = Grade Point Average
1250 WHILE GPA <> 1E+15
1300    IF C$ = "GC" THEN PRINT N$
1350    READ N$,C$,GPA
1400 WEND
1500    DATA Matt,GC,3.7
1600    DATA Keisha,IT,3.4
1700    DATA Sara,GC,2.8
1800    DATA 1E+15,1E+15,1E+15
Ok
SAVE"A:SELECT3↵
Ok
RUN↵
Matt
Sara
Ok
```

When data flags are used, the proper output is obtained

The **WHILE** statement in line **1250** instructs the computer to execute the statements inside the loop while the value of **GPA** is not equal to **1E+15**. When the value of **GPA** finally does equal **1E+15**, the loop is exited and the program terminates. Note that we could have just as easily used the condition **N$ <> "1E+15"** or **C$ <> "1E+15"** in the **WHILE** statement (in this case the quotation marks around **"1E+15"** are needed because the variables are strings); it makes no difference which variable is used in the condition in the **WHILE** statement. The new line of data, **1800**, contains a full set of data (three values) because the **READ** statements assign values to three variables at a time. If only one value had been entered in line **1800**, an **Out of Data** error message would have been displayed because the computer would try to **READ** three pieces of data when there was only one left.

Data Flags and the Payroll Program

On page B80, a payroll program, **WAGES2**, was developed that read employee names, rates of pay, and hours worked and calculated their pay for a given week. **FOR** and **NEXT** statements were used to define the beginning and end of the processing loop and to tell the computer the number of times the loop was to be processed.

In order to tell the computer how many times to process the loop, the number of sets of data (two in this case) had to be counted and then that number had to be entered into the **FOR** statement. This extra bit of work can be eliminated by using a data flag and either a **FOR/NEXT** loop in conjunction with an **IF/THEN/ELSE** statement or a **WHILE/WEND** loop. In each case, the computer will determine when it has reached the last piece of information in a data list (the data flag) and then exit the loop.

First, modify the program by using an **IF/THEN/ELSE** statement in the **FOR/NEXT** loop so that the loop is exited when the last set of data is read. You need to perform three tasks (see the program listing on the following page):

1. Add a **DATA** statement with a set of data flags.
2. Add an **IF/THEN/ELSE** statement right after the **READ** statement in line **2700** to check to see if the data flag has been read. If it has, control should be transferred outside the loop to line **3100**. If not, the processing should continue inside the loop.
3. Change the terminating value in the **FOR** statement in line **2600** so that the loop will be executed more than four times. Because the loop will be exited right after the data flag has been read, it really does not matter what is chosen for the terminating value as long as it is more than the number of sets of data in the **DATA** statement.

In the modified program listed below, the new **DATA** statement at line **4000** contains three pieces of data, even though only one piece is used as the data flag. Three pieces of data must be added because the **READ** statement in line **2700** reads three pieces of data at a time. If only one piece of data were added, the computer would assign that to the variable **EMPLOYEE$** and then immediately try to assign a value to **RATE**. Because there would be no more values, an **Out of DATA** error message would result.

HOURS was chosen arbitrarily as the variable to hold the data flag. The variables **EMPLOYEE$** or **RATE** could have been chosen to obtain the same result. **LOAD** the new version of the program, **LIST** it, **SAVE** it to your *BASIC Data* diskette, and then **RUN** it as shown on the next page:

```
LOAD"C:\BA\WAGES3 ↵
Ok
LIST ↵
1100 REM Program to compute wages given total hours worked and pay rate
1200 REM Douglas Robertson (373-4026), created 1 Mar 91
1300 REM Define variables:
1400 REM   EMPLOYEE$ = name in form LastName Space First (e.g., Roberts Matt)
1500 REM        RATE = rate of pay in dollars per hour (e.g.,  3)
1600 REM       HOURS = total number of hours worked for pay period (e.g., 50)
1700 REM         PAY = total pay earned for pay period (e.g., 150)
1800 REM Begin processing
1900    REM Define PRINT USING images
2000      IMAGE1$ = "Employee        Pay Rate       Hours    Total Pay"
2100      IMAGE2$ = "--------        --------       -----    ---------"
2200      IMAGE3$ = "\              \   $##.##        ##.#      $####.##"
2300      IMAGE4$ = "All data read, processing complete"
2400    PRINT IMAGE1$                          'Display header
2500    PRINT IMAGE2$                          'Display header
2600      FOR NUM = 1 TO 100                   'For each person do the following
2700        READ EMPLOYEE$,RATE,HOURS          'Assign values to name, rate, hours
2710        IF HOURS = 1E+15 THEN 3100         'Check for end of data flag
2800        PAY = RATE*HOURS                   'Calculate pay using formula
2900        PRINT USING IMAGE3$;EMPLOYEE$,RATE,HOURS,PAY
3000      NEXT NUM                             'Repeat loop for next person
3100    PRINT
3200    PRINT IMAGE4$                          'Display footer
3300 REM End processing
3400 REM Define DATA list in form:
3500 REM DATA NAME          ,RATE,HOURS
3600      DATA Roberts Matt,   4,   30
3700      DATA Sim Keisha  ,   3,   50
3800      DATA Tech Sara   ,   6,   21
3900      DATA Well Vanessa,   5,   40
4000      DATA 1E+15,1E+15,1E+15,1E+15
Ok
SAVE"A:WAGES3 ↵
Ok
RUN ↵
Employee        Pay Rate       Hours    Total Pay
--------        --------       -----    ---------
Roberts Matt     $ 4.00         30.0     $120.00
Sim Keisha       $ 3.00         50.0     $150.00
Tech Sara        $ 6.00         21.0     $126.00
Well Vanessa     $ 5.00         40.0     $200.00

All data read, processing complete
Ok
```

Even though the above program serves the purpose for which it was intended, it does not follow proper programming style because it uses the **IF/THEN/ELSE** statement to exit a loop. While the **IF/THEN/ELSE** statement is logical and easy to employ in simple programs, programmers try to use it as little as possible to exit loops because it leads to confusion in more complex programs. The more jumping around in a program, the more difficult it is for humans to follow and understand the flow of the program. This type of jumping around can lead to what is called *spaghetti code* (Fig. 1) because trying to follow the logical flow of the program is like trying to follow a single strand of pasta in a plate of spaghetti from one end to the other.

FIGURE 1

"Spaghetti code" makes programs difficult to follow.

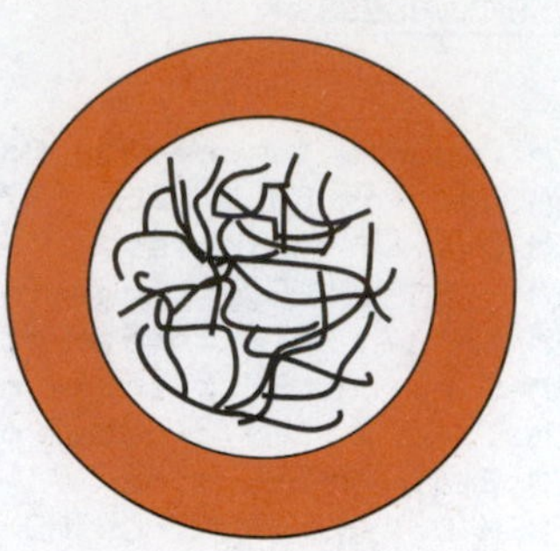

The **WHILE/WEND** statements can be used to construct loops that can be exited logically and easily without the use of the **IF/THEN/ELSE** statement. Accomplish this by performing the following steps (see the program listing on the next page):

1. Line **2600**, which contains the **FOR** statement, is deleted.
2. Line **2710**, which contains the **IF/THEN/ELSE** statement, is changed into a **WHILE** statement (notice how the condition in the **IF/THEN/ELSE** statement becomes a part of the **WHILE** statement).
3. Line **3000** is modified by changing **NEXT** into **WEND**.
4. A second **READ** statement is inserted at line **2910**, just before the **WEND**. Notice that there will be two **READ** statements: one is needed just before the loop (line **2700**) to assign the first set of data to the variables before the **WHILE** condition is executed. The **READ** is needed at the end of the loop to assign all the other sets of data to the variables while the loop is executing. This may seem a bit more complicated than using **FOR/NEXT**, but it is better programming practice because it involves less jumping around within the program. As your programs get longer and more complex, this structure will make things easier for you. **LOAD** the new version of the program, **LIST** it, **SAVE** it to your *BASIC Data* diskette, and then **RUN** it as shown on the next page:

```
LOAD"C:\BA\WAGES4
Ok
LIST
1100 REM Program to compute wages given total hours worked and pay rate
1200 REM Douglas Robertson (625-1075), created 1 Jul 90
1300 REM Define variables:
1400 REM   EMPLOYEE$ = name in form LastName Space First (e.g., Roberts Matt)
1500 REM        RATE = rate of pay in dollars per hour (e.g.,  3)
1600 REM       HOURS = total number of hours worked for pay period (e.g., 50)
1700 REM         PAY = total pay earned for pay period (e.g., 150)
1800 REM Begin processing
1900   REM Define PRINT USING images
2000     IMAGE1$ = "Employee        Pay Rate       Hours    Total Pay"
2100     IMAGE2$ = "--------        --------       -----    ---------"
2200     IMAGE3$ = "\             \   $##.##        ##.#      $####.##"
2300     IMAGE4$ = "All data read, processing complete"
2400   PRINT IMAGE1$                         'Display header
2500   PRINT IMAGE2$                         'Display header
2700     READ EMPLOYEE$,RATE,HOURS           'Assign values to name, rate, hours
2710   WHILE HOURS <> 1E+15                  'For each person do the following
2800     PAY = RATE*HOURS                    'Calculate pay using formula
2900     PRINT USING IMAGE3$;EMPLOYEE$,RATE,HOURS,PAY
2910     READ EMPLOYEE$,RATE,HOURS           'Assign values to name, rate, hours
3000   WEND                                  'Repeat loop for next person
3100   PRINT
3200   PRINT IMAGE4$                         'Display footer
3300 REM End processing
3400 REM Define DATA list in form:
3500 REM DATA NAME        ,RATE,HOURS
3600     DATA Roberts Matt,   4,   30
3700     DATA Sim Keisha  ,   3,   50
3800     DATA Tech Sara   ,   6,   21
3900     DATA Well Vanessa,   5,   40
4000     DATA 1E+15,1E+15,1E+15,1E+15
Ok
SAVE"A:WAGES4
Ok
RUN
Employee        Pay Rate       Hours    Total Pay
--------        --------       -----    ---------
Roberts Matt      $ 4.00        30.0      $120.00
Sim Keisha        $ 3.00        50.0      $150.00
Tech Sara         $ 6.00        21.0      $126.00
Well Vanessa      $ 5.00        40.0      $200.00

All data read, processing complete
Ok
```

Counters

Counters are variables that are used to keep track of the number of times something is done and to find sums of numbers. A statement that counts by ones might look like the following:

NUM = NUM + 1

This is a strange statement—it is not a proper algebraic equation but then we are not doing algebra. This is called an *assignment* or *replacement* statement because the quantity on the right side of the equal sign is calculated and the result is assigned to (i.e., replaces the value of) the variable indicated on the left. The statement **NUM = NUM + 1** says to add 1 to the present value of **NUM** and then to store this sum at variable location **NUM**. The effect is to increase the current value of **NUM** by 1 (i.e., to count by 1). Rather than using an equal sign here, it would be clearer if we could use an arrow, ←, showing that the quantity on the right is replacing the quantity on the left. However, a statement such as **NUM ← NUM + 1** is not legal in BASIC and, therefore, **NUM = NUM + 1** must be used.

As an example of counters, modify the college selection program, **SELECT3**, so that it keeps track of the number of sets of data read from the data list. To do this, three statements need to be added to the program:

- Line **1100** is added to initialize the value of the counter to zero. Because most versions of BASIC automatically initialize all numeric variables to zero, this statement is not absolutely necessary, but it is good practice to include it just in case.
- Line **1260** is added to do the counting. Each time this statement is executed, the value of **NUM** is increased by 1.
- A **PRINT** statement is added at line **1450** to display the result of the counting process. **LOAD** the new version of the program, **LIST** it, **SAVE** it to your *BASIC Data* diskette, and then **RUN** it as shown below:

```
LOAD"C:\BA\SELECT4
Ok
LIST
1100 NUM = 0                  'Initializes the value of NUM to 0
1200 READ N$,C$,GPA           'N$ = name, C$ = college, GPA = Grade Point Average
1250 WHILE GPA <> 1E+15
1260   NUM = NUM + 1
1300   IF C$ = "GC" THEN PRINT N$
1350   READ N$,C$,GPA
1400 WEND
1450 PRINT "Number of data sets read is"NUM
1500   DATA Matt,GC,3.7
1600   DATA Keisha,IT,3.4
1700   DATA Sara,GC,2.8
1800   DATA 1E+15,1E+15,1E+15
Ok
SAVE"A:SELECT4
Ok
RUN
Matt
Sara
Number of data sets read is 3
Ok
```

Line Numbers	Comments
1100	Creates a storage location called **NUM** and assigns a value of **0** to that location.
1260	Takes the current value of **NUM** (which is **0**), adds 1 to it, and assigns the new value (**1**) to storage location **NUM** (the value of **NUM** is increased by 1). This process is repeated until the data flag is read and the loop is exited.

The entire run of the program can be summarized as follows:

Memory Assignments for Program `SELECT4`

Line no.	NUM	N$	C$	GPA	
					Variable names
	0			0	Default values
1100	0				Assigned values
1200		Matt	GC	3.7	
1250					Loop entered
1260	1 ← 0 + 1				Calculated value
1300		Matt			Output
1350		Keisha	IT	3.4	Assigned values
1400					Return to top of loop
1250					Loop continued
1260	2 ← 1 + 1				Calculated value
1300					No output
1350		Sara	GC	2.8	Assigned values
1400					Return to top of loop
1250					Loop continued
1260	3 ← 2 + 1				Calculated value
1300		Sara			Output
1350		1E+15	1E+15	1E+15	Assigned values
1400					Return to top of loop
1250					Loop exited
1450	3				Output

The following program uses replacement statements to count by two's. Note that in order to save space, the output was printed horizontally rather than vertically. This was done by placing a comma at the end of the **PRINT** statement at line **30**.

```
NEW
Ok
10 COUNT = 2                              'Initialize COUNT to 2
20   FOR N = 1 TO 10                      'Begin loop
30     PRINT COUNT,                       'Display value of COUNT
40     COUNT = COUNT + 2                  'Increase COUNT by 2
50   NEXT N                               'End loop
RUN
 2            4             6             8             10
 12           14            16            18            20
Ok
```

How should line **40** be changed in order to double each value rather than increase it by two? Doubling means to multiply by two. Thus, the **+** sign needs to be replaced by an *.

```
10 COUNT = 2                              'Initialize COUNT to 2
20   FOR N = 1 TO 10                      'Begin loop
30     PRINT COUNT,                       'Display value of COUNT
40     COUNT = COUNT * 2                  'Double COUNT
50   NEXT N                               'End loop
RUN
 2            4             8             16            32
 64           128           256           512           1024
Ok
```

Finding an Average

To find the average of a set of numbers, the numbers are added and then this sum is divided by the number of numbers in the set. The following program finds the average of a set of numbers read in from **DATA** statements. **LOAD** the program, **LIST** it, **SAVE** it to your *BASIC Data* diskette, and then **RUN** it as shown below:

```
LOAD"C:\BA\AVE1
Ok
LIST
1100 NUM = 0                'Number of values read
1200 SUM = 0                'Sum of all numbers read
1300 READ X                 'Assigns first value in DATA to X
1400 WHILE X <> 1E+15       'Begin loop
1500   NUM = NUM + 1        'Counts number of values read
1600   SUM = SUM + X        'Adds value of X to current total
1700   READ X               'Assigns next value in DATA to X
1800 WEND                   'End loop
1900 PRINT NUM"numbers read from DATA.  Sum is"SUM" and average is"SUM/NUM
2000 DATA 5,11,8,1E+15
Ok
SAVE"A:AVE1
Ok
RUN
 3 numbers read from DATA.  Sum is 24  and average is 8
Ok
```

Line Numbers	Comments
1100	Creates a storage location called **NUM** and assigns a value of **0** to that location.
1200	Creates a storage location called **SUM** and assigns a value of **0** to that location.
1300	Creates a storage location called **X** and assigns the first value in the data list (**5**) to that location.
1400	Begins the loop. Because the value of **X** is not **1E+15**, the statements inside the loop are executed.
1500	Increases the value of **NUM** by 1 and stores the result (**0 + 1 = 1**) at location **NUM**.
1600	Increases the value of **SUM** by **X**. The current value of **X** (which is **5**) is added to the current value of **SUM** (which is **0**) and the result (**0 + 5 = 5**) is stored at location **SUM**.
1700	Assigns the next value in the data list (**11**) to variable **X**.
1800	Returns control to the beginning of the loop.
1400	Checks the value of **X**. Because the value of **X** is not **1E+15**, the statements inside the loop are executed.
1500	Increases the value of **NUM** by 1 and stores the result (**1 + 1 = 2**) at location **NUM**.
1600	Increases the value of **SUM** by **X**. The current value of **X** (which is **11**) is added to the current value of **SUM** (which is **5**) and the result (**5 + 11 = 16**) is stored at location **SUM**.
1700	Assigns the next value in the data list (**8**) to variable **X**.
1800	Returns control to the beginning of the loop.
1400	Checks the value of **X**. Because the value of **X** is not **1E+15**, the statements inside the loop are executed.
1500	Increases the value of **NUM** by 1 and stores the result (**2 + 1 = 3**) at location **NUM**.
1600	Increases the value of **SUM** by **X**. The current value of **X** (which is **8**) is added to the current value of **SUM** (which is **16**) and the result (**8 + 16 = 24**) is stored at location **SUM**.
1700	Assigns the next value in the data list (**1E+15**) to variable **X**.
1800	Returns control to the beginning of the loop.
1400	Checks the value of **X**. Because the value of **X** is **1E+15**, the loop is exited.
1900	Displays the values of **NUM**, **SUM**, and the average of the numbers (**SUM/NUM**).

The entire run of the program can be summarized as follows:

Memory Assignments for Program AVE1

Line no.	NUM	SUM	X	
	0	0	0	Default values
1100	0			Assigned values
1200		0		
1300			5	
1500	1 ← 0 + 1			Calculated values
1600		5 ← 0 + 5		
1700			11	Assigned value
1500	2 ← 1 + 1			Calculated values
1600		16 ← 5 + 11		
1700			8	Assigned value
1500	3 ← 2 + 1			Calculated values
1600		24 ← 16 + 8		
1700			1E+15	Assigned value
1900	3	24		Calculated values

(Variable names: NUM, SUM, X)

Calculating a Standard Deviation

The average of a set of data usually provides a good piece of summary information but it can be misleading. For example, suppose you are interested in two companies where the average wage of the employees in each company is $25,000 per year. Do the employees of both companies make comparable wages? Let's say the data for the companies are as follows:

Company 1

Worker classification	Salary
Production	1,000
Production	1,000
Production	1,000
President	97,000
Average Salary	25,000

Company 2

Worker classification	Salary
Production	20,000
Production	20,000
Production	20,000
President	40,000
Average Salary	25,000

As you can see, even though the average salary in both companies is the same there is quite a difference in the salaries paid to the production workers versus the presidents—the salaries are much more varied in Company 1 than in Company 2. Recall from the discussion on page L65 that the standard deviation can be used to measure this type of variability. One formula for the standard deviation of a population that contains **n** pieces of data is given on the next page:

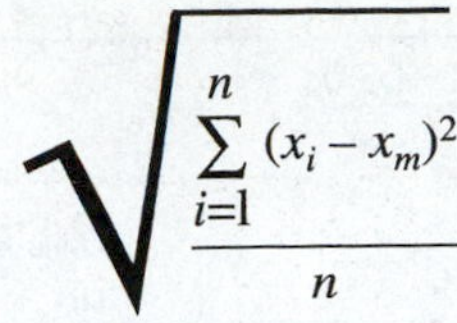

where x_i = a single value
x_m = the average (mean) of all the values
n = the number of values in the set of data
Σ = a symbol that says to sum up the values

For our purposes, the details of the formula are not important. However, it can be shown that the above formula is equivalent to the following:

$$\sqrt{\frac{\sum_{i=1}^{n} x_i^2 - nx_m^2}{n}}$$

This version of the formula is used to do the actual calculations by following the steps given below:

1. Find the sum of the squares of each value (Σx_i^2).
2. Find the product of the number of values used and the square of the average (nx_m^2).
3. Subtract the result in step 2 from the result in step 1 ($\Sigma x_i^2 - nx_m^2$).
4. Divide the result found in step 3 by the number of values used (n).
5. Find the square root of the result found in step 4. In BASIC, the square root of a number (e.g., *X*) is found using the **`SQR(X)`** function.

While the process may seem complicated it is quite easy to modify the program **`AVE1`** so that it calculates the standard deviation in addition to the average. One statement (see line **`1610`**) needs to be added to the **`WHILE/WEND`** loop so that the sum of the squares of the individual values is calculated (this is step 1 above). The next four steps in the calculation are performed at the bottom of the program (lines **`1930`** through **`1970`**). **`LOAD`** the new version of the program, **`LIST`** it, **`SAVE`** it to your *BASIC Data* diskette, and then **`RUN`** it as shown on the next page:

```
LOAD"C:\BA\STD-DEV1 ↵
Ok
LIST ↵
1100 NUM = 0               'Number of values read
1200 SUM = 0               'Sum of all numbers read
1210 SUMSQ = 0             'Sum of squares of all numbers read
1300 READ X                'Assigns first value in DATA to X
1400 WHILE X <> 1E+15      'Begin loop
1500   NUM = NUM + 1       'Counts number of values read
1600   SUM = SUM + X       'Adds value of X to current total
1610   SUMSQ = SUMSQ + X^2    'Adds square of value of X to current total
1700   READ X              'Assigns next value in DATA to X
1800 WEND                  'End loop
1900 PRINT NUM"numbers read from DATA.  Sum is"SUM" and average is"SUM/NUM
1910 REM Calculate standard deviation
1920   STEP1 = SUMSQ              'Find sum of squares of each value
1930   STEP2 = (SUM/NUM)^2*NUM    'Find square of average times number of values
1940   STEP3 = STEP1 - STEP2      'Subtract result in step 2 from result in step 1
1950   STEP4 = STEP3/(NUM)        'Divide by the number of values
1960   STD.DEV = SQR(STEP4)       'Find square root of result found in step 4.
1970   PRINT "Standard deviation is "STD.DEV
2000 DATA 5,11,8,1E+15
Ok
SAVE"A:STD-DEV1 ↵
Ok
RUN ↵
 3 numbers read from DATA.  Sum is 24  and average is 8
Standard deviation is  2.44949
Ok
```

You can see how the standard deviation reflects the true differences between the salary structures of the two companies by running the program using the salaries mentioned above.

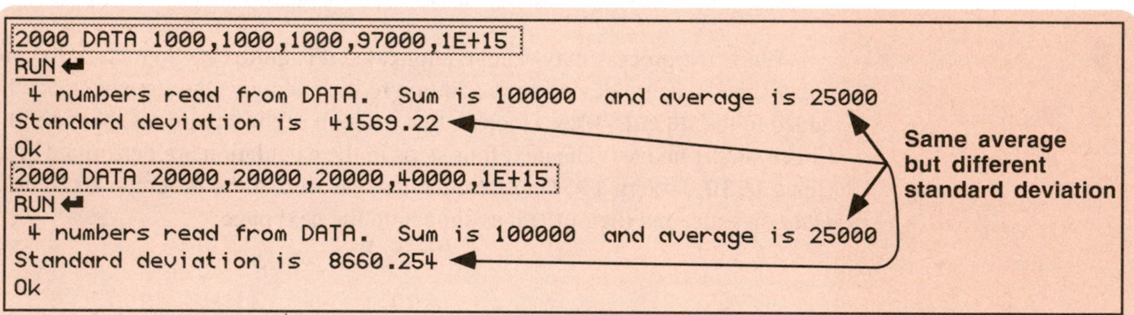

```
2000 DATA 1000,1000,1000,97000,1E+15
RUN ↵
 4 numbers read from DATA.  Sum is 100000  and average is 25000
Standard deviation is  41569.22
Ok
2000 DATA 20000,20000,20000,40000,1E+15
RUN ↵
 4 numbers read from DATA.  Sum is 100000  and average is 25000
Standard deviation is  8660.254
Ok
```


Combining Selection and Counting

The ideas of counting and selection can be combined to produce a program that selects data with certain characteristics and then generates some statistics on only the selected data. As an example of this, let's modify the college selection program, **SELECT4**, so that it calculates the average GPA of only those students in the General College (**GC**). Three parts have to be added to the program:

1. At line **1100**, the counter for the sum of the GPAs is initialized to 0.
2. At line **1300**, counters are added for the number of students in GC (**NUM**), and the sum of their GPAs (**SUM**). It is at this line that the college of the student is checked to see if it is equal to **GC**. If it is, the value of **NUM** is increased by 1 and the value of **GPA** is added to the value of **SUM** (in the following program these statements are combined on one line through the use of colons (**:**) to make the program easier to read and understand). If the student is from some college other than **GC**, the **THEN** part of line **1300** is not executed and the student's values are not included in the variables **NUM** and **SUM**.
3. A **PRINT** statement is added at line **1450** to display the results. **LOAD** the new version of the program, **LIST** it, **SAVE** it to your *BASIC Data* diskette, and then **RUN** it as shown on the next page:

```
LOAD"C:\BA\SELECT5↵
Ok
LIST↵
1100 NUM = 0 : SUM = 0      'Initialize counters
1200 READ N$,C$,GPA          'N$ = name, C$ = college, GPA = Grade Point Average
1250 WHILE GPA <> 1E+15
1300   IF C$ = "GC" THEN PRINT N$ : NUM = NUM + 1 : SUM = SUM + GPA
1350   READ N$,C$,GPA
1400 WEND
1450 PRINT "Average GPA of the"NUM"GC students is"SUM/NUM
1500   DATA Matt,GC,3.7
1600   DATA Keisha,IT,3.4
1700   DATA Sara,GC,2.8
1800   DATA 1E+15,1E+15,1E+15
Ok
SAVE"A:SELECT5↵
Ok
RUN↵
Matt
Sara
Average GPA of the 2 GC students is 3.25
Ok
```

TO TAKE A BREAK Type **SYSTEM** ↵, remove diskette(s). To resume (hard disk): Insert *Data* diskette, type **A:** ↵, **C:\BA\BASICA** ↵. To resume (two drive): Insert diskettes, type **A:** ↵, **B:\BASICA** ↵.

Subroutines

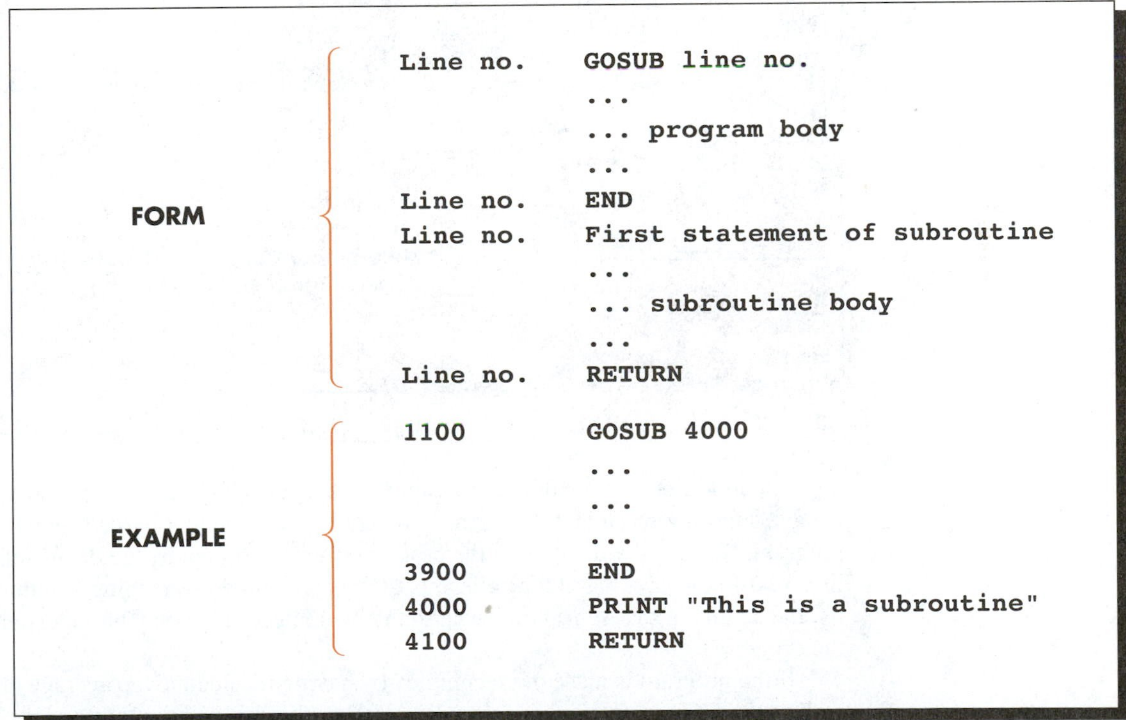

Subroutines are parts of programs that are, themselves, programs. They usually do a specific task, such as a computation, and usually are required to do that task more than once during the execution of a program.

Many times, subroutines are used to write complex programs in segments called modules. This allows programmers to write and test particular parts of a whole program as individual units and then to put the units together to construct a larger program. Because this allows a complex problem to be broken up into a series of simple problems, it is a powerful technique to use when working on large problems or when more than one programmer is working on a particular task. This idea of breaking up a complex problem into a number of simpler ones is used in many different areas. For example, an automaker will manufacturer the components of a car (engine, transmission, radio, etc.), test each part to be sure it runs properly, and then assemble the parts into one product. This makes the task much simpler and more efficient.

Let's revise the college selection program, **SELECT5**, so that it uses a subroutine to do the computations.

Subroutines are called through the use of a **GOSUB** statement such as **GOSUB 2100**, where **2100** is the line number of the first statement of the subroutine. The subroutine statements are located at the end of the main program, just after the **END** statement at line **2000**. It is good practice to begin a subroutine with a **REM** statement that indicates the purpose of the subroutine (see line **2100**). A subroutine must always end with a **RETURN** statement. This statement tells the computer to return control to the line just after the **GOSUB** statement that initiated the execution of the subroutine. In the following program, the **RETURN** statement returns control to line **1350**. **LOAD** the new version of the program, **LIST** it, **SAVE** it to your *BASIC Data* diskette, and then **RUN** it as shown below:

```
LOAD"C:\BA\SELECT6
Ok
LIST
1100 NUM = 0 : SUM = 0      'Initialize counters
1200 READ N$,C$,GPA         'N$ = name, C$ = college, GPA = Grade Point Average
1250 WHILE GPA <> 1E+15
1300    IF C$ = "GC" THEN GOSUB 2100   <-- Calls subroutine at line 2100
1350    READ N$,C$,GPA
1400 WEND
1450 PRINT "Average GPA of the"NUM"GC students is"SUM/NUM
1500    DATA Matt,GC,3.7
1600    DATA Keisha,IT,3.4
1700    DATA Sara,GC,2.8
1800    DATA 1E+15,1E+15,1E+15
2000 END
2100 REM SUBROUTINE to print GC student names and compute average GPA
2200    PRINT N$
2300    SUM = SUM + GPA
2400    NUM = NUM + 1
2500 RETURN   <-- Returns control to line directly after GOSUB (i.e., to line 1350)
Ok
SAVE"A:SELECT6
Ok
RUN
Matt
Sara
Average GPA of the 2 GC students is 3.25
Ok
```

The modified version of the program does the same thing as the original version. The advantage of using a subroutine is that it places the computations all together in their own module at the end of the program. Notice how the flow of the program is uninterrupted by the details of the computations (i.e., line **1300** now says that if the college is **GC** then go and do something—at this point we do not want to list the details of that something because that would get in the way of understanding the overall logic of the program).

If the program is made more complex by having it calculate the average of the non-GC students as well as the GC students, using subroutines makes the modification quite easy. All that needs to be done is to add another subroutine to do the extra computations and then change the **IF/THEN/ELSE** and **PRINT** statements accordingly. **LOAD** the new version of the program, **LIST** it, **SAVE** it to your *BASIC Data* diskette, and then **RUN** it as shown on the next page:

```
LOAD"C:\BA\SELECT7
Ok
LIST
1100 NUM = 0 : SUM = 0 : NUM2 = 0 : SUM2 = 0    'Initialize counters
1200 READ N$,C$,GPA       'N$ = name, C$ = college, GPA = Grade Point Average
1250 WHILE GPA <> 1E+15
1300   IF C$ = "GC" THEN GOSUB 2100 ELSE GOSUB 2600
1350   READ N$,C$,GPA
1400 WEND
1450 PRINT "Average GPA of the"NUM"GC students is"SUM/NUM
1460 PRINT "Average GPA of the"NUM2"non-GC students is"SUM2/NUM2
1500   DATA Matt,GC,3.7
1600   DATA Keisha,IT,3.4
1700   DATA Sara,GC,2.8
1800   DATA 1E+15,1E+15,1E+15
2000 END
2100 REM SUBROUTINE to print GC student names and compute average GPA
2200   PRINT N$
2300   SUM = SUM + GPA
2400   NUM = NUM + 1
2500 RETURN
2600 REM SUBROUTINE to compute average GPA of non-GC students
2700   SUM2 = SUM2 + GPA
2800   NUM2 = NUM2 + 1
2900 RETURN
Ok
SAVE"A:SELECT7
Ok
RUN
Matt
Sara
Average GPA of the 2 GC students is 3.25
Average GPA of the 2 non-GC students is 3.4
Ok
```

The changes allow the programmer to see that when the condition at line **1300** is true a group of statements is executed (the statements within the subroutine beginning at line **2100**) and when that condition is not true a different group of statements is executed (the statements within the subroutine beginning at line **2600**). This makes it easier for the programmer to understand the logic of the program. As the programs become longer and more complex, using subroutines in this way allows the programmer to concentrate on the overall flow of logic of the program or, if the programmer chooses, to concentrate on the details of smaller modules of the program.

More Complex Decisions

Sometimes decisions must be based on a number of different conditions. For example, suppose you have data on a group of people that includes the name, phone number, ZIP code, age, and political party affiliation of each person in the group. You have been asked to develop a program that can be used to organize volunteers in the community to help a Democratic Party candidate campaign for an upcoming election. To do this the program should print the names and phone numbers of people who are Democrats and who live in a certain geographical location (e.g., they have ZIP codes between 55100 and 56999). The program should also list the person's age so that someone of similar age could contact the prospective volunteer to ask for help.

• *The Task* •

Write a program that will read information from a database and display the names, phone numbers, and ages of Democrats whose ZIP codes are between 55100 and 56999.

• *Step 1: Justify Using the Computer* •

The computer is needed to sort through a large set of data.

• Step 2: Define the Problem •

Output For the data specified below, the output would look like the following:

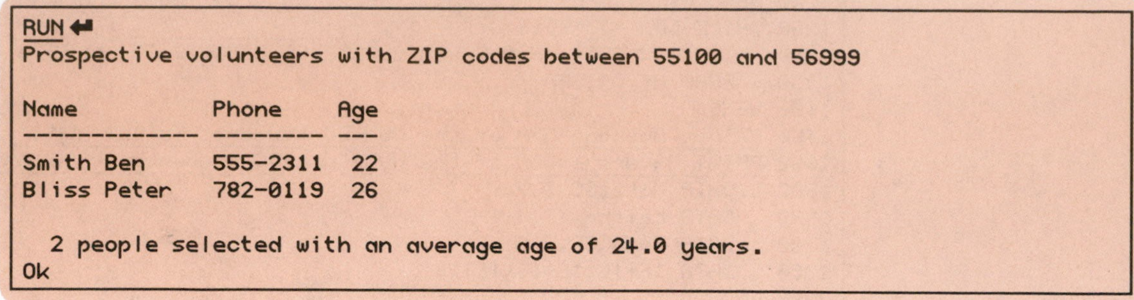

RUN
Prospective volunteers with ZIP codes between 55100 and 56999
Name Phone Age
Smith Ben 555-2311 22
Bliss Peter 782-0119 26
2 people selected with an average age of 24.0 years.
Ok

Sample data:

Name	*Phone number*	*ZIP code*	*Age*	*Party*
Smith Ben	555-2311	55110	22	D
Benson Amy	555-3401	55201	34	R
Mack Sara	541-3321	55011	55	D
Bliss Peter	782-0119	55202	26	D
Pander Pam	333-4266	55101	43	R

Processing Structurally, the document can be viewed as follows:

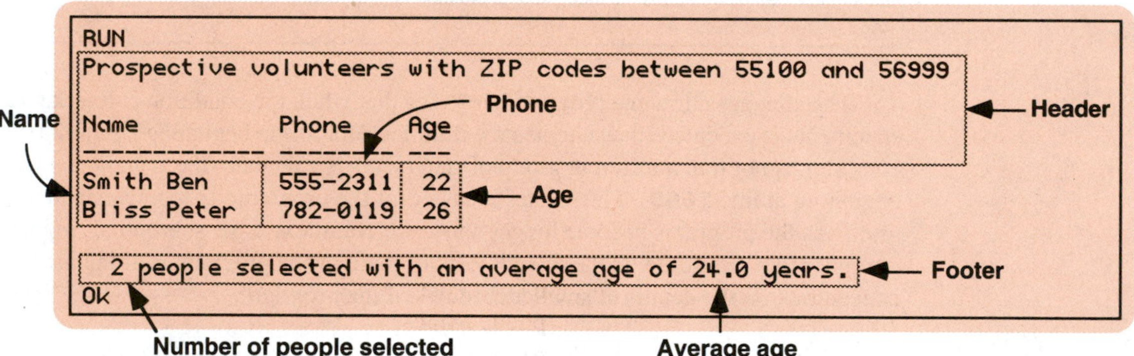

Each piece of information in the output can be defined as follows:

Header: Descriptive information about the document, including column headings.

Name: The name of the person (read from the **DATA** list) in the form **LastName** Space **FirstName**

Phone: The phone number of the person (read from the **DATA** list) in the form **xxx-xxx**.

Age: The age (in years) of the person (read from the **DATA** list).

Number of people selected: The number of people read from the **DATA** list that meet the specified criteria for selection (they have a ZIP code between 55100 and 56999 and their party type is Democratic). This is calculated using a counter.

Average age: The average age of the people selected (calculated from the sum of the ages of those selected divided by the number of people selected). Note that in order to calculate this, the sum of the ages first must be calculated (see below).

Footer: Descriptive information about the document including the number of people selected and the average age of the people selected.

In addition to the information found on the output, the program also needs to operate with some other pieces of data in order to properly select the people and perform the calculations:

Party preference: Even though the political party of each person is not displayed, this information is needed in order to select the proper names from the list. The party preference is read from the **DATA** list.

ZIP code: Like the party preference, the ZIP code of each person is not displayed, but this information is needed in order to select the proper names from the list. The ZIP code is read from the **DATA** list.

Sum of ages: The sum of the ages of the people selected (calculated from the ages of those selected) is needed to calculate the average age. This is calculated using a counter.

Input Data needed for processing are name, phone number, age, ZIP code, and party affiliation.

• *Step 3: Define the Program Variables* •

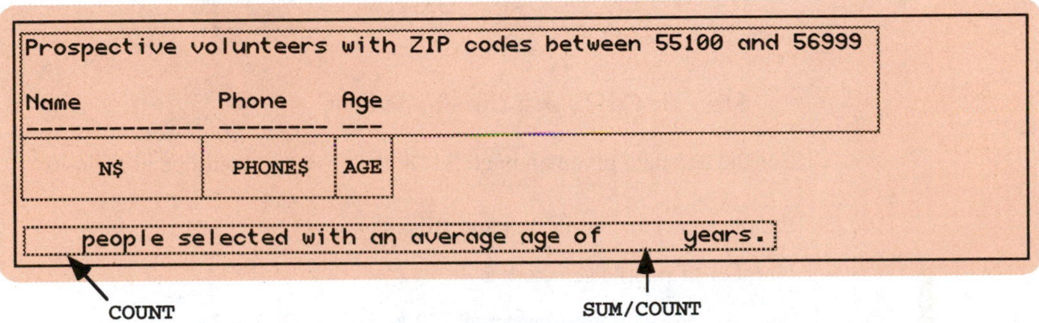

where the following are read from the database:

N$ = name in the form **LastName** space **FirstName** (data)
PHONE$ = phone number
ZIP = postal ZIP code
AGE = age in years
PARTY$ = party (**R** = Republican, **D** = Democrat, **N** = other)

and the following are calculated using counters:

COUNT = number of people selected
SUM = sum of the ages of the people selected

• *Step 4: Construct the Pseudocode* •

Try constructing the pseudocode yourself. Then compare your pseudocode with that given below (your code may be different but just as correct).

```
Begin processing
        Define PRINT USING images
        Initialize counters (COUNT and SUM)
        Display header
        Assign values to first set of variables (N$, PHONE$, ZIP, AGE, PARTY$)
        Begin loop—while the value of ZIP is not the data flag, do the following:
                Check PARTY$ and ZIP: If PARTY$ is D and ZIP is between 55100 and 56999
                        THEN  Display N$, PHONE$, AGE
                              Add 1 to COUNT
                              Add AGE to SUM
                        ELSE  Continue
                Assign values to next set of variables (N$, PHONE$, ZIP, AGE, PARTY$)
        End loop
        Display footer
End processing
```

• *Step 5: Calculate the Answers* •

For the test data given on page B118, the answers would be as follows:

People selected: Smith Ben and Bliss Peter

Number of people selected: 2

Average age of people selected: (22 + 26)/2 = 48/2 = 24

• *Step 6: Translate the Pseudocode into BASIC* •

Now try to translate the pseudocode into a proper BASIC program. One version of the BASIC code is as follows. Notice the use of subroutines to do the processing of the several parts of the program. The large number of **REM** statements make the program seem longer than it really is. The most important statement is line **2700**, which actually selects the people by evaluating two conditions connected by the logical connector **AND**. Remember, with **AND** all conditions must be true for the statement to be true. With **OR** only one of the conditions needs to be true for the statement to be true.

```
LOAD"C:\BA\PARTY1
Ok
LIST
1100 REM Program displays names of democrats living in a certain area
1200 REM Douglas Robertson (373-4026), created 1 Mar 91
1300 REM Define variables:
1400   REM       N$ = name in form LastName space FirstName
1500   REM   PHONE$ = phone number in form 373-4026
1600   REM      ZIP = postal ZIP code in form 55455
1700   REM      AGE = age in years
1800   REM   PARTY$ = party preference (R = republican, D = Democrat, N = other)
1900   REM    COUNT = number of people selected
2000   REM      SUM = sum of the ages of the people selected
2100 GOSUB 3300                         'Define images for PRINT USING
2200 GOSUB 4000                         'Initialize counters
2300 GOSUB 4400                         'Display header
2400 READ N$,PHONE$,ZIP,AGE,PARTY$      'Assign values to first set of variables
2500 REM Begin loop (exit data flag is 1E+15)
2600   WHILE ZIP <> 1E+15
2700     IF PARTY$ = "D" AND ZIP >= 55100! AND ZIP =< 55699! THEN GOSUB 5000
2800     READ N$,PHONE$,ZIP,AGE,PARTY$  'Assign values to next set of variables
2900   WEND
3000 REM Display footer
3100   GOSUB 5500
3200 END
3300 REM ***** SUBROUTINE to define images for PRINT USING:
3400   I1$ = "Prospective volunteers with ZIP codes between 55100 and 56999"
3500   I2$ = "Name             Phone     Age"
3600   I3$ = "-------------- --------- ---"
3700   I4$ = "\            \ \      \ ###"
3800   I5$ = "### people selected with an average age of ##.# years."
3900 RETURN
4000 REM ***** SUBROUTINE to initialize variables
4100   COUNT = 0
4200     SUM = 0
4300 RETURN
4400 REM ***** SUBROUTINE to display header
4500   PRINT I1$
4600   PRINT
4700   PRINT I2$
4800   PRINT I3$
4900 RETURN
5000 REM ***** SUBROUTINE to display and count volunteers
5100   PRINT USING I4$; N$,PHONE$,AGE
5200   COUNT = COUNT + 1
5300   SUM = SUM + AGE
5400 RETURN
5500 REM ***** SUBROUTINE to display footer
5600   PRINT
5700   PRINT USING I5$; COUNT, SUM/COUNT
5800 RETURN
5900 REM DATA has form Lastname space FirstName,phone,ZIP,age,party
6000   DATA Smith Ben,   555-2311,55110,   22,D
6100   DATA Benson Amy,  555-3401,55201,   34,R
6200   DATA Mack Sara,   541-3321,55011,   55,D
6300   DATA Bliss Peter,782-0119,55202,   26,D
6400   DATA Pander Pam,  333-4266,55101,   43,R
6500   DATA 1E+15,      1E+15,   1E+15,1E+15,1E+15
Ok
SAVE"A:PARTY1
Ok
```

Program ends here and subroutines begin

• Step 7: Type the Program •

Load (or type) the above program and save it using the name **PARTY1**.

• Step 8: Run the Program •

Run the program for the data given.

```
RUN ↵
Prospective volunteers with ZIP codes between 55100 and 56999

Name           Phone     Age
-------------- --------- ---
Smith Ben      555-2311  22
Bliss Peter    782-0119  26

  2 people selected with an average age of 24.0 years.
Ok
```

• Step 9: Check the Computer's Results •

Check the output of the above test run to see if the answers obtained by hand are the same as those provided by the computer.

• Step 10: Debug the Program •

Because the answers check, debugging is not needed.

Replacement Statements

As was noted earlier, the meaning of the *equal* sign in BASIC is different than in algebra. Algebraically speaking, expressions such as **A = B** and **B = A** have the same meaning. In BASIC, however, **A = B** means *replace the current value of* **A** *with the current value of* **B**, while **B = A** means the reverse (i.e., *replace the current value of* **B** *with the value of* **A**). The two programs below illustrate this point:

```
NEW ↵
Ok
10 A = 5
20 B = 3
30 PRINT A,B
40 A = B              ◄— Replace the current value of A with the current value of B
50 PRINT A,B
RUN ↵
 5             3
 3             3 ◄— Both A and B now have original B value
Ok
```

Line Numbers	Comments
10	Creates a storage location called **A** and assigns a value of **5** to that location.
20	Creates a storage location called **B** and assigns a value of **3** to that location.
30	Displays the current values of **A** and **B**.
40	Replaces the current value of **A** with the current value of **B**. The effect is to change the value of **A** from **5** to **3**.
50	Displays the current values of **A** and **B**.

If line **40** is changed to **40 B = A**, a different result is displayed:

```
NEW ←
Ok
10 A = 5
20 B = 3
30 PRINT A,B
40 B = A              ← Replace the current value of B with the current value of A
50 PRINT A,B
RUN ←
 5            3
 5            5       ← Both A and B now have original value of A
Ok
```

The reason for the new result is that line **40** now says to replace the current value of **B** with the current value of **A**. When this is done, both **A** and **B** have the original **A** value.

Study the above programs until you are sure you understand why they work the way they do. That idea will be used in the next two sections.

Largest Number in a List

Replacement statements can be employed to write a simple program that will find the largest number in a given list of numbers. Before you try to write the program, think about how you would determine the largest number on a list if you had to do it by hand. For example, what is the largest number in the list of numbers 3, 4, 2? All you have to do is look at the list for one second and the answer, 4, pops into your head. Now try to figure out how to tell the computer to do the same task. Finding the solution in your head is so simple and you did it so fast that it is probably difficult for you to write down the steps you followed. It may help for you to try to solve a more difficult problem. For example, find the largest number in the following list: 35, 23, 12, 67, 43, 67, 3, 4, 66, 43, 34, -45, 3.53, 12, 65, 32, 35.66, 34, 25. Now finding the solution takes more time and you have to be systematic in your approach. One way of solving the problem is outlined in the pseudocode given on the next page.

Variables: **BIG** = largest number on the list so far
NUM = a new number read from the data list

Begin processing
    Assign very small value to largest number so far
    Assign value of first piece of data to **NUM**
        While **NUM** is not the data flag, do the following
            Compare new number to largest so far: If **NUM** is larger than **BIG**
                THEN **NUM** is largest so far. Replace **BIG** with **NUM**
                ELSE **BIG** is still largest so far, so continue
            Assign next value in data list to **NUM**
        End loop
    Display value of **BIG** (largest number on list)
End processing

The program that corresponds to this pseudocode is given below. Study how the program was translated from the pseudocode into BASIC code. **LOAD** the program, **LIST** it, **SAVE** it to your *BASIC Data* diskette, and then **RUN** it as shown below:

```
LOAD"C:\BA\BIG1↵
Ok
LIST↵
1100 BIG = -1E+15                         'Assign small value to largest # so far
1200 READ NUM                             'Assign value of first data set to NUM
1300   WHILE NUM <> 1E+15                 'Begin loop
1400     IF NUM > BIG THEN BIG = NUM      'Compare new number to largest so far
1500     READ NUM                         'Assign next value to NUM
1600   WEND                               'End loop
1700 PRINT "Largest number on list is" BIG
1800 DATA 7,5,2,8,6,1E+15
Ok
SAVE"A:BIG1↵
Ok
RUN↵
Largest number on list is 8
Ok
```

Notice that line **1100** initially assigns a very small value to **BIG**. Doing so will guarantee that the first time line **1400** is executed, the value of **BIG** will be replaced by the value of **NUM**. For this particular set of data, line **1100** is not really needed because all the data are positive and the initial value of **BIG** would be, by default, zero. However, if the data were all negative, then line **1100** is needed or the computer will give the value **0** as the largest number on the list. The example below shows what happens when line **1100** is deleted and the data are changed to negative numbers.

```
1100 BIG = -1E+15                         'Assign small value to largest # so far
1200 READ NUM                             'Assign value of first data set  to NUM
1300   WHILE NUM <> 1E+15                 'Begin loop
1400     IF NUM > BIG THEN BIG = NUM      'Compare new number to largest so far
1500     READ NUM                         'Assign next value to NUM
1600   WEND                               'End loop
1700 PRINT "Largest number on list is" BIG
1800 DATA -7,-5,-2,-8,-6,1E+15
Ok
RUN↵
Largest number on list is-2   <-- Program runs correctly
Ok
1100↵                         <-- When line 1100 removed, program gives wrong answer
RUN↵
Largest number on list is 0   <--
Ok
```

Smallest Number in a List

How could the above program be changed to find the smallest number on the list? Clearly, the variable called **BIG** should be changed into a variable called **SMALL** (this is only a cosmetic change—the computer does not care what the variables are called).

More importantly, note that line **1400** is where the comparison is made between the new value just read from the list (**NUM**) and the largest number so far on the list (**BIG**). **BIG** was to be replaced by **NUM** if the new number was larger than the largest number so far. Thus, line **1400** was written as:

```
1400  IF NUM > BIG THEN BIG = NUM
```

Now **SMALL** is to be replaced by **NUM** if the new number read is *smaller than* the smallest number so far. Thus, the greater than symbol **>** is replaced with a less than symbol **<** and line **1400** has the form:

```
1400  IF NUM < SMALL THEN SMALL = NUM
```

If the above changes are made, a **RUN** of the program would produce the following:

```
1100 SMALL = -1E+15                          'Assign small value to smallest# so far
1200 READ NUM                                'Assign value of first data set  to NUM
1300   WHILE NUM <> 1E+15                    'Begin loop
1400     IF NUM < SMALL THEN SMALL = NUM'Compare new number to smallest so far
1500     READ NUM                            'Assign next value to NUM
1600   WEND                                  'End loop
1700 PRINT "Smallest number on list is" SMALL
1800 DATA 7,5,2,8,6,1E+15
Ok
RUN
Smallest number on list is-1E+15  <--- Answer is incorrect
Ok
```

The answer is not correct. The computer says that the smallest number is **-1E+15**, which is not even on the data list! Where did the value **-1E+15** come from? In line **1100** the value of **SMALL** was initialized in the same way that the value for **BIG** was initialized. If you start off with **SMALL** being equal to a very small number, then it will remain that value because none of the numbers on the data list is smaller than the initial value assigned to **SMALL**. This can be fixed by changing the initial value of **SMALL** to a very large number, such as **1E+15**.

```
1100 SMALL =  1E+15                          'Assign large value to smallest # so far
1200 READ NUM                                'Assign value of first data set  to NUM
1300   WHILE NUM <> 1E+15                    'Begin loop
1400     IF NUM < SMALL THEN SMALL = NUM'Compare new number to smallest so far
1500     READ NUM                            'Assign next value to NUM
1600   WEND                                  'End loop
1700 PRINT "Smallest number on list is" SMALL
1800 DATA 7,5,2,8,6,1E+15
SAVE"A:SMALL1
Ok
RUN
Smallest number on list is 2 <--- With proper initialization of SMALL, answer is correct
Ok
```

You should carefully go through both programs. Be sure that you understand why **SMALL** must be initialized to a very large number in the above program and why **BIG** must be initialized to a very small number in the previous program. Also, be sure you understand the difference between **SMALL = NUM** and **NUM = SMALL**.

Finding the Largest Wage Paid

Let's modify the payroll program, **WAGES4** (p. B107), so that it finds both the largest and smallest pay checks earned for all employees listed. The important part of this modification is the addition of two **IF/THEN/ELSE** statements: one to keep track of the largest wage paid and the other to keep track of the smallest. Before looking at the program listing below, try to figure out on your own what statements need to be added. Then, **LOAD** the new version of the program, **LIST** it, **SAVE** it to your *BASIC Data* diskette, and **RUN** it as shown below:

```
LOAD"C:\BA\WAGES5↵
Ok
LIST↵
1100 REM Program to compute wages given total hours worked and pay rate
1200 REM Douglas Robertson (373-4026), created 1 Mar 91
1300 REM Define variables:
1400 REM   EMPLOYEE$ = name in form LastName Space First (e.g., Roberts Matt)
1500 REM        RATE = rate of pay in dollars per hour (e.g.,  3)
1600 REM       HOURS = total number of hours worked for pay period (e.g., 50)
1700 REM         PAY = total pay earned for pay period (e.g., 150)
1800 REM Begin processing
1900   REM Define PRINT USING images
2000     IMAGE1$ = "Employee       Pay Rate       Hours    Total Pay"
2100     IMAGE2$ = "--------       --------       -----    ---------"
2200     IMAGE3$ = "\            \  $##.##         ##.#      $###.##"
2300     IMAGE4$ = "Largest wage paid is $###.## and smallest is $###.##"
2400   PRINT IMAGE1$                              'Display header
2500   PRINT IMAGE2$                              'Display header
2510   GOSUB 4200                                 'Initialize var for large & small
2700   READ EMPLOYEE$,RATE,HOURS                  'Assign values to name, rate, hours
2710     WHILE HOURS <> 1E+15                     'For each person do the following
2800       PAY = RATE*HOURS                       'Calculate pay using formula
2810       GOSUB 4600                             'Calculate largest & smallest wage
2900       PRINT USING IMAGE3$;EMPLOYEE$,RATE,HOURS,PAY
2910       READ EMPLOYEE$,RATE,HOURS              'Assign values to name, rate, hours
3000     WEND                                     'Repeat loop for next person
3100   PRINT
3200   PRINT USING IMAGE4$; BIG,SMALL             'Display footer
3300 REM End processing
3400 REM Define DATA list in form:
3500 REM DATA NAME          ,RATE,HOURS
3600     DATA Roberts Matt,  4,   30
3700     DATA Sim Keisha  ,  3,   50
3800     DATA Tech Sara   ,  6,   21
3900     DATA Well Vanessa,  5,   40
4000     DATA 1E+15,1E+15,1E+15,1E+15
4100 END
4200 REM ***** SUBROUTINE to initialize counters for largest and smallest wages
4300   BIG   = -1E+15
4400   SMALL =  1E+15
4500 RETURN
4600 REM ***** SUBROUTINE to calculate largest & smallest wage
4700   IF PAY > BIG   THEN BIG   = PAY
4800   IF PAY < SMALL THEN SMALL = PAY
4900 RETURN
Ok
SAVE"A:WAGES5↵
Ok
RUN↵
Employee       Pay Rate       Hours    Total Pay
--------       --------       -----    ---------
Roberts Matt    $ 4.00         30.0      $120.00
Sim Keisha      $ 3.00         50.0      $150.00
Tech Sara       $ 6.00         21.0      $126.00
Well Vanessa    $ 5.00         40.0      $200.00

Largest wage paid is $200.00 and smallest is $120.00
Ok
```

Notice the two subroutines that were added. The first subroutine initializes the counters for **BIG** and **SMALL** to the proper values. The second subroutine contains the two **IF/THEN/ELSE** statements (lines **4700** and **4800**) that actually carry out the replacements. Also notice that an **END** statement was added at line **4100** in order to separate the main program from the subroutines.

TO TAKE A BREAK Type **SYSTEM** ↵, remove diskette(s). To resume (hard disk): Insert *Data* diskette, type **A:** ↵, **C:\BA\BASICA** ↵. To resume (two drive): Insert diskettes, type **A:** ↵, **B:\BASICA** ↵.

Homework Exercises

For each of the following homework exercises, use the programming process to develop a BASIC program that will produce the output described. Each program should contain enough **REM** statements to clearly document the program. Unless instructed to do otherwise, produce a hard copy of a **LIST** and a **RUN** of each of your final working programs. Also, save each program using a name such as **HWB4-01** for future reference. Your instructor may also ask you to hand in other materials related to the development of the programs such as the variable definitions, pseudocodes, etc.

---

① In Exercise 6 of Chapter 3 you wrote a program that calculated the charges for electricity usage for the month of August for three residences. Modify that program so that the charges are computed for the month of May for the same three residences. From October through May, Northern States Power Company charges $.05392 per kilowatt hour (KWH) for the first 1,000 KWH of electricity used by a residential customer and $.04942 per KWH for electrical use in excess of 1,000 KWH. It also charges a flat fee of $6.00 per month to help defray the costs of the power system such as reading the electric meter and keeping accounts. Added to the bill is a city tax of 1.5% and a state tax of 6.0% on both the energy charge and the flat fee.

Your program should employ **PRINT USING** to display a table showing the total monthly electric bill for the three houses listed below. Note that the sum of the items for **5 Elm Street** is displayed as **24.13** but, if you add up the numbers in the table, you get **24.14**. This is because the computer does the calculations to a precision of 14 decimal places but the **PRINT USING** statement rounds off the numbers to two decimal places when it displays them. Hence, the difference of **.01** is due to round-off error. The actual values that the computer uses in its calculations are:

Item to compute	*Computation*	*Computed value*	*Value displayed*
Basic charge	305*.05392 =	16.4456	16.45
Flat fee	6	6.00	6.00
City tax	(16.4456 + 6)*.015 =	0.336684	0.34
State tax	(16.4456 + 6)*.06 =	1.346736	1.35
Total charge	sum of above =	24.12902	24.13

but the sum of the values displayed is 24.14

The output from your program should look like the following (the values in the boxes should be calculated by the computer):

Continued . . .

```
Homework B4-01                        Joe Computer                      1 Mar 91

Electric Residential costs for February, 1991

                              Basic
                              Energy     Flat     City    State    Total
Address                KWH    Charge      Fee      Tax      Tax    Charge
----------------     ----    -------   ------   ------   ------   -------
5 Elm Street           305   $ 16.45   $ 6.00   $ 0.34   $ 1.35   $ 24.13
8 Perry Court         1902   $ 98.50   $ 6.00   $ 1.57   $ 6.27   $112.33
2 Adams Avenue        1001   $ 53.97   $ 6.00   $ 0.90   $ 3.60   $ 64.47
Ok
```

② Use the programming procedure to develop a program that will read from a **DATA** statement the name, sex, and age of individuals, count the number of children under 5 years of age and count the total number of people on the list. Use the following data (the values are listed as name, sex, age):

Sue,F,3,Sara,F,2,Pete,M,20,Brian,M,30,Amy,F,20,Steve,M,22

The output from your program should look like the following (the values in the box should be calculated by the computer):

```
Homework B4-02                        Joe Computer                      1 Mar 91

6 people on the list.
2 children under 5 years of age.
```

③ Extend the program you wrote for Exercise 2 so that in addition to counting the number of people and the number of children under 5, it also counts the number of males, the number of females, and finds the average age of all the males between the ages of 18 and 26, inclusive. Use the same data as in Exercise 2.

The output from your program should look like the following (the values in the box should be calculated by the computer):

```
Homework B4-03                        Joe Computer                      1 Mar 91

6 people on the list.
2 children under 5 years of age.
3 males on the list.
3 females on the list.
21 is the average age of all males between 18 and 26.
```

④ Extend the program you wrote for Exercise 3 so that the user is asked to enter the selection criterion for age (i.e., use an **INPUT** statement to allow the user to input the age cutoff for those people selected). This means that you will have to create a variable to store the maximum age and then use that variable in the **IF/THEN/ELSE** statement.

Run the program using a maximum age of 21. The output from your program should look like the following (the values in the box should be calculated by the computer):

```
Homework B4-04                    Joe Computer                    1 Mar 91

Enter maximum age for children to be counted? 21 ↵
 6 people on the list.
 4 children under 21 years of age.
 3 males on the list.
 3 females on the list.
 21 is the average age of all males between 18 and 26.
```

⑤ As was stated in Exercise 1 of Chapter 3, for young adults, the approximate relationship between height and weight is given by the formula $W = 5.5(H - 40)$ where W is weight in pounds and H is height in inches.

Use the programming procedure to develop an interactive program that will determine if a person is underweight, overweight, or just right according to the above formula. Do this by asking the person to input his or her height and weight and then, if the weight is more than 10% above or below the value given by the formula, print ideal weight and the number of pounds over or under the ideal weight (rounded off to the nearest whole pound). Have the program loop back and continue to ask for the data until the user exits the program by entering a data flag (such as **1E15**) for his or her height.

The output from your program should look like the following (the values in the boxes should be calculated by the computer):

```
Homework B4-05                    Nguyen Dang                    1 Mar 91

Enter height in inches, weight in pounds or 1E15,1E15 to quit? 62,200 ↵
Your ideal weight is 121 pounds.  You are 79 pounds overweight.

Enter height in inches, weight in pounds or 1E15,1E15 to quit? 62,100 ↵
Your ideal weight is 121 pounds.  You are 21 pounds underweight.

Enter height in inches, weight in pounds or 1E15,1E15 to quit? 62,125 ↵
Your ideal weight is 121 pounds.  You are within 10% of this.

Enter height in inches, weight in pounds or 1E15,1E15 to quit? 1E15,1E15 ↵

Thank you for your time.
```

⑥ Barb and Karl own a small stationary store and want to keep their price list on the computer. They sell the following items:

Stock number	Item name	Manufacturer	Unit Price
27365	Paper	Xerox	29.95
83288	Ink	Smithson	12.34
21560	Pencils	Farber	2.34
18332	Copy fluid	Xerox	18.50
29335	File folders	Smithson	19.00

Continued . . .

CHAPTER FOUR

Use the programming procedure to develop a program that displays the above information in table form. The program should use **READ** and **DATA** statements to assign values to variables, **WHILE** and **WEND** statements for the loop, a counter to count the number of items read, and **PRINT USING** statements. In addition, if the manufacturer is **Smithson**, the program should display **@@** to the right of the price. The output should look like the following:

```
Homework B4-06                     Joe Computer                     1 Mar 91

      Stock
Num   Number  Item Description  Manufacturer  Price
---   ------  ----------------  ------------  ------
 1    27365   Paper             Xerox         $29.95
 2    83288   Ink               Smithson      $12.34 @@
 3    21560   Pencils           Farber        $ 2.34
 4    18332   Copy fluid        Xerox         $18.50
 5    29335   File folders      Smithson      $19.00 @@
---   ------  ----------------  ------------  ------
```

---

⑦ On page L101 a Lotus 1-2-3 worksheet was developed that computed the shipping charges for mail order products purchased from Turkey Feather Electronics. As you recall, the charges are based on the weight of the item and the postal zone. The following rules apply:

Weight in pounds	***Shipping charges in dollars***
Under 5	5 + (weight)* (postal zone)
5–10	10 + (weight in excess of 5 pounds)*(postal zone)
over 10	15 + (weight in excess of 10 pounds)*(postal zone)

Use the programming procedure to develop a program that computes the shipping charges for the items listed. The output from your program should look like the following (the values in the box should be calculated by the computer):

```
Homework B4-07                     Joe Computer                     1 Mar 91

Stock              Postal    Shipping
Number   Weight     Zone     Charges
 4398       2         3       $11.00
 3402       6         5       $15.00
 1743      12         2       $19.00
 3452       8         3       $19.00
 6545      20         1       $25.00

                Total         $89.00
                Average       $17.80
                Maximum       $25.00
                Minimum       $11.00
                Number           5
```

Which do you think was easier to do: construct the BASIC program or create the Lotus 1-2-3 worksheet?

⑧ On page L142 you created a Lotus 1-2-3 worksheet that displayed the sales performances of the employees of MicroMania Computers, Inc. Use the programming procedure to develop a program that accomplishes the same task. The output from your program should look like the following (the values in the boxes should be calculated by the computer):

```
Homework B4-08                    Joe Computer                    1 Mar 91

MicroMania Computers, Inc., Sales Summary
        Date:  03-01-1991
        Time:  17:18:09

Num Employee    Hardware    Software Total Sales
--- --------- ---------- ---------- -----------
  1 Sherri    $22,357.92  $1,052.83  $23,410.75
  2 Mary      $13,862.31  $2,832.09  $16,694.40
  3 Lawrence  $10,154.00  $1,502.00  $11,656.00
--- --------- ---------- ---------- -----------
      Totals: $46,374.23  $5,386.92  $51,761.15
    Averages: $15,458.08  $1,795.64  $17,253.72
```

For this exercise, use simple strings to display the date (**03-01-1991**) and the time (**17:18:09**). Which do you think was easier to do: construct the BASIC program or create the Lotus 1-2-3 worksheet? Which do you think would be easier to expand to include 500 employees?

---

⑨ On page L143) you created a Lotus 1-2-3 worksheet that displayed the sales performances of the employees of MicroMania Computers, Inc. and that also calculated and displayed their commissions and total earnings. Recall that employees earn a base salary of $10,000 per year plus a commission on items they sell. The commissions are computed as follows:

Hardware Sales Employee earns a 10% commission on hardware sales up to the first $20,000 worth of equipment sold, and then 12% on all hardware sales over $20,000.

Software sales Employee earns 8% on all sales.

Modify your program from Exercise 8 so that it accomplishes the same task as the Lotus 1-2-3 worksheet. The output from your program should look like the following (the values in the boxes should be calculated by the computer):

```
Homework B4-09                    Joe Computer                    1 Mar 91

MicroMania Computers, Inc., Sales Summary
        Date:  03-01-1991
        Time:  17:46:52

Num Employee    Hardware    Software Total Sales Commission    Earnings
--- --------- ---------- ---------- ----------- ---------- ----------
  1 Sherri    $22,357.92  $1,052.83  $23,410.75  $2,367.18 $12,367.18
  2 Mary      $13,862.31  $2,832.09  $16,694.40  $1,612.80 $11,612.80
  3 Lawrence  $10,154.00  $1,502.00  $11,656.00  $1,135.56 $11,135.56
--- --------- ---------- ---------- ----------- ---------- ----------
      Totals: $46,374.23  $5,386.92  $51,761.15  $5,115.54 $35,115.54
    Averages: $15,458.08  $1,795.64  $17,253.72  $1,705.18 $11,705.18
```

Which do you think was easier to do: construct the BASIC program or create the Lotus 1-2-3 worksheet? Which do you think would be easier to expand to include 500 employees?

CHAPTER FOUR

Advanced Loops

Objectives *After you have completed this chapter, you should be able to*

- Use complex **FOR/NEXT** loops.
- Use **TRACE** to display line numbers as statements are executed.
- Use **DATE$** and **TIME$** to time stamp program runs.
- Be able to modify an already existing program in a systematic way.
- Use **INT** to determine whether or not one number is a factor of another number.

CHAPTER 5

- Use **INT** to round numbers to a specified level of precision.
- Explain what verification codes are and use them to check the accuracy of input data.
- Use **BEEP**, **SOUND**, and **PLAY** to instruct the computer to produce audio output.
- Use **CHR$** and **STRING$** to create special effects in programs.
- Use **LOCATE** to position the cursor anywhere on the screen.

Introduction

In previous chapters we saw that looping is the process of telling the computer to execute the same set of statements over and over again. This was accomplished by using **FOR/NEXT** and **WHILE/WEND** statements. In this chapter the notion of looping is extended to more complex examples.

Also in this chapter is a discussion of three more BASIC functions: **INT**, **BEEP**, and **SOUND**. The **INT** function returns the integer part of a number (this can be used to see whether or not a number has a decimal part) while **BEEP** and **SOUND** allow the programmer to instruct the computer to produce different sounds on the speaker of the system unit.

FOR and NEXT Statements

FORM

```
Line no.   FOR lv = initial val TO term val STEP inc val
           .
           . loop body
           .
Line no.   NEXT lv
```

where

lv	=	loop variable (any legal numeric variable name).
initial val	=	the value that the loop variable will begin with.
terminal val	=	the value that the loop variable will go up to.
inc val	=	increment used to change the value of the loop variable each time the loop is executed.

EXAMPLE

```
1100       FOR J = 1 TO 4 STEP 3
1200         PRINT J
1300       NEXT J
```

As was discussed in Chapter 3, the **FOR** and **NEXT** statements allow the programmer to control the number of times a particular set of instructions will be carried out. These statements can also be used for generating number sequences. For example, suppose you want to display the sequence of numbers 2, 4, 6. This is easily done by setting up a **FOR/NEXT** loop with the following **FOR** statement:

```
10 FOR J = 2 TO 6 STEP 2
```

This says to execute the statements in the **FOR/NEXT** loop beginning with the value of **J** equal to 2 (**FOR J = 2**) until the value of **J** exceeds 6 (**TO 6**). Each time the loop is processed, the value of **J** is incremented by 2 (**STEP 2**). The full program would look like the following:

```
NEW
Ok
10 FOR J = 2 TO 6 STEP 2
20   PRINT J
30 NEXT J
40 PRINT "Value of J is " J
RUN
 2
 4
 6
Value of J is  8
Ok
```

Line Numbers	Comments
10	Creates a storage location called **J** and assigns a value of **2** to that location. Then this value is checked to see if it exceeds the terminal value of **6**. If it does, the loop is skipped and control is transferred to the statement directly after the **NEXT** statement (i.e., control is transferred to line number **40**). If the current value of **J** does not exceed the terminal value, control is transferred to the statement directly after the **FOR** statement (i.e., control is transferred to line number **20**). Because 2 =< 6 is a true statement, line number **20** is executed next.
20	The value of **J** (which is **2**) is displayed.
30	The **STEP** (which is **2**) is added to the current value of **J** (which is **2**) making the new value of **J** equal to **4**. Control is then transferred back to the **FOR** statement at line number **10**.
10	The current value of **J** (which is **4**) is checked to see if it exceeds the terminal value (**6**). If it does, the loop is exited and control is transferred to the statement directly after the **NEXT** statement (i.e., control is transferred to line number **40**). If the current value of **J** does not exceed the terminal value, control is transferred to the statement directly after the **FOR** statement (i.e., control is transferred to line number **20**). Because 4 =< 6 is a true statement, line number **20** is executed next.
20	The value of **J** (which is **4**) is displayed.
30	The **STEP** (which is **2**) is added to the current value of **J** (which is **4**) making the new value of **J** equal to **6**. Control is then transferred back to the **FOR** statement at line **10**.
10	Again, the current value of **J** (now **6**) is compared to the terminal value. Because 6 =< 6 is a true statement, line **20** is executed next.
20	The value of **J** (which is **6**) is displayed.
30	The **STEP** (which is **2**) is added to the current value of **J** (which is **6**) making the new value of **J** equal to **8**. Control is then transferred back to the **FOR** statement at line **10**.
10	Again, the current value of **J** (now **8**) is compared to the terminal value. Because 8 =< 6 is a false statement, the loop is exited and control passes to the statement directly after the **NEXT** statement (i.e., control passes to line **40**).
40	The final value of **J** (which is **8**) is printed.

The entire run of the program can be summarized as follows:

Memory Assignments for Sample FOR/NEXT Program

Line no.	J	
	0	Default value
10	2	Assigned value
	2 =< 6 is true, so execute statements inside loop	Decision
20	2	Output
30	4 ⬅ 2 + 2	Calculated value
10	4 =< 6 is true, so execute statements inside loop	Decision
20	4	Output
30	6 ⬅ 4 + 2	Calculated value
10	6 =< 6 is true, so execute statements inside loop	Decision
20	6	Output
30	8 ⬅ 6 + 2	Calculated value
10	8 =< 6 is false, so exit loop	Decision
40	8	Output

(J: Variable name)

Look at the following program and try to figure out what the output will be before you look at the **RUN**:

```
NEW ↵
Ok
10 FOR K = 9 TO 16 STEP 3
20   PRINT K
30 NEXT K
40 PRINT "Value of K is "K
RUN ↵
 9
 12
 15
Value of K is  18
Ok
```

Line Number	Value of K	Comments
10	9	Creates a storage location called **K** and assigns a value of **9** to that location. Also, the value of **K** (which is **9**) is compared to the terminal value (**16**). Because 9 =< 16 is true, the statements inside the loop are processed.
20	9	Displays current value of **K**.
30	9 + 3 = 12	The **STEP** (which is **3**) is added to the current value of **K** (which is **9**) to create a new value for **K** (which is **12**). Control passes back to the **FOR** statement at line number **10**.
10	12	Because 12 =< 16 is true, the statements inside the loop are processed.
20	12	Displays current value of **K**.
30	12 + 3 = 15	The **STEP** (which is **3**) is added to the current value of **K** (which is **12**) to create a new value for **K** (which is **15**). Control passes back to the **FOR** statement at line **10**.
10	15	Because 15 =< 16 is true, the statements inside the loop are processed.
20	15	Displays current value of **K**.
30	15 + 3 = 18	The **STEP** (which is **3**) is added to the current value of **K** (which is **15**) to create a new value for **K** (which is **18**). Control passes back to the **FOR** statement at line number **10**.
10	18	Because 18 =< 16 is false, the loop is skipped and control passes to line number **40**.
40	18	The value of **K** is displayed.

If the **STEP** is not explicitly stated, it is assumed to be 1. For example:

```
NEW ←
Ok
10 FOR K = 3 TO 5        ← The word STEP is left off so the STEP is assumed to be 1
20   PRINT K
30 NEXT K
40 PRINT "Value of K is "K
RUN ←
 3
 4
 5
Value of K is  6
Ok
```

FOR/NEXT loops may be used to increment values from low to high (this happens when the **STEP** is positive) or from high to low (this happens when the **STEP** is negative). When the **STEP** is negative the ending value must be smaller than the beginning value.

```
NEW ↵
Ok
10 FOR K = 5 TO -2 STEP -3
20   PRINT K
30 NEXT K
40 PRINT "Value of K is "K
RUN ↵
 5
 2
-1
Value of K is -4
Ok
```

Line Number	Value of K	Comments
10	**5**	Creates a storage location called **K** and assigns a value of **5** to that location. Also, the value of **K** (which is **5**) is compared to the terminal value (which is **–2**). Because 5 >= –2 is true, the statements inside the loop are processed. Notice how the inequality sign is the reverse of the previous example because the **STEP** is negative rather than positive.
20	**5**	Displays current value of **K**.
30	**5 + –3 = 2**	The **STEP** (which is **–3**) is added to the current value of **K** (which is **5**) to create a new value for **K** (which is **2**). Control passes back to the **FOR** statement at line **10**.
10	**2**	Because 2 >= –2 is true, the statements inside the loop are processed.
20	**2**	Displays current value of **K**.
30	**2 + –3 = –1**	The **STEP** (which is **–3**) is added to the current value of **K** (which is **2**) to create a new value for **K** (which is **–1**). Control passes back to the **FOR** statement at line **10**.
10	**–1**	Because –1 >= –2 is true, the statements inside the loop are processed.
20	**–1**	Displays current value of **K**.
30	**–1 + –3 = –4**	The **STEP** (which is **–3**) is added to the current value of **K** (which is **–1**) to create a new value for **K** (which is **–4**). Control passes back to the **FOR** statement at line **10**.
10	**–4**	Because –4 >= –2 is false, the loop is skipped and control passes to line number **40**.
40	**–4**	The value of **K** is displayed.

The trace function can be used to help the programmer follow the order in which the lines are being executed. To turn tracing on, type **TRON ↵** (**TR**ace **ON**) or press the **[F7]** key. After the trace has been turned on the computer will display each line number as that line is executed. For example:

```
NEW ↵
Ok
10 FOR K = 5 TO -2 STEP -3
20   PRINT K
30 NEXT K
40 PRINT "Value of K is "K
RUN ↵
 5
 2                            ◄── RUN without trace turned on
-1
Value of K is -4
Ok
TRON ↵                        ◄── Turns on tracing function
Ok
RUN ↵
[10][20] 5
[30][20] 2                    ◄── RUN with trace turned on
[30][20]-1
[30][40]Value of K is -4
Ok
```

Line numbers are displayed in square brackets as the statements are executed

To turn off the trace function, type **TROFF ↵**, or press **[F8]**, or begin a new program by typing **NEW ↵**.

What happens if the parameters of the **FOR/NEXT** loop are incorrect? For example, what happens if the terminal value is larger than the initial value but the **STEP** is negative?

```
NEW ↵
Ok
10 PRINT "Before loop, value of K is "K
20   FOR K = 2 TO 5 STEP -2
30     PRINT "Inside loop, K = "K
40   NEXT K
50 PRINT "After loop, value of K is "K
TRON ↵
Ok
RUN ↵
[10]Before loop, value of K is  0
[20][50]After loop, value of K is  2
Ok
```

Inconsistent parameters in FOR statement cause the loop to be skipped (lines 30 and 40 are never executed)

Line Numbers	Comments
10	Displays the default value of **K** (recall that the default value of a numeric variable is **0**).
20	Creates a storage location called **K** and assigns a value of **2** to that location. Also, the value of **K** (i.e., **2**) is compared to the terminal value (i.e., **5**). The **STEP** is negative and so the comparison to be used is 2 > = 5. Because this is false, the loop is skipped and control passes to line number **50**.
50	The value of **K** is displayed.

Another way that the loop parameters can be inconsistent is to have the beginning value larger than the terminal value (which implies that the loop will start high and go low) but the step is a positive number (which implies that the loop will start low and go high). Study the following example:

```
NEW
Ok
10 PRINT "Before loop, value of K is "K
20   FOR K = 5 TO 2 STEP 2
30     PRINT "Inside loop, K = "K
40   NEXT K
50 PRINT "After loop, value of K is "K
TRON
Ok
RUN
[10]Before loop, value of K is  0
[20][50]After loop, value of K is  5
Ok
```

Inconsistent parameters in FOR statement cause the loop to be skipped (lines 30 and 40 are never executed)

In this case, when line **20** is executed, the value of **K** is set to **5**. Then, that value is compared to the terminal value, **2**. The value of **K** (i.e., **5**) exceeds the terminal value (i.e., **2**) and the step is positive so the loop is not executed. Notice that only lines **10** (**PRINT**), **20** (**FOR**), and **50** (**PRINT**) are executed.

The values for the parameters of the **FOR** statement may be variables or variable expressions as the next example shows:

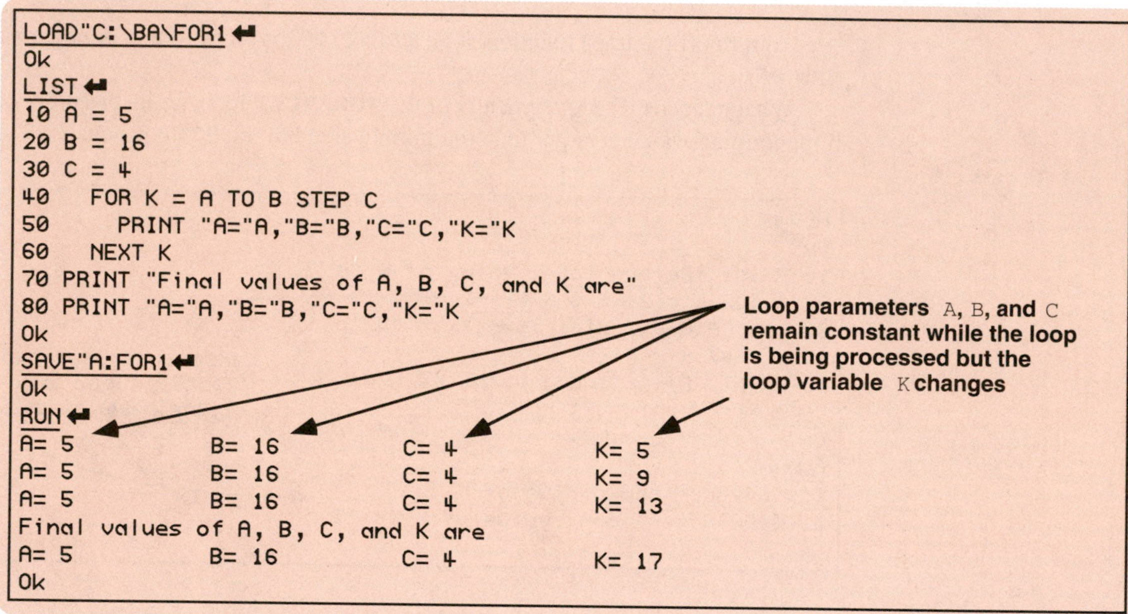

```
LOAD"C:\BA\FOR1
Ok
LIST
10 A = 5
20 B = 16
30 C = 4
40   FOR K = A TO B STEP C
50     PRINT "A="A,"B="B,"C="C,"K="K
60   NEXT K
70 PRINT "Final values of A, B, C, and K are"
80 PRINT "A="A,"B="B,"C="C,"K="K
Ok
SAVE"A:FOR1
Ok
RUN
A= 5           B= 16          C= 4           K= 5
A= 5           B= 16          C= 4           K= 9
A= 5           B= 16          C= 4           K= 13
Final values of A, B, C, and K are
A= 5           B= 16          C= 4           K= 17
Ok
```

Loop parameters A, B, and C remain constant while the loop is being processed but the loop variable K changes

Notice how the initial value (**A = 5**), the final value (**B = 16**), and the increment (**C = 4**) remain constant throughout the loop while the loop variable (**K**) changes each time the loop is processed.

The loop parameters can be decimals as well as integers. However, round-off errors sometimes occur with decimals (as was discussed on p. B44). For example:

```
NEW
Ok
10 FOR J = 4 TO 5 STEP .3
20   PRINT J
30 NEXT J
RUN
 4
 4.3
 4.600001
 4.900001
Ok
```

Because the **FOR** statement initializes the value of **J** to **4** and uses a **STEP** of **.3**, the computer should display **4**, **4.3**, **4.6**, and **4.9**. However, because of the round-off error, **4.600001** is displayed instead of **4.6**, and **4.900001** is displayed instead of **4.9**.

Of course, **PRINT USING** could be employed to display the numbers rounded off to one decimal place:

```
NEW↵
Ok
10 FOR J = 4 TO 5 STEP .3
20   PRINT USING "##.#"; J
30 NEXT J
RUN↵
 4.0
 4.3
 4.6
 4.9
Ok
```

A Metric Conversion Table

Let's use a **FOR/NEXT** loop in a program that prints a table showing the relation between inches, centimeters, and meters. (Recall that 1 inch = 2.54 centimeters and that 100 centimeters = 1 meter.) The chart is to begin at 0 inches and go up to a maximum of 12 inches in steps of 4 inches (i.e., the conversion should be done **FOR INCH** beginning at **0** inches up **TO** a maximum of **12** inches and in **STEP**s of **4** inches). **LOAD** the program, **LIST** it, **SAVE** it to your *BASIC Data* diskette, and then **RUN** it as shown below:

```
LOAD"C:\BA\METRIC1↵
Ok
LIST↵
1100 A$ = "Inches  Centimeters  Meters"
1200 B$ = "  ##        ##.##      ##.##"
1300   PRINT A$
1400     FOR INCH = 0 TO 12 STEP 4
1500       PRINT USING B$;INCH,2.54*INCH,2.54*INCH/100
1600     NEXT INCH
Ok
SAVE"A:METRIC1↵
Ok
RUN↵
Inches  Centimeters  Meters
  0         0.00      0.00
  4        10.16      0.10
  8        20.32      0.20
 12        30.48      0.30
Ok
```

The program can be made more flexible by allowing the user to specify where the chart is to begin, to end, and how to increment the inches. This feature can be added to the program through the use of an **INPUT** statement at line **1250** and by changing the parameters of the **FOR** statement so that they are variables:

```
1100 A$ = "Inches   Centimeters   Meters"
1200 B$ = "  ##          ##.##       ##.##"
1250 INPUT "Enter values for beginning, ending, and increment"; LOW,HI,INCR
1300   PRINT A$
1400     FOR INCH = LOW TO HI STEP INCR
1500       PRINT USING B$;INCH,2.54*INCH,2.54*INCH/100
1600     NEXT INCH
SAVE"A:METRIC2
Ok
RUN
Enter values for beginning, ending, and increment? 0,12,4
Inches  Centimeters  Meters
   0        0.00       0.00
   4       10.16       0.10
   8       20.32       0.20
  12       30.48       0.30
Ok
```

The program can be expanded further by allowing the user to make more than one chart each time the program is run. This can be done by placing the bulk of the program inside a **WHILE/WEND** loop and adding an **INPUT** statement that asks the user if he or she would like to run the program again. Line **1240** of the program listed below says that while the value of **ANSWER$** is **YES** or **yes**, the statements in the loop are to be processed. When the value of **ANSWER$** becomes anything other than **YES** or **yes**, the loop is exited and the program terminates.

```
1100 A$ = "Inches   Centimeters   Meters"
1200 B$ = "  ##          ##.##       ##.##"
1220 ANSWER$ = "YES"
1240 WHILE ANSWER$ = "YES" OR ANSWER$ = "yes"
1250 INPUT "Enter values for beginning, ending, and increment"; LOW,HI,INCR
1300   PRINT A$
1400     FOR INCH = LOW TO HI STEP INCR
1500       PRINT USING B$;INCH,2.54*INCH,2.54*INCH/100
1600     NEXT INCH
1700   INPUT "Would you like to make another chart"; ANSWER$
1800 WEND
SAVE"A:METRIC3
Ok
RUN
Enter values for beginning, ending, and increment? 0,12,4
Inches  Centimeters  Meters
   0        0.00       0.00
   4       10.16       0.10
   8       20.32       0.20
  12       30.48       0.30
Would you like to make another chart? YES
Enter values for beginning, ending, and increment? 6,0,-2
Inches  Centimeters  Meters
   6       15.24       0.15
   4       10.16       0.10
   2        5.08       0.05
   0        0.00       0.00
Would you like to make another chart? Yes
Ok
```

Why does program terminate here? Doesn't the computer understand English?

Why were both **YES** and **yes** included in the **WHILE** condition in line **1240**? Remember that the computer does not speak English. Therefore **YES** and **yes** are considered to be two completely different strings and so each must be checked. What happens when the user responds with **Yes** (or **yeah** or **SURE**)? The loop is exited when line **1240** is executed because the condition in the **WHILE** statement is false. This type of problem is one that programmers and computer users face all the time when working with interactive programs. Possible solutions to this problem are discussed on page B172–74.

Interest on Money Deposited or Borrowed

When money is borrowed to buy a house or a car, the bank charges interest on that money until it is paid back. In effect, the bank is being paid by the borrower for the privilege of using the bank's money to buy goods or services. Similarly, when money is deposited in a savings account, the bank pays the account holder for the use of that money while it is in the account.

Interest on money borrowed or loaned can be computed in many different ways. For example, to compute what is known as *simple interest* on money deposited in a savings account the following formula is used:

$$I = P*R*T$$

where I = Interest (the amount of money earned).

P = Principal (the amount of money deposited).

R = Rate (the interest rate paid per year). This is sometimes called the APR or Annual Percentage Rate.

T = Time (the number of years the money is left in the account).

When the money is withdrawn from the account, the bank pays the depositor the interest earned (I) plus the original deposit (P). For example, this formula can be used to compute the simple interest paid on $1000 invested at a rate of 10% per year for 5 years as follows:

$$I = P*R*T$$
$$I = (1000)*(.10)*(5)$$
$$I = 500$$

Thus, at the end of 5 years, the bank would pay the depositor $500 in interest, plus the original deposit of $1000, for a total of $1500.

The computer can be used to calculate the simple interest earned for different deposits, rates, and numbers of years. Using a **FOR/NEXT** loop in such a program is useful because the computer can be instructed to calculate the interest (evaluate the formula) for any number of years. For example, the following program calculates and displays the value of an investment for any length of time in steps of 1 year. **LOAD** the program, **LIST** it, **SAVE** it to your *BASIC Data* diskette, and then **RUN** it as shown below:

```
LOAD"C:\BA\INVEST1↵
Ok
LIST↵
10 INPUT "Enter principal, rate, time";P,R,T
20   FOR YEAR = 1 TO T  ◄— Defines range of values for YEAR (time)
30     I = P*R*.01*YEAR  ◄— Calculates interest using simple interest formula
40     VALUE = P + I     ◄— Calculates value of investment
50     PRINT USING "Value after ## years is $$######,.##";YEAR,VALUE
60   NEXT YEAR
Ok
SAVE"A:INVEST1↵
Ok
RUN↵
Enter principal, rate, time? 1000,10,5↵
Value after  1 years is    $1,100.00
Value after  2 years is    $1,200.00
Value after  3 years is    $1,300.00
Value after  4 years is    $1,400.00
Value after  5 years is    $1,500.00
Ok
```

The program can be made a bit more realistic by changing the formula from simple interest to compound interest. Compounding the interest means that the simple interest will be computed for a given period of time and then this interest will be added to the principal for the next period, and so on. Thus, interest is earned on interest. For example, let's do the same problem as above, but this time compound the interest each year. This means that every year the interest is computed and added to the principal. Doing this by hand for 5 years would mean five computations (one computation per year for 5 years).

The computations can be simplified by using the following formula for compound interest:

$$\text{Value} = P*(1 + R/C)^{(T*C)}$$

where

Value = Value of the money at the end of a certain number of years (this includes the original deposit plus any interest earned).

P = Principal (the amount of money deposited).

R = Rate (the interest rate paid per year).

C = Compounding (the number of times per year the interest is computed and then added to the principal).

T = Time (the number of years the money is left in the account).

To have the computer do the calculations, two changes need to be made to the program. First, the user must be asked for the number of times per year the interest is to be compounded (i.e., a new variable **C**, which represents the number of compoundings, must be added to line **10**). Second, the new formula must be used in place of lines **30** and **40**. Let's make the changes and run this new program using the same data as before but with compounding at the end of each year (i.e., the number of times the interest is compounded per year is 1).

```
10 INPUT "Enter principal, rate, time, compounding";P,R,T,C
20    FOR YEAR = 1 TO T
40       VALUE = P*(1 + R*.01/C)^(YEAR*C)  ◄— New formula to calculate value of investment
50       PRINT USING "Value after ## years is $$######,.##";YEAR,VALUE
60    NEXT YEAR
SAVE"A:INVEST2↵
Ok
RUN↵
Enter principal, rate, time, compounding? 1000,10,5,1↵
Value after  1 years is      $1,100.00
Value after  2 years is      $1,210.00
Value after  3 years is      $1,331.00
Value after  4 years is      $1,464.10
Value after  5 years is      $1,610.51
Ok
```

The value after 1 year is the same as without compounding. However, the value at the end of the second year with compounding is $1,210 rather than $1,200 without compounding. The extra $10 is the interest earned on the interest from the first year (the interest from the first year is $100 and the interest on $100 after 1 year at a rate of 10% is $10). With compounding each year an extra $110.51 is earned by the end of the fifth year.

Now let's see the effect of compounding quarterly (4 times per year):

```
RUN↵
Enter principal, rate, time, compounding? 1000,10,5,4↵
Value after  1 years is      $1,103.81
Value after  2 years is      $1,218.40
Value after  3 years is      $1,344.89
Value after  4 years is      $1,484.51
Value after  5 years is      $1,638.62
Ok
```

Notice that by compounding four times per year, rather than one time per year, an extra $28.11 is earned after 5 years.

Let's see the effect of compounding daily (365 times per year). Note: The formula given is not quite right for daily compounding because banks pretend that a year has 360 days when compounding the interest, but pay the interest over the full 365 days, not including leap year. The difference is negligible for our purposes.

```
RUN ↵
Enter principal, rate, time, compounding? 1000,10,5,365 ↵
Value after  1 years is    $1,105.15
Value after  2 years is    $1,221.35
Value after  3 years is    $1,349.76
Value after  4 years is    $1,491.69
Value after  5 years is    $1,648.53
Ok
```

With daily compounding, rather than quarterly compounding, an extra $9.91 is earned over the 5-year period.

As a final example, let's say that you want the output displayed every 10 years rather than every year. This can be accomplished by using a **STEP 10** in the **FOR** statement in line **20**. If this is done, the program can be used to solve the following problem: Suppose right now you are 20 years old and you plan on retiring at age 70. Also, let's say that you spend $50 on a wonderful date with the person of your dreams. What would be the value of that $50 if you were to place it into a savings account at, say, 5.5% interest, compounded quarterly for fifty years rather than spending it on the date?

```
10 INPUT "Enter principal, rate, time, compounding";P,R,T,C
20   FOR YEAR = 10 TO T STEP 10
40     VALUE = P*(1 + R*.01/C)^(YEAR*C)
50     PRINT USING "Value after ## years is $$######,.##";YEAR,VALUE
60   NEXT YEAR
Ok
RUN ↵
Enter principal, rate, time, compounding? 50,5.5,50,4 ↵
Value after 10 years is      $86.34
Value after 20 years is     $149.09
Value after 30 years is     $257.44
Value after 40 years is     $444.53
Value after 50 years is     $767.61
Ok
```

Thus, the value of the $50 spent today would be $767.61 in 50 years. Of course, who knows what $767.61 will be able to buy in 50 years!

TAKE A BREAK Type **SYSTEM ↵**, remove diskette(s). To resume (hard disk): Insert *Data* diskette, type **A: ↵**, **C:\BA\BASICA ↵**. To resume (two drive): Insert diskettes, type **A: ↵**, **B:\BASICA ↵**.

Payroll Program Extended

On page L36 you created a Lotus 1-2-3 worksheet that calculated the wages earned by employees based on their rates of pay, the number of regular hours they worked, and the number of overtime hours they worked. Let's now write a BASIC program that will accomplish the same task (this program will really be an extension of **WAGES4**, which was discussed on p. B107).

The output from **WAGES4** was the following:

```
LOAD"C:\BA\WAGES4 ↵
Ok
LIST ↵
1100 REM Program to compute wages given total hours worked and pay rate
1200 REM Douglas Robertson (373-4026), created 1 Mar 91
1300 REM Define variables:
1400 REM   EMPLOYEE$ = name in form LastName Space First (e.g., Roberts Matt)
1500 REM        RATE = rate of pay in dollars per hour (e.g.,  3)
1600 REM       HOURS = total number of hours worked for pay period (e.g., 50)
1700 REM         PAY = total pay earned for pay period (e.g., 150)
1800 REM Begin processing
1900   REM Define PRINT USING images
2000     IMAGE1$ = "Employee        Pay Rate       Hours    Total Pay"
2100     IMAGE2$ = "--------        --------       -----    ---------"
2200     IMAGE3$ = "\            \   $##.##         ##.#      $###.##"
2300     IMAGE4$ = "All data read, processing complete"
2400   PRINT IMAGE1$                          'Display header
2500   PRINT IMAGE2$                          'Display header
2700       READ EMPLOYEE$,RATE,HOURS          'Assign values to name, rate, hours
2710     WHILE HOURS <> 1E+15                 'For each person do the following
2800       PAY = RATE*HOURS                   'Calculate pay using formula
2900       PRINT USING IMAGE3$;EMPLOYEE$,RATE,HOURS,PAY
2910       READ EMPLOYEE$,RATE,HOURS          'Assign values to name, rate, hours
3000     WEND                                 'Repeat loop for next person
3100   PRINT
3200   PRINT IMAGE4$                          'Display footer
3300 REM End processing
3400 REM Define DATA list in form:
3500 REM DATA NAME          ,RATE,HOURS
3600       DATA Roberts Matt,   4,   30
3700       DATA Sim Keisha  ,   3,   50
3800       DATA Tech Sara   ,   6,   21
3900       DATA Well Vanessa,   5,   40
4000       DATA 1E+15,1E+15,1E+15,1E+15
Ok
RUN ↵
Employee        Pay Rate       Hours    Total Pay
--------        --------       -----    ---------
Roberts Matt     $ 4.00         30.0      $120.00
Sim Keisha       $ 3.00         50.0      $150.00
Tech Sara        $ 6.00         21.0      $126.00
Well Vanessa     $ 5.00         40.0      $200.00

All data read, processing complete
Ok
```

A **LIST** and **RUN** of the modified program, **WAGES6**, are given on the next three pages. Note that two extra employees were added to make the data in **WAGES4** identical to that of the Lotus 1-2-3 worksheet. Also, recall that employees are paid time and a half for hours worked in excess of 40. **LOAD** the new version of the program, **LIST** it, **SAVE** it to your *BASIC Data* diskette, and then **RUN** it as follows:

```
LOAD"C:\BA\WAGES6 ↵
Ok
LIST ↵
1100 REM Program to compute wages given total hours worked and pay rate
1200 REM Douglas Robertson (373-4026), created 1 Mar 91
1300 REM Define variables:
1400 REM   EMPLOYEE$ = name in form LastName Space First (e.g., Roberts Matt)
1500 REM        RATE = rate of pay in dollars per hour (e.g.,  3)
1600 REM       HOURS = total number of hours worked for pay period (e.g., 50)
1700 REM         PAY = total pay earned for pay period (e.g., 150)
1705 REM         REG = regular pay earned
1710 REM          OT = overtime pay earned
1715 REM         NUM = number of sets of data read from DATA list
1720 REM       TRATE = sum of RATE
1725 REM        THRS = sum of HOURS
1730 REM        TREG = sum of REG
1740 REM         TOP = sum of OT
1750 REM        TPAY = sum of PAY
1760 REM       ARATE = average of RATE
1770 REM        AHRS = average of HOURS
1780 REM        AREG = average of REG
1790 REM        ATOP = average of OT
1795 REM        APAY = average of PAY
1800 REM Begin processing
1850 GOSUB 4500                               'Initialize counters
1900 GOSUB 5000                               'Define PRINT USING images
2400 GOSUB 6000                               'Display header
2700   READ EMPLOYEE$,RATE,HOURS              'Assign values to first set of data
2710     WHILE HOURS <> 1E+15                 'For each person do the following
2720       IF HOURS =< 40 THEN GOSUB 7000 ELSE GOSUB 7500  'Calc reg & OT pay
2800       PAY = REG + OT                     'Calculate pay
2850       NUM = NUM + 1                      'Count data sets displayed
2900       PRINT USING I6$;NUM,EMPLOYEE$,RATE,HOURS,REG,OT,PAY
2905       GOSUB 8000                         'Calculate sum for each variable
2910       READ EMPLOYEE$,RATE,HOURS          'Assign values to name, rate, hours
3000     WEND                                 'Repeat loop for next person
3050   GOSUB 9000                             'Calculate averages
3200   GOSUB 9650                             'Display footer
3300 REM End processing
4100 END
4500 REM ***** SUBROUTINE to initialize counters
4510     NUM = 0
4520   TRATE = 0
4530    THRS = 0
4540    TREG = 0
4550     TOP = 0
4560    TPAY = 0
4570 RETURN
```

Continued . . .

```
5000 REM ***** SUBROUTINE to define PRINT USING images
5100   I1$ = "Puter Pals, Inc., Payroll Summary"
5200   I2$ = "Date: \            \"
5300   I3$ = "Time: \            \"
5400   I4$ = "Num  Employee        Pay Rate  Hours  Reg Pay   OT Pay  Total Pay"
5500   I5$ = "---  --------------  --------  -----  -------  -------  ---------"
5600   I6$ = " ##  \            \    $##.##  ###.#  $####.##  $###.##  $#####.##"
5700   I7$ = "     Totals                    ###.#  $####.##  $###.##  $#####.##"
5800   I8$ = "     Averages          $##.##  ###.#  $####.##  $###.##  $#####.##"
5900 RETURN
6000 REM ***** SUBROUTINE to display header
6100   PRINT I1$
6200   PRINT USING I2$; DATE$
6300   PRINT USING I3$; TIME$
6400   PRINT
6500   PRINT I4$
6600   PRINT I5$
6700 RETURN
7000 REM ***** SUBROUTINE to calculate reg and overtime pay for 40 or less hours
7100   REG = HOURS*RATE                      'Regular pay for 40 or less hours
7200    OT = 0                               'Overtime pay for 40 or less hours
7300 RETURN
7500 REM ***** SUBROUTINE to calculate regular and overtime pay for over 40 hour
7600   REG = 40*RATE                         'Regular pay for over 40 hours
7700    OT = (HOURS - 40)*RATE*1.5           'Overtime pay for over 40 hours
7800 RETURN
8000 REM ***** SUBROUTINE to calculate sum for each variable
8100   TRATE = TRATE + RATE
8200    THRS = THRS  + HOURS
8300    TREG = TREG  + REG
8400     TOP = TOP   + OT
8500    TPAY = TPAY  + PAY
8600 RETURN
9000 REM ***** SUBROUTINE to calculate averages for each variable
9100   ARATE = TRATE/NUM
9200    AHRS =  THRS/NUM
9300    AREG =  TREG/NUM
9400    ATOP =   TOP/NUM
9500    APAY =  TPAY/NUM
9600 RETURN
9650 REM ***** SUBROUTINE to display footer
9700   PRINT I5$
9750   PRINT USING I7$;THRS,TREG,TOP,TPAY
9800   PRINT USING I8$;ARATE,AHRS,AREG,ATOP,APAY
9850 RETURN
10100 REM Define DATA list in form:
10200 REM DATA NAME          ,RATE,HOURS
10300      DATA Roberts Matt,   4,   30
10400      DATA Sim Keisha  ,   3,   50
10500      DATA Tech Sara   ,   6,   21
10600      DATA Well Vanessa,   5,   40
10700      DATA Taylor David,   4,   35
10800      DATA Peters Bill,    4,   50
10900      DATA 1E+15,1E+15,1E+15,1E+15
Ok
```

Continued . . .

```
RUN ←
Puter Pals, Inc., Payroll Summary
Date: 03-01-1991
Time: 19:47:19

Num  Employee          Pay Rate  Hours  Reg Pay    OT Pay   Total Pay
---  ---------------  --------  -----  -------   -------   ---------
  1  Roberts Matt       $ 4.00   30.0  $120.00   $  0.00   $ 120.00
  2  Sim Keisha         $ 3.00   50.0  $120.00   $ 45.00   $ 165.00
  3  Tech Sara          $ 6.00   21.0  $126.00   $  0.00   $ 126.00
  4  Well Vanessa       $ 5.00   40.0  $200.00   $  0.00   $ 200.00
  5  Taylor David       $ 4.00   35.0  $140.00   $  0.00   $ 140.00
  6  Peters Bill        $ 4.00   50.0  $160.00   $ 60.00   $ 220.00
---  ---------------  --------  -----  -------   -------   ---------
     Totals                     226.0  $866.00   $105.00   $ 971.00
     Averages           $ 4.33   37.7  $144.33   $ 17.50   $ 161.83
Ok
```


Carefully examine the output of the new program. In order to make the needed changes, two questions have to be answered:

- How will the new information be created (e.g., how do you program the computer to find the sum of a set of numbers)? We will create a new subroutine for each new process (defining new image statements, defining a new header, finding totals and averages, calculating regular and overtime pay, and counting the number of employees).
- When will the new processes be carried out (e.g., where in the program must the subroutine be called that will find the sums of the numbers)?

The modifications to the original program, **WAGES4**, were accomplished by following the steps given below.

Step 1 The overall look of the output has been changed to accommodate the new information to be displayed by modifying the **PRINT USING** image statements. This part of the output is produced by calling the following subroutine at line **1900**:

```
5000 REM ***** SUBROUTINE to define PRINT USING images
5100    I1$ = "Puter Pals, Inc., Payroll Summary"
5200    I2$ = "Date: \          \"
5300    I3$ = "Time: \          \"
5400    I4$ = "Num  Employee          Pay Rate  Hours  Reg Pay   OT Pay   Total Pay"
5500    I5$ = "---  ---------------  --------  -----  -------   -------   ---------"
5600    I6$ = " ##  \              \   $##.##  ###.#  $####.##  $####.##  $#####.##"
5700    I7$ = "     Totals                     ###.#  $####.##  $####.##  $#####.##"
5800    I8$ = "     Averages          $##.##  ###.#  $####.##  $####.##  $#####.##"
5900 RETURN
```

Notice how the image statements look like an abbreviated version of the actual output.

Step 2 A heading has been added that includes the company name, the date, and the time. The **DATE$** function is used to display the current date in the form **MM-DD-YYYY** where **MM** is the month, **DD** is the day, and **YYYY** is the year (e.g., 1 March 1991 would be displayed as **03-01-1991**). The **TIME$** function is used to display the current time in the form **HH:MM:SS** where **HH** is hours, **MM** is minutes, and **SS** is seconds. This part of the output is produced by calling the following subroutine at line **2400**:

```
6000 REM ***** SUBROUTINE to display header
6100    PRINT I1$
6200    PRINT USING I2$; DATE$
6300    PRINT USING I3$; TIME$
6400    PRINT
6500    PRINT I4$
6600    PRINT I5$
6700 RETURN
```

Step 3 Three new columns were added for the number of employees, regular pay earned, and overtime pay earned.

The column labeled **Num** is used to display the number of employees. A counter is needed to count the number of data sets read from the **DATA** statements. A variable called **NUM** is used for this counter. To accomplish this, the following line is added just before the **PRINT** statement at line **2900**, which displays the individual data for each person:

```
2850        NUM = NUM + 1                         'Count data sets displayed
```

The column labeled **Reg Pay** is used to display the regular pay earned. This is the pay for 40 or fewer hours of work per week. The rate for this will be the regular pay rate. This is really the difficult part of the modification. In order to determine the regular and overtime pay the computer must first determine whether or not the person has worked over 40 hours. The decision logic for this part was discussed on page L95:

Select the proper formula for regular pay:

IF **HOURS** =< 40

THEN Calculate regular pay using **REG = HOURS*RATE**

ELSE Calculate regular pay using **REG = 40*RATE**

The column labeled **OT Pay** is used to display the overtime pay. This is the pay for more than 40 hours of work per week. The rate for these hours will be 1.5 times the regular pay rate. The decision logic for this part was discussed on page L94:

Select the proper formula for overtime pay:

IF **HOURS** =< 40

THEN Calculate overtime pay using **OT = 0**

ELSE Calculate overtime pay using **OT = (HOURS - 40)*RATE*1.5**

To calculate both **REG PAY** and **OT PAY** above, the following **IF/THEN/ELSE** statement was added to select the proper subroutine:

```
2720        IF HOURS =< 40 THEN GOSUB 7000 ELSE GOSUB 7500  'Calc reg & OT pay
```

Notice how this statement selects one of two subroutines depending on whether or not the person has worked overtime hours. If the person has not worked overtime (i.e., **HOURS =< 40** is a true statement), the following subroutine is called to calculate both the regular and overtime pay:

```
7000 REM ***** SUBROUTINE to calculate reg and overtime pay for 40 or less hours
7100    REG = HOURS*RATE                        'Regular pay for 40 or less hours
7200     OT = 0                                 'Overtime pay for 40 or less hours
7300 RETURN
```

If the person has worked overtime (i.e., **HOURS =< 40** is a false statement), the following subroutine is called to calculate both the regular and overtime pay:

```
7500 REM ***** SUBROUTINE to calculate regular and overtime pay for over 40 hour
7600    REG = 40*RATE                           'Regular pay for over 40 hours
7700     OT = (HOURS - 40)*RATE*1.5             'Overtime pay for over 40 hours
7800 RETURN
```

Step 4 The total pay is calculated using the sum of the regular pay and the overtime pay. The following line was modified:

```
2800        PAY = REG + OT                      'Calculate pay
```

Step 5 A new row has been added to display the totals of the columns. This means that five new counters are needed (one for each column to be totaled) as follows:

TRATE = sum of **RATE** (pay rate) of all employees.

THRS = sum of **HOURS** (hours worked) of all employees.

TREG = sum of **REG** (regular pay) of all employees.

TOP = sum of **OT** (overtime pay) of all employees.

TPAY = sum of **PAY** (total pay) of all employees.

This part of the program is produced by calling the following subroutine at line **2905**:

```
8000 REM ***** SUBROUTINE to calculate sum for each variable
8100    TRATE = TRATE + RATE
8200     THRS = THRS  + HOURS
8300     TREG = TREG  + REG
8400      TOP = TOP   + OT
8500     TPAY = TPAY  + PAY
8600 RETURN
```

Of course, counters should be initialized (usually to 0) before they are used. This part of the program is produced by calling the following subroutine at line **1850**:

```
4500 REM ***** SUBROUTINE to initialize counters
4510      NUM = 0
4520    TRATE = 0
4530     THRS = 0
4540     TREG = 0
4550      TOP = 0
4560     TPAY = 0
4570 RETURN
```

Step 6 A new row has been added to display the averages of the columns. This means that five new variables are needed (one for each column to be averaged). These averages need to be calculated by dividing the sum of the totals by the number of data sets read:

ARATE = **TRATE/NUM** = average pay rate.

AHRS = **THRS/NUM** = average hours worked.

AREG = **TREG/NUM** = average regular pay.

ATOP = **TOP/NUM** = average overtime pay.

APAY = **TPAY/NUM** = average total pay.

This part of the program is produced by calling the following subroutine at line **3050**:

```
9000 REM ***** SUBROUTINE to calculate averages for each variable
9100   ARATE = TRATE/NUM
9200    AHRS =  THRS/NUM
9300    AREG =  TREG/NUM
9400    ATOP =   TOP/NUM
9500    APAY =  TPAY/NUM
9600 RETURN
```

Step 7 The two new rows that make up the footer were produced by calling the following subroutine at line **3200**:

```
9650 REM ***** SUBROUTINE to display footer
9700   PRINT I5$
9750   PRINT USING I7$;THRS,TREG,TOP,TPAY
9800   PRINT USING I8$;ARATE,AHRS,AREG,ATOP,APAY
9850 RETURN
```

Although this is a long program, there is really nothing new in the individual statements. It may be instructive to look at the overall structure of the program to get an idea of how the program is put together on a global scale. Being consistent and logical in the way programs are put together makes programming a lot easier and takes up less time in the long run because fewer errors are made.

The structure can be viewed as follows. Note the extensive use of subroutines to define specific small tasks.

Line Numbers	*Comments*
1100–1795	**REM** statements stating what the program does, who wrote it, and defining the variables.
1850	Subroutine call to set the initial value of all counters to 0.
1900	Subroutine call to define images to be used by **PRINT USING** statements.
2400	Subroutine call to display the document header.
2700	Assigns the first set of data to the variables.
2710–3000	The loop where the data are processed. Note the use of subroutines to do many of the calculations.
2720	The **IF/THEN/ELSE** statement that selects which formulas to use, based on the number of hours the person has worked.
2800	Calculates the total pay. If the calculation had been more complex (e.g., if federal, state, and social security taxes had been calculated) this would have been put in a subroutine.

Continued . . .

Line Numbers	Comments
2850	Counts the number of data sets displayed.
2900	Displays the values for each employee.
2905	Subroutine call to calculate sums.
2910	Assigns the next set of data to the variables.
3050	Subroutine call to calculate averages. Note that this is outside the loop because all the data must have been processed before averages can be calculated.
3200	Subroutine call to display the document footer.
4100	End of the main program.
4500–4570	Subroutine to initialize counters.
5000–5900	Subroutine to define **PRINT USING** images.
6000–6700	Subroutine to display header.
7000–7300	Subroutine to calculate regular and overtime pay for people who worked 40 or less hours.
7500–7800	Subroutine to calculate regular and overtime pay for people who worked over 40 hours.
8000–8600	Subroutine to calculate sum for each variable.
9000–9600	Subroutine to calculate average for each variable.
9650–9850	Subroutine to display footer.
10100–10900	**DATA** statements.

INT *Function*

FORM	Line no.	V = INT (x)
EXAMPLE	1100	Y = INT(X)

The **INT** function returns the largest integer that is less than or equal to the value of a given number. It is useful when you want to see if one number is evenly divisible by another number. Consider the following program:

```
NEW ↵
Ok
10 PRINT "INT( 5.2) = " INT( 5.2),"INT( 5.6) = " INT( 5.6)
20 PRINT "INT(-5.2) = " INT(-5.2),"INT(-5.6) = " INT(-5.6)
RUN ↵
INT( 5.2) =  5              INT( 5.6) =  5
INT(-5.2) = -6              INT(-5.6) = -6
Ok
```

In line **10**, the value of **INT(5.2)** is displayed as **5** because **5** is the largest integer that does not exceed **5.2**. Similarly, **INT(5.6)** is **5** because **5** is the largest integer that does not exceed **5.6**. Note that the **INT** function does not round off numbers but finds the largest integer part of a number.

Negative numbers follow the same rule as positive numbers but the results may be surprising. Line **20** displays the value of **INT(–5.2)** as **–6** because **–6** is the largest integer that does not exceed **–5.2**. The answer cannot be **–5** because **–5** is larger than **–5.2** (i.e., it is to the right of **–5.2** on a number line).

The following program uses the **INT** function to determine if one number is evenly divisible by another number:

```
LOAD"C:\BA\INT1↵
Ok
LIST↵
10 INPUT "Enter the two numbers";X,Y
20 IF X/Y  = INT(X/Y) THEN PRINT X "is evenly divisible by" Y
30 IF X/Y <> INT(X/Y) THEN PRINT X "is NOT evenly divisible by" Y
Ok
SAVE"A:INT1↵
Ok
RUN↵
Enter the two numbers? 12,3↵
 12 is evenly divisible by 3
Ok
RUN↵
Enter the two numbers? 12,5↵
 12 is NOT evenly divisible by 5
Ok
```

Keystroke	Action Resulting from Keystroke
10	Assigns values supplied by user to variables **X** and **Y**.
20	Checks to see if the quotient **X/Y** is the same as the integer value of that quotient. If it is, it means that the quotient has no decimal part (i.e., **X** is evenly divisible by **Y**) and the **PRINT** statement saying so is executed. For the first two numbers given, the condition would be: **12/3 = INT(12/3)**; **4 = INT(4)**; **4 = 4**, so the condition is true. For the second set of numbers, the condition would be: **12/5 = INT(12/5)**; **2.4 = INT(2.4)**; **2.4 ≠ 2,** so the condition is false.
30	This statement is similar to the statement in line **20** except that the condition is just the opposite. If the quotient **X/Y** is *not* the same as the integer value of **X/Y**, then **X** is *not* evenly divisible by **Y** and the **PRINT** statement saying so is executed.

Lines **20** and **30** could have been combined into one line as follows:

```
20 IF X/Y = INT(X/Y) THEN PRINT X "is evenly divisible by" Y ELSE
PRINT X "is not evenly divisible by" Y
```

Modifying Output Using INT

Program **METRIC1** (p. B141) computed and displayed a table of metric conversions. The **INT** function can be used to make the table more readable as it gets larger by inserting column headings at appropriate locations in the output. For example, if the following line is added:

```
1550 IF INCH/5 = INT(INCH/5) THEN PRINT : PRINT A$
```

the computer will print a blank line and the column heading stored in **A$** every time the value of **INCH** is a multiple of **5** (recall that the colon **:** is used to enter two or more statements on the same line). This makes the table easier to read. **LOAD** the new version of the program, **LIST** it, **SAVE** it to your *BASIC Data* diskette, and then **RUN** it as shown below:

```
LOAD"C:\BA\METRIC4 ↵
Ok
LIST ↵
1100 A$ = "Inches  Centimeters  Meters"
1200 B$ = "  ##        ##.##      ##.##"
1300   PRINT A$
1400     FOR INCH = 1 TO 12 STEP 1
1500       PRINT USING B$;INCH,2.54*INCH,2.54*INCH/100
1550       IF INCH/5 = INT(INCH/5) THEN PRINT : PRINT A$
1600     NEXT INCH
Ok
SAVE"A:METRIC4 ↵
Ok
RUN ↵
Inches  Centimeters  Meters
   1        2.54      0.03
   2        5.08      0.05
   3        7.62      0.08
   4       10.16      0.10
   5       12.70      0.13

Inches  Centimeters  Meters
   6       15.24      0.15
   7       17.78      0.18
   8       20.32      0.20
   9       22.86      0.23
  10       25.40      0.25

Inches  Centimeters  Meters
  11       27.94      0.28
  12       30.48      0.30
Ok
```

Rounding Numbers

By using a clever mathematical trick, the **INT** function can be used to round off numbers to any number of decimal places. Let's say that you want the number 2.39 rounded off to one decimal place. The following statement will do just that:

```
1100 X = INT(.5 + 2.39*10)/10
```

Below are the steps that the computer follows when doing the calculations:

1. The calculation **2.39*10** yields **23.9** (remember, the order of operations requires that multiplication is done before addition). The multiplication by 10 simply moves the decimal point one place to the right.
2. The calculation **.5 + 23.9** yields **24.4**. Adding **.5** to the answer in step 1 is needed because the number should be rounded up if the digit to the right of the place value of interest is 5 or more but the number should remain the same if the digit is under 5.

3. The calculation **INT (24.4)** yields **24**.
4. The calculation **24/10** yields **2.4**. This step essentially *undoes* the first step (multiplying by 10).

In a similar fashion, a number may be rounded off to two decimal places by multiplying and dividing by 100 and to three decimal places by multiplying and dividing by 1000 and so on. Study the following program:

```
LOAD"C:\BA\ROUND1
Ok
LIST
10 X = 2.39312
20 PRINT X, INT(.5 + X*10)/10
30 PRINT X, INT(.5 + X*100)/100
40 PRINT X, INT(.5 + X*1000)/1000
50 PRINT X, INT(.5 + X*10000)/10000
60 PRINT X, INT(.5 + X*100000!)/100000!
Ok
SAVE"A:ROUND1
Ok
RUN
 2.39312       2.4
 2.39312       2.39
 2.39312       2.393
 2.39312       2.3931
 2.39312       2.39312
Ok
```

Remember, the exclamation point means that the number is a single-precision number

Value of X rounded off

Actual value of X

Note that rounding off numbers using the **INT** function is different from employing **PRINT USING** to *display* the values of numbers rounded off. The **INT** function can be used to actually change the value of a number that will be used in a later calculation, whereas the **PRINT USING** statement only changes the way the number is displayed.

Verification Codes

The **INT** function can be used in a program that will check input from a keyboard or terminal to see if it contains typographical errors. Let's say that you are a supermarket manager and that you have entered into your computer an item identification number and the price for every item you sell. For example, a *Green Giant* ®15-ounce can of corn might have an ID number of 10 and a price of 39 cents. To check for typographical errors when these data are entered, you could add on a special *verification code*. This code will be chosen so that the sum of the item identification number, the price, and the verification code is evenly divisible by a particular number (i.e., the quotient has no decimal part). In this case, let's say that the sum must be evenly divisible by 29 (you can pick any number for this). Thus, the verification code will be 9 because 10 + 39 + 9 = 58 which is divisible by 29. If either the item identification number, the price, or the verification code is incorrectly typed, the sum will probably not be evenly divisible by 29 and the computer can issue a caution message.

The following program uses this verification code scheme:

```
LOAD"C:\BA\VER1
Ok
LIST
1100 INPUT "Enter item number, price, verification";ITEM,PRICE,VER
1200   SUM = ITEM + PRICE + VER
1300   IF SUM/29 = INT(SUM/29) THEN PRINT "Entry OK" ELSE PRINT "Input error"
1400 END
Ok
SAVE"A:VER1
Ok
RUN
Enter item number, price, verification? 10,93,9
Input error
Ok
RUN
Enter item number, price, verification? 10,39,9
Entry OK
Ok
```

There is an error in the input data (the 93 should be 39)

The input data are correct

Line Numbers	***Comments***
1100	Asks the user to enter the values for the item number, price, and verification code and stores those values at variable locations **ITEM**, **PRICE**, and **VER**.
1200	Adds the values of **ITEM**, **PRICE**, and **VER** and stores the sum at variable location **SUM**.
1300	Checks to see if the value of **SUM** is evenly divisible by **29**. If it is (i.e., if **SUM/29 = INT(SUM/29)** is true), the first **PRINT** statement acknowledges that the entry was correct. If the sum is not evenly divisible by **29**, the **PRINT** statement after **ELSE** indicates that an error has occurred.

This type of data checking is done automatically at the checkout counters in many larger stores. The process is made even more efficient through the use of machine readable codes printed right on the items. The next time you go shopping at a supermarket, look closely at the label of one of the items you buy (e.g., *Campbell's® Vegetable Beef* soup). You will see a set of white and black stripes (called the UPC or Universal Product Code) on the label, which looks something like the following:

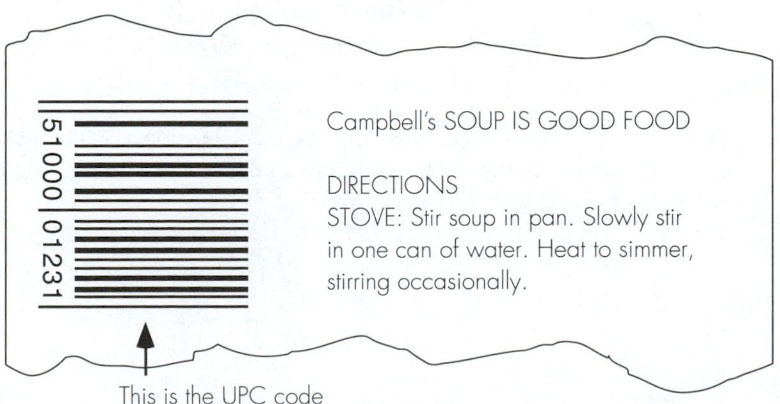

51000 01231
Campbell's SOUP IS GOOD FOOD
DIRECTIONS
STOVE: Stir soup in pan. Slowly stir in one can of water. Heat to simmer, stirring occasionally.
This is the UPC code

The check-out clerk will run the label through a scanner, which reads the stripes, and then a computer will decode the information. The last two bars are a verification code that the computer uses to check to see if the first part of the code was correctly read. If it was, the price of the item is entered onto the sales slip. If the computer detects an error, a beep will sound and the clerk will have to run the can through the scanner again.

BEEP *Function*

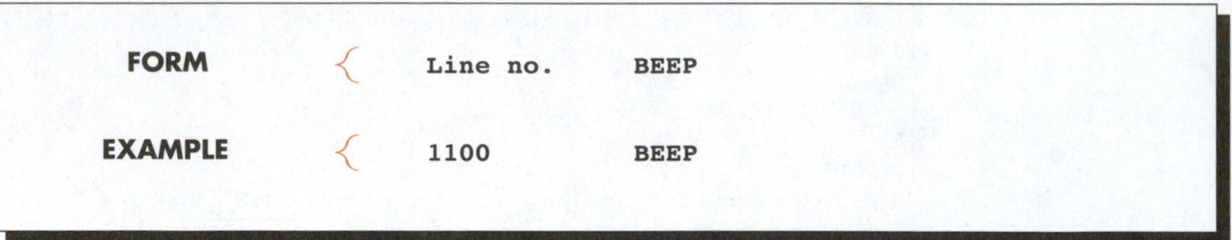

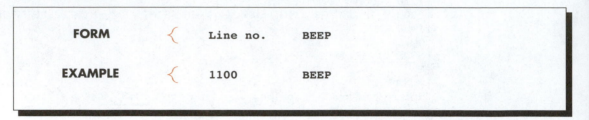

FORM	Line no.	BEEP
EXAMPLE	1100	BEEP

This function causes the speaker of the system unit to make a sound (a beep with a frequency of 800 Hertz) for 1/4 second. It is used to alert the user that something important has occurred. For example, in the verification code program, you may want to have the computer **BEEP** when an error has been detected. This can be done by adding a subroutine that contains the **BEEP** statement. The screen display is the same as before, but the speaker will sound after the words **Input error** are displayed.

```
LOAD"C:\BA\VER2←
Ok
LIST←
1100 INPUT "Enter item number, price, verification";ITEM,PRICE,VER
1200   SUM = ITEM + PRICE + VER
1300   IF SUM/29 = INT(SUM/29) THEN PRINT "Entry Ok" ELSE GOSUB 1500
1400 END
1500 REM SUBROUTINE to display error message and BEEP
1600   PRINT "Input error"
1700   BEEP
1800 RETURN
Ok
SAVE"A:VER2←
Ok
RUN←
Enter item number, price, verification? 10,93,9←
Input error  ←── Listen to the BEEP
Ok
RUN←
Enter item number, price, verification? 10,39,9←
Entry Ok  ←── No BEEP sounded
Ok
```

The **BEEP** statement could be placed inside a **FOR/NEXT** loop to make it sound longer. For example, in the following program lines **1610** to **1710** make the beep last for 10 seconds (1/4 seconds * 40 beeps = 10 seconds of beeping):

```
LOAD"C:\BA\VER3
Ok
LIST
1100 INPUT "Enter item number, price, verification";ITEM,PRICE,VER
1200   SUM = ITEM + PRICE + VER
1300   IF SUM/29 = INT(SUM/29) THEN PRINT "Entry Ok" ELSE GOSUB 1500
1400 END
1500 REM SUBROUTINE to display error message and BEEP
1600   PRINT "Input error"
1610   FOR N = 1 TO 40
1700     BEEP
1710   NEXT N
1800 RETURN
Ok
SAVE"A:VER3
Ok
RUN
Enter item number, price, verification? 10,93,9
Input error   <-- Listen to the BEEP for 10 seconds
Ok
RUN
Enter item number, price, verification? 10,39,9
Entry OK   <-- No BEEP sounded
Ok
```

SOUND *Function*

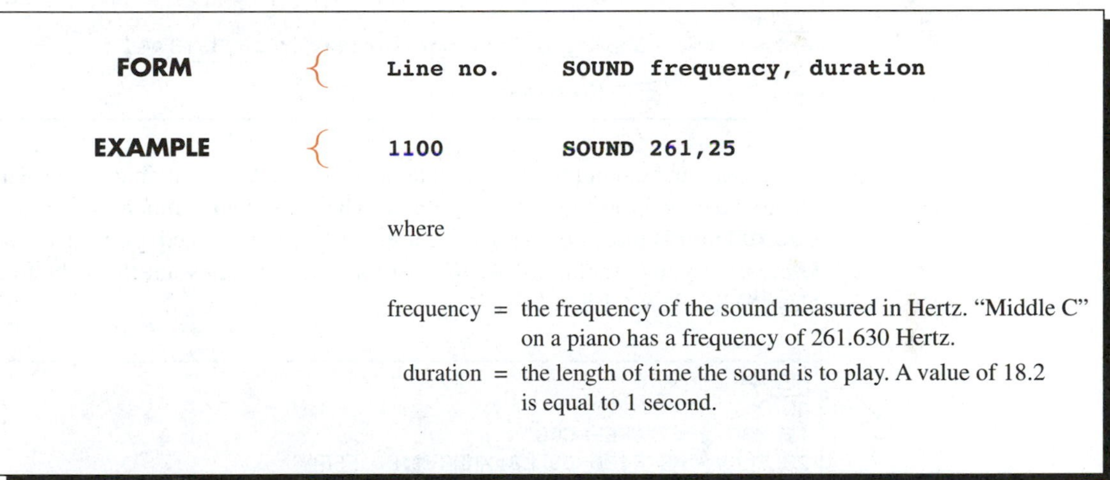

FORM	`Line no.`	`SOUND frequency, duration`
EXAMPLE	`1100`	`SOUND 261,25`

where

frequency = the frequency of the sound measured in Hertz. "Middle C" on a piano has a frequency of 261.630 Hertz.

duration = the length of time the sound is to play. A value of 18.2 is equal to 1 second.

This function causes the speaker in the system unit to make a sound of the specified frequency and duration. The **SOUND** function can be used like **BEEP** to get the attention of the computer user.

For example, let's modify the verification program **VER2** to make a more interesting sound when an error is encountered. This can be done by replacing the **BEEP** function with the **SOUND** function in the error subroutine. **LOAD** the new version of the program, **LIST** it, **SAVE** it to your *BASIC Data* diskette, and then **RUN** it as follows:

```
LOAD"C:\BA\VER4↵
Ok
LIST ↵
1100 INPUT "Enter item number, price, verification";ITEM,PRICE,VER
1200   SUM = ITEM + PRICE + VER
1300   IF SUM/29 = INT(SUM/29) THEN PRINT "Entry Ok" ELSE GOSUB 1500
1400 END
1500 REM SUBROUTINE to display error message and BEEP
1600   PRINT "Input error"
1610     FOR FREQ = 500 TO 1200 STEP 10    'Begins low and goes up
1620       SOUND FREQ,.182                 'Sound duration is 1/100 sec
1630     NEXT FREQ
1640     FOR FREQ = 1200 TO 500 STEP -10   'Begins high and goes down
1650       SOUND FREQ,.182                 'Sound duration is 1/100 sec
1660     NEXT FREQ
1670     FOR LOOP = 1 TO 3                 'Repeat next 2 sounds 3 times
1680       SOUND 1000,9.100001             'High sound for 1/2 second
1690       SOUND  500,9.100001             'Low sound for 1/2 second
1700     NEXT LOOP
1800 RETURN
Ok
SAVE"A:VER4↵
Ok
RUN↵
Enter item number, price, verification? 10,93,9↵
Input error  ◄── Listen to the sound
Ok
RUN↵
Enter item number, price, verification? 10,39,9↵
Entry OK  ◄── No sound
Ok
```

There is another sound producing statement called **PLAY**, which can be used to actually play music provided in a coded form in a string variable. This statement is much more powerful and flexible than **SOUND** but it is more complicated to use. If you are interested, you can consult the *BASIC Reference Manual* for your version of BASIC. Just for fun, you may want to try the following program, which plays "Mary Had a Little Lamb":

```
NEW↵
Ok
10 MARY$ = "GFE-FGGG"
20 PLAY "MB T100 O3 L8;XMARY$;P8 FFF4"
30 PLAY "GB-B-4; XMARY$; GFFGFE-..."
SAVE"A:MARY1↵
Ok
RUN↵
Ok        ◄── Listen to the song
```

Using Special Characters

BASIC assigns a numeric value (ASCII code) to every character that can be sent to an output device (e.g., the screen or a printer). For example, the ASCII code for the uppercase **Y** is 089 while the ASCII code for the lowercase **y** is 121. It is for this reason that BASIC considers lowercase letters to be different from uppercase letters (remember from the discussion on p. B142 that **Yes** and **yes** are two different strings).

The **CHR$** function can be used to display the ASCII codes assigned by BASIC. For example, the following program will display all the printable ASCII codes (some codes, such as ringing the bell (007), the line feed (010), and the carriage return (013), are not printable). A complete listing of the codes may be found in the *BASIC Reference Manual*. **LOAD** the program **CODE1**, **LIST** it, **SAVE** it to your *BASIC Data* diskette, and then **RUN** it as shown below:

```
LOAD"C:\BA\CODE1↵
Ok
LIST↵
10 FOR CODE = 1 TO 6
20    PRINT USING "[###] \  \";CODE,CHR$(CODE);
30 NEXT CODE
40 FOR CODE = 14 TO 27
50    PRINT USING "[###] \  \";CODE,CHR$(CODE);
60 NEXT CODE
70 FOR CODE = 32 TO 255
80    PRINT USING "[###] \  \";CODE,CHR$(CODE);
90 NEXT CODE
Ok
SAVE"A:CODE1↵
Ok
RUN↵
[  1] ☺   [  2] ☻   [  3] ♥   [  4] ♦   [  5] ♣   [  6] ♠   [ 14] ♫   [ 15] ☼
[ 16] ►   [ 17] ◄   [ 18] ↕   [ 19] ‼   [ 20] ¶   [ 21] §   [ 22] ▬   [ 23] ↨
[ 24] ↑   [ 25] ↓   [ 26] →   [ 27] ←   [ 32]     [ 33] !   [ 34] "   [ 35] #
[ 36] $   [ 37] %   [ 38] &   [ 39] '   [ 40] (   [ 41] )   [ 42] *   [ 43] +
[ 44] ,   [ 45] -   [ 46] .   [ 47] /   [ 48] 0   [ 49] 1   [ 50] 2   [ 51] 3
[ 52] 4   [ 53] 5   [ 54] 6   [ 55] 7   [ 56] 8   [ 57] 9   [ 58] :   [ 59] ;
[ 60] <   [ 61] =   [ 62] >   [ 63] ?   [ 64] @   [ 65] A   [ 66] B   [ 67] C
[ 68] D   [ 69] E   [ 70] F   [ 71] G   [ 72] H   [ 73] I   [ 74] J   [ 75] K
[ 76] L   [ 77] M   [ 78] N   [ 79] O   [ 80] P   [ 81] Q   [ 82] R   [ 83] S
[ 84] T   [ 85] U   [ 86] V   [ 87] W   [ 88] X   [ 89] Y   [ 90] Z   [ 91] [
[ 92] \   [ 93] ]   [ 94] ^   [ 95] _   [ 96] `   [ 97] a   [ 98] b   [ 99] c
[100] d   [101] e   [102] f   [103] g   [104] h   [105] i   [106] j   [107] k
[108] l   [109] m   [110] n   [111] o   [112] p   [113] q   [114] r   [115] s
[116] t   [117] u   [118] v   [119] w   [120] x   [121] y   [122] z   [123] {
[124] |   [125] }   [126] ~   [127] ⌂   [128] Ç   [129] ü   [130] é   [131] â
[132] ä   [133] à   [134] å   [135] ç   [136] ê   [137] ë   [138] è   [139] ï
[140] î   [141] ì   [142] Ä   [143] Å   [144] É   [145] æ   [146] Æ   [147] ô
[148] ö   [149] ò   [150] û   [151] ù   [152] ÿ   [153] Ö   [154] Ü   [155] ¢
[156] £   [157] ¥   [158] ₧   [159] ƒ   [160] á   [161] í   [162] ó   [163] ú
[164] ñ   [165] Ñ   [166] ª   [167] º   [168] ¿   [169] ⌐   [170] ¬   [171] ½
[172] ¼   [173] ¡   [174] «   [175] »   [176] ░   [177] ▒   [178] ▓   [179] │
[180] ┤   [181] ╡   [182] ╢   [183] ╖   [184] ╕   [185] ╣   [186] ║   [187] ╗
[188] ╝   [189] ╜   [190] ╛   [191] ┐   [192] └   [193] ┴   [194] ┬   [195] ├
[196] ─   [197] ┼   [198] ╞   [199] ╟   [200] ╚   [201] ╔   [202] ╩   [203] ╦
[204] ╠   [205] ═   [206] ╬   [207] ╧   [208] ╨   [209] ╤   [210] ╥   [211] ╙
[212] ╘   [213] ╒   [214] ╓   [215] ╫   [216] ╪   [217] ┘   [218] ┌   [219] █
[220] ▄   [221] ▌   [222] ▐   [223] ▀   [224] α   [225] ß   [226] Γ   [227] π
[228] Σ   [229] σ   [230] µ   [231] τ   [232] Φ   [233] Θ   [234] Ω   [235] δ
[236] ∞   [237] φ   [238] ε   [239] ∩   [240] ≡   [241] ±   [242] ≥   [243] ≤
[244] ⌠   [245] ⌡   [246] ÷   [247] ≈   [248] °   [249] ∙   [250] ·   [251] √
[252] ⁿ   [253] ²   [254] ■   [255]
Ok
```

ASCII code

Corresponding character

The last character is a blank

The **STRING$** function can be used to print strings of specific lengths and with specific characters. This function has the following form:

FORM

```
Line no.     V$ = STRING$(n,m)
        or
Line no.     V$ = STRING$(n,X$)
```

where

n = the number of times the character is to be repeated.
m = the ASCII code of the character you want displayed.
X$ = a string (only the first character is displayed).

EXAMPLE

```
1100         Y$ = STRING$(10,100)
```

Suppose you wanted to display a double line across the page. The following program would do just that:

```
NEW ↵
Ok
20 PRINT STRING$(80,205)          'Displays 80 double dashes (ASCII code 205)
RUN ↵
═══════════════════════════════════════════════════════════════════════════════
Ok
```

The **LOCATE** function can be used in conjunction with the **STRING$** function to display characters in particular locations on the screen. This function has the following form:

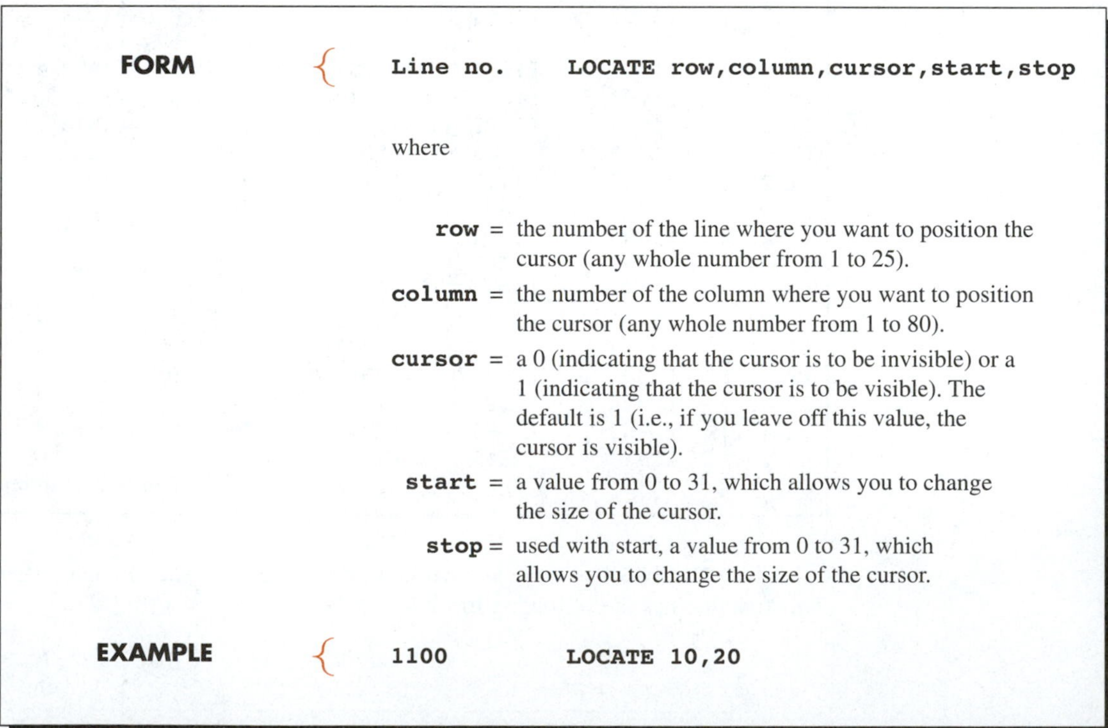

FORM

```
Line no.     LOCATE row,column,cursor,start,stop
```

where

row = the number of the line where you want to position the cursor (any whole number from 1 to 25).
column = the number of the column where you want to position the cursor (any whole number from 1 to 80).
cursor = a 0 (indicating that the cursor is to be invisible) or a 1 (indicating that the cursor is to be visible). The default is 1 (i.e., if you leave off this value, the cursor is visible).
start = a value from 0 to 31, which allows you to change the size of the cursor.
stop = used with start, a value from 0 to 31, which allows you to change the size of the cursor.

EXAMPLE

```
1100         LOCATE 10,20
```

Suppose you wanted to display a double line across the center of the page. The statement **LOCATE 13,1** can be used to position the cursor at column **1** of line **13** (i.e., midway between lines 1 and 25) and the statement **STRING$(80,205)** would display 80 double dashes.

```
10 LOCATE 13,1                          'Positions cursor at line 13, column 1
20 PRINT STRING$(80,205)                'Displays 80 double dashes (ASCII code 205)
RUN←



════════════════════════════════════════════════════════════════════════════════

Ok
_







1LIST  2RUN←  3LOAD"  4SAVE"  5CONT←  6,"LPT1  7TRON←  8TROFF←  9KEY  0SCREEN
```

The output displayed by the verification program, **VER2**, could be dressed-up somewhat by using the **LOCATE** and **STRING$** functions. For example if the input is incorrect, the program could be instructed to clear the screen (using **CLS** and **KEY OFF**) and then display the error message in the center of the screen inside a box. To make a box you need an upper left-hand corner (218), a horizontal line (196), an upper right-hand corner (191), a vertical line (179), a lower left-hand corner (192), and a lower right-hand corner (217). **LOAD** the program **VER5**, **LIST** it, **SAVE** it to your *BASIC Data* diskette, and then **RUN** it as shown below:

```
LOAD"C:\BA\VER5←
Ok
LIST←
1100 INPUT "Enter item number, price, verification";ITEM,PRICE,VER
1200   SUM = ITEM + PRICE + VER
1300   IF SUM/29 = INT(SUM/29) THEN PRINT "Entry Ok" ELSE GOSUB 1500
1400 END
1500 REM SUBROUTINE to display error message and BEEP
1510   CLS : KEY OFF                                          'Clear the screen
1520   LOCATE 11,30                                           'Cur to ln 11, col 30
1530   PRINT STRING$(1,218);STRING$(13,196);STRING$(1,191) 'Display box top
1545   LOCATE 12,30                                           'Cur to ln 12, col 30
1600   PRINT STRING$(1,179);" Input error ";STRING$(1,179) 'Display message
1610   LOCATE 13,30                                           'Cur to ln 13, col 30
1620   PRINT STRING$(1,192);STRING$(13,196);STRING$(1,217) 'Display box bottom
1630   LOCATE 14,30                                           'Cur to ln 14, col 30
1700   BEEP
1800 RETURN
Ok
SAVE"A:VER5←
Ok
RUN←
Enter item number, price, verification? 10,93,9
```

Just before [Enter] **is pressed**

Just after **[Enter]** is pressed, the speaker will beep and the screen will look as follows:

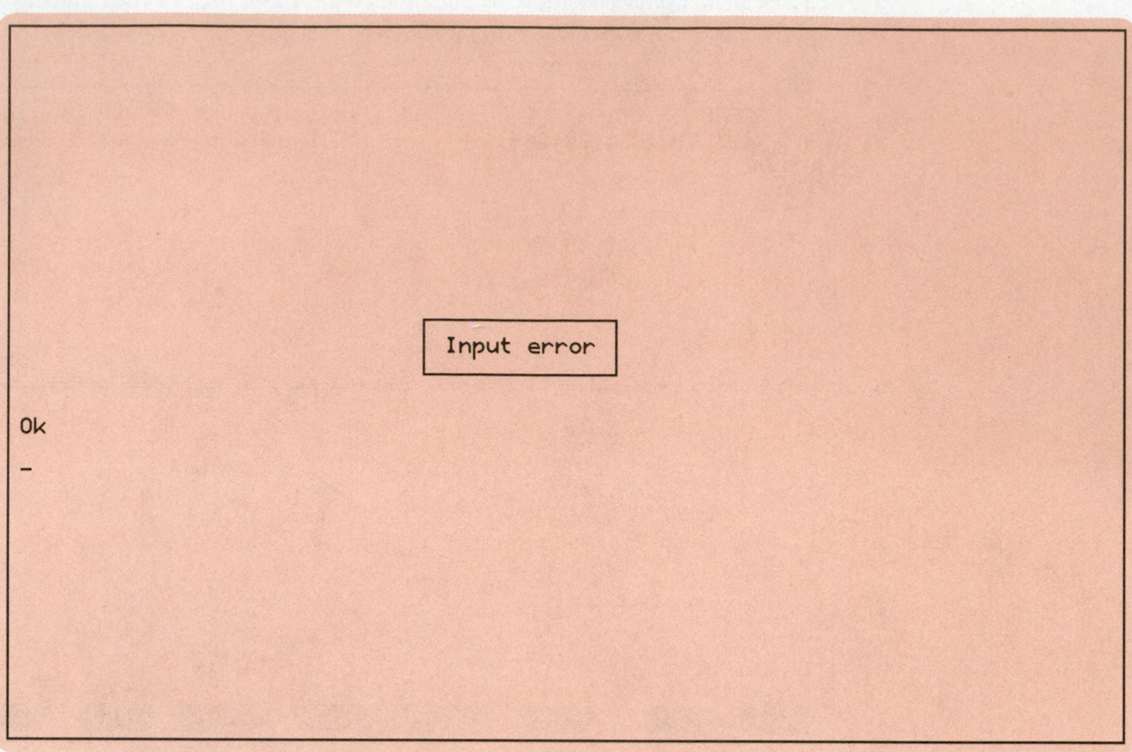

To display the menu again at the bottom of the screen, type **KEY ON** and press **[Enter]**.

You need to be careful when *dressing-up* the output of a program. You can spend a considerable amount of time getting the output to look exactly the way you want it. Sometimes this is worth the effort, but often you could use your time more efficiently working on something else. Don't be too compulsive! Always ask yourself, Is the fancy appearance of the output worth the extra effort?

TO TAKE A BREAK Type **SYSTEM** ↵, remove diskette(s). To resume (hard disk): Insert *Data* diskette, type **A:** ↵, **C:\BA\BASICA** ↵. To resume (two drive): Insert diskettes, type **A:** ↵, **B:\BASICA** ↵.

Homework Exercises

For each of the following homework exercises, use the programming process to develop a BASIC program that will produce the output described. Each program should contain enough **REM** statements to clearly document the program. Unless instructed to do otherwise, produce a hard copy of a **LIST** and a **RUN** of each of your final working programs. Also, save each program using a name such as **HWB5—01** for future reference. Your instructor may also ask you to hand in other materials related to the development of the programs such as the variable definitions, pseudocodes, etc.

---

① Kathy is interested in finding out how much time it will take her to drive the 16 miles from her house to Liberty High School at different speeds on the highway.

Use the programming procedure to write a program that displays a chart indicating the time it would take to travel 16 miles on a freeway at different driving speeds. Begin the chart with a speed of 65 miles per hour and continue down to a speed of 40 miles per hour in steps of 5 miles per hour. Use a **FOR/NEXT** loop and **PRINT USING** to round off the times to one decimal place. The output from your program should look like the following (the values in the box should be calculated by the computer):

```
Homework B5-01                  Joe Computer                    1 Mar 91

              The following times (rounded to nearest 1/10 minute)
              are needed to travel 16 miles at the speeds indicated:

                          Count      MPH       Minutes
                          -----      ---       -------
                            1         65        14.8
                            2         60        16.0
                            3         55        17.5
                            4         50        19.2
                            5         45        21.3
                            6         40        24.0
```

---

② Kelly runs a flower shop. By looking at the records of past sales, she determined that her profits are related to the amount of money she spends on advertising by the following formula:

$$\text{Profit} = -.1A^2 + 60A - 3100$$

where A = the number of dollars she spends on advertising each week.

Use the programming procedure to write a program that uses **FOR/NEXT** and **PRINT USING** to display the profits of her shop for an advertising budget that ranges from $0 per week to $700 per week in increments of $100. The output from your program should look like the following (the values in the box should be calculated by the computer):

Continued . . .

CHAPTER FIVE

```
Homework B5-02                    Joe Computer                    1 Mar 91

              Profit versus advertising for Kelly's Flower Shop
              Amounts are dollars per week

                          Advertising        Profit
                          -----------      -----------
                          $   0.00         $ -3,100.00
                          $ 100.00         $  1,900.00
                          $ 200.00         $  4,900.00
                          $ 300.00         $  5,900.00
                          $ 400.00         $  4,900.00
                          $ 500.00         $  1,900.00
                          $ 600.00         $ -3,100.00
                          $ 700.00         $-10,100.00
```

③ Kelly is interested in determining what amount she should spend on advertising for her flower shop so that her profits will be the highest possible.

Modify the program you wrote for Exercise 2 so that the computer also displays the largest profit made and the amount of advertising dollars needed to attain that profit. Be careful! This might be trickier than it seems. You will have to use a variable that stores the largest profit and another variable that stores the corresponding advertising expenditure. The output from your program should look like the following (the values in the boxes should be calculated by the computer):

```
Homework B5-03                    Joe Computer                    1 Mar 91

              Profit versus advertising for Kelly's Flower Shop
              Amounts are dollars per week

                          Advertising        Profit
                          -----------      -----------
                          $   0.00         $ -3,100.00
                          $ 100.00         $  1,900.00
                          $ 200.00         $  4,900.00
                          $ 300.00         $  5,900.00
                          $ 400.00         $  4,900.00
                          $ 500.00         $  1,900.00
                          $ 600.00         $ -3,100.00
                          $ 700.00         $-10,100.00

              Largest profit on this list is $5,900.00
Corresponding amount spent on advertising is   $300.00
```

CHAPTER FIVE

④ Shirley, chief executive officer of the Renton Nut Company, wants to have small group meetings with her top sales people. Each group should have no more than three people.

Use the programming procedure to write a program that will read the names and weekly sales figures for the employees, select only those employees with sales greater than $1000 per week, and display their names in groups with a maximum of three people per group.

Use the following **DATA** statements:

```
DATA Don,1010
DATA Willey,840
DATA Brad,2000
DATA Mike,1300
DATA Max,200
DATA Kathy,1050
DATA Annie,1340
DATA 1E15,1E15          ← Data flags
```

The output should look like the following:

```
Homework B5-04                    Joe Computer                   1 Mar 91

Top Salespeople Groups

Group  1     Number    Name
               1       Don
               2       Brad
               3       Mike

Group  2     Number    Name
               4       Kathy
               5       Annie
```

One way of doing this problem is to use the **INT** function to determine when the **Number** in the above chart is 1 or 4 or 7, etc. This can be done using the following condition in an **IF/THEN/ELSE** statement:

```
IF (NUMBER—1)/3 = INT((NUMBER—1)/3)
```

When this statement is true, the next name selected should be placed in the next group by calling a subroutine that displays the group heading.

---

⑤ Use the programing process to write a program that will determine whether or not a number is prime. Recall that a prime number is a whole number greater than 1 that is evenly divisible only by itself and 1. The program should request the number to be examined, check to see if it is a whole number, check to see if it is greater than 1, and then check to see if it is divisible by any other whole number less than itself. Use the **INT** function to do the checking.

The output from your program should look like the following (run the program using the values given in the output displayed on the next page):

Continued . . .

```
RUN ↵
Homework B5-05                    Joe Computer                    1 Mar 91

What is the number you wish tested? -1 ↵
Sorry, the number must be more than 1.
Ok
RUN ↵
Homework B5-05                    Joe Computer                    1 Mar 91

What is the number you wish tested? 2.3 ↵
Sorry, the number must be a whole number.
Ok
RUN ↵
Homework B5-05                    Joe Computer                    1 Mar 91

What is the number you wish tested? 7 ↵
The number is prime.
Ok
RUN ↵
Homework B5-05                    Joe Computer                    1 Mar 91

What is the number you wish tested? 8 ↵
The number is not prime - it is divisible by  2
Ok
```

---

⑥ In Exercise 6 of Part II, Chapter 1, you constructed a Lotus 1-2-3 worksheet that calculated the grade point average (GPA) for the courses a student had completed in her first quarter of college.

Use the programming procedure to write a BASIC program that will accomplish the same task using the data provided below. Make this program a little more general by having the computer assign the proper numeric value to a grade after it has been read from a **DATA** statement (an **A** has a value of 4, a **B** has a value of 3, a **C** has a value of 2, and a **D** has a value of 1). The program should use a **WHILE/WEND** loop to display the course, number of credits, grade, grade value, and the product of the value times the number of credits. The total number of credits and the GPA should also be calculated and displayed. Use **PRINT USING** to round the displayed value of the GPA to one decimal place.

```
DATA GC 1571,5,A
DATA GC 1421,4,B
DATA GC 1211,5,D
DATA PE 1122,1,C
DATA 1E15,1E15,1E15    ⟵ Data flags
```

Using the above **DATA** statements, the output should look like that given below (the values in the boxes should be calculated by the computer):

```
Homework B5-06                    Joe Computer                    1 Mar 91

 Course        Credits       Grade     Value     Val*Cr
GC 1571           5            A         4         20
GC 1421           4            B         3         12
GC 1211           5            D         1          5
PE 1122           1            C         2          2

Total Cr         15
     GPA        2.6
```

C H A P T E R   F I V E

⑦ Modify the program you wrote for Exercise 6 by using the **LOCATE** and **STRING$** functions to place boxes around different parts of the output. The output from the program should look like the following:

```
Homework B5-07                  Joe Computer                    1 Mar 91

 Course      Credits       Grade     Value     Val*Cr
GC 1571         5            A         4         20
GC 1421         4            B         3         12
GC 1211         5            D         1          5
PE 1122         1            C         2          2

 Total Cr  |   15
      GPA  |  2.6
```

Error Checking and Nested Loops

Objectives *After you have completed this chapter, you should be able to*

- Use **WHILE/WEND** loops in checking for errors in data.
- Expand an already existing program to include error checking.
- Use error flags to determine whether or not certain information should be displayed.
- Explain the structure of nested loops.

CHAPTER 6

- Create tables using nested **FOR/NEXT** loops.
- Create nested loops that employ both **WHILE/WEND** and **FOR/NEXT**.
- Use the programming procedure to create complex programs.

Introduction

There is an old saying in the computer field: *Garbage in/Garbage out*—in other words, the output from a computer is only as good as the data and programs fed into the computer. In the programs discussed so far, it was assumed that all the data entered were correct. Making this assumption allowed us to concentrate on the process of writing programs to do specific tasks without having to worry about taking care of strange or false data. However, in real-life settings the data are almost never completely correct. Perhaps the data-entry person made a typographic error, such as misspelling a word or reversing the digits in a number, or the data-entry person misunderstood or misread the data, or the data-entry person was given the wrong data to begin with. No matter what the cause, if the data are incorrect, the output from the computer will be incorrect. The first part of this chapter discusses different ways that can be used to instruct the computer to check the *reasonableness* of input data and to instruct the computer to take appropriate action when a strange piece of data is detected. The second half of the chapter deals with programs that contain complex loops.

WHILE and WEND in Error Checking

The **WHILE** and **WEND** statements are convenient to use for some error-checking routines. For example, at the end of the metric conversion program, **METRIC3** (see p. B142), the computer asked if the user would like to make another chart. If the response was **YES** or **yes**, the statements inside the **WHILE/WEND** loop were executed and another chart was produced. If the person said something other than **YES** or **yes**, the loop was exited and the computer terminated the program.

```
LOAD"C:\BA\METRIC3↵
Ok
LIST↵
1100 A$ = "Inches  Centimeters  Meters"
1200 B$ = "  ##         ##.##      ##.##"
1220 ANSWER$ = "YES"
1240 WHILE ANSWER$ = "YES" OR ANSWER$ = "yes"
1250 INPUT "Enter values for beginning, ending, and increment"; LOW,HI,INCF
1300   PRINT A$
1400     FOR INCH = LOW TO HI STEP INCR
1500       PRINT USING B$;INCH,2.54*INCH,2.54*INCH/100
1600     NEXT INCH
1700   INPUT "Would you like to make another chart"; ANSWER$
1800 WEND
Ok
RUN↵
Enter values for beginning, ending, and increment? 0,12,4↵
Inches  Centimeters  Meters
   0        0.00      0.00
   4       10.16      0.10
   8       20.32      0.20
  12       30.48      0.30
Would you like to make another chart? Yes↵
Ok
```

In the preceding program, why is the loop not processed again when the user responds with **Yes** to the question? The problem is that at line **1240** the computer was told to execute the loop if **ANSWER$** was equal to **YES** or **yes** but not to **Yes**. Because the computer does not speak English, it could not tell that **Yes** and **YES** mean the same thing.

To remedy this situation the computer could be instructed to check to see if either **YES** or **NO** was entered. If neither was entered, the computer would ask the user to respond with either **YES** or **NO**. To do this, a few new lines of code need to be added at the bottom of the program. **LOAD** the new version of the program, **LIST** it, **SAVE** it to your *BASIC Data* diskette, and then **RUN** it as shown on the next page:

```
LOAD"C:\BA\METRIC5↵
Ok
LIST↵
1100 A$ = "Inches  Centimeters  Meters"
1200 B$ = "  ##       ##.##      ##.##"
1220 ANSWER$ = "YES"
1240 WHILE ANSWER$ = "YES" OR ANSWER$ = "yes"
1250 INPUT "Enter values for beginning, ending, and increment"; LOW,HI,INCR
1300   PRINT A$
1400     FOR INCH = LOW TO HI STEP INCR
1500       PRINT USING B$;INCH,2.54*INCH,2.54*INCH/100
1600     NEXT INCH
1700   INPUT "Would you like to make another chart"; ANSWER$
1750   GOSUB 2100                           'Checks for errors in user response
1800 WEND
1900 END
2000 REM ***** Subroutine to check for errors in user response
2100   WHILE ANSWER$ <> "YES" AND ANSWER$ <> "NO"
2200     PRINT "Please answer YES or NO (all uppercase letters)"
2300     INPUT "Would you like to make another chart";ANSWER$
2400   WEND
2500 RETURN
Ok
SAVE"A:METRIC5↵
Ok
RUN↵
Enter values for beginning, ending, and increment? 0,12,4↵
Inches  Centimeters  Meters
  0        0.00       0.00
  4       10.16       0.10
  8       20.32       0.20
 12       30.48       0.30
Would you like to make another chart? Yes↵
Please answer YES or NO (all uppercase letters) ←—— Produced by error subroutine
Would you like to make another chart? YES↵
Enter values for beginning, ending, and increment? 6,0,-2↵
Inches  Centimeters  Meters
  6       15.24       0.15
  4       10.16       0.10
  2        5.08       0.05
  0        0.00       0.00
Would you like to make another chart? NO↵
Ok
```

If the value of **ANSWER$** is not exactly equal to **YES** or **NO**, the statements in the **WHILE/WEND** loop (lines **2100** – **2400** in the error-checking subroutine) will be executed. If **ANSWER$** is exactly **YES** or exactly **NO**, the statements in the error-checking subroutine loop will not be executed and control will return to line **1800**. Notice how the **WHILE/WEND** statements define the beginning and end of the loop in a simple and convenient way.

The above example shows that the **WHILE/WEND** statements are very useful when you want to remain in a loop until a correct form of the data is entered. This, of course, could be frustrating to someone who is unfamiliar with the operation of the program. For example, suppose the person does not know what *uppercase* means. The person may not know how to exit the loop and would not be able to terminate the program properly.

To make the program more *user friendly* (i.e., easier for a human to use), a few more statements could be added in order to exit the error-checking loop after it has been executed a specified number of times and then to display a help message. In the screen dump that follows, the statements in the dotted boxes were added to accomplish this task. **LOAD** the new version of the program, **LIST** it, **SAVE** it to your *BASIC Data* diskette, and then **RUN** it as shown on the next page:

```
LOAD"C:\BA\METRIC6
Ok
LIST
1100 A$ = "Inches  Centimeters  Meters"
1200 B$ = "  ##        ##.##      ##.##"
1220 ANSWER$ = "YES"
1240 WHILE ANSWER$ = "YES" OR ANSWER$ = "yes"
1250 INPUT "Enter values for beginning, ending, and increment"; LOW,HI,INCR
1300   PRINT A$
1400     FOR INCH = LOW TO HI STEP INCR
1500       PRINT USING B$;INCH,2.54*INCH,2.54*INCH/100
1600     NEXT INCH
1700   INPUT "Would you like to make another chart"; ANSWER$
1750   GOSUB 2100           'Checks for errors in user response
1800 WEND
1900 END
2000 REM ***** Subroutine to check for errors in user response
2050   COUNT = 0                          'Tracks # times loop is executed
2100   WHILE ANSWER$ <> "YES" AND ANSWER$ <> "NO"
2140     COUNT = COUNT + 1                'Counts # of times this loop is executed
2150     IF COUNT = 3 THEN GOSUB 2600     'Subroutine to display help message
2200     PRINT "Please answer YES or NO (all uppercase letters)"
2300     INPUT "Would you like to make another chart";ANSWER$
2400   WEND
2500 RETURN
2600 REM ***** Subroutine to display help messasge if user gets stuck
2700   PRINT
2800   PRINT "  ***********************************************"
2900   PRINT "  *     There is a problem with your responses     *"
3000   PRINT "  *  Please call Joe Computer at 373-4026 for help *"
3100   PRINT "  ***********************************************"
3200   END
Ok
SAVE"A:METRIC6
Ok
RUN
Enter values for beginning, ending, and increment? 0,12,4
Inches  Centimeters  Meters
   0        0.00      0.00
   4       10.16      0.10
   8       20.32      0.20
  12       30.48      0.30
Would you like to make another chart? Yes
Please answer YES or NO (all uppercase letters)
Would you like to make another chart? Yeah
Please answer YES or NO (all uppercase letters)
Would you like to make another chart? Sure

  ***********************************************
  *     There is a problem with your responses     *
  *  Please call Joe Computer at 373-4026 for help *
  ***********************************************
Ok
```

In line **2140**, note the use of the counter and in line **2150** the **IF/THEN/ELSE** statement that examines the value of the counter each time the error loop is executed. When the loop executes for the third time, control is sent to a subroutine that provides the user with a way of getting help from a human. Having a human available to users is important because working with computers can be very frustrating. Sometimes you just cannot figure out what you are doing wrong and you need a human who can assist you (and maybe offer a sympathetic pat on the back or a shoulder to cry on).

Checking Data in the Insurance Premium Program

On page B98, the program **INSURE1** was developed, which would compute a car insurance premium based on a person's age and the number of accidents he or she had had. The program was written under the assumption that all the data would be correct. To refresh your memory, a sample run of the program is given below:

```
RUN
                    What is your age? 30
How many accidents have you had? 2
                      Base premium: 50
                Additional premium: 100
                     Total premium: 150
Ok
```

Now let's consider some *unreasonable* data that might be entered into the program. For example, what should the computer do if the following data were entered?

- Age = –5: Can a person be a negative number of years old?
- Age = 10: Would you give car insurance to a 10 year old?
- Age = 120: Would you give car insurance to a 120 year old?
- Number of Accidents = –2: Can someone have –2 accidents? (Sure. I am such a great defensive driver that I would have had 2 accidents if I had not skillfully avoided them. Therefore, I have had -2 accidents.)
- Number of Accidents = .5: Can someone have one half of an accident? (Sure. I was involved in an accident and the other person and I decided we were equally at fault. Thus, we each claimed one half of the blame.)
- Number of Accidents = 50: Would you insure someone who has had 50 accidents? (Probably not!)

For each of the above cases, the program would have to tell the computer what to do. If the program does not specifically say what to do, the computer will do something, but what?

On page B99, the program was run for a 5 year old who claimed to have had –8 accidents. The output was the following:

```
RUN
                    What is your age? 5
How many accidents have you had? -8
                      Base premium: 100
                Additional premium:-100
                     Total premium: 0
Ok
```

The total premium for this person is **0** because the additional premium was calculated to be **-100** and this exactly cancels the base premium. Clearly, the program needs to be adjusted so that it takes such problems into account. Note that the first piece of data is not really an error (the true age of the person running the program may, in fact, be 5) but the data are not appropriate for our purposes. Such errors are called *range errors*, meaning that the values may be correct but they are out of the range of values we want to consider.

The computer could be told to check the data right after each **INPUT** statement (using an **IF/THEN/ELSE** statement) and to issue an error message (in a subroutine) if a range error occurs. Let's modify the program in this way so that the computer will only accept ages between 18 and 65, inclusive. **LOAD** the new version of the program, **LIST** it, **SAVE** it to your *BASIC Data* diskette, and then **RUN** it as shown on the next page:

```
LOAD"C:\BA\INSURE2
Ok
LIST
1100 REM Program computes semi-annual insurance premium given
1200 REM  person's age and number of accidents
1300 REM Douglas Robertson (625-1075), created 1 Jul 90
1400 REM Define variables:
1500 REM    AGE = person's age in years
1600 REM    NUM = number of accidents person has had
1700 REM   BASE = value of base premium
1800 REM    ADD = value of additional premium
1900 REM    TOT = total premium to be paid
2000 REM Input data on age and number of accidents
2100   INPUT "                    What is your age";AGE
2150   IF AGE < 18 OR AGE > 65 THEN GOSUB 3400     'Checks age for range error
2200   INPUT "How many accidents have you had";NUM
2300 REM Check age to determine base premium.
2400   IF AGE =< 20 THEN BASE = 100 ELSE BASE = 50
2500 REM Check # accidents to determine additional premium.
2600   IF NUM = 0 THEN ADD = 0 ELSE ADD = 60 + 20*NUM
2700 REM Compute total premium
2800   TOT = BASE + ADD
2900 REM Display results
3000   PRINT "                        Base premium:"BASE
3100   PRINT "                  Additional premium:"ADD
3200   PRINT "                       Total premium:"TOT
3300 END
3400 REM ***** Subroutine to issue error message for AGE out of range
3500   PRINT
3600   PRINT "Sorry, your age must be between 18 and 65"
3700   PRINT "Your BASE and TOTAL premiums cannot be properly calculated"
3800   PRINT
3900 RETURN
Ok
SAVE"A:INSURE2
Ok
RUN
                   What is your age? 5

Sorry, your age must be between 18 and 65
Your BASE and TOTAL premiums cannot be properly calculated

How many accidents have you had? -8
                        Base premium: 100
                  Additional premium:-100
                       Total premium: 0
Ok
```

The program now detects the error but still does the computations using the incorrect information. The program could be made more practical by adding an error flag (such as **AGE.ERROR**) to the subroutine so that if an unacceptable value for age were entered, the variable **AGE.ERROR** would be set to 1. But if a correct value were entered, the variable **AGE.ERROR** would remain at its default value of 0. The computer would be instructed to display the results for the base premium and the total only if the value of **AGE.ERROR** were 0 (i.e., only if there were no errors in the data). The bottom of the program would now look as follows:

```
3000    IF AGE.ERROR = 0 THEN PRINT "                    Base premium:"BASE
3100                          PRINT "              Additional premium:"ADD
3200    IF AGE.ERROR = 0 THEN PRINT "                   Total premium:"TOT
3300 END
3400 REM ***** Subroutine to issue error message for AGE out of range
3500    PRINT
3600    PRINT "Sorry, your age must be between 18 and 65"
3700    PRINT "Your BASE and TOTAL premiums cannot be properly calculated"
3800    PRINT
3850    AGE.ERROR = 1
3900 RETURN
Ok
SAVE"A:INSURE3↵
Ok
RUN↵
                What is your age? 5↵

Sorry, your age must be between 18 and 65
Your BASE and TOTAL premiums cannot be properly calculated

How many accidents have you had? -8↵
                Additional premium:-100
Ok
```

A similar procedure could be employed to check the values for the number of accidents. In that case, an **IF/THEN/ELSE** statement would be added at line **2250** to call a subroutine at line **4000**.

LOAD the new version of the program, **INSURE4**, **LIST** it, **SAVE** it to your *BASIC Data* diskette, and then **RUN** it as shown on the next page.

```
2000 REM Input data on age and number of accidents
2100   INPUT "               What is your age";AGE
2150   IF AGE < 18 OR AGE > 65 THEN GOSUB 3400     'Checks age for range error
2200   INPUT "How many accidents have you had";NUM
2250   IF NUM < 0 OR NUM > 5 OR NUM <> INT(NUM) THEN GOSUB 4000    'Checks NUM
2300 REM Check age to determine base premium.
2400   IF AGE =< 20 THEN BASE = 100 ELSE BASE = 50
2500 REM Check # accidents to determine additional premium.
2600   IF NUM = 0 THEN ADD = 0 ELSE ADD = 60 + 20*NUM
2700 REM Compute total premium
2800   TOT = BASE + ADD
2900 REM Display results
3000   IF AGE.ERROR = 0 THEN PRINT "                    Base premium:"BASE
3100   IF NUM.ERROR = 0 THEN PRINT "              Additional premium:"ADD
3200   IF AGE.ERROR = 0 AND NUM.ERROR = 0 THEN
                     PRINT "                   Total premium:"TOT
3300 END
3400 REM ***** Subroutine to issue error message for AGE out of range
3500   PRINT
3600   PRINT "Sorry, your age must be between 18 and 65"
3700   PRINT "Your BASE and TOTAL premiums cannot be properly calculated"
3800   PRINT
3850   AGE.ERROR = 1
3900 RETURN
4000 REM ***** Subroutine to issue error message for NUM out of range
4100   PRINT
4200   PRINT "Sorry, number of accidents must be a whole number between 0 and 5"
4300   PRINT "Your ADDITIONAL and TOTAL premiums cannot be properly calculated"
4400   PRINT
4500   NUM.ERROR = 1
4600 RETURN
Ok
SAVE"A:INSURE4 ↵
Ok
RUN ↵
               What is your age? 5 ↵

Sorry, your age must be between 18 and 65
Your BASE and TOTAL premiums cannot be properly calculated

How many accidents have you had? -8 ↵

Sorry, number of accidents must be a whole number between 0 and 5
Your ADDITIONAL and TOTAL premiums cannot be properly calculated

Ok
```

Notice how the use of subroutines simplifies the extension of a program. To add a new part you simply add a new subroutine call and associated subroutine.

Checking for Errors in the Payroll Program

Let's add some error checking to the data for the extended payroll program, **WAGES6**, from page B147. For example, let's say that the rate of pay must be between $4 and $7 per hour, inclusive, and that the hours worked must be between 0 and 60, inclusive. This can be done by adding a subroutine to check for input errors. The subroutine call (i.e., the **GOSUB**) would be entered at the beginning of the loop that does the calculations (see line **2715** in the program listing on the next page). The subroutine would have four **IF/THEN/ELSE** statements, one for each type of error (rate too low, rate too high, hours too few, hours too many). If an error is detected, the computer should display a warning stating that an error has occurred.

Also, as in the previous example, there must be a way of telling the computer not to do the calculations if an error has been detected. This can be done, again, using an error flag. When the subroutine is entered, the error flag is set to 0 (see line **9870**), indicating that no errors have been detected so far. Then, if an error is detected, the error flag is set to 1 (see lines **9880** through **9910**). When control is returned to the main program, other **IF/THEN/ELSE** statements are used to check the value of the error flag. The calculation and display statements are to be executed only if the value of the error flag is 0 (see lines **2850** through **2905**).

A **LIST** and a **RUN** of the complete modified program is shown on the next three pages. Two pieces of data were changed to provide incorrect data. **LOAD** the new version of the program, **LIST** it, **SAVE** it to your *BASIC Data* diskette, and then **RUN** it as shown below:

```
LOAD"C:\BA\WAGES7↵
Ok
LIST↵
1100 REM Program to compute wages given total hours worked and pay rate
1200 REM Douglas Robertson (373-4026), created 1 Mar 91
1300 REM Define variables:
1400 REM   EMPLOYEE$ = name in form LastName Space First (e.g., Roberts Matt)
1500 REM        RATE = rate of pay in dollars per hour (e.g.,  3)
1600 REM       HOURS = total number of hours worked for pay period (e.g., 50)
1700 REM         PAY = total pay earned for pay period (e.g., 150)
1705 REM         REG = regular pay earned
1710 REM          OT = overtime pay earned
1715 REM         NUM = number of sets of data read from DATA list
1720 REM       TRATE = sum of RATE
1725 REM        THRS = sum of HOURS
1730 REM        TREG = sum of REG
1740 REM         TOP = sum of OT
1750 REM        TPAY = sum of PAY
1760 REM       ARATE = average of RATE
1770 REM        AHRS = average of HOURS
1780 REM        AREG = average of REG
1790 REM        ATOP = average of OT
1795 REM        APAY = average of PAY
1798 REM        EFLG = flag for range errors (0 = no errors, 1 = error)
1800 REM Begin processing
1850 GOSUB 4500                               'Initialize counters
1900 GOSUB 5000                               'Define PRINT USING images
2400 GOSUB 6000                               'Display header
2700   READ EMPLOYEE$,RATE,HOURS              'Assign values to first set of data
2710     WHILE HOURS <> 1E+15                 'For each person do the following
2715       GOSUB 9860                         'Checks for errors in data
2720       IF HOURS =< 40 THEN GOSUB 7000 ELSE GOSUB 7500  'Calc reg & OT pay
2800       PAY = REG + OT                     'Calculate pay
2820       IF EFLG = 1 THEN PRINT USING I9$; EMPLOYEE$,RATE,HOURS,REG,OT,PAY
2850       IF EFLG = 0 THEN NUM = NUM + 1     'Count correct data sets
2900       IF EFLG = 0 THEN PRINT USING I6$;NUM,EMPLOYEE$,RATE,HOURS,REG,OT,PAY
2905       IF EFLG = 0 THEN GOSUB 8000        'Calculate sum for each variable
2910       READ EMPLOYEE$,RATE,HOURS          'Assign values to name, rate, hours
3000     WEND                                 'Repeat loop for next person
3050   GOSUB 9000                             'Calculate averages
3200   GOSUB 9650                             'Display footer
3300 REM End processing
4100 END
4500 REM ***** SUBROUTINE to initialize counters
4510     NUM = 0
4520   TRATE = 0
4530    THRS = 0
4540    TREG = 0
4550     TOP = 0
4560    TPAY = 0
4570 RETURN
```

Continued . . .

```
5000 REM ***** SUBROUTINE to define PRINT USING images
5100   I1$ = "Puter Pals, Inc., Payroll Summary"
5200   I2$ = "Date: \            \"
5300   I3$ = "Time: \            \"
5400   I4$ = "Num  Employee          Pay Rate  Hours  Reg Pay   OT Pay   Total Pay"
5500   I5$ = "---  --------------    --------  -----  -------   -------  ---------"
5600   I6$ = " ##  \              \    $##.##  ###.#  $###.##  $###.##  $####.##"
5610   I9$ = "    [\              \]  [$##.##][###.#]    N/A      N/A        N/A  "
5700   I7$ = "     Totals                       ###.#  $###.##  $###.##  $####.##"
5800   I8$ = "     Averages             $##.##  ###.#  $###.##  $###.##  $####.##"
5900 RETURN
6000 REM ***** SUBROUTINE to display header
6100   PRINT I1$
6200   PRINT USING I2$; DATE$
6300   PRINT USING I3$; TIME$
6400   PRINT
6500   PRINT I4$
6600   PRINT I5$
6700 RETURN
7000 REM ***** SUBROUTINE to calculate reg and overtime pay for 40 or less hours
7100   REG = HOURS*RATE                    'Regular pay for 40 or less hours
7200    OT = 0                             'Overtime pay for 40 or less hours
7300 RETURN
7500 REM ***** SUBROUTINE to calculate regular & overtime pay for over 40 hours
7600   REG = 40*RATE                       'Regular pay for over 40 hours
7700    OT = (HOURS - 40)*RATE*1.5         'Overtime pay for over 40 hours
7800 RETURN
8000 REM ***** SUBROUTINE to calculate sum for each variable
8100   TRATE = TRATE + RATE
8200    THRS = THRS  + HOURS
8300    TREG = TREG  + REG
8400     TOP = TOP   + OT
8500    TPAY = TPAY  + PAY
8600 RETURN
9000 REM ***** SUBROUTINE to calculate averages for each variable
9100   ARATE = TRATE/NUM
9200   AHRS =  THRS/NUM
9300   AREG =  TREG/NUM
9400   ATOP =   TOP/NUM
9500   APAY =  TPAY/NUM
9600 RETURN
9650 REM ***** SUBROUTINE to display footer
9700   PRINT I5$
9750   PRINT USING I7$;THRS,TREG,TOP,TPAY
9800   PRINT USING I8$;ARATE,AHRS,AREG,ATOP,APAY
9850 RETURN
```

Continued . . .

```
9750   PRINT USING I7$;THRS,TREG,TOP,TPAY
9800   PRINT USING I8$;ARATE,AHRS,AREG,ATOP,APAY
9850 RETURN
9860 REM ***** SUBROUTINE to check for errors in data
9870   EFLG = 0   'Set error flag to 0 to show no errors so far for this data
9880   IF RATE  <  4 THEN PRINT EMPLOYEE$" skipped: RATE = " RATE"<  4":EFLG = 1
9890   IF RATE  >  7 THEN PRINT EMPLOYEE$" skipped: RATE = " RATE">  7":EFLG = 1
9900   IF HOURS <  0 THEN PRINT EMPLOYEE$" skipped: HOURS ="HOURS"<  0":EFLG = 1
9910   IF HOURS > 60 THEN PRINT EMPLOYEE$" skipped: HOURS ="HOURS"> 60":EFLG = 1
9930  RETURN
10100 REM Define DATA list in form:
10200 REM DATA NAME          ,RATE,HOURS
10300     DATA Roberts Matt,   4,   30
10400     DATA Sim Keisha   ,  41,   50
10500     DATA Tech Sara    ,   6,   21
10600     DATA Well Vanessa,   5,   40
10700     DATA Taylor David,   4,   35
10800     DATA Peters Bill,    4,   62
10900     DATA 1E+15,1E+15,1E+15,1E+15
Ok
SAVE"A:WAGES7↵
Ok
RUN↵
Puter Pals, Inc., Payroll Summary
Date: 03-01-1991
Time: 19:49:14

Num  Employee         Pay Rate  Hours  Reg Pay   OT Pay   Total Pay
---  --------------   --------  -----  -------  -------   ---------
  1  Roberts Matt      $ 4.00   30.0  $120.00  $  0.00   $ 120.00
Sim Keisha skipped: RATE =  41 >  7
    [Sim Keisha    ]  [$41.00][ 50.0][$%1640.00][$615.00][$2255.00]
  2  Tech Sara         $ 6.00   21.0  $126.00  $  0.00   $ 126.00
  3  Well Vanessa      $ 5.00   40.0  $200.00  $  0.00   $ 200.00
  4  Taylor David      $ 4.00   35.0  $140.00  $  0.00   $ 140.00
Peters Bill skipped: HOURS = 62 > 60
    [Peters Bill   ]  [$ 4.00][ 62.0][$160.00][$132.00][$ 292.00]
---  --------------   --------  -----  -------  -------   ---------
     Totals                    126.0  $586.00  $  0.00   $ 586.00
     Averages          $ 4.75   31.5  $146.50  $  0.00   $ 146.50
Ok
```

When the program was run, the errors in the new data were detected and appropriate error messages displayed. The rate of pay for Keisha Sim was way too high. It was probably supposed to be $4.10, but the data entry person forgot to key in the decimal point. Thus, her pay rate was entered as $41 per hour. If the data had not been checked for errors, Keisha would have been paid $2,255 for the week! Would she have called to the boss and said "Hey, I cannot accept this, you paid me too much" or would she have cashed the check and thought that the boss was finally paying her what she was really worth? Notice that the image statement for her values is too small and therefore a **%** was added to the left-hand side of the value for her regular pay (for more information on this type of **PRINT USING** problem, see page B39).

The number of hours worked for Bill Peters may have been, in fact, correct. However, it was out of the range of normal hours for a typical person and so the program was set up to flag it. At this point, a human would have to look at the data and decide whether or not the value is legitimate and take appropriate action.

Study the new parts of this program very carefully. The four main points are:

- The use of **IF/THEN/ELSE** statements to check for range errors (see the subroutine at lines **9860 – 9930**).
- The use of a data flag (**EFLG**) to indicate whether or not an error has occurred (see the subroutine at lines **9860 – 9930**).
- The use of **IF/THEN/ELSE** statements to check to see if a value should be printed or not (see lines **2820** and **2900**).
- The use of **IF/THEN/ELSE** statements to check to see if counters should be incremented (see lines **2850** and **2905**).

Nested FOR/NEXT Loops

More complex loops can be created using *nested* loops. Nested means that one loop is completely inside another loop (think of nested canisters). To see how nested loops work, carefully examine the following program:

```
LOAD"C:\BA\NEST1
Ok
LIST
10 FOR OUTER = 1 TO 2
20   FOR INNER = 1 TO 3              ⎤ Inner
30     PRINT OUTER,INNER             ⎥ loop          Outer
40   NEXT INNER                      ⎦               loop
50   PRINT "OUTER loop changes. OUTER ="OUTER" and INNER ="INNER
60 NEXT OUTER
70 PRINT "Value of OUTER is now "OUTER
Ok
SAVE"A:NEST1
Ok
RUN
 1             1
 1             2
 1             3
OUTER loop changes. OUTER = 1  and INNER = 4
 2             1
 2             2
 2             3
OUTER loop changes. OUTER = 2  and INNER = 4
Value of OUTER is now  3
Ok
```

Line Numbers	Comments
10	**OUTER** is assigned the value **1**. Because this value does not exceed the terminal value (**2**), the statements in the loop are executed and control passes to line **20**.
20	**INNER** is assigned the value **1**. Because this value does not exceed the terminal value (**3**) for this loop, the statements in the loop are executed (i.e., control passes to line **30**).
30	The values of **OUTER** (which is **1**) and **INNER** (which is **1**) are displayed
40	The **STEP** (which is **1**) for the inside loop is added to the current value of **INNER** (which is **1**) and control is sent back to the **FOR** statement at line **20**.
20	The new value (1 + 1 = 2) of **INNER** is checked to see if it exceeds the terminal value (which is **3**) for this loop. Because this value does not exceed the terminal value (which is **3**) for this loop, the statements in the loop are executed (i.e., control passes to line **30**).
30	The values of **OUTER** (which is **1**) and **INNER** (which is **2**) are displayed.
40	The **STEP** (which is **1**) for the inside loop is added to the value of **INNER** (which is **2**) and control is sent back to the **FOR** statement at line **20**.
20	The new value (2 + 1 = 3) of **INNER** is checked to see if it exceeds the terminal value (which is **3**) for the loop. Because this value does not exceed the terminal value (which is **3**) for this loop, the statements in the loop are executed (i.e., control passes to line **30**).
30	The values of **OUTER** and **INNER** are displayed.
40	The **STEP** (which is **1**) for the inside loop is added to the value of **INNER** (which is **3**) and control is sent back to the **FOR** statement at line **20**.
20	The new value (3 + 1 = 4) for **INNER** is checked to see if it exceeds the terminal value (which is **3**) for the loop. Because it does exceed the terminal value, the loop is exited (i.e., control passes to the statement directly after **NEXT INNER**).
50	The values of **OUTER** and **INNER** are displayed.
60	The **STEP** (which is **1**) for the *outside* loop is added to the value of **OUTER** (which is **1**) and control is sent back to the **FOR** statement at line **10**.
10	The new value (1 + 1 = 2) for **OUTER** is checked to see if it exceeds the terminal value (which is **2**) for this loop. Because this value does not exceed the terminal value (which is **2**) for this loop, the statements in the loop are executed (i.e., control passes to line **20**).
20	The inside loop is executed all over again. Because the last statement executed was not a **NEXT INNER** statement, the variable **INNER** is assigned the value **1** again, rather than being incremented by the **STEP** for the inside loop. Because the value for **INNER** (which is **1**) does not exceed the terminal value (which is **3**) for this loop, the statements in the loop are executed (i.e., control passes to line **30**).
	(And so on until the program terminates.)

Notice that the **OUTER** loop changes at a slower rate than does the **INNER** loop. This is because a particular value of **OUTER** remains constant while the entire **INNER** loop is run through. In this sense, the outer loop changes more slowly than the inner loop. The entire run of the program can be summarized as follows:

Memory Assignments for Program NEST1

Line no.	OUTER	INNER	
	0	0	Variable names / Default values
10	1 1 =< 2 true, so execute outer loop		Assigned value Decision
20		1 1 =< 3 true, so execute inner loop	Assigned value Decision
30	1	1	Output
40		2 ← 1 + 1	Calculated value
20		2 =< 3 true, so execute inner loop	Decision
30	1	2	Output
40		3 ← 2 + 1	Calculated value
20		3 =< 3 true, so execute inner loop	Decision
30	1	3	Output
40		4 ← 3 + 1	Calculated value
20		4 =< 3 false, so exit inner loop	Decision
50	1	4	Output
60	2 ← 1 + 1		Calculated value
10	2 =< 2 true, so execute outer loop		Decision
20		1 1 =< 3 true, so execute inner loop	Assigned value Decision
30	2	1	Output
40		2 ← 1 + 1	Calculated value
20		2 =< 3 true, so execute inner loop	Decision
30	2	2	Output
40		3 ← 2 + 1	Calculated value

Continued . . .

Memory Assignments for Program NEST1

20		3 =< 3 true, so execute inner loop	Decision
30	2	3	Output
40		4 ⬅ 3 + 1	Calculated value
20		4 =< 3 false, so exit inner loop	Decision
50	2	4	Output
60	3 ⬅ 2 + 1		Calculated value
10	3 =< 2 false, so exit outer loop		Decision
70	3	4	Output

Study the example given below and try to predict what the output will be before looking at the **RUN**:

```
LOAD"C:\BA\NEST2↵
Ok
LIST↵
10 FOR K = 1 TO 5 STEP 3                                        ┐
20    FOR J = 9 TO 2 STEP -4  ┐ Inner                           │ Outer
30      PRINT K,J             │ loop                            │ loop
40    NEXT J                  ┘                                 │
50    PRINT "After NEXT J statement, K ="K" and J ="J           ┘
60 NEXT K
70 PRINT "Final values are: K ="K" and J ="J
Ok
SAVE"A:NEST2↵
Ok
RUN↵
 1            9
 1            5
After NEXT J statement, K = 1  and J = 1
 4            9
 4            5
After NEXT J statement, K = 4  and J = 1
Final values are: K = 7  and J = 1
Ok
```

With nested loops, one loop must be entirely within the other loop. The loops may not be overlapped as the example on the next page:

```
NEW ↵
Ok
10 FOR K = 1 TO 5
20   FOR J = 1 TO 3
30     PRINT K,J
40   NEXT K
50 NEXT J
SAVE"A:NEST3 ↵
Ok
RUN ↵
NEXT without FOR in 50
Ok
```

Outer loop

Inner loop

Improperly nested loops cause a misleading error message

Notice that the error message is misleading. The computer thinks that there is a **NEXT** statement without a corresponding **FOR** statement. However, the **FOR** and **NEXT** statements are correctly paired but they are not in the proper order.

TO TAKE A BREAK Type **SYSTEM** ↵; remove diskette(s). To resume (hard disk): Insert *Data* diskette, type **A:** ↵, **C:\BA\BASICA** ↵. To resume (two drive): Insert diskettes, type **A:** ↵; **B:\BASICA** ↵.

Interest Earnings

The program **INVEST2** (see p. B144) was designed to compute the value of money invested at a given rate of interest for a given number of years. This program can be modified so that it calculates and displays the value of the deposit for a number of different rates of interest. The original program is listed and run below:

```
LOAD"C:\BA\INVEST2 ↵
Ok
LIST ↵
10 INPUT "Enter principal, rate, time, compounding";P,R,T,C
20   FOR YEAR = 1 TO T
40     VALUE = P*(1 + R*.01/C)^(YEAR*C)
50     PRINT USING "Value after ## years is $$######,.##";YEAR,VALUE
60   NEXT YEAR
Ok
RUN ↵
Enter principal, rate, time, compounding? 1000,10,5,1 ↵
Value after  1 years is    $1,100.00
Value after  2 years is    $1,210.00
Value after  3 years is    $1,331.00
Value after  4 years is    $1,464.10
Value after  5 years is    $1,610.51
Ok
```

The only major change that has to be made is to add a loop inside the **YEAR** loop to compute the value of the investment for different rates of interest (e.g., the rates are to range from 6 to 12 percent in steps of 2 percent). In addition, minor changes need to be made to the **INPUT** statement so that it does not ask for the rate and to the **PRINT** statement so that the interest rate is displayed also. **LOAD** the new version of the program, **LIST** it, **SAVE** it to your *BASIC Data* diskette, and then **RUN** it as shown on the next page:

```
LOAD"C:\BA\INVEST3
Ok
LIST
10 INPUT "Enter principal, time, compounding";P,T,C
20   FOR YEAR = 1 TO T
30     FOR R = 6 TO 12 STEP 2
40     VALUE = P*(1 + R*.01/C)^(YEAR*C)
50     PRINT USING "Value = $$####,.##, Year = #  Rate = ##";VALUE,YEAR,R
55     NEXT R
60   NEXT YEAR
Ok
SAVE"A:INVEST3
Ok
RUN
Enter principal, time, compounding? 1000,5,1
Value =  $1,060.00, Year = 1  Rate =  6
Value =  $1,080.00, Year = 1  Rate =  8
Value =  $1,100.00, Year = 1  Rate = 10
Value =  $1,120.00, Year = 1  Rate = 12
Value =  $1,123.60, Year = 2  Rate =  6
Value =  $1,166.40, Year = 2  Rate =  8
Value =  $1,210.00, Year = 2  Rate = 10
Value =  $1,254.40, Year = 2  Rate = 12
Value =  $1,191.02, Year = 3  Rate =  6
Value =  $1,259.71, Year = 3  Rate =  8
Value =  $1,331.00, Year = 3  Rate = 10
Value =  $1,404.93, Year = 3  Rate = 12
Value =  $1,262.48, Year = 4  Rate =  6
Value =  $1,360.49, Year = 4  Rate =  8
Value =  $1,464.10, Year = 4  Rate = 10
Value =  $1,573.52, Year = 4  Rate = 12
Value =  $1,338.23, Year = 5  Rate =  6
Value =  $1,469.33, Year = 5  Rate =  8
Value =  $1,610.51, Year = 5  Rate = 10
Value =  $1,762.34, Year = 5  Rate = 12
Ok
```

New loop

Notice how the outer loop (the time in years, **YEAR**) is held constant while the inner loop (the rate of interest, **R**) runs through all its values. For example, the value of **YEAR** is set to 1 and then the answers are calculated for rates (**R**) of 6, 8, 10, and 12 percent. Then, the value of **YEAR** is changed to 2 and the answers are calculated again for rates (**R**) of 6, 8, 10, and 12 percent. In a like manner, the answers for years 3, 4, and 5 are calculated.

As it stands, the output takes up more room on the screen than is needed. The output can be made more compact by adding statements that will display the information across the screen in a table form. To do this, two new **PRINT** statements (lines **15** and **25**) need to be added to display a header for the table and the **PRINT** statement at line **50** needs to be adjusted accordingly. Also, in order to display the output across the screen, a semicolon needs to be added to the end of the **PRINT** statement at line **50** and another **PRINT** statement needs to be added at line **58** to *undo* the semicolon (without this extra **PRINT** statement the output would continue across the page rather than going to the next line when the value of **YEAR** changes). **LOAD** the new version of the program, **LIST** it, **SAVE** it to your *BASIC Data* diskette, and then **RUN** it as shown on the next page:

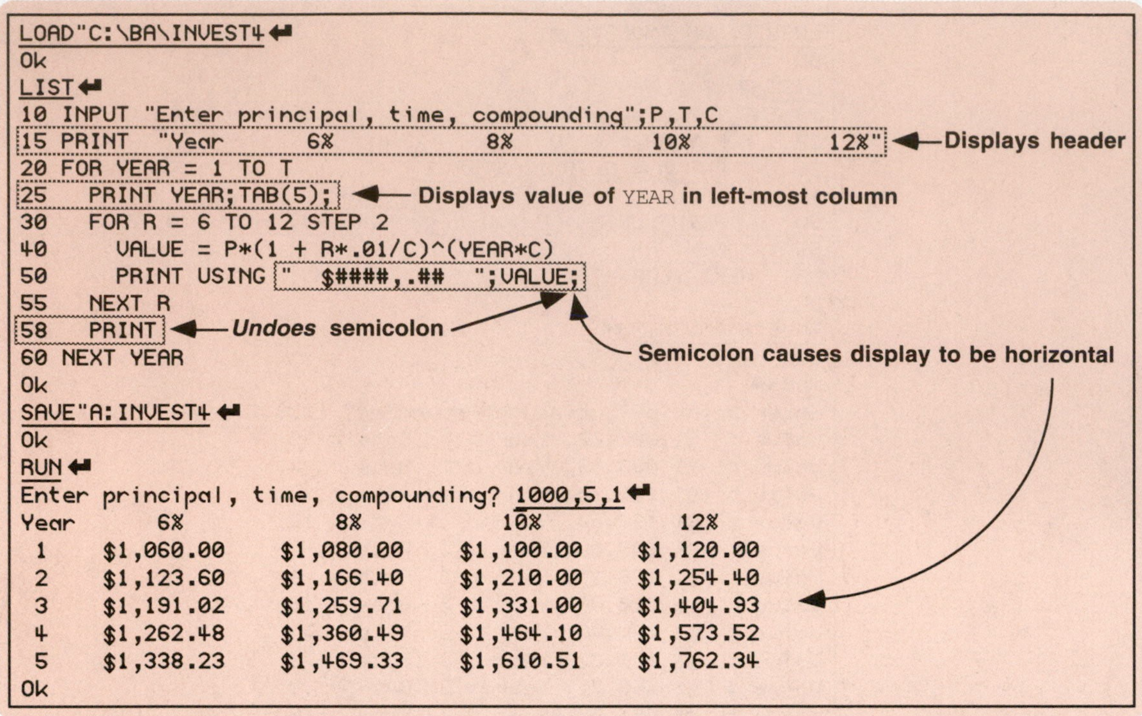

```
LOAD"C:\BA\INVEST4
Ok
LIST
10 INPUT "Enter principal, time, compounding";P,T,C
15 PRINT  "Year        6%              8%              10%             12%"
20 FOR YEAR = 1 TO T
25    PRINT YEAR;TAB(5);
30    FOR R = 6 TO 12 STEP 2
40       VALUE = P*(1 + R*.01/C)^(YEAR*C)
50       PRINT USING "  $####,.##  ";VALUE;
55    NEXT R
58    PRINT
60 NEXT YEAR
Ok
SAVE"A:INVEST4
Ok
RUN
Enter principal, time, compounding? 1000,5,1
Year      6%           8%           10%          12%
 1     $1,060.00    $1,080.00    $1,100.00    $1,120.00
 2     $1,123.60    $1,166.40    $1,210.00    $1,254.40
 3     $1,191.02    $1,259.71    $1,331.00    $1,404.93
 4     $1,262.48    $1,360.49    $1,464.10    $1,573.52
 5     $1,338.23    $1,469.33    $1,610.51    $1,762.34
Ok
```


It is important for you to study the structure of this program. Notice how the outer loop (**YEAR**) is held constant (e.g., at **YEAR** = 1) while the inner loop (**R**) ranges from 6 to 12 and the value of **VALUE** is displayed across the page. Then the outer loop (**YEAR**) changes by 1 (e.g., **YEAR** becomes 2) and the inner loop (**R**) again goes through all of its values and displays the output across the page again. This pattern continues for the rest of the program.

Histogram

Let's examine a program that has almost the same structure as the previous program (i.e., nested loops) but carries out a completely different task. This new program uses a **FOR/NEXT** loop nested inside a **WHILE/WEND** loop to display a frequency pattern (i.e., a histogram) of a set of data. Histograms are often used to help researchers understand the general characteristics of a set of data.

For this example, a histogram is to be constructed for a set of data that contains people's names and ages. As you study the program below, note how the name is held constant (just like the year in the investment program) while the computer displays the proper number of X's (just like the values for different rates in the investment program) across the page. **LOAD** the program, **LIST** it, **SAVE** it to your *BASIC Data* diskette, and then **RUN** it as shown on the next page:

```
LOAD"C:\BA\HIST1↵
Ok
LIST↵
1100 REM Program creates simple histogram (displayed sideways)
1200 REM Douglas Robertson (373-4026), created 1 Mar 91
1300 REM Define variables:
1400 REM      N$ = person's name
1500 REM     AGE = person's age in years
1600 REM    YEAR = loop variable counting year from 1 to AGE
1700 REM Begin Processing
1800 GOSUB 3300                         'Define images for PRINT USING statements
1900 PRINT IMAGE1$                      'Display column heading
2000 READ N$,AGE                        'Enter name and age of first person
2100   WHILE AGE <> 1E+15               'Begin loop
2200     PRINT USING IMAGE2$;N$,AGE;
2300       FOR YEAR = 1 TO AGE
2400         IF YEAR/5 = INT(YEAR/5) THEN PRINT "*"; ELSE PRINT "X";
2500       NEXT YEAR
2600     PRINT                          'Cancel ; at end of PRINT
2700     READ N$,AGE                    'Enter name and age of next person
2800   WEND                             'End loop
2900 REM Display scale at bottom of histogram
3000   PRINT IMAGE3$
3100   PRINT IMAGE4$
3200 END
3300 REM ***** Subroutine to define images for PRINT USING statements
3400   IMAGE1$ = "Name       Quan      Frequency Count                   "
3500   IMAGE2$ = "\        \  [##]      "
3600   IMAGE3$ = "                      1234567890123456789012345678901234567890"
3700   IMAGE4$ = "                               1         2         3         4"
3800 RETURN
3900 REM End processing and begin DATA statements
4000   DATA Terry,37
4100   DATA Jeff,18
4200   DATA Tom,22
4300   DATA Steve,35
4400   DATA Nobody,1E+15
Ok
SAVE"A:HIST1↵
Ok
RUN↵
Name       Quan      Frequency Count
Terry      [37]      XXXX*XXXX*XXXX*XXXX*XXXX*XXXX*XXXX*XX
Jeff       [18]      XXXX*XXXX*XXXX*XXX
Tom        [22]      XXXX*XXXX*XXXX*XXXX*XX
Steve      [35]      XXXX*XXXX*XXXX*XXXX*XXXX*XXXX*XXXX*
                     1234567890123456789012345678901234567890
                              1         2         3         4
Ok
```

Line Numbers	Comments
1100-1600	**REM** statements defining the program and the variables.
1800	Calls the subroutine to define the images for the **PRINT USING** statements.
1900	Displays the column heading.
2000	Enters name and age of the first person on the list.
2100-2800	Defines the loop where the processing occurs.
2200	Displays the name and age of the person. Note the semicolon at the end of the line. This is needed to cause the **X**s displayed by line **2400** to begin printing on the same line as the person's name.
2300	Begins the inner loop by assigning the value 1 to variable **YEAR**. The value of **YEAR** begins at 1 and ends at **AGE**. Each time this loop is executed an **X** or an ***** is displayed horizontally across the screen. Thus, the number of **X**'s and *****'s is equal to the age of the person.
2400	If the value of **YEAR** is a multiple of 5, an asterisk (*****) is displayed. If the value is not a multiple of 5, an **X** is displayed. Displaying the ***** every fifth number helps to make the histogram more readable. Note the semicolon at the end of each **PRINT** statement on this line. This will ensure that each part of the histogram is displayed on the same line (horizontally) rather than on separate lines (vertically).
2500	Adds the **STEP** (which is **1**) to the value of **YEAR** and passes control to the beginning of the loop (the **FOR** statement).
2300	If the new value of **YEAR** is more than the value of **AGE**, the inner loop is exited and control passes to line **2600**. If the new value of **YEAR** is equal to or less than **AGE**, the statements within the inner loop are executed again.
2600	This statement counteracts the semicolon at the end of line **2400**. After line **2600** has been executed, printing will resume on the next line of the output. Thus, when the name of the next person is displayed, it will appear at the beginning of a new line rather than on the end of the current one.
2700	Enters the name and age of the next person.
2800	Marks the end of the outer loop. Control is transferred back to the **WHILE** statement in line **2100** where the value of **AGE** is compared with **1E+15**. If the values are equal, the loop is exited and control passes to line **2900**. If the values are not equal, the statements within the loop are executed again.
3000-3100	Displays a scale at the bottom of the output for reference purposes.

The graph could be made a bit nicer by using the **STRING$** function to replace the *****s and the **X**s with special characters (see p. B162). To do this, only line **2400** needs to be modified:

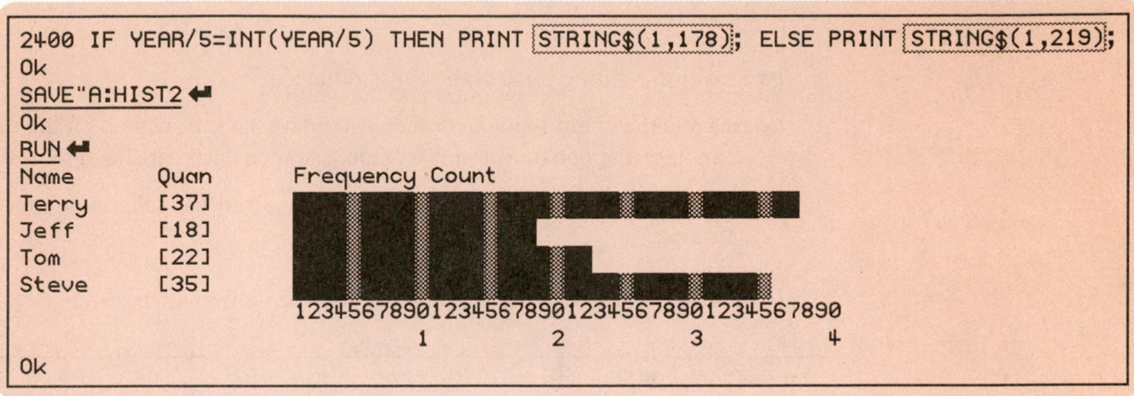

```
2400 IF YEAR/5=INT(YEAR/5) THEN PRINT STRING$(1,178); ELSE PRINT STRING$(1,219);
Ok
SAVE"A:HIST2
Ok
RUN
Name        Quan        Frequency Count
Terry       [37]
Jeff        [18]
Tom         [22]
Steve       [35]
                        1234567890123456789012345678901234567890
                                 1         2         3         4
Ok
```

Sales Records

As a final example of complex loops, consider the following problem. A car dealer wants to keep track of the cars sold by each employee and the total cars sold for the company. Let's use the programming process to develop a computer program that will accomplish this task.

As you work through the process, be sure to focus your attention on how each step is accomplished. Remember, you are trying to learn how to write programs in general and not how to do this particular program. This is a complex problem; you should expect to spend a lot of time on it.

• The Task •

Write a program that will read information from a database and display the names and sales data for each salesperson in the company.

• Step 1: Justify Using the Computer •

The computer is needed to sort through and keep track of the data on a weekly basis for each sales person. Doing this by hand would take too long.

• Step 2: Define the Problem •

Output For the data specified below, the output should look like the following:

```
RUN
Syosset Chrysler Dealership
Sales record as of 03-01-1991 at 13:14:52

Num  Employee  Num     Price   Commis   Dealer    Vehicle      Date
---  --------  ---    ------   ------   ------   --------    ------
 1)  Sara
                1)    $10000     $700    $9300    Caravan    24 Jun
                2)     $9000     $630    $8370    Colt       26 Jun
                3)     $9500     $665    $8835    Charger    28 Jun
    --------------    ------   ------   ------
            Totals    $28500    $1995   $26505

 2)  Matt
                1)    $15000    $1050   $13950    LeBaron    25 Jun
                2)     $6000     $420    $5580    Century    29 Jun
    --------------    ------   ------   ------
            Totals    $21000    $1470   $19530

==================     Price   Commis   Dealer  =================
|| Company Totals     $49500    $3465   $46035                 ||
=================================================================
Ok
```

In the table,

`Price` is the selling price of the car in dollars.

`Commis` is the commission in dollars earned by the salesperson on the sale of this car (in this example, the person gets a 7% commission on each car she or he sells).

`Dealer` is the dollars that the dealer receives from the sale. Note that **`Comm`** + **`Dealer`** = **`Price`**.

Processing Structurally, the document can be viewed as follows:

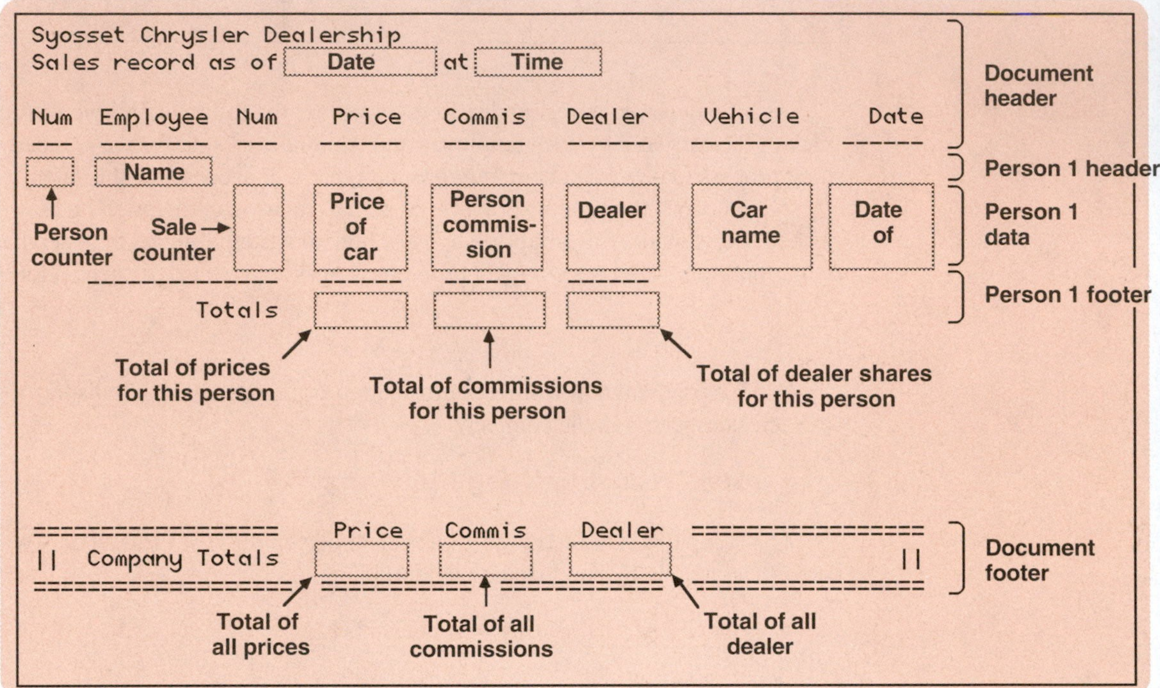

Each piece of information in the output can be defined as follows:

Document header: Descriptive information including company name and date and time program was run.

> **Date**: The date on the system clock when the program was run (produced using the **`DATE$`** function).
>
> **Time**: The time on the system clock when the program was run (produced using the **`TIME$`** function).

Person header: Descriptive information about this person including a counter and the person's name.

> **Person counter**: Counts the number of different people read from the **`DATA`** list (calculated by a counter of the form **`NUM = NUM + 1`**).
>
> **Name**: The first name of the person (read from the **`DATA`** list).

Person data: Descriptive information about the sales of this person including the number of sales, the price of each car sold, the commission earned, the dealer's share, the name of the car sold, and the date of the sale.

> **Sale counter**: Counts the number of sales for this person read from the **`DATA`** list (calculated by a counter of the form **`NUM = NUM + 1`**).
>
> **Price of car**: The selling price of the car in dollars (read from the **`DATA`** list).

Person commission: The commission earned by the person on the sale of the car (calculated by taking 7% of the selling price of the car).

Dealer share: The part of the price of the car that goes to the dealer (calculated by taking 93% of the selling price of the car—the person's commission and the dealer's share must add up to the price of the car).

Car name: Name of the car sold (read from the **DATA** list).

Date of sale: The day and month the car was sold (read from the **DATA** list).

Person footer: Descriptive information about the sales of this person including the totals for the car prices, commissions, and dealer shares.

Total of prices for this person: The sum of the values under **Price** (calculated).

Total of commissions for this person: The sum of the values under **Commis** (calculated).

Total of dealer shares for this person: The sum of the values under **Dealer** (calculated).

Document footer: Descriptive information about all sales people including sums for the prices, commissions, and dealer shares.

Total of all prices: The sum of all the individual prices under the column **Price** (calculated).

Total of all commissions: The sum of all the individual commissions under the column **Commis** (calculated).

Total of all dealer shares: The sum of all the individual dealer shares under the column **Dealer** (calculated).

Input: The data needed for processing are the name of each sales person, and for each car sold, the price, the car name, and the date sold.

• *Step 3: Define the Program Variables* •

The variables may be defined as follows:

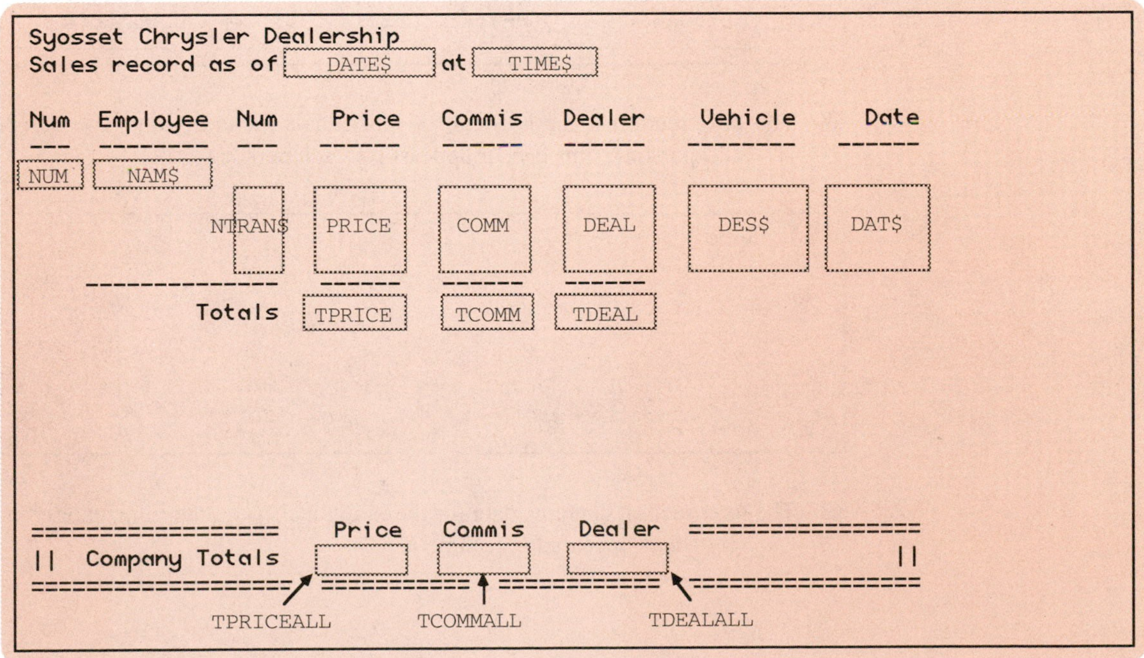

DATE$ is current date generated by computer.

TIME$ is current time generated by computer.

NUM is number of person.

NAM$ is name of person.

NTRANS is number of transaction for this person.

PRICE is purchase price of individual car sold by this person.

COMM is commission earned by person on this car (7% of price).

DEAL is share of price retained by dealer for this transaction (93% of price).

DES$ is description of vehicle.

DAT$ is date of transaction.

TPRICE is total of purchase prices of all cars sold by this person.

TCOMM is total of commissions earned by this person.

TDEAL is total dealer share of sale by this person.

TPRICEALL is total of prices of all cars sold by all people.

TCOMMALL is total of commissions earned by all people.

TDEALALL is total of dealer shares of all sales by all people.

• Step 4: Construct the Pseudocode •

Before writing the pseudocode for this problem, let's look at the general structure of the output:

- The top five lines are the document header and contain information that refers to the document as a whole:

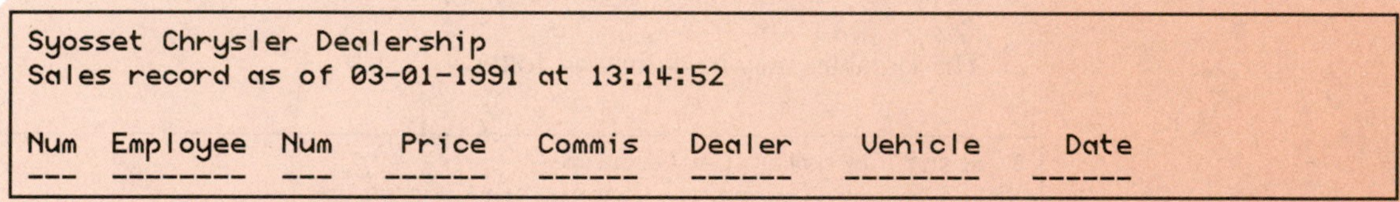

```
Syosset Chrysler Dealership
Sales record as of 03-01-1991 at 13:14:52

Num  Employee  Num    Price   Commis   Dealer   Vehicle    Date
---  --------  ---   ------   ------   ------   --------   ------
```

- The next section is the headers for individuals (actually, only the number and name of the salesperson). This header appears for each person.

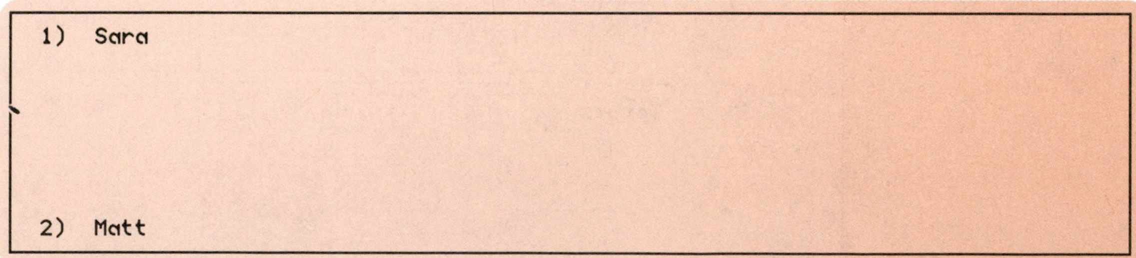

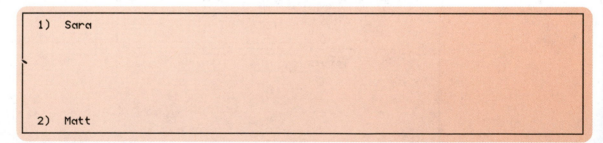

```
  1)  Sara





  2)  Matt
```

- The next section contains data for the individuals (i.e., the information on the cars sold). This set of data appears for each person.

```
   1)   $10000     $700    $9300     Carivan    24 Jun
   2)    $9000     $630    $8370     Colt       26 Jun
   3)    $9500     $665    $8835     Charger    28 Jun



   1)   $15000    $1050   $13950     LeBaron    25 Jun
   2)    $6000     $420    $5580     Century    29 Jun
```

The next section contains footers for individuals (these summarize the information for an individual). This data appears for each person.

```
 --------------   ------   ------   ------
         Totals   $28500    $1995   $26505



 --------------   ------   ------   ------
         Totals   $21000    $1470   $19530
```

The structure repeats itself for each person until all the data have been entered and displayed. Finally, there is a document footer, which summarizes the information in the entire document.

```
==================     Price   Commis    Dealer   ================
||  Company Totals    $49500    $3465   $46035                  ||
==================================================================
```

The output can be represented structurally in the following way:

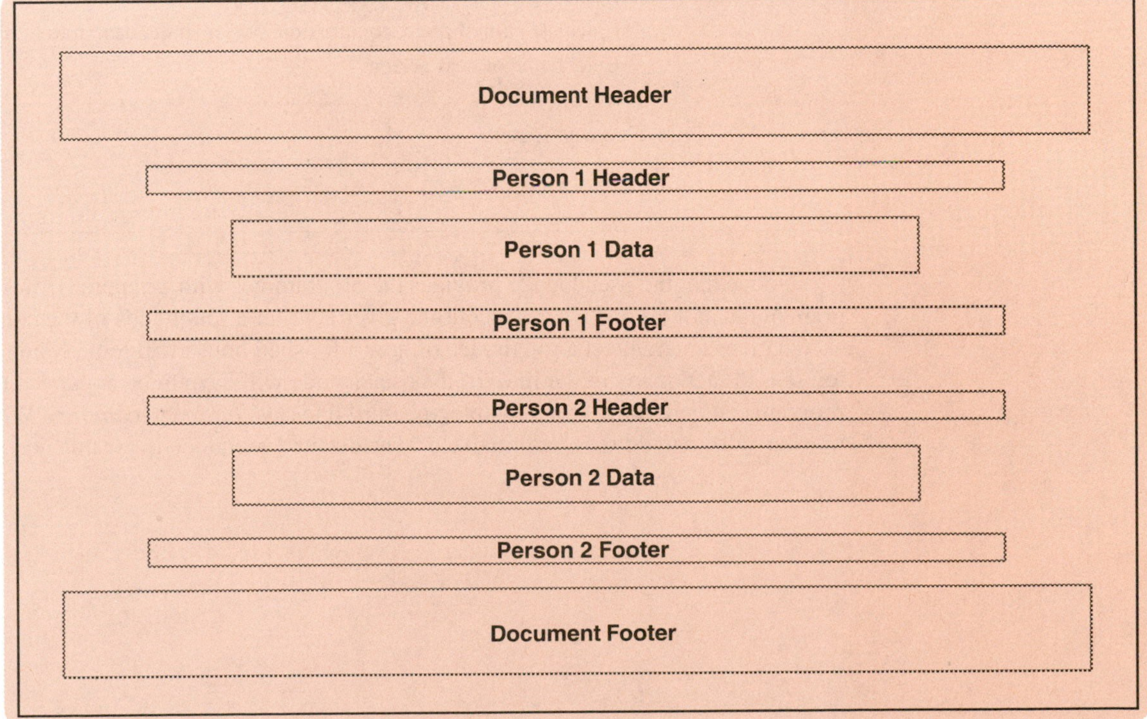

Because this structure appears in many programs, you should study it carefully to be sure that you understand it completely. After the document header has been displayed, the outer loop holds a salesperson constant while all the data for that person are read, processed, and displayed by the inner loop. Then the outer loop changes and enters the name of the next person and the inner loop is processed all over again using that new person's data. Finally, when all the data have been processed, the document footer is displayed.

Now try to construct the pseudocode by yourself. Then compare your pseudocode with that given below (your code may be different but just as correct).

```
Begin processing
    Define images for PRINT USING
    Initialize counters
    Display document header
    Enter name of first person
        For each person, do the following
            Update counter for number of people read
            Initialize counters for person
            Display number and name of person
            Enter price of first sale
                For each sale, do the following
                    Update counter for number of sales for this person
                    Compute commission for person
                    Compute dealer's share
                    Read description and date
                    Display data for this person
                    Display transaction
                    Update counters for sums for this person
                    Enter price for next sale
                End sales loop for this person
            Display person footer
            Calculate sum of price, commission, dealer share, description, date for all people
            Enter name of next person
        End person loop
    Print document footer
End processing
```

Notice that the pseudocode provides the programmer with a general view of the flow of the program in much the same way as an outline gives a writer a rough idea of the contents of a paper or a sketch gives an architect a rough idea of how a finished house will look. Many of the details have been left out. In fact, many of the lines of the pseudocode will have to be expanded (detail added) before the program can be written. For example, the third line says *Initialize counters*. What are the counters and to what value should they be initialized? The detailed pseudocode for this line might be the following:

```
Initialize counters
    Begin processing
        Set total of all prices to 0
        Set total of all commissions to 0
        Set total of all dealer shares to 0
End processing
```

This small module can be easily translated into BASIC code as a subroutine. In fact, many of the lines of the pseudocode will be translated into subroutines. Writing the program in this way helps the programmer keep track of the logic of the overall program as well as the details.

• Step 5: Calculate the Answers •

For the test data given above, the answers would be as follows:

For Sara, sale #1:
    Commission = 10000*.07 = 700
    Dealer = 10000*.93 = 9300

For Sara, sale #2:
    Commission = 9000*.07 = 630
    Dealer = 9000*.93 = 8370

For Sara, sale #3:
    Commission = 9500*.07 = 665
    Dealer = 9500*.93 = 8835

Totals for Sara:
    Price = 10000 + 9000 + 9500 = 28500
    Commission = 700 + 630 + 665 = 1995
    Dealer = 9300 + 8370 + 8835 = 26505

For Matt, sale #1:
    Commission = 15000*.07 = 1050
    Dealer = 15000*.93 = 13950

For Matt, sale #2:
    Commission = 6000*.07 = 420
    Dealer = 6000*.93 = 5580

Totals for Matt:
    Price = 15000 + 6000 = 21000
    Commission = 1050 + 420 = 1470
    Dealer = 13950 + 5580 = 19530

Totals for the entire company (actually, just Matt and Sara):
    Price = 28500 + 21000 = 49500
    Commission = 1995 + 1470 = 3465
    Dealer = 26505 + 19530 = 46035

• Step 6: Translate the Pseudocode into BASIC •

Now try to translate the pseudocode into a proper BASIC program. One version of the BASIC code is given on the next two pages. Notice the use of subroutines to do the processing of the several parts of the program and the large number of **REM** statements that are almost identical to the actual pseudocode. When one of the authors created this program, he wrote out the variable definitions (step 3) and the pseudocode (step 4) on a word processor and then used the editing features of the word processor to convert the text to BASIC code (i.e., he added line numbers, the words **REM**, **PRINT**, **GOSUB**, etc.). Then he saved the file as a text (ASCII) file, entered the BASIC environment, and used the **LOAD** command to access the program. This saved a considerable amount of typing.

```
LOAD"C:\BA\SALES1↵
Ok
LIST↵
1100 REM Program produces sales data for individual salespersons
1200 REM Douglas Robertson (373-4026), created 1 Mar 91
1300 REM Define variables:
1400   REM    MONTH$ = Month data were collected
1500   REM     DATE$ = Current date generated by computer
1600   REM      CLK$ = Current time generated by computer
1700   REM       NUM = Number of person
1800   REM      NAM$ = Name of person
1900   REM    NTRANS = Number of transaction for this person
2000   REM     PRICE = Purchase price of individual car sold by this person
2100   REM      COMM = Commission earned by person on this car (7% of price)
2200   REM      DEAL = Share of price retained by dealer for this transaction
2300   REM      DES$ = Description of vehicle
2400   REM      DAT$ = Date of transaction
2500   REM    TPRICE = Total of purchase prices of all cars sold by this person
2600   REM     TCOMM = Total of commissions earned by this person
2700   REM     TDEAL = Total dealer share of sale by this person
2800   REM TPRICEALL = Total of prices of all cars sold by all people
2900   REM  TCOMMALL = Total of commissions earned by all people
3000   REM  TDEALALL = Total of dealer shares of all sales by all people
3100   GOSUB 5700                             'Define images for PRINT USING
3200 REM Begin processing
3300   GOSUB 7000                             'Initialize counters to zero
3400   GOSUB 7500                             'Display document header
3500   READ NAM$                              'Assign name of first person
3600   WHILE NAM$ <> "NOBODY"                 'For each person do the following
3700     NUM = NUM + 1                        'Count number of people read
3800     TPRICE=0:TCOMM=0:TDEAL=0:NTRANS=0    'Initialize counters for person
3900     PRINT USING I5$; NUM, NAM$           'Display name of person
4000     READ PRICE                           'Enter price of first sale
4100       WHILE PRICE <> 1E+15               'Begin individual sales loop
4200         NTRANS = NTRANS + 1              'Count # sales for this person
4300         COMM = PRICE*.07                 'Compute commission for person
4400         DEAL = PRICE*.93                 'Compute dealer's share
4500         READ DES$,DAT$                   'Read description and date
4600         PRINT USING I6$; NTRANS, PRICE, COMM, DEAL, DES$, DAT$
4700         GOSUB 8200                       'Calculate sums for this person
4800         READ PRICE                       'Enter price for next sale
4900       WEND                               'End sales loop for this person
5000     GOSUB 8700                           'Display person footer
5100     GOSUB 9100                 'Sum price, comm, dealer share for all people
5200     PRINT
5300     READ NAM$                            'Enter name of next person
5400   WEND
5500   GOSUB 9600                             'Print document footer
5600  END                                     'End main program
```

Continued . . .

```
5700 REM ***** Subroutine to define images for PRINT USING statements
5800   I1$ = "Syosset Chrysler Dealership"
5900   I2$ = "Sales record as of \        \ at \      \"
6000   I3$ = "Num  Employee  Num    Price   Commis   Dealer    Vehicle      Date"
6100   I4$ = "---  --------  ---   ------   ------   ------   --------   ------"
6200   I5$ = "##)  \      \"
6300   I6$ = "               ##)  $$#####  $$#####  $$#####    \      \   \   \"
6400   I7$ = "    --------------   ------   ------   ------                    "
6500   I8$ = "            Totals  $$#####  $$#####  $$#####                    "
6600   I9$ = "==================    Price   Commis    Dealer   ================="
6700  I10$ = "||  Company Totals  $$#####  $$#####  $$#####                  ||"
6800  I11$ = "================================================================="
6900 RETURN
7000 REM ***** Subroutine to initialize counters to zero
7100   TPRICEALL = 0
7200   TCOMMALL = 0
7300   TDEALALL = 0
7400 RETURN
7500 REM ***** Subroutine to display document header
7600     PRINT I1$
7700     PRINT USING I2$; DATE$,TIME$
7800     PRINT
7900     PRINT I3$
8000     PRINT I4$
8100 RETURN
8200 REM ***** Subroutine to calculate sums for this person
8300   TPRICE = TPRICE + PRICE              'Sum net price for this person
8400   TCOMM = TCOMM + COMM                 'Sum commission for this person
8500   TDEAL = TDEAL + DEAL                 'Sum dealer share for this person
8600 RETURN
8700 REM ***** Subroutine to display person footer
8800   PRINT I7$
8900   PRINT USING I8$; TPRICE, TCOMM, TDEAL
9000 RETURN
9100 REM ***** Subroutine to sum price, commission, and dealer share for company
9200   TPRICEALL = TPRICEALL + TPRICE
9300   TCOMMALL = TCOMMALL + TCOMM
9400   TDEALALL = TDEALALL + TDEAL
9500 RETURN
9600 REM ***** Subroutine to display document footer
9700   PRINT I9$
9800   PRINT USING I10$;TPRICEALL,TCOMMALL,TDEALALL
9900   PRINT I11$
10000 RETURN
10100 REM Begin DATA statements
10200   REM DATA flag for each person is 1E+15 for PRICE
10300   REM DATA flag for entire data set is NOBODY for N$
10400   DATA Sara
10500     DATA 10000
10600     DATA Caravan,24 Jun
10700     DATA 9000
10800     DATA Colt,26 Jun
10900     DATA 9500
11000     DATA Charger,28 Jun
11100     DATA 1E+15
11200   DATA Matt
11300     DATA 15000
11400     DATA LeBaron,25 Jun
11500     DATA 6000,Century,29 Jun
11600     DATA 1E+15
11700 REM Data flag is NOBODY
11800   DATA NOBODY
Ok
```

• Step 7: Type the Program •

Load (or type) the program into the computer and save it on your *BASIC Data* diskette using the name **SALES1**.

• Step 8: Run the Program •

When the program is run, the following output will be generated:

```
RUN ↵
Syosset Chrysler Dealership
Sales record as of 03-01-1991 at 13:14:52

Num  Employee  Num    Price   Commis   Dealer    Vehicle     Date
---  --------  ---   ------   ------   ------   --------   ------
 1)  Sara
                1)   $10000     $700    $9300    Caravan   24 Jun
                2)    $9000     $630    $8370    Colt      26 Jun
                3)    $9500     $665    $8835    Charger   28 Jun
     --------------  ------   ------   ------
             Totals  $28500    $1995   $26505

 2)  Matt
                1)   $15000    $1050   $13950    LeBaron   25 Jun
                2)    $6000     $420    $5580    Century   29 Jun
     --------------  ------   ------   ------
             Totals  $21000    $1470   $19530

==================    Price   Commis    Dealer   =================
|| Company Totals    $49500    $3465   $46035                  ||
==================================================================
Ok
```

• Step 9: Check the Computer's Results •

Check the output of the above test run to see if the answers obtained by hand are the same as those provided by the computer.

• Step 10: Debug the Program •

Because the answers check, debugging is not needed.

TO TAKE A BREAK Type **SYSTEM** ↵, remove diskette(s). To resume (hard disk): Insert *Data* diskette, type **A:** ↵, **C:\BA\BASICA** ↵. To resume (two drive): Insert diskettes, type **A:** ↵, **B:\BASICA** ↵.

Homework Exercises

For each of the following homework exercises, use the programming process to develop a BASIC program that will produce the output described. Each program should contain enough **REM** statements to clearly document the program. Unless instructed to do otherwise, produce a hard copy of a **LIST** and a **RUN** of each of your final working programs. Also, save each program using a name such as **HWB6-01** for future reference. Your instructor may also ask you to hand in other materials related to the development of the programs such as the variable definitions, pseudocodes, etc.

---

① Use the programming process to write a program that displays a chart indicating the time of travelling different distances on a freeway at different driving speeds. Employ **PRINT USING** to line up the decimal points and to round off the answers to the nearest tenth of a minute. The output from your program should look like the following (the values in the box should be calculated by the computer):

```
Homework B6-01                   Joe Computer                   1 Mar 91

                  Miles per hour

          45        50        55        60        65
Miles    ----      ----      ----      ----      ----
   5      6.7       6.0       5.5       5.0       4.6
  10     13.3      12.0      10.9      10.0       9.2
  15     20.0      18.0      16.4      15.0      13.8
  20     26.7      24.0      21.8      20.0      18.5
  25     33.3      30.0      27.3      25.0      23.1
  30     40.0      36.0      32.7      30.0      27.7
```

This problem is very similar to the histogram problem discussed in this chapter and should employ nested **FOR/NEXT** loops. However, there are no data to read (all the values are generated by the computer) so **READ** and **DATA** statements should not be used. The outer loop will be the miles driven while the inner loop will be the miles per hour (i.e., hold the distance constant and calculate the times for different speeds. Then change the distance by 5 miles and calculate the times for all the different speeds again). Remember, to have the computer **PRINT** across the page (rather than down the page) you must use a semicolon at the end of the **PRINT** statements (as was done in line **2400** of program **HIST1** on p. B189).

---

② In Exercise 6 of Chapter 5 you wrote a program that was designed to compute the grade point average (GPA) of a set of courses. In this exercise, your task is to modify that program so that it checks for the following errors in the data:

a. The grade for a course must be A, B, C, D, or F. If an illegal grade is entered, the computer must print an error message similar to the following:

```
GC 1237          4              Q
    Error in Grade for GC 1237
    Grade = Q but must be A, B, C, D, or F
    Grade & credits not included in GPA or totals
```

b. The number of credits for a course must be a whole number between 0 and 5, inclusive. If the number of credits for a course is not correct, the computer must print an error message similar to the following:

Continued . . .

CHAPTER SIX

```
GC 1411          2.50          A
     Error in number of credits for GC 1411
     Credits =  2.5  but must be whole numbers from 0 to 5
     Grade & credits not included in GPA or totals
```

Use the **DATA** statements given below. The data are in the order course, credits, grade.

```
DATA GC 1571,5,A
DATA GC 1237,4,Q
DATA GC 1421,4,B
DATA GC 1211,5,D
DATA PE 1122,1,C,
DATA GC 1411,2.5,A
DATA GC 1171,9,B
DATA 1E15,1E15,1E15   ←Data flags
```

Using the above **DATA**, the output from your program should look like the following (the values in the boxes should be calculated by the computer):

```
Homework B6-02                   Joe Computer                       1 Mar 91

Computation or Grade Point Average

 Course        Credits         Grade       Value     Val*Cr
GC 1571          5               A          4           20

GC 1237          4               Q
    Error in Grade for GC 1237
    Grade = Q but must be A, B, C, D, or F
    Grade & credits not included in GPA or totals

GC 1421          4               B          3           12
GC 1211          5               D          1            5
PE 1122          1               C          2            2

GC 1411          2.50            A
    Error in number of credits for GC 1411
    Credits =  2.5  but must be whole numbers from 0 to 5
    Grade & credits not included in GPA or totals

GC 1171          9.00            B
    Error in number of credits for GC 1171
    Credits =  9  but must be whole numbers from 0 to 5
    Grade & credits not included in GPA or totals

Total number of credits is 15 (based on 4 courses)
Grade point average (GPA) is 2.6
```

③ Kelvins Department Store has a catalog sales department where people can phone in an order and pick up the merchandise the next day. When people arrive at the store they must find the bin number where their packages are stored and then take the packages to the checkout counter. Use the programming algorithm to write a program that will help people locate their packages. The program should ask for the phone number of the customer, locate the data for the customer with that phone number, and then display the number of packages and the bin number (location) of the packages. If the phone number is not on the list in the store's database (a set of **DATA** statements in this example) the program should display a message asking the user to try again or to get help from a clerk. Use the follow-

CHAPTER SIX

ing **DATA** statements (the data are listed in the order phone number, number of packages, bin location):

```
DATA 626-1001,2,E17
DATA 373-4026,3,F34
DATA 624-9223,1,A12
DATA 1E15,1E15,1E15
```
←**Data flags**

The output from your program should look like the following for those phone numbers that are found on the data list:

```
Homework B6-03                  Joe Computer                    1 Mar 91

Enter your phone number? 373-4026↵
You have 3 parcel(s) in bin F34

Thank you for shopping at Kelvins Department Store.
```

Do a second run of the program to show that it works when the phone number cannot be found:

```
Homework B6-03                  Joe Computer                    1 Mar 91

Enter your phone number? 555-5555↵
Sorry, I could not locate your parcels.
Please try again or ask a clerk for help.

Thank you for shopping at Kelvins Department Store.
```

---

④ In Exercise 8 of Part II, Chapter 1 (p. L174), you constructed a Lotus 1-2-3 worksheet that displayed a chart of the diving performances of members of a swim team. Use the programming procedure to write a BASIC program that will accomplish the same task using the data provided below. The output should include each diver's name and scores from the judges and the average score for each diver. In the sample output displayed on the next page, the formula for the **Score** for each diver should be constructed as follows:

- The sum of the judges' scores for a person is calculated first.
- Then the lowest score is subtracted from that sum.
- Then the highest score is subtracted from that value.
- Finally, the value is divided by the number of scores used.

Using the following **DATA** statements, the output should look like that given on the next page (the values in the box should be calculated by the computer):

```
DATA Matt,9.0,9.1,9.6,8.9
DATA Juan,9.9,9.3,8.9,9.0
DATA David,9.7,9.3,9.4,8.9
DATA Erich,9.5,9.1,9.6,9.0
DATA Amit,9.0,8.9,9.1,8.4
DATA 1E15,1E15,1E15,1E15,1E15
```
←**Data flags**

Continued . . .

CHAPTER SIX

```
Homework B6-04                    Joe Computer                    1 Mar 91

           Scores by Individual Judges          Average
         Judge 1   Judge 2   Judge 3   Judge 4    Score
Divers   -------   -------   -------   -------    -----
Matt       9.0       9.1       9.6       8.9       9.0
Juan       9.9       9.3       8.9       9.0       9.1
David      9.7       9.3       9.4       8.9       9.3
Erich      9.5       9.1       9.6       9.0       9.3
Amit       9.0       8.9       9.1       8.4       9.0
```

Due to round-off errors, these answers are not correct (arrows point to 9.0, 9.1 and 9.3 for Matt, Juan and David)

Notice that three of the calculated average scores in the above output are not correct. This is due to round-off error encountered when BASIC converted the decimal numbers into their binary representations (see p. B44 for more discussion of round-off errors). In the screen dump below, the image for the average score was changed to display 8 decimal places. As you can see, the rounding is correct but the calculated value is not.

```
Homework B6-04                    Joe Computer                    1 Mar 91

           Scores by Individual Judges          Average
         Judge 1   Judge 2   Judge 3   Judge 4    Score
Divers   -------   -------   -------   -------    -----
Matt       9.0       9.1       9.6       8.9     9.04999900
Juan       9.9       9.3       8.9       9.0     9.14999900
David      9.7       9.3       9.4       8.9     9.34999900
Erich      9.5       9.1       9.6       9.0     9.30000000
Amit       9.0       8.9       9.1       8.4     8.95000100
```

The actual calculated values (arrows point to the values for Matt, Juan and David)

Some versions of BASIC will give you the correct answers because they automatically correct for this round-off error while other versions do not. Thus, to be sure of your output, always check your answers.

---

⑤ Sally's Stationary Store sells school supplies. Use the programming process to write a program that will produce an invoice for her customers. The program should use **READ/DATA** to input the names of items purchased, the prices of those items, and the quantities ordered. Use the following **DATA** statements (the data are listed in the order item name, price in cents, quantity ordered):

```
DATA Pen,105,3

DATA Paper,110,2

DATA Paper clips,104,5

DATA Ruler,123,4

DATA Eraser,89,3

DATA Tape,299,4

DATA Staples,46,5

DATA 1E15,1E15,1E15        ⟵ Data flags
```

Have the program calculate the cost of the the items and display the items in groups of three to a page, with appropriate headers and footers. At the bottom of each page, display the subtotal for that page.

This program has the same structure as the car sales program discussed in this chapter. Think about the structure carefully as you go through the programming process. Careful planning will save you a lot of time in the long run.

Using the above data, the output from your program should look like the following (the values in the boxes should be calculated by the computer):

```
Homework B6-05                  Joe Computer                    1 Mar 91

Sally's Stationary Store                       Date of order: 03-01-1991
2560 North Fourth Street SE                    Time of order: 12:37:37
Minneapolis, MN  55414 (373-4026)                       Page: 1

Number    Item            Price     Quan    Item Cost
------    ------------    ------    ----    ---------
   1      Pen             $ 1.05     3      $    3.15
   2      Paper           $ 1.10     2      $    2.20
   3      Paper clips     $ 1.04     5      $    5.20
                                            ---------
                                Subtotal    $   10.55

Sally's Stationary Store                       Date of order: 03-01-1991
2560 North Fourth Street SE                    Time of order: 12:37:40
Minneapolis, MN  55414 (373-4026)                       Page: 2

Number    Item            Price     Quan    Item Cost
------    ------------    ------    ----    ---------
   4      Ruler           $ 1.23     4      $    4.92
   5      Eraser          $ 0.89     3      $    2.67
   6      Tape            $ 2.99     4      $   11.96
                                            ---------
                                Subtotal    $   19.55

Sally's Stationary Store                       Date of order: 03-01-1991
2560 North Fourth Street SE                    Time of order: 12:37:58
Minneapolis, MN  55414 (373-4026)                       Page: 3

Number    Item            Price     Quan    Item Cost
------    ------------    ------    ----    ---------
   7      Staples         $ 0.46     5      $    2.30
                                            ---------
                                Subtotal    $    2.30

                                            ---------

                                    Tax:    $    1.94
                             Amount Due:    $   34.34
```

⑥ Susan wants to keep track of her checking account using the computer. Each month she gets a statement from her bank that lists the deposits she has made to her account, the checks she has written that have cleared the bank, and the final balance of her account as of the day the statement was produced. Of course, by the time Susan gets her bank statement in the mail, she has made other deposits and written other checks. Therefore, she wants to develop a program that will allow her to use the bank balance from the bank statement and the deposits and checks that do not appear on the bank statement to determine her true balance (this process is called reconciling a checkbook).

Use the programming process to develop a program that will reconcile Susan's checkbook. The program should be general enough to work for any number of outstanding deposits and outstanding checks. To do this, put a data flag at the end of the list of deposits to indicate the end of the deposits and the beginning of the checks. The program should input the data from **DATA** statements, display the value of each outstanding check and deposit, compute the total value of all outstanding checks, compute the total value of all outstanding deposits, count the number of outstanding checks, count the number of outstanding deposits, and display the current checkbook balance (closing balance plus total deposits minus total checks).

Continued . . .

The program should check for the following errors:

- The bank balance (obtained from the monthly bank statement) must be between $0 and $1000, inclusive.
- The value of each outstanding deposit (obtained from Susan's records) must be between $0 and $500, inclusive.
- The value of each outstanding check (obtained from Susan's records) must be between $0 and $400, inclusive.
- Data input should have no more than 2 decimal places (e.g., 10.123 would be considered an error). The **INT** function may be used to check for this error.

If an error is detected, the program should ask the user if the value should be included in the totals anyway (i.e., the value may be unusual [out of the normal range] but still correct). If the user says **YES**, the value should be included; if the user says **NO**, the value should be ignored.

To test the program, use the following data (the 1E15 is a data flag):

Bank Balance (from the monthly bank statement): 827.33

Outstanding deposits: 12.34,156.20, –3,5000,10.123,15,1E15

Outstanding checks: 44.50,80,4000,1E15

Using the above data, the output from your program should look like the following (the values in the boxes should be calculated by the computer):

```
Homework B6-06                    Susan Gorman                    1 Mar 91

Checkbook Balancing Program

Beginning bank balance from bank statement
 $827.33

Listing of Deposits Outstanding
  $12.34
 $156.20
  -$3.00  Value out of range (0-500), include anyway? NO
$5000.00  Value out of range (0-500), include anyway? YES
  $10.12  Value 10.123 has too many decimal places, include anyway? NO
  $15.00
--------  -----------------------------------------------------
$5183.54  Total of outstanding deposits

Listing of Checks Outstanding
  $44.50
  $80.00
$4000.00  Value out of range (0-400), include anyway? YES
--------  -----------------------------------------------------
$4124.50  Total of outstanding checks

=================================================================

Summary of Transactions
 $827.33  Bank balance from bank statement
$5183.54  Value of deposits not cleared (based on 4 deposits)
$4124.50  Value of checks   not cleared (based on 3 checks)
--------  -----------------------------------------------------
$1886.37  Current checkbook balance (as of 03-01-1991 at 08:19)
```

To show that the program can handle different sets of data, run it again using the new set of data given below (again, the 1E15 is a data flag):

Bank Balance (from the monthly bank statement): 550

Outstanding deposits: None

Outstanding checks: 30,50,1E15

This problem will take careful planning so be sure to use the programming process to help you organize your thoughts. To get you started, below is a sample of how the image statements and some of the variables for this problem might be set up:

```
                  I0$ = "Homework B6-06                    Susan Gorman                    1 Mar 91

                  I1$ = "Checkbook Balancing Program

                  I2$ = "Beginning bank balance from bank statement
BGN.BAL           I3$ = "$$###.##

                  I4$ = "Listing of Deposits Outstanding
DEPOSIT           I5$ = "$$###.##
                          $156.20
ANSWER$                    -$3.00  Value out of range (0-500), include anyway? NO
                         $5000.00  Value out of range (0-500), include anyway? YES
                           $10.12  Value 10.123 has too many decimal places, include anyway? NO
                           $15.00
                  I6$ = "--------  ----------------------------------------------------
TOT.DEP           I7$ = "$$###.##  Total of outstanding deposits

                  I8$ = "Listing of Checks Outstanding
CHECK                      $44.50
                           $80.00
                         $4000.00  Value out of range (0-400), include anyway? YES
                         --------  ----------------------------------------------------
TOT.CHK           I9$ = "$$###.##  Total of outstanding checks

                  I10$ = "=================================================================

                  I11$ = "Summary of Transactions
BGN.BAL           I12$ = "$$###.##  Bank balance from bank statement
TOT.DEP,NUM.DEP   I13$ = "$$###.##  Value of deposits not cleared (based on # deposits)
TOT.CHK,NUM.CHK   I14$ = "$$###.##  Value of checks   not cleared (based on # checks)
                  I15$ = "--------  ----------------------------------------------------
DATE$,TIME$       I16$ = "$$###.##  Current checkbook balance (as of \        \ at \    \)
```

External Data Files

Objectives *After you have completed this chapter, you should be able to*

- Define what is meant by an external data file.
- Create external data files that can be accessed by BASIC programs.
- Explain the similarities and differences in assigning values to variables using **LET**, **READ/DATA**, **INPUT**, and external data files.
- Use **OPEN** to define **INPUT**, **OUTPUT**, and/or **APPEND** type data files for use within a BASIC program.

CHAPTER 7

- Use **INPUT #** to assign values input from an external data file to variables.
- Modify an existing BASIC program so that it reads data from an external data file.
- Use **PRINT #** and **PRINT # USING** to write information to an external data file.
- Update an existing external data file.

Introduction

To this point, you have been able to assign values to variables in BASIC programs using the **LET**, **READ/DATA**, and **INPUT** statements. In this chapter, a fourth method, which employs external data files, is discussed. An external data file is a file (i.e., a collection of information) that is external to (i.e., completely separate from) a program and contains data for the program to analyze. The databases created by dBASE are examples of external data files.

External data files enable you to completely separate the program, which provides instructions on how to process data, from the actual data itself. This means that you can write a single program to do a specific task (e.g., calculate wages) and then use that program to analyze many different sets of data without altering the program itself.

Ways of Assigning Values to Variables

The programs discussed so far have assigned values (data) to variables and then done some sort of processing with those variables. The data were entered into the RAM memory of the computer either through assignment statements (e.g., **10 LET A = 2**) or **READ/DATA** statements (e.g., **10 READ A . . . 20 DATA 2**) or **INPUT** statements (e.g., **10 INPUT A**). Once a variable had been assigned a value (e.g., once the variable **A** was assigned the value **2**), it no longer mattered how the assignment was made; the computer would just process the variable using the value in memory. There are, however, reasons for entering data in different ways:

- The **LET** statement attaches the data to the variable name within a single line of the program. This is convenient for those values that remain the same each time the program is run (e.g., initializing values of counters).
- The **READ/DATA** statements list the variables in one statement and the data in another. Because the variables and the data are separate, the data can be grouped together at the end of the program, so the data can be found easily and changed, without having to reenter the names of the variables. This is useful for data that will be processed only by one program (i.e., the data are not needed by other programs).
- The **INPUT** statement also separates the names of the variables from the actual data but allows the data to be entered by the user while the program is executing. This allows the program to acquire data during processing in a straightforward manner.

When thinking about how data are acquired by the computer, it might help to think of a human analogy. Humans have five senses: sight, smell, touch, hearing, and taste. We use those senses to gather data from the outside world, we process that data in some way and then we take action based on the data and the processing. Once the data have been entered via one of our senses (e.g., we see a train coming, or we hear it coming) it really does not matter to our processing what the source was—what matters is that we have information in memory, it is meaningful to us, and we know how to process it. For example, if I am at a railroad crossing and I need to decide whether or not to cross the tracks, I can use different senses to help me make a decision. I can look down the tracks to see if a train is coming. If it is very foggy and I cannot see, I can listen for the sound of the train. If there is a strong wind blowing and it is very noisy and difficult to hear, I can try to feel a rumble in the ground that would indicate a train approaching. I might even be able to smell the train (the exhaust from the diesel engine) if the wind is blowing in the right direction. In each case, my objective is to collect data from whatever source is appropriate to help me determine whether or not a train is coming and to take appropriate action based on that determination. If a train is coming (I see it, hear it, feel it, or smell it) I remain where I am; otherwise, I cross the tracks.

Entering data into the computer is similar to this. Each method of data entry has a purpose and, in particular situations, one method may be preferred over the others. However, once the variables have been assigned values, it is then irrelevant how those values were entered into the computer (by **LET** or **READ/DATA** or **INPUT**). Each of these ways of assigning values to variables requires that the data be attached to the program in some way or entered during execution and, therefore, the data cannot be used by other programs without reentering it into those programs. A fourth method of assigning values to variables, using external data files, overcomes this difficulty. Think of these external data files as databases that hold data that can be used by more than one program. You have already experienced this type of situation when working with dBASE. That program was designed to manipulate data from any database that had the proper format. In this chapter you will write programs using BASIC that have a similar capability.

Having the data completely separate from the program is useful because it allows you to store a set of data (a database) and then analyze that data in many different ways using different programs. For example, you might have a database on employees that contains information such as name, address, phone number, sex, education, and yearly salary. In one instance, you may want to print out a mailing list of all employees sorted by ZIP code in order to send out a mailing at a reduced postage rate. In another instance, you may want to compute the average salary for males and females of equal educational background, experience, and rank to see if males and females are being treated equally with regards to salary. In a third instance, you may want to select employees who have a college degree and consider them for management training. In each case, the same set of data is analyzed but the programs used to complete the analysis would be different.

Creating, Opening, and Inputting Data from External Data Files

We have already discussed how to create uncoded (ASCII or text) external data files using the *Text In/Out* feature of WordPerfect (see p. W113), the **COPY CON** command of DOS (see p. W202), the *Print File* feature of Lotus 1-2-3 (see p. L42), and the *Copy File Type SDF* feature of dBASE. Files saved in ASCII format in any of these ways can be read or modified by BASIC programs. The process is fairly straightforward: (1) tell the BASIC program the name and location of the external data file using the **OPEN** statement; (2) assign values in the file to variable names using the **INPUT #** statement or write values to the file using the **PRINT #** statement. The **INPUT #** statement is similar to the **INPUT** statement discussed on page B58 except that **INPUT #** requests data from an external data file rather than displaying a question mark and requesting the data from the user. Likewise, the **PRINT #** statement is similar to the **PRINT** statement except that **PRINT #** writes data on an external data file rather than displaying it on the screen.

For example, let's process some of the information from the file **PHONES**, which you created using **COPY CON** on p. W202. You may copy the file **PHONES** from your *WPD-BU* disk to your *BASIC Data* diskette by using the **COPY** command or use **COPY CON** to create it again. The copy process would look like the following on a hard-disk system with one floppy drive (the single floppy drive will act as both the A: and B: drive):

```
C:\BA>COPY A:PHONES B:↵
Insert diskette for drive B: and press any key when ready
↵
       1 File(s) copied

C:\BA>TYPE A:PHONES↵

Insert diskette for drive A: and press any key when ready
↵
Smith,   Jim,       555-2132
Benson,  Geri,      553-3224
Perez,   Juan,      545-8912
Daniels, Matt,      555-6672
Wheeler, Vanessa,   505-6540

C:\BA>_
```

Place the *WPD-BU* diskette in drive A: and type this command

Place the *BASIC Data* diskette in drive A: and press [Enter]

Just press [Enter] — the *BASIC Data* diskette is already in drive A:

After copying **PHONES** to your *BASIC Data* diskette, access BASIC and then load the following program, **LIST** it, **SAVE** it to your *BASIC Data* diskette, and then **RUN** it as shown on the next page. The program is designed to read the information from the file **PHONES** and display it.

```
LOAD"C:\BA\FILE1↵
Ok
LIST↵
1100 OPEN "A:PHONES" FOR INPUT AS #1
1200   WHILE NOT EOF(1)
1300     INPUT #1, LAST$, FIRST$, PHONE$
1400     PRINT LAST$, FIRST$, PHONE$
1500   WEND
1600 CLOSE #1
Ok
SAVE"A:FILE1↵
Ok
RUN↵
Smith         Jim           555-2132
Benson        Geri          553-3224
Perez         Juan          545-8912
Daniels       Matt          555-6672
Wheeler       Vanessa       505-6540
Ok
```

Let's examine the four new statements in program **FILE1**.

```
1100 OPEN "A:PHONES" FOR INPUT AS #1
```

This statement gives the computer information about the external data file that the program will use:

OPEN is a key word that tells BASIC to look for an external data file and open it up so the contents can be used by the program—think of the external data file as a file folder that is being opened up so the contents can be seen.

"A:PHONES" is the specification of the file to be opened (**A:** means the file is on the disk in the A: drive and **PHONES** is the name of the file).

FOR INPUT means that the data on the file will be used by an **INPUT #** statement to assign the values to variables (i.e., information from the file will be *input* into the main memory of the computer).

AS #1 means that during the execution of this program the file is to be referred to as **#1**. This is important because the computer can access more than one external data file at a time and assigning a number to each file helps the computer to identify each individual file. The number assigned to the file is immaterial; it can be any whole number from 1 to the maximum number of external data files allowed by the computer system (usually 3).

```
1200   WHILE NOT EOF(1)
```

This statement is just like the **WHILE** statement discussed on page B100 except that the condition **NOT EOF(1)** is unfamiliar. The **EOF(1)** means **E**nd **O**f **F**ile number **1**. The **WHILE NOT EOF(1)** means that the loop should be processed while the end of file number 1 has not yet been reached. In other words, the statements inside the loop will be processed until the last piece of data has been read from file number 1. When the end of the file has been detected, the loop will be exited.

```
1300     INPUT #1, LAST$, FIRST$, PHONE$
```

INPUT #1 means to request values for the variables from file number 1 (rather than asking the user for the values). The computer knows which file is **#1** because of the **OPEN** statement. The first value read from file 1 is assigned to the variable **LAST$**, the second value is assigned to **FIRST$**, and the third value is assigned to **PHONE$**.

```
1600 CLOSE #1
```

The **CLOSE** statement is the opposite of the **OPEN** statement. It tells the computer that the external data file **#1** will no longer be needed by the program and so it can be released (closed).

Notice that the original data file, **PHONES**, has commas separating the last name, first name, and phone number. Recall that the comma is used to delimit (separate) different pieces of data that are on the same line. The commas are not really a part of the data and, therefore, are not stored in the variables. Thus, no commas were displayed by the **PRINT** statement.

As you shall see, there are occasions when the information from the data file should be stored exactly as it appears in the file, including commas and any spaces. You can ask the computer to do this by replacing the **INPUT #** statement with a **LINE INPUT #** statement. The **LINE INPUT #** statement tells the computer to input an entire line of data, including any commas and spaces that might be present. For example, change **INPUT #** to **LINE INPUT #** in line **1300**. Note that because the entire line from the data file is being input at one time, the variable list **LAST$, FIRST$, PHONE$** must be changed into a single variable, such as **TEMP$**.

```
1100 OPEN "A:PHONES" FOR INPUT AS #1
1200   WHILE NOT EOF(1)
1300     LINE INPUT #1, TEMP$
1400     PRINT TEMP$
1500   WEND
1600 CLOSE #1
SAVE"A:FILE2
Ok
RUN
Smith,    Jim,        555-2132
Benson,   Geri,       553-3224
Perez,    Juan,       545-8912
Daniels,  Matt,       555-6672
Wheeler,  Vanessa,    505-6540
Ok
```

With LINE INPUT **the commas are considered data and so are displayed**

Wages Program Using an External Data File

Let's modify the payroll program, **WAGES4** (see p. B107) so that it uses an external data file and **INPUT #** rather than **READ/DATA** to assign values to variables. To do this, follow the five steps outlined below:

1. Create a data file that contains the data. This file can be created using the **COPY CON** command (see p. W202) or a word processor. The data file should look just like the **DATA** statements in **WAGES4** except that the line numbers and the word **DATA** must be removed. Also, because the end of a file can be detected using the **EOF** statement, the data flags (**1E+15**) at the end of the data list are no longer needed.

   Let's create the data file using the **COPY CON** command and call it **WAGES.DTA**. If you are currently in the BASIC environment, return to DOS by typing **SYSTEM** and pressing **[Enter]**. Then type the following when the system prompt appears:

```
C:\BA>COPY CON A:WAGES.DTA
Roberts Matt,    4,    30
Sim Keisha  ,    3,    50
Tech Sara   ,    6,    21
Well Vanessa,    5,    40^Z        ← Press [F6] and then [Enter] to exit from COPY CON
        1 File(s) copied

C:\BA>TYPE A:WAGES.DTA               ← Checks to see if the file was entered correctly
Roberts Matt,    4,    30
Sim Keisha  ,    3,    50
Tech Sara   ,    6,    21
Well Vanessa,    5,    40
C:\BA>_
```

2. Enter the BASIC environment, load the payroll program, **WAGES4**, and then list it.

3. Delete the **DATA** statements at the bottom of the program by typing **DELETE 3400-4000** and pressing **[Enter]**.

4. Change the **READ** statement at line **2700** into an **INPUT #** statement. Be careful! If you just change the word **READ** to the word **INPUT** and run the program, the following output would result:

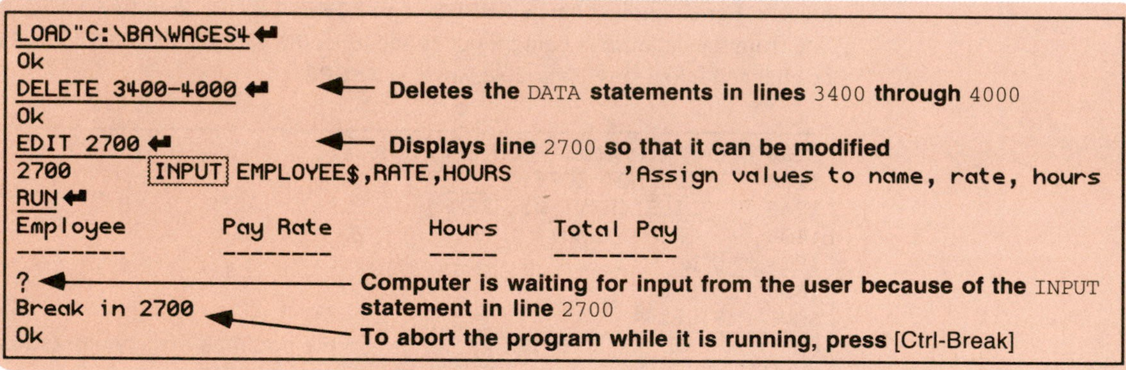

LOAD"C:\BA\WAGES4
Ok
DELETE 3400-4000
Deletes the DATA statements in lines 3400 through 4000
Ok
EDIT 2700
Displays line 2700 so that it can be modified
2700 INPUT EMPLOYEE$,RATE,HOURS 'Assign values to name, rate, hours
RUN
Employee Pay Rate Hours Total Pay
-------- -------- ----- ---------
?
Computer is waiting for input from the user because of the INPUT statement in line 2700
Break in 2700
Ok
To abort the program while it is running, press [Ctrl-Break]

The computer will wait for the user to enter the data requested at line **2700**. Unless you tell it differently, the computer will always assume that the **INPUT** statement should request data from the user. However, in this case, you want the computer to get the information from the data file **WAGES.DTA**, which you just created. To do this, **#1**, must be added to the right of the word **INPUT**.

When this correction is made and the program is run, the following is displayed:

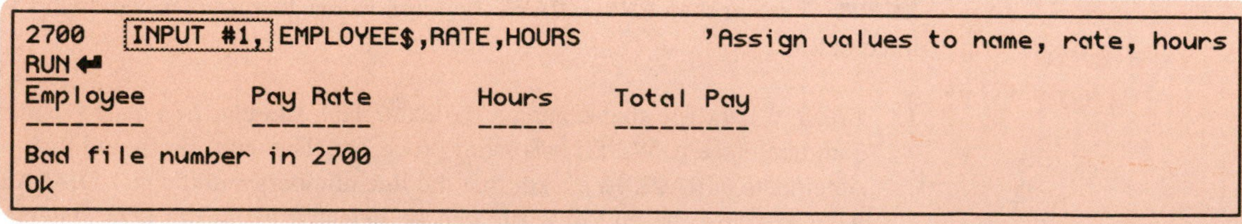

2700 INPUT #1, EMPLOYEE$,RATE,HOURS 'Assign values to name, rate, hours
RUN
Employee Pay Rate Hours Total Pay
-------- -------- ----- ---------
Bad file number in 2700
Ok

The error message **Bad file number in 2700** says that line **2700** told the computer to input the values for variables **EMPLOYEE$**, **RATE**, and **HOURS** from an external data file with reference number **#1**. However, the computer does not know the name of that file because the program does not have an **OPEN** statement. The **OPEN** statement tells the computer that the program will use an external data file, gives the name of that file, indicates what type of file it is, and assigns a number to the file. The statement to be added is the following:

```
1850 OPEN "A:WAGES.DTA" FOR INPUT AS #1
```

This statement produces the information about the external data file that the program will use:

OPEN is the key word that refers to an external data file.

"A:WAGES.DTA" is the specification of the file to be opened (**A:** means the file is on the disk in the A: drive, **WAGES** is the name of the file, and **DTA** is an extension that indicates that the file is a **D**a**TA** file).

FOR INPUT means that the data on the file will be used by an **INPUT #** statement to assign the values to variables (i.e., data will be input from the file):

AS #1 means to always refer to the file as **#1**.

5. Because the data file does not contain the data flags **1E+15**, a different condition must be used in the **WHILE** statement at line **2710**.

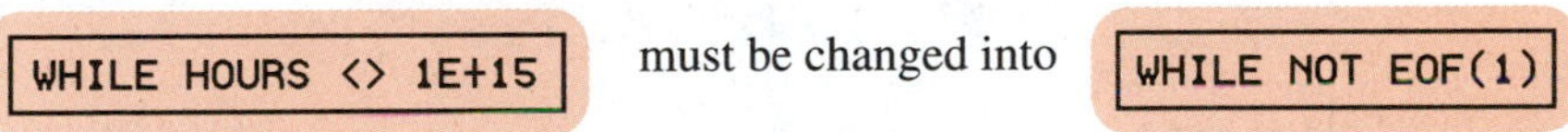

WHILE HOURS <> 1E+15
must be changed into
WHILE NOT EOF(1)

The **EOF(1)** means **E**nd **O**f **F**ile number **1**. Therefore, **WHILE NOT EOF(1)** means that the loop will be executed while the end of the file has not been reached. When the **WHILE** statement is executed and the computer detects the end of file number one (i.e., when the last piece of data has been read), the loop will be exited.

The location of the **INPUT #** statement must be changed from just before the **WHILE** statement (line **2700**) to just after it (line **2720**) and the **READ** statement at line **2910** must be removed. This is done because there is no data flag in the data file (as there was in the **DATA** statements) and so the loop must be executed for all sets of data, including the last set. Moving the **INPUT #** statement to line **2720** will accomplish this.

This program should be saved using the name **WAGES8**. A list and run of the modified program appear on the next page. Notice that the output is identical to that of program **WAGES4**.

```
LOAD"C:\BA\WAGES8
Ok
LIST
1100 REM Program to compute wages given total hours worked and pay rate
1200 REM Douglas Robertson (373-4026), created 1 Mar 91
1300 REM Define variables:
1400 REM   EMPLOYEE$ = name in form LastName Space First (e.g., Roberts Matt)
1500 REM        RATE = rate of pay in dollars per hour (e.g.,  3)
1600 REM       HOURS = total number of hours worked for pay period (e.g., 50)
1700 REM         PAY = total pay earned for pay period (e.g., 150)
1800 REM Begin processing
1850   OPEN "A:WAGES.DTA" FOR INPUT AS #1
1900   REM Define PRINT USING images
2000     IMAGE1$ = "Employee        Pay Rate        Hours    Total Pay"
2100     IMAGE2$ = "--------        --------        -----    ---------"
2200     IMAGE3$ = "\             \  $##.##          ##.#      $###.##"
2300     IMAGE4$ = "All data read, processing complete"
2400   PRINT IMAGE1$                            'Display header
2500   PRINT IMAGE2$                            'Display header
2710     WHILE NOT EOF(1)                       'For each person do the following
2720       INPUT #1, EMPLOYEE$,RATE,HOURS       'Assign values to name, rate, hours
2800       PAY = RATE*HOURS                     'Calculate pay using formula
2900       PRINT USING IMAGE3$;EMPLOYEE$,RATE,HOURS,PAY
3000     WEND                                   'Repeat loop for next person
3100   PRINT
3200   PRINT IMAGE4$                            'Display footer
3300 REM End processing
Ok
SAVE"A:WAGES8
Ok
RUN
Employee        Pay Rate        Hours    Total Pay
--------        --------        -----    ---------
Roberts Matt     $ 4.00          30.0     $120.00
Sim Keisha       $ 3.00          50.0     $150.00
Tech Sara        $ 6.00          21.0     $126.00
Well Vanessa     $ 5.00          40.0     $200.00

All data read, processing complete
Ok
```

Gas Mileage Program Using an External Data File

Let's modify the gas mileage program, **GAS4** (see p. B60), so that it reads the data from an external data file rather than from **DATA** statements. Here are the things that must be done:

1. Use **COPY CON** or WordPerfect to create an external data file that contains the data and call it **GAS.DTA**. Using **COPY CON**, the process would look as follows:

```
SYSTEM

C:\BA>COPY CON A:GAS.DTA
01 June,300,15,120
08 June,250,10,125
15 June,207, 9,120^Z          ← Press [F6] and then [Enter] to exit from COPY CON
        1 File(s) copied

C:\BA>_
```

Of course, because the above data are already in the program, **GAS4**, you could simply edit that program using WordPerfect rather than retyping the information using **COPY CON**. If you wanted to use WordPerfect, you could enter WordPerfect and then use **[Ctrl-F5]** to retrieve the BASIC program **GAS4.BAS** as a DOS text file. Remember, however, that BASIC saves files in compressed binary format and, therefore, if you load a BASIC program into WordPerfect (or any other program) it will appear in coded form. The WordPerfect screen would look like the following:

```
Define variables:(^Sx^EÅ   WEEK$ = week data were
collectedO^S_^EÅ   MILES = miles driven that week)^S@^FÅ     GAL
= gallons of gas used that week«^Sñ^FÅ   PRICE = price in cents
per gallon of gasΦ^S^H^GÅ     MPG = computed value of miles per
gallon of gas^TI^GÅ Define images for PRINT USING:U^T╨^G  IMAGE1$
γ "    Week     Miles     Gallons     Price     Miles/Gallon"¥^T╪^H
IMAGE2$ γ "  ------     -----     -------     -----
------------"β^Tÿ^H  IMAGE3$ γ "  \    \     ###.#      ##.#
$##.##        ##.#"^Uⁿ^HÅ Display column headings:^P^U'       æ
IMAGE1$ ^U─      æ IMAGE2$1^U(
Å Begin loopG^Uî
  é ENTRY γ ^R ╠ ^TI^U≡
    Å Assign values to variablesÄ^UT       Ç
WEEK$,MILES,GAL,PRICE»^U^\
================================================================================
    Å Calculate gas mileage:╓^UÇ
================================================================================
      MPG γ MILES∞GALπ^UΣ
================================================================================
    Å Display results^V^VH       æ ╫
IMAGE3$;WEEK$,MILES,GAL,PRICE∞^Od,MPG$^Vz  â ENTRY3^VäÅ End
loopO^V¼Å Begin DATA statementsi^V^P^N  ä 1 June,300,15,120â^Vt^N
ä 8 June,250,10,125¥^V╪^N  ä 15 June,207,9,120_

A:\GAS4.BAS                                   Doc 1 Pg 4 Ln 1.5" POS 5.6"
```

The data appear in the last two lines of the file along with many other pieces of information in coded form. The WordPerfect standard editing techniques could be used to modify the file so that it looks the way you want it to.

If you had saved the BASIC program in ASCII (text) format (by typing, for example, **SAVE"A:GAS4ASC",A** while in the BASIC environment), very little editing would be necessary when the file was retrieved by WordPerfect. In that case, the file would look like that found on the following page when in WordPerfect.

```
Miles/Gallon"
2100   IMAGE2$ = "  ------    -----    -------    -----
------------"
2200   IMAGE3$ = "  \    \    ###.#     ##.#    $##.##
##.#"
2300 REM Display column headings:
2400   PRINT IMAGE1$
2500   PRINT IMAGE2$
2600 REM Begin loop
2700   FOR ENTRY = 1 TO 3
2800     REM Assign values to variables
2900       READ WEEK$,MILES,GAL,PRICE
3100     REM Calculate gas mileage:
3200       MPG = MILES/GAL
3300     REM Display results
3400       PRINT USING IMAGE3$;WEEK$,MILES,GAL,PRICE/100,MPG
3450   NEXT ENTRY
3460 REM End loop
3500 REM Begin DATA statements
3600   DATA 1 June,300,15,120
3700   DATA 8 June,250,10,125
3800   DATA 15 June,207,9,120

A:\GAS4ASC.BAS                              Doc 1 Pg 1 Ln 6.5" POS 1"
```

This file could be easily edited but then it would have be saved as a text file again using the *Text In/Out* feature.

Because the amount of data is very small, it is probably easier and faster in this example to use **COPY CON** and type in the data.

2. Enter the BASIC environment, load the gas mileage program, **GAS4**, and then list it.
3. Delete the **DATA** statements at the bottom of the program by typing **DELETE 3500-3800** and pressing **[Enter]**.
4. Change the word **READ** in line **2900** into **INPUT #1,** so that the data are input from the data file rather than from the **DATA** statements.
5. Add the following statement, which opens the external data file and assigns it the number 1:

```
1810 OPEN "A:GAS.DTA" FOR INPUT AS #1
```

6. Change the **FOR/NEXT** loop to a **WHILE/WEND** loop by entering the following two statements:

```
2700 WHILE NOT EOF(1)

3450 WEND
```

The modified program would look like the following:

```
LOAD"C:\BA\GAS5
Ok
LIST
1100 REM Calculates gas mileage given miles driven and gal of gas used
1200 REM Douglas Robertson (373-4026), created 1 Jul 90
1300 REM Define variables:
1400 REM   WEEK$ = week data were collected
1500 REM   MILES = miles driven that week
1600 REM     GAL = gallons of gas used that week
1700 REM   PRICE = price in cents per gallon of gas
1800 REM     MPG = computed value of miles per gallon of gas
1810 OPEN "A:GAS.DTA" FOR INPUT AS #1
1900 REM Define images for PRINT USING:
2000   IMAGE1$ = "  Week     Miles     Gallons     Price     Miles/Gallon"
2100   IMAGE2$ = "  ------   -----     -------     -----     ------------"
2200   IMAGE3$ = "  \    \   ###.#      ##.#     $##.##          ##.#"
2300 REM Display column headings:
2400   PRINT IMAGE1$
2500   PRINT IMAGE2$
2600 REM Begin loop
2700   WHILE NOT EOF(1)
2800     REM Assign values to variables
2900       INPUT #1, WEEK$,MILES,GAL,PRICE
3100     REM Calculate gas mileage:
3200       MPG = MILES/GAL
3300     REM Display results
3400       PRINT USING IMAGE3$;WEEK$,MILES,GAL,PRICE/100,MPG
3450   WEND
3460 REM End loop
Ok   <---- DATA statements deleted
SAVE"A:GAS5
Ok
RUN
    Week     Miles     Gallons     Price     Miles/Gallon
  ------     -----     -------     -----     ------------
  01 Jun     300.0       15.0     $ 1.20         20.0
  08 Jun     250.0       10.0     $ 1.25         25.0
  15 Jun     207.0        9.0     $ 1.20         23.0
Ok
```

Writing Information to External Data Files

Information can be written to external data files using the **PRINT #** or **PRINT # USING** statements. To illustrate the use of **PRINT #**, let's make some modifications to the payroll program, **WAGES7**, from page B179. In that program, a subroutine was used to check for errors in the input data. The rate of pay had to be in the range 4 through 7 and the hours worked had to be in the range 0 through 60.

```
LOAD"C:\BA\WAGES7
Ok
RUN
Puter Pals, Inc., Payroll Summary
Date: 03-01-1991
Time: 08:24:28

Num  Employee          Pay Rate  Hours  Reg Pay   OT Pay   Total Pay
---  --------------    --------  -----  -------   -------  ---------
  1  Roberts Matt      $ 4.00    30.0   $120.00   $  0.00  $ 120.00
Sim Keisha skipped: RATE =  41 >  7
    [Sim Keisha    ]  [$41.00][ 50.0][$%1640.00][$615.00][$2255.00]
  2  Tech Sara         $ 6.00    21.0   $126.00   $  0.00  $ 126.00
  3  Well Vanessa      $ 5.00    40.0   $200.00   $  0.00  $ 200.00
  4  Taylor David      $ 4.00    35.0   $140.00   $  0.00  $ 140.00
Peters Bill skipped:  HOURS = 62 > 60
    [Peters Bill   ]  [$ 4.00][ 62.0][$160.00][$132.00][$ 292.00]
---  --------------    --------  -----  -------   -------  ---------
     Totals                      126.0  $586.00   $  0.00  $ 586.00
     Averages          $ 4.75    31.5   $146.50   $  0.00  $ 146.50
Ok
```

The error checking works well but the output is confusing because the errors are listed in the middle of the chart. It would be nice if the errors could be collected and then displayed at the bottom of the chart, after all the correct information was displayed.

The errors can be collected in an external data file by converting the **PRINT** statements that display the error messages into **PRINT #** statements. The **PRINT #** statement works exactly the same as the **PRINT** statement except that the output is written to an external data file rather than to the screen. The only change to the existing **PRINT** statements is the addition of **#1**, just to the right of the word **PRINT**. The modified statements will look like the following:

```
2820       IF EFLG = 1 THEN PRINT #1, USING I9$; EMPLOYEE$,RATE,HOURS,REG,OT,PAY
9880    IF RATE < 4 THEN PRINT #1, EMPLOYEE$" skipped: RATE= " RATE"<  4":EFLG=1
9890    IF RATE > 7 THEN PRINT #1, EMPLOYEE$" skipped: RATE= " RATE">  7":EFLG=1
9900    IF HOURS< 0 THEN PRINT #1, EMPLOYEE$" skipped: HOURS="HOURS"<  0":EFLG=1
9910    IF HOURS>60 THEN PRINT #1, EMPLOYEE$" skipped: HOURS="HOURS"> 60":EFLG=1
```

Of course, in order to use an external data file, an **OPEN** statement must be added stating that the program will use an external data file (e.g., **OPEN**), providing the complete specification for that file (e.g., **A:ERROR.DTA**), indicating what type of file it is (e.g., **OUTPUT**), and assigning a number to the file (e.g., **#1**). The statement given below does just this. Notice that rather than being an **INPUT** file (one that will *input* data to the program) this data file will be an **OUTPUT** file (one that will receive *output* from the program).

```
1810 OPEN "A:ERROR.DTA" FOR OUTPUT AS #1
```

The output of the modified program will be the following:

```
LOAD"C:\BA\WAGES7
Ok
1810 OPEN "A:ERROR.DTA" FOR OUTPUT AS #1     ◄— Added line
LIST 2820
2820        IF EFLG = 1 THEN PRINT #1, USING I9$; EMPLOYEE$,RATE,HOURS,REG,OT,PAY
Ok                                            Modified lines
LIST 9880-9910
9880    IF RATE < 4 THEN PRINT #1, EMPLOYEE$" skipped: RATE= " RATE"<  4":EFLG=1
9890    IF RATE > 7 THEN PRINT #1, EMPLOYEE$" skipped: RATE= " RATE">  7":EFLG=1
9900    IF HOURS< 0 THEN PRINT #1, EMPLOYEE$" skipped: HOURS="HOURS"<  0":EFLG=1
9910    IF HOURS>60 THEN PRINT #1, EMPLOYEE$" skipped: HOURS="HOURS"> 60":EFLG=1
Ok
SAVE"A:WAGES9
Ok
RUN
Puter Pals, Inc., Payroll Summary
Date: 03-01-1991
Time: 08:29:28

Num  Employee          Pay Rate  Hours  Reg Pay   OT Pay   Total Pay
---  --------------    --------  -----  -------   -------  ---------
  1  Roberts Matt      $ 4.00     30.0  $120.00   $  0.00  $ 120.00
  2  Tech Sara         $ 6.00     21.0  $126.00   $  0.00  $ 126.00
  3  Well Vanessa      $ 5.00     40.0  $200.00   $  0.00  $ 200.00
  4  Taylor David      $ 4.00     35.0  $140.00   $  0.00  $ 140.00
---  --------------    --------  -----  -------   -------  ---------
     Totals                      126.0  $586.00   $  0.00  $ 586.00
     Averages          $ 4.75     31.5  $146.50   $  0.00  $ 146.50
Ok
```

The error messages for **Keisha Sim** and **Bill Peters** do not appear on the screen. They have been *printed on* (written to) the file **ERROR.DTA** rather than *displayed on* (written to) the screen. In order to display the error messages at the bottom of the output, the file **ERROR.DTA** must first be closed (using the **CLOSE #** statement) as an **OUTPUT** file (you no longer want to write *output* to this file) and then re-opened as an **INPUT** file (you now want to *input* data from this file). Then, the data from the file must be input and displayed. The subroutine call and subroutine on the next page will accomplish this:

```
3250 GOSUB 9940                          'Calls subroutine for displaying file contents
9940 REM SUBROUTINE to display contents of file ERROR.DTA
9945   PRINT
9950   PRINT "The following people have data errors"
9952   PRINT
9953   PRINT I4$
9954   PRINT I5$
9955   CLOSE #1
9960   OPEN "A:ERROR.DTA" FOR INPUT AS #1
9965     WHILE NOT EOF(1)
9970       LINE INPUT #1, TEMP$
9975       PRINT TEMP$
9980     WEND
9985 RETURN
SAVE"A:WAGES10
Ok
RUN
Puter Pals, Inc., Payroll Summary
Date: 03-01-1991
Time: 08:39:28

Num  Employee         Pay Rate  Hours  Reg Pay    OT Pay   Total Pay
---  ---------------  --------  -----  -------   -------   ---------
  1  Roberts Matt      $ 4.00   30.0   $120.00   $  0.00   $ 120.00
  2  Tech Sara         $ 6.00   21.0   $126.00   $  0.00   $ 126.00
  3  Well Vanessa      $ 5.00   40.0   $200.00   $  0.00   $ 200.00
  4  Taylor David      $ 4.00   35.0   $140.00   $  0.00   $ 140.00
---  ---------------  --------  -----  -------   -------   ---------
     Totals                     126.0  $586.00   $  0.00   $ 586.00
     Averages          $ 4.75   31.5   $146.50   $  0.00   $ 146.50

The following people have data errors

Num  Employee         Pay Rate  Hours  Reg Pay    OT Pay   Total Pay
---  ---------------  --------  -----  -------   -------   ---------
Sim Keisha skipped: RATE=  41 >  7
     [Sim Keisha     ]  [$41.00][ 50.0][$%1640.00][$615.00][$2255.00]
Peters Bill skipped: HOURS= 62 > 60
    [Peters Bill    ]  [$ 4.00][ 62.0][$160.00][$132.00][$ 292.00]
Ok
```

Lines 9945–9954: Displays a header for the listing of the error messages

- 9955: Closes file #1 as an OUTPUT file
- 9960: Re-opens file #1 as an INPUT file
- 9965: Do the following until the end of the file
- 9970: Inputs entire lines of data at a time
- 9975: Displays the data input at line 9970
- 9980: Returns to the beginning of the loop

The correct data and processed information now are separate from the erroneous data and information. Note the use of **LINE INPUT #** in line **9970** rather than **INPUT #**. The **LINE INPUT #** statement takes the entire line written on the data file, including all leading and trailing blank spaces and treats commas as data rather than as delimiters. If **INPUT #** had been used in line **9970** the leading spaces would have been ignored in the second and fourth lines of the file **ERROR.DTA**. This would have caused the column headings to not match up with the data.

The word LINE was removed from this statement

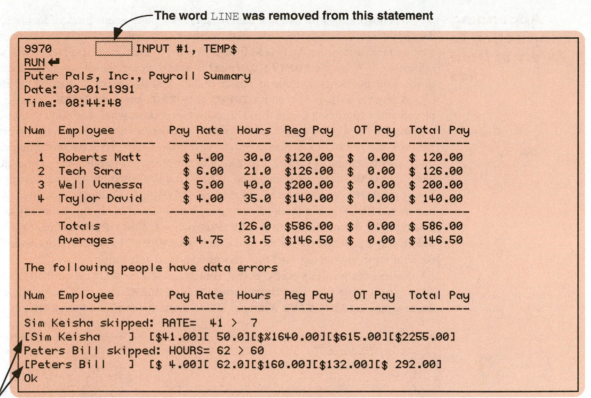

```
9970          INPUT #1, TEMP$
RUN ↵
Puter Pals, Inc., Payroll Summary
Date: 03-01-1991
Time: 08:44:48

Num  Employee        Pay Rate  Hours  Reg Pay    OT Pay   Total Pay
---  --------------  --------  -----  -------    -------  ---------
  1  Roberts Matt     $ 4.00    30.0  $120.00  $  0.00  $ 120.00
  2  Tech Sara        $ 6.00    21.0  $126.00  $  0.00  $ 126.00
  3  Well Vanessa     $ 5.00    40.0  $200.00  $  0.00  $ 200.00
  4  Taylor David     $ 4.00    35.0  $140.00  $  0.00  $ 140.00
---  --------------  --------  -----  -------    -------  ---------
     Totals                    126.0  $586.00  $  0.00  $ 586.00
     Averages         $ 4.75    31.5  $146.50  $  0.00  $ 146.50

The following people have data errors

Num  Employee        Pay Rate  Hours  Reg Pay    OT Pay   Total Pay
---  --------------  --------  -----  -------    -------  ---------
Sim Keisha skipped: RATE=  41 >  7
[Sim Keisha     ]  [$41.00][ 50.0][$%1640.00][$615.00][$2255.00]
Peters Bill skipped: HOURS= 62 > 60
[Peters Bill    ]  [$ 4.00][ 62.0][$160.00][$132.00][$ 292.00]
Ok
```

When INPUT # rather than LINE INPUT # is used, the leading blank spaces are ignored. This causes the data written to the file ERROR.DTA to not line up with the column headings.

To see the actual contents of the file **ERROR.DTA**, you can return to DOS by typing **SYSTEM** ↵ and then use the **TYPE** command as follows:

```
A>TYPE A:ERROR.DTA↵
Sim Keisha skipped: RATE=  41 >  7
    [Sim Keisha     ]  [$41.00][ 50.0][$%1640.00][$615.00][$2255.00]
Peters Bill skipped: HOURS= 62 > 60
    [Peters Bill    ]  [$ 4.00][ 62.0][$160.00][$132.00][$ 292.00]

A>_
```

Because the erroneous and correct data have been listed separately, the two sections could be sent to two different people. For example, perhaps the correct data summary is to be used by a department manager for budgeting purposes and the list of data errors is to be sent to the payroll department to correct the errors.

Of course, because the erroneous data now are in a separate data file, that file could be sent electronically to anyone who needs it (rather than sending a hard copy by mail). And, if all the **PRINT** statements were changed to **PRINT #** statements, the correct information could also be distributed electronically. This is very useful when time pressures are extreme and the information is to be used by people in different physical locations (buildings, cities, or even countries). For example, one of the authors of this book lives in Minnesota, the other lives in Washington, and the editor lives in California. When deadlines are tight, we can electronically connect our computers (over regular telephone lines) and then send each other files that contain modified versions of the manuscript. Even with overnight mail, this process can save days of time and may even be cheaper.

Appending Information to External Data Files

When working with external data files, the computer keeps track of its place in the file by using a data pointer, which is very similar to the pointer used with **READ/DATA** statements (see p. B62). Each time a piece of information is read from or written to the file, the pointer moves to the next piece of information. When the **EOF(#)** statement is used to detect the end of a file, the computer really checks to see if the pointer is pointing at a piece of data or at the marker located at the end of the file.

Whenever a file is opened for **INPUT** or **OUTPUT** using the **OPEN** statement, the data pointer is placed at the beginning of the file. This causes a problem when you want to add data to the end of an existing file. If you tell the computer to open an existing file for output, the original information on the file will be written over (replaced by) the new information. To solve this problem, the **APPEND** option of the **OPEN** statement is used. **APPEND** tells the computer to place the pointer at the end of the file when the **OPEN** statement is executed. When a file is opened for append, the information written on the file by a **PRINT #** statement is added to the end of the file rather than written over (replacing) information on the file. You can think of writing information to a file in the same way as recording music on a tape recorder. Using the **INPUT** or **OUTPUT** options of the **OPEN** statement is like rewinding the tape before playing it (**INPUT**) or recording on it (**OUTPUT**). The **APPEND** option is like finding the last piece of music on the tape and then recording after that location.

As an example, let's access BASIC and examine a program called **ADD1**, which adds information to an existing data file. The program uses the file **PHONES** (see p. B211) as the external data file. **LOAD** the program, **LIST** it, **SAVE** it to your *BASIC Data* diskette, and then **RUN** it as shown below:

```
LOAD"C:\BA\ADD1 ↵
Ok
LIST ↵
1100 INPUT "Enter name of file";FILE$
1200 OPEN FILE$ FOR APPEND AS #1
1300 PRINT "Begin entering data.  Enter DONE to stop data entry mode."
1400 LINE INPUT "Type data:";NEWDATA$
1500   WHILE NEWDATA$ <> "DONE"
1600     PRINT #1, NEWDATA$
1700     LINE INPUT "Type data:";NEWDATA$
1800   WEND
1900 CLOSE #1
Ok
SAVE"A:ADD1 ↵
Ok
RUN ↵
Enter name of file? A:PHONES ↵
Begin entering data.  Enter DONE to stop data entry mode.
Type data:Smith,   Douglas,  348-0922 ↵
Type data:Marlin,  Greg,     522-8335 ↵
Type data:DONE ↵
Ok
SYSTEM ↵                    ◄── Returns to DOS environment so file can be displayed


A>TYPE A:PHONES ↵
Smith,   Jim,      555-2132
Benson,  Geri,     553-3224
Perez,   Juan,     545-8912
Daniels, Matt,     555-6672
Wheeler, Vanessa,  505-6540
Smith,   Douglas,  384-0922 ◄─┐
Marlin,  Greg,     230-4431 ◄─┴─ Names added to the file PHONES

A>_
```

Line Numbers	Comments
1100	Asks the user to type in the name of the external data file to be used by the program. The name of the file is assigned to the variable **FILE$**. Asking the user for the name of the file allows you to use the same program on any data file without having to write the name of the data file in the **OPEN** statement.
1200	Opens the external data file whose name is stored in variable **FILE$** as an **APPEND** type file and assigns the number 1 to that file. **APPEND** instructs the computer to position the pointer at the end of the external data file so that when a **PRINT #** statement is executed the new information is added to the end of the file rather than writing over information already in the file.
1400	The new information is entered by the user and stored in variable **NEWDATA$**. Note the use of **LINE INPUT** rather than **INPUT**. This means that the comma will not be interpreted as a delimiter and, therefore, the entire line of data typed by the user will be entered into the data file as a single entry.
1600	The information in variable **NEWDATA$** is written at the end of the file **PHONES** (i.e., the new information is appended to the file **PHONES**).
1900	The data file is closed and the information is actually written to the disk. If this statement is not present (and there is no **END** statement), the appended information is not physically written to the disk and, therefore, the new data that was typed in would be lost.

Note what happens if the file is mistakenly opened for **INPUT** in line **1200** but then an attempt is made to **PRINT** onto the file (don't do this!).

```
1200 OPEN FILE$ FOR INPUT  AS #1
RUN
Enter name of file? A:PHONES
Begin entering data.  Enter DONE to stop data entry mode.
Type data:Bast,     Sueann,    334-6654
Bad file mode in 1600
Ok
```

The error message **Bad file mode in 1600** is caused by the fact that line **1200** opened the file for **INPUT** but line **1600** tried to use it for **OUTPUT**.

Also, note what happens if the file is opened for **OUTPUT** rather than for **APPEND** (don't do this!).

```
1200 OPEN FILE$ FOR OUTPUT AS #1
RUN
Enter name of file? A:PHONES
Begin entering data.  Enter DONE to stop data entry mode.
Type data:Bast,     Sueann,    334-6654
Type data:DONE
Ok
SYSTEM

A>TYPE A:PHONES
Bast,     Sueann,    334-6654

A>_
```

No error message appears, but the data in the original file **PHONES** was erased and replaced by the single line of data just entered. This is because the file was opened for **OUTPUT** rather than for **APPEND**. Opening for **OUTPUT** instructs the computer to place the pointer at the beginning of the file before writing to the file. Be careful! This mistake can cause you to lose a lot of data.

When appending information to external data files it is generally a good practice to give the user some information on the file being modified. This is important because the more files you have to work with the more likely it is to make mistakes such as appending information to the wrong file. The above program can be made more useful by making the following modifications:

1. Ask the user whether or not to examine the file to be appended. If the file is large, examining it may take some time (seconds or minutes). The confident (or careless) user may not want to do this.
2. Count the number of lines of data on the file to be appended. This can be done by first opening the file for **INPUT**, inputting all the lines in the file, and counting each line as it is input.
3. Display the last line in the data file.
4. Ask the user whether or not to continue the append process. This gives the user an opportunity to select a different file if needed. If the program is to be continued, the file can then be opened for **APPEND** and the process completed.

An easy way of accomplishing the modification is to call a subroutine to do the task right after the user has indicated the name of the file. Type **BASICA ↵**, if necessary, **LOAD** the program, **ADD2**, **LIST** it, **SAVE** it to your *BASIC Data* diskette, and then **RUN** it as shown on the next page:

```
LOAD"C:\BA\ADD2 ↵
Ok
LIST ↵
1100 INPUT "Enter name of file";FILE$
1120 GOSUB 2000                                      'Examines file to be appended
1200 OPEN FILE$ FOR APPEND AS #1
1300 PRINT "Begin entering data.  Enter DONE to stop data entry mode."
1400 LINE INPUT "Type data:";NEWDATA$
1500   WHILE NEWDATA$ <> "DONE"
1600     PRINT #1, NEWDATA$
1700     LINE INPUT "Type data:";NEWDATA$
1800   WEND
1900 CLOSE #1
1950 END
2000 REM ***** Subroutine to examine the file to be appended
2100   INPUT "Do you want to examine this file before appending"; ANS$
2200   IF ANS$ = "NO" THEN RETURN
2300   OPEN FILE$ FOR INPUT AS #1
2400     WHILE NOT EOF(1)
2500       LINE INPUT #1, TEMP$
2600       COUNT = COUNT + 1
2700     WEND
2800   PRINT
2900   PRINT FILE$ " contains "COUNT" lines.  The last line on the file is:"
3000   PRINT "[" TEMP$"]"
3100   PRINT
3200   INPUT "Do you wish to continue with the append process";ANS$
3300   IF ANS$ = "YES" THEN RETURN
3400 END
Ok
SAVE"A:ADD2 ↵
Ok
RUN ↵
Enter name of file? A:PHONES ↵
Do you want to examine this file before appending? YES ↵

A:PHONES contains  7  lines.  The last line on the file is:
[Marlin,  Greg,     522-8335]

Do you wish to continue with the append process? NO ↵
Ok
```

One more modification might be of interest. Suppose you wanted to append information to the file but you wanted to keep a copy of the original file, perhaps as a backup. This can be accomplished by having the computer make a copy of the file under a new name before the modification process takes place. The following changes need to be made to the program:

- The user should be asked to specify whether or not a backup file is desired (see lines **2110** and **2120** in the program below). If the answer is **YES**, the name of the backup file should be requested (see line **4100** in the program below).
- The backup file should be opened (see line **4200** in the program below) and the lines from the original file printed onto it (see line **2550** in the program below). **LOAD** the new version of the program, **LIST** it, **SAVE** it to your *BASIC Data* diskette, and then **RUN** it as shown below:

```
LOAD"C:\BA\ADD3↵
Ok
LIST↵
1100 INPUT "Enter name of file";FILE$
1120 GOSUB 2000                              'Examines file to be appended
1200 OPEN FILE$ FOR APPEND AS #1
1300 PRINT "Begin entering data.  Enter DONE to stop data entry mode."
1400 LINE INPUT "Type data:";NEWDATA$
1500   WHILE NEWDATA$ <> "DONE"
1600     PRINT #1, NEWDATA$
1700     LINE INPUT "Type data:";NEWDATA$
1800   WEND
1900 CLOSE #1
1950 END
2000 REM ***** Subroutine to examine the file to be appended
2100   INPUT "Do you want to examine this file before appending"; ANS$
2110   INPUT "Do you want to BACKUP  this file before appending"; ANS2$
2120   IF ANS2$ = "YES" THEN GOSUB 4000          'Defines backup file
2200   IF ANS$ = "NO" THEN RETURN
2300   OPEN FILE$ FOR INPUT AS #1
2400     WHILE NOT EOF(1)
2500       LINE INPUT #1, TEMP$
2550       IF ANS2$ = "YES" THEN PRINT #2, TEMP$  'Writes data to backup file
2600       COUNT = COUNT + 1
2700     WEND
2800   PRINT
2900   PRINT FILE$ " contains "COUNT" lines.  The last line on the file is:"
3000   PRINT "[" TEMP$"]"
3100   PRINT
3200   INPUT "Do you wish to continue with the append process";ANS$
3300   IF ANS$ = "YES" THEN RETURN
3400 END
4000 REM ***** Subroutine to define the backup file
4100   INPUT "Type name for backup file (letters & digits only)"; FILE2$
4200   OPEN FILE2$ FOR OUTPUT AS #2
4300   ANS$ = "YES"
4400 RETURN
Ok
SAVE"A:ADD3↵
Ok
RUN↵
Enter name of file? A:PHONES↵
Do you want to examine this file before appending? NO↵
Do you want to BACKUP  this file before appending? YES↵
Type name for backup file (letters & digits only)? A:PHONES.BK1↵

A:PHONES contains  7  lines.  The last line on the file is:
[Marlin,  Greg,      522-8335]

Do you wish to continue with the append process? NO↵
Ok
```

To see the contents of the backup file, exit BASIC by typing **SYSTEM** and tapping **[Enter]**:

```
SYSTEM ↵

A>TYPE A:PHONES.BK1↵
Smith,   Jim,      555-2132
Benson,  Geri,     553-3224
Perez,   Juan,     545-8912
Daniels, Matt,     555-6672
Wheeler, Vanessa,  505-6540
Smith,   Douglas,  348-0922
Marlin,  Greg,     522-8335

A>_
```

TO TAKE A BREAK Type **SYSTEM** ↵, remove diskette(s). To resume (hard disk): Insert *Data* diskette; type **A:** ↵; **C:\BA\BASICA** ↵. To resume (two drive): Insert diskettes, type **A:** ↵, **B:\BASICA** ↵.

Homework Exercises

For each of the following homework exercises, use the programming process to develop a BASIC program that will produce the output described. Each program should contain enough **REM** statements to clearly document the program. Unless instructed to do otherwise, produce a hard copy of a **LIST** and a **RUN** of each of your final working programs. Also, save each program using a name such as **HWB7-01** for future reference. Your instructor may also ask you to hand in other materials related to the development of the programs such as the variable definitions, pseudocodes, etc.

CHAPTER SEVEN

① As you recall from Exercise 6 of Chapter 4 (p. B129), Barb and Karl own a small stationary store and want to keep track of their inventory on the computer. They sell the following items:

Stock number	*Item name*	*Manufacturer*	*Unit price*
27365	Paper	Xerox	29.95
83288	Ink	Smithson	12.34
21560	Pencils	Farber	2.34
18332	Copy fluid	Xerox	18.50
29335	File folders	Smithson	19.00

Use **COPY CON** (or a word processor) to create an ASCII (text only) external data file called **HWB7-01.DTA** that contains the above information. Use a comma to delimit each piece of information.

---

② Modify the program you wrote for Exercise 6 of Chapter 4, p. B129 so that the data for the program are read from the external data file, **HWB7-01.DTA**, which you just created in Exercise 1. The output from your program should look the same as before (except for the homework number printed in the upper-left corner of the output):

```
Homework B7-02                    Joe Computer                1 Mar 91

      Stock
Num   Number  Item Description   Manufacturer   Price
---   ------  ----------------   ------------   ------
 1    27365   Paper              Xerox          $29.95
 2    83288   Ink                Smithson       $12.34 @@
 3    21560   Pencils            Farber         $ 2.34
 4    18332   Copy fluid         Xerox          $18.50
 5    29335   File folders       Smithson       $19.00 @@
---   ------  ----------------   ------------   ------
```

---

③ Modify the program you wrote in Exercise 2 so that if the manufacturer is **Smithson** the program writes the **Stock Number**, **Item Description**, and **Price** on an external data file caled **HWB7-03.TMP** in addition to displaying it in the chart. After the program has run, use the **SYSTEM** command to exit BASIC and the command **TYPE A:HWB7-03.TMP** to list the contents of the newly created file. Do a screen dump of the result.

---

④ In Exercise 9 of Chapter 4 (p. B131), you constructed a BASIC program that calculated the total sales of employees of MicroMania Computers, Inc. Modify that program so that it will input the raw data from an external data file rather than from **DATA** statements. Create the external data file using **COPY CON** and call it **HWB7-04.DTA**. The output from the program should be the same as before (except for the homework number in the upper-left corner of the output):

```
Homework B7-04                    Joe Computer                1 Mar 91

MicroMania Computers, Inc., Sales Summary
        Date:  03-01-1991
        Time:  17:56:55

Num Employee     Hardware    Software Total Sales  Commission   Earnings
--- ---------  ----------  ---------- -----------  ----------  ----------
  1 Sherri     $22,357.92  $1,052.83   $23,410.75  $2,367.18  $12,367.18
  2 Mary       $13,862.31  $2,832.09   $16,694.40  $1,612.80  $11,612.80
  3 Lawrence   $10,154.00  $1,502.00   $11,656.00  $1,135.56  $11,135.56
--- ---------  ----------  ---------- -----------  ----------  ----------
     Totals:   $46,374.23  $5,386.92   $51,761.15  $5,115.54  $35,115.54
   Averages:   $15,458.08  $1,795.64   $17,253.72  $1,705.18  $11,705.18
```

Continued . . .

CHAPTER SEVEN

⑤ In Exercise 2 of Chapter 6 (p. B201), you modified a program that was designed to calculate a grade point average so that it would check for and display errors in the data. In this exercise, your task is to further modify that program so that the messages for errors in the data are listed at the end of the output rather than within the body of the printed table. To do this, you may want to use an external data file in a fashion similar to that discussed on pages B221–23. The output from your program should look like the following:

```
Homework B7-05                    Joe Computer                    1 Mar 91

Computation of Grade Point Average

 Course       Credits       Grade     Value     Val*Cr
GC 1571          5            A         4         20
GC 1421          4            B         3         12
GC 1211          5            D         1          5
PE 1122          1            C         2          2

Total number of credits is 15 (based on 4 courses)
Grade point average (GPA) is 2.6

================================================================

The following errors were detected in the data:

 Course  Credits  Grade  Error
-------  -------  -----  ------------------------------
GC 1237    4.0      Q    Grade but must be A B C D or F
GC 1411    2.5      A    Credits must be a whole number
GC 1171    9.0      B    Credits may not be more than 5
```

---

⑥ Modify the checkbook reconcillation program you developed for Exercise 6 of Chapter 6 (p. B205) so that it inputs the values of the bank balance, outstanding deposits, and outstanding checks from a data file instead of from **DATA** statements. The program should ask the user for the name of the data file to be used. The program should also update another external data file by appending the current bank balance, date, and time to the file. This data file will contain a chronological history of the bank balance. The program should ask the user for the name of this file. Run the program two times using the same data as you did in Chapter 6. Then use the **SYSTEM** command to return to DOS and the **TYPE** command to display the contents of the two data files. The output from the first run of the program should look like the following (the new parts are enclosed in the boxes):

CHAPTER SEVEN

```
Homework B7-06                    Susan Gorman                    1 Mar 91

Enter the name of the input data file? A:HWB7-06.DT1

Checkbook Balancing Program

Beginning bank balance from bank statement
 $827.33

Listing of Deposits Outstanding
  $12.34
 $156.20
  -$3.00  Value out of range (0-500), include anyway? NO
$5000.00  Value out of range (0-500), include anyway? YES
  $10.12  Value 10.123 has too many decimal places, include anyway? NO
  $15.00
--------  ----------------------------------------------------
$5183.54  Total of outstanding deposits

Listing of Checks Outstanding
  $44.50
  $80.00
$4000.00  Value out of range (0-400), include anyway? YES
--------  ----------------------------------------------------
$4124.50  Total of outstanding checks

==============================================================

Summary of Transactions
 $827.33  Bank balance from bank statement
$5183.54  Value of deposits not cleared (based on 4 deposits)
$4124.50  Value of checks   not cleared (based on 3 checks)
--------  ----------------------------------------------------
$1886.37  Current checkbook balance (as of 03-01-1991 at 10:10)

Should current balance, date, & time be appended to a data file? YES
Enter file name? A:HWB7-06.BAL

A:HWB7-06.BAL was updated
```

The data file **HWB7-06.BAL** should look like the following after the second run:

```
A>TYPE A:HWB7-06.BAL
1886.37,"03-01-1991","10:11:56"  ◄── Data from first run
470,"03-01-1991","10:14:25"      ◄── Data from second run

A>_
```

⑦ Ms. Nielson is the supervisor of student records at Willow Lane University. The president of the university has asked her to produce a list of students who work in her office so that he can form a student advisory committee that will meet with him on a regular basis. The committee should have a mix of students based on their sex and college of registration. Ms. Nielson has collected the following information on the students:

Continued . . .

CHAPTER SEVEN

Last name

First name

Sex (F = female and M = male)

College (GC = General College, IT = Institute of Technology, CLA = College of Liberal Arts, ED = College of Education)

Age in years

The actual data are listed below:

Ascot,Chad,M,GC,18

Jackson,Sara,F,GC,18

Linn,Jason,M,IT,20

Marston,Dan,M,CLA,23

Morales,Tina,F,GC,20

Schwartz,Keith,M,CLA,34

Wheeler,Vanessa,F,ED,19

Use the programming process to develop a program that will display the students' names arranged by sex and then again by college and that will also list the names of all males between the ages of 18 and 25, inclusive.

One way of constructing this program is to use IF/THEN/ELSE statements to determine which category an individual belongs to and then to write that person's name to an external data file for that category. For example, if the sex of a particular person is **F**, then append that person's name to a file called **FEMALE** or, if the sex is **M**, then append that person's name to a file called **MALE**. Follow a similar procedure for grouping the names by college. After all the raw data have been processed, the individual files can be opened for input and the contents read and displayed. If you use this method of temporary data files, be sure that the files are emptied at the beginning of a run (use a statement like **OPEN "FEMALE" FOR OUTPUT AS #2 : CLOSE #2**). If you do not do this, each time the program is run more and more names will be added to the temporary file but never deleted from it.

The output from your program should look like the following:

```
Homework B7-07                    Joe Computer                    1 Mar 91

Enter name of data file? A:HWB7-07.DTA↵

Student Services Personnel

Listing by Sex:
  Females:
    Sara Jackson
    Tina Morales
    Vanessa Wheeler

  Males:
    Chad Ascot
    Jason Linn
    Dan Marston
    Keith Schwartz

Listing by College
  General College
    Chad Ascot
    Sara Jackson
    Tina Morales

  College of Liberal Arts
    Dan Marston
    Keith Schwartz

  Other Colleges
    Jason Linn (IT)
    Vanessa Wheeler (ED)

Listing of males between 18 and 25 years old, inclusive
    Chad Ascot ( 18 )
    Jason Linn ( 20 )
    Dan Marston ( 23 )
```

Subscripted Variables

Objectives *After you have completed this chapter, you should be able to*

- Use **MID$** to select portions of strings for processing.
- Use **VAL** to convert string representations of numbers into numeric representations.
- Access and process databases created by other applications.
- Use subscripted variables to store data.

CHAPTER 8

- Use the bubble sort to arrange a set of data in a database.
- Explain why the computer sometimes sorts data in nonstandard ways.
- Develop complex programs that use multiple data files, process arrays, and update already-existing data files.

Introduction

This chapter begins by discussing two new BASIC functions: **MID$** and **VAL**. The **MID$** function allows programmers to select and process any portion of a string while the **VAL** function permits the conversion of strings that contain only digits into numbers that can be used in computations.

A new type of variable called a *subscripted variable* is also introduced. Such variables allow programmers to store each individual piece of data using individual variable names and then to easily access the individual pieces of data in a random fashion.

MID$ and VAL Functions

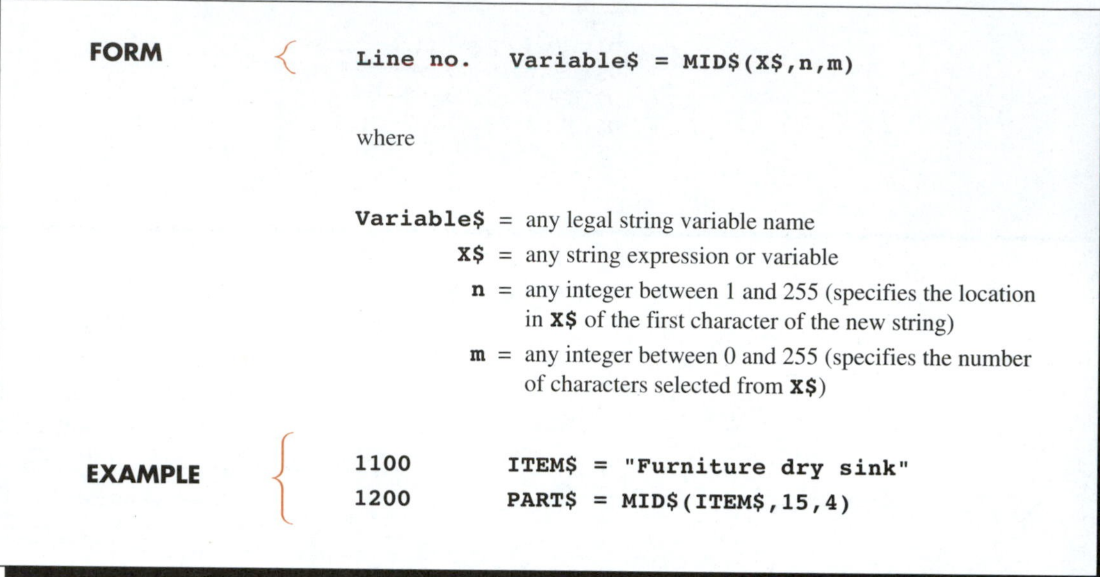

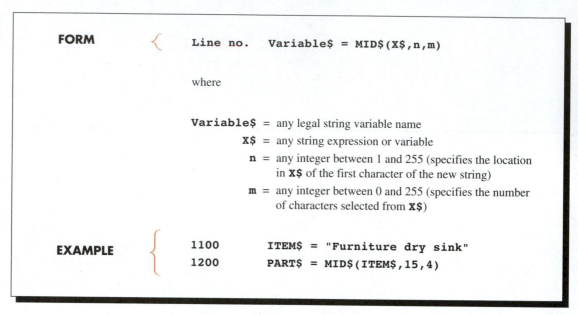

FORM { `Line no.   Variable$ = MID$(X$,n,m)`

where

Variable$ = any legal string variable name
X$ = any string expression or variable
n = any integer between 1 and 255 (specifies the location in **X$** of the first character of the new string)
m = any integer between 0 and 255 (specifies the number of characters selected from **X$**)

EXAMPLE
```
1100        ITEM$ = "Furniture dry sink"
1200        PART$ = MID$(ITEM$,15,4)
```

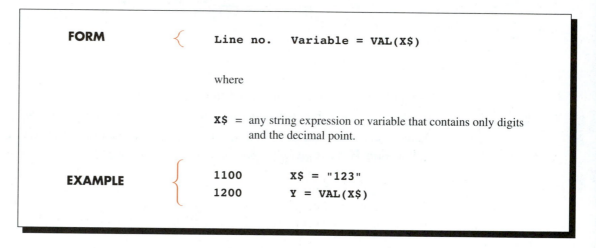

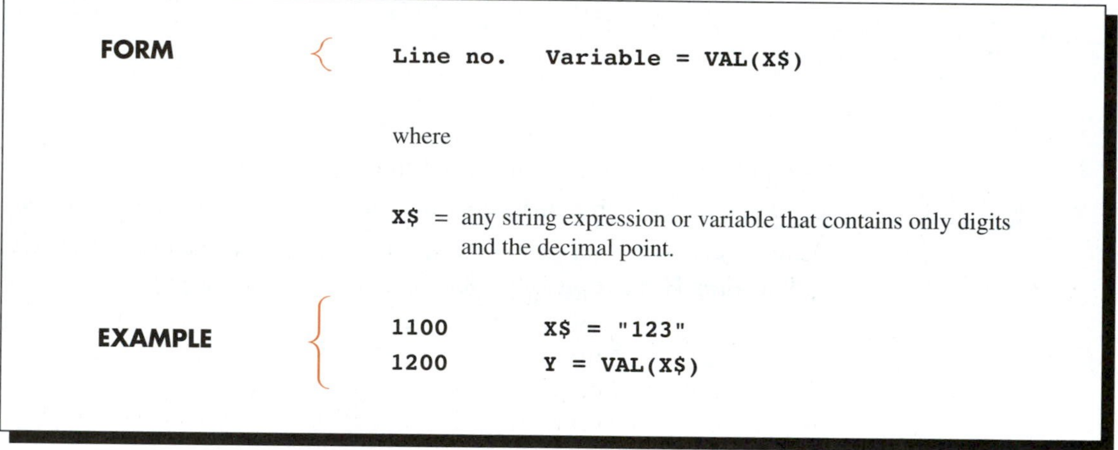

FORM { `Line no.   Variable = VAL(X$)`

where

X$ = any string expression or variable that contains only digits and the decimal point.

EXAMPLE
```
1100        X$ = "123"
1200        Y = VAL(X$)
```

First, let's examine the **MID$** function, which allows the programmer to select a portion of a specified string. For example, recall the home inventory database that was discussed in Part III, Chapter 1. The ninth record in that database was for a dry sink:

Field width →	1234567890	123456789012345	123456789012	1234567890	12345678	12345678
Field name →	CATEGORY	NAME	MANUFACT	SERIAL_NUM	DATE	VALUE
Record # 9 →	Furniture	Dry sink	Hand made	---	04/12/87	500.00

Suppose this data were available to a BASIC program in a **LET** statement such as:

```
10 REC$ = "Furniture Dry sink        Hand made    ---        04/12/87  500.00"
```

Let's say that you want to display the name of the item (**Dry sink**) in reverse order (**sink, Dry**) and the value of the item (**500.00**). To do this, the **MID$** function would be used to select pieces of the string and then a **PRINT** statement would be used to display those pieces individually.

The following program does just that. **LOAD** the program, **LIST** it, **SAVE** it to your *BASIC Data* diskette, and then **RUN** it as shown below:

```
LOAD"C:\BA\MID1↵
Ok
LIST↵
10 REC$ = "Furniture Dry sink        Hand made    ---         04/12/87  500.00"
20 PART1$ = MID$(REC$,15,4) ◄— Begin at column 15 and select 4 columns (i.e., 15,16,17,18)
30 PART2$ = MID$(REC$,11,3) ◄— Begin at column 11 and select 3 columns (i.e., 11,12,13)
40 PART3$ = MID$(REC$,56,8) ◄— Begin at column 56 and select 8 columns (i.e., 56 - 63)
50 PRINT "Item is " PART1$  ", "  PART2$ " and value is " PART3$
Ok
SAVE"A:MID1↵
Ok
RUN↵
Item is sink, Dry and value is   500.00
Ok
```

The program uses

```
20 PART1$ = MID$(REC$,15,4)
```

to select the 15th, 16th, 17th, and 18th characters from the string **REC$** (i.e., it selects **sink**) and assigns that value to the variable **PART1$**. Then, it uses

```
30 PART2$ = MID$(REC$,11,3)
```

to select the 11th, 12th, and 13th characters from the string **REC$** (i.e., selects **Dry**) and assigns that value to the variable **PART2$**. Then, it uses

```
40 PART3$ = MID$(REC$,56,8)
```

to select the 56th, 57th, 58th, 59th, 60th, 61st, 62nd, and 63rd characters from the string **REC$** (i.e., it selects **500.00**) and assigns that value to the variable **PART3$**. Finally, it displays the values of **PART2$**, **PART1$**, and **PART3$**. The effect is to reverse the words **Dry sink** so that they are displayed as **sink, Dry**, and to display the value of the item.

Now, suppose you want to do an arithmetic calculation on the number **500.00** in the string **REC$**. For example, to calculate a 6% sales tax on that item the value of **PART3$** is multiplied by .06.

```
10 REC$ = "Furniture Dry sink        Hand made    ---         04/12/87  500.00"
20 PART1$ = MID$(REC$,15,4)
30 PART2$ = MID$(REC$,11,3)
40 PART3$ = MID$(REC$,56,8)
50 PRINT "Item is " PART1$  ", "  PART2$ " and value is " PART3$
60 PRINT "6% sales tax is " PART3$*.06
SAVE"A:MID2↵
Ok
RUN↵
Item is sink, Dry and value is   500.00
6% sales tax is
Type mismatch in 60
Ok
```

The message, **Type mismatch in 60** is caused by **PART3$*.06** in the **PRINT** statement at line **60**. The computer cannot use a string in an arithmetic computation. Of course, you can easily see that **PART3$** is really a number, but the dollar sign at the end of the variable name tells the computer that it is a string. In situations like this, where a number has been stored in a string variable, the **VAL** function can be used to tell the computer that the value in the string is really a number. To do this, change **PART3$** into **VAL(PART3$)** as the following program shows:

```
10 REC$ = "Furniture Dry sink        Hand made    ---        04/12/87  500.00"
20 PART1$ = MID$(REC$,15,4)
30 PART2$ = MID$(REC$,11,3)
40 PART3$ = MID$(REC$,56,8)
50 PRINT "Item is " PART1$  ", "  PART2$ " and value is " PART3$
60 PRINT "6% sales tax is " VAL(PART3$)*.06
SAVE"A:MID3
Ok
RUN
Item is sink, Dry and value is   500.00
6% sales tax is  29.99999932944775
Ok
```

The VAL function returns the value of a string so that it can be used in an arithmetic calculation

Note that if you try to take the **VAL** of a string that does not contain a number, the computer returns the value 0.

```
10 REC$ = "Furniture Dry sink        Hand made    ---        04/12/87  500.00"
20 PART1$ = MID$(REC$,15,4)
30 PART2$ = MID$(REC$,11,3)
40 PART3$ = MID$(REC$,56,8)
50 PRINT "Item is " PART1$  ", "  PART2$ " and value is " PART3$
60 PRINT "6% sales tax is " VAL(PART3$)*.06
70 PRINT VAL(PART1$)
SAVE"A:MID4
Ok
RUN
Item is sink, Dry and value is   500.00
6% sales tax is  29.99999932944775
 0
Ok
```

The VAL of a string that does not contain a number is 0

The **MID$** and **VAL** functions are useful for extracting information from databases created by dBASE or other applications.

Accessing Databases Using a BASIC Program

Entering large amounts of data into data files or **DATA** statements is time consuming and, therefore, expensive. Up to this point, commas or carriage returns were used in data lists as delimiters to separate individual pieces of data. Using the comma as a delimiter is fine for small data sets, but as the amount of data increases the comma is undesirable for two reasons: it takes time to type and it takes up space in the memory of the computer.

For example, suppose you have a set of data that consists of 40 single-digit numbers. Using commas as delimiters would require 80 keystrokes to enter the data into the computer (40 keystrokes for the actual data plus 39 keystrokes for the commas used as delimiters plus one final keystroke for the carriage return). In addition, the computer would have to store 80 characters in its memory. If the data could be entered without commas, the entry time and data storage requirement would be cut in half.

With commas as delimiters, 80 keystrokes are needed and 80 characters must be stored.

```
1,2,3,4,5,6,7,8,9,0,1,2,3,4,5,6,7,8,9,0,1,2,3,4,5,6,7,8,9,0,1,2,3,4,5,6,7,8,9,0
1234567890123456789012345678901234567890
```

Without commas as delimiters, only 41 keystrokes need to be entered and 41 characters need to be stored.

The problem with leaving out the comma delimiters is that there needs to be a way of identifying the individual pieces of data. One solution is to employ *data fields* in the same way as they were used with dBASE. Recall from Part III, Chapter 1 that a data field is a position in the records of a database file that always contains the same type of information. For example, we created a dBASE database, **HOMEINV1.DBF**, with the following structure:

Field name	*Length*	*Columns*	*Sample entry*
Category	10	01-10	Furniture
Name	15	11-25	Dry sink
Manufact	12	26-37	Hand made
Serial_Num	10	38-47	—
Date	8	48-55	04/12/87
Value	8	56-63	500.00

Recall that you saved this database using the regular dBASE format and also in ASCII format under the name **HOMEINV1.TXT**. You should copy that file to your *BASIC Data* disk now.

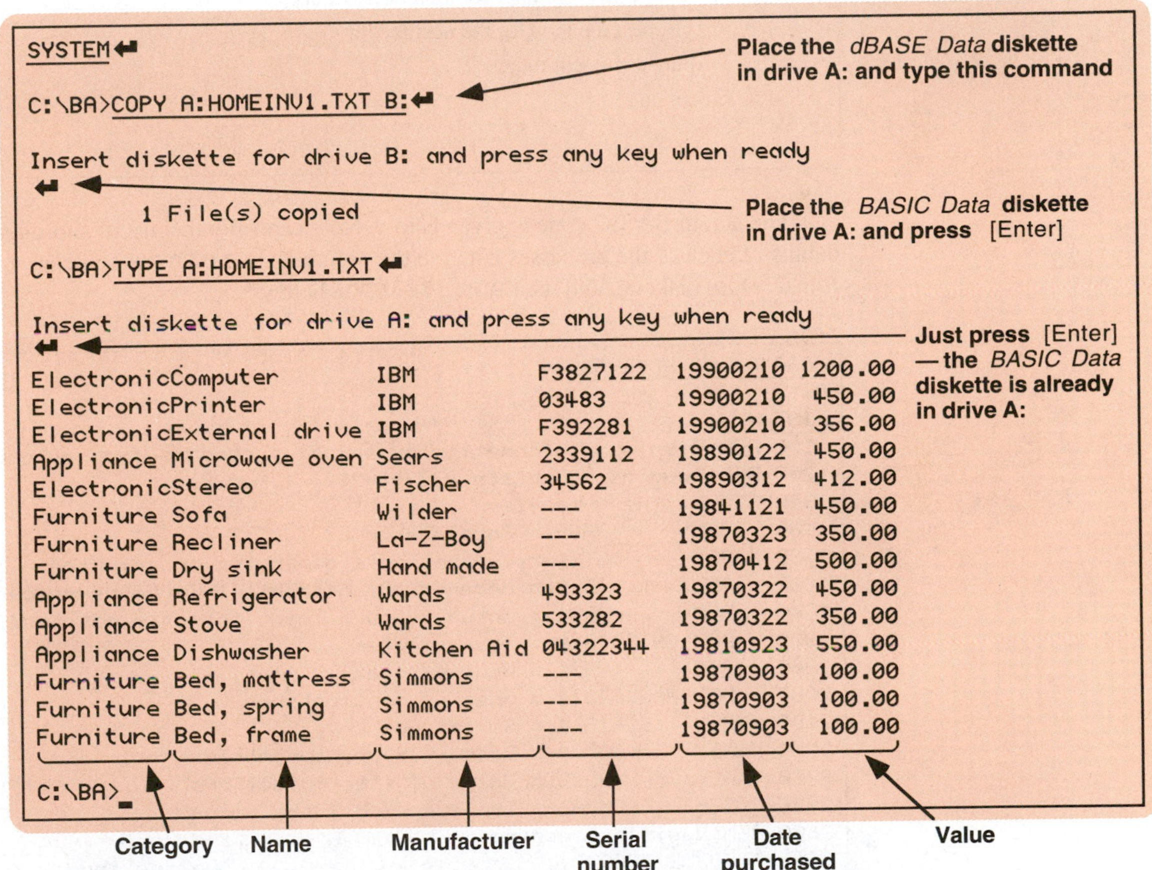

The field widths are defined as they were in dBASE and the data are exactly the same except that the values for the dates are in the form **YYYYMMDD** (i.e., the first four characters, **YYYY**, represent the year; the next two characters, **MM**, represent the month; and the last two characters, **DD**, represent the day). For example, the date for the first record is **19900210**. This means the year is **1990**, the month is **02**, and the day is **10**. This represents February 10, 1990. The date is written in this form to make it easy to compare two dates.

Now let's discuss a BASIC program that can access the information in the database **HOMEINV1.TXT** and process it in the same way as did dBASE. The program will display a report similar to the one you produced in dBASE that contains the category, name, and value of all items in the database.

The BASIC program will be quite simple. For each record (line of data) in the database, the program will input the information from the external data file, **HOMEINV1.TXT**, and display the strings in columns 1–10 (category), columns 11–25 (name), and columns 56–63 (value). The program will also display the total of all the values of the selected items.

One version of the pseudocode for the program is given below:

```
Begin processing
    Define images for PRINT USING
    Initialize counters
    Define external data file
    Display document header
        For each record in the database, do the following
            Assign data for record to variable REC$
            Break up REC$ into individual pieces of data
            Display category, name, and value
            Update counter for total of all values
        Repeat the loop for the next record
    Display document footer
End processing
```

The actual BASIC code is given below. Note carefully the use of subroutines to carry out the details of each of the processes listed in the pseudocode. **LOAD** the program, **LIST** it, **SAVE** it to your *BASIC Data* diskette, and then **RUN** it as shown below:

```
LOAD"C:\BA\HOMEANA1
Ok
LIST
1100 REM Displays information on selected records from database
1200 REM Douglas Robertson (373-4026), 1 Mar 91
1300 REM Define variables
1400   REM      PAGE = Page number
1500   REM     DATE$ = Current date generated by computer
1600   REM       DB$ = Name of the database file to be processed
1700   REM      REC$ = Actual record input from the database
1800   REM CATEGORY$ = Type of item
1900   REM      NAM$ = Name of item
2000   REM MANUFACT$ = Name of manufacturer
2100   REM   SERIAL$ = Serial number
2200   REM     DATP$ = Date item was purchased
2300   REM     VALUE = Value of item in dollars
2400   REM    SUMVAL = The sum of all the values
2500 REM Begin processing
2600   GOSUB 3900                               'Define images for PRINT USING
2700   GOSUB 5300                               'Initialize counters
2800   GOSUB 5700                               'Define external data file
2900   GOSUB 6100                               'Display document header
3000   REM For each record in the database, do the following
3100     WHILE NOT EOF(1)
3200       GOSUB 7600                           'Assign data of each record to REC$
3300       GOSUB 7900                           'Break up REC$ into individual data
3400       GOSUB 8700                           'Calculate summary information
3500       GOSUB 9000                           'Display information
3600     WEND                                   'Repeat the loop for the next record
3700   GOSUB 9300                               'Display document footer
3800 END
```

Continued . . .

```
3900 REM ***** Subroutine to define images for PRINT USING
4000    I1$ = "Page No. #####                                                  "
4100    I2$ = "\        \                                                      "
4200    I3$ = "                               Home Inventory                   "
4300    I4$ = "                     All records from HOMEINV1 selected "
4400    I5$ = "                             Douglas Robertson                  "
4500    I6$ = "Category   Name                 Dollar                          "
4600    I7$ = "   of        of                  Value                          "
4700    I8$ = "  Item      Item                   of                           "
4800    I9$ = "                                 Item                           "
4900   I10$ = "\         \ \               \ ####.##                           "
5000   I11$ = "*** Total ***                                                   "
5100   I12$ = "                                ####.##                         "
5200 RETURN
5300 REM ***** Subroutine to initialize counters
5400     PAGE = 1
5500   SUMVAL = 0
5600 RETURN
5700 REM ***** Subroutine to define external data file
5800   INPUT "Enter name of dababase to be analyzed"; DB$
5900   OPEN DB$ FOR INPUT AS #1
6000 RETURN
6100 REM ***** Subroutine to display document header
6200   PRINT USING I1$; PAGE
6300   PRINT USING I2$; DATE$
6400   PRINT       I3$
6500   PRINT       I4$
6600   PRINT
6700   PRINT       I5$
6800   PRINT
6900   PRINT       I6$
7000   PRINT       I7$
7100   PRINT       I8$
7200   PRINT       I9$
7300   PRINT
7400   PRINT
7500 RETURN
7600 REM ***** Subroutine to assign data of each record to REC$
7700   LINE INPUT #1, REC$
7800 RETURN
7900 REM ***** Subroutine to break up REC$ into individual data items
8000   CATEGORY$ = MID$(REC$,1,10)                        'Type of item
8100        NAM$ = MID$(REC$,11,15)                       'Name of item
8200   MANUFACT$ = MID$(REC$,26,12)                       'Name of manufacturer
8300     SERIAL$ = MID$(REC$,38,10)                       'Serial number
8400       DATP$ = MID$(REC$,48,8)                        'Date item was purchased
8500       VALUE = VAL(MID$(REC$,56,8))                   'Value of item in dollars
8600 RETURN
8700 REM ***** Subroutine to calculate summary information
8800   SUMVAL = SUMVAL + VALUE
8900 RETURN
9000 REM ***** Subroutine to display information
9100   PRINT USING I10$;CATEGORY$,NAM$,VALUE
9200 RETURN
9300 REM ***** Subroutine to display document footer
9400   PRINT I11$
9500   PRINT USING I12$;SUMVAL
9600 RETURN
Ok
SAVE"A:HOMEANA1↵
Ok
```

Continued . . .

```
RUN
Enter name of dababase to be analyzed? A:HOMEINV1.TX
Page No.     1
03-01-1991
                              Home Inventory
                        All records from HOMEINV1 selected

                             Douglas Robertson

Category   Name                 Dollar
   of       of                   Value
  Item     Item                     of
                                  Item


Electronic Computer           1200.00
Electronic Printer             450.00
Electronic External drive      356.00
Appliance  Microwave oven      450.00
Electronic Stereo              412.00
Furniture  Sofa                450.00
Furniture  Recliner            350.00
Furniture  Dry sink            500.00
Appliance  Refrigerator        450.00
Appliance  Stove               350.00
Appliance  Dishwasher          550.00
Furniture  Bed, mattress       100.00
Furniture  Bed, spring         100.00
Furniture  Bed, frame          100.00
        *** Total ***
                              5818.00
Ok
```

The above output is similar to that produced by dBASE. Using dBASE to produce the report was faster, but using high-level programming languages such as BASIC generally provides more flexibility and control over the processing and the form of the output. You may find that, after you become proficient at programming, many tasks are easier to accomplish using BASIC rather than a spreadsheet or database management program.

Let's modify the program so that it displays information for those items whose values are over $400 and which were purchased in 1989. To do this operation using dBASE, the following command would be issued at the dot prompt:

```
REPORT FORM A:EXP1989 FOR VALUE > 400 .AND. DATE >= CTOD('01/01/89')
              .AND. DATE <= CTOD('12/31/89')
```

In the BASIC program, only lines **3400** and **3500** need to be modified to include the appropriate **IF/THEN/ELSE** statement.

```
3400       IF VALUE > 400 AND DATP$ >= "19890101" AND DATP$ <= "19891231"
             THEN GOSUB 8700               'Calculate summary information
3500       IF VALUE > 400 AND DATP$ >= "19890101" AND DATP$ <= "19891231"
             THEN GOSUB 9000               'Display information
```

Notice that the statement that does the selection in BASIC is very similar to the dBASE statement:

dBASE	BASIC
REPORT FORM A:EXP1989	**PRINT USING I10$;CATEGORY$,NAM$,VALUE**
FOR VALUE > 400	**IF VALUE > 400**
.AND.	**AND**
DATE >= CTOD ('01/01/89')	**DATP$ >= "19890101"**
.AND.	**AND**
DATE <= CTOD ('12/31/89')	**DATP$ <= "19891231"**

If lines **3400** and **3500** are modified as indicated, the program will produce the following output:

```
LOAD"C:\BA\HOMEANA2
Ok
LIST 3400-3500
3400        IF VALUE > 400 AND DATP$ >= "19890101" AND DATP$ <= "19891231"
              THEN GOSUB 8700                    'Calculate summary information
3500        IF VALUE > 400 AND DATP$ >= "19890101" AND DATP$ <= "19891231"
              THEN GOSUB 9000                    'Display information
Ok
SAVE"A:HOMEANA2
Ok
RUN
Enter name of dababase to be analyzed? A:HOMEINV1.TXT
Page No.     1
03-01-1991
                                Home Inventory
                         All records from HOMEINV1 selected

                               Douglas Robertson

Category    Name                Dollar
   of        of                 Value
  Item      Item                   of
                                 Item


Appliance  Microwave oven       450.00
Electronic Stereo               412.00
*** Total ***
                                862.00
Ok
```

Arrays (Subscripted Variables)

An *array* is defined as a list or table of values that is stored using a single variable name. Each value in the array is called an *element* and each of the elements is given a unique number or set of numbers for reference purposes. The reference numbers are called *subscripts.*

Subscripted variables are often used when describing sets of data. For example, suppose you have a group of five people and you want to assign the first name of each person to its own variable called **F**. You could set up the table shown on the next page:

Data number	Student name	Name variable
1	Jim	F_1
2	Geri	F_2
3	Juan	F_3
4	Matt	F_4
5	Vanessa	F_5

Each name will be stored using the variable **F** and each **F** has a subscript that uniquely assigns it to a particular name. For example, F_3 contains the name **Juan** while F_1 contains the name **Jim**.

Because it is difficult to display this type of subscript notation on computer screens the developers of BASIC decided to use a different notation. Instead of writing the subscript one half space below the variable name (e.g., F_1) the subscript is written inside parentheses (e.g., **F(1)**). Thus, the BASIC version of the variable names would be the following (note that the **$** is needed because these are string variables):

Data number	Student name	Name variable
1	Jim	F$(1)
2	Geri	F$(2)
3	Juan	F$(3)
4	Matt	F$(4)
5	Vanessa	F$(5)

As a simple example, let's modify the program **FILE1** (see p. B212) so that it uses subscripted variables in place of its regular variables. As you recall, **FILE1** accessed data from the external data file **PHONES** and displayed the information on the screen. A list and run of the original program are given below:

```
LOAD"C:\BA\FILE1↵
Ok
LIST↵
1100 OPEN "A:PHONES" FOR INPUT AS #1
1200   WHILE NOT EOF(1)
1300     INPUT #1, LAST$, FIRST$, PHONE$
1400     PRINT LAST$, FIRST$, PHONE$
1500   WEND
1600 CLOSE #1
Ok
RUN↵
Smith          Jim            555-2132
Benson         Geri           553-3224
Perez          Juan           545-8912
Daniels        Matt           555-6672
Wheeler        Vanessa        505-6540
Ok
```

To employ subscripted variables, the following changes need to be made.

1. A counter needs to be added so that variables can be assigned unique numbers as the data are input from the file. Call the counter **NUM**.
2. The variable names need to be changed as follows:

Old name	*New name*
LAST$	**LAST$(NUM)**
FIRST$	**FIRST$(NUM)**
PHONE$	**PHONE$(NUM)**

3. A new type of statement called **DIM** must be added. **DIM** stands for **DIM**ension and is used to specify the maximum number of subscripts that will be used with each subscripted variable. The computer needs this information in order to allocate its memory efficiently during execution.

As you will see, using subscripted variables will make the program more flexible because it will enable you to assign each piece of data (each element of each array) to its own variable rather than having to reuse variables every time a new set of data is entered. **LOAD** the new version of the program, **LIST** it, **SAVE** it to your *BASIC Data* diskette, and then **RUN** it as shown below:

```
LOAD"C:\BA\SUB1
Ok
LIST
1100 OPEN "A:PHONES" FOR INPUT AS #1
1150 DIM LAST$(6), FIRST$(6), PHONE$(6)
1200   WHILE NOT EOF(1)
1250     NUM = NUM + 1
1300     INPUT #1, LAST$(NUM), FIRST$(NUM), PHONE$(NUM)
1400     PRINT LAST$(NUM), FIRST$(NUM), PHONE$(NUM)
1500   WEND
1600 CLOSE #1
Ok
SAVE"A:SUB1
Ok
RUN
Smith         Jim           555-2132
Benson        Geri          553-3224
Perez         Juan          545-8912
Daniels       Matt          555-6672
Wheeler       Vanessa       505-6540
Ok
```

Line Numbers	Comments
1100	Opens the file **PHONES** as an input file and assigns it the number 1.
1150	Specifies the maximum number of elements for each subscripted variable. When this line is executed, the computer sets up the following array in its main memory:

Variable	Value
LAST$(0)	
LAST$(1)	
LAST$(2)	
LAST$(3)	
LAST$(4)	
LAST$(5)	
LAST$(6)	

Variable	Value
FIRST$(0)	
FIRST$(1)	
FIRST$(2)	
FIRST$(3)	
FIRST$(4)	
FIRST$(5)	
FIRST$(6)	

Variable	Value
PHONE$(0)	
PHONE$(1)	
PHONE$(2)	
PHONE$(3)	
PHONE$(4)	
PHONE$(5)	
PHONE$(6)	

Continued . . .

The subscripts begin at 0 and go to a maximum of 6 in steps of 1. This means that each of the variables can hold a total of 7 values at one time. Note also that each value is set to the default value for the variable (i.e., all elements in string variables are set to the null string (a string that contains no characters) and all elements in numeric variables are set to 0).

1200 The loop is entered.

1250 The counter **NUM** is changed from 0 (its default value) to 1.

1300 The first piece of data is assigned to **LAST$(1)**, the second to **FIRST$(1)**, and the third to **PHONE$(1)**.

Variable	Value
LAST$(0)	
LAST$(1)	**Smith**
LAST$(2)	
LAST$(3)	
LAST$(4)	
LAST$(5)	
LAST$(6)	

Variable	Value
FIRST$(0)	
FIRST$(1)	**Jim**
FIRST$(2)	
FIRST$(3)	
FIRST$(4)	
FIRST$(5)	
FIRST$(6)	

Variable	Value
PHONE$(0)	
PHONE$(1)	**555-2132**
PHONE$(2)	
PHONE$(3)	
PHONE$(4)	
PHONE$(5)	
PHONE$(6)	

1400 Displays the values of **LAST$(1)**, **FIRST$(1)**, and **PHONE$(1)**.

1500 Repeats the loop for the next set of data. The process continues until the end of the data file is reached.

1600 The data file is closed. At this point, all the data have been read and assigned to variables as follows:

Variable	Value
LAST$(0)	
LAST$(1)	**Smith**
LAST$(2)	**Benson**
LAST$(3)	**Perez**
LAST$(4)	**Daniels**
LAST$(5)	**Wheeler**
LAST$(6)	

Variable	Value
FIRST$(0)	
FIRST$(1)	**Jim**
FIRST$(2)	**Geri**
FIRST$(3)	**Juan**
FIRST$(4)	**Matt**
FIRST$(5)	**Vanessa**
FIRST$(6)	

Variable	Value
PHONE$(0)	
PHONE$(1)	**555-2132**
PHONE$(2)	**553-3224**
PHONE$(3)	**545-8912**
PHONE$(4)	**555-6672**
PHONE$(5)	**505-6540**
PHONE$(6)	

One advantage of using subscripted variables is that once the data have been entered by a **READ**, **LET**, **INPUT**, or **INPUT #** statement, they can be randomly accessed by the user. For example, let's modify the above program by adding statements that make it interactive. The user is asked to enter the student's ID number (what we called the subscript and stored in the variable **NUM**) and then that person's name and phone number are displayed. The **PRINT** statement at line **1400** has been removed so that all the data are not displayed (it is not a big deal for the small set of data we are using, but if we had 10,000 sets of data we would not want all of them displayed every time the program is run). **LOAD** the new version of the program, **LIST** it, **SAVE** it to your *BASIC Data* diskette, and then **RUN** it as follows:

```
LOAD"C:\BA\SUB2
Ok
LIST
1100 OPEN "A:PHONES" FOR INPUT AS #1
1150 DIM LAST$(6), FIRST$(6), PHONE$(6)
1200   WHILE NOT EOF(1)
1250     NUM = NUM + 1
1300     INPUT #1, LAST$(NUM), FIRST$(NUM), PHONE$(NUM)
1500   WEND
1600 CLOSE #1
1800 ANSWER$ = "YES"
1900   WHILE ANSWER$ = "YES"
2000   PRINT
2100   INPUT "Enter ID number of person whose phone number you want"; NUM
2200   PRINT "Phone number of " FIRST$(NUM) " " LAST$(NUM) " is " PHONE$(NUM)
2300   INPUT "Would you like another phone number";ANSWER$
2400 WEND
Ok
SAVE"A:SUB2
Ok
RUN

Enter ID number of person whose phone number you want? 5
Phone number of Vanessa Wheeler is 505-6540
Would you like another phone number? YES

Enter ID number of person whose phone number you want? 3
Phone number of Juan Perez is 545-8912
Would you like another phone number? NO
Ok
```

PRINT at line 1400 was deleted

Notice how this program accomplished the same thing as the dBASE command **DISPLAY FOR RECNO()=5**.

The program has data for people with ID numbers 1 through 5. What happens if an ID number that is not one of those is entered?

```
RUN

Enter ID number of person whose phone number you want? 6
Phone number of   is
Would you like another phone number? YES

Enter ID number of person whose phone number you want? 7
Phone number of
Subscript out of range in 2200
Ok
```

When ID number 6 was entered, the computer responded with **Phone number of   is**. No data were available for ID number 6 and so the computer used the default values of the three strings (the default value for string variables is the null string—i.e., a string that has no characters).

When ID number 7 was entered, the computer responded with **Subscript out of range in 2200**. There is an error because the **DIM** statement told the computer that the maximum value for the subscripts of the three variables would be 6 but the user asked it to use a seventh value. When you try to use a subscript that is either too large or negative, the computer will display an error message and abort the program.

If the **DIM** statement is omitted, subscripted variables are assumed to have a dimension of 10. However, it is considered bad form to omit **DIM** statements, so always include them when using subscripted variables. Also, the maximum number of subscripts for an array is approximately 255, depending on the version of BASIC you are using.

Sorting with Subscripted Variables

Subscripted variables can be used in a program to sort (arrange or alphabetize) data in some predetermined way (called the collating sequence). There are many different methods that can be used to sort a list of strings but, unfortunately, there is no one best method (best meaning fastest and most efficient). One of the simplest methods of sorting is the *bubble sort.* In the bubble sort, a list of strings is sorted by comparing pairs of strings and then exchanging the strings if the first string is larger than the second. This process is done for all pairs of strings and then repeated until the list is properly sorted. During this procedure, the strings that belong at the top of the list rise (bubble up) to the top like a gas bubble in a glass of soda pop. For example, let's do a bubble sort on the following list of four names:

`Nessa     Kathy     Carol     Annie`

The first pair, **`Nessa`** and **`Kathy`**, are compared and, because they are not in alphabetical order, they are swapped. The list now looks like this:

`Kathy     Nessa     Carol     Annie`

The next pair, **`Nessa`** and **`Carol`**, are compared and, because they are not in alphabetical order, they are swapped.

`Kathy     Carol     Nessa     Annie`

Finally, the last pair, **`Nessa`** and **`Annie`**, are compared and, because they are not in alphabetical order, they are swapped.

`Kathy     Carol     Annie     Nessa`

Now, go to the beginning of the list and follow the same procedure again (each pair is compared and, if they are not in the correct order, they are swapped). The next pass through the list would look like the following:

Begin here:	**`Kathy`**	**`Carol`**	**`Annie`**	**`Nessa`**
`Kathy and Carol` swapped:	**`Carol`**	**`Kathy`**	**`Annie`**	**`Nessa`**
`Kathy and Annie` swapped:	**`Carol`**	**`Annie`**	**`Kathy`**	**`Nessa`**
`Kathy and Nessa` remain where they are:	**`Carol`**	**`Annie`**	**`Kathy`**	**`Nessa`**

The final pass would look as follows:

Begin here:	**`Carol`**	**`Annie`**	**`Kathy`**	**`Nessa`**
`Carol and Annie` swapped:	**`Annie`**	**`Carol`**	**`Kathy`**	**`Nessa`**
`Carol and Kathy` remain where they are:	**`Annie`**	**`Carol`**	**`Kathy`**	**`Nessa`**
`Kathy and Nessa` remain where they are:	**`Annie`**	**`Carol`**	**`Kathy`**	**`Nessa`**

The list is now in alphabetical order. Notice how, for example, Annie began at the bottom of the list and then *bubbled up* to the top:

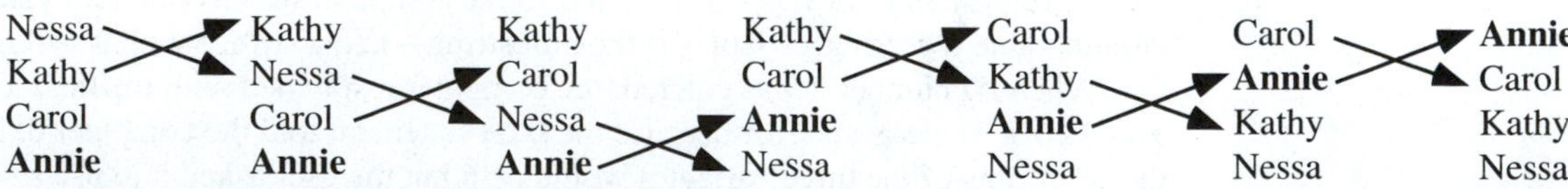

Let's create a data file called **`ALFDAT1`** that contains the above four names and then write a program that will sort the data on the file. Typing **`SYSTEM`** will return control to the DOS environment and then you can use the **`COPY CON`** command to create the data file. Do the following:

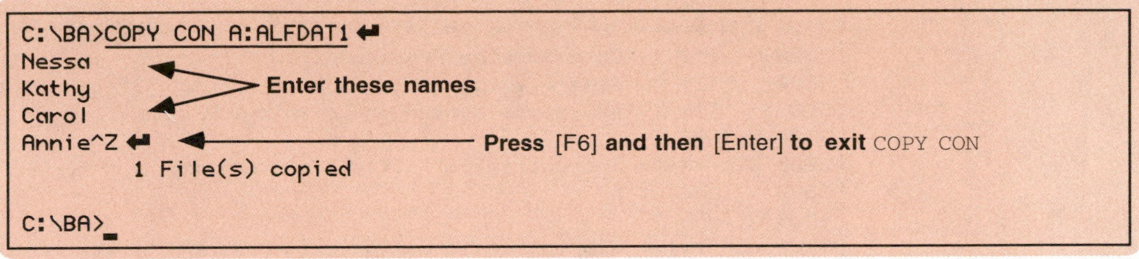

C:\BA>COPY CON A:ALFDAT1
Nessa
Kathy
Carol
Annie^Z
1 File(s) copied
C:\BA>_
Enter these names
Press [F6] and then [Enter] to exit COPY CON

One version of the pseudocode for the sorting program is listed below:

```
Begin processing
    Define dimensions for variables
    Define images for PRINT USING
    Initialize counters
    Define external data file
    Display document header
        For each record in the database, do the following
            Assign data for record to ITEM$
        Repeat the loop for the next record
    Arrange the data using bubble sort
    Display sorted list
End processing
```

The BASIC program to do the sorting is listed below. It follows the same procedure as was just discussed. **LOAD** the program, **LIST** it, **SAVE** it to your *BASIC Data* diskette, and then **RUN** it as shown below:

```
LOAD"C:\BA\SORT1
Ok
LIST
1100 REM Sorts data input from database
1200 REM Douglas Robertson (373-4026), 1 Mar 91
1300 REM Define variables
1400   REM     DATE$ = Current date generated by computer
1500   REM     TIME$ = Current time generated by computer
1600   REM   ITEM$() = Array to hold input data
1700   REM     INDEX = Counter to assign subscripts
1800   REM       FLG = Swap flag (=0 for no swap; =1 for swap
1900   REM       NUM = Loop variable for FOR/NEXT
2000 REM Begin processing
2100   DIM ITEM$(100)                     'Define dimensions for variables
2200   GOSUB 3300                         'Define images for PRINT USING
2300   GOSUB 3800                         'Initialize counters
2400   GOSUB 4100                         'Define external data file
2500   GOSUB 4500                         'Display document header
2600   REM For each record in the database, do the following
2700     WHILE NOT EOF(1)
2800       GOSUB 5000                     'Assign data for record to ITEM$()
2900     WEND                             'Repeat the loop for the next record
3000   GOSUB 5400                         'Bubble sort routine
3100   GOSUB 6300                         'Display sorted list
3200 END
```

Continued . . .

```
3300 REM ***** Subroutine to define images for PRINT USING
3400    I1$ = "Data Sorting Program"
3500    I2$ = "Generated on \        \ at \      \ from database \            \"
3600    I3$ = "### items sorted and displayed"
3700 RETURN
3800 REM ***** Subroutine to initialize counters
3900   INDEX = 0
4000 RETURN
4100 REM ***** Subroutine to define external data file
4200   INPUT "Enter name of dababase to be analyzed"; DB$
4300   OPEN DB$ FOR INPUT AS #1
4400 RETURN
4500 REM ***** Subroutine to display document header
4600   PRINT        I1$
4700   PRINT USING I2$;DATE$,TIME$,DB$
4800   PRINT
4900 RETURN
5000 REM ***** Subroutine to assign data for record to ITEM()$
5100   INDEX = INDEX + 1             'Count number of items input from database
5200   LINE INPUT #1, ITEM$(INDEX)
5300 RETURN
5400 REM ***** Subroutine to carry out Bubble Sort
5500   FLG = 0                       'Set swap flag to 0 (a swap has taken place)
5600   WHILE FLG = 0
5700     FLG = 1                     'Set swap flag to 1 (no swap has taken place)
5800     FOR NUM = 1 TO INDEX - 1    'Begin loop for swapping pairs
5900       IF ITEM$(NUM)>ITEM$(NUM+1) THEN SWAP ITEM$(NUM),ITEM$(NUM+1): FLG = 0
6000     NEXT NUM
6100   WEND
6200 RETURN
6300 REM ***** Subroutine to display sorted list
6400   FOR NUM = 1 TO INDEX
6500     PRINT ITEM$(NUM),           'Trailing comma causes horizontal display
6600   NEXT NUM
6700   PRINT
6800   PRINT USING I3$;INDEX
6900 RETURN
Ok
SAVE"A:SORT1 ↵
Ok
RUN ↵
Enter name of dababase to be analyzed? A:ALFDAT1 ↵
Data Sorting Program
Generated on 03-01-1991 at 10:59:23 from database A:ALFDAT1

Annie          Carol          Kathy          Nessa
  4 items sorted and displayed
Ok
```

Line Numbers	***Comments on the Bubble Sort Subroutine***
5400	Begins the bubble sort subroutine.
5500	Sets a swap flag to 0. This flag is used to determine when the list is finally in order. When the computer passes through the entire list of names and has not done any more swaps, the list is sorted and the value of **FLG** will be 1. This causes the loop to be exited and then control is returned to the main program.
5600	Begins the swap loop. This loop is executed while the value of the swap flag, **FLG**, is 0 (i.e., until all swaps have been done).

Continued . . .

Line Numbers	Comments on the Bubble Sort Subroutine
5700	The swap flag, **FLG**, is set to 1. If this value is not changed by the **IF/THEN/ELSE** statement in line **5900**, the loop will be exited because the list is in the correct order.
5800	Begins the comparison loop. This loop is executed up to the last item on the list.
5900	The values of a pair of items are compared and, if the first item is greater than the second item, the items are exchanged by the **SWAP** statement (i.e., the first item becomes the second and the second item becomes the first). Also, if two items are swapped, the value of the swap flag, **FLG**, is set to 0 ensuring that the **WHILE** loop will be executed at least one more time. If no swaps have occurred, the value of the swap flag, **FLG**, remains 1 and the loop is exited when the **WHILE** statement at line **5600** is executed.

Let's use the above program, **SORT1**, to sort the entries on a data file called **ALFDAT2**. First, return to DOS and copy the data file to your *BASIC Data* diskette as shown below (or use **COPY CON** to create the data file):

```
SYSTEM ↵

C:\BA>TYPE ALFDAT2 ↵
Allen
Barb
STEVE
Sara
PROG1
PROG2
2.3
-2
100
-3
0
Zoo
ZOO
ann
Britt

C:\BA>COPY ALFDAT2 A:↵
        1 File(s) copied

C:\BA>_
```

After the file has been created, return to BASIC, load the program **SORT1**, and then run it.

```
LOAD"C:\BA\SORT1↵
Ok
RUN ↵
Enter name of dababase to be analyzed? A:ALFDAT2↵
Data Sorting Program
Generated on 03-01-1991 at 11:11:58 from database A:ALFDAT2

-2             -3             0              100            2.3
Allen          Barb           Britt          PROG1          PROG2
STEVE          Sara           ZOO            Zoo            ann

 15 items sorted and displayed
Ok
```

Examine the output carefully. The computer does not do the sorting as you might expect. In line 1 of the output, notice that the **-2** comes before the **-3**, but –2 is not less than –3. The problem is caused by the fact that the program stored the numbers –2 and –3 using the string variable **ITEM$()** (see line **5200**). Because a string variable was used, the computer treated the characters as strings rather than as numbers. Thus, the computer compared the first characters of **-2** and **-3** (i.e., the negative signs) and, because they were the same, the computer then compared the second characters (i.e., the **2** and the **3**). The **2** was *smaller* than the **3**, so the **-2** was placed before the **-3**. The same thing happens with the **0**, **100**, and **2.3**. They are in order according to their first characters: **0**, **1**, **2**.

The second line of output looks reasonable, but there is a problem in the third line. **STEVE** comes before **Sara** in the list, but this is not correct alphabetical order. Again, the computer saw the same first character (i.e., **S**) in **STEVE** and **Sara** and so compared the second characters (i.e., the **T** in **STEVE** and the **a** in **Sara**). This time the computer had to decide which was larger, an uppercase **T** or a lowercase **a**. It made the decision based on the ASCII codes of the characters. As you recall from the discussion on page B160, all characters that can be sent to an external device are assigned a unique number called an ASCII code. When BASIC compares two characters it simply compares their ASCII codes to tell which is the larger. The ASCII code for the uppercase letter **T** is 84 while the ASCII code for the lowercase letter **a** is 97. Hence, the letter **T** comes before the letter **a** when the computer sorts characters.

If all the characters from the keyboard were entered into a data file called **ALFDAT3** and then the sorting program was run, the following output would be displayed (the comma at the end of line **6500** was changed to a semicolon in order to save space on the output):

The semicolon compresses the output

```
LOAD"C:\BA\SORT1
Ok
LIST 6500
6500     PRINT ITEM$(NUM);          'Trailing comma causes horizontal display
RUN
Enter name of dababase to be analyzed? C:\BA\ALFDAT3
Data Sorting Program
Generated on 03-01-1991 at 11:20:51 from database C:\BA\ALFDAT

 !"#$%&'()*+,-./0123456789:;<=>?@ABCDEFGHIJKLMNOPQRSTUVWXYZ[\]^_'abcdefghijklmn
opqrstuvwxyz{|}~
 93 items sorted and displayed
Ok
```

Notice that the collating sequence is exactly the same as that used by dBASE. In general, you can expect data to be sorted as follows:

Blank space:	
Special characters:	**!"#$%&'()*+,-./**
Digits:	**0123456789**
Special characters:	**:;<=>?@**
Uppercase letters:	**ABCDEFGHIJKLMNOPQRSTUVWXYZ**
Special characters:	**[\]^_'**
Lowercase letters:	**abcdefghijklmnopqrstuvwxyz**
Special characters:	**{|}**

Variables with Two Subscripts: Consumer Survey

In the previous examples of arrays each variable had a single subscript. However, arrays may contain up to a maximum of 255 subscripts. In general, each subscript may be used to describe or keep track of a specific attribute of a given variable.

For example, suppose you made a survey of a number of nearby supermarkets in order to determine the prices of various items in the stores. A program that uses two dimensional arrays (i.e., variables with two subscripts) could be designed to keep track of the prices of the items sold in the stores and to determine which store has the best prices.

For this example, let's use the data given below (of course, in a real survey, there would be many more stores and many more items). The supermarkets are listed across the top of the chart, the items are listed along the left-hand side, and the prices of the items in the stores are in the body of the table.

	CUB Market	Country Store	Super Value
Corn	$ .39	$.43	$.41
Hamburger	$ .79	$.75	$.83
Cheese	$1.10	$1.20	$1.15
Milk	$1.40	$1.39	$1.35

Each price has two attributes: *Item name* and *Store name*. For example, to determine the price of cheese in any store, you need to locate the row that contains cheese (i.e., row 3). Similarly, to determine the price of any item in CUB Market, you would need to locate the column that contains CUB (i.e., column 1). To determine the price of cheese at CUB Market, you must locate the value at row 3 and column 1 (the price is $1.10).

A group of numbers arranged in a chart like this is sometimes called a *matrix*. Each number in the matrix is called an *element* and can be identified by giving its row number first and then its column number. In BASIC, variables with two subscripts can be used to store the values for the numbers in a matrix. For example, the variable that holds the price of cheese in CUB supermarket could be written as **PRICE(3,1)**. **PRICE** is the variable name, **3** is the row number, and **1** is the column number.

When using two dimensional subscripted variables, always give the row first and then the column (remember RC as in RC Cola). Note that this is just the opposite of plotting a point on a rectangular graph in algebra. There, coordinates of points are given as (X,Y) pairs where the X is the horizontal component (i.e., the column) and the Y is the vertical component (i.e., the row).

Let's examine a program that assigns a variable name to each piece of data in the chart and then computes the average price of milk in all the stores. If you are in the BASIC environment, return to DOS and copy the data file **FOOD2** to your *BASIC Data* diskette (or use **COPY CON** to create the data file):

```
SYSTEM ↵

C:\BA>TYPE FOOD2 ↵
CUB Market,Country Store,Super Value,1E15
Corn      , 39, 43, 41
Hamburger, 79, 75, 83
Cheese    ,110,120,115
Milk      ,140,139,135
C:\BA>COPY FOOD2 A: ↵
        1 File(s) copied

C:\BA>_
```

Notice how the data file has the same structure as the chart (store names are listed along the top and then each subsequent row contains an item name followed by the prices of the items). This arrangement helps keep the data straight as they are entered. The first row ends with a data flag, **1E15** so that the computer will know when the store names have ended and the item names and prices will begin. The remaining rows do not need data flags because they will each have one item name followed by the same number of prices as there are stores.

A pseudocode for the overall program is listed on the next page:

```
Begin processing
    Define images for PRINT USING
    Initialize counters
    Define external data file
    Define dimensions of arrays
    Display document header
    Input store names
    Input item names and prices
    Display input data in table form
    Calculate average price
    Display average price
End processing
```

Notice how the above pseudocode describes the overall flow of the program. Each line of the pseudocode will become a subroutine in the actual program. Some of those subroutines are quite simple (e.g., Define images for **PRINT USING**) while others will involve more complex processing (e.g., Display input data in table form). For example, the table to be displayed should look like the following:

	CUB Market	Country Store	Super Value
Corn	$ 0.39	$ 0.43	$ 0.41
Hamburger	$ 0.79	$ 0.75	$ 0.83
Cheese	$ 1.10	$ 1.20	$ 1.15
Milk	$ 1.40	$ 1.39	$ 1.35

A pseudocode to display the table is given on the next page. Before looking at it, try to develop one yourself. Think of how the computer will display the information and then try to think of the instructions it needs to accomplish that task. Remember, the **PRINT** statements display output from left to right and from top to bottom. Therefore:

- The store names must be displayed first,
- Then the first item name,
- Then the prices of that item,
- Then the second item name,
- Then the prices of that item.

and so on until all the item names and prices have been processed.

One version of the pseudocode is given below:

```
Begin processing of display of table
    Move cursor to column 15 in preparation for displaying store names
    For each store, do the following
        Display the store name
    Repeat for next store
    For each item, do the following
        Display the item name
        For each store, do the following
            Display the price for this item at this store
        Repeat for next store
    Repeat for next item
End processing of display of table
```

One version of the BASIC subroutine that follows this pseudocode is given below. Notice how closely it follows from the pseudocode:

```
7300 REM ***** Subroutine to display input data
7400   PRINT TAB(15);
7500     FOR ENTRY = 1 TO STORE.NUM
7600       PRINT USING "   \            \"; STORE$(ENTRY);
7700     NEXT ENTRY
7800   PRINT
7900     FOR ITEM = 1 TO ITEM.NUM
8000       PRINT ITEM$(ITEM);TAB(13);
8100         FOR STORE= 1 TO STORE.NUM
8200           PRINT USING "       $##.##    ";PRICE(ITEM,STORE)/100;
8300         NEXT STORE
8400       PRINT
8500     NEXT ITEM
8600   PRINT
8700 RETURN
```

The entire program used to analyze the data is listed on the next two pages. **LOAD** the program, **LIST** it, **SAVE** it to your *BASIC Data* diskette, and then **RUN** it as shown below:

```
LOAD"C:\BA\CONS4
Ok
LIST
1100 REM Displays price and name of supermarket items stored in database
1200 REM Douglas Robertson (373-4026), 1 Mar 91
1300 REM Define variables
1400   REM      DATE$ = Current date generated by computer
1500   REM   STORE$() = store names
1600   REM  STORE.NUM = number of stores input
1700   REM    ITEM$() = item names
1800   REM   ITEM.NUM = number of items input
1900   REM PRICE(ITEM.NUM,STORE.NUM) = price of item ITEM.NUM in store STORE.NUM
2000   REM   MILK.TOT = total of all prices of milk
2100 REM Begin processing
2200   GOSUB 3200                              'Define images for PRINT USING
2300   GOSUB 3600                              'Initialize counters
2400   GOSUB 4300                              'Define external data file
2500   GOSUB 4900                              'Define dimensions of arrays
2600   GOSUB 5200                              'Display document header
2700   GOSUB 5700                              'Input store names
2800   GOSUB 6400                              'Input item names & prices
2900   GOSUB 7300                              'Display input data
3000   GOSUB 8800                              'Calculate and display average price
3100 END
3200 REM ***** Subroutine to define images for PRINT USING
3300    I1$ = "Supermarket Item Survey"
3400    I2$ = "Generated on \        \ at \      \ from database \          \"
3500 RETURN
3600 REM ***** Subroutine to initialize counters
3700     STORE.ID = 0
3800      ITEM.ID = 0
3900     MILK.TOT = 0
4000   NUM.STORES = 0
4100    NUM.ITEMS = 0
4200 RETURN
4300 REM ***** Subroutine to define external data file
4400   REM In data file, store names are entered first, then 1E15 data flag,
4500   REM   then item1 name and prices, then item2 name and prices, etc.
4600     INPUT "Enter name of database to be analyzed"; DB$
4700     OPEN DB$ FOR INPUT AS #1
4800 RETURN
4900 REM ***** Subroutine to define dimensions of arrays
5000   DIM ITEM$(10), STORE$(5), PRICE(10,5)
5100 RETURN
5200 REM ***** Subroutine to display document header
5300   PRINT     I1$
5400   PRINT USING I2$;DATE$,TIME$,DB$
5500   PRINT
5600 RETURN
5700 REM ***** Subroutine to input store names
5800   WHILE STORE$(STORE.NUM) <> "1E15"
5900     STORE.NUM = STORE.NUM + 1           'Count number of store names input
6000     INPUT #1, STORE$(STORE.NUM)         'Assign store name to array
6100   WEND
6200   STORE.NUM = STORE.NUM - 1  'Don't count last entry (1E15) in # of stores
6300 RETURN
6400 REM ***** Subroutine to input item names & prices
6500   WHILE NOT EOF(1)                      'Loop to enter item names & prices
6600     ITEM.NUM = ITEM.NUM + 1             'Count number of items input
6700     INPUT #1, ITEM$(ITEM.NUM)           'Assign item name to array
6800       FOR STORE = 1 TO STORE.NUM        'Loop to enter prices
6900         INPUT #1, PRICE(ITEM.NUM,STORE)
7000       NEXT STORE
7100   WEND
7200 RETURN
```

Continued . . .

```
7300 REM ***** Subroutine to display input data
7400   PRINT TAB(15);
7500     FOR ENTRY = 1 TO STORE.NUM
7600       PRINT USING "   \            \"; STORE$(ENTRY);
7700     NEXT ENTRY
7800   PRINT
7900     FOR ITEM = 1 TO ITEM.NUM
8000       PRINT ITEM$(ITEM);TAB(13);
8100         FOR STORE= 1 TO STORE.NUM
8200           PRINT USING "       $##.##    ";PRICE(ITEM,STORE)/100;
8300         NEXT STORE
8400       PRINT
8500     NEXT ITEM
8600   PRINT
8700 RETURN
8800 REM ***** Subroutine to calculate average price of milk
8900   ITEM = 4
9000   TOTAL = 0
9100     FOR STORE = 1 TO STORE.NUM
9200       TOTAL = TOTAL + PRICE(ITEM,STORE)
9300     NEXT STORE
9400   PRINT "Average price of "ITEM$(ITEM) " is ";
9500   PRINT USING "$##.##";TOTAL/100/STORE.NUM
9600 RETURN
Ok
SAVE"A:CONS4←
Ok
RUN←
Enter name of dababase to be analyzed? A:FOOD2←
Supermarket Item Survey
Generated on 03-01-1991 at 11:26:55 from database A:FOOD2

                     CUB Market       Country Store    Super Value
Corn                   $ 0.39           $ 0.43           $ 0.41
Hamburger              $ 0.79           $ 0.75           $ 0.83
Cheese                 $ 1.10           $ 1.20           $ 1.15
Milk                   $ 1.40           $ 1.39           $ 1.35

Average price of Milk is $ 1.38
Ok
```

Line Numbers	Comments
1100 - 2000	**REM** statements describing the purpose of the program and defining the variables.
2100 - 3100	The main program. Notice that the main program is almost identical to the pseudocode and consists of calls to many subroutines. Breaking up the program into smaller sections like this allows the programmer to concentrate on the details of each section without having to worry about the details of the other sections. The more complicated the programs are, the more useful (and necessary) this technique becomes.
5700 - 6300	Subroutine to input the names of the stores. Carefully analyzing the structure of the data file is important because the program must follow that structure when it inputs the data. The first set of data contains the names of the stores, followed by a data flag, **1E15**, to mark the end of the store name list. The **WHILE** loop reads those names until the data flag is reached.

Continued . . .

Line Numbers	Comments
5900	Notice that the program could be run with any number of stores because line **5900** counts the store names as they are entered. This saves the user the trouble of doing this and makes the program more general.
6200	In the **WHILE/WEND** loop, the data flag **1E15** was counted as a store name and so to obtain the true number of stores 1 must be subtracted from the value of **STORE.NUM**.
6400 - 7200	Subroutine to assign the item names and prices to variables. Notice the nesting of the **FOR/NEXT** loop, which inputs the prices, inside the **WHILE/WEND** loop, which inputs the item names. In essence, the outer loop (**WHILE/WEND**) inputs the name of an item and then holds this name constant while the inner loop (**FOR/NEXT**) inputs all the prices for the item. This concept was discussed in detail on page B182 (nested loops), page B187 (compound interest program), page B188 (histogram program), and page B195 (car dealership program).
6600	Counts the number of items input.
6700	Inputs the name of the item.
6800-7000	Inputs the prices for the item at each store.
7100	Passes control back to the **WHILE** statement in line **6500** where the process is repeated until the end of the data file has been reached.
7300 - 8700	Subroutine to display the raw data in a chart. Displaying the raw data gives the user the opportunity to check the data to see if they are correct. Remember, you should always assume that there are errors in the data! It is usually a good idea to display all or some of the raw data so that a visual check can be made. If there are thousands of data items, you might want to display only a few items to see if they look reasonable (you could do this by adding a **STEP** to the **FOR** statements in lines **7900** and **8100**).

8800 - 9600	Subroutine to calculate and display the average price of milk (item 4) in the stores. To calculate and display the average price of a different item (e.g., corn) line **8900** would be changed to indicate that item number (e.g., for corn it would be **ITEM = 1**). To calculate and display the average price of all items in all stores, a **FOR/NEXT** loop could be used (e.g., **8900 FOR ITEM = 1 TO ITEM.NUM**). Similarly, to find the sum of the prices of all the items in each store (to see which store had the cheapest overall prices), the inner and outer loops could be exchanged. For example:
	`8900 FOR STORE = 1 TO STORE.NUM`
	`9100   FOR ITEM = 1 TO ITEM.NUM`
	You will have the opportunity to try this in homework Exercise 6.

This program is long and complicated and took many hours to develop. Study it carefully and use it as a model as you write increasingly complex (and useful) programs.

Arrays and Files: Inventory Updating

As a final example, let's examine a program designed to help a store manager with inventory control. The program keeps a record of which items are in stock and which items are sold, updates the inventory file automatically, and displays a reorder message when the inventory of a particular item is reduced to a predetermined level.

Three data files are needed by this program:

1. The file **ID1** contains the item descriptions. For this example, the store sells only three items, which are coded as follows:

Item code	Description
1	red shirt
2	blue shirt
3	yellow shirt

If you are in the BASIC environment, return to DOS and then copy the file to your *BASIC Data* diskette:

```
C:\BA>TYPE ID1↵
Item names and codes last updated on 02-28-1991 at  8:04:31
 1,Red shirts
 2,Blue shirts
 3,Yellow shirts
C:\BA>COPY ID1 A:↵
        1 File(s) copied

C:\BA>
```

The first line contains the date and time when the file was last updated. The remaining lines contain the item codes, a comma to serve as a delimiter, and then the item descriptions.

2. The file **INV1** contains information on the quantity of each item currently in stock. Copy the file to your *BASIC Data* diskette:

```
C:\BA>TYPE INV1↵
Inventory last updated on 02-28-1991 at 10:05:11
 1   6
 2  55
 3  11
C:\BA>COPY INV1 A:↵
        1 File(s) copied

C:\BA>_
```

The first line contains the date and time when the file was last updated. The remaining lines contain the actual inventory. Each record (line) contains up to six characters. The first two characters contain the item code **1** or **2** or **3**, then there is a space, and the last three characters represent the number of that type of item left in stock. For example, the code **1   6** represents a red shirt (the first two characters are a space and a 1, which stands for red shirt) of which there are 6 currently in stock. Thus, the above data file indicates that there are 6 red shirts, 55 blue shirts, and 11 yellow shirts.

3. The file **SOLD1** contains information on the quantity and price of each item sold. Copy the file to your *BASIC Data* diskette:

```
C:\BA>TYPE SOLD1↵
Sales last updated on 02-28-1991 at 11:04:31
11599
12321
31011
20999
31566
22324
23224
22244
21552
21244
21112
21001
21311
21211
21244
21626
31323
30988
21323
21332
21233
21542
C:\BA>COPY SOLD1 A:↵
        1 File(s) copied

C:\BA>_
```

The first line contains the date and time when the file was last updated. The remaining lines contain the actual sales data. Each record (line) contains five digits. The first digit represents the item code and the last four digits represent the price of the shirt in cents. For example, **11599** represents a red shirt (the first digit is a **1**, which represents a red shirt) that was sold for $15.99 (the last four digits are **1599**).

Now, let's examine the program that will analyze the above data files. A pseudocode for the overall program is listed on the next page:

```
Begin processing
    Define images for PRINT USING
    Define array dimensions
    Initialize counters
    Define external data files
    Input last modification date/time of each data file
    Display document header
    Input ID numbers and item descriptions for each item in the file ID1
    Input ID numbers and number in inventory for each item in file INV1
    Input ID numbers and prices of items sold from file SOLD1
    For each item, update counters for number sold and money taken in
    For each item, update inventory counters
    Display data in table
    Display document footer
    For each item, check to see if number in stock is <5
        If so, display a warning message and sound beep
        If not, continue processing
    Ask if new inventory file should be created
        If yes:   Ask for name for new file
                      Define new file
                      Write date and time of update to new file
                      For each item, write new inventory numbers to new file
                      Display message stating that new file was created
        If no:    Display message that inventory was not updated
End processing
```

As with the previous example, most of the lines in the pseudocode will correspond to separate subroutines. Each of those subroutines will contain a number of processes. For example, a more detailed pseudocode can be written for the following two lines:

```
Input ID numbers and prices of items sold from file SOLD1
For each item, update counters for number sold and money taken in
```

These two processes can be combined as shown on the next page:

```
Begin processing for entering ID numbers and prices and updating counters
    While there is still more data in the file SOLD1, do the following
        Input a record
        Define the first character in the record as the item code
        Define the last four characters in the record as the price
        Increment the number counter for this item
        Increment the price counter for this item
    Repeat for next record
End processing for entering ID numbers and prices and updating counters
```

One version of the BASIC subroutine that follows this pseudocode is given below. Notice how closely it follows the pseudocode:

```
12000 REM ***** Subroutine to input ID# & price from sales file & update counter
12100   WHILE NOT EOF(2)
12200     INPUT #2, SALE$                        'item code and price
12300     ID = VAL(MID$(SALE$,1,1))              'item code
12400     PRICE = VAL(MID$(SALE$,2,4))           'price of item ID
12500     NUM.SOLD(ID) = NUM.SOLD(ID) + 1        'counts # of item ID sold
12600     MONEY(ID) = MONEY(ID) + PRICE/100      'sums money from item ID
12700   WEND
12800 RETURN
```

The complete BASIC program is given below and on the following three pages. **LOAD** the program, **LIST** it, **SAVE** it to your *BASIC Data* diskette, and then **RUN** it.

```
LOAD"C:\BA\UPDATE7
Ok
LIST
1100 REM Displays inventory and sales data and updates inventory file
1200 REM Douglas Robertson (373-4026), 1 Mar 91
1300 REM Define variables
1400   REM           DATE$ = Current date generated by computer
1500   REM           TIME$ = Current time generated by computer
1600   REM      INVENFILE$ = Name of inventory input data file
1700   REM      SALESFILE$ = Name of sales input data file
1800   REM      ITEMSFILE$ = Name of item names input data file
1900   REM INVEN.UPDATE$ = Date and time of last update of Inventory file
2000   REM SALES.UPDATE$ = Date and time of last update of Sales file
2100   REM ITEMS.UPDATE$ = Date and time of last update of Items file
2200   REM              ID = Item identification number (stock number)
2300   REM         OLDINV$ = Record from Inventory file (ID & # in stock)
2400   REM           SALE$ = Record read from Sales file (ID & price)
2500   REM    NUM.SOLD(ID) = Number of items sold with stock number (ID)
2600   REM       MONEY(ID) = Money received for items with stock number (ID)
2700   REM    OLDSTOCK(ID) = Number of items with #ID before sales
2800   REM    NEWSTOCK(ID) = Number of items with #ID after sales
2900   REM        ITEM$(ID) = Name of item with stock number (ID)
3000   REM        TOT.SOLD = Total number of all items sold
3100   REM             MAX = Maximum ID number
3200   REM         TOT.NEW = Total number of all items left in stock
3300   REM         TOT.OLD = Total number of all items previously in stock
```

Continued . . .

```
3400 REM Begin processing
3500   GOSUB 5100                          'Define images for PRINT USING
3600   GOSUB 6700                          'Define array dimensions
3700   GOSUB 7000                          'Initialize counters
3800   GOSUB 8000                          'Define external data files
3900   GOSUB 8800                          'Input last modification date/time
4000   GOSUB 9300                          'Display document header
4100   GOSUB 10700                         'Enter ID# & names from data file
4200   GOSUB 11300                         'Input ID# & # in stock from inven
4300   GOSUB 12000                         'Input ID# & price from sales file
4400                                       '  and update counters
4500   GOSUB 12900                         'Update counters and display table
4600   GOSUB 13900                         'Display document footer
4700   GOSUB 14400                         'Check to see if # in stock is < 5
4800   GOSUB 14900                         'Ask if new inven file to be created
4900   IF A$ = "YES" THEN GOSUB 15700 ELSE GOSUB 16800
5000 END
5100 REM ***** Subroutine to define images for PRINT USING
5200     IM1$ = "White Bear Shirt Shoppe Inventory Report"
5300     IM2$ = "Report Generated on \         \ at \      \"
5400     IM3$ = "Inventory file [\      \] updated on \        \"
5500     IM4$ = "    Sales file [\      \] updated on \        \"
5600     IM5$ = "     Item file [\      \] updated on \        \"
5700     IM6$ = "Item               Previous    Number    Dollars     Current"
5800     IM7$ = "Description          Stock      Sold      Earned      Stock"
5900     IM8$ = "------------       --------    ------    -------    -------"
6000     IM9$ = "\            \       ####      ####    $####.##      ####"
6100    IM10$ = "Totals:              ####      ####    $####.##      ####"
6200    IM11$ = "Inventory last updated on \        \ at \      \"
6300    IM12$ = "Reorder \                \, # left in stock"
6400    IM13$ = "File [\      \] saved on \        \ at \      \"
6500    IM14$ = "Inventory file has not been updated."
6600 RETURN
6700 REM ***** Subroutine to define array dimensions
6800   DIM NUM.SOLD(99), MONEY(99), OLDSTOCK(99), NEWSTOCK(99), ITEM$(99)
6900 RETURN
7000 REM ***** Subroutine to initialize counters
7100   MAX = 5
7200   FOR ID = 1 TO MAX
7300     NUM.SOLD(ID)   = 0
7400     MONEY(ID)      = 0
7500     OLDSTOCK(ID)   = 0
7600     NEWSTOCK(ID)   = 0
7700     ITEM$(ID)      = "N/A"
7800   NEXT ID
7900 RETURN
8000 REM ***** Subroutine to define external data files
8100   INPUT "Enter the name of the inventory data file:"; INVENFILE$
8200   INPUT "    Enter the name of the sales data file:"; SALESFILE$
8300   INPUT "Enter the name of the item name data file:"; ITEMSFILE$
8400   OPEN INVENFILE$ FOR INPUT AS #1       'Inventory file
8500   OPEN SALESFILE$ FOR INPUT AS #2       'Sales records file
8600   OPEN ITEMSFILE$ FOR INPUT AS #3       'Item ID and names file
8700 RETURN
8800 REM ***** Subroutine to input last modification of date and time
8900   INPUT #1, INVEN.UPDATE$
9000   INPUT #2, SALES.UPDATE$
9100   INPUT #3, ITEMS.UPDATE$
9200 RETURN
```

Continued . . .

```
9300 REM ***** Subroutine to display document header
9400   CLS
9500   PRINT
9600   PRINT IM1$
9700   PRINT USING IM2$;DATE$,TIME$
9800   PRINT
9900   PRINT USING IM3$; INVENFILE$,RIGHT$(INVEN.UPDATE$,22)
10000   PRINT USING IM4$; SALESFILE$,RIGHT$(SALES.UPDATE$,22)
10100   PRINT USING IM5$; ITEMSFILE$,RIGHT$(ITEMS.UPDATE$,22)
10200   PRINT
10300   PRINT IM6$
10400   PRINT IM7$
10500   PRINT IM8$
10600 RETURN
10700 REM ***** Subroutine to enter ID numbers and item names from data file
10800   WHILE NOT EOF(3)
10900     INPUT #3, ID, ITEM$(ID)
11000   WEND
11100   CLOSE #3
11200 RETURN
11300 REM ***** Subroutine to input ID# and number in stock from inventory file
11400   WHILE NOT EOF(1)
11500     INPUT #1, OLDINV$                        'item code and # in stock
11600     ID = VAL(MID$(OLDINV$,1,2))              'item code
11700     OLDSTOCK(ID) = VAL(MID$(OLDINV$,3,4))'number of item ID in stock
11800   WEND
11900 RETURN
12000 REM ***** Subroutine to input ID# & price from sales file & update counter
12100   WHILE NOT EOF(2)
12200     INPUT #2, SALE$                          'item code and price
12300     ID = VAL(MID$(SALE$,1,1))                'item code
12400     PRICE = VAL(MID$(SALE$,2,4))             'price of item ID
12500     NUM.SOLD(ID) = NUM.SOLD(ID) + 1          'counts # of item ID sold
12600     MONEY(ID) = MONEY(ID) + PRICE/100        'sums money from item ID
12700   WEND
12800 RETURN
12900 REM ***** Subroutine to update counters and display information in chart
13000   FOR ID = 1 TO MAX
13100     NEWSTOCK(ID) = OLDSTOCK(ID) - NUM.SOLD(ID)
13200     IF ITEM$(ID) <> "N/A" THEN PRINT USING IM9$; ITEM$(ID), OLDSTOCK(ID),
                                  NUM.SOLD(ID),MONEY(ID), NEWSTOCK(ID)
13300     TOT.SOLD  = TOT.SOLD  + NUM.SOLD(ID) 'total # of items sold (all IDs)
13400     TOT.MONEY = TOT.MONEY + MONEY(ID)    'total of all revenue taken in
13500     TOT.NEW   = TOT.NEW   + NEWSTOCK(ID) 'total # of items left in stock
13600     TOT.OLD   = TOT.OLD   + OLDSTOCK(ID) 'tot # items previously in stock
13700   NEXT ID
13800 RETURN
13900 REM ***** Subroutine to display document footer
14000   PRINT IM8$
14100   PRINT USING IM10$; TOT.OLD,TOT.SOLD,TOT.MONEY,TOT.NEW
14200   PRINT
14300 RETURN
```

Continued . . .

```
14400 REM ***** Subroutine to check to see if number in stock is under 5
14500   FOR ID = 1 TO MAX
14600     IF NEWSTOCK(ID) < 5 AND ITEM$(ID) <> "N/A"
            THEN PRINT USING IM12$; ITEM$(ID),NEWSTOCK(ID) : BEEP
14700   NEXT ID
14800 RETURN
14900 REM ***** Subroutine to ask user if new inventory file is to be created
15000   PRINT
15100   INPUT "Should new Inventory file be created";A$
15200     WHILE A$ <> "YES" AND A$ <> "yes" AND A$ <> "NO" AND A$ <> "no"
15300       PRINT "Please answer either YES or NO"
15400       INPUT "Should new Inventory file be created";A$
15500     WEND
15600 RETURN
15700 REM ***** Subroutine to create new inventory file
15800   INPUT "Enter name for new inventory file"; NEWINV$
15900   OPEN NEWINV$ FOR OUTPUT AS #3
16000   PRINT #3,USING IM11$;DATE$,TIME$
16100     FOR ID = 1 TO MAX
16200       IF ITEM$(ID) <> "N/A" THEN PRINT #3,USING "## ###";ID,NEWSTOCK(ID)
16300     NEXT ID
16400   CLOSE 1,2,3
16500   PRINT USING IM13$; NEWINV$,DATE$,TIME$
16600   END
16700 RETURN
16800 REM ***** Subroutine to end program without updating inventory file
16900   PRINT IM14$
17000   END
17100 RETURN
Ok
SAVE"A:UPDATE7↵
Ok
RUN↵
Enter the name of the inventory data file:? A:INV1↵
    Enter the name of the sales data file:? A:SOLD1↵
Enter the name of the item name data file:? A:ID1↵
```

At this point, the screen is cleared

```
White Bear Shirt Shoppe Inventory Report
Report Generated on 03-01-1991 at 16:28:37

Inventory file [A:INV1  ] updated on 02-28-1991
    Sales file [A:SOLD1 ] updated on 02-28-1991
     Item file [A:ID1   ] updated on 02-28-1991

Item            Previous    Number    Dollars    Current
Description      Stock       Sold      Earned     Stock
-------------   ---------   ------    -------    -------
Red shirts           6          2     $  39.20       4
Blue shirts         55         16     $ 245.22      39
Yellow shirt        11          4     $  48.88       7
-------------   ---------   ------    -------    -------
Totals:             72         22     $ 333.30      50

Reorder Red shirts      , 4 left in stock

Should new Inventory file be created? YES
Enter name for new inventory file? A:INV2
File [A:INV2  ] saved on 03-01-1991 at 16:30:02
Ok
SYSTEM                                          <-- Returns to DOS


C:\BA>TYPE A:INV2                               <-- Lists contents of new inventory file
Inventory last updated on 03-01-1991 at 16:30:01
 1   4
 2  39
 3   7

C:\BA>_
```

Line Numbers	Comments
6700–6900	The dimensions of the arrays are set to 99.
7100	The maximum number of different types of items the program will analyze is set to 5 for this simple example. This number can be anything up to the value in the dimension (99), but it cannot exceed that value.
7200–7800	The initial values of the arrays are set. Note that **ITEM$()** is set to **N/A**, which stands for **N**ot **A**vailable, for each element of the array. This will serve as a flag to signal the program to do the computations only for those ID numbers that have associated items (see lines **13200**, **14600**, and **16200**).
11300–11900	Enters the ID numbers and quantity left in stock of each item.
11600	Defines the ID number of the item just input. Notice that since the item ID numbers and quantity left it stock are set up using data fields rather than separated by commas, **MID$** is used to break apart the two pieces of information. Also, the different parts will be used as numbers and, therefore, **VAL** is used to inform the computer that the characters of the string are really numbers and that they will be used as numbers later in the program.
11700	Defines the number of items in stock in the same way as the ID numbers were defined.

Continued . . .

Line Numbers	Comments
12000–12800	Enters the ID numbers and the prices from the sales file and updates the counters. Because the information on the sales file is coded in much the same way as that from the inventory file, the loop is similar in structure to the previous loop. **MID$** and **VAL** are used in the same way also.
12900–13800	Displays the information in the chart and updates the counters. Note that line **13200** only displays the information for items that actually exist (i.e., if the value of **ITEM$()** is **N/A**, the **PRINT** statement is not executed).
14900–15600	Asks the user if a new inventory file should be created. The user is asked for the name of the new inventory file because it may be desirable to create a new file and leave the old inventory file intact. For example, the sales file may have errors that were not detected when the program was run. If the inventory file was replaced by an incorrect updated version, it would be difficult or impossible to recover the old file and run the program again with the correct data. Also, copies of old inventory files may provide important information on how the inventory has changed over time.
15700–16700	Creates the new inventory file. Notice how the information is copied to (written on) the new file using the same structure as the old inventory file.

The above program illustrates the use of more than one file at a time and one way of updating files. This program is long and complex but shows many important programming techniques. Be sure to study it carefully. You may be able to use the same type of structure in programs you write in the future.

TO TAKE A BREAK Type **SYSTEM** ↵; Remove diskette(s). To resume (hard disk): Insert *Data* diskette, type **A:** ↵, **C:\BA\BASICA** ↵. To resume (two drive): Insert diskettes, type **A:** ↵, **B:\BASICA** ↵.

Homework Exercises

For each of the following homework exercises, use the programming process to develop a BASIC program that will produce the output described. Each program should contain enough **REM** statements to clearly document the program. Unless instructed to do otherwise, produce a hard copy of a **LIST** and a **RUN** of each of your final working programs. Also, save each program using a name such as **HWB8-01** for future reference. Your instructor may also ask you to hand in other materials related to the development of the programs such as the variable definitions, pseudocodes, etc.

---

① Max owns a lawn service company and wants to survey his customers with regards to their satisfaction with his operation. He has mailed out the following questionnaire:

```
Max's Lawn Service Customer Satisfaction Survey

Please answer each of the following questions by circling the
   response that best describes how you feel today about our
   lawn service.

1. Employees are courteous:
   a) Strongly disagree  b) Disagree  c) No opinion  d)  Agree
   e) Strongly agree

2. Service is completed on time:
   a) Strongly disagree  b) Disagree  c) No opinion  d)  Agree
   e) Strongly agree

3. Service is of high quality:
   a) Strongly disagree  b) Disagree  c) No opinion  d)  Agree
   e) Strongly agree

4. Materials used (fertilizer and seeds) are of high quality:
   a) Strongly disagree  b) Disagree  c) No opinion  d)  Agree
   e) Strongly agree

5. Prices are reasonable:
   a) Strongly disagree  b) Disagree  c) No opinion  d)  Agree
   e) Strongly agree
```

Use the programming process to develop a program that employs subscripted variables to analyze the responses to the questionnaire and displays the questions, the number of each response for each question, and a weighted average response for each question. To compute the average response, count an **a** as **1**, **b** as **2**, **c** as **3**, **d** as **4**, and **e** as **5**. The average will be:

$$\frac{(\#\ \mathbf{a}\text{'s})*1 + (\#\ \mathbf{b}\text{'s})*2 + (\#\ \mathbf{c}\text{'s})*3 + (\#\ \mathbf{d}\text{'s})*4 + (\#\ \mathbf{e}\text{'s})*5}{\text{total \# of responses for this question}}$$

CHAPTER EIGHT

Enter the following raw data into a data file called **HWB8-01.DTA**. The first line indicates what the survey is about and the date the data were recorded. The next five lines provide a brief outline of the questions. These can be input directly into the program and used in the output (this would enable you to use the same program with a different set of questions by simply changing the data file). The seventh line indicates the possible responses. Beginning with line eight, each line represents a record (i.e., responses from a single questionnaire) and each column corresponds to a particular question (i.e., column 1 contains the responses to question 1, column 2 is for question 2, and so on).

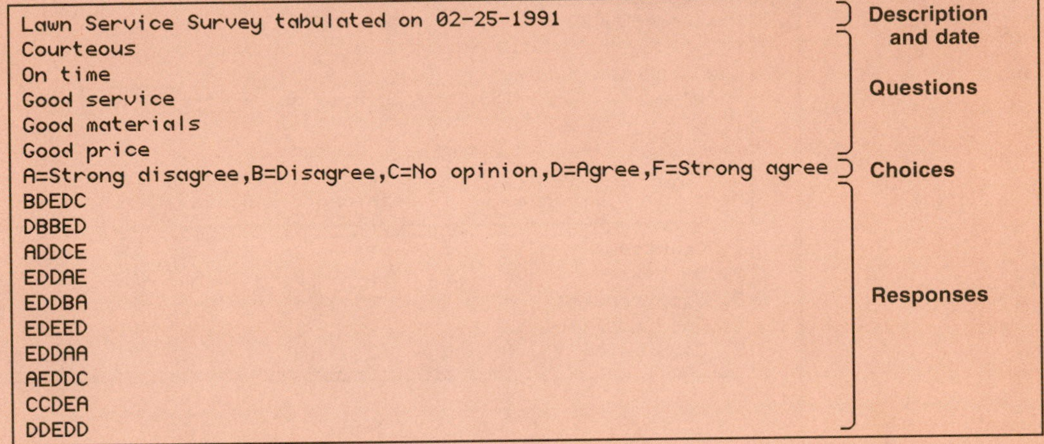

```
Lawn Service Survey tabulated on 02-25-1991                               } Description
                                                                            and date
Courteous
On time
Good service                                                              } Questions
Good materials
Good price
A=Strong disagree,B=Disagree,C=No opinion,D=Agree,F=Strong agree          } Choices
BDEDC
DBBED
ADDCE
EDDAE
EDDBA                                                                     } Responses
EDEED
EDDAA
AEDDC
CCDEA
DDEDD
```

Using the above raw data, the output from your program should look like the following (the values in the boxes should be calculated by the computer):

```
Homework B8-01                    Joe Computer                    1 Mar 91

Lawn Service Survey
Recorded on 02-25-1991 and printed on 03-01-1991 at 09:10

                          Disagree       Agree
                 Strongly     |     No      |  Strongly
No               Disagree     |  Opinion    |   Agree    Num    Ave
-- ----------------+----+------+------+-----+-------++---+++-
1. Courteous        2     1      1      2     4       10    3.5
2. On time          0     1      1      7     1       10    3.8
3. Good service     0     1      0      6     3       10    4.1
4. Good material    2     1      1      3     3       10    3.4
5. Good price       3     0      2      3     2       10    3.1
```

② Modify the program you developed for Exercise 1 by checking for incorrect data. If a response is not a 1 or 2 or 3 or 4 or 5 then it should be counted as a *no-response* and its value should not be included in the number of responses nor in the weighted average. Also, if the number of no-responses is greater than 10% of the total number of responses, print two **@@** symbols on the same line as the question. This will alert someone reading the summary that there is possibly a problem with those questions (the responses may not be representative of the true feelings of the customers or the questions may be confusing or unanswerable).

Continued . . .

To show that the program is able to detect errors, add the following two lines to the data file from Exercise 1:

```
QDDXA
8EDDC
```

The output from your program should look like the following (the values in the boxes should be calculated by the computer):

```
Homework B8-02                    Joe Computer                    1 Mar 91

Lawn Service Survey
Recorded on 02-25-1991 and printed on 03-01-1991 at 15:06

                   Disagree       Agree
            Strongly    |    No     |  Strongly               No
No          Disagree    |  Opinion  |   Agree   Num    Ave   Resp
-- ---------------+----+-----+-----+-----+------++---+++----+-
1. Courteous       2    1     1     2     4      10    3.5    2  ee
2. On time         0    1     1     8     2      12    3.9    0
3. Good service    0    1     0     8     3      12    4.1    0
4. Good material   2    1     1     4     3      11    3.5    1
5. Good price      4    0     3     3     2      12    2.9    0
```

---

③ On pages L61–66 and pages L101–108 we developed a Lotus 1-2-3 worksheet that kept track of student grades for a particular class. For this exercise, use the programming process to develop a BASIC program that will do the same task. Use the same data and grade calculations as in the Lotus 1-2-3 example:

- Drop the lowest quiz score from the quiz average (i.e., determine the lowest quiz score for a student and do not count this score in the quiz average for that student). For a hint on finding the smallest number on a list, see page B125.
- Calculate the total points using the following formula:

  Total = .20*Quiz average + .15*Homework + .30*Midterm + .35*Final exam

- Determine the letter grade for each student using the following grading curve (see p. L103 for a hint on the decision logic):

Total points	Letter grade
90–100	A
80–89	B
70–79	C
65–69	D
00–64	F

The program should read the data from a data file and employ subscripted variables. The output from your program should look like the following (the values in the boxes should be calculated by the computer):

CHAPTER EIGHT

```
Homework B8-03                     Joe Computer                       1 Mar 91

    Course: GC 1571 Introduction to Microcomputer Applications
Instructor: Professor Moothedan
      Term: Fall, 1991

Student    Qu 1  Qu 2  Qu 3  Qu 4  Q Av   HW    Mt   Fin   Tot   Gra
-------    ----  ----  ----  ----  ----  ----  ----  ----  ----  ----
Matt        89    95    90    80    91   100   100    95    97    A
Lindsay     76    98    83    85    89    90    80    75    81    B
Angela      83    85    78    80    83    90    90    80    85    B
Ian         70    80    75    80    78    95    98    80    87    B
Britt       95    90    90    85    92    95    90    90    91    A

Average     83    90    83    82    87    94    92    84    88
Std Dev      9     7     6     2     5     4     7     7     5
Number       5     5     5     5     5     5     5     5     5
```

---

④ Modify the bubble sort program (see p. B249) so that it is interactive. It should allow the user to specify the name of the file to be sorted, which columns the sort should be based on (use the **MID$** function), whether the sort should be in ascending or descending order, and whether the sort should be alphabetical or numerical (use the **VAL** function).

As the data for the program, use the file **HWW3-02T**, which you created in Part I, Chapter 3. That file looked like the following:

```
Column 1           Column 20      Column 35 Column 45
↓                  ↓              ↓         ↓
Bliss Bill,        NSP,           555-2311, 15221.00
Wheeler Katie,     Land O'Lakes,  555-2213, 25111.00
Moony Hal,         Geosyncronics, 555-0054, 15455.00
Bast Peg,          UNISYS,        555-6672, 12110.00
```

Run the program so that the data are sorted by last name (columns 1 through 19) in descending order. In that case, the output should look like the following:

```
Homework B8-04                     Joe Computer                       1 Mar 91

Data Sorting Program
Generated on 03-01-1991 at 17:48:01 from database

                  Enter the name of the file to be sorted? A:CONTACTS↵
              Enter the column number where sort is to begin? 1↵
              Enter number of columns to be used as sort key? 19↵
Sort in ascending (enter 1) or descending (enter 2) order? 2↵
   Are data numerical (enter 1) or alphabetical (enter 2)? 2↵

Wheeler Katie,     Land O'Lakes   555-2213, 25111.00
Moony Hal,         Geosyncronics, 555-0054, 15455.00
Bliss Bill,        NSP,           555-2311, 15221.00
Bast Peg,          UNISYS,        555-6672, 12110.00

  4 items sorted and displayed
```

Continued . . .

CHAPTER EIGHT

Run the program again but sort the items in ascending order by total sales (columns 45–52):

```
Homework B8-04                    Joe Computer                      1 Mar 91

Data Sorting Program
Generated on 03-01-1991 at 17:49:22 from database

                 Enter the name of the file to be sorted? A:CONTACTS←
             Enter the column number where sort is to begin? 45←
             Enter number of columns to be used as sort key? 8←
Sort in ascending (enter 1) or descending (enter 2) order? 1←
   Are data numerical (enter 1) or alphabetical (enter 2)? 1←

Bast Peg,           UNISYS,           555-6672, 12110.00
Bliss Bill,         NSP,              555-2311, 15221.00
Moony Hal,          Geosyncronics,    555-0054, 15455.00
Wheeler Katie,      Land O'Lakes      555-2213, 25111.00

  4 items sorted and displayed
```

---

⑤ Modify the student records office program of Exercise 7 in Chapter 7 so that the names are listed in reverse alphabetical order within each category. Hint: Use the bubble sort in a subroutine to arrange the database in reverse alphabetical order before it is processed by the program.

---

⑥ Modify the consumer survey program presented in this chapter to do the following:

a. Display the chart (the program already does that).

b. Calculate and display the average price of each item.

c. Calculate and display the total cost of the items in each store.

d. Rank the stores in ascending order on the basis of total cost of all items in each store. It may be easiest to write the store names and total costs onto a temporary external data file and then use the bubble sort to arrange the records on this file in ascending order by the value of the total cost in each store.

Use the raw data given in the example to make the output from your program look like the following (the values in the boxes should be calculated by the computer):

Homework B8-05 Joe Computer 1 Mar 91

Supermarket Item Survey
Generated on 03-01-1991 at 14:08:03 from database FOOD2 ↵

	CUB Market	Country Store	Super Value
Corn	$ 0.39	$ 0.43	$ 0.41
Hamburger	$ 0.79	$ 0.75	$ 0.83
Cheese	$ 1.10	$ 1.20	$ 1.15
Milk	$ 1.40	$ 1.39	$ 1.35

Item Name	Average Price
Corn	$ .41
Hamburger	$ .79
Cheese	$1.15
Milk	$1.38

Store Name	Total Cost
CUB Market	$3.68
Country Store	$3.77
Super Value	$3.74

Store Ranking, Lowest to Highest Total Cost

Store Name	Total Cost
CUB Market	$3.68
Super Value	$3.74
Country Store	$3.77

APPENDIX: Summary of Selected BASIC Features

The following is a brief description of many BASIC commands, statements, and functions with reference to pages in the text. Items with N/C in place of a page number were not specifically covered in the text but are provided for your information. Consult the *BASIC Reference Manual* for more details.

In the summary that follows, items enclosed in brackets **[ ]** are optional, **ln** stands for **l**ine **n**umber, and **filespec** stands for **file spec**ification (i.e., the directory, name, and extension of a file).

Quick Review

Page	Commands	Description
B7	**BASICA** ↵	Access BASIC from the DOS environment.
B53	**NEW** ↵	Clear the screen without saving the current program.
B50	**DELETE X-Y** ↵	Delete a range of statements (specify the line numbers **X** through **Y**).
B49	**LIST X-Y** ↵	Display a range of statements (specify the line numbers **X** through **Y**).
B53	**SYSTEM** ↵	Exit BASIC without saving current program and return to DOS.
B10	**LLIST** ↵	Print a complete listing of program.
B50	**LOAD"filespec** ↵	Retrieve the BASIC program called **filespec**.
B10	**SAVE"filespec** ↵	Save the BASIC program called **filespec**.
B30	**ln LPRINT...**	A BASIC statement which sends the program output to the printer instead of the screen (use **PRINT** to display output on the screen).

Cursor Control and Editing

Page	Keystrokes	Description
B15	↵	Complete editing a statement and accept the changes made to the current line.
B16	↑	Move the cursor one line **up**.

Continued . . .

Page	Keystrokes	Description
B16	⬇	Move the cursor one line **down**.
B16	⬅	Move the cursor one character **left**.
B16	➡	Move the cursor one character **right**.
B18	**[Ctrl ➡]**	Move the cursor to the next word on the **right**.
B18	**[Ctrl ⬅]**	Move the cursor to the next word on the **left**.
B18	**[End]**	Move the cursor to the last character of the line.
B18	**[Home]**	Move the cursor to the upper-left corner of the screen.
B18	**[Ctrl-Home]**	Move the cursor to the upper-left corner of the screen and clear the screen.
N/C	**[Ctrl-Enter]**	Move the cursor to the beginning of the next screen line (this is not the same as **[Enter]** because it does not signal the end of the statement line).
N/C	**[Tab]**	Move the cursor one tab stop to the right. Tab stops are automatically set every eight columns.
B18	**[Backspace]**	Delete one character to the left of the cursor.
B18	**[Delete]**	Delete one character at the cursor.
B18	**[Ctrl-End]**	Delete all characters to the end of the current line.
B18	**[Esc]**	Delete all characters on the line containing the cursor.
B10	**[Ctrl-PrintScreen]**	Toggle between only displaying characters on the screen and sending characters to the printer as well as displaying them on the screen.
B18	**[Insert]**	Toggle between insert and typeover modes.
N/C	**[Ctrl-C]**	Cancel changes made to the current line or exit auto line numbering mode.

Summary of Selected Commands

Page		Command/Comment
B45	Command:	**`AUTO`** Display line numbers each time **[Enter]** is pressed. Press **[Ctrl-C]** to exit Auto mode.
	Form:	**`AUTO [first line number][,increment]`**
	Example:	**`AUTO 1100,100`** Display line number **`1100`**, then **`1200`**, then **`1300`**, etc.
N/C	Command:	**`CHDIR`** Change the default directory.
	Form:	**`CHDIR "pathname"`**
	Example:	**`CHDIR "A:\"`** Change the default directory to the root directory of the diskette in drive A:.

Continued . . .

Page		Command/Comment
B10	Command:	**CLS** Clear (blank) the screen and return the cursor to the upper-left corner. Has the same effect as pressing **[Ctrl-HOME]**.
	Form:	**CLS**
	Example:	**CLS**
B21	Command:	**CONT** Continue program execution after a break (from **STOP**, **END**, or **[Ctrl-Break]**).
	Form:	**CONT**
	Example:	**CONT**
B50	Command:	**DELETE** Delete specified lines of the program. If no line numbers are specified, the entire program is deleted.
	Form:	**DELETE [line#1][-line#2]**
	Example:	**DELETE 600-900** Delete all program lines from **600** through **900**.
N/C	Command:	**EDIT** Display for editing the line whose number is specified.
	Form:	**EDIT ln**
	Example:	**EDIT 1100** Display line **1100** for editing.
B52	Command:	**FILES** Display a listing of files in a specified directory (similar to the **DIR** command in DOS)
	Form:	**FILES ["filespec]**
	Example:	**FILES "A:*.BAS"** Display the names of all files on the diskette in A: drive that contain the extension **.BAS**.
B53	Command:	**KILL** Erase specified files from the disk (similar to the **DEL** command in DOS).
	Form:	**KILL "filespec**
	Example:	**KILL "A:F1.BAS** Erase file **F1.BAS** from the diskette in drive A:.
B49	Command:	**LIST** Display specified program statements on the screen. If no line numbers are specified, entire program is listed.
	Form:	**LIST [line #1] [-line #2]**
	Example:	**LIST 10-30** Display all statements from line **10** through line **30**.
B10	Command:	**LLIST** Print specified program statements on the printer.
	Form:	**LLIST [line #1] [-line #2]**
	Example:	**LLIST 10-30** Print all statements from line **10** through line **30**.
B50	Command:	**LOAD** Load a program stored on a disk into RAM memory.
	Form:	**LOAD "filespec**
	Example:	**LOAD "A:F1.BAS"** Load program **F1.BAS** from the diskette in drive A: into memory.

Continued . . .

Page		Command/Comment
N/C	Command:	**MERGE** Merge lines of a program, which was saved in ASCII format, into the current program.
	Form:	**MERGE "filespec**
	Example:	**MERGE "A:F1"** Merge the file **F1** with the current file. Note that **F1** must have been saved in an ASCII format (e.g., saved using **SAVE "A:F1",A**).
N/C	Command:	**NAME** Change the name of a file (similar to the **RENAME** command in DOS).
	Form:	**NAME "filespec1" AS "filespec2"**
	Example:	**NAME "A:F1.BAS" AS "A:F2.BAS"** Change the name of file **F1.BAS** into **F2.BAS**.
B53	Command:	**NEW** Erase the current program from RAM memory.
	Form:	**NEW**
	Example:	**NEW**
B50	Command:	**RENUM** Renumber the lines in a program.
	Form:	**RENUM [new begin ln],[ln to begin renumbering],[increment]**
	Example:	**RENUM 100,,50** Renumber all lines. The first line number is set to **100**, the second to **150**, the third to **200**, etc.
N/C	Command:	**RMDIR** Delete a subdirectory from the disk.
	Form:	**RMDIR "pathspec"**
	Example:	**RMDIR "A:\BEANS"** Remove the subdirectory **BEANS** from the root directory of the diskette in drive A:.
B50	Command:	**RUN** Execute the statements contained in a program.
	Form:	**RUN [line number]**
	Example:	**RUN 20** Begin execution of the program at line **20**.
B10	Command:	**SAVE** Write a copy of the current program to disk.
B14	Form:	**SAVE "filespec [",A]**
	Example:	**SAVE "A:F1"** Save a copy of the program **F1** on the diskette in drive A:.
B53	Command:	**SYSTEM** Exit BASIC and return control to DOS.
	Form:	**SYSTEM**
	Example:	**SYSTEM**
B51	Command:	**TRON** and **TROFF**. Turn on (or off) the tracing of program execution.
	Form:	**TRON** or **TROFF**
	Example:	**TRON** As each statement is executed, the corresponding line number is displayed .

Page		Statement/Comment
B158	Statement:	**BEEP** Generate a sound of frequency 800 Hertz for one quarter of a second.
	Form:	`ln BEEP`
	Example:	`10 BEEP`
B213	Statement:	**CLOSE** Terminate the association between a file and its file number.
	Form:	`ln CLOSE [#1] [,#2] [,#3] ...`
	Example:	`10 CLOSE #1, #2` Close file #1 and file #2.
B163	Statement:	**CLS** Clear (blank) the screen during program execution.
	Form:	`ln CLS`
	Example:	`10 CLS`
N/C	Statement:	**COLOR** Allow the user to select the foreground, background, and border colors of the screen. This will have different effects depending on the hardware being used.
	Form:	`COLOR [foreground #][,background #][,border #]`
	Example:	`10 COLOR 1,3,3` Display dark blue text on a light blue background.
B62	Statement:	**DATA** Store string and numeric constants for use by **READ** statements.
	Form:	`ln DATA constant #1 [,constant #2, constant #3, ...]`
	Example:	`10 DATA Matt,4.5,Britt,5.6`
B149	Statement:	**DATE$** Return the current date as a ten-character string in the form mm-dd-yyyy.
	Form:	`DATE$`
	Example:	`10 D$ = DATE$` Store the current date in variable **D$**.
N/C	Statement:	**DEF FN** Allow the user to define a function.
	Form:	`DEF FNname(arguments) = expression`
	Example:	`10 DEF FNDIST(X,Y) = SQR(X^2 + Y^2)`. The function **FNDIST** is defined as the square root of the value of **X** squared plus the value of **Y** squared. The function may later be evaluated in a statement such as `20 PRINT FNDIST(3,4)` (the result, **5**, would be displayed).
B245	Statement:	**DIM** Specify the maximum number of elements in an array (subscripted variable).
	Form:	`ln DIM variable#1(num1), variable#2(num2), ...`
	Example:	`10 DIM A(15),B$(20,30)` Reserve 16 places (labeled 0 through 15) for the elements of variable **A** and 651 (i.e., 21 x 31) places for the elements of variable **B$**.

Continued . . .

Page	Statement/Comment

B40 Statement: **END** Terminate program execution and close all files (may be placed anywhere in the program).

Form: **ln END**

Example: **10 IF X = 2 THEN END** Terminate program execution if the value of **X** is 2.

B134 Statement: **FOR** and **NEXT** Pair of statements that control execution of a loop. **FOR** begins the loop and **NEXT** ends the loop.

Form: **ln FOR variable = initial val TO terminal val [STEP increment]**

...

... loop statements

...

ln NEXT variable

Example: **10 FOR X = 1 TO 6 STEP 2**

...

50 NEXT X Executes the statements inside the loop 3 times (for X = 1, 3, and 5).

B115 Statement: **GOSUB** Transfer control to a specified subroutine. See also **RETURN**.

Form: **GOSUB linenumber**

Example: **10 GOSUB 50** Transfer control to a subroutine that begins at line **50**.

N/C Statement: **GOTO** Transfer control to the specified line number.

Form: **GOTO ln**

Example: **10 GOTO 50** Transfer control to line number **50**.

B92 Statement: **IF/THEN/ELSE** Conditionally execute (or transfer control to) one of two statements (or line numbers).

Form: **ln IF condition THEN statement or ln [ELSE statement or ln]**

Example: **10 IF X < 3 THEN GOSUB 50 ELSE PRINT "Hours worked too large"** If the value of **X** is less than 3, control is transferred to the subroutine beginning at line **50**. Otherwise, the string is printed.

B58 Statement: **INPUT** Input values from the keyboard and assign those values to variables in the variable list.

Form: **ln INPUT ["prompt";] variable [, variable#2, variable#3, ...]**

Example: **10 INPUT "Enter name, rate";NAM$,RATE** Display the string and then pause until the user enters values for **NAM$** and **RATE** and presses **[Enter]**.

B213 Statement: **INPUT #** Input values from a file and assign those values to variables in the variable list.

Form: **ln INPUT # variable [, variable#2, variable#3, ...]**

Example: **10 INPUT #1 NAM$,RATE** Assigns the first value in file #1 to **NAM$** and the next value to **RATE**.

Continued . . .

Page	Statement/Comment	
B26	Statement:	**LET** Evaluate an expression and assign a value to a variable.
	Form:	**ln [LET] variable = expression**
	Example:	**10 A$ = "Hello"** Note that the word **LET** is optional.
		20 B = X + Y
B225	Statement:	**LINE INPUT** Input an entire line from the keyboard, ignoring delimiters.
	Form:	**LINE INPUT ["prompt";] string variable**
	Example:	**10 LINE INPUT "Enter name";NAM$** Input an entire line from the keyboard and assign it to variable **NAM$**.
B213	Statement:	**LINE INPUT #** Input an entire line from a specified file, ignoring delimiters.
	Form:	**LINE INPUT #, string variable**
	Example:	**10 LINE INPUT #1, NAM$** Input an entire line from file #1 and assign it to variable **NAM$**.
B162	Statement:	**LOCATE** Move the cursor to a specified location on the screen.
	Form:	**LOCATE [ROW][,[COLUMN][,[CURSOR][,[START][,STOP]]]]**
	Example:	**10 LOCATE 1,1** Move the cursor to column 1 row 1 (i.e., to the upper-left corner of the screen).
B10	Statement:	**LPRINT** Send output to printer without displaying on screen.
	Form:	**LPRINT [strings and/or variables]**
	Example:	**10 LPRINT "Pay = "RATE*HOURS**
N/C	Statement:	**LPRINT USING** Like **LPRINT** but the output is formatted by an image string.
	Form:	**LPRINT USING image string; list of variables**
	Example:	**10 LPRINT USING "Pay = $##.##"; RATE*HOURS**
B134	Statement:	**NEXT** See **FOR/NEXT**
B212	Statement:	**OPEN** Allow a file to be used for input or output.
	Form:	**OPEN filespec [FOR mode] AS [# filenumber]**
	Example:	**10 OPEN "A:F1" FOR OUTPUT AS #1** Allow the file **F1** to accept output from the program.
B160	Statement:	**PLAY** Play music designated by a string.
	Form:	**PLAY string**
	Example:	**10 PLAY "MB CDEFGAB"**
B30	Statement:	**PRINT** Display output on the screen.
	Form:	**PRINT strings and/or variables**
	Example:	**10 PRINT "Pay = "RATE*HOURS**

Continued . . .

Page	Statement/Comment	
B219	Statement:	**PRINT #** Write output to a specified file.
	Form:	**PRINT # strings and/or variables**
	Example:	**10 PRINT #1 "Pay = "RATE*HOURS** Write output to file #1 (this file must have already been opened for input or append by an **OPEN #** statement).
B35	Statement:	**PRINT USING** Like **PRINT** but output is formatted by an image string.
	Form:	**PRINT USING image string; list of variables**
	Example:	**10 PRINT USING "Pay = $##.##"; RATE*HOURS**
B219	Statement:	**PRINT # USING** Like **PRINT #** but output is formatted by an image string.
	Form:	**PRINT # USING image string; list of variables**
	Example:	**10 PRINT #1 USING "Pay = $##.##"; RATE*HOURS** Write the output to file #1.
B62	Statement:	**READ** Assign values in **DATA** statements to variables.
	Form:	**READ variable list**
	Example:	**10 READ A, B$, C**
B45	Statement:	**REM** Non-executable statement containing a remark.
	Form:	**REM remark**
	Example:	**10 REM Program finds pay from hours worked and rate of pay**
N/C	Statement:	**RESTORE** Allow data in **DATA** statements to be reread by **READ** statements.
	Form:	**RESTORE [ln]**
	Example:	**10 RESTORE** The next **READ** statement accesses the first item of data in the first **DATA** statement.
B116	Statement:	**RETURN** Terminate a subroutine and return control to the main program.
	Form:	**RETURN**
	Example:	**50 RETURN**
N/C	Statement:	**SHELL** Load and execute another program while the current program is in memory.
	Form:	**SHELL [command string]**
	Example:	**SHELL "DIR"** Display a directory of the default disk.
B159	Statement:	**SOUND** Produce a sound on the speaker.
	Form:	**SOUND frequency, duration**
	Example:	**10 SOUND 523,100** Play a *middle C* note for about 5 seconds.

Continued . . .

Page | **Statement/Comment**

N/C

Statement: **STOP** Terminate program execution and produce the message **Break in line nnnn**.

Form: **STOP**

Example: **10 STOP**

B251

Statement: **SWAP** Exchange the values of two variables.

Form: **SWAP variable1, variable2**

Example: **10 SWAP X,Y** Exchange the values of **X** and **Y**.

B149

Statement: **TIME$** Return the current time in the form **hours:minutes:seconds**

Form: **TIME$**

Example: **10 PRINT TIME$** Display the current time as recorded on the system clock.

B100

Statements: **WHILE** and **WEND** Define the beginning and end of a program loop.

Form:

```
ln WHILE condition
...
... loop statements
...
ln WEND
```

Example:

```
10 WHILE X <> 0
20   INPUT "Enter cost of item";X
30   PRINT "Tax is " .06*X
30 WEND
```

N/C

Statement: **WRITE** Like **PRINT** except that commas are inserted between items, strings are enclosed in quotation marks, and no blank is inserted to the left of positive numbers.

Form: **WRITE strings and/or variables**

Example: **10 WRITE "Pay = ";RATE*HOURS**

N/C

Statement: **WRITE #** Like **PRINT #** except that commas are inserted between items, strings are enclosed in quotation marks, and no blank is inserted to the left of positive numbers.

Form: **WRITE # strings and/or variables**

Example: **10 WRITE #1 "Pay = ";RATE*HOURS** Write output to file #1 (this file must have already been opened for input or append by an **OPEN #** statement).

Page		Function/Comment
N/C	Function:	**ABS** Return the absolute value of an expression.
	Form:	**ABS(expression)**
	Example:	**10 PRINT ABS(X)** Display the absolute value of **X**.
N/C	Function:	**ATN** Return the trigonometric arctangent of a value expressed in radians.
	Form:	**ATN(expression)**
	Example:	**10 PRINT ATN(X)** Display the arctangent of **X**.
N/C	Function:	**ASC** Return the ASCII code for the first character of a string.
	Form:	**ASC(string)**
	Example:	**10 PRINT ASC(S$)** Display the ASCII code for the first character of the string **S$.**
B161	Function:	**CHR$** Convert an ASCII code into the equivalent character.
	Form:	**CHR$(code)**
	Example:	**10 PRINT CHR$(65)** Display the character equivalent of ASCII code number 65 (i.e., display the upper case letter **B**).
N/C	Function:	**COS** Return the trigonometric cosine of a value expressed in radians.
	Form:	**COS(X)**
	Example:	**10 PRINT COS(X)** Display the cosine of **X**.
B212	Function:	**EOF** Indicate the end of a data file.
	Form:	**EOF(filenumber)**
	Example:	**10 WHILE NOT EOF(1)** Execute a loop until the end of file number 1 has been reached.
N/C	Function:	**EXP** Return the power of *e* (the base of natural logarithms).
	Form:	**EXP(X)**
	Example:	**10 PRINT EXP(X)** Display the value of e^X.
B153	Function	**INT** Return the largest integer that does not exceed the given value.
	Form:	**INT(value)**
	Example:	**10 PRINT INT(X)** Display the largest integer not exceeding the value of **X**.
N/C	Function	**LEFT$** Return a specified number of characters from the left-hand side of a string.
	Form:	**LEFT$(string,number)**
	Example:	**10 A$ = LEFT$(T$,5)** Assign the five left-most characters in **T$** to **A$**.

Continued . . .

Page		Function/Comment
N/C	Function	`LEN` Return the length (number of characters) of a specified string.
	Form:	`LEN(string)`
	Example:	`10 A = LEN(T$)` Assign the number of characters in `T$` to `A`.
N/C	Function:	`LOG` Return the natural logarithm of a value. The value must be greater than zero.
	Form:	`LOG(X)`
	Example:	`10 PRINT LOG(X)` Display the natural logarithm of `X`.
B236	Function	`MID$` Return a specified portion of a string.
	Form:	`MID$(string,bgn,number)`
	Example:	`10 PRINT MID$(T$,10,4)` Display the tenth through thirteenth characters of `T$`.
N/C	Function	`RIGHT$` Return a specified number of characters from the right-hand side of a string.
	Form:	`RIGHT$(string,number)`
	Example:	`10 A$ = RIGHT$(T$,5)` Assign the five right-most characters in `T$` to `A$`.
N/C	Function	`RND` Generate a random number in the range 0 to 1.
	Form:	`RND[(X)]`
	Example:	`10 PRINT RND` Display the next number on the random number list.
N/C	Function:	`SIN` Return the trigonometric sine of a value expressed in radians.
	Form:	`SIN(X)`
	Example:	`10 PRINT SIN(X)` Display the sine of `X`.
B35	Function	`SPC` Skip the specified number of spaces in a `PRINT` statement.
	Form:	`SPC(number)`
	Example:	`10 PRINT "Hi" SPC(25) "Matt"`
B113	Function:	`SQR` Return the square root of a value.
	Form:	`SQR(X)`
	Example:	`10 PRINT SQR(X)` Display the square root of `X`.
N/C	Function	`STR$` Return the string representation of a given value.
	Form:	`STR$(value)`
	Example:	`10 X$ = STR$(6)` Convert the numeric value **6** into a string.
B161	Function	`STRING$` Return a string of specified characters.
	Form:	`STRING$(num,code)`
	Example:	`10 PRINT STRING$(80,205)` Display 80 characters with ASCII code 205.

Continued . . .

Page		Function/Comment
B34	Function	**TAB** Move the cursor to a specified horizontal location.
	Form:	**TAB(number)**
	Example:	**10 PRINT "Hi" TAB(10) "Matt"**
N/C	Function:	**TAN** Return the trigonometric tangent of a value expressed in radians.
	Form:	**TAN(X)**
	Example:	**10 PRINT TAN(X)** Display the tangent of **X**.
N/C	Function:	**TIMER** Return the number of seconds since midnight or since a system reset.
	Form:	**variable = TIMER**
	Example:	**X = TIMER**
B236	Function	**VAL** Return the numerical value of a specified string.
	Form:	**VAL(string)**
	Example:	**PRINT VAL(X$)** Display the numeric value of **X$**.

Variable Declarations

Page	Indicator	Description
B26	**$**	On the end of a variable name, indicates a string variable (e.g., **X$**).
N/C	**%**	On the end of a variable name, indicates an integer (i.e., a whole number between –32768 and +32767 such as 23). For example, **X%**.
B13	**!**	On the end of a variable name, indicates a single precision value (i.e., a decimal number of seven or fewer digits such as 48.4). For example, **X!**.
B13	**#**	On the end of a variable name, indicates a double precision value (i.e., a number with eight or more digits such as 3.141593173). For example, **X#**.

Relational Operators

Page	Operator	Description
B41	**=**	Equal to.
B41	**<>**	Not equal to.
B41	**>**	Greater than.
B41	**<**	Less than.

Continued . . .

Page	Operator	Description
B41	>=	Greater than or equal to.
B41	<=	Less than or equal to.

Mathematical Operators

Page	Operator	Description
B41	+	Addition.
B41	-	Subtraction.
B41	*	Multiplication.
B41	/	Division.
B41	^	Exponentiation (e.g., 5^2 is written as **5^2**).
B41	( )	Parentheses (for grouping or to change the order in which mathematical operations are to be performed).

Logical Operators

Page	Operator	Description
B94	**AND**	Used to connect two conditions, both of which must be true for the entire condition to be true.
B94	**OR**	Used to connect two conditions, either one of which may be true for the entire condition to be true.
N/C	**NOT**	Returns the opposite of the given value (i.e., true becomes false and false becomes true).

Using Flowcharts

A flowchart is a visual representation of the logic of a program. The flowchart does in graphic form what the pseudocode does in words. Some programmers like to use flowcharts because flowcharts show pictorially how the pieces of the program fit together.

Many standard symbols are used to construct flowcharts. However, flowcharts for most programs can be constructed using only six symbols. For example, on page B76, the following flowchart was presented for a program that calculates employee wages:

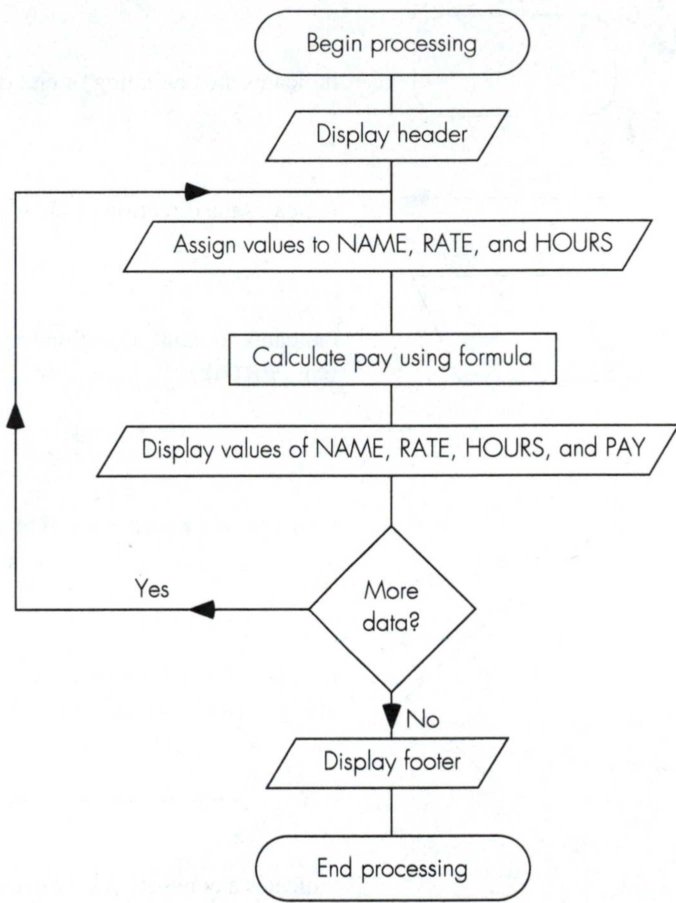

Each flowchart symbol has a specific meaning so that the programmer can quickly see the general type of operation that is to be carried out at each step in the program:

Name	Symbol	Use in Flowchart
Oval	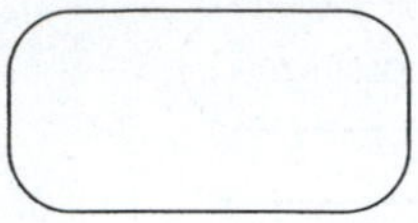	Indicates the beginning or end of the program.
Flow line		Indicates the direction of the logic flow in the program.
Parallelogram	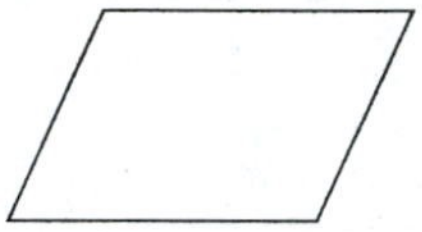	Indicates an input operation (e.g., **`INPUT, READ`**) or an output operation (e.g., **`PRINT`**).
Rectangle	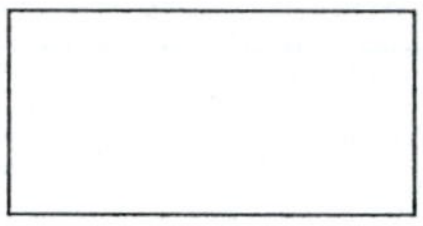	Indicates that a process is to be carried out (e.g., a calculation).
Diamond	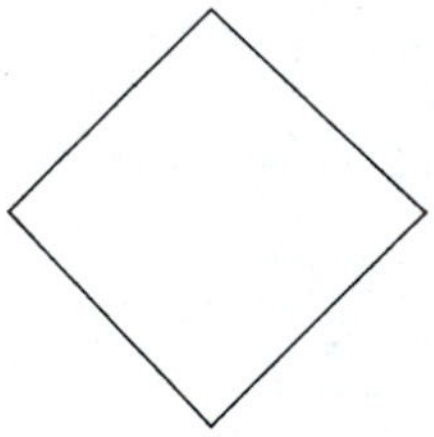	Indicates that a decision is to be made and that the program should continue along one of two routes (e.g., **`IF/THEN/ELSE`**).
Circle	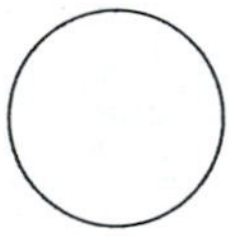	Indicates a connection between separate parts of the program. This is used when the flowchart is too large to fit on a single sheet of paper or when the complexity of a program makes it difficult to draw flow lines.

Flowcharts are intended to make the development of a program easier for the programmer and to make the logic flow of a program more easily determined by other programmers. Like pseudocode, flowcharts are an aid to the programming process and not an end in themselves. If you decide to use flowcharts, be sure that they are clear and convey the meaning that you intend.

Abort To stop a command, program, or procedure before it is completed. For example, to abort a DOS command, tap **[Ctrl-C]**.

Absolute cell reference (see *cell reference*).

Absolute tab (see *tab stop*).

Access (see *load*).

Active cell In Lotus 1-2-3, the cell currently being worked on. Synonymous with *current cell*.

Algorithm A well-defined procedure that ends in a finite number of steps.

Alignment character In WordPerfect, a character that will be used to line up text when the **[Tab]** key is pressed. The default alignment character is the decimal point, but this can be changed by the user.

Alphanumeric characters Characters that can be entered via the keyboard including letters, digits, punctuation, and special symbols.

American Standard Code for Information Interchange (see *ASCII*).

Application A program such as WordPerfect, Lotus 1-2-3, or dBASE that can be used to accomplish a specific task.

Applications software Programs such as WordPerfect, Lotus 1-2-3, and dBASE that enable the computer to analyze and manipulate data under the direction of the computer user.

Array In BASIC, an organized list or table of values that is stored using a single variable name. Each value in the array is called an *element* and each of the elements is given a unique reference number or set of numbers called its *subscript*. Variables in a *one-dimensional array* contain a single subscript as in **H(1)**, **H(2)**, and **H(3)**, and are referred to as *singly subscripted variables*. Variables in a *two-dimensional array* contain two subscripts as in **H(1,1)**, **H(1,2)**, and **H(1,3)** and are referred to as *doubly subscripted variables*. The two-dimensional arrays can be thought of as a table where the rows are labeled by the first subscript and the columns are indicated by the second subscript (note that this is the reverse of the order used in Lotus 1-2-3 cell addresses where the column letter is given first and the row number is given second).

Arrow keys The four keys that have arrows pointing in different directions that are used to position the cursor on the screen. Synonymous with *cursor control keys*.

ASCII (American Standard Code for Information Interchange) A standard coding scheme developed in 1968 for English-language computers. A file saved in ASCII by one application (e.g., Lotus 1-2-3) can be used by most other applications (e.g., WordPerfect), although some special codes (e.g., margins, character enhancements) will be lost. ASCII files are sometimes referred to as *text-only* files because they have been stripped of all of their special codes.

ASCII code In BASIC, a numeric value assigned to every character that can be sent to an output device (e.g., the screen or a printer). For example, the ASCII code for the upper case *Y* is 089 while the ASCII code for the lowercase *y* is 121.

AUTOEXEC.BAT In DOS, a file that is executed automatically when the computer is booted. This file usually contains commands such as **PATH**, **BUFFERS**, or **FILES** that the user wants executed every time the computer is turned on.

Automatic recalculation In Lotus 1-2-3, a mode of operation where the values of all formulas are recalculated when data in the worksheet are changed. This is the opposite of *manual recalculation*.

Backup To make a copy of a file for archival purposes or as insurance against data loss.

BASIC Acronym for Beginners All-purpose Symbolic Instruction Code. A high-level computer language developed in the early 1960s by John Kemeny and Thomas Kurtz as a vehicle for teaching programming skills.

BASICA The advanced version of BASIC distributed by IBM on the DOS diskette included with IBM computers. This is virtually identical to GW-BASIC.

Batch file A file that contains a list of individual commands that are to be executed.

Binary digit (or *bit* for short) The smallest unit that can be used to store data in the binary number system. A binary digit is either a 0 or a 1.

Bit (see *binary digit*).

Block A selected portion of the screen. This may include text or graphics.

Block operation An operation on a block of text or graphics such as copying, deleting, moving, cutting or pasting.

Boldface Text that is darker than normal (**like this**).

Boolean operator (see *logical operator*).

Boot To start a computer by transferring instructions (usually part of the operating system) from a storage device into the computer's memory. A *cold boot* occurs when the electrical power to the computer must be turned on in order to start the machine. If the power is already on, the startup process is called a *warm boot*.

Branch In BASIC, the execution of program statements in a nonsequential fashion. A *conditional branch* changes the order of statement execution based on whether a condition is true or false. For example, **IF X = 2 THEN 300 ELSE 400** transfers control to line **300** if the value of **X** is **2** and to line **400** if the value of **X** is not **2**. An *unconditional branch* changes the order of statement execution whenever the branching statement is executed, regardless of any conditions. For example, **GO TO 400** is an unconditional branching statement that transfers control to line **400** whenever the **GO TO** statement is executed.

Bubble sort A simple algorithm designed to sort a list. The bubble sort is easy to understand and works well but is not very efficient.

Buffer A part of memory used to hold data on a temporary basis.

Bug An error, usually within a program, that causes the computer to produce incorrect results, behave erratically, or crash. The term was coined in the late 1940s when a moth became entangled in one of the electric circuits of the ENIAC computer.

Byte Typically, eight bits bundled together. A byte is a unit used to indicate the amount of data that can be stored on a disk or in the memory of a computer. A byte represents one character (letter, digit, punctuation mark, etc.).

Calculated field In dBASE, a field that contains the results of calculations performed on constants or on other fields.

Case insensitive operation An operation that is carried out without regard to the case of the letters in the command. DOS commands are case insensitive (e.g., **COPY** and **copy** have the same meaning) but searches in dBASE are generally case sensitive (e.g., **Furniture** and **FURNITURE** are considered two different words).

Catalog In dBASE, a database that contains the names of a group of related files. Like DOS subdirectories, catalogs are used as an organizational aid for hard disks that contain many files.

Cell In Lotus 1-2-3, a location within a worksheet used to store a single piece of information. Cells, which are similar to the variables used in computer languages such as BASIC, may contain numbers, text (also called labels or titles), or formulas. A cell is one column wide and one row high.

Cell address In Lotus 1-2-3, the code that identifies the location of a cell. For example, **D3** is the address of the cell in column **D** of row **3**.

Cell definition In Lotus 1-2-3, the true contents of a cell as it was typed into a worksheet on the entry line. This may be a formula, label, or value and may be different from that which is displayed in the body of the worksheet at the cell address (especially in the case of a formula).

Cell format In Lotus 1-2-3, the way the contents of a cell are to appear on the screen. For example, values might be displayed with a specified number of decimal places, commas, the dollar sign, or the percent sign. A cell format does not affect the contents of the cell, only the way it appears on the screen.

Cell pointer In Lotus 1-2-3, a rectangular block on the screen, usually in reverse video (black on white rather than white on black), that indicates which cell is currently active.

Cell reference In Lotus 1-2-3, a cell or cell range used in a formula. For example, the formula **@SQRT(D3)** finds the square root of the value whose cell reference is **D3**. A *relative cell reference* is one that is interpreted relative to the current cell location. For example, if a certain formula contains **A3** and that formula is copied to a different cell, the **A3** will be adjusted to make sense in the new location. An *absolute cell reference* is one that always remains the same, even if the formula is copied to another cell location. These references are indicated using a dollar sign to the left of the column letter and/or row number. For example, if a certain formula contains **A3** and that formula is copied to a different cell, the **A3** will not be adjusted to fit the new location.

Cell width In Lotus 1-2-3, the number of characters a cell can display.

Center justification (see *justification*).

Central processing unit (CPU) In a microcomputer, the integrated circuit contained in the microprocessor that carries out arithmetic and logical operations and controls the operations of the computer.

CGA (see *Color Graphics Adapter*).

Character enhancements Changes to characters that alter their appearance such as superscript (e.g., the 2 in X^2), boldface (e.g., **like this**), italic (e.g., *like this*), subscript (e.g., the 2 in H_2O) and underline (e.g., like this).

Child of a directory In DOS, the directory that is immediately below the active directory. The directory immediately above the active directory is called the *parent* of the active directory.

Click To tap one of the buttons of a mouse while holding the mouse perfectly still.

Code In BASIC, (1) the act of constructing programming statements (as in *It takes a long time to code a complex program*) (2) the programming statements themselves (as in *Your code is very efficient*).

Codes In WordPerfect, codes are hidden markers that instruct the program to perform various tasks such as setting margins, line spacing, character enhancements, and line justification.

Cold boot (see *boot*).

Color Graphics Adapter (CGA) A low-resolution monitor driver that can display four colors at one time. See also *EGA* and *VGA*.

Command An instruction given to the computer by the user (e.g., **DIR**).

COMMAND.COM The DOS system file that contains the command processor which must be present when the computer is booted.

Comparison operator An operator such as **=**, **>**, and **<** that instructs the computer to compare the values of two quantities. Synonymous with *relational operator*.

Compiler A program that converts statements from a high-level computer language such as BASIC into a form that can be used directly by the computer. A compiler translates all the statements before it executes any of them (compare with *interpreter*).

Compressed binary format The coding scheme used by BASIC to store programs and data. This code is unreadable by humans.

Computer An electronic device capable of receiving data, manipulating the data arithmetically and logically according to prescribed internally-stored instructions, and then supplying the results of those manipulations. A *microcomputer* is a small, low-priced computer driven by a microprocessor that contains both the arithmetic logic unit and control unit. Microcomputers are designed to meet the needs of a single user but can be networked to share information and programs. Also known as *micros*, *personal computers*, or *PCs*. A *minicomputer* is larger and more expensive than a microcomputer and can be used by more than one person at a time; designed to meet the needs of small groups of people working on similar tasks. A *mainframe* computer is large and expensive but can process large amounts of data at high speed and can be used by more than one person at a time; generally designed to meet the needs of a large organization. *Supercomputers* are the largest and most expensive computers and can process billions of instructions per second; designed for users who must perform extremely high-speed calculations.

Computer system All the components needed to use a computer, including the user (human operator), hardware (physical components), software (programs), storage devices (disks), and data.

Concatenation Connecting two pieces of data into a single piece by appending one onto the end of the other. For example, in BASIC if `A$ = "Super"`, `B$ = "man"`, and `C$ = A$ + B$` then the strings stored in `A$` and `B$` would be concatenated and the value of `C$` would be `Superman`.

Conditional branch (see *branch*).

`CONFIG.SYS` A DOS file that contains commands such as **`FILES`** and **`BUFFERS`** for configuring the DOS environment of a computer session.

Coordinates (see *cell address*).

Counter In BASIC, a variable incremented by a fixed amount. For example, the statement `X = X + 1` will increment the value of `X` by `1` each time the statement is executed. The `X` is a counter.

CPU (see *central processing unit*).

Crash The termination of a computer session in an abnormal way. A crash may be caused by hardware failure, software errors, or incompatibility of hardware and software components. It usually results in the monitor and/or keyboard freezing up or in the computer acting strangely. To recover from a crash, the machine usually has to be booted again.

Current cell (see *active cell*).

Cursor A character (usually a blinking line) on the screen that indicates where other characters will be displayed when typing begins.

Cursor control keys (see *arrow keys*).

Cut To remove a selected block of text or graphics and save a copy of the block in the memory of the computer. This is different from deleting text because the text can be retrieved from memory at a later time.

Cut and paste (see *move*).

Data The raw, unorganized facts and figures which, when correctly processed and interpreted, become information. The word *data* technically is a plural (as in *these data are correct*); the singular version is datum. *Numeric* data consist of values (numbers) that can be used in arithmetic calculations. *Alphanumeric* data consist of text (letters), digits, punctuation, and other special characters that can be stored, but which are not used in arithmetic calculations.

Data assignment In BASIC, to assign a value to a variable (i.e., to replace the current value of a variable with a new value). For example, the statement `X = 10` assigns the value `10` to variable `X`; the statement `X = X + 1` assigns the value `X + 1` to variable `X` (i.e., the old value of `X` is increased by `1` and the resulting value is stored at variable location `X`).

Data error (see *error*).

Data file A file that contains raw data versus a program file, which contains instructions.

Data flag In BASIC, a piece of data that could not possibly be a piece of data. Data flags are used as signals (flags) in programs to indicate the end of a data list or to show when one set or type of data has ended and another is to begin.

Data pointer In BASIC, a marker that keeps track of which data item will be assigned to a variable by the next **`READ`** statement.

Data structure In BASIC, the organization or logic of a set of data.

Database A collection of related data that is organized in such a way that it can be easily accessed and modified.

Database management Tasks related to collecting, organizing, modifying, maintaining, and retrieving data stored in databases.

Database management program A computer program that is designed to help users create, organize, modify, maintain, and provide access to databases. dBASE is a database management program.

Database structure In dBASE, the organization of a database that includes the names, order, widths, and types of data fields contained in a database.

Debug To locate and remove errors in a computer program.

Default An assumption made by the computer system when the user has not indicated a specific choice. A default *drive* is the disk drive assumed by the computer system unless the user specifies a specific drive. A default *value* is a quantity that is assumed unless otherwise specified.

Delete To remove (erase) a character or group of characters.

Delimiter A character used to separate (delimit) one part of a command from another or a character used to separate two pieces of data. In DOS, the space is the usual delimiter, while in BASIC the comma is the usual delimiter.

Device Hardware such as a printer, monitor, or mouse that can send and/or receive data.

Dimension In BASIC, the maximum value a subscript may use in an array.

Directory A listing of the names of files and/or other directories stored on a disk or part of a disk.

Directory path (see *path*).

Disk (see *diskette*).

Disk drive A secondary storage mechanical device used to read data from disks and write data on disks. A floppy disk drive uses removeable $3\frac{1}{2}$-inch square or $5\frac{1}{4}$-inch square diskettes while a hard-disk drive uses nonremovable (fixed) disks.

Disk operating system (DOS) A set of programs stored on disk that act as the interface between the user and the computer hardware for IBM and IBM-compatible microcomputers.

Diskette A small (usually $3\frac{1}{2}$ or $5\frac{1}{4}$ inches square), thin ($\frac{1}{8}$ of an inch high), flexible piece of plastic that is coated with an iron oxide capable of being magnetized and encased within a flexible vinyl cover or a stiff plastic case. Diskettes are used as secondary storage devices. Synonymous with *floppy diskette*, *flexible diskette*, *floppy*, and *disk*.

Document A file such as a memo, letter, or report created by WordPerfect.

DOS (see *disk operating system*).

DOS command An instruction given to the disk operating system of the computer. *Internal* DOS commands such as **DIR**, **COPY**, and **TYPE** are built into the **COMMAND.COM** file and loaded into the memory of the computer when the system is booted. *External* DOS commands such as **DISKCOPY**, **FORMAT**, and **SORT** are stored in separate files whose names are listed in the DOS directory and whose contents must be read from the disk into memory before they can be executed. Files with the extensions **COM**, **EXE**, or **BAT** usually contain external DOS commands.

DOS prompt Usually, a letter such as **A**, **B**, or **C** that indicates the current default disk drive followed by a "greater than" symbol (e.g., **C>**). The display of the DOS prompt indicates that the computer is ready to receive DOS commands. The DOS prompt can be changed using the **PROMPT** command.

Dot leader A line of dots inserted between characters when the **[Tab]** key is pressed. Dot leaders are typically used between subjects and corresponding page numbers in tables of contents.

Dot matrix printer A type of printer that constructs images and text by printing small dots on the paper. The dots are formed by a vertical column of pins in a moving print head striking a piece of paper through an inked ribbon.

Dot prompt In dBASE, the command-driven mode of operation.

Double precision variable (see *variable*).

Doubly subscripted variable (see *array*).

Drag To slide a mouse while one of the buttons is held down.

Drop to DOS To suspend the operation of the active application in order to execute DOS commands. In WordPerfect, this is called the *Shell* feature.

Dump To transfer the contents of the screen (screen dump) or the computer's memory (memory dump) to a printer or a file.

Dvorak keyboard arrangement An efficient keyboard arrangement that reduces the distance fingers have to travel by a factor of about sixteen when compared to the standard QWERTY arrangement. The arrangement was developed in 1936 by August Dvorak.

Edit To modify (change, add to, or delete) a document or part of a document.

EGA (see *enhanced graphics adapter*).

Element (see *array*).

Enhanced Graphics Adapter A medium-resolution monitor driver that can display up to 16 colors at one time. See also *CGA* and *VGA*.

Environment The context within which you are working. When in the DOS environment, the system prompt, **C:\>** is displayed and you can execute DOS commands such as **DIR**. Likewise, when in the WordPerfect environment the status line is displayed and you may execute WordPerfect commands but not DOS commands.

Equation editor In WordPerfect, a feature that allows users to create complex mathematical equations.

Error In BASIC, a program or data element that is not correct. A *logic error* is a mistake in the logic of a program; a *syntax error* is a mistake in the rules of grammar that govern the programming language (e.g., using a comma instead of a semicolon or omitting a needed quotation mark); a *data error* is an incorrect or inappropriate piece of data; a *range error* is a value that is out of the range of values specified by the programmer.

Executable program statement In BASIC, a statement that contains program instructions such as **LET**, **PRINT**, or **FOR** that are carried out during program execution. A *non-executable statement* is one that is not processed by the computer during execution. **REM** and **DATA** are non-executable statements.

Execute (see *run*).

Exit a file To close a file (e.g., a WordPerfect document) while still remaining within the environment of the application.

Exit a program To leave a program and return to the DOS environment.

Exponential notation A compact way of expressing very large or very small numbers. Using this notation, numbers are written with a decimal part that ranges between 1 and 10 (including 1 but not including 10), the letter *E* to signal an exponent, and an integer representing the number of places the decimal point of the original number has been moved (positive for numbers greater than 1 and negative for numbers between 0 and 1). For example, **1.2E5** represents 120000 while **1.2E-5** represents .000012.

Export To output data from one application in a form that can be used by another application.

Extension A one-, two-, or three-character label added to the end of a DOS file name. In **FORMAT.COM**, the word **FORMAT** is the name of the file and **COM** is the extension.

External DOS command (see *DOS command*).

Field In dBASE, a group of characters within a record that are meaningful. Fields are used to describe characteristics or attributes of sets of data.

File A collection of related information that is stored as a logical unit in the memory of the computer (e.g., a letter written in WordPerfect or a Lotus 1-2-3 worksheet).

File specification The complete designation for a file including the disk drive where the file resides, the directory path to the file, the name of the file, and the file name extension (e.g., **C:\WP51\WPDOCS\MRMPREP.V1**).

Filter A program or command such as **SORT** or **MORE** that reads data from a file or input device (e.g., the keyboard), modifies the data (e.g., alphabetizes it), and then sends the modified data to another file or output device (e.g., the monitor).

Finite loop (see *loop*).

Fixed drive (see *hard disk*).

Flag (see data *flag*).

Floppy diskette (see *diskette*).

Flow chart A visual representation of the logic of a computer program. Flow charts use standard symbols for operations including the parallelogram for input data, the rectangle for calculations, and the diamond for decision making. The symbols are connected with *flow lines* that indicate the order in which the operations will be performed.

Flow lines (see *flow chart*).

Flush left (see *justification*).

Flush right (see *justification*).

Font A complete set of characters using a certain typeface. In monospaced fonts, all characters are the same width. In proportionally spaced fonts, characters have varying widths depending on their shapes.

Footer A portion of a document that automatically appears at the bottom (foot) of each page.

Format a diskette In DOS, to prepare the magnetic material on a disk so that it matches the way in which data are stored by a given brand of computer. For example, a diskette formatted for use with an IBM PS/2 cannot be used in an Apple Macintosh without reformatting it for that machine. Synonymous with *initialize a diskette*.

Format a document In WordPerfect, to make a document look a certain way including spacing, pagination, character enhancements, margin settings, headers, and footers.

Formula In Lotus 1-2-3, a mathematical expression or logical expression within a worksheet that can include both numbers and cell coordinates. For example, **`B3/100 + C3`** means that the contents of cell **`B3`** will be divided by **`100`**, then the quotient will be added to the contents of cell **`C3`** and then the result will be displayed in the active cell.

Full justification (see *justification*).

Function A formula for a predetermined operation. For example, in Lotus 1-2-3 **`@AVG(A1.A5)`** will calculate the average of all the numbers in cells **`A1`**, **`A2`**, **`A3`**, **`A4`**, and **`A5`**.

Function keys Keys labeled F1, F2, etc. that enable the user to perform specific tasks such as saving, printing, and formatting with a single keystroke.

Garbage in/garbage out In BASIC, a saying that means that the output from a computer is only as good as the data and programs fed into the machine.

Gb Abbreviation for gigabyte.

Generation A phase of development in the evolution of computers. First generation (1951–1958) computers used vacuum tubes to process information, magnetic drums to store internal data and instructions, and punched (Hollerith) cards to store data externally. Second generation (1959–1964) computers used transistors in place of vacuum tubes and magnetic cores instead of magnetic drums. Third generation (1965–1970) computers used integrated circuits in place of many transistors and other electronic components. In addition, remote typewriter-like terminals were developed that allowed many users to interact with a single computer at one time. Fourth generation (1971–present) computers use LSI (large-scale integration) and VLSI (very large-scale integration) technology to place hundreds of thousands to millions of electronic components on a single silicon chip. Also, the magnetic core memory system has been replaced by much more reliable and smaller silicon chip memory systems.

Gigabyte A unit of storage equal to 2^{30} = 1,073,741,824 or about one billion bytes. A gigabyte is abbreviated 1 Gb or 1 gig.

GIGO (see *garbage in/garbage out*).

Global An operation that affects an entire file at one time.

Global character A character (**`?`** or **`*`**) that can take the place of one or more other characters in a command. Synonymous with *wild card*.

Graphics Nontext material such as pictures, tables, or charts.

Graphics Tablet A device that consists of a pencil-like stylus and a flat surface that can record the location of the stylus in relation to a grid. The stylus may be used to draw graphic images that are then encoded into binary data and sent to the computer to be stored as a graphic image.

GW-BASIC A version of BASIC developed by Microsoft Corporation (the *GW* stands for *Gee Whiz*). This version of BASIC is virtually identical to *IBM BASIC*.

Hanging indent (see *hanging paragraph*).

Hanging paragraph A paragraph whose first line begins to the left of the left margin. The remainder of the text in the paragraph is indented. Synonymous with *hanging indent* and *outdent*.

Hard copy Printed computer output.

Hard disk A mechanical device that includes the magnetic disk and disk drive as a permanent hermetically sealed unit. Hard disks can store millions to billions of bytes of data and the computer can access data much faster from a hard disk than from a floppy diskette. Synonymous with *hard drive* and *fixed disk*.

Hard drive (see *hard disk*).

Hard page break (see *page break*).

Hard return In WordPerfect, a code that indicates where the **[Enter]** key was pressed. A hard return is used to counteract the effects of word wrap and to insert blank lines.

Hardware The physical components that make up a computer system including the system unit, monitor, keyboard, disk drive, and printer.

Header Text such as a title or page number that appears at the top of each page of a document.

Headword In WordPerfect, words that can be looked up in the thesaurus.

Help key A key that when tapped provides on-screen access to information about the program in use. *Context sensitive* help means that the information displayed is related to the current operation. **[F3]** is the help key for WordPerfect while **[F1]** is the help key for Lotus 1-2-3 and dBASE.

High-level programming language A computer programming language such as BASIC or Pascal that allows users to write program code using simplified statements (such as **`PRINT`**) rather than machine-readable code.

Highlight To make a menu selection, block of text, graphic, or other element on the screen look different from the other elements. Highlighted items typically appear in reverse video, boldface, or a different color.

IBM BASIC A version of BASIC developed by IBM Corporation. This version of BASIC is virtually identical to *GW BASIC*.

Image string In BASIC, a string that exactly describes the way output will be displayed or written to a file. For example, the image string **###.##** in **PRINT "###.##";A** indicates that the value of variable **A** will be displayed using a maximum of three digits to the left of the decimal point and with exactly two digits to the right of the decimal point.

Import To input data created by one application into another application.

Infinite loop (see *loop*).

Initialize a diskette (see *format a diskette*).

Initialize a variable In BASIC, to assign a value to a variable for the first time. The default initialization of a string variable is the null string whereas the default initialization of a numeric variable is 0.

Inkjet printer A type of printer that shoots tiny drops of ink from a cartridge in the print head onto the paper. The location of the dots of ink is controlled by electric fields generated in the print head.

Input data In BASIC, data assigned to variables during program execution.

Input device A device such as a keyboard used to enter data into the computer.

Insert To add (insert) a character or group of characters without replacing others. As the new characters are inserted, all characters to the right of the cursor are moved accordingly.

Integer variable (see *variable*).

Intel 80486 A powerful microprocessor introduced in 1989 for IBM and compatible microcomputers that includes a full 32-bit data bus structure and memory partitioning so that more than one program can be run at one time. This microprocessor contains more than one million transistors on a silicon chip only $\frac{1}{4}$-inch square. Less powerful Intel microprocessors include the 80386 (introduced in 1986), the 80286 (introduced in 1984), and the 8088 (introduced in 1978 and used in the original IBM PC).

Interface The connection between the computer and some external device such as a printer or a modem. Three popular types of interfaces currently in use in microcomputers are the serial interface, the parallel interface, and the small computer system interface. Synonymous with *port*.

Internal DOS command (see *DOS command*).

Interpreter Similar to a compiler, an interpreter translates statements from a high-level computer language such as BASIC into a code that can be used directly by the computer. An interpreter executes a statement as soon as it translates it rather than translating all statements in a program and then executing them as a compiler does.

Justification The alignment of text to one or both edges of a paragraph. *Left justification* aligns the left edge of the paragraph while leaving the right edge ragged; *right justification* aligns the right edge of the paragraph while leaving the left edge ragged; *full justification* aligns both the left and right edges of a paragraph by adding blank spaces between words; *center justification* (centering) centers lines of text within the defined margins.

K Abbreviation for kilobyte.

Key word (see *reserved word*).

Kilobyte A unit of storage equal to 2^{10} = 1,024 bytes or about one thousand bytes. One kilobyte is abbreviated 1 K.

Label In Lotus 1-2-3, a text entry such as a name or a column heading. Entries are considered labels unless they begin with **0 1 2 3 4 5 6 7 8 9 - + . (@ #** or **$**. Numeric or formula entries are referred to as *values*.

Label prefix In Lotus 1-2-3, a character that is added to the left end of a label to indicate how the label should be aligned when displayed in a cell. Three common label prefixes are **'** (flush left), **"** (flush right), and **^** (center).

Laser printer A type of printer that is similar to a dot matrix printer in that it forms images by printing dots. However, instead of using mechanical pins and an inked ribbon, a laser printer uses a highly-focused laser beam to electrostatically charge extremely small dots on a photosensitive drum and then applies small black plastic dots to the charged locations.

Left justification (see *justification*).

LET statement (see *replacement statement*).

Load To read a program or data file from disk and place a copy into the memory of the computer so that it can be used. Synonymous with *access* and *retrieve*.

Logic error (see *error*).

Logical formula In Lotus 1-2-3, one of three types of formulas (logical, string, and numeric). Logical formulas use logical operators to evaluate a condition in order to determine if it is true or false.

Logical operator A symbol used in a logical formula to make a comparison or to create complex formulas that combine two or more formulas into one. The logical operators include **=**, **<**, **>**, **<=**, **>=**, **<>**, **AND**, **OR**, and **NOT**.

Loop A set of programming statements that is repeated. In BASIC, *conditional loops* (i.e., those processed while a particular condition is true) are formed using **WHILE** and **WEND** statements whereas *unconditional loops* (i.e., those processed a specified number of times) are formed using **FOR** and **NEXT** statements. A *finite loop* is one that is executed a finite (countable) number of times. An *infinite loop* is one that is executed without end. For example, the program statement **10 GO TO 10** is an infinite loop because once the statement is executed the program will never move to another statement and hence never end.

Loop variable In BASIC, the variable used to control a **FOR/NEXT** loop. Synonymous with *loop counter*.

Lowercase letters Small letters such as a, b, c. Compare with uppercase.

Machine language The fundamental language of a computer in which instructions can be directly carried out by the computer's central processing unit. This language consists of a series of 0s and 1s making it unreadable by humans.

Macro A program (set of instructions) that is created to work within an application to accomplish a specific task. In their simplest form, macros are just a series of keystrokes that the user has told the computer to memorize and that can be implemented with a single keystroke.

Magnetic disk (see *diskette*).

Mail merge (see *merge*).

Main directory (see *root directory*).

Main memory (see *random access memory*).

Main storage (see *random access memory*).

Mainframe computer (see *computer*).

Manual recalculation In Lotus 1-2-3, a mode of operation where the values of formulas are only recalculated when the user instructs the program to do so. This is the opposite of *automatic recalculation*.

Mathematical operators The symbols used to indicate mathematical operations including addition (+), subtraction (-), multiplication (*), division (/), and exponentiation (^).

Matrix (see *array*).

Mb Abbreviation for megabyte.

Megabyte A unit of storage equal to 2^{20} = 1,048,576 or about one million bytes. A megabyte is abbreviated 1 Mb or 1 meg.

Megahertz A unit of measurement equal to one million cycles per second. Megahertz are used to compare the speeds of microprocessors. For example, the Intel 80386 runs at a clock speed of between 16 and 33 megahertz. A higher clock speed means a faster computer.

Menu A list of choices presented on the screen.

Menu bar In WordPerfect, the top line of the screen that displays a set of pull down menus. The menu bar is accessed by tapping **[Alt=]**.

Merge To combine data from two files in some way. In WordPerfect and dBASE, data from one file, called a secondary file or a database, are inserted into another file, usually a form letter called a primary file or a report form, at locations specified by special merge codes. Because this process is used to produce individualized mass mailings it is often referred to as *mail merge*.

Microcomputer (see *computer*).

Microprocessor An integrated circuit that contains the central processing unit (the brain) of a computer. It determines the overall characteristics of the computer including performance and cost. The Intel 80486 and Motorola 68030 are examples of microprocessors.

Minicomputer (see *computer*).

Modem An electronic device that converts between digital signals (produced by a computer) and analog signals (used on most telephone lines). Modems enable users to transfer data between computers over telephone lines. The word modem is short for *modulator/demodulator*.

Module In BASIC, a group of related program statements that carries out a narrowly defined function in a more or less independent fashion. Complex programs usually are broken up into modules that can be conceptualized, developed, coded, tested, and run independently of other modules. Writing programs in this fashion provides structure that can be easily understood and modified by other programmers.

Motherboard The main circuit board of a computer that houses electronic parts such as the microprocessor, coprocessor, and RAM memory chips.

Mouse A small electronic device, about the size of a common field mouse, that is used to position a cursor on the screen by sliding the device across a desktop. The mouse is used in place of, or in addition to, the cursor control keys.

Mouse cursor In WordPerfect, an element on the screen that shows the position of the mouse.

Move In WordPerfect, to copy a selected block of text or graphics, then delete it from its current location in a document, and finally insert the copy at a new location. Synonymous with *cut and paste*.

Nested program loops In BASIC, **FOR/NEXT** or **WHILE/WEND** loops where one loop is contained completely inside another loop.

Network A group of computers connected to each other so that they can share hardware, software, and data.

Non-executable program statement (see *executable program statement*).

Null string In BASIC, a string that contains no characters (not even 0 or a blank space). The null string is indicated by two quotation marks side by side as in "". The null string is the default value of string variables.

Numeric formula In Lotus 1-2-3, one of three types of formulas (logical, string, and numeric). Numeric formulas perform calculations on numbers, functions, and other formulas. These formulas use the numeric operators ^, *, /, +, and -.

Numeric keypad The set of keys on the right side of a computer keyboard that looks like a calculator keypad. These keys are used for entering numeric data, inserting and deleting characters, and moving the cursor to different locations on the computer display.

Numeric variable (see *variable*).

On-line help A feature that enables the user to gain on-screen access to helpful information about an application while it is running. See also, *help key*.

One-dimensional array (see array).

Operating system Instructions (programs) that monitor and control the internal operations of the system and allow some control over the operations by the user.

Orphan The first line of a multi-line paragraph that appears alone at the bottom of a page.

Outdent (see *hanging paragraph*).

Output Information sent from the computer to the outside world, usually by displaying it on the screen or by printing it.

Output device A device such as a monitor or printer that is used to produce output.

Page break In WordPerfect, a location in a document that tells the printer to continue printing on a new sheet of paper. A hard page break is one that is inserted by the user; a soft page break is one that is automatically inserted by the application when it determines that the bottom of a page has been reached.

Page format The way a printed page will appear including the margins, text justification, headers, and footers.

Paginate To break up a document into pages of a specified size and to number the pages sequentially.

Parallel interface An interface that transmits data in parallel streams of bits.

Parameter An option or value that can be changed by the user when a command is given in order to customize the command to follow the exact wishes of the user. If a parameter is left off, a default value will be used.

Parent directory In DOS, the directory that is immediately above the active directory. Directories immediately below the active directory are called *children* of the directory.

Paste To insert at the cursor a block of text or graphics that had been copied to the memory of the computer.

Path The route that must be followed in order to access a file on a disk. The *path name* is the name of the subdirectory where a file resides. For example, if there is a subdirectory called **WPDOCS**, which is a child of the subdirectory **WP51**, which is a child of the root directory on the C drive, then the path name for the subdirectory **WPDOCS** would be **C:\WP51\WPDOCS**.

PC (see *computer*).

Peripheral An external device, such as a printer or a modem, that can be attached to the computer.

Personal computer (see *computer*).

Pipe The symbol **|** that is used to capture the output from one command and use it as the input of the next command. For example, **DIR | SORT** sends the output from the **DIR** command to the **SORT** command rather than to the screen. The result is a sorted listing of the default directory.

Pixel A dot (picture element) on the screen that is used to construct text and graphic images.

Pointer (see *data pointer*).

Port (see *interface*).

Printer driver A set of instructions that tells an application how to send output to a specific type of printer.

Program A set of instructions written in a computer language such as BASIC that tells the computer to carry out certain tasks.

Program file A file that contains instructions, versus a data file, which contains raw data.

Program module (see *module*).

Program statement (see *statement*).

Programming language A translator such as BASIC that provides the interface between human language (e.g., English) and the electronic language used by the computer (e.g., machine language).

Prompt (see *system prompt*).

Pseudocode The set of English-like phrases that describe what a program will do.

Pull-down menu A menu that may be opened (pulled down) from a menu bar. The process is visually similar to pulling down a window shade.

QBE In dBASE, QBE stands for Query By Example and is a method of constructing queries where the user enters search criteria into a pre-defined template.

Query In dBASE, a set of instructions that tells the program how to retrieve records that meet specific criteria.

QuickBASIC A version of BASIC developed by Microsoft Corporation.

QWERTY keyboard arrangement The typical arrangement of keys on a keyboard. QWERTY gets its name from the arrangement of the letters of the keys in the upper left-hand side of the second row. See also *Dvorak keyboard arrangement*.

RAM (see *random-access memory*).

Random-access memory (RAM) A part of the memory of the computer that temporarily holds instructions and data that can be directly accessed by the computer's central processing unit. The contents of RAM can be changed by the computer user but RAM is erased when the power to the computer is turned off.

Range In Lotus 1-2-3, one or more cells that form a rectangular area on the screen. Ranges can be rectangular groups of cells, entire columns or rows of cells, or single cells. Ranges are identified using the coordinates of two opposite corners of the range separated by one or two periods. For example, the range **A1.A1** includes only cell **A1**; the range **A3.D3** includes all cells in row **3** from column **A** through column **D** (i.e., cells **A3**, **B3**, **C3**, and **D3**); the range **G1.G31** includes all cells in column **G** from row **1** through row **31** (i.e., cells **G1**, **G2**, **G3**, . . . **G31**).

Range error (see *error*).

Read-only memory (ROM) A part of the memory of the computer that permanently holds instructions. The contents of ROM cannot be changed by the user but ROM is not erased when the power to the computer is turned off.

Read/write head The assembly of a disk drive that contains electromagnets attached to a moveable access arm. The read/write head is used to detect the magnetic fields on a disk during a read operation (to retrieve data) or to alter magnetic patterns during a write operation (to store data).

Reboot (see *warm boot*).

Record In dBASE, a group of fields that are related in some way. Each record of a database contains the same fields.

Record pointer In dBASE, a number that is used to keep track of the active record in the database.

Redirection In DOS, to instruct a program or command to receive its input from (or send its output to) some device other than the keyboard (for input) or the monitor (for output). The symbol **<** redirects input while the symbol **>** redirects output. For example, **DIR > PRN** redirects the listing of the directory from the monitor to the printer.

Reference In WordPerfect, words listed under head words in the thesaurus.

Reformat In WordPerfect, changing the form of a paragraph so that all characters fall between the right and left margins. This is accomplished by pressing an **[arrow key]** or the **[Insert key]**.

Relational operator (see *comparison operator*).

Relative cell reference (see *cell reference*).

Relative tab (see *tab stop*).

Replacement statement In BASIC, a statement that assigns a value to a variable through the use of the equal sign. For example **A = B** is a replacement statement that replaces the value of **A** with the value of **B**. Compare this with **B = A**, which is the reverse because it replaces the value of **B** with the value of **A**. Other examples of replacement statements are **X = X + 1**, which replaces the current value of **X** with one more than that value, and **A$ = "Alec"** which replaces the current value of **A$** with the string **Alec**. All **LET** statements are replacement statements.

Report In dBASE, selected and organized output from a database that is usually sent to the printer.

Reserved word A special word that is recognized by an application. For example, **PRINT** is a reserved word in BASIC. Synonymous with *key word.*

Retrieve (see *load*).

Reveal codes window In WordPerfect, the lower portion of the screen, which displays text and hidden codes, when using the *Reveal Codes* feature.

Reverse video Part of a display where the colors are inverted (e.g., if the display normally shows white letters on a black background then reverse video would show black letters on a white background).

RGB monitor A monitor that forms colors through the use of three electron guns, one each for red, green, and blue. The electron beams are aligned to strike three-color phosphors on the screen at the same location and by altering the intensity of the individual beams they may produce many different colors.

Right justification (see *justification*).

ROM (see *read-only memory*)

Root directory The single main directory of a disk that is created when the disk is formatted.

Round-off error An error that occurs when a number has to be rounded off to a specified number of decimal places. For example, the fraction $\frac{2}{3}$ cannot be expressed exactly using decimal notation. It can be rounded off to approximate values such as .7, or .67, or .667, or .6667, etc.

Run To execute (follow the instructions given in) the statements in a computer program.

Save a file Write a copy of a file to an external storage device such as a disk or tape.

Scanner A device that can be used to convert graphics or text into a form that can be stored and/or interpreted by the computer.

Screen dump A printed copy of the exact contents of the screen.

Screen Editor A type of text editor that enables the user to go to and change any character on the screen.

Scroll (1) The movement of text or graphics off the top of the screen as new material is added to the bottom. (2) To move vertically or horizontally within a document in order to display parts not presently visible on the screen.

SCSI (see *small computer system interface*).

Search To scan a document for a specific set of characters such as words or phrases.

Search and replace To scan a document for a set of characters and replace the characters with another set.

Select To choose an option for action. Usually, items are highlighted in some way first and then are selected for action.

Serial interface A computer interface that transmits data in a stream one bit at a time. The RS-232 is a standard serial interface used by many microcomputers.

Single-precision variable (see *variable*).

Singly subscripted variable (see *array*).

Small computer system interface A fast computer interface often used to connect external hard disks or laser printers to computers. Synonymous with *SCSI* (pronounced scuzzy).

Soft page break (see *page break*).

Soft return In WordPerfect, a code that indicates the end of a line of text. Soft returns are inserted automatically by WordPerfect to show where word wrap has automatically moved text to the next line.

Software The set of instructions that direct the operation of the computer hardware. Applications such as WordPerfect and Lotus 1-2-3 are software.

Sort To arrange data according to a specified sequence such as alphabetical order.

Source code Computer program statements written in a high-level language like BASIC.

Spaghetti code Programming code that jumps around so much that logical paths cannot be easily followed by human programmers. Such programs lack proper structure and this makes them difficult to read or modify.

Spell checker A program or program feature that checks spelling by comparing the words in a document with those in a dictionary. When a match cannot be found, the user is alerted and then can make a decision concerning the fate of the flagged word.

Spreadsheet (see *worksheet*).

Spreadsheet program A computer program such as Lotus 1-2-3 that displays a matrix of rows and columns, much like an electronic ledger, and which allows users to enter text, numeric data, and formulas and then to manipulate them to construct summary information or make projections.

Statement In BASIC, a line within a program.

Status line In WordPerfect, the bottom of the edit screen that provides information on the location of the cursor and the name of the document being edited.

Storage device A device such as a hard disk used to store data on a permanent basis.

String A sequence of characters that is treated as a single unit. A string can be an English word such as **beans**, a group of alphanumeric characters such as **HWW201**, or a group of letters, digits, blank spaces, and punctuation such as **wow @#$! 23**.

String formula In Lotus 1-2-3, one of three types of formulas (logical, string, and numeric). A string formula works on groups of characters (e.g., text and punctuation) using the string operator **&** (ampersand) and/or special functions. For example, if cell **A3** contains the label **Harlan**, then the string formula **+"Dear Ms. "&A3** would display **Dear Ms. Harlan**.

String variable (see *variable*).

Structured programming A way of constructing computer programs that breaks up complex procedures into smaller logical units that can be conceptualized, developed, coded, and tested independently of other units. Structured programming seeks to make the overall logic of a program as visible as possible through the use of program *modules* and the avoidance of *spaghetti code*.

Subdirectory A listing of the files (i.e., a directory) that have been grouped together under a single heading. The directory just above the active subdirectory is called its *parent* while the directories just below the active subdirectory are called its *children*.

Submenu A menu derived from another menu.

Subroutine A set of programming instructions, which can be called from anywhere within a main program, whose function is to perform some specialized task. For example, a group of statements to find the average of a set of numbers might form a subroutine in a BASIC program.

Subscript (see *array*).

Subscripted variable (see *array*).

Supercomputer (see *computer*).

Switch An option in a DOS command that indicates how the command is to be carried out. Switches are always preceded by a **/**. For example, in the DOS command **DIR /P**, the **/P** is a switch that tells DOS to display the directory listing one screen-full at a time.

Syntax The set of rules that govern how instructions must be given to the computer including the arrangement and style of key words, parameters, and punctuation. This is similar to the grammar of a human language.

Syntax error (see *error*).

System prompt (see *DOS prompt*).

System unit The main part of a microcomputer that contains the central processing unit (CPU), disk drives, power supply, and memory. For IBM computers, the system unit is the box that the monitor sits upon. For the original Macintosh, the system unit also includes the monitor.

Tab ruler In WordPerfect, the middle portion of the screen, which displays a ruler containing the locations of tab stops and margins, when using the *Reveal Codes* feature.

Tab stop A marker that indicates where the cursor will be located when the **[Tab]** key is tapped. *Absolute* tabs position the cursor in relation to the left edge of the page while *relative* tabs position the cursor in relation to the left margin.

Text file (see *ASCII file*).

Text window In WordPerfect, the upper portion of the screen, which displays text, when using the *Reveal Codes* feature.

Title (see *label*).

Toggle To switch between two modes. For example, in WordPerfect, the **[Insert]** key toggles between insert mode and typeover mode. The **[CapsLock]** and **[NumLock]** keys are also toggle keys.

Touch screen A device that fits over the front of a computer's screen that allows the computer operator to select objects or commands on the screen by pointing with his/her finger. The location of the tip of the finger is recorded by measuring its horizontal and vertical coordinates, which then are interpreted by a microprocessor.

Trackball A cursor positioning device that is similar to an upside-down mouse with an oversized ball. With this device, the ball is rotated by the fingers of the user while the trackball case remains stationary. It performs the same function as a mouse.

True BASIC A version of BASIC developed by Kemeny and Kurtz, the inventors of the language.

Truncate To cut off data at a specified point. For example, if the string **ABCDEFG** were truncated at four characters, the result would be **ABCD**; if the number **3.4567** were truncated to four characters, the result would be **3.45** (notice that this is different from rounding off the number).

Two-dimensional array (see *array*).

Typeover To replace (type over) one character with another.

Unconditional branch (see *branch*).

Undo To reverse the action of a previous command. In Lotus 1-2-3, the undo command is initiated by tapping **[Alt-F4]**.

Uppercase letters Capital letters such as A, B, C. Compare with lowercase.

User friendly Applications designed to be easy to learn and operate.

User interface The point of meeting between the computer and the computer user.

Vaccine (see *virus*).

Value In Lotus 1-2-3, a numeric entry such as a rate of pay or a formula such as for the calculation of total pay earned. Entries are considered values if they begin with **0 1 2 3 4 5 6 7 8 9 - + . (@ #** or **$**. Text entries are referred to as *labels*.

Variable A named part of memory that can hold different values. In BASIC, string variables, which are identified with a dollar sign suffix, may contain letters, digits, or punctuation whereas numeric variables may contain only values or numeric expressions. Numeric variables that contain integer values between –32768 and +32767, inclusive are termed *integer variables* and are given the suffix **%**. Numeric variables that are not integers but contain seven or fewer digits are termed *single-precision variables* and are given the suffix **!**. Numeric variables that contain 8 or more digits are termed *double-precision variables* and are given the suffix **#**.

VGA (see *video graphics array*).

Video Graphics Array A medium resolution monitor driver that can display up to 256 colors at one time. See also *CGA* and *EGA*.

View feature A WordPerfect feature that allows the user to see on the screen how a document will look when printed.

View query In dBASE, the display of data from a database that meets criteria defined in a query.

Virus A program written to replicate itself and then secretly attach the copy to another program or data file. Some viruses are intended only as jokes but others are designed to damage computer software. Virus checking programs, called *vaccines*, have been designed to detect and eliminate some viruses.

Volume In DOS, a one to eleven character name given to a diskette in order to identify it. The **LABEL** command is used to change the name of a volume.

Warm boot (see *boot*).

Widow The last line of a multi-line paragraph that appears alone at the top of a page.

Wild card (see *global character*).

Window A portion of the screen that is dedicated to a specific purpose.

Word-processing program A computer program such as WordPerfect that enables a user to enter, manipulate, store, and print documents such as memos and reports.

Word wrap A word processing feature that automatically adjusts the number of words in a line so that a word that would be displayed past the right margin of the line is placed at the left margin of the next line without the user having to tap the **[Enter]** key.

Worksheet The matrix of rows and columns, including any data that has been entered, displayed by a spreadsheet program. Synonymous with *spreadsheet.*

Write protect To configure a diskette so that it is write protected (i.e., so that it may not be written to or erased by the computer). To write protect a $5\frac{1}{4}$-inch diskette, cover the write-enable notch. To write protect a $3\frac{1}{2}$-inch diskette, open the write-enable window.

Write-enable notch A notch cut in the upper-right edge of a $5\frac{1}{4}$-inch diskette that is used to determine whether or not information may be written to the diskette. If the notch is open, permission to write to the diskette is granted. If the notch is covered, the diskette is said to be *write-protected* and permission to write to the diskette is denied. Synonymous with *write-protect notch.*

Write-enable window A hole in the upper-right corner of a $3\frac{1}{2}$-inch diskette that is used to determine whether or not information may be written to the diskette. If the hole is covered, permission to write to the diskette is granted. If the hole is open, the diskette is said to be *write-protected* and permission to write to the diskette is denied.

WYSIWYG An acronym for *What-You-See-Is-What-You-Get.* WYSIWYG programs display on the screen exactly what will be printed including all character enhancements such as boldface, underline, and font.

Zap In dBASE, to erase the contents of a database.

This index is divided into two sections: **Section 1** provides the names, page references, and a brief description of each file created in the body of the book or as a homework exercise. The file names are listed alphabetically within each application (WordPerfect, Lotus 1-2-3, dBASE, and BASIC). **Section 2** provides an alphabetical listing of topics covered in the book.

Remember that in order to distinguish between the different parts of the book, page numbers have been given one of the following letter prefixes:

Part		***Letter prefix***
Getting Started:	Concepts	C
Part I	WordPerfect and DOS	W
Part II	Lotus 1-2-3	L
Part III	dBASE	D
Part IV	BASIC	B

Section 1: Index of Sample and Homework Files

• Part I: WordPerfect •

ALTH.WPM (macro to set up ruler), W189
ALTR.WPM (macro to set margins and tabs), W151
ANXIETY.CON (index concordance file), W184
ANXIETY.FIN (modified **ANXIETY9**—pagination fixed), W176
ANXIETY.NDX (modified **ANXIETY.TOC**—index added), W186
ANXIETY.TOC (modified **ANXIETY.FIN**—table of contents added), W183
ANXIETY1 (term paper title and thesis statement), W161
ANXIETY2 (modified **ANXIETY1**—outline added), W164
ANXIETY3 (modified **ANXIETY2**—**m1** replaced with **mathematics**), W167
ANXIETY4 (modified **ANXIETY3**—title formatted), W167
ANXIETY5 (modified **ANXIETY4**—outline page formatted), W169
ANXIETY6 (modified **ANXIETY5**—headers and footers added), W171
ANXIETY7 (modified **ANXIETY6**—footnote added), W172
ANXIETY8 (modified **ANXIETY7**—section titles formatted), W174
ANXIETY9 (modified **ANXIETY8**—references formatted), W176
CONTACTS (names and addresses of business contacts), W214
CONTACTS.BAK (copy of **CONTACTS**), W214
CONTACTS.BK2 (copy of **CONTACTS.BAK**), W215
CONTRIB (database for *Merge* feature), W132
DOCU1BU (copy of **MEMO1BU**—name changed using **RENAME** command), W209
DOCU2BU (copy of **MEMO2BU**—name changed using **RENAME** command), W209
DOCU3BU (copy of **MEMO3BU**—name changed using **RENAME** command), W209
DOCU4BU (copy of **MEMO4BU**—name changed using **RENAME** command), W209
EQ-V1 (contains equations), W140
EQ-V2 (modified **EQ-V1**—second equation added), W140
HWTOP.WPM (macro to display homework header), W189
HWW1-02 (personal letter to a friend), W38
HWW1-05 (memo to parking services), W39
HWW1-06 (modified **HWW1-05**—business form), W40
HWW1-08 (résumé), W40–41
HWW2-01 (KeepGreen complaint letter), W102
HWW2-03 (modified **HWW2-01**—new margins), W102
HWW2-05 (modified **HWW2-01**—double spaced), W102
HWW2-06 (modified **HWW2-01**—reversed reasons), W103
HWW2-08 (modified **HWW2-01**—line numbering), W103
HWW2-09 (tutor advertisement), W103
HWW2-10 (modified **HWW2-09**—uppercase letters), W103
HWW2-11 (modified **HWW2-10**—underline and boldface), W103
HWW2-12 (modified **HWW2-01**—hard page break), W103
HWW2-13 (modified **HWW2-12**—header and footer), W103
HWW3-02R (names of business contacts—WordPerfect format), W187
HWW3-02T (names of business contacts—ASCII format), W187
HWW3-03 (memo complimenting subordinate), W187
HWW3-04 (modified **HWW3-03**—file **HWW3-02T** added), W187
HWW3-05 (modified **HWW2-09**—file **HWW3-02R** added), W187
HWW3-06 (modified **HWW3-02R**—names sorted), W188
HWW3-07 (modified **HWW3-02R**—**555** replaced with **999**), W188
HWW3-08D (database for merge), W188
HWW3-08L (form letter for merge), W188
HWW3-09 (essay with graphic), W188
HWW3-10 (document with mathematics formula), W188
HWW3-13 (outline for term paper), W189
HWW3-14 (three-page term paper), W189
HWW3-15 (modified **HWW3-14**—index added), W189
HWW3-15C (concordance file for term paper index), W189
LETTER (form letter for *Merge* feature), W134
MEMO1 (memo about computer purchases), W14
MEMO1BU (copy of **MEMO1** using **COPY** command), W206
MEMO2 (modified **MEMO1**—edited text), W31
MEMO2BU (copy of **MEMO2** using **COPY** command), W206
MEMO3 (modified **MEMO2**—text inserted), W120
MEMO3.FIG (modified **MEMO3**—figure inserted), W140

• Part II: Lotus 1-2-3 •

• Part III: dBASE IV •

• *Part IV: BASIC* •

Section 2: Index of Contents

A 1
B 2
C 3
D 4
E 5
F 6
G 7
H 8
I 9
J 0